ENCYCLOPEDIA OF PSYCHOLOGY

EDITORS

ENCYCLOPEDIA OF PSYCHOLOGY

Alan E. Kazdin

Editor in Chief

VOLUME 2

AMERICAN
PSYCHOLOGICAL
ASSOCIATION

OXFORD
UNIVERSITY PRESS

2000

AMERICAN
PSYCHOLOGICAL
ASSOCIATION

Washington, D.C.

OXFORD
UNIVERSITY PRESS

Oxford   New York

Athens   Auckland   Bangkok   Bogotá   Buenos Aires   Calcutta
Cape Town   Chennai   Dar es Salaam   Delhi   Florence   Hong Kong   Istanbul
Karachi   Kuala Lumpur   Madrid   Melbourne   Mexico City   Mumbai
Nairobi   Paris   São Paulo   Singapore   Taipei   Tokyo   Toronto   Warsaw

and associated companies in
Berlin   Ibadan

Copyright © 2000 by American Psychological Association and Oxford University Press, Inc.

Published by American Psychological Association
750 First Street, NE, Washington, D.C. 20002-4242
www.apa.org
and
Oxford University Press, Inc.
198 Madison Avenue, New York, New York 10016
www.oup.com

Oxford is a registered trademark of Oxford University Press.

Library of Congress Cataloging-in-Publication Data
Encyclopedia of psychology / Alan E. Kazdin, editor in chief
p.   cm.
Includes bibliographical references and index.
1. Psychology—Encyclopedias.   I. Kazdin, Alan E.
BF31 .E52   2000   150'.3—dc21   99-055239
ISBN 1-55798-187-6 (set); ISBN 1-55798-651-7 (vol. 2)

AMERICAN PSYCHOLOGICAL ASSOCIATION STAFF

Gary R. VandenBos, Ph.D., *Publisher*
Julia Frank-McNeil, *Commissioning Editor*
Theodore J. Baroody, *Senior Development Editor*
Adrian Harris Forman, *Project Editor*

OXFORD UNIVERSITY PRESS STAFF

Karen Casey, *Publisher*
Claude Conyers, *Commissioning Editor*
Marion Osmun, *Senior Development Editor*
Matthew Giarratano, *Managing Editor*
Peri Zeenkov and Norina Frabotta, *Project Editors*
Nancy Hoagland, *Production Manager*
Jessica Ryan and Will Moore, *Production Editors*
AEIOU, Inc., *Index Editor*
AEIOU, Inc., Linda Berman, Denise McIntyre,
Space Coast Indexers, Inc., Linda Webster, *Indexers*
Suzanne Holt, *Book Design*
Joan Greenfield, *Cover Design*

3 5 7 9 8 6 4 2

Printed in the United States of America
on acid-free paper

C

CALKINS, MARY WHITON (1863–1930), American psychologist and philosopher. An eminent psychologist and philosopher and the first woman elected president of both the American Psychological Association (in 1905) and the American Philosophical Association (in 1918), Mary W. Calkins devoted most of her career to developing, defending, and promoting a system of self-psychology. From the time she first presented her system in 1900 until her death in 1930 she became increasingly convinced that the proper subject matter of the science of psychology was the self in relation to its social and physical environment.

In the 1890s, Calkins was among the first generation of women in the United States to pursue graduate study in the new scientific psychology, a discipline just beginning to establish itself within the academy. Institutions that offered graduate training in psychology were few, and fewer still were those that were willing to admit women as students. Calkins was teaching Greek at Wellesley College, an undergraduate college for women outside of Boston, when she was offered a newly created position in experimental psychology contingent upon her studying the subject for 1 year. In 1890, she turned to nearby universities, Harvard and Clark, for graduate instruction in psychology, but neither was willing to admit women as candidates for advanced degrees. After extended negotiations with the Harvard authorities, Calkins was granted permission to attend the seminars of William James and Josiah Royce but as a guest of the university, not as a student. At Clark, she made arrangements to study experimental psychology privately with Edmund C. Sanford. Calkins returned to Harvard in 1892 for further graduate training in psychology under the direction of Hugo Munsterberg and in the next 3 years completed all the requirements for the Ph.D., a degree that Harvard never granted her because she was a woman.

By the fall of 1891, Calkins had set up a psychological laboratory at Wellesley College, the first in the United States in an undergraduate institution, in conjunction with the new course she was teaching in experimental psychology. Over the decade of the 1890s, she conducted numerous empirical investigations on a variety of topics at Harvard, Clark, and in the Wellesley laboratory. Two of these have special significance—her studies of association and of dreams.

Calkins began to study the association of ideas in the seminar she took with William James and continued her work with experiments on the topic in Munsterberg's laboratory at Harvard. It was while conducting this research that she invented a memory technique that came to be known as the method of paired-associates, a method in use to the present day. With themselves as the sole experimental subjects, Calkins and Sanford carried out an early dream study, which he reported on at the first annual meeting of the American Psychological Association in 1892. Calkins published a paper on their joint dream study in 1893 and in 1896 published the results of some further dream research carried out by two of her undergraduate students at Wellesley College, Florence Hallam and Sarah Weed. Soon after, in his monumental work *The Interpretation of Dreams*, Sigmund Freud cited both of Calkins's published contributions on dreams with approval as providing empirical support for his own subjective impressions.

Calkins's involvement in empirical research came to an end around 1900; thereafter her energies were focused on theoretical and philosophical work. This shift has been attributed to Calkins's increasing dissatisfaction with the then dominant Wundtian and Titchenerian school of psychology and, in particular, with its limitation of the contents of psychology to elemental sensations, emotions, and images. Coming to view this atomistic approach as flawed because it excluded psychological phenomena that to her were basic facts of everyday experience, namely conscious selves, Calkins in 1900 proposed her own system, a self-psychology that was a departure from the reigning school.

In regard to the origins of her approach, Calkins identified several sources. She attributed her emphasis on the social nature of the self to James Baldwin and Josiah Royce and credited William James and the English psychologist James Ward with having exerted an influence on her formulation of psychology as the study of conscious selves. Calkins initially adopted Hugo Munsterberg's position, called the double standpoint view in psychology, that every experience can be treated from both the atomistic and the self-psychological perspectives. By 1910, she became convinced that psychology was better conceived as solely the study of conscious selves, and dropped the consideration of elemental mental events because she doubted the significance and disapproved of the abstractness of this approach.

For 30 years, Calkins developed her system of self-psychology, which remained essentially as she first presented it in 1900. Her efforts were directed to clarifying, modifying, and defending her system against the challenges posed by competing systems including structuralism, functionalism, behaviorism, hormic psychology, Gestalt psychology, and psychoanalysis. Calkins described her self-psychology as a form of introspectionist psychology opposed to varieties of behaviorism that denied self and consciousness. Furthermore, the kind of introspectionist psychology she espoused was personal—studying conscious, experiencing beings—rather than impersonal—ignoring the self to focus on, for example, the contents of consciousness or ideas. Finally, she allied herself with a strictly psychological rather than biological approach to personalistic psychology, insisting that the self is not constituted by a body, but rather that the self has a body.

During Calkins's career in psychology, the focus of the field changed from the study of consciousness to an attempt to explain it away. Calkins commented critically in 1915 about the tendency among laboratory psychologists to arrange their experiments so that evidence of the conscious self was eradicated from their results. Through the 1920s, in the face of a militant behaviorism that was overtaking American psychology, Calkins remained steadfast in her commitment to the belief that psychology should be conceived as the science of the self. In fact, shortly before her death in 1930 and soon after her retirement from Wellesley College, she claimed that with each year she lived, with each book she read, and with each observation she made, she became more convinced of the correctness of her position.

Bibliography

Works by Calkins

Calkins, M. W. (1893). Statistics of dreams. *American Journal of Psychology, 5,* 311–343. Report of the dream study conducted by Calkins and E. C. Sanford.

Calkins, M. W. (1896). Association: An essay analytic and experimental. *Psychological Review Monograph Supplement Number 2,* 1–56. Contains a description of the technique of paired-associates invented by Calkins to study memory.

Calkins, M. W. (1900). Psychology as science of selves. *Philosophical Review, 9,* 490–501. Calkins's first presentation of her self-psychology.

Calkins, M. W. (1901). *An introduction to psychology.* New York: Macmillan. Textbook in which Calkins treats psychology from a dual standpoint as both a science of selves and a science of mental processes.

Calkins, M. W. (1906). A reconciliation between structural and functional psychology. *Psychological Review, 13,* 61–81. Presidential address delivered at the meeting of the American Psychological Association in 1905.

Calkins, M. W. (1909). *A first book in psychology.* New York: Macmillan. Textbook in which Calkins abandons the dual standpoint in favor of treating psychology exclusively as the study of conscious selves.

Calkins, M. W. (1915). The self in scientific psychology. *American Journal of Psychology, 26,* 495–524. Article in which Calkins criticized the tendency among psychologists to deny or ignore the self.

Calkins, M. W. (1930). Mary Whiton Calkins. In C. Murchison (Ed.), *A history of psychology in autobiography* (Vol. 1, pp. 31–62). Worcester, MA: Clark University Press. Posthumously published chapter divided evenly between an account of Calkins's career in psychology and an argument for her system of self-psychology.

Works about Calkins

Heidbreder, E. (1972). Mary Whiton Calkins: A discussion. *Journal of the History of the Behavioral Sciences, 8,* 56–68. Discussion of Calkins's system of self-psychology considering the ways in which it resembles a Kuhnian paradigm and the similarities between it and her treatment of philosophical and psychological problems more generally.

Furumoto, L. (1990). Mary Whiton Calkins (1863–1930). In A. N. O'Connell & N. F. Russo (Eds.), *Women in psychology: A bio-bibliographic sourcebook* (pp. 57–65). Westport, CT: Greenwood Press.

Furumoto, L. (1991). From "paired-associates" to a psychology of the self: The intellectual odyssey of Mary Whiton Calkins. In G. A. Kimble, M. Wertheimer, & C. White (Eds.), *Portraits of pioneers in psychology* (pp. 57–72). Washington, DC: American Psychological Association & Hillsdale, NJ: Erlbaum.

Scarborough, E., & Furumoto, L. (1987). *Untold lives: The first generation of American women psychologists.* New York: Columbia University Press. Contains a chapter on Calkins's pursuit of graduate training in psychology and the institutional barriers she encountered at Harvard and Clark universities.

Laurel Furumoto

CAMPBELL, ANGUS (1910–1980), American psychologist. Campbell was director of the Institute for Social Research and professor of psychology, political science, and law at the University of Michigan. Both as a leader of the Institute and as a research scholar, he was a major figure in the development of survey methods and their application to social problems.

Campbell was born in Indiana, but in his boyhood the family moved to Portland, Oregon. He graduated from the University of Oregon in 1931 and in the following year received his master's degree in psychology, after which he began doctoral work in experimental psychology at Stanford University. His major professor there was E. R. Hilgard, but Campbell also became interested in social psychology, probably influenced by Kurt Lewin, who spent a short time at Stanford as a visiting professor. In 1936, having just received his Ph.D., Campbell was appointed to the faculty of Northwestern University. There his interest in the social aspects of his field was further stimulated by discussions with the social anthropologist Melville Herskovits, and in 1939 Campbell received a postdoctoral fellowship in anthropology from the Social Science Research Council.

His plan had been to spend the fellowship year at Cambridge University, but shortly after his arrival there the entry of Great Britain into World War II forced a change in plan. Campbell moved to the Virgin Islands, where he conducted a study of the black population, an activity that furthered his commitment to social psychology and began his long involvement in survey research. His return to Northwestern, at the end of the fellowship year, was brief; the United States was entering the War and Campbell moved to Washington, where he joined Rensis Likert and the group of social scientists who were creating in the Department of Agriculture the survey facility that was later recreated at the University of Michigan as the Survey Research Center and the Institute for Social Research.

The range of Campbell's research interests and the importance of his contributions are especially exemplified in three of the many books of which he was author or co-author: *The American Voter* (1960), *White Attitudes Toward Black People* (1971), and *The Sense of Well-Being in America* (1980). *The American Voter* set a conceptual and methodological standard for the study of national politics that has been followed ever since. *White Attitudes Toward Black People*, published at a time when America had only begun to acknowledge the persisting problems of race relations, described unflinchingly the depth of white prejudice. Campbell's last book, *The Sense of Well-Being in America*, summed up his work on measuring the experienced quality of life.

Campbell's scientific and professional contributions were widely recognized during his lifetime. He received the Distinguished Achievement Award of the American Association for Public Opinion Research (1962), an honorary LL.D. from the University of Strathclyde (1970), the Distinguished Scientific Contribution Award of the American Psychological Association (1974), the Lazarsfeld Award of the Council for Applied Research (1977), and the Lasswell Award of the International Society of Political Psychology (1980). He was elected to the American Academy of Arts and Sciences in 1961 and to the National Academy of Sciences in 1980.

Bibliography

Campbell, A., Converse, P. E., Miller, W. E., & Stokes, D. E. (1960). *The American voter*. New York: Wiley.

Campbell, A. (1971). *White attitudes toward Black people*. Ann Arbor, MI: Institute for Social Research, The University of Michigan.

Campbell, A. (1980). *The sense of well-being in America: Recent patterns and trends*. New York: McGraw-Hill.

Kahn, R. L. (1981). Angus Campbell (1910–1980). *American Psychologist, 36*, 1450–1451.

Robert L. Kahn

CAMPBELL, DONALD THOMAS (1916–1996), American psychologist. Campbell was a social psychologist by training and intellectual identification, but his scholarly contributions were pandisciplinary. During his distinguished career, his influence extended to researchers and theorists in all of the social sciences, education, philosophy, and law. His field of study was, in essence, the study of science itself.

Campbell was born in 1916 in Michigan, but was raised and educated in California. He earned his bachelor's degree in 1939 at the University of California, Berkeley, where he worked with both Edward Tolman and Egon Brunswik, and earned his Ph.D. there in 1947. Following completion of his graduate work, Campbell took his first faculty position at the Ohio State University (1947–1950) and then moved to the University of Chicago (1950–1953). But the majority of his academic career was spent in the department of psychology at Northwestern University (1953–1979). It was during his 26-year tenure at Northwestern that he made his mark on psychology, and published the best-known of his more than 200 scholarly papers.

Campbell's areas of research and scholarship included measurement, experimental design, applied social experimentation, cross-cultural psychology, epistemology, and sociology of science. His most widely cited scholarly publications were methodological. In 1959, he published with Donald W. Fiske the article "Convergent and Discriminant Validation by the Multitrait-Multimethod Matrix" (Campbell & Fiske, 1959), which provided a conceptual and methodological framework for defining and assessing the construct validity of psychological measures. This was followed a few years later by a paper with Julian Stanley entitled "Experimental and Quasi-Experimental Designs for Research on Teaching," which was initially published as a chapter in the 1963 *Handbook for Research on Teaching* and later reprinted as a separate volume (Campbell & Stanley, 1966). This seminal paper introduced the concepts of internal and external validity as different criteria for evaluating the conclusions that can be drawn from an experimental study, particularly the validity of any inferences about causal relationships that might be claimed. Campbell and Stanley's monograph also introduced the logic of quasi-experimentation for field research in the social sciences, becoming the classic text for teaching principles of research design and methodology to generations of social scientists.

As a social scientist, Campbell was committed to multidisciplinary and multimethodological research. His own substantive research efforts ranged from laboratory experiments on perceptual contrast effects to cross-cultural studies of ethnocentrism and intergroup relations. He was convinced that some of the greatest achievements of the social sciences were methodologies that could be applied to analyzing and solving social problems. He was among the earliest proponents of the use of randomized experiments to evaluate the effectiveness of social programs, while at the same time recognizing the need for innovative variations of experimental design to fit the needs and constraints of research in the world of social policy and social change. His methodological prescriptions for social research were presented in the influential article "Reforms as Experiments" (Campbell, 1969), a paper that helped to launch the nascent field of program evaluation research.

Campbell's methodological contributions represented just one manifestation of his broader interests in epistemology and philosophy of science. His writings on the acquisition of knowledge through perception, trial-and-error, and vicarious learning culminated in his model of evolutionary epistemology (Campbell, 1974), which drew the admiration of such prominent philosophers as Karl Popper. Drawing analogies with Darwin's theory of evolution of species, Campbell's model identified processes of variation and selective retention as the fundamental principles of learning in individuals and in social systems.

Campbell closed a chapter in his academic and personal life when he left Northwestern University in 1979 to accept a position as the Albert Schweitzer Professor at the Maxwell School of Syracuse University. In 1982, he moved again to become University Professor of Social Relations, Psychology, and Education at Lehigh University until his quasi-retirement in 1994. Campbell spent much of the later part of his scholarly career studying science as a social system.

The many honors and awards that Campbell accrued over his productive career reflect the range of his contributions to educational, experimental, and social psychology, as well as to the social sciences more generally. He served as president of the American Psychological Association in 1973 and was an elected member of the National Academy of Sciences and the American Academy of Arts and Sciences. He received distinguished scientist awards from the American Psychological Association, American Psychological Society, American Educational Research Association, American Evaluation Society, Society for Experimental Social Psychology, and Society for the Psychological Study of Social Issues. Although Campbell was nearly 80 when he died in May 1996, his death put a premature end to a still active and fruitful scholarly career.

Bibliography

Brewer, M. B., & Collins, B. E. (Eds.). (1981). *Scientific inquiry and the social sciences: A volume in honor of Donald T. Campbell.* San Francisco: Jossey-Bass. Papers written as a *festschrift* to Campbell in recognition of his contributions to social science methodology and epistemology. The final chapter is a retrospective written by Campbell on his own scholarly career.

Campbell, D. T. (1969). Reforms as experiments. *American Psychologist, 24,* 409–429. Campbell's seminal paper on program evaluation research.

Campbell, D. T. (1974). Evolutionary epistemology. In P. A. Schilpp (Ed.), *The philosophy of Karl Popper* (pp. 413–463). La Salle, IL: Open Court. Campbell's best-known contribution to the philosophy of science.

Campbell, D. T. (1988). *Methodology and epistemology for social science: Selected papers* (E. S. Overman, Ed.). Chicago: University of Chicago Press. A selection of Campbell's papers on measurement, research design, social experimentation, epistemology, and sociology of science. Includes some previously unpublished works, such as his 1971 paper on "the experimenting society" and excerpts from his 1977 William James Lectures at Harvard University.

Campbell, D. T., & Fiske, D. W. (1959). Convergent and discriminant validation by the multitrait-multimethod matrix. *Psychological Bulletin, 56,* 81–105.

Campbell, D. T., & Stanley, J. C. (1966). *Experimental and quasi-experimental design for research.* Chicago: Rand McNally. The paperback version of Campbell and Stanley's famous treatise on field research methodology and validity.

Cook, T. D., & Campbell, D. T. (1979). *Quasi-experimentation: Design and analysis issues for field settings.* Chicago: Rand McNally. An expansion and elaboration of the quasi-experimental designs and statistics first introduced by Campbell and Stanley.

LeVine, R. A., & Campbell, D. T. (1972). *Ethnocentrism: Theories of conflict, ethnic attitudes and group behavior.* New York: Wiley. A collaborative work with anthropologist Robert LeVine that compiles and integrates social science theories of intergroup relations, as a blueprint for a large-scale comparative cross-cultural study of ethnocentrism.

Marilynn B. Brewer

CANADA. With an area of nearly 4 million square miles, Canada is the world's second largest country, after Russia. Nearly two thirds of its 30 million residents live within 200 miles of Canada's southern border with the United States, the "world's longest undefended border." Canada was populated by indigenous, aboriginal peoples before the seventeenth century, with subsequent European colonization by two "charter" or founding groups: the French, beginning in the early seventeenth century, and later the English, who militarily defeated the French in 1759. Today, approximately 25% of Canada's population identifies French as its mother tongue, with most French-speaking Canadians living in the province of Quebec. Sixty percent of Canadians identify English as their mother tongue; and 15%, a language other than English or French.

In the twentieth century, Canada's English and French cultures have been characterized as "two solitudes," a metaphor referring to the lack of contact, interaction, and mutual understanding between two cultures speaking different languages. Although Canada became officially bilingual (English-French) in 1969, an enduring political tension exists between predominantly French-speaking Quebec and the other nine Canadian provinces, in which English predominates. Feeling that Canada has been unresponsive to its demands for political autonomy and support for its distinctive Francophone culture within North America, Quebec has held referenda seeking independence and secession from Canada on two occasions. The second of these, in 1995, failed by less than 1% of the vote. The likelihood that such referenda will be held again means that the prospects for Canada's existence as a unified country remain uncertain.

Like the United States, Canada is also a "nation of immigrants," but it receives more immigrants per capita than the United States does. In contrast to the assimilationist, "melting pot" ethic in the United States, however, Canada subscribes to a "mosaic" approach, in which immigrant and ethnic groups are encouraged to retain their cultural heritage while participating in Canada's "host" or mainstream culture. Canada's "mosaic," together with its federal multiculturalism policy, has resulted in considerable ethnocultural diversity throughout Canada, especially in its cities. In the 1990s, more than 30% of Canada's population reported ethnic backgrounds other than English or French.

In Canada, the provinces and territories have jurisdiction over health, education, and the regulation of professions (including "professional" psychologists, as defined below). Canada also provides its residents universal medical care, with the federal government insuring national health care standards and universal access. From 1994 to 1999, Canada annually ranked first among the world's nations on the United Nations' Human Development Index, a social indicator reflecting the overall quality of life a country provides its citizens and residents.

Canadian Psychology: A Concise History

The roots of psychology in Canada were first formed in university philosophy departments of the early nineteenth century. Nova Scotia's Dalhousie University can claim Canada's first psychology course in 1838 and its first "official" psychologist, William Lyall, who held Dalhousie's Chair of Psychology and Metaphysics in 1866. The first "modern" psychologist in Canada, however, was James Mark Baldwin from the United States, who held the Metaphysics Professorship from 1889 to 1893 at the University of Toronto, where he established Canada's first psychology laboratory in 1891 and supervised psychological research. During his Canadian sojourn, Baldwin was a founding member of the American Psychological Association (conceived originally as a "continental" association for North America) in 1892. He arranged for August Kirschmann from Wundt's laboratory in Germany to succeed him in directing the psychological laboratory. Kirschmann made Toronto's laboratory an active center for psychological research (especially in vision) from 1893 to 1909, after which he returned permanently to Germany.

E. A. Bott, a philosophy undergraduate when Kirschmann left, inherited Kirschmann's zeal for laboratory research in psychology and subsequently nurtured the birth and growth of the University of Toronto's psychology department over 40 years. During World War I, Bott turned the psychological laboratory into a soldiers' rehabilitation clinic, reflecting the University of Toronto's strong applied psychology orientation from then until after World War II. In the 1930s, University of Toronto psychologists focused on mental health and child study, while Montreal's McGill University psychologists investigated psychological effects of the Depression. Having previously polled his colleagues about forming a national psychological organization in Canada, Bott convened a meeting in Ottawa in June 1938 that created the Canadian Psychological Association (CPA), with 38 founding members and Bott as its first president. For his many achievements, Bott has been called the "dean of Canadian psychology." CPA's inaugural meeting occurred in April 1939, the eve of World War II.

Canadian psychologists greatly assisted the Allied effort in World War II by devising the Canadian armed forces' classification tests for recruits, developing scientific procedures for selecting and training British Commonwealth pilots and aircrew, training child care workers in Canada and England, and exploring ways to improve morale. Several years after the war, CPA successfully secured several funding sources from the Canadian federal government for psychological research. However, CPA encountered difficulties and less success in developing standards and certification procedures for "professional" psychologists, partly because statutory recognition and regulation of professions was (and remains) a provincial rather than a national prerogative. These divergent outcomes were the first signs of a developing tension between "scientific psychology" (i.e., research oriented, university based) and "professional psychology" (i.e., practice oriented, emphasizing applied psychology and providing psychological services to clients) in Canada that has since endured.

Until the 1970s, CPA favored scientific over professional psychology, owing to Robert MacLeod's (1955) report, commissioned by the Canadian Social Science Research Council. MacLeod, a distinguished Canadian psychologist then at Cornell, surveyed psychology in Canadian universities and colleges of the early 1950s. His report, published in 1955, became Canadian psychology's first overview and evaluation. Given the limited resources then available to psychology in Canada, MacLeod specifically warned against "premature professionalization," suggesting that efforts to establish professional psychology undermined scientific psychology, where he believed the future of Canadian psychology lay. MacLeod recommended that CPA convene a conference to define psychological research, norms for training in psychological research, and the scientific basis for psychological applications. The resulting 1960 Opinicon Conference, attended by 41 psychologists in Canada, dealt exclusively with teaching and research training for scientific psychology but advocated a scientist-practitioner model for professional psychologists.

Canada's professional psychologists responded to Op-

inicon, some angrily, by demanding that CPA convene a conference on professional psychology. The 1965 Couchiching Conference was mandated to define professional psychology, specify its objectives, and design a program to meet them. It produced 89 resolutions that defined applied psychology, academic requirements for professional practice, and training objectives for various categories of professional psychologists.

Although CPA responded to Canadian professional psychologists primarily through its regional and professional affairs committees in the 1960s, professional psychologists generally perceived CPA as more interested in creating an infrastructure for scientific psychology and basic psychological research in university settings than in promoting professional psychology. Meanwhile, provincial psychology association representatives agreed in 1967 to form an organization, now called the Council of Provincial Associations of Psychologists (CPAP), to represent their strong interest in professional psychology independent of CPA. CPAP's membership includes representatives from collegial and regulatory organizations of psychologists from Canadian provinces and territories, as well as from CPA.

Since 1970, CPA has taken a more inclusive attitude toward professional psychology. In 1977, CPA's leadership narrowly averted an action by practitioners to create a separate Canadian national association for professional psychologists by accommodating and acting on their demands. CPA's 1984 State of the Discipline Review represented both professional and scientific psychology in Canada by treating research, teaching, and service delivery. Also, in the mid-1980s, the lack of a national credentialing body for professional psychologists in Canada was addressed, in good part, by establishing the Canadian Register of Health Service Providers in Psychology (CRHSPP), a goal CPAP and CPA both promoted.

CPA's tilt toward professional psychology alienated some scientifically oriented psychologists in Canada, especially those working in biological and experimental psychology, who withdrew from CPA in the late 1980s to form an exclusively scientific and experimentally oriented psychological organization of their own called the Canadian Society for Brain, Behavioural, and Cognitive Science (CSBBCS). The establishment of CSBBCS eroded scientists' representation within CPA. About 13% of CPA's 1996 membership categorized themselves as "scientists," whereas "practitioners" and "scientist-practitioners" each accounted for 43%. Today, many of CPA's current "scientist" members come primarily from social, personality, developmental, and educational psychology. Since 1996, CPA and CSBBCS have cooperated to pursue common scientific goals.

In sum, a continuing dialectic between science and practice is a prominent, if not defining, theme in the history of Canadian psychology since World War II. Canadian psychology reflects several features of Canada's complex sociopolitical context. Like the English-French "solitudes," scientific and professional psychology in Canada have often been two separate and clashing "cultures" (science and humanism). Also, tensions between national and provincial organizations of psychologists as regards representing professional psychologists mirror federal-provincial government conflicts within Canada's political system.

Canada's lack of national cohesion and unity is also parallelled by a multiplicity of competing psychological associations in Canada—an arguably expensive, somewhat redundant, and complex organizational infrastructure for fewer than 20,000 psychologists. (Although the total number is not known exactly, there are an estimated 13,000 "regulated" professional psychologists in Canada, half of these in Quebec alone, and perhaps no more than several thousand scientific psychologists in academia and other research settings.) The siren call of its U.S. neighbor, with many scientific and professional psychology organizations available to Canadians to join, further complicates the project of creating a highly representative organizational infrastructure for Canada's diverse psychologists.

Yet the lack of a single dominant psychology organization in Canada and competition between organizations within both scientific and professional psychology requires that Canada's psychological societies work together on common projects and form collaborative partnerships in order to succeed and even survive. In fact, several coalitions or partnerships have evolved among Canada's psychological organizations. CPA, CPAP, and CRHSPP have collaborated successfully toward several goals, such as getting exemption from the federal government's Goods and Services Tax for professional psychologists who are listed with CRHSPP, forming a National Professional Psychology Consortium, and reducing mobility restrictions for professional psychologists. Likewise, CPA, CSBBCS, and the Council of Canadian Departments of Psychology (CCDP) have frequently cooperated to promote scientific psychology in Canada. Representing both scientific and professional psychology and having its head office in Canada's capital in Ottawa, Ontario, CPA is uniquely positioned to speak on behalf of Canada's psychologists and to work collaboratively with scientific and professional psychology organizations inside and outside Canada.

Psychology Organizations in Canada

As suggested above, Canada has spawned a diverse array of psychology organizations that can be categorized as academic or scientifically oriented, professional or practitioner oriented, or both scientist and practitioner oriented. National organizations of academic or scientifically oriented psychologists include the Canadian So-

ciety for Brain, Behavioural, and Cognitive Science (CSBBCS) and the Council of Canadian Departments of Psychology (CCDP). The Société Québécoise pour la Recherche en Psychologie (SQRP) represents Francophone psychologists and psychology students in Quebec's universities and elsewhere in Canada.

CSBBCS, known as BBCS within Canada, promotes Canadian research in experimental psychology (e.g., learning, perception, cognition, biological psychology, and neuroscience). Toward this end, it liaises with major granting agencies in order to influence Canadian science policy and funding for scientific psychological research within its domains and promotes scientific research to the public and press. Its annual meetings are often held around the time of CPA's annual convention or in conjunction with other scientific psychology organizations. Established around 1989–1990, CSBBCS included more than 600 members by 1996. Canadian scientists working in a behavioral research setting in Canada or abroad are eligible for CSBBCS membership.

CCDP is a national organization of chairs or heads representing academic psychology departments within chartered Canadian universities. Member departments must also belong to one of four regional organizations (representing the Atlantic provinces, Quebec, Ontario, and the West) to qualify for membership in CCDP. Founded at a chairs' meeting during CPA's 1991 convention, CCDP's inaugural meeting occurred at CPA's 1992 convention. Though independent of CPA and CSBBCS, CCDP usually holds its national meeting at CPA's annual convention site.

Based primarily in Quebec, SQRP is a French-speaking organization that promotes scientific research in all psychology subfields, advocates for psychological research with Quebec's granting agencies and the public, and supports student involvement in scientific research. SQRP had 350 members in 1997, the majority of whom were psychology graduate students. SQRP publishes a French-language journal for scholarly research, the *Revue Québécoise de Psychologie*, and holds annual meetings for research and other presentations.

Practitioner oriented organizations include regulatory bodies and/or collegial organizations of psychologists within each of the 10 provinces and the Northwest Territories. At the national level, provincial organizations for professional psychologists are represented by delegates to the Council of Provincial Associations of Psychologists (CPAP). For further reference see also *Psychology in Canada: Provincial/Territorial Organizations*. CPAP brings the concerns and interests of provincial/territorial organizations of psychologists to one another and to the attention of national organizations for professional psychology, especially CPA and CRHSPP.

In the late 1990s, CPAP has played a leading role, along with CPA and CRHSPP, in ensuring that mobility requirements for professional psychologists across provinces conform to Canada's Agreement on Internal Trade (AIT), a "free trade" agreement signed in 1995 by the federal and provincial governments. Between 1960 and 1991, each Canadian province and the Northwest Territories passed legislation regulating the practice of psychology. Since the acts differ considerably in regard to standards of academic entry requirements, supervised experience, and competency examinations for psychologists, problems and delays in certification sometimes arise for professional psychologists moving from one province to another when requirements differ. AIT's intent is to reduce such obstacles to professional mobility in Canada.

CRHSPP is a nonprofit, national credentialing organization that vets professional psychologists providing health services in Canada so that they may receive payments for their services from third parties, such as insurance companies, employee assistance programs, and quality assurance agencies. As Canada's counterpart to the National Register of Health Service Providers in Psychology in the United States, CRHSPP lists more than 3,000 members in its annual directory, mainly clinical practitioners providing psychotherapy and diagnosis as their main professional activities. Eligibility for CRHSPP membership and directory listing depends upon training, experience, and statutory recognition as a psychologist by an appropriate regulatory body. CRHSPP promotes professional psychology as a health profession in Canada and cooperates with other professional psychology and health profession organizations.

Founded in 1977 by the late Park Davidson, the Canadian Council of Professional Psychology Programmes (CCPPP) is a professionally oriented national organization representing doctoral psychology programs in Canadian universities and internship settings for training clinical psychologists, counseling psychologists, and clinical neuropsychologists. CCPPP included 69 member programs by the mid-1990s. CCPPP fosters communication between university training programs and internship sites, facilitates student placements at internship sites, publishes a Canadian Internship Directory for students and program directors, compiles a registry of faculty who supervise students' clinical research, surveys the annual number of internships and interns placed, and organizes program directors' workshops during CPA's annual conventions. CCPPP supports and encourages accreditation standards for professional psychologists in Canada but is not itself an accrediting body. CCPPP also represents Canadian professional psychology training programs within and outside Canada and cooperates with similar organizations in the United States, such as the Association of Psychology Postdoctoral and Internship Centers (APPIC).

Representing both scientific and professional psychology, since 1989 CPA has consistently had more than four thousand members, who may also belong to one or more of its 23 sections and two interest groups. [*See* Canadian Psychological Association.] CPA lobbies the Canadian federal government's ministries and research agencies on behalf of psychologists (often with consortia of other academic, scientific, health, and professional organizations in Canada), holds annual conventions, liaises with other psychological organizations in and out of Canada, and coordinates periodic conferences concerning professional and/or scientific psychology in Canada.

CPA publishes a quarterly newspaper, *Psynopsis*, and three scholarly refereed journals that publish articles in both English and French concerning professional and/or scientific psychology. *Canadian Psychology*, CPA's official journal, publishes "broad interest" articles concerning both professional and scientific issues and the development of psychology within Canada. The *Canadian Journal of Experimental Psychology* publishes research reports in general experimental psychology dealing with cognition, learning, motivation, and perception in humans and animals. The *Canadian Journal of Behavioural Science* publishes original research contributions in personality, social, cross-cultural, developmental, educational, counseling, community, environmental, and industrial-organizational psychology, as well as applied psychology generally.

Through its accreditation panel, CPA accredits professional psychology training programs in Canada and, in 1998, listed 17 doctoral programs in clinical psychology and 25 predoctoral internship programs (22 in clinical psychology, 2 in counseling psychology, and 1 in clinical neuropsychology). Professional psychology training programs in Canada may also seek accreditation from the American Psychological Association (APA), as well as joint CPA-APA accreditation. As of mid-1997, 14 doctoral programs and 19 internship programs in Canada had joint APA-CPA accreditation, and 2 internship programs had APA accreditation only.

Established in 1985, the Canadian Association of School Psychologists (CASP) is a national organization for school psychologists, both scientist and practitioner oriented, with 175 members in 1998. CASP publishes the *Canadian Journal of School Psychology* and a newsletter, both appearing twice annually. CASP holds an annual national conference in conjunction with an annual meeting of one of the provincial psychological associations.

Research Centers, Institutes, Networks, and Conferences

Most psychological research in Canada is conducted in its universities. Significant research in psychology is conducted at each of the 55 psychology departments (33 with graduate psychology programs) at Canadian universities, though space limitations preclude listing each department and its faculty's achievements. Since at least 1970, however, the University of Toronto's psychology department has been Canada's premier facility for psychological research and is "world class" in stature. Two international comparisons of Canadian, U.S., and British or European university psychology departments in the mid-1970s and early 1990s, respectively, placed the University of Toronto in the top 10 on citation counts (i.e., the frequency its faculty's research publications were cited in other publications), a well-validated index of eminence.

Canada also has important psychological research facilities outside university psychology departments; the following list is illustrative rather than exhaustive. The National Research Council (NRC), with research institutes across Canada, is the federal government's agency for intramural research in science and technology. NRC's Institute for Information Technology investigates computer interactions, virtual reality, neural network models, integrated reasoning, and visual information technology. Psychologists at NRC's Institute for Research in Construction study design and operating requirements of "optimal indoor environments" and building occupants' behavior during emergencies. NRC's Institute for Biodiagnostics conducts psychological research in neuroscience and neuropsychology.

Toronto and Montreal, as Canada's largest and most populous urban centers, have the most psychological research and training facilities, in addition to their universities. Toronto's Baycrest Centre for Geriatric Care established the Rotman Research Institute of Baycrest Centre in 1989. The Rotman Institute explores cognitive and behavioral changes in elderly people, focusing on memory and brain functioning in normal aging and aging-related medical conditions such as Alzheimer's and strokes. It enjoys close collaborative relationships with several University of Toronto faculties and affiliates: the psychology department, the faculty of medicine, and the Clarke Institute of Psychiatry. Endowed university chairs in cognitive neuroscience and neuropsychology, respectively, are associated with the Rotman Institute, which also hosts periodic meetings on current topics with international representation.

Other psychological research centers associated with the University of Toronto are the Clarke Institute of Psychiatry and the Institute for Child Study. Established in 1966, the Clarke Institute combines a research institute, teaching hospital, and leading educational facility for mental health. Due to a health services restructuring in Ontario in the late 1990s, the Clarke was merged with the Addiction Research Foundation and two other facilities to form the Centre for Addiction and Mental Health (CAMH). Established in 1926, the Institute for Child Study, with its multidisciplinary Laidlaw Research Centre, promotes research and professional education in child development.

The Addiction Research Foundation (ARF) and the C. M. Hincks Institute and Treatment Centre are other Toronto facilities for psychological research and treatment. ARF, an Ontario Ministry of Health agency since 1949 and a World Health Organization collaborating center since 1977, is a leading research facility in addictions to tobacco, alcohol, and other substances, combining research with treatment and prevention programs for addictions. The Hincks Institute focuses on children's and adolescents' mental health; its research includes infant development and intervention, adolescent depression, language disorders, and school-based services. The Hincks Treatment Centre offers different types of psychotherapy services to the young and their families.

Montreal also has several important psychological research and training centers, in addition to those in its universities. The Montreal Neurological Institute (MNI), a McGill University affiliate, is devoted to studying the brain and nervous system and renowned for epilepsy treatment and research. Its cognitive neuroscience unit explores how the brain's neural mechanisms process and represent information. Its McConnell Brain Imaging Centre investigates brain structure, physiology, and function using high-technology scanners.

Other Montreal centers for psychological research and practice include the Sir Mortimer B. Davis–Jewish General Hospital, a McGill University teaching hospital with a culture and mental health research unit. The Royal Victoria Hospital, another McGill University teaching hospital, has both a psychology department and a psychiatric wing, the Allan Memorial Institute, with psychological research and practice functions. The Psychosocial Research Unit of the Douglas Hospital Research Centre focuses on epidemiology, the course of severe mental illnesses, evaluation of mental health services, and international studies of community mental health. Research at the Centre de Recherche Philippe Pinel de Montréal focuses on social maladaptation and mental health.

Research networks are geographically dispersed teams focused on a common issue that meet periodically. Two networks that include psychologists are the Canadian Aging Research Network (CARNET), one of Canada's Centres of Excellence networks between 1990 and 1995, and the ongoing network on early childhood of the Canadian Institute for Advanced Research.

Canada has hosted two of the twentieth century's quadrennial International Congresses of Psychology devoted to basic research: the fourteenth in 1954 and the twenty-sixth in 1996. Annual psychology conferences held in Canada include the Banff Annual Symposium in Cognitive Science (BASICS) in Alberta and the Lake Ontario Visionary Establishment (LOVE) in Niagara Falls, Ontario, for psychologists interested in perception and cognition. A biennial developmental psychology conference has been held at the University of Waterloo in Ontario from the mid-1980s to 2000.

Research Granting Agencies

Three granting agencies, funded and administered by the Canadian government, financially support most psychological research and training fellowships in Canada: the Natural Sciences and Engineering Research Council (NSERC), the Social Sciences and Humanities Research Council (SSHRC), and the Medical Research Council (MRC). These agencies each award research grants annually to individuals and teams after rigorous peer review and adjudication by committees of respected scholars in their domains.

By contrast to its counterpart U.S. granting agencies, which have enjoyed annual increases in their budgets during the 1990s, Canadian granting agencies have seen their budgets decreased in the 1990s as Canada's federal government attempted to balance its budget. These decreases resulted in reduced research funding and lower applicant success rates. NSERC, SSHRC, and MRC's budgets were "increased" back to their 1994 levels in early 1998.

Supporting university research and training for Canadian scientists and engineers, NSERC is Canada's largest research granting council, with a 1998 budget of approximately $500 million Canadian for all its disciplines. Psychologists' grant applications for basic research in perception, cognition, biopsychology, cognitive science, and neuroscience are considered by NSERC's Grant Selection Committee (GSC-12, Psychology: Brain and Behavior). For NSERC's 1998 competition, the GSC-12 success rates were 60% for new applicants and 88.4% for renewal applications. SSHRC funds Canadian university-based research and student training in the social sciences and humanities, with a total 1998 budget of nearly $100 million Canadian. SSHRC's Committee 10 (Psychology) reviews research in social, personality, clinical, and developmental psychology and related areas. Its 1998 "success" rate for psychology applicants for standard research grants was approximately 35%. The Medical Research Council funds biomedical and health sciences research in Canada, with a 1998 budget of more than $250 million Canadian, and an overall 1997 success rate of 28% for new and continuing applicants. The committees of the MRC that are most relevant to psychology include the Behavioral Sciences A and B Committees, respectively; the Psychosocial and Behavioral Research Committee; and the Health Services Research Committee.

MRC, NSERC, and SSHRC also recently collaborated in establishing a uniform ethics code concerning human research participation called the Tri-Council Policy Statement, which is to be implemented at newly created Research Ethics Boards (REBs) in Canadian universities, research centers, and institutes beginning in 1999. This policy resulted from consultation rounds among agencies, drafting groups, and Canadian research communities (including psychology organizations).

Funds for psychological research and training are also available from provincial sources—the Ontario Mental Health Foundation and Quebec's Fonds FCAR (Formation de Chercheurs et l'Aide à la Recherche) being the largest—and intramurally within universities, colleges, and research centers.

Major Figures and Achievement: A Sampler of Excellence

Reflecting Canada's considerable achievements in psychology, 33 psychologists were listed in 1998 as Fellows in the Royal Society of Canada, a national society recognizing Canadian excellence in the sciences and humanities. Several Canadian psychologists have become Fellows of London's Royal Society, and some have been awarded the American Psychological Association's prestigious prizes.

Space limitations preclude listing the many outstanding Canadian psychologists and their research achievements, though Adair, Paivio, and Ritchic's (1996) comprehensive review of Canadian psychology provides an excellent overview for the interested reader. Instead, a sampler of Canadian psychology's most important figures and their research contributions at several research oriented universities and institutes are highlighted below.

Montreal's McGill University claims several major figures in psychology, the late Donald Hebb being perhaps the most important. Viewing psychology as a biological science, Hebb made McGill into Canada's first modern research oriented psychology department in the late 1940s. Called the "father of neuropsychology" for proposing neurobiological concepts to understand the rules of behavioral organization in humans and animals, Hebb's "synapse rule" (that repeated neuronal connections are modified and strengthened) remains central in neural network models and neoconnectionism. His view of the mind and brain as being identical anticipated developments in cognitive psychology and neuroscience. Hebb's emphasis on the brain's arousal center contributed to James Olds and Peter Milner's discovery of "reward centers" in the 1950s. Hebb also mentored distinguished Canadian psychologists such as Brenda Milner, whose subsequent research on the neural basis of memory disorders and the effects of brain lesions on cerebral organization, among other things, have made her a major figure in neuropsychology. Both

CPA's and CSBBCS's prestigious prizes in scientific psychology are named after Hebb.

McGill's Ronald Melzack implicated brain processes in the understanding of pain. Melzack and Patrick Wall's gate control theory, proposed in the 1960s and now widely accepted, shows that the brain, the spinal cord, and psychological factors are all relevant to pain and its control. Melzack explains "phantom limb" phenomena (feeling pain in an amputated limb) by postulating a conceptual nervous system in which the brain's neural processes underlie the experience of a unified "body self" and generate perceptual experiences in the absence of external inputs. The University of British Columbia's Kenneth Craig and Dalhousie's Patrick McGrath have also made important contributions to understanding pain.

McGill's Wallace Lambert made the bilingualism and multiculturalism of Canada his research interests and made Canadian psychology a world leader in those areas. His research revealed the cognitive, educational, and social advantages to being or becoming bilingual, and his pioneering "immersion education" system for second-language learning is now widely used throughout Canada, the United States, and Europe. Moreover, Canadian and American ethnic minority members, he found, generally prefer the "multiculturalism" option of maintaining their heritage culture to assimilating into the dominant culture. Canadian research on the social psychology of language has been further advanced by Robert Gardner of the University of Western Ontario and research on multiculturalism by Queen's University's John Berry and others.

Innovative research and theorizing about human memory and cognitive processes, especially by Endel Tulving and Fergus Craik, are the principal foundations for the University of Toronto's international prominence in psychology since the 1960s. Among his many contributions, Tulving has proposed that human memory is organized hierarchically into several systems—procedural memory (for behaviors), semantic memory (for factual knowledge about the world), and episodic memory (for personally experienced events)—along with a separate perceptual representation system interacting with them. PET scan studies by Tulving and his associates reveal different cortical regions for encoding versus retrieving episodic memories.

Craik's eminence stems from research and theorizing concerning "levels of processing" and memory changes with aging, respectively. According to the levels of processing framework proposed by Craik with Robert Lockhart in 1972 and still highly influential, the memory trace is best understood in terms of processing depth, with "deeper" processing (i.e., more cognitive analysis) begetting better memory retention. Craik also showed that memory decrements with aging arise mainly on tasks involving self-initiated processing.

Toronto's York University claims two major figures in psychology: Norman Endler and David Regan. Endler has promoted interactional psychology, a major model of personality and social behavior, and showed that person-situation interactions explain more behavior across many domains than either personality or situational factors separately. Endler also developed multidimensional personality tests for assessing facets of anxiety and coping, respectively.

Regan's eminence in psychology comes from his highly regarded research into human vision and hearing and exceptional technical skills in relating visual and auditory perception to brain activity by techniques such as brain recording and neural modeling. Regan has also applied his perception research to diagnosing medical disorders and understanding the perceptual feats required of airplane pilots and highly trained athletes such as cricket batsmen.

Future Prospects

Canadian psychology resembles U.S. psychology in the tensions between scientific and professional psychology and in the increasing public demands upon psychology in the latter twentieth century. However, funding for both scientific and professional psychology now and in the past has been more austere in Canada than in the United States. The 1990s have witnessed severe cutbacks by both federal and provincial governments in Canada in funding health, education, and scientific research, which in turn have negatively affected both professional and scientific psychology.

Canadian psychology's future prospects unquestionably depend on federal and provincial governments providing stable, and preferably increasing, funding for research, education, and health care. Canadian national conferences for professional and scientific psychology in 1994 and 1997, respectively, have independently emphasized the importance of advocacy for psychology with the Canadian federal and provincial governments and public. Canadian psychologists, like their U.S. counterparts, need to "sell" effectively the worthiness of their discipline, science, and profession in order to prosper into the twenty-first century. In so doing, scientific and professional psychologists in Canada may find common ground. Psychological practice and applications without a sound scientific basis are potentially charlatanism, whereas scientific psychology without any practical implications now or in the future is potentially sterile and unlikely to interest the public, whose tax dollars mostly underwrite psychology in Canada. With adequate funding, the future of psychology in Canada is bright indeed.

[See also Canadian Psychological Association; Regional Psychological Associations; and the biographies of Baldwin, Hebb, and Olds.]

Bibliography

Adair, J. G., Paivio, A., & Ritchie, P. (1996). Psychology in Canada. *Annual Review of Psychology, 47,* 341–370. Comprehensively reviews Canadian contributions to basic and applied psychology and much more.

Conway, J. B. (1984). Clinical psychology training in Canada: Its development, current status, and the prospects for accreditation. *Canadian Psychology, 25,* 177–191. A thoughtful article chronicling the development and status of clinical (and professional) psychology in Canada by the early 1980s.

Conway, J. B. (1992). A world of differences among psychologists. *Canadian Psychology, 33,* 1–24. A presidential address to the Canadian Psychological Association eloquently describing the two separate "cultures" of scientific and professional psychology in Canada and elsewhere.

Dobson, K., & Dobson, D. (Eds.). (1993). *Professional psychology in Canada.* Toronto: Hogrefe & Huber. The single best source describing the development and current status of professional psychology in Canada as of the early 1990s.

Dobson, K. S., & King, M. C. (Eds.). (1995). *The Mississauga conference on professional psychology.* Ottawa, Ontario: Canadian Psychological Association. The final report of the 1994 national conference on professional psychology in Canada.

Fentress, J. C. (1987). D. O. Hebb and the developmental organization of behavior. *Developmental Psychobiology, 20,* 103–109. A fond reminiscence of Donald Hebb and his contributions to psychology.

Gauthier, J. G., & Phillips, A. G. (Eds.). (1998). *National conference on psychology as a science.* Ottawa, Ontario: Canadian Psychological Association. The final report of the 1997 national conference on scientific psychology in Canada.

Hoff, T. L. (1992). Psychology in Canada one hundred years ago: James Mark Baldwin at the University of Toronto. *Canadian Psychology, 33,* 683–694. The full story behind the founding of Canada's first psychology laboratory.

MacLeod, R. B. (1955). *Psychology in Canadian universities and colleges: A report to the Canadian Social Science Research Council.* Ottawa, Ontario: Canadian Social Science Research Council. The famous report that launched Canadian psychology onto a strongly scientific path from 1955 to 1970.

Ritchie, P. L.-J., & Sabourin, M. E. (1992). Sous un même toit: Canada's functional-structural approach to the unity of psychology. *International Journal of Psychology, 27,* 311–325. Describes the internal/external and unifying/diversifying forces operating upon psychology in Canada as of the early 1990s.

Valentine, E. R. (1989). Neural nets: From Hartley to Hebb to Hinton. *Journal of Mathematical Psychology, 33,* 348–357. A short, informative historical survey about neural networks and neural models for the novice.

Wand, B. (1993). The unity of the discipline: A challenge for the profession. *Canadian Psychology, 34,* 124–134. A professional psychologist reviews the tensions between scientific and professional psychology in Canada and identifies factors that could unify them.

Wright, M. J. (1974). CPA: The first ten years. *Canadian Psychologist, 15,* 112–131.

Wright, M. J., & Myers, C. R. (1982). *History of academic psychology in Canada.* Toronto, Ontario, Canada: Hogrefe. Describes Canadian psychology's evolution from philosophy into its own separate academic department in universities offering doctorates in psychology before 1960.

Kenneth L. Dion

CANADIAN PSYCHOLOGICAL ASSOCIATION. The Canadian Psychological Association (CPA) was founded in 1939 by a handful of psychologists whose first goal was to negotiate with the government of Canada for psychological services to be used in the war effort. The first officers were E. A. Bott, president; George Humphrey, secretary; Roy Liddy, treasurer; and J. M. MacEachran, honorary president. A test construction committee was immediately established to develop a general selection test for use by the Canadian army. The first official annual meeting was held in Montreal in 1940, when D. O. Hebb became editor of the first bulletin. Other psychologists prominent during the war years included C. R. Myers, W. Line, K. S. Bernhardt, and W. E. Blatz.

When the psychologists returned from their wartime personnel selection duties to their academic positions, most of the energies of CPA were directed toward establishing two things: a dependable financial base to support research and training and structures to control the quality of psychological services offered to the public. CPA is a national voluntary association with its roots in academic psychology, whereas the regulatory control of the profession is the mandate of provincial or territorial jurisdictions that developed several years after the formation of CPA. It was not until the 1980s that CPA began to balance its scientific interests with attention to concerns of practitioners.

The motto of the Canadian Psychological Association is "Advancing psychology for all." Its mission statement is "to lead, advance and promote psychology as a science and as a profession for the benefit of humanity; to provide leadership in psychology in Canada; to promote a sense of identity among psychologists; to promote the advancement, dissemination, and practical application of psychological knowledge; to develop standards and ethical principles for education, training, science, and practice in psychology." Today the membership of CPA numbers more than 4,000 scientists and practitioners from all 12 provinces and territories in the country, as well as a few psychologists who live outside Canada. CPA and the American Psychological Association (APA) have a reciprocal agreement whereby psychologists who pay full membership fees in the country in which they reside may belong to the other association at one half the usual fee. CPA maintains liaisons with the APA and with the Association of State and Provincial Psychology Boards.

The organization of CPA was restructured in 1989 and again in 1996 in order to enhance its ability to meet the aspirations expressed in its bylaws. The board of directors is elected by the members and consists of three presidential officers, three directors at large, and three section-nominated directors, one for each category of scientist, scientist-practitioner, and practitioner. The term of office is three years. The two dozen sections reflect a dynamic diversity of interests. As a national voluntary association, CPA serves its members well and also provides leadership on issues that affect the work of psychologists who are not members. For example, many scientists are affiliated with other academic and scientific organizations, and it is mandatory for practitioners to be licensed by provincial or territorial jurisdictions. CPA is also a member of the Council of Provincial Associations of Psychologists, which represents the provincial regulatory and voluntary associations. Special interests are represented in the organizational structure of CPA, and affiliations with a wide range of related associations enhance the ability of the Association to represent Canadian psychology in all its diversity.

CPA publications include the *Canadian Journal of Psychology, Canadian Journal of Behavioural Science, Canadian Psychology,* and the official newspaper *Psynopsis,* all of which appear quarterly. Electronic in-house publication is well advanced, with increasing amounts of material available on CPA's home page on the World Wide Web. A national convention is held in June of each year, and awards are presented for distinguished contributions in the fields of science, practice, and education and training, as well as a humanitarian award for an organization that has made a significant contribution to society. CPA has developed a number of guidelines, standards, and position papers; of these, the greatest demand is for the uniquely formatted *Canadian Code of Ethics for Psychologists* (1991) and the *Companion Manual to the Canadian Code of Ethics for Psychologists* (1992).

The Canadian Psychological Association provides assistance to government and other organizations concerned with social and national problems such as education, health, and corrections. CPA has firm liaisons with the national research funding bodies. CPA was instrumental in the development of the Canadian Register of Health Service Providers in Psychology and of the accreditation of doctoral programs and internships in professional psychology. Strong coalitions to lobby the federal government to maintain financial support for research, education, and health are maintained. A government lobby to exclude health service providers in psychology from the new Goods and Services Tax was successful. A major conference or state-of-the-discipline review on the future of Canadian psychology was held in 1984. The future of professional psychology was the topic of the Mississauga Conference on Professional Psychology in 1994. The future of psychology as a science was the topic of a special conference in 1997.

Major concerns involve questions of how to increase the association's capacity to advocate effectively on behalf of both the scientific and professional interests of psychology. The development of nondues income has become important in maintaining a sound financial base. Publications, continuing education, and public education are increasing in importance. There is a constant effort to maintain a high level of collaboration among psychologists who are diverse in geography, language, culture, and special interests. The Canadian Psychological Association is dynamic and diverse in providing national leadership and coordination on issues of common concern to psychologists in all jurisdictions.

[*See also* Canada; *and* Regional Psychological Associations.]

Bibliography

Canadian Psychological Association [On-line]. http://www.cpa.ca. The World Wide Web home page of the CPA.

Dobson, K., & Dobson, D. (Eds.). (1993). *Professional psychology in Canada.* Toronto, Ontario: Hogrefe & Huber.

Myers, C. R. (1972). *Transcript of interviews: Oral history of psychology in Canada* (Vol. 26, File 26–1). Ottawa, Ontario: National Archives of Canada, Manuscript Division.

Wright, M. J. (1974). CPA: The first ten years. *Canadian Psychologist, 15,* 112–131.

Wright, M. J., & Myers, C. R. (Eds.). (1982). *History of academic psychology in Canada.* Toronto, Ontario: Hogrefe.

Jean L. Pettifor

CANCER. The human cost of cancer is staggering. Each year in the United States more than 1.4 million individuals are diagnosed and another half million people—one person every 90 seconds—die of the disease (Parker, Tong, Bolden, & Wingo, 1997). Although much of the increase in cancer incidence and mortality over the years appears related to advances in early detection, as well as to the general aging of the population (age is a risk factor), it has been noted that cancer death rates may now be slightly decreasing (a drop of 1–3%) in the United States.

Cancers vary in their prevalence and mortality. Tables 1 and 2 display data from the United States on the incidence and death rates by specific sites and genders. These data indicate, for example, that the most common diagnosis for women is breast cancer and for men, prostate cancer, but that lung cancer is the number one killer for both. There is, however, variability across countries. For example, age-adjusted death rates per 100,000 people across sites and gender for 1990–1993 ranged from a high of 385 in Hungary to a low of 139 in Albania; the rate for the United States was 276 (Parker et al., 1997). In short, cancer is a significant medical problem that affects the health status of millions of people worldwide.

Research on the psychological, social, and behavioral aspects of oncology began in the early 1950s; however, our knowledge base has significantly expanded during the last 20 years. In particular, research has clarified relationships between psychological responses (e.g., personality, mood, coping style, relationships), social factors (e.g., presence/absence of partner, size of social network, level of social support), and behavioral variables (e.g., compliance with treatment, diet, exercise). Contemporary research incorporates these variables and biological systems (e.g., immune and endocrine) to examine and test their effects on disease course. Of interest to researchers has been the connections between stress and immunity/endocrine function.

A Biobehavioral Model of Cancer Stress and Disease Course

The stability of many cancer mortality rates, particularly those with the highest incidence, such as lung and breast, makes it imperative that new, innovative steps be taken to improve survival and enhance quality of life. We know that psychological interventions result in significant improvements in quality of life (see Andersen, 1992, for a review). Furthermore, summaries of the psychoneuroimmunology (PNI) literature conclude that stress and psychological distress are reliably associated with negative changes in immunity (see Herbert & Cohen, 1993, for a review). Thus addressing the mental health needs of those with cancer has important implications for patient welfare. Figure 1 provides a representation of a model with the psychological and behavioral factors and biological mechanisms by which disease or health outcomes might be influenced.

Stress and Quality of Life. The model first considers the occurrence of stress and lowered quality of life that come with diagnosis and treatment. These are

CANCER. Table 1. 1997 estimates of cancer incidence by site and gender for the five leading sites

Male (Total est. 785,800)		Female (Total est. 506,000)	
Site	Number (%)	Site	Number (%)
Prostate	334,500 (43%)	Breast	180,200 (30%)
Lung	98,300 (13%)	Colon/Rectum	79,800 (13%)
Colon/Rectum	48,100 (8%)	Lung	50,900 (11%)
Bladder	39,500 (5%)	Uterus	34,900 (6%)
Lymphoma	30,300 (4%)	Ovary	26,800 (4%)

The data are from *Cancer Statistics 1997*, American Cancer Society. Copyright 1997 by the American Cancer Society. Adapted with permission.

objective, negative events, and although negative events do not always produce stress and lowered quality of life, data from many studies document severe, acute stress at diagnosis. It is also possible that lengthy cancer treatments and the disruptions the disease causes in family, social, economic, and/or occupational functioning produce chronic stress. For example, sexual problems and/or sterility may affect intimate relationships and social support, and unemployment, underemployment, job discrimination, and difficulty in obtaining health insurance can lower income and standards of living. Therefore, these things can become chronic stressors resulting in a lowered level of quality of life for people with cancer and their families.

Behavioral Factors. An increase in negative health behaviors and/or a decrease in positive ones can occur (see Figure 1). There are many circumstances that can result in negative health behaviors. Individuals who are depressed and/or anxious are more likely to self-medicate with alcohol and other drugs, and, in addition, alcohol abuse can potentiate distress. Distressed individuals often have appetite disturbances or dietary changes that are manifested in eating less often or in eating meals of lower nutritional value. Distressed individuals may report sleep disturbances, such as early-morning awakening, sleep-onset insomnia, and middle-of-the-night insomnia. Cigarette smoking and caffeine use, which often increase during periods of stress, can intensify the physiological effects of psychosocial stress, such as increasing the release of stress hormones. Conversely, individuals who are stressed may not begin or may abandon their previous positive health behaviors, such as engaging in regular physical activity.

The model suggests that health behaviors may, in turn, affect immunity (see Figure 1). Problematic health behaviors can have direct as well as interactive effects on immunity. For example, substance abuse has direct effects on immunity, as well as indirect effects via alterations in nutrition, and poor nutrition is associated with a variety of immunological impairments. Conversely, there is growing evidence that positive health behaviors such as physical activity can have positive consequences for both the immune and endocrine systems, even among individuals with chronic diseases. In summary, these data suggest that distressed individuals tend toward negative health behaviors that may potentiate their stress and concurrently exert negative immune effects. Furthermore, positive health behaviors, such as exercise, may have the converse effect.

The model suggests that health behaviors may be directly related to disease progression (see Figure 1). Considering all the health behaviors noted above, the strongest case can be made for the importance of nutrition and diet in a number of cancers (e.g., breast, gastrointestinal). For example, a variety of data link nutrition and dietary factors to risk for breast cancer recurrence (increased fat intake, obesity at diagnosis, and weight gain during treatment), and lower fiber intake has been related to the occurrence of gastrointestinal cancers.

The second behavioral factor noted in the model is compliance or noncompliance with treatment (see Figure 1). Compliance problems cross a wide range of diseases, therapies, and individual patient characteristics. With cancer, some patients become discouraged and fail to complete treatment. The model presumes that a range of compliance behaviors may be relevant, as different treatments may produce different behavioral difficulties. The model suggests that poor compliance can affect either local or metastatic control of the disease or both, and which route is selected depends on the treatment regimen, as well as on the characteristics of an individual's noncompliance.

The model specifies that the processes governing compliance and health behaviors may interact (see Figure 1) or even be synergistic. That is, those who are compliant with treatment may expect better health outcomes and thus may comply with diet, exercise, sleep, or other behaviors indicative of "good health."

Biological Pathways. Stress sets into motion important biological effects involving the autonomic, endocrine, and immune systems. Stress may be routed to the immune system by the central nervous system (CNS) via activation of the sympathetic nervous system or through neuroendocrine-immune pathways (i.e., the release of hormones; see Figure 1). In the latter case, a variety of hormones that are released under stress have been implicated in immune modulation (e.g., catecholamines, cortisol, prolactin, and growth hormone).

Without any stress pathway (effect) to immunity, there is evidence for the importance of the immune responses in host resistance against cancer progression; thus the arrows in Figure 1 go in both directions, from immunity to local and metastatic disease. Experts in the

CANCER. Table 2. 1997 estimates of cancer mortality by site and gender for the five leading sites

Male (Total est. 294,100)		Female (Total est. 265,900)	
Site	Number (%)	Site	Number (%)
Lung	94,400 (32%)	Lung	66,000 (25%)
Prostate	41,800 (14%)	Breast	43,900 (17%)
Colon/Rectum	27,000 (9%)	Colon/Rectum	27,900 (10)
Pancreas	13,500 (5%)	Pancreas	14,600 (5%)
Lymphoma	12,400 (4%)	Ovary	14,200 (5%)

The data are from *Cancer Statistics 1997*, American Cancer Society. Copyright 1997 by the American Cancer Society. Adapted with permission.

immunology/cancer area cite the following important findings with regard to the specific importance of natural killer (NK) cell activity: patients with a variety of solid malignancies and large tumor burdens have diminished NK cell activity in the blood; low NK cell activity in cancer patients is significantly associated with the development of distant metastases; and in patients treated for metastatic disease, the survival time without metastasis correlates with NK cell activity.

In considering these mechanisms, a central issue is whether an immune response can be affected by stress, and if it can, whether or not the magnitude of the effect has any biological significance. Both time-limited (acute) and chronic stressors can produce immunological changes in relatively healthy individuals. Some of the largest effects, usually found in NK cell assays, occur with lengthy stressors and/or ones that have interpersonal components. Many of the qualities of chronic stressors (continued emotional distress, disrupted life tasks such as employment, and social relationships) are associated with decrements in quality of life reported by cancer patients. The relationship between stress and immunity has been tested by Andersen and her colleagues (Andersen et al., 1998). They have found that the physiological effects of stress inhibit a number of cellular immune responses, including cancer-relevant NK cell cytotoxicity and T cell responses in newly diagnosed breast cancer patients.

Disease Course. Are there adverse health (illness) consequences of stress? There are few data on this important issue, and the majority come from healthy (but stressed) adults. It has been found that rates of both respiratory infection and clinical colds increase in a dose-response manner with increases in psychological stress across at least five different strains of cold viruses and that caregivers of Alzheimer's patients showed slower healing of arm wounds than noncaregivers. These relationships remain to be studied with cancer patients, but these experimental data from stressed but

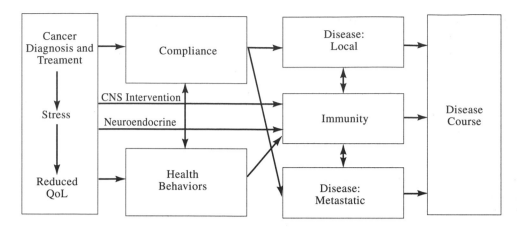

CANCER. Figure 1. A biobehavioral model of the psychological (stress and quality of life), behavioral (compliance and health behaviors), and biologic pathways from cancer stressors to disease course. CNS = central nervous system. (From Andersen, Kiecolt-Glaser, & Glaser (1994), copyright 1994 by the American Psychological Association.)

otherwise healthy samples suggest the covariation of stress and selected health outcomes.

Specific Psychological, Social, and Behavioral Responses: From Symptoms to Disease Outcomes

In view of the magnitude of the cancer problem and the potential for life threat, it is puzzling that some individuals delay in seeking medical treatment for symptoms; yet delay is a surprisingly common circumstance (see Andersen, Cacioppo, & Roberts, 1995, for a model of delay). First, the development of malignancy and the appearance of cancer symptoms are oftentimes protracted, and a complex and changing symptom picture can be typical, unlike the presentation of many other serious medical problems (e.g., myocardial infarction). Symptoms can also vary with the site and extent of the disease. For example, ovarian cancer has varied presentations—pelvic cramping, low back pain, pain or bleeding with intercourse, and urinary frequency irregularities, among others. Moreover, as the disease progresses regionally or systemically, it can involve other bodily systems, and the symptom picture can then change from specific or localized complaints (e.g., vaginal discharge/bleeding) to diffuse ones (e.g., loss of appetite, nausea, "flu" symptoms). Finally, although cancer is a life-threatening disease, it is a low-probability one for many individuals. Thus delay may lengthen as people think it unlikely that their symptoms would indicate a condition as serious as cancer.

Diagnosis. Specific emotions—sadness (depression), fear (anxiety), and confusion—can characterize the diagnostic period. It is not surprising that depressive symptoms are the most common affective problem. Al-

though it has been estimated that approximately 50% of cancer patients meet the American Psychiatric Association's criteria for a formal psychiatric disorder, the clear majority of these diagnoses represent adjustment disorders (i.e., emotional and/or behavioral problems) related to a known transient stressor—cancer (see Tope, Ahles, & Silberfarb, 1993, for a review). Specific clinical diagnoses for depression and anxiety are 13% and 4%, respectively.

It should be emphasized that the clinical problem of diagnostic and treatment-related distress can be alleviated through psychological interventions (see Andersen, 1992, and Spiegel, 1996, for reviews). A comprehensive example of such an effort is the study of Fawzy and colleagues (1990a, b). They reduced distress, improved coping, and enhanced immune functioning in newly diagnosed melanoma patients via a structured group support intervention that included health education, illness-related problem solving, relaxation training, and group support. Six weekly sessions of group treatment were provided. Improvements such as these in mood and coping are all the more impressive because they are often achieved with brief, cost-effective interventions (e.g., 10 hours of therapy with delivery in a group format).

Treatment. A certain component of the emotional distress that occurs at diagnosis is due to the anticipation of treatment. Cancer therapies include surgery, radiotherapy/radiation, chemotherapy, and/or hormonal therapy (e.g., tamoxifen). Bone marrow transplant, one of the most rigorous of treatments, once reserved for metastatic disease, is now being used in combination as a primary therapy not only for hematological malignancies but for solid tumors (e.g., breast and ovary) as well. Regardless of the protocol, however, all treatments are preceded or followed by physical examinations, tumor surveys, and/or laboratory studies. Thus, after an often long diagnostic period, the receipt of treatment is filled with further multiple medical stressors.

The data are consistent in their portrayal of more distress (particularly fear and anxiety), slower rates of emotional recovery, and, perhaps, higher rates of other behavioral difficulties (e.g., food aversions, continued fatigue and malaise) in cancer patients in comparison with individuals undergoing non-cancer-related medical treatment. Nonetheless, the emotional crisis that characterizes the diagnostic period lessens as time passes, and studies find that as treatments end and recovery begins there is an emotional rebound.

Psychological and behavioral efforts to reduce patients' treatment anxiety have been incorporated into routine care. Such efforts include procedural information (e.g., how the surgery or radiotherapy is done), sensory information on the actual physical sensations of the surgery or preparatory events, behavioral coping instructions, cognitive coping interventions, relaxation, hypnosis, and emotion-focused interventions. These interventions produce many benefits—such as decreases in ratings of negative affect and pain, in amount of pain medication, in length of hospital stay, in behavioral recovery, and in physiological indices.

Although there are many disease-related and treatment-related complications, efforts have focused on three specific ones. First, a primary side effect of cancer treatment is fatigue, which is the most commonly reported symptom of people having been diagnosed with and treated for cancer. Fatigue and associated symptoms—feeling tired, lacking energy, sleepy, confused—have been related to other cancer morbidities (e.g., decreased quality of life) and poor treatment compliance (e.g., stopping treatments). Psychological and behavioral interventions for fatigue have focused on alleviating or increasing tolerance to fatigue through preparatory information on side effects and activity/rest cycle recommendations (such as naps), increasing tolerance to fatigue through exercise, coping efforts (such as planning and scheduling activities, decreasing nonessential activities, relying on others for assistance as needed), and interventions aimed at improving and maintaining nutritional status.

Second, appetite and weight changes, either loss or gain, can represent different problems for patients based on their diagnoses and treatments. Appetite and weight loss are significant clinical problems for those cancer patients who are susceptible to tumor-induced metabolism or taste changes, who have tumor-related obstructions (often diagnosed as primary cachexia/anorexia), or who are receiving gastrointestinal-toxic chemotherapy or abdominal radiotherapy (secondary cachexia/anorexia). Importantly, malnutrition is associated with increased morbidity and mortality. Food aversions learned in connection with chemotherapy may affect up to 50% of these patients. Although food aversions may not involve appetite or weight loss per se, patients may unknowingly develop aversions to their favorite foods, and this can, in turn, affect their daily routine and perceived quality of life. Researchers have begun to investigate morbidity and mortality related to weight gain in breast cancer patients. It is clear that treatment-related weight gain, especially for those women receiving chemotherapy or hormone therapy, is subjectively distressing to many breast cancer patients and may result in decreased quality of life and poorer self-esteem. Furthermore, it has been suggested that weight gain during therapy for breast cancer may be associated with increased recurrence and decreased survival.

Third, compliance with treatment remains important, as the expectation and/or experience of unpleasant side effects such as those described here can diminish a patient's quality of life. Furthermore, such side effects can at times be so discouraging or annoying that a patient may be reluctant to continue treatment or may even want to terminate treatment prematurely. Noncompliance with treatment has been related to increased emotional distress, increased hostility and guilt, and severity of treatment side effects (e.g., nausea and vomiting). Even when patients are responsible for self-administration of therapy, such as taking their chemotherapy at home in order to reduce the number of hospital visits, their noncompliance may continue. In short, noncompliance is a behavioral problem that can have direct impact on the effectiveness of cancer therapy.

Psychological interventions to improve patient compliance have focused on a variety of techniques, including appointment reminders, clearly written and specific treatment communications, home visits, and medication-taking shaping interventions. In addition, hospital-based interventions, such as offering a tour of the oncology clinic, videotape presentations about the therapy, discussion and question sessions, and take-home information, have been employed as well. Preparatory information can improve patients' ability to cope with treatment.

Recovery and Long-Term Survival. The most important cancer endpoints have been treatment response rates, length of disease-free interval, and survival. There has been increased attention to quality of life for long-term survivors of cancer. The term *survivor* frequently refers to individuals surviving at least 5 years, as the probability of late recurrence declines significantly after that time for most sites. Research data indicate that if the disease is controlled, by 1 year after treatment the severe distress of diagnosis will have dissipated, and emotions will have stabilized. Thus we note that global adjustment problems do not occur for the majority of individuals diagnosed with cancer; a more likely scenario is the occurrence of specific problem areas. An exception to this positive trajectory may be the circumstances of bone marrow transplant (BMT) survivors, who experience, in general, a somewhat slower recovery due to the many difficult aspects of BMT (e.g., intensive chemotherapy, possible whole-body radiation, long recovery time, hospital isolation).

Lingering emotional distress from the "trauma" of a cancer diagnosis, treatment, and, more generally, life threat is similar to the distress experienced by individuals who have experienced other traumatic events (for example, natural disasters or physical assault). In fact, the residual distress from the diagnosis and treatment of a life-threatening illness or disorder (such as cardiac arrest, burns, or cancer) is now included as one of the circumstances that may precipitate posttraumatic stress disorder (PTSD), a disorder characterized by intrusive thoughts, avoidant behavior, and hyperarousal surrounding the traumatic event (American Psychiatric Association, *Diagnostic and Statistical Manual of Mental Disorders*, 1994). However, it is highly unlikely that such a diagnosis would be made for the "average" cancer patient. Risk factors for cancer-related PTSD may include undergoing the most difficult of treatment regimens (e.g., BMT), having treatments with life-altering and/or disfiguring effects (e.g., limb amputations, pelvic exenteration, laryngectomies), having a history of anxiety disorder and/or being exposed to previous traumatic events, and reporting a lower quality of life.

Some cancer survivors may need to cope with the expected but nevertheless troubling sequelae that may be consequences of the disease or treatment and may be permanent. For example, coping with altered cognitive and physical abilities (e.g., changes in memory and attention due to chemotherapy or radiation or loss of natural speech following laryngectomy) and/or changes in organ functions (e.g., infertility) may require adjustment that demands new behaviors or emotions. Others may have to cope with losses (such as adjusting to a sexual relationship that does not include intercourse). Finally, late side effects of cancer treatment—for example, a bowel dysfunction that is traced to pelvic radiotherapy—can occur and change health status, as well as affect mood and coping.

One life area that undergoes disruption for many cancer survivors is sexuality. All cancer patients with solid tumors (approximately 85% of adult patients) and many treated for hemotological malignancies are vulnerable to sexual dysfunction. Across sites, estimates range from 10% (for breast cancer patients treated with lumpectomy) to 70 to 90% (for women with vulva cancer treated with modified radical vulvectomy) to 100%

(for men with prostate cancer treated with radical prostatectomy), with the distribution skewed toward greater levels of disruption. Among the hematological malignancies, estimates are in the range of 20% (Andersen & Lamb, 1995). Although it is clear that the sexual problems are psychologically distressing, disease and treatment sequelae are the primary reasons for the sexual problems (e.g., nerve dissection occurring during some prostatectomies, vaginal discharge and bleeding, irregular menses related to long-term adjuvant tamoxifen therapy for breast cancer). Despite the emotional distress and, for some, the accompanying sexual disruption that couples experience, the majority of marriages remain intact and satisfactory.

Still, families are not immune to the cancer experience (see Baider, Cooper, & Kaplan De-Nour, 1996, for a review), and the kin's distress may approach that of the patient. Family strain appears to be affected by illness variables (e.g., prognosis, stage and duration of illness, caregiving demands, patient's distress), family variables (e.g., age and gender of family members, socioeconomic status, other family stressors), and relational variables (e.g., quality of marriage, marital communication, family stage, and social support; see Sales, Schulz, & Biegel, 1992, for a review). When the wife has cancer and young children are still in the home, couples may be at heightened risk for relationship difficulties.

Recurrence and Death. Cancer recurrence is devastating; the magnitude of distress is even greater than that found with the initial diagnosis. In fact, cancer recurrence has been conceptualized as a "traumatic event" with the potential to induce stress-response symptoms such as intrusive thoughts, behavior aimed at avoiding cancer-related stimuli, and hyperarousal. Patients recently told of their cancer recurrence have reported being less hopeful and more discouraged and having increased thoughts of death and dying, as well as feelings of guilt and regret about their previous treatment decisions.

There are two frequent complications of advanced disease: delirium and pain. Delirium is the second most commonly diagnosed psychiatric disorder in cancer patients and is characterized by acute perceptual and behavioral disturbances, such as impairment of attention, orientation, and memory. Approximately 75% of patients with metastatic cancer meet criteria for delirium as compared with 8% of all cancer patients. Delirium in cancer patients can be caused by a number of factors, including treatment side effects (e.g, type and dosage of chemotherapy), medications (e.g., narcotics), disease progression (e.g, brain metastases), and other treatment- or disease-related complications (e.g, metabolic and endocrine disorders; Tope et al., 1996). Although delirium is a reversible brain disorder, it is often misunderstood and underdiagnosed by medical personnel, with symptoms often being attributed to depression and anxiety.

Although it might be one of the first symptoms of cancer or might be present when disease is localized, pain is more common and less controllable for those with metastatic disease. Eighty percent of patients with recurrent cancer report moderate to severe pain, as compared with 40% of patients in earlier stages (see Ashburn & Lipman, 1993, for a review). The major cause of cancer pain, accounting for roughly 70% of the cases, is due to direct tumor involvement (such as nearby metastatic bone disease or nerve compression), and the remainder is usually due to medical therapy (such as postoperative pain or radiation-induced pain). Thus the pain experienced by cancer patients can be any combination of acute malignant pain, chronic malignant pain, and/or chronic nonmalignant pain.

With this variable presentation, it is important that a pain assessment be completed before and during treatment for pain control (Ashburn & Lipman, 1993). Besides medical considerations, other factors are also important in assessing the patient's experience of pain. For instance, pain is associated with depression, anxiety, and delirium. If pain worsens or is difficult to control, quality of life deteriorates, and emotional distress increases; physical mobility may decline, and social interactions may suffer. It is striking that inadequately controlled pain has been cited as a primary reason for requests of physician-assisted suicide among cancer patients (Foley, 1995). The most difficult circumstance of pain control occurs when chronic pain accompanies disease progression. Treatment combinations of antitumor therapy, anesthetic blocks, and behavioral approaches are considered. When palliative therapy is of little use and/or brings further debilitation, psychological interventions may provide support and pain control and, secondarily, may treat pain sequelae (e.g., sleep disturbances, reduced appetite, irritability).

Psychological interventions offered to terminal patients appear to have the effect of enhancing their quality of life. Spiegel and colleagues (Spiegel & Bloom, 1983; Spiegel, Bloom, & Yalom, 1981), for example, studied a group support intervention that included discussion of death and dying, family problems, communication problems with physicians, living fully with terminal breast cancer, and using hypnosis. Women reported significantly fewer phobic responses and lower anxiety, fatigue, and confusion than women not in a support group. Furthermore, women receiving hypnosis reported no change in their pain sensations during the year, whereas pain sensations significantly increased for those women who did not receive hypnosis. The most startling data from this project were reported in a survival analysis, which found that intervention partici-

pants lived an average of 18 months longer than non-intervention participants (Spiegel, Bloom, Kraemer, & Gottheil, 1989).

Conclusions

Significant progress has been made in understanding the psychological, social, and behavioral aspects of cancer. More is known about the psychological processes in and reactions to the diagnosis and treatment of cancer than is known about any other chronic illness. Breast cancer patients (see Glanz & Lerman, 1992, for a review) have been well studied, but the study of other disease sites, of men, and of children is becoming more common. Research data can be used for models that predict which patients might be at greatest risk for adjustment difficulties and lowered quality of life (see Andersen, 1994, for a discussion). The above is an important step toward designing interventions tailored to the difficulties and circumstances of cancer patients. The mental health community emphasizes the need to reduce stress and prevent deterioration in quality of life for those with cancer. The importance of such efforts is underscored by three contextual factors. First, the stability of many cancer mortality rates, particularly those with the highest incidence, such as lung and breast, makes it imperative that new, innovative treatments be developed to improve survival rates. Second, research has demonstrated that psychological interventions result in significant improvements in quality of life (Andersen, 1992). Third, summaries of the psycho-neuroimmunology literature conclude that psychological distress and stressors (e.g., negative life events, both acute and chronic) are reliably associated with negative changes in immunity. Thus addressing the mental health needs of those with cancer will have important quality of life benefits, and the possibility of positive biological or health consequences is raised as well. Finally, the biobehavioral model offered here provides a theoretical framework for examining questions of the interaction of psychological, behavioral, and biological variables and the course of disease.

Bibliography

American Psychiatric Association. (1994). *Diagnostic and statistical manual of mental disorders* (4th ed.). Washington, DC: Author.

Andersen, B. L. (1992). Psychological interventions for cancer patients to enhance the quality of life. *Journal of Consulting and Clinical Psychology, 60*, 552–568.

Andersen, B. L. (1994). Surviving cancer. *Cancer, 74*, 1484–1495.

Andersen, B. L., Cacioppo, J. T., & Roberts, D. C. (1995). Delay in seeking a cancer diagnosis: Delay stages and psychophysiological comparison processes. *British Journal of Social Psychology, 34,* 33–52.

Andersen, B. L., Farrar, W. B., Golden-Kreutz, D., Kutz, L. A., MacCallum, R., Courtney, M. E., & Glaser, R. (1998). Stress and immune response following surgical treatment for regional breast cancer. *Journal of the National Cancer Institute, 90,* 30–36.

Andersen, B. L., Kiecolt-Glaser, J. K., & Glaser, R. (1994). A biobehavioral model of cancer stress and disease course. *American Psychologist, 49,* 389–404.

Andersen, B. L., & Lamb, M. A. (1995). Sexuality and cancer. In A. I. Holleb, D. Fink, & G. P. Murphy (Eds.), *American Cancer Society textbook of clinical oncology* (2nd ed., pp. 699–713). Atlanta, GA: American Cancer Society.

Ashburn, M. A., & Lipman, A. G. (1993). Management of pain in the cancer patient. *Anesthesia Analog, 76,* 402–416.

Baider, L., Cooper, C., & Kaplan De-Nour, A. (1996). *Cancer and the family.* UK: Wiley.

Fawzy, F. I., Cousins, N., Fawzy, N., Kemeny, M. E., Elashoff, R., & Morton, D. (1990a). A structured psychiatric intervention for cancer patients: I. Changes over time in methods of coping and affective disturbance. *Archives of General Psychiatry, 47,* 720–725.

Foley, K. M. (1995). The relationship of pain and symptoms management to patient requests for physician-assisted suicide. *Journal of Pain and Symptom Management, 6,* 289–297.

Glanz, K., & Lerman, C. (1992). Psychosocial impact of breast cancer: A critical review. *Annals of Behavioral Medicine, 14,* 204–212.

Herbert, T. B., & Cohen, S. (1993). Depression and immunity: A meta-analytic review. *Psychological Bulletin, 113,* 472–486.

Parker, S., Tong, T., Bolden, S., & Wingo, P. (1997). Cancer Statistics, 1997. *CA: A Cancer Journal for Clinicians, 47,* 5–27.

Sales, E., Schulz, R., & Biegel, D. (1992). Predictors of strain in families of cancer patients: A review of the literature. *Journal of Psychosocial Oncology, 10,* 1–26.

Spiegel, D. (1996). Cancer and depression. *British Journal of Psychiatry, 168,* 109–116.

Spiegel, D., & Bloom, J. R. (1983). Group therapy and hypnosis reduce metastatic breast carcinoma pain. *Psychosomatic Medicine, 45,* 333–339.

Spiegel, D., Bloom, J. R., Kraemer, H. C., & Gottheil, E. (1989). Effect of psychosocial treatment on survival of patients with metastatic breast cancer. *Lancet, 2,* 888–891.

Spiegel, D., Bloom, J. R., & Yalom, I. (1981). Group support for patients with metastatic cancer: A randomized outcome study. *Archives of General Psychiatry, 38,* 527–533.

Tope, D. A., Ahles, T. A., & Silberfarb, P. M. (1993). Psycho-oncology: Psychological well-being as one component of quality of life. *Psychotherapy and Psychosomatics, 60,* 129–147.

Barbara L. Andersen, Deanna M. Golden-Kreutz, and Vicki DiLillo

CANNON, WALTER BRADFORD (1871–1945), physician and research physiologist, born on 19 October 1871, in Prairie du Chien, Wisconsin, and attended St. Paul High School in Minnesota before entering Harvard College in 1892. He received the A.B. summa cum laude in 1896, an A.M. in 1897, and an M.D. from Harvard Medical School in 1900. He then rose from instructor in physiology to become the George Higgenson Professor of Physiology at Harvard Medical School in 1906, a position which he held with distinction until his retirement in 1942. In 1901, he married Cornelia James, and from this union produced one son and four daughters.

Cannon's entire career was marked by a succession of spectacular achievements. During his first year as a student at Harvard Medical School, using primitive apparatus and Roentgen's discovery that the salts of heavy metals are opaque to the newly discovered X ray, Cannon fed bismuth subnitrate to animals and was the first to study gastric motility without anesthesia or surgery. He summarized years of work on this subject in *The Mechanical Factors in Digestion* (1911). In his senior year as a medical student, 1900, he borrowed an idea from his roommate, a law student, and proposed the case teaching method in medicine. This was immediately taken up in the medical school departments of surgery, obstetrics, neurology, and gynecology, and led to the development of the clinical case conferences at the Massachusetts General Hospital, which were still a regular feature in the *New England Journal of Medicine*. During his early years as the Higgenson professor, Cannon studied the effects of intense emotional states on the body, which led him to the experimental identification of adrenaline and noradrenaline and articulation of the fight/flight reflex. He summarized this work in *Bodily Change in Pain, Hunger, Fear, and Rage* (1915).

During World War I, Cannon was chairman of the National Research Council's committee on physiology and served overseas with the Harvard Hospital Unit (1917–1919). He worked as a physiologist at the central laboratory for the U.S. Army Base Hospital no. 5. He was detached for service with the British army and then discharged as a lieutenant colonel. During this period he made major contributions to the understanding of wound shock.

Cannon' early study of the effects of the emotional disturbances of cats under X-ray examination of intestinal movements led to a large body of research on the emergency function of sympathetic-adrenal mechanisms. In the 1920s, this led him to the search for chemical mediators in the transmission of the electrical impulse across the synapse, presaging major developments now taking place in the neurosciences. He also became involved with the sociology of Vilfredo Pareto, and, taking the larger philosophical view in physiology, first articulated the concept of homeostasis in another pioneering work, *The Wisdom of the Body* (1934). During this later period, perhaps his most well-known work was his study of voodoo death, with Walter Alvarez.

Numerous accolades were heaped upon Cannon. As a major figure in American medicine, he was president of the American Physiological Society (1913–1916), a member of the National Academy of Sciences, acting dean of Harvard Medical School (1926–1927), member of the Permanent Committee for the International Congresses of Physiology (1935–1938), and became one of the first foreign members of the Russian Academy of Science (1942). He also held honorary doctorates from Yale University, Wittenberg College, Boston University, and the universities of Liege, Strasbourg, Paris, and Harvard.

Regarding Cannon's intellectual lineage, his first and foremost influence as an undergraduate was William James. Other classmates who also shared James's attention included Boris Sidis, Gertrude Stein, William Healy, Robert Woodworth, Mary Calkins, and W. E. B. DuBois. Immediately after publication of James's monumental *Principles of Psychology*, one of Cannon's major assignments for James was to summarize the James-Lange theory of the emotions and collect the various critiques of it throughout the psychological literature in preparation for James's formal response, which appeared in 1894. At one point Cannon had contemplated a career in philosophy, but James warned him away from it. While Cannon later described himself as the grandson of Ludwig and the son of Bowditch, two of the greatest names in turn-of-the-century experimental physiology, there can be little doubt of the Jamesean influence on Cannon's choice of subject matter in the basic sciences. In addition, Harvard Medical School student notebooks still extant from 1902, and various anecdotes still circulated among the older faculty at the medical school whom he taught much later, reveal that Cannon occasionally even lectured on hypnosis and suggestibility from a Jamesean point of view and was himself an adept at the techniques of subconscious suggestion.

A resident of Cambridge his entire professional life, Cannon and his wife were neighbors and close friends with the Jameses and the Royces, as well as Ralph Barton and Rachel Perry, Ernest and Mabel Southard, Edwin B. Holt, Hugo Münsterberg, Richard and Ella Cabot, and Robert and Ada Yerkes. With Cannon, many of these male friends were also members of the Wicht Club, an informal gathering enamored with the German intellectual tradition. This group overlapped considerably with the Royce circle, a knot of devotees around Josiah Royce that included Richard Cabot, L. J. Henderson, Cannon, and others destined to become major power brokers in medicine, science, and politics at Harvard in the 1920s.

Cannon's impact on psychology, while broad and deep, was overshadowed by the behaviorists' emphasis in the 1930s on the so-called black-box theory—that as long as the causal relation between stimulus and response could be measured, psychologists had no need for the physiological explanations of behavior. His influence is therefore more obvious in subfields such as physiological psychology, although every introductory psychology textbook still discusses the Cannon-Bard theory of the emotions.

Nevertheless, Cannon was directly associated with psychology in several ways. Along with his membership in various professional societies, he was also a member of the American Psychological Association. Also, there can be no doubt that he established a thorough and rigorous standard for exacting laboratory research in physiology, which influenced comparative animal psychologists such as Robert Yerkes and protobehaviorists such as E. B. Holt. In addition, by identifying the neurohumoral correlates of the fight/flight reflex and the hypothalamus as the emotional center in the brain, he articulated a neurophysiological theory of emotions that remains the current standard in the biological sciences, one that not only has withstood the physiological nihilism of the behaviorists but is again attracting the attention of psychologists as the neuroscience revolution continues to medicalize psychology. Through his teacher Henry Pickering Bowditch, and beginning with his publications in 1898, Cannon also drew the attention of an entire generation of younger psychologists to the earliest work of Pavlov on conditioned reflexes. Finally, Cannon remains one of the great pioneers in psychosomatic medicine, psychophysiology, and behavioral medicine. And, according to cardiologist Herbert Benson, (1975), whose original studies were conducted in Cannon's laboratory under the late Clifford Barger, Cannon's work was a primary influence in the development of the relaxation response.

In 1945, Cannon published an autobiographical account of his life's research, entitled *The Way of an Investigator*. He died that same year, on 1 October, in Franklin, New Hampshire.

Bibliography

Benison, S., Barger, & Wolfe, E. (1987). *Walter B. Cannon: The life and times of a young scientist*. Cambridge, MA: Belknap Press of Harvard University Press.

Benson, H. (1975). *The relaxation response*. New York: Morrow.

Brooks, C. M., Koizumi, K., & Pinkston, J. O. (Eds.). (1975). *The life and contributions of Walter Bradford Cannon, 1871–1945: His influence on the development of physiology in the twentieth century*. Papers delivered at a centennial symposium held at the State University of New York

Downstate Medical Center, 25–26 May 1972. Albany, NY: State University of New York Press.

Cannon, W. B. (1911). *The mechanical factors in digestion.* New York: Longmans, Green.

Cannon, W. B. (1915). *Bodily change in pain, hunger, fear, and rage.* New York: Appleton.

Cannon, W. B. (1923). *Traumatic shock.* New York: Appleton.

Cannon, W. B. (1932). *The wisdom of the body.* New York: Norton.

Cannon, W. B. (1945). *The way of an investigator.* New York: Norton.

Cannon, W. B., & Rosenblueth, A. (1937). *Autonomic neuro-effector systems.* New York: Macmillan.

Eugene Taylor

CAREER. [*This entry comprises four articles. The first three articles provide discussions on the role of psychology and psychologists in assisting one's career choice, career development, and career assessment. The fourth article reviews the interventions that psychologists have developed to address problems in one's career. For related discussions, see also* Career Counseling; *and* Careers in Psychology.]

Career Choice

Most individuals have an interest in or affinity toward certain career fields or occupations. Such aspirations and preferences are formed early in life and are a product of genetics, socioeconomic status, gender, personality, and learning history. These early hopes and dreams are modified (positively and/or negatively) by forces in society that act upon individuals and groups of individuals as they make career-related decisions (e.g., labor market constraints, competitive admission to schools and programs, opportunities provided by special programs, etc.). Career choices result when individual aspirations and preferences are reexamined in light of the constraining forces imposed by the social environment in which that individual lives. It is possible to differentiate several levels of career choice based upon the degree to which that choice has been subjected to the limitations of societal constraints. An individual may begin with a *preference* for a career—for example, medicine—that does not imply the weathering of any particular stress constraint, or crisis. A *choice* implies the completion of some actions or successful steps, and the *attainment* of a career is the final outcome of the career choice process. The distinction among these three constructs—preference, choice, and attainment—is important to a comprehensive understanding of career choice. Although there is some evidence that young women may anticipate societal constraints and adjust their preferences in advance, societal constraints have little effect on career preferences but exert increasing influence as the individual moves further along in the selection process. Thus career choices and career attainments are affected substantially by the limits and pressures of a limited labor market, as well as by other barriers and constraints that society imposes.

Research suggests that early occupational aspirations are similar across widely divergent social groups (Mexican, African American, White; cf. Arbona & Novy. 1991). Even though early career aspirations are similar, the resources and opportunities needed to implement such early choices are distributed very unevenly across these same social groups. Considerable evidence now confirms that some social groups, when faced with barriers, will have lower aspirations than others (Phillips & Imhoff, 1997). Minority group members, for example, face more pervasive social constraints than their nonminority counterparts, and women face more constraints than do men.

Before moving to theories and models of career choice, the reader should understand that the term "career" generally implies more than a single instance of selection. Careers involve a series of choices or sets of preferences, choices, and attainments with the goal of increasing level of responsibility or learning with each successive job position. Thus careers develop, change, and cumulate over time. Careers promote identity development, interpersonal development, and personal meaning, as well as financial compensation.

Two opposing theoretical models have dominated thinking about career choice, beginning with the publication of "Choosing an Occupation" (Boston, 1909) by Frank Parsons, a Boston social reformer. These two models, the search model and the compromise or developmental model, account for the majority of research, theory, and intervention in the career choice process.

Search Models

This model, earlier termed the *trait-factor view*, maintains that individuals search for a career option in which the working environment is a reasonable fit with their personal qualities—interests, skills, personality, and so forth. Modern trait-factor theorists have described dynamic systems of person-environment fit—principal among them is John Lewis Holland (1997). Holland describes six relatively stable personality dispositions (realistic, investigative, artistic, social, enterprising, conventional) that develop early in life and direct the individual's search for a career that will enhance that disposition. Occupational environments are classified using the same six types (realistic, investigative, artistic, social, enterprising, conventional). Individuals are then rated as congruent or incongruent based upon the similarity between their personality type and the type of environment in which they work. Incongruent individuals are more inclined to report job dissatisfaction and/or to change jobs more often (eventually to a more congruent option). Career choice according to the search model, then, is a relatively straightforward process in which the individual attempts to implement a career that is a reasonable fit with his or her interests and personal qualities in the face of societal constraints. Research support for the search model is found in a large body of literature that demonstrates the stability of occupational interests over time (Swanson, in press) and the correlates of person-environment fit.

It now appears that a few common human traits or dispositions may underlie personality, intelligence, and interest measures (Ackerman & Heggestad, 1997). Stated another way, there is considerable overlap among measures of personality, interests, and even ability in the same individual. The search model has received new support from studies that find that the genetic component of occupational interests may be as large as 50% (Betsworth et al., 1994) and that career choice, although it certainly has a developmental component, may be partially "hard-wired" early in life. Less change in the individual is presumed in search models than is implied in compromise or developmental models, but a modern person-environment fit theory is a complex and appropriate way of thinking about career choice that does involve a dynamic interaction between individuals and their occupational environments.

Compromise Models

Compromise models of career choice reason that individuals change and adapt over time by integrating career interactions into a developing self or ego identity. This identity cumulates over time. According to the developmental or compromise view, individuals evolve predictably over time through a series of identifiable stages or phases that eventually cumulate and culminate into a career. The principal proponents of this compromise view (Gottfredson, 1981; Super, 1957; Vondracek, Lerner, & Schulenberg, 1986) argue that the portion of individual career aspirations that changes over time is as crucial as (sometimes more crucial than) the portion that remains stable. Growth and development relevant to career choice begins quite early in life, accelerates during adolescence, and continues at a reduced rate through adulthood.

Support for the compromise/developmental view comes from large-scale longitudinal studies that followed participants through the stages and phases of career development (Gribbons & Lohnes, 1982). Career maturity is a concept central to the development view. Individuals who complete the developmental tasks essential to each stage are judged to be career mature. Several inventories have been constructed to measure progress through career stages in adolescents and adults. The developmental model draws upon research in mainstream psychology on human development. Compromise or developmental models, then, imply incremental, predictable, and substantial growth in the individual's career identity, rather than the more stable, transactional model implied in search models of career choice.

Anxiety, Neurosis and Career Decisions

Anxiety plays a role in many career decisions and may serve as a constructive motivator if the levels of anxiety are low or moderate. At higher levels, however, anxiety exacerbates career indecision and will make it more difficult for the individual to make and implement a career choice. Likewise, what Costa and McCrae (1985) have dubbed "neurosis"—or repeated instances of nonconstructive or self-defeating behaviors—appears to play more of a role in career choice problems than social scientists first imagined. These twin problems, anxiety and nonconstructive behaviors, may affect an individual's ability to persist following a failure experience, as well as the ability to recover and revise his or her self-image in the face of serious environmental constraints.

Gender and Career Choice

The career choices of women is one of the most popular topics in modern psychology. The literature from the past decade (Phillips & Imhoff, 1997) reveals that career choices of women involve a complex consideration of personal characteristics, labor market constraints, family plans, and self-efficacy. This literature repeatedly demonstrates that even though gender stereotyping of careers and occupations is lessening, many women continue to lower their career aspirations in the face of pervasive societally imposed barriers—in many cases before those barriers are even encountered. Unfortunately, successful attempts to intervene in this lowering of aspirations are few and rarely successful (Phillips & Imhoff, 1997). Stress resulting from multiple roles, work-family conflict, and primary care giving (for children and aging parents) is high. Efforts to reduce this stress, in contrast to the aspiration research, have been promising. Sexual harassment appears to be a growing problem that can act to further constrain women's participation and advancement in the workplace. It seems fair to conclude that career choice is a complicated process for women that continues to defy simple explanatory models. The literature seems to be emerging from its focus on negative aspects of women's career development and emphasizing instead the benefits derived from maintaining strong social networks at work and at home. More research is needed on how best to assist women in managing complex career decisions and on theoretical models to explain those decisions.

Self-Efficacy and Career Decisions

Considerable research has focused on the self-relevant thinking engaged in about careers. Called self-efficacy or personal agency, research in this area examines the beliefs that individuals harbor about the probability that they can and will succeed in various occupations. This research literature draws upon Bandura's self-efficacy theory and emphasizes math self-efficacy as it relates to women's career choices. Self-efficacy, then, is a hypothetical construct that explains the mediating effects of social constraints and barriers upon individual career choices. An unusually compelling review and application of this work in the field of interest measurement can be found in Betz (1999). Self-efficacy research continues to exert an influence on both the compromise and the search models of career choice.

Intervening in the Career Choice Process

Substantial progress has been made over the past 50 years in our understanding of how to assist individuals who are struggling with career choices. Several therapeutic ingredients are essential to a successful career intervention (Holland, Magoon, & Spokane, 1981). These ingredients are:

- *Cognitive rehearsal of occupational aspirations.* Rehearsal involves thinking about, talking about, and clarifying career aspirations. In the face of difficult or anxiety-provoking career choices, most individuals avoid this crucial rehearsal component.
- *Social support from family, friends, advisors, counselors, or instructors.* Parents and peers are especially helpful during career choices so long as the discussions remain positive.
- *Information about self and the world of work.* This information includes information about one's personal qualities, talents, and strengths, as well as information about the nature and requirements of jobs.
- *An accurate cognitive framework for organizing and filtering information.* Many individuals report that they do not know how to go about making a career decision. Learning how to do so, then, is an important component of any career intervention.
- *Mobilization of constructive career behaviors.* These behaviors include adequate exploratory behavior and persistence in job finding and follow through.

Summary

Career choice is a complex process of balancing personal characteristics with societal constraints in an effort to clarify and implement a series of career decisions over time. These decisions taken in sum are a career. Two theoretical models, the search model and the compromise model, account for most of the research on how the career selection process occurs. Although intervention and counseling research has advanced considerably since the early 1990s, attempts to conduct career intervention research may be less frequent than they once were—thus slowing progress. Case study or individual case research offers a promising new avenue for studying the career intervention process. Questions of gender, anxiety, and self-efficacy are important contemporary topics for study.

[*See also* Career Assessment; Career Development; *and* Career Interventions.]

Bibliography

Ackeman P. L., & Heggestad, E. D. (1997). Intelligence, personality and interests: Evidence for overlapping traits. *Psychological Bulletin, 121,* 219–245.

Arbona, C., & Novy, D. M. (1991). Career aspirations and expectations of Black, Mexican American and White students. *Career Development Quarterly, 39,* 231–239.

Betsworth, D., Bouchard, T. J., Jr., Cooper, C., Grotevant, H., Hansen, J., Scarr, S., & Weinberg, R. (1994). Genetic and environmental influences on vocational interests assessed using adoptive and biological families and twins reared apart and together. *Journal of Vocational Behavior, 44,* 263–278.

Betz, N. E. (1999). Getting clients to act on their interests: Self-efficacy expectations as mediators of the implementation of vocational interests. In M. L. Savickas & A. R. Spokane (Eds.), *Occupational interests: Their meaning, measurement, and counseling use.* (pp. 327–344). Palo Alto: CA: Davies Black.

Costa, P. T., Jr., & McCrae, R. R. (1985). *The NEO Personality Inventory manual.* Odessa, FL: Psychological Assessment Resources.

Gottfredson, L. S. (1981). Circumscription and compromise: A developmental theory of occupational aspirations. *Journal of Counseling Psychology, 28,* 549–579.

Gribbons, W., & Lohnes, P. R. (1982). *Careers in theory and experience: A twenty-year longitudinal study.* Albany: State University of New York Press.

Holland, J. L. (1997). *Making vocational choices: A theory of vocational personalities and work environments* (3rd ed.). Odessa, FL: Psychological Assessment Resources.

Holland, J. L., Magoon, T. M., & Spokane, A. R. (1981). Counseling psychology: Career interventions, research, and theory. *Annual Review of Psychology, 32,* 279–300.

Parsons, F. (1909). *Choosing a vocation.* Boston: Houghton Mifflin.

Phillips, S. D., & Imhoff, A. R. (1997). Women and career development: A decade of research. *Annual Review of Psychology, 48,* 31–59.

Super, D. E. (1957). *The psychology of careers.* New York: Harper & Row.

Vondracek, F. W., Lerner, R. M., & Schulenberg, J. E. (1986). *Career development: A life-span development approach.* Hillsdale, NJ: Erlbaum.

Arnold R. Spokane

Career Development

Career development is a lifelong process involving psychological, educational, economic, sociological, and physical factors, as well as chance factors, that interact to influence the career of an individual. Cultural influences have not been adequately considered in theories of career development. However, research suggests that there are important factors among cultural groups in areas such as work values and career decision-making attitudes (Leong, 1995). Therefore, cultural factors should be included in the list of influences upon the career development of individuals.

Despite the importance and apparent complexity of the career development process, the latest survey by the National Career Development Association (NCDA; Hoyt & Lester, 1995) revealed that only about one third of the adults in the United States were in their current jobs as a result of conscious planning. Thus the majority of adults entered their jobs because of chance circumstances. In addition, 28% of those surveyed indicated that they would change their jobs within 3 years. Assisting an individual through the career development process is a primary task of a vocational psychologist.

There are a great number of techniques and interventions a vocational psychologist may use to facilitate an individual's career development. These techniques and interventions include individual and group career counseling, workshops, mentoring, testing (e.g., ability, interests, needs), job shadowing (i.e., following a worker in a desired job around for a day), interviews with various people (e.g., employers, workers, college admissions personnel), apprenticeships, internships, school-to-work transition services, and use of career resources. One major career resources is the *Dictionary of Occupational Titles* (U.S. Department of Labor, 1991), which defines and classifies occupations and the characteristics of workers in each occupation. Typically, there are three major outcomes for these interventions: the making of a career choice; the acquisition of decision skills; and/or enhanced general adjustments to the work situation, such as job satisfaction and success. The use of a theory of career development serves as a guide for the psychologist in the selection of assessment tools and techniques. Psychologists have developed several useful theories of career development.

Theories of Career Development

The following theories are generally considered to be the most influential theories of career choice and development in terms of research and practice. Theories explaining career behavior provide the psychologist with a conceptual map and describe the purposes for which career counseling, career education, and other career interventions should be implemented.

Trait-and-Factor. Among the early theorists on career development, Frank Parsons in *Choosing a Vocation* (Boston, 1909) argued that a wise vocational choice was made first by studying the individual, second by understanding the relevant characteristics of occupations, and finally by matching the individual with the occupation. This process, called the *trait-and-factor theory*, became the foundation for many career counseling programs and is still in use today. It has led to the development of assessment instruments, as well as to the study of individual job requirements. This theory focuses on individual traits but does not account for changes in values, interest, skills, achievement, and personality over the course of a lifetime. Thus, although assessments based on the trait-and-factor approach are quite useful in career counseling, this theory is generally considered to be quite limited.

Ginzberg. In contrast to the static approach of the trait-and-factor theory, Ginzberg, Ginsburg, Axelrad, and Herma (1951) were the first to view career development as a lifelong process, with an emphasis on very early development. Ginzberg and associates outline three distinct stages or periods in the career-choice process, each of which is divided into substages. During the fantasy stage (childhood before age 11), play gradually becomes work oriented and reflects initial preferences for certain types of activities. The second period, called tentative, is divided into four substages (interest, capacity, values, and transition) and lasts from ages 11 to 17. During the tentative period, the individual becomes more aware of work requirements and of his or her own abilities and values and makes decisions regarding vocational likes and dislikes. At the realistic stage (ages 17 to young adult), there is further integration of perceived abilities and occupational interests, as the person first narrows his or her choices to a few possibilities and then makes a commitment by selecting a job or entering specialized training. Ginzberg (1984) reemphasized that career development is lifelong process for those who seek to attain major job satisfaction. As changing work goals occur, a person will reassess how to improve the fit with the work environment.

Super. Donald Super's (1953) life span developmental theory includes five major stages. The first, growth, occurs from birth to ages 14 or 15 and is characterized by the development of attitudes, interests, needs, and aptitudes associated with self-concept. During the exploratory stage (ages 15 through 24), occupational choices are narrowed, and the establishment stage (ages 25 through 44), is characterized by work experience. From ages 45 to 65 the person experience a continual adjustment process to improve the working situation. Finally, during the decline phase (ages 65 and over) there is reduced work output and eventual retirement. Super's theory has been expanded and refined over the years. Super's (1996) theory has increasingly been viewed as the most comprehensive of the developmental approaches.

Roe. Roe's (1956) theory focuses on early relations within the family and their subsequent influence on career choice. Roe classifies occupations into two major categories: person oriented and non–person oriented. Empirical investigations of Roe's theory have generally failed to provide validation, and the theory itself is difficult to implement in research terms. Roe's major contribution appears to be her emphasis of the impact of childhood experiences on career development and her job classification system.

Holland. The theory that has generated the most research and has the most influence on the career practice of psychologists and counselors is the work of John Holland. According to Holland (1985), the choice of a career is an extension of one's personality into the world of work. Individuals choose careers that satisfy their preferred personal orientations. Holland developed six modal personal styles and six matching work environments: realistic, investigative, artistic, social, enterprising, and conventional. A person is attracted to the particular role demand of an occupational environment that meets his or her needs. For example, someone who is socially oriented would seek out a work environment that provides interactions with others, such as nursing in a hospital setting. Holland and his colleagues have developed a number of instruments (e.g., the Self-Directed Search) designed to assist in identifying individual personality traits and matching those traits to occupational groups. Holland's theory assesses each individual in terms of two or three most prominent personality types and matching each type with the environmental aspects of potential careers. It is predicted that the better the match, the better the congruence, satisfaction, and persistence (Holland, 1985).

Krumboltz. Krumboltz's (1979) theory of career development is grounded in social learning theory and in classical behaviorism. It also incorporates the more recent ideas from self-efficacy theory (Bandura, 1977) and cognitive-behavioral theory (Beck, 1976; Ellis, 1970). This theory incorporates many factors, each of which has a different impact on the person in his or her career decision making. First, genetic endowment may expand or limit options for each individual. Included in genetic endowment are set factors (sex, race, developmental disabilities), as well as those innate talents that a person can choose to develop. Second, career decisions are influenced by environmental conditions and events beyond a person's control, such as cultural norms and economy. The third factor is individual learning, which can occur both instrumentally (e.g., being rewarded for writing may lead to an interest in being a journalist) and associatively (e.g., watching

a movie in which a policeman is seriously injured may reduce the desire to go into law enforcement). Learning experiences include acquiring (or failing to acquire) work habits and problem-solving skills. Finally, Krumboltz highlights the importance of what he calls self-observation generalizations. That is, people compare their own performance, skills, and abilities with some standard and draw conclusions about their competence and worth. These conclusions are used in making responses to future situations. If the conclusions reached are not reasonable but rather unrealistic or inappropriate, their images of themselves as workers, may be damaged. For example, a girl may not believe that she could be capable in math, and so she avoids math-related activities and career possibilities. In summary, Krumboltz sees career development as unique for the individual and believes that most of the influences on career development and career choice (e.g., interests, self-concept) are capable of being altered at any point in life.

Other Noteworthy Theories. Other theories of career development include the work of Tiedemann and his colleagues (Tiedemann & O'Hara, 1963) on the career decision-making process; a psychoanalytic approach (Bordin, Nachmann, & Segal, 1963); the theory of work adjustment (Lofquist & Dawis, 1969); and a theory of circumscription and compromise in career aspirations (Gottfredson, 1981). Tiedemann's theory has had little empirical support, but his ideas have served to highlight the importance of self-awareness in career decision making. The approach of Bordin and his colleagues (Bordin, Nachmann, & Segal, 1963) proposed that psychoanalytically developed dimensions of need that are established by the age of 6 influenced career choice. The major contribution of this theory is the attention directed to the early developmental processes and early child-parent relationships. In the theory of work adjustment, the main construct of interest is correspondence, which is the fit between the individual's attributes and those required by an occupation. High correspondence should correlate with longer tenure and greater satisfaction and performance (Dawis & Lofquist, 1984). Gottfredson's (1981) theory postulates that occupational preferences emerge from the complexities that accompany mental and physical growth. One unique feature of her theory is that the range of aspirations narrows according to sex type and prestige during self-concept development. Also, a person may compromise by settling for less compatible but more accessible career choices. In general, persons are less willing to compromise in job level and sex type because these factors are closely associated with self-concept.

Convergence of Theories. In 1990, Osipow suggested that the major career development theories are converging as empirical evidence about vocational behavior accumulates and as the theories are continuously revised. His analysis of four major theories include those of Super, Holland, Lofquist and Davis, and Krumboltz. Osipow identified common themes among those theories: biological factors, parental influences, personality, outcomes, and life-stage influences.

Hackett, Lent, and Greenhaus (1991) have also argued the need to work toward unifying career decision theories to bring together conceptually related constructs (e.g., self-efficacy and self-concept), to more fully explain outcomes that are common to a number of career theories (e.g., satisfaction), to account for the relations among seemingly diverse constructs (e.g., interests, needs, abilities), and to identify the major variables crucial to a comprehensive theory of career development. If career development theory is to be comprehensive and useful, it must include some variables that have received relatively little attention or that are even omitted in current theories. These include the influence of life roles (e.g., sex role, racial identity), what opportunities are available to a person within a particular geographic area, and economic influences. It must be noted, however, that all-encompassing theories are likely to pose barriers to research and practice because of the increased number of constructs and the complex network of interrelationships among them.

Career Development Needs of Special Groups

There are some groups of people for whom circumstances or conditions require some adjustment in the usual career development process. Although the career development process must be somewhat individualized for each person due to unique characteristics and circumstances, there are commonalities generally shared by others within groups of people. Groups that may face some different experiences in the career development process include women, ethnic and racial minority groups, persons with disabilities, delayed entrants into the work force (e.g., displaced homemakers, returning military personnel, prior offenders), midlife changers (voluntary or involuntary), older workers, and gay, lesbian, and bisexual individuals.

Compared with men, women experience special problems in their career development that have not been adequately addressed in the major career development theories. Some progress has been made, as reflected in the work of Hackett and Betz (1981), Farmer (1985), and Fassinger (1985), for example. It is suggested by these writers and others that women's career issues are much more complex than are those facing men.

Different cultures may have different conceptions of the family, gender roles, and work-family relationships. For example, "career" may have a collective, not an individual meaning. Although it is important to understand the meaning work and related concepts have for an individual's racial or ethnic group, it is also important to assess the salience of membership in a cultural group to better understand a person's career behavior.

A person with disabilities is one who is usually considered different physically or psychologically from a normal person because of birth, devolpmental problems, accident, or disease. These disabilities may or may not be a vocational hindrance. An important recent development relating to individuals with disabilities and work is the passage of the Americans with Disabilities Act (ADA) of 1990. In this act, a distinction is made between essential and nonessential job functions, and an employer may only consider the former when hiring or promoting. In vocational rehabilitation, psychologists and counselors will engage in all or some of the following activities when working with a client: vocational testing, situational assessment (work sampling, vocational evaluation), skills training, employment preparation, counseling, job referral and placement, work adjustment training, and postplacement counseling.

It must be noted that the identification of group differences and cultural and environmental influences in the emergence of those differences cannot be translated into definite conclusions about individuals who are members of identifiable groups. All individuals are influenced to varying degrees by their environment, but psychological research has shown that differences between persons within a particular group typically exceed the degree of difference between groups. Therefore, although the exploration of group influences can advance the understanding of career development, it is important for the vocational psychologist not to extend these findings rigidly when working with individual clients.

Career Development Issues

A vocational psychologist studies many important issues that people might encounter in their career development process. Often these same issues are what prompt an individual to seek the assistance of a psychologist or career counselor. These issues include career transitions (i.e., school to work, midlife changes, and work to retirement), work and well-being, job satisfaction, career advancement, career coping strategies, networking, work motivation, and stress and burnout. Motivation and stress are two of the most common issues of importance to the career development process.

Motivation to work varies from person to person. For many people, work is more than earning a wage. Most individuals share the basic human need for self-fulfillment through meaningful work. Choosing a particular career may fulfill other needs, such as status, security, or satisfaction. The type of tasks required for a particular occupation, the working conditions (both physical and interpersonal), and the working hours required (e.g., shift work) may also influence motivation to work.

The work environment and the demands of work have the potential to be stressors that may interact with stressors outside work (e.g., family stressors). These stressors, as frequently cited in the literature, include poor physical working conditions (e.g., excess heat), work overload or underload, home and work pressures, job dissatisfaction, shift work, and poor relationships with colleagues or management. Stressors may also stem from the person. For example, a Type A personality is characterized by excessive competitiveness and ambition, which may cause the person to experience greater occupational stress. Stress overload may result in burnout, which is the depletion of physical and mental resources that results in nonproductive behavior, job dissatisfaction, boredom, accidents, or interpersonal conflicts.

Current Trends in Career Development

The world of work has been changing rapidly in the last few decades due to new technology, changes in the organization of work, shifting requirements for worker knowledge and skill, and a global labor surplus (Herr & Cramer, 1996). All these changes affect the career development of individuals over the life span. Current trends for the area of career development include the following:

1. Substantial changes will continue to occur in the occupational, economic, industrial, and social environments and structures, and these changes will influence individual career development. For example, the use and sophistication of technology have increased dramatically. New jobs are created, and the need for other jobs is reduced or even eliminated, thus requiring more workers to change jobs or even move to another occupational group.

2. As job opportunities shift, there will be more participation in retraining programs.

3. There is a greater need for a better educated work force. There are fewer opportunities for an unskilled work force because the jobs they do are done for less money in underdeveloped countries. A survey by the National Alliance of Business (1990) found that 64% of the companies responding were dissatisfied with the reading, writing, and reasoning skills of today's entering work force.

4. Flexibility in work schedules (e.g., job sharing, part-time work) will likely increase, giving more options to workers with particular needs.

5. There will be even greater attention to the career development of a more diverse population. The work force today includes more women, members of racial and ethnic groups, openly homosexual and bisexual individuals, and persons with various types of disabilities.

6. There is a greater awareness of the need to attend to career development issues across the life span.

7. As the "baby boom" cohort approaches the traditional retirement age, there is an increasing interest in research concerning the decision to retire. Although financial status is a critical factor in the decision to retire, physical limitations and health problems and psychological factors such as satisfaction with career attainment and anxieties about separation from the workplace also play a role.

Bibliography

Bandura, A. (1977). Self-efficacy: Toward a unifying theory of behavioral change. *Psychological Review, 84,* 191–215.

Beck, A. T. (1976). *Cognitive therapy and emotional disorders.* New York: International University Press.

Bordin, E. S., Nachmann, B., & Segal, S. J. (1963). An articulated framework for vocational development. *Journal of Counseling Psychology, 10,* 107–116.

Brown, D., & Brooks, L. (1996). *Career choice and development: Applying contemporary theories to practice* (3rd ed.). San Francisco, CA: Jossey-Bass.

Crites, J. O. (1981). *Career counseling: Models, methods, and materials.* New York: McGraw-Hill.

Dawis, R. V., & Lofquist, L. H. (1984). *A psychological theory of work adjustment: An individual differences model and its applications.* Minneapolis: University of Minnesota Press.

Ellis, A. (1970). *The essence of rational psychotherapy: A comprehensive approach to treatment.* New York: Institute for Rational Living.

Farmer, H. S. (1985). Model of career and achievement motivation for women and men. *Journal of Counseling Psychology, 32,* 363–390.

Fassinger, R. E. (1985). A casual model of college women's career choice. *Journal of Vocational Behavior (Monograph), 27,* 123–153.

Ginzberg, E. (1984). Career development. In D. Brown and L. Brooks (Eds.) *Career choice and development: Applying contemporary theories to practice.* San Francisco, CA: Jossey-Bass.

Ginzberg, E., Ginsburg, S. W., Axelrad, S., & Herma, J. L. (1951). *Occupational choice: An approach to general theory.* New York: Columbia University Press.

Gottfredson, L. S. (1981). Circumscription and compromise: A development theory of occupational aspirations. *Journal of Counseling Psychology, 28,* 545–579.

Hackett, G., & Betz, N. E. (1981). A self-efficacy approach to career development of women. *Journal of Vocational Behavior, 18,* 326–339.

Hackett, G., Lent, R. W., & Greenhaus, J. (1991). *Journal of Vocational Behavior, 38,* 3–38.

Herr, E. L., & Cramer, S. H. (1996). *Career guidance and*

counseling through the lifespan (5th ed.). New York: HarperCollins.

Hoffman, M. A. (1997). HIV disease and work: Effect on the individual, workplace, and interpersonal contexts. *Journal of Vocational Behavior, 51,* 163–201. This article reviews the literature on the effect of HIV disease on the career of the person with the disease, as well as on the careers of informal care givers.

Holland, J. L. (1985). *Making vocational choices: A theory of vocational personalities and work environments* (3rd ed.). Odessa, FL: Psychological Assessment Resources.

Hoyt, K. B., & Lester, J. L. (1995). *Learning to work: The NCDA Gallup survey.* Alexandria, VA: NCDA.

Isaacson, L. E., & Brown, D. (1997). *Career information, career counseling, and career development* (6th ed.). Boston, MA: Allyn & Bacon.

Krumboltz, J. D. (1979). A social learning theory of career decision making. In A. M. Mitchell, G. B. Jones, & J. D. Krumboltz (Eds.), *Social learning and career decision making.* Cranston: RI: Carroll Press.

Leong, F. T. L. (1995). *Career development and vocational behavior of racial and ethnic minorities.* Mahwah, NJ: Erlbaum. Examines research related to career development theory and assessment for African Americans, Asian Americans, Hispanic Americans, and Native Americans.

Lofquist, L. II., & Dawis, R. V. (1969). *Adjustment to work.* New York: Appleton-Century-Crofts.

Lowman, R. L. (1993). *Counseling and psychotherapy of work dysfunctions.* Washington, DC: American Psychological Association. Work dysfunctions refers to psychological conditions in which there is a significant impairment in the ability to work due to the personality of the person or the interaction of the work environment with the characteristics of the person. Lowman's book focuses on the psychological treatment of these work dysfunctions.

McDaniels, C., & Gysbers, N. C. (1992). *Counseling for career development: Theories, resources, and practice.* San Francisco, CA: Jossey Bass.

National Alliance of Business (1986). *Employment practices: Looking to the year 2000.* Washington, DC: Author.

Osipow, S. H. (1990). Convergence in theories of career choice and development: Review and prospect. *Journal of Vocational Behavior, 36,* 37–42. Osipow identified the following common themes among four major career theories: biological factors, parental influences, personality, outcomes, and life-stage influences.

Roe, A. (1956). *The psychology of occupations.* New York: Wiley.

Savickas, M. L., & Lent R. W. (Ed.). (1994). *Convergence in career development theories.* Palo Alto, CA: Consulting Psychologists Press.

Super, D. E. (1953). A theory of vocational development. *American Psychologist, 30,* 88–92.

Super, D. E. (1996). A life-span, life-space approach to career development. In D. Brown & L. Brooks (Eds.). *Career choice and development: Applying contemporary theories to practice* (2nd ed., pp. 197–261). San Francisco, CA: Jossey-Bass.

Szymanski, E. M., & Parker, R. M. (Eds.). (1996). *Work and disability: Issues and strategies in career development and job placement.* Austin, TX: Pro-Ed.

Tiedeman, D. V., & O'Hara, R. P. (1963). *Career development: Choice and adjustment.* New York: College Entrance Examination Board.

Walsh, W. B., & Osipow, S. H. (Eds.). (1995). *Handbook of vocational psychology: Theory, research, and practice.* Mahwah, NJ: Erlbaum.

Karen D. Multon

Career Assessment

Career assessment is the process of gathering information that is used to better understand a client and his or her educational or career situation. Psychological instruments and structured questions are typically used in career assessment. The assessment provides information that can be used in the initial stages of counseling to inform the counselor about the client (diagnostic information), as well as in the intervention stage of counseling to increase the client's self-understanding, especially in relation to educational or work settings.

Career assessment has been in use since the early 1900s. Frank Parsons (1909) was one of the first proponents of using assessment for the purpose of guidance, and in 1927 E. K. Strong, Jr., developed the first interest inventory, the Strong Vocational Interest Blank. The use of career assessment instruments, such as interest inventories, has been and continues to be a core feature of career counseling and development. Since the onset of World War I, the use of career assessment for the purpose of selection and placement has been a common practice in educational, government, and business settings. During the 1970s the utility and fairness of assessment practices and tools were questioned, especially in regard to the assessment of women and minority groups. This period of criticism led to refinements, including development of guidelines for the competent delivery of career assessment services to diverse groups, and to closer scrutiny of the reliability and accuracy of instruments for all persons. Today, many counseling, school, and industrial/organizational psychologists use testing on a regular basis for educational and career counseling, career development, and educational and occupational selection and placement. The goal of assessment might be to help clients understand how their interests compare with others in different occupational areas (counseling) or to help organizations identify who might perform best in a competitive program (selection). It is predicted that the use of career assessment will increase in the future (Seligman, 1994).

Career assessment in general, and testing in particular, typically occurs within the context of a counseling relationship. Counselors and clients work together to establish the goals of counseling and the type of assessment that is most appropriate for the client. Counselors are responsible for using instruments that are consistent with the goals of counseling and valid for the client. This means that psychologists who engage in the practice of career assessment must have a good working knowledge of career counseling so they can determine the clients' needs and select the instruments that best meet those needs. They must also have a good working knowledge of measurement so that they can evaluate the quality of instruments and make interpretations that do not exceed the limits of the instruments. An educational casebook that illustrates responsible test use, including examples of career assessment, has been published by the American Psychological Association (Eyde et al., 1993).

Topics of Career Assessment

Previous authors (Betz, 1992; Hackett & Watkins, 1995) have divided topics of career assessment into individual difference variables (ability/aptitude, interest, and work values), career-process variables (decision making and career maturity), and career-related cognitions (career beliefs and self-efficacy). Although there is some overlap among categories, this is a useful framework.

Individual Difference Measures. Achievement, aptitude, ability, and intelligence tests are all designed to measure performance. In career assessment, aptitude and ability testing are used regularly, and they measure knowledge acquired through learning and innate abilities, respectively. Ability and aptitude tests provide information about probable success in different training programs or occupational settings. This information can be used by clients to help them develop educational or career plans or by institutions to inform candidate selection. For example, most students in the United States take the Scholastic Aptitude Test or American College Testing Program examination for admission to college and the Graduate Record Examination for admission to graduate programs. The Differential Aptitude Test and General Aptitude Test battery are well-known examples of multiple aptitude assessment batteries.

The use of ability and aptitude testing has been widely debated, with proponents advocating the predictive accuracy or efficiency of educational or employment testing and critics raising concerns about culture, race, and gender bias. The use of ability and aptitude testing extends from issues with individual clients to social policy issues, such as adverse impact. Given the impact that aptitude and ability testing can have on clients, it is essential that psychologists understand the nature of norm-referenced testing, the use of appropriate norms, the impact of the testing context, and principles of measurement, especially estimation and measurement error.

Interest assessment is the most popular type of career assessment and is a standard part of educational and career counseling. Interests refer to what people like, and they can be measured using hands-on tools, such as card sorts, or, more typically, through psychometrically developed interest measures (e.g., Self-Directed Search, Strong Interest Inventory). The purpose of interest assessment is to help people understand their general interest patterns (e.g., artistic activities) and their specific interests (e.g., writing) and to provide a comparison of their interests with people in different occupations (e.g., interests similar to those of commercial artists). Thus a psychologist would use interest assessment to help a client identify broad interest patterns and specific interests to better understand both work and leisure preferences. Interest assessment enhances self-knowledge, helps relate personal interests and work environments, and helps people prioritize different educational or occupational areas for further exploration. Issues of particular concern to interest inventories include predictive validity (to insure that interests predict future occupational choices) and nonbiased (particularly nonsexist) results.

Values, or needs, is another topic that is frequently addressed in career assessment. Work values can be differentiated from interests in that the former refer to "what is important" and the latter refer to "what is liked." Work values are qualities important to an individual that can be met through work and that generate work satisfaction. Achievement, autonomy, security, comfort, and altruism are examples of higher order work values (Dawis & Lofquist, 1984). When a work environment offers people who value achievement an opportunity to achieve, they tend to be more satisfied with their work. Thus psychologists would engage in work values assessment to help clients understand factors that lead to work adjustment.

Values assessment can extend beyond the work environment to include multiple life areas. The increased number of dual-career families has led many people to engage in career/life planning, a process in which people examine the salience of different life roles and how values are met across family, work, and community activities. The Salience Inventory is one example of an assessment instrument that measures values across life roles. In general, values assessment and clarification is an important part of both life and career planning. Of particular concern for values measures is the need to balance inclusiveness (capturing a broad array of values) and functionality (maintaining a parsimonious framework for meaningful interpretation).

Career Process Variables. Career process variables describe the way in which people make educational and career decisions and the person's stage of career development, including level of development within a stage. The most frequently studied career process variables are career decision making and career development or maturity. It should be noted that career decision making can also be an individual difference variable. Sometimes counselors simply want to assess level of career indecision. In this case, instruments (e.g., Career Decision Scale, Career Factors Inventory) are used to estimate individual differences in career indecision and to identify possible sources of career indecision. For example, career choice anxiety often interferes with someone's ability to make a decision. From an individual difference perspective, a high level of career choice anxiety is a cue, or diagnostic indicator, for the counselor that affective antecedents of career indecision need to be addressed.

Process-oriented career decision measures are used in the context of career development to provide feedback on level of career decision-making readiness. The best example of this type of measure is the Assessment of Career Decision Making, which measures stages of career decision making (e.g., awareness, planning, commitment, implementation), as well as individual differences in decision-making styles (e.g., rational, intuitive, dependent). Career process assessment would be used to identify areas in which a person needs to enhance developmental skills, and intervention would be designed to increase skills and help that person move to the next stage of career decision making.

Career development measures are sometimes referred to as career maturity measures, but the word "maturity" can have pejorative connotations. Career development instruments measure career development competencies, such as occupational knowledge and career planning skills. They are typically used by psychologists who are working from a developmental orientation. The Career Maturity Inventory and the Career Development Inventory are the most widely recognized instruments of this type, and they are typically used as part of a career intervention to help students ascertain their readiness to engage in effective educational and career planning or to evaluate the effectiveness of an intervention (i.e., pre- and posttesting). Collectively, career development measures are potentially very useful, but some concern has been raised about their psychometric adequacy.

Cognitive Measures. Over the last 15 years, career counseling has devoted increased attention to the influence of cognitions on career development. Assessment tools have focused on confidence or self-efficacy and on beliefs that may impede the attainment of career goals. One notable trend has been the inclusion of confidence scales in interest inventories. For example, both the Campbell Interest and Skills Inventory and the Strong Interest and Skills Inventory include a component in which people report their level of skills or confidence, respectively, across different general occupational areas. These scales are then used in tandem with interest scales to identify areas of high interest and confidence, as well as areas of high interest but low confidence. This type of information can help counselors understand a client's hesitation or reluctance to explore certain educational or occupational areas.

Sometimes the beliefs or stereotypes that people hold interfere with their ability to achieve career goals. Recently, instruments have been developed that assess people's beliefs about themselves and work. Most notably, the Career Beliefs Inventory and the Career Thoughts Inventory assess beliefs related to self, work, and decision making. In the social cognitive tradition, these belief scales are relatively specific and measure constructs that are conceptually distinct from more global personality or trait constructs. This type of assessment works particularly well for psychologists who prefer to work from a cognitive-behavioral orientation or learning-based theory. Interventions focus on examining the beliefs in relation to career goals and ascertaining their validity.

Summary

Career assessment is commonly used by counseling, school, and industrial/organizational psychologists, as well as by other counseling professionals. Although some career assessment instruments are designed for self-directed use, most instruments and assessments should be used selectively (i.e., appropriately for the client) and in conjunction with other information. Further, it is imperative that psychologists have a thorough understanding of instrument development and a psychometric understanding of a particular instrument before using it. Interpretations, which can be immensely helpful or hurtful, are based on an understanding of the client, the assessment tool, and the situation. The advent of enhanced computer technology is creating a need to reevaluate principles of responsible career assessment within a new medium. In summary, these trends suggest that career assessment will be a thriving but more complex area within psychology.

Bibliography

Betz, N. E. (1992). Career assessment: A review of critical issues. In S. D. Brown & R. W. Lent (Eds.), *Handbook of counseling psychology* (2nd ed., pp. 453–484). New York: Wiley. A review of major issues in the field.

Dawis, R. V. & Lofquist, L. (1984). *A psychological theory of work adjustment.* Minneapolis: University of Minnesota Press. A theory of work focusing on the adjustment process.

Eyde, L. D., Robertson, G. J., Krug, S. E., Moreland, K. L., Robertson, A. G., Shewan, C. M., Harrison, P. L., Porch, B. E., Hammer, A. L., & Primoff, E. S. (1993). *Responsible test use : Case studies for assessing human behavior.* Washington, DC: American Psychological Association. A review of ethical issues.

Hackett, G., & Watkins, C. E., Jr. (1995). Research in career assessment: Abilities, interests, decision making, and career development. In W. B. Walsh & S. H. Osipow (Eds.), *Handbook of vocational psychology* (2nd ed., pp. 181–216). Mahwah, NJ: Erlbaum. A review of relevant research.

Parsons, F. (1909). *Choosing a vocation.* Boston: Houghton Mifflin. The forming of a foundation in career assessment.

Savickas, M. L., & Walsh, W. B. (Eds.). (1996). *Handbook of career counseling theory and practice.* Palo Alto, CA: Davis-Black. A comprehensive review of career counseling theory and practice.

Seligman, L. (1994). *Developmental career counseling and assessment* (2nd ed.). Thousand Oaks, CA: Sage. Career counseling and assessment from a developmental perspective.

Special Issue (1997). Career assessment for women: Theory into practice. *Journal of Career Assessment, 5,* 355–474.

Special Issue (1997). Career assessment, multicultural diversity, and individual differences. *Journal of Career Assessment, 5,* 115–252.

Judy M. Chartrand and W. Bruce Walsh

Career Interventions

Career interventions have been developed to address a range of problems over the life span. Corresponding to the developmental tasks of exploring, selecting, implementing, and adjusting to career choices, career interventions are directed toward the particular problems encountered at different life stages. Career interventions have been developed for the needs of children, adolescents and young adults, and adults.

Career Interventions for Children

At the elementary school level, career interventions focus on developing children's basic self-knowledge and their awareness of different occupations. Specific career interventions and education designed to match the developmental levels of the students are usually infused into the traditional academic curriculum. In terms of self-knowledge, even very young children can begin to develop an understanding of their individual differences in interests and abilities. Many psychologists have also argued that elementary-school age is a developmentally ideal time to help children understand and overcome sex-role stereotypes. Through exposure to nontraditional role models in the school or community and through biographical reading assignments, children can learn about people who have had successful

and interesting nontraditional careers. At these early stages, career interventions are intended to help children develop a clear, positive self-concept that is not restricted by gender or cultural bias.

Career interventions also introduce elementary-school children to different kinds of work environments. Popular activities for schoolchildren include taking field trips to local businesses, industries, and agencies, inviting speakers into the classroom from different occupational areas, and using films and games to understand different types of jobs. Elementary-school children are taught how to explore career information independently. Projects that encourage use of libraries, career centers, and other school and community resources can help children build their skills at occupational research. Children at this age are often encouraged to interview someone who holds a job in which they are interested. This can develop their skills in conducting interviews, generating interview questions, and reporting on what they learned. Career intervention and education are also frequently integrated with writing assignments to help students synthesize what they have learned about the world of work, while simultaneously building basic writing skills.

Through researching careers and learning about individual preferences, elementary-school students can begin to appreciate the idea that different people are best suited to different jobs. Many schools have used Holland's occupational classification system (*Making Vocational Choices*, Englewood Cliffs, NJ, 1997) to help students think about career options and types of people. Young students have also benefited from instruction in basic decision making and goal setting.

Critics have argued that infusion of career development into school curricula might encourage children to make premature decisions about career options. However, this contention is not clearly supported by the research, and, in fact, empirical evidence suggests that career education has important positive outcomes (e.g., enhanced academic achievement) that may broaden students' career options.

Career Interventions for Adolescents and Young Adults

Needs for career interventions intensify during the adolescent and young adult years. Partly because of their proximity to entering the work force, individuals' choices made during these years can have a substantial impact on their career options. Gender stereotyping of occupational alternatives and diminished self-efficacy for activities (such as math or science) that will act as a critical filter for later options need to be addressed promptly. Further, many of the choices that are called for during these years are made by young people with relatively little assistance or supervision, and it is critical that they be prepared to make such choices. The targets of career intervention during these years, then, include further clarification and testing of individuals' self-awareness, gathering accurate and useful information about the world of work, and developing skills in decision making and planning that would enable them to formulate and execute wise career choices. In addition, work force preparation is essential, including such skills as self-presentation, communication, work habits, and interpersonal relationship management. Strategies for career interventions that address these targeted attitudes and behaviors include curriculum infusion and freestanding career intervention programs. Research on these strategies has provided strong support for the effectiveness of these career interventions.

Curriculum infusion is most commonly used as a career intervention strategy in secondary-school settings. As with the strategies used for interventions with children, the methods by which the targeted attitudes and behaviors are introduced into the classroom are widely varied. They may include modules and assignments that relate the particular curriculum area to work and careers, the introduction of the notion of work families or career clusters, and projects that help students get practice in profiling themselves and their options and in generating plans for implementing particular choices. Specific decision-making games and simulations have been developed to aid in the acquisition of mature career attitudes and behaviors.

Freestanding career intervention programs are frequently used at both the secondary and the postsecondary levels and are found both in the school setting and in community service agencies such as libraries, clubs, and activity organizations. Beyond individual career counseling, these interventions include a broad array of workshops, groups, courses, experiential learning, and computer-assisted information and guidance systems. [See Career Counseling.]

Workshops, groups, and courses all draw upon the resources of peer involvement, social support, and discussion that are available in a group setting. These efforts typically include planned exposure to or instruction about information about the participants, the world of work, and decision making and planning. They may be quite brief (e.g., three contacts) or, for greater effectiveness, may include more extended and comprehensive contact. Within these activities, the methods of intervention used might include standardized and self-administered tests, exercises, discussions, exploration projects, and role playing. More specialized programs have been designed to foster particular aspects of career development, such as nontraditional occupational options or specific job-hunting skills (e.g., resume writing, interviewing). Both broad and specific programs may be directed to special groups (e.g., athletes, at-risk youth, the gifted), and in that context, they are improved by including attention to the array of re-

lated problems or concerns for that group. Alternately, programs such as these may be embedded in a larger student development project that attends to multiple fronts of development. Typically, the program participant is the adolescent or young adult; however, some programs specifically involve parents in promoting the career development of the young people with positive results.

Experiential learning includes such activities as structured observation of role models, work shadowing (accompanying an individual at work), cooperative education, internships, or work-study programs. These programs are in use in both secondary and collegiate settings and serve to provide detailed information about opportunities in the work force. Ranging from "career days" or "career fairs" to actual work activity, these programs provide the developing individual with hands-on exposure to a particular sector of the world of work. These opportunities provide not only work experience but also enhanced self-knowledge, more detailed knowledge about specific occupations, and reality-based work force preparation skills. They are best accompanied by participation in a counseling or mentoring arrangement to aid in helping the individual's broad-based learning and career development.

Computer-assisted information and guidance systems draw upon the information sorting and retrieval capacities of the computer to provide individuals with rapid access to data about themselves or the workplace. Furthermore, following programmed exercises in self-exploration and values clarification, the information retrieval activity can be tailored to an individual's particular characteristics. The more comprehensive computer-assisted information and guidance systems (such as SIGI PLUS or DISCOVER; see Sampson & Reardon, 1990) provide the user with modules covering a variety of self-assessment topics, as well as access to specific occupational, educational, and financial information. More circumscribed computer programs focus on a single aspect of career development, such as values clarification, resume writing, or financial aid. Although research has demonstrated generally positive outcomes of the use of computers in career interventions, there is also general consensus that computer-assisted systems are best used in connection with a human-based counseling or guidance program.

Career Interventions for Adults

Career interventions for adults, often presented in a group format, typically include a combination of three essential features. The first is self-assessment, designed to increase participants' awareness of their interests, skills, working styles, and personality types. The second component is the provision of career information; participants learn to access information about different occupational options and educational or entry requirements. The third feature of many career interventions for adults is a skill development component to strengthen participants' skills in job hunting, networking, interviewing, goal setting, planning, and decision making. Often, these interventions incorporate some training in stress reduction and time management, as well.

Career development programs may be provided through community resources, such as mental health clinics and career centers, or at the workplace itself. In the workplace, some employers offer structured interventions such as career workshops, whereas other employers foster employee career development by encouraging continued education (e.g., through educational cost reimbursement programs) or by providing continued vocational training (e.g., through training seminars).

Another type of career intervention that may be offered through employers is outplacement, targeting employees who have been terminated. Outplacement programs are generally designed to promote reemployment by helping participants assess their skills, evaluate job alternatives, and develop effective job search strategies. Programs that include an element of social support and focus specific attention on coping with negative emotional reactions to job loss appear to be particularly beneficial to terminated employees.

Many employers offer career interventions in the form of employee assistance programs (EAPs). EAPs are distinct from the more broadly based career development interventions and are specifically designed to enhance employees' personal adjustment at work. Narrowly defined, EAPs have focused on identifying and assisting workers with substance abuse problems. More comprehensively defined, these programs provide assistance for any problem that might impair an employee's performance on the job (e.g., managing demands of work and family, absenteeism, coping with conflicts among employees), often serving as an in-house referral system to community resources. EAPs respond to workers' needs in times of job change (such as demotions or promotions), change in the organizational structure (such as acquisitions or mergers) or points of personal crisis (such as substance abuse or family crises). Several reviewers agree that rigorous outcome research is sparse in the EAP literature, making it difficult to evaluate objectively the effectiveness of these programs.

Outside the workplace, community-based career interventions often focus on adult career changers. In this capacity, interventions are designed to guide participants through reexamination of values and identification of special skills derived from past work experiences. Interventions that help individuals evaluate career alternatives with consideration of other important life roles can be especially useful. Many of these interventions are supplemented by computer-based guidance and information systems and individual counseling. In addition, specialized career interventions have been developed for individuals with disabilities, cultural and ethnic minorities, low-income students, and others with unique career development needs. These programs rely heavily on identification of the particular problems and needs of diverse groups and development of programmatic features that recognize cultural values or special needs.

Bibliography

Herr, E. L., & Cramer, S. H. (1992). *Career guidance and counseling through the lifespan: Systematic approaches.* (4th Ed.) New York: HarperCollins. Provides a comprehensive overview of developmentally geared career interventions.

Kirk, J. J. (1994). Putting outplacement in its place. *Journal of Employment Counseling, 31,* 10–18. Introduces a model of outplacement services that includes three critical components and that is concise and typical of other models.

Lubin, B., Shanklin, H. D., & Sailors, J. R. (1992). The EAP literature: Articles and dissertations, 1970–1990. *Employee Assistance Quarterly, 8*(1), 47–90. Provides a bibliography of the literature in employee assistance, organized by topic.

Phillips, S. D. (1992). Career counseling: Choice and implementation. In S. Brown & R. Lent (Eds.), *Handbook of counseling psychology* (2nd ed., pp. 513–547). New York: Wiley. Provides an analysis of the career intervention literature, together with a summary of the underlying rationale for different interventions.

Sampson, J. P., & Reardon, R. C. (1990). Evaluating computer assisted career guidance systems: Synthesis and implications. *Journal of Career Development, 17,* 143–149. Summarizes a special issue of this journal devoted to the analysis and evaluation of using computers in career interventions.

Spokane, A. R., & Oliver, L. W. (1983). The outcomes of vocational intervention. In W. B. Walsh & S. H. Osipow (Eds.) *Handbook of vocational psychology: Vol. 2. Applications* (pp. 99–136). Hillsdale, NJ: Erlbaum. Provides a comprehensive analysis of the effectiveness of career interventions.

Susan D. Phillips and Anne R. Imhoff

CAREER COUNSELING. In the broad arena of vocational life, career counseling can play an important role in assisting individuals to select careers, achieve their vocational potential, and succeed in managing multiple demands in society. Since the inception of career counseling in the early 1900s, its definition has been refined to reflect the dynamic role career counseling can play in meeting the changing needs of individuals and of society. In the late 1980s, for example, the National Career Development Association defined career counseling as a set of activities performed by an individual specifically trained in career counseling and working with such issues as occupations, career planning, and decision making. Since that time, many writers have refined and added to that definition of career counseling to include mention of the importance of career counseling over the life span. In addition, there has been increased recognition of the relationship between career counseling and social and emotional counseling, in order to emphasize the interrelated roles of a person's vocational life and overall identity and psychological well-being. Thus writers have stressed that career counseling occurs over the lifetime and involves not only choosing a career but also adjusting and advancing in the career as well. In addition, some writers contend that career counseling not only fosters career development but also facilitates personal and psychological adjustment. Thus these definitions emphasize the role of career counseling in assisting individuals across the life span with career-related issues and the myriad intersecting social and emotional issues that converge in a person's life.

History of Career Counseling

The roots of career counseling can be found in the late 1800s and early 1900s, which was a time of great turmoil and transition in the United States. This economic turmoil and demographic change were coupled with dramatic changes brought on by the Industrial Revolution in Europe and the United States. Social services of the time were designed to help the influx of European immigrants find their place in this vast country. At that time, there was much worker abuse, poverty, and discrimination in employment.

It was within this social and historical context that Frank Parsons, who is sometimes referred to as the "father of career development," began his work as director of the Breadwinner's Institute in 1905. The Breadwinner's Institute was under the umbrella of the Civic Service House in Boston, which was designed to provide educational programs for immigrants seeking employment. In working with immigrants, Parsons developed a systematic guidance procedure that was to have a profound and lasting effect on the field of career counseling. He outlined his three-step procedure in his book *Choosing a Vocation* (Boston, 1909), which was published posthumously. Parsons believed that there were three primary factors in choosing a vocation: a clear understanding of oneself, including one's aptitudes, abilities, interests, and limitations; a knowledge of the requirements, advantages, disadvantages, and prospects of different types of jobs; and the ability to reason regarding the relation of these two sets of facts. This

three-step procedure had lasting impact on the way career counseling was conducted for a long period of time in the United States and continues to be influential in current-day practice.

Shortly after Parsons's influential book was published, the First National Conference on Vocational Guidance was held in Boston in 1910. This organization became the National Vocational Guidance Association in 1913; today it is called the National Career Development Association (NCDA). This organization continues to provide leadership in the advancement of career counseling.

Also important to the growth of career counseling were developments in related fields. Vernon Zunker, in his text *Career Counseling: Applied Concepts of Life Planning* (Pacific Grove, California, 1994), outlines the following as important influences: scientists in Europe, such as Francis Galton, Wilhelm Wundt, Alfred Binet, and V. Henri, who were publishing studies on human abilities and individual differences; scientists in the United States, such as G. Stanley Hall, James Cattell, and John Dewey, who were contributing in the areas of mental characteristics of children, mental tests, and educational reforms, respectively; the development of intelligence testing in France, the U.S. Army Alpha and Beta testing, and the publishing of the Strong Vocational Interest Blank in 1927; and the federal government, which passed a number of pieces of legislation between 1917 and 1940 and published the *Dictionary of Occupational Titles* in 1939.

Career Development Theories

The growth of the practice of career counseling ran parallel to the creation of theories of occupational choice and career development. The earliest of these theories were being formulated in the 1920s and 1930s. Building on Parsons's model, trait and factor approaches to career counseling were developed and continue to have major influence on the field. Parsons's influence, for example, can be seen in E. G. Williamson's early conceptualization of counseling as having six steps: analysis, synthesis, diagnosis, prognosis, counseling, and follow-up. Although the trait-and-factor approach continued to dominate the practice of career counseling through the 1930s, Carl Rogers's client-centered approach provided a challenge to the directive style of trait-and-factor theory in the early 1940s. Rogers's client-centered approach also opened the way for a variety of theoretical applications of psychological theories to career counseling. For example, in the 1950s, four major scholars developed theories that would advance the field. Eli Ginzberg was perhaps the first to conceptualize the career development process as lifelong and subject to compromise. Edward Bordin developed a career counseling approach grounded in psychoanalytic theory, and Ann Roe formulated a theory based on Abraham Maslow's hierarchy of needs and personality types. Donald Super drew from both personal construct theory and the literature in human development to articulate a theory that emphasized that career development is a process and not a choice made at one point in time. All these approaches continue to influence the way career counseling is understood and researched today.

None of these theories, however, has had as much influence on career research and practice as the work of John Holland. With ideas from his comprehensive trait-and-factor model in the 1950s, Holland published his theory in book form in 1973 (*Making Vocational Choices*) and published revisions in 1985 and 1997. Holland's theory has spurred a vast amount of research and the development of several frequently used instruments and has profoundly changed the practice of career counseling. In brief, Holland's theory proposes that people can be categorized into six personality types, and work environments can also be categorized as fitting those six types. His theory maintains that people will search for and find the greatest satisfaction in environments that match their personalities.

In the past few decades, a number of new theories have been developed that derive from the theories of the earlier part of the century. In the 1960s Lofquist and Dawis published a theory of work adjustment. In the 1970s, Krumboltz published a theory using social learning theory to understand career decision making. In the 1980s Gottfredson published a theory about the processes of circumscription and compromise in career choice. And in the 1990s Lent, Brown, and Hackett developed a social-cognitive theory of career choice. In the past decade there has been considerable attention given to the role of convergence in career theories, with scholars attempting to find common points among the most influential theories.

Career Counseling: Process and Outcome

In research, the term *career counseling* has often been used to describe a great variety of different interventions. Thus some studies have investigated individual career counseling, whereas others have examined group interventions, classes, one-time workshops, or use of computerized career information and guidance systems. This lack of clear and specific definition led to confusion about what is actually known about the process and outcome of career counseling. To understand more about the actual effectiveness of career interventions, Laurel Oliver and Arnold Spokane (1988) used meta-analytic procedures to examine effect sizes for various career interventions. They reported a mean effect size for all career interventions of 0.85 and determined that career counseling demonstrated a high level

of effectiveness given the duration of treatment needed. This important meta-analytic study (*Journal of Counseling Psychology*, 1988, 35, 447–462) supports individual empirical investigations in concluding that career counseling appears to be highly effective.

Which specific components of career counseling are effective, however, remains considerably less clear. Researchers are just beginning to examine what aspects of the career counseling process lead to the most effective outcomes. Methodologies are being developed and others modified from psychotherapy process research, and it seems clear that there is much rich territory to explore within the process dimension of career counseling.

Trends in Career Counseling

The workplace is changing in fundamental ways, and thus the role of career counseling becomes increasingly important. Increases in unemployment, increased diversity in the work force, people living and working longer, all have an influence on the future of career counseling. Trends for the field include the following.

1. There is a greater awareness of the need for career counselors to develop competencies to work with increasingly complex issues. In recognition of this complexity, the National Career Development Association has developed a list of competencies for career counselors. The list contains a diverse array of skills, ranging from individual and group counseling skills to legal and ethical issues in the field.

2. Career counselors have a greater need to be aware and knowledgeable in working with a much more diverse clientele than ever before. The work force is changing and includes more members of racial and ethnic minority groups, more women and especially single mothers, more openly gay, lesbian, and bisexual individuals, and individuals with various forms of disability. The profession is responding with increased training and a variety of new resources to help build competence.

3. Greater attention must be given to effective ways of integrating personal and career counseling. There appears to be growing consensus that it is unproductive to try to dichotomize the concerns individuals bring to counseling as either career concerns or social and emotional concerns. Instead, there is recognition that individuals come to career counseling with an array of interrelated concerns and that the career counselor should be competent in handling social and emotional issues as well as strictly career issues.

4. Greater diagnostic specificity is needed in determining what would be the most helpful interventions for specific client problems. Assessment of an individual's personality, interest, skills, and values has always been at the heart of career counseling. There will likely

be greater emphasis on career counselors' ability to provide helpful data to clients and to further target and refine interventions based on client assessment data.

5. Increased research is needed to investigate the important elements of career counseling and what specifically contributes to positive outcome.

6. There must be greater integration of constructs from other disciplines to enrich our understanding of the career development process. There have already been a number of lines of research that have drawn on constructs from related disciplines and fruitfully applied them to the area of career counseling, including self-efficacy theory, models of information processing, attachment theory, and the role of the working alliance.

7. Greater use of technological advances can help to bring the most up-to-date information and resources to clients in the most accessible manner.

[See also Career.]

Bibliography

Gysbers, N. C., Heppner, M. J., & Johnston, J. J. (1998). *Career counseling: Process, issues, and techniques.* Boston: Allyn & Bacon. Focuses specifically on the process of career counseling and how this process can be helpful in expanding the life choices of women, men, racial and ethnic minorities, and individuals with disabilities.

Holland, J. L. (1997). *Making vocational choices: A theory of vocational personalities and work environments* (4th ed.). Odessa, FL: Psychological Assessment Resources. A thorough explanation of Holland's theory of occupational choice and an integrated review of research conducted on the theory.

Leong, F. T. L. (1995). *Career development and vocational behavior of racial and ethnic minorities.* Mahwah, NJ: Erlbaum. A discussion of the research related to career development theory and assessment related to the four major racial and ethnic minority groups in the United States: Native Americans, Asian Americans, African Americans, and Hispanic Americans.

National Career Development Association (1992). NCDA reports: Career counseling competencies. *Career Development Quarterly, 40,* 379–386. An article outlining the competencies that are deemed critical for effective career counseling by the National Career Development Association.

Savickas, M. L., & Lent, R. W. (Eds.). (1994). *Convergence in career development theories.* Palo Alto, CA: Consulting Psychologists Press. A text in which scholars explore the prospects of convergence among theories of career choice and development.

Walsh, W. B., & Osipow, S. H. (Eds.). (1994). *Career counseling for women.* Hillsdale, NJ: Erlbaum. An edited volume of articles on a range of issues related to the career development of women, including assessment, dual career issues, racial and ethnic minority women's issues, women in science and engineering, gifted girls and women.

Walsh, W. B., & Osipow, S. H. (Eds.). (1995). *Handbook of vocational psychology: Theory, research, and practice.* Mahwah, NJ: Erlbaum. An edited volume in which authors review the most salient research and theoretical literature in a range of career development topics, such as women's career development, career process and outcome research, and the relationship of career counseling to personal adjustment.

Mary J. Heppner

CAREER SERVICE OFFICERS. *See* Military Service.

CAREERS IN PSYCHOLOGY. Both as a science and as a discipline of professional practice, psychology is concerned with why people behave the way they do. Psychologists produce scientific knowledge about behavior and apply that knowledge to a wide variety of areas. The field of psychology makes significant contributions to national and individual needs in areas ranging from health and education to industry and technology. People seek careers in psychology for many reasons. Some have specific goals: They wish to help people experiencing duress and illness. Some dream of identifying the basis for cognitive processes or developing a model to predict school performance or to make personnel decisions. Still others imagine building companies that capitalize on the newest knowledge about neuroscience or organizational systems. Some choose careers in psychology because they are curious about behavior and how the mind works; they are motivated by the excitement and beauty of the intellectual world and hope to formulate theories that will lead to new ways of thinking about our world. Others imagine educating people about the discipline of psychology or may want to shape public policy on issues of direct relevance to individuals, schools, groups, and society. Many psychologists will work in several of these domains across their careers.

As the techniques, knowledge, and applications of psychology become better known to the general public, the discipline is recognized as relevant to more and more careers. Today, psychologists can be counted among professionals in the realms of health, business, education, and government.

Employment status varies greatly by educational level achieved. The highest paid and greatest range of jobs directly in the field of psychology are available to those with doctoral degrees. Unemployment rates for doctoral psychologists (1.3% in 1993) are slightly below the average for other doctoral scientists and engineers, which ranged from a low of 1% for computer and information scientists to a high of 3% in geology and oceanography that same year (National Science Foundation, 1995). At least some of the unemployment reported by those with baccalaureate (24%) and master's (6%) degrees is a consequence of the larger numbers graduating each year with bachelor's (72,083 in 1994) and master's (13,921 in 1994) degrees in psychology. Also, these degrees are stepping stones to other careers rather than terminal points or degrees permitting entry into a psychology position.

Sources of Data

The primary sources of data about careers in psychology are the Bureau of Labor Statistics (BLS), the National Science Foundation (NSF), and the Research Office of the American Psychological Association (APA). Each of these sources has strengths and limitations. The BLS data are self-reports by employers who are asked to provide the number of psychologists they employ and by employees who are asked to self-report their occupations. The major limitation of these data is the definition of what constitutes a psychologist, which can range across degree level and job activity. Data from individuals collected as part of the U.S. Census are limited in this way as well since they depend on individuals' definitions of their occupations.

The NSF data provide a different view of careers because they are collected from doctoral students upon graduation and from samples of doctoral graduates throughout their careers. However, these data do not include psychologists with the doctor of psychology (Psy.D.) or doctor of education (Ed.D.) degrees and most often are reported in predetermined, combined categories (e.g., social sciences or psychology), making it difficult to observe patterns desegregated by subfields of psychology.

The APA data from new doctorates, including Psy.D.s and Ed.D.s, are a measure of jobs as self-reported by graduates within a year of their graduation. APA also collects information from its members about a variety of factors, including salaries and career paths. These data are limited by the characteristics of association membership.

Combined, these data give us important answers to the larger question we ask; however, no one source is without limitations. Each has been designed for different uses and with different target populations and each has different assumptions about the field of psychology. The composite picture must be viewed within the constraints that form it.

Doctoral Graduates

The most recent (1998) and best estimate of the number of doctoral-level psychologists in the United States is approximately 105,000. This figure was compiled by the APA Research Office from the National Science Foundation (NSF) Survey of Doctorate Recipients (SRS), augmented to include Psy.D. and Ed.D. recipients. Based on what we know about Ph.D. psychologists, 90% are employed; fewer than 1% are unemployed and seeking employment. Of the employed psychologists, 79% are working full time; of those not employed, 2% are in postdoctoral positions and 5%, approximately 4,000 people, are retired. Combining all sources of information on careers in 1995 (Wicherski & Kohout, 1997), it is estimated that a majority (39.3%) of psychologists are employed in business settings, either as self-employed professionals or in business and incorporated private practices primarily in the service of health care delivery. Slightly fewer psychologists are employed in university and college (34.6%) or other educational settings (5.3%). The remaining psychologists are scattered among federal, state, and local government (11.6%) and private nonprofit settings (9%). Looking at employment settings of psychologists since 1973, the APA Research Office documents the dramatic shift in career paths away from academic settings primarily engaged in teaching (37%) and research (15%) to careers in professional services, primarily as health providers. By 1995, 53% of doctoral-level psychologists reported being involved in professional services, 14% in management, and about equal proportions in teaching (17%) and research (16%). In today's volatile marketplace, much speculation continues about changing career patterns for the discipline. The interim between 1993 and 1995 suggests a beginning upward trend toward psychologists in academic settings (i.e., colleges, universities, and medical schools) when compared proportionally, not in absolute numbers, with a concomitant drop in those in the for-profit and self-employed settings. Such a pattern is echoed in an analysis of *APA Monitor* job placement advertising for the academic year 1997–1998 and anecdotally by many practitioners. Other categories of job settings appear to have remained proportionally stable over this same 25-year period.

The number of new psychologists entering the marketplace each year for the last decade has remained relatively stable at approximately 4,000. Between 1973 and 1983, the number per year grew quickly, from approximately 2,500 per year to 3,500 per year. But the most dramatic growth in the discipline occurred between 1930, when about 100 new doctorates emerged in the marketplace each year, and 1960, when that number had grown to about 1,000 per year. The vast majority of psychologists are awarded the Ph.D. degree, which constituted 76% of all new degrees in 1995; the remaining new psychologists in 1995 were awarded a professional degree, doctor of psychology (22%) or doctor of education (2%).

One of the strengths of the discipline is the range of subfields in which a psychologist can focus his or her interests and expertise, a range broadly described by the 52 divisions presently recognized within the American Psychological Association. By far the most popular subfield in the discipline is clinical psychology, which captured 40% of new doctorates in 1995. Yet, in the most recent comparison of proportional employment status across subfields (as reported by the APA Research Office), 85% of new doctorates in industrial/organizational psychology were employed full time compared with 81% of those with new degrees in social and personality psychology, 64% in health service providing subfields, 62% in developmental and educational psychology, and 50% in physiological and experimental psychology. The relatively low full-time employment numbers of those with newly minted degrees in physiological and experimental psychology is countered by their relatively high proportion (40%) in postdoctoral positions, a pattern common to other sciences, such as chemistry and physics. Consistent with these interests, the primary employment settings of new 1995 doctoral graduates is predominately in health service positions, including managed care (45%), followed by academic and education and school settings (37%) and business, government, and other similar settings (18%).

In spite of the relatively good job market for psychologists, new doctoral recipients' perceptions of their career opportunities has become substantially more negative over the past decade. During this period, the proportion reporting an excellent perception declined from 12% in 1989 to 3% in 1995. Although the reported perception varies by subfield, declines have been reported for all subfields of the discipline. Yet the time reported to be necessary to find employment has improved slightly during this same time period; a contradiction perhaps best understood by the increase of those reporting that they are "involuntarily out of field or underemployed." Unfortunately, because this measure is self-reported, we are unable to determine if it represents an observable pattern of unexpected career paths or idiosyncratic choices.

An important aspect of careers, both to the individual and as a measure of social status and value, is earning power. Mean annual salaries of doctoral-level psychologists in 1997, as reported by the APA Research Office, mirror, albeit imperfectly, the trend observed in the subfield interests of new doctorates. Average annual salaries range from a low of $48,000 for those in faculty positions to a high of $80,000 for those in industrial/organizational psychology. Between these extremes are the health service providers, who earn on average between $60,000 in Veterans Administration hospitals or other direct human service positions and $74,000 in independent practice. Research administrators likewise earn salaries averaging $70,000 per year,

whereas those in research positions report average annual salaries of $50,000. Starting salaries mirror these patterns in more restricted ranges, from $37,000 to $54,000. These salaries are achieved after a long period of formal education averaging more than seven years, an education that in 1996 brought 67% of new doctoral recipients significant debt levels; of these, fewer than 35% reported debt levels less than $10,000, whereas 13% report debt levels more than $40,000.

Given the current volatility in jobs and the futurists' predicted paradigm shift in the very definition of a job, when peering into the future of careers in psychology it is important to listen to what our new doctoral recipients say about their education. In general, these new psychologists report that the most useful learning they acquired include quantitative skills, teaching abilities, and administrative and communication expertise. Our new health service providers point to the business and management skills they need to begin their practices, knowledge of health care delivery systems, and short-term and brief therapy intervention techniques. We should be cognizant as well that when a sample of graduate students from all disciplines was asked which skills developed in graduate school are most valuable in the outside world, some of the most popular responses include: the ability to work productively with difficult people, the ability to work in high-stress environments, persistence, and circumventing the rules (Fiske, 1997)—not what faculty likely knew they were imparting but perhaps an important peek at both the marketplace and our preparation for it.

Master's Graduates

A master's degree in psychology provides the educational background relevant to a number of employment opportunities. The results of the most recent APA survey of 1996 master's graduates is consistent with earlier reports that nationally the single greatest area of employment opportunity exists in human service agencies (50% of respondents). These settings include community mental health centers, clinics, retardation or substance abuse facilities, psychiatric hospitals, and other community social service agencies. But career options for master's degree holders are limited by state licensing and certification regulations. The doctoral degree is recognized by all states as the academic degree level required for licensure as a psychologist in independent practice. There are some states that license at the master's degree level, but it usually is a restricted practice license. Master's graduates working in health delivery settings also conduct applied research to evaluate and/or manage programs.

A second major setting for employment of those with master's degrees in psychology is in the schools and educational system (20% of respondents). Jobs in these environments include student guidance and counseling, psychoeducational testing, and working with special-needs children. Many master's graduates in psychology also work in business, government, or other nonprofit organizations (15% of respondents). Jobs in these settings include research, consulting, program evaluation, employment testing, needs assessment, training and development, public policy analysis, and human resources management. And some master's graduates (12% of respondents) are employed in universities, colleges, and community colleges in work such as teaching, research, or career counseling.

Increasingly, graduates of master's programs are employed in settings not traditionally considered to be part of psychology. These include architectural and legal firms; the entertainment industry; and advertising and marketing companies that conduct applied behavior research, for example, on driving behavior, health compliance, product use, or workplace safety. The critical thinking, behavioral observation, research, and interpersonal skills learned in a master's program prepare graduates for many areas not generally labeled psychological but utilizing the kinds of knowledge and skills common to the discipline of psychology.

Median starting annual salaries reported by 1996 master's graduates range from $26,000 for direct human service positions to $35,000 for applied and administrative positions. Like doctoral graduates, a large proportion of new master's graduates report some cumulative debt level (60%) from their education years. Among those with debt, these levels are lower than for their doctoral counterparts: 16% report levels under $5,000, whereas 30% report debt in excess of $20,000.

Bachelor's Graduates

Some people stop their formal education with a bachelor's degree in psychology and find work related to their college major. They may be assistants in rehabilitation centers; or, if they meet state certification requirements, they can teach psychology in high school. But the study of psychology at the bachelor's level is mostly preparation for other careers. Most baccalaureate graduates find jobs in administrative support, public affairs, education, business, sales, service industries, health, the biological sciences, and computer programming. They work as employment counselors, correction counselor trainees, interviewers, personnel analysts, probation officers, and writers. Two thirds of those surveyed by the APA Research Office believe their jobs are closely or somewhat related to their psychology background and that their jobs hold career potential. As one banker with a bachelor's degree in psychology commented: "Once you learn the principles of human behavior, they are always at the top of your mind, ready to be used."

Because of the changing education and career landscape of baccalaureate recipients, the best view of careers of these graduates is provided by the APA Research Office's Psychology Baccalaureate Survey (1997), which follows 1992 degree recipients at points in time after their graduations and extends the Baccalaureate and Beyond study done in 1993 by the National Center for Education Statistics. In 1994, 75% of these graduates were employed, a rate somewhat lower than that of other college graduates. Yet, of those unemployed, only 5% were seeking work. Most likely, these statistics reflect the likelihood that undergraduate psychology degree holders seek further education. Over half of the 1992 baccalaureate respondents were enrolled in or planned to continue their education. Of those having begun or having completed their graduate study by 1995, 39% reported psychology as their chosen field. Counseling (11%), education (10%), and social work (9%) were the next most popular fields of study, after which medicine (7%), law (5%), and business (2%) drew significant numbers.

Changing Demographic Patterns in Psychology

The shortage of minority researchers, practitioners, and college faculty in psychology is acute (APA, 1996). Only about 8% of psychological researchers and other behavioral scientists are members of minority groups, compared with 15% in the biological and life sciences, 17% in the physical sciences, and 18% in computer sciences and mathematics (Thurgood & Clarke, 1995).

Although minority groups make up 26% of the general population (U.S. Bureau of the Census, Washington, D.C., 1995), APA's Research Office estimates that only 10% of all psychologists are members of minority groups. In 1993, there were 2,240 Black psychologists practicing as health providers out of 33 million Black Americans; 1,640 practicing Hispanic psychologists out of 23 million Hispanic Americans; 1,110 practicing Asian psychologists out of 9 million Asian Americans; and 410 practicing Native American psychologists out of 2.2 million Native Americans (NSF, 1995). This is troubling because research has shown that minority psychologists can treat clients from their own racial and ethnic groups more effectively than nonminority psychologists can (Meyers, Wohlford, Guzman, & Echemendia, 1991).

Today, 19% of college graduates who majored in psychology are from minority groups. At the graduate level, 16% are minority students, but only 8% of these students obtained doctoral degrees in 1998. This constricting pipeline for minority groups is of great concern. One solution is to bolster the diversity of college faculty in general and of psychology departments in particular. Of all college faculties, 12% are from minority groups, and of psychology faculty, 9% (National

Center for Educational Statistics, 1993). This situation is particularly troubling given data showing that the presence of minority faculty is positively correlated with the recruitment and retention of minority students (Guzman & Messenger, 1991). Moreover, minority students are most likely to graduate if minority faculty members are available to serve as their mentors and role models (Striker et al., 1990).

The discipline has fared much better in attracting women. In the last 25 years, the number of women at all levels of education has grown significantly, currently accounting for 73% of bachelor's degrees and 69% of new doctorates. Yet, although the pipeline is quite full, the concomitant success of these women remains elusive, as measured by salary level or job advancement (e.g., tenure) achieved.

The Future

Predictions about long-term needs for psychological expertise suggest a rosy future (Branch, 1995; U.S. Department of Labor, 1994–1995). There are few areas of national or individual need to which psychological knowledge or skill cannot apply. Moreover, history demonstrates the ability of psychologists to shift areas in which to pursue the discipline, to apply their knowledge and skills, and to find employment. Whereas the discipline was once thought of in terms of teaching and research, it is now thought of in terms of application. But success will require continuing transformations, new applications, and career paths not yet identified.

[*See also* Career; Licensure; Private Practice; *and* Public Service.]

Bibliography

American Psychological Association, Commission on Ethnic Minority Recruitment, Retention, and Training in Psychology. (1996). *Visions and transformations.* Washington, DC: Author.
Branch, S. (1995). The most lucrative degrees. *Money Guide 1995.*
Grocer, S., & Kohout, J. (1997). *The 1995 APA survey of 1992 psychology baccalaureate recipients.* Washington, DC: American Psychological Association.
Guzman, L. P., & Mersenger, L. C. (1991). *Recruitment and retention of ethnic minority students and faculty: A survey of doctoral programs in psychology.* Washington, DC: American Psychological Association.
Myers, H. F., Wohlford, P., Guzman, L. P., & Echemendia, R. J. (1991). *Ethnic minority perspective in clinical training and services in psychology.* Washington DC: American Psychological Association.
National Science Foundation. (1995, March 15). *Survey of doctoral recipients* (Data Brief, Vol. 2, No. 5). Washington, DC: Author.
Striker, G., Davis-Russell, E., Bourg, E., Daran, E., Hammand, W. R., McHolland, H., Polite, K., & Vaughn, B. E. (1990). *Towards ethnic diversification in psychology education and training.* Washington, DC: National Council of Schools of Professional Psychology.
Thurgood, D. H., & Clarke, J. E. (1995). *Summary report 1993: Doctorate recipients from United States universities.* Washington, DC: National Academy Press.
U.S. Department of Education, Office of Educational Research and Improvement, National Center for Education Statistics. (1993). *Occupational and educational outcomes of recent college graduates 1 year after graduation: 1991.* (NCES No. 93–162). Washington DC: U.S. Government Printing Office.
U.S. Department of Labor, Bureau of Labor Statistics. (1994–1995). *Social scientists and legal occupations* (Bulletin 2450–5). Washington DC: U.S. Government Printing Office. Reprinted from the *Occupational Outlook Handbook.* 1994–1995.
Wicherski, M., & Kohout, J. (1997). *1995 doctorate employment survey.* Washington, DC: American Psychological Association.

Jill N. Reich

CARMICHAEL, LEONARD (1898–1973), American psychologist and administrator. Leonard Carmichael was born the son of a successful physician-father and a well-educated mother in the Germantown section of Philadelphia, Pennsylvania. In the family tradition, he did his undergraduate work at Tufts University, completing a senior research project on the embryology of eye muscles in sharks. He then attended graduate school at Harvard University, where he was influenced by Walter Dearborn, G. H. Parker, Edwin G. Boring, Leonard Troland, and William McDougall. He completed his Ph.D. degree in psychology in 1924 with a dissertation that was a theoretical-historical survey of the heredity-environment problem.

Carmichael joined the faculty at Princeton University in 1924. There he did his best known research, dealing with the development of behavior in larval salamanders and frog tadpoles. He raised the animals in a mild concentration of the anesthetic chloretone so that they grew normally but were immobilized. To his surprise, Carmichael found that when removed from the anesthetic the experimental animals swam as well as did controls reared under normal conditions. Although Carmichael continued to stress the interaction of nature and nurture, these results were important in demonstrating the role of maturation without practice and thus of hereditary factors in the development of behavior. At Princeton, Carmichael also worked on issues of theory and philosophy and formed a dinner discussion group named in honor of Charles Bell, an early contributor to physiological psychology.

Carmichael moved to Brown University in 1927. There he conducted research on the development of behavior in mammalian fetuses. He also taught many sections of introductory psychology, becoming a very popular instructor, and pioneered early work with the electroencephalogram.

In 1936 Carmichael became a professor and dean of the Faculty of Arts and Sciences at the University of Rochester, New York. Two years later he returned to Tufts as the university president. Carmichael made important contributions to the World War II effort, especially in his role as the director of the National Roster of Scientific and Specialized Personnel, which helped in placing scientists in positions where they could be most effective.

In 1953 Carmichael was called to the secretaryship of the Smithsonian Institution in Washington. He remained for 11 years and was instrumental in adding several buildings and in getting the annual congressional appropriation raised from $2.5 to $13 million. When he retired from the Smithsonian in 1964, Carmichael became the vice-president for research and exploration of the National Geographic Society. There, he was able to facilitate much research, especially that on primate behavior, including the efforts of Jane Goodall.

Carmichael edited two editions of the *Manual of Child Psychology* (New York, 1946, 1954) and wrote an introductory textbook, *Basic Psychology* (New York, 1957). He received 23 honorary degrees, orders of merit from four foreign countries, and numerous other honors. He was elected to the American Academy of Arts and Sciences in 1932, the American Philosophical Society in 1942, and National Academy of Sciences in 1943. He was president of the American Philosophical Society from 1970 to 1973 and of the American Psychological Association in 1940. He served on the boards of numerous scientific organizations including the Yerkes Laboratories of Primate Biology. A dormitory at Tufts and a lecture hall at Brown are named in his honor.

[*Many of the people mentioned in this article are the subjects of independent biographical entries.*]

Bibliography

Works by Carmichael

Carmichael, L. (1925). Heredity and environment: Are they antithetical? *Journal of Abnormal and Social Psychology, 20,* 245–260.

Carmichael, L. (1926). The development of behavior in vertebrates experimentally removed from the influence of external stimulation. *Psychological Review, 33,* 51–58.

Carmichael, L. (1926). Sir Charles Bell: A contribution to the history of physiological psychology. *Psychological Review, 33,* 188–217.

Carmichael, L. (1941). The experimental embryology of the mind. *Psychological Bulletin, 38,* 1–28.

Carmichael, L. (1968). Some historical roots of present-day animal psychology. In B. B. Wolman (Ed.), *Historical roots of contemporary psychology* (pp. 47–76). New York: Harper & Row.

Works about Carmichael

Carmichael, L. (1967). Leonard Carmichael. In E. G. Boring & G. Lindzey (Eds.), *A history of psychology in autobiography* (Vol. 5, pp. 29–56). New York: Appleton-Century-Crofts.

Mead, L. C. (1974). Leonard Carmichael: 1898–1973. *American Journal of Psychology, 87,* 517–525.

Pfaffmann, C. (1980). Leonard Carmichael, November 9, 1898–September 16, 1973. In *Biographical Memoirs, National Academy of Sciences of the United States of America* (Vol. 51, pp. 25–47). Washington, DC: National Academy of Sciences.

Donald A. Dewsbury

CARR, HARVEY A. (1873–1954), American psychologist. Carr was born on an Indiana farm and grew up in a community that "firmly believed in the value of book learning" (C. Murchison, Ed., *History of Psychology in Autobiography*, Worcester, Mass., 1936, p. 69). He began his undergraduate work at DePauw University and continued at the University of Colorado, where he studied psychology with Arthur Allin, earning his bachelor's degree in 1901 and master's degree in 1902. He went on to the University of Chicago to study experimental psychology with John Dewey, James Rowland Angell, and John B. Watson. He was awarded a doctorate in 1905, having written a dissertation on the topic of a visual illusion of motion during eye closure. Finding no university position, Carr taught high school in Texas and at the State Normal School in Michigan in 1905 and 1906, then at the Pratt Institute in Brooklyn until 1908, when he was invited to replace Watson at Chicago. He remained there until his retirement in 1938.

Carr served as chairman of the department of psychology at Chicago from 1926 to 1938. He was elected president of the American Psychological Association in 1926 and of the Midwestern Psychological Association in 1937. He was advisory editor for the *Journal of Experimental Psychology* from 1916 to 1925 and associate editor of the *Journal of General Psychology* from 1929 to 1954. He also served for many years as general editor of Longman's psychology series.

Carr is usually regarded as having succeeded Angell as torchbearer for the Chicago school of American functionalism. Edna Heidbreder wrote: "The work of Carr represents functionalism when it had settled down and become a recognized school, and was no longer a renaissance and a reformation" (*Seven Psychologies*, New York, 1933, p. 219). But Carr's functionalism was more austere than Angell's, which had sought to "discern and portray the typical *operations* of consciousness under actual life conditions" (*Psychological Review*, 1907, *14*, p. 61). Although he did not deny consciousness and subjectivity, as Watson had done in his version of behaviorism, Carr paid them little direct attention, preferring instead to speak of the adaptive activities of the organism and their conditions. These were analyzed in terms of causal relations between stimuli and responses, which were studied objectively and, when possible, experimentally. "Personality, mind, and self," he wrote, "are conceptual objects that can be studied only indirectly through their manifestations" (*Psychology: A Study of Mental Activity*, New York, 1925, p. 4). Carr's functionalism thus differed from strict behaviorism in granting that mental processes existed, of which behavior could be understood as a manifestation. This idea did not, however, extend to animals. In his APA presidential address, he wrote: "I am somewhat of a behaviorist in the field of animal psychology, although I do not class myself as such so far as human psychology is concerned" (Carr, *Psychological Review*, 1927, *34*, p. 104).

Carr took charge of the animal laboratory at Chicago and continued Watson's study of the senses albino rats used to get through mazes. Vision, he learned, was by far the most important to them. In the course of this work, Carr invented an improved maze that became widely adopted for experiments of this sort. He had admired Watson's animal work and encouraged his students to choose thesis topics in comparative psychology. He supervised 18 theses in that field over the span of his career. He was disappointed, however, that students tended to avoid comparative psychology because they felt that identification with it "would be detrimental to their professional placement and advancement" (C. Murchison, Ed., *History of Psychology in Autobiography*, Worcester, Mass., 1936, p. 79).

He was still less successful in persuading students to share his enthusiasm for the problems of space perception. Over his career only five theses were produced on this problem. Carr attributed this largely to the "technicalities of the subject" (C. Murchison, Ed., *History of Psychology in Autobiography*, Worcester, Mass., 1936, p. 79). It remained an important topic for him, however. He continued work on it and near the end of his career published his textbook on the subject, *An Introduction to Space Perception* (New York, 1935).

Student response to his interest in learning was more gratifying. Over his thirty years as professor at Chicago, he supervised 29 theses on memorization, perceptual-motor learning, and the conditions affecting

acquisition of adaptive behaviors. Carr was a sharp critic of popular research practices in the field of learning. He alleged that psychologists made "illicit use of mathematics" (*Psychological Review*, 1933, *40*, pp. 514–532) and sought oversimplified answers to their questions.

Carr had a reputation for being a cautious but tolerant thinker and was universally admired by his students. It is said that his main influence on psychology came through his students and manifested itself more in attitude and style than, as Helen Koch put it, in any "specific content of their preachments" (Koch, *Psychological Review*, 1955, *62*, p. 82).

Bibliography

Carr, H. A. (1930). Functionalism. In C. Murchison (Ed.), *Psychologies of 1930* (pp. 59–78). Worcester, MA: Clark University Press. A vigorously mounted defense against the allegation that functionalists cannot agree on their use of the term "function."

Pillsbury, W. B. (1955). Harvey A. Carr: 1873–1954. *American Journal of Psychology*, *68*, 149–151. An obituary with biographical information.

Whitely, P. L. (1976). A new name for an old idea? A student of Harvey Carr reflects. *Journal of the History of the Behavioral Sciences*, *12*, 260–274. A warm tribute to Carr by an appreciative former student. Reprinted in D. A. Owens & M. Wagner (Eds.) (1992). *Progress in modern psychology: The legacy of American functionalism*. Westport, CT: Praeger.

Charles W. Tolman

CASE LAW. It is commonly acknowledged that psychology advances science and promotes human welfare through research and the perfection of methods of assessment and intervention. In the past quarter century, however, the field has begun to recognize that the courts have a powerful role to play in formulating sound scientific and mental health policy.

There are many sources of law. The United States Constitution, of course, is the ultimate wellspring of fundamental legal principles. Congress and state legislatures, however, are the major, though by no means the sole, producers of enforceable obligations that control almost every aspect of day-to-day functioning. Administrative agencies within the executive branch of government, through the promulgation of regulations that have the force of law, implement and particularize these statutes.

Another major source of legal duties is case law developed by federal and state judges. The traditional roles of courts are to determine whether laws meet constitutional requirements; to interpret statutes and rules; to adjudicate disputes between parties, both in civil and criminal contexts; and, in appropriate cases, to advance civil law by creating new duties or obligations where the legislature has not specifically delineated them.

The courts have had a profound effect in staking out the scope of psychology and in formulating public policy that is undergirded by empirical social science findings. For example, in the past half century, the courts, among many other far-reaching decisions, have interpreted the federal rules of evidence to qualify psychologists as expert witnesses in trial settings, as well as to determine the admissibility of social science and forensic psychological evidence and the extent to which confidential therapeutic communications are protected from disclosure to third parties in legal proceedings. They have also provided protections for psychologist-researchers from defamatory comments by legislators and have delineated the proper use of assessment devices in employment settings.

In addition, the courts, particularly the U.S. Supreme Court, have been enmeshed in some of the most significant issues of social policy to which psychology may make important contributions. Some of these are: the psychological sequelae of abortion; the effectiveness of the death penalty; the size, composition, and attitudes of juries in civil and criminal trials; the trial and execution of people with mental disabilities; the duty of mental health professionals to protect unsuspecting private third parties from their violent patients; the right of the public to choose their own mental health provider; and the right of involuntarily committed mental patients to refuse certain kinds of proposed interventions, including psychotropic medication.

Scientific, educational, and professional organizations such as the American Psychological Association need not be simply the passive recipients of judicial decisions. These kinds of organizations can have a significant influence on the decisions of state and federal courts, including the Supreme Court, by submitting *amicus curiae* ("friend of the court") briefs in appropriate cases. Carefully crafted, well-written, and scientifically sound *amicus* briefs play a crucial role in shaping judicial decisions. Frequently, because of a persuasive *amicus* brief, the holdings of judicial opinions and thus their precedential value can be narrowed or broadened despite the outcome urged by the parties. Alternatively, there may be issues of little concern to the parties but of great importance to an *amicus*. Occasionally, a case will be decided on a ground suggested only by the *amicus* association. Since their lone and initial use in 1823, about two thirds of all cases decided by a written opinion of the U.S. Supreme Court have involved *amicus curiae* briefs.

An *amicus* brief filed by a scientific and professional association can take one of several forms. First, because

the Supreme Court takes fewer than 5% of the cases petitioners ask them to hear, an *amicus* brief on behalf of a petitioner noting the national importance of the issue may influence the Court to take a case it ordinarily would not decide.

Second, it can help the party the association is supporting to flesh out arguments that the party is forced to make in summary form. Strict space limitations are imposed on the parties to a case, and they are often compelled to argue some of their points in rather abbreviated form. For example, *Price Waterhouse v. Hopkins* (490 U.S. 228, 1989) was a case in which the sole claim of employment discrimination was based on the allegation that the employer refused to promote the employee because of sex stereotyping. The party representing the employee was limited in the number of pages that could be devoted to the social science literature on gender stereotyping. Despite the central importance of stereotyping to a finding of discrimination, the employee had other legal, nonempirical issues she needed to address in her 50-page brief that were a result of the nature of the lower court decisions. In the *amicus* brief APA filed in this case, however, APA was able to spend all of its allotted 30 pages informing the Supreme Court about the extensive research on stereotyping, citing more than 100 articles.

Third, an *amicus* brief can make arguments that the party wants to but cannot make in a tenable manner. A professional association can provide data that can inform the Court's decision with greater credibility than a lay party can, as long as the data are within the scope of the association's expertise. For example, in a case that involved a state law mandating that only physicians provide abortion counseling (*City of Akron v. Akron Center for Reproductive Health*, 462 U.S. 416, 1983), the party devoted almost no space to arguing against this narrow requirement. But the APA marshaled empirical studies to show why counseling by nonphysicians would help to promote truly informed consent, and the Supreme Court agreed.

Fourth, one of the most common forms of *amicus* support is to inform the court of interests other than those represented by the parties and to focus the court's attention on the broader implications of various rulings. Far more than other courts, the Supreme Court issues decisions that have consequences beyond those affecting the involved parties. Thus the Supreme Court is more sensitive than most other courts to the implications of its rulings for society at large. An *amicus* brief can inform the Court of those implications. For example, in a case concerning the immunity from antitrust liability of peer review committees that decide on hospital privileges (*Patrick v. Burget*, 486 U.S. 94, 1988), APA argued against absolute immunity. It did so primarily on the ground that absolute immunity would insulate peer review committees composed only of physicians from claims of restraint of trade when psychologist-competitors were arbitrarily and irrationally denied hospital privileges. The Supreme Court agreed and adopted the position that there was no basis for granting absolute immunity to peer review groups.

Further, as an *amicus*, there is the opportunity for working closely with counsel for the party the association is supporting. This can sharpen and improve the approach the party takes in its brief and oral arguments. Some associations, such as APA, organize sophisticated moot courts at which the lawyer who will argue for the party that the *amicus* is supporting can work with experts knowledgeable about the Supreme Court to develop concise and persuasive answers to hard questions the Court may ask during oral argument. Although such informal assistance has a lower profile than the *amicus* brief itself, this kind of assistance to the party can make the difference between a victory or defeat in the Supreme Court.

Between 1962 and 1997, the APA submitted 82 *amicus curiae* briefs in federal and state courts, 33 of them in the U.S. Supreme Court. The cases have involved such widely varied subject matter as reproductive rights; animal research; child abuse; civil commitment; confidentiality; the right of the defendant to expert assistance from mental health professionals in criminal cases; the death penalty; the duty of psychologists to protect third parties from their patients' predicted violence; the insanity defense; discrimination against certain protected groups, such as minorities, women, and gay men and lesbian women; hospital privileges; the use of assessment devices in employment settings; and the rights of those with mental disabilities. In many of these cases, the data supplied or the arguments made by the APA were cited in the Supreme Court's decision, reflecting their salience and significance. An *amicus* brief is a potentially powerful means of exerting substantial influence on issues of national importance.

Perhaps the case with the most profound impact on psychologists, particularly those scientists and professionals who are called upon to testify as expert witnesses, had on its surface nothing to do with psychology. Nor was it one in which APA submitted an *amicus* brief. In that case, *Daubert v. Merrell Dow Pharmaceuticals, Inc.* (509 U.S. 579, 1993), the Supreme Court delineated the proper test that federal judges must use in determining the admissibility of scientific evidence.

The issue of admissibility first arose in 1923, when a federal court of appeals held that, at least with respect to novel scientific evidence, such evidence "must be sufficiently established to have gained general scientific acceptance in the field in which it belongs" (*Frye v. United States*, 293 F. 1013, 1014, D.C. Cir. 1923). In 1975 the Federal Rules of Evidence were adopted. Under Rule 702, "scientific, technical, or other specialized knowledge" is admissible if "it will assist the trier of fact to understand the evidence or to determine a fact in issue. . . ." Although Rule 702 is, on its face, silent as to whether it incorporates *Frye*, several lower courts held that Rule 702 had to be interpreted in light of the *Frye* test; several others ruled that *Frye* was irrelevant. The Supreme Court, in *Daubert*, decided to resolve this sharp division among the lower courts.

Although the precise issue in *Daubert* concerned the admissibility of epidemiological studies in the context of a product liability case, the issue before the Court was not limited to such evidence. The Court held, after studying Rule 702 and reviewing the debates in Congress preceding its adoption, that the "austere [*Frye*] standard, absent from, and incompatible with, the Federal Rules of Evidence, should not be applied in federal trials" (*Daubert*, 1993, p. 589).

In addition, the Court presented a framework for federal judges to use in analyzing the admissibility of scientific evidence. The Federal Rules require that the trial judge serve as a gatekeeper and evaluate the proffered scientific evidence to ensure that it is both valid and relevant before it is admitted (see also *General Electric Co. v. Joiner*, 118 S. Ct. 512, 1997). To help judges determine whether such evidence was indeed scientific, the Court created a nonexclusive list of factors to be considered. The first factor is whether the theory or technique serving as the foundation for the testimony is testable, that is, capable of generating hypotheses that can be falsified through experimentation. The second factor is the known or potential rate of error of the particular scientific technique at issue and the existence and maintenance of standards controlling the operation of the technique. The third and fourth factors are peer review (and publication) and general acceptance. Though not direct measures of scientific validity, the Court considered these factors as proxies for the determinative inquiry. Since this decision, the majority of states have followed the Supreme Court's lead and applied Rule 702 to the consideration of scientific evidence in state trials, discarding the *Frye* test. It is clear that both federal and state courts are scrutinizing the admissibility of forensic psychological and social science evidence under *Daubert* principles.

Judicial decisions are now readily and almost instantaneously accessible on computer databases, with LEXIS and Westlaw the major providers of this service. Given the impact of case law on the functioning of psychologists, it is becoming increasingly important and valuable for members of the profession to maintain reasonable familiarity with decisions that affect the science and practice of psychology. At times, as in *Tarasoff v. Board of Regents*, 551 P.2d 334 (1976)—the case in which the California supreme court held that psychologists have a duty to protect private third parties from their patients' violence—a court may identify a new duty that can have a profound impact on practice or research. Without access to some source of current legal information, it is possible that psychologists will fall short of providing the most ethical and legal services needed by clients and research participants.

Bibliography

Bersoff, D. N., & Glass, D. J. (1995). The not-so "Weisman": The Supreme Court's continuing misuse of social science research. *University of Chicago Law School Roundtable, 2,* 279–302. The most recent discussion of cases on point, including those in which the APA contributed an *amicus* brief.

Bersoff, D. N., & Ogden, D. W. (1991). APA *amicus curiae* briefs: Furthering lesbian and gay male civil rights. *American Psychologist, 46,* 950–956.

Ennis, B. J. (1984). Effective *amicus* briefs. *Catholic University Law Review, 33,* 603–609. A short but pithy compilation of pointers.

Saks, M. J., & Baron, C. (1980). *The use/nonuse/misuse of applied social research in the courts.* Cambridge, MA: Abt Books. A comprehensive evaluation of extant cases and issues; now a bit dated.

Sales, B. D., & VandenBos, G. R. (Eds.). (1994). *Psychology in litigation and legislation.* Washington, DC: American Psychological Association. A compilation of master lectures on law and psychology.

Schierer, C. J., & Hammonds, B. J. (Eds.). (1983). *The master lecture: Vol. 2. Psychology and the law.* Washington, DC: American Psychological Association. A compilation of master lectures on law and psychology.

Tomkins, A., & Oursland, K. (1991). Social and social scientific perspectives in judicial interpretation of the Constitution: A historical view and an overview. *Law and Human Behavior, 15,* 101–120.

Tremper, C. R. (1987). Organized psychology's efforts to influence judicial policymaking. *American Psychologist, 42,* 496–501. Summarizes APA's contributions to important case law, with major focus on Supreme Court decisions.

Donald N. Bersoff

CASE STUDY. The term *case study* refers in general to the in-depth examination of an individual, as in a clinical case study, as well as to the investigation of a group of individuals with shared characteristics, as in an anthropological case study. The former provides a detailed description and analysis of an individual, usually including the treatment of the person's problems. This is a time-honored clinical research method in psychology and allied health disciplines. A comprehensive case study typically includes family history, health and illness background, educational history, details of significant personal relationships such as marriage and children, information on development and personality, and the individual's current life circumstances. As with other methods of knowledge gathering and dissemination, the kinds of information and interpretation found in a case study are heavily influenced by the clinical researcher's theoretical perspective. For example, psychoanalytic case histories emphasize child development factors relating to unconscious conflicts, whereas case studies reported by behaviorally oriented clinicians focus on such variables as reinforcement patterns and cognitive distortions.

As Arnold A. Lazarus and I proposed (A. E. Bergin & S. L. Garfield, Eds., *Handbook of Psychotherapy and Behavior Change*, New York, 1971), there are several characteristics unique to case studies that earn for them a firm place in psychological research:

1. A case study may cast doubt upon a general theory.
2. A case study may serve as a valuable heuristic method furthering subsequent and better controlled research.
3. Although it is poorly controlled, a case study may permit the investigation of rare but important phenomena.
4. A case study can provide the opportunity to apply principles and notions in entirely new ways.
5. A case study can, under certain circumstances, provide enough experimenter control over a phenomenon to furnish scientifically acceptable information.
6. A case study can assist in fleshing out a theory.

First, the successful handling of a particular case may underscore an important exception to a theory. For example, a given theory may hold that a certain kind of problem is untreatable or should not be approached in a particular way. If a therapist succeeded in making a favorable impact on the problem, this would cast doubt upon the tenets of the theoretical viewpoint under consideration. Examples can be found in the literature on exposure-based behavior therapy treatments for phobias, such as systematic desensitization research inspired by Joseph Wolpe's *Psychotherapy by Reciprocal Inhibition* (Stanford, Calif., 1958). Classical psychoanalytic theory regards phobias as defenses against the expression of repressed conflicts. Direct elimination or reduction of the phobia without resolving the putative unconscious conflict would be expected to result in a worsening of the patient's clinical status. The many clinical and experimental reports of successful elimination of unwarranted avoidances without dealing with repressed conflicts cast serious doubt on the general analytic theory and prompted some to revise it to account for the positive findings.

Second, case studies in clinical psychology are probably best known for suggesting new directions that can be pursued systematically in controlled investigations. In fact, it has been suggested that they play a unique and essential role in science by virtue of their heuristic value in generating hypotheses and new ideas. Through exposure to the life histories of patients, clinicians can gain experience in understanding and interpreting complex clinical phenomena. Hypotheses arising from such clinical observations may well elude the investigator who deals only with controlled studies of groups of people.

Examples of the heuristic value of case studies and of clinical experience more generally are legion. In his clinical work with disturbed children, Leo Kanner (*Nervous Child*, 1943, 2, 217–250) noticed that some of them showed a similar constellation of symptoms, including failure to develop appropriate language and extreme isolation from people. He induced from these observations a new syndrome, which he called infantile autism, that many years later became a part of the *Diagnostic and Statistical Manual of Mental Disorders*. Another example is seen in the clinical insights of Sigmund Freud and his followers, writings that spawned generations of research examining various propositions put forward by these pioneering clinicians through their reporting of individual cases. Similarly, the cognitive behavior therapy movement of the later 1960s that extends into the present is derived largely from the clinical reports and theoretical propositions first propounded by clinical innovators such as Albert Ellis in *Reason and Emotion in Psychotherapy* (New York, 1962) and Aaron T. Beck in *Depression: Clinical, Experimental, and Theoretical Aspects* (New York, 1967).

The case study embodies what Gordon Allport in *Personality: A Psychological Interpretation* (New York, 1937) called the idiographic study of the individual case, an epistemological approach that he deemed an essential complement to the nomothetic approach taken by most social scientists (wherein general laws are sought or constructed to explain phenomena across individuals).

Third, human beings are capable of harming themselves and others in the most unusual ways. It is the practicing clinician who is most likely to encounter the vagaries of human conduct. Unusual case reports from "field observers" can add to clinical and experimental knowledge. A well-known example is the classic case of dissociative identity disorder reported by C. H. Thigpen and H. Cleckley in *The Three Faces of Eve* (Kingsport, TN, 1954). A subsequent disputing of this report in *I'm Eve* (Garden City, NY, 1977) by the patient herself, however, points up a central problem with the case study—namely, the potential for biased and incomplete description on the part of the authors.

Fourth, the clinical setting affords the opportunity and challenge to develop new procedures based on techniques and principles already in use in order to fit the idiographic demands of a particular patient. It is a truism that one will look in vain for the "textbook case." Clinicians are often faced with problems for which existing procedures seem unsuitable or insuffi-

cient. At the same time, certain aspects of a particular clinical problem may call for a new way of relating old principles and procedures to the resolution of the problem. Clinical innovation implies the discovery that "old" methods can be applied to new problems, as well as the discovery of new methods for overcoming common but seemingly intractable syndromes. This issue is not unrelated to the sixth point below.

Fifth, we have at least implicitly accepted thus far the commonly held view that case reports are intrinsically uncontrolled and cannot provide knowledge of value in establishing cause-effect relationships. However, one can look to the work of the Skinnerians in both laboratories and clinical settings for disproof of this point of view. As has been documented in many places, one can establish a reliable baseline for the occurrence of a given behavior in an individual case and then demonstrate changes that follow the alteration of a particular contingency. Then we may return the behavior to its original level by changing the contingency once again. This is the familiar A-B-A design; numerous and ingenious variations on the basic reversal design have been described elsewhere and represent a unique method for understanding causes and effects within the study of the individual case. [*See* Single-Case Experimental Design.]

Sixth, as mentioned earlier, the theoretical notions to which clinicians subscribe bear importantly on the specific decisions made in a particular case. Clinicians in fact approach their work with a given set, a framework for ordering the complex data that are their domain. But frameworks are insufficient. The clinician, like any other applied scientist, must flesh out the theoretical abstraction. Individual cases present problems that always call for knowledge beyond basic psychological principles. For example, a decision to try to increase the frequency of a particular behavior via positive reinforcement requires that the therapist understand what it is that the patient finds desirable and is willing to expend effort to obtain.

Thus the case study is useful and important for these several reasons. Except for reversal designs, the fifth point discussed, it falls short in establishing general laws and principles, and it is also incapable of providing evidence for cause-effect relationships. For creating these kinds of understanding, research methods that allow one to study groups of people under controlled observational and laboratory conditions are required.

[*See also* Research Methods, *article on* Concepts and Practices.]

Bibliography

Davison, G. C., & Lazarus, A. A. (1994). Clinical innovation and evaluation: Integrating practice with inquiry. *Clin-*

ical Psychology: Science and Practice, 1, 157–168. A discussion of the complex interplay of clinical discovery and controlled evaluation and of the strengths and limitations of case studies and of group designs in comparative therapy research.

Kazdin, A. E. (1992). *Research design in clinical psychology* (2nd ed.). Boston: Allyn & Bacon. Discussion of the case study and single-case research designs, along with other methodological topics in clinical research.

Ragin, C. C., & Becker, H. S. (Eds.). (1992). *What is a case? Exploring the foundations of social inquiry.* Cambridge, England: Cambridge University Press. Essays examining the meaning of the term "case study," which is shrouded in ambiguity.

Wachtel, P. L. (1997). *Psychoanalysis, behavior therapy, and the relational world.* Washington, DC: American Psychological Association. A treatise on the history and nature of psychoanalysis and how it can be integrated at the theoretical as well as the procedural level with behavior therapy.

Gerald C. Davison

CATEGORY ACCESSIBILITY. A category cannot be activated, or brought to a person's mind, unless it is present in that person's memory. Category availability refers to whether or not a category is actually stored in memory. Category accessibility refers to the activation potential of an available category (Higgins, 1996). The term *potential* in the definition of accessibility captures the fact that an accessible category is capable of being activated (and then used) but that it exists in a latent rather than in an active state. The "potent" root of "potential" captures the property of accessibility in that it contributes to the likelihood that a category will be used in judgments, inferences, and other cognitive outputs. The term *potential* also includes notions of energy or effectiveness from chemical or electrical properties or from the position of a piece of matter in an arrangement, and these notions cover the range of metaphors that have been used to understand the nature of accessibility.

The accessibility of an available category can be increased temporarily by priming or activating it prior to the situation in which the category might be used. Many studies have found that prior exposure to a category-related word in one situation increases the likelihood that the category will be used several minutes later to make a judgment in a different situation. An early study by Higgins, Rholes, and Jones (1977), for example, initially exposed participants to one or another set of trait-related constructs as an incidental aspect of a "perception" task. Later these participants were asked to characterize the ambiguous behaviors of a target person in a supposedly unrelated "reading comprehension" task. The participants were more likely to use the trait-related categories primed in the first task to categorize the target person's behaviors in the second task than participants who had not had these categories primed. Such effects of priming on later categorization do not require conscious awareness (Bargh Pietromonaco, 1982; Smith, Stewart, & Buttram, 1992).

A stored category can be primed once recently or many times over a longer period. By the early nineteenth century, if not before, psychologists recognized that both recent exposure and frequent exposure influenced the likelihood that stored knowledge would be used in response to current input. Srull and Wyer (1979) showed that priming effects on categorization are stronger and more long lasting as the frequency of prior exposure to the category increases. If the exposure is frequent enough, then a category can become chronically accessible, which means that the category remains highly accessible for periods of months or years.

There are personality, developmental, and cultural differences in chronic accessibility (Bruner, 1957). To date, studies of chronically accessible categories have been mostly concerned with individual differences in categories related to traits or attitudes. The most common measure of individuals' chronically accessible person categories involves asking an individual to list the traits of a type of person that he or she likes, dislikes, seeks out, avoids, and frequently encounters. Chronic accessibility is defined in terms of output primacy and/or frequency. For a given trait-related category, individuals would be "chronic" on a construct if they listed that category first in response to one or more questions and/or if they listed it frequently in response to the questions. Individuals would be "nonchronic" if they did not list the category in response to any question. Studies have found that chronically accessible person categories can be relatively stable for years and that they influence memory, impressions, and behavior.

The most common measure of attitude accessibility involves asking people about their attitudes, such as asking them to evaluate whether each attitude object is "good" or "bad," and measuring the speed with which each person responds to the inquiry. The faster the response, the higher the accessibility. Higher attitude accessibility, in turn, predicts greater consistency between a person's attitude toward some object and his or her behavior toward that object. The accessibility of attitudes can also be increased by frequent evaluation of the attitude objects. In a study by Fazio, Chen, McDonel, and Sherman (1982), for example, half of the participants evaluated each puzzle in a set of puzzles three different times, and the remaining participants evaluated each puzzle only once. Later, the repeated-expression participants were quicker than the single-expression participants to say whether they found each puzzle interesting or not, and their attitudes toward each puzzle better predicted time spent with each puzzle during free play.

Two basic types of models (or metaphors) have been used to understand the nature of category accessibility and its effects—mechanistic models and excitation transmission models. Mechanistic models understand accessibility in terms of the arrangement and the working of stored component parts. In contrast, excitation transmission models understand accessibility in terms of the heightening and the dissipation of excitation (or energy levels) from stimulation and decay. These models differ in their assumptions about the interrelations among accessibility, activation, and stimulus input. In mechanistic models, a category that has been recently or frequently activated has a position within the structural arrangement of categories that makes it likely to be retrieved first. A mechanistic "bin" model, for example, postulates that when a category has just been used, it is returned to the top of the storage bin of categories, where it will be found first in subsequent top-down retrieval processing (Wyer & Srull, 1989). Once retrieved or activated, the category is then compared to the stimulus input, and its use in categorization depends on there being a reasonably good fit between the category and the input. If the fit is good, the category will be used to categorize the input. If the fit is poor, the top-down retrieval process will continue until a suitable category is found.

In excitation transmission models, the accessibility of the category and the input features that match the category both contribute to the excitation level of the category that determines whether it is activated in the first place. If a category has very low accessibility, then the fit between the category and the input must be very good to activate the category. But if a category has very high accessibility, then the fit between the category and the input need not be good to activate the category because the accessibility will compensate for the poor fit. Indeed, a study by Higgins and Brendl (1995) found that people for whom a category was chronically high in accessibility and who also had had this category recently primed spontaneously used the category to form an impression of another person even though they received only extremely vague information about the person.

Many variables determine which category is used to respond to a stimulus. Surprisingly, the prior accessibility of a category can be as important to categorization as the actual features of the stimulus. This fact has profound implications for the accuracy and validity of human judgment and inference (Higgins, 1996; Sedikides & Skowronski, 1991).

Bibliography

Bargh, J. A., & Pietromonaco, P. (1982). Automatic information processing and social perception: The influence of trait information presented outside of conscious awareness on impression formation. *Journal of Personality & Social Psychology, 43,* 437–449.

Bruner, J. S. (1957). On perceptual readiness. *Psychological Review, 64,* 123–152.

Fazio, R. H., Chen, J.-M., McDonel, E. C., & Sherman, S. J. (1982). Attitude accessibility, attitude-behavior consistency, and the strength of the object-evaluation association. *Journal of Experimental Social Psychology, 18,* 339–357.

Higgins, E. T. (1996). Knowledge activation: Accessibility, applicability, and salience. In E. T. Higgins & A. W. Kruglanski (Eds.), *Social psychology: Handbook of basic principles* (pp. 133–168). New York: Guilford Press.

Higgins, E. T., & Brendl, M. (1995). Accessibility and applicability: Some "activation rules" influencing judgment. *Journal of Experimental Social Psychology, 31,* 218–243.

Higgins, E. T., Rholes, W. S., & Jones, C. R. (1977). Category accessibility and impression formation. *Journal of Experimental Social Psychology, 13,* 141–154.

Sedikides, C., & Skowronski, J. J. (1991). The law of cognitive structure activation. *Psychological Inquiry, 2,* 169–184.

Smith, E. R., Stewart, T. L., & Buttram, R. T. (1992). Inferring a trait from a behavior has long-term, highly specific effects. *Journal of Personality & Social Psychology, 62,* 753–759.

Srull, T. K., & Wyer, R. S. (1979). The role of category accessibility in the interpretation of information about persons: Some determinants and implications. *Journal of Personality & Social Psychology, 37,* 1660–1672.

Wyer, R. S., & Srull, T. K. (1989). *Memory and cognition in its social context.* Hillsdale, NJ.: Erlbaum.

E. Tory Higgins

CATHARSIS is the discharge or release of repressed emotions resulting in the alleviation of psychological tension and associated symptoms. It is believed by some to be a central goal in psychotherapy. However, the role of cathartic emotional expression as a curative factor is the subject of considerable debate.

The concept of catharsis was originally proposed by Aristotle in the *Poetics* to explain the effect that tragic theater has on an audience. According to Aristotle, the vicarious experience of tragic events in the drama arouses in the spectator feelings of pity and fear. This was believed to result in a purgation or cleansing of those feelings from the spectator.

Cathartic rituals in magic and religion have long been recorded. However, its formal use as a therapeutic tool originated with the early work of Sigmund Freud and Josef Breuer. Breuer, a Viennese physician, discovered and developed a cathartic technique while treating a 21-year-old hysterical patient whom he identified as "Anna O." Anna O. suffered from various physical symptoms with no discernible physical basis, including paralysis, sight and speech disturbances, food aversion, and a nervous cough. Breuer noticed that Anna O. experienced partial relief from her symptoms following a detailed recounting of traumatic incidents from her life. Her recollections, which initially occurred during self-induced trancelike states, were later encouraged under induced hypnosis. Breuer referred to his method of treatment as "catharsis," or, as Anna O. termed it, the "talking cure."

Freud, strongly influenced by Breuer, advanced a treatment for hysteria that relied heavily on catharsis. These early efforts mark the beginning of psychoanalysis and modern emotive therapy. Freud believed that symptoms of hysteria were rooted in experiences of emotional trauma that occurred under circumstances that prevented the normal expression of affect. His treatment of these patients involved evoking vivid recollections of early traumas to facilitate a discharge of associated feelings. This direct expression of previously repressed emotion, which Freud referred to as "abreaction," was considered to be the key element of the cathartic method. Freud and Breuer described their theory of catharsis and proposed an early psychoanalytic theory of neurosis in *Studies on Hysteria*, first published in 1895.

Although Freud initially expressed confidence in the cathartic method, he became dissatisfied with its temporary results. He eventually abandoned catharsis and shifted the emphasis of psychoanalysis to the more intellectual dimensions of early memories. Insight became the primary goal of psychoanalysis, and Freud came to view affect as merely incidental to the analytic work.

Although orthodox psychoanalytic thought shifted away from the use of catharsis, interest in cathartic theory and methods continued. Wilhelm Reich, a Viennese psychoanalyst who studied under Freud, advanced a therapy that emphasized emotional catharsis. The release of emotions and the relaxation of muscular tension associated with those emotions were central to his theories, and he has been credited with pioneering modern cathartic methods in psychotherapy.

Controversy over the efficacy of catharsis as a therapeutic agent has continued, with the split traditionally occurring between advocates of experiential therapies (e.g., psychodrama, Gestalt, primal therapy), who emphasize cathartic methods, and psychoanalytic therapists, who tend to rely more heavily on interpretation and insight. One important area of disagreement involves the degree to which catharsis is understood to be an active process. Early psychoanalysts were critical of the passive nature of catharsis. However, J. L. Moreno, a leading figure in the early history of group therapy, argued that catharsis is an active process and is essential to therapy. He suggested that psychoanalysts failed to use catharsis effectively because of their inability to find workable techniques. This disagreement over the nature of catharsis underscores a major reason for the continued controversy surrounding catharsis—namely, widely divergent views on how the construct is defined, interpreted, and used.

Problems related to ambiguous interpretations of catharsis are particularly salient in comparisons between social learning approaches and clinical approaches. According to social learning theory, behavior is learned through reinforcement or imitation. Social learning theorists have long held that catharsis is unnecessary for behavior change and is frequently counterproductive. They propose an alternate model to explain emotions, particularly anger. According to the frustration–aggression hypothesis, anger and aggression result from interference in obtaining expected gratification. Berkowitz suggests that a therapeutic focus on the discharge of emotion is misplaced, particularly since the outward expression of anger tends to intensify rather than reduce anger. Advocates of this position (e.g., Lewis & Bucher, 1992) point to a large body of research that demonstrates that individuals who are allowed to express anger overtly benefit little and frequently become more aggressive rather than less so. The hypothesis that catharsis reduces aggression has been further attacked on the basis of research that indicates that watching television violence increases rather than decreases aggressive behavior. Based on these research findings, some psychologists conclude that catharsis should be abandoned as a therapeutic tool.

Conclusions based on nonclinical research findings have been strongly criticized. Kosmicki and Glickauf-Hughes (1997), Scheff (1979), and others argue that much of the social psychological research in this area relies on distorted conceptual definitions of catharsis and employs inappropriate "cathartic" interventions. For example, studies frequently define catharsis as something that occurs through aggressive or retaliatory behaviors. Some challenge this definition and question the relevance of research findings to clinical settings. Studies that assume that passive viewing of television violence constitutes catharsis have been similarly challenged by Scheff (1979).

Despite controversy over the use of cathartic techniques in therapy, catharsis continues to have many adherents. Emotional discharge in itself is generally not considered curative in the absence of other variables. Pierce, Nichols, and DuBrin (1983), Kosmicki and Glickauf-Hughes (1997), Scheff (1979), and others emphasize the importance of the therapeutic context in which catharsis is used. A placement of catharsis in a proper therapeutic context has become increasingly problematic because of the disagreement over how catharsis is defined and because of the inadequate integration of various theoretical frameworks. Nonetheless, much of the clinical literature on the role of emotion in therapy converges on some broad conceptual factors. One of these is the idea that for catharsis to be useful, it must be an active rather than a passive process. There is also wide support for the importance of a related cognitive component in cathartic work. Several theorists (Nichols & Zax, 1977; Pierce et al., 1983; Scheff, 1979) advocate models of therapy in which emotional expression is combined with some type of cognitive processing or focusing. Finally, it is commonly assumed that in order for catharsis to be used effectively, it should occur in a safe environment and in the context of a therapeutic relationship.

[See also Abreaction; Emotion; Violence and Aggression; and the biographies of Breuer and Freud.]

Bibliography

Berkowitz, L. (1970). Experimental investigations of hostility catharsis. *Journal of Consulting & Clinical Psychology, 35,* 1–7. This is a report on early empirical research questioning the value of catharsis of anger.

Berkowitz, L. (1989). Frustration-aggression hypothesis: Examination and reformulation. *Psychological Bulletin, 106,* 59–73. This article provides a modern conceptualization of the frustration-aggression hypothesis.

Kosmicki, F. X., & Glickauf-Hughes, C. (1997). Catharsis in psychotherapy. *Psychotherapy, 34* (2), 154–159. This article addresses the problem of trying to find a workable definition of catharsis amid divergent views on what constitutes catharsis. The authors are critical of social learning approaches and suggest a placement of catharsis in an appropriate therapeutic context.

Lewis, W. A., & Bucher, A. M. (1992). Anger, catharsis, the reformulated frustration-aggression hypothesis, and health consequences. *Psychotherapy, 29* (3), 385–392. The authors of this article are critical of cathartic approaches. The article provides a concise review of more recent research in the area in the context of the frustration-aggression hypothesis. The authors conclude that catharsis should be abandoned as a therapeutic tool.

Nichols, M., & Zax, M. (1977). *Catharsis in therapy.* New York: Gardner Press. This book provides a useful historical overview of catharsis and therapy.

Pierce, R. A., Nichols, M. P., & DuBrin, J. R. (1983). *Emotional expression in psychotherapy.* New York: Gardner Press. The authors advocate the use of catharsis and view it as a central component of therapy. They discuss effective and useful ways of working with emotional expression in therapy.

Safran, J. D., & Greenberg, L. S. (Eds.). (1991). *Emotion, psychotherapy, and change.* New York: Guilford Press. This book presents various current theories about the use of emotions in psychotherapy. Diverse perspectives, including cognitive-behavioral views, psychodynamic views, and experiential views, are all represented, and attempts are made to synthesize the different theories on the role of emotion in therapy.

Scheff, T. J. (1979). *Catharsis in healing, ritual, and drama.* Berkeley: University of California Press. This book provides broad coverage on the importance of catharsis in psychology, culture, and the arts. Scheff's theory about proper distancing from emotional experience is of particular interest. He also addresses some of the criticisms leveled against catharsis.

Frank X. Kosmicki

CATHEXIS. Freud made frequent use of the word *besetzen,* a common German verb meaning to occupy or possess, to refer to a person's motivational investment in an idea, image, or symbol. The word *besetzen* is readily understandable to any German reader. The British translators of Freud's work decided to replace Freud's ordinary language terms with obscure Greek and Latin terms such as *id* and *scopophilia.* Thus the term *cathexis,* a word with no links of any kind to any but the most erudite reader of English, was adopted to translate *Besetzung* (the noun form, "occupation" or "possession"). *Cathexis* was used only once by Freud himself in the many years following its introduction. Freud's use of *Besetzung* has its roots in his early neurological theorizing, in which an amount of energy was considered to fill and thus energize a neuron. Any theory of motivation needs some way to account for variations in motivational levels, and in Freud's later theory *Besetzung* indicates the degree or intensity of a person's interest. For a person who has an obsessional idea—say, that his hands are dirty no matter how clean they are objectively—the idea of having dirty hands is said to be highly *besetzt.* How the idea got that way, and with what kind of libidinal interest, is the subject matter of the theory of instincts and of neurosis.

Beyond its role as an indicator of the intensity of interest or motivation, the *Besetzung* concept is key in Freud's theory of "mental energy," which Freud called the "economic" theory. Here it is used to describe the processes by which the degree of interest or motivation is raised or lowered ("variations in cathectic potential"), how different interests can combine on one object or action, and how one motive can interfere with another and to explain the differences between kinds of thinking, such as dreaming and problem solving.

To briefly outline this complex theory (see also Holt, 1962; Rapaport, 1959), there are basically three varieties of mental energy. The first variety is the "bound" cathexes of the waking, rational mind (the ego). The energy processes—"cathectic processes"—of waking thought follow what Freud called the secondary process. Secondary-process thought is realistic and logical, and the energy that sustains it is restrained—not impulsive, not wasting itself on the easiest route to pleasure.

The energy of the unconscious (the id) functions according the primary process and is called *freely mobile cathexis*. In displacement, the cathexis of one idea shifts to another, making minor details overly important, as in dreams and obsessional preoccupations. In condensation, energy from several ideas joins together in a single idea, which then represents several ideas at once, as observed, for example, in dreams when one image combines features of several people. More generally, logical sequences are broken up and reassembled irrationally, as unbound cathexes seek discharge by the quickest available paths.

Secondary-process, conscious thought can only occur when an idea has sufficient energy to reach consciousness. On the other hand, this energy must be "bound" energy, since primary-process thinking is not permitted in the conscious ego. In order for ideas arising in the unconscious to reach consciousness, they must attach (bind) themselves to word representations, which are governed by the secondary process.

The third type of mental energy, called *attention cathexis* or *hypercathexis*, is a mobile form of energy available for use by the conscious mind or ego. Attention cathexis helps previous ideas or memories gain sufficient energy to reach consciousness (for example, trying to remember where you put your keys).

The ego may block unacceptable wishes from consciousness by means of an opposing energy called *anticathexis*, a process called *defense*. Freud suggested that the common lack of energy for life seen in persons with neuroses can be due to their expending excessive amounts of their store of mental energy on anticathexes. Loss of interest of all kinds—in ideas, people, goals—is attributed either to defense or to "decathexis," the actual withdrawal of interest.

Much work was done by psychoanalytic theorists on the energy theory in the period 1930–1960. The resulting complex economic theory began to seem unwieldy in the late 1950s and early 1960s (Kubie, 1947; Apfelbaum, 1959) and has essentially disappeared from contemporary psychoanalytic theory, although some (Shengold, 1988, for example) continue to use the concept of traumatic overstimulation (being flooded by unmanageable levels of cathexis). The need still remains, however, to characterize the varying intensity of the individual's interest in ideas, wishes, and other people. Contemporary analytic theorists and therapists now tend to think not in terms of a general theory of energy but in more specific terms of affective intensity, emotional investment, and the motivational force of wishes, fears, and ideals. Sometimes "cathexis" and "decathexis" are used in an informal way to refer to these concepts.

[*See also* Attachment; *and* Psychoanalysis, *article on* Theories.]

Bibliography

Apfelbaum, B. (1959). Some problems in contemporary ego psychology. *Journal of the American Psychoanalytic Association, 10*, 526–537. A critique of the economic theory, suggesting alternative approaches.

Holt, R. R. (1962). A critical examination of Freud's concept of bound vs. free cathexis. *Journal of the American Psychoanalytic Association, 10*, 475–525. A thorough discussion of the various meanings and uses of cathexis in Freud's work.

Kubie, L. S. (1947). The fallacious use of quantitative concepts in dynamic psychology. *Psychoanalytic Quarterly, 16*, 507–518.

Ornston, D. (1985). The invention of 'cathexis' and Strachey's strategy. *International Review of Psychoanalysis, 12*, 391–400. A study of Strachey's invention of new terms for Freud's original German words.

Rapaport, D. (1959). The structure of psychoanalytic theory: A systematizing attempt. In Sigmund Koch (Ed.), *Psychology: A study of a science. Study I. Conceptual and systematic. Vol. 3. Formulations of the persona and the social context* (pp. 55–183). New York: McGraw-Hill. A systematic presentation of the fully developed energy (economic) theory.

Shengold, L. (1988). *Halo in the sky: Observations on anality and defense.* New York: Guilford Press.

Robert L. Hatcher

CAT SCAN. *See* Brain Imaging Techniques.

CATTELL, JAMES McKEEN (1860–1944), American psychologist and editor. Cattell was born in Easton, Pennsylvania, the son of William C. Cattell, a Presbyterian minister and later longtime president of Lafayette College in Easton, and Elizabeth McKeen, the daughter of James McKeen, the college's most generous benefactor. He grew up as the scion of Easton's leading family, and even as a student at Lafayette (bachelor of arts, 1880), he came to expect the deference of others. His father doted on his mother, and his family's closeness led him to study the ethics of Comtean positivism, which idealized the mother's sacrifice in childbirth as the model of all altruistic (and hence ethical) behavior. At Lafayette, the teaching of world-renowned philologist Francis Andrew March—especially his emphasis on the philosophy of Francis Bacon—impressed Cattell greatly. He developed an approach to science that combined a Comtean emphasis on quantification with a Baconian appreciation for the hypothesis-free collection of empirical "facts" and the ultimate utility of science. Throughout his career he thus adopted methods that produced quantitative data about (potentially applicable) psychological phenomena, even if he often could not explain them.

Hoping to emulate March's scholarly career, Cattell studied at the universities of Göttingen and Leipzig before his father secured for him a fellowship at Johns Hopkins University in 1882. There Cattell's experimental talent first emerged, and he modified standard laboratory instruments to time individuals' reading of letters and words. He claimed that his results showed that people naturally read whole words, rather than syllables. (Early-twentieth-century psychologists who studied reading—such as E. B. Huey—extended Cattell's approach, and their work led many later reading teachers to abandon phonics for the "whole word" approach.) In 1883, Cattell lost his fellowship in part because he complained that Johns Hopkins president Daniel Coit Gilman had "not taken as much interest in me as he might have." He returned to Leipzig, where he designed several new instruments (such as what soon became known as the Cattell Gravity Chronometer) and modified others (such as the standard Hipp Chronoscope). In 1886 he became the first American to earn a German doctorate with Wilhelm Wundt in the new experimental psychology. For his dissertation, he measured reaction times under varying conditions more precisely than any previous investigator and (despite Wundt's preference) made no use of *Selbstbeobachtung* (often translated as "introspection"). These Comtean-influenced experiments thus emphasized their participants' behavior and set a precedent that many later psychologists followed. More immediately, their extreme precision and the instruments Cattell designed helped convince many commentators of the new psychology's status as a science.

Unable to find a suitable American position, Cattell became a fellow-commoner at St. Johns College, Cambridge, in 1886. While in England, he assimilated into his approach to science Francis Galton's concern for differences among individuals. For Galton, these differences were the variations that made natural selection possible, and he developed this concern into a program of positive eugenics, which called for intelligent men and women to marry each other and have many children. This idea, with its emphasis on the family, resonated with Cattell's early Comtean-reinforced notions of family life. In 1888, he married Josephine Owen, an Englishwoman who had studied voice at the Mendelssohn Conservatory in Leipzig. They enjoyed an exceptionally close marriage and had seven children.

In 1889, Cattell assumed a professorship at the University of Pennsylvania, where he performed (with colleagues) two elaborate series of experiments. With biologist Charles S. Dolley, he continued and extended his reaction-time studies in an attempt to measure the velocity of the nervous impulse. With philosopher George S. Fullerton, he extended traditional psychophysical techniques whose proponents claimed they measured the relation between (physical) stimulus and (mental) sensation. Cattell and Fullerton studied individuals' ability to control arm movements, and they used their results to argue against any mentalistic interpretation of their (or others') experiments. For example, instead of claiming that their experiments measured just-noticeable differences, they argued that they measured errors of observation. The extreme precision of this work again impressed others, especially scientists previously unfamiliar with experimental psychology.

Cattell moved to Columbia University in 1891, where he developed an influential program of "mental tests." He and his collaborators used standard laboratory procedures—which measured (among other traits) reaction times, short-term memory, and the keenness of the senses—to gather quantitative data on psychological differences. Their work attracted much attention from professional educators, who hoped that Cattell's procedures would help them develop techniques to "Americanize" the flood of immigrant children then flocking to urban schools. But Cattell lacked a functional view of how the traits he measured helped people live their lives, and his tests produced no useful results. In 1901, Clark Wissler, one of his students, showed that the results of none of Cattell's tests correlated with the results of any other nor with any other measure or estimate of academic performance or potential. Most psychologists thus soon abandoned Cattell's tests, and he abandoned the laboratory. But in the same year his earlier experimental achievement led to his election as the first psychologist to join the National Academy of Sciences. In 1904, in a formal address at the St. Louis World's Fair, he explicitly urged his colleagues to apply their science to practical problems. In the years that followed, many psychologists who developed a clearly applied psychology cited Cattell's address as their inspiration.

From 1894 (when he founded *The Psychological Review* with Princeton colleague James Mark Baldwin), Cattell owned, edited, and (eventually) published many major scientific journals. These publications usually had professional goals; *The Psychological Review* challenged Clark University president G. Stanley Hall's leadership of the American psychological community. Cattell, however, was often as interested in their profitability, as his Columbia salary could not support his family in the style in which he had been raised. In late 1894 he took control of the failing weekly *Science*, and in 1900 it became (though still privately owned) the official journal of the American Association for the Advancement of Science (AAAS). This arrangement greatly increased AAAS membership, *Science*'s circulation, and Cattell's advertising income. Before 1920, he used *Science* to set the terms of and draw participants into debates over major policy issues, including the activities of federal scientific bureaus, plans for the Carnegie Institution of Washington's $10 million endowment, and the governance of higher education. After 1915, *Science* emphasized serious discussions about support for scientific research, and both the National Research Council and the AAAS's own Committee of One Hundred on Scientific Research. These concerns attracted additional readers, and this growing readership (and its weekly publication schedule) in turn led many American scientists to publish their best work in *Science*.

Cattell took over another failing journal, *The Popular Science Monthly*, in 1900, and used his editorship of *Science* to attract prominent contributors. (In 1915, he sold the journal's name but continued it as the *Scientific Monthly*.) In 1903, Cattell began collecting data for what emerged (in 1906) as the first edition of *American Men of Science*, a directory of the country's scientific workers. He also used these data in his studies of the psychology of scientific eminence, through which he identified (with stars at their entries in the directory) the 1,000 most eminent American scientists. He repeated these procedures (with modifications) for the later *American Men of Science* editions he oversaw, and other psychologists adapted his "order of merit" techniques for use in their own research on, for example, the efficacy of advertisements. In 1904, he sold his share of *The Psychological Review*, and he took over *The American Naturalist* in 1907. Though he initially hoped that the *Naturalist* would encourage positive eugenics, he soon came to rely on the editorial guidance of Columbia colleague Thomas H. Morgan, and the journal instead promoted Mendelian genetics. In 1915, he founded *School and Society* to serve educators as *Science* served scientists. He edited these publications through the late 1930s—and *Science* through the early 1940s—and they defined his position in the American scientific community.

Though American scientists respected Cattell's scientific and editorial achievements, they resented his approach to others, and in 1909 a Columbia colleague wrote that "Cattell is chronically opposed nowadays to anything that anybody does." This opposition at times emerged as a defense against what he saw as violations of academic freedom, and in 1913 he collected a series of *Science* articles on the topic in a volume, *University Control* (Garrison, NY). But Cattell's actions in such cases often included ad hominem attacks on others that cost him friends. When Columbia president

Nicholas Murray Butler tried to force Cattell to retire in 1913, these friends admitted his personal shortcomings but rushed to defend his professorship. Their maneuvering saved his position. But in the years that followed, Cattell gradually alienated most of them, including such longtime supporters at Columbia as anthropologist Franz Boas and philosopher John Dewey. In 1917, when the university finally fired Cattell, ostensibly for opposing U.S. conscription policy during World War I, he found few supporters. He sued Columbia for libel, and in a 1922 out-of-court settlement won an annuity in lieu of a regular pension. He used Columbia's lump-sum payment of installments due from 1917 to found the Psychological Corporation, through which he tried to implement his interest in applied psychology. Cattell, however, emphasized the firm's organization and never could explain just how psychologists could actually apply their science. The corporation thus floundered until 1926, when psychologists with significant experience with "real world" problems assumed its control.

Cattell continued to edit his journals through the 1920s and 1930s, founded the Science Press to publish them, chaired the AAAS Executive Committee, and acted as psychology's grand old man. But his last years proved disappointing. *Science* grew duller and attracted fewer readers, younger scientists found the stars in *American Men of Science* less meaningful than their predecessors had, and Cattell continued to alienate others. For example, under his leadership the AAAS hired and fired four permanent secretaries through the 1930s, and his public personal attack (as president of the 1929 International Congress of Psychology) on Duke University researcher William McDougall scandalized American psychologists. In 1941, other AAAS influentials forced him to yield the chair of the Association's executive committee, which he had held for 21 years. He died at age 83 in Lancaster, Pennsylvania, where he had moved to oversee the Science Press.

Bibliography

Poffenberger, A. T. (Ed.). (1947). *James McKeen Cattell: Man of science* (2 vols.). Lancaster, PA: Science Press. Includes many of Cattell's most important scientific papers.

Sokal, M. M. (1971). The unpublished autobiography of James McKeen Cattell. *American Psychologist, 26,* 626–635.

Sokal, M. M. (Ed.). (1981). *An education in psychology: James McKeen Cattell's journal and letters from Germany and England, 1880–1888.* Cambridge, MA: MIT Press.

Sokal, M. M. (1981). The origins of the Psychological Corporation. *Journal of the History of the Behavioral Sciences, 17,* 54–67.

Sokal, M. M. (1982). James McKeen Cattell and the failure

of anthropometric mental testing, 1890–1901. In W. R. Woodward and M. G. Ash (Eds.), *The problematic science: Psychology in nineteenth-century thought* (pp. 322–345). New York: Praeger.

Sokal, M. M. (1984). James McKeen Cattell and American psychology in the 1920s. In J. Brozek (Ed.), *Explorations in the history of psychology in the United States* (pp. 273–323). Lewisburg, PA: Bucknell University Press.

Sokal, M. M. (1987). James McKeen Cattell and mental anthropometry: Nineteenth-century science and reform and the origins of psychological testing. In M. M. Sokal (Ed.), *Psychological testing and American society, 1890–1930* (pp. 21–45). New Brunswick, NJ: Rutgers University Press.

Sokal, M. M. (1990). Life-span developmental psychology and the history of science. In E. Wolfe (Ed.), *Beyond history of science: Essays in honor of Robert E. Schofield* (pp. 67–80). Bethelehem, PA: Lehigh University Press.

Sokal, M. M. (1994). James McKeen Cattell, the New York Academy of Sciences, and the American Psychological Association, 1891–1902. In H. E. Adler & R. W. Rieber (Eds.), *Aspects of the history of psychology in America: 1892–1992* (pp. 13–35). New York: New York Academy of Sciences.

Sokal, M. M. (1995). Stargazing: James McKeen Cattell, *American Men of Science*, and the reward structure of the American scientific community, 1906–1944. In F. Kessel (Ed.), *Psychology, science, and human affairs: Essays in honor of William Bevan* (pp. 64–86). Boulder, CO: Westview Press.

Sokal, M. M. (1997). Baldwin, Cattell, and the *Psychological Review*: A collaboration and its discontents. *History of the Human Sciences, 10,* 57–89.

Michael M. Sokal

CATTELL, RAYMOND B. (1905–1998), English psychologist. Cattell was born on 20 March 1905 in Hilltop, a village on the outskirts of Birmingham, England. He was the second of three sons of Alfred Cattell and Mary Field Cattell, both of whom were born in Hilltop, as was the paternal grandfather. The family moved to the seaside town of Torquay in south Devonshire when Cattell was 6 years old. There he won a scholarship to Torquay Boys' Grammar School and, in 1921, a county scholarship to University College, London, where he earned a bachelor of science degree with first-class honors in chemistry in 1924. He then turned his studies principally to psychology. He entered the doctoral program at King's College in 1924. His dissertation topic was "The Subjective Character of Cognition and the Pre-sensational Development of Perception," for which he received a doctorate in 1929. Also from the University of London he earned a master's degree in education in 1932 and an honorary doctor of science degree in 1939.

Thinking back on his early education, Cattell wrote:

My interests in boyhood recapitulated the history of the sciences—from astronomy to physics to chemistry and to biology. In 1921 I found myself in science at the University of London in the midst of the ferment of social and political ideas that broke out after World War I. Shaw, Wells, Huxley, Haldane, and Russell were our prophets. Oddly, as I see it now, I was able to meet them all! I was lucky also in having Charles Spearman, developing the logic of factor analysis, on one side of the college yard at University College and Fisher, developing analysis of variance, on the other. Interpreting these two poles of statistics technically, but more interested in social and political implications, was Sir Cyril Burt. Soon, I thought I saw the possibility of reaching in human affairs beyond the traditional rules of thumb into radical improvements based on a science of psychology. (Cattell, 1984, pp. 122–123)

From 1927 to 1932 Cattell taught at Exeter University and served as an advisory psychologist at Dartington Hall, a progressive school that was much discussed in the 1930s. From 1932 through 1936 he served as director of the City of Leicester Child Guidance Clinic. In 1937 E. L. Thorndike offered him a research associate position at Columbia University. Cattell accepted the offer, expecting to stay in the United States no more than two years. But in 1938 he won an appointment to the G. Stanley Hall professorship in genetic psychology at Clark University. He moved from there to a lectureship at Harvard in 1941, where he remained until 1945, when he was appointed to a newly created research professorship in psychology at the University of Illinois. He remained in that post until 1973, when university policy forced his retirement. In 1974 he moved to Honolulu, where he was appointed to adjunct professorships at the University of Hawaii and the Hawaii School of Professional Psychology. He continued to publish more than four articles per year and two books per decade through the 1970s and 1980s and remained active in writing even as he became sick with colon cancer, prostate cancer, and heart disease in the 1990s. He died of congestive heart failure in his sleep at his home in Honolulu on 2 February 1998.

The effects of one person's research and writings on a discipline as broad as psychology are difficult to identify, but it seems clear that Raymond Cattell must rank at the top among those who have most influenced scientific psychology in the twentieth century. In more than 50 books and 400 articles he developed a comprehensive theory based on evidence derived from empirical research that has become the base of modern theory of personality. He also developed designs for research, methods for analysis (particularly multivariate analysis), and measurement operations that have become basic to behavioral science research.

The rudiments of Cattell's theory emerged in the 1920s and 1930s in 27 published studies that were largely devoted to construction of measures of temperament and cognitive capabilities. Between 1940 and 1950 he and his coworkers produced some 41 studies of objective-test, behavioral-rating, and self-report indicators of personality. The main results of this work were put together in a highly influential 1950 book, *Personality: A Systematic, Theoretical, and Factual Study,* which provided an organizational and developmental explanation of individual differences in cognition, motivation, and temperament. Some 48 additional studies were carried out between 1950 and 1957, and again the results were synthesized in a major theoretical treatise, *Personality and Motivation Structure and Measurement* (1957). Pulling together evidence from studies of group behavior, behavior genetics, and both cross-sectional and longitudinal analyses of self-reports, ratings, and objective tests, this book was widely used throughout the world as a guide for the design of research on personality. Cattell's laboratory continued to produce much research through the 1960s and 1970s. More than 200 studies came from his laboratory, the results of which also were merged into advancements in theory in monographs that were published every three to seven years. These include *The Meaning and Measurement of Neuroticism and Anxiety* (with I. Scheier, 1961), *Personality Factors in Objective Test Devices* (with J. Hundleby and K. Pawlik, 1965), *Objective Personality and Motivation Tests* (with F. Warburton, 1967), *The Prediction of Achievement and Creativity* (with R. Butcher, 1968), *Handbook for the Sixteen Personality Factor Questionnaire* (with H. Eber and M. Tatsuoka, 1970), *Motivation and Dynamic Structure* (with D. Child, 1975), *The Scientific Analysis of Personality and Motivation* (1977), and *Personality and Learning Theory* (two volumes, 1979, 1980).

The theory that emerged from all this empirical work provides a basis for describing the uniqueness of individuals. It has been classified in introductory textbooks as trait theory, but it deals with much more than merely the enduring characteristics whereby one person can be distinguished from another; it is also an account of states and systematic changes in behavior brought about through motivation and learning. It provides a description of short-term and lifelong changes in behavior associated with neurophysiological, genetic, familial, social, and cultural factors. It is a comprehensive theory of human behavior. Most remarkably, it is steadfastly anchored to empirical evidence. The plan of attack of this work for building understanding of personality set the course of research on personality from the 1940s onward. The regularities indicated in Cattell's research, now appearing in many guises, remain among the principal contributions to theoretical analysis of personality. Many self-report measures of personality stem from his Sixteen Personality Factor Questionnaire (16PF), for example.

Cattell also made several rather nuclear contributions that are important to the science of psychology.

He pioneered in developing the theory of fluid and crystallized intelligence, the multiple abstract variance analysis (MAVA) model for sampling and distinguishing genetic and environmental influences, and the distinction between state and trait anxiety. He invented the covariation chart, also known as the data box, for specifying research designs and analyses, and the scree test for number of factors in factor analysis. He brought together outstanding authors in edited books, for example, the widely used *Handbook of Multivariate Experimental Psychology* (Chicago, 1966; 2nd ed., New York, 1988). He was instrumental in founding the Society of Multivariate Experimental Psychologists and in establishing the journal of this society, *Multivariate Behavioral Research.*

Cattell also produced work that was severely criticized. In one line of such work, he argued that evidence generally supports the hypothesis that individual differences in intelligence are genetically determined. He then found evidence consistent with the hypothesis that people of lower intelligence were producing more children than people of higher intelligence and concluded that it was important to encourage a higher birth rate of the more intelligent and lower birth rate of the dull. In a second line of work that was much criticized he argued that morality is a branch of natural science, that evolutionary ethics provides the true universal morality, and that religions—in particular Christianity—have uncritically and falsely failed to recognize this. He reasoned that ethics that apply within groups do not apply between groups. Competitiveness should exist between groups, but the development of large political organizations is inimical to advancement of the human species. Humans should organize into small independent communities that peacefully compete in advancing particular views about the correct way to live. A principle of survival of the fittest communities would then operate to enable human societies to adapt and improve. The more successful of such communities would adopt eugenic policies. Mechanisms that can most safely, effectively, and intelligently control such groups can be created, put in place, and maintained only by a government of scientists. Science must become a highly organized major function of national and international life. Criticized as impetuous, not well based on evidence, illogical, impractical, elitist, and racist, these writings led some to question Cattell's credibility and to dismiss or ignore his other work.

[*See also* Sixteen Personality Factor Questionnaire.]

Bibliography

Cattell, R. B. (1937). *The fight for our national intelligence.* London: King.

Cattell, R. B. (1950). *Personality: A systematic, theoretical, and factual study.* New York: McGraw-Hill.

Cattell, R. B. (1957). *Personality and motivation structure and measurement.* New York: World Book.

Cattell, R. B., (1965). *Personality and social psychology: Collected papers.* San Diego, CA: Knapp.

Cattell, R. B. (1971). *Abilities: Their structure, growth, and action.* Boston: Houghton Mifflin.

Cattell, R. B. (1972). *A new morality from science: Beyondism.* New York: Pergamon.

Cattell, R. B. (1980). *Personality and learning theory: Vol. 2. A systems theory of maturation and structured learning.* New York: Springer.

Cattell, R. B., & Butcher, R. J. (1968). *The prediction of achievement and creativity.* Indianapolis, IN: Bobbs-Merrill.

Cattell, R. B., Eber, H. W., & Tatsuoka, M. (1970). *Handbook for the Sixteen Personality Factor Questionnaire.* Champaign, IL: IPAT.

Cattell, R. B., Hundleby, J. D., & Pawlik, K. (1965). *Personality factors in objective test devices.* San Diego, CA: Knapp.

Cattell, R. B., & Scheier, I. H. (1961). *The meaning and measurement of neuroticism and anxiety.* New York: Ronald Press.

John Horn

CENTER FOR ADVANCED STUDY IN THE BEHAVIORAL SCIENCES.

In 1954, the Center for Advanced Study in the Behavioral Sciences (CASBS) was established by the Ford Foundation on a hilltop overlooking Stanford University and San Francisco Bay. Since then it has provided 40 to 50 residential postdoctoral fellowships per year to scholars in the traditional behavioral sciences (anthropology, economics, history, linguistics, political science, psychology, and sociology), as well as a wide array of related disciplines such as biology, computer science, education, geography, law, literature, philosophy, psychiatry, and statistics.

Although the Center is committed to interdisciplinary research, it has always been strongly associated with the field of psychology. The chairman of its founding board of trustees was Frank Stanton, a psychologist and former president of Columbia Broadcasting System. The first director of the Center was Ralph Tyler, a distinguished educational psychologist, who served for 13 years; the third director, Gardner Lindzey, who served for 14 years, is also a psychologist. Moreover, the nearly 2,000 former fellows of the center include more psychologists than representatives of any other discipline.

Each fellowship offers 9 to 12 months of complete freedom from the usual demands of teaching, meetings, and committee work. Fellows use their time to pursue whatever paths of research or study they choose. They are encouraged to minimize travel during their period of residence and to take advantage of the many opportunities to interact with their counterparts in other fields. Numerous occasions for interaction are built into the routine of the center, including weekly formal seminars, spontaneous reading and discussion groups, and daily lunches in an appealing and congenial setting.

A majority of the most eminent psychologists of the past half century have been fellows at the center. Their contributions are partially documented in the bibliography of the Ralph Tyler Collection, which includes only books and monographs that contain specific reference to the role of the center in the initiation, preparation, or completion of the fellows' publications. Space limitations preclude any attempt at spelling out the importance of the more than 1,300 volumes of the Tyler Collection. Nevertheless, it is possible to point to some areas of psychology in which the center has been influential and to individual fellows who were particularly important in their growth. An illustrative list follows:

Behavior genetics
Irving I. Gottesman, Jerry Hirsch, Gardner Lindzey, Robert Plomin, Kurt Schlesinger, J. Paul Scott

Clinical psychology
W. Stewart Agras, Albert Bandura, Bruno Bettelheim, Alan Kazdin, Isaac Marks, Stanley Rachman, Martin E. P. Seligman, G. Terence Wilson, Irvin Yalom

Cognitive psychology
Richard C. Atkinson, Gordon Bower, William K. Estes, George A. Miller, Ulric Neisser, Donald Norman

Cultural psychology
Michael Cole, Roy G. D'Andrade, Hazel R. Markus, Robert A. LeVine, Richard A. Shweder, John W. M. Whiting

Developmental psychology
Paul B. Baltes, John J. Conger, Erik H. Erikson, Willard Hartup, Jerome Kagan, William Kessen, Eleanor Maccoby, Paul H. Mussen, Robert R. Sears

Educational psychology
Lee J. Cronbach, Nathaniel L. Gage, Robert Gagne, Howard E. Gardner, Arthur R. Jensen

Forensic psychology
Phoebe C. Ellsworth, Reid Hastie, Elizabeth F. Loftus, John Monahan

Mathematical psychology
Richard C. Atkinson, William K. Estes, R. Duncan Luce, Frederick Mosteller, Patrick Suppes

Social psychology
Robert P. Abelson, Elliot Aronson, Leon Festinger, Harold B. Gerard, Irving L. Janis, Harold H. Kelley, Paul Lazarsfeld, Gardner Lindzey, Theodore M. Newcomb, Robert Zajonc

Center fellows are selected through a series of evaluations and ratings. Anyone is entitled to nominate an accomplished or highly promising scholar for consideration as a fellow, but most nominations come from well-known professors, academic administrators, former fellows, and directors of the center's summer institutes for younger scholars. Decisions on fellowships are made by the center's board of trustees, typically with heavy reliance on panel ratings and letters of reference. Nominees are judged on the basis of their previous work and potential contributions to their field rather than on specific project proposals. The stipends for fellows, combining sabbatical allowances with center funds, are designed to spare fellows financial hardship and to leave them at liberty to study and work with unrestricted freedom. An experienced staff provides professional services to support research productivity.

Aspects of the fellowships that have seemed most important to former fellows include the following:

- the opportunity to devote an extended period of time to intellectual development at an advanced level, free from normal routines and from the responsibilities of the home institution;
- the stimulating company of other leading scientists and scholars from a variety of disciplines, under circumstances that maximize the likelihood of easy and rewarding interactions and the acquisition of new skills;
- freedom to set one's own schedule and direct one's own activities in ways that enhance scholarly development and productivity;
- secretarial, library, statistical, and editorial services and help with computing and photocopying;
- arrangements for financial support at a level that protects fellows from serious financial sacrifice and enables their families to participate in the fellowship year;
- a physical environment for fellows' work that is agreeable year round and a congenial community setting for their families;
- the proximity of many distinguished scholars and scientists at nearby institutions, such as Stanford University and several campuses of the University of California.

In an era of funding constraints on basic research in the behavioral and social sciences, the center is almost unique in not requiring prospective fellows to submit a proposal for a specific project. Indeed, unexpected intellectual discovery and embarking on new and unanticipated projects are among the most cherished benefits of a fellowship year. CASBS publishes an annual report and the Tyler Collection bibliography, which are available on request.

Gardner Lindzey

CENTER FOR EPIDEMIOLOGIC STUDIES DEPRESSION SCALE. The Center for Epidemiologic Studies Depression Scale (CES-D; Radloff, 1997) was originally developed by Ben Locke and Peter Putnam to assess the severity of depressive symptoms in community-residing adults. The CES-D is a self-report measure that consists of 20 items assessing depressed mood, lack of positive affect, somatic symptoms, and interpersonal difficulties. Items are rated on a 4-point scale according to the frequency with which symptoms were experienced during the preceding week. The scale was initially validated by Lenore Radloff (Radloff, 1977) and has been translated into several languages, including German, French, Spanish, Russian, and Italian, as well as Chinese, Japanese, and Korean, and has been used with children, adolescents, adults, and elderly persons. Although initially developed to assess the severity of depression, one of the primary uses of the CES-D has been to estimate the prevalence of depression in large epidemiological samples and to screen for depressive illness in medical settings.

Psychometric Properties

Psychometric studies have shown that the CES-D is internally consistent, moderately stable over several weeks ($rs \approx 0.57$; cf. Radloff, 1977) and months ($rs \approx 0.50$; cf. Lewinsohn, Hoberman, & Rosenbaum, 1988) and correlates strongly with many other measures of depression. Confirmatory factor analyses support the existence of four factors, initially identified in the original validation sample (Radloff, 1977), but subsequent research has demonstrated that a single higher order factor may account for responses to individual items equally well. Other studies have suggested that the CES-D may not effectively discriminate between clinical depression and other psychiatric conditions and may be related to both depressed and anxious mood states. Psychometric analyses based on item response models (Santor, Zuroff, Ramsay, Cervantes, & Palacios, 1995) have shown that the CES-D may be better at discriminating among individual differences in depressed mood in nonclinical populations than the Beck Depression Inventory, originally designed for use with clinical populations. Short forms consisting of 4, 8, 10, and 11 items have appeared, and a variety of improvements to the scoring methods have been recommended (Santor & Coyne, 1997). Few studies have examined the degree to which gender bias may be observed in individual responses to items.

Initial studies conducted with clinical populations suggested that individuals scoring 16 or more on the scale could be designated as depressed (Radloff, 1977); this score has been adopted as the conventional cutoff score in most community based and epidemiological studies. However, studies specifically examining the efficiency of conventional cutoff scores have suggested that higher cutoff scores are required. Recommended cutpoints have ranged as high as 19 in chronic pain patients, 21 in the elderly, and 27 in adolescents and medical patients.

Evaluating the efficiency of cutoff scores on CES-D focused initially on measures of sensitivity and specificity, namely, the effectiveness of the CES-D at detecting individuals who are depressed, as well as ruling out those who are not. Estimates of the sensitivity and specificity for most cutpoints used with the CES-D generally exceed 0.80. Only more recently has attention focused on other measures of efficiency, such as the positive and negative predictive value of various cutoff scores, which research has shown are substantially lower (Fechner-Bates, Coyne, & Schwenk, 1994; Santor & Coyne, 1997). Studies have focused on the test-retest reliability of cutoff scores; however, few studies have explicitly examined the reliability of either conventional or alternate cutoff scores. Consequently, most clinically depressed individuals obtain scores exceeding standard cutpoints; however, a substantial number of depressed persons will not (Santor & Coyne, 1997). Moreover, most persons obtaining high scores will not meet formal diagnostic criteria for depression. Given the unavoidable tradeoff between maximizing either sensitivity or positive predictive value, the costs of using the CES-D as a screening tool either to improve the detection of cases of depression in primary care or to identify research samples should be considered carefully.

Concerns Regarding Use of the CES-D

Two related issues involving the use of the CES-D remain controversial, namely, the suitability of the CES-D as a tool for identifying clinically depressed individuals and the use of the CES-D as a measure of depressive symptomatology. Problems of overdiagnosing the prevalence of depression with the CES-D have been well documented in medical patients (Fechner-Bates et al., 1994), adolescents (Roberts, Andrews, Lewinsohn, & Hops, 1990), college students (Santor et al., 1995), and community-residing adult populations (Myers & Weissman, 1980). Estimates with standard cutpoints in similar populations vary from 9% to well over 40%, raising concerns about the use of self-report measures such as the CES-D as screening tools for depression (Roberts, Lewinsohn, & Seeley, 1991; Santor & Coyne, 1997; United States Preventive Services Task Force, 1996).

Attempts to improve the efficiency of the CES-D have been numerous. Detecting the presence or absence of a depressive disorder was never the criterion by which individual items were included or excluded from the original scale. Indeed, assessing the severity of distress (a continuum) and detecting cases of depression (a category) require scales with very different psychometric properties. Most attempts to improve the CES-D have relied on adjusting cutoff scores rather than on identifying effective items; however, even after identifying effective items, limitations of the CES-D as a self-report screening measure persist (Santor & Coyne, 1997). Although research has demonstrated that elevated scores on the CES-D are associated with a variety of psychosocial difficulties and may represent some small risk for a depressive disorder (Lewinsohn et al., 1988), caution must be exercised in viewing the CES-D as a measure of depression (Coyne, 1994). Items are assessed with respect to the past week and therefore may measure only transient distress; many items do not correspond to actual symptoms of depression; and most individuals scoring high on the CES-D will not become depressed (Lewinsohn et al., 1988). Individuals may score high on the CES-D by endorsing a large number of items at relatively mild levels of dysphoria that may not be long lasting. In summary, evidence supports the CES-D as an excellent measure of general distress and dysphoria rather than as a tool for identifying cases of depression.

Bibliography

Coyne, J. C. (1994). Self-reported distress: Analog or ersatz depression? *Psychological Bulletin, 116,* 29–45.

Fechner-Bates, S., Coyne, J. C., & Schwenk, T. L. (1994). The relationship of self-reported distress to depressive disorders and other psychopathology. *Journal of Counseling and Clinical Psychology, 62,* 550–559.

Lewinsohn, P. M., Hoberman, H. M., & Rosenbaum, M. (1988). *Journal of Abnormal Psychology, 97,* 251–264.

Myers, J. K., & Weissman, M. M. (1980). Use of a self-report symptom scale to detect depression in a community sample. *American Journal of Psychiatry, 137,* 1081–1084.

Radloff, L. S. (1977). The CES-D Scale: A self-report depression scale for research in the general population. *Applied Psychological Measurement, 1,* 385–401.

Roberts, R. E., Andrews, J. A., Lewinsohn, P. M., & Hops, H. (1990). Assessment of depression in adolescent using the Center for Epidemiologic Studies Depression Scale. *Psychological Assessment, 2,* 122–128.

Roberts, R. E., Lewinsohn, P. M., & Seeley, J. R. (1991). Screening for adolescent depression: A comparison of scales. *Journal of the American Academy of Child Adolescent Psychiatry, 30,* 58–66.

Santor, D. A., & Coyne, J. C. (1997). Shortening the CES-D to improve its ability to detect cases of depression. *Psychological Assessment, 9,* 233–243.

Santor, D. A., Zuroff, D. C., Ramsay, J. O., Cervantes, P., & Palacios, J. (1995). Examining scale discriminability in the BDI and CES-D as a function of depressive severity. *Psychological Assessment, 7,* 131–139.

United States Preventive Services Task Force (1996). *Guide to preventive services* (2nd ed.). Baltimore: Williams & Wilkins.

Darcy A. Santor

CHARCOT, JEAN-MARTIN (1825–1893), French neurologist. Born the son of a Parisian carriage maker in 1825, Charcot obtained his medical degree from the University of Paris in 1848 and was promoted to an internship at the Salpêtrière, a large charitable hospital that housed several thousand of Paris's poorest women. He saw this as an opportunity to study diseases of the nervous system, and, after a brief foray into histology, Charcot turned his attention to neurological categorization. He believed that it was possible to relate specific neurological diseases to distinctive physical lesions and began a career of neurological nosology (classification) that led to international recognition as the "father of neurology." Charcot was particularly successful in research dealing with spinal cord disorders, subcortical brain organization, and cortical localization. In this connection, he made significant contributions to the understanding of amyotrophic lateral sclerosis, locomotor ataxia, multiple sclerosis, and Parkinson's disease.

In the years between the mid-1860s and the mid-1870s, Charcot gradually acquired local celebrity and international fame. By 1872, when he was appointed professor of pathological anatomy on the faculty of the Paris Medical School, he had already achieved a reputation as a remarkable teacher, and his classes were extremely popular. On Tuesday mornings at the Salpêtrière he taught his "clinical lessons," in which he was able to get patients, singly and in groups, to display neurological symptoms to his audience of physicians and medical students; these displays were followed by an incisive analysis of the symptoms and a diagnosis of the disorder. Then on Friday mornings Charcot delivered his formal lectures, which were carefully worked out, dramatically spiced presentations of his current ideas; a novel feature of these spellbinding lectures was his use of photographic projections as teaching aids. Both the clinical lessons and the lectures eventually came to be so well known that they were frequently attended by renowned visitors from other countries.

Although he delivered his first lecture on hysteria in 1870, Charcot's specific formulation of the nosology of that condition developed between 1872 and 1878. Charcot's view of hysteria may be gleaned from the pages of a work by his pupil Paul Richer (1849–1933) entitled *Études cliniques sur la grande hystérie ou hystéro-épilepsie* (Paris, 1881). Here are depicted Charcot's four phases of the prototypical form of hysteria, which Charcot called *grande hystérie*. Charcot asserted that

these phases were found everywhere, in all countries and all races, and therefore represent a universal pathological structure analogous to a disease entity.

In 1878, Charcot turned his attention to hypnotism and began a series of experiments intended to scientifically establish its nature and effects. Drawing his experimental subjects from among his most gifted female hysterics, he identified what he believed to be recurring and predictable hypnotic phases. Charcot concluded that hypnotism, like hysteria, took a consistent structured form. This form could be represented as three successive stages: catalepsy, lethargy, and somnambulism. Each stage of this prototypical *grande hypnotisme* had its specific, unvarying characteristics. Catalepsy was characterized by contractions in which the subject's limbs remained in the position they were in when he or she was hypnotized or in the position given them by the hypnotizer. In this stage the subject is susceptible to suggestion. Lethargy was characterized by what appeared to be profound sleep with total limpness of the body. In this stage, consciousness disappeared, and the subject was unable to feel pain. The somnambulistic stage was characterized by a sleeplike state, much like lethargy, with a similar absence of pain perception. The difference was that somnambulists could converse with the hypnotist, and, although susceptible to suggestion, as were cataleptics, they did not act as automatons but could ask questions about the hypnotizer's commands.

In 1882 Charcot read a paper presenting his findings on hypnotism to the Académie des Sciences. His international stature had the effect of immediately giving hypnotism a legitimacy in the academic community and stimulating innumerable articles on the subject in scientific journals.

Charcot's work on psychologically caused paralysis also had far-reaching influence in the medical world. He set out to demonstrate that through hypnosis he could produce states of bodily paralysis that mimicked those of organic origin. He claimed that this "psychic paralysis" could be connected to psychological trauma that remained outside the patient's conscious awareness, establishing the notion of a posttraumatic paralysis. Charcot classified hysterical, posttraumatic, and hypnotic paralyses as "dynamic" paralyses, as opposed to lesion-produced "organic" paralyses.

Charcot believed that these and other experiments proved that hypnotism must be seen as a manifestation of hysteria and that the three stages of *grande hypnotisme* were closely related to the four phases of *grande hystérie*. Charcot's views about hypnotism were espoused by his students and colleagues at the Salpêtrière hospital and were the central tenets of what came to be called the Salpêtrière School of hypnotism.

This school was opposed by the Nancy School of hypnotism, founded by Hippolyte Bernheim (1840–1919), which held that hypnotism was a state that could be induced in normal people and that the three stages of the Salpêtrière School were artifacts created through suggestions unwittingly conveyed by the hypnotizer. The Nancy School held that the concept of suggestion was central to understanding hypnotism and that suggestion was the principal means for inducing the hypnotic state.

In 1895, two years after Charcot's death, Pierre Janet (1859–1947) delivered a thoughtful but devastating criticism of Charcot's work on hysteria and hypnotism. Janet pointed out that, over time, Charcot lost contact with what was going on with his patients on the wards, where incompetent assistants were hypnotizing them often and unwittingly training them to reproduce the phases of *grande hystérie* and the stages of *grande hypnotisme*. Janet believed that the closed institutional community of the Salpêtrière of the time preserved the delusion of the universality of these characteristics and made those workers blind to the mental contagion that flourished there.

Although Charcot's contributions to neurological nosology endured, his experiments with hysteria and hypnotism did not have a lasting influence. The suggestion oriented approach of the Nancy School of hypnotism was clearly victorious over the views of the Salpêtrière School. However, the controversy between the two schools had the beneficial effect of bringing the central issues of hypnotism to public awareness and creating a broad interest in hypnotic research.

Bibliography

Ellenberger, H. (1970). *The discovery of the unconscious*. New York: Basic Books.

Gauld, A. (1992). *A history of hypnotism*. Cambridge, England: Cambridge University Press.

Goetz, C. G., Bonduelle, M., & Gelfand, T. (1995). *Charcot: Constructing neurology*. New York: Oxford University Press.

Guillain, G. (1959). *J.-M. Charcot (1825–1893): His life—his work*. London: Pitman Medical.

Janet, P. (1895). J.-M. Charcot. Son oeuvre psychologique. *Revue philosophique, 39*, 569–604.

Laurence, J.-R., & Perry, C. (1988). *Hypnosis, will and memory*. New York: Guilford Press.

Micale, M. S. (1995). *Approaching hysteria: Disease and its interpretation*. Princeton, NJ: Princeton University Press.

Owen, A. R. G. (1971). *Hysteria, hypnosis and healing: The work of J.-M. Charcot*. London: Dobson.

Adam Crabtree

CHILD ABUSE AND NEGLECT. At least three decades of research have focused on child abuse since Henry Kempe first categorized the term *battered child syndrome*.

In 1994 more than 3.1 million reports of child abuse were made, of which more than one million can be substantiated by sufficient evidence. Approximately one half of all substantiated child abuse reports were of neglect; 21% involved physical abuse, and 11% sexual abuse. About 3% occurred in the newer category of emotional abuse. Although there has been a significant increase in the reporting of child abuse, the percentage of adults who have experienced child abuse (varying from approximately 25 to 33%) has not changed significantly during these last few decades. Most children who are victims of child abuse still never come to the attention of physicians, social workers, or other professionals, which is costly given the significant impact on the mental and medical health care systems and given the increasing number of abused and neglected children (which has doubled in the years 1986–1993; Alexander, 1995).

Epidemiology

A number of epidemiological studies have been done to define the demographic characteristics of those children who have been abused, as well as of the abusers. In one study (Jessee & Rieger, 1996), one in every five substantiated cases of child abuse and over 50% of child abuse–related deaths were the result of physical injuries. Approximately 90% of all cases involved children 5 years old or younger, with 60% being less than 2 years of age. The results of this study suggested that age was an important factor in the location, type, and severity of injuries due to the physical abuse of a child. Another study focused on gender (MacMillan et al., 1997). In that retrospective study, a greater percentage of females reported a history of severe sexual abuse (11%) than males (4%). A history of child physical abuse was reported more often by males (31%) than females (21%), whereas sexual abuse during childhood was more commonly reported by females (13%) than males (4%). The severity of physical abuse was reported by similar proportions of males (11%) and females (9%).

Reporting

Reporting has been a central issue in child abuse because of its questionable reliability and history of presumed underreporting. Generally, the literature conflicts on this issue, although there is consensus that reporting is becoming increasingly reliable. In one study (Crenshaw et al., 1995) the reporting tendency and the reporting rate were unrelated to the gender of the victim or of the respondent, and the reporting tendency was unrelated to the profession of the educator (i.e., principal, counselors, etc.), although certain types of abuse were suspected and/or reported significantly less often by classroom teachers. Educators were uniform in their high level of awareness of mandatory reporting laws, although they expressed the need for additional training on how to report child abuse. In another study therapists and child-protection workers were interviewed regarding their experiences with mandated reporting. The results indicated widespread disagreement between the groups about the nature of appropriate reports, the requirements of the law, and the processes designed to protect the children and help families (Deisz, Doueck, & George, 1996). Figures have varied between approximately 69% and 88% of hospital personnel nationwide reporting documented episodes of abuse.

Injuries

Research has shown that one half to two thirds of child abuse injuries are inflicted on the head and neck region. For this reason it is mandatory that dentists are sensitive to these signs. Common signs of physical abuse include fractures of the teeth or of the maxilla, mandible, and other facial bones; facial burns; lacerations of the lips; and bite marks on the face and neck (Jessee, 1995). In another study (McMahon, Grossman, Gaffney, & Stanitski, 1995), 92% of the children had soft-tissue injuries, and only 9% had a fracture. Whereas children under 9 months of age had an average of one soft-tissue injury, the children between 10 months and 3 years of age had an average of two soft-tissue injuries. Of those children older than 10 months, 85% had injuries involving the head or face, and 15% were burned.

More Subtle Signs

Drawings have been used in many clinical conditions in which signs are more subtle. Young children, fortunately, are able to communicate their feelings very often in their drawings. In one study, the family drawings of abused and neglected preschool children could be differentiated from those of other children who were not abused or neglected (Carpenter, Kennedy, Armstrong, & Moore, 1997). These findings were confirmed by another group (Petersen, Hardin, & Nitsch, 1995), who showed that sexually molested children could be discriminated from those nonmolested by their human figure drawings and kinetic family drawings (Petersen et al., 1995).

Another more subtle indicator is sleep. As in many stressors of childhood, sleep is the first behavior to be significantly affected by the stress. This seems to be true for abuse as well. In a recent study by Glod, Teicher, Hartman, and Harakal (1997), 19 children with documented abuse were compared with 15 nonabused normal controls and 10 depressed children. Ambulatory activity monitoring was used to evaluate sleep-related activities for three consecutive nights. Data were analyzed for nocturnal activity. The abused children were twice as active at night as normal and depressed children, and they emitted a greater percentage of their total daily activity during the night. The actigraph-derived sleep measures suggested that the abused children have prolonged sleep latency and decreased sleep efficiency. Physically abused children have more impaired sleep efficiency than sexually abused children. These data are similar to those of Sadeh and colleagues (Sadeh et al., 1995), who reported that nonabused and sexually abused children had better sleep quality than physically abused children.

Brain waves also discriminate children who have been abused from those who have not. In a study using EEG coherence and MRI (Teicher et al., 1997), there was suggestive evidence for abnormal cortical development in physically and sexually abused children. In a related study on event-related potentials (McPherson, Newton, Ackerman, Oglesby, & Dykman, 1997), the abused participants showed abnormal P2-N2 evoked responses to tones.

Problems in Later Development

The problem of child abuse, of course, is the risk for later developmental problems. In many studies, a host of problems have been identified, ranging from feelings of shame (versus pride), sexually inappropriate behavior, sibling incest, symptoms of bipolar personality disorder, and, in adulthood, homelessness. An example of the range of problems that can be experienced is illustrated in a study by Flisher and colleagues (Flisher et al., 1997). In this study on a community based probability sample of children and adolescents aged 9 to 17 years, 26% of the sample reported having a history of physical abuse. Physical abuse was significantly associated with global impairment, poor social competence, major depression, conduct disorder, oppositional defiant disorder, agoraphobia, overanxious disorder, and generalized anxiety disorder. In several studies internalizing and externalizing characteristics have been reported for sexually and physically abused children, including a study by Dykman and colleagues (Dykman et al., 1997). In this study the externalizing scores were significantly higher than the internalizing scores in the abused children, and posttraumatic stress disorder was diagnosed in 50% of the abused children. In another study (Dodge, Pettit, Bates, & Valente, 1995), early abuse increased the risk of teacher-rated externalizing outcomes in third and fourth grades fourfold. In contrast, in another study abused children with co-occurring high levels of internalizing problems exhibited significantly higher levels of aggression as rated by parents, suggesting that internalizing problems combined with abuse may have more significant outcomes than externalizing problems combined with abuse (Scerbo & Kolko, 1995). More serious psychotic symptoms, including symptoms of schizophrenia, have been reported in children who have been physically and sexually abused (Ellason & Ross, 1997).

Longer Term Problems

Longer term problems have been determined retrospectively by interviewing adults who have been sexually or physically abused. In a study by Silverman, Reinherz, and Giaconia (1996), approximately 80% of the young adults who had been abused as children met *DSM–III–R* criteria for at least one psychiatric disorder at age 21. As compared with their nonabused colleagues, they demonstrated more significant impairments in functioning at both ages 15 and 21, including more depressive symptomatology, anxiety, psychiatric disorders, emotional-behavioral problems, suicidal ideation, and suicide attempts. Longer term consequences have been reported by many others, including Mullen, Martin, Anderson, Romans, and Herbison (1996), who reported increased rates of psychopathology, sexual difficulties, decreased self-esteem, and personal problems. In addition to more lifetime occurrences of episodes of depression, posttraumatic stress and substance abuse were also reported in adults who experienced child abuse (Duncan, Saunders, Kilpatrick, Hanson, & Resnick, 1996). The problem extends to crime and most particularly violent crime, which was noted in a study by Maxfield and Widom (1996). In their study they found that children who were abused were more likely than those in a control group to have a juvenile or adult arrest for any nontraffic offenses and for violent crimes.

Interventions

A wide range of treatments has been used with children, the most popular being therapeutic day care with emphasis on improving developmental skills. Although most programs showed some improvement with treatment, many have very short or no follow-up to determine whether improvement was sustained (Oates & Bross, 1995). Hospitalization is rarely used for child abuse and represents a very small fraction of total pediatric admissions and of child protective services reports. The rate of hospitalization for child abuse is approximately 10 children per 100,000 per year. However, in a study in which children at risk for abuse were matched on demographic characteristics with children not at risk for abuse, significantly more high-risk children were hospitalized (40% versus 22%), and the high-risk children were hospitalized for a mean of 9 days versus a mean of 3.8 days for the comparison children. For admissions for medical problems, 28% of hospital days in the high-risk group were considered inappropriate versus 8% in the comparison group (Leventhal, Pew, Berg, & Garber, 1996). Thus it would appear that considerable resources are spent on these high-risk children, many for protective services. It is interesting in this light that even though elderly abuse is only slightly less common than child abuse (46% of reported abuse involves elders), the states on average spend about $22 per child but only $2.90 per elder for protective services. The most cost-effective intervention, of course, would be prevention programs that could target those children most at risk for child abuse. Identifying the most predictive risk factors has been the most complex problem in the entire field of child abuse and is perhaps the one that has shown the least progress in the research arena.

Frequently Targeted Risk Factors

Mothers of abused children have been the most frequently targeted risk factor. Most of the studies on mothers have focused on those who are substance abusers. In one study, for example, social and demographic variables were found to be limited predictors of maltreatment, whereas substance disorders were strongly associated with the onset of both abuse and neglect and depression was found to be a strong risk factor for physical abuse (Chaffin, Kelleher, & Hollenberg, 1996). In contrast to most studies on child abuse that have been limited by self-report data, these data were based on the National Institute of Mental Health epidemiological catchment area survey of 7,103 parents in which a significant number of factors were explored with no reliance on self-report data. In addition to social and demographic factors, several psychiatric disorders, including substance abuse and depression, were examined, and risk models were developed using hierarchical logistic regression in which physical abuse and neglect were found to have distinct sets of risk factors with minimal overlap between the groups. Similar findings were noted in a study using mother and teacher ratings of behavior problems in abused and nonabused children (Kinard, 1995). Based on the Achenbach Child Behavior Checklist, abused children were noted to have greater behavior problems than nonabused children, with abused boys having more problems than abused girls. Regardless of abuse status, there were no significant differences by rater. The combination of abuse and maternal depressed mood resulted in the greatest problems for children.

More Subtle Risk Factors

Some research has looked more closely at the more subtle characteristics of mothers who have abused their children. In one study, mothers who had physically abused their children were compared with nonabusing mothers of chronic problem children. The mothers' coping was measured by several methods. In comparison with the nonabusive mothers, independent ratings indicated that abusive mothers exhibited a pattern of coping characterized by greater use of emotion-focused strategies and less use of effective problem-focused strategies. Using self-report ratings of coping, abusive mothers perceived their coping to be more ineffective than the nonabusive mothers did. In another study (Milner, Halsey, & Fultz, 1995), empathetic responsiveness and affective reactivity to infant stimuli were assessed in mothers who were at high or low risk for physical abuse. Compared with baseline, high-risk mothers reported no change in empathy across different infant conditions (baseline, infant smiling, infant quiet, and infant crying), whereas low-risk mothers reported an increase. Previous studies had shown that child abusers were less empathetic and more hostile in response to a crying child. The findings support aggression models that suggest a lack of empathy in the presence of negative affectivity preceding abusive behavior (Milner et al., 1995).

In an extensive review of the literature on primate species and on different cultures, Field (1983) explored environmental stressors—including early separation between parents and infants, environmental changes, social isolation and lack of a support system, crowding, and poverty—that were often implicated as contributing to child abuse in the literature. Child characteristics implicated in the literature were also explored, including birth order, sex of the child, age of the child, and the "problem" child (the child who has a handicapping condition or is generally "difficult"). The parents' characteristics were also explored, including the mother's age, physical and mental health, substance abuse, and other psychopathology. Finally, the early socialization and child-rearing practices in different primate groups and in different cultures were explored. A summary of the data reviewed in this article supported a working hypothesis that abuse happens to an undersocialized child interacting with parents whose discipline is inconsistent in a culture in which accepted forms of discipline are ambiguous or not transmitted by cultural traditions. This profile is thought to constitute a primary constellation of vulnerability for idiosyncratic (out-of-control) abuse as we know it in the United States.

Future Research

The lion's share of research has yielded very little new information over the past two decades. Closer analysis of the literature, such as the study conducted by Field (1983), and examination of more subtle factors, such as the imposition of inconsistent discipline on an undersocialized child that leads to idiosyncratic abuse and parents' lack of empathy during early interactions with their infants, may move the field closer to understanding the dynamics of the abusing parent-abused child interaction that lead to the abuse.

[See also Domestic Violence; Family Violence; Mandated Reporting; and Violence and Aggression.]

Acknowledgments. This research was supported by NIMH Research Scientist Award #MH00331 and NIMH Research Grant #MH46586 to the author and a grant from Johnson & Johnson to the Touch Research Institute of the University of Miami School of Medicine.

Bibliography

Alexander, R. C. (1995). Current and emerging concepts in child abuse. *Comprehensive Therapy, 21*(12), 726–730.

Carpenter, M., Kennedy, M., Armstrong, A. L., & Moore, E. (1997). Indicators of abuse or neglect in preschool children's drawings. *Journal of Psychosocial Nursing and Mental Health Services, 35*(4), 10–17.

Chaffin, M., Kelleher, K., & Hollenberg, J. (1996). Onset of physical abuse and neglect: Psychiatric, substance abuse, and social risk factors from prospective community data. *Child Abuse and Neglect, 20*(30), 191–203.

Crenshaw, W. B. et al. (1995). When educators confront child abuse: An analysis of the decision to report. *Child Abuse and Neglect, 19*(9), 1095–1113.

Deisz, R., Doueck, H. J., & George, N. (1996). Reasonable cause: A qualitative study of mandated reporting. *Child Abuse and Neglect, 20*(4), 275–287.

Dodge, K. A., Pettit, G. S., Bates, J. E., & Valente, E. (1995). Social information-processing patterns partially mediate the effect of early physical abuse on later conduct problems. *Journal of Abnormal Psychology, 104*(4), 632–645.

Duncan, R. D., Saunders, B. E., Kilpatrick, D. G., Hanson, R. F., & Resnick, H. S. (1996). Childhood physical assault as a risk factor for PTSD, depression, and substance abuse: Findings from a national survey. *American Journal of Orthopsychiatry, 66*(3), 437–448.

Dykman, R. A., McPherson, B., Ackerman, P. T., Newton, J. E., Mooney, D. M., Wherry, J., & Chaffin, M. (1997). Internalizing and externalizing characteristics of sexually and/or physically abused children. *Integrative Physiological and Behavioral Science, 32*(1), 62–74.

Ellason, J. W., & Ross, C. A. (1997). Childhood trauma and psychiatric symptoms. *Psychological Reports, 80*(2), 447–450.

Field, T. (1983). Child abuse in monkeys and humans: A comparative perspective. *Child Abuse: The Nonhuman Primate Data*, pp. 151–174.

Flisher, A. J., Kramer, R. A., Hoven, C. W., Greenwald, S., Alegria, M., Bird, H. R., Canino, G., Connell, R., & Moore, R. E. (1997). Psychosocial characteristics of physically abused children and adolescents. *Journal of the American Academy of Child and Adolescent Psychiatry, 36*(1), 123–131.

Glod, C. A., Teicher, M. H., Hartman, C. R., & Harakal, T. (1997). Increased nocturnal activity and impaired sleep maintenance in abused children. *Journal of the American Academy of Child and Adolescent Psychiatry, 36*(9), 1236–1243.

Jessee, S. A. (1995). Child abuse and neglect curricula in North American dental schools. *Journal of Dental Education, 59*(8), 841–843.

Jessee, S. A., & Reiger, M. (1996). A study of age-related

variables among physically abused children *ASDC Journal of Dentistry for Children, 63*(4), 275–280.

Kinard, E. M. (1995). Mother and teacher assessments of behavior problems in abused children. *Journal of the American Academy of Child and Adolescent Psychiatry, 34*(8), 1043–1053.

Leventhal, J. M., Pew, M. C., Berg, A. T., & Garber, R. B. (1996). Use of health services by children who were identified during the postpartum period as being at high risk of child abuse or neglect. *Pediatrics, 97*(3), 331–335.

MacMillan, H. L., Fleming, J. E., Trocme, N., Boyle, M. H., Wong, M., Racine, Y. A., Beardslee, W. R., & Offord, D. R. (1997). Prevalence of child physical and sexual abuse in the community. Results from the Ontario Health Supplement. *JAMA, 278*(2), 131–135.

Maxfield, M. G., & Widom, C. S. (1996). The cycle of violence. Revisited 6 years later. *Archives of Pediatrics and Adolescent Medicine, 150*(4), 390–395.

McMahon, P., Grossman, W., Gaffney, M., & Stanitski, C. (1995). Soft-tissue injury as an indication of child abuse. *Journal of Bone and Joint Surgery—American Volume, 77*(8), 1179–1183.

McPherson, W. B., Newton, J. E., Ackerman, P., Oglesby, D. M., & Dykman, R. A. (1997). An event-related brain potential investigation of PTSD and PTSD symptoms in abused children. *Integrative Physiological and Behavioral Science, 32*(1), 31–42.

Milner, J. S., Halsey, L. B., & Fultz, J. (1995). Empathic responsiveness and affective reactivity to infant stimuli in high- and low-risk for physical child abuse mothers. *Child Abuse and Neglect, 19*(6), 767–780.

Mullen, P. E., Martin, J. L., Anderson, J. C., Romans, S. E., & Herbison, G. P. (1996). The long-term impact of the physical, emotional, and sexual abuse of children: A community study. *Child Abuse and Neglect, 20*(1), 7–21.

Oates, R. K., & Bross, D. C. (1995). What have we learned about treating child physical abuse? A literature review of the last decade. *Child Abuse and Neglect, 19*(4), 463–473.

Peterson, L. W., Hardin, M., & Nitsch, M. J. (1995). The use of children's drawings in the evaluation and treatment of child sexual, emotional and physical abuse. *Archives of Family Medicine, 4*(5), 445–452.

Sadeh, A., McGuire, J. P., Sachs, H., Seifer, R., Tremblay, A., Civita, R., & Hayden, R. M. (1995). Sleep and psychological characteristics of children on a psychiatric inpatient unit. *Journal of the American Academy of Child and Adolescent Psychiatry, 34*(6), 813–819.

Scerbo, A. S. & Kolko, D. J. (1995). Child physical abuse and aggression: Preliminary findings on the role of internalizing problems. *Journal of the American Academy of Child and Adolescent Psychiatry, 34*(8), 1060–1066.

Silverman, A. B., Reinherz, H. Z. & Giaconia, R. M. (1996). The long-term sequelae of child and adolescent abuse: A longitudinal community study. *Child Abuse and Neglect, 20*(8), 709–723.

Teicher, M. H., Ito, Y., Glod, C. A., Andersen, S. L., Dumont, N., & Ackerman, E. (1997). Preliminary evidence for abnormal cortical development in physically and sexually abused children using EEG coherence and MRI. *Annals of the New York Academy of Sciences, 821*, 160–175.

Tiffany Field

CHILD AND ADOLESCENT PSYCHOTHERAPY. Psychotherapy consists of treatments that are designed to decrease distress and emotional and behavioral problems and to improve adaptive and prosocial functioning. Psychotherapy draws on psychological or psychosocial processes such as learning, persuasion, conflict resolution, and interpersonal interaction to influence how individuals feel (affect), think (cognition), and act (behavior). Psychotherapy is distinguished from biological interventions, such as medication or psychosurgery, that also may be used to influence emotional and behavioral problems.

Psychotherapy is usually applied in clinical settings, including mental health services, clinics, health maintenance organizations, psychiatric hospitals, and private practice, to which children and adolescents are referred for treatment. Problems for which children are often referred for psychotherapy include oppositional, aggressive, and antisocial behavior, hyperactivity, anxiety, depression, parent-child conflict, and adjustment problems in response to stressful events, such as divorce or loss of a parent. Many of these problems are delineated as psychiatric disorders in contemporary systems of diagnosis such as the *Diagnostic and Statistical Manual of Mental Disorders* (DSM–IV, American Psychiatric Association, 1994). The impetus for initiating treatment is usually recognition by parents, teachers, or school counselors that the child's functioning in everyday life is impaired.

Special Characteristics of Treating Children and Adolescents

Psychotherapy with children and adolescents raises special challenges. First, many emotional and behavioral problems that are treated in therapy (e.g., aggression, hyperactivity, anxiety) are often evident in less extreme forms as part of normal development. For most youths, these behaviors decrease and do not portend maladjustment or psychiatric disorders in adulthood. Psychological treatment may be warranted when the symptoms are extreme, form part of a larger constellation of behaviors, interfere with functioning in everyday life, and do not attenuate with maturation. Whether and when to intervene raises special challenges, because many of the seemingly problematic behaviors may represent short-lived problems or perturbations in development rather than signs of lasting clinical impairment.

Second, children and adolescents, unlike adults, rarely refer themselves for treatment or identify themselves as experiencing stress or symptoms. Problems most commonly referred for treatment are disruptive behaviors, such as aggression and hyperactivity, that are disturbing to others (parents, teachers) who initiate the treatment process. Emotional problems that are less disruptive, such as depression, anxiety, and withdrawal, are more likely to be overlooked by parents and teachers. Whether referred for behavioral or emotional problems, children may not see their symptoms as a "problem" in need of treatment. The challenge is to involve the child in treatment and to work toward a change that the child may not view as necessary or important.

Third, the dependence of children on adults makes them particularly vulnerable to multiple influences over which they have little control. Parent mental health, marital and family functioning, stress in the home, difficult living circumstances, and socioeconomic disadvantage are a few of the factors that can influence the nature and severity of child impairment and the likelihood of therapeutic change. Psychotherapy for the child is often only a part of the intervention; significant efforts may be required to address parent and family dysfunction that may contribute to or maintain adjustment problems of the child.

Fourth, in the prototypic image of therapy, a client is seen individually in treatment sessions by a mental health practitioner (usually a psychologist, psychiatrist, or social worker). Yet in child therapy, parents, teachers, siblings, and peers, alone and in various combinations, can play an ancillary, supplementary, supportive, or even primary role in administering treatment. Challenges come from working with others, such as parents, who deliver aspects of treatment aimed at changing child behavior. Parent and family problems, such as major depression, substance abuse, or violence in the home, may directly impede delivery of treatment.

Fifth, assessing child and adolescent emotional and behavioral problems raises its own set of challenges. Questionnaires and interviews often ask subtle questions about the onset, duration, and intensity of emotional and behavioral problems. Whether young children (e.g., younger than 6 or 7 years) can report on these characteristics is not well established. In most studies, multiple informants (parents, teachers, children) are used to evaluate emotional and behavioral problems of the child. Measures from different informants often yield different views about the severity and scope of the problems.

Historical Overview

The development of psychoanalysis in the late 1800s by Sigmund Freud is a landmark in the development of psychotherapy. In psychoanalysis as a form of therapy, talk serves as the medium of exchange between the therapist and patient. The exchanges are designed to reveal and help resolve internal conflicts and unexpressed or inappropriately expressed psychic impulses, those mechanisms that Freud proposed to explain the emergence of psychological problems such as anxiety. A key psychoanalytic tenet is that the underpinnings of emotional problems in adults develop during childhood. Although almost all of Freud's work was with adult patients, his approach underscored the importance of early child development.

Beginning in the 1920s, psychoanalytic treatment was extended to children. Anna Freud (Sigmund Freud's daughter) and Melanie Klein are key figures in the history of child psychotherapy because they adapted psychoanalytic treatment to children. Because young children are less able to talk about inner psychological processes than are adults, treatment was modified for children. Play, rather than talk, was used as a way of evoking emotional and unconscious expressions of the child and to help the therapist understand the child's thoughts, feelings, and sources of conflict.

Research has not supported the notion that psychic conflicts, as proposed by Freud, are the basis for the development of emotional and behavioral problems. Even so, psychoanalysis has had an enormous impact on the development of psychotherapy. Many other psychotherapy techniques have developed from challenging the assumptions of psychoanalysis and from theories and research on the nature of emotional and behavioral problems.

In the 1950s, the effectiveness of psychotherapy came into sharp focus in a provocative article by Hans Eysenck ("The effects of psychotherapy: An evaluation," *Journal of Consulting Psychology*, 1952, 16, 319–324). Eysenck reviewed the scant research with adults and children and concluded that there was no persuasive evidence that psychotherapy was effective. By Eysenck's calculation, the proportion of people who improved with treatment (about two thirds of the cases) was equal to the proportion that improved without any treatment at all. The review was quite controversial. Among the conclusions on which all could agree was that there was a paucity of firm evidence in carefully controlled studies that supported the effectiveness of psychotherapy. In the late 1950s and early 1960s, separate reviews of evidence for the treatment of children and adolescents led to the same conclusion. The net effect of these reviews and of the climate they fostered was to generate increased research. In the 1960s and 1970s, research on psychotherapy in the treatment of adults increased considerably.

Advances in psychotherapy depend on many other areas of research, including investigation of the nature and characteristics of various psychological or psychiatric disorders; of the biological, psychological, and other characteristics in the population with which various problems are associated; and of factors that lead to onset and long-term course of the dysfunction. Until recently, research on psychotherapy and the areas on which treatment advances depend (e.g., diagnosis and assessment of clinical disorders) focused primarily on adults. Only within the past 20 years has research accelerated on child and adolescent disorders and their treatment.

Diversity of Treatments

Currently, more than 500 forms of psychotherapy that are applied to children and adolescents can be identified. Traditionally, the treatments have been classified by their approaches to therapy. Major approaches include psychoanalytic and psychodynamic, client-centered, experiential, family, humanistic, existential, behavioral, and cognitive-behavioral therapy. These groupings are based on broad conceptual orientations regarding how clinical problems come about or can be ameliorated. For example, psychoanalytic and psychodynamic treatments emphasize the child's psychological processes and conflicts and how they may contribute to the problem or be altered in treatment; family therapies emphasize the child in the context of the family and how family communication, interpersonal roles, and structure contribute to symptoms in the child. The broad groupings are minimally useful in discussing therapy because within a given approach many different treatments can be identified. These treatments often reflect different, and indeed conflicting, views about treatment and focus on different clinical problems. Also, many treatment techniques, such as play therapy or family-based treatment, encompass multiple theoretical approaches.

Treatments can vary in many ways, such as in the focus of treatment (the emotional life of the child, child-parent relations), in the activities in which the child and therapist engage (talk, play, role playing, games), in the time period that is emphasized during treatment (past or current influences on the child), and in the degree to which potential participants (child, parent, all of the family) are incorporated into the treatment process. For example, in parent management training, treatment focuses on child behaviors and parent reactions to those behaviors. Didactic instruction, role playing, and feedback are used to develop new ways for parents to interact with their children. The focus of parent management training is on current behaviors of the child at home, at school, and in the community, and, in addition to the parents, other adults in frequent contact with the child (teachers, relatives living in the home) may be incorporated into treatment.

For a given therapy technique, the treatment sessions may differ as a function of the age of the child. For example, psychodynamic therapy for young children is likely to rely on play to reveal processes and conflicts, whereas for older children and adolescents, it is more likely to rely on talk as a medium of exchange between the therapist and client. Adapting treatment to the developmental level of the child or adolescent is required, but guidelines on how to do this are not well studied.

Effectiveness of Treatment

The main criteria for evaluating the effectiveness of treatment is the extent to which it reduces emotional and behavioral problems and associated impairment and improves adaptive functioning in everyday life. Several hundred studies have been completed evaluating the effectiveness of child and adolescent psychotherapy. The research relies heavily on randomized, controlled clinical trials in which children or adolescents are assigned randomly to various conditions within the experiment, such as treatment or no treatment, two or more variations of a given treatment, or two or more different treatments. Reviews of the research have used meta-analysis, a statistical procedure that permits summarization, integration, and quantification of results from several different studies. The conclusions have been consistent in noting that psychotherapies for children and adolescents are effective when compared to no treatment. In general, behavioral and cognitive-behavioral treatments have tended to produce greater effects than more traditional approaches, such as psychodynamic and client-centered treatments. However, differences in the effectiveness of different treatment orientations are less clear because of the paucity of studies on traditional treatment approaches and because of differences in the treatment foci of studies that use different treatment techniques. Also a given approach, such as cognitive-behavioral treatment, may encompass many different treatments that vary in their effectiveness. Hence discussing treatments at the level of broad approaches is not helpful in making recommendations for treatment.

General conclusions about the overall effectiveness of psychotherapy are useful as a broad summary, but researchers and practitioners are more concerned about the effects of specific treatments as they are applied to specific problems at specific points in development. More specific conclusions can be reached about selected treatment techniques. For example, variations of cognitive-behavioral treatment have been found to be effective in treating anxiety and aggressive behavior among children and depression in both children and adolescents. Parent management training, one of the more well-studied treatments, is supported by extensive evidence for the treatment of oppositional, aggressive, and antisocial children. Parent management training has been applied to many problem domains, including child compliance, tantrums, enuresis, tics, eating disorders, hyperactivity, and adherence to medical regimens, and to diverse populations. The populations include preschool children, as well as adolescents, with such diagnoses as autism, mental retardation, learning disability, conduct disorder, and attention-deficit/hyperactivity disorder.

There are limitations in the evidence of treatment effectiveness, in spite of the excellent progress in child and adolescent therapy research. Most studies of psychotherapy focus on children and adolescents who are recruited or solicited, rather than referred, for treatment. Nonreferred youths are less likely to show severe clinical impairment or the multiple problems and psychiatric disorders that are characteristic of youths who are referred for treatment and seen in outpatient clinics. Also, in research, treatments tend to be relatively brief, to involve only one technique rather than a combination of different techniques, and to be implemented under highly controlled and carefully monitored experimental conditions. These conditions depart from the conditions in which treatment is implemented in clinical practice. Research in clinical settings has been shown to be effective, but relatively few carefully controlled studies are available in this context.

Key Issues and Future Directions

Treatment of children and adolescents has progressed greatly in a relatively short time span. Nevertheless, several fundamental issues remain to be addressed. First, psychotherapy research for children and adolescents has focused on a relatively narrow range of treatment techniques. Currently, behavioral and cognitive-behavioral techniques dominate and, indeed, account for approximately one half of the treatment outcome studies. Other more traditional techniques, such as psychoanalysis, psychodynamic therapy, family therapy, and play therapy, are much less frequently studied, even though they are often used in clinical practice. In clinical practice, therapists often draw on multiple approaches to treat a particular child or adolescent, an approach referred to as eclecticism or eclectic psychotherapy. Very little research has studied how treatments are combined in clinical work and whether combinations improve treatment outcome.

Second, most treatment studies have focused on whether treatment is more effective than no treatment or on the relative effectiveness of two or more treatments for the same problem. In addition to these questions, it is important to evaluate the components and characteristics of the treatment that contribute to therapeutic change; whether combinations of treatment are more effective than a particular treatment administered by itself; what factors or processes during therapy facilitate or impede therapeutic change; and how

characteristics of the child, parent, and family, as well as of the therapist, may influence treatment outcome. Research has not adequately addressed these questions.

Third, the long-term effects of treatment are not well studied. Long-term follow-up assessment is needed to evaluate whether treatment effects are maintained and whether later functioning in adolescence and adulthood is enhanced by treatment in childhood. Long-term follow-up information is very difficult to obtain because of the difficulty of remaining in contact with cases and also because many influences other than treatment can intervene in the ensuing years. Beneficial effects of some treatments are maintained up to several months or one year later, but more attention is needed to evaluate longer term follow-up.

Fourth, there is keen interest in identifying validated or empirically supported treatments so that these can be used in clinical practice. Validated treatments refer to techniques that have been studied in controlled research and shown to be effective in more than one study when tested with clinical samples. Most treatments in use in clinical settings have not been well validated, and most techniques that are well validated are not in use in clinical settings. Identifying treatments that have been well studied in research reflects interest in disseminating these treatments to clinical settings and evaluating whether the effects can be obtained under conditions in which treatment delivery is less easily monitored and controlled.

Fifth and finally, a critical priority for treatment research is greater attention to the treatment and mental health needs of minority groups, including children and adolescents who are African American, Hispanic American, Asian American, and Native American. For many youths, minority-group status is also associated with low socioeconomic status, higher incidence of clinical dysfunction, and poor access to health and mental health services. Minority youth are underrepresented in treatment research and clinical practice. An important challenge is to identify culturally sensitive, relevant, and acceptable treatments and to evaluate their effectiveness.

Conclusions

Research on child and adolescent psychotherapy has made significant progress in the past two decades. Evaluations of treatment outcome research have shown that treatments produce beneficial effects. This general conclusion is important in view of historical challenges regarding the effectiveness of therapy.

There are many challenges that confront the development of effective treatments. First and foremost, the task is to understand child development, the emergence of childhood and adolescent disorders, and the conditions that contribute to adjustment and maladjustment. Basic research is needed on the development of affect, cognition, and behavior and how variations of development increase or decrease the likelihood of later clinical dysfunction. Some advances have been made already. For example, harsh child-rearing practices, as reflected in the excessive use of corporal punishment, influence the development of oppositional and aggressive behavior in children. Even though this is only one of many influences, treatment that alters parent-child interactions and parent discipline practices (parent management training) reduces oppositional and aggressive behavior. As this example illustrates, advances in understanding factors that promote behavioral problems can provide important leads for treatment.

Second, a challenge for research is to understand why treatment does and does not work and for whom treatment is and is not effective. Identifying optimally effective treatments will depend on knowing more about how changes are made with treatment. Also, individuals may vary in responsiveness to treatment. Understanding the conditions that influence responsiveness will help improve treatment outcome and direct children and adolescents to treatments that are most likely to be effective. Child and adolescent psychotherapy research remains a very active area of study in light of the wide range of disorders that youths experience, the relatively high prevalence rates of many disorders, and the impact that disorders can have on child and family functioning.

[See also Play Therapy; and Psychotherapy.]

Bibliography

Durlak, J. A., Wells, A. M., Cotten, J. K., & Johnson, S. (1995). Analysis of selected methodological issues in child psychotherapy research. *Journal of Clinical Child Psychology, 24,* 141–148.

Hibbs, E., & Jensen, P. (Eds.). (1996). *Psychosocial treatment research of child and adolescent disorders: Empirically based strategies for clinical practice.* Washington, DC: American Psychological Association.

Kazdin, A. E. (2000). *Psychotherapy for children and adolescents.* New York: Oxford University Press. This book reviews the current status of child and adolescent therapy and directions for future research.

Kazdin, A. E., & Weisz, J. R. (1998). Identifying and developing empirically supported child and adolescent treatments. *Journal of Consulting and Clinical Psychology, 66,* 19–36.

Kratochwill, T. R., & Morris, R. J. (Eds.). (In press). *Handbook of psychotherapy with children and adolescents* (2nd ed.). Needham Heights, MA: Allyn & Bacon. This book reviews research on the treatment of child and adolescent disorders.

Mash, E. J., & Barkley, R. (Eds.). (In press). *Treatment of childhood disorders* (2nd ed.). New York: Guilford Press. This book reviews research on the treatment of child and adolescent disorders.

Weisz, J. R., Donenberg, G. R., Han, S. S., & Weiss, B. (1995). Bridging the gap between laboratory and clinic in child and adolescent psychotherapy. *Journal of Consulting and Clinical Psychology, 63,* 688–701. This paper notes some of the major differences between therapy as it is conducted in research and in clinical practice and the implications of these differences.

Weisz, J. R., Weiss, B., Han, S. S., Granger, D. A., & Morton, T. (1995). Effects of psychotherapy with children and adolescents revisited: A meta-analysis of treatment outcome studies. *Psychological Bulletin, 117,* 450–468.

Alan E. Kazdin

CHILD BEHAVIOR CHECKLIST. The Child Behavior Checklist (CBCL) is one of a family of standardized instruments for assessing behavioral and emotional problems and competencies. Parents fill out the CBCL to describe their children's functioning. Separate versions are available for ages 2 to 3 and 4 to 18. Related self-administered instruments include the Caregiver-Teacher Report Form for ages 2 to 5; Teacher's Report Form for ages 5 to 18; Youth Self-Report for ages 11 to 18; Young Adult Behavior Checklist for ages 18 to 30; Young Adult Self-Report for ages 18 to 30; Adult Self-Report for ages 30 to 59; and Older Adult Self-Report for ages 60 to 90. For use by clinical interviewers, there is the Semistructured Clinical Interview for Children and Adolescents. And for use by observers who see children in classrooms and other group settings, there is the Direct Observation Form.

All the instruments embody an empirically based approach to assessment and taxonomy. This approach starts with numerous items chosen for their hypothesized association with needs for mental health or special education services. Large samples of relevant criterion groups are then rated by the appropriate informants. Scores on the items are analyzed to identify those that discriminate between normative and deviant groups. The items are also analyzed to identify those that co-occur to form syndromes. Scales are constructed for scoring each syndrome, groupings of correlated syndromes designated as internalizing and externalizing, and all the problem items. The scales are displayed on profiles and are normed to provide a basis for comparing the problems reported for individuals with those reported for gender- and age-specific normative samples.

Extensive reliability and validity data have been published. More than 3,000 publications also report diverse research and clinical applications. Translations are available in 58 languages (Vignoe et al., 1999).

The empirically based instruments have been used to derive syndromal constructs from patterns of problems that are found in both genders across multiple developmental periods, as rated by different types of informants. The following seven cross-informant constructs have been found for ages 4 to 30: *aggressive behavior, anxious/depressed, attention problems, delinquent behavior, somatic complaints, thought problems*, and *withdrawn*. For ages 4 to 18, an additional cross-informant construct is designated as *social problems*, and for ages 18 to 30, an additional construct is designated as *intrusive*.

To take account of differences in the problems reported by different types of informants, the scales and standard scores for measuring a particular syndromal construct differ somewhat from one type of informant to another. Computer programs are available for entering data from different types of informants, printing profiles scored from each informant for the same subject, and comparing item and scale scores obtained from each informant (Arnold & Jacobowitz, 1993, 1997).

Bibliography

Achenbach, T. M. (1991). *Manual for the Child Behavior Checklist/4–18 and 1991 Profile*. Burlington: University of Vermont, Department of Psychiatry. This comprehensive manual presents details of the development of the Child Behavior Checklist, construction of scales for scoring it, reliability, validity, and relations to other instruments. It also illustrates diverse practical and research applications.

Achenbach, T. M. (1995). Empirically based assessment and taxonomy: Applications to clinical research. *Psychological Assessment, 7*, 261–274. This article outlines the empirically based paradigm for assessment and taxonomy of psychopathology and presents diverse research findings that have been generated by this paradigm.

Achenbach, T. M. (1997). *Manual for the Young Adult Behavior Checklist and Young Adult Self-Report*. Burlington: University of Vermont, Department of Psychiatry. This manual presents extensions of empirically based assessment to ages 18 to 30. It includes detailed descriptions of the young-adult instruments, construction of scales for scoring them, reliability and validity data, and illustrations of applications.

Achenbach, T. M., & McConaughy, S. H. (1996). Relations between *DSM-IV* and empirically based assessment. *School Psychology Review, 25*, 330–342. This article highlights similarities and differences between the *DSM-IV* and empirically based approaches to behavioral and emotional problems. A case example illustrates applications of both approaches.

Achenbach, T. M., & McConaughy, S. H. (1997). *Empirically based assessment of child and adolescent psychopathology: Practical applications* (2nd ed.). Thousand Oaks, CA: Sage. This book provides detailed case illustrations of how various empirically based procedures are applied to children with diverse problems, as seen in diverse contexts.

Arnold, J., & Jacobowitz, D. (1993). *Cross-Informant Program for the CBCL/4–18, YSR, and TRF*. Burlington: University of Vermont, Department of Psychiatry.

Arnold, J., & Jacobowitz, D. (1997). *Cross-Informant Program for the YASR and YABCL*. Burlington: University of Vermont, Department of Psychiatry.

Crijnen, A. A. M., Achenbach, T. M., & Verhulst, F. C. (1997). Comparisons of problems reported by parents of children in 12 cultures: The CBCL/4–18 syndrome constructs. *Journal of the American Academy of Child and Adolescent Psychiatry, 156*, 569–574. This study reports comparisons of behavioral and emotional problems reported on the Child Behavior Checklist for children in 12 cultures. Most cultures showed minimal deviations from the mean of the problem scores obtained by averaging problem scores across all the cultures.

Vignoe, D., Berube, R. L., & Achenbach, T. M. (1997). *Bibliography of published studies using the Child Behavior Checklist and related materials: 1997 edition*. Burlington: University of Vermont, Department of Psychiatry.

Thomas M. Achenbach

CHILD CARE. *See* Day Care.

CHILD CUSTODY. Until the nineteenth century, child custody in divorce was presumed to be the right of the father under the legal doctrine of *patria potestas*. The child was considered property, and the father, as natural protector, had absolute control over his children. The development of the *parens patriae* doctrine in the mid-nineteenth century recognized the state's right to abridge the power of the father to ensure his children's well-being, but fathers were still usually awarded custody. Around 1900, social changes yielded the "tender years" concept of the mother as primary physical and psychological caretaker, especially during the child's "early years." Initially, fathers, who bore financial responsibility for the child's well-being, were expected to obtain custody when the child became older; however, mothers soon became the favored custodians of all ages. The legal development of child support provisions enhanced these views.

The "welfare of the child" standard was first expressed in *Chapsky v. Wood* (26 Kan. 650 1881) and was labeled the "best interests" standard in *Finlay v. Finlay* (240 N.Y. 429, 433, 148 N.E. 624 1925). As the tender-years presumption became established, best interests almost always led to mother custody. To gain custody, a father had to prove the mother was unfit (usually based on immorality such as adultery) or incompetent (usually due to mental illness or alcoholism). Judges also tended to enforce the notion that the parent most culpable for the divorce was less deserving of custody.

Moreover, the readily accepted "parent-natural-rights" doctrine had and still has the effect of ensuring that in disputes with other caretakers, the natural parents usually win. Until the early 1980s, the best-interests standard was usually formulaic: The tender-years presumption favored the mother in divorce, and the biological presumption favored the natural parent(s) when custody involved another caretaker.

In the 1960s and 1970s, rising divorce rates, enactment of no-fault divorce laws, and the increase of women in the work force changed society's, including men's, conceptions of fatherhood. The courts are more willing to grant custody to fathers, especially if the father can establish himself as the primary caretaker. In addition, as the concept that the child is an independent person with needs and rights has become more accepted, most courts believe that an older (ten and above) child's preference of custodial parent should be considered.

In 1973, Goldstein, Freud, and Solnit, in their extremely influential book, *Beyond the Best Interests of the Child*, suggested that because of the inherent ambiguities in the best-interests standard, a more realistic consideration was the "least detrimental alternative for safeguarding the child's growth and development" (p. 53). To ensure that a child will be placed with the adult who is now or who is likely to become the child's "psychological parent," they elaborated three criteria:

1. Continuity of relationship with the psychological (custodial) parent should be safeguarded. Psychological parenthood is determined by emotional attachments, the results of daily care, and social, psychological, and emotional interactions and is often synonymous with the primary caretaker. This has become a critical consideration in most custody assessments.
2. Custody adjudication should proceed in consideration of the child's sense of time to decrease possible psychological harm. Prolonged custody litigation needs to be avoided.
3. The incapacity of the state to supervise interpersonal relationships and the limits of making long-range predictions about the future needs of children and parents argues for the importance of family autonomy and the private ordering of relationships within the family. This criterion emphasizes the benefits of limited interference by the state.

These proposals offer comprehensive, determinate standards for adjudicating custody decisions, and, in large part, have been adopted by the courts. Unfortunately, the validity of these assumptions is questionable at best and potentially harmful at worst. For example, had these guidelines been followed strictly, the alternative of joint legal custody that has emerged over the past 20 years would not have been possible because of Goldstein and colleagues' insistence on regarding a single parent as primary caretaker. Joint legal custody provides both parents equal power and authority with regard to their children's upbringing, education, and general welfare and often appears to be in the best interests of children. Advocates claim that joint custody promotes cooperation and reduces conflict, and this option is now readily available and/or encouraged in most states.

Joint legal custody is popular with the courts because judges need not choose between fit parents; its goal is for the child to lose neither parent (a frequent occurrence in sole custody cases). Research suggests that continued contact with both parents is beneficial but only in the absence of significant interpersonal conflict between the parents; this circumstance appears to be more important to the child's postdivorce adjustment than either father absence or disruption of parental relationship. Even with cooperating parents, joint physical custody is more problematic. A sizeable minority of older youth are not satisfied when the arrangement means changing households regularly.

Another recent development is the frequently endorsed intervention known as "mediation," which is designed to decrease the adversarial process of court. Research suggests that this intervention is very positive for many divorcing families; however, the mediator must be skilled enough to keep one parent from using the custody decision to put the other parent at a disadvantage in other areas, such as financial support.

The noted forensic psychologist Thomas Grisso has described custody evaluations as involving, first, a description of the functional abilities, behaviors, and capacities of the parents, emphasizing those recognized as critical for child rearing and meeting the needs of children; second, explanations for any functional deficits within the limits of clinical methods; and third, an interactive comparison between the parents' abilities and the child's needs. While providing this information, psychologists must be careful not to "overreach" in their recommendations. They should not offer conclusions on legal issues, exceed the limitations of their scientific or clinical database, or use inappropriate and irrelevant assessment strategies. In sum, although psychological input can be valuable in helping the court to render a decision, psychologists must exercise caution, because their testimony may determine the course of a child's future upbringing and infringe on a parent's fundamental right to raise his or her children.

[*See also* Adoption; *and* Mandated Reporting.]

Bibliography

American Psychological Association (1994). Guidelines for child custody evaluations in divorce proceedings. *American Psychologist, 49*, 677–680.

Emery, R. E. (1994). *Renegotiating family relationships: Divorce, child custody and mediation.* New York: Guilford Press. Reviews demographic information, legal context, and psychological research related to divorce and child custody, focusing on changes in interparental and parent-child relationships, and describes the theoretical rationale for and effects of mediation in custody decisions on legal involvement, parent satisfaction, and parent and child well-being.

Goldstein, J., Freud, A., & Solnit, A. (1973). *Beyond the best interests of the child.* New York: Free Press. Very influential and controversial psychoanalytic conceptualization of children's needs in custody situations, with recommendations for the court and mental health professionals.

Grisso, T. (1986). *Evaluating competencies: Forensic assessments and instruments.* New York: Plenum Press. Reviews objectives, techniques, and instruments available for divorce custody assessments and other forensic issues.

Maccoby, E., & Mnookin, R. (1992). *Dividing the child: Social and legal dilemmas of custody.* Cambridge, MA: Harvard University Press. Investigates 933 divorcing couples in California and discusses types of interventions, such as litigation, mediation, and negotiation, and types of custody options.

Weithorn, L. A. (Ed.). (1987). *Psychology and child custody determinations: Knowledge, roles, and expertise.* Lincoln, NE: University of Nebraska Press. Reviews the legal context of child custody evaluations, the state of scientific knowledge pertinent to the court's inquiries in divorce custody cases, the boundaries of clinical expertise, and the conflicts inherent in particular roles, emphasizing both the strengths of psychology in contributing to the legal resolution of custody disputes and the limitations that should constrain psychological input in divorce custody cases.

Nicholas Dickon Reppucci

CHILDREN'S EYEWITNESS TESTIMONY. The accuracy of children's eyewitness testimony has been of concern in psychology and in society in general for over a century. The earliest research concluded that children were highly suggestible, dangerous witnesses—not competent to give court testimony. After years of inattention, there was a resurgence in children's testimony research in the early 1980s, mainly in response to the increased reporting of child abuse, which, in turn, brought about rising numbers of legal investigations involving child witnesses.

Children are most likely to testify in child sexual abuse cases, in which their testimony is crucial because there is often little other corroborative evidence. In such cases, two goals are paramount: guarding against false accusations against innocent adults and detecting actual abuse so that children can be protected from future

risk. Modern child-witness research has been framed in controversy, largely emanating from researchers' varying degrees of attention to these goals. Today, however, a growing body of empirical evidence is beginning to bring consensus about factors that influence children's accuracy and suggestibility and, with consensus, the realization that these goals are compatible.

Research reveals that children are not as suggestible as once thought, particularly when questioned about meaningful events under optimal reporting conditions. Children typically provide the most accurate information when they freely recall information in response to open-ended nonleading questions (e.g., "What happened while you were in the house?"); however, they report very little information in response to such questions. Therefore, in legal investigations, more specific or focused questions are often needed to determine what a child witnessed or whether a child experienced abuse (e.g., "Did you ride in Uncle Bill's car?"). But asking such questions raises the issue of suggestibility: Will children agree with an adult's misleading (inaccurate) suggestion? Research finds that younger children, particularly preschoolers, are generally more suggestible than older children and adults. Their accuracy is particularly likely to suffer when interviewed by biased, coercive, or intimidating interviewers; when questioned with developmentally inappropriate language; when questioned repeatedly with misleading questions; when interviewed after a long delay; when interviewed about events that were not central or meaningful or about events they did not directly experience; and when asked to identify strangers from target-absent photographic lineups (lineups that do not include the stranger's picture). Importantly, such factors may or may not affect children's actual memory; rather, they may only affect children's reports. For example, like adults, children may be reluctant to report a well-remembered embarrassing or traumatic event or an event they are motivated to keep secret.

Findings from children's testimony research have been used to formulate recommendations about optimal forensic interview techniques. Over the past decade, forensic investigators have heeded these policy recommendations, and interviewing techniques have improved, ensuring more accurate reports from children. Even so, child-interview protocols are still evolving, because there are still many unanswered questions about children's eyewitness abilities.

Thus there has been a great deal of research investigating the accuracy of children's testimony. Another area of children's testimony research has focused on adults' perceptions of children's accuracy. This research is driven by the fact that although children's actual accuracy may never be known in a legal context, children's testimony must be evaluated by forensic investigators, jurors, and judges. This research finds that adults may not be very accurate themselves in determining children's accuracy and that their perceptions are influenced by a number of factors. These include case factors, such as evidence strength and the presence of a corroborating child witness; child-witness factors, such as age, race, and whether the child is a bystander or victim witness; and characteristics of the adults themselves, such as gender, attitudes, and biases, level of empathic concern, and personal history of abuse.

Courts have been cautiously responsive to the results of psychological research on children's testimony, and court reform based on research findings has been implemented in some jurisdictions. Perhaps the most important reforms include the development of special programs to prepare children for the task of testifying in court and innovations aimed at removing children from the potentially stressful courtroom altogether. These innovations include replacing children's in-court testimony with testimony given either via closed circuit television, in the form of hearsay testimony from another witness, or via videotaped pretrial forensic interviews. In determining whether such innovations should be used, the constitutional rights of the accused must be carefully considered and weighed against potential trauma to the child witness. These considerations are highlighted in the U.S. Supreme Court's reasoning in *Maryland v. Craig* (110 S. Ct. 3157, 1990). Psychological research is beginning to reveal that although children's actual accuracy may be increased when their testimony is presented via alternative modes, their perceived credibility may suffer in the eyes of the jury.

Child-witness researchers have striven to achieve high standards of ecological validity in their research to facilitate the generalization of their findings to legal contexts in which the research has considerable application. The study of children's testimony has brought about significant theoretical advances that cross several subdisciplines of psychology (e.g., developmental, cognitive, social). For example, the research has yielded important basic knowledge about developmental changes in children's memory abilities and models for understanding the impact of stress and social influences on children's memory. Future child-witness research is likely to yield even more ecologically valid methods and, in turn, more generalizable results and also more exciting theoretical breakthroughs. Researchers face formidable empirical issues, including the needs to design forensic interview practices that maximize disclosures of real abuse while minimizing false reports; to understand psychological mechanisms underlying accurate and inaccurate reports of past events; to untangle current mixed findings regarding the role of trauma and stress in children's memory; to determine how to distinguish true from false reports; and to identify individual differences, such as attachment style or temperament, that might affect children's testimony (a paramount question in the eyes of the court, which is concerned about the accuracy of specific children in specific cases).

[*See also* Eyewitness Testimony.]

Bibliography

Edited Volumes

Each of the following books is composed of research-based chapters on a broad range of topics, from children's memory and suggestibility to jurors' perceptions of children's testimony. Chapters are written by recognized experts in the field.

Bottoms, B. L., & Goodman, G. S. (Eds.). (1996). *International perspectives on child abuse and children's testimony: Psychological research and law.* Newbury Park, CA: Sage.

Ceci, S. J., Ross, D. F., & Toglia, M. P. (Eds.). (1991). *Perspectives on the child witness.* New York: Springer-Verlag.

Dent, H., & Flin, R. (Eds.). (1992). *Children as witnesses.* Chichester, England: Wiley.

Goodman, G. S., & Bottoms, B. L. (Eds.). (1993). *Child victims, child witnesses: Understanding and improving testimony.* New York: Guilford Press.

Zaragoza, M., Graham, J., Hall, G., Hirschman, R., & Ben-Porath, Y. S. (Eds.). (1995). *Memory and testimony in the child witness.* Newbury Park, CA: Sage.

Other Works

Ceci, S. J., & Bruck, M. (1993). The suggestibility of the child witness: A historical review and synthesis. *Psychological Bulletin, 113,* 403–439.

Goodman, G. S., Emery, R., & Haugaard, J. (1998). Developmental psychology and law: Divorce, child maltreatment, foster care, and adoption. In W. Damon (Series Ed.), & I. Siegel & A. Renninger (Vol. Eds.), *Handbook of child psychology: Vol. 4. Child psychology in practice* (pp. 775–876). New York: Wiley. In the context of a discussion of other issues related to developmental psychology and law, these authors provide an excellent review of factors influencing children's accuracy and suggestibility, with emphasis on implications for policy regarding forensic interviews.

Koocher, B., Goodman, G. S., White, S., Friedrich, W., Sivan, A., & Reynolds, C. (1995). Psychological science and the use of anatomically detailed dolls in child sexual abuse assessments. *Psychological Bulletin, 118,* 199–222. A complete review of psychological research on the advantages and disadvantages of using anatomically detailed dolls as a tool to aid children's reports during forensic interviews.

Myers, J. E. B. (1992). *Evidence in child abuse and neglect cases.* New York: Wiley. A thorough compilation of U.S. law governing children's evidence in legal proceedings. Includes extensive commentary that makes the law accessible to legal novices.

Bette L. Bottoms

CHINA. Psychological understanding in China, in some senses, is as old as its civilization. The teachings of Confucius, Mencius, Lao Zi, and their followers are based on philosophies that deal with the concepts of humanity, development, and appropriate forms of conduct (Mote, 1971). But the common and diverse views contained within them did not have an impact on or explicitly inform the modern Western discipline until 1978, when Chinese psychologists, in the wake of another political upheaval, took it upon themselves to link modern psychology to their own historical and philosophical past (Gao, 1985; Zhao, Lin, & Zhang, 1989).

Since the turn of the last century, psychology's development in China has been buffeted by enormous political upheavals, and these have had a strong and mixed influence. Chinese psychology, or rather psychology in China, thereby stands as an acute example of a discipline peculiarly sensitive to ideological influence. [*See* Hong Kong; *and* Taiwan.]

For a variety of reasons psychology was seen from the beginning of its importation to be a foreign discipline, initially American-European, later Marxist, and later still, Soviet. In the second decade of the People's Republic of China, psychology became progressively Maoist in outlook, only to be outlawed as a bourgeois discipline (Munro, 1977). It subsequently reemerged with broadened scope and aims as China once again became receptive to ideas from inside and outside the culture.

Problems of Translation

Western psychology's entrance to China can be said to date from 1889 with the Chinese translation by Y. K. Yen (Yan Yongjin) of Joseph Haven's *Mental Philosophy* (Kodama, 1991). Yen was also the first to encounter the difficulty of translating psychology and of finding appropriate equivalent terms in Chinese that do not distort the original meanings. Having no prior term to refer to, he chose three characters not previously conjoined: *xin ling xue* [心靈學], which translates back into English as "pneumatology," the study of spirit, a far remove from its present understanding. But his choice of the character *ling* [靈], for spirit, was in keeping with the theme of Haven's book, that behavior is a derivative of the soul, and in Chinese culture the soul is considered a primary element of mind and nature (Zhao, 1983).

By the time of the appearance in China of the next prominent Western psychology text, Wang Guowei's translation of Harald Hoffding's *Outlines of Psychology* in 1907, the term for psychology, probably relying on the Japanese translation, had become *xin li xue* [心靈學], *li* [理] replacing *ling*. Whereas the modern simple back-translation renders this phrase as "knowledge of the heart," both *xin* and *li* have long "histories of meaning, including, from the time of Mencius, ethical principles of conduct arising out of competing views on human nature—from the Confucian ethic of intrinsic goodness, to the heart's propensity for evil, in the writings of Xun Zi [荀子] (Creel, 1954). The heart-mind's major role was to make evaluations of how one should act in relation to others. These understandings have generally framed the Chinese intellectual outlook and help to explain why traditionally there has been no sophisticated philosophical or psychological system of mind and why distinctions between conscious and unconscious thought are not emphasized (Munro, 1969, 1977; Petzold, 1987).

Early Institutional Developments

Psychology texts were introduced to China as an aid to moral instruction after the Imperial examinations were abolished and schools became established in the first decade of the twentieth century. Teaching about the mind was not so much to understand its workings *per se* as to foster the notion of a healthy mind that would instigate correct patterns of behavior. Although some teaching came by way of church-sponsored organizations, some Japanese intellectuals were also invited to lecture in China's universities. One, Hattori Unokichi, taught at the newly opened College of Education at Peking's Capital [now Beijing Normal] University in 1902 and delivered what were probably the first lectures on psychology (Zhao, 1992).

However, the first psychology laboratory was not established until 1917 at Peking National University under the urging of the democratic reformer Cai Yuanpei, who had studied under Wundt in Leipzig (Petzold, 1987). The advent of the May Fourth Movement in 1919 that gave the impetus for expanding the curriculum in China's universities to include psychology among other Western disciplines as students campaigned vigorously for improvements to society based on science and democracy (known at the time as "Mr. Science" and "Mr. Democracy"; Chow, 1964; Israel, 1966).

Many of the intellectuals of this period had studied abroad in Europe or America, and many of the first-generation Chinese psychologists were American-trained. The first psychology department was opened at Southeastern University in Nanking in 1920. Within ten years, other departments opened at universities in Guangzhou, Shanghai, Qinqhua, Amoy, and Tientsin (Chou, 1927, 1932). By 1928, the Institute of Psychology was founded within the Chinese Academy of Sciences. A Chinese Psychological Society was formally established in 1921. The following year it began publishing the *Chinese Journal of Psychology*, whose main emphasis reflected the contemporary mainstream of psychology in the West in which many of the Chinese students educated abroad had been steeped. The outlook was primarily behavioristic, and educational testing and measurement formed a large part of the initial concerns (Chou, 1927a,b). Between 1922 and 1940, some 370 papers on psychology were published (Pan, Chen, Wang, & Chen, 1980).

These developments did not pose any threat to fundamental values, since they were seen as tools in the service of the greater good of society. The behaviorism and functionalism that the American-educated students brought back to China with them could be accommodated within the new pragmatic view of the need for Western science, even if their essentially deterministic conceptions could arguably be seen as a challenge to Confucian notions of mind. This leniency was not accorded to psychoanalysis, however. Chinese intellectuals trod warily through some of the more radical aspects of this theory as they attempted to exalt Freud for the purposes of education and social reform. Some translations of Freud resulted in layers of censorship introduced by his translators in order to downplay what they took to be his pansexualism and to make his ideas more palatable. Oedipal theory, for example, was subverted into a social theory of family conformity (Blowers, 1994, 1995).

By the late 1920s and early 1930s, not only universities but also many teacher's colleges were instructing their pupils in the ideas of Freud, Watson, McDougall, Piaget, Lewin, and Kohler using translated texts and critical essays (Bauer & Hwang, 1982). Unfortunately, these ideas did not aid the modernization of the country in the way the student movement had hoped (see Pye, 1992, for a lucid account).

The war against the Japanese at the end of the 1930s and the political upheavals that accompanied the Communist revolution brought developments in psychology to a halt. Institutions teaching the subject or engaged in psychological research were closed down or evacuated to Taiwan. The Psychological Society suspended practically all its activities, including publication (Lee & Petzold, 1987).

Psychology in the People's Republic of China

Following the founding of the People's Republic of China in 1949, a broad program of socialist reform was ushered in. At this time it was widely held that psychology had to be revised to fit better into the new social and political milieu. Like other intellectuals, psychologists had to study Marxist philosophy, and their discipline had to be practiced in accordance with two principles—that psychological phenomena are a product or function of the brain and that mind is a reflection of outer reality. These were drawn from Lenin's theory of reflection in his *Materialism and Empiriocriticism* and Mao Zedong's *On Contradiction* and *On Practice* (Ching, 1980). Soviet psychology had to be studied, and Western psychology, in its various schools, had to be critically examined for its failings (Lee & Petzold, 1987). Most of the allowable textbooks in psychology were translations from the Russian (Petzold, 1984).

Russian educationalists came to China in the early 1950s to teach in Beijing, advocating a new foundation for the acquisition of knowledge. Inspired by the work of Lev Vygotsky, Alexander Luria, and Aleksei Leont'ev, dialectical materialism became the central philosophy underlying all permissible psychology. From this position, consciousness was a historically and developmentally formed mental product, so that its objects could not be thought of as separate from the reflection process, *fan she* [反射], which brings them into being. This contrasted with certain idealist tendencies in Western psychology that were predicated on a separation of subject and object, or mental image and objective reality. Mental processes, then, could not be studied apart from the contexts in which they occur (Chin & Chin, 1969).

In spite of the tendency to theorize all psychological activity in these terms, Chinese psychologists, following the reopening of the Psychological Society, fought for their own views. This was made possible in the brief period of liberal reform, known as the One Hundred Flowers Movement, of 1957. During this period, psychologists questioned the status of much reductionistic psychology, arguing that it was becoming divorced from reality (Zhao et al., 1989) and should have a practical or applied component. This argument led many psychologists to give up laboratory work and seek out applications in factories, hospitals, and schools.

Early Suppression

However, this period of open debate and questioning was quickly counteracted in the Antirightist or Criticism Movement that followed in August of 1958. Psychology was banned as "bourgeois pseudoscience," and many psychologists were persecuted.

The political justification of this suppression was as follows: by concentrating on the biological foundations of behavior and the experimental isolation of variables, psychologists were guilty of abstracting entities from their social context. As the study of consciousness, psychology was class bound. Psychologists essentially dehumanized the class nature of their activities. This line of thinking, quite unfounded, denied the possibility of there being any common or universal features of the mind that were worthwhile objects of study.

Following the failure of the Great Leap Forward a year later, these criticisms were stopped, and discussions among psychologists led to an integration of the viewpoints of psychology as both a natural and social science (Cao, 1959). In the early 1960s, educational and developmental psychology became the most productive areas of the discipline, so that by 1963, at the first annual meeting of the Chinese Psychological Society, they represented more than three fourths of the 203 papers presented. Other papers were in the applied areas of personnel and clinical psychology.

Later Suppression

This hiatus of productivity was short-lived, however, as attacks on the discipline soon came from students and young cadres in the wake of the Cultural Revolution. Mao encouraged the country's youth in anarchic activities against the more progressive elements of the Party, which had been content to accede a certain autonomy to intellectuals (whom Mao believed would lead the country to failure). Attacks on many academic disciplines occurred. Psychology was especially targeted by a leading figure of the party, Yao Wenyuan. As minister of propaganda, writing an editorial under a pseudonym in the newspaper *Renmin Ribao*, Yao attacked an article by Chen Li and Wang Ansheng, on color and form preferences in children for much the same reasons that had motivated the outbursts during the earlier Criticism Movement: the experiments abstracted the lived realities of people from their actual social contexts and were not therefore legitimate objects of research. Because of Yao's influential position, his editorial fueled the flames of a growing attack on the discipline as a whole, forcing it to be shut down by 1966, with the banning of psychology books and journals and the ceasing of its teaching in universities and research institutes.

Rehabilitation

At the third plenary session of the Party Congress in 1978, however, the discipline became respectable again. The first meeting of the Chinese Psychological Society held during this period reelected Pan Shu—an American-trained psychologist—as its president. Along with a contemporary of his generation, Gao Juefu, he was invited to write histories of Chinese and Western psychology (Gao, 1985; Pan & Gao, 1983). Also at the meeting there were many opportunities for the denunciation of the previous injustices perpetrated by Yao Wenyuan. These were led by Wang Ansheng, who had been the coauthor of the original psychology paper that Yao had attacked (Blowers, 1995, 1998; Chen & Wang, 1981; Petzold, 1987). In this more favorable post-Mao climate, psychologists were called upon to contribute to the modernization program, as China once again became receptive to the West. Intellectuals of various persuasions began visiting, and exchanges were and continue to be encouraged.

The Outlook

However, the prospects for the development of psychology in China are far from rosy. To begin with, there is the enormous gap in continuity of education created by the closing of the university doors for ten years and the loss of intellectual development of a whole generation of actual and potential students. In addition, there are less than a dozen universities throughout the whole of China at which a student can get a degree in psychology, although it is taught in many of China's "normal" universities, or teacher-training institutes, as a subject allied to education. In the practical spheres of education, health, and industry, there is still much demand for the subject matter, but the local database is sparse as a result of political disruption to research activities.

Dialogue with Western psychological authorities continues, through visits and reciprocal arrangements for study periods. Since 1980, China has been a member of the International Union of Psychological Science (IUPS). However, the development of an appropriate theoretical perspective for Chinese psychology has yet to emerge. Although much present-day Western psychology is welcomed for its utilitarian value, there is little evidence that the metaphysical assumptions of its rigid determinism (as seen in radical behaviorism and psychoanalysis) and its individualism (in personality and intellectual assessment) are embraced in any fundamental way by Chinese people. Western psychology seemingly provides skills training in helping society solve a myriad of problems in child development, health, and industry, but it is nevertheless used in the service of an authoritarian collectivist culture. There is all the more reason, therefore, for the Chinese themselves to develop a specifically Chinese framework for future study (Pan, 1980). Whether this framework will ultimately materialize will depend upon, among other things, the number of students that China is willing to accommodate for university training in the discipline and the opportunities for postgraduate research in its institutes.

In some areas of the discipline, notably social psychology, the justification for pursuing indigenous lines of research is strong, given the cultural influence over social processes. In areas more traditionally aligned to natural sciences, for example, experimental and cognitive psychology, Chinese psychologists are likely to continue imitating their Western counterparts. Funding for experimentally based projects continues from the Chinese government itself and from other countries. Given that funding is often tied to academic exchanges among those with mutual interests, there will likely be a tendency to develop more studies in partnership with psychologists in the West and therefore to strengthen more traditional areas of the discipline. These financial considerations will continue to affect Chinese psychologists both in and outside of China.

Two unfortunate trends go against any immediate

prospects for expansion. In the present inflationary economy, graduates and young teachers are leaving the universities in droves, lured by the opportunities to earn a decent standard of living by entering joint venture businesses. Many others are seeking study in the United States and elsewhere with a view not only to obtaining higher degrees, but also to securing residence in their host countries for employment purposes. These opportunities are granted to only a relatively few in each case, but they highlight an underlying dissatisfaction that mobilizing those remaining within the discipline is unlikely to eradicate.

Beyond these economic constraints, there is the difficulty of writing research reports and papers in English as a second language, an activity that is necessary for the advancement of the discipline in the international community, as well as for the academic promotion of the individual. This requirement poses an added strain, since one's standard will have to be good enough to pass muster in the editorial offices of leading overseas journals. But since writing academic psychology can be seen as the exhibition of one's latest conjectures, it poses a problem for those exceptionally concerned about negative evaluations. A typical solution to this problem leads many to adopt an ultraconventional style of writing, as seen, for example, in the format of the experimental report with its attention to technical detail at the expense of conjecture and reflection and its often "variable vague" view of the behavior of its studies' participants (Billig, 1994). This practice is also a recurrent problem for many psychologists schooled in the West, so that, unless and until psychology curricula in their tertiary institutes include evaluation of the knowledge base as a core activity and cultural critique and interpretative stance become the accepted tools of the trade, Chinese psychologists are likely to continue to emulate what they see as the still-dominant positivist mode of mainstream Western psychology.

Bibliography

Bauer, W., & Hwang, S. C. (1982). *German impact on modern Chinese intellectual history*. Wiesbaden, Germany: Franz Steiner Verlag.

Billig, M. (1994). Repopulating the depopulated pages of social psychology. *Theory and Psychology, 4*, 307–335.

Blowers, G. H. (1994). Freud in China: The variable reception of psychoanalysis. In G. Davidson (Ed.), *Applying psychology: Lessons from Asia-Oceania* (pp. 35–49). Victoria: Australian Psychological Society.

Blowers, G. H. (1995). Gao Juefu: China's interpreter of Western psychology. *World Psychology, 1* (3), 107–121.

Blowers, G. H. (1998). Chen Li: China's elder psychologist. *History of Psychology 1*(4), 315–330.

Cao, R. C. (1959, June 10). Canjia Xinlixue xueshu taolun de tihui [Experiences learned from the symposium on psychology]. *Renmin Rebao*, p. 6.

Chen, L., & Wang, A. S. (1981). Hold on to scientific explanation in psychology. In L. B. Brown (Ed.), *Psychology in contemporary China* (pp. 151–156). New York: Pergamon.

Chin, R., & Chin, A. L. S. (1969). *Psychological research in Communist China 1949–1966*. Cambridge, MA: MIT Press.

Ching, C. C. [Jing Qicheng]. (1980). Psychology in the People's Republic of China. *American Psychologist, 35*, 1084–1089.

Chow, T. T. (1964). *The May Fourth Movement: Intellectual revolution in modern China*. Cambridge, MA: Harvard University Press.

Chou, S. G. K. (1927a). The present status of psychology in China. *American Journal of Psychology, 38*, 664–666.

Chou, S. G. K. (1927b). Trends in Chinese psychological interest since 1922. *American Journal of Psychology, 38*, 487–488.

Chou, S. G. K. (1932). Psychological laboratories in China. *American Journal of Psychology, 44*, 372–374.

Creel, H. G. (1954). *Chinese thought from Confucius to Mao Tse Tung*. London: Eyre & Spottiswoode.

Gao, J. F. (Ed.). (1985). *Zhongguo Xinlixueshi* [History of psychology in China]. Beijing: Renmin Jiaoyu Chubanshe.

Hoffding, H. (1891). *Outlines of Psychology* (Mary E. Lowndes, trans.) London: Macmillan.

Israel, J. (1966). *The rise of student nationalism, 1927–1937*. Stanford, CA: Stanford University Press.

Kodama, S. (1991). Life and work of Y. K. Yen, the first person to introduce Western psychology to modern China. *Psychologia, 34*, 213–226.

Lee, H. W., & Petzold, M. (1987). Psychology in the People's Republic of China. In G. H. Blowers & A. M. Turtle (Eds.), *Psychology moving East: The status of Western psychology in Asia and Oceania* (pp. 105–125). Boulder, CO: Westview Press.

Mote, F. (1971). *Intellectual foundations of China*. New York: Knopf.

Munro, D. J. (1969). *The concept of man in early China*. Stanford, CA: Stanford University Press.

Munro, D. J. (1977). *The concept of man in contemporary China*. Ann Arbor: University of Michigan Press.

Pan, S. (1980). On the investigation of basic theoretical problems of psychology. *Chinese Sociology and Anthropology, 12*, 24–42.

Pan, S., Chen, L., Wang, J. H., & Chen, D. R. (1980). Weilian Fengte yu Zhongguo xinlixue. [Wilhelm Wundt and Chinese psychology]. *Xinli Xuebao, 12*, 367–376.

Pan, S., & Gao, J. F. (Eds.). (1983). *Zhongguo grudai xinlixue sixiang yanjiu* [The study of psychology in ancient China]. Nanshong, China: Jiangxi Renmin Chubanshe.

Petzold, M. (1984, July). The history of psychology in the People's Republic of China. *ASIEN Serial* (Journal of the German Association for Asian Studies), *12*.

Petzold, M. (1987). The social history of Chinese psychology. In M. G. Ash & W. R. Woodward (Eds.), *Psychology in twentieth century thought and society* (pp. 213–231). Cambridge, England: Cambridge University Press.

Pye, L. W. (1992). *The spirit of Chinese politics* (Rev. ed.). Cambridge, MA: Harvard University Press.

Zhao, L. R. (1983). Youguan xinlinxue yi shudi yanjiu. [Pneumatology: A Chinese translation of Joseph Haven's *Mental Philosophy*], Xinli Xuebao, 15, 380–388.

Zhao, L. R. (1992). *Xinlixue dongtai: Zhongguo xiandal xinlixue deqi yuanhe fazhan* [The status of psychology: The origin and development of modern psychology in China]. Beijing: Institute of Psychology.

Zhao, L. R., Lin, F., & Zhang, S. Y. (1989). *Xinli xueshi* [History of Psychology]. Beijing: Tungyi Chubanshe.

Geoffrey H. Blowers

CHRISTIANITY AND PSYCHOLOGY. All religions contain inherent, if not explicit, understandings of human nature. Christianity has always had a psychology, or, better said, psychologies, called *theological anthropology.* Early in Christian history two divergent psychological commentaries appeared, one based on Jesus' Sermon on the Mount (Matthew 5–7) and the other on Paul's letter to the Romans. Any discussion of Christian psychology must take into account these differing views of human nature.

In the spirit of the eighth-century BC prophets, Jesus called for an ideal standard of ethical behavior that went significantly beyond the demands of the Jewish law. In the Sermon on the Mount (Matthew 5–7) Jesus suggested that his followers were to be the "salt of the earth." He encouraged them to forgive their enemies, to turn the other cheek, and to love their neighbors as themselves. Contained within such mandates was a fundamentally optimistic view of human nature and its potential. Paul, on the other hand, saw human beings as self-centered, sinful, and unable to live up to such high ideals. According to Paul, even humans' good deeds were ironically directed toward their own self-interest. Although predating the establishment of psychology as a science by many centuries, this debate on human nature has been repeated throughout Christian history and continues even into the modern era. In Patristic times (100–400 CE), the church sided with Paul in declaring humans basically sinful and unable to do good without God's help. The more optimistic viewpoint, in accord with Jesus, was advocated by the monk Pelagius—a view that was eventually labeled heresy. The Protestant Reformation in the 1500s at its heart concerned this issue. Luther reasserted the classical position that humans could be redeemed only by God's good will, not by their own efforts. This was in contrast to the implicit conviction within Roman Catholicism and the Orthodox wing of Christianity that some good could come from human action.

This same dialogue occurred two hundred years later in John Wesley's reaction to Martin Luther's doctrine of the "grace of God." Luther contended that even though human beings could be redeemed by accepting God's good will, or grace, in conversion, only God's way of looking at people changed, not people themselves. No change of character occurred; rather, God simply looked at them differently by filtering his judgment through the lens of Christ's death. Wesley, the founder of Methodism, countered Luther. Although he, too, agreed that salvation came from God's action, not human effort, he was convinced that the grace of God was more than a perceptual change on God's part. The grace of God, which was given to persons in conversion, was like a seed planted in the human heart. Grace, like seeds, could grow and develop. Change toward goodness was possible and was expected. Thus Wesley could be said to side with Jesus' view of human beings, whereas Luther agreed with Paul.

This quasi-psychological discussion about human nature can be seen within Christianity in the twentieth century: (1) in the debate over social gospel versus personal salvation, (2) in the "Death of God" explosion, and (3) in the dialogue between theologians Karl Barth and Emil Brunner. In the later nineteenth and early twentieth centuries, the conviction that social conditions, not original sin, were the causes of evil led many Christians to become involved in acts of human welfare and social justice. Resistance to this so-called "social gospel" led others to reassert the Pauline/Lutheran view that environment would not change people. Only by accepting God's salvation would evil be abolished. To some extent, this difference of opinion still separates liberal and conservative churches and is a modern version of the two psychologies that have permeated Christianity through the centuries.

The second example of the continuing impact of this difference of viewpoint can be seen in the mid-century "Death of God" movement. Thomas Altizer in *The Gospel of Christian Atheism* (Philadelphia, 1966) spoke for a number of thinkers who resolved their post-Enlightenment agnosticism by asserting that the Pauline/Christian God was dead and a new God, who was aligned with human potentiality, was alive. Although this movement never had significant impact on local congregations, it was heavily debated in theological circles. It was viewed as an extension of Friedrich Nietzsche's ideas about the nature of human power and self-assertion. As such, in a circuitous manner, it reflected Jesus' optimism about human beings and was a counter to the Pauline point of view.

Although there have been other examples of the continuing discussion about human nature within Christianity, the debate between theologians Emil Brunner and Karl Barth serves both as a final illustration of this phenomenon and an entree into the relationship psychology has had with Christianity since it became a science. Barth and Brunner were German theologians who reacted differently to the situation in Europe between World Wars I and II. Barth has been labeled a *neo-orthodox* thinker who reasserted the classical point of view that only God could save humans from their finite condition. According to Barth, not only were humans powerless to save themselves or do good, but they were also so depraved that they were not even able to ask for God's help. Therefore, in Jesus, God took the initiative, as well as the power, to save people from their sins. The only thing that people could do, according to Barth, was to wait patiently for God to act in their behalf. On the other hand, Brunner has been labeled an *existentialist* thinker who emphasized the fact that, although God had the power to redeem human beings, humans would never know it unless they felt a need and asked for God's help. Human anxiety, not God's initiative, was the stimulus that established a contact between human need and divine action. Barth said God made His own point of contact with humans, whereas Brunner said human anxiety was the point of contact.

The Barth–Brunner debate leads naturally into a discussion of the relationship between psychology and Christianity since psychology became a science. Unquestionably, modern psychology has viewed human behavior as motivated by internal desires, not supernatural interventions. Psychology, even the Freudian point of view, has seen persons as able to make changes in their lives. Thus psychology has affirmed Brunner's point of view.

Commencing with Edwin Starbuck, who in the late 1890s wrote the first American dissertation relating psychology and Christianity, psychology had entered into the fundamental discussion concerning human nature. In his study of adolescent conversion, Starbuck, a student of William James, viewed conversion as a transforming force that could integrate the personality. G. Stanley Hall, the first president of the American Psychological Association, contributed a two-volume work, *Jesus, the Christ, in Light of Psychology* (New York, 1917), and encouraged discussion by gathering a number of researchers together in what came to be known as the "Clark School of Religious Psychology." As its influence expanded, a necessary dialogue was initiated between Christianity and psychology, as both proffered answers to the fundamental questions concerning human nature.

The personal discourse between Sigmund Freud and Oskar Pfister was one early example. Embedded within their literary conversation, one finds Freud siding with Paul's pessimistic view of human potential and Pfister forwarding Jesus' hope in human goodness. Other commentaries, such as Carl Jung's *Modern Man in Search of a Soul* (New York, 1933), Paul Tournier's *The Meaning of Persons* (New York, 1955), O. Hobart Mowrer's *The Crisis in Psychiatry and Religion* (Princeton, New Jersey, 1961), and *The Courage to Be* by existentialist theologian Paul Tillich (Princeton, New Jersey, 1952), examined human nature, drawing upon psychological and Christian perspectives. In Tillich can be seen the acceptance of the psychoanalytic critique of religion coupled with a psychodynamic understanding of the process of faith. He combined this analysis with a Pauline acknowledgment of human depravity attached to an affirmation of Jesus as the actualization of human potential. Tillich asserted that true religion resulted in courage. These works advanced and popularized scholarship that drew upon and often integrated psychological and Christian views.

Within the integration literature one finds texts that aim to bring into dialogue psychology *and* religion, as well as volumes that intend to offer a psychology *of* religion. The former most often contribute to the long-standing discussion of human nature and draw upon psychological and religious, including explicitly Christian, sources in considering issues such as personal meaning, sin, and salvation. Paul Pruyser's *A Dynamic Psychology of Religion* (New York, 1968) and W. W. Meissner's *Life and Faith: Psychological Perspectives on Religious Experience* (Washington, D.C., 1987) serve as examples. Studies in the psychology of religion apply empirical methods to the subject of religious, including Christian, affiliation, belief, practice, and experience. Other contributions, such as John McDargh's *Psychoanalytic Object Relations Theory and the Study of Religion* (Lanham, Maryland, 1983), provide both a psychology of religion and a discourse between theology and psychology. Still others, such as Rebecca L. Propst's *Psychotherapy in a Religious Framework: Spirituality in the Emotional Healing Process* (New York, 1988), concern clinical application. Central within this literature are multiple Christian psychologies that describe humanity's relationship with God and the prescriptions for salvation.

Bibliography

Brunner, E., & Barth, K. (1987). *Natural theology: Comprising "nature and grace."* London: Centenary Press. This volume contains the seminal debate between these two Protestant theologians regarding human nature and the power of God. Brunner contends that humans only reach for God when they are anxious. This provides a "point of contact." Barth exclaims "No!" to this presumption and insists that humans are not able to reach out to God. God, in turn, has made his own "point of contact" by reaching out to humans in the person of Jesus the Christ.

Collins, G. (1988). *Christian counseling: A comprehensive guide.* Dallas, TX: Word. Presents a model of Christian counseling involving explicit integration.

Journal of Psychology and Christianity. Published by the Christian Association for Psychological Studies, this publication provides a forum for discussion of clinical and theoretical issues across mental health disciplines.

Journal of Psychology and Theology. Established by the Rosemead Graduate School of Psychology, this publication provides a forum for discussion of explicit integration, including theological commentaries and issues in clinical practice.

Meyers, D. G., & Jeeves, M. A. (1987). *Psychology through the eyes of faith*. San Francisco: Harper & Row. Presents a comprehensive discussion of psychology from a Christian perspective.

Richards, P. S., & Bergin, A. E. (1997). *A spiritual strategy for counseling and psychotherapy*. Washington, DC: American Psychological Association. A comprehensive discussion of psychological treatment, integrating a theistic position. Considers the ethics, treatment approaches, and techniques in treatment in which a spiritual perspective is integrated.

H. Newton Malony

CHRONIC FATIGUE SYNDROME (CFS) is an illness diagnosed by exclusion. For many people, CFS begins after an acute infection, such as a cold, bronchitis, hepatitis, or an intestinal bug. For some, it follows a bout of mononucleosis that temporarily saps the energy of teenagers and young adults. In others, CFS develops more gradually, with no clear triggering event. Often a patient reports that the illness emerged during a period of high stress. It is currently defined (Fukada et al., 1994) as a syndrome in which the patient suffers from sore throat, tender lymph nodes, fatigue, headaches, muscle and joint aches, and cognitive impairments. To be diagnosed with CFS, the patient must not have a psychiatric disorder or any other medical illness that can account for these symptoms. There must be at least a 50% impairment in ability to function in a work situation for at least 6 months or longer. This syndrome does not have a delineated biological marker, although dysregularities in the sympathetic-hypothalamic systems are often noted. The symptoms overlap with those of other diseases such as multiple sclerosis, lupus, fibromyalgia, and chemical sensitivities. In other countries, the syndrome may be known as myalgic encephalomyelitis, postviral fatigue syndrome, and immune dysfunction syndrome.

Many physicians have been skeptical about legitimizing this disease, as 21% of patients come into primary care settings with complaints about fatigue. Therefore, in addition to suffering an amorphous and often unrelenting series of bouts, patients are denied the legitimacy of having a serious illness. Thus we need to examine psychosocial factors that mediate how these individuals respond to pain and fatigue.

In the large epidemiological studies conducted on referred patients, only 4 to 10 cases per 100,000 adults have been noted. However, the prevalence approaches 12% in community studies (Friedberg & Jason, 1998). Three times as many women as men are given this diagnosis, despite the fact that in community studies the prevalence is equally reported in both sexes. Women and men engage in social roles, role expectations, and burdens that have distinct impact on health. Imbalances in social roles and subsequently in power, equality, and control are likely to affect women's health adversely. Since women tend to seek medical diagnoses more often than men and suffer candidiases (yeast infections), also characterized by weakness and fatigue, more frequently, they are more likely to be diagnosed with CFS.

The recommended treatment combines cognitive restructuring, coping skills training, stress management, and behavioral modification in terms of coping strategies and activity levels. The increased-activity treatment is thought to help break the cycle of avoidance. In patients who attribute chronic symptoms to a physical problem, the prognosis is not as good as it is in those who see a link with stress. For most people, CFS symptoms plateau early in the course of the illness and thereafter wax and wane. Some people improve but do not get completely better. By helping patients focus on what they can do, not on what they cannot do, depression and inertia can be overcome. The increase in activity levels may also change the physiological and neurochemical levels in the body to facilitate improvement. On the other hand, patients need to conserve energy so as not to experience overexertion relapse. Thus an appropriate level of activity needs to be established for each individual, taking into account both perceived energy and expended energy. At the same time that researchers identify subgroups of patients who experience this illness, individual programs of emotional support and counseling should be used to help patients and their loved ones cope with the uncertain prognosis and ups and downs of the illness.

Medical approaches that have reported successes in small numbers of patients include antivirals, antidepressants, and immunomodulators. Patients have also benefited from other kinds of antidepressants, including the newer serotonin reuptake inhibitors. Therapeutic doses of antidepressants often increase fatigue in CFS, so doctors may have to escalate the dosage very slowly. In addition, some patients benefit from the benzodiazepines, a class of drugs used to treat acute anxiety and sleep problems. The lack of any proven effective treatment can be frustrating to both patients and their physicians. Experts recommend that people with CFS try to maintain good health by eating a balanced diet and getting adequate rest. Physical conditioning should be preserved by exercising regularly but without causing more fatigue. It is important that people with CFS learn to pace themselves—physically, emotionally, and intellectually—since too much stress may aggravate the symptoms (National Institute of Allergy and Infectious Diseases [NIAID], 1995).

Bibliography

Friedberg, F., & Jason, L. (1998). *Understanding chronic fatigue syndrome: A guide to assessment and treatment.* Washington, DC: American Psychological Association.

Fukado, K., Strauss, S. E., Hickie, I., Sharpe, M., Dobbins, J. G., & Komaroff, A. (1994). Chronic fatigue syndrome: A comprehensive approach to its definition and study. *Annals of Internal Medicine.*

National Institute of Allergy and Infectious Diseases (1997). *Chronic fatigue syndrome: Information for physicians.* Washington, DC: U.S. Government Printing Office.

Barbara G. Melamed

CHRONIC OBSTRUCTIVE PULMONARY DISEASE.
The American Thoracic Society (1995) defines chronic obstructive pulmonary disease (COPD) as

> a disease state characterized by the presence of air flow obstruction due to chronic bronchitis or emphysema. The air flow obstruction is generally progressive, may be accompanied by airway hyperreactivity and may be partially reversible. (p. 578)

Chronic bronchitis, emphysema, and asthma are the three diseases that contribute to the diagnosis of COPD. These diseases are similar because they all are disorders of expiration associated with obstruction of air flow out of inflated lungs; however, they differ in the nature of the airway obstruction. It is most common for patients to have components of two or more of these diseases.

Obstructive Lung Diseases

Until recently, the diagnosis separating emphysema from chronic bronchitis was anatomic and typically made at the time of autopsy. However, newer techniques in radiology have made it possible to separate emphysema from chronic bronchitis in living people. Emphysema is caused by the loss of elastic recoil and overinflation of the lung. These changes are typically associated with destruction of the alveolar walls, which are the walls of the small sacs in the lung that inflate and deflate during breathing. Emphysema is a chronic condition that develops over many years and is characterized by progressive shortness of breath on activity. The disease process is largely irreversible and results in considerable disability for affected individuals, as well as high morbidity and mortality.

The consequences of chronic bronchitis are similar. However, chronic bronchitis is defined as the presence of a persistent cough and sputum production that last at least three months in two consecutive years. This results in continuing inflammation of the bronchi, which are the cell linings of the breathing passages. Asthma is a reversible airway narrowing that may occur in response to stimuli such as infection, allergy, cold air, or cigarette smoke. The narrowing of the airway might be caused by a spasm of smooth muscle, inflammation, or the oversecretion of mucus. Chronic asthma occurs when the narrowing persists over the course of time. Chronic asthma and bronchitis often coexist, resulting in a diagnosis of "asthmatic bronchitis."

COPD is a major cause of death and disability. In 1990, COPD was the fourth leading cause of death in the United States, and it was associated with more than 90,000 deaths in 1991. For older adults, aged 55 to 74, COPD is the third leading cause of death for men and the fourth leading cause of death for women. In contrast to heart disease, which has shown a decreasing incidence in the last few decades, deaths from COPD increased by 38% between 1979 and 1991.

What Causes COPD?

Most of the causes and consequences of COPD are behavioral. It has been estimated that 90% of cases of COPD are directly attributable to the use of cigarettes. Compared to people who do not smoke cigarettes, current smokers are 10 times more likely to develop COPD. The risks are approximately equal for men and women. For many years it was assumed that COPD was a disease of men. However, in recent years, as women have increased their cigarette use, rates of COPD have been escalating for females.

Genetic factors also play an important role in the development of COPD. Even among cigarette smokers, only about 15 to 20% develop significant COPD. However, some individuals may be genetically susceptible, leaving them at much greater risk if they are exposed to cigarette smoke or other irritants. There is still debate about whether or not secondary smoke is a significant risk factor for COPD. However, there is evidence suggesting that environmental exposures, such as air pollution and exposure to dusts and fumes in the workplace, may exacerbate underlying lung disease and may increase the risks of developing COPD.

Medical and Surgical Treatment

Medical management of COPD involves the use of medications to stabilize and/or improve airway function and symptoms and strategies to minimize the consequences and prevent complications of the disease. Patients with COPD often use bronchodilator medicines to maximize airway size. In addition, some patients may use corticosteroids to reduce inflammation. Further, medications are often used to control secretions. This is sometimes achieved by consumption of several glasses of fluid per day. Antibiotics are commonly used to control infections. Vaccinations against influenza and certain types of bacteria are used to prevent and to reduce the risk of pneumonia. For patients with severe reductions in oxygen levels in their blood, continuous oxygen therapy has been shown to improve survival and reduce complications of the disease.

Considerable evidence suggests that some patients may be genetically susceptible to the development of emphysema. Some of these individuals have an identified genetic abnormality that causes deficiency of a protective enzyme called α_1 antitrypsin. There has been experimentation with methods that replace the deficient protein in people affected by this condition. However, this treatment remains experimental, and the drug costs can exceed $25,000 per year.

A recent development in the treatment of severe emphysema is lung volume reduction surgery. Patients with emphysema have areas of damaged lung that lose elasticity, become overinflated, and compress areas of better functioning lung. Surgical techniques have been developed to remove these diseased sections from the lungs. However, evidence for the effectiveness of this surgery is still accumulating, and the National Institutes of Health, in conjunction with the Health Care Financing Administration, is conducting a major clinical trial to evaluate the risks and benefits of these procedures.

Behavioral Interventions

Patients with COPD can benefit from three areas of behavioral intervention. First, cigarette smoking is the major cause of COPD, and those who carry this diagnosis must stop smoking. The National Heart, Lung and Blood Institute has conducted large clinical trials demonstrating that those who stopped smoking retarded the decline in lung function. Individuals susceptible to the effects of smoking might not ever develop symptomatic obstructive lung disease if they quit smoking early in adulthood.

Exercise has also been shown to produce significant benefits for patients with COPD. This has been typically demonstrated through comprehensive rehabilitation programs that emphasize physical activity along with education about lung disease and management strategies. Systematic experimental trials have shown that rehabilitation programs that include a physical activity component are successful at increasing exercise performance and reducing symptoms. Unfortunately, maintenance of these changes is often difficult. Newer research is investigating the application of behavioral interventions designed to maintain these changes over the course of time. In addition to improvement in phys-

ical activity, comprehensive rehabilitation programs have been shown to improve symptoms of breathlessness and ratings of self-efficacy.

Finally, patients with chronic lung disease often experience psychological, emotional, and social problems. Depression, anxiety, and problems with sexual function are common complaints among patients with obstructive lung diseases, who struggle to cope with the smothering sensation of breathlessness. Further, studies have shown that patients with COPD sometimes have difficulties in cognitive and neuropsychological functioning. These changes might be associated with chronic deficiencies of oxygen to the brain. Some evidence suggests that supportive psychological therapy is helpful for patients with COPD, and comprehensive rehabilitation programs typically include a psychosocial component. In addition, psychoactive drugs might be prescribed to alleviate the depression commonly experienced by patients with this condition.

Bibliography

American Thoracic Society. (1995). Standards for the diagnosis and care of patients with chronic obstructive pulmonary disease (COPD) and asthma. *American Review of Respiratory Disease, 152,* S78–S121.

Atkins, J. C., Kaplan, R. M., Timms, R. M., Reinsch, S., & Lofback, K. (1984). Behavioral exercise programs in the management of chronic obstructive pulmonary disease. *Journal of Consulting and Clinical Psychology, 52,* 591–603.

Creer, T., & Kaptein, A. A. (1999). Only the lonely: Doing behavioral research on respiratory disorders. In A. A. Kaptein & T. Creer (Eds.), *Behavioral Sciences and Respiratory Disorders.* London: Harwood Academic.

Eakin, E. G., Resnikoff, P. M., Prewitt, L. M., Ries, A. L., & Kaplan, R. M. (1998). Validation of a new dyspnea measure: The UCSD shortness of breath questionnaire. *Chest, 113,* 619–624.

Grodner, S., Prewitt, L. M., Jaworski, B. A., Myers, R., Kaplan, R. M., & Ries, A. L. (1996). The impact of social support in pulmonary rehabilitation of patients with chronic obstructive pulmonary disease. *Annals of Behavioral Medicine, 18,* 139–145.

Hodgkin, J., Connors, G. L., & Bell, C. W. (Eds.). (1993). *Pulmonary rehabilitation: Guidelines to success* (2nd ed.). Philadelphia: Lippincott.

Kaplan, R. M., Atkins, C. J., & Timms, R. (1984). Validity of a quality of well-being scale as an outcome measure in chronic obstructive pulmonary disease. *Journal of Chronic Diseases, 37,* 85–95.

Kaplan, R. M., Ries, A. L., & Atkins, C. J. (1985). Area review: Behavioral management of chronic obstructive pulmonary disease. *Annals of Behavioral Medicine, 7,* 5–10.

Kaplan, R. M., Ries, A. L., Prewitt, L. M., & Eakin, E.

(1994). Self-efficacy expectations predict survival for patients with chronic obstructive pulmonary disease. *Health Psychology, 13*, 366–368.

Kaptein, A. A. (1997). Behavioral interventions in COPD: A pause for breath. *European Respiratory Review, 7*, 88–91.

Ries, A. L. (1990). Scientific basis of pulmonary rehabilitation: Position paper of the American Association of Cardiovascular and Pulmonary Rehabilitation. *Journal of Cardiopulmonary Rehabilitation, 10*, 418–441.

Ries, A. L., Kaplan, R. M., Limberg, T. M., & Prewitt, L. M. (1995). Effects of pulmonary rehabilitation on physiologic and psychosocial outcomes in patients with chronic obstructive pulmonary disease. *Annals of Internal Medicine, 122*, 823–832.

Toshima, M. T., Blumberg, E., Ries, A. L., & Kaplan, R. M. (1992). Does rehabilitation reduce depression in patients with chronic obstructive pulmonary disease? *Journal of Cardiopulmonary Rehabilitation, 12*, 261–269.

Toshima, M. T., Kaplan, R. M., & Ries, A. L. (1992). Self-efficacy expectancies in chronic obstructive pulmonary disease rehabilitation. In R. Schwarzer (Ed.), *Self-efficacy: Thought control of action* (pp. 325–354). Washington, DC: Hemisphere.

Robert M. Kaplan and Andrew L. Ries

CHURCH-BASED INTERVENTIONS. *See* Interventions Based in Religious Congregations.

CIRCADIAN RHYTHMS. [*This entry comprises two articles. The first article provides an overview of circadian rhythms, including physiological and behavioral manifestations. The companion article discusses circadian rhythm disorders.*]

An Overview

The term *circadian* was coined in the 1950s by the American physiologist Franz Halberg. Its derivation is from the Latin *circa dies*, meaning "about a day." Thus circadian rhythms are variations in human or animal physiology and psychology that repeat themselves with a period of about one day. Circadian rhythms are primarily driven by the "biological clock" or "circadian pacemaker," which is a small area in the hypothalamus labeled the suprachiasmatic nuclei (SCN). However, most observed circadian rhythms also reflect an additional influence from the cycle of rest and activity. As an example, Figure 1 shows the circadian rhythm in core body temperature of people when they are asleep at night and awake during the day (top panel) and when they are kept continuously awake but in bed (bot-

tom panel). A circadian rhythm appears in both cases, but the size of the rhythm (amplitude) is greater and the trough lasts longer when sleep at night is permitted.

The "about" part of the term *circadian* is important because biological clocks typically do not run with a period of exactly 24 hours unless acted upon by time cues that "entrain" the pacemaker. These are referred to as *zeitgebers* (German for "time givers"). The most powerful *zeitgeber* for human beings (and most other species) is the alternation of daylight and darkness caused by the rotation of our planet. When humans live for many weeks isolated from all *zeitgebers*, they usually settle on a day length that varies between 24 and 25 hours, depending upon the individual and the experimental conditions. This behavior is referred to as "free-running" and indicates the "natural" period length of the circadian pacemaker.

Under a normal routine of sleep at night and wakefulness during the day, the *zeitgebers* of daylight and darkness, as well as other 24-hour *zeitgebers* from one's surroundings, keep the circadian pacemaker running at a period of exactly 24 hours. Under these conditions the pacemaker fulfills its function of preparing the individual for restful sleep at night and active wakefulness during the day. Thus, for example, while one is still asleep, body temperature and cortisol production are rising, so that one can "hit the ground running" even before the alarm clock goes off. Similarly, a few hours before bedtime, the pineal hormone melatonin is being produced, and body temperature is falling, so that the individual is ready for sleep. More important, functions such as thirst, appetite, and the need to void are suppressed by the circadian pacemaker so that a restful seven or eight hours of sleep can be obtained.

Perhaps because of this preparatory function of the circadian pacemaker, circadian rhythms also exist in the psychological variables of subjective alertness and performance efficiency. These rhythms are, like most physiological rhythms, a composite mixture of those effects that stem directly from the circadian pacemaker and those that are a function of how long the individual has been awake. Also, like physiological rhythms, performance and alertness rhythms show a smooth function covering the entire 24 hours and are of nontrivial magnitude. This is illustrated nicely by Drew Dawson and Kathryn Reid (*Nature*, 1997, *388*, p. 235), who expressed circadian fluctuations in performance (under the condition of continuous wakefulness from 8 a.m.) on a tracking task using a metric defined in terms of alcohol impairment (Figure 2). Thus the impairment after 17 hours awake (at 3 a.m.) was equivalent to that associated with the "legal limit" of alcohol in many countries. Not all tasks show the same performance rhythm, and though many tasks do show a broad parallelism with the body temperature rhythm,

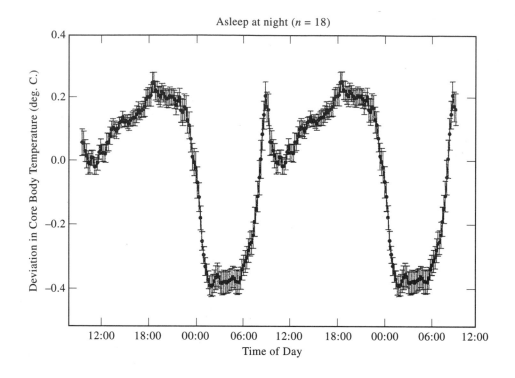

Asleep at night ($n = 18$)

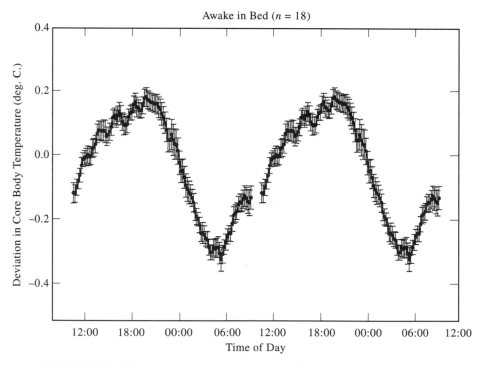

Awake in Bed ($n = 18$)

CIRCADIAN RHYTHMS: An Overview. Figure 1. Mean deviation in core body temperature (from the participant's own twenty-four-hour mean) double plotted as a function of time of day ($+/-$ one s.e.m.) for eighteen healthy young adults (nine male, nine female). *Top*: awake during the day, asleep at night; *Bottom*: constant wakeful bed rest. (Previously unpublished graphs from the author's laboratory.)

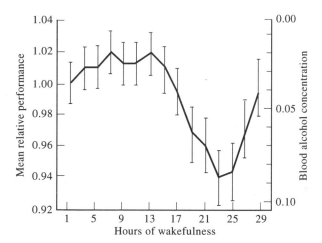

CIRCADIAN RHYTHMS: An Overview. Figure 2. Performance during sustained wakefulness from 8 a.m. (+/− one s.e.m.) expressed as mean relative performance and the percentage of blood alcohol concentration equivalent ($n = 40$). (Reprinted with permission from Dawson & Reid (1997), in *Nature*, copyright 1997 Macmillan Magazines Ltd.)

some do not, particularly in terms of peak timing. Although body temperature typically peaks at about 8 p.m., subjective alertness typically peaks at about noon, and short-term or immediate memory typically peaks in the morning hours. However, when people are kept awake all night, the troughs of temperature, performance, and alertness all seem to occur at about the same time of night (between 4 and 7 a.m.).

Unfortunately for those who fly across time zones or who are forced to work at night, the circadian pacemaker is slow to adjust to a change in routine. Thus for several days there may be a mismatch between what the circadian pacemaker is "expecting" and the pattern of rest and activity the individual is trying to live by. This mismatch results in sleep disruption, performance impairments, malaise, and fatigue, a collection of symptoms referred to as "jet lag" or "shift lag." There are three main causes: the individual is trying to be awake and perform during the "down" phase of the cycle; sleep is disrupted and shortened because the circadian pacemaker has not prepared the individual by shutting down processes such as appetite and the need to void; and the normal harmony of the component circadian rhythms is lost, resulting in circadian desynchrony. Thus, even if sleep is artificially improved by the use of sleeping pills, performance and mood may still be impaired. In the shift-work situation, these circadian problems may be exacerbated by social and domestic stressors connected with the need to work while others are asleep and to be asleep while others are awake. In some cases several decades of exposure to shift work may lead to an increased risk of major de-

pressive disorder. Besides sleep disorders, the other major health risks connected with shift work are gastrointestinal distress and cardiovascular disorders.

A misaligned circadian system may also occur in some people who are not flying across time zones or working at night. Advancing age is often associated with a change in the timing of the circadian pacemaker. Thus most older people go to bed and wake up earlier than they did when they were younger adults. For some older people, this can be problematic, because they fall asleep in the early evening, missing out on social opportunities, and wake in the very early hours of the morning, when there is no one to talk to and little to do. This problem may require treatment with bright lights to delay the circadian pacemaker to a later time. Another group of individuals who are troubled by early-morning awakening are those suffering from major depression. Here, however, the evidence for a simple phase advance of the circadian pacemaker is less clear. [See Depression.]

In conclusion, the circadian system renders people very different, in both their physiology and their psychology, from one time of day to another. When the circadian system is misaligned, problems can arise in sleep, alertness, mood, performance, and health.

[See also Sleep.]

Bibliography

Aschoff, J., Hoffman, K., Pohl, H., & Wever, R. A. (1975). Re-entrainment of circadian rhythms after phase-shifts of the *zeitgeber. Chronobiologia, 2,* 23–78.

Campbell, S. S., Dawson, D., & Anderson, M. W. (1993). Alleviation of sleep maintenance insomnia with timed exposure to bright light. *Journal of the American Geriatric Society, 41,* 829–836.

Dijk, D. J., Duffy, J. F., & Czeisler, C. A. (1992). Circadian and sleep/wake dependent aspects of subjective alertness and cognitive performance. *Journal of Sleep Research, 1,* 112–117.

Folkard, S., & Monk, T. H. (1985). Circadian performance rhythms. In S. Folkard & T. H. Monk (Eds.), *Hours of work: Temporal factors in work scheduling* (pp. 37–52). New York: Wiley.

Halberg, F. (1969). Chronobiology. *Annual Review of Physiology, 31,* 675–725.

Monk, T. H., & Folkard, S. (1992). *Making shift work tolerable.* London: Taylor & Francis.

Moore, R. Y. (1982). The suprachiasmatic nucleus and the organization of a circadian system. *Trends in Neurosciences, 5*(11), 404–407.

Wehr, T. A., & Goodwin, F. K. (1983). *Circadian rhythms in psychiatry.* Pacific Grove, CA: The Boxwood Press.

Wever, R. A. (1979). *The circadian system of man: Results of experiments under temporal isolation.* New York: Springer-Verlag.

Timothy H. Monk

Circadian Rhythm Disorders

Circadian (24-hour) rhythms are ubiquitous in human physiology and behavior. As one example, deep body temperature reaches a peak typically at about 6–7 p.m. and a trough at about 4–5 a.m. The amplitude (difference between peak and trough) of the measured rhythm usually includes an exogenous component driven mainly by daytime physical activity and nighttime sleep. However, when the exogenous components are removed or controlled under constantly inactive, wakeful conditions, an endogenous component remains, with an amplitude of about 0.3–0.5 degrees Celsius.

Effect of Circadian Rhythms on Sleepiness

The timing of the endogenous temperature rhythm is strongly related to performance on various types of cognitive tasks and on general alertness. Experimental studies using an enforced sleep/wake cycle markedly shorter or longer than 24 hours have shown that the time taken to fall asleep varies markedly across the phases of the endogenous circadian body temperature rhythm. The time of maximum sleepiness is centered around the time of the minimum body temperature, which for most people is around 3–7 a.m. Then, coincident with an increase of body temperature and metabolic rate, there is increasing alertness. There is some controversy as to whether a secondary period of sleepiness in the early afternoon, apparently more prevalent in some cultures and age groups, is part of the endogenous circadian rhythm. Maximum alertness is reached at about the time of the maximum endogenous body temperature, which for most people is around 6–9 p.m. and has been named the "wake-maintenance zone" for its inhibition of sleep onset.

Delayed Sleep Phase Syndrome (DSPS)

This syndrome is indicated by an inability to initiate sleep until very late in the night (e.g., later than 2–4 a.m.). However, once sleep is initiated, it is normal in quality and duration, resulting in a very late final awakening (e.g., 10 a.m.–1 p.m.). Attempts to advance the sleep period with earlier awakenings usually result in reduced total sleep time, since earlier bedtimes do not result in earlier sleep onsets. DSPS is associated with delayed circadian rhythms that inhibit the onset of sleep until very late, when body temperature and metabolic rate are declining rapidly.

This syndrome is more prevalent in the adolescent and young adult population than in the elderly. Although extreme cases are relatively uncommon (e.g., sleep onset time later than 5 a.m.), a milder form has been found in up to 20% of a university student pop-ulation. For extreme cases of DSPS, "chronotherapy" (delaying bedtime by two hours on consecutive days until the desired target bedtime is reached) has been a successful, if arduous, therapy. For mild DSPS (e.g., typical sleep onset time between 1 a.m. and 3 a.m.), bright light therapy in the mornings and the administration of melatonin several hours before bedtime can be used to phase advance the circadian rhythms and enable earlier sleep onsets.

Sleep-onset insomnia, which afflicts an estimated 5% of the population, is the chronic tendency for sleep to be delayed by at least 45 minutes following the desired bedtime. Since it has been shown to be associated with a delayed circadian temperature rhythm, it may also be treated as a mild form of DSPS.

Advanced Sleep Phase Syndrome (ASPS)

ASPS is indicated by inconveniently early sleep onsets and final awakenings (e.g., 2–4 a.m.). Although apparently rare, it is more prevalent in the elderly than in young adults. Attempts simply to delay bedtime seem ineffective in resolving this difficulty and simply result in reduced total sleep. Advanced chronotherapy has been attempted on single cases with some benefit.

A mild form of ASPS, including phase advanced temperature and melatonin rhythms, is evident in early-morning-awakening insomnia and is associated with insufficient total sleep time and deficits in daytime functioning. It has been treated effectively with evening bright light stimulation, which phase delays circadian rhythms.

Non-24-Hour Sleep-Wake Syndrome

This syndrome is usually the result of an endogenous circadian rhythm period longer than 24 hours that fails to remain synchronized with the 24-hour world. It is relatively common in totally blind individuals, presumably because of the lack of synchronizing effect of visual stimulation on the "body clock," the suprachiasmatic nucleus in the hypothalamus. Individuals who must maintain a daily occupation experience alternations between good and poor nocturnal sleep and daytime functioning as the circadian system drifts respectively in and out of synchrony with the fixed bedtimes and wake times. In individuals with no daytime commitments, the syndrome is often indicated by progressively delayed sleep-onset and wake-up times when sleep and wakeful quality are satisfactory but at periodically inconvenient times.

Rigorous adherence to a 24-hour sleep/wake schedule with evening melatonin and, in the case of sighted individuals, morning bright light have been suggested as treatments.

[*See also* Sleep Disorders.]

Bibliography

Coleman, R. M. (1986). *Wide awake at 3:00 a.m.: By choice or by chance?* New York: Freeman. A very readable coverage of the effects of circadian rhythms on sleep and daytime functioning and the problems caused by shift work and jet lag. It also has a nicely illustrated description of chronotherapy.

Graeber, R. C. (1994). Jet lag and sleep disruption. In M. H. Kryger, T. Roth, & W. C. Dement (Eds.), *Principles and practice of sleep medicine* (2nd ed., pp. 463–470). London: Saunders.

Lack, L., Mercer, J., & Wright, H. (1996). Circadian rhythms of early morning awakening insomniacs. *Journal of Sleep Research, 5,* 211–219. Evidence that a common type of insomnia in older individuals, that of early morning awakening, is associated with circadian rhythms timed earlier than normal.

Lack, L., & Wright, H. (1993). The effect of evening bright light in delaying the circadian rhythms and lengthening the sleep of early morning awakening insomniacs. *Sleep, 16,* 423–443.

Monk, T. (1994). Shift work. In M. H. Kryger, T. Roth, & W. C. Dement (Eds.), *Principles and practice of sleep medicine* (2nd ed., pp. 471–476). London: Saunders.

Morris, M., Lack., L., & Dawson, D. (1990). Sleep-onset insomniacs have delayed temperature rhythms. *Sleep, 13,* 1–14.

Roehrs, T., & Roth, T. (1994). Chronic insomnia associated with circadian rhythm disorders. In M. H. Kryger, T. Roth, & W. C. Dement (Eds.), *Principles and practice of sleep medicine* (2nd ed., pp. 477–481). London: Saunders.

Wagner, D. R. (1990). Circadian rhythm sleep disorders. In M. J. Thorpy (Ed.), *Handbook of sleep disorders* (pp. 493–527). New York: Dekker. An excellent detailed coverage of all the topics included in this article.

Leon C. Lack

CITIZEN PARTICIPATION is defined as "a process in which individuals take part in decision making in the institutions, programs, and environments that affect them" (Heller, Price, Reinharz, Riger, & Wandersman, 1984, p. 339). Advocates of citizen participation propose that multiple benefits result from citizen participation: (1) participation improves the quality of the environment, program, or plan because the people who are involved in implementation or usage have special knowledge that contributes to quality; (2) participation increases feelings of control over the environment and helps individuals develop a program, plan, or environment that better fits with their needs and values; and (3) participation increases feelings of helpfulness and responsibility and decreases feelings of alienation and anonymity.

Citizen participation plays an important role in many different settings in our society, including (1) work settings, where the largest amount of participatory research has been performed, especially as Japanese business success in the 1980s increased U.S. interest in quality circles and participative management; (2) health care programs, where citizen participation in decision making may occur at multiple levels including doctor-patient or community; (3) neighborhood planning and rehabilitation, where resident participation in neighborhood improvement and renewal has received considerable attention in many countries during the last two decades; (4) human service agencies, where participation may be by staff in organizational policy and program development or by the clients served by the organization; and (5) political participation, the type often referred to by political scientists and government officials, where participation includes voting, working for a political party, or rallying around a particular issue.

Central Issues in Citizen Participation

The areas listed above provide a glimmer of the vast interest in citizen participation. However, citizen participation is neither easy nor a panacea for problems. It is a complex issue, and it is often difficult to successfully accomplish. While there are hundreds of empirical studies in the area of participation (many of them in sociology, political science, and social work), they have left us with three basic issues that can be stated as questions: (1) what are the characteristics of people who participate? Why do they participate? Who are the people who do not participate and why do they not participate? (2) what are the characteristics of organizations or environments that facilitate or inhibit effective participation? (3) what are the effects of different forms of participation? What are the impacts on individuals who participate? How does participation affect the program or community in which it occurs? Wandersman and his colleagues have developed frameworks to help clarify the important concepts in citizen participation in several content areas: participation in planning environments, participation in community organizations, participation in community mental health centers, participation in research, and participation in community organizations formed in response to toxic hazards. In all of these areas, the frameworks describe the antecedents of participation, the process of participation, and the effects of participation.

Individual Participation

Despite the desirable outcomes proposed as consequences of participation, relatively few people participate in government-initiated efforts or in grassroots groups. The literature pertinent to individual characteristics and participation can be divided into demographic research and into social psychological research. Demographic variables (e.g., age, race, and sex) have been used in political science, sociology, and psychological studies to predict participation. For example, higher income and educational and occupational status have often been associated with greater participation, presumably because these social positions provide access to resources such as time and access that is relevant to participation. With regard to race, after income has been statistically controlled, blacks are more likely to participate in neighborhood associations than whites. However, demographic variables have small predictive power. Two studies that used multiple demographic variables to predict participation predicted only 9% of the variance or less. Based on extensive review of the literature, Widmer (1984) concluded that many of the studies on why citizens participate actually focus on the characteristics of who participates but have little to say about the motives of participants and the benefits they receive. According to this view, personality and social psychological variables offer more opportunities to understand and predict the process of participation than do demographic variables. For example, a belief that one can influence one's environment, defined variously as an internal locus of control, psychological empowerment, or political efficacy, has been associated with participatory behavior in several settings. Chavis and Wandersman (1990) demonstrated in a longitudinal study that a sense of community could serve as a catalyst for participation in block associations, and Checkoway (1991) found that more active members and leaders in neighborhood associations rated community problems as more severe. Over 25 years ago, Mischel (1973) suggested five cognitive social learning variables as potentially useful in conceptualizing how the qualities of the person influence the impact of situations and how each person generates distinct patterns of behavior in interaction with the conditions of his or her life. Florin and Wandersman (1984) operationalized Mischel's cognitive social learning variables to predict participation in community settings. A set of cognitive social learning variables was compared with a larger set of traditional demographic and personality trait variables for the ability to discriminate members from nonmembers, and they accounted for more of the variance in participation.

Another approach to the issue of why people participate is represented by the political economy theory. The theory suggests that a social exchange takes place in organizations in which participants will invest their energy in the organization, only if they expect to receive some benefits. Wandersman, Florin, Friedmann, and Meier (1987) investigated the benefits and costs of participation in a cross-cultural study. They found two benefit factors (helping others and personal gains) and two cost factors (opportunity costs and organizational frustration). The absolute ratings suggested that both members and nonmembers agree that the greatest benefits are in making a contribution and helping others rather than in self-interest or personal gains. In regard to costs, nonmembers perceived more costs than members reported.

Organizational Characteristics and Participation. Organizational characteristics such as the structure, decision-making style, and social climate of a group have been related to members' participation. Studies have found that members in structured organizations were more involved and spent more time working for the organization outside of meetings, increased participation in decision-making was related to the amount of time members spent working for the organization, and members spent more time volunteering in block associations that used a democratic decision-making process. Finally, the social climate or "collective personality" of an organization as perceived by its members has been related to participation. Higher average time involvement of members was related to a social climate that is (1) higher in cohesion; (2) lower in tolerance for independent action that is uncoordinated with the group; (3) higher in encouragement for sharing personal feelings and information; and (4) higher in tolerance for negative feelings or disagreements.

Effects of Citizen Participation. Systematic research examining the effects of participation is limited. In general, it consists primarily of case studies and rarely employs quasi-experimental or experimental designs. Here we review selected effects in three domains: (1) impacts on the participating individuals; (2) impacts on interpersonal relationships; and (3) impacts on physical and social conditions.

Impacts on the Participating Individuals. Individual impacts such as changes in attitudes and beliefs, or increases in skills may occur during the process of participation. Participation may result in changed attitudes and beliefs about various aspects of the environment, including attitudes toward one's neighbors, municipal services, or government in general. For example, some studies indicate that participation will increase individual satisfaction with one's neighborhood and also help to develop more positive attitudes toward other community members. Chavis and Wandersman (1990) found that participation increased individuals' sense of community. Advocates have long promoted participation as increasing confidence and efficacy while reducing alienation and powerlessness. Studies of general participation in community organizations and studies of specific participation programs have, indeed, found that participants have stronger feelings of personal and political efficacy than nonparticipants. Empirical studies of participation, thus, suggest a strong association between participation and feelings about the self, but the cross-sectional nature of the data in most studies does not allow us to rule out the possibility that such associations may be the cause of rather than the effect of participation. Most likely these variables both influence the decision to participate and are then themselves amplified in the participatory process in a reciprocal spiral of causality.

Impacts on Interpersonal Relationships. Impacts of participation in neighborhood organizations on interpersonal relationships include changes in socializing and mutual assistance among residents. This may be viewed as a secondary goal of community development or as the means to an end (e.g., promoting neighboring to increase mutual assistance toward the goal of reducing crime). Many studies have found a relationship between participation in formal community organizations and informal interactions among residents.

A few studies have found an increase in neighboring as an effect of participation. Results suggest that block associations do increase neighboring among residents but only for those residents who participate. Participation, it appears, is not a spectator sport, and there are only minor spillover effects for nonparticipants.

Impacts on Physical and Social Conditions. The majority of neighborhood community development efforts have primary goals that focus on concrete conditions affecting neighborhood residents and there are many case examples in the literature of neighborhood organizations successfully changing local physical conditions. Such impacts range from relatively simple cleanup and beautification programs to home repair and improvement programs to more ambitious building projects. Several studies indicate that community crime prevention programs do reduce crime rates but that the effects of crime prevention programs on fear of crime is less clear-cut. Some studies have found that fear of crime was reduced; others found that it increased. Still other studies found no relationship between participation and fear. Such discrepant findings indicate a complex relationship with the need to study types of programs, severity of local crime, neighborhood makeup, and other situational factors as mediating variables. Neighborhood community development can also address social services provided to local residents. The actual mechanisms used to improve social service delivery have varied greatly. Some neighborhood organizations organize and deliver their own social services provided entirely by volunteers. For example, neighborhood organizations have provided day care and baby-sitting cooperatives, and designed and delivered programs for youth (e.g., summer employment programs) and the aged (e.g., senior escort services and home visits). Neighborhood organizations may also influence various arrangements made by their city to decentralize and/or coordinate municipal services at the neighborhood level. The actual structural arrangements may range from task forces to multiservice centers to neighborhood councils. Yin and Yates (1974) reviewed 215 case studies of decentralization and concluded that service delivery improved in 72% of the cases. Moreover, they found that such improvement of services happened most often in those decentralization programs in which residents had the most direct governing control over the service provided. In the same vein, McMillan et al. (1995) found that community coalitions that generated higher levels of participation and empowerment among their members were more successful in influencing the policies and resource allocation of key community decision makers (e.g., town council chairs, police chiefs, superintendents of schools) one year later.

The noted black educator Benjamin Mays said that "nobody is wise enough, nobody is good enough, and nobody cares enough about you, for you to turn over to them your future or your destiny." Citizen participation offers the potential to make schools, neighborhoods, and other institutions, environments, and services responsive to individuals and families.

Bibliography

Chavis, D. M., & Wandersman, A. (1990). Sense of community in the urban environment: A catalyst for participation and community development. *American Journal of Community Psychology, 18*(1), 55–81.

Checkoway, B. (1991). Neighborhood needs and organizational resources: New lessons from Detroit. Nonprofit and voluntary sector quarterly. *Nonprofit and Voluntary Sector Quarterly, 20*(2), 173–189.

Florin, P., & Wandersman, A. (1984). Cognitive social learning and participation in community development. *American Journal of Community Psychology, 12,* 689–708.

Gibbs, L. (1982). *Love Canal: My story.* Albany, NY: State University of New York Press.

Heller, K., Price, R., Reinharz, S., Riger, S., & Wandersman, A. (1984). *Psychology and community change: Challenges of the future.* Homewood, IL: Dorsey Press.

McMillan, B., Florin, P., Stevenson, J., Kerman, B., & Mitchell, R. E. (1995). Empowerment praxis in community coalitions. *American Journal of Community Psychology, 23,* 699–727.

Mischel, W. (1973). Toward a cognitive social learning reconceptualization of personality. *Psychological Review, 80,* 252–283.

Wandersman, A., Florin, P., Friedmann, R., & Meier R. (1987). Who participates, who does not, and why? An analysis of voluntary neighborhood organizations in the United States and Israel. *Sociological Forum, 2,* 534–555.

Widmer, C. (1984). *An incentive model of citizen participation applied to a study of human service agency boards of directors.* Unpublished doctoral dissertation, Cornell University, Ithaca, NY.

Yin, R. K., & Yates, D. (1974). *Street-level governments: Assessing decentralization and urban services.* Santa Monica, CA: Rand.

Abraham Wandersman

CITIZENSHIP. *See* Groups; Intergroup Relations; *and* Political Behavior.

CLAIRVOYANCE. *See* Parapsychology.

CLAPARÈDE, ÉDOUARD (1873–1940), Swiss psychologist. Claparède, born in the French-speaking Swiss city of Geneva in an aristocratic Protestant family, was an important figure in the professional establishment of child psychology and education. A physician by training, he wrote on clinical neurology, perception, animal psychology, hypnosis, hysteria, psychological methodology, the association of ideas, sleep, play, emotions, the empirical control of mediums, and the genesis of hypotheses. He pioneered the use of film in psychology and the psychological investigation of judicial testimony, and contributed to introduce psychoanalysis to the French-speaking world. He was educational consultant to several governments. In the late 1930s, he argued that psychology, by throwing light on politics, could help advance international cooperation and combat the rise of Fascism. *Archives de Psychologie,* which he founded in 1901 with Théodore Flournoy (1854–1920), was for many years a chief European psychological journal. Claparède taught at the University of Geneva from 1908 to 1940.

Claparède's reputation and influence rest on two achievements. One is his book *Experimental Pedagogy and Psychology of the Child,* translated into 12 European languages. In it, Claparède synthesized the history, problems, and methods of the field, and argued that pedagogy should be based on the scientific knowledge of the child. His other books in educational psychology dealt with the school "made to the child's measure," aptitude testing, and "functional education" (*L'école sur mesure,* 1920; *Comment diagnostiquer les aptitudes des écoliers,* 1924; *L'éducation fonctionnelle,* 1931); they exist in several languages but not in English.

Claparède's second major accomplishment was the creation in 1912 of the Jean-Jacques Rousseau Institute of Geneva, a center for teacher education, educational experimentation, and developmental research that became a model for similar institutions throughout the world. Claparède claimed that the school should adapt to the child, and that education should be based on the child's development, needs, and activity. Although, unlike Ovide Decroly (1871–1932) or Maria Montessori (1870–1952), he was not a creator of pedagogical methods, he became a key figure in the child-study and progressive education (*école active*) movements.

Claparède's thought is characterized by the "functional" approach he first elaborated as a critique of associationism. He postulated that all behavior has an adaptive function, and applied this premise to diverse areas of psychology, including the development of intelligence. A key notion of Claparède's functionalism was the "law of the grasp of consciousness," according to which the more a type of behavior has been used automatically, the harder it is to become aware of it. The idea that taking cognizance of one's intellectual operations plays a crucial role in the growth of intelligence later became a central notion in Piaget's developmental psychology.

Thanks to his publications, consulting, and the Rousseau Institute, Claparède gave a significant impetus to developmental and pedagogical studies in Europe and beyond. By reinforcing psychologists' roles as experts on child development and mental testing, he contributed to strengthen their authority in the field of education. Claparède's main intellectual heir was Jean Piaget (1896–1980), whose career took place mainly in the Rousseau Institute.

Bibliography

Berchtold, A. (1974). Édouard Claparède et son temps. *Revue suisse de psychologie, 33,* 286–304.

Claparède, É. (1912–13). *Experimental pedagogy and psychology of the child.* Translated by M. Louch and H. Holman. New York: Longman. Original: *Psychologie de l'enfant et pédagogie expérimentale.* Geneva: Kündig, 1905. The book went through eight editions, some of them expanded and/or with new prefaces. The English version, translated from the fourth (1911) edition, first appeared in England (London: Arnold, 1911).

Claparède, É. (1930). Autobiography. In C. Murchison (Ed.). *A history of psychology in autobiography* (vol. 1, pp. 63–97). Worcester, MA: Clark University Press. A candid self-portrait. The best initiation to the man and his work.

Hameline, D. (1986). Édouard Claparède (1873–1940). *Prospects. Quarterly Review of Education* (UNESCO), *16,* 397–404.

Trombetta, C. (1989). *Édouard Claparède psicologo.* Rome: Armando. The second of two books on Claparède by the same author. The first one, published in 1976, was biographical; this one focuses on Claparède's psychological writings. Both contain extensive bibliographies.

Fernando Vidal

CLARK, KENNETH BANCROFT (1914–), an American psychologist whose research helped bring about the Supreme Court's 1954 ruling against public school racial segregation. Referred to as "the scholar of the civil rights movement," Clark's research findings concerning the development of consciousness of self and racial identification in all students became the backbone of the Court's ruling. Early in his research career, social psychologist Kenneth Clark teamed with his wife, psychologist Mamie Phipps Clark, to investigate the relationship between self-esteem and skin color in preschool children. So significant was Clark's research that he became the first recipient of the American Psychological Association (APA) award for Distinguished Contributions to Psychology in the Public Interest (1959). Later, he was elected president of APA's Society for the Psychological Study of Social Issues (SPSSI). In 1971, Clark became the seventy-ninth president of the American Psychological Association. In doing so, he became the first African American to achieve this distinction.

Born in the Panama Canal Zone, the son of Arthur and Miriam (Hanson), Clark came to the United States at the age of 7. He received his public school education in New York City and enrolled at Howard University in 1929. Several years later he became a naturalized citizen. Studying under Francis Sumner, Clark received his B.S. from Howard in 1935. He enrolled at Columbia University and while a graduate student was a research assistant for Gunnar Myrdal's comprehensive study, *An American Dilemma* (1944). Clark was awarded a Ph.D. in psychology in 1940. He joined the faculty at City College in the City University at New York in 1946 and eventually attained the status of distinguished university professor. He became professor emeritus in 1975.

In 1954 Clark charged the New York City school system with allowing de facto segregation in some of its schools. He rejected the theory that heredity played a predominant role in determining intellectual abilities and thus underscored the importance of environmental factors in academic attainment. For a time, Clark headed Harlem Youth Opportunities Unlimited (HAR-YOU), a program designed to help reduce the number of unemployed youngsters, school dropouts, and juvenile delinquents. In 1955 he published *Prejudice and Your Child*, in which he analyzed the effects of racial discrimination upon black and white children and proposed certain remedies. This book was nationally praised for its "comprehensiveness and clean objectivity." His prize-winning analysis, *Dark Ghetto: Dilemmas of Social Power* (1965), was published in six different languages. He coauthored, with Jeannette Hopkins, *The Relevant War Against Poverty* (1968) and, with Talcott Parsons, *The Negro American* (1968). In 1974 he wrote *Pathos of Power*. He has contributed many articles to scholarly journals and is the founding president of the Metropolitan Applied Research Center (MARC), which was established as a catalyst for change and as an advocate for the poor and powerless in American cities. Clark has received numerous honorary doctoral degrees, the Sidney Hillman Prize Book Award, APA's Kurt Lewin Memorial Award, and the National Association for the Advancement of Colored People (NAACP) Springarn Medal.

Bibliography

Clark, K. B. (1965). *Dark ghetto: Dilemmas of social power*. New York: Harper and Row.

Guthrie, R. V. (1998). *Even the rat was white: A historical view of psychology* (2nd ed.). Boston: Allyn and Bacon. Includes Clark's background and collaborations with Mamie Phipps Clark. Discusses Clark's contributions to the 1954 Supreme Court decision regarding public school racial integration.

Kinsman, C. D. (Ed.). (1976). *Contemporary authors* (Vols. 33–36). Detroit, MI: Gale Research.

Marquis Who's Who. (1976–1977). *Who's who in America*. Chicago: Author.

Robert V. Guthrie

CLASSICAL CONDITIONING, also known as Pavlovian conditioning, refers to the class of procedures and the outcomes of those procedures, named for the Russian physiologist I. P. Pavlov, in whose laboratory they were first systematically explored. In the late nineteenth century, Pavlov directed a large laboratory engaged in studying the functioning of the digestive glands, among them the salivary glands. He assigned a physician named Vul'fson the task of understanding how dogs salivated when various edible and inedible substances were placed in their mouths. Vul'fson noted that when a dog had repeatedly been fed a particular food that made it salivate, then the mere sight of that food would evoke similar salivation, which was at first called a "psychic secretion."

Pavlov's Formulation

Within a few years, Pavlov was using very different language to describe this salivation in response to the sight of food. Hungry dogs salivated to food in the mouth from the outset of the experiment. Pavlov called this stimulus-response relation an unconditioned or unconditional reflex. The dogs did not salivate, however, at the sight of food until they had repeatedly been shown the food prior to eating it. Pavlov called salivation in response to the sight of food a conditional reflex, one that depended on the existence of certain conditions; foremost among them, for Pavlov, was that the sight of food signaled food in the mouth. Pavlov saw in this phenomenon the beginnings of a program for studying how individuals acquire new reflexes, and as he became convinced that conditioned salivary reflexes were lawful, and thus would produce interpretable results, he made them the focus of his research program.

Pavlov's initial formula for conditioning entailed presenting one stimulus, for example, the ticking of a metronome, which did not at first evoke the salivary response he wanted to condition, followed after a short interval by a second stimulus, for example, meat powder introduced into the dog's mouth, which did evoke salivation from the outset. The first stimulus is called the conditional or conditioned stimulus (CS). The second stimulus is called the unconditional or unconditioned stimulus (US or UCS), and the salivary response to that stimulus is called the unconditional or unconditioned response (UR or UCR). When, after a number of CS–US pairings, or conditioning trials, presented at intervals of a few minutes, the dog does salivate upon hearing the metronome, that salivation is called the conditioned or conditional response (CR). It is a hallmark of the Pavlovian procedure that the unconditioned stimulus is presented whether the organism responds to the conditioned stimulus or not. The food is not a reward given to the dog when it salivates in response to the metronome; rather salivation to the metronome is engendered as a consequence of the temporal arrangement of metronome and food.

Pavlov's nearly 40-year-long research program on salivary conditioning and much of modern research on Pavlovian conditioning can be thought of as an exploration of how variations in the arrangement of conditioned and unconditioned stimuli in time and space affect the development of conditioned responses. Although nearly all the experiments in Pavlov's laboratory were on salivary conditioning of dogs, Pavlov's interest was in acquired reflexes in general, and he seemed to believe that his formula would apply across species and for all CSs, USs, and URs. That is, he maintained that as long as some stimulus (US) reliably evokes some response (UR) from the start of an experiment and as long as that stimulus is repeatedly preceded by some other stimulus (CS) that the organism perceives but that does not initially evoke the response, then conditioning will occur—the CS will come to evoke a response similar to the UR.

Generality of Pavlovian Conditioning

Pavlov is regarded as a major figure in the history of conditioning in part because his formulation has been shown to apply far beyond salivary conditioning of dogs. Autonomic responses, such as changes in heart rate, skin conductance, and blood pressure, can be conditioned to stimuli that precede USs that evoke these responses. Conditioned stimuli that precede an air puff to the cornea (US), which evokes an eye blink, will themselves evoke eye blinks after repeated pairings with the US. Other defensive reflexes, such as leg or toe flexion in response to a painful stimulus, are similarly conditionable. Even the sea slug's response of bending back a part of its respiratory apparatus (called the siphon) in response to tail shock (US) can readily be conditioned to a tactile stimulus (CS) that repeatedly precedes the US.

In the 1960s, it was discovered that such simple reflexes are not the only motor behaviors that can be conditioned in a Pavlovian fashion. If a hopper full of birdseed is placed within reach of a hungry pigeon, the bird will peck at the hopper, picking up grains. Now suppose that a small disk mounted on the wall is illuminated (CS) five seconds before each presentation of food (US). With repeated presentations of this CS–US sequence, the bird will learn to approach and peck the disk whenever it lights up, though food will be presented whether it pecks or not. The significance of this phenomenon, called sign tracking, is that not only does a CS that can be approached and contacted come to evoke a CR like the UR, but the CR is directed at the CS. When water instead of food is the US, the CR includes sipping movements directed at the illuminated disk. In these cases, the CR looks like the UR, but in some cases of sign tracking the form of the response directed at the conditioned stimulus is different from the form of the unconditioned response. In one experiment, illumination of a light bulb (CS) repeatedly preceded the availability of a food pellet (US), which dogs consumed avidly. The dogs did not learn to bite at the CS; one dog learned to direct a food-begging response to the illuminated bulb, and another learned to sight point at the bulb. Perhaps the CRs took these particular forms because the dogs had a history of directing such responses at natural signals for food.

Pavlovian conditioning of emotional responses has been a major focus of research on learning for many years, with fear and anxiety the most widely studied examples because of their relevance for the understanding and treatment of human anxiety disorders. Fear-conditioning experiments with the rat typically entail occasional presentations of an auditory or visual CS followed by a brief, painful foot shock (US), which evokes a brief burst of activity. Within a few trials, onset of the conditioned stimulus evokes behavior indicative of fear, for example, freezing (remaining motionless and rigid). This is another instance in which the forms of the unconditioned and conditioned responses are quite different.

Sexual arousal has also been shown to be conditionable in a Pavlovian fashion. Male rats were placed in a distinctive environment (CS) for ten minutes each day just before being placed near a sexually receptive female that was out of reach. After eight such conditioning trials, the male was again exposed to the CS for ten minutes and then placed with the female. If the CS evoked sexual arousal, then the male should have ejaculated sooner than would a control male that had not been aroused just before being placed with the female. That is what happened; the latency of ejaculation was fifteen minutes for the control male and six minutes for the experimental one.

Over the last few decades Pavlovian conditioning based on drug USs has been a major focus of research. The administration of a drug, whether in a medical or abuse setting, is typically preceded by stimuli, for example, the sight of the syringe or the drug preparation ritual, that could act as Pavlovian CSs. In 1975 Shepard Siegel (Evidence from rats that morphine tolerance is a learned response, *Journal of Comparative and Physiological Psychology, 89*, 498–506) proposed that since organisms tend to maintain homeostasis, conditionable organisms would be expected to do so by making compensatory conditioned responses to CSs for drugs. These responses would allow an organism to compensate in advance for the onslaught of a drug. For example, if a drug increases heart rate, one might expect a decrease in heart rate to be conditioned to a CS that signals that drug. This view predicts that, as the compensatory conditioned response grows over trials, it will more and more effectively oppose the drug effect. Thus tolerance, a diminished response to a drug after repeated administrations, should be observed if the effect of the drug is assessed in the presence of the conditioned stimulus, but there should be no tolerance if the effect is assessed in the absence of the CS. This prediction was first confirmed for the analgesic effects of morphine and has also been confirmed for other responses to a variety of drugs. Currently, there is little doubt that associative learning is important for some instances of drug tolerance, though there remains dispute about whether conditioned compensatory responses are responsible for the effect. It has also been suggested that the very same conditioned responses that are responsible for tolerance constitute withdrawal symptoms when a morphine-paired CS is not followed by administration of the drug. Conditioned withdrawal responses can be evoked by drug-associated cues and, in the laboratory setting, also by cues that have been associated with agents that themselves induce withdrawal, for example, the morphine antagonist naloxone.

Some Fundamental Determinants of Pavlovian Conditioning

The determinant of Pavlovian conditioning that has received the most attention over the years is the temporal arrangement of CS and US. Pavlov found that conditioning would occur only if the CS could signal the US, that is, only if the CS preceded the US on a trial. More-

over, he observed that the CS–US interval should be relatively brief; otherwise a CS followed after a long delay by a US would signal "no food for a while." Such a CS would actually evoke inhibition of salivation, which would give way to a salivary conditioned response as the time of food drew near. As research on conditioning expanded to other laboratories, organisms, and response systems, it became clear that CS–US intervals that are effective for some responses may be ineffective for others. For example, eye blink conditioning fails to occur with intervals of more than a second or two, but fear conditioning and conditioning of sexual arousal are successful with intervals of several minutes, and aversions may be conditioned to flavors that precede illness by several hours. We now know that conditioning can occur when CS and US begin simultaneously and even when US precedes CS, if only we assess that conditioning in an appropriate way. It has also been demonstrated that the form of the conditioned response may depend on the CS–US interval. The time between successive conditioning trials is also important. For a given CS–US interval, conditioning is more effective with longer intertrial intervals than with shorter ones.

Other Phenomena of Pavlovian Conditioning

The first few years of Pavlov's research on conditioning saw the discovery of many fundamentally important phenomena. "Extinction" refers both to the procedure in which following conditioning the CS is repeatedly presented without the US and to the gradual disappearance of the CR that results. Extinction, even when conducted until the CS no longer evokes the CR, does not wipe out all traces of conditioning, for if the animal is allowed a vacation for some days after extinction, when it is returned to the laboratory the CS will evoke the conditioned response on the very first trial, without any further conditioning. Pavlov called this phenomenon "spontaneous recovery" and inferred from it that the extinction procedure engendered an inhibitory conditioned response. In the case of his dogs, this was an active tendency not to salivate that opposed the previously conditioned tendency to salivate, thus reducing the magnitude of the observed salivary response. For Pavlov, conditioned inhibition was an important determinant of behavior whenever some conditioned stimulus was not followed by the US in a situation where the US otherwise occurred.

"Stimulus generalization" refers to the finding that the effect of conditioning to one conditioned stimulus generalizes to other stimuli. For example, if a pure tone of a certain frequency precedes food on many occasions, not only will that CS evoke salivation, but tones of other frequencies will also do so. Moreover, the magnitude of the conditioned response will decline in an orderly fashion as the similarity of the frequencies of the conditioning and test tones declines. Such a finding implies that the organism must have been paying attention to the dimension of auditory frequency during conditioning. Thus the study of stimulus generalization has been a useful way to learn about attention.

Stimulus generalization can be construed as a process that extends the range of stimuli that evokes a particular conditioned response. Opposing generalization is "discrimination," which in Pavlov's laboratory resulted from repeatedly presenting one conditioned stimulus followed by food, while on other occasions presenting a different CS without food. If the two stimuli are fairly similar, then there will be initial generalization; the animal will at first respond indiscriminately to both CSs. However, as conditioning progresses, while the CR to the signal for food is maintained, the CR to the stimulus presented alone will wither, reflecting for Pavlov the conditioning of inhibition to that CS. When this happens the animal is said to be discriminating between the two stimuli or responding discriminatively. The discrimination procedure has been used to assess organisms' ability to distinguish stimuli; if they respond differently to two stimuli, they must be able to tell them apart. In the early days of conditioning, Russian investigators used this method to advance our knowledge of the human infant's ability to distinguish different sounds.

Recent Research and Current Directions

Research on Pavlovian conditioning in North America began to flourish in the 1960s, largely because of discoveries that arose from the introduction of novel arrangements of CSs and USs, only two of which will be mentioned here. Leon Kamin (Selective association and conditioning. In N. J. Mackintosh and W. K. Honig, Eds., *Fundamental issues in associative learning.* Halifax, Canada: Dalhousie University Press, 1969) gave rats many pairings of one CS with an aversive US, until the CS reliably evoked a fear response. Then, a second CS was added to the first, and the pairings continued as before. Finally, the second CS was presented alone, to see whether it evoked any fear. It did not, and additional research showed that this failure of conditioning, called "blocking," depended on the prior conditioning of the first CS. So it was not enough that the added CS reliably preceded the US by an otherwise appropriate time interval; for conditioning to occur it apparently had to inform the animal about the occurrence of the aversive US. In this case, the added CS was redundant. In an experiment in 1966, Robert Rescorla (Predictability and number of pairings in Pavlovian fear conditioning. *Psychonomic Science, 4,* 383–384) showed that a regimen of CS–US pairings that would otherwise lead to conditioning would not do so if enough additional presentations of the US by itself were given so that the US

was equally likely in a given interval of time whether the CS had just occurred or not. In other words, it appeared that for conditioning to occur the CS not only had to be paired with the US, but it also had to signal an increased likelihood of US presentation, relative to the background level.

The next stage of theoretical development in this area, the Rescorla–Wagner model, provided an explanation for these two phenomena. The core of this model is the assertion that a given US can promote only so much conditioning, and that conditioning will be shared among any CSs that precede a US on a trial. This model treated the experimental situation or context like any other conditioned stimulus, except that context was always present. From this perspective, (1) Kamin's blocking effect occurred because all the conditioning that the US could promote accrued to the first CS, so that when the second CS was added there was none left for it, and (2) the extra USs in Rescorla's experiment acted to condition a response to the context, so that when the CS and context together were followed by the US, the context blocked conditioning to the CS. Although the Rescorla-Wagner model explained a vast amount of data, its inability to explain certain important outcomes led to the development of a number of alternative formal models, and such developments continue today.

Pavlov maintained that conditioning was adaptive in the sense that an organism that could be conditioned would be able to use signals (CSs) for biologically important events (USs) whenever the environment provided them, and this would give it an advantage over an organism that could not be conditioned. This was a plausible supposition but only that. Indeed, if we assume that the adaptive value of some characteristic is a function of its contribution to reproductive success, then the contribution of Pavlovian conditioning to sexual behavior may be the best place to look for conditioning's adaptive value. We have already seen that conditoned sexual arousal can facilitate ejaculation of male rats, and plausible accounts about how this facilitation has adaptive value could be constructed. But only in the late 1990s was there a demonstration that conditioning is important for the number of offspring produced. Male blue gourami fish have to be aggressive to defend territories, but such aggression has the cost of repelling females. Karen Hollis and her students ("Classical conditioning provides paternity advantage for territorial male blue gouramis," *Journal of Comparative Psychology*, 1997, 111, 219–225) gave an experimental group of male gouramis repeated trials on which a visual stimulus (CS) was followed 10 seconds later by visual access to a female (US); control fish received the CS and US 4 to 6 hours apart. In a subsequent test, all males were presented with the CS and then were allowed to interact with a novel female for six days. Not only did the males in the experimental group, for which the CS had become a signal for a female, behave less aggressively than controls to the new female, but experimental males spawned with females sooner and produced many more young than controls. This is just one of many research programs that are exploring the adaptive value of Pavlovian conditioning.

The study of the neural mechanisms of Pavlovian conditioning is flourishing. This area includes research on simple systems like the defensive reflex of the sea slug described earlier, as well as investigations of diverse mammalian preparations, such as fear conditioning in the rat and eye blink conditioning in the rabbit. The work is being driven forward by advances in anatomical, physiological, biochemical, and genetic techniques. The emergence of research groups with expertise in learning theory as well as neuroscience bodes well for a rapid advance of knowledge.

Bibliography

Brown, P. L., & Jenkins, H. M. (1968). Auto-shaping of the pigeon's key peck. *Journal of the Experimental Analysis of Behavior, 11,* 1–8. The first demonstration of sign-tracking.

Cunningham, C. L. (1998). Drug conditioning and drug-seeking behavior. In W. O'Donohue (Ed.), *Learning and behavior therapy.* Needham Heights, MA: Allyn & Bacon. Written for those who are primarily concerned with clinical issues.

Domjan, M. (1998). *The principles of learning and behavior* (4th ed.). Pacific Grove, CA: Brooks/Cole. A leading textbook for a university course on conditioning and learning. Includes a discussion of the Rescorla-Wagner model and other formal models of classical conditioning.

Hollis, K. L. (1997). Contemporary research on Pavlovian conditioning: A "new" functional analysis. *American Psychologist, 52,* 956–965. Describes contemporary research with a functional or adaptive perspective, including work on antipredator defense, courtship and reproduction, and drug tolerance and addiction. Also describes contemporary research with an associative or cognitive perspective, arguing that such research benefits from attention to adaptive function.

LeDoux, J. (1996). *The emotional brain.* New York: Touchstone. Includes accounts of how emotional conditioning occurs and how the human brain functions to produce that conditioning.

Ohman, A., Dimberg, U., & Ost, L.-G. (1995). Animal and social phobias: Biological constraints on learned fear responses. In S. Reiss & R. R. Bootzin (Eds.), *Theoretical issues in behavior therapy.* New York: Academic Press. Argues provocatively that humans are predisposed to acquire, through Pavlovian conditioning, animal and social phobias.

Pavlov, I. P. (1927). *Conditioned reflexes.* Oxford: Oxford University Press. Describes virtually all of Pavlov's impor-

tant experiments on conditioning and provides his interpretation of them.

Rescorla, R. A. (1988). Pavlovian conditioning: It's not what you think it is. *American Psychologist, 43,* 151–160. A clearly written summary of modern data and theory in classical conditioning, focusing on the circumstances that produce conditioning and the content of conditioning.

Rescorla, R. A., & Wagner, A. R. (1972). A theory of Pavlovian conditioning: Variations in the effectiveness of reinforcement and nonreinforcement. In A. H. Black & W. F. Prokasy (Eds.), *Classical conditioning II: Current research and theory.* New York: Appleton-Century-Crofts. This is probably the most influential theoretical paper on conditioning, and it is extraordinarily well written.

Todes, D. P. (1997). From the machine to the ghost within: Pavlov's transition from digestive physiology to conditional reflexes. *American Psychologist, 52,* 947–955. A new account of the transition from "psychic secretion" to "conditional reflex"; very different from Pavlov's description.

Zamble, E., Hadad, G. M., Mitchell, J. B., & Cutmore, T. R. H. (1985). Pavlovian conditioning of sexual arousal: First- and second-order effects. *Journal of Experimental Psychology: Animal Behavior Processes, 11,* 598–610. A full report of the research on conditioning of sexual arousal in the male rat.

Vincent M. LoLordo

CLASSROOMS. [*This entry comprises two articles. The first article describes the nature of the classroom (process and management). The second article discusses the various types, the role, and the use of technology in the classroom and their impact on learning.*]

Processes and Management

At one time, only the children of the rich received formal education, typically in the form of private tutoring. Such tutoring would be the method of choice for most educational purposes, because the curriculum can be individualized and the teacher can provide the student with sustained personalized attention. However, private tutoring is beyond the means of most families. Consequently, as systems for mass education developed, one constant feature has been an arrangement whereby each teacher works with many students.

Colonial times featured the one-room schoolhouse, in which students of all ages were instructed in all subjects by a single teacher, who had few if any commercially prepared texts or curriculum materials. Instruction featured recitations and memory exercises. With the Industrial Revolution and the shift of population to cities, schools became larger and education became more standardized and formalized. Age grouping became the basis for assigning students to classes, curriculum guidelines were established for each grade level, and teachers began using commercial textbooks and tests. Certain practices for organizing and managing instruction became well established and have continued through the present as the traditional model of classroom teaching: (1) the lock-step curriculum with its grade-level sequencing, division of the school day into periods for teaching different subjects, and division of instruction in each subject into units and lessons; (2) group pacing, in which the whole class is moved through the same curriculum at roughly the same speed using largely the same materials and methods; and (3) whole-class instructional methods, in which the teacher typically begins a lesson by reviewing prerequisite material, then introduces and develops new concepts or skills, then leads the group in a recitation or supervised practice or application activity, and then assigns work for students to do on their own. Some teachers may teach small groups rather than the whole class (especially for beginning reading instruction), may provide a degree of individualized instruction when "making the rounds" during independent work times, or may arrange for students to work on assignments in pairs or groups rather than individually. With these and other minor variations, the basic whole-class instruction/recitation/independent work model has persisted as the dominant approach to teaching, despite frequent criticism and calls for reform (Cuban, 1993).

Given that most teachers must work with classes of 15 to 45 students, this method may be the best compromise available, allowing teachers to meet more of the needs of more of their students than they could meet using any other method. However, the traditional method clearly has weaknesses. Two major ones are that the majority of students must work without close supervision whenever teachers work with small groups or individuals, and teachers cannot get around to each student often enough to provide effective individualized instruction.

Many adaptations to the traditional model have been proposed as methods of increasing the individualization of instruction. Usually these suggested reforms call for shifting responsibility for planning and accomplishing learning from the teacher to the student and for shifting responsibility for communicating content from the teacher to the instructional materials, because it is not possible for one teacher to meet the needs of all students in a class simultaneously (Jackson, 1985). Certain elements of some of these suggested innovations have been assimilated into traditional schooling, but the innovations have not been retained as complete packages to supplant traditional methods. Typically, this has been because reformers made unwarranted assumptions about students' capabilities for independent goal setting

and learning, produced materials that focused on low-level and isolated skills, or required too much testing or managerial complexity. These same problems have plagued recent attempts to individualize by relying on computerized instruction.

Slavin (1984) suggested that, for any kind of instruction to be effective, four conditions must be satisfied: (1) instruction must be high in quality, (2) instruction must be appropriate to students' levels, (3) students must be motivated to work on tasks, and (4) students must have adequate time to learn. He argued that individualized instructional programs have not lived up to expectations because they have concentrated on increasing the appropriateness of instruction but have not addressed the other three essential conditions. Quality of instruction is reduced because students are not taught directly by the teacher but instead are required to learn on their own. They are not adequately motivated because working through individualized programs often is boring and seldom offers incentives for progressing rapidly. Finally, much classroom time is spent on procedural matters (passing out material, waiting for the teacher to check work, taking tests), to the point that time for learning is reduced. It appears that approaches that call for teachers to provide individualized instruction simultaneously to all students in a class are not feasible unless the teachers are working in very small classes or get significant help from aides or other adults (Good & Brophy, 2000).

A widely used variation on the whole-class teaching model, especially in elementary schools, is within-class grouping of students according to ability or prior achievement levels. This makes it easier for teachers to provide intensive small-group instruction in content and skills that are closely matched to the current achievement levels of the students in each group, and a meta-analysis indicated trivial-to-small positive effects of within-class grouping on student achievement (Kulik & Kulik, 1989). However, grouping arrangements complicate classroom management, because provisions must be made to keep the rest of the students profitably occupied whenever the teacher is busy instructing a small group. Furthermore, ability grouping tends to exaggerate preexisting differences in achievement by accelerating the progress of students in the top groups but slowing the progress of students in the bottom groups, and it tends to segregate students along social class and racial lines, both in and out of the classroom. Good and Brophy (2000) suggested guidelines for using within-class grouping in ways that exploit its advantages but minimize its disadvantages.

Management of Traditional Classrooms

Managing a classroom effectively is a complex task. The teacher must not only establish a management system that works but also must keep it working by monitoring events continually and responding quickly when breakdowns threaten. Sometimes this involves resorting to quick fix measures that are less than ideal but make it possible for the system as a whole to continue functioning. The complexities involved can be reduced considerably through planning and preparation. Teachers can help ensure the success of planned activities by arranging for an appropriate seating pattern, having materials ready for efficient distribution to students, and preparing thoroughly enough to be able to instruct effectively without having to stop to consult a lesson plan or teacher's guide. Further simplification is achieved by developing routines and heuristics for handling commonly occurring situations. Routines are standardized methods of handling recurring situations that can be taught to students as rules or procedures. These routines simplify the complexities of life in classrooms for both teachers and students by imposing structures that make events more predictable. This reduces the students' needs to seek direction and the teachers' needs to make decisions or give specific instructions concerning everyday events.

In addition to routines, teachers use heuristics (implicit rules of thumb) for monitoring classroom events and making decisions about whether and how to respond to emerging conditions. For example, teachers learn to identify cues (the identities of the students involved, the specific nature of their misbehavior) to help them predict which undesirable behaviors can be safely ignored and which may require intervention because they threaten to become disruptive. Teachers who identify such cues and develop appropriate response routines that function automatically when triggered by the cues are better able than other teachers to optimize their classroom management by intervening only when necessary, yet intervening effectively when intervention is needed.

Early, anecdotally based advice to teachers about classroom management was of the "Don't smile until Christmas" variety, with emphasis on control or discipline. However, such advice became more systematic and theory driven as classroom management began to receive scholarly attention. There was some early emphasis on humanistic psychology notions, such as supporting students' self-concepts, and depth psychology notions, such as interpreting the underlying reasons for students' symptomatic behavior. However, primary emphasis was given to the theoretical concepts and techniques for bringing behavior under stimulus control that had been developed by applied behavior analysts and other behaviorists who emphasized controlling behavior by manipulating its consequences (particularly, by applying or withholding reinforcement). Early behavioristic formulations were overly focused on specific

behaviors and emphasized rather wooden and rigid technique prescriptions ("rules, praise, and ignoring") or converting classroom reward structures into token economy systems. As behaviorism developed and began to take into account human intentions and cognitions, behavioristic advice to teachers retained its emphasis on reinforcement but became more realistic, featuring techniques such as social skills training and negotiated goal setting with students formalized through behavioral contracts. Also, emphasis shifted from a focus on eliminating particular forms of misbehavior to shaping desired behavior (high-quality engagement in lessons and learning activities).

Behavioristic approaches are still emphasized in school psychology (which focuses on treatments for individual students), in special education (where teachers work in classes with small student/teacher ratios), and in sources offering suggestions about dealing with students who present persistent and severe behavioral problems. In addition, some popular approaches to regular classroom management, most notably assertive discipline (Canter & Canter, 1992), rely heavily on behavioristic principles.

For the most part, however, approaches to regular classroom management based on the principle of using reinforcement to bring behavior under stimulus control have been supplanted by more eclectic approaches based on replicated findings obtained by several research teams working independently in different parts of the country. These approaches emphasize strategies that are applied to the class as a whole more than to individual students and focus on launching and maintaining the momentum of lessons and learning activities more than on manipulating behavior through incentives and sanctions. The foundations for these approaches were laid by Jacob Kounin (1970), based on his analyses of videotapes taken in well-managed and poorly managed classrooms. Influenced by the "discipline" orientation dominant at the time, Kounin's initial analyses focused on the teachers' handling of disruptive incidents. Surprisingly, these analyses failed to produce consistent results. Effective managers did not differ in systematic ways from ineffective managers when they were responding to student misbehavior. However, Kounin noticed that effective managers differed from ineffective managers in other ways. Followup analyses indicated that the effective managers displayed certain key behaviors:

- *"Withitness."* Remaining aware of what is happening in all parts of the classroom at all times by continuously scanning the classroom, even when working with small groups or individuals, and demonstrating this "withitness" to students by intervening promptly and appropriately when their disengaged behavior threatens to become disruptive. This minimizes timing errors (failing to notice and intervene until an incident has already become disruptive) and target errors (mistakes in identifying the students responsible for the problem).

- *Overlapping.* Doing more than one thing at a time, such as responding to the needs of individuals while sustaining a group activity or using eye contact or physical proximity to restore inattentive students' attention to a lesson while continuing the lesson itself without interruption.
- *Signal continuity and momentum during lessons.* Teaching well-prepared and well-paced lessons that focus students' attention by providing a continuous academic signal, which is more compelling than the noise of competing distractions, and by sustaining the momentum of this academic signal throughout the lesson.
- *Challenge and variety in assignments.* Encouraging students' engagement in independent work by providing assignments that are optimal in difficulty level (easy enough to allow success with reasonable effort but new or difficult enough to provide challenge) and varied enough to sustain interest.

Kounin showed that effective managers succeed not so much because they are good at handling disruption when it occurs but because they are good at preventing disruption from occurring in the first place. These teachers do not focus on preventing disruption; instead, they focus on establishing the classroom as an effective learning environment, preparing and teaching good lessons, and monitoring students as they work on good follow-up assignments.

Related Findings

Evertson and Emmer (1982) replicated and extended Kounin's findings through their studies of how teachers establish an effective management system at the beginning of the year and sustain it thereafter. These studies demonstrated the importance of showing and telling students what to do. Clarity about rules and routines is crucial, supported, if necessary, by demonstrations of desired behavior.

In the lower grades, effective managers spend a great deal of time in the early weeks of school explaining expectations and modeling classroom routines and procedures. If necessary, they provide their students with opportunities to practice and receive feedback concerning matters such as when and how to use the pencil sharpener or how to manage the transitions between reading groups. In the upper grades, there is less need to teach daily routines (the students are already familiar with most of them or can understand them sufficiently from verbal explanations), but it is just as important to be clear and detailed in describing expected behavior.

At all grade levels, teachers need to ensure that students follow the desired procedures by providing additional reminders or feedback as needed. Effective managers consistently monitor compliance with rules and demands, enforce accountability procedures (for example, penalties for late or unacceptable work), and are prepared to punish students for repeated misconduct, if necessary. However, their emphasis is positive and prescriptive, not threatening and punitive. Effective management primarily involves teaching students what to do before the fact rather than applying discipline following misconduct.

Doyle (1984) focused on teachers' managerial activities during independent work times. He found that successful managers establish an activity system early in the year and closely supervise it, ushering it along and protecting it from intrusion or disruption. In the early weeks, contacts with individual students during independent work time were brief, and the teachers circulated around the room to maintain a whole-group perspective. In response to disruption, less successful managers tended to focus public attention on misbehavior through frequent reprimands, causing the majority of the students in the class to stop working. In contrast, successful managers tended to push the curriculum and talk about getting work done rather than talk about the misbehavior. After a month or two, these teachers had established a work system that itself imposed order in the class, and teachers were able to spend less time orchestrating the total class and more time with individuals.

Subsequent studies by other investigators have elaborated on these findings, especially as they apply to the whole-class instruction/recitation/independent work approach that has dominated traditional K–12 teaching. Major management elements of this approach include preparing the classroom as a physical environment suited to the nature of the planned learning activities, developing and implementing a workable set of housekeeping procedures and conduct rules, maintaining students' attention to and participation in lessons and activities, and monitoring the quality of their engagement in assignments and their progress toward intended achievement outcomes. These broader management goals are accomplished through procedures and routines concerning aspects such as:

- storing supplies and equipment
- establishing traffic patterns
- setting general expectations and rules at the beginning of the year
- starting and ending each class period smoothly
- managing transitions between activities
- keeping activities going once they are started by stimulating involvement and minimizing interruptions
- giving directions for and getting the class started on assignments
- circulating to monitor progress and to meet the needs

of individual students as they work on the assignments

The major findings from observational research on classroom management agree that teachers who emphasize establishing and maintaining effective learning environments are more successful than teachers who emphasize their roles as authority figures or disciplinarians. Teachers *are* authority figures and must require their students to follow certain rules and procedures. However, these rules and procedures are not ends in themselves. They are the means for organizing the classroom as an environment that supports learning.

The key to successful management is the teacher's ability to maximize the time students spend actively engaged in worthwhile academic activities and to minimize the time they spend waiting for activities to get started, making transitions between activities, sitting with nothing to do, or engaging in misconduct. Good classroom management does not just imply that the teacher elicits the students' cooperation in minimizing misconduct and intervenes effectively when misconduct occurs; it also implies that worthwhile learning activities occur more or less continuously and that the management system as a whole is designed to maximize students' engagement in those activities. Learning activities are planned and implemented effectively, and management interventions support their continuity and impact by maintaining student engagement in learning activities in ways that do not disrupt the flow of the activities themselves (Brophy, 1988; Good & Brophy, 1995, 1997; Jones, 1996).

When all of these features of effective classroom management are implemented simultaneously, they create a classroom that reveals organization, planning, and scheduling. The room is divided into distinct areas equipped for specific activities. Frequently used equipment is stored where it can be accessed easily, and each item has its own place. Traffic patterns facilitate movement around the room and minimize crowding or bumping. Transitions between activities are accomplished efficiently following a brief signal or a few directions from the teacher, and students know where they are supposed to be, what they are supposed to be doing, and what equipment they will need. Students are attentive to presentations and responsive to questions. Lessons and other group activities are structured so that subparts are discernible and separated by clear transitions. When students are released to work on their own or with peers, they know what to do and settle quickly into doing it. Usually they continue the activity through to completion without difficulty and then turn to some new approved activity. If they need help, they can get it from the teacher or from some other source and then resume working.

Adapting Established Management Principles to Social Constructivist Teaching

Most of the research that established these principles was done in rooms that featured transmission approaches to teaching. Recently, however, views on good teaching and learning have shifted from transmission views toward social construction or learning community views (see Table 1). When knowledge is socially constructed, classroom discourse emphasizes reflective discussion of networks of connected content. Questions are divergent, designed to stimulate and scaffold students' thinking and help them develop understanding of powerful ideas that anchor the knowledge networks. Students are expected to strive to make sense of what they are learning by relating it to their prior knowledge and by discussing it with others. Instead of working mostly alone, practicing what has been transmitted to them, they act as a learning community that constructs shared understandings.

The management principles identified through research done primarily in transmission classrooms also are applicable to social constructivist classrooms, if they are interpreted and implemented as principles for establishing effective learning communities and not just as techniques for eliciting students' compliance with teachers' demands. Teachers who intend to socialize their students into learning communities that share values and follow procedures that support the social construction of knowledge will have to prepare their students to take on a broader range of roles than is required of students in more traditional transmission settings (see Table 2).

Leaders in research on social constructivist approaches to teaching have emphasized the importance of instructing students not only in how to pay attention during lessons and work alone on assignments but also in how to participate in collaborative dialogues and to work together in cooperative learning activities (Cohen, 1994; Palincsar & Brown, 1989; Rogers & Freiberg, 1994). Collaborative knowledge construction means not only taking turns talking, listening politely, and keeping criticism constructive but also responding thoughtfully to what others have said, making contributions that will advance the discussion, and citing relevant arguments and evidence to support one's position. When students work in pairs or small groups, collaboration includes making sure that everyone in the group understands the goals of the activity, participates in carrying it out, and gets the intended learning benefits from this participation.

Ensuring that students learn to participate optimally still requires the familiar management principles of articulating clear expectations, modeling or providing instruction in desired procedures, cuing students when these procedures are needed, and applying sufficient

CLASSROOMS: Processes and Management. Table 1. Teaching and learning as transmission of information versus as social construction of knowledge

Transmission View	Social Constructivist View
Knowledge consists of a fixed body of information transmitted from teacher or text to students	Knowledge results from developing interpretations constructed through discussion
Texts and teachers serve as authoritative sources of expert knowledge to which students defer	Authority for constructed knowledge resides in the arguments and evidence cited in its support by students as well as by texts or teacher; everyone has expertise to contribute
Teacher is responsible for managing students' learning by providing information and leading students through activities and assignments	Teacher and students share responsibility for initiating and guiding learning efforts
Teacher explains, checks for understanding, and judges correctness of students' responses	Teacher acts as discussion leader who poses questions, seeks clarifications, promotes dialogue, helps group recognize areas of consensus and of continuing disagreement
Students memorize or replicate what has been explained or modeled	Discourse emphasizes reflective discussion of networks of connected knowledge; questions are more divergent but designed to develop understanding of the powerful ideas that anchor these networks; focus is on eliciting students' thinking
Activities emphasize replication of models or applications that require following step-by-step algorithms	Activities emphasize applications to authentic issues and problems that require higher-order thinking
Students work mostly alone, practicing what has been transmitted to them in order to prepare themselves to compete for rewards by reproducing it on demand	Students collaborate by acting as a learning community that constructs shared understandings through sustained dialogue.

From Good, T. L., & Brophy, J. E. (2000). *Looking in classrooms* (8th ed.). New York: Longman.

pressure to compel changes in behavior when students have failed to respond to more positive methods. The teacher still retains ultimate control in the classroom and when necessary exerts authority by articulating and enforcing managerial guidance. However, this guidance emphasizes thoughtful, goal-oriented learning not mindless compliance with rules.

Recent work on issues related to classroom management has emphasized the value of extending the socialization that occurs within classrooms to the level of the school as a whole. For example, research by Gottfredson, Gottfredson, and Hybl (1993) demonstrated the value of a schoolwide management program that focused on clarity of school rules, consistency of rule

enforcement, improving classroom organization, and increasing communication with parents regarding student behavior. Other work also supports the conclusion that management efforts within classrooms are likely to be most effective when norms for the school as a whole support communication and collaboration among the principal, the teachers, the parents, and the students in establishing the school as a learning community (Rogers & Freiberg, 1994).

Conclusion

Three basic classroom management principles appear to apply across all potential instructional approaches. First, management that emphasizes clarifying what stu-

CLASSROOMS: Processes and Management.
Table 2. Student roles that might guide classroom
management efforts in social constructivist classrooms

Role Competencies Featured in Knowledge Transmission
Classrooms that Also Apply in Social Constructivist
Classrooms

  1. Be in class/seat on time
  2. Store personal belongings in their proper place
  3. Handle classroom supplies and materials carefully and re-
     turn them to their proper place after use
  4. Have desk cleared and be ready to learn when lessons begin
  5. Pay attention during lessons and learning activities
  6. Participate by volunteering to answer questions
  7. Work carefully on in-school and homework assignments
  8. If you get stuck, try to work out the problem on your own
     before asking for help, but do ask for help if you need it
  9. Turn in assignments completed and on time
  10. Confine conversations to approved times and forms
  11. Treat others with politeness and respect

Additional Role Competencies that Need to Be Developed
in Social Constructivist Classrooms

  1. In whole-class settings, participate as a member of the
     group as we develop new understandings
  2. Recognize that everyone has something to contribute, and
     you are here to learn as well as to help others learn; act
     accordingly
  3. Listen carefully to what others say and relate it to your
     own knowledge and experience (Do you agree? Why or why
     not?)
  4. If you are not sure what others mean, ask for clarification
  5. In putting forth your own ideas, explain your reasoning by
     citing relevant evidence and arguments
  6. In challenging others' ideas and responding to challenges to
     your ideas, focus on the issues and on trying to reach
     agreement; do not get personal or engage in one-upmanship
  7. When working in pairs or small groups, see that each per-
     son's ideas are included and that everyone accomplishes the
     goal of the activity
  8. When helping partners or fellow group members, do not
     just do the work for them; instead, make sure that they
     learn what they need to know

Adapted from Brophy, J., & Alleman, J. (1998). Classroom management in
a social studies learning community. *Social Education, 62*(I), 56–58.

dents will be expected to do, helping them learn to do it, and cuing them when it is time to do it is likely to be more effective than management that focuses on misbehavior and places more emphasis on after-the-fact discipline than on before-the-fact socialization and prevention.

Second, management systems need to support instructional systems. A management system that orients students toward passivity and compliance with rigid rules will undercut the potential effects of an instructional system that is designed to emphasize active learning, higher order thinking, and the social construction of knowledge (McCaslin & Good, 1992).

Third, managerial planning should begin by identifying the student outcomes that constitute the goals of instruction, then considering what these outcomes imply about desired learning activities and about the knowledge, skills, values, and behavioral dispositions that students will need to acquire in order to engage in these learning activities most profitably. This planning process should yield clear articulation of desired student roles, which then become the goal and the rationale for the teacher's management system. The management system will function most smoothly and support the instructional system most effectively if it features clear articulation of desired student roles, supported by whatever structuring and scaffolding may be needed to enable students to learn these roles and to begin to display them on their own when appropriate.

Bibliography

Brophy, J. (1988). Educating teachers about managing classrooms and students. *Teaching and Teacher Education, 4,* 1–18.

Brophy, J., & Alleman, J. (1998). Classroom management in a social studies learning community. *Social Education, 62*(1), 56–58.

Canter, L., & Canter, M. (1992). *Assertive discipline: Positive behavior management for today's classroom* (2nd ed.). Santa Monica, CA: Lee Canter & Associates.

Cohen, E. (1994). *Designing group work: Strategies for heterogeneous classrooms* (2nd ed.). New York: Teachers College Press.

Cuban, L. (1993). *How teachers taught: Constancy and change in American classrooms, 1890–1990* (2nd ed.). New York: Longman.

Doyle, W. (1984). How order is achieved in classrooms: An interim report. *Journal of Curriculum Studies, 16,* 259–277.

Evertson, C. (1987). Managing classrooms: A framework for teachers. In D. Berliner & B. Rosenshine (Eds.), *Talks to teachers* (pp. 54–74). New York: Random House.

Evertson, C., & Emmer, E. (1982). Effective management at the beginning of the school year in junior high classes. *Journal of Educational Psychology, 74,* 485–498.

Good, T., & Brophy, J. (1995). *Contemporary educational psychology* (5th ed.). White Plains, NY: Longman.

Good, T., & Brophy, J. (2000). *Looking in classrooms* (8th ed.). New York: Longman.

Gottfredson, D., Gottfredson, G., & Hybl, L. (1993). Managing adolescent behavior: A multi-year, multi-school study. *American Educational Research Journal, 30,* 179–215.

Hallinan, M., & Sorensen, A. (1985). Ability grouping and student friendships. *American Educational Research Journal, 22,* 485–499.

Jackson, P. (1985). Private lessons in public schools: Remarks on the limits of adaptive instruction. In M. Wang & H. Walberg (Eds.), *Adapting instruction to individual differences* (pp. 66–81). Berkeley, CA: McCutchan.

Jones, V. (1996). Classroom management. In J. Sikula, T. Buttery, & E. Guyton (Eds.), *Handbook of research on teacher education* (Vol. 2, pp. 503–521). New York: Macmillan.

Kounin, J. (1970). *Discipline and group management in classrooms.* New York: Holt, Rinehart & Winston.

Kulik, J., & Kulik, C. (1989). Meta-analysis in education. *International Journal of Educational Research, 13,* 221–340.

McCaslin, M., & Good, T. (1992). Compliant cognition: The misalliance of management and instructional goals in current school reform. *Educational Researcher, 21,* 4–17.

Palincsar, A., & Brown, A. (1989). Classroom dialogues to promote self-regulated comprehension. In J. Brophy (Ed.), *Advances in research on teaching* (Vol. 1, pp. 105–151). Greenwich, CT: JAI.

Rogers, C., & Freiberg, J. (1994). *Freedom to learn* (3d ed.). Columbus, OH: Merrill.

Slavin, R. (1984). Component building: A strategy for research-based instructional improvement. *Elementary School Journal, 84,* 255–269.

Jere Brophy

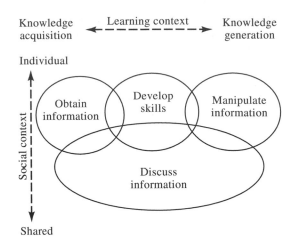

CLASSROOMS: Technology. Figure 1. Student learning activities facilitated by classroom technology.

Technology

Taken most broadly, technology refers to the application of knowledge for practical ends, and the field of technology studies considers the role technology plays in society and the ethical issues and social consequences of its use. Such a comprehensive view of technology, however, is too broad for the purposes of this article. Consequently, the following discussion restricts the definition of classroom technology to electronic devices, usually programmable, used by teachers and students to understand the subject matter and to develop the cognitive skills defined by a curriculum or course of study.

Student Cognitive Activities and the Contexts of Classroom Technology Use

Although available classroom technology encompasses a vast number of software programs, computer platforms, peripheral devices, and electronic interconnections, the common thread among these technologies is the way in which they are used in the classroom. Technology is a tool that can facilitate students' learning. Although it can be its own subject of study (for example, courses in computer programming or in the use of specific software), it is more frequently used to help students learn about something else. It can be controlled by the teacher or the student (or both) and can be used in the service of diverse learning objectives.

Figure 1 presents a heuristic diagram that organizes classroom technology use according to four cognitive activities and the social and learning contexts that define its application. Students and teachers use classroom technology to obtain, manipulate, or discuss information. Students also use technology to help them develop skills necessary for learning about and understanding the world. These four functions are indicated by the overlapping circles in Figure 1, which also denotes the social and learning contexts of technology use. These contexts define with whom technology will be used and the nature of the learning activities undertaken. Classroom learning is often complex and combines a number of discrete cognitive activities or social arrangements. Consequently, the precise placement of a learning activity on one or the other context continuum is often difficult. We speak then of emphases rather than typologies.

Technology can be used by an individual student in a solitary social context, such as a library workstation or a private area of the classroom, or, through the use of computer networks, images and information can be shared by many, displayed nearly simultaneously throughout the world. These usage patterns are distinguished by their social context. Similarly, classroom assignments can require students to acquire specific knowledge, develop cognitive skills, or to generate new knowledge. An example of knowledge acquisition is when students read how different eyewitnesses described the bombing of Pearl Harbor. Students develop skills when they memorize math facts or become competent chess players. Knowledge generation occurs when students are called on to solve problems for which the answer is unknown or for which there are multiple correct answers. An assignment that requires knowledge generation might ask students to investigate pollution in nearby streams and identify its source.

Although classroom technology may facilitate the completion of some types of assignments and extend classroom resources, by itself, it has little or no impact on student learning, just as a hammer has little impact on the style of a house being constructed. The content students learn is defined by the learning tasks and social conditions implicitly and explicitly organized by the teacher. Classroom technology should always be considered in conjunction with the teacher's pedagogical intent, the nature of the material being learned, the cognitive activities necessary to complete the learning, and the social context within which it is used.

Obtaining Information. Although educators increasingly emphasize the importance of helping students to think critically and to solve complex problems, there remains a common canon of knowledge that students must understand and remember. This information includes, for example, important dates in history, the periodic table of elements, and the story of the decline of the Roman Empire. Technology can be used by the teacher to enhance didactic presentations, or it can be used to engage student learning and supplement (or supplant) traditional teaching.

Teachers have long used overhead projectors to display lecture notes or diagrams. An earlier generation of instructors accompanied their lectures with sixteen-millimeter motion pictures. Today, teachers frequently rely on classroom video—both live and prerecorded—to complement their instruction or to provide students with new information. Such programs break down the classroom walls and bring distant experts or events inside. Presentation software programs and projection devices enable teachers to use graphic diagrams, animations, and sound to communicate information.

As with books, students can use classroom technology to obtain knowledge directly without teacher intervention. Multimedia CD-ROMs make reference works come alive by mixing text, animation, and video with accompanying narration and musical background. The World Wide Web provides an array of multimedia websites dedicated to specific topics and subject areas that incorporate sound, animation, and video.

Developing Skills. Information is a necessary ingredient of learning, but it is also an inert one. If students are to use—rather than simply recall—information, they must develop cognitive skills. These include learning the rules and regularities of mathematics, the structure and syntax of good writing, the ability to recognize the central ideas in written passages, and the relationships among musical notes. Although many have been enthusiastic about the potential of technology to "teach" students these and many other skills, the success of using computers as "teaching machines" has not been adequately measured.

There are many software programs designed to teach students basic academic skills. Often disguised as games, these programs provide extensive opportunities for student drill and practice. Integrated Learning Systems (ILS) are more sophisticated versions of these drill-and-practice programs and utilize net-worked computer systems to deliver instruction. They not only provide individual instruction to students on a specific set of concepts and skills, they test students' concept acquisition and modify future instruction on the basis of whether students were successful in learning earlier concepts. By so doing, an ILS can provide slower students with additional tutoring and skip rapidly through concepts with students who catch on immediately.

Research on the effectiveness of ILS presents ambiguous results. Becker (1992) concludes that students in elementary and middle grades "generally do at least somewhat better using ILS than they would be expected to do" but points out that such results are often contingent on the ability of the teacher to understand student gaps in learning and to integrate classroom and ILS instruction. Although ILS systems are often argued to be especially beneficial to low-achieving students, Hativa and Lesgold (1996) found that high-achieving students are the greatest beneficiaries. They observed high-achieving students master material that was two or more grade levels above their current grade. While low-achieving students reported dissatisfaction with ILS instruction and fell behind. It appears that ILS work best with motivated learners who are more focused on the learning goal than on the experience of learning and who perceive repetitive tutoring by machine as a tolerable means to a valued end.

Manipulating Information. In the previous sections, classroom technology was discussed as a support or substitute for didactic instruction. Although such technology use can be pedagogically effective, it does not exploit technology's unique strength as a tool to manipulate information and thereby enable students to generate new knowledge.

Many readers are familiar with the power of word processing software to manipulate text and desktop publishing software to manipulate graphics and design documents. Drawing, graphics, or presentation software programs enable individuals to create and change images. Calculator, spreadsheet, and statistical analysis software programs allow students to manipulate numbers and to perform complex calculations. Simulation software enables students to create scenarios and then test these situations against specified criteria. Modeling programs help students use their observations and measurements to create mathematical models or graphical representations of phenomena and their relationships.

These examples demonstrate how classroom technology enables students to manipulate information and to accomplish tasks more readily and with greater precision than was possible before the introduction of computers. Whether this enhanced ability to manipulate information results in greater student learning and the generation of new knowledge, however, depends on the nature of classroom learning tasks and expectations for student performance, as well as the learning goals students pursue. When classroom technology is a tool for knowledge generation, teachers' instructional strategies change. Assigned tasks become more complex and more loosely defined. Problems are confronted for which there is not a single correct answer. Lessons often take longer to complete as assignments become projects with multiple participants, numerous steps, and unusual and idiosyncratic outcomes (working models of phenomena, statistical projections, animated or illustrated narratives).

Although such complex uses of classroom technology are often advocated on the basis of helping students to gain learning-to-learn and problem-solving skills, for such progressive pedagogy to be successful, students must be self-disciplined and motivated, and teachers must be skilled in structuring student learning and governing classroom behavior. As students are given increasing responsibility for defining and carrying out loosely structured learning activities, the possibility of entropic disintegration increases, and key learning opportunities are often restricted to the brightest or most verbal students. To realize the possibilities afforded by classroom technology and associated project-oriented instruction, teachers must model appropriate behavior, continually assess student performance, manipulate task and group assignments, and scaffold and guide student learning.

Discussing Information. With the ability to translate text, pictures, sound, video, and animations into digital data and the increasing connection of classrooms to the Internet, teachers and students have the opportunity to use computer-mediated communication to share and discuss information. Digital documents can include essays, video, sound files, and scanned drawings and graphics and can be shared asynchronously (individuals communicate at different times and store their messages in a central computer) or synchronously (individuals communicate instantaneously, in "real time"). Synchronous video conferencing provides an opportunity for multiple groups of students in schools dispersed around the world to share and dispute findings, much as if they were sitting in the same classroom. These discussions can be augmented by software that creates a virtual whiteboard, which allows participants to display, annotate, or modify graphic diagrams. Although computer networks allow students and teachers to converse across vast distances, conversations by themselves have limited pedagogical usefulness. When student learning is the desired outcome, discourse is most useful when it engenders student reflection and consideration of ideas. Consequently, the purpose of computer-mediated discussions and the structure in which they take place are key factors in maximizing student learning.

A more humble way classroom technology enables students and teachers to discuss information is through the use of listservs, software programs that automatically copy a contributor's e-mail message to all members of the list. Members then have the opportunity to read or to reply to other member's postings. Newsgroups and Web-based message boards provide a similar opportunity for discussion and debate on specific topics, or "threads." Discussions can last for weeks and are generally archived and made available to those who missed the original exchanges. There are now thousands of listservs and newsgroups focusing on every conceivable topic. For example, students (or teachers) can join in discussions of Thomas Jefferson with amateur history buffs and professional historians or discuss international politics with members in other countries.

Although listservs, newsgroups, and message boards provide the infrastructure to create worldwide virtual communities in which individuals discuss matters of mutual interest, their contribution as tools for learning depends completely on the nature of these discussions and the way they are integrated into course demands and expectations.

Future Trends

Technology is becoming cheaper and more pervasive in classrooms and in homes. Digital information sources on Internet servers continue to proliferate. As a consequence, information is more easily accessible, and students increasingly turn to computers, rather than to books, for information. The ready availability of information enables teachers to reorganize their instructional role, moving primarily from that of knowledge expert to manager of student learning. Whether the majority of teachers will make significant shifts in their instructional role, however, is not clear. Cuban (1986) has documented how little new classroom technologies have changed teaching in the last 70 years. This is not surprising. It is not technology that will change classrooms but teachers and students. Students will have to take increasing responsibility for their own learning, and teachers will have to revise traditional classroom behavior and conceive new ways to challenge, scaffold, guide, and support student learning, if the educational opportunities afforded by technology's ability to manipulate information are to be realized. Such a fundamental change in the interlocking roles of students and teachers is not easy. It will require pedagogical reform, not merely the addition of computers.

Bibliography

Becker, H. J. (1992). Computer-based integrated learning systems in the elementary and middle grades: A critical review and synthesis of evaluation reports. *Journal of Educational Computing Research, 8* (1), 1–41. Many evaluations of Integrated Learning Systems were commissioned by manufacturers to "prove" that computer-based instruction was effective. Others were conducted by researchers interested in the usefulness of this new technology. Becker examines these reports and concludes that although ILS can be useful tools to increase student achievement, they are not a panacea.

Cuban, L. (1986). *Teachers and machines: The use of classroom technology since 1920.* New York: Teachers College Press. Cuban describes how visionaries predicted new classroom technologies of film, radio, television, and computers would significantly change the nature of schooling and then shows how similar today's schools and classrooms are to those of the past. This is a sobering book for those advocating the revolutionary impact of classroom technology.

Hativa, N., & Lesgold, A. (1996). Situational effects in classroom technology implementations: Unfilled expectations and unexpected outcomes. In S. T. Kerr (Ed.), *Technology and the future of schooling: Ninety-fifth yearbook of the National Society for the Study of Education* (pp. 131–171). Chicago: University of Chicago Press. Hativa and Lesgold provide interesting case studies of students and teachers using Integrated Learning Systems and describe how the contexts of schools and classrooms lead to unanticipated and adverse results.

Means, B. (Ed.). (1994). *Technology and educational reform: The reality behind the promise.* San Francisco: Jossey-Bass. Means and her coauthors describe how technology can be used to support and extend school reform by portraying successful examples of classroom technology being used to change the traditional classroom and to accomplish new goals. The authors speculate on how technology can be most effective in increasing student learning and improving teacher training.

Scardamalia, M., Bereiter, C. V., & Lamon, M. (1994). CSILE: Trying to bring students into the world 3. In K. McGilley (Ed.), *Classroom lessons: Integrating cognitive theory and classroom practice* (pp. 201–228). Cambridge, MA: MIT Press. CSILE is a networked computer environment that enables students to share information, questions, and hypotheses while seeking answers to a common problem. As students pursue their investigations, they enter their thoughts into a common database that can be searched by keyword, author, date, or topic. All entries are public and can be linked to other entries, thus forming discussion threads and stimulating further exploration. The article provides good examples of how classroom technology can be used to stimulate thinking and discussion.

Schank, R. C., & Cleary, C. (1995). *Engines for education.* Hillsdale, NJ: Erlbaum. Schank and Cleary provide a thoughtful consideration of how computers can be used in innovative ways to change the basic structure of teaching and learning. There are concrete examples of software programs and instructional strategies that make use of technology to manipulate information and to make students more responsible for their own learning.

U.S. Congress, Office of Technology Assessment. (1995). *Teachers and technology: Making the connection* (OTA-EHR-616). Washington, DC: U.S. Government Printing Office. (http://www.ota.nap.edu/pdf/data/1995/9541. PDF). This national study was commissioned by Congress to explore how teachers were using technology in 1994 and to consider the roles of schools, states, the private sector, and the federal government in integrating technology into the classroom. It provides good statistics about the prevalence of computers and computer use by teachers and students and contains several vignettes about exemplary teacher training programs in school districts and colleges of education.

U.S. Congress, Office of Technology Assessment. (1995). *Education and technology: Future visions* (OTA-BP-EHR-169). Washington, DC: U.S. Government Printing Office. (http://www.ota.nap.edu/pdf/data/1995/9522. PDF). Five distinguished educators describe their own scenarios about the future of education and technology. Some scenarios require significant changes in schools and the way they operate. Others are more cautious regarding the changes computer technology can and will bring to classrooms and schools. The document also summarizes key points of discussions held among the authors.

John R. Mergendoller

CLIENT-CENTERED THERAPY or person-centered therapy is an approach that focuses on the client as an individual who has self-actualizing potential. The fundamental assumption is that if therapists provide the facilitative conditions of empathy, unconditional positive regard (warmth), and genuineness (congruence), clients will come to accept themselves and will be able to unblock their natural growth tendencies. Hence, therapists are not the authorities with the answers but people who care deeply about clients and trust them to set their own goals and come up with their own answers. Client/person-centered therapy fits within the tradition of humanistic and experiential therapy and philosophy (for examples, the work of Binswanger, Boss, Bugenthal, Frankl, May, Perls, Yalom) because of its beliefs in phenomenology, an actualizing or growth tendency, self-determination, and respect for the person.

History and Development

Client-centered therapy arose in reaction to the diagnostic, prescriptive, impersonal, authoritarian tradition of psychological treatment in the United States in the 1930s. During this period, the role of therapists was to understand and interpret client dynamics, whereas only minor attention was given to therapist behavior. Another important historical influence was the American culture of optimism and the valuing of scientific evidence.

The first period of client-centered therapy began with Carl R. Rogers listening to his clients and trying to follow each client's lead. His theoretical propositions followed from his experiences doing counseling and psychotherapy. Rogers presented his initial ideas in his book *The Clinical Treatment of the Problem Child* (1939), in a 1940 address to the Psi Chi chapter at the University of Minnesota on "Some Newer Concepts of Psychotherapy," and in *Counseling and Psychotherapy* (1942). He proposed that therapists be "nondirective," acting as midwives to establish a permissive, noninterpretive atmosphere of acceptance and clarification. Furthermore, he suggested that therapists respond to feelings rather than to content and accept whatever feelings are expressed, with the goal of allowing clients to achieve insight into their own situations.

The second period began with the publication of *Client-Centered Therapy* in 1951. During this period, Rogers shifted from thinking about the use of techniques (such as clarification of feelings) to suggesting that therapists must possess a facilitative attitude or orientation of acceptance. Rogers increasingly attended to the client's phenomenological experience as the only reality. He believed that self-actualization was possible if therapists could unconditionally prize and attend to the client's frame of reference. Rogers (1957) formulated six propositions about necessary and sufficient conditions for therapeutic change: (a) the client and therapist must be in psychological contact, (b) the client must be in a state of incongruity, (c) the therapist must be in a state of congruity for this client, (d) the therapist must feel unconditional positive regard for the client, (e) the therapist must feel empathy for the client, and (f) the client must experience the therapist as congruent, unconditional in regard, and empathic. Rogers still viewed therapists as mirrors in that their primary role was to reflect to clients what they heard and experienced from them in an effort to help clients develop congruence of self-concept and experience.

The third period was introduced by the publication of *On Becoming a Person* (Boston, 1961). In this stage, client-centered therapy was relabeled person-centered therapy because its principles were being applied to education, groups, industry, and other human relations contexts. In addition, Rogers reconceptualized the role of therapists as he came to believe that therapists could be more effective if they were more spontaneous and expressive of their own feelings, which he postulated would lead to greater mutuality in the relationship.

The fourth period evolved in the later years of Rogers's life and was characterized by Rogers's move into more global issues, such as world peace and conflict resolution. During this period, a number of counselor training programs for teaching specific helping skills based on Rogers's theory were developed (for example, by Carkhuff, Egan, Ivey, Kagan, Truax). Extensions of the theory were also made by Thomas Gordon to teaching skills to parents and teachers, by Bernard Guerney to family therapy, by Virginia Axline to play therapy, by Eugene Gendlin to experimental therapy, and by Robert Carkhuff to helping skills training.

Although interest in client-centered therapy declined during the 1980s, perhaps because of its association with the encounter group and counterculture movement in the 1960s and 1970s, interest appears to be reviving. Rogers had discouraged the institutionalization of client-centered therapy, so it was only during the late 1970s that a journal (*Person-centered Review*) was started. An international organization started in 1988.

The main change has been that client-centered principles have been absorbed into almost every form of therapy, such that most therapies now consider the facilitative conditions to be necessary although not always sufficient. Furthermore, recent theoretical and empirical innovations, particularly by Leslie Greenberg and associates (e.g., Greenberg, Rice, & Elliott, 1993), have created a merger between client-centered and Gestalt therapies such that the facilitative conditions set the foundation for the implementation of specific interventions.

Theory of the Development of Personality

Client-centered theory postulates that children are born with a natural curiosity and a striving for self-actualization. They evaluate events in their environment through an organismic valuing process (OVP), which indicates to them which things enhance their organism and which do not.

Rogers postulated that children, at birth, do not have a "self" but develop a sense of self as they distinguish themselves from others. Rogers also believed that children have a need for positive regard from others, in that they need to be accepted, respected, and loved. If children feel prized, they can go on to fulfill their blueprint for self-actualization. If parents, however, put a lot of conditions of worth of their children, the children will start trying to please their parents instead of following their OVP. Heeding the conditions of worth leads them to grow apart from their internal experiences. Hence, conditions of worth can lead to a split between the real and ideal self.

A person feels "threat" when she or he perceives an incongruity between experience and self-concept and feels "anxiety" when the self is in danger. Too many feelings of anxiety lead to the development of defenses, which serve to reduce incongruity and anxiety. Two typical defenses are perceptual distortion (which alters the way that experience is perceived) and denial (which disavows the experience). Defenses keep the incongruent experiences out of awareness and allow the self to function. However, if the distortions and denial cause the person to get too far from his or her internal experience, the person can disintegrate.

For reintegration to occur, the person must reduce conditions of worth and/or increase positive self-regard. When the person gets unconditional positive regard from another person, the conditions of worth lose their significance, and the person can become more open to his or her experience. Rogers believed that a person usually needs a helping relationship to reintegrate.

Techniques and Practices of Therapy

Rather than using specific techniques, client-centered therapists rely on a facilitative attitude or orientation toward attending and listening carefully to the client. Client-centered therapists believe that if they accept clients at a deep level, clients will come to accept themselves. Empathy, or trying to understand the person from the person's frame of reference, is the most fundamental and important attitude. Rogers (1951) described almost merging with clients in an effort to understand what they are thinking and feeling and to help them explore and verbalize these thoughts and feelings. Thus, at a deep level, empathy enables therapists to feel their clients' feelings. Unconditional positive regard means valuing the client's experience without judgment. Congruence means not having discrepancies between experience and expression, and, relatedly, genuineness means being able to be who one truly is with clients. Through empathy, unconditional positive regard, and congruence (or genuineness), the goal is to reduce the discrepancy between clients' real and ideal selves, to help clients experience more of their inner feelings, and to help clients gain insight and unleash their creative potential. In summary, if therapists accept clients, clients can come to accept themselves. The organismic valuing process is unblocked, and clients can heal themselves.

Client-centered therapists do not generally diagnose or interpret. The goal of client-centered therapists is not to be the authority who figures out problems and tells clients what to do; instead, the goal is to unblock the clients' natural capacities so that they can begin to solve their own problems.

The goal for clients is to move along a continuum of growth, facilitated by therapists who accept them as they are. At the lowest end of the continuum, clients have a rigidity of perception and feel no need to change themselves. Clients begin to have a dim perception of their problems, often seeing problems as residing in others rather than in themselves. In the next step, clients treat the self as an object and do not own their feelings. Then, clients have a partial recognition and greater flexibility of feelings but still are often in the past rather than involved in present feelings. As they progress, clients have an improved recognition of feel-

ings and want to be the "real me." Clients move to being able to accept feelings with richness. Finally, new feelings are experienced fully in the present moment, and clients are flexible, trustworthy, and capable of growth and change.

Research Findings

One of Rogers's major contributions was his insistence on examining therapy empirically. Earl F. Zinn developed methods of recording therapy sessions so that they could be studied (a radical change from the sanctuary of the closed doors of practicing therapists). Initial research by Elias Hull Porter (1943), Frank R. Robinson (1950), and William V. Snyder (1945) focused on developing taxonomies and rating scales of therapist and client behaviors and then examining the interactions between therapists and clients. Butler and Haigh developed a Q-sort technique, which allows people to make comparative judgments about themselves, as a way of investigating discrepancies between the perceived and ideal self. Godfrey J. Barrett-Lennard (1962) developed the Relationship Inventory, which has been widely used to investigate the effects of the facilitative conditions. A major project that Rogers was involved in applied client-centered principles to treatment of schizophrenics and found that the facilitative conditions were also important in this population (Rogers, Gendlin, Kiesler, & Truax, 1967). One of the major fruits of this research was the development of the Experiencing Scale (Klein, Mathieu-Coughlan, & Kiesler, 1986) and the Vocal Quality Scale (Rice & Kerr, 1986) to assess the process of client change.

The major findings from this body of research involve the evidence that the therapist-offered facilitative conditions are positively related to therapy outcome. Whether the facilitative conditions are necessary and sufficient or whether they are necessary but not sufficient has been a matter of controversy in the field. Furthermore, although a relationship has been established between the facilitative conditions and outcome, evidence for a cause-effect relationship between facilitative conditions and outcome is still lacking. In addition, some researchers suggest that the facilitative conditions are important for all clients, whereas others argue that the facilitative conditions may be applicable only to client-centered therapy or only for mild conditions rather than severe disorders. A number of critical reviews of the literature have found client-centered therapy to be equivalent to (neither better nor worse than) other theoretical approaches.

The recent emphasis in research has shifted away from the therapist facilitative conditions to the therapeutic relationship. Researchers have become aware that client characteristics and the therapist-client alliance contribute to the relationship, so examining the therapist conditions alone is not sufficient. Research suggests that the relationship may be more important than therapist techniques in facilitating client change.

Conclusions

Client-centered therapy has made a major impact on the field of psychology. Initially, it, along with other humanistic theories, was considered so different from psychoanalytic and behavioral therapies that it was considered the third force in psychotherapy. Client-centered therapy forced therapists to rethink the way they did therapy, to focus more on their behaviors and the climate they established in the therapeutic relationship. It also fostered a healthy appreciation of the need for research on the effective components of psychotherapy. Currently, the client-centered principles of empathy, unconditional positive regard, and genuineness have been included as foundations for almost every form of therapy. Furthermore, client-centered principles have had an impact on many other fields, such as education, parenting, and conflict resolution.

[See also the biography of Rogers.]

Bibliography

Barrett-Lennard, G. T. (1962). Dimensions of therapist response as causal factors in therapeutic change. *Psychological Monographs, 76* (43, Whole No. 562).

Greenberg, L. S., Rice, L. N., & Elliott, R. (1993). *Facilitating emotional change.* New York: Guilford Press.

Klein, M. H., Mathieu-Coughlan, P., & Kiesler, D. J. (1986). The Experiencing Scale. In L. S. Greenberg & W. M. Pinsof (Eds.), *The psychotherapeutic process: A research handbook* (pp. 21–72). New York: Guilford Press.

Porter, E. H. Jr. (1943). The development and evaluation of a measure of counseling interview procedures. *Educational and Psychological Measurement, 3,* 105–126.

Raskin, N. J., & Rogers, C. R. (1995). Person-centered therapy. In R. J. Corsini & D. Wedding (Eds.), *Current psychotherapies* (5th ed., pp. 128–161). Itasca, IL: Peacock Publishers.

Rice, L. N., & Greenberg, L. S. (1992). Humanistic approaches to psychotherapy. In D. K. Freedheim (Ed.), *History of psychology: A century of change* (pp. 197–224). Washington DC: American Psychological Association.

Rice, L. N., & Kerr, G. P. (1986). Measures of client and therapist vocal quality. In L. S. Greenberg & W. M. Pinsof (Eds.), *The psychotherapeutic process: A research handbook* (pp. 73–106). New York: Guilford Press.

Robinson, F. R. (1950). *Principles and procedures in student counseling.* New York: Harper.

Rogers, C. R. (1951). *Client-centered therapy: Its current practice, implications, and theory.* Boston: Houghton Mifflin.

Rogers, C. R. (1957). The necessary and sufficient conditions of therapeutic personality change. *Journal of Consulting Psychology, 21,* 95–103.

Rogers, C. R. (1964). In retrospect: Forty-six years. *American Psychologist, 29,* 115–123.

Rogers, C. R. (1967). Carl R. Rogers. In E. G. Boring & G. Lindzey (Eds.), *A history of psychology in autobiography* (Vol. 5). New York: Appleton-Century-Croft.

Rogers, C. R., Gendlin, E. T., Kiesler, D. J., & Truax, C. B. (1967). *The therapeutic relationship and its impact: A study of psychotherapy with schizophrenics.* Madison, WI: University of Wisconsin Press.

Snyder, W. U. (1945). An investigation of the nature of nondirective psychotherapy. *Journal of General Psychology, 33,* 193–223.

Truax, C. B., & Mitchell, K. M. (1971). Research on certain therapist interpersonal skills in relation to process and outcome. In A. E. Bergin and S. L. Garfield (Eds.), *Handbook of psychotherapy and behavior change* (pp. 299–344). New York: Wiley.

Zimring, F. M., & Raskin, N. J. (1992). Carl Rogers and client/person-centered therapy. In D. K. Freedheim (Ed.), *History of psychology: A century of change* (pp. 629–656). Washington DC: American Psychological Association.

Clara E. Hill

CLINICAL GEROPSYCHOLOGY might also be called the clinical psychology of later life. The theoretical substance of clinical geropsychology derives from the concepts of general psychology, and much of its content derives from the multidisciplinary field of gerontology. Clinical geropsychology represents the application of psychological knowledge to the assessment and treatment of psychopathological conditions and, more broadly, to efforts to improve quality of life by changing the behavior, cognition, affect, and contexts of older people.

History

There have been four major directions of effort in this area: assessment, psychotherapy, life enhancement, and programmatic and environmental intervention. Among these, assessment of older people was one of the earliest directions of interest in geropsychology, including the assessment of cognitive and motor skills, memory, psychomotor functions, neuropsychological testing, and differential intelligence test performance, as embedded in Wechsler's measures of intelligence. By contrast, psychotherapy for older people was rarely addressed until the 1990s, a delay no doubt strongly influenced by Freud's conviction that older people were unable to benefit from psychoanalysis. Clinical geropsychology was absent from the first *Handbook of Aging and the Individual* (Birren, 1959), the first book on aging, published by the American Psychological Association (APA) (Anderson, 1959), and was so poorly represented in the field by the time the 1973 APA book (Eisdorfer & Lawton, 1973) was published that a question mark was included in the section title: "Clinical Psychology?" The

Eisdorfer and Lawton book and a subsequent book by Storandt, Siegler, and Elias (1978) helped coalesce the effort to recognize and define a clinical psychology of later life.

The American Psychological Association and its Division 20 (Adult Development and Aging) and more recently section 2 (Aging) of Division 12 (Clinical Psychology) constituted a major force in responding to the needs of its own members in advancing the development of geropsychology. In 1981, the "Older Boulder" conference was convened, whose theme was training and practice in clinical geropsychology. This meeting included foci on the knowledge base in psychology, the technologies of assessment, psychotherapy, and other interventions, and the first detailed consideration of training at multiple levels (undergraduate, graduate, internship, professional, continuing education, and credentialing issues). This conference was described in detail in an APA publication, *Psychology and the Older Adult*, edited by Santos and VandenBos (1982). A follow-up conference was held by APA in 1992 (Knight, Teri, Wohlford, & Santos, 1995) whose general tone was one of dissatisfaction with the progress made since Older Boulder in advancing the professionalization of clinical geropsychology and specifically in funding training at the undergraduate, graduate, and professional levels. In 1997 the APA was in the process of strengthening its administrative structure in support of both general geropsychology and clinical geropsychology. The 1997 annual meeting under APA president Norman Abeles sponsored the first aging miniconvention, entitled "Psychology and the Aging Revolution." Other formal organizations serving the clinical geropsychologist include Psychologists in Long Term Care, which has a more limited but very active presence in this area. The Gerontological Society of America sponsors a multi-disciplinary interest group, Mental Health and Aging. The Department of Veteran's Affairs, the largest employer of psychologists, has engaged in a number of activities that have benefited the growth of clinical geropsychology.

Theoretical and Knowledge Base

The four major application areas of geropsychology have their roots in four theoretically distinct domains: Perceptual-motor and cognitive psychology, developmental psychology and personality, social stress and support, and environmental psychology. All four classic streams of research contributed, in varying degrees, to each of the areas of application in addition to those most direct influences.

Like general psychology, geropsychology began with the study of perceptual-motor performance, learning, memory, and intelligence. One sees the direct descendants of this research in contemporary activities related to cognitive training, memory training, behavior therapy, and cognitive therapy. Current clinical neuropsychology drew on these research origins, as well as from neuroscience. Clinical assessment was strongly influenced by the extensive use of the Wechsler-Bellevue Scale and the analysis of subtest profiles by age, continuing into the present in general clinical assessment and functional assessment. The thrust of much of this research was to demonstrate an age decline in many such functions, a conclusion that came to be greatly moderated by research stemming from the developmental approach.

Although "developmental psychology" does not denote a psychological function in the sense that cognition does, it came to represent the most important worldview in this discipline. That is, the inclusion of adulthood and aging as stages of biopsychological growth represents a breakthrough in general psychology for which geropsychology was responsible. The general developmental theories of Piaget and Erikson led to the seminal contributions by Charlotte Bühler, Warner Schaie, Klaus Riegel, and Paul Baltes. Schaie's formulation of age, cohort, and time-related effects made plain the social and intrapersonal sources of possible change in the life trajectories of people and the incomplete picture that cross-sectional age comparisons provided in the study of any psychological phenomenon. One of the central latent variables in human development is the concept of motivation to achieve one's purpose in life. For example, the phenomenon that Baltes et al. (1984) called selective optimization with compensation was consistent with continuity theory in its explanation of how people preserve what is valued most in their personalities, while relinquishing less valued behaviors. This dynamism has obvious uses in various forms of psychotherapy. Recognition of the relative stability of personality structure is essential to good therapy. The dialectics of change and stability in the individual are particularly well illustrated in the work of Bernice Neugarten, Robert Havighurst, and their colleagues at the University of Chicago in the 1960s. Kastenbaum provided an early contribution to the dynamics of death as a personal and social issue as well as recognition of a number of subjective phenomena (1964). The most evident set of pathways to modern geropsychological practice stemmed from the early research on social processes and social stress and adaptation. Research on social attitudes toward aging by both older and younger people that was pioneered by Tuckman and Lorge (1952) and was continued in the research of Kogan (1961) strongly influenced current concepts of positive mental health. Virtually every individually oriented intervention has included in its approaches the basic ideas of dealing with age stereotyping and rejection versus acceptance of one's own aging.

Social stress, broadly speaking, came to the fore in

several early gerontologists' work. Chronologically first was Cumming and Henry's (1961) disengagement theory, which, despite its major intrapsychic developmental emphasis, focused equally on the pressure exerted by society to dislodge the aging person from some of its supportive structures. Some of the richest applications of Henry Murray's (1938) personology are combined with a transactional view of society's interplay with the individual in Cumming and Henry's (1961) detailing of these processes in *Growing Old*.

Another branch of the University of Chicago enterprise was exemplified by the explicit focus on institutionalization as a source of stress for frail elders, seen in the program of research undertaken by Lieberman and Tobin (1983). Among the many contemporary messages from their work are two thoughts essential to every interventionist. First, stressed elders, even those with diminished resources, cope with stress and find new, usually acceptable, modes of adaptation. Second, the expectation of change is as potent, if not more potent, a stressor as change itself. Residential change and adaptation remain salient concerns for the clients of many practitioners.

The third important stream, like the others, wedded social stress to the interior of the person. Marjorie Fiske (then Lowenthal) contributed an empirically derived concept that has not only stimulated an immense amount of later research but also become embedded in virtually every variety of individual or program intervention. Social isolation is a risk factor for mental illness in old age, and the existence of an intimate relationship can moderate the negative effects of other stressors on mental health (Lowenthal & Haven, 1968). The substantial literature on caregiver services and support groups of all kinds is based on knowledge regarding both normal social attitudes, social support, and stress related outcomes. Specialized interventions for clinical mental health problems and for many stress-induced situations short of clinical pathology depend heavily on these early investigators' work. Finally, geropsychologists' participation in self-actualization and quality of life–enhancement endeavors for elders in general has been heavily influenced by this intellectual tradition.

The application of stress theory informed by physiological and biological psychology is seen in health psychology and preventive programs applied to elders. Interventions such as exercise, nutrition, education, and illness-focused support groups represent applications of geropsychology that are not limited to clinical psychopathology.

Environmental psychology is the fourth intellectual thread to be followed in the history of geropsychology. Welford (1958) provided the earliest gerontological research of the human-factors type, though his interest was more strongly in the human skill aspect than in the task or the person-machine interface. The contributions of Fozard (1981) were required to turn gerontology's attention formally into the human factors arena. Kleemeier (1959), Carp (1966), and Lawton and Nahemow (1973) provided conceptual structures for comprehending person-environment transactions. These and later contributions eventuated in a very active set of related endeavors in applying knowledge of person-environment principles in later life to a number of focal areas: planned housing, home rehabilitation, institutional design (including specialized settings for Alzheimer's disease patients), product design, adaptive devices, work and transportation environments, and various forms of programmatic psychosocial intervention that might be called milieu therapies, such as the early work of Wilma Donahue on the geriatric wards of a mental hospital.

This brief sketch of the major types of knowledge in geropsychology illustrates that a far more general base of knowledge than that of clinical psychology alone was required to provide the expertise utilized by clinical geropsychologists. The same knowledge base that afforded insights into the process of normal adult development was what created clinical expertise. Applications of such knowledge underlie the contributions of psychology to the betterment of the lives of both normal and pathological and endowed and deprived people as they move through later developmental periods of life.

Contemporary Clinical Geropsychology

The major arenas of activity, in addition to research, are in clinical practice, life enhancement, training, and policy regarding psychological services for older people. Clinical practice consists of clinical assessment, therapy, and programmatic and environmental intervention.

Assessment. Clinical assessment refers to psychological evaluation of the individual performed by fully professionally trained clinicians, while functional assessment refers to structured evaluative measures of behavioral and psychological attributes of behavioral and psychological attributes that may be administered by nonclinicians as screening devices prior to clinical assessment.

Two compelling clinical needs currently drive the practice of clinical assessment: assessing cognitive function and assessing depression. Advances in neuroscience have led psychologists to the continued improvement of formal neuropsychological testing methods focused on specific nervous system functions that in turn aid in neurological differential diagnosis. Public awareness of Alzheimer's disease (AD), combined with the absence of definitive *in vivo* biological diagnostic signs of AD, have made the neuropsychological test battery a necessary and often routine part of the diagnostic battery for older people in many settings. There is extensive use of neuropsychological testing in forensic science, age and employment issues, and in the determination of legal competence. Perhaps the greatest usefulness of cognitive testing is its ability to track change over time from a baseline level.

Assessing depression is often accomplished through brief screening measures that are related to diagnoses of the American Psychiatric Association's *Diagnostical and Statistical Manual of Mental Disorders* (Washington, D.C., 1994) but do not reproduce clinical diagnoses of depression. Other types of personality assessment are relatively infrequently used. Over the years a trickle of published papers have appeared in the literature dealing with the use of structured tests such as the Minnesota Multiphasic Personality Inventory (MMPI and MMPI-2), or projective tests. Because long-term psychotherapy is infrequently reimbursed and therefore infrequently used with older clients, in-depth personality assessment is also infrequent.

Psychologists have taken a major role in the development of functional assessment tools for use in both mental health and non–mental health service settings. Functional assessment is often performed for screening cognitive function, activities of daily living, health, and physical symptoms, social engagement and quality, depression, life satisfaction, affect quality, and many other clinically relevant attributes. The skills of the geropsychologist have been applied in both the psychometric design of such measures and the supervision and clinical use of the findings from functional assessment.

In light of the expertise and knowledge available to clinicians regarding neuropsychological, clinical, and functional assessment, it is surprising that no commercially published "how-to" manual or handbook has yet appeared to guide the clinician through the process of selecting measures, applying them to elders, and using them in treatment. The best available books (e.g., LaRue, 1992; Carstensen, Edelstein, & Dornbrand, 1996; Edelstein, in press) are more like source books than manuals. The journal *Clinical Gerontologist* is most likely to be useful to the practicing clinician. The *Journal of Mental Health and Aging* and the *Journal of Clinical Geropsychology* are focused more on empirical clinical research reports than on assessment or therapy in practice. None of these is limited to an audience of psychologists; three other nominally psychiatric journals (*Aging and Mental Health*, the *International Journal of Geriatric Psychiatry*, and *International Psychogeriatrics*) publish material written by and appropriate for most mental health professionals. Indeed, the multidisciplinary character of gerontology in general is nowhere better illustrated than in the frequent collaboration of psychologists, physicians, nurses, social workers, and others in both assessment and other mental health activities. Limited circulation guides for assessment techniques and legal competence assessment have been produced by the Department of Veterans' Affairs' National Center on Cost Containment.

Therapy. Traditional dynamic psychotherapy has been slow to develop and only very recently can be said to have developed an identity of its own in the field of aging. It must be acknowledged that a definitive case has yet to be made for age-specific psychotherapy. Nonetheless, many age-specific issues may be identified in the course of psychotherapy. Interest in this topic was increased by the publication of Knight (1996), which guides the therapist through therapeutic processes and is supplemented with copious case material. This work, along with Zarit and Knight (1996), marks the point at which psychotherapy with elders became defined as a speciality. Individual therapy based on cognitive-behavioral models has also been widely applied and reported, particularly in late-life depression.

Not surprisingly, psychological expertise in behaviorally oriented approaches to change has seen very wide application to older people. Such methods have been ideally suited to improving ADL performance, treating incontinence, and dealing with behavior problems, especially in the nursing home. Carstensen et al. (1996), Hersen and VanHasselt (1996), and Wisocki (1991) document a number of approaches to behavior therapy with elders.

Programmatic and environmental intervention includes a wide variety of interventions broadly designed to treat multiple individuals, frequently including environmental and milieu-oriented features in the treatment. Some early work in institutional token economies was performed, but more recently approaches such as caregiver education, caregiving support, family therapy, group therapy, "special-care units" for people with dementia, and staff training in reinforcing independent behavior have been applied. Again, these are areas where the psychologist has special expertise but also where an interdisciplinary mode of care delivery has often been central to the success of the intervention.

Life Enhancement and Adaptation

Beyond dealing with clinical assessment and treatment issues, psychology has a major consultative role in the design of policies and delivery of services that enhance quality of life for all older people and their caregivers. Such roles have been enacted in the organization of institutional care, residential programs for elders, community-based non-mental health services, health and preventive services, age discrimination, workplace design and practices, and many other arenas where ordinary older people are found. Many services to stressed elders, such as socially supportive program groups based on health-psychological knowledge and self-actualization, have been initiated and conducted by geropsychologists.

Training in Clinical Geropsychology

Doctoral-level training in clinically relevant aspects of geropsychology has been available for some time at the University of Southern California, West Virginia University, Washington University, and other centers; the medical school of Northwestern University was in the vanguard of this effort, under David Gutmann's leadership from 1977 to 1990. The number is slowly growing. It has been very difficult for such training to gain full status within the formal structures of organizations such as universities and associations of psychologists. Incremental growth in the number and quality of such opportunities occurred beginning with the Older Boulder conference. Many training issues are discussed by Santos and Vanden Bos (1982) and Knight et al. (1996). Included are recommendations favoring federal funding for training at all levels (still rarely available) and the establishment of standards for specialization in clinical geropsychology.

Public Policy Issues in Clinical Geropsychology

Health care constitutes a very special arena for the practice of clinical geropsychology. Professional psychology has had an influential voice in current issues revolving around the question of how to pay for mental health services to the aged. The APA, state psychological associations, and many other groups have worked to make mental health services as accessible to elders as other medical services under both Medicare and Medicaid, although such parity is in constant jeopardy. A second issue, specific to psychology, concerns the establishment of practice and reimbursement privileges that are equal to those of other professionals. Issues such as which types of psychotherapy delivered to a dementia patient may be reimbursed remain to be resolved. A third issue is whether special credentialing for clinical psychologists who wish to feature their expertise with older clients is necessary or desirable. A fourth issue concerns managed care. Making mental health services available to a broad range of elders and providing services beyond those sanctioned as quick and minimal is a challenge for the first decade of the twenty-first century.

The Future of Clinical Geropsychology

The demography of the age structure will increase greatly the sheer numbers as well as proportions of potential older consumers of mental health services. Another very important factor in increasing demand is the current entry into the over-65 age cohort of the first group of people whose early socialization included exposure to psychological and mental-health concepts. One would think that a commensurate spurt in the use of geropsychologists to deliver these services might oc-

cur. Forces operating against such change are substantial, however. Among them are the constant pressures to reduce costs by using less well paid personnel (bachelor-level nonprofessionals), to substitute truncated screening assessment for more complete psychological and neuropsychological assessment, or to make therapy shorter, less skilled, and even overreported and overcharged. Thus the need for training at all levels, the continued feeding of research findings into practice, respect for objective measurement, use of practice data for planning both individual treatment and larger programs, explicit treatment protocols, and monitoring of outcomes is extremely important. As psychology and clinical psychology in particular have grown in size, the Boulder model of the scientist-clinician has become increasingly rare. If geropsychological practice is to maintain its scientific and ethical quality, modes for perpetuating these goals for the scientist-clinician need to be fortified.

[*See also* Gerontology.]

Bibliography

American Psychiatric Association. (1994). *Diagnostic and statistical manual of mental disorders* (4th ed.). Washington, DC: Author.

Anderson, J. E. (Ed.). (1956). *Psychological aspects of aging.* Washington, DC: American Psychological Association.

Baltes, P. B., Dittmann-Kohli, F., & Dixon, R. A. (1984). New perspectives on the development of intelligence in adulthood. In P. B. Baltes & O. G. Brim (Eds.), *Life-span development and behavior, 6* (pp. 33–76). New York: Academic Press.

Birren, J. E. (Ed.). (1959). *Handbook of aging and the individual.* Chicago: University of Chicago Press.

Carp, F. (1966). *A future for the aged.* Austin, TX: University of Texas Press.

Carstensen, L. L., Edelstein, B. A., & Dornbrand, L. (Eds.). (1996). *The practical handbook of clinical gerontology.* Thousand Oaks, CA: Sage.

Cumming, E., & Henry, W. (1961). *Growing old.* New York: Basic Books.

Edelstein, B. (Ed.). (in press). *Clinical geropsychology,* Vol. 7 in A. S. Bellack & M. Hersen (Eds.), *Comprehensive clinical psychology.* New York: Pergamon.

Eisdorfer, C., & Lawton, M. P. (Eds.). (1973). *The psychology of adult development and aging.* Washington, DC: American Psychological Association.

Erikson, E. H. (1963). *Childhood and society.* New York: Norton.

Fozard, J. L. (1981). Person-environment relationships in adulthood: Implications for human factors engineering. *Human Factors, 23,* 7–27.

Goldstein, K., & Scheerer, M. (1941). Abstract and concrete behavior. *Psychological Monographs, 53,* 1–151.

Hersen, M., & Van Hasselt, V. B. (Eds.). (1996). *Psychological treatment of older adults.* New York: Plenum Press.

Kastenbaum, R. (Ed.). (1964). *Contributions to the psychobiology of aging.* New York: Springer.

Kleemeier, R. W. (1959). Behavior and the organization of the bodily and the external environment. In J. E. Birren (Ed.), *Handbook of aging and the individual* (pp. 400–451). Chicago: University of Chicago Press.

Knight, B. G. (1996). *Psychotherapy with older adults,* 2nd ed. Thousand Oaks, CA: Sage.

Knight, B. G., Teri, L., Wohlford, P., & Santos, J. (Eds.). (1995). *Mental health services for older adults.* Washington, DC: American Psychological Association.

Kogan, N. (1961). Attitudes toward old people in an older sample. *Journal of Abnormal and Social Psychology, 62,* 616–622.

LaRue, A. (1992). *Aging and neuropsychological assessment.* New York: Plenum Press.

Lawton, M. P., & Nahemow, L. (1973). Ecology and the aging process. In C. Eisdorfen & M. P. Lawton (Eds.), *Psychology of adult development and aging* (pp. 619–674). Washington, DC: American Psychological Association.

Lieberman, M. A., & Tobin, S. S. (1983). *The experience of old age.* New York: Basic Books.

Lowenthal, M. F., & Haven, C. (1968). Interaction and isolation: Intimacy as a critical variable. *American Sociological Review, 33,* 20–30.

Piaget, J. (1972). Intellectual evaluation from adolescence to adulthood. *Human Development, 15,* 1–12.

Storandt, M., Siegler, I. C., & Elias, M. F. (Eds.). (1978). *The clinical psychology of aging.* New York: Plenum Press.

Tuckman, J., & Lorge, I. (1952). The best years of life: A study in ranking. *Journal of Psychology, 34,* 137–149.

Welford, A. (1958). *Ageing and human skill.* London, UK: Oxford University Press.

Wisocki, P. A. (Ed.). (1991). *Handbook of clinical behavior therapy with the elderly.* New York: Plenum Press.

Zarit, S. H., & Knight, B. G. (Eds.). (1996). *A guide to psychotherapy and aging.* Washington, DC: American Psychological Association.

M. Powell Lawton

CLINICAL PSYCHOLOGY. [*This entry comprises four articles: an overview of the broad history of the field from its inception to the present; a survey of the principal theories that have determined the course of development of the field; a general descriptive review of assessments used in (or unique to) the field; and a profile of interventions employed in the field. For discussions related to clinical psychology, see the entries on* Counseling Psychology; Personality Psychology; Psychoanalysis; Psychology; *and various independent entries on specific psychosocial interventions.*]

History of the Field

Clinical psychology is a broad discipline concerned with the scientific study of psychopathology and with the assessment and treatment of persons with emotional, cognitive, and behavioral problems. It is perhaps the most common psychological specialty in the world (Sexton & Hogan, 1992), although it is defined and organized somewhat differently from one country to another.

Its Relation to Other Disciplines

Clinical psychology overlaps considerably with the neighboring field of psychiatry, especially in terms of the subject matter of its research. The distinction between the two is in terms of education, training, and scope of professional practice. Clinical psychologists receive more exposure to the behavioral sciences and have greater expertise in psychometrics (Anastasi & Urbina, 1997) and in behavioral approaches to treatment (Kazdin, 1978). Psychiatrists are medically trained and have more expertise in the biological aspects of psychopathology and in psychopharmacology (Shorter, 1997).

Clinical psychology was the first of many practice-oriented specialties that developed within psychology. Several other such specialties were originally part of clinical psychology and then split off from it and became more independent areas of practice. Thus at least a part of school psychology began as clinical psychology in a school setting. Part of counseling psychology began as clinical psychology in rehabilitation facilities or university guidance centers. Clinical health psychology was another spin-off field, applying similar concepts and assessment and intervention methods to the psychological problems associated with physical health conditions. Clinical neuropsychology works closely with the medical field of neurology and is concerned with the precise analysis of brain-behavior relationships. Psychoanalytic psychology was officially named as a specialty once psychologists achieved the legal right to be trained within psychoanalytic institutes in the United States in the 1980s.

Origins

The first known use of the term *clinical psychology* was in a 1907 article by Lightner Witmer in the inaugural issue of *Psychological Clinic,* the journal he edited. The field has roots as an area of professional practice somewhat separate from those as an academic endeavor. Witmer founded the first psychology clinic in 1896 at the University of Pennsylvania (Witmer, 1897) and was one of the first to advocate the use of psychology in order to help people rather than only to carry out research. His clinic focused on work with school-aged children with academic and behavioral problems, including difficulties with reading and spelling, mental retardation, and what would today perhaps be labeled as childhood autism. At times it extended into the adult age range. Clients were examined at this psychological clinic using procedures adapted from the laboratory psychology of the day and the results were used primarily to direct remedial teaching to try to overcome the difficulties presented. Witmer trained many doctoral students in psychology at the University of Pennsylvania in such clinical methods. He encouraged them to seek more intensive training in the form of full-time internships at such nearby sites as the Training School at Vineland, New Jersey, a residential institution for persons with mental retardation. He traced the intellectual origins of his work to such European figures as Rodriguez Perreira (a Portuguese-French teacher of the deaf) and J. M. G. Itard (the French physician who had worked to try to socialize the Wild Boy of Aveyron). He identified others who influenced him as the physician Edouard Seguin, who founded a school in Paris to try to rehabilitate children with mental retardation, and the physician-educator Maria Montessori, who developed innovative educational procedures for use with slum children in Rome. Despite the historical importance of Witmer in relation to clinical psychology, the work he did resembles the diagnostic teaching done by special educators more than it does the activities of present-day clinical psychologists.

The fields of abnormal psychology and psychotherapy, which are key parts of present-day clinical psychology, had a much more ancient origin. The study of psychopathology can be traced back at least to the medical writings attributed to Hippocrates dating from the fifth century BCE and to the work of philosophers such as Democritus who were not physicians (Routh, 1998). The precise origins of psychotherapy are more elusive. According to Jerome Frank's (1961) influential book, *Persuasion and Healing*, such practices may be ubiquitous in human societies.

The involvement of psychologists in the study of psychopathology and its treatment obviously had to wait until the late nineteenth century, when a formal discipline of psychology developed, but research on psychopathology soon became a part of this new field. The neurologist Charcot appointed Pierre Janet to direct a psychology laboratory at the Salpêtrière Hospital in Paris in 1890 to study the female patients with hysteria there. Alfred Binet was another early French psychologist who worked with Charcot and was greatly influenced by him. The German psychiatrist Emil Kraepelin spent time working with the psychologist Wilhelm Wundt at the University of Leipzig. Kraepelin was an influential figure in the development of descriptive psychopathology and of psychopharmacology. He later carried out psychological research in his psychiatry service at the University of Munich.

In the United States beginning toward the end of the nineteenth century, there was great interest in abnormal psychology and psychotherapy among many of the early psychologists, including William James, G. Stanley Hall, Boris Sidis, and Morton Prince. James presented the Lowell lectures on exceptional mental states in Boston in 1896 (Taylor, 1982) and was interested in research on automatic writing. Hall at one point served as the lay superintendent of a mental hospital in Maryland and later taught psychology to psychiatry residents at Worcester State Hospital in Massachusetts. Morton Prince, a psychologically oriented physician, studied a famous case of a woman with multiple personality. He established the *Journal of Abnormal Psychology* in 1906, and he founded the Harvard Psychological Clinic in 1926. What might be termed the Boston school of abnormal psychology and psychotherapy was active in the 1890s and at the turn of the century, though it tended to be absorbed by the psychoanalytic movement after the first decade of the new century.

Clinical psychology also had significant roots in psychoanalysis. The two fields have shared a century-long history and have a continuing relationship. Breuer and Freud published the book that established psychoanalysis, *Studies in Hysteria*, in 1895. From the beginning, Freud expressed the wish that psychoanalysis not be simply a medical specialty and was willing to train analysts with various backgrounds, including psychology. The psychoanalysts who were professional psychologists included Otto Rank, Theodore Reik, and many others.

One complication was that the American Psychoanalytic Association wished to restrict the practice of psychoanalysis and especially access to its training programs to psychiatrists only. For many years, psychologists in the United States who wanted to be trained and supervised in psychoanalysis had to achieve this in irregular or devious ways. This restrictive policy was not overcome until four clinical psychologists lead by Bryant L. Welch sued the American Psychoanalytic Association for antitrust violations and won an out-of-court settlement in the 1980s.

Principal Figures

In a field that is hardly more than a century old, the choice of a few individuals as principal figures is bound to be a bit arbitrary. We will confine this discussion to persons who are no longer living. One of these pioneers was Alfred Binet, the codeveloper of the first valid intelligence test (Binet & Simon, 1905). This test significantly distinguished children with mental retardation from their typically developing peers, and various versions of it have been in continuous clinical use ever since that time. This line of research was significantly advanced by Lewis M. Terman (1916), who standardized Binet's test and published norms for it using sizable groups of children of different ages. Terman (1925; Terman & Oden, 1947) went on to demonstrate the long-term reliability of this test and its predictive utility not only in relation to academic performance but also other life achievements. Then Jean W. Macfarlane of the University of California at Berkeley had the wisdom to convert a flawed study of the effects of clinical guidance of children into a life-span study of development within the general population. She and her colleagues (including Erik Erikson) paid attention not only to cognitive development but also to aspects of personality and social adjustment.

Carl R. Rogers in the 1940s helped move the field of clinical psychology from an overly exclusive preoccupation with mental testing toward a more balanced emphasis on psychotherapeutic intervention as well (Rogers, 1951). Rogers' client-centered or person-centered approach to psychotherapy was original with him but was indirectly influenced by Freud as interpreted by the psychologist-psychoanalyst Otto Rank and the social worker Jessie Taft. Rogers had the boldness to carry out tape recordings of actual therapy sessions and to initiate controlled research on psychotherapy process and outcome.

Clinical psychological assessment came to encompass personality and psychopathology as well as cognitive functioning. One of the most innovative ventures in this domain was developed by Starke R. Hathaway, who was a coauthor of the Minnesota Multiphasic Personality Inventory (MMPI; Hathaway & McKinley, 1943). In contrast to earlier questionnaire measures of psychopathology, the MMPI was empirically validated using groups of patients with particular psychiatric diagnoses compared to normal control subjects. In addition, the MMPI provided novel "validity" scales enabling the psychologist to detect subjects' attempts to dissemble or to present themselves in an unduly favorable or unfavorable light. The validity scales also detected patterns of incomprehension, confusion, or random responding. The MMPI continues to be one of the most widely used measures of its kind and has been translated into many different languages.

George A. Kelly developed some original approaches to assessing how individuals construed their social world. His personal construct theory (Kelly, 1955) was also the basis of an approach to intervention that was perhaps the first example of cognitive therapy, presently one of the most widely used kinds of treatment.

In the United Kingdom, Hans Eysenck founded a Department of Psychology within the Institute of Psychiatry at the University of London. Eysenck devised his own questionnaires for the assessment of personality and psychopathology that were widely used and influential. He published a critique of the effectiveness of psychotherapy that, though not without its own flaws, spurred research on psychosocial intervention throughout the world (Eysenck, 1952). Eysenck was also a pioneer in promoting behavioral approaches to therapy. These emerged as a strong influence on clinical psychology beginning in the 1960s.

Major Areas of Research

The focus of the work of the principal figures in clinical psychology discussed above was primarily on assessment and treatment. Clinical psychology has also emphasized research on psychopathology throughout its existence. The research program of David Shakow, begun at Worcester State Hospital, for example, concerned attentional difficulties in schizophrenia (e.g., Shakow, 1962). He used the classic experimental paradigm of reaction time to demonstrate difficulties patients with schizophrenia have in maintaining "set." They are easily distracted and may be overly influenced, for example, by the timing of the RT signal on the immediately preceding trial. Paul E. Meehl (1962), another clinical psychologist whose research often focused on schizophrenia, elaborated an influential theory about how genetic factors are involved in this group of disorders. Meehl defined "schizotaxia" as the hypothetical genetic factors hypothesized to be necessary but not sufficient for the development of schizophrenia. Meehl used the term "schizotypy" to refer to the corresponding phenotype. A schizotype is thus a person at risk for schizophrenia and might manifest traits such as interpersonal aversiveness and subclinical cognitive slippage. Given an adverse environment, for example, perinatal difficulties or other stresses, the schizotype might manifest the clinical disorder of schizophrenia.

In another domain of psychopathology research, clinical psychologist Martin E. P. Seligman (1975) translated his basic research on "learned helplessness" in dogs into a prototype for understanding how clinical depression might develop in human beings. The dog, in a shuttle apparatus, learns that nothing it can do will avoid episodes of electric shock. Similarly, a human might acquire a predisposition to depression in the form of the habit of making internal, stable, and global attributions for failure ("I failed because that is just the way I am, I will always be that way, and this applies to every domain of my life").

Other Significant Professional Concerns

A concern of clinical psychology throughout its existence as an organized specialty group has been with the credentialing of practitioners. The purposes of these efforts are to give public recognition to psychologists qualified to offer their services to the public and to discourage practice by others not so qualified. Beginning in 1919, the American Psychological Association attempted to implement a plan to certify individuals who met certain criteria as "consulting psychologists." This plan did not prove to be functional. Only 25 psychologists were ever so certified, and the scheme had to be discontinued after only a few years (Routh, 1994).

During the period after World War II, from 1945 to

1977, every U.S. state passed legislation certifying or licensing psychologists to practice independently. Certification generally refers to the protection of the title "psychologist," while licensing usually refers to protection of the practice itself. These laws typically required possession of a doctoral degree in psychology, plus two years of supervised experience in the field, one of which could be predoctoral. All Canadian provinces, the United Kingdom, most countries in the British Commonwealth, and the Scandinavian countries implemented similar licensing schemes, though not necessarily with the requirement of training at the doctoral level. Other countries in Europe and Latin America appear to be on the road to developing similar legislation, but this is far from a worldwide development. There are wide variations from one country to another in the legal qualifications for the independent practice of psychology. Such laws, where they exist, are usually generic to psychology and do not refer to clinical psychology separately by name.

In 1947, the organization presently known as the American Board of Professional Psychology was established and soon began to examine candidates for its diploma signifying advanced competence in clinical psychology. This process was intended to be the equivalent of board certification in psychiatry or other medical specialties.

Clinical psychologists in independent practice in the United States have fought a long, extensive battle for recognition by hospitals, insurance companies, and third-party payers. This has led to the establishment of a National Register of Health Service Providers in Psychology to provide insurance companies with the names of practitioners who have training at the doctoral level, active state licensure, and a formal internship involving at least a year of full-time clinical training.

Training Requirements

The University of Pennsylvania, among other academic institutions, has been training clinical psychologists for over 100 years, but for most of that time there was no public agreement on exactly what the curriculum in the field should be. As mentioned already, the tradition of a 1-year, full-time internship was established within 12 years after the field was founded, and by about 1920 there was an informal consensus that this was a necessary part of training for clinical psychologists who wished to provide services to the public. Besides the internship at Vineland, others were established at the Boston Psychopathic Hospital and elsewhere.

After World War II, there was a move to standardize training in clinical psychology in both North America and in parts of the United Kingdom and northern Europe. At that time, clinical psychology became part of the national health care system in the United Kingdom

and several other countries that had such systems. At that time in the United States, both the Veterans' Administration (VA) and the newly established National Institute of Mental Health (NIMH) began to offer training grants in clinical psychology. These organizations requested the American Psychological Association to set up a formal system for accrediting training in clinical psychology, and it did so. An APA committee on training in clinical psychology, headed by David Shakow, wrote up recommendations for such training. They were essentially ratified by a national conference held in Boulder, Colorado, in 1949. Thus was born the "Boulder" or scientist-practitioner model of clinical training. Clinical psychologists were to be trained at the Ph.D. level, including a required predoctoral internship in the third year, with the expectation that upon graduation they would go into careers involving both research and service, either in universities or in public sector positions in the VA, state hospitals, child guidance centers, and the like. A separate accreditation program was set up by the APA for internship programs. Graduates of Boulder-model clinical psychology programs deviated from the above expectations in two ways. Many of them did little research, and eventually quite a number of them went into private practice.

By the end of World War II, some university psychology departments already had long traditions of training clinical psychologists primarily for research rather than service activities. These universities included many elite schools such as Harvard, Columbia, the University of Chicago, and Stanford, who either never endorsed this new accredited training model or gradually dropped away from participating in it. They tended to resist the standardization demanded by the new APA accreditation system but continued to train at least some psychologists interested in the scientific study of psychopathology.

On the other end of the academic spectrum, some programs arose that offered training for professional practice, perhaps involving a doctor of psychology of Psy.D. degree (originally suggested by Hollingworth, 1918), rather than for both research and practice. Eventually, a national conference at Vail, Colorado, in 1973 endorsed this "practitioner" training model (Korman, 1974). In the United Kingdom, the pattern has now grown up of offering professional training and awarding Doctor of Clinical Psychology (D.Clin.Psych.) degrees. Elsewhere in the world, training for practice takes place in master's degree or 6-year undergraduate "licenciado" programs, with doctoral level training being reserved for academics.

Professional Organizations

The first professional organization in this field was the American Association of Clinical Psychologists (AACP), founded in 1917. This group met in Pittsburgh, Pennsylvania, on the campus of the Carnegie Institute of Technology in connection with the APA meeting going on there at the time (Routh, 1994). Its founders were motivated by the wish to establish professional standards, in particular in the administration of the Binet test, which at the time was being inappropriately given and interpreted by school teachers untrained in psychology on the one hand, and by academic psychologists with no clinical experience on the other. The AACP was absorbed back into the APA two years later in 1919, becoming the "Clinical Section" of the APA. In 1937, the Clinical Section of the APA dissolved itself because of distress at the restrictions put by the APA on its continued attempts to promote professional standards. It reconstituted itself as the Clinical Section of a new organization known as the American Association for Applied Psychology (AAAP). Then, in 1945, the AAAP and the APA merged. The Clinical Section became APA Division 12, originally called the Division of Clinical and Abnormal Psychology.

Similar clinical psychology organizations were formed in Canada, the United Kingdom, and various other countries, typically as a division or section of the national psychological organization. Many are also affiliated with regional organizations such as the European Federation of Professional Psychology Associations (EFFPA).

Major Publications

One of the most prestigious peer-reviewed scholarly journals in clinical psychology is the *Journal of Abnormal Psychology*. It was founded by Boston physician Morton Prince in 1906 and later given by him to the American Psychological Association. This journal was known for a number of years as the *Journal of Abnormal and Social Psychology* but then reverted to its original name and scope. In addition to research on psychopathology, this journal has always provided a niche for articles on hypnotism or dissociative phenomena, in line with Prince's research interests. Prince was the same man who founded the Harvard Psychological Clinic (a research-oriented facility rather than one concerned mainly with service delivery), expressing his view that the study of psychopathology belonged to the liberal arts rather than the medical school. True to form, he had also founded the American Psychopathological Association as an organization for researchers in the field of psychopathology, including psychologists as well as psychiatrists.

A second high-prestige journal in clinical psychology is the *Journal of Consulting and Clinical Psychology*, also now published by the APA. It was founded under the name, *Journal of Consulting Psychology* and was published for its first ten years as a "house organ" by the AAAP. Upon the merger of the AAAP and the APA, it became a peer-reviewed scholarly journal.

The *British Journal of Clinical Psychology* is also a highly respected journal and is one of those published by the British Psychological Society. Many other scholarly journals devoted to clinical psychology exist in various countries.

Future Directions

Research in psychopathology, including its assessment and treatment, has greatly accelerated during the past 100 years. Much more research in this field has been published during the twentieth century than in all previous centuries (Routh, 1998). Research funding is available from various private foundations, from the National Institutes of Health in the United States, the Medical Research Council in the United Kingdom, and other such governmental organizations. Thus, clinical psychology, psychiatry, and other disciplines involved in research in this domain are in a relatively healthy state.

In the domain of the delivery of professional services in mental health, however, powerful trends are under way to cut costs, improve efficiency, and transform the field into a more businesslike operation. In the United States, these efforts go on under the heading of managed care. Since a large share of health costs is taken up by the salaries and fees paid to relatively expensive professionals, including psychiatrists and clinical psychologists, their incomes are now under threat. Psychotherapy can be delivered by social workers and others with master's degrees or even more modest levels of training. Similarly, prescriptions for psychotropic medications can, in many cases, be written by primary-care physicians without the need for psychiatric referral. Thus, there is some possibility that what happened to the primary-care specialty of neurology at the beginning of the twentieth century could happen to clinical psychology and psychiatry now. They might come to exist as fields primarily consisting of researchers, teachers, and high-level consultants and not be so much involved in everyday mental health care. Whatever the outcome, it is clear that the situation will be much changed even within the next decade.

Bibliography

Anastasi, A., & Urbina, S. (1997). *Psychological testing* (7th ed). Upper Saddle River, NJ: Prentice Hall.

Binet, A., & Simon, T. (1905). A new method for the diagnosis of intellectual level of abnormal persons. *Annee psychologique, 11,* 191–244.

Breuer, J., & Freud, S. (1986). *Studies in hysteria.* In J. Strachey (Ed.), *The standard edition of the complete psychological works of Sigmund Freud. Vol. 2.* London: Hogarth Press and the Institute of Psychoanalysis. (Original work published 1895)

Eysenck, H. J. (1952). The effects of psychotherapy: An

evaluation. *Journal of Consulting Psychology, 16*, 319–324.

Frank, J. D. (1961). *Persuasion and healing.* Baltimore: Johns Hopkins University Press.

Hathaway, S. R., & McKinley, J. C. (1943). *The Minnesota Multiphasic Personality Inventory.* New York: Psychological Corporation.

Hollingworth, L. S. (1918). Tentative suggestions for the certification of practicing psychologists. *Journal of Applied Psychology, 2*, 280–284.

Kazdin, A. (1978). *History of behavior modification: Experimental foundations of contemporary research.* Baltimore: University Park Press.

Korman, M. (1974). National conference on levels and patterns of professional training in psychology: The major themes. *American Psychologist, 29*, 441–444.

Kelly, G. (1955). *The psychology of personal constructs.* New York: Norton.

McReynolds, P. (1997). *Lightner Witmer: His life and times.* Washington, DC: American Psychological Association.

Meehl, P. E. (1962). Schizotaxia, schizotypy, schizophrenia. *American Psychologist, 17*, 827–838.

Rogers, C. R. (1951). *Client centered therapy.* Boston: Houghton Mifflin.

Routh, D. K. (1994). *Clinical psychology since 1917: Science, practice, and organization.* New York: Plenum Press.

Routh, D. K. (1998). Hippocrates meets Democritus: A history of psychiatry and clinical psychology. In C. E. Walker (Ed.), *Foundations of clinical psychology.* Oxford, UK: Elsevier Science.

Seligman, M. E. P. (1975). *Helplessness: On depression, development, and death.* San Francisco: W. H. Freeman.

Sexton, V. S., & Hogan, J. D. (1992). Epilogue. In V. S. Sexton & J. D. Hogan (Eds.), *International psychology: Views from around the world* (pp. 467–477). Lincoln, NE: University of Nebraska Press.

Shakow, D. (1962). Segmental set: A theory of the formal psychological deficit in schizophrenia. *Archives of General Psychiatry, 6*, 1–17.

Shorter, E. (1997). *A history of psychiatry.* New York: Wiley.

Taylor, E. I. (1982). *William James on exceptional mental states: Reconstruction of the 1896 Lowell lectures.* New York: Scribner's Sons.

Terman, L. M. (1916). *The measurement of intelligence.* Boston: Houghton Mifflin.

Terman, L. M. (1925). *Genetic studies of genius. Vol. 1.* Stanford, CA: Stanford University Press.

Terman, L. M., & Oden, M. H. (1947). *The gifted child grows up: Twenty-five years' follow-up of a superior group.* Stanford, CA: Stanford University Press.

Witmer, L. (1897). The organization of practical work in psychology. *Psychological Review, 4*, 116.

Witmer, L. (1907). Clinical psychology. *Psychological Clinic, 1*, 1–9.

Donald K. Routh

Theories

Clinical psychology represents that branch of psychology concerned with deviations in personality functioning, or behavior we term as abnormal or pathological. The study of behavior in its abnormality is important in our search for understanding normal human behavior, just as in medicine the study of pathological tissues has contributed to the understanding of how normal cells function.

The field of clinical psychology has come to represent at least two major areas of endeavor. One area centers on the science of the field—the study of behavior in its abnormality. The science of clinical psychology is conducted mainly in universities, medical schools, and large public and private clinical facilities, often supported by governmental grants. The researchers, predominately with Ph.D. degrees in psychology, have been trained in experimental methods and are devoted to the pursuit of scientific inquiry.

The second area is the practice of the field—the application of a whole range of techniques designed to evaluate and alleviate mental and emotional problems. The practice of psychology takes place primarily in hospitals, community mental health centers, or private clinical settings by clinical psychologists as well as a wide range of other mental health professionals, including psychiatrists, social workers, psychiatric nurses, and mental health counselors. A mental health clinician's educational background varies according to the particular academic or professional field, but must involve at least graduate work at the master's level and the possession of a state license. For psychologists to practice independently in the field and to be full members of the national professional association (American Psychological Association), they must earn a doctorate.

Professionals who chose both to do research and to practice in the field of clinical psychology have traditionally earned Ph.D. degrees in programs dedicated to the "scientist-professional" or Boulder model of training, emphasizing both scientific and professional areas, as delineated at a conference in Boulder, Colorado, in 1949. Other models emphasizing various aspects of clinical psychology, such as the role of clinical training in dealing with school and community problems in the area of mental health, have been developed over the years. Most recently, there has been a rapid growth of doctor of psychology or Psy.D. programs, which place heavier emphasis on the application of clinical skills over the research of clinical problems.

Whatever the path of training or the degree obtained, the clinical psychologist is an applied scientist or a scientist practitioner who utilizes scientific knowledge in the field to beneficial ends.

Before discussing the current theories in clinical psychology, let us briefly explore the theoretical frameworks that have guided the discipline as it has evolved through the ages. From earliest historical times, humans have been fascinated by deviant behavior and have attempted to develop theories for explaining the phenomena. As expected, most theories have been in keeping with the prevailing cultural and intellectual context of the times. Whenever new theories differ from the accepted contemporary beliefs, they are often ridiculed, rejected, or even condemned. Whether a new theoretical avenue is a true breakthrough or a cul-de-sac may be determined only with time.

The earliest conceptualizations of aberrant behavior attributed abnormality to magical causes, spirits within the brain, or punishment for sins (Walker, 1991). Evidence for these theories appears in early findings of skulls and in writings going back to the Babylonians in 2100 BCE. In keeping with the beliefs of those times, in order to rid an individual of the abnormality, holes were made in the skull (trepanning), appeals were made to the gods by medicine men, or persons with such behavior were made spectacles of, or even banished from society.

During the Golden Age of Greek Enlightenment (500–300 BCE), abnormal behavior or mental illness was conceived of as emerging from within the corpus of the person, mainly as excesses of certain bodily humors in the blood and other fluids. Because aberrant behavior was viewed as a physical condition, the treatment of such illness came within the province of the emerging medical profession. However, philosophers at the time also distinguished the mind from the body and attempted to understand "disordered thought" in terms of irrational thinking. Thus, the mind/body or biological versus psychological dilemma over the causes of abnormality was argued from the onset of rational thinking.

This early dichotomous theorizing about the foundations of abnormal behavior—organic vs. functional—remains with us today in the still unresolved determination of the etiology of many behavioral pathologies.

Those who have pursued the theory of organic origins of mental illness, mainly psychiatrists and neurologists, have experimented with shock treatments, brain surgery, diet regimes, and medications. Today there are a number of effective psychotropic drugs that alter emotions, thinking, and behavior in mentally distressed persons. These remedies have not resolved the questions on the origins of the mental illness, although they may go a long way in alleviating much of the suffering of persons with mental disorders.

Clinical psychology has developed many theories attempting to explain behavior aberration as a function of psychological interactions or reactions to stressful events. For the most part, these theoretical formulations have been divided into three main movements in the mental health field.

The first major efforts in the modern era to conceptualize mental and emotional distress in functional terms were undertaken by psychoanalysts. The founder of the movement and the most articulate of this point of view was Sigmund Freud (1856–1939), who determined that the interactions of the child with parents during crucial stages of maturational development were the significant elements in the eventual personality functioning of the adult. In the late nineteenth century this was a radical departure from the emphasis on organic factors as causes of mental illness, and many of Freud's theories—especially those involving early "sexual" feelings in children—drew much criticism and derision from the medical community as well as the public at large.

The theories of personality deviation based on dynamic relationship factors were supported by reports of case studies, using the psychoanalytic method of treatment. The technique called for the patient to "free associate" (say whatever came to mind) in a session with an analyst. As the patient reviewed his or her (interestingly, women were the predominant ones in treatment) history of relationships, the therapist came to represent various significant figures in the patient's life. The feelings associated with the earlier relationships were transferred to the analyst. Through the reliving of early emotional experiences, the patient gained insight into the sources of emotional distress and conflict, released the psychic energy used to cover up or repress the stressful memories, and was then able to function normally.

Today, the technique of psychoanalysis has been modified greatly to include the patient's functioning in everyday life—not just childhood—and the earlier requirement for long (four to five years), intensive (four to five days a week) sessions has been reduced to shorter, more practical terms.

At the time of Freud's early writings, psychologists were just emerging from the philosophical and physiological departments of universities, studying basic human phenomena such as reaction time and perceptual awareness. It was not until 1896 that Lightner Witmer (1861–1956), a member of the psychology faculty at the University of Pennsylvania, started a clinic for treating educational and behavioral problems. Eleven years later he founded a journal called *The Psychological Clinic*, which contained articles describing the work of the clinic and a new "clinical" approach to dealing with learning deficiencies and behavioral dysfunctioning. Witmer determined that both biological and psychological factors contributed to such problems. Known as the father of clinical psychology, Witmer is still a model for the present-day clinician who considers all the physical and psychological aspects of the individual in assessing and treating persons with dysfunctional behavior.

The second wave of theoretical conceptions of personality development bearing on the field of clinical psychology was initiated in the mid-1920s by the behaviorists, led by J. B. Watson (1878–1958) and B. F. Skinner (1904–1990). They viewed behavior as responses to the rewards and punishments experienced by individuals as they grew. The behavior might be reflexive, based on physiological or psychological stimuli; or more complex, due to the instrumental acts in seeking to meet needs (drives).

The behavioral school placed the issues of abnormal behavior squarely in the realm of the clinical psychologist, who studied the science of behavior and applied the knowledge gained to understand and reduce deviant behavior. In the middle of the twentieth century, clinical psychology flourished with exciting experiments demonstrating the effects of stimuli on responses, establishing the principles of generalization and discrimination gradients, and developing desensitization techniques that rapidly altered thinking and modified behavior. Manuals for child training, personality enhancement, and control of aberrant behavior based on behavioral techniques were popular with the profession as well as with the public at large. At last, clinical psychology had techniques based on scientific evidence tested under controlled, laboratory conditions, instead of reports of case studies and theorizing. As with psychoanalysis, behavior theory today has evolved and modified to include cognitive factors and greater complexity in approaching clinical problems (Fishman & Franks, 1992).

The third wave of clinical theorizing came in the 1940s, with leaders in the Gestalt field, such as Fritz Perls (1893–1970) and in the client-centered field, singularly led by Carl Rogers (1902–1987). The movement was partly a reaction to the somewhat authoritarian psychoanalytic approach and the sterile precision of the behavioral approach. A number of psychologists began to view the human condition in more existentialist, humanistic terms. The new approach to psychological problems included greater acceptance of individuality, sharing of feelings, and genuine regard for the person, whatever the behavior. Mental problems came to be understood as the failure to realize the fullness of one's humanity (Richly, 1981) and thus were treated with compassion and acceptance. The effectiveness of therapy relied on the human encounter between the therapist and the patient, who changed due to trust and the belief in the genuineness of the regard for the patient. Without emphasis on insight or behavioral regimes, the patient was enabled to exercise freedom of choice with maturity, independence, and responsibility (Brems, Thevenin, & Routh, 1991).

These three major theoretical frameworks of clinical psychology are broad representatives of many variants they have spawned and the myriad formulations of personality that clinical psychology embraces. Recent attempts to integrate theories (Arkowitz, 1992) and to treat emotional and behavioral problems with more eclectic approaches have gained in popularity. The So-ciety to Explore Psychotherapy Integration sponsors a journal and holds international conferences each year to discuss developments in the theoretical and practice approaches to understanding and treating psychological problems.

Clinical psychology along with the other mental health professions has expanded its study and work into many areas, including marital and family conflict, career changes, addictive behaviors, conflict resolution, natural and accidental disaster response, and living situations that require emotional coping skills. The knowledge obtained through research is invaluable in guiding the interventions necessary to meet these demands. And the experiences from the endeavors of mental health helpers provide important material for guiding the research and eventual theory building that is the work of clinical psychology.

Bibliography

Arkowitz, H. (1992). Integrative theories of therapy. In D. K. Freedheim (Ed.), *History of psychotherapy: A century of change* (pp. 261–303). Washington, DC: American Psychological Association. A good overview of eclectic and integrative approaches to psychotherapy and clinical psychology.

Brems, C., Thevenin, D. M., & Routh, D. K. (1991). The history of clinical psychology. In C. E. Walker (Ed.), *Clinical psychology: Historical and research foundations* (pp. 3–35). New York: Plenum Press. Introduction and overview of the roots of clinical psychology.

Freedheim, D. K. (1992). *History of psychotherapy: A century of change.* Washington, DC: American Psychological Association. Historical and current perspectives on the field of clinical psychology and psychotherapy.

Fishman, D. B., & Franks, C. M. (1992). Evolution and differentiation within behavior therapy: A theoretical and epistemological review. In D. K. Freedheim (Ed.), *History of psychotherapy: A century of change* (pp. 159–196). Washington, DC: American Psychological Association. A scholarly exposition of behavioral theory and its applications.

Garfield, S. L. (1982). *Clinical psychology* (2nd ed.). New York: Aldine. Basic text of the major systems and fields of clinical psychology.

Miller, R. B. (Ed.). (1992). *The restoration of dialogue: Readings in the philosophy of clinical psychology.* Washington, DC: American Psychological Association. An excellent collection of essays on the foundations and philosophies guiding the mental health movement over the centuries.

Richly, J. (1981). *Introduction to personality and psychotherapy.* Dallas, TX: Houghton Mifflin.

Walker, C. E. (1991). *Clinical psychology: Historical and research foundations.* New York: Plenum Press. A good overview of models in the field, various psychological conditions, and treatment approaches.

Wolman, B. B. (Ed.). (1965). *Handbook of clinical psychology*. New York: McGraw-Hill. Classic edited text covering the field of clinical psychology into the 1960s.

Donald K. Freedheim

Assessment

Traditionally, assessment has been one of the most important functions in clinical psychology. Clinical assessment is a procedure by which clinicians, using observation, interviews, and psychological tests, develop a summary of the client's symptoms and problems in order to develop treatment and other decisions. In clinical assessment, the clinician attempts to identify the main sources and dimensions of a client's problems and to predict the likely course of events under various conditions. It is at this initial stage that crucial decisions have to be made, such as what, if any, treatment approach is to be offered, whether the problems will require hospitalization, to what extent family members might need to be included in treatment, and so on. Sometimes these decisions might need to be made quickly, as in emergency conditions, and without access to critical information that would probably become available with extended client contact.

Mental health patients may present with behavioral, emotional, or physical discomfort that is often difficult for a clinical practitioner to understand initially. Usually, in mental health settings a clinical psychologist attempts to understand the nature and extent of the patient's problem by a process of inquiry that is similar to the way a detective might approach a case by collecting evidence and using inductive and deductive logic to focus on the most likely factors. Assessment of mental disorders is usually more difficult, more uncertain, and more protracted than it is for evaluation of many physical diseases. Yet, early assessment of mental health problems is extremely important in clinical practice. No rational, specific treatment plan can be instituted without at least some general notion of what problems need to be addressed.

In order for psychological assessment to proceed effectively, the person being evaluated must feel a sense of rapport with the clinician. The assessor needs to structure the testing situation so that the person feels comfortable. Important components of a good relationship in a clinical assessment situation include the following: Clients need to feel that the testing will help the practitioner gain a clear understanding of their problems and to understand how the tests will be used and how the psychologist will incorporate them in the clinical evaluation.

What does a clinician need to know in psychological assessment? First, of course, the problems must be identified. Are they of a situational nature? That is,

have they been precipitated by some environmental stressor, or are the problems more pervasive and long-term? Or is it perhaps some combination of the two? Is there any evidence of recent deterioration in cognitive functioning? How long has the person had the symptoms and how are they dealing with the problem? What, if any, prior help has been sought? Are there indications of self-defeating behavior or low self-esteem, or is the individual using available personal and environmental resources in a good effort to cope? How has the problem affected the person's performance of important social roles? Does the individual's symptomatic behavior fit any of the diagnostic patterns in the current diagnostic and statistical nomenclature (American Psychiatric Association, *Diagnostic and statistical manual of mental disorders*, 4th ed.).

It may be important to have an adequate diagnostic classification of the presenting problem for a number of reasons. Knowing a person's type of disorder can help in planning and managing the appropriate treatment. However, diagnosis alone is insufficient for most clinical evaluations. Psychological assessment or diagnosis can be an ongoing process that proceeds along with, rather than only preceding, treatment efforts. An important function of pretreatment assessment is that of establishing observational baselines for various psychological functions to be part of the treatment plan. Having a baseline of information about a client's problems and behaviors allows the clinician to assess changes that might come about in therapy. Several factors that are important to address in clinical assessment are:

Personal History

It is important to have a basic understanding of the individual's history and development, family history (whether the person has relatives with a history of mental illness), intellectual functioning, personality characteristics, and environmental pressures and resources. For example, how does the person characteristically respond to other people? Are there excesses in behavior, such as eating or drinking too much? Are there notable deficits, as, for example, in social skills? Does the person show any inappropriate behavior?

Personality Factors

Assessment needs to include a description of any relevant long-term personality characteristics. Has the person behaved in deviant or bizarre ways in particular situations, for example, circumstances requiring submission to legitimate authority? Do there seem to be personality traits or behavior patterns that predispose the individual to behave in maladaptive ways across a broad range of situations? Does the person tend to become dependent on others to the point of losing his or her identity? Is the person able to accept help from others? Is the person capable of accepting appropriate responsibility for others' welfare? Such questions are necessarily at the heart of many assessment efforts.

Social Situations

It is also important to evaluate the social contexts in which the individual functions. What environmental demands do they face? What emotional support or special stressors exist in the person's life?

The diverse information about the individual's personality traits, behavior patterns, and environmental demands need to be integrated into a consistent and meaningful picture often referred to as a dynamic formulation, because it describes the current situation and provides hypotheses about what is driving the person to behave in maladaptive ways. For example, the clinician should try to arrive at a plausible explanation for why a normally passive and mild-mannered man suddenly flew into a rage and became physically abusive toward his wife. The formulation will allow the clinician to develop hypotheses that might explain the client's future behavior. What is the likelihood that the person would get worse if the problems are left untreated? Which behaviors should be the initial focus of change, and what treatment methods are likely to be most efficient in producing this change? What changes might reasonably be expected if the person were provided a particular type of therapy?

Clients who are being assessed in a clinical situation are usually highly motivated to be evaluated and usually like to know the results of the testing. They usually are eager to give some definition to their discomfort. In many situations, it is important to incorporate information from a medical evaluation in the psychological assessment in order to rule out physical abnormalities that may be causing or contributing to the problem.

Clinical assessment attempts to provide a comprehensive picture of an individual's psychological functioning and the stressors and resources in his or her life situation. In the early stages of the process, the assessment psychologist attempts to obtain as much information about the client as possible—including present feelings, attitudes, memories, demographic facts, important formative life events—and tries to fit the diverse pieces together into a meaningful pattern. Starting with a global technique, such as a clinical interview, clinicians may later select more specific assessment tasks or tests. The following procedures are some of the methods that may be used to obtain the necessary data.

Assessment Interview

The assessment interview is usually the initial and often the central information source in the assessment process. This is usually a face-to-face interaction in which information about various aspects of a patient's situation, behavior, past history characteristics, and personality is acquired. The initial interview may be relatively open in format, with an interviewer deciding about his or her next question based on the client's answers to other ones, or it may be more structured so that a planned set of questions is followed. In structured interviewing, the clinician may choose from a number of possible interview formats whose reliability has been established in research. The structured interviewing approach is likely to be more reliable but may be less spontaneous than the free-response interview.

Clinical interviews can be subject to error because they rely upon human judgment to choose the questions and process the information. The assessment interview can be made more reliable by the use of rating scales that serve to focus inquiry and quantify the interview data. For example, the person may be rated on a 3-, 5-, or 7-point scale with respect to suicide potential, violence potential, or other personality characteristics, depending upon the goals of the assessment.

Clinical Observation

One of the most useful assessment techniques that a clinician has for gaining patient-relevant information is direct observation. Observation can enable the clinician to learn more about the person's psychological functioning, for example, personal hygiene, emotional responses, and pertinent behaviors including depression, anxiety, aggression, hallucinations, or delusions. Clinical observation is probably more effective if conducted in the natural environment (such as classroom or home). However, it is more likely to take place upon admission or in the clinic or hospital ward.

Rating Scales. Clinical observation can provide more valuable information in the clinical situation if it is objectively structured, for example, by using structured rating scales. The most useful rating scales are those that enable a rater to indicate not only the presence or absence of a particular behavior but also its prominence. Standard rating scales can provide a quantifiable format for rating clinical symptoms. For example, the Hamilton Anxiety Rating Scale (M. Hamilton, "The assessment of anxiety states by rating," *British Journal of Medical Psychology*, 1959, 32, 50–55) specifically addresses behavior related to the experience of intense anxiety and has become almost the standard in this respect for assessing anxiety states. Observations made in clinical settings by trained observers can provide behavioral data useful in ongoing clinical management of patients, for example, to focus on specific patient behaviors to be changed.

Psychological Tests

Psychological tests are standardized sets of procedures or tasks for obtaining samples of behavior. A client's responses to the standardized stimuli are compared with those of other people having comparable demographic characteristics, usually through established test norms or test score distributions. Psychological tests are useful diagnostic tools for clinical psychologists in much the same way that blood tests or X-ray films are useful to physicians in diagnosing physical problems. In all these procedures, problems may be revealed in people that would otherwise not be observed. The data from tests allow a clinician to draw inferences about how much the person's psychological qualities differ from those of a reference norm group, typically a sample of "normal" persons. Psychological tests have been developed to measure many psychological attributes in which people vary. Tests have been devised to measure such characteristics as coping patterns, motive patterns, personality factors, role behaviors, values, levels of depression or anxiety, and intellectual functioning.

Two types of psychological tests are typically incorporated in psychological assessments in clinical practice: intelligence tests and personality tests.

Intelligence Tests. In many cases, it is important to have an evaluation of the person's level of intellectual functioning. The clinician can assess intellectual ability with a wide range of intelligence tests. For example, if the patient is a child, the Wechsler Intelligence Scale for Children-Revised or WISC-III (Psychological Corporation, *Wechsler Intelligence Scale for Children [WISC III] manual*, San Antonio, Texas, 1992) and the current edition of the Stanford–Binet Intelligence Scale (Terman, L. M. *The Stanford–Binet [4th Ed.]. Standard–Binet Intelligence Scale: Manual for the 4th Ed.*, Boston, 1997) might be used for measuring the child's intellectual abilities. For measuring adult intelligence, the Wechsler Adult Intelligence Scale-Revised or WAIS-III (Psychological Corporation, *WAIS-III manual*, San Antonio, Texas, 1997) is the most frequently used measure.

Individually administered intelligence tests—such as the WISC-R, the WAIS-III, and the Stanford–Binet—are labor intensive and typically require 2 to 3 hours to administer, score, and interpret. The information obtained about the cognitive functioning of patients, however, can provide useful hypotheses about the person's intellectual resources and capability of dealing with problems.

Personality Tests. The clinician would likely employ several tests designed to measure personal characteristics. Personality tests are of two general types: projective and objective.

Projective Techniques. Projective techniques are unstructured tasks, for example, ambiguous stimuli such as incomplete sentences, which the person is asked to complete. The individual's responses to these ambiguous materials are thought to reveal a great deal about their personal problems, conflicts, motives, coping techniques, and personality traits. One important assumption underlying the use of projective techniques is that individuals (in trying to make sense out of vague, unstructured stimuli) tend to "project" their own problems, motives, and wishes into the situation, because they have little else on which to rely in formulating their responses to these materials. Projective tests are considered to be valuable in providing clues as to an individual's past learning and personality. The three most frequently used projective tests are the Sentence Completion Test, the Thematic Apperception Test (TAT), and the Rorschach. Due to space considerations we will examine in detail only the Rorschach and the TAT.

The *Rorschach test* was developed by the Swiss psychiatrist Hermann Rorschach in 1911. The test uses ten inkblot pictures the person is instructed to look at and respond to in terms of "what it looks like or reminds you of." After the initial responses to all the cards are recorded, the examiner then goes back through the responses to determine "what about the inkblot made it look the way it did." Once the responses are obtained, the clinician must then interpret what they mean. This normally involves scoring the protocol according to a standard method in order to determine what the responses mean. The most widely used and reliable scoring system is the Exner Comprehensive System (Exner & Weiner, 1993). The indexes resulting from the scoring summary are then employed to explore the literature to determine the meaning of the responses. Experience with the instrument is extremely important in arriving at useful hypotheses about clients.

The THEMATIC Apperception Test (TAT) was introduced in 1935 by C. D. Morgan and H. A. Murray ("A method for investigating fantasies," *Archives of Neurology and Psychiatry*, 1935, 34, 289–306) as a means of studying personality traits. The TAT uses a series of pictures about which a subject is instructed to make up stories. The content of the pictures is highly ambiguous as to actions and motives, so that people tend to project or attribute their own conflicts and worries into their stories. Interpretation of the stories is impressionistic. The interpreter reads the constructions and rationally determines what potential motives as behavioral tendencies the respondent might have in "seeing" the pictures in the ways they did. The content of the TAT stories is thought to reflect the person's underlying traits, motives, and preoccupations.

Projective tests, like the Rorschach and TAT, can be valuable in many clinical assessment situations, particularly in cases where the task involves obtaining a comprehensive picture of a person's personality makeup. The great strengths of projective techniques are their unstructured nature and their focus on the unique aspects of personality. However, this is also a weakness because their interpretation is subjective, unreliable, and difficult to validate. In addition, projective tests typically require a great deal of time to administer and advanced skill to interpret. The clinician also needs to employ more objective tasks in order to put the client's symptoms and behavior in an appropriate perspective.

Objective Personality Scales: The MMPI-2. Objective tests are *structured* in that they use questions or items that are carefully phrased. In giving alternative responses as choices, they provide a more quantifiable format than projective instruments and, thus, are more objective. This provides greater response, which in turn enhances the reliability of test outcomes. The most widely used of the major structured inventories for personality assessment is the Minnesota Multiphasic Personality Inventory (MMPI), now the MMPI-2 after a revision in 1989 (J. N. Butcher, W. G. Dahlstrom, J. R. Graham, A. Tellegen, & B. Kaemmer, *Minnesota Multiphasic Personality Inventory-2 (MMPI-2): Manual for administration and scoring,* Minneapolis, 1989). It is described here because in many ways it is the most successful test in this class of instruments and because it is the most widely studied test.

The MMPI was introduced for general use in 1943 by S. R. Hathaway and J. C. McKinley; it is today the most widely used personality test for both clinical assessment and psychopathologic research in the United States and is the assessment instrument most frequently taught in graduate clinical psychology programs. Moreover, translated versions of the MMPI-2 are widely used internationally (J. N. Butcher, *International adaptations of the MMPI-2,* Minneapolis, 1996). The MMPI-2 consists of 567 items covering topics ranging from physical symptoms and psychological problems and social attitudes. Normally, subjects are encouraged to answer all of the items either *true* or *false.*

The MMPI-2 is interpreted by scoring scales that have been devised to measure clinical problems. The MMPI clinical scales were originally developed by an empirical item selection method. The pool of items for the inventory was administered to a large group of normal and several quite homogeneous groups of clinical patients who had been carefully diagnosed. Answers to the items were then analyzed to see which ones differentiated the various groups. On the basis of the findings, the clinical scales were constructed, each consisting of the items that were answered by one of the patient groups in the direction opposite to the predominant response of the normal group. This method of item selection, known as empirical keying, produced scales that were valid in predicting symptoms and behavior. If a person's pattern of true/false responses closely approximates that of a particular group, such as depressed patients, it is a reasonable inference that

he or she shares other psychiatrically significant characteristics with the group, and may, in fact, be functioning "psychologically" like others in that group.

Each of these "clinical" scales measures tendencies to respond in psychologically deviant ways. Raw scores of a client are compared with the scores of the normal population, many of whom did (and do) answer a few items in the critical direction, and the results are plotted on the standard MMPI-2 profile form. By drawing a line connecting the scores for the different scales, a clinician can construct a profile that shows how far from normal a patient's performance is on each of the scales. The schizophrenia scale, for example, is made up of the items that schizophrenic patients consistently answered in a way that differentiated them from normal individuals. People who score high (relative to norms) on this scale, though not necessarily schizophrenic, often show characteristics typical of the schizophrenic population. For instance, high scorers on this scale may be socially withdrawn, have peculiar thought processes, may have diminished contact with reality, and in severe cases may have delusions and hallucinations.

One extremely useful feature of the MMPI-2 is that it contains a number of scales to evaluate test-taking attitudes. It includes a number of validity scales to detect whether a patient has answered the questions in a straightforward, honest manner. For example, there is one scale that detects lying or claiming extreme virtue, and several scales to detect faking or malingering. Extreme endorsement of the items on any of these measures may invalidate the test.

The MMPI-2 is used in several ways to evaluate a patient's personality characteristics and clinical problems. The traditional use of the MMPI-2 is as a diagnostic standard. The individual's profile pattern is compared with profiles of known patient groups. If the client's profile matches a particular group, information about patients in this group can suggest a broad descriptive diagnosis for the patient under study. A second approach to MMPI interpretation is referred to as content interpretation. This approach is used to supplement the empirical interpretation by focusing on the content themes in a person's response to the inventory. For example, if an individual endorses an unusually large number of items about depression, a clinician might well conclude that the subject is preoccupied with low mood.

Applications of Clinical Assessment

Psychological assessment methods have found applicability in a broad range of settings. Three diverse applications will be highlighted to illustrate their use.

Assessment in Mental Health Settings. Most clinical assessment is undertaken in medical, psychiatric, or prison settings to evaluate the mental health status of people undergoing problems. The practitioner would administer, score, and interpret the battery of tests, usually at the beginning of the clinical contact, and develop an integrated report. The report would likely focus on such tasks as developing mental health treatment plans (L. E. Beutler & M. R. Berran, *Integrative Assessment of Adult Personality*, 1995).

Psychological Assessment in Forensic or Legal Cases. One of the fastest-growing applications of psychological tests involves their use in evaluating clients in court cases. Psychological tests have been found to provide valuable information for forensic evaluations, particularly if they contain a means of assessing the person's test-taking attitudes (such as the MMPI-2, which contains several measures that provide an appraisal of the person's cooperativeness or frankness in responding to the test items). Many litigants or defendants in criminal cases attempt to present themselves in a particular way (for example, to appear disturbed in the case of an insanity plea or impeccably virtuous when trying to present a false or exaggerated physical injury), and their motivations to "fake good" or "fake bad" tend to result in noncredible test patterns.

Because of their scientific acceptability, well-known psychological tests, such as the WAIS-III and MMPI-2, are widely accepted by courts as appropriate assessment instruments. In order for a test to be allowed into testimony, it must be shown to be an accepted scientific standard. The primary means of assuring that tests are appropriate for court testimony is that they are standardized and are not experimental procedures (J. Ogloff, The legal basis of forensic application of the MMPI-2. In Y. S. Ben-Porath, J. R. Graham, G. C. N. Hall, R. D. Hirschman, & M. S. Zaragoza (Eds.), *Forensic applications of the MMPI-2*, Thousand Oaks, CA, 1995). Psychological assessments in court cases can provide information about the mental state of felons on trial, to assess the psychological adjustment of litigants in civil court cases and to aid in the determination of child custody in divorce cases.

Use of Psychological Tests in Personnel Screening

Personality tests in testing employment screening have a long tradition. Actually, the first formal use of a standardized personality scale in the United States was implemented to screen out World War I draftees who were psychologically unfit for military service (R. S. Woodworth, *The Personal Data Sheet*, Chicago, 1920). Today, personality tests are widely used for personnel screening in occupations that require great public trust. Some occupations such as police officers, airline flight crews, firefighters, nuclear power plant workers, and certain military specialties require greater emotional stability than most other jobs. Maladaptive personality traits or behavior problems in such employees can result in public safety concerns. For example, someone who behaves in an irresponsible manner in a nuclear power plant control room could significantly endanger the operation of the facility and the surrounding community. The potential for problems can be so great in some high-stress occupations that measures need to be taken in the hiring process to evaluate applicants for emotional adjustment.

Personnel screening for emotional stability and potentially irresponsible behavior requires a somewhat different set of assumptions than clinical assessment. One assumption is that personality or emotional problems, such as poor reality contact, impulsivity, or pathological indecisiveness, would adversely affect the way in which a person would function in a critical job. Psychological tests should not be the sole means of determining whether a person is hired. Psychological tests are more appropriately used in the context of an employment interview, a background check, and a careful evaluation of previous work records.

Summary

Psychological assessment is one of the most important and complex activities undertaken by clinical psychologists. The goals of psychological assessment include identifying and describing the individual's symptoms and possible causes and severity of the problem, as well as exploring the individual's personal resources, which might be valuable in the decisions to be made.

A broad range of psychological assessment methods is used for gathering relevant psychological information for clinical decisions about people. The most flexible assessment methods are the clinical interview and behavior observation. These methods can provide a wealth of clinical information. Psychological tests are used to measure personality by employing standardized stimuli for collecting behavior samples that can be compared with other individuals through test norms. Two different personality testing methods have been employed: projective tests, such as the Rorschach, in which unstructured stimuli are presented to a subject, who then "projects" meaning or structure onto the stimulus, thereby revealing "hidden" motives, feelings, and so on; and objective tests, or personality inventories, in which a subject is required to read and respond to itemized statements or questions. Objective personality tests usually provide a cost-effective way of collecting personality information. The MMPI-2 provides a number of clinically relevant scales for describing abnormal behavior. Psychological tests are widely used for making clinical decisions in mental health settings, forensic applications, and personnel screening for positions that require emotionally stable employees.

Bibliography

American Psychiatric Association. (1994). *Diagnostic* and statistical manual of mental disorders (4th ed.). Washington, DC: Author.

Butcher, J. N. (1991). Screening for psychopathology: Industrial applications of the Minnesota Multiphasic Personality Inventory-2 (MMPI-2). In J. Jones, B. D. Steffey, & D. Bray (Eds.), *Applying psychology in business: The manager's handbook* (pp. 835–850). Boston: Lexington Books.

Exner, J. E., & Weiner, I. (1995). *The Rorschach: A comprehensive system. Vol. 3. Assessment of children and adolescents.* (2nd ed.). New York: Wiley.

Ogloff, J. R. P. (1995). The legal basis of forensic application of the MMPI-2. In Y. S. Ben-Porath, J. R. Graham, G. C. N. Hall, R. D. Hirschman, & M. S. Zaragoza (Eds.), *Forensic applications of the MMPI-2* (pp. 18–47). Thousand Oaks, CA: Sage.

Piotrowski, C., & Keller, J. W. (1992). Psychological testing in applied settings: A literature review from 1982–1992. *Journal of Training and Practice in Professional Psychology, 6*(2), 74–82.

Piotrowski, C., & Zalewski, C. (1993). Training in diagnostic testing in APA approved PsyD and PhD clinical psychology programs. *Journal of Personality Assessment, 61*(2), 394–405.

James N. Butcher

Interventions

Interventions in clinical psychology are behavioral or verbal actions taken by a professional with the intention of altering the emotions, thoughts, or actions of a client in the direction of greater health or adaptiveness. We often think of interventions as synonymous with psychotherapy, and of this psychotherapy as taking place in the office of the professional. On both counts, this is only an approximation of the truth. Interventions occur in private offices, but they also occur in public outpatient settings as well as in a wide range of inpatient settings, and can also take place in facilities within the community at large. These interventions include psychotherapy, perhaps as the most prominent example, but also include many other actions by trained professionals. It should also be noted that there are important interventions currently outside the scope of clinical psychology, such as the use of psychotropic drugs to alter emotions, thoughts, and actions. Finally, interventions can be used by psychologists in fields other than clinical psychology, and by professionals in disciplines other than psychology. This entry will be restricted to the activities of clinical psychologists, with all the caveats implied above, and with full recognition of the great breadth of interventions that are available to the professional community.

Perhaps the best way of organizing the approaches to intervention is derived from public health, and consists of distinguishing among various levels of prevention (Caplan, 1964). The most basic level, *primary prevention*, refers to efforts to reduce the incidence of psychosocial problems, and thus is geared toward preventing the occurrence of the target problem. In a medical setting, vaccination would be a good example of a primary prevention effort. Next is *secondary prevention*, an attempt to reduce the duration of difficulties that already have occurred, directed toward the early identification and treatment of an existing problem so as to minimize its potential for damage to the client. Medically, screening that allows early detection of illness, such as X-rays to detect tuberculosis, would qualify as secondary prevention. Finally, there is *tertiary prevention*, or the treatment of an already existing disorder so as to reduce the severity of its impact. Seeking the services of a physician after developing the symptoms of a disorder is the usual tertiary prevention effort we see in the medical community.

Clearly, the use of the term *prevention* is different in this technical sense than it is in common parlance, as tertiary prevention is much more commonly associated with treatment than with prevention. Additionally, there are many approaches to secondary prevention. The approaches that identify problems in their earliest stages are consistent with our usual thoughts about prevention; however, approaches that address existing acute problems in their early stages might also be thought of as treatment rather than as prevention oriented. Regardless of these difficulties, we will use these distinctions as an organizing framework, and will not attend further to whether activities are truly preventative or more nearly therapeutic.

Although it is not the topic of this entry, mention must be made of the role of evidence in psychological interventions. Many interventions are based on clinical experience rather than on a solid scientific footing, much as is the case in medicine. However, the importance of using whatever evidence exists, and of contributing to the body of knowledge that does exist, cannot be gainsaid. It is encouraging to note that a growing number of psychological interventions are rooted in a substantial knowledge base (Roth & Fonagy, 1996), and this should influence practice in future years. In evaluating existing evidence, it also is critical to recognize the distinction between efficacy and effectiveness. Briefly, efficacy refers to evidence gathered in a research environment, allowing for all of the controls that are necessary to generate sound findings. Effectiveness refers to evidence gathered in a clinical setting, with all of the naturalistic variables at play that serve to reduce the ability to implement the best of experimental designs, but that do encourage generalizability to the setting in which the intervention is to be used. The two sources of evidence are not in competition with one another, but should complement each other in developing a clear sense of which findings have a sound scientific foundation, and to whom they apply.

Primary Prevention

Primary prevention efforts can be directed toward the community as a whole, or toward specific groups of individuals within the community. Thus, the focus can be on the environment or on the individual. Although it may seem as though psychologists would be most interested in the individual, there are several examples of psychologically based, environmentally oriented prevention programs. For example, an attempt to establish job training programs, or a remedial education program, within a disadvantaged community is an example of a service that is intended to have an impact on an entire community that may be viewed as at risk, and should serve to ameliorate some of the sources of risk. A more focussed approach that is similar to this is when specific groups are identified on the basis of their developmental status, and programs are developed to be helpful to them. Examples of such programs include well baby clinics, premarital counseling programs, and retirement counseling efforts. In these cases, there are no specific identified patients, and there are no symptoms that have been developed yet, but individuals at those stages of life are viewed as being at risk for the development of symptoms, and attempts to help them can prevent the difficulty before it occurs. Other, less developmentally based programs focus on conditions that often lead to difficulty, but do so before the difficulty begins. Programs for children of alcoholics or for people who have been victimized by a natural disaster can anticipate the stress of these circumstances and provide assistance before the stress begins to take its toll. Finally, primary prevention programs not only can serve to reduce the incidence of emotional problems, they also can be designed so as to enhance functioning in otherwise well-functioning individuals.

There are many examples of primary prevention programs, but one exemplar must suffice at this point. The best known of all the primary prevention programs, in all likelihood, is Project Head Start (Zigler & Valentine, 1979). Head Start was a massive and politically charged federal program that was developed in order to increase the ability of disadvantaged children to express social competence. It is a classic example of primary prevention, in that attention was focused on preschool children who were at risk for social difficulties in order to forestall those difficulties with a preemptive psychological and educational intervention. The project has been subjected to a great deal of evaluation research because of its political implications, and probably has been overly praised by its defenders and overly criticized by its detractors. Nonetheless, the results appear to indicate that children in the program, as compared to those who were not, showed clear benefits. They also demonstrated gains on preschool achievement tests (not the focus of the project), but these dissipated over time (and may have been maintained if there had been adequate follow-up, either at home or in the schools). It is not necessary to pursue the political agendas that have greeted evaluations of Project Head Start to note that it was an effort directed at children at risk and, at least on some levels, the children benefited, thereby demonstrating the potential advantage of a primary prevention intervention.

Secondary Prevention

Secondary prevention efforts have a clearly defined target, unlike primary prevention, which is directed toward populations rather than people, because signs of difficulty already are present when secondary prevention becomes appropriate. These signs may be in the early stages of a disorder, or they might be more extreme and occur in the acute phase of the disorder. In either case, the goal of secondary prevention is to assure that the disorder is arrested at an early stage so that the long-term consequences for the client are minimized.

Secondary prevention programs that target early stages of potentially damaging disorders are similar to the high-risk interventions of primary prevention, but incipient signs of difficulty already are present. The establishment of hot lines to provide access to services for people who feel in need, such as suicide hot lines, is a good example of such an effort. Attempts to provide counseling and other services for preadolescents with some behavioral problems in school also can be classified as secondary prevention. These efforts do have the danger of overprediction, as many identified high-risk people will not develop the feared condition. However, in a serious matter such as suicide, providing services for many people who would not need them is a small price to pay for offering such services to the very few who would go on to make an attempt on their life.

The exemplar we will describe for secondary prevention is the Primary Mental Health Project (PMHP; Cowen et al., 1996). Primary refers to the grade of the children being studied and not to the level of prevention, as this is a secondary prevention project directed at high-risk children. The PMHP originated more than 40 years ago and has both undergone continuous evolution and spawned multiple attempts to duplicate its success in other school districts. Of particular note, not only has the project provided service to many needy children, it also has been subject to critical research scrutiny, so that the apparent success can be well documented.

The heart of the program is a massive screening effort with 6-year-old children in school. Children who displayed either actual signs of maladjustment or a high probability that it would develop were identified by the placement of a red tag on their school folders. These children, left to their own devices, developed in a more dysfunctional manner than their non-red-tagged peers. The introduction of a comprehensive mental health program in the school led to a significant improvement in all of the children in the school, including those who otherwise seemed destined for multiple problems. This ability to intervene at an early stage and reduce the severity of subsequent pathology is an excellent example of secondary prevention.

Tertiary Prevention

Tertiary prevention only can be considered prevention under the nomenclature that we have adopted. It ordinarily would be viewed as treatment, and as the stereotypic view of what psychological intervention consists of. When we think of clinical psychological intervention, we usually think of individual psychotherapy delivered by a clinical psychologist to a single client in a private office setting. This is tertiary prevention, but it is not all of tertiary prevention activities. Tertiary prevention, or psychotherapy, can take place in many settings with many modalities and many orientations. Many are described at greater length separately, so we will simply review the large number of possibilities that fall under this rubric.

Let us first address some of the modalities of psychotherapy that exist. Many clients are seen individually, but other possibilities also exist. Small groups, such as couples, can be seen. Typically, these couples are heterosexual married couples who seek help with a dysfunctional relationship. However, dysfunctional relationships can exist in other groupings, so that we also have couples therapy for unmarried couples, for homosexual couples, for adult parent and child, and for unrelated couples such as business partners. The group can become larger if the entire family is seen, and family therapy, too, can be offered to families of many types. In even larger groups, therapy can be used to help unrelated people gathered together, or these people may be related by a common concern, such as alcoholism. The groups often have professional leadership, but many 12-step programs are leaderless, or are led by nonpsychologists. In another variation, some groups have more than one leader. In some cases, the intention of the group is not to correct psychopathology but rather to enhance functioning and promote growth, but such groups would not be considered tertiary prevention activities (groups also can be used for primary and secondary prevention).

The venue in which intervention is offered can be a private office, but it is not limited to that setting. Much intervention occurs in public facilities, such as community mental health centers. The most seriously impaired of clients frequently are treated, at least initially, in an inpatient hospital setting, from which they may go on to a partial care setting such as a day hospital, and then may be returned to the community for individual treatment. Much intervention of value is delivered within a school setting. Within hospitals, treatment can be offered as a liaison to medical services, such as psychotherapy intended to reduce the anxiety of a patient with a serious medical illness, or in anticipation of a stressful procedure such as surgery. The settings in which psychotherapy is offered, and the combinations of clients who may be seen, are limited only by the imagination of the clinical psychologist. However, with all these variants possible, it remains critical for research programs to document the success (or failure) of each effort.

Estimates of the number of orientations to psychotherapy vary from a very small number to well over 400. The larger estimates confer the title of orientation on every variation of technique that exists, and probably are using the term orientation improperly. Two very common, and much smaller, estimates of the number of orientations are two and three. The two orientations consist of action and reflection, with some approaches geared toward active attempts to change behavior and thought, and other approaches focused primarily on increasing self-reflection and self-knowledge. It is likely that active changes in the client will lead to some changes in self-regarding attitudes, and that greater insight will lead to some behavioral change, so that the division between the two is not as clean as it may seem. Often the three orientations are seen as psychodynamic, behavioral, and humanistic. Psychodynamic approaches are the oldest, and clearly fit in the reflection category. They place a premium on self-understanding, with the implicit (or sometimes explicit) assumption that increased self-understanding will produce salutary changes in the client. Behavioral approaches are geared toward action, with a clear attempt to mobilize the resources of the client in the direction of change, whether or not there is any understanding of the etiology of the problem or the ramifications of the change. Humanistic approaches also aim toward increased self-understanding, often in the direction of personal growth, but use treatment techniques that often are much more active than are likely to be employed by the psychodynamic clinician.

These very broad categories each describe what may be seen as a pure-form orientation. However, more and more, clinicians are following hybrid approaches that attempt to combine the best of the various approaches, either as guided by an attempt to select whatever works best (eclecticism) or in a manner that is guided by theory (psychotherapy integration). Because of the importance of the psychotherapy integration movement (Stricker & Gold, 1993), we will describe it in much greater detail as an important contemporary development in tertiary prevention.

Psychotherapy Integration. Psychotherapy integration includes various attempts to look beyond the confines of single-school, pure-form approaches in order to see what can be learned from other perspectives. It is characterized by an openness to various ways of integrating diverse theories and techniques. The term *psychotherapy integration* has been applied to a common-factors approach to understanding psychotherapy, to assimilative integration (a combination of treatments drawn from different approaches but guided by a unitary theoretical understanding), and to theoretical integration (an attempt to understand the patient by developing a superordinate theoretical framework that draws from a variety of different frameworks).

Common factors refer to aspects of psychotherapy that are present in most, if not all, approaches to treatment. Most practicing psychotherapists appear to be aware of this common core and, as a result, we can expect that more experienced therapists will make greater use of the common factors. Although there is no fixed, established list of common factors, consensus suggests that such a list would include the development of a therapeutic alliance, exposure of the patient to prior difficulties followed by a new corrective emotional experience, expectations by the therapist and by the patient for positive change, beneficial therapist qualities such as attention, empathy, and positive regard, and the provision to the patient of a rationale for problems. For those therapists who are impressed by the mutative role of the common factors, the critical question is how much any specific technique or theoretical understanding adds to the benefit provided by these common factors. It is for this reason that the inclusion of a control group that provides the common factors is critical in any definitive psychotherapy research program.

Assimilative integration is an approach in which a solid grounding in one theoretical position is accompanied by a willingness to incorporate techniques from other therapeutic approaches. It probably is the single most practiced approach to psychotherapy integration, although many practitioners may not have the terminology to refer to it as such. Whatever the theoretical preference of the therapist may be, it is not unusual to incorporate techniques from other approaches, and this constitutes an attempt to assimilate these other approaches into the one defined by the dominant preference. This also leads to a challenge to the dominant theory, as the therapist must then think about why this effective approach is not suggested by the preferred theory, and what the success means in terms of possible needed revisions to the theory.

Theoretical integration is the most difficult level at which to achieve integration, for it requires bringing together concepts from disparate approaches, some of which may differ in their fundamental worldview. Thus, for example, the possible integration of psychoanalysis and behavior therapy (Wachtel, 1977) requires an integration of an approach that sees people as unwitting victims of their history with another that views people as actively capable of altering their fate and making it work out well in the end. It also requires finding an appropriate balance between the reflection favored by one and the action preferred by the other. It is much easier to assimilate the techniques of either approach into the theory of the other than it is to develop a true integrative theory that combines such disparate assumptions and roots.

An eclectic approach, in contrast to psychotherapy integration, is one in which the therapist chooses interventions because they work, without the need for a theoretical basis for, or understanding of, or necessary concern with, the reason for using the technique other than the one of efficacy. Psychotherapy integration differs from eclecticism in that it attends to the relationship between theory and technique. However, several practitioners of eclecticism feel that they do employ theory, and this distinction may be one that is more reliant on terminology then on genuine difference.

The general point to be made is that there is a clear value to the role of theory in the combination of therapeutic techniques, whether or not the process is called psychotherapy integration. This is true whether the theory is the level at which integration occurs, the framework that governs the choice of a breadth of technical interventions, or the organizing principle for understanding the common factors that are present in all psychotherapy.

Bibliography

Bongar, B., & Beutler, L. E. (Eds.). (1995). *Comprehensive textbook of psychotherapy: Theory and practice.* New York: Oxford University Press.

Caplan, G. (1964). *Principles of preventive psychiatry.* New York: Basic Books.

Cowen, E. L., Hightower, A. D., Pedro-Carroll. J. L., Work, W. C., Wyman, P. A., & Haffey, W. G. (1996). *School-based prevention for children at risk: The Primary Mental Health Project.* Washington, DC: American Psychological Association.

Freedheim, D. K. (Ed.) (1992). *History of psychotherapy: A century of change.* Washington, DC: American Psychological Association.

Gurman, A. S., & Messer, S. B. (Eds.). (1995). *Essential psychotherapies: Theory and practice.* New York: Guilford Press.

Roth, A., & Fonagy, P. (1996). *What works for whom?: A critical review of psychotherapy research.* New York: Guilford Press.

Stricker, G., & Gold, J. (Eds.). (1993). *Comprehensive handbook of psychotherapy integration.* New York: Plenum Press.

Wachtel, P. L. (1977). *Psychoanalysis and behavior therapy: Toward an integration.* New York: Basic Books.

Zigler, E., & Valentine, J. (Eds.). (1979). *Project Head Start: A legacy of the war on poverty.* New York: Free Press.

George Stricker

COCAINE. In nature, cocaine occurs in the leaves of two species of the *Erythroxylum* shrub, which flourish along the eastern slopes of the Andes (*E. coca*) and the Caribbean coast (*E. novogranatense*) of South America. The leaves have been chewed by native civilizations for centuries to elicit feelings of energy and euphoria. When cocaine was isolated from coca leaves in 1860, it became popular in Europe and the United States as a tonic and stimulant. Enterprising businesses added it to liquers, soft drinks, wines, and even cigarettes and cheroots. By the early 1900s, problems of cocaine abuse became increasingly common, and legislation soon emerged to restrict the sale and distribution of cocaine as well as other narcotics. Cocaine use went underground and largely remained there until the 1970s when changing social attitudes, coupled with an incomplete understanding of the consequences of cocaine dependence, helped fuel a modern cocaine epidemic. It began with the spread of cocaine to the middle class, which used the drug as a water-soluble hydrochloride salt mainly for sniffing. The epidemic changed shape in the late 1980s with the widespread availability of cocaine free base, or crack, a readily smokable form of cocaine hydrochloride. Because crack is cheap, its use spread rapidly among the urban poor. As a further complication, crack shortened the time lag for the development of addiction from months or years to weeks. Almost 3 million cocaine users in the United States are estimated to be in need of treatment.

Pharmacodynamics

Although the central actions of cocaine are the same regardless of the route of administration, a rapid entry into the brain appears to enhance both the "rush" that cocaine users report and the likelihood of abuse. Such entry is assured when cocaine hydrochloride is injected intravenously or the free base form is smoked. With either of these routes of administration, arterial plasma levels of cocaine peak within 15 seconds. Correspondingly, intravenous and smoked cocaine are associated with a high incidence of abuse. The pattern of abuse is irregular, characterized by a binge of readministration, often at progressively higher doses, every 10 to 30 minutes for many hours or even days. Cocaine and its metabolites are generally eliminated from the body within a few days after a binge, though in abstinent chronic users, traces may remain for up to three weeks.

Clinical and Behavioral Characteristics

Perhaps the most widely reported response to the first administration of cocaine is a state of alertness accompanied by a sense of heightened well-being. Both addicts and laboratory subjects describe a cocaine-induced magnification of most normal pleasures, while anxiety and social inhibitions decline. These and other perceived effects may vary with environment and other nonpharmacological factors, though research on this topic is sparse. Cocaine is known to increase cardiac load by increasing blood pressure and heart rate, while reducing the flow of blood to the heart. Cocaine also acts as a local anesthetic and is still used medicinally to anesthetize the upper respiratory tract. In some cases, the cardiovascular complications, which can be exacerbated by a local anesthetic action, are fatal.

With continued cocaine use, addiction and dependence develop over a highly variable time course. Addiction is characterized by high-dose, long-duration binging, the goal of which is to regain a state of euphoria that becomes increasingly elusive as tolerance sets in. Behavior becomes focused on acquiring more cocaine. Psychotic manifestations also emerge, most notably paranoia, hallucinations, delusions, and a compulsive, stereotyped pattern of movement and thinking. Although the psychosis often dissipates soon after cessation of use, some symptoms have been reported to persist. Complete cessation is difficult. The intense dysphoria that accompanies withdrawal triggers memories of the cocaine-induced euphoria, prompting a return to the drug.

In animals, cocaine induces behavioral hyperactivity, which shows signs of sensitization with repeated treatment, a form of reverse tolerance much like the binge-induced psychosis in humans. Both the hyperactivity and the psychosis are attenuated by antipsychotic drugs. Amphetamine, a synthetic stimulant with a longer duration of action, elicits many of the same clinical and behavioral effects as cocaine but without the profound local anesthesia.

Neurobiology and Treatment

Cocaine has a clearly defined action on the major monoamine transmitters in the brain: dopamine (DA), norepinephrine (NE), and serotonin (5-HT). It binds to the membrane proteins responsible for removing these transmitters from the synapse, the so-called transporter proteins. This action disables an important monoamine-regulating mechanism, resulting in abnormally high levels of synaptic monoamines. Although the effects of cocaine on NE and 5-HT transmission play a role in behavioral responding, the DA transporter is considered the primary site of cocaine action.

Dopamine neurons not only innervate portions of the basal ganglia, which regulate sensorimotor functioning, but also cortical and limbic areas thought to control pleasure or reward. In animals, electrical self-stimulation of the mesocorticolimbic DA system induces reward-seeking behavior that closely matches that of cocaine self-administration. The behavior, moreover, occurs in conjunction with an increase in mesocorticolimbic DA transmission and is attenuated by lesions of this system or by DA receptor antagonists. By blocking DA transport, therefore, cocaine appears to gain access to a neuronal system critical for reward. Brain-imaging studies in humans have confirmed that the doses used by cocaine abusers do, in fact, block the DA transporter and that this blockade correlates with the euphoric effects of cocaine. Although many other drugs of abuse do not act directly on the DA transporter, they all share an ability to increase mesocorticolimbic DA transmission. This neurochemical response also occurs during natural behavior considered to have rewarding effects, including feeding, novelty-seeking, and sex.

Although cocaine is closely linked to DA and reward, addiction to cocaine involves many behavioral changes, including cognitive dysfunction and loss of control as well as compulsive drug intake. In addition, repeated cocaine administration triggers complex neuroadaptations not only in the mesocorticolimbic DA system but in other neuronal systems as well, further complicating the search for a neurobiological substrate. Thus, the prospect of an effective treatment for cocaine addiction remains elusive. At present, the most successful measures involve peer-support groups, education sessions, and individual therapy, but relapse remains a common problem. The search continues for a pharmacotherapy based on cocaine-induced changes in neuronal function. Such therapy, used in conjunction with effective behavioral interventions, holds the best hope for treating the problem of cocaine dependence.

[See also Drug Abuse.]

Bibliography

Di Chiara, G. (1995). The role of dopamine in drug abuse viewed from the perspective of its role in motivation. *Drug and Alcohol Dependence, 38,* 95–137.

Fischman, M. W., & Johanson, C. E. (1996). Cocaine. *Pharmacological Aspects of Drug Dependence, Handbook of Experimental Pharmacology, 118,* 159–195.

Gawin, F. H. (1991). Cocaine addiction: psychology and neurophysiology. *Science, 251,* 1580–1586.

Hyman, S. E. (1996). Addiction to cocaine and amphetamine. *Neuron, 16,* 901–904.

Koob, G. F., Caine, S. B., Parsons, L., Markou, A., & Weiss, F. (1997). Opponent process model and psychostimulant addiction. *Pharmacology, Biochemistry and Behavior, 57,* 513–521.

Robinson, T. E., & Berridge, K. C. (1993). The neural basis of drug craving, an incentive-sensitization theory of addiction. *Brain Research Reviews, 18,* 247–291.

Schindler, C. W. (1996). Cocaine and cardiovascular toxicity. *Addiction Biology, 1,* 31–47.

Self, D. W., & Nestler, E. J. (1995). Molecular mechanisms of drug reinforcement and addiction. *Annual Review of Neuroscience, 18,* 463–495.

White, F. J. (1996). Synaptic regulation of mesocorticolimbic dopamine neurons. *Annual Review of Neuroscience, 19,* 405–436.

Wise, R. A. (1996). Neurobiology of addiction. *Current Opinion in Neurobiology, 6,* 243–251.

George V. Rebec

COERCION. *See* Violence and Aggression.

COGNITION. The word "cognitive" comes from the Latin word "cognare," which means "to know." Hence, cognitive psychology is the study of the behavior of knowing or thought. Although experimental psychologists have long studied issues relevant to this topic, this area gained considerable impetus during the late 1950s and early 1960s when psychologists (along with linguists, computer scientists, and neuroscientists) began providing empirical evidence and theoretical models that support the distinctions among qualitatively distinct mental operations. For example, all memories are not the same, that is, short-term memories seem to be qualitatively distinct from long-term memories.

In order to carve out a niche for this burgeoning area of research, Neisser (1967) defined cognitive psychology as the study of all processes by which "a sensory input is transformed, reduced, elaborated, stored, recovered, and used." One might argue that such a definition may be too inclusive, because all processes that are involved from the input of a stimulus to some response by the individual are under the auspices of this definition. In fact, there are now thriving fields such as social cognition, cognitive development, and cognitive neuroscience that illustrate the extension of the cognitive perspective into historically distinct areas of experimental psychology. Moreover, because there is no clear specification that cognition need only involve humans, there is a subfield of experimental psychology referred to as animal cognition. But surely, once one takes this step, then one might question the utility of the label, if indeed all experimental psychologists are at some level cognitive psychologists.

Instead of specifying the processes that cognitive psychologists are interested in, one might specify the (a) major content areas, (b) theoretical assumptions, and (c) modes of study. Regarding content areas, cognitive psychologists have been interested in the study of all processes by which objects are recognized, attended, remembered, imagined, and linguistically elaborated. These basic processes also feed into higher-order decision making and complex problem-solving behavior. Although each of these areas involves a rich and unique set of experimental findings and theoretical developments, the last three decades of research have also indicated that there is considerable overlap across content areas. For example, in developing models of memory, cognitive psychologists must also be sensitive to developments in the area of attention, and vice versa.

Turning to the theoretical assumptions, most cognitive theories still have some resemblance to information processing models, in which earlier stimulus encoding operations lead to (and interact with) more elaborate processes, which eventually lead to some response execution. The stimulus could either be externally presented (such as a picture or a word) or internally generated (such as in a visual image of a picture or an object represented by a word). The first wave of theoretical models developed in cognitive psychology were in large part metaphorical models, e.g., boxes in flow charts reflecting memory stores. However, recent advances in cognitive neuroscience and in computational modeling have produced a second wave of theories that show the promise of being more neurally plausible and computationally specific.

Turning to the method of research, cognitive psychologists rely most heavily on the experimental method in which data are most often gathered in laboratories. Researchers investigate the influence of some independent variable, while controlling for possible extraneous nuisance variables, on a well-characterized dependent measure. Measures of accuracy, response bias, verbal report, and response latency are often the primary dependent measures. In mathematically tractable models, simulations sometimes provide insights into underlying processes. Finally, recent advances in brain imaging now afford researchers an opportunity to measure neural activity (reflected in blood flow changes in areas of the brain or evoked electrical potentials) while individuals are engaged in a cognitive experiment.

In sum, the experimental study of mental processes has extended into a number of diverse fields of psychology along with other disciplines. Although this extension has taken place, cognitive psychology can be defined by a set of targeted areas of study, types of theoretical approaches, and methods of experimental study.

Bibliography

Neisser, U. (1967). *Cognitive psychology.* New York: Appleton-Century Crofts.

David A. Balota

COGNITIVE-AFFECTIVE THEORY. *See* Personality Psychology, *article on* Theories.

COGNITIVE ANTHROPOLOGY. The cognitive revolution has brought to anthropology a series of limited but highly significant changes. Substantive, theoretical, and methodological in character, these developments transpired within a specialty that in the 1980s and 1990s became known as *cognitive anthropology.* (Earlier, from the 1950s through the 1970s, the field was variously termed *ethnoscience, ethnosemantics, folk science,* or *the new ethnography.*) Originally a movement that was attempting to apply advanced linguistic methodology to the study of not only language but all of culture, the early efforts centered on substantive domains of traditional anthropological interest, as, for example, on kinship and the plant and animal worlds. The main aspects of this program of investigation into the structure of categorization systems are presented in the first section below. As categorization research proceeded, dissatisfaction with some of its assumptions about word meaning prompted fruitful theoretical proposals concerning the idea of the *schema,* and of its relationship to cultural knowledge. The second section, on cultural models, outlines recent conceptual advances in thinking about schemas and models. In the final section, culture as consensus, a third area of activity in cognitive anthropology is described. While a unique contribution of culture as consensus has been the clarification and resolution of certain critical issues in method and measurement, generous elements of theory-driven progress will also be found within this area.

Categorization

The study of natural systems of classification and categorization manifested in language has been a primary interest in cognitive anthropology, not only as a way of understanding culture (especially from the native's viewpoint), but also of answering questions about the specificity or universality of human thought processes (see Casson, "Cognitive Anthropology," in Bock, Ed., *Handbook of Psychological Anthropology*, Westport, CT, 1994, pp. 61–96). Early research focused on kinship and ethnobotanical classifications, which were found, respectively, to exhibit paradigmatic and taxonomic organizations. Research in other classification domains, for example, the ethnoanatomical, revealed hierarchical but nontaxonomic structures. At this point, a "feature theory" of meaning was employed in which category members shared a given set of features in contrast to opposing category members that lacked certain features.

Early research on kinship classification, concerned with establishing the "psychological reality" of the paradigm, also developed a variety of formal validating procedures, for example, through the multidimensional scaling of similarity judgments among category members. Scaling results were found to be related to reaction times and to clustering in memory. Continuing research in ethnobotanical classification finds that "natives" classify plants and animals very similarly to the way scientists do, lending strong support to the "bottom-up" argument that certain features of objects in the world are perceptually salient, leading to similar groupings of objects by novices and experts alike (Malt, "Category coherence in cross-cultural perspective," *Cognitive Psychology*, 1995, *29*, 85–148).

Investigation in the domain of color terminology in various languages, once thought to be capricious and arbitrary, also revealed more orderliness than previously suspected. Berlin and Kay (*Basic Color Terms: Their Universality and Evolution*, Berkeley, CA 1969/1991) identified eleven basic color terms that are added to languages in a sequence related to cultural complexity. Basic color term categories are organized around "best" examples, or *focal* colors, upon which there is wide agreement across individuals and languages, although their range of extension is highly variable. Further research has linked this finding to the neurophysiology of color vision, particularly to opponent-process theory. The discovery of categorical "best examples" was also important for the development of *prototype* theory, in which category membership was hypothesized to be graded on the basis of resemblance to the prototype rather than on the principle of all-or-none inclusion.

Cultural Models

The pursuit of questions about the structure of categorization systems eventually led, in the 1970s and early 1980s, to concerns with the ways in which knowledge becomes organized. With this shift, as Naomi Quinn has noted ("'Commitment' in American marriage," *American Ethnologist*, 1982, *9*, 775–798), cognitive anthropology began to converge with the new multidisciplinary field of cognitive science. Cognitive anthropology's contribution to the quest has been to try to elucidate the role of culture in the representation of knowledge.

The concept of the *schema* as a knowledge structure stored in memory was appropriated from cognitive science and applied by anthropologists to a broad array of phenomena. But rather than using the schema concept to understand individual cognition, cognitive anthropologists have employed it as a means to investigate shared mental constructs, that is, *cultural* knowledge. Examples of schemas in U.S. culture would be *romance* or *friendship*. More complex schemas are often labeled "models," and examples of these would be the traditional navigational system used by islanders in Micronesia, or the American model of marriage. For the latter, Quinn has shown (in Holland & Quinn, Eds., *Cultural Models in Language and Thought*, Cambridge, U.K., 1987) that eight characteristics—sharedness, lastingness, mutual benefit, compatibility, difficulty, effort, success/failure, and risk—summarized the key ways her informants talked about marriage. Even broader knowledge systems, for example, grammars of folktales, have also been identified.

Recent theoretical argument, borrowing from connectionist theory in cognitive science, holds that models and schemas are patterns of activation learned from experience, and that they may be constrained by limitations on plasticity, yet be flexible enough to adapt to new or ambiguous situations, and missing or incorrect information. They are also argued to be intimately connected with motives and emotions, so that behavioral outcomes frequently, though not ineluctably, issue from such ideation. Finally, though cultural models and schemas are susceptible to historical change, they are often held to be durable and stable, and not constantly contested (see Strauss & Quinn, *A Cognitive Theory of Cultural Meaning*, Cambridge, U.K., 1997).

Culture as Consensus

The development of "consensus" theory and methodology represents a third major direction in cognitive anthropology. The theory is based on the idea that culture consists of shared meaning and knowledge systems acquired by individuals through experience as members of families, communities, and/or interest groups (Romney, Weller, & Batchelder, 1986). Moreover, the theory posits that this kind of learning and cognitive sharing is not only adaptive but also necessary for the survival of the human species, since no survival information is coded in the human genome. The theory also recognizes that culture is not perfectly shared or homogeneous among all members of a group, and that, in fact, wide intracultural variability exists. In addition, some areas or "domains" of culture may be more widely known than others. Kinship provides an example of a widely known domain compared with knowledge of healing practices, which may be limited to "expert" practitioners. Thus the social distribution of knowledge may be accounted for by numerous factors including gender, age, social status, occupational specialization, and the division of labor in society.

Consensus theory is distinguished in cognitive anthropology by the development of a quantitative methodology to measure consensus, including the overall strength of the pattern of agreement among individuals as well as estimates of individual knowledge. A collection of formal mathematical models has been developed to analyze respondent-item response data where the "correct" answer to each item is unknown in advance, but rather is estimated from the pattern of agreement among individuals, with more weight given to the responses of individuals who agree with each other (Batchelder & Romney, "Test theory without an answer key," *Psychometrika*, 1988, 53, 71–92). It is assumed that individuals will agree with each other in their responses if they hold similar knowledge in common. Psychologists will quickly recognize that this is reliability theory applied to respondents rather than test items, and indeed consensus methodology utilizes much of the accumulated knowledge of traditional psychometric test theory. In applying consensus methodology, the choice of the proper model is dependent on the format of the original questions, with methods developed to analyze true-false (binary), rank order, multiple choice, and fill-in-the-blank formats.

Consensus theory and methodology have been successfully applied in a number of diverse areas including the study of folk medical beliefs, knowledge of specific illnesses, social intelligence, occupational prestige, beliefs among American environmentalists, and social network analysis. It should be noted that successful application of the model usually assumes some preliminary ethnographic interviewing on the researcher's part in order to select a well-ordered domain for analysis as well as to construct questions that are salient and meaningful to informants.

Conclusion

Cognitive anthropology promises to contribute significantly to the study of culture and behavior, not least because it possesses a precision in theory and an explicitness in methodology that are unusual in sociocultural inquiry. Areas that have been less intensively studied in cognitive anthropology and deserve greater attention include the development of cultural models in children and memory processes. But the accomplishments of this subdisciplinary specialty have some already noted implications for psychological theory and research, especially with respect to questions concerning natural category systems, and the problem of the relationship between individual cognition and cultural knowledge.

Bibliography

Atran, S. (1990). *Cognitive foundations of natural history.* Cambridge, England: Cambridge University Press. History and evidence regarding classifications of natural kinds.

Berlin, B. (1992). *Ethnobiological classification.* Princeton, NJ: Princeton University Press. Comparative examination of the indigenous classifications of plants and animals.

Colby, B. N., & Colby, L. M. (1981). *The daykeeper: The life and thought of an Ixil diviner.* Cambridge, MA: Harvard University Press. With data from a Maya diviner, one of the first attempts to apply schema theory to ethnographic material.

D'Andrade, R. G. (1995). *The development of cognitive anthropology.* New York: Cambridge University Press. A definitive history of the field by a leading cognitive anthropologist of our time.

Hutchins, E. (1996). *Cognition in the wild.* Cambridge, MA: MIT Press. Analysis of shipboard navigation. Focuses on the ways human cognition (outside the laboratory) is socially distributed and shaped by culturally constituted activities.

Kempton, W., Boster, J. S., & Hartley, J. A. (1995). *Environmental values in American culture.* Cambridge, MA: MIT Press. A comparative study of different groups of American environmentalists, utilizing cultural models and consensus theory and methodology.

Kronenfeld, D. B. (1996). *Plastic glasses and church fathers: Semantic extension from the ethnoscience tradition.* New York: Oxford University Press. Attempts to explain both the usefulness of language's variability and the mechanisms which enable us to understand each other in spite of the variability.

Romney, A. K. (1994). Cultural knowledge and cognitive structure. In M. M. Suarez-Orozco, G. Spindler, & L. Spindler (Eds.), *The making of psychological anthropology II.* (pp. 254–283). Fort Worth, TX: Harcourt Brace. A personal and professional statement about the value of science and methodology in cognitive anthropology in opposition to postmodernist theory in contemporary anthropology.

Romney, A. K., Boyd, J. P., Moore, C. C., Batchelder, W. H., & Brazil, T. J. (1996). Culture as shared cognitive representations. *Proceedings of the National Academy of Sciences, 93,* 4699–4705. The most recent work on American-English kinship terminology, including current multivariate scaling techniques and utilizing consensus theory and methodology.

Romney, A. K., Weller, & Batchelder, W. H. (1986). Culture as consensus: A theory of culture and informant accuracy. *American Anthropologist, 88,* 313–338.

Taylor, J. R. (1995). *Linguistic categorization: prototypes in linguistic theory* (2nd ed.). New York: Oxford University Press. An overview of prototype theory from a "cognitive linguistic" perspective, with a review of recent research in the field.

Weller, S. C., Pachter, L. M., Trotter, R. T., & Baer, R. D. (1993). *Empacho* in four Latino groups: A study of intra- and inter-cultural variation in beliefs. *Medical Anthropology, 15,* 109–136. Comparative study of folk illness beliefs among four Hispanic groups, utilizing consensus methodology.

Weller, S. C., & Romney, A. K. (1988). *Systematic data collection. Newbury Park, CA: Sage. Introduces consensus theory and other structured data-collection techniques.

Carmella C. Moore and Robert L. Munroe

COGNITIVE-BEHAVIORAL THERAPY (CBT) is integrative, uniting theories of cognition and learning with treatment techniques derived from the cognitive and behavioral therapies. Cognitive-behavioral therapies assume that cognitive, emotional, and behavioral variables are functionally interrelated; therefore, altering one system (such as avoidant behavior) can lead to changes in others (such as dysfunctional thoughts). This model posits that learning is cognitively mediated: individuals respond to cognitive representations of environmental events rather than the events themselves. In other words, not only the situation, but also what one *thinks* of the situation drives his or her response. Consequently, cognitive factors such as expectancies, attributions, and self-talk are targeted along with behaviors such as avoidance in efforts to correct, predict, and understand behavioral and emotional dysfunction.

Historical Precis

As one might presume from the name, cognitive-behavioral theories evolved from bidirectional movements in the existing fields of cognitive psychology and behavioral science. Beginning in the 1950s, there was a rise in psychological therapies based upon behavioral theories. These therapies were unlike the existing psychoanalytic or psychodynamic therapies: they were based on principles of learning, shorter in duration, and relied greatly upon empirical findings. However, in the early 1970s some dissatisfactions arose with strict behavioral therapies. Social learning theorists proposed a central role of an individual's perceptions of events in influencing behaviors and emotional responses, rather than simply the events themselves. Cognitive research demonstrated that people are often biased processors of information and that these biases may be leading to maladaptive behavior, as well as disturbances in affect. There was an associated rise in cognitive therapies that sought to alter cognition as a path to induce behavioral and affective change. This movement, often said to have been led by Aaron Beck, a Philadelphia-area psychiatrist who developed a cognitive treatment for depression (Beck, Rush, Shaw, & Emery, 1979), and Albert Ellis, a New York psychologist who presented his own rational emotive therapy (RET) (now REBT; rational emotive behavior therapy; e.g., Ellis, 1962), expanded rapidly and cognitive therapies were soon developed to treat various client populations.

During the times of expansion, researchers and clinicians alike reported that cognitive factors could be viewed as behavior and, therefore, could be manipulated using techniques related to conventional behavior therapies. Behavioral techniques, such as modeling and reinforcement, could be used to teach clients cognitive strategies and explore the validity of their inferences. Cognitive restructuring techniques and behavioral techniques such as modeling and problem-solving were reconceptualized as cooperative tools for achieving cognitive as well as behavioral changes. In addition, the rise of the critical role of empiricism, which began with the behaviorist movement, was maintained and continues to be a central element of cognitive-behavioral therapies today.

Basic Features

Cognitive-behavioral therapy differs from other psychotherapies in several ways. Unlike traditional psychoanalysis and other psychodynamic approaches, CBT is typically time limited and often requires the therapist to be active and directive (Kendall, 1991). The therapist collaborates with the client, helping him or her solve problems, and helps the client identify effective strategies for coping with difficult situations. Cognitive-behavioral treatments may range from 6 sessions to 30, but they rarely exceed 7 or 8 months. Often, these treatments are based on treatment manuals that indicate specific goals for each session, and recommend techniques to accomplish these goals. The benefits of manual-based treatments are twofold: first, they provide the clinician with a set of guidelines from which to administer the treatment most effectively; and second, they allow for empirical examination because they can be administered consistently across therapists, clients, and settings. The availability of CBT manuals has facilitated empirical research, and in turn, has allowed for adjustments to be made to treatment procedures based upon empirical findings. This emphasis on careful research evaluation and the resultant modification of treatment in accord with the data (focus on empirical support) is not often found in psychodynamic approaches.

Unlike traditional behavior therapies, such as a token economy or systematic desensitization, cognitive-behavioral therapy places greater importance on an individual's cognitive functioning and the role of cognitive processing in influencing behavior and affect. For example, a behavior therapist might treat a socially phobic person by exposing the client to social activities for several sessions. This treatment would be appropriate and likely effective. A cognitive-behavioral therapist would also employ exposure, but might, in addition, identify the client's thoughts (self-talk) concerning social events, teach the client strategies to modify these thoughts, and discuss the thinking that took place before, during, and after the exposure exercises. Similar to cognitive therapies, one aim of CB therapies is to modify or alter maladaptive self-talk and reinforce and support more adaptive and useful ways of thinking. However, in cognitive-behavioral therapies this is accomplished through the use of behavioral techniques such as exposure, modeling, reinforcement, and homework, in addition to cognitive strategies such as coping skills training. In fact, these names (e.g., cognitive therapy, behavioral therapy, cognitive-behavioral therapy) are often used somewhat interchangeably, thus leading to confusion and occasional disagreements.

Cognitive-behavioral therapy focuses on social information processing—how the individual thinks about himself or herself and his or her environment. There are two ways in which a client's thoughts may be maladaptive: distortion or deficiency (Kendall, 1991). Individuals who experience *distorted* thinking often misinterpret their environment and social interactions (e.g., Beck's illogical thinking; Ellis's irrational beliefs). In contrast, deficiencies in thinking such as a lack of forethought or acting impulsively, are associated with a lack of behavioral control. During CBT, clients learn to identify elements of distorted thinking or ways of approaching a problem to overcome deficiencies in thinking, and opportunities to practice these new ways of thinking are provided. For instance, a depressed client who inaccurately blames himself or herself for negative outcomes of events could practice first identifying this habit and then considering and testing alternative explanations.

Cognitive-behavioral therapy uses various strategies to help clients identify maladaptive thoughts and behavior and to foster change. There are basic categories of cognitive interventions, such as coping skills, cognitive restructuring, and problem-solving, as well as behavioral techniques, such as relaxation training, pleasant events scheduling, and reinforcement. Some behavioral techniques allow the client to practice new skills and develop a sense of mastery in the therapy session (role-plays) whereas others involve teaching the client a new skill (i.e., relaxation training, self-reinforcement).

Cognitive restructuring is a phrase linked to cognitive therapies—it describes the process by which the therapist helps the client increase his or her accurate appraisal of information by altering aspects of his or her cognitive structure or belief system. A first step is to help the client identify his or her maladaptive (distorted) perceptions and thoughts. Next, the therapist teaches the client to modify these thoughts and adopt new views and strategies that may be more facilitative and constructive.

Coping skills training helps the client develop new ways to adapt to stressful circumstances, encouraging the generation and evaluation of alternatives by the client. For example, in stress-inoculation training (Mei-chenbaum, 1986) clients learn to cope with increasingly challenging amounts of stress.

Problem-solving therapy (D'Zurilla & Nezu, 1999) actively engages clients in solving their own problems. Problem-solving is a process in which the client works to formulate the problem and the major goals for the solution. The client generates alternative solutions, considers each of these alternatives in terms of how well they will help the client achieve his or her goal, and selects a solution to test out. The final step is to verify and evaluate the success of the outcome.

Contingent reinforcement, a cornerstone of behavior therapy, allows the therapist to help shape behavior, as well as cognitive factors. Learning to behave more adaptively involves carving the desired outcome into smaller, more manageable steps (i.e., shaping by successive approximations). The client is rewarded with either tangible or social rewards for the performance of a target behavior or for abstaining from a negative behavior. In addition, the client learns the importance and usefulness of self-reward in his or her everyday life.

The process of modeling allows clients to witness and participate in difficult situations, try alternative ideas, and observe and experience the emotional and behavioral outcomes. There are several different ways for a therapist to use modeling. For example, symbolic modeling involves videotapes or audiotapes of someone performing a task that the client finds difficult, allowing him or her to observe how someone else might cope with a difficult situation. Live modeling requires the therapist or another person to demonstrate coping to and with the client. Modeling can take different emphases; the therapist may demonstrate mastery in which a successful outcome is shown, or coping, in which the therapist models the client's problem and takes steps to cope with obstacles. Coping modeling is often preferred because it allows the client to witness the actual implementation of problem-solving skills, and shows the client that although problems or mistakes will and do happen, coping with them is a preferred outcome.

Like behavior therapy, a central step in cognitive-behavioral therapies (particularly those for anxiety disorders) is the exposure of the client to stress-producing situations. Exposure allows the client to practice newly learned coping skills in anxiety-producing situations with the support of the therapist. Exposure tasks are usually implemented in a graduated manner, whereby the client is initially presented with a mildly difficult situation, followed by exposure to increasingly stressful ones. The graduated process proceeds at a pace that is comfortable for both the client and therapist—the tasks are emotionally challenging and therefore, if the client is not ready for a particular exposure task, he or she may mistakenly misperceive the situation as a failure. Imaginal exposures (imagining the stressful situation while describing thoughts and feelings and the implementation of coping skills) may be employed if real exposure would be too distressing, or if the nature of the concerns ethically prohibits actual exposure.

Cognitive-behavioral therapy uses homework to encourage the client to experiment with (test out) and practice material discussed in sessions. Oftentimes a client may be asked to maintain a journal of thoughts, emotions, or behavior, to keep a record of relationships between these elements, and to identify change as it occurs. Homework assignments may also include the testing of hypotheses concerning irrational beliefs. For example, a client may insist that everyone else at work received better evaluations than he or she did. The cognitive-behavioral therapist may recommend an assignment whereby the client tests this hypothesis by asking others about their evaluations.

Cognitive-Behavioral Therapies and Their Empirical Support

We have, thus far, described a series of components that are a part of numerous cognitive-behavioral therapies. These components of CBT, however, are typically implemented in varying amounts and in different ways within particular programs. They have been studied in their own right and several have been combined and found to be efficacious for a range of adult disorders, including depression, anxiety disorders, eating disorders, sexual dysfunctions, and substance or alcohol abuse and dependence (see DeRubeis & Crits-Christoph, 1998), as well as a number of childhood disorders (Kazdin & Weisz, 1998). CBT also has successful applications in behavioral medicine (e.g., smoking cessation, migraine headaches; Compas et al., 1998). In general, the empirical literature indicates that CBT is superior to no-treatment or placebo conditions and that, additionally, for particular disorders, CBT may be more efficacious than comparable drug or psychosocial treatments.

Cognitive-behavioral therapy is among those considered to be an effective treatment for depressed individuals (see Hollon & Beck, 1994). Cognitive-behavioral therapy for depression focuses on the negative thoughts, beliefs, and appraisals that maintain depression and teaches patients to become aware of these negative thoughts. In addition, the client is taught to investigate and challenge underlying beliefs and assumptions through the use of cognitive restructuring techniques. Behavioral experiments are designed and performed to test out the truth of the client's beliefs. Homework tasks may include these behavioral experiments as well as self-monitoring of thoughts, behavior, and emotions. Problem solving, social skills training, pleasant activity monitoring and scheduling, and training in self-reinforcement are often incorporated.

Empirical studies have provided support for the efficacy of cognitive-behavioral therapies for the treatment of depression. For example, several studies have compared CBT to medications and have found that whereas in the short-term, CBT has a comparable effect (as did tricyclics) on ratings of depression (Hollon et al., 1992), it is especially impactive in preventing subsequent relapses. Several studies have documented the efficacy of CBT for depressed school-aged children and adolescents (e.g., Birmaher, Ryan, Williamson, & Brent, 1996), however the long-term effects of CBT for depressed youth have received mixed support.

Cognitive-behavioral therapy has emerged as a front-runner in the treatment of anxiety disorders. It has been applied in the treatment of generalized anxiety disorder (GAD), social phobia, panic disorder, and obsessive compulsive disorder (OCD). Cognitive-behavioral therapy with an anxious client often consists of an amalgam of behavioral techniques (e.g., exposure) and strategies designed to achieve cognitive change. For example, in the treatment of panic disorder, the therapist challenges the client's misappraisals of physical symptoms through cognitive restructuring, educates the client about the nature of anxiety, and facilitates interoceptive exposure (inducing feared sensations such as hyperventilation) (Clark, 1986; Barlow & Cerny, 1988). Behavioral experiments are designed to help patients end avoidance and disconfirm negative beliefs. Accordingly, CBT for GAD includes cognitive restructuring and behavioral experiments aimed at modifying dysfunctional beliefs about worrying (for example, the belief that worry is uncontrollable). Cognitive-behavioral therapy for social phobia (e.g., Heimberg, Liebowitz, Hope, & Sohneier, 1995) focuses on misappraisals of ambiguous social situations and catastrophic interpretations of negative social interaction and performance. Cognitive restructuring addresses the client's increased self-focused attention and extreme reliance on self-evaluative thoughts (most often negative thoughts) in social situations. Avoidance and safety behaviors are challenged through role plays, exposure, and homework assignments, and videotaped or audiotaped feedback is employed to help patients develop more realistic appraisals of their performance.

Cognitive-behavioral therapy has demonstrated efficacy in the treatment of several of the anxiety disorders in both adults and children. Researchers have found significant effects of CBT on social phobia, although the superiority of combined CBT over exposure alone has not been consistently demonstrated. For the treatment of panic disorder, CBT has been found to be superior to waitlist control conditions and to other active psychosocial treatments, as well as pharmacological treatments (for a review, see Barlow, 1997). Studies indicate that CBT is also efficacious for GAD, with one review of nine studies reporting a strong average effect size in comparisons with controls. Controlled clinical trials with children have found that compared to wait-list control, CBT can be effective in reducing self-reported and parent-reported anxiety and diagnoses of an anxiety disorder (e.g., Kendall et al., 1997).

Studies have found cognitive-behavioral therapies to be effective for other psychological disorders besides anxiety and depression. For example, CBT for bulimia strives to correct distorted beliefs about weight and food and negative self-perceptions, and modify disturbed eating habits. Outcome studies have found CBT to be useful. In addition, CBT has been found to be superior to pharmacological treatments alone, although it has not been consistently shown to be more effective than other psychosocial treatments (Wilson & Fairburn, 1993).

With regards to CBT for childhood disorders, outcome studies have been conducted with aggressive, conduct-disordered youth (for a review, see Lochman, 1990). In several instances, children receiving CBT displayed greater decreases in externalizing and aggressive behavior, and increases in prosocial behavior and adjustment, than did children receiving nondirective relationship therapy or a control condition. Although CBT's emphasis on cognitive and social problem-solving appears to be promising, results are not entirely supportive. Long-term follow-ups suggest that decreases in aggressive or delinquent behavior are often not maintained over time or do not generalize across situations.

Issues for Future Consideration

Although CBT has been supported by empirical evaluations of its merits with several adult and childhood disorders, issues critical to the further development of the field merit consideration. Relevant issues include (a) treatment flexibility; (b) treatment dismantling; and (c) the transportability of treatment.

Although manual-based, CBT therapy is not rigid. Rather, CBT is a pragmatic and flexible approach aimed at addressing the particular needs of each client. Although manual-based treatments act as guidelines to follow in meeting treatment goals, therapist flexibility and creativity are required in tailoring specific tasks and strategies to the client.

Cognitive-behavioral therapy encompasses diverse techniques and strategies. Given the recent onus on the field to develop shorter, and more cost-effective therapies, the question has been raised as to which therapy components are the truly active and necessary ingredients. In other words, can certain aspects of treatment be removed while maintaining an efficacious intervention? In order to answer this question, further research is needed to explore the individual components of current cognitive-behavioral therapies.

Demonstrating treatment efficacy within a research setting is an essential first step—but it may not be sufficient. It is also important for an effective treatment to be transportable outside the research clinic and into service-oriented clinics (Kendall & Southam-Gerow, 1996). Although most evaluations of CBT have been conducted in research settings, and patients have often been real clients (i.e., with comorbid diagnoses) work needs to be done to successfully transport the treatments. In one example, CBT was transported successfully: CBT for panic disorder provided in a community mental health center (Wade, Treat, & Stuart, 1998) produced favorable outcomes comparable to those reported from the research clinics. More research is needed to evaluate those client and therapist factors that may be involved in successful transportation of effective treatments—with the potential of closing the gap between research and clinical practice.

[*See also* Behavior Therapy; *and* Cognitive Therapy.]

Bibliography

Barlow, D. H. (1997). Cognitive-behavioral therapy for panic disorder: Current status. *Journal of Clinical Psychiatry, 58* (Suppl. 2), 32–37.

Barlow, D. H., & Cerny, J. A. (1988). *Psychological treatments of panic.* New York: Guilford Press.

Beck, A. T., & Emery G. (1985). *Anxiety disorders and phobias: A cognitive perspective.* New York: Basic Books.

Beck, A. T., Rush, A. J., Shaw, B. F., & Emery, G. (1979). *Cognitive therapy of depression.* New York: Guilford Press.

Birmaher, B., Ryan, N. D., Williamson, D. E., & Brent, D. A. (1996). Childhood and adolescent depression: A review of the past 10 years, Part II. *Journal of the American Academy of Child and Adolescent Psychiatry, 35,* 1575–1583.

Clark, D. M. (1986). A cognitive approach to panic. *Behaviour Research and Therapy, 24,* 461–470.

Compas, B. E., Haaga, D. A., Keefe, F. J., Leitenberg, H., & Williams, D. A. (1998). Sampling of empirically supported psychological treatments from health psychology: Smoking, chronic pain, cancer, and bulimia nervosa. *Journal of Consulting and Clinical Psychology, 66,* 89–112.

DeRubeis, R. J., & Crits Christoph, P. (1998). Empirically supported individual and group psychological treatments for adult mental disorders. *Journal of Consulting and Clinical Psychology, 66,* 37–52.

D'Zurilla, T., & Nezu, A. (1999). *A problem solving approach to therapy.* New York: Springer Publishing.

Ellis, A. (1962). *Reason and emotion in psychotherapy.* New York: Stuart.

Heimberg, R. G., Liebowitz, H., Hope, D., & Schneier, A. (1995). *Social phobia: Diagnosis, assessment, and treatment.* New York: Guilford Press.

Hollon, S. D., & Beck, A. T. (1994). Cognitive and cognitive–behavioral therapies. In A. E. Bergin & S. L. Garfield (Eds.), *Handbook of psychotherapy and behavior change* (4th ed., pp. 428–466). New York: Wiley.

Hollon, S. D., DeRubeis, R. J., Evans, M. D., Wiemer, M. J., Garvey, M. J., Grove, W. M., & Tuason, V. B. (1992). Cognitive therapy and pharmacotherapy for depression:

Singly and in combination. *Archives of General Psychiatry, 49,* 774–781.

Kazdin, A. E., & Weisz, J. R. (1998). Identifying and developing empirically supported child and adolescent treatments. *Journal of Consulting and Clinical Psychology, 66,* 19–36.

Kendall, P. C. (1991). Guiding theory for therapy with children and adolescents. In P. C. Kendall (Ed.), *Child and adolescent therapy: Cognitive-behavioral procedures* (pp. 3–22). New York: Guilford Press.

Kendall, P. C., & Southam-Gerow, M. A. (1996). Long term follow-up of a cognitive-behavioral therapy for anxious youth. *Journal of Consulting and Clinical Psychology, 64,* 724–730.

Kendall, P. C., Flannery-Schroeder, E., Panichelli-Mindel, S. M., Southam-Gerow, M., Henin, A., & Warman, M. (1997). Therapy for youths with anxiety disorders: A second randomized clinical trial. *Journal of Consulting and Clinical Psychology, 65,* 366–380.

Lochman, J. E. (1990). Modification of childhood aggression. In M. Hersen & R. M., Eisler et al. (Eds.), *Progress in behavior modification* (Vol. 25, pp. 47–85). Newbury Park, CA: Sage Publications.

Meichenbaum, D. (1986). *Stress inoculation training.* New York: Pergamon Press.

Wade, W. A., Treat, T. A., & Stuart, G. L. (1998). Transporting an empirically supported treatment for panic disorder to a service clinic setting: A benchmarking strategy. *Journal of Consulting and Clinical Psychology, 66,* 231–240.

Wilson, T. G., & Fairburn, C. G. (1993). Cognitive treatments for eating disorders. *Journal of Consulting and Clinical Psychology, 61,* 261–269.

Philip C. Kendall, Amy L. Krain, and Aude Henin

COGNITIVE CONSISTENCY THEORIES, emphasizing people's need to keep coherence among their thoughts, feelings, and actions, is one of numerous partial views of the person used by psychologists, each making use of one basic aspect of the person (e.g., the person as a consistency-maximizer, meaning-giver, ego-defender, sensation-seeker, tension-reducer, etc.). These mutually supplementary views differ (McGuire, 1985) as regards what provokes human action: (1) whether to maintain one's current homeostasis or to grow, and (2) whether triggered by internal forces or by environmental forces—and as regards what terminates human action: (3) whether attaining a cognitive or an affective state, and (4) whether attaining relations among components of the self or between self and environment. On these four dimensions, consistency theories emphasize the person's being triggered to action by the need to maintain the current homeostasis rather than to grow, and by internal forces (need to maintain intrapersonal consistency) rather than by environmental presses; and as terminating action by attaining cognitive rather than affective states, and states within the self rather than between self and environment.

Origins and Variants of Consistency Theories

That humans have some need for consistency has been long recognized but became especially popular in the 1950s and 1960s. Heider's (1946, 1958) P–O–X balance theory influenced qualitative consistency theories such as Newcomb's (1953) symmetry theory and Festinger's (1957) theory of cognitive dissonance. More independent quantitative approaches include Abelson and Rosenberg's (1958) psycho-logic theory utilizing matrix algebra, Osgood and Tannenbaum's (1955) congruity theory using the semantic differential, Cartwright and Harary's (1956) structural balance approach employing graph theory, and McGuire's (1960) probabilogical approach using a probability-calibrated formal logic. They agree that people's cognitive systems operate partly on logical consistency (e.g., the product of two negatives is a positive as in "my enemy's enemy is my friend"), partly on hedonic consistency (e.g., wishful thinking, that assimilates an event's judged likelihood to its desirability), and partly on economizing heuristics (e.g., selective salience).

Modes of Resolving Inconsistencies

Consistency theorists identify multiple modes of reducing inconsistencies such as repressing one of a set of conflicting cognitions, bolstering one cognition to submerge conflicting cognitions, using subdivision (e.g., explaining that evolutionary theory conflicts with the literal but not figurative meaning of the Bible), redefinition (e.g., reinterpreting politician to mean statesman rather than ward heeler or making a *credo quia absurdum* virtue of inconsistency, as in Emerson's "A foolish consistency is the hobgoblin of little minds"). The laity may accept an inconsistency believing that experts can resolve it; experts sometimes live with an inconsistency as an interim working accommodation (e.g., physicists accepting both wave and particle theories of light). Consistency theorists have identified interaction variables that affect tolerance for inconsistency, when various modes of inconsistency reduction are used, and which among conflicting cognitions are most likely to change (e.g., those least involving, cathected, committed, volitional, anchored, or positive). Unresolved is whether people minimize connectedness in cognitive systems, so lessening the possibility that inconsistency will arise (indicating that inconsistency per se is aversive), or whether people maximize connectedness, so increasing the availability of resolvable inconsistencies (indicating that what is rewarding is reducing inconsistencies rather than not having any).

Issues Confronted in
Consistency Theorizing

Methodological issues needing further study include the validity of dichotomous versus continuous scales, the use of graph theory versus matrix algebra for quantifying cognitive consistency, a measure of felt inconsistency to serve as a mediator, whether inconsistency is better calibrated as a ratio or difference, how to handle the availability of multiple modes of inconsistency reduction, and replication problems caused by complex and ambiguous inconsistency manipulations such as role playing, hypnosis, and vignettes. Conflicting results require more study of how inconsistency is affected by awareness, felt discomfort, volition, commitment, temporal interval, and active participation.

Consistency theories have been honed via confrontation with alternative theories, some of which derive consistency needs from broader perspectives (e.g., Daniel Katz from functional theory and Irving Sarnoff from psychoanalytic theory). Other theorists supplement consistency theories by analyzing the same relations from another perspective (e.g., Vernon N. Allen from role theory and Harry Upshaw from judgment theory). Still others provide alternative explanations for consistency theory findings (e.g., Barry E. Collins so used reinforcement theory and Daryl Bem, radical behaviorism). Other theories critically confront consistency theory by making conflicting predictions (e.g., Salvatore Maddi's need-variety position and Daniel E. Berlyne's collative approach).

Paradoxically, when consistency theories flourished in the 1960s, so did antithetical novelty-seeking theories. Consistency theories depict people as striving for confirmation, stability, redundancy, familiarity, avoidance of the new and unexpected; the coflourishing novelty-seeking theories (put forth by James Bieri, Salvatore Maddi, Henry Fowler, Marvin Zuckerman, etc.) emphasize opposite curiosity needs such as stimulation, surprise, novelty, varied experience, exploration, stimulus hunger, unpredictability, excitement. Such contemporaneous coexistence of contrary partial views of the person can provide thesis and antithesis for a higher synthesis, here implying that people strive for a manageable intermediate level of consistency, somewhere between completely redundant confirmation and totally unpredictable novelty. The optimal-level inflection point of the resulting nonmonotonic inverted-U relation can then be shown to shift adaptively with personal and situational interacting variables.

Applications of
Consistency Theories

Consistency theories have suggested who communicates to whom, why, and with what effects (e.g., selective exposure to belief-supporting messages; increased proselytizing for a belief after disconfirmation). They have inspired work on changing attitudes by the Socratic method of asking salience-enhancing questions (without presenting new information), and on changing attitudes on related issues not explicitly mentioned in the persuasive message, and on producing resistance to persuasion via anchoring (McGuire & McGuire, 1991). Consistency theory has produced rich bodies of research on how action change may cause as well as be caused by belief change, on how evaluations of alternatives are affected by choosing among them, and on when increasing the incentive for counterattitudinal advocacy reduces versus enhances internalized belief change. Most richly, consistency theories have advanced study of the content, structure, and functioning of thought systems.

Bibliography

Abelson, R. P., Aronson, E., McGuire, W. J., Newcomb, T. N., Rosenberg, M. J., & Tannenbaum, P. H. (Eds.). (1968). *Theories of cognitive consistency.* Chicago: Rand-McNally. An exhaustive report on the status of consistency theories at the height of their popularity.

Beauvois, J.-L., & Joule, R.-V. (1996). *A radical dissonance theory.* Bristol, PA: Taylor and Francis. A revisionist but sympathetic review of dissonance theory, the most popular consistency theory.

Berlyne, D. E. (1960). *Conflict, arousal, and curiousity.* New York: McGraw-Hill. Integrates consistency theories with antithetical novelty theories.

Festinger, L. (1957). *A theory of cognitive dissonance.* Stanford, CA: Stanford University Press. An initial statement of dissonance theory, the most popular, easily grasped consistency approach.

Heider, F. (1958). *The psychology of interpersonal relations.* New York: Wiley.

McGuire, W. J. (1966). The current status of cognitive consistency theories. In S. Feldman (Ed.), *Cognitive consistency* (pp. 1–46). New York: Academic Press. A succinct overview of consistency theory issues.

McGuire, W. J. (1985). Attitudes and attitude change. In G. Lindzey & E. Aronson (Eds.), *Handbook of social psychology* (pp. 233–346). Describes consistency theories in the context of 15 supplementary partial views of the person.

McGuire, W. J., & McGuire, C. V. (1991). The content, structure, and operation of thought systems. In R. S. Wyer, Jr., & T. K. Srull (Eds.), *Advances in social cognition* (Vol. 4, pp. 1–78).

Osgood, C. E., Suci, G. J., & Tannenbaum, P. H. (1957). *The measurement of meaning.* Urbana, IL: University of Illinois Press.

William J. McGuire

COGNITIVE DISSONANCE. The theory of cognitive dissonance, invented by Leon Festinger in 1957, is generally considered to be social psychology's most important and most provocative theory. Simply stated, cognitive dissonance is a state of tension that occurs whenever an individual simultaneously holds two cognitions (ideas, attitudes, beliefs, opinions) that are psychologically inconsistent with each other. Two cognitions are dissonant if, considering these two cognitions alone, the opposite of one follows from the other.

Because the experience of cognitive dissonance is unpleasant, people are motivated to reduce it either by changing one or both cognitions in such a way as to render them to be more compatible (more consonant) with each other, or by adding more cognitions that help bridge the gap between the original cognitions. For example, the cognition that I smoke cigarettes would be dissonant with my knowledge that cigarette smoking causes cancer. The most direct way to reduce dissonance would be to stop smoking; but suppose I have tried to stop smoking and have been unsuccessful. How might I reduce dissonance? I might try to convince myself that smoking isn't that bad—by criticizing the scientific data, or by coming to believe that filters trap most of the harmful substances, or by focusing my attention on Sam Caruthers who smokes two packs a day and is 93 years old and still going strong. All of these cognitions help reduce some of the dissonance associated with smoking, by suggesting that smoking might not be as harmful as generally believed. Consistent with this reasoning, Gibbons et al. (1997) found that heavy smokers who attended a smoking cessation clinic, quit smoking for a while, and then relapsed into heavy smoking, subsequently succeeded in lowering their perception of the dangers of smoking.

Basic Research on Dissonance Theory

Dissonance theory has produced a wide array of interesting and provocative findings. The following is a list of just a few of the classic experiments.

1. *Post-decision dissonance.* The theory suggests that, whenever we make a difficult decision, we will experience dissonance because all negative aspects of the chosen alternative are dissonant with having chosen it; similarly, all positive aspects of the rejected alternative are dissonant with having rejected it. Brehm (1956) demonstrated that within a few minutes after making a difficult decision, people reduced dissonance by spreading apart their evaluation of the two alternatives—convincing themselves that the chosen alternative is more attractive than they originally thought—and that the rejected alternative was less attractive than they originally thought.

2. *Effort and dissonance.* The theory suggests that,

all other things being equal, the harder we work for something, the more we will like it. The cognition, "I worked hard for something" is dissonant with anything negative about it. To reduce dissonance we will try to distort our perception of the item in a positive direction. Aronson & Mills (1959) found that individuals who went through a severe initiation in order to gain admission to a boring discussion group, rated that group as more attractive than people who gained admission to the group with little or no effort.

3. *Induced compliance.* If individuals are induced to make a statement opposite to their actual beliefs, the smaller the inducement offered, the greater will be the change in their actual belief in the direction of the statement they have made (Festinger & Carlsmith, 1959; Nel, Helmreich, & Aronson, 1969). This occurs because the greater the inducement (in the form of rewards or punishments), the less the dissonance. Thus, if people are paid only $1 for telling a lie they will experience more dissonance than if they are paid $20. To reduce dissonance they will convince themselves that the statement they made was actually close to their real beliefs.

Evolution of the Theory

The theory of cognitive dissonance caused a great stir in psychology, in part because it showed the limitations of conventional wisdom, which had been based primarily on reinforcement theory. In effect, the new wisdom became: If you want to get someone to do something unpleasant, high rewards will be helpful, as reinforcement theory suggests; but if you want that person to like what he is doing or to believe in the truth of what he is saying, the lowest possible reward will produce the greatest change.

As with most theories, dissonance theory has evolved in the years since its inception. Perhaps the most fundamental change had to do with the notion of the self-concept (Aronson, 1960, 1992, 1998; Aronson & Carlsmith, 1962). Aronson argued that, in any dissonant situation, dissonance is not produced by any two cognitions being discrepant (as Festinger believed). Rather it is the cognition about a particular behavior that is dissonant with a person's self-concept. For example, in the Festinger-Carlsmith experiment, the researchers hypothesized that the cognition, "I believe X," was dissonant with the cognition "I said Not-X." According to the self-concept notion, the dissonance exists between the cognition: "I am a person of integrity," and the cognition "I told a lie."

The change in emphasis has had many ramifications. On a conceptual level, it clarified the theory by delineating where it did and did not apply. On a generative level it opened the door to a wide array of research and theorizing on self-behavior disparities such as Swann's (1991) work on self-verification, Steele's (1988) work on self-affirmation, and Aronson's (1992) work on hypocrisy.

Applications of Dissonance Theory

From its inception, the applications of the theory to real world issues were apparent (see Festinger, Riecken & Schachter, 1956). This applicability continues to the present day. Dissonance theory has been used successfully to help find a solution to a diverse array of problems, such as curing snake phobias (Cooper, 1980), convincing sexually active teenagers to use condoms (Stone et al. 1994), inducing college students to conserve water by taking shorter showers (Dickerson, Thibodeau, Aronson, & Miller, 1992), and reducing prejudice among college students (Leippe & Eisenstadt, 1994).

Bibliography

Aronson, E. (1992). The return of the repressed: Dissonance theory makes a comeback. *Psychological Inquiry*, 3, 303–311. A brief history and analysis of the growth, eclipse and reemergence of dissonance theory.

Aronson, E. (1998). Dissonance, hypocrisy, and the self concept. In E. Harmon-Jones E. & J. S. Mills (Eds.), *Cognitive dissonance theory: Revival with revisions and controversies*. Washington, DC: American Psychological Association Books. An analysis of the self-concept model of dissonance theory.

Festinger, L. (1957). *A theory of cognitive dissonance*. Evanston: Row Peterson. The original statement of dissonance theory—brilliant, clear and concise.

Harmon-Jones, E., & Mills, J. S. (1998). *Cognitive dissonance theory: Revival with revisions and controversies*. Washington, DC: American Psychological Association Books. The most recent compilation of current research and conceptual issues on dissonance theory. Contributors include several of the most active researchers in the area.

Elliot Aronson

COGNITIVE ELECTROPHYSIOLOGY. In 1929, German neurologist Dr. Hans Berger published a paper in which he described recording electrical activity from the surface of the scalp in humans. Although electrical activity had been previously observed in animals, Berger was the first to report the phenomenon in humans, and he coined the term *electroencephalography*—literally, "electric brain writing," or EEG as it is now commonly called. His findings were based on very simple tasks, such as the opening and closing of the eyes, but they were the first in a continuing attempt to uncover the relationship between the body's electrical impulses and the phenomenal experience of mind. This discovery of systematic neuroelectric activity that was responsive to external stimuli initiated a search for the mechanism the brain uses to translate physically based signals into the mental experiences we call "mind." That search has developed along both scientific and clinical paths; this article reviews the main themes that shaped the use of brainwaves over the last 70 years since their discovery.

After Berger's initial reports were verified by other neurologists and the findings published in English in the 1930s, the potential use of EEG as a clinical tool became apparent and a variety of neurologic and psychiatric patients were examined with the new procedure. Although clear signs of abnormal EEG patterns were found in many different patients—especially when their disorder was severe enough to disrupt cognitive and behavioral functioning—the specificity of EEG activity in terms of where and how it is generated remains a major area of active investigation. However, as electronic technology was developed from the 1940s to 1950s, standardization of EEG measurement in clinical and scientific situations evolved. During this period the location of electrode placements, amplification procedures, and EEG data analysis techniques were standardized and became more reliable as the clinical applications of brainwave measures became more widely used.

High-Tech EEG

Today, advanced recording and measurement capabilities for neuroelectric activity are being adopted at an increasing rate because the spatial and temporal resolution achieved by modern signal-processing techniques can produce striking images of cognition. A major new technique is topographic "brain mapping," in which a large number of electrodes (e.g., one hundred or more) are placed over the entire scalp by means of small disks embedded in an "electrode cap." The cap is fitted on the head, and a conductive gel is placed between the scalp and electrode. The small EEG signal then travels through wires from the cap to amplifiers, and the microvolt electrical measures are converted into a digital or numeric format by computer processing. These numbers are then analyzed, and the voltage variation over the scalp can be portrayed in an integrative fashion so that responses from different parts of the brain can be viewed appositionally. Equipment and software to produce these sorts of images are becoming readily available, although the scientific evaluation of large electrode arrays is still an ongoing process. It is likely that both scientific and clinical laboratories of the near future will be able to easily produce such images as the technology becomes more widely available.

Sensory Evoked Potentials

Several decades after the discovery of human EEG signals, a new technique was developed by presenting subjects with a series of stimuli and then averaging the poststimulus EEG responses. The brainwave potentials obtained from signal averaging procedures yield waveform patterns that directly reflect how a stimulus affects the nervous system. These patterns were called *evoked potentials*, or EPs, because they were evoked by the stimulus in the concurrent EEG. Most of these EPs occur well within one second after stimulus presentation, so only relatively short segments of electrical activity have to be acquired and averaged to observe EPs; the number of stimuli needed to extract a clear EP varies with the strength of the neuroelectric signal elicited by the stimulus.

In the early 1960s, EPs became relatively easy to record and began to provide useful information about sensory processes. These methods have become very important because they are a neuroelectric definition of human sensory capabilities. As such, they have been developed as clinical tools to help isolate and identify aberrations in sensory information transmission such as those that can occur with neurologic disorders. Many of the basic findings and attributes of these brainwave patterns were described in the 1970s and 1980s, so they are now well accepted as both clinical and basic sensory investigative tools. A listing of the major sensory EPs is presented in Table 1. Different modalities and types of stimuli produce different types of sensory potentials, and these are labeled according to their electrical polarity (positive- or negative-going) and timing (by serial order or in milliseconds).

In general, the size, or amplitude, and the timing, or latency, of each peak define the measurement attributes of interest. It is assumed that a potential's amplitude reflects increased activity of the neurons that produce the peak, and the potential's latency reflects the amount of time required for the potential to obtain maximum amplitude. Each modality uses various types of stimuli (e.g., tones, checkerboard pattern, mild electric shock, etc.), and basic science researchers have employed these techniques to ascertain how the human sensory system works by manipulating stimulus strength and other parameters. In general, these potentials all reflect the neural activity that underlies sensory processing and are typically measured using only one or few electrodes on the scalp. In contrast to the more complex and broadly defined EEG signal, EPs have proven quite useful because they indicate the underlying neurophysiology of the sensory response.

Although their application to the basic research issues of auditory, visual, and somatic processes is ongoing, the most recent advances have involved olfactory evoked potentials (gustatory or taste EPs are not yet a practical reality). Technological developments that permit the precise timing and presentation of a distinct olfactory stimulus (e.g., the smell of ammonia) by means of computer-controlled air flow mechanisms have opened the way for the application of the electrophysiological assessment of olfaction. The changing sensitivity of the olfactory system to normal aging and disease or trauma and as an index of olfactory memory is proving accessible with olfactory EPs, which hold significant promise for future development.

Because each potential is thought to be generated by a specific brain area, clinical neurologists were quick to recognize the diagnostic utility of EPs as a means of assessing sensory system integrity. To use EPs in this way, the normative value of a potential's size or amplitude and its timing or latency is established. If a lesion or other abnormality occurs along the sensory pathway, then the amplitude and/or latency of a specific potential will be altered, thereby revealing that some sort of processing deficit is present. For example, in multiple sclerosis, the timing of the P100 potential elicited by a pattern-shift checkerboard stimulus is appreciably delayed beyond the normal value of 100 ms. In patients suspected of having this disorder, the P100 can be elicited using standardized clinical procedures to determine if the individual's peak latency is longer than normal for their age and sex, with an abnormal value taken as supporting evidence for the diagnosis. This same logic has been applied to the other sensory EPs, and their application as neurological diagnostic tools has been of substantial benefit in the last 20 years. Finally, clinical applications of olfactory EPs are currently under development for the assessment of anosmia from trauma and disease, and the evaluation of normal sensory aging.

Cognitive Brain Potentials

The development of sensory EP techniques spurred a variety of studies attempting to use similar methods to investigate the mental or cognitive processes that Berger originally sought. Unfortunately, many of the initial reports employed relatively unsophisticated operational definitions of cognition that resulted in a large number of specious findings. However, in the 1960s the influence of the rat-based stimulus-response psychology waned and cognitive psychology focused on human mental function. In conjunction with these theoretical and methodological developments, the computer processing of electrical signals became more sophisticated so that EEG responses from different stimulus categories could be averaged separately. By instructing subjects to respond to stimuli in a psychological task, the mental events required to perform the task would manifest themselves in the averaged EEG. Because the resulting waveforms reflected mental events originating with task performance, these procedures produced a new type of electrical brain response that was dubbed an event-related potential, or ERP. Thus, unlike simple sensory EPs, which index averaged EEG activity to a repeated stimulus, ERPs reflect the neuroelectric activity of the

COGNITIVE ELECTROPHYSIOLOGY. Table 1. Major sensory-evoked potentials, or EPs, organized by modality and primary peaks*

Modality	Latency Range		
	0–10 ms	10–50 ms	50–250 ms
Auditory			
Name	Brainstem	Middle Latency	Long Latency
Components	Waves I–VII	No, Po, Na, Pb	N1, P2, N2
Visual			
Name	Flash Potentials		Checkerboard-Shift
Components	P1, N2, P2		P100
Somatosensory			
Name	Somatosensory (mild electric shock)		
Components	P/N13, N19, P22		
Olfactory			
Name	Olfactory Evoked Potentials		
Components	N1, P2, N2, P3		

*The most commonly used names for each of the major components are presented for each modality and latency range. The N or P refers to either negative- or positive-going amplitude, and the number or letter refers to the order of component location or average latency.

mental operations produced when a subject is engaged in a cognitive act.

Table 2 lists the primary cognitive ERPs along with their theoretical interpretations. In general, each potential, or ERP component, is elicited with a specific laboratory task, or paradigm. Each paradigm presents a series of stimuli typically in the auditory or visual modality, and the subject is required to respond—usually by pressing a button. Hence, the stimulus sequence and specific information-processing task are designed to elicit a particular mental response from the subject. Figure 1 illustrates the P300 component as an example. A series of tones is presented to which the subject just listens—the standard stimulus. A target tone is presented infrequently, to which the subject is instructed to respond (by pressing a button, mentally counting, etc.). When the EEG to each stimulus type is averaged, the standard stimuli will evoke only sensory EPs, whereas the target stimuli will elicit those same sensory potentials plus an additional component (labeled P300 in Figure 1) that reflects the identification of that tone type as the target stimulus event. Therefore, such psychological or discrimination activities produce changes in the ongoing EEG that can be observed after signal averaging is applied to the EEG segments that follow each of the different stimuli. Again, the amount of EEG required to observe these cognitive brain potentials is relatively short, and most can be obtained within 1 second after stimulus onset. Thus, cognitive brain potentials are determined by the mental operations required to process stimulus and task-related information in highly controlled circumstances.

Computer-based signal processing and averaging software became readily available in the mid-1970s, and it was at about this time that cognitive brain potentials became viable tools in the assessment of human-information processing. This research endeavor continues vigorously today, and the influence of the initial studies helped form the burgeoning field of cognitive neuroscience, that is, the investigation of what brain parts produce the neural activity that underlies mental experiences—the very same problem that prompted Berger's initial brainwave study. As Table 2 indicates, different cognitive operations have been associated with the amplitude and latency of specific ERP components. Indeed, relatively comprehensive literatures exist for each of these components, and the findings are pointing the way toward greater specificity of the spatial and, in particular, temporal aspects of human cognition. Toward this end, the theoretical background and empirical findings for the P300 ERP component will be reviewed to illustrate the primary approaches of the field as a whole.

P300 and Cognition. Examples of ERP wave forms are shown in Figure 1, which schematically illustrates the "oddball" paradigm often used to elicit the P300 (or P3) ERP component. In a typical application of this procedure, auditory stimuli are presented such that a designated standard (S) tone elicits the N100, P200, and N200 potentials that reflect the initial sensory and attentional processing of the stimulus by the auditory cortex. When a different, or "oddball," target tone (T) stimulus is randomly presented within the stimulus series and the subject is instructed to respond by silently counting or pressing a button to each target, the same components observed for the standard are produced

COGNITIVE ELECTROPHYSIOLOGY. Table 2. Major cognitive event-related potentials, or ERPs, organized by timing and the mental activity they primarily reflect.

Component Name	Cognitive Interpretation
N100/P200	Selective attention
N200	Target detection
P300	Attention allocation/memory updating
N400	Semantic evaluation
Contingent Negative Variation (CNV)	Response preparation
Lateralized Readiness Potential (LRP)	Motor response preparation

The N or P refers to either negative- or positive-going amplitude, and the number refers to the modal or typical latency.

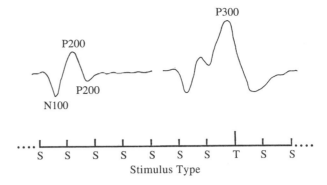

COGNITIVE ELECTROPHYSIOLOGY. Figure 1. Schematic illustration of the "oddball" paradigm that is often used to elicit the P300 event-related brain potential (ERP). A series of stimuli are presented into the subject every one to three seconds. The subject is instructed to ignore the more common "standard" (S) stimuli and to respond by mentally counting or pressing a button to the infrequent "target" (T) stimuli. When the EEG that occurs for about one second after each stimulus is averaged, the standard stimuli elicit sensory evoked potentials (EPs), whereas the target stimuli elicit the P300 component in addition to the sensory responses. The P300 ERP is thought to reflect attentional and immediate memory operations and has been a focus of contemporary brainwave research.

with a positive-going P300 potential also elicited. The P300 was first reported by Samuel Sutton and his colleagues in 1965, and this brainwave component has become a major focus of ERP research.

Because ERPs provide specific information about the precise timing and, given appropriate caveats, location of mental events, cognitive brain potentials can yield data about mental operations not readily derived from behavioral measures. As indicated in Table 2, the P300 component is thought to reflect attentional resource allocation and memory-updating operations. This theoretical perspective is based on a number of related findings and has been articulated most effectively by Emanuel Donchin and his colleagues. Put simply, the P300 is produced whenever the mental representation of the stimulus environment is changed. Thus, when a target tone stimulus occurs and the subject discriminates it from the preceding standard tone during the oddball paradigm, attention is allocated to the incoming stimulus and the immediate working memory for the previous standard stimulus is changed, or "updated," as a consequence. The amplitude of the P300 component reflects these operations. Furthermore, P300 latency is defined by the timing of the peak's maximum amplitude relative to stimulus onset and has been interpreted as a direct index of stimulus evaluation and categorization time. This property makes P300 latency a chronometric measure of cognitive processes that is independent of manual response time, but sensitive to factors that affect stimulus encoding and task performance, as well as individual differences in cognitive capability. Even though it is derived from a relatively simple psychological act—the discrimination of one stimulus from another—the P300 ERP is a manifestation of the neural events underlying fundamental mental processes that affect a wide range of cognitive activities.

Applied Uses of P300. Because the P300 component is a neuroelectric manifestation of basic cognitive

events, it has been used as a measure of cognition in experimental and applied settings. Moreover, the findings from basic studies are used to guide clinically oriented ERP investigations, since P300 can be employed to measure general information-processing efficacy and is correlated with individual differences in cognitive capability (e.g., shorter P300 latencies are associated with superior performance on mental tasks across individuals). These variables have become important in the development of neuroelectric diagnostic methods for cognitive dysfunction originating from neurologic and psychiatric disorders. Additional applications involve its use as a measure of mental processing efficiency in research concerned with how humans process complex displays of information. For example, procedures are available in which P300 amplitude can provide a direct index of attentional resource allocation when stimulus information and task requirements are varied from easy to hard, such as those required when complex display systems are monitored (e.g., the instrument panel in a jet plane). Thus, the real-world application of the various ERPs in Table 2 is providing considerable insight into human mental operations in both clinical and daily contexts.

As a concrete example, Alzheimer's disease is a well-known cause of dementing illness, with its major

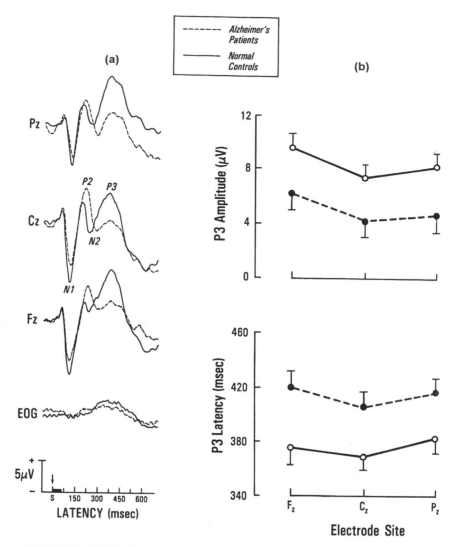

COGNITIVE ELECTROPHYSIOLOGY. Figure 2. (a) ERP waveforms from an easy auditory discrimination task performed by normal elderly control subjects and Alzheimer patients. Note that the amplitude of the P3(oo) component is larger for the controls compared to Alzheimer patients. (b) Mean (+ 1 standard error of the mean) P3(oo) component amplitude (top) and latency (bottom) from the same normal elderly subjects and Alzheimer patients plotted as a function of the midline electrode positions. The normal controls have larger amplitudes and shorter P3(oo) latencies compared to the Alzheimer patients. These type of procedures are being developed for diagnostic and prognostic applications in a wide range of neurologic and psychiatric patients.

symptom of immediate memory loss. Currently, its diagnosis is based on the exclusion of all other possible reasons for a decline in cognitive function. In an elderly person, this procedure is often a difficult medical evaluation to make because of the complicating effects of minor strokes, depression, medications, and the general decline in cognitive capability associated with advanced aging. However, the P300 has been found to be much smaller and have appreciably longer latencies in individuals who appear to be in the early stages of Alzheimer's disease compared to normal control subjects. Furthermore, its peak latency increases systematically with increases in the mental disability caused by dementia. Figure 2 illustrates P300 results for Alzheimer patients in the early stages of the disease compared to normal elderly control subjects. Note the amplitude and latency difference between the Alzheimer patients and normal controls was obtained with the relatively easy task. These findings have sparked the search for more sensitive ERP paradigms in order to enhance the diagnostic utility of the P300 and other components for the study of dementia, as well as such disorders as schizophrenia, depression, alcoholism, and autism, to name a few.

Conclusion. The assessment of mental function with EEG has advanced substantially since the time of Hans Berger, but many important problems remain. Chief among these is the localization of the neural generators for cognitive potentials and how the various components are related neurophysiologically. Although ERP brain mapping techniques are helping to uncover these associations, experimentally determined functional relationships are still very much needed to guide the search for the underlying brain mechanisms which produce the potentials observed at the scalp. However, it is exactly for this reason that ERPs will continue to play a major role in the development of cognitive science: they are an important bridge between psychological function and neural structures. Indeed, if the increasing number of ERP laboratories in psychology and related departments is any indication, cognitive brain potentials are becoming more and more important as a means for understanding the connection between mind and body.

Bibliography

Donchin, E., Karis, D., Bashore, T. R., Coles, M. G. H., & Gratton, G. (1986). Cognitive psychophysiology and human-information processing. In M. G. H. Coles, E. Donchin, & S. W. Porges (Eds.), *Psychophysiology: Systems, processes, and applications* (pp. 244–267). New York: Guilford Press.

Gevins, A., Leong, H., Smith, M. E., Le, J., & Du, R. (1995). Mapping cognitive brain function with modern high-resolution electroencephalography. *Trends in Neuroscience, 18,* 427–461.

Hillyard, S. A., & Picton, T. W. (1986). Electrophysiology of cognition. In S. R. Geiger (Ed.), *Handbook of physiology: A critical, comprehensive presentation of physiological knowledge and concepts* (Vol. 5, Section 1: The nervous system, pp. 519–584). New York: American Physiology Association.

Polich, J. (1993). Cognitive brain potentials. *Current Directions in Psychological Science, 2,* 175–179.

Polich, J. (1998). P300 clinical utility and control of variability. *Journal of Clinical Neurophysiology, 15,* 14–33.

John Polich

COGNITIVE MAPS are internal representations of spatial environments that permit the planning and execution of movement within them. In the 1930s

and 1940s, the behavioral psychologist Edward Tolman ("Cognitive maps in rats and men," *Psychological Review,* 1948, 55, 189–208) showed that rats had something like a map of places in space, rather than a fixed routine for moving through it based on their history of reinforcement. The rats demonstrated spatial learning after exploration even in the absence of reward, and they readily followed novel, previously unreinforced pathways to a goal when their usual routes were blocked. Tolman's ideas were controversial in the 1930s, the era of stringent behaviorism, but it is now widely accepted that humans and lower animals have representations of space that support purposive action.

Basic questions about cognitive mapping by humans include: Are cognitive maps like mental pictures, that is, internalized versions of real space? How accurate are cognitive maps in preserving the distances and directions between locations in space, and from what sources do inaccuracies arise? Do cognitive maps differ according to the nature of spatial learning, for example, active exploration versus viewing a physical map? What are the physiological bases for cognitive mapping? Are children's cognitive maps different from adults? Can blind people have cognitive maps? These topics are discussed in the current entry.

Reliance of Cognitive Maps on Perceptual and Cognitive Processes

One avenue of substantial research has been concerned with the spatial accuracy of cognitive maps, for example, whether the mentally represented distance between points constitutes a Euclidean metric. A unit of measurement is called a metric if it follows certain rules. One requirement of a metric for measuring distance is that judgments should be symmetric; that is, the distance from A to B should be equal to the distance from B to A. Violations of metric principles commonly occur in cognitive mapping.

Exclusive concerns with the geometric properties of cognitive maps have yielded to a realization that they have nonspatial as well as spatial components and that they are influenced by processes of perception, learning, and meaningful interpretation. Research has been directed toward the underlying causes of systematic errors in cognitive mapping. These errors arise from numerous sources, because multiple psychological processes enter into the formation of cognitive maps and the retrieval of information from them.

Humans can form cognitive maps by viewing physical maps, but more commonly, they form spatial representations by perceiving and interacting with their environment. They use manipulation and locomotion as well as vision, thereby involving the haptic modality (purposive touch) and proprioception (sensing via the muscles, tendons, joints, and vestibular system). The modalities of audition and olfaction can also signal environmental features that are incorporated into cognitive maps.

The accuracy of spatial representation is limited by perceptual processes. For example, the perception of an object's distance from a viewer when it is viewed with reduced cues—with one eye, or in the absence of spatial context such as walls or other objects—tends to be systematically distorted, and the cognitive map that results from such restricted viewing will share the distortions. Processes of perceptual organization also shape cognitive maps. A perceptual bias—to see offset points in a visual display as more regularly arranged than they actually are—results in a tendency to represent cities or countries that were viewed on a map as more aligned than they actually are. By means of this alignment bias, we tend to think of South America as lying due south of North America, when it is considerably east (B. Tversky, "Distortions in memory for maps," *Cognitive Psychology*, 1981, *13*, 407–433).

The way in which a cognitive map is learned affects people's ability to use the information it conveys. A physical map represents space with a fixed orientation (for example, north is portrayed upward). When people learn about a spatial layout from a map and then try to perform actions within it—like figuring out the direction of the rest rooms while standing in front of the grocery store—they do better when their position within the space matches the orientation of the map. The confusion that results from mismatched alignment is a common experience, one that arises when people stand at a "you-are-here" map that is oriented differently from their facing direction. A common tendency is to reorient themselves or the map. Orientation-specific learning also arises when people view a large-scale space from a fixed perspective, but it is alleviated when they can actively explore within it.

Processes that meaningfully interpret spatial layouts and relate them to higher-level knowledge can induce systematic errors in cognitive maps. In judging the distance and direction between two points, people may apply knowledge about the superordinate units in which the points reside. It surprises them to find that Seattle is further north than Montreal; after all, Canada is north of the United States (A. Stevens & P. Coupe, "Distortions in judged spatial relations," *Cognitive Psychology*, 1978, *10*, 422–437). People may use knowledge about the difficulty of getting from one location to another when judging the distance between them; thus barriers or indirect routes inflate distance estimates. Similar tendencies have been found for large-scale space explored on foot and small-scale space explored with a fingertip, suggesting the sources of error are in highly general cognitive processes.

Egocentric and Allocentric Maps

A distinction has been made between cognitive maps that localize points relative to one's own self, and those that localize points relative to external reference frames. The former are called egocentric, and the latter are most commonly called allocentric. According to the scientist C. R. Gallistel (1990), egocentric representations are more primitive in animal navigation, in that when an animal explores a new space, it first learns where points are relative to itself, then derives the locations relative to one another

Studies of children's development of cognitive maps, using a procedure introduced by L. Acredolo ("Infant mobility and spatial development," in Stiles-Davis et al., 1998) also suggest a progression from egocentric to allocentric representations. When an infant is exposed to a rewarding event at a rightward location and then turned around to look from the opposite direction, it will tend to persist in looking rightward, rather than turning left to face the previously rewarding location. The infant has coded the rewarding location relative to its body, rather than as a fixed location in space. This egocentric tendency diminishes as the infant grows older and has more experience with exploring space under its own control.

People appear to be very good at registering the locations of objects egocentrically, or relative to themselves. Adults can briefly view a target location as much as 20 meters away, then close their eyes and walk to it accurately. The accuracy persists when they walk to the target indirectly, for example, when they view two locations and walk first to one, then to the other, all with eyes closed. This shows that people can maintain accurate knowledge of the locations of the points relative to their own body, even over a period where they move around in the space without vision. But if people are asked to judge the distance between two points without moving to one of them, they are being asked to make an allocentric judgment, one that is independent of their own location. Allocentric judgments are less accurate than judgments of distances relative to the body, indicating that people can have an egocentric map but not have adequate psychological processes for determining the distances between locations on it (Loomis et al., 1996).

Physiological Basis of Cognitive Maps

The complexity of processing that leads to formation of a cognitive map strongly suggests that there is no one location in the brain for cognitive mapping. Studies of lower organisms similarly reveal that multiple locations with different functions are required to support the animal's ability to navigate.

For example, in studies that record electrical signals from neurons in the brain, rats have been found to have some neurons that become active when the rat is in a particular place in a familiar space. The firing pattern does not depend on the direction in which the rat is facing or on the particular landmarks currently within its field of view. These so-called place cells have been found in an area of the brain called the hippocampus (J. O'Keefe and L. Nadel, *The Hippocampus as a Cognitive Map*, Oxford, 1978). Other cells, called head direction cells, fire when the animal faces in a particular direction but do not depend on its precise location in the space; these cells have been found in several areas within the rat brain.

Place cells have been found to fire even when the animal navigates in a dark environment. Because in this case the cells cannot be driven by visual cues, the animal must have some other way of tracking its position and knowing that it is a familiar place. The process by which it does so is known as path integration. By using path integration, an animal takes its velocity or acceleration into account, in order to track changes in its position. Path integration has been extensively studied in insects, birds, and lower mammals, and there is also work with humans. Some species—but not humans—show great accuracy in keeping track of their position by movement-based cues alone, without vision. Some even keep track of positional changes when they are moved passively rather than under self-control. In the rodent, path integration is likely to involve multiple sites within the brain.

Cognitive maps are the representation not only of abstract places or directions, but also of particular objects that reside in space and serve as landmarks to define places and head direction. The neural pathways that are involved in object representation and recognition have been extensively studied; Milner and Goodale (1995) provide an overview that relates object perception to spatial action.

Cognitive Maps in the Congenitally Blind

That congenitally blind people have maps of space should be obvious when we consider that like sighted individuals, they manipulate objects and locomote within a richly featured, three-dimensional environment. They rely on their knowledge of spatial layout for mobility and independent travel. The lack of vision does, however, limit the access that a blind person has to environmental cues at any point in time. In the absence of special equipment, the cues must be near enough to be sensed with the limbs or a long cane, unless they are communicated from distant sources (like heat from the sun, the whistle of a remote train, or a breeze from a lake).

The ability of blind people to perform many spatial tasks has been found to be equivalent to that of sighted individuals. Studies of path integration in humans have assessed the ability of blind and sighted to com-

plete simple pathways by returning "home." A group of researchers studying spatial cognition in the blind found that congenitally blind individuals who demonstrated independent mobility in their everyday lives performed equivalently to sighted, blindfolded participants in a task of completing a triangle after being guided through the first two legs (J. Loomis, R. Klatzky, R. Golledge, J. Cicinelli, J. Pellegrino, and P. Fry, "Nonvisual navigation by blind and sighted: Assessment of path integration ability," *Journal of Experimental Psychology: General*, 1980, *122*, 73–91).

When a sighted individual moves through space under visual guidance, the optic flow patterns produced by objects and textures provide strong cues to changes in the individual's spatial location. When people close their eyes and travel through a familiar space, they are able to update their position even without the optic flow field, as indicated by their being able to point to the locations of objects as they move. The behavioral scientists J. Reiser, D. Guth, and E. Hill ("Sensitivity to perspective structure while walking without vision," *Perception*, 1986, *15*, 173–188) found that sighted individuals tend to have greater difficulty updating when they imagined moving than when they were moved physically. They also found that unlike the sighted, at least some blind subjects had difficulty updating under physical movement as well as imagined movement. However, the evidence on this point is mixed, and Loomis and associates in the 1996 study already cited found that some blind people appear to update position when they move as effectively as do blindfolded, sighted individuals.

In assessing the results of visual impairment, the nature of the impairment must be taken into account. Some causes of blindness produce a reduction in the size of the field of view but leave the ability to resolve details relatively intact. Other causes of blindness cause a reduction in visual acuity throughout the visual field. A reduction in the visual field is more damaging to spatial learning than the reduction in acuity throughout the field (J. Rieser, E. Hill, C. Talor, A. Bradfield, and S. Rosen, "Visual experience, visual field size, and the development of nonvisual sensitivity to the spatial structure of outdoor neighborhoods explored by walking," *Journal of Experimental Psychology: General*, 1992, *121*, 210–221). When the visual field is reduced, the experience becomes like seeing through a tunnel. Features that would normally be seen simultaneously must be retained in memory and integrated over time, which impairs the ability to form a cognitive map.

Bibliography

Eilan, N., McCarthy, R., & Brewer, B. (1993). *Spatial representation*. Oxford: Basil Blackwell. Discusses philosophical issues related to spatial representation, with contributions from behavioral and neural scientists.

Etienne, A. S., Maurer, R., & Séguinot, V. (1996). Path integration in mammals and its interaction with visual landmarks. *Journal of Experimental Biology, 199,* 201–209.

Gallistel, C. R. (1990). *The organization of learning.* Cambridge, MA: MIT Press. An extensive discussion of animal navigation and path integration.

Loomis, J., DaSilva, J., Philbeck, J., & Fukusima, S. (1996). Visual perception of location and distance. *Current directions in psychological science, 5,* 72–76. Describes experiments differentiating the perception of egocentric and nonegocentric spatial properties.

Loomis, J. M., Klatzky, R. L., Golledge, R. G., & Philbeck, J. W. (in press). Human navigation by path integration. In R. Golledge (Ed.), *Wayfinding: Cognitive mapping and spatial behavior.* Baltimore: Johns Hopkins University Press.

Milner, A. D., & Goodale, M. A. (1995). *The visual brain in action.* Oxford: Oxford University Press. Relates object perception to spatial action from a cognitive neuroscience perspective.

Paillard, J. (1991). *Brain and space.* Oxford: Oxford University Press. Discusses neurophysiological and behavioral approaches to space perception and action, including models of space representation and the role of the hippocampus in spatial memory.

Portugali, J. (Ed.). (1996). *The construction of cognitive maps.* The Hague: Kluwer.

Stiles-Davis, J., Kritchevsky, M., & Bellugi, U. (Eds.). (1998). *Spatial cognition: Brain bases and development.* Mahwah, NJ: Erlbaum.

Touretzky, D. S, & Redish, A. D. (1996). Theory of rodent navigation based on interacting representations of space. *Hippocampus, 6,* 247–270. Presents a computational theory encompassing place cells, head-direction cells, and other functional units in the rodent's navigational system.

Tversky, B. (1992). Distortions in cognitive maps. *Geoforum, 23,* 131–138.

Roberta L. Klatzky

COGNITIVE NEUROPSYCHOLOGY. *See* Neuropsychology.

COGNITIVE PSYCHOLOGY. [*This entry comprises three articles: an overview of the broad history of the field from its inception to the present; a survey of the principal theories that have determined the course of development of the field; and a review of the research methods that have been employed in this field. For discussions related to cognitive psychology, see the entries on* Animal Learning and Behavior; Experimental Psychology; *and* Perception and Action.]

History of the Field

Strange as it may seem, the present changes the past; and, as the focus and range of psychology shift in the present, new parts of the past enter into its history and other parts drop out.

E. G. Boring
A History of Experimental Psychology

At the beginning of the twenty-first century, cognitive psychology is a broad field concerned with memory, perception, attention, pattern recognition, consciousness, neuroscience, representation of knowledge, cognitive development, language, thinking, and, human and artificial intelligence. But contemplation about the source of knowledge, how people think, solve problems, and perceive their world is as ancient as human history and has occupied a venerated position in the musings of philosophers, theologians, mystics, and scientists for as long as we can tell. These notions started to be tested empirically during the latter part of the nineteenth century and throughout the twentieth century and became known in the history of science as cognitive psychology.

The history of cognitive psychology can be parsed into four periods: philosophical, early experimental, the cognitive revolution, and modern cognitive psychology.

Philosophical Period

Ancient Egyptian hieroglyphics suggest that thoughtful people were concerned with processes such as thought, memory, and most of all the ka, or soul. Great energy was directed toward preserving the soul but also some theorized that knowledge was localized in the heart. Greek philosophers were obsessed with knowledge and cognitive matters and current models of cognition often have some ties to ancient Greece. Aristotle's views on the locus of knowledge were similar to the Egyptians. However, Plato postulated that the brain was the true locus of knowledge. Renaissance scholars considered thinking, logic, and the nature of the soul and, although divergent views were expressed, the locus of the knowledge and rationality was thought to be in the brain.

During the eighteenth century, philosophic debate over the source of knowledge took place between the empiricist and the nativist. A British empiricist believed knowledge came from experience. However, the nativist believed knowledge was innate and based on structural characteristics and properties inherent in the brain. Modern cognitive psychologists continue to argue these matters, although usually with scientific data.

The philosophic period provided a context for understanding the mind and its processes. In addition, these early thinkers identified some major theoretical issues that would later be studied empirically using scientific research methods.

Early Experimental Period

Cognition has been studied scientifically since the end of the nineteenth century. In 1879, the philosophical aspects of mental processes gave way to empirical observations when Wundt founded the first psychological laboratory in Germany in 1879. Psychology began to break away from philosophy and form a discipline based on objective science rather than on speculation, logic, and conjecture. Many forces propelled the break with moral philosophy, but certainly the development of new methods that allowed for the examination of mental events changed the way cognition was studied. Introspection, or looking within, was one such method that allowed the observer to examine consciousness and the structure of mental representation by breaking down an experience into sensations and images. By detecting patterns within introspective reports, the mind's contents were presumed to be revealed.

Theories of knowledge representation became divided between introspectionists who studied observable sensations, and act psychologists, led by Brentano, who studied the activities of the mind. Brentano considered internal representations meaningless to psychology and chose to study mental acts of comparing, judging, and feeling physical objects.

By the beginning of the twentieth century American psychology was beginning to take a distinctive form with a wide range of topics under investigation. Leading this expanded experimental psychology was William James, the first president of the American Psychological Association. His ideas on philosophy, religion, and psychology shaped the intellectual history of these topics throughout the twentieth century. No less important were his thoughts about attention and memory, and his distinction of a dichotomy memory store—primary and secondary memory—led directly to experiments in the 1960s on that topic. Clearly, James's ideas were important in shaping modern cognitive psychology.

During this time, American psychologists became interested in educational matters and were greatly influenced by the objective nature of act psychology. Psychologists such as Thorndike were concerned with the effects of reward and punishment on learning and less concerned with consciousness. The introspective technique, in which a subject asks himself what sensations he might experience, for example, were considered by American psychologists as being sterile and leading to inconsistent results. There was, argued many, a need for a purely objective and scientific psychology in which

mental processes, such as memory, sensations, and learning, could be reliably measured. Behaviorism, led by John Watson, was predicated on the idea that overt behavior could be objectively observed, offered an attractive scientific approach to psychology, and was an appropriate foil to the rapidly developing interest in psychoanalysis.

Despite interest in overt behavior, cognitive process were not totally neglected. During the early 1900s Donders and Cattell were conducting perception experiments on imageless thought using brief visual displays to examine the time required for mental operations to take place and using reaction time data as dependent measures.

In several laboratories in America interesting research was being done on memory, attention, perception, language, concept formation, and problem solving that was the preformal stage of cognitive psychology. In addition to these efforts within psychology, several forces outside of traditional experimental psychology helped shape cognitive psychology. Among these forces are the considerable influence of the Swiss psychologist, Jean Piaget, whose central idea was that there are distinctive cognitive stages through which children develop. In Russia, the brilliant young savant, Lev Vygotsky, suggested a model of development psychology in which learning precedes development. Another important influence was the work of Frederic Bartlett, from England, who investigated memory from a naturalistic viewpoint and was particularly concerned with the remembering of stories. From recall of stories, Bartlett hypothesized that memory is largely determined by schemata, or the way knowledge is organized and represented in the brain. Even some animal studies were beginning to embrace cognitive themes. In 1932, Tolman, a well-known behavioral psychologist, observed that rats learned a cognitive map of their environment while learning to run a maze.

Although cognition was not the dominant school of psychological thought in America during this time, some experimental psychologists demonstrated that scientific methodology could be used in the study of mental events. The techniques, subject matter, procedures, and even the interpretations used by these researchers anticipated the emergence of a cognitive discipline.

Concepts such as sensation, thinking, and mental imagery were anathema under the behaviorist's influence, as they were considered subjective. Internal states were considered intervening variables and not necessary to understand human behavior. Psychology had been concentrated on observable behaviors and human subjects were largely replaced with rats and pigeons.

Gestalt psychology offered an alternative way to study sensory perception to the problematic method of introspection that diffused the research on cognition.

Concurrently the behaviorists attempted to create a purely objective psychology by successfully attacking the cognitive psychologists and Gestaltists as well.

Cognitive Revolution

Cognitive psychology began to take form as a new way of understanding the science of the mind during the late 1950s. These formative events were spurred on by research discoveries in memory, learning, and attention as well as ideas outside of the mainstay of experimental psychology, such as communication theory, developmental psychology, social psychology, linguistics, and computer science, which gave cognitive psychologists additional breadth to deal with the complexity of human information processing and thinking.

The reemergence of cognitive psychology during this period is commonly referred to as the Cognitive Revolution, emerging in 1956 with a conference on communication theory at Massachusetts Institute of Technology (MIT) (Solso, 1998) in which seminal papers were presented by Noam Chomsky, Jerome Bruner, Allen Newell and Herbert Simon, and George Miller. The coalescence of cognitive psychology during this period was probably not due to a single group of people (and certainly no precise date of a movement is possible) but was a reflection of a larger zeitgeist in which psychologists appreciated the complexity of the thinking human. At the same time, cognitive psychologists rejected the traditional, simplistic theories of the mind, but in many cases held on to the scientific methodology as had developed in the early part of the twentieth century. The paradigm that offered a pertinent methodology and embraced a sufficiently wide latitude of intellectual topics was cognitive psychology, which enjoyed widespread acceptance and growth.

Research in verbal learning and semantic organization led to the development of testable models of memory and cognition, providing another empirical base for the study of mental processes. George A. Miller made a distinction between short-term and long-term memory and his influential paper *The Magic Number Seven, Plus or Minus Two* (Miller, 1956) addressed the limited capacity of short-term memory and introduced the concept of chunking—the idea that the limits of short-term memory could be extended by grouping information into larger units of information. In 1958, Peterson and Peterson in America and John Brown in England found a rapid loss or decay of memory after the study of nonsense syllables after a few seconds when verbal rehearsal was absent, thus promoting the idea of a separate stage of short-term memory. In 1960, Sperling showed that a very transitory memory (or information storage system) held information for a very brief period of time. This discovery further advanced the notion that humans were complex information-processing creatures who processed incoming information through a series of stages. That simple idea was a perfect model for researchers and theorists interested in memory, and several models appeared about this time by Atkinson and Shiffrin, Waugh and Norman, and later by Craik and Tulving.

Prior to this period, information theory was introduced by Shannon and Weaver, who used box diagrams to describe how information is communicated and transformed along a series of stages. Donald Broadbent, a psychologist at Cambridge, began applying Shannon and Weaver's ideas to selective attention processes and introduced the concept of information flow to psychology and used box diagrams to describe cognitive processes. Broadbent's information flow referred to the series of operations that analyze, transform, or change mental events such as memory encoding, forgetting, thinking, concept formation, etc. As such, Broadbent provided "a language to talk about what happened inside a man which was not a mentalistic introspective language" (Cohen, 1986, p. 23).

Elsewhere, technological advances in computer science called for reexamination of basic postulates of cognition. In 1955, Simon and Newell developed a computer capable of solving a mathematical proof. Cognitive psychologists were excited that machines could simulate human thought and computers could possibly be operating according to the same rules and procedures as the human mind. Furthermore, since computers were seen as intelligent, it required us to analyze our own intelligence so that the intelligence of a machine could be determined. As a result the hypothetical Turing test was devised to determine if observers could discriminate the output of a computer from that of human responses.

Meanwhile, the behaviorists came under attack from Chomsky, a linguist from MIT, who developed a method of analyzing the structure of language. Chomsky argued that language was too complicated to learn and produce via behavioral principles of reinforcement and postulated the existence of a cognitive structure of an innate language acquisition device.

Another influence that aided cognitive psychology's foothold was World War II. Financial support in areas of military interest became readily available during the war. Because of the military's interest in developing and using new technology, research in vigilance, creativity, and human factors was encouraged. One outcome was a seminal report in 1954 by Tanner and Swets on signal detection demonstrating that cognitive processes can have a mediating effect on sensory thresholds. Another outcome of the war was that many soldiers suffered from brain injuries. A vast amount of clinical data in perception, memory, and language was a by-product of these victims' afflictions.

In the 1950s, interest turned to attention, memory, pattern recognition, images, semantic organization, language processes, thinking, and even consciousness (the most dogmatically eschewed concept), as well as other cognitive topics once considered outside the boundary of experimental psychology. Behaviorism and its dogma failed to account for the richness and diversity of human experience. Behaviorists could not account for the results found by Piaget's and Chomsky's developmental studies. And information theory and computer science gave psychologists new ways to conceptualize and discuss cognition.

Modern Cognitive Psychology

By the 1960s, cognitive psychology had experienced a renaissance. *Cognitive Psychology*, which systematized the new science, was written by Ulric Neisser and was published in America (1967). Neisser's book was central to the solidification of cognitive psychology as it gave a label to the field and defined the topical areas. Neisser used the computer metaphor for selecting, storing, recovering, combining, outputting, and manipulating information. And in 1966 Hilgard and Bower introduced a chapter in their *Theories of Learning* (New York) that developed the idea of using computer programs to serve as models on theories of cognition.

The 1970s saw the emergence of professional journals devoted to cognitive psychology such as *Cognitive Psychology, Cognition, Memory & Cognition*, and a series of symposia volumes, including the *Loyola Symposium on Cognition* edited by Solso and the Carnegie-Mellon series edited by Chase and others, based on the Carnegie Symposium on Cognition. In the 1970s and 1980s cognitive laboratories were beginning to be built, symposia and conferences appeared at national and regional meetings, courses in cognitive psychology and related topics were being added to curricula, grants were awarded to people investigating memory, language processing, attention, and like topics, new textbooks were written on the theme of cognition, and universities recruited professors of cognitive psychology to replace those of traditional experimental psychology. In the 1980s and 1990s serious efforts were made to find corresponding neural components that were linked to cognitive constructs. Thus, the cerebral location for a word, like *hammer*, as a noun, might be far different than the location for the same word if the word were used as a verb. Furthermore, influential memory theories (such as Tulving's semantic and episodic memory theory) were manifest in cerebral localization experiments using brain imaging technology. The science of human cognition is still undergoing transformation due to major changes in computer technology and brain science. As a result cognitive psychology has converged with computer science and neuroscience to create a new discipline called cognitive science.

Finally, with the advent of new ways to see the brain (e.g., functional magnetic resonance imaging [fMRI],

positron emission tomography [PET], electroencephalogram [EEG]) cognitive psychologists have expanded their operations to neuroscience, which promises to empirically display the parts of the brain involved in cognition that were hypothesized by twentieth-century psychologists.

Bibliography

Anderson, J. R. (1985). *Cognitive psychology and its implications* (2nd ed.). San Francisco: Freeman.

Baars, B. J. (1986). *The cognitive revolution in psychology*. New York: Guilford Press.

Boring, E. G. (1950). *A history of experimental psychology*. New York: Appleton-Century-Crofts.

Gardner, H. (1985). *The mind's new science: A history of the cognitive revolution*. New York: Basic Books.

Hilgard, E. R. (1987). *Psychology in America: A historical survey*. New York: Harcourt Brace.

Knapp, T. J., & Robertson, L. C. (Eds.). (1986). *Approaches to cognition: Contrasts and controversies*. Hillsdale, NJ: Erlbaum.

Neisser, U. (1967). *Cognitive psychology*. New York: Appleton-Century-Crofts.

Solso, R. L. (1998). *Cognitive psychology* (5th ed.) Boston: Allyn and Bacon.

Solso, R. L. (Ed.). (1975). *Information processing and cognition: The Loyola symposium*. Hillsdale, NJ: Erlbaum.

Robert L. Solso and Otto H. MacLin

Theories

The primary goal of cognitive psychology is to provide an understanding of mental activity via the use of the scientific method. Because mental activity mediates between stimuli presented to a person and the person's response, and is therefore not directly observable, cognitive science is heavily theory laden. Theories attempt to provide an explanation of the results from a large number of studies and to provide predictions that can be directly tested. A good theory should reduce complex behavior to a limited set of principles that explain why some phenomena may occur in some circumstances and may not occur in others. However, there are some general limitations to theories that are noteworthy. For example, because most cognitive theory is based on experimentation, in which independent variables are manipulated and their influence is measured on dependent variables, there is always a limitation of building the model of the structures and processes intervening between the manipulations and behavior. In fact, Anderson (1976) has argued that behavioral data may not allow one to distinguish between theories that assume very different representations and processes. Theories must then be guided by other criteria such as parsimony, effectiveness, generality, and accuracy.

Given the difficulty in cognitive theory development, how does one build confidence in a theory? Converging operations is a method that has been used extensively by cognitive scientists to discriminate among alternative theoretical accounts of particular patterns of data (Garner, Hake, & Eriksen, 1956). Converging operations reflect the use of two or more experimental operations that eliminate an alternative theoretical account of a set of data. If Theory A is consistently supported after being pitted against reasonable competing theoretical accounts of a set of data, then there is increased confidence in Theory A.

In order for the reader to gain some appreciation for cognitive theories, a brief overview of some of the theoretical issues that have been addressed in cognitive psychology will presented. Obviously, it would be impossible to cover the richness of theory development in such a limited space. Therefore, we have chosen to provide a brief overview of some of the theoretical issues that have stirred controversy in the field.

Bottom-up Versus Interactive Models of Pattern Recognition

Models of perception attempt to explain, in large part, how patterns are recognized. Our intuitions might suggest the following "bottom-up" stream of events: patterns in the environment activate sensory receptive systems (e.g., ears and eyes) and these systems provide signals that are transformed into higher-level representations that provide information regarding the identity of a stimulus pattern. For example, the pandemonium model of letter recognition (Selfridge & Neisser, 1960) is a classic example of a bottom-up feature detection model in which stimuli first activate a set of feature detectors (e.g., vertical lines, horizontal lines, oblique patterns, diagonals), and these feature detectors are combined to activate relevant letters (e.g., the letter E would be activated by the presence of three horizontal lines and one vertical line). Ultimately, the most activated letter is selected as the target to report. Interestingly, not long after Selfridge's theoretical model was introduced, results from electrophysiological studies provided some converging evidence for feature-like detectors in nonhuman species (e.g., Hubel & Wiesel, 1962).

Although evidence for feature detectors exists, and the bottom-up approach is intuitively appealing, there is also support for an alternative perspective, called the interactive model, which assumes that pattern recognition is not simply controlled by the stimulus but is aided by preexisting memory representations. For example, one of the classic findings in support of an interactive position is the word superiority effect, i.e., letters embedded within words are better perceived than letters embedded in nonwords or presented in isolation. The theoretical conundrum that this finding presents

is: How can the word representation influence the letters that make up the word because the letters must have been already identified in route to recognizing the word? These findings led McClelland (1979) to propose that higher order mental representations influence recognition via a processing cascade. Specifically, early in perception before letter recognition has occurred, letter units begin receiving activation, and partial activation is transferred to higher-order representations (e.g., words). These higher-order representations then transmit partial activation back down to the relevant letter representations, which actually helps constrain the perception of those letters.

The interactive perspective with both bottom-up and top-down processes has been very influential because it suggests that the stimulus is not the only source of information, but rather the perceiver adds information across time to the stimulus information to construct the perceptual experience. It is precisely this type of added information that provides a way of understanding perceptual illusions and potentially memories of events that never occurred. Our perceptions and memories involve an elaborate interaction between the external stimulus and preexisting knowledge.

One of the major theoretical debates that has arisen in this area is the extent to which there are interactions among distinct systems within the processing system. According to the modular approach (e.g., Fodor, 1983), there are dedicated systems that only provide feedforward information from lower-level systems to higher-level systems. On the other hand, some theorists believe that there is almost complete interactivity across systems. For example, an area of research that has amassed a considerable amount of empirical and theoretical debate concerns the processes by which the appropriate meanings of ambiguous words are resolved in sentence contexts. The modular approach suggests that when processing an ambiguous word (e.g., the word *organ* can refer to musical instrument or bodily organ), a prior sentence context such as, "The musician played both the piano and organ," does not influence which meaning becomes initially activated (i.e., both the musical instrument meaning and the body meaning of *organ* would become initially activated). In contrast, the interactive approach suggests that prior sentence context should control which meaning becomes initially activated (i.e., only the contextually relevant meaning becomes activated). Although the original research in this area strongly supported the modular approach, more recent work has indicated that a strong sentence context can influence the initial interpretation of ambiguous linguistic structures.

In summary, one goal of cognitive theory is to explain how patterns are recognized. Early models were primarily bottom-up processors, i.e., from the sensory systems to higher-level systems. However, the results of cognitive research and theory development suggest that pattern recognition is influenced by top-down conceptual processes that reflect the interactive nature of the processing architecture.

Attentional Selection: Early or Late

One of the most difficult issues that cognitive scientists have had to grapple with is how to empirically address and theoretically model human attention. For example, how do people at a crowded party ignore distracting information and focus on (i.e., attend to) one conversation? As in pattern recognition, we all have intuitions regarding attention, but how does one develop a theory of attention based on experimental studies? Researchers have used metaphors such as attentional filters, switches, reservoirs of capacity, spotlights, executive processors, and many others. Although attention research ultimately touches on all areas of cognitive psychology, most researchers work on specific aspects of attention such as the locus of attentional selection, its relationship to consciousness, and aspects of attentional control and automaticity.

Much of the early theoretical debate focused on the extent to which unattended stimuli are processed. Early selection models postulated that selection occurs at a relatively early level in the system, before meaning has been extracted. The initial support for this notion was classic studies using the dichotic listening task in which listeners were given a very demanding primary task to one ear (verbally repeating the information presented over headphones, i.e., shadowing), while information was simultaneously presented to the other ear (e.g., Cherry, 1953). The results suggested that participants noticed little of the information presented to the unattended ear, e.g., did not even notice a switch to a different language. However, researchers soon realized that attentional selection was not an all-or-none phenomenon. For example, if one is presented with a highly relevant stimulus in the unattended channel (such as the person's name), then in fact the person could recall information presented to the unattended channel (Moray, 1959). Returning to the crowded party example presented earlier, one would be able to tune out most of the other conversations at the party, but if one hears something that is highly relevant to the person (e.g., his or her own name), then it is likely that the person would attend to this information. Hence, although it appears that there may be some attenuation of unattended information, it is still possible for some signal to get through, and such a signal can push highly relevant stimuli over the threshold. The topic of attentional selection has invoked rather widespread interest not only in studies of healthy young adults, but also in the neuropsychological literature, because in some patient populations (such as attention-deficit dis-

orders and schizophrenia), there may be a breakdown in the amount of information getting into the system (i.e., a breakdown in the attentional selection system), thereby overloading any limited capacity aspect of the processing system.

Related to the issue of attentional selection is the control of attention. Again, our intuitions would suggest that we have control over what we attend. However, researchers have become interested in situations where effects of variables are outside of the individual's attentional control. One classic example of this is the Stroop task, wherein one is asked to name the color that words are printed in. When words are printed in incongruent colors, e.g., the word *red* printed in blue, there is considerable slowdown in color naming, compared to naming the color of a neutral word such as *run*. Some researchers have argued that this interference occurs because words invoke a qualitatively distinct type of processing, referred to as automatic processing, in which words automatically activate their meaning (outside of attentional control), and this automatic processing produces conflict when the color and word information are inconsistent. Automatic processes reflect those processes that are well practiced and under consistent stimulus-to-response mappings, e.g., the processing of the meaning of the word *blue* is consistent and highly processed. Because these processes have in some sense been wired into the system, they are outside the scope of attentional control. Researchers have addressed theoretically interesting questions regarding the development of automaticity such as the role of conscious control, the time course, the influence of practice, and even the neurophysiological substrates. Thus, the distinction between automatic and attentional control processes has been a central theme in current theory development.

Separate Versus Unitary Memory Systems

Our intuitions would suggest that there are a number of distinct types of memory systems. For example, rehearsing a telephone number until it is dialed seems to be quite distinct from recalling what one had for breakfast, which also seems quite distinct from providing the definition of the low-frequency word orb from memory. Indeed, there is a rich history of memory research that has been viewed as supporting distinct types of memory systems such as short-term, long-term, implicit, explicit, etc. Are these types of memory reflective of distinct memory systems or are they best understood in terms of a single system that utilizes different processes? The debate over memory types has had a long tradition in cognitive psychology. For example, Atkinson and Shiffrin (1968) introduced an information-processing model comprised of sensory, short-term, and long-term memory stores. However, shortly thereafter, Craik and Lockheart (1972) advanced a unitary view of memory referred to as depth of processing. The idea was that the level at which information is initially processed determines how well it will be encoded in memory. Memory for information processed at a shallow level (e.g., visual features) differs from memory processed at a deep (e.g., meaning) level. Thus, the distinction between short- and long-term memory could also be viewed as a distinction between different types of processes that vary in the quality of memory-trace strength.

In addition to the distinction between short- and long-term memory systems, distinctions have been made between declarative/explicit (directly recollecting an earlier experience) and procedural/implicit (the benefit from an earlier exposure to a stimulus on an indirect measure) memory systems. For example, manipulations of encoding condition that lead to a particular result on explicit measures (e.g., recall of a list of words) can produce opposite effects on implicit measures (e.g., perceptual identification of a visually degraded word) (e.g., Jacoby, 1983). These dissociations would appear to support distinct memory systems. However, this evidence was challenged by Roediger, Weldon, and Challis (1989), who argued that many of the dissociations that appear in the literature could also be accommodated within the transfer-appropriate-processing (TAP) framework. This approach emphasizes the match between encoding operations and retrieval operations. They noted that studies of implicit memory often emphasized data-driven processes, whereas studies of explicit memory often emphasized conceptually driven processes. They also argued that if dissociations were the criterion for separate systems, we would need many more than just two or three distinct systems.

Finally, even the dissociation between abstract category information and individual episodic experiences has been challenged. Specifically, Posner and Keele (1968), among others, have argued for a distinct representation for prototypes/categories (e.g., dog, which represent the common attributes of members within a category, e.g., collie, poodle, beagle). More recent work by Hintzman (1986) and Barsalou (1991) has demonstrated that the evidence in support of qualitatively distinct representations for instances and categories can be accommodated by a model that assumes only one type of instance based memory system. These theorists argue that the apparent distinction between category and instances falls quite naturally from correlations among the features across members within a category. That is, collies, poodles, and beagles all have four legs, bark, have fur, are good pets, etc. It is the similarity across these features that produces the dog category.

Although there is still theoretical debate regarding distinct memory systems versus distinct processing engaged by different tasks, it is important to note that there is evidence for some memory-system distinctions. For example, results indicate that amnesics perform poorly on explicit memory tasks, while their performance on implicit tasks is often normal. Thus, the lesion produced in these individuals would appear to be primarily affecting one system while leaving the other system intact (Squire, 1987). Moreover, evidence from brain-imaging studies is beginning to provide evidence for distinct memory systems (Nyberg, Cabeza, & Tulving, 1996). Thus, although it is clearly the case that some memory-system dissociations are more apparent than real, it is also the case that some system dissociations are in fact real.

Analog Versus Propositional Representations of Mental Images

Humans have little difficulty imagining stimuli that are typically perceived via the senses. For example, we have little difficulty imagining a shiny red apple or a yellow school bus. The theoretical issue that has concerned researchers in this area is the form of representation to generate these images. For example, do mental images demand a qualitatively different form of representation than the representation that we use to process language?

One popular notion of imagery posits that the mental code retains the spatial and sensory properties of the external stimuli we perceive in analog form. For example, an analog representation of the neighborhood in which we live would preserve the relative distances between houses and their sizes. Accordingly, the time it takes to mentally scan between two objects in a mental image should reflect their relative distance to each other. Many experiments have demonstrated this to be the case (e.g., Kosslyn & Pomerantz, 1977). The alternative view of imagery posits that mental images are represented as abstract propositions. According to this account, mental images, language, and other information relies on one primitive code that the brain uses to process all types of information (i.e., *The Language of Thought*, Fodor, 1975). The generation of images occurs after this primitive code is accessed.

Recently there has been some progress in this theoretical debate. Much of the support has actually arisen from studies of the neuropsychological underpinnings of mental imagery. For example, Kosslyn, Thompson, Kim, and Albert (1995) have demonstrated, via brain-imaging studies, that not only do visual images activate areas of the brain dedicated to visual processing, but activations within neural systems across perception and imagery appear to be correlated across stimuli that vary in size. Thus, there appears to be a link between the neural systems that underlie imagery and the actual visual perception of the stimulus. Moreover, studies of individuals with brain lesions have produced dissociations between different aspects of visual imagery such as the spatial versus the visual nature of the image (e.g., Farah,

Hammond, Levine, & Calvanio, 1988). Thus, it is clear that important constraints have been placed on theories of visual imagery based on both behavioral and neuropsychological evidence.

Connectionist Versus Symbolic Representations

One issue that has recently received a considerable amount of attention is the level of description needed for models of higher-level cognition such as language processing and problem solving. For example, how might one build a theory of orthography, phonology, or syntax within a language? Based on linguistic theory, one might assume a set of rules that specify how the constituents can be combined within a language. For example, a rule might specify that the vowel that precedes the letter "e" at the end of a word, as in gave, should be elongated. Such rules provide a descriptive account of many phenomena in language processing. Unfortunately, as in most rules, there are many exceptions. For example, according to the above rule, the word have should be pronounced differently. Thus, linguistic models are often forced to provide a separate processing route for such exceptions.

Within the past decade, there has been an increased appreciation for an alternative way of modeling aspects of human cognition, i.e., connectionist modeling. Connectionist models typically assume a relatively simple set of processing units that are in distinct layers, with all the processing units within a layer connected to all the processing units in adjacent layers. These models do not assume any rules, and are mathematically specified. Knowledge of a domain is contained in the values of weighted connections linking units that are either built into the models or are adjusted according to a gradual learning algorithm that updates activation patterns based on the frequency of exposure to a given stimulus and the deviation of the correct response to the current output. Interestingly, the general principles of connectionist modeling have been used to account for many aspects of cognitive processes (i.e., pattern recognition, speech production, category learning).

Clearly there has been some tension between symbolic rule-based theories and connectionist theories (e.g., Fodor & Pylyshyn, 1988). One might argue that the symbolic models reflect the first wave of cognitive theorizing. These models are often metaphorical in nature, i.e., performance can be modeled by a specific set of stages and a specific set of rules at each stage. These models remain central in current theories of human cognition. On the other hand, connectionist models have a level of computational specificity that is quite appealing. Moreover, there is at least some sense of neural plausibility within such connectionist models (i.e., the simple processing units have some surface level resemblance to neurons, whereas rules are difficult to

envisage within a neural network). Ultimately, the adequacy of such models may lie in their ability to provide new insights into understanding a set of empirical observations. Because both types of models have advantages, it is likely that both first wave metaphorical models, and second wave connectionist models will continue to be central to theoretical accounts of human cognition (Spieler & Balota, 1997).

Summary

The present article provides a brief overview of a few of the theoretical controversies and issues that have been the focus of theory development in cognitive psychology. In each of these areas we have shown how basic research in cognitive psychology has allowed one to distinguish between alternative theories. Cognitive psychology has made considerable progress in understanding mental activity and is now in the excellent position of taking advantage of new technologies (e.g., connectionist modeling, neuroimaging) to provide important advances in theory development.

Bibliography

Anderson, J. R. (1976). Arguments concerning representations for mental imagery. *Psychological Review, 85,* 249–277.

Atkinson, R. C., & Shiffrin, R. M. (1968). Human memory: A proposed system and its control processes. In W. K. Spence & J. T. Spence (Eds.), *The psychology of learning and motivation: Advances in research and theory* (Vol. 2, pp. 89–195).

Barsolou, L. W. (1991). Deriving categories to achieve goals. In G. H. Bower (Ed.), *The psychology of learning and motivation* (Vol. 27, pp. 1–64).

Cherry, E. C. (1953). Some experiments on the recognition of speech, with one and two ears. *Journal of the Acoustical Society of America, 25,* 975–979.

Craik, F. I. M., & Lockhart, R. S. (1972). Levels of processing: A framework for memory research. *Journal of Verbal Learning and Verbal Behavior, 11,* 671–684.

Farah, M. J., Hammond, K. M., Levine, D. N., & Calvanio, R. (1988). Visual and spatial mental imagery: Dissociable systems of representation. *Cognitive Psycholgy, 20,* 439–462.

Fodor, J. A. (1975). *The language of thought.* New York: Crowell.

Fodor, J. A. (1983). *Modularity of mind.* Cambridge, MA: MIT Press.

Fodor, J. A., & Pylyshn, Z. W. (1997). *Mind design II: Philosophy, psychology, artificial intelligence.* Cambridge, MA: MIT Press.

Garner, W. R., Hake, H. W., & Eriksen C. W. (1956). Operationism and the concept of perception. *Psychological Review, 63,* 149–159.

Hintzman, D. L. (1986). "Schema abstraction" in a multiple-trace memory model. *Psychological Review, 93,* 411–427.

Hubel, D. H., & Wiesel, T. N. (1962). Receptive fields, binocular interaction, and functional architecture in the cat's visual cortex. *Journal of Physiology, 160*, 106–154.

Jacoby, L. L. (1983). Remembering the data: Analyzing interactive processes in reading. *Journal of Verbal Learning and Verbal Behavior, 22*, 485–508.

Kosslyn, S. M., & Pomerantz, J. P. (1977). Imagery, propositions, and the form of internal representations. *Cognitive Psychology, 9*, 52–76.

Kosslyn, S. M., Thompson, W. L., Kim, I. J., & Alpert, N. M. (1995). Topographical representations of mental images in primary visual-cortex. *Nature, 378*, 496–498.

McClelland, J. L. (1979). On the time relations of mental processes: An examination of systems of processes in cascade. *Psychological Review, 86*, 287–330.

Moray, N. (1959). Attention in dichotic listening: Affective cues and the influence of instructions. *Quarterly Journal of Experimental Psychology, 11*, 56–60.

Nyberg, L., Cabeza, R., & Tulving, E. (1996). PET studies of encoding and retrieval: The HERA model. *Psychonomic Bulletin & Review, 3*, 135–148.

Posner, M. I., & Keele, S. W. (1968). On the genesis of abstract ideas. *Journal of Experimental Psychology, 77*, 353–363.

Roediger, H. L., Weldon, M. S., & Challis B. H. (1989). Explaining dissociations between implicit and explicit measures of retention: A processing account. In R. L. Roediger & F. I. M. Craik (Eds.), *Varieties of memory and consciousness* (pp. 3–41). Hillsdale, NJ: Erlbaum.

Selfridge, O. G., & Neisser, U. (1960). Pattern recognition by machine. *Scientific American, 203*, 60–68.

Spieler, D. H., & Balota, D. A. (1997). Bringing computational models of word naming down to the item level. *Psychological Science, 8*, 411–416.

Squire, L. R. (1987). *Memory and brain.* New York: Oxford University Press.

David A. Balota and Michael J. Cortese

Research Methods

The methods used by cognitive psychologists have been developed to experimentally tease apart mental operations. At the onset, it should be noted that cognitive psychologists rely most heavily on the experimental method, in which independent variables are manipulated and dependent variables are measured to provide insights into the cognitive architecture. In order to statistically evaluate the results from such experiments, cognitive researchers rely on standard hypothesis testing, along with inferential statistics (e.g., analyses of variance) to provide estimates of the likelihood of a particular pattern of results occurring if they were occurring only by chance.

The methodological tools that cognitive psychologists use depend in large part upon the area of study. Thus, we provide an overview of the methods used in a number of distinct areas including perception, memory, attention, and language processing, along with some discussion of methods that cut across these areas.

Perceptual Methods

During the initial stage of stimulus processing, an individual encodes/perceives the stimulus. Encoding can be viewed as the process of translating the sensory energy of a stimulus into a meaningful pattern. However, before a stimulus can be encoded, a minimum or threshold amount of sensory energy is required to detect that stimulus. In psychophysics, the method of limits and the method of constant stimuli have been used to determine sensory thresholds. The method of limits converges on sensory thresholds by using sub- and suprathreshold intensities of stimuli. From these anchor points, the intensity of a stimulus is gradually increased or decreased until it is at its sensory threshold and is just detectable by the participant. In contrast, the method of constant stimuli converges on a sensory threshold by using a series of trials in which participants decide whether a stimulus was presented or not, and the experimenter varies the intensity of the stimulus. At the sensory threshold, participants are at chance of discriminating between the presence and absence of a stimulus.

Although sensory threshold procedures have been important, these methods fail to recognize the role of nonsensory factors in stimulus processing. Thus signal detection theory was developed to take into account an individual's biases in responding to a given signal in a particular context (Green & Swets, 1966). The notion is that target stimuli produce some signal that is always available in a background of noise and that the payoffs for hits (correctly responding "yes" when the stimulus is presented) and correct rejections (correctly responding "absent" when the stimulus is not presented) modulate the likelihood of an individual reporting that a stimulus is present or absent. One example of this has been a sonar operator in a submarine hearing signals that could be interpreted as an enemy ship or background noise. Because it is very important to detect a signal in this situation, the sonar operator may be biased to say "yes" another ship is present, even when the stimulus intensity is very low and could just be background noise. This bias will not only lead to a high hit probability, but it will also lead to a high false-alarm probability (i.e., incorrectly reporting that a ship is there when there is only noise). Signal detection theory allows researchers to tease apart the sensitivity that the participant has in discriminating between signal and signal plus noise distributions (reflected by changes in a statistic called d prime) and any bias that the individual may bring into the decision making situation (reflected by changes in a statistic called beta).

Signal detection theory has been used to illustrate the independent roles of signal strength and response bias not only in perceptual experiments, but also in other domains such as memory and decision making. Consistent with the distinction between sensitivity and bias, variables such as subject motivation and the proportion of signal trials have been shown to influence the placement of the decision criterion but not the distance between the signal plus noise and noise distributions on the sensory energy scale. On the other hand, variables such as stimulus intensity have been shown to influence the distance between the signal plus noise and noise distributions but not the placement of the decision criterion.

Memory Methods

One of the first studies of human cognition was the work of Ebbinghaus (1885/1913) who demonstrated that one could experimentally investigate distinct aspects of memory. One of the methods that Ebbinghaus developed was the *savings-in-learning* technique in which he studied lists of nonsense syllables (e.g., puv) to a criterion of perfect recitation. Memory was defined as the reduction in the number of trials necessary to relearn a list relative to the number of trials necessary to first learn a list. Since the work of Ebbinghaus, there has been considerable development in the methods used to study memory.

Researchers often attempt to distinguish between three different aspects of memory: encoding (the initial storage of information), retention (the delay between storage and the use of information), and retrieval (the access of the earlier stored information). For example, one way of investigating encoding processes is to manipulate the participants' expectancies. In an intentional memory task, participants are explicitly told that they will receive a memory test. In contrast, during an incidental memory test, participants are given a secondary task that may vary with respect to the types of processes engaged (e.g., making a deep semantic decision about a word versus simply counting the letters). Hyde and Jenkins (1969) found that both the intentionality of learning and the type of encoding during incidental memory tasks influenced later memory performance.

Studies of the retention of information most often involve varying the delay between study and test to investigate the influences of the passage of time on memory performance. However, researchers soon realized that it is not simply the passage of time that is important but also what occurs during the passage of time. In order to address the influence of interfering information, researchers developed retroactive interference paradigms, in which the similarity of the information presented during a retention interval was ma-

nipulated. Results from such studies indicate that interference is a powerful modulator of memory performance (see Anderson & Neely, 1996, for a review).

There are two general classes of methods used in memory research to tap into retrieval processes. On an explicit memory test, the participants are presented a list of materials during an encoding stage, and at some later point in time they are given a test in which they are asked to retrieve the earlier presented material. There are three common measures of explicit memory: recall, recognition, and cued recall. During a recall test (akin to a classroom essay test), participants attempt to remember material presented earlier either in the order that it was presented (serial recall) or in any order (free recall). Researchers often compare the order of information during recall to the initial order of presentation (serial recall functions) and also the organizational strategies that individuals invoke during the retrieval process (measures of subjective organization and clustering). In order to investigate more complex materials such as stories and discourse processing, researchers sometimes measure the propositional structure of the recalled information. The notion is that in order to comprehend a story, individuals rely on a network of interconnected propositions. A proposition is a flexible representation of a sentence that contains a predicate (e.g., an adjective or a verb) and an argument (e.g., a noun or a pronoun). By looking at the recall of the propositions, one can provide insights into the representation that the individuals may have gleaned from a story (Kintsch & van Dijk, 1978).

Of course, there may be memories available that the individual may not be able to produce in a free recall test. Thus, researchers sometimes employ a cued recall test, which is quite similar to free recall, with the exception that the participant is provided with a cue at the time of recall that may aid in the retrieval of the information that was presented earlier. In a recognition task (akin to a classroom multiple choice test), participants are given the information presented earlier and are asked to discriminate this information from new information. The two most common types of recognition tests are the forced choice recognition test and the free choice or yes/no recognition test. On a forced choice recognition test, a participant chooses which of two or more items is old. On a yes/no recognition test, a participant indicates whether each item in a large set of items is old or new.

A second general class of memory tests has some similarity to Ebbinghaus's classic savings method. These are called implicit memory tests. The distinguishing aspect of implicit tests is that participants are not directly asked to recollect an earlier episode. Rather, participants are asked to engage in a task where performance often benefits from earlier exposure to the stimulus items. For example, participants might be presented with a list of words (e.g., elephant, library, assassin) to name aloud during encoding, and then later they would be presented with a list of word fragments (e.g., __le__a__t) or word stems (e.g., ele__) to complete. Some of these fragments or stems might reflect earlier presented items while others may reflect new items. In this way, one can measure the benefit (also called priming) of previous exposure to the items compared to novel items. Interestingly, amnesics are often unimpaired in such implicit memory tests, while showing considerable impairment in explicit memory tests, such as free recall.

Chronometric Methods

In addition to relying on experiments to discriminate among mental operations, cognitive psychologists have attempted to provide information regarding the speed of mental operations. Interestingly, this work began over a century ago with the work of Donders (1868/1969) who was the first to use reaction times to measure the speed of mental operations. In an attempt to isolate the speed of mental processes, Donders developed a set of response time tasks that would appear to differ only in a simple component of processing. For example, task A might require Process 1 (stimulus encoding), whereas, task B might require Process 1 (stimulus encoding) and Process 2 (binary decision). According to Donder's subtractive method, cognitive operations can be added and removed without influencing other cognitive operations. This has been referred to as the assumption of pure insertion and deletion. In the previous example, the duration of the binary decision process can be estimated by subtracting the reaction time in task A from the reaction time in task B.

Sternberg (1969) pointed out that the pure insertion assumptions of subtractive factors have some inherent difficulties. For example, it is possible that the speed of a given process might change when coupled with other processes. Therefore, one cannot provide a pure estimate of the speed of a given process. As an alternative, Sternberg introduced additive factors logic. According to additive factors logic, if a task contains distinct processes, there should be variables that selectively influence the speed of each process. Thus, if two variables influence different processes, their effects should be statistically additive. However, if two variables influence the same process, their effects should statistically interact. In this way, additive factor methods allow one to use studies of response latency to provide information regarding the sequence of stages and the manner in which such processes are influenced by independent variables.

Unfortunately, even additive factors logic has some difficulties. Specifically, additive factors logic works if one assumes a discrete serial stage model of information processing in which the output of a processing stage is not passed on to the next stage until that stage is complete. However, there is a second class of models that assume that the output of a given stage can begin exerting an influence on the next stage of processing before completion. These are called cascade models to capture the notion that the flow of mental processes (like a stream over multiple stones) can occur simultaneously across multiple stages. McClelland (1979) has shown that if one assumes a cascade model, then one cannot use additive factors logic to unequivocally determine the locus of the effects of independent variables.

One cannot consider reaction time measures without considering accuracy because there is an inherent tradeoff between speed and accuracy. Specifically, most behaviors are less accurate when completed too quickly (e.g., consider the danger associated with driving too fast, or the errors associated with solving a set of arithmetic problems under time demands). Most chronometric researchers attempt to ensure that accuracy is quite high, most often above 90% correct, thereby minimizing the concern about accuracy. However, Pachella (1974) has developed an idealized speed-accuracy tradeoff function that provides estimates of changes in speed across conditions and how such changes might relate to changes in accuracy. The importance of Pachella's work is that at some locations of the speed-accuracy tradeoff function, very small changes in accuracy can lead to large changes in response latency and vice versa. More recently, researchers have capitalized on the relation between speed and accuracy to empirically obtain estimates of speed-accuracy functions across different conditions. In these deadline experiments, participants are given a probe that signals the participant to terminate processing at a given point in time. By varying the delay of the deadline, one can track changes in the speed-accuracy function across conditions and thereby determine if an effect of a variable is in encoding and/or retrieval of information (see Meyer, Osman, Irwin, & Yantis, 1988, for a review).

It is important to note that although the temporal dynamics of virtually all cognitive processes can (and probably should) be measured, studies of attention and language processing are the areas that have relied most heavily on chronometric methods. For example, in the area of word recognition, researchers have used the lexical decision task (participants make word/nonword judgments) and speeded naming performance (speed taken to begin the overt pronunciation of a word) to develop models of word recognition. These studies have looked at variables such as the frequency of the stimulus (e.g., orb versus dog), the concreteness of the stimulus (e.g., faith versus truck), or the syntactic class (e.g., dog versus run). In addition, eye-tracking methods have been developed that allow one to measure how long the reader is looking at a particular word (e.g., fixation and gaze measures) while they are engaged in more natural reading. Eye-tracking methods have allowed important insights into the semantic and syntactic processes that modulate the speed of recognizing and integrating a word with other words in the surrounding text.

Researchers in the area of attention have also relied quite heavily on speeded tasks. For example, two common techniques in attention research are interference paradigms and cueing paradigms. In interference paradigms, at least two stimuli are presented that compete for output. A classic example of this is the Stroop task in which a person is asked to name the ink color of a printed word. Under conditions of conflict, that is, when the word green is printed in red ink, there is a considerable increase in response latency compared to nonconflict conditions (e.g., the word deep printed in red ink). In the second class of speeded attention tasks, individuals are presented with visual cues to orient attention to specific locations in the visual field. A target is either presented at that location or at a different location. The difference in response latency to cued and uncued targets is used to measure the effectiveness of the attentional cue.

Cross-Population Studies

Although cognitive psychologists rely most heavily on college students as their target sample, there is an increasing interest in studying cognitive operations across quite distinct populations. For example, there are studies of cognition from early childhood to older adulthood that attempt to trace developmental changes in specific operations such as memory, attention, and language processing. In addition, there are studies of special populations that may have a breakdown in a particular cognitive operation. Specifically, there has been considerable work attempting to understand the attentional breakdowns that occur in schizophrenia and the memory breakdowns that occur in Alzheimer's disease. Thus, researchers have begun to explore distinct populations to provide further leverage in isolating cognitive activity.

Case Studies

After a trauma to the brain, there are sometimes breakdowns in apparently isolated components of cognitive performance. Thus, one may provide insights into the cognitive architecture by studying these individuals and the degree to which such cognitive processes are isolated. For example, there is the classic case of H M in memory research. H M are the initials of an individual who, because of an operation to relieve epilepsy, acquired severe memory loss on explicit tests, although performance on implicit memory tests was relatively intact. In addition, there are classic dissociations across individuals with different types of language breakdowns. For example, Broca's aphasics have relatively spared comprehension processes but difficulty producing fluent speech. In contrast, Wernicke's aphasics have impaired comprehension processes but relatively fluent speech production.

Measures of Brain Activity

With the increasing technical sophistication from the neurosciences, there has been an influx of studies that measure the correlates of mental activity in the brain (Posner & Raichle, 1994). Although there are other methods that are available, we will only review the three most common here. The first is the evoked potential method. In this method, the researcher measures the electrical activity of systems of neurons (i.e., brain waves) as the individual is engaged in some cognitive task. This procedure has excellent temporal resolution, but the specific locus in the brain that is producing the activity can be relatively equivocal.

An approach that has much better spatial resolution is positron emission tomography (PET). In this approach, the individual receives an injection of a radioactive isotope that emits signals that are measured by a scanner. The notion is that there will be increased blood flow (which carries the isotope) to the most active areas of the brain. In this way, one can isolate mental operations by measuring brain activity under specific task demands. Typically, these scans involve about a minute of some form of cognitive processing (e.g., generating verbs to nouns), which is compared to other scans that involve some other cognitive process (e.g., reading nouns aloud). Given the window of time necessary for such scans, the PET approach has some obvious temporal limitations.

A third more recent approach is functional magnetic resonance imaging (fMRI). This procedure is less invasive because it does not involve a radioactive injection. Moreover, there has been some progress made in this area, which suggests that one can look at a more fine grained temporal resolution in fMRI, at least compared to PET techniques. Ultimately, the wedding of evoked potential and fMRI signals may provide the necessary temporal and spatial resolution of the neural signals that underlie cognitive processes.

Computational Modeling

Most models of cognition, although grounded in the experimental method, are metaphorical and noncomputational in nature, e.g., short-term versus long-term memory stores. However, there is also an important method in cognitive psychology that uses computationally explicit models. One example of this approach is connectionist/neural network modeling in which relatively simple processing units are often layered in a highly interconnected network (Rumelhart & Mc-Clelland, 1986). Activation patterns across the simple processing units are computationally tracked across time to make specific predictions regarding the effects of stimulus and task manipulations. Computational models are used in a number of ways to better understand the cognitive architecture. First, these models force researchers to be very explicit regarding the underlying assumptions of metaphorical models. Second, these models often can be used to help explain differences across conditions. Specifically, if a manipulation has a given effect in the data, then one may be able to trace that effect in the architecture within the model. Third, these models can provide important insights into different ways of viewing a given set of data. For example, as noted earlier, McClelland (1979) demonstrated that cascadic models can handle data that were initially viewed as supportive of serial stage models.

Summary

The goal of this article is to provide an encapsulated review of some of the methods that cognitive psychologists use to better understand mental operations. Researchers in cognitive psychology have developed a set of research tools that are almost as rich and diverse as cognition itself.

Bibliography

Anderson, M. C., & Neely, J. H. (1996). Interference and inhibition in memory retrieval. In E. L. Bjork & R. A. Bjork (Eds.), *Memory*. New York: Academic Press.

Donders, F. C. (1969). On the speed of mental processes. Translated by W. G. Koster in W. G. Koster (Ed.), *Attention and performance* (Vol. 2). Amsterdam: North Holland Press. (Original work published in 1868)

Ebbinghaus, H. (1913). *Memory: A contribution to experimental psychology*. New York: Columbia University Press. (Original work published in 1885)

Green, D. M., & Swets, J. A. (1966). *Signal detection theory and psychophysics*. New York: Wiley.

Hyde, T. S., & Jenkins, J. J. (1969). Differential effects of incidental tasks on the organization of recall of a list of highly associated words. *Journal of Experimental Psychology, 82*, 472–481.

Kintsch, W., & van Dijk, T. A. (1978). Toward a model of text comprehension and production. *Psychological Review, 85*, 363–394.

McClelland, J. L. (1979). On the time relations of mental processes: An examination of systems of processes in cascade. *Psychological Review, 86*, 287–330.

Meyer, D. E., Osman, A. M., Irwin, D. E., & Yantis, S. (1988). Modern mental chronometry. Special issue: Event related potential investigations of cognition. *Biological Psychology, 26*, 3–67.

Pachella, R. G. (1974). The interpretation of reaction time in information-processing research. In B. H. Kantowitz (Ed.), *Human information processing—Tutorials in performance and cognition*. Hillsdale, NJ: Erlbaum.

Posner, M. I., & Raichle, M. E. (1994). *Images of mind*. New York: Scientific American Library.

Rumelhart, D. E., McClelland, J. L., & the PDP Research Group (1986). *Parallel distributed processing: Explorations in the microstructure of cognition: Vol. 1. Foundations*. Cambridge, MA: MIT Press.

Sternberg, S. (1969). The discovery of processing stages: Extensions of Donders' method. In W. G. Koster (Ed.), *Attention and performance* (Vol. 2). Amsterdam: North Holland Press.

David A. Balota and Jason M. Watson

COGNITIVE SCIENCE SOCIETY. The Cognitive Science Society brings together researchers from many fields who hold a common goal: understanding the nature of the mind. Its members include psychologists, computer scientists, linguists, anthropologists, neuroscientists, and philosophers. The society's primary activities are to publish the journal *Cognitive Science* and to hold an annual cognitive science conference. The proceedings of each conference are published, and those from most years are available from Lawrence Erlbaum Associates. Membership in the society includes a subscription to *Cognitive Science*. The society is a member of the Federation of Behavioral, Psychological and Cognitive Sciences.

The planning meeting to organize the society was held on 17 March 1979, in the Dallas-Fort Worth airport. A resulting conference on cognitive science was held at La Jolla, California, on 13 August 1979, at which time the society formally came into being. The society was incorporated in Massachusetts later that year. The organizing committee included Roger Schank, Allan Collins, Donald Norman, and a number of other scholars from psychology, linguistics, computer science, and philosophy. A conference has been held annually since the society's founding.

The society currently has more than 1,000 members, including a significant number from countries other than the United States. The society maintains a World Wide Web site with information on its activities, the annual meeting, other conferences in the cognitive sciences, graduate programs in cognitive science, and research and employment notices.

The journal *Cognitive Science* was organized by Ablex Publishing Corporation in 1975 and began publication in 1976. It was later turned over to the society by Ablex, which continues to publish the journal for the society.

The Society has a 12-member board of governors, who annually elect a chair. Its affairs are managed by an executive officer, currently Professor Colleen Seifert.

Previous executive officers were Donald Norman, Kurt VanLehn, and Alan Lesgold.

The annual proceedings of the Cognitive Science Society Conference represent a major source of information on new work and new ideas in the scientific study of thinking. In 1990, the society, with help from an anonymous donor, established the David Marr Prize to be awarded for the best student paper at each annual meeting.

The Web site for the Cognitive Science Society is http://www.umich.edu/~cogsci/

Alan M. Lesgold

COGNITIVE STYLES. [*This entry comprises two articles:* Intelligence *and* Personality.]

Intelligence

In psychology, the idea of style was formally introduced by Gordon Allport (1937), when he referred to style as a means of identifying distinctive personality types or types of behavior. Allport's understanding of styles was rooted in Jung's (1923) theory of psychological types and Adler's notion of styles of life. Since Allport's time, the term has been modified and imbued with different meanings, but the core definition of style—that is, its reference to habitual patterns or preferred ways of doing something (e.g., thinking, learning, teaching) that are consistent over long periods of time and across many areas of activity—remains virtually the same.

Psychologists' interest in styles in cognition emerged in part because psychometric research on abilities and intelligence failed to reflect and interpret the processes generating individual differences. Disappointed with IQ as a construct and motivated by their frustration with the psychometric view of intelligence, psychologists in the 1950s and 1960s searched for new concepts. A small group of experimental psychologists set out to explore and describe individual differences in cognitive functioning (for more history of the field, see Cantor & Kihlstrom, 1987; Kagan & Kogan, 1970). Collectively, these efforts led to a school of thought in cognitive psychology, designated *new look*, that developed a number of stylistic constructs. Among the cognitive styles identified and investigated in the early *new-look* days were constricted-flexible control (an ability to disregard one of two conflicting cues; Smith & Klein, 1953); sharpening-versus-leveling styles (tendency to be hypersensitive to minutiae, to respond excessively to fine nuances and sharpen small differences [sharpening] versus tendency to maximize assimilation effects in such a way that the fine shades of distinctions among individual elements are lost [leveling]; Klein, 1970);

equivalence range (a way of spontaneous differentiation of heterogeneous items into a complex of related groups; Gardner, 1953); tolerance for unrealistic experiences (the readiness to accept and report experiences at variance with conventional reality or with what they knew to be true; Klein & Schlesinger, 1951); and field dependence-independence (the individual differences expressed as a degree of dependence on the structure of a prevailing visual field; Witkin et al., 1954). Later entries include reflection-impulsivity (the degree of subjective consideration of alternative hypotheses with minimal reliance on their probable validity; Kagan, 1958) and category width (the degree of subjective urge to act on or ignore an awareness of differences, Pettigrew, 1958), among many others. These approaches were based loosely on a definition of cognitive styles as, "the characteristic, self-consistent models of functioning which individuals show in their perceptual and intellectual activities" (Witkin, Oltman, Raskin, & Karp, 1971, p. 3). The essence of style as a construct was its reflection of individual differences in cognition (memory, reasoning, perception, attention, thinking, and concept formation). The reader interested in a complete listing and description of cognitive styles should consult reviews by Goldstein and Blackman (1978), Kagan and Kogan (1970), Kogan (1976), and Messick (1976). As justifiably stated by Kogan (1994), a substantial portion of the field of styles in cognition is now primarily of historical value. Accordingly, this presentation is limited to general points and illustrative examples.

The conceptualization of each cognitive style was accompanied by the development of one (or several) corresponding instrument(s). For example, two widely known cognitive-style instruments used for assessing field dependence-independence are the Rod and Frame Test (RFT) and the Embedded Figures Test (EFT). In the RFT individuals must ignore a visual and/or postural context to locate a true vertical. In the EFT (Witkin et al., 1971), the individual must locate a previously seen simple figure within the context of a larger, more complex figure that has been purposely designed to embed and obscure the simple figure. People who are able to locate a simple figure or a vertical position in a complex context are said to be field-independent; those who have difficulty with such tasks are said to be field-dependent. Another well-known instrument is the Matching Familiar Figure Test (MFFT), which has been most frequently used to measure the construct of reflection-impulsivity (Block, Block, & Harrington, 1974; Butter, 1979; Das, 1983; Kagan, 1966). The MFFT is a perceptual task, in which a person is required to select, from among several alternatives, the one that exactly matches a standard. The number of errors and the time to complete the test are measured, and the median point is viewed as a cutoff for categorizing individuals. People with faster response times and relatively more errors are called impulsive; those with longer response times and longer latencies are called reflective. Two other groups include the minority of fast accurates and slow inaccurates.

Between the late 1950s and early 1980s researchers carried out a great deal of work on different cognitive styles. Hundreds of papers addressing different issues, ranging from developmental mechanisms of styles to cross-comparisons of styles, were published. By the early 1980s, however, enthusiasm for studying styles tapered off. To summarize the luminous body of literature that had been created, researchers (Goldstein & Blackman, 1978; Kogan, 1973; Messick, 1976, Wardell & Royce, 1978) organized the work involving cognitive styles into a number of schemes. Messick (1976) identified a total of nine groups of cognitive styles from the range of nineteen registered in the literature. His review consists of thorough definitions and major findings associated with each style. Kogan and Saarni (1990) updated the review and conducted a slightly more detailed examination of selected styles.

Kogan (1973, 1983) offered a threefold classification based on the distance of a style from the domain of abilities and on the nature of the measurement operations employed in the assessment of a style. A Type I is closest to the ability domain, because performance on the operational index of the style can be described as more or less veridical. For example, an individual described as field-independent is more proficient in setting the rod to the vertical in the rod-and-frame test than the field-dependent person. Because the task requirement is to set the rod at the true vertical, field independence necessarily implies a superior level of performance.

In Type II cognitive styles, the question of veridicality of performance does not arise and the issues of accuracy and efficiency are not considered. Nevertheless, there is still an implicit assumption of the greater value of one specific kind of performance relative to another. Such a value choice is sometimes made on purely theoretical grounds—one style is postulated to be "developmentally more advanced" than another. Moreover, value also comes into play when the styles in question correlate with ability measures. If, out of the two compared styles, one positively correlates (or correlates significantly higher) with ability indexes, whereas an alternative style does not (or correlates significantly lower), the first style tends to be endowed with greater value. Typical of the Type II category are the conceptual styles described by Kagan, Moss, and Sigel (1963). Although an analytic style in no sense represents a higher level of performance than a thematic-relation style, there is an implicit assumption of the greater value of the former.

Type III is the only category in which styles are nei-

ther ranked nor synonymous with ability. For example, a broad versus narrow style of categorization (Pettigrew, 1958) was initially advanced in largely value-neutral terms. Since that time, investigators have not found a consistent pattern of correlations to suggest that either broad or narrow categorizers have a consistent cognitive advantage (Kogan, 1971).

Yet another attempt to summarize the vast literature on styles was undertaken by Wardell and Royce (1978). In his multifactorial framework, Royce (1973) defined style as a characteristic mode or way of manifesting cognitive and/or affective phenomena. This definition suggests that styles are essentially stable traits, designating consistent modes of cognitive and affective processings. Furthermore, the combination of styles of any individual constitutes that individual's style subsystem. Royce defined the style subsystem as a multidimensional, organized sub-system of processes by means of which an organism manifests cognitive and/or affective phenomena. According to this definition, styles can be seen as higher order traits in that they influence the way cognitive abilities and affective traits are related to individual behavior. Based on this definition, Royce's analysis distinguishes three major types of stylistic constructs: cognitive styles, affective styles, and cognitive-affective styles. The first two are concerned with functional consistencies in the relationships between styles and, respectively, ability factors or affective traits. Cognitive-affective styles are concerned with consistent ways in which styles simultaneously integrate ability and affective traits. Within this model, there are three general styles—rational, empirical, and metaphoric—which reflect three different ways in which cognition and affect are integrated. Through meta-analysis, Wardell and Royce identified seven cognitive and four affective styles corresponding to the general styles. The cognitive and affective styles reflect some degree of construct validity based on extensive empirical research performed mostly in the framework of the new look.

Although styles in cognition have been studied extensively, and the results of this work have been presented in hundreds of publications, there are empirical and conceptual problems related to the very concept of style.

The empirical problem in this field goes beyond usual general complaint regarding the fragmentary nature of research and the lack of meta-theoretical analysis. In this case, there are at least as many specific measurement instruments as there are styles, but there are only a few studies linking various "styles of . . ." together and cross-referencing both different constructs and different measures.

The conceptual problems derive from the proliferation of definitions of style. Of greatest concern are the relation of styles to intelligence, the closeness of the concepts of style and strategy, and the nature of styles themselves. Since its very appearance, the theory of styles in cognition has had a complicated relationship with the theory of intelligence. The concern of inbreeding is well grounded because several cognitive styles have ability-like properties, which are especially apparent because of the value-laden character of some styles. Indeed, just as higher abilities are preferred over lower abilities, some styles (e.g., field dependence-independence) are desired and supported more than their counterparts.

As for the relationships between style and strategy, some authors (e.g., Luchins & Luchins, 1970) claim that the two concepts have different theoretical foundations and encompass functional differences, whereas others (e.g., Cronbach & Snow, 1977) use these terms interchangeably. The consensus today is that styles and strategies differ on (1) degree of awareness—styles operate without conscious effort, whereas strategies involve a conscious choice of alternatives; (2) degree of stability—strategy is used for task- or context-dependent situations, whereas style implies a higher degree of stability; and (3) specificity of adaptation—styles are viewed as adaptational control mechanisms mediating relations between the need state and the environment (Wallach & Kogan, 1965), whereas strategies are viewed as adaptational mechanisms aimed at the minimization of errors in decision-making processes.

Regarding the nature of styles, many theorists place them at the interface of intelligence and personality, defining them as the ways in which personalities choose to exploit their intelligence (Sternberg, 1997). There are, however, exceptions. Gustafson and Kallen (1989) distinguish cognitive styles from personality styles. Myers (1988) refers to a hierarchy of styles of cognition, defining personality as a source of individual variation within styles. Developed to ascertain the element of affect in cognition, the construct of style has never been clearly distinguished from either ability (intelligence) or personality.

Based on the frequency of relevant publications, only two major styles, field dependence-independence and reflection-impulsivity, survived the general ebb of research in the field. Theory and research on both of these styles continue to be a center of interest for many psychologists (Globerson & Zelniker, 1989; Grigorenko & Sternberg, 1995; Wapner & Demick, 1991). Currently, the cognitive-style movement appears, once again, to be gaining some attention and entering mainstream psychological research (Sternberg & Grigorenko, 1997). The concept of style in cognition has reemerged under the term *thinking style*, coined in Sternberg's Theory of Mental Self-Government (Sternberg, 1997). This theory defines a style of thought as a preferred way of thinking or expressing one or more abilities. When applied to intelligence, the concept of mental self-government—that is how intelligence is organized or directed—generates 13 thinking styles.

Styles have provided and continue to provide a much needed interface between research on cognition and research on personality. Unlike many psychological constructs, styles are easy to describe and quantify, and, throughout their history, they have lent themselves to operationalization and direct empirical tests. Moreover, styles predict performance over and above individual differences in abilities. Finally, styles are more flexible and modifiable than abilities and so can provide information about the ways individuals interact with and adapt to environments.

Bibliography

Allport, G. W. (1937). *Personality, a psychological interpretation.* New York: Henry Holt and Co.

Block, J., Block, J. H., & Harrington, D. M. (1974). Some misgivings about the Matching Familiar Figures Test as a measure of reflection-impulsivity. *Developmental Psychology, 11*, 611–632.

Butter, E. (1979). Visual and haptic training and cross-modal transfer of reflectivity. *Journal of Education Psychology, 72*, 212–219.

Cantor, N., & Kihlstrom, J. F. (1987). *Personality and social intelligence.* Englewood Cliffs, NJ: Prentice Hall.

Cronbach, L. J., & Snow, R. E. (1977). *Aptitudes and instructional methods.* New York: Wiley.

Das, P. (1983). Impulsive behavior and assessment of impulsivity with hospitalized adolescents. *Psychological Reports, 53(3–1)*, 764–766.

Gardner, R. (1953). Cognitive style in categorizing behavior. *Perceptual and Motor Skills, 22*, 214–233.

Globerson, T., & Zelniker, T. (Eds.). (1989). *Cognitive style and cognitive development.* Norwood, NJ: Ablex.

Goldstein, K. M., & Blackman, S. (1978). *Cognitive style.* New York: Wiley.

Grigorenko, E. L., & Sternberg, R. J. (1995). Thinking styles. In D. H. Saklofske & M. Zeidner (Eds.), *International handbook of personality and intelligence* (pp. 205–229). New York: Plenum Press.

Gustafson, R., & Kallen, H. (1989). Alcohol effects on cognitive and personality style in women with special reference to primary and secondary process. *Alcoholism: Clinical and Experimental Research, 13*, 644–648.

Jung, C. (1923). *Psychological types.* New York: Harcourt Brace.

Kagan, J. (1958). The concept of identification. *Psychological Review, 65*, 296–305.

Kagan, J. (1966). Reflection-impulsivity: The generality and dynamics of conceptual tempo. *Journal of Abnormal Psychology, 71*, 17–24.

Kagan, J., & Kogan, N. (1970). Individual variation in cognitive processes. In P. A. Mussen (Ed.), *Carmichael's manual of child psychology* (Vol. 1, pp. 1273–1365). New York: Wiley.

Kagan, J., Moss, H. A., & Sigel, I. E. (1963). Psychological significance of styles of conceptualization. *Monographs of the Society for Research in Child Development*.

Klein, G. S. (1970). *Perception, motives, and personality*. New York: Knopf.

Klein, G. S., & Schlesinger, H. J. (1951). Perceptual attitudes toward instability: I. Prediction of apparent movement experiences from Rorschach responses. *Journal of Personality, 19*, 289–302.

Kogan, N. (1971). Educational implications of cognitive styles. In G. S. Lesser (Ed.), *Psychology and educational practice* (pp. 242–292). Glenview, IL: Scott, Foresman.

Kogan, N. (1973). Creativity and cognitive style: A life span perspective. In P. Baltes & K. W. Schaie (Eds.), *Life span developmental psychology: Personality and socialization* (145–178). New York: Academic Press.

Kogan, N. (1976). *Cognitive styles in infancy and early childhood*. New York: Wiley.

Kogan, N. (1983). Cognitive styles as moderators of competence: A commentary. In E. D. Neimark, R. DeLisi, & J. L. Newman (Eds.), *Moderators of competence* (pp. 175–189). Hillsdale, NJ: Erlbaum.

Kogan, N. (1994). Cognitive styles. In R. J. Sternberg (Ed.) *Encyclopedia of intelligence* (Vol 1., pp. 266–273). New York: Macmillan.

Kogan, N., & Saarni, C. (1990). Cognitive style in children: Some evolving trends. In O. N. Saracho (Ed.), *Cognitive style and early education* (pp. 3–31). New York: Gordon & Breach.

Luchins, A. S., & Luchins, E. H. (1970). Effects of preconceptions and communications on impressions of a person. *Journal of Social Psychology, 81(2)*, 243–252.

Messick, S. (1976). Personality consistencies in cognition and creativity. In S. Messick et al. (Eds.), *Individuality in learning* (pp. 4–22). San Francisco: Jossey-Bass.

Myers, P. L. (1988). Paranoid pseudocommunity beliefs in a sect milieu. *Social Psychiatry and Psychiatric Epidemiology, 23*, 252–255.

Pettigrew, T. F. (1958). The measurement of category width as a cognitive variable. *Journal of Personality, 26*, 532–544.

Royce, J. R. (1973). The conceptual framework for a multi-factor theory of individuality. In J. R. Royce (Ed.), *Contributions of multivariate analysis to psychological theory*. London: Academic Press.

Smith, G. J. W., & Klein, G. S. (1953). Cognitive controls in serial behavior patterns. *Journal of Personality, 22*, 188–213.

Sternberg, R. J. (1997). *Thinking styles*. New York: Cambridge University Press.

Sternberg, R. J., & Grigorenko, E. L. (1997). Are styles still in style? *American Psychologist, 52*, 700–712.

Wallach, M., & Kogan, N. (1965). *Modes of thinking in young children*. New York: Holt, Rinehart & Winston.

Wapner, S., & Demick, J. (Eds.). (1991). *Field dependence-independence: Cognitive style across the life span*. Hillsdale, NJ: Erlbaum.

Wardell, D. M., & Royce, J. R. (1978). Toward a multi-factor theory of styles and their relationships to cognition and affect. *Journal of Personality, 46*, 474–505.

Witkin, H. A., Oltman, P. K., Raskin, E., & Karp, S. A. (1971). *Embedded Figures Test, Children's Embedded Figures Test, Group Embedded Figures Test*. Manual. Palo Alto, CA: Consulting Psychologists Press.

Witkin, H. A., Lewis, H. B., Hertzman, M., Machover, K., Meissner, P. B., & Wapner, S. (1954). *Personality through perception*. New York: Harper.

Elena L. Grigorenko

Personality

In thinking about thinking, most researchers are intrigued by the basic mechanisms of how all human minds work: for example, how early and later information affects our conclusions, how we evaluate evidence, how we predict probable outcomes of a situation, how we choose among different strategies and decisions, how the amount, clarity, and reliability of information are assessed, and the relationship between what goes on in the mind and what goes on in the brain. All of these are aspects of cognition, and cognitive scientists try to find universal patterns in how human beings deal with such issues.

The Cognitive Aspect of Personality

The area of cognitive styles has a different focus from cognition as such. Cognitive styles refers to the overlap between aspects of all human thinking and aspects of individual personalities: differences among individuals in their stable, long-lasting, and pervasive tendencies to process information in particular ways.

The recognition that people think differently from each other goes back into the myths of antiquity—the subtle, perhaps even convoluted thought patterns of Odysseus, for example, contrasting with the straightforward simple reactions of Achilles. But systematic studies of cognitive style date from the early part of the twentieth century. At that time, researchers were intrigued by such questions as how people differed in their use of environmental cues and information as opposed to internal standards for decisions (field dependence).

In the immediate aftermath of World War II, there was a seminal attempt to explain why some people are likely to embrace political movements built upon oppression and violence—such as the ones just defeated at untold cost and suffering (Adorno, Frenkel-Brunswick, Levinson, & Sanford, 1950). These authors proposed that the foundation of an authoritarian personality was what we would now call a cognitive style: the tendency to think in clear-cut, unchanging categories.

This concept was elaborated by later theorists, and a more tightly specified format became particularly influential in cognitive styles research. Among the hypothesized styles derived from it are rigidity, dogmatism, and intolerance of ambiguity, all of which contribute to a combined dimension of open- to closed-mindedness (Rokeach, 1960).

Rigidity refers to difficulty in modifying an existing strategy or belief even when there is strong evidence that it is incorrect or dysfunctional. Rigid people persist in trying to solve problems in a particular way even after their continued failure is obvious, or hew to an opinion even after there are strong reasons to judge it as mistaken.

Dogmatism, like rigidity, involves resistance to intellectual change; but dogmatism refers to difficulty in dealing with information that would require a change in one's system of beliefs or attitudes. Such information may be ignored, reinterpreted to reduce its impact, disbelieved, or explained away; the result is that the existing cognitive structure can be maintained as is.

Intolerance of ambiguity is a basic cognitive style. In fact, rigidity and dogmatism may merely be ways of averting ambiguity (or, conversely, ways of maintaining clarity, certainty, and closure). People who are intolerant of ambiguity need definite and clear ideas, opinions, and solutions, and are uncomfortable with uncertainty and doubt. Thus, they may ignore contradictory information; persevere with what to observers may be obviously unsuccessful strategies; jump to and then defend premature conclusions; prefer problems and tasks with solutions that are obviously either right or wrong, good or bad (rather than, say, alternatives with some good and some bad aspects); and hold on to mutually contradictory thoughts and beliefs—e.g., believing that members of some other ethnic group are simultaneously too ambitious and too lazy—by refusing to see the contradictions.

Open-mindedness in turn has become the foundation for more recent theories and research. It is a central feature in the study of cognitive or conceptual complexity. Complexity incorporates flexibility of thinking, receptivity to new information, the ability to see shades of gray rather than only black or white, and the avoidance of premature closure. Although this approach offers causal explanations, measures, and applications that are very different from those of Adorno and his colleagues, the similarities are obvious. Complexity is a function of the tendency to perceive and consider different ways of assessing a situation (differentiation) and to combine these ways so as to reach valid conclusions (integration). Research has shown that individual level of complexity is related to self-perception, decision-making in a great variety of contexts, student-teacher interactions, child-rearing practices and outcomes, and the performance of managers and their organizations (Siegfried Streufert and Susan C. Streufert in *Behavior in the Complex Environment*, Washington, D.C., 1978).

Other recent theorists have developed categories of cognitive styles very similar to open-mindedness and complexity. In addition, some have proposed an emotional component of enjoyment of, or aversion to, cognitive effort generally (need for cognition; J. T. Cacioppo, et al., *Psychological Bulletin*, 1996, *119*, 197–253): and more specifically, positive or negative reactions to "playing" with new ideas, contradictory information, and creative thought. One theory labels this uncertainty orientation, a characteristic of people who seek out new information and enjoy discovering, exploring, and mastering uncertainty—as opposed to avoiding uncertainty and adhering to what is already known (certainty orientation; chapter by Sorrentino and others in Smith, 1991). Another theorist, Arie Kruglanski (for example, in A. W. Kruglanski & D. W. Webster, *Psychological Review*, 1996, *103*, 263–283), argues that people differ in the desire to have definite knowledge about whatever situation or task they are facing (need for closure). Michael J. Apter's concept of telic dominance (*Reversal Theory*, London, 1989) posits related dimensions of serious-mindedness (goal-directedness), planning orientation (thinking ahead), and arousal avoidance. The opposite pole, paratelic dominance, describes individuals whose style is characterized by intrinsic motivation, spontaneity, and arousal-seeking.

Some cognitive style theories include more dimensions. Robert J. Sternberg's analysis (*Thinking Styles*, New York, 1997) invokes the metaphor of governmental structure. His concept of "mental self-government" recognizes legislative, executive, and judicial functions, which respectively describe preferences for planning, implementing, and evaluating; styles labeled as monarchic (a tendency to pursue one goal at a time), hierarchic (multiple goals with different priorities), oligarchic (multiple, equally important, goals), and anarchic (unstructured, random problem-solving); global and local levels (preferring to think about large, abstract issues versus concrete details); internal and external scope (related to introversion/extroversion, social skills, and cooperativeness); and conservative (rule-based) versus progressive (creative, change-oriented) leanings. Although these categories overlap with open-mindedness, orientation to ambiguity, and complexity, they also incorporate other characteristics, not all of them cognitive.

Several recent theories are built upon the recognition that the ability to cope successfully with stressful situations depends at least to some extent on how one thinks about them. Cognitive styles that predict healthy and positive coping—self-efficacy, hardiness, sense of coherence, optimistic explanatory style—include thinking that one has significant control over events, understanding the meaning of what is happening and how it fits into one's life, viewing difficulties as challenges to be met and planning how to meet them, explaining failures as resulting from specific, remediable causes rather than from pervasive and permanent flaws in oneself, and both persevering to solve problems and being resilient in exploring new solutions if needed.

Measuring Cognitive Styles

The assessment of cognitive styles has concerned theorists right from the beginning, and a great many methods have been invented and used. They have included paper-and-pencil scales, interviews, complicated dynamic simulations of decision-making situations, measures of how the person interprets ambiguous stimuli, searching for patterns in biographical data, and analyses of the individual's written or spoken utterances for evidence concerning their underlying thought processes.

The measures differ widely for several reasons. One, of course, is that the theorized cognitive styles themselves differ, as do the conditions under which they are thought to affect observable behavior. Another is that not all methods are equally feasible for all groups being studied: the cognitive styles of famous people, for example, are unlikely to be measured by scales or simulations because researchers seldom have access to such people. The use of multiple methods makes comparison difficult, but it has an advantage as well in that when consistent findings are produced, the variability of the measurement itself makes the results more credible.

The Status of Cognitive Styles Research

It is difficult to separate differences in how people process information—that is, patterns of intellectual functioning—from their characteristic motives, moods, and general personality traits. As we have seen, some cognitive style theories themselves incorporate emotional and motivational components; there are also theories of personality traits or types, such as optimism–pessimism and attributional or explanatory style, that include cognitive style components. At the other side of the cognition-personality intersection, it is quite likely that some characteristics considered to be universal may in fact show stable individual differences: for example, cognitive dissonance, which is a theorized unpleasant state arising from the recognition of ambiguity or self-contradiction, may be consistently more aversive for some people than for others (and therefore may be a stronger motivator of steps to reduce it among the former group).

There is also a problem in separating "ways" of thinking from the content of thought. One of the most vigorous criticisms of *The Authoritarian Personality* (Adorno, Frenkel-Brunswick, Levinson, & Sanford, 1950) has been based on its assumption that closed-mindedness is necessarily linked with right-wing politi-

cal ideology. This confusion has persisted in more recent incarnations of authoritarianism theory, such as Bob Altemeyer's *Right-Wing Authoritarianism* (Winnipeg, 1981).

A similar problem arises with regard to separating thinking styles from abilities. Most theorists would agree that intelligence is not a cognitive style, but there are styles that do seem related to sheer intellectual power (for example, conceptual complexity is moderately but consistently correlated with IQ score). Moreover, some psychologists such as Robert Sternberg equate different kinds of thinking—which many experts would categorize as cognitive styles—with different kinds of intelligence.

How to test whether a tendency to think in a given way is really stable, long-lasting, and pervasive across topics and problems is another challenge to scientists. Research linking cognitive styles to actual behavior has had encouraging results: cognitive style measures do predict, or at least are correlated with, a wide variety of responses such as attitude stability, reactions to persuasive attempts, the search for or avoidance of new information and the processing of information in making decisions, compatibility with teaching methods, choosing among vocational and avocational activities, approaches to social interaction, making judgments about other people, stress resistance, and preferences in politics, religion, philosophy, aesthetics, and abstract ideas. The fact that one measure, administered one time, shows relationships with so many behavioral outcomes supports the idea that cognitive styles are in fact stable over time and pervasive across contexts, situations, and tasks.

However, some theorists now view cognitive style factors, including open-mindedness, complexity, vigilance, and even authoritarianism, as having both trait (personality) and state (temporary) components. The trait level predisposes the person to think within a limited range of levels of the factor, and the state level—established by situational influences—determines the actual level that is activated at a given time or in a specific situation. For example, someone may generally approach problems using highly complex strategies; but just how complex a strategy will be used for a specific problem will be affected by such factors as the person's energy and stress levels, the importance of the problem, the difficulty of solving it, and so on (chapter by Suedfeld and others, in Smith; 1991).

A large and growing research literature has applied such concepts not only to customary groups of research participants but also to political and military leaders, business executives, and other elite decision-makers. The goal is to analyze the conditions under which people are more or less likely to think in open-versus closed-minded, or complex versus simple, ways, and to unravel the connections between such styles of thinking and the likely outcomes of decisions, with greater predictive power than is obtained through a one-time assessment of cognitive style. The idea that behavior is best predicted and understood by considering the interaction between trait and state aspects of cognition may bring the field new achievements and insights.

[See also Field Dependence and Independence; and Optimism and Pessimism.]

Bibliography

Adorno, T. W., Frenkel-Brunswick, E., Levinson, D. J., & Sanford, R. N. (1950). *The authoritarian personality*. New York: Harper & Row. A seminal work in cognitive styles as well as general political psychology and personality theory.

Goldstein, K. M., & Blackman, S. (1978). *Cognitive style: Five approaches and relevant research*. New York: Wiley. Reviews five of the most important early theories of cognitive styles and evaluates their measurement techniques and predictive ability.

Rokeach, M. (1960). *The open and closed mind*. New York: Basic Books. The first detailed analysis of rigidity and dogmatism as cognitive styles.

Rosenbaum, M. (Ed.). (1990). *Learned resourcefulness: On coping skills, self-control, and adaptive behavior*. New York: Springer. An excellent overview of major theories relating cognitive styles (and other relevant factors) to coping with stressful events.

Smith, C. P. (Ed.). (1991). *Motivation and personality: Handbook of thematic content analysis*. New York: Cambridge University Press. Theoretical and research summaries, and detailed assessment manuals, of personality variables including several cognitive styles.

Peter Suedfeld

COGNITIVE THERAPY is a treatment approach based on the notion that dysfunctional thinking plays a role in a number of psychological disorders. According to cognitive theory, the way an individual interprets life events determines in part his or her response to those events in terms of both affect and behavior. In cognitive therapy, the therapist helps the patient learn to identify the maladaptive information processing styles that lead to dysfunctional beliefs and to systematically test their accuracy.

History of the Approach

Cognitive therapy grew out of work by Aaron T. Beck in the early 1960s examining the psychodynamic notion that depression is a consequence of anger turned inward. In a series of studies, Beck found little evidence of retroflected anger in the dreams and free associations of depressed patients. Instead, he found the same themes of loss and personal inadequacy that dominated their conscious ruminations. Moreover, both mood and performance improved with concrete evidence of success on simple behavioral tasks, something that should not have happened if depression represented an unconscious need to fail.

This led him to conclude that depression is more a manifestation of consciously accessible negative thinking and maladaptive information processing than retroflected anger or masochistic drives. He further noted that the thinking of depressed patients was dominated by a negative view of the self, the personal world, and the future (the negative cognitive triad) and marked distortions in logic and information processing. This led him to articulate a model of change that incorporated an interrelated set of cognitive and behavioral strategies designed to systematically identify and test those dysfunctional beliefs and distortions in information processing.

Core Concepts and Therapeutic Strategies

Cognitive therapy rests on the principle of collaborative empiricism. Patients are encouraged to gather data and conduct experiments to test the accuracy of their beliefs. It relies on a process of guided discovery, in which a series of questions are used in a Socratic fashion to encourage the patient to examine his or her beliefs and to relate them to prior experience. In this regard, cognitive therapy differs from Ellis's Rational Emotive Therapy (RET), which also emphasizes the primacy of beliefs, but relies on reason and persuasion to encourage patients to adopt a more Stoic philosophy. Similarly, although cognitive therapy incorporates a number of behavioral strategies and techniques, it does so within a larger conceptual model that emphasizes the importance of empirical hypothesis testing of beliefs. In this sense, it more fully integrates behavior change strategies within a larger cognitive conceptualization than other related cognitive-behavioral interventions.

In essence, cognitive therapists teach their patients to operate like scientists, regarding beliefs as hypotheses (not facts) that can be systematically tested and discarded if found to be inaccurate. Patients are trained to differentiate thoughts from feelings and to look for those hot cognitions most closely linked to affective response. These are often found among the patient's automatic thoughts, specific negative interpretations that rise unbidden in the ongoing stream-of-consciousness in the form of either verbal ruminations or visual images. Automatic thoughts are typically related to more generic attitudes and beliefs that form the core of the larger meaning system. These dysfunctional attitudes and core beliefs may not always be manifest in conscious awareness, but usually can be readily accessed with simple probes.

This larger meaning system operates in a schematic fashion. Schemas are interrelated meaning structures that determine how incoming information is processed and provide a set of heuristics for making judgments under uncertainty. Erroneous core beliefs distort information in a maladaptive fashion and generate inaccurate perceptions and inferences in specific situations. For some disorders, like recurrent depression, the problematic schemas operate like latent diatheses, lying inert until activated by negative life events. For other disorders, like the personality disorders, the problematic schemas appear to be chronically hypervalent and represent the only way the patient has to think about the self or the world. In these latter instances, treatment tends to take considerably longer.

A variety of strategies and techniques are used to identify and correct dysfunctional thinking. These include the use of Socratic questioning to generate alternative explanations for problematic events and to review the available evidence speaking to the validity and implications of the respective hypotheses. Patients are encouraged to conduct behavioral experiments to test the accuracy of their beliefs. These simple interventions are often sufficient for dealing with patients with less complex disorders. In recent years, considerable attention has been devoted to developing strategies for exploring and modifying the conditional assumptions and core beliefs at the heart of the larger meaning system. This emphasis on the process of cognitive conceptualization represents a major advance in the treatment of more complex and chronic problems.

Clinical Indications

As described by the authors in a recent review in the *Handbook of Psychotherapy and Behavior Change* (Hollon & Beck, 1994), cognitive therapy has been applied to a wide variety of disorders. One of its earliest applications was to the treatment of depression. Beginning in the late 1970s, a series of studies suggested that cognitive therapy was at least as efficacious as drugs in the treatment of depressed outpatients and possibly more enduring. Although antidepressant medications tend to be effective as long as they are taken, they do little to reduce subsequent risk once they are discontinued. Several studies have shown that patients treated to remission with cognitive therapy were considerably less likely to relapse following treatment termination than patients treated to remission pharmacologically.

This same pattern is evident in the treatment of panic disorder. As for depression, cognitive therapy appears to be at least as efficacious as drugs (and behavioral interventions) and quite possibly longer lasting. The central notion of the cognitive model of panic is that patients fall prey to catastrophic misinterpretations of relatively benign physical or psychological events. That is, they interpret normal signs of physiological arousal as signs of an impending medical or psychiatric emergency. In cognitive therapy, the therapist encourages the patient to test those catastrophic misinterpretations by inducing an actual panic attack. The patient can then test the notion that he or she will die or go crazy as a consequence of becoming aroused.

Treatment of agoraphobia retains the emphasis on identifying and testing catastrophic thoughts, but also encourages patients to enter situations that they previously avoided, devoting careful attention to collecting data about their expectations in that regard. Treatment of phobia follows a similar theme, with a clear recognition that it is important to assess precisely what the patient thinks might happen while in the phobic situation. Phobic avoidance of flying based upon a fear of crashing needs to be approached differently from fear of flying based on concerns over becoming airsick, and patients frequently cannot access their problematic beliefs unless they are in the actual situation. Although clearly efficacious, it is not clear how cognitive therapy compares with more purely behavioral interventions in the treatment of simple phobias.

Cognitive therapy has yet to be tested in the treatment of social phobia, although closely related cognitive-behavioral interventions have been shown to be effective. As with other anxiety disorders, the key lies in examining the catastrophic misperceptions expected to occur as a consequence of engaging in normal social interactions. According to David Clark at Oxford University, the most troublesome beliefs often appear in the form of visual images regarding one's own ineptitude, concerns that are only magnified by efforts to engage in safety behaviors designed to forestall public humiliation. As in the treatment of panic, patients are encouraged to test their beliefs by observing the consequences of dispensing with those safety behaviors. Similar self-protective strategies appear to maintain exaggerated concerns about physical illness in hypochondriasis and also appear to yield to cognitive interventions.

Cognitive therapy has also been applied to the treatment of obsessive-compulsive disorder with generally good results, as long as it retains an emphasis on exposure and response prevention. Whether its benefits exceed those provided by exposure alone remains to be determined, although each is clearly more effective than traditional dynamic interventions. Similarly, cognitive therapy has shown considerable promise in the treatment of posttraumatic stress disorder, particularly when patients are encouraged to relive traumatic experiences in the service of coming to grips with the "hot cognitions" engendered by those events.

The treatment of bulimia represents yet another area in which cognitive therapy and related cognitive-behavioral interventions are rapidly becoming the standard of treatment. Concerns about shape and weight (often based upon underlying concerns about desirability) appear to drive excessive dieting, which in turn sets the stage for binge eating and subsequent efforts to purge. Given this causal chain, there is considerable opportunity for cognitive intervention and recent studies suggest that these approaches are at least as efficacious and longer lasting than other current alternatives. Moreover, recent studies suggest that cognitive interventions may even be effective in the treatment of anorexia nervosa, which is further complicated by the effects of self-starvation.

Cognitive therapy has been adapted to the treatment of impulse control disorders, with promising results. Recent studies suggest that the notion that impulses demand immediate gratification can be tested like any other belief and that patients can learn to extend their behavioral repertoire to include strategies that are less damaging than using drugs or acting out. Although no panacea, it appears that cognitive therapy can play a useful role in the treatment of alcohol and substance abuse, as well as other problems of impulse control such as family violence.

Closely related are recent advances in the treatment of the personality disorders. This represents an area of major activity over the last decade, one that has led to particular growth and maturation in the underlying approach. Many of these patients first presented for treatment of axis I symptoms and simply failed to get better as rapidly as patients without underlying axis II disorders. In learning to cope with such patients, strides were made to articulate more fully the relation of core beliefs and conditional assumptions to specific automatic thoughts and to develop strategies to address more effectively those underlying beliefs. In particular, attention was given to the role of compensatory strategies, repetitive patterns of behavior that serve to protect patients from the consequences of their perceived deficits (core beliefs) but at the expense of undermining the quality of their interpersonal relationships. In essence, a conceptual framework was developed that related the maladaptive behavior patterns found in the personality disorders to underlying beliefs and attitudes so that each could be examined and tested via a combination of rational and empirical means.

Finally, great strides have been made in recent years to extend cognitive therapy to the treatment of severe psychiatric disorders, including schizophrenia and bipolar affective disorder. Although not a substitute for appropriate pharmacological management, cognitive interventions do appear to reduce belief in delusions and lower the probability of acting out in an impulsive fashion. The key is to not confront the patient directly with respect to specific delusions, but rather to view the ideation as an effort to make sense out of troublesome or puzzling experiences. The patient is encouraged to review the nature of those experiences and is invited to consider alternative explanations for their occurrences. Evidence is then examined regarding the accuracy of both the original delusion and the alternative formulation.

Conclusions

Cognitive therapy appears to be applicable to the treatment of a variety of disorders. It is among the most efficacious interventions for such disorders as depression, panic, and bulimia, and appears to have an enduring effect not found with medications. It is also effective in the treatment of a number of related anxiety and somatic disorders and shows considerable promise in the treatment of substance abuse and the personality disorders, which are often difficult to treat. Finally, recent studies suggest that it might even have a role to play in the treatment of anorexia nervosa and the psychoses, disorders that traditionally have not been considered amenable to this approach. Clearly, cognitive therapy is based on a flexible model that lends itself to the articulation of strategies and techniques that can be shaped to the needs of a broad array of different disorders.

[See also Cognitive-Behavioral Therapy.]

Bibliography

Beck, A. T. (1976). Cognitive therapy and the emotional disorders. New York: International Universities Press. A comprehensive introduction to the role of beliefs and information processing in a variety of disorders and an early articulation of the basic principles of cognitive therapy as applied to those disorders.

Beck, A. T. (1988). Love is never enough. New York: Harper & Row. A description of cognitive theory and therapy as it applies to problems in relationships and written for both lay and professional audiences.

Beck, A. T. (1991). Cognitive therapy: A 30-year retrospective. American Psychologist, 46(4), 368–375. An overview of the history and development of both cognitive theory and cognitive therapy over its formative years.

Beck, A. T., & Emery, G. (1985). Anxiety disorders and phobias: A cognitive perspective. New York: Basic Books. An application of cognitive theory and therapy to the etiology and treatment of anxiety disorders.

Beck, A. T., Freeman, A., & Associates. (1990). Cognitive therapy of personality disorders. New York: Guilford Press. This text extends the cognitive model to the treatment of personality disorders, emphasizing the role of core beliefs, conditional assumptions, and compensatory strategies.

Beck, A. T., Rush, A. J., Shaw, B. F., & Emery, G. (1979). Cognitive therapy of depression. New York: Guilford Press. The original treatment manual describing cognitive therapy for depression; it remains a classic in the field.

Beck, J. (1995). *Cognitive therapy: Basics and beyond*. New York: Guilford Press. An excellent overview and update of the basic approach that serves as the primary source for recent advances in cognitive therapy.

Burns, D. D. (1980). *Feeling good: The new mood therapy*. New York: Morrow. The first and one of the best of the many self-help manuals based on cognitive therapy and written for a lay audience.

Hollon, S. D., & Beck, A. T. (1994). Cognitive and cognitive-behavioral therapies. In A. E. Bergin & S. L. Garfield (Eds.), *Handbook of psychotherapy and behavior change* (4th ed., pp. 428–466). New York: Wiley. A recent review of the efficacy of cognitive and cognitive-behavioral interventions for a variety of psychological disorders.

Kingdon, D. G., & Turkington, D. (1994). *Cognitive-behavioral therapy of schizophrenia*. New York: Guilford Press. An interesting description of the application of cognitive therapy to the treatment of schizophrenic patients.

Steven D. Hollon and Aaron T. Beck

COGNITIVE UNDERSTANDING LEVELS. Many physical, chemical, biological, and social science concepts, such as heat, electrical current, diffusion, natural selection, and supply and demand have been incredibly hard for students to understand. Many reasons have been offered for their difficulties; these reasons fall into the following four major types. One proposed explanation is that concepts of this kind are complicated, involving many subcomponents, including subconcepts and mathematics. Such a complicated view would propose that if instruction removed the mathematics and focused on clarifying the subconcepts, then learning and understanding would be facilitated. A second explanation is that many of these concepts are abstract often not visible to perception. A remedy then would be to design instruction that could reveal the nonperceptible parts of the concept, or make these concepts more concrete by providing hands-on experiences, or situating the concept in an everyday context. A third explanation is that these concepts tend to be dynamic, whereas our ways of describing and symbolizing phenomena in the world tend to employ static representations. Instructional interventions might facilitate understanding by using dynamic computerized displays. A fourth explanation is that students have naive intuitive understanding that is incorrect, and such naive incorrect understanding hinders their learning of the correct understanding. Such an intuitive knowledge view would propose that instruction should build upon students' existing intuitive understanding, in order to scaffold the students gradually from the naive understanding to the correct understanding. However, all of these instructional tactics, as a whole, have not led to correct and deeper understanding of these complicated, abstract, and dynamic (CAD) concepts, thus calling into question the viability of these four explanations. These kinds of CAD concepts are particularly difficult to learn, because there is an incommensurability between the categorical structure or schema to which students attempt to assimilate these concepts and the veridical categorical structure or schema to which they ought to assimilate them. The role of incommensurability in the development of scientific understanding can be illustrated with an analysis of the concept of diffusion.

The CAD concepts cited above are not concepts of concrete objects, nor of causal events, but rather, they are concepts of processes of a specific kind. They are all a kind of process for which the observable perceptual global phenomenon emerges from an intrinsically distinct underlying local interacting processes. Take the simplest example of the process of diffusion, say between a red-colored liquid and a blue-colored liquid, initially separated in a flask by a barrier. When the barrier between them is removed, the process of diffusion begins. What one sees is that the red liquid seems to be moving toward the blue liquid and the blue liquid seems to be moving toward the red liquid. When the liquid ends up looking uniformly purple, then the movement seems to stop. Thus, what the students see is the flow of red liquid to the blue liquid area, and vice versa. Moreover, the entire flow seems to stop when equilibrium is reached.

This perception is consistent with the students' interpretation of a text. One high school text explains diffusion (of gases and nutrients in the human circulatory system) in the following way:

> Diffusion of gases and nutrients take place across the thin capillary walls from areas of greater concentration to areas of lesser concentration.

Thus, students do think of diffusion as a process (so they do not have difficulty understanding dynamic concepts per se), whereby molecules move from an area of greater concentration to an area of lesser concentration, until the concentration of the two areas are equal. Moreover, they are perfectly capable of understanding and imagining the molecules underlying the liquid, so it's not as if they have trouble imagining the abstract concept in terms of concrete molecular components. Finally, the complicated view would say that students may not understand diffusion because they do not understand the subconcepts of concentration and equilibrium. However, students often do understand these subconcepts. For example, when asked, "What does concentration mean?" one student from our study (Chi, de Leeuw, Chiu, & LaVancher, 1994) can correctly reply:

One side is more dense and the other side is less dense. It's trying to get from more dense to less dense. The molecules are farther apart on the lesser side and closer together on the greater side, and there are more of them.

Students can also correctly define equilibrium as when the number of molecules are equal on each side. Thus, students' understanding of the component subconcepts do not appear to be the source of difficulty for their failure to understand the target concept (e.g., diffusion) deeply.

In sum, students are failing to understand these CAD concepts not because they are complicated, abstract, and dynamic. The only remaining explanation left is that students have naive intuitive knowledge that is incorrect and hinders understanding. The question is, Why does this intuitive knowledge prevent deep correct understanding of these CAD concepts? The problem with their "intuitive" conception is that they attribute the following properties to the process of diffusion:

They attribute causality to why the molecules move in the direction they do (usually the cause is limited space or crowding). They attribute intentionality to the process (such as "it's trying to get from more dense to less dense"), as if there is an agent directing the molecules to move in a certain direction, or the idea that there is a goal to be reached (the equilibrium state is often thought of as the goal). And they attribute sequentiality and/or chronology to the process (from areas of high concentration to areas of low concentration). They attribute *distinct actions* to the blue and red liquid (or molecules making up the liquid), as if the blue molecules move in one direction and the red molecules move in another direction. They also believe that the process is *bounded*, so that there is a beginning, defined as the onset, the point at which the barrier in the flask is removed, and an end, the point at which the liquid turns into a uniform bluish purple color; and finally, related to the notion of boundedness is the idea of *termination* of the process of diffusion when no perceptible motion of the blue and red liquid is detected.

From students' naive explanations (see Ferrari & Chi, 1998, for another CAD concept, natural selection), we can see a pattern of attributions that can be succinctly summarized as consisting of the following set of related attributes: distinct actions; sequential/chronological; bounded/terminates; and contingent/causal/intentional/goal-directed (Chi, 1992, 1997; Slotta, Chi & Joram, 1995; Ferrari & Chi, 1998; Slotta & Chi, 1996).

Such a pattern of attribution fits the attributes of a causal schema. For instance, a causal event (such as a baseball game) has the properties of having a beginning and an end, it has distinct actions (some players hit the balls, some catch the balls), its subcomponents

occur sequentially or chronologically in a contingent and causal way (a player must get to the first base before s/he may try for the second base), each event has an external and explicit goal (trying to get as many runs as possible), and the event terminates when there is no more visible movement (no one else is coming to bat nor running). In contrast, the schema that describes the CAD concepts has an alternative contrastive set of attributes. A process such as diffusion has no beginning and end, instead it is *ongoing*. Diffusion is the net effect of multiple *independent, simultaneous, uniform,* and *local* actions (such as the random movement of molecules). The actions are *not goal directed.* This means a red liquid molecule, over time, from random movement, may migrate into the blue liquid location; likewise, blue molecules may migrate into the red liquid location, after the barrier is removed. Over time, the net effect is that there are just as many red molecules in the blue liquid location as there are blue molecules in the red liquid location. Hence, there is no intentionality or causality, nor is the movement of any molecule contingent upon the movement of any other molecules. Instead, all actions are independent (rather than contingent); simultaneous (rather than sequential or chronological); and uniform (rather than distinct), in that they all have the same action, which is to move about randomly. Moreover, the molecules continue to move even though equilibrium (the obvious stopping of motion of flow) has been reached.

Although researchers often attribute the concept of random movement as a source of difficulty deterring students' understanding of the concept of diffusion, the claim here is that random movement per se is not an attribute of this kind of process, and therefore is also not a source of students' difficulty in understanding diffusion. Random movement happens to be an attribute of molecular motion, which is the particular action of this concept of diffusion. For an alternative concept such as natural selection (of the English peppered moth), the individual action is the eating of a moth by a bird, and not random motion. What is important and difficult to understand is the attribute of multiple, independent, *simultaneous,* and uniform local interactions, the totality of which manifests itself in a global phenomenon.

Hence, diffusion is a process that has a set of attributes (noncontingent/acausal; unbounded and ongoing; simultaneous, independent, and uniform actions resulting in a net effect) that is ontologically different from the attributes of a causal event (Chi, 1997). The fact that diffusion is really a global process resulting from multiple local interactions, and yet students misconceive of it as an event-like causal process, means that students' naive understanding is embedded in a schema that is incommensurate (or ontologically distinct) with the concept's veridical schema (we have called it various names in the past, but let's refer to it here as the emergent schema). When this occurs, that is, when the students misattribute properties of one schema (the causal schema) to concepts from another ontologically distinct schema (the emergent schema), then students will never understand the concepts deeply. This is because attributes from two incommensurate schemas cannot modify each other's concepts in a meaningful way.

The example above shows incommensurability between a causal schema and an emergent schema. Incommensurability can occur between various other schemas: substance versus processes (Chi, Slotta, & de Leeuw, 1994), static versus dynamic, artifacts versus natural kind (Gelman, 1988), and animate versus inanimate.

Students' naive attributions of characteristics of diffusion, as stated above, are neither haphazard, random, inconsistent, simplistic, peculiar, nor piecemeal. (In fact, these attributions are shared by the majority of the students that we have examined, so that they may be universal.) Rather, these characteristics fit the attributes of a causal, event-like schema. What makes students appear to be inconsistent, either within an individual or among individuals, is that they draw upon any one of the attributes from either the substance or the event schema to generate an explanation, so that they appear to have knowledge in pieces that are inconsistent and contradictory (diSessa, 1993). But in fact, they are extremely coherent and consistent, when one views their responses from the standpoint of a specific schema.

A similar framework has been proposed by Gelman (in press). Gelman distinguishes between core domains and noncore domains. A core domain is an innate skeletal structure that predisposes children to perceive the world in terms of its skeletal features. The existence of innate core domains can be seen by the way very young infants are sensitive to certain environmental inputs and not others. For example, one-month-old infants can discriminate and categorize speech sounds (Juscyck, 1996), and five-month-old infants believe that one solid object cannot pass through another solid object (Baillargeon, Spelke, & Wasserman, 1985). These kinds of evidence suggest that there already exist mental structures that predispose infants to be sensitive to environmental inputs that are relevant to these structures. In our framework, we might say that the nature of students' naive conceptions, in mistakenly conceiving of CAD concepts as either causal events or concrete substances, arise from the erroneous assimilation of these processes into existing core domains. In order to learn a non-core domain, such as a CAD concept, specific formal instruction may be required. However, since the skeletal structure of a non-core domain is not in-

nately available, one can only expect correct understanding and deep learning if the domain-relevant content knowledge (such as diffusion or natural selection) is taught after the domain-relevant skeletal structure (the emergent schema) is already in place, so that the learners can assimilate inputs into existing skeletal structures. We have proceeded in exactly this vein, and achieved surprising deep understanding, in the context of learning about the CAD concept of electrical current (Slotta & Chi, 1996).

To summarize, CAD concepts are hard to learn not because they are complicated, abstract and dynamic per se, nor because students have naive intuitive notions that are incorrect. Rather, CAD concepts are hard to learn because the students' naive intuitive notions are not merely incorrect, but more important, they are incorrect in that they are subsumed within a schema that is incommensurate with the schema to which they should be correctly subsumed. Thus, instructional intervention should focus on creating and activating the appropriate emergent schema to embed understanding of CAD concepts, rather than building from their existing naive conceptions that have been embedded in an incommensurate schema.

Bibliography

Baillargeon, R., Spelke, E. S., & Wasserman, S. (1985). Object permanence in five-month-old infants. *Cognition, 20*, 191–208.

Chi, M. T. H. (1992). Conceptual change within and across ontological categories: Examples from learning and discovery in science. In R. Giere (Ed.), *Cognitive models of science: Minnesota Studies in the Philosophy of Science* (pp. 129–186). Minneapolis: University of Minnesota Press.

Chi, M. T. H. (1997). Creativity: Shifting across ontological categories flexibly. In T. B. Ward, S. M. Smith, R. A. Finke & J. Vaid (Eds.), *Creative thought: An investigation of conceptual structures and processes* (pp. 209–234). Washington, DC: American Psychological Association.

Chi, M. T. H., de Leeuw, N., Chiu, M. H., & LaVancher, C. (1994). Eliciting self-explanations improves understanding. *Cognitive Science, 18*, 439–477.

Chi, M. T. H., Slotta, J. D., & de Leeuw, N. (1994). From things to processes: A theory of conceptual change for learning science concepts. *Learning and Instruction, 4*, 27–43.

diSessa, A. (1993). Toward an epistemology of physics. *Cognition and Instruction, 10*, 105–225.

Ferrari, M., & Chi, M. T. H. (1998). The nature of naive explanations of natural selection. *International Journal of Science Education, 20*, 1231–1256.

Gelman, R. (in press). Domain specificity in cognitive development: Universals and non-universals. *International Journal of Psychology*.

Gelman, S. (1988). The development of induction within

natural kind and artifact categories. *Cognitive Psychology, 20,* 65–90.

Juscyck, P. (1996). *The discovery of spoken language.* Cambridge, MA: MIT/Bradford Books.

Slotta, J. D., & Chi, M. T. H. (1996). Understanding constraint-based processes: A precursor to conceptual change in physics. In G. W. Cottrell (Ed.), *Proceedings of the eighteenth annual conference of the Cognitive Science Society* (pp. 306–311). Mahwah, NJ: Erlbaum.

Slotta, J. D., Chi, M. T. H., & Joram, E. (1995). Assessing students' misclassification of physics concepts: An ontological basis for conceptual change. *Cognition and Instruction, 13,* 373–400.

Michelene T. H. Chi

COHORT EFFECTS. A *cohort* refers to a group of people who have experienced a significant life event (birth, marriage, etc.) at the same period of time. Usually a cohort is defined as a birth cohort, or generation. The essential purpose of cohort analysis is to describe the nature of the changes and the differences over time in the social and behavioral characteristics under study in terms of three key variables: age (getting older), period (changing historical circumstances), and cohort (successive generations). Point of departure of the analysis is the cohort table in which the information about the pertinent dependent characteristic (e.g., intelligence quotient, or IQ) is rendered in a particular way for several cohorts, several age categories, and several periods of observation. A cohort table may take the form of an A(ge) × P(eriod) table (see Table 1), an A(ge) × C(ohort) table, or a C(ohort) × P(eriod) table, resulting from what the developmental psychologist K. Warner Schaie called a time-sequential design, a cohort-sequential design, and a cross-sequential design, respectively. What makes Table 1 into a cohort table is that because of the correspondence between the spacing of the moments of observation (here: five-year intervals) and the length of the age intervals (here: five years), all observations within a particular cell can be uniquely and completely assigned to one particular cohort.

If the cells in Table 1 had contained observations of IQ, comparisons of the rows would have provided information on age differences with regard to IQ, column-wise comparisons on period differences, and comparisons of the diagonals on cohort differences. However, these differences would not have reflected the relevant age, period, and cohort effects. As can be clearly seen, the age differences within a particular column result from both age and cohort effects. In a similar way, the period differences reflect both period and cohort effects. When a particular cohort is followed over time, age and period effects are confounded, or mixed together. [*See*

COHORT EFFECTS. Table 1. Cohort Table; Time-sequential Design; A × P table

Age	Period of Observation		
	1990	1995	2000
15–20	C4	C5	C6
20–25	C3	C4	C5
25–30	C2	C3	C4
30–35	C1	C2	C3

Randomized Experiments.] It turns out to be impossible to disentangle the effects of age, cohort, and period (called the identification problem) without making additional assumptions, discussed by John R. Nesselroade, Jacques A. Hagenaars, and many others.

These assumptions may be found by recognizing that age, period, and cohort are often used as surrogates for other theoretical variables. For example, *age* is a variable that is of central interest to developmental psychologists and refers to the way people mature and to all relevant biological, psychological, and social phenomena that go together with it. *Period* refers to everything that is happening in society during the period of observation; it may also refer to such trivial circumstances as different testing procedures at the different moments of observation. *Cohort* is a surrogate variable for generational characteristics such as cohort size, educational practices, or nutritional habits; it also refers to age-period interactions in the sense that certain events happen at a certain age and may have a lasting impact on a particular cohort.

Given the complex and somewhat loose meanings of the three operational key concepts, cohort analysis will mainly serve exploratory purposes. The least it will then accomplish is to describe how the developmental curve regarding some dependent characteristic (e.g., IQ) based on cross-sectional age differences at one point in time differs from the curve obtained when following a particular cohort over time and differs for several cohorts. In this way a cohort analysis can often give the researcher a much better insight into what exactly has to be explained than other, less complicated designs and may prevent the researcher from drawing naive or even misleading conclusions about processes of individual change.

[*See also* Longitudinal Research.]

Bibliography

Glenn, N. D. (1977). *Cohort analysis.* Beverly Hills: Sage. Short monograph, providing an excellent introduction to cohort analysis not requiring statistical knowledge above the very basic level.

Hagenaars, J. A. (1990). *Categorical longitudinal data: Log-linear panel, trend, and cohort analysis.* Newbury Park: Sage. Provides a thorough treatment of the several proposals that have been made to solve the identification problem, along with an extended empirical example, using log-linear models.

Mason, W. A., & Fienberg, S. E. (Eds.). (1985). *Cohort analysis in social research: Beyond the identification problem.* New York: Springer. A thorough and extensive treatment of cohort analysis, dealing with the many methodological issues surrounding cohort analysis and providing many interesting applications, however, at a rather sophisticated statistical level.

Nesselroade, J. R., & Von Eye, A. (Eds.). (1985). *Individual development and social change: Explanatory analysis.* Orlando: Academic Press. Covers a wide range of topics on "human development" and contains treatments of cohort analyses from a methodological as well as a substantive point of view; the chapters not dealing directly with cohort analyses are worthwhile because they provide the necessary framework for a correct administration and interpretation of cohort analyses.

Schaie, K. W. (1970). A reinterpretation of age related changes in cognitive structure and functioning. In L. R. Goulet & P. Baltes (Eds.), *Life-span developmental psychology: research and theory* (pp. 486–507). New York: Academic Press. One of the most influential writers on cohort analysis in developmental psychology describes here his "sequential designs." Although they could not—as he once mistakenly thought and here argues—directly solve the identification problem, his expositions of cohort analysis, as well as his applications to intelligence research are exemplary.

Jacques A. Hagenaars

COLLECTIVISM AND INDIVIDUALISM. Cultural syndromes (Triandis, 1996) are patterns of shared meaning found among those who speak a particular language dialect, and live in a specific geographic region during a particular time period. Cultural syndromes can be identified by discovering shared attitudes, beliefs, self-definitions, role definitions, norms and values, that are organized around a theme.

Collectivism is a cultural syndrome organized around the importance of collectives (family, coworkers, tribe, religious group, political group, philosophic viewpoint, nationality, social class, race). Individualism is a cultural syndrome organized around the importance of individuals in social life.

History

The cultural patterns of collectivism and individualism have been discussed in the social sciences for several hundred years, but they became the focus of intensive research after Hofstede's (1980) book was published. Macfarlane (1978) reported that individualism developed in England after the twelfth century. German sociologists contrasted *Gemeinschaft* (community) and *Gesellschaft* (society) early in this century. Kagitcibasi (1997) has provided an excellent review of the literature concerning these constructs.

Defining Attributes

The two syndromes can be contrasted by considering four defining attributes:

1. The definition of the self. The self is defined as interdependent or independent (e.g., Markus & Kitayama, 1991).
2. The structure of goals. The priority of in-group or personal goals would be examples (e.g., Triandis, 1990; Yamaguchi, 1994).
3. The importance of in-group norms. Social behavior is determined by in-group norms. In collectivism norms and attitudes are equally important determinants of social behavior, while in individualism attitudes are extremely important and norms are of minor importance as determinants of social behavior (e.g., Bontempo & Rivero, 1992).
4. Emphasis on relatedness versus rationality. In collectivism, valuing in-group relationships has priority over computations of the rewards and costs of social relationships (Kim, 1994). In individualism one computes the costs relative to the benefits of a relationship, and if the costs are too high one drops the relationship, even when it is important to members of the in-group (e.g., marriage). A parallel distinction was made by Mills and Clark (1982) who discussed communal and exchange relationships.

Other Attributes

Each culture has its own kind of collectivism or individualism. For example, Korean collectivism has much in common with Japanese collectivism but also has purely Korean attributes. Swedish individualism has some elements in common with American individualism but also has unique Swedish attributes.

Some attributes are emphasized in one culture more than they are stressed in other cultures, so that unique configurations of collectivism and individualism emerge. One of the more important distinctions between types of collectivism and individualism is their horizontal or vertical aspects (Triandis, 1995).

Horizontal individualists emphasize equality and their uniqueness and independence from groups. Vertical individualists emphasize that they are "the best" and value competitions that will demonstrate their high status. Horizontal collectivists emphasize their interdependence with others who are equal to them. Vertical collectivists accept the hierarchy that may exist in their in-group, and they are willing to sacrifice themselves so that their in-group may reach its goals.

Collectivists often attribute their success to the help they have received from others and their failure to their own lack of sufficient effort. Individualists often attribute their success to their own abilities and their failure to the difficulty of the task or to their bad luck.

Collectivists remember a lot more about others than about themselves, while the opposite is true of individualists. Collectivists think of achievement primarily as group achievement, and they emphasize cooperation, endurance, order, and self-control. Individualists think of personal achievement, and they emphasize self-glory, competition, exhibition, and power.

Collectivists experience little cognitive dissonance when their behavior is inconsistent with their attitudes, because they consider it appropriate that behavior should be consistent with norms and that attitudes are of no importance. Individualists experience considerable dissonance when their behavior does not match their attitudes.

The emotions of collectivists tend to be other-focused (e.g., sympathy), while those of individualists tend to be self-focused (e.g., anger). Modesty is valued by collectivists while self-enhancement and optimism are important characteristics of individualists.

It is possible to make a person temporarily collectivist by asking the person to think for two minutes what he or she has in common with family and friends. Conversely, by priming what makes the person different from family and friends one can increase individualism (Trafimow, Triandis, & Goto, 1991).

Individualists tend to attribute social behavior to internal factors much more than to external factors, while collectivists use both internal and external factors in making their attributions.

Collectivist cognitions are context dependent, and collectivist communication tends to depend on context and to be indirect. Individualist cognitions are context-independent, and the emphasis is on the exact meaning of words presented directly. Collectivists use more "we," "perhaps," and "maybe" in their conversations, and use many action verbs, while individualists use "I" very frequently, tend to exaggerate (this is "the best," "the greatest"), and use adjectives more frequently in their communication (Zwier, 1997).

The values of collectivists stress cooperation, security, obedience, duty, in-group harmony, hierarchy, and intimacy. The values of individualists emphasize pleasure, achievement, competition, freedom, autonomy, and fairness. The greatest calamity for collectivists is ostracism; for individualists it is dependence.

In-groups are perceived as homogeneous by collectivists and as heterogeneous by individualists. They are defined by collectivists most frequently on the basis of similarity of ascribed attributes such as kinship, caste, race, village, and nationality. Individualists define them occasionally in that way also, but most frequently on the basis of occupation, beliefs, preferences, and values.

Social behavior is very different when the other person is an out-group as opposed to an in-group member in the case of collectivists, and not so different in the case of individualists. Among collectivists, reciprocity of social behavior tends to be long term and does not require that it involve the same resource (e.g., if I give you status, you might give me a letter of recommendation). Among individualists reciprocity is short term and tends to require the use of the same resource (e.g., I invited you, you invite me very soon after).

When distributing resources to in-group members, collectivists tend to use equality or need as the bases for the distribution; individualists tend to use equity (to each according to contribution). However, collectivists use equity when distributing resources to out-groups.

Collectivists have few skills for entering new groups. It is difficult to become friends with a member of a collectivist culture if one is an outsider, but if one succeeds in becoming a friend, the friendship is likely to become intimate, and loyalty is greatly valued. Individualists usually have skills for entering new groups. It is easy to establish superficial relationships with members of individualist cultures, but these relationships are rarely intimate or long lasting.

Collectivists are likely to lie when that saves the face of the other person or promotes the goals of their in-group. Individualists value authenticity (Trilling, 1972), and feel embarrassed about lying. Collectivists are concerned about saving both their own face and the face of the other person. Individualists are not especially concerned with saving the face of the other person.

Collectivists often engage in activities that reflect togetherness, such as co-dating or skiing in groups, while individualists often engage in solitary activities that emphasize privacy.

Collectivists choose spouses that will be loyal family members and often require that their spouse be a virgin. Individualists emphasize sexual and physical attraction and an exciting personality, while they do not consider virginity an important factor in mate selection.

Measurement

Triandis (1995, appendix) listed more than 20 ways in which the constructs can be measured. The most common ways to measure them have been attitude items with Likert-type answer formats or scenarios followed by several options in multiple-choice format.

It is important to distinguish measurements at the cultural level from measurements at the individual level. For example, if 200 members in each of 10 cultures have responded to 30 attitude items, one can do a factor analysis of the 30 by 30 matrix based on 2,000 observations per variable. That is known as a pancultural factor analysis. It will often give different results from an analysis that begins with the sums of the responses of the 200 people in each culture. Here the 30 by 30 matrix would be based on 10 (the number of cultures) observations per variable. This is an analysis at the cultural level. Alternatively, one can analyze the data culture by culture, for example do a factor analysis of the 30 by 30 matrix based on 200 observations. This would be an individual level analysis. Triandis et al. (1993) presented an analysis of individualism and collectivism that explicitly examined the results when different levels of analyses were used. One can detect both strong and weak culturally universal themes, as well as themes that occur in one culture but not in others (e.g., Indonesian women expressed anxiety when they were far from their in-groups, but this factor was not observed in other cultures).

Antecedents

Collectivism is usually found in homogeneous societies that are relatively isolated from other cultures, where interdependence is functional, and where population density requires the development of many rules and norms for social behavior. Individualism on the other hand, is most often found in societies that are heterogeneous, that are at the intersection of major cultures, where people can do their own thing without offending others, and where low population density or an urban setting allows people to ignore some norms of social behavior.

Collectivism is more common in societies that are economically undeveloped, where survival requires the help of the group, that are traditional, and where religion is emphasized. The lower social classes in most societies are high in collectivism. Individualism is more common in segments of the population in which people are affluent, socially mobile, and under the influence of U.S.-made television programs. Upper social class is correlated with individualism in all societies.

Consequences

Collectivist child rearing emphasizes duty, obedience, and conformity; individualist child rearing emphasizes exploration, creativity, and achievement.

Personality and Situational Factors

All humans are assumed to have both collectivist and individualist predispositions. Corresponding to collectivism is a personality type called allocentrism; corresponding to individualism is a personality type called idiocentrism (Triandis, Leung, Villareal, & Clark, 1985). [See Allocentrism-Idiocentrism.] These predispositions are activated by different situations. For example, when the in-group is threatened, all humans become collectivists; when people interact with collectivists and wish to have a good relationship with them they are more likely to activate collectivist cognitions. When people interact with individualists and wish to have a good relationship with them, they are likely to activate individualist cognitions. Cooperative situations activate collectivism, and competitive situations often activate individualism.

Allocentrics tend to define most situations the way collectivists define situations, and idiocentrics tend to define most situations the way individualists define situations.

Applications of the Constructs

Individuals who travel from an individualist culture to a collectivist culture need to be trained to understand the point of view of the collectivist culture. For example, they should be trained not to boast and to present themselves modestly. They should not consider having fun a very important goal. They should expect that collectivists will have more difficulty than individualists in making decisions, and they will try to make decisions after extensive consultation with their in-groups. They should expect people to behave not according to what they like to do, but rather according to what is their duty. They should learn that they are expected to establish intimate and long-lasting relationships. They must be more patient, take more time to build relationships, and not get on the task as early as is typical in their own culture.

Conversely, people from collectivist cultures who visit individualist cultures should learn to excuse individualists when they appear arrogant, with very high self-esteem and optimism. They should learn to tolerate exaggerations in statements (e.g., "that is terrific"). They should expect that individualists will stress having fun. Happiness is very important for them. They can expect individualists to decide quickly and with minimal consultation with others. They can expect individualists to place great value on consistency, and they must be careful that they will not be perceived as hypocrites when they act inconsistently with their own attitudes. They must be careful not to lie because no matter how good their intentions, and how beneficial this behavior may be for their in-group, they will not be excused by individualists who detect the lie. They should learn that individualists do not make a very sharp distinction between private and public behavior, which is very common among collectivists. They can expect individualists to do what is fun rather than what is conventionally important. They must learn that individualists will communicate directly and will not depend much on the context of communication. They should change the way they communicate; otherwise they will be perceived as indecisive, unable to make up their mind. They need to learn to boast a bit about their accomplishments. They should expect relationships to be relatively superficial and to last a short time.

Bibliography

Bontempo, R. & Rivero, J. C. (1992, August). *Cultural variation in cognition: The role of self-concept in the attitude-behavior link.* Paper presented at the meeting of the American Academy of Management in Las Vegas, Nevada.

Hofstede, G. (1980). *Culture's consequences.* Beverly Hills, CA: Sage.

Kagitcibasi, C. (1997). Individualism and collectivism. In J. W. Berry, M. H. Segall, & C. Kagitcibasi (Eds.), *Handbook of cross-cultural psychology* (2nd ed., Vol. 3, pp. 1–50) Boston: Allyn & Bacon.

Kim, U. (1994). Individualism and collectivism: Conceptual clarification and elaboration. In U. Kim, H. C. Triandis, C. Kagitcibasi, S-C. Choi, & G. Yoon (1994). *Individualism and collectivism: Theory, method, and applications* (pp. 19–40). Thousand Oaks, CA: Sage.

Macfarlane, A. (1978). *Origins of English individualism: The family, property, and social transition.* New York: Cambridge University Press.

Markus, H. & Kitayama, S. (1991). Culture and self: Implications for cognition, emotion, and motivation. *Psychological Review, 98,* 224–253.

Mills, J., & Clark, M. S. (1982). Exchange and communal relationships. In L. Wheeler (Ed.), *Review of personality and social psychology* (Vol. 3, pp. 121–144). Beverly Hills, CA: Sage.

Trafimow, D., Triandis, H. C., & Goto, S. (1991). Some tests of the distinction between the private and collective self. *Journal of Personality and Social Psychology, 60,* 649–655.

Triandis, H. C. (1990). Cross-cultural studies of individualism and collectivism. In J. Berman (Ed.), *Nebraska Symposium on Motivation, 1989,* (pp. 41–133). Lincoln: University of Nebraska Press.

Triandis, H. C. (1995). *Individualism and collectivism.* Boulder, CO: Westview Press.

Triandis, H. C. (1996). The psychological measurement of cultural syndromes. *American Psychologist, 51,* 407–415.

Triandis, H. C., Leung, K., Villareal, M., & Clack, F. L. (1985). Allocentric vs. idiocentric tendencies: Convergent and discriminant validation. *Journal of Research in Personality, 19,* 395–415.

Triandis, H. C., McCusker, C., Betancourt, H., Iwao, S., Leung, K., Salazar, J. M., Setiadi, B., Sinha, J. B. P., Touzard, H., Wang, D., & Zaleski, Z. (1993). An etic-emic analysis of individualism and collectivism. *Journal of Cross-Cultural Psychology, 24,* 366–383.

Trilling, L. (1972). *Sincerity and authenticity.* London: Oxford University Press.

Yamaguchi, S. (1994). Empirical evidence on collectivism among the Japanese. In U. Kim, H. C. Triandis, C. Kagitcibasi, S-C. Choi, & G. Yoon (1994). *Individualism and collectivism: Theory, method, and applications* (pp. 175–188). Thousand Oaks, CA: Sage.

Zwier, S. (1997). *Patterns of language use in individualistic and collectivistic cultures.* Unpublished doctoral dissertation, Free University of Amsterdam, Netherlands.

Harry C. Triandis

COLLEGE TEACHING AND LEARNING. The psychological study of teaching and learning in college includes many topics that have been investigated with a range of methodologies.

Students

The characteristics of college students that affect learning and teaching have been the focus of extensive investigation. Although theory and research in psychology and education are moving toward more contextual models and away from perspectives that focus primarily on the individual, several more traditional psychological perspectives have proved useful in understanding college students' cognitive and social development. Perhaps the most influential and frequently applied are the stage theories of Swiss psychologist Jean Piaget (cognitive development), American psychologist William Perry (epistemological development), and German American psychoanalyst Eric Erikson (psychosocial development).

Like many theories of cognitive and psychological development, Piaget's theory suggests that individuals move from ways of thinking and solving problems that are simple, concrete, and tied to physical reality to ways that are complex, abstract, and based on mental manipulation of multiple possibilities. College students are assumed to be at Piaget's fourth and final stage, formal operations, and thus able to think abstractly about propositions and concepts, reason hypothetically about combinations of variables, and reflect on their own thinking and problem-solving processes (Piaget & Inhelder, 1973). Many courses in college require these cognitive capabilities. Some research has shown however, that about half of college freshman are not able to apply formal operations consistently (Pascarella & Terenzini, 1991). Students are more likely to use formal thinking in their major field of study (De Lisi & Staudt, 1980). Thus, the strong stage theories of Piaget are giving way to more contextual and domain-specific understandings of cognitive development. A number of these theories suggest that there are levels of development in thinking beyond formal operations, and that these stages are influenced by experience.

Perry (1970) identified nine positions (similar to stages) that characterize college-age students' beliefs about the nature of knowledge and the role of authorities in defining and conveying knowledge. These positions range from beliefs that all questions have one right or best answer that is known by authorities, to a sense that there are some unanswered questions in some areas, to a belief in relativism (many answers are equally valid, but also equally flawed), and finally to a conscious commitment to one idea or stance after a careful consideration of the alternatives. Formal operational thinking is assumed to play a role in reaching the final position of commitment. Beliefs about knowledge influence college students' expectations about the subjects they study and their professors' roles—moving from the expectation that professors will explain the facts of the field to a sense that learning involves a consideration of alternatives and evidence, with professors serving as more experienced seekers of understanding who can guide and support learning. Perry's work has been influential in the design of college courses, but his theories have been challenged. In the widely cited book, *Women's Ways of Knowing*, for example, Belenky and her colleagues (1986) suggest that women move through positions that have more to do with the source of knowledge, rather than its nature.

Erikson's (1980) theory of psychosocial development suggests that college students are in the stage of identity versus role diffusion. Identity refers to the organization of the individual's drives, abilities, beliefs, and history into a consistent image of self. It involves deliberate choices and decisions, particularly about vocation, sexual orientation, and a "philosophy of life" (Marcia, 1987). If adolescents fail to integrate all of these aspects and choices, or if they feel unable to choose at all, there is the possibility of role confusion. Elaborating on Erikson's work, Marcia and his colleagues have suggested that there are four alternatives for adolescents as they confront themselves and their choices: identity achievement, identity foreclosure (committing to the goals, values, and lifestyles of others, usually parents), identity diffusion (no firm direction), and moratorium (a very common, and probably healthy, delay in deciding).

Nature of Learning in College

Much of the research on learning in college has focused on students' knowledge and use of learning strategies, their metacognitive skills, and their ability to be self-regulated. Weinstein and Mayer (1986) identified three types of learning strategies among college students: (a) basic rehearsal (e.g., recopying notes, underlining in texts), (b) elaboration (building internal connections with images, summaries, analogies, etc.), and (c) organization (outlining, diagramming, networking, etc.). Meta-cognitive strategies include planning, monitoring, and self-regulation. The latter two are related; as students monitor their comprehension of a difficult text, for example, they may regulate their reading speed to improve comprehension.

There are many theories of self-regulated learning, but all assume that student achievement increases as students learn to regulate their cognition, motivation, and behavior. Courses and techniques designed to teach learning strategies, develop metacognitive awareness and skill, and enhance self-regulatory abilities have proved successful, but a number of unanswered questions remain. Should the teaching of these strategies be integrated into subject courses or taught as a separate course? Does the application of newly learned strategies and self-regulation transfer to other courses and tasks? Do student differences such as those described by Perry, Belenky, or Piaget interact with the learning or application of strategies?

College Teaching

The study of teaching at the college level reflects many of the issues and trends in the study of precollege teaching. Early research, from about the mid-1920s to the 1960s, focused on the effects of class size, teaching format (often lecture versus discussion), group-centered discussion (growing out of Kurt Lewin's group dynamics and Carl Rogers's nondirective counseling), and independent study or peer learning. In general, smaller class sizes were found to be associated with superior retention and problem solving and more positive attitudes toward the subject. Students in larger classes, however, tend to be taught through lectures and evaluated with objective methods such as multiple-choice; discussion and written work are limited, therefore effects of class size are confounded with effects of teaching and assessment methods. Effective lectures are characterized by clarity of presentation, organized structure, and lecturer expressiveness. Lecture methods tend to be associated with more learning for less well-prepared students and with greater recall of facts for all students, whereas discussion appears to be generally superior for higher-level outcomes such as problem solving (McKeachie, 1990). Evidence suggests that typical lectures are limited in their impact on the most important instructional objectives.

Research on student-centered discussions has advanced the study of college teaching by expanding outcome measures to include affective and social as well as cognitive indices, and by noting that students with different aptitudes respond differently to varying teaching methods. It is the work on independent study and peer learning, however, that bridges research on college teaching from the 1960s to the present. Early studies of independent and peer learning were encouraged by the need to absorb more students after World War II and by the popularity of the T-group movement in business. A number of structures, such as the learning cell, Keller Plan, and peer tutoring, were developed for students to work in pairs or small groups. Of these, the Keller Plan, which involved dividing material to be learned into units, demonstrating mastery of each unit before moving to the next, and having advanced students serve as proctors for learning groups as they progress through the units, proved most effective. With the exception of the Keller Plan, many of these individual and group structures are best utilized together with other approaches such as lecture rather than being the only format for teaching a class.

With the work on individual and group learning, researchers moved from looking only at outcomes to examining the processes through which outcomes are achieved (McKeachie, 1990). The outcomes achieved depend on what actually happens in the study groups and the cognitive engagement of the participants. For example, research on peer tutoring indicates that the deeper processing of material that is necessary to teach the material explains the common finding that the tutor learns more than the tutee (Webb & Palincsar, 1996).

Cooperative or small group learning is incorporated into many college courses today, for one or more assignments or as a structure for the entire class. Research on cooperative learning suggests that this process can be effective for both cognitive learning and for developing social skills and tolerance. However, the positive outcomes are not automatic (Webb & Palincsar, 1996). Group membership and tasks must be established such that all students are actively engaged in appropriate cognitive activities. Some level of conflict or controversy may also facilitate learning.

In addition to cooperative learning, college and university courses today may include case-based or problem-based learning, project methods, laboratory or field experiences, simulations, and other innovations. Many of the innovations are attempts to encourage active as opposed to passive learning. Chickering and Gamson (1991) developed "seven principles for good practice in undergraduate education" that emphasize active learning, which have been widely disseminated. Previous research on college teaching methods found that innovative approaches, for the most part, are slightly superior to conventional teaching, with the exception of the Keller Plan, which is markedly superior. This research also demonstrates, however, that different approaches are appropriate for different learning goals.

The most influential innovations of the present and future could be those involving electronic technologies. Although there are many claims that electronic technologies will radically change higher education, there is little systematic research on how these innovations affect teaching and learning. Existing research is consistent with studies of other innovations—achievement is at least as good using these approaches compared to conventional teaching and may be superior for some learning goals, particularly more complex, higher-order tasks (Emerson & Mosteller, 1998). Research is needed on the processes as well as the outcomes of electronically mediated teaching and learning, particularly on interactions between teacher(s) and student(s) and the changing roles of each.

[See also Learning; and Teachers.]

Bibliography

Belenky, M. F., Cinchy, B. M., Goldberger, N. R., & Tarule, J. M. (1986). *Women's ways of knowing: The development of self, voice, and mind.* New York: Basic Books.

Chickering, A. W., & Gamson, Z. F. (Eds.). (1991). Applying the seven principles for good practice in undergraduate education. *New Directions for Teaching and Learning*, No. 47.

De Lisi, R., & Staudt, J. (1980). Individual differences in college students' performance on formal operations tasks. *Journal of Applied Development Psychology, 1,* 201–208.

Emerson, J. D., & Mosteller, F. (1998). Interactive multimedia in college teaching. Part I: A ten year review of reviews. *Educational Media and Technology Yearbook, 23,* 43–58.

Erikson, E. H. (1980). *Identity and the life cycle* (2nd ed.). New York: Norton.

Marcia, J. (1987). Ego identity development. In J. Adelson (Ed.), *The handbook of adolescent psychology.* New York: Wiley.

McKeachie, W. J. (1990). Research on college teaching: The historical background. *Journal of Educational Psychology, 82,* 189–200.

Pascarella, E. T., & Terenzini, P. T. (1991). *How college affects students.* San Francisco: Jossey Bass.

Perry, W. G. (1970). *Forms of intellectual and ethical development in the college years: A scheme.* New York: Holt, Rinehart, & Winston.

Piaget, J., & Inhelder, B. (1973). *Memory and intelligence.* London: Routledge & Kegan Paul.

Sutherland, T. E., & Bonwell, C. C. (Eds.). (1996). Using active learning in college classes: A range of options for faculty. *New Directions for Teaching and Learning*, No. 67.

Webb, N. M., & Palincsar, A. S. (1996). Group processes in the classroom. In Berliner, D. & Calfee, R. (Eds.), *Handbook of educational psychology* (pp. 841–873). New York: Macmillan.

Weinstein, C. E., & Mayer, R. F. (1986). The teaching of learning strategies. In M. Wittrock (Ed.), *Third handbook of research on teaching* (pp. 315–326). New York: Macmillan.

Wigfield, A., Eccles, J. S., & Pintrich, P. R. (1996). Development between the ages of 11 and 25. In D. Berliner & R. Calfee (Eds.), *Handbook of educational psychology* (pp. 148–185). New York: Macmillan.

Anita Woolfolk Hoy

COLOMBIA. Colombia has one of the oldest training programs for psychologists in Latin America, founded in 1947 by the Spanish psychologist Mercedes Rodrigo (1891–1982) at the National University of Colombia. Furthermore, there is a long history of research into aspects of psychology that predates the first university departments or faculties of psychology. These research interests include the functioning of the brain, developmental retardation, hypnosis, old age, cognitive development, neuropsychology, psychological testing and assessment, and social psychology.

The development of psychology in Colombia as a profession (in the modern sense) has passed through three stages: between 1947 and 1960 there was an emphasis in psychometrics; between 1960 and 1970 the emphasis was on psychoanalysis; and from 1970, the emphasis has been on experimental psychology. The development of psychology as a profession in Colombia started with the creation of training programs at the National University of Colombia in 1947, and the Javeriana University in 1962. Other universities in cities such as Barranquilla. Medellín, Manizales, and Cali followed with their own programs. Now, in the late 1990s with universities developing their own curricula, there are 30 centers for training psychologists, most of them being university faculties of psychology located in most of the major cities. In 1999 there were about 20,000 students and 12,000 professional psychologists in Colombia.

There is a greater emphasis in applied and professional psychology than in research. Approximately 94% of Colombian psychologists consider themselves professionals, working in areas such as clinical (42%), educational (21%), industrial and organizational (18%), and applied social psychology (5%), and fewer in sport, gerontological, forensic, health, and clinical neurpsychology. The 6% involved in research are mainly focused in the areas of experimental analysis of behavior and social psychology. However, there has been important work done in other fields such as learning, biofeedback, clinical research, physiological psychology, measurement and psychometrics, personality, health psychology, cognitive development, community, and social psychology. There are ongoing research programs financed by Colciencias, a governmental institution that supports and funds scientific research, as well as in universities and various private foundations. As in many Latin American countries, there is a great interest in the relevance of psychology to solving the social problems associated with developing nations, such as violence, aggression, destruction of natural resources, inequalities of wealth distribution, etc.

The profession of psychology was granted legal status in 1983 (Ley 58/1983), and requires a training period of 5 years, similar to some European countries such as Germany and Spain. It is very different from the programs offered by universities in the United States, where there are different levels of academic and professional recognition, such as B.A., B.S., M.A., M.S., and Ph.D. or Psy.D. The profession of psychologist is highly regarded, and several psychologists have held important government posts, including minister of health, minister of education, and even minister of justice. Others have been senators, held high posts in universities and in other organizations, and have obtained international recognition for their scientific research.

There are various professional associations, the most important being the Colombian Society of Psychology that organizes the Colombian Congress of Psychology. It is part of the Colombian National Committee of Psychology that represents Colombia on the International Union of Psychological Science, as well as representing the interests of psychologists and the profession with the government and other official agencies. It publishes a *Bulletin* that contains news relating to the profession.

There are other specialized associations such as the Colombian Association of Clinical Psychologists and Psychotherapists, the Colombian Association of Health Psychology, and the Association of Sports Psychologists, as well as those for graduates of some universities (e.g., the Association of Javeriana Psychologists, the Association of Uniandes Psychologists, etc.).

Colombian psychologists have produced many books that have been published internationally in Spain, Mexico, Argentina, and other Latin American countries. The *Revista Latinoamericana de Psicología* [Latin American Journal of Psychology], founded in 1969, and *Avances en Psicología Clínica Latinoamericana* [Advances in Latin American Clinical Psychology], founded in 1982, are two journals that are widely distributed throughout the Spanish-speaking world.

Bibliography

Ardila, R. (Ed.). (1993). *Psicología en Colombia. Contexto social e histórico* [Psychology in Colombia. Social and historical context]. Bogotá: Tercer Mundo Editores.

Rubén Ardila

COLOR VISION is the aspect of visual sensation beyond perceived intensity (dim to bright). Hue and saturation describe this aspect of vision. The hues seen in a rainbow or in light refracted by a prism include red, yellow, green, and violet. Saturation is the perceived difference between a color and white. Pink, for example, is less saturated than red.

Color is not in light. Color vision is a mental phenomenon, not a physical one. The pattern of neural responses, not the wavelength of light that generates them, mediates color vision.

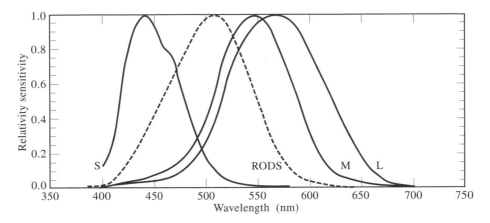

COLOR VISION. Figure 1. Spectral sensitivity functions of the S, M, and L cones (plotted from values in DeMarco, Pokorny, & Smith (1992) and the rods.

Light is defined as the part of the physical electromagnetic spectrum to which the eye is sensitive; this is the wavelength range between 375 and 750 nanometers (nm). Light results in the colors we see because it selectively and unequally stimulates the several distinct types of photoreceptors within the eye. When a single wavelength is viewed alone, the pattern of neural responses from these receptors results in the color percept of violet (wavelengths below 450 nm), blue (near 470 nm), blue-green (480–495 nm), green (near 500 nm), yellow-green (520–560 nm), yellow (near 580 nm), orange (600–630 nm), or red (above 640 nm). Despite common usage, it is incorrect to speak of blue light or yellow light because blue or yellow is in the mind rather than the light.

Any lights that generate the identical pattern of neural responses will result in the same color experience. For example, a 550 nm light appears a shade of green, while a 700 nm light appears red. Superimposed on one another, their mixture appears yellow and is indistinguishable from the color seen with only 580 nm light. No physical principle can explain why a mixture of 550 nm light and 700 nm light is visually identical to 580 nm. A physicist would say, correctly, that 580 nm is unrelated to a mixture of 550 and 700 nm. The mixture appears identical to 580 nm because the neural (mental) representations are the same.

Trichromacy

The neural representation of color is trivariate in humans; that is, a particular color that one experiences depends on responses in each of three distinct neural pathways. If two different physical lights have spectral energy distributions that result in the same triple of neural responses then the unequal lights are visually indistinguishable. The trivariate feature of color vision is called trichromacy. The three distinct neural

signals are due to three types of light receptors in the eye, called cones because of their shape. Each of the three types of cone responds to a broad range of wavelengths but has a specific wavelength of greatest sensitivity: approximately 440, 540 or 565 nm for the short-wavelength (S), middle-wavelength (M) or long-wavelength (L) sensitive cone, respectively (Figure 1).

The trichromatic neural representation of color is the reason that a mixture of 550 and 700 nm appears identical to 580 nm. The mixture gives the same triple of neural responses as 580 nm. Trichromacy implies further that an infinite number of different wavelength mixtures can give rise to any particular color percept. For example, the yellow appearance of 580 nm light is identical also to the appearance of a mixture of 570 and 600 nm, or a mixture of every wavelength between 550 and 650 nm in suitable amounts, or any other mixture of wavelengths resulting in the same trivariate neural representation as for 580 nm. Physically different lights that appear identical are called *metamers*.

The color white does not result from any single wavelength but rather is experienced with a physical stimulus composed of all wavelengths of light at equal energy. Any mixture of two or more wavelengths that results in the same triple of neural responses also appears white.

Rod Photoreceptors

The rods, a fourth class of photoreceptor, are intermingled with the cones in the eye. Rods are more sensitive to light than cones and therefore can mediate vision in dimly lit environments, such as moonlight, where the cones are not responsive. The spectral sensitivity of rods is broad so most wavelengths can stimulate them (dashed line, Figure 1). Rods are of only one type so rod mediated vision (cones unresponsive) produces only a single neural response at each location. Accordingly, rods cannot carry information about the stimulating light's spectral distribution because any stimulating wavelength can produce the same rod neural response by adjusting the light's intensity. The single neural dimension of rod-mediated vision gives rise to achromatic percepts that vary in only brightness, regardless of stimulus wavelengths. Rod-mediated vision further demonstrates that color is in the mental representation of the light entering the eye, not in the light itself. [Prove this to yourself by placing a glossy color magazine under a dining room fixture controlled by a dimmer switch. Slowly reduce the light illuminating the magazine until the color in the picture disappears (this must be done at night or in a room without windows so the magazine is in near darkness when the fixture is turned off). With dim illumination the picture is still visible, which shows the wavelengths of light from the fixture are reaching the eye, but the light is too feeble to generate the neural signals from cones necessary for color vision.]

Defective Color Vision

Abnormal color vision is common though true color blindness, which is the complete inability to distinguish lights based on hue, is very rare (less than 0.01% of the population). Inherited genes carried by the X chromosome cause most abnormalities of color vision. These genes affect the M or L cone but not the S cone, which is normal. About 8% of men lack either a functional M cone or a functional L cone in the central part of the eye. This is the part of the eye with greatest acuity, as required for reading, and the part normally examined in color vision testing. About a quarter of these men (approximately 2% of all men), who are called *dichromats*, have color vision mediated by only two neural pathways rather than the normal three (for example, only S-cone and M-cone neural responses). Dichromats fail to distinguish many colors that are obviously different to color normals who differentiate the colors by the neural-signal difference in the third pathway that is missing in dichromats. The remaining three quarters of these men, approximately 6% of all men, are trichromats who lack either a functional M cone or L cone but who have two distinct types of cone with very similar spectral sensitivities in addition to the normal S cone. These two cones' peaks are separated by only a few nanometers and are always near the peak of either the normal M cone or the normal L cone (for example, a person may have S cones, M cones, and a third type of cone very similar to the M cone). These color defective individuals are called *anomalous trichromats* because their color vision depends on three neural pathways, as in normal color vision, but their metamers are different from those perceived by the vast majority of the population.

Color deficiency in women is much rarer than in men, occurring in less than 1% of the female population. A woman's two X chromosomes, compared to a man's single one, tend to protect her from color deficiency because color vision is essentially normal if either of her X chromosomes has normal color vision genes. A woman with normal genes on one X chromosome and defective genes on the other can transmit color deficiency to her offspring even though her own color vision is normal. Rarer forms of congenital and acquired color vision abnormality have many other causes.

Unique Hues

The number of distinguishably different colors runs to the millions, but a fundamental property of color vision is the minimal set of hues, called *unique hues*, that alone or in combination can describe all hue percepts. The unique hues are red, green, yellow, and blue. Each unique hue refers to the perceptual experience of that hue alone; for example, unique yellow is the percept of yellow with no hint of red (approaching orange) or green (approaching lime green). By definition, no unique hue can be described by a combination of the others; orange, for example, is not a fifth unique hue because it can be described as yellowish red. All hues can be described as red, green, yellow, or blue, or by four of the six possible combinations of the unique hues: yellow-red, blue-red, yellow-green, or blue-green (examples of these combinations are, respectively, orange, purple, lime green, or turquoise).

The four unique hues logically allow two other combinations, red-green and yellow-blue, but neither of these combinations is experienced in human vision. This observation is the cornerstone of *opponent colors theory*, which posits two bipolar dimensions: one from green (negative values) to red (positive values) with a central zero-point for colors with no reddish or greenish content (that is, unique yellow, unique blue, or white); and a second one from blue to yellow with a central zero-point for colors with no bluish or yellowish content (that is, unique red, unique green, or white). White is perceived with a zero value on both bipolar dimensions. The specifics of classical opponent colors theory are in question, but bipolar coding of chromatic neural signals is well established.

Context

Trichromacy implies that the color one sees is not sufficient to specify the physical light stimulus. Postreceptoral neural processes cause the inverse: knowing the physical stimulus is not sufficient to determine the color appearance of the light. The appearance of a particular light depends on the context of other lights also in view. An example (in black and white) is shown in Figure 2, where six identical ovals are presented, each one on a different background. The ovals appear to be

COLOR VISION. Figure 2. An example of chromatic induction. Each of the six ovals above are presented on different backgrounds. The ovals appear to be different sizes even though they are all identical.

different from each other though all six of them are identical physically. A similar phenomenon occurs in color. For example, a light that appears white when viewed alone appears tinged with red when seen within a green-appearing surround, or appears tinged with yellow when seen within a blue-appearing surround. The change in one light's perceived color due to other light in a neighboring area is called *chromatic induction*.

Color Surfaces

Directly viewed sources of light such as traffic signals and televisions are the exception even in our modern world. We mostly see colors of surfaces and objects, which are visible only when illuminated by an external light source. Common illuminants are the sun, an electric lamp, or a candle. Surfaces reflect some of the illuminating light; the reflected light enters the eye. The color of a surface results from selectively greater reflection of some wavelengths than others. For example, a surface that appears blue reflects short wavelengths more than longer ones, while a surface that appears red reflects long wavelengths more than shorter ones.

All light that illuminates a surface is either reflected or absorbed, so selective reflection of wavelengths implies that the complement of the reflected light is selectively absorbed. Spectrally selective absorption of light explains the colors seen when two paints are combined. Both paints in the mixture absorb light so the light reflected from the mixture, which is what one sees, is that light not absorbed by either paint. For example, a paint that predominantly reflects long wavelengths (>600 nm), which appears red, when mixed with a paint that predominantly reflects somewhat shorter wavelengths (560–610 nm), which appears yellow, yields a mixture that most strongly reflects wavelengths between 600 and 610 nm, which appears orange. Combining paints is an example of *subtractive mixture* because the mixture reduces the amount of light reaching the eye compared to one of the components in the

mixture. By comparison, the *additive mixture* of wavelengths discussed earlier results in more light at the eye than from either component alone. The color one perceives with either type of mixture depends on the relative amounts of each wavelength in the visual stimulus, though a subtractive mixture can appear quite dark if all wavelengths are absorbed strongly.

Color Constancy

The light from an object that reaches the eye depends both on the spectrally selective surface reflectance of the object and on the spectral distribution of the illuminating light. Surface reflectance is quite stable over time, but the illuminating light can vary considerably. Natural daylight illumination changes spectrally from morning to noon to sunset. Artificial illuminants such as electric lamps expand the variety of common spectral energy distributions. Consider the light reflected from a white eggshell viewed at noon under daylight at an outdoor farm market. If the light reflected from the eggshell completely determines its color, then the same eggshell would appear orangish on a kitchen table illuminated by a screw-in light bulb. Of course this does not happen. The eggshell remains white, which implies that color perception does not depend on only the trivariate neural representation of the light reflected from the object. *Color constancy* is the perceived stability of the color of objects and surfaces, despite changes in the light illuminating them and thus despite changes in the spectral distribution of light that reaches the eye.

The human visual system discounts the particular light illuminating objects, substantially if not completely, so that each object appears a nearly stable color under all but the most extreme illuminants (an example of an extreme illuminant is sodium lighting sometimes used along highways, which gives a yellowish cast). Color constancy reveals again that color is a psychological percept rather than a property of physical light.

[*See also* Vision and Sight.]

Bibliography

Chevreul, M. E. (1839). *The principles of harmony and contrast of colors and their applications to the arts.* (First English translation 1854, republished 1967.) New York: Reinhold.

DeMarco, P., Pokorny, J., & Smith, V. C. (1992). Full-spectrum cone sensitivity functions for X-chromosome-linked anomolous trichromats. *Journal of the Optical Society of American A*, 9, 1465–1476.

Hering, E. (1920). *Outlines of a theory of the light sense.* (English translation by L. M. Hurvich & D. Jameson, 1964.) Cambridge, MA: Harvard University Press.

Hurvich, L. M. & Jameson, D. (1957). An opponent-process theory of color vision. *Psychological Review*, 6, 384–404.

Kaiser, P. K. & Boynton, R. M. (1996). *Human color vision* (2nd ed.). Washington, DC: Optical Society of America.

Pokorny, J., Smith, V. C., Verriest, G., & Pinckers, A. J. L. G. (Eds.). (1979). *Congenital and acquired color vision defects.* New York: Grune & Stratton.

Shevell, S. K (Ed.) (2000). *The science of color* (2nd ed.). Washington, DC: Optical Society of America.

Wyszecki, G. & Stiles, W. S. (1982). *Color science: Concepts and methods, quantitative data and formulae* (2nd ed.). New York: Wiley.

Steven K. Shevell

COMBAT. One of the ironies of effective military performance is that it is most essential precisely when it is most difficult. Combatants face the proximate threat, violent death and injury, witness the sudden bloody deaths of their comrades, and are expected to inflict the same brutal death and injury on the enemy. They are required to perform exhausting, and at times, complex tasks under the most trying physical conditions, from extremes of climate through the ear-piercing noise of shelling and the fumes of smoke and toxins. Sometimes they must endure utter isolation, at other times suffocating crowding, burdened by the cumbersome weight of heavy weapons and protective devices.

These and other stresses of the battlefield are implicated in measurable physiological effects, such as increased heart beat, trembling, and labored breathing. In addition, cognitive changes such as cue restriction, narrowing of the perceptual field, decreased search behavior, longer reaction time to peripheral cues, and behavioral impairments, including decreased vigilance, degraded problem solving, performance rigidity, and others may be experienced. Under these and innumerable other hardships of the battlefield, there is an ever present danger of serious error. Risk is incorrectly gauged and managed, performance precision declines, and crucial information is ignored (Driskell & Eduardo, 1991).

Military performance is further jeopardized by the many emotional effects of the stress. First and foremost is the inevitable anxiety. Anxiety is a perfectly normal response to imminent threat and, in moderate levels, functional in combat, in that it heightens vigilance where that is needed. At the same time, as observed by Marshall (1978) in World War II and repeatedly confirmed since, all but a small percentage of combat troops are too paralyzed by anxiety to fire their weapons during battle. Most experience other stress-induced symptoms as well. Nonetheless, the vast preponderance of soldiers remain psychologically intact despite the awesome destructiveness of modern warfare. They continue to function as soldiers. They are not a danger to themselves or their fellow fighters and do not insist upon being evacuated.

A small but not insignificant percentage of soldiers are overwhelmed by their anxiety. They perceive the stress as so intense, prolonged, and uncontrollable that they feel totally vulnerable and powerless. This marks the psychological breakdown known as *combat stress reaction* (CSR). A CSR occurs when the soldier is stripped of his defenses and feels so overwhelmed by the threat that he becomes powerless to counteract or distance himself from it and is inundated by feelings of utter helplessness and existential insecurity. In this state, he is a danger to himself and his unit and is no longer able to perform any military duties.

In the view of current military psychology, whether the soldier withstands or succumbs to the stresses of battle depends on the resolution of the inner dilemma of fight or flight that is inherent in every life-threatening experience (Noy, 1991). The danger of combat is formidable, ever present, and impossible to totally ignore or deny, giving rise to the desire, whether conscious or unconscious, to flee. On the other hand, the soldier's personality, motivation, military assignment and standing in his unit all affect his perception and interpretation of the danger and his assessment of his ability to cope with it. Numerous counterforces keep him fighting. These include his soldierly pride and self image; his ties to his buddies and officers; dependence on, identification with, and sense of belonging in his unit; and his belief in the justice and aims of the war he is fighting. The soldier's emotional ability to withstand the threat depends on the balance of his fear and of these counterforces (Kardiner & Spigel, 1947). So long as the latter outweigh the former, he will continue to fight. When the perception of danger increases and/or the sustaining convictions and moral and personal ties weaken, his anxiety mounts, until it overwhelms him and he can no longer continue to fight.

Combat Stress Reaction

Combat stress reaction (CSR) is the most severe of the psychological responses to the stress of combat. It is marked by a large range of polymorphic and labile symptoms. Somatic symptoms range from loss of bladder and bowel control, trembling, stuttering, and vomiting to conversion reactions such as blindness and paralysis without organic causes. Cognitive symptoms include confusion, problems in perception, memory, and judgment, and disorientation. In extreme cases, the soldier may not know who or where he is. The main emotional symptoms are paralyzing anxiety and deep depression, which often alternate. The behavioral symptoms are the manifestations of these emotions: great agitation, on the one hand, apathy and withdrawal on the other. Some of them are quite bizarre. There are CSR soldiers who tear off their uniforms and run amok in sight of the enemy; others may become frozen in their tracks, refuse to shower or cling to a piece of clothing or other talisman. These manifestations change as rapidly as the emotional states that underlie them, and the rapidity is quite perplexing to observers. The result of these symptoms is the soldier's total inability to continue to perform his battlefield duties and the necessity of evacuating him.

With minor variations, this clinical picture has been repeatedly observed at different times, in different armies, different wars, and different cultures. Nonetheless, the great variability and lability of the reaction make it difficult to arrive at an agreed upon clinical definition. For practical purposes, armies the world over use a functional definition. In the formulation of Kormos (1978), this is that "combat stress reaction consists of behavior by a soldier under conditions of combat, invariably interpreted by those around him as signaling that the soldier, although expected to be a combatant, has ceased to function as such."

The multiplicity and variability of the symptoms, both within a single soldier and from casualty to casualty, make it very difficult to capture the elusive nature of CSR. This difficulty is reflected in the succession of appellations the phenomenon has borne, each encapsulating a different conception of what it is (Mangelsdorf, 1985). For example, the term "shell shock" used in World War I expressed the belief that it is a disorder of the central nervous system caused by exposure to intense shelling and bombing. In the postwar vogue of Freudian thought, the favored term became "war neurosis," conveying the view that CSR is caused by reawakening of subconscious childhood conflicts. The term currently used by most armies, combat stress reaction (Mullins & Glass, 1973), expresses the conviction that the breakdown is the result of the massive stress to which the soldier is exposed. It makes no distinction between soldiers who are unable to fight and those who are unwilling to fight, and it avoids moral judgment.

Identification. Despite its seemingly simple functional definition and sometimes bizarre manifestation, CSR is usually difficult to identify. For one thing, conduct on the battlefield is generally disorganized and non-normative in everyday life. For example, the loss of bladder, and even bowel control is quite common. This blurs the identification threshold. Moreover, those who would make the identification, the afflicted soldier's commanders and buddies, are themselves caught up in the stresses and anxiety of the situation and their judgment is not at peak capacity. Furthermore, there is a tendency to retain popular soldiers and to evacuate ones who are less well liked (Moses & Cohen, 1984).

Prevalence. The reported prevalence of CSR varies considerably both within and among wars (Noy, 1991). Rates in World War II ranged from a low of 10% to a high of 48%. In the Vietnam War, rates were substantially lower, with official figures putting the number at 12 per 1,000 fighters (Bourne, 1970). In the Yom Kippur War (1973) the official count in Israel was 10% of all those wounded in action, but in some units it reached up to 70% of the wounded. In the Lebanon War (1982), the official figure was 23% of those wounded in action.

These figures have been challenged as underestimates. The growing number of cases of delayed onset following the Vietnam War led to charges of denial and under-reporting. Similar charges were made with regard to the initial figures for the Yom Kippur War, where some put the rate closer to 40% of the wounded.

The variations derive from differences in the identification and counting of CSR cases, as well as from differences in the battlefields. All in all, however, the reported rates clearly indicate that CSR is an inevitable and common consequence of war. Most armies recognize it as a major source of manpower loss, which can contribute to an army's defeat. Glass (1973), for example, noted that in 1942 evacuations due to psychological breakdown alone outnumbered the numbers that the U.S. army could mobilize at the time.

The Course of CSR. Combat stress reaction does not necessarily end with the psychological breakdown on the battlefield. For many casualties, it is followed by long-enduring, disruptive sequela. The most common is post-traumatic stress disorder (PTSD). Follow-up studies of Israeli psychiatric casualties of the Lebanon War (1992) (Solomon, 1993) indicate that 61% of identified CSR casualties suffered from diagnosable PTSD one year after their participation in combat, 56% two years after, and 43% three years later. Longer follow-ups revealed somewhat lower but yet substantial rates (Solomon, 1993). These men also suffered considerable impairment in social, family, and work functioning, high rates of somatic complaints, and elevated levels of general psychiatric symptoms.

Moreover, even when the casualty seems to recover, he remains more vulnerable than other veterans to subsequent stress. He is more likely to break down in a subsequent war and to suffer adverse reactions to stressful life events. Such events, especially events reminiscent of the original traumatic event, may lead to the reactivation or exacerbation of the original CSR. Reactivated symptomatology has been observed when traumatized veterans attend war memorials and other public ceremonies that remind them of their combat experiences. When reactivation occurs in a subsequent war, the symptoms tend to be more intense and recovery more difficult than in a first time reaction.

In addition, some soldiers who apparently function well in combat and are asymptomatic develop combat-related stress disorders later on. These disorders were first recognized to be widespread after the Vietnam War. The official CSR rates for that war were among the lowest recorded, but in the years following, the steadily growing stream of veterans with ascribed war-related stress reactions became a major public health problem. Some clinicians (e.g., Pitman, Sparr, Saunders & Mc-Farlane, 1996) have questioned the validity of this diagnosis, claiming that malingering, fictitious symptoms, drug abuse, and precombat psychopathology were mistakenly diagnosed as delayed CSR. Furthermore, there is a question as to whether it is the onset or the identification that is delayed. Follow-ups of soldiers in the Lebanon War revealed that fifteen years later, the number of revealed cases is triple that of immediate onset, and still growing. But close scrutiny of these cases indicates that only 10% of them were delayed onset and the rest were instances of delayed help-seeking and identification. The symptoms of delayed onset tend to be less intense and functioning is less impaired than that of acute CSR and recovery is more rapid (Solomon, 1993).

[*See also* War and Conflict, *article on* Effects on Military Personnel.]

Bibliography

Bourne, P. G. (1970). Military psychiatry and the Vietnam experience. *Journal of the Royal Army Medical Corps, 127,* 123–130.

Driskell, E.J., & Salas, E. (1991). Overcoming the effects of stress on military performance: Human factors, training, and selection strategies. In R. Gal., & A. D. Mangelsdorff (Eds.), *Handbook of military psychology* (pp. 491–506). New York: Wiley.

Glass, A. J. (Ed.). (1973). *Neuropsychiatry in World War II, Vol. II: Overseas Theaters.* (W. S. Mullins, Ed.). Washington, DC: Office of the Surgeon General, Department of the Army, U.S. Army.

Kardiner, A., & Spiegel, H. (1947). War, stress and neurotic illness. New York: Hoeber.

Kormos, H. R. (1978). The nature of combat stress. In C. R. Figley (Ed.), *Stress disorders among Vietnam veterans* (pp. 3–22). New York: Brunner/Mazel.

Mangelsdorff, A. D. (1985). Lessons learned and forgotten:
The need for prevention and mental health interventions in disaster preparedness. *Journal of Community Psychology, 13,* 239–257.

Marshal, S. L. A. (1978). *Men against fire: The problem of battle command in future war.* Gloucester, MA: Peter Smith.

Moses, R. & Cohen, I. (1984). Understanding and treatment of combat neurosis: The Israeli experience. In H. Schwartz (Ed.), *Psychotherapy of the combat veteran.* (pp. 269–304). New York: Medical Scientific Books.

Noy, S. (1991). *I am not anymore.* Israel: Israel Ministry of Defense.

Noy, S. (1991). Combat stress reaction. In R. Gal., & A. D. Mangelsdorff (Eds.), *Handbook of military psychology.* (pp. 491–506). New York: Wiley.

Pitman, R., Sparr, L., Sounderes, L., & McFarlane, A. Y. (1996). Legal issues in post-traumatic stress disorder. In B. Van-Der-Kolk, A. McFarlane, & L. Weisaeth (Eds.), *Traumatic stress: The effect of overwhelming experience on mind, body, and society.* New York: Guilford Press.

Solomon, Z. (1993). *Combat stress reaction: The enduring toll of war.* New York: Plenum Press.

Zahava Solomon

COMMITMENT. The concept of commitment is used in several distinct ways (e.g., Brickman, 1987; Klinger, 1995, Tubbs, 1993) and has been applied in numerous distinct settings. In all of its motivational uses, commitment refers to some aspect of a person's determination to pursue goals. In Brickman's (1987) words, "commitment is whatever it is that makes a person engage or continue in a course of action when difficulties or positive alternatives influence the person to abandon the action" (p. 2). However, these general formulations encompass a number of discrete meanings. Thus, in one usage, commitment refers to the momentary event of deciding to pursue any particular goal (Klinger, 1977)—tantamount to choosing a goal (M. L. Tubbs, *Journal of Applied Psychology, 78,* 86–97, 1993) and to forming an intention to pursue it (Heckhausen & Kuhl, 1985). In another usage, it refers to publicly expressing one's intention to perform some act (Kiesler, 1971). More often, the term *commitment* refers to the strength of one's intention to pursue the goal or one's actual adherence to its pursuit. Finally, it can refer to an individual's characteristic engagement with life or society by pursuing significant goals (Brickman, 1987) or socially compatible goals—the opposite of alienation (K. Kenniston, *American Scholar, 38,* 97–112, 1968).

The several motivational meanings of commitment thus range from momentary events to strength of an intention over time to enduring personality traits. Unfortunately, the field has so far failed to develop a nomenclature that might distinguish these different meanings. Instead, they must be surmised from the context in which the term is used, particularly the assessment methods.

Psychologists have applied the concept of commitment to many settings and varying kinds of goals, such as commitment (in the sense of pledges) to particular tasks (e.g., Kiesler, 1971), close relationships (e.g., Sternberg, 1986), religious beliefs or practices (e.g., R. L. Dudley, *Adolescence*, 1993, *28*, 21–28; Liu, 1988), employment in general (e.g., M. H. Banks and P. Henry, 1993, *Journal of Occupational and Organizational Psychology*, *66*, 177–184), particular careers (e.g., K. D. Carson and A. G. Bedeian, 1994, *Journal of Vocational Behavior*, *44*, 237–262), assigned projects, labor unions, and safe sex (G. M. Breakwell, L. J. Millward, and C. Fife-Schaw, 1994, *Journal of Applied Social Psychology*, *24*, 189–217).

Methods for Assessing Commitment

Psychologists' conceptions of commitment are best understood by examining the methods they use to assess it. One of the earliest such methods is a scale on the Motivational Structure Questionnaire and its predecessors (Klinger, 1987), dating to the 1970s. This measure is a single six-point rating scale that runs from 6 "*I fully intend to if I possibly can (or I would if I could)*" to 1 "*I do not (or would not) intend to (get, keep, etc.) the thing*" (Klinger, Cox, & Blount, 1995). This scale assesses whether a commitment to a specific goal has taken place and the degree of determination to attain it. Perhaps the most widely used general methods for assessing commitment are those of J. R. Hollenbeck, H. J. Klein, A. M. O'Leary, and P. M. Wright (*Journal of Applied Psychology*, 1989, *74*, 951–956). Their scales are composed of items such as "*It's hard to take this goal seriously*" and "*I am strongly committed to pursuing this goal*," to which respondents mark their agreement or disagreement.

Additionally, there are numerous more specific scales. For example, there is a measure of commitment to one's labor union (M. E. Gordon, J. W. Philpot, R. E. Burt, C. A. Thompson, and W. E. Spiller, 1980, *Journal of Applied Psychology*, *65*, 479–499) whose four intercorrelated factors are loyalty and responsibility to the union, willingness to perform work for it, and belief in unionism. A sport commitment scale asks, for example, about dedication to a particular sports program and about willingness and determination to keep playing in it (T. K. Scanlan, J. P. Simons, P. J. Carpenter, and G. W. Schmidt, 1993, *Journal of Sport and Exercise Psychology*, *15*, 16–38). A measure of career commitment (K. D. Carson and A. G. Bedeian, 1994, *Journal of Vocational Behavior*, 1994, *44*, 237–262) contains such factors as degree of identification with a particular career, doubts about whether it is worth the trouble, and the extent of planning for it.

Significance of the Commitment Construct in Psychology

The significance of the commitment concept derives from the centrality of goal-striving in psychology and, indeed, in zoology. Survival of animals depends on their successful pursuit of their necessary nutrients, mates, and environmental conditions. Thus, animal life consists of an endless series of goal pursuits. Because species survive according to how well individuals succeed in attaining their goals, evolution must have selected all animal features, both physical and behavioral, for their usefulness in promoting successful goal-striving. In this sense, motivational processes are at the center of animal and human evolution, including its psychological facets.

Each goal pursuit must have a beginning and a continuing guidance mechanism to maintain goal orientation. It is the initiation of a goal pursuit and the vigor with which it is pursued that are called commitment. Thus, commitment covers essential aspects of goal-striving and hence motivation.

Evidence in Support of the Commitment Construct

The preceding statements assume that commitment constitutes a valid construct. In contradiction to the logical, evolution-based argument for its inevitability, one might argue that behavior simply flows from one phase to another according to contemporaneous factors acting on individuals, without requiring a discrete construct such as commitment (e.g., J. W. Atkinson and D. Birch, *Dynamics of Action*, New York, 1970). However, there is empirical evidence to support its validity in at least four forms.

First, factors that influence behavior do so differently after a commitment to a goal from before. Thus, suppose a person discovers that obstacles to attaining a goal—perhaps a certain career or relationship—are greater than originally expected. Before having become committed to the goal, this new realization would tend to discourage the person from pursuing the goal; coming after commitment, it would invigorate pursuit of the goal and increase its subjective value (Klinger, 1977; Lydon & Zanna, 1990). Furthermore, people who make an assigned task a personal goal perform better the more difficult the task; but if they perform the task without this inner commitment, but simply to comply with somebody's directions, the more difficult the task the more poorly they perform (M. Erez and I. Zidon, *Journal of Applied Psychology*, 1984, *69*, 69–78). Information about how well others do on an assigned task also affects performance of highly committed people differently from performance of the weakly committed (B. A. Martin and D. J. Manning, *Journal of Management*, 1995, *21*, 65–80).

Second, people's attention, recall, and thought and dream contents differ after a commitment as compared with before one. People react disproportionately to stimuli associated with their goal pursuits, which affects what they dream about at night and also what they daydream about (Klinger, 1990, 1996a, 1996b; and affects the focus of their day-to-day activities (J. Brunstein, *Journal of Personality and Social Psychology*, 1993, 65, 1061–1070; Klinger, 1987; Roberson, *Organizational Behavior and Decision Processes*, 1989, 44, 345–367).

Third, people attend, recall, and think thoughts differently when they are focused in a given moment on deliberating about forming a commitment from when they are focused on carrying out a commitment already made, even with respect to material irrelevant to the particular commitment. Thus, when people were experimentally induced to stop short of a commitment to a certain task but were still in a deliberative mind-set, they displayed different memory spans for task-irrelevant material and the endings of their task-irrelevant stories were different from situations where they had first been induced to undertake the commitment and adopt an implemental mind-set (Gollwitzer, 1990).

Finally, once a commitment is made, it cannot simply be terminated without special psychological processing and costs (J. Beckmann, *Motivation and Emotion*, 1994, 18, 317–334; Klinger, 1977). Particularly when a goal pursuit is abandoned, people go through a reasonably regular sequence of phases entailing invigoration, anger, depression, and eventual recovery. These phases are accompanied by corresponding mental activity regarding the lapsed goal.

Determinants and Correlates of Commitment

As a broad general principle, the best predictors of commitment to a goal are the individual's sense of the satisfactions the goal is capable of bringing and its attainability. These factors, which have long been main components of Expectancy X Value theories, crop up in a wide variety of settings. For example, the combination of these variables predicted commitment to laboratory tasks and mediated the influence of other personal and situational factors (H. J. Klein and P. M. Wright, *Journal of Applied Social Psychology*, 1994, 24, 95–114; M. E. Tubbs and J. G. Dahl, *Journal of Psychology*, 1992, 126, 181–188; J. C. Wofford, V. L. Goodwin, and S. Premack, *Journal of Management*, 1992, 18, 595–615). In accordance with an *investment model* of close relationships (C. E. Rusbult and B. P. Buunk, *Journal of Personal and Social Relationships*, 1993, 10, 175–204; see also S. Sprecher, *Social Psychology Quarterly*, 1988, 51, 318–328), people stay in a relationship according to their level of satisfaction with it, the quality of relationships alternative to it, and the amount of psychic and other investment in it. These factors are then subjectively experienced as commitment to the relationship. In a study of sports performance, the difficulty of the goals people set for themselves were predicted by their estimates of satisfaction in performance and self-efficacy (Y. Theodorakis, *Journal of Applied Sport Psychology*, 1996, 8, 171–182). Farmers' commitment to farming was "contingent on the intrinsically rewarding aspects of both farm and nonfarm work" (C. M. Coughenour, *Social-Science-Research*, 1995, 24, p. 367).

There are also other ways to express essentially the same concepts, as in Lydon's (1996) view that commitment is especially strong to goals that represent an individual's "core beliefs, values, and identities" (p. 196). Others have explored the specific meaning of such factors in exceptional moral commitment (e.g., Colby and Damon, *The Moral Self*, 1993, Cambridge, Mass.). However, some individuals (the *state-oriented*) are less able to distinguish commitments they undertook entirely by themselves from commitments they adopted when requested by others (J. M. Kuhl and M. Kazén, *Journal of Personality and Social Psychology*, 1894, 66, 1103–1115).

Behavioral Effects of Commitment

A wide variety of experimental studies (reviewed by R. Katzev and T. Wang, *Journal of Social Behavior and Personality*, 1994, 9, 13–26) have shown that when people become committed to a goal of changed behavior (in the sense of pledging to someone that they will attain it), they are much more likely to actually change their behavior than under alternative conditions, such as having merely received information about the desirability of doing so. Many of these studies were field studies on such actions as energy conservation, use of public transit, or watching someone else's belongings to prevent theft. Simply making the commitment appeared as effective as receiving various incentives, and the behavior was sometimes shown to stay changed.

Bibliography

Brickman, P. (1987). *Commitment, conflict, and caring.* Englewood Cliffs, NJ: Prentice Hall.

Gollwitzer, P. (1990). Action phases and mind-sets. In E. T. Higgins & R. M. Sorrentino (Eds.), *Handbook of motivation and social cognition* (pp. 53–92). New York: Guilford Press.

Heckhausen, H., & Kuhl, J. (1985). From wishes to action: The dead ends and short cuts on the long way to action. In M. Frese & J. Sabini (Eds.), *Goal directed behavior: The concept of action in psychology* (pp. 134–195). Hillsdale, NJ: Erlbaum.

Kiesler, C. A. (1971). *The psychology of commitment: Experiments linking behavior to belief.* New York: Academic Press.

Klinger, E. (1977). *Meaning and void: Inner experience and the incentives in people's lives.* Minneapolis: University of Minnesota Press.

Klinger, E. (1987). The Interview Questionnaire technique: Reliability and validity of a mixed idiographic-nomothetic measure of motivation. In J. N. Butcher & C. D. Spielberger (Eds.), *Advances in personality assessment* (Vol. 6, pp. 31–48). Hillsdale, NJ: Erlbaum.

Klinger, E. (1990). *Daydreaming.* Los Angeles: Jeremy Tarcher.

Klinger, E. (1995). Selbstverpflichtungs-Theorien [Commitment theories]. In J. Kuhl (Ed.), *Enzyklopädie für Psychologie: Vol. 4. Motivation, Volition, Handlung: Motivation und Emotion* [Encyclopedia of psychology: Vol. 4. Motivation, volition: Motivation and emotion]. (pp. 469–483). Göttingen: Hogrefe.

Klinger, E., Cox, W. M., & Blount, J. P. (1995). The Motivational Structure Questionnaire. In J. P. Allen (Ed.), *Assessing alcohol problems: A guide for clinicians and researchers* (pp. 399–411). Bethesda, MD: National Institute on Alcohol Abuse and Alcoholism.

Kuhl, J., & Kazén, M. (1994). Self-discrimination and memory: State orientation and false self-ascription of assigned activities. *Journal of Personality and Social Psychology, 66*(6), 1103–1115.

Liu, O. C. (1988). *Commitment to religion: Definition, measurement, and correlates.* Unpublished doctoral dissertation, Stanford University, Stanford, CA.

Locke, E. A., Latham, G. P., & Erez, M. (1988). The determinants of goal commitment. *Academy of Management Review, 13,* 23–39.

Lydon, J. (1996). Toward a theory of commitment. In C. Seligman, J. M. Olson, & M. P. Zanna (Eds.), *The psychology of values: The Ontario symposium* (Vol. 8, pp. 191–213). Mahwah, NJ: Erlbaum.

Lydon, J. E., & Zanna, M. P. (1990). Commitment in the face of adversity: A value-affirmation approach. *Journal of Personality and Social Psychology, 58,* 1040–1047.

Mottaz, C. J. (1988). Determinants of organizational commitment. *Human Relations, 41,* 467–482.

Sternberg, R. J. (1986). A triangular theory of love. *Psychological Review, 93,* 119–135.

Eric Klinger

COMMUNAL RELATIONSHIP. *See* Friendship.

COMMUNITY ECOLOGY. Community dynamics refer to the interplay of forces in the community that give it its distinctive character. These forces emerge from such factors as community history, ethnic composition, crime rate, degree of poverty, and sense of cohesion in the community. Community dynamics both shape the experiences of individuals in communities and are the objects of varied kinds of interventions focusing on differing aspects of the community itself. Examples of both research and intervention directed to understanding and changing community forces to promote the well-being of citizens are presented below.

Theories of Communities

While there is no consensus in defining the concept of community, varying operational definitions have evolved. Warren (1977) provides the definitive overview in outlining six contrasting images of the community: (1) the community as space, typified in studies of rural and urban communities; (2) the community as people, the community's population defined by the kinds of demographic data found in census tracts such as the number and percentages of people in different ethnic and racial groups and their age and sex distributions; (3) the community as shared institutions and values, the kind of total pattern of living often studied by anthropologists in understanding a particular culture; (4) the community as interaction, focusing on the association of individuals with each other and the behavior associated with community institutions such as churches, schools, and the family; (5) the community as a distribution of power, based on an assessment of who in the community exerts more influence over what happens in that community than others and how those with power are themselves interrelated; and (6) the community as a social system, the emerging current image which focuses on a variety of community processes, including communication patterns, boundary maintenance, systemic linkage or interdependence of units in the community, socialization processes, mechanisms of social control, and the institutionalization or predictability of organization and social actions in the community. These six images not only draw attention to differing aspects of communities; they provide a framework for comparing communities in terms of similarities and differences.

Theories of neighborhoods, the building blocks or subcomponents of larger communities, have also received attention. Burton, Price-Spratlen, and Spencer (in press) have differentiated four approaches to the concept of neighborhood that echo many of the images specified by Warren: neighborhood as site, as perception, as social network, and as culture. Neighborhood as site reflects Warren's space concept, focusing on spatial and geographical definitions and defining neighborhoods in terms of such aggregate characteristics as ethnic and racial composition and percentage of children living in poverty. Neighborhood as perception draws attention to the perceived environment of the neighborhood, something one cannot accurately infer from its demographics alone (see J. C. Buckner, "The development of an instrument to measure neighborhood cohesion," *American Journal of Community Psychology*, 1988, *16*, 771–791).

Defining neighborhoods in terms of social networks focuses on one aspect of Warren's notion of interaction; the interpersonal linkages among people in the neighborhood. This draws attention to the neighborhood as an interpersonal environment (see Duck, 1997). Finally, neighborhood as culture parallels Warren's notion of shared institutions and values, emphasizing the shared rituals, meanings, traditions, and histories that characterize neighborhoods over time.

Methods, Research Strategies, and Select Findings

Each of the varying definitions of communities and neighborhoods are operationalized using diverse assessment methods. The community or neighborhood as space or site most frequently rests on objective data gathered from census tracts, while the neighborhood as perception approach and the social network analysis involve the solicitation of citizen input through structured questionnaires. However, a variety of other methods have been employed as well. Thus, ethnography, field observations, cognitive maps drawn by children and adolescents, and focus groups have also been employed.

From these methods have come important findings relating community characteristics to community dynamics. For example, Sampson, Raudenbush, and Earls ("Neighborhoods and violent crime: A multilevel study of collective efficacy," *Science*, 1997, *277*, 918–924) found a negative relationship between collective efficacy, defined as social cohesion among neighbors combined with their willingness to intervene on behalf of the common good, such as monitoring the play of children in the neighborhood, and various indices of neighborhood violence.

The role of neighborhood dynamics in the socialization of children has also been investigated. Much of this work acknowledges the impact of William Julius Wilson's 1987 book *The Truly Disadvantaged* (Chicago), which provided a rich conceptual analysis of how structural changes in postindustrial society contributed to the number of poor and jobless people in inner-city neighborhoods. From a quantitative perspective, Brooks-Gunn, Duncan, Klebanov, and Sealand ("Do neighborhoods influence child and adolescent development?" *American Journal of Sociology*, 1993, *99*, 353–395) used two existing data sets to study the effects of neighborhoods on childhood IQ, teenage births, and dropout rates. While family-level differences within neighborhoods affected developmental outcomes of children, neighborhood differences also influenced child and adolescent behavior.

Ethnographic research has likewise provided important findings relating community dynamics to family and child adaptation. In a classic work, Stack (1972) portrayed the impact of poverty and racism on the form and function of kinship networks in a small and rural African American community. Her work showed how the kinds of relations among family and fictive kin reflected an intricate adaptive network for the raising of children and the survival of the community. Burton, Obeidallah, and Allison (1996) used ethnographic data from an inner-city African American community to cast doubt on the generality of the assumption that adolescence is itself a discrete developmental stage. They show how the vicissitudes of community dynamics cause adolescents in high-risk neighborhoods to develop an accelerated life course based on the expectation of a foreshortened life expectancy as well as grow up in an age-condensed family structure with a typical age between generations of 13 to 17 years. These forces truncate and indeed transform the nature of adolescence in ways seldom accounted for by existing developmental theory.

A somewhat different perspective on community dynamics is found in literature on immigrant and refugee families. Portes and Rumbaut (1990) discuss how the immigrant experience in the new community is shaped by the relationship between the "contexts of exit" and "contexts of reception." The former refers to circumstances surrounding the leaving of their native country, such as whether it was forced or unforced, and the latter refers to policies, labor markets factors, and the availability of ethnic communities comprised of coculturals. In their analysis, the experience of newcomers is greatly influenced by the presence or absence of an existing ethnic community in which they may locate. The presence of an ethnic community provides readily available networks of culturally similar individuals and is a source of information about jobs and coping in the new culture. However, such a community may make less immediate the acculturative demands of language acquisition and the development of a bicultural style.

Intervention in Communities

Most interventions in communities as conducted by psychologists involve work in varied community settings such as schools, with little attention to the broader effects of these interventions on the community. However, varied interventions have been described that involve the dynamics between community groups and community settings. One such area involves initiatives to enhance school-parent relationships. Trickett ("Developing an ecological mind-set on school-community collaboration," in J. L. Swartz & W. E. Martin, Eds., *Applied Ecological Psychology for Schools within Communities*, Mahwah, N.J., 1997) employed an ecological perspective on school-community interdependence to illustrate how the dynamics of parent-school interaction are affected by such community factors as poverty and crime and such school factors as receptivity to parent involvement and commitment to multiculturalism in immigrant and refugee communities.

However, in addition to these more delimited interventions there have been a number of models of community intervention and empirical reports of interventions at the community level. Rothman ("The interweaving of community intervention approaches," *Journal of Community Practice*, 1996, *3*, 3–4, 69–99) provides examples of his three-pronged model of community intervention involving locality development, social action, and social planning policy. Locality development stresses participatory and self-help mechanisms in the community, while social action emphasizes the redistribution of power to disempowered segments of the community. The social planning approach, in contrast, emphasizes technical bureaucratic responses to local needs. He describes the interweaving of these different models in interventions designed to affect the well-being of the community.

Steuart (1994) provides another model of community intervention beginning with the identification of gross community units of identity such as ethnicity. From there he emphasizes working from within the community frame of reference. He distinguishes between community-oriented strategies and community-centered ones, preferring the latter because of the emphasis on social and cultural considerations in the design and evaluation of community interventions.

A third model is the neighborhood or community-based empowerment model in which local leadership and local ownership of initiatives is fostered. These initiatives have taken a variety of forms, ranging from problem-solving coalitions of local agencies to university-community collaborations. With respect to the former, for example, Nelson ("The development of a mental health coalition: A Case Study," *American Journal of Community Psychology*, 1994, *22*(2), 229–256) uses resource mobilization theory to document the effectiveness of a mental health coalition's 6-year effort to influence housing and community support programs for psychiatric consumers/survivors (see also Zimmerman and Perkins, "Empowerment theory, research, and application," *American Journal of Community Psychology*, 1995, *23*(5)). McHale and Lerner ("University-Community Collaborations on Behalf of Youth," *Journal of Research on Adolescence*, 1996, *6*(1), 1–86) provide a compendium of projects and perspectives on university-community collaborations on behalf of youth. Included here are ideas and examples of how intervention projects and research, if conducted in a collaborative manner, can be a resource for community development and changes in community dynamics between individuals and community institutions. Examples of community participation in coping with community issues such as neighborhood rehabilitation and dealing with toxic contaminants are found in Altman and Wandersman (1987).

Empowerment has taken on special salience in efforts to intervene in immigrant and refugee communities because of the relative poverty and lack of social resources in many of these communities. Sitka and Tip ("Empowering the silent ranks: The southeast Asian experience," *American Journal of Community Psychology*, 1994, *22*(4), 497–530) focus on three themes related to the Southeast Asian experience and community-based interventions aimed at empowerment: (1) the importance of understanding the cultural dimensions of the Southeast Asian experience as it relates to the suitability of Western approaches to intervention; (2) the importance of understanding trauma and the hardship associated with immigration, particularly forced immigration, and (3) the urgency of adopting multifaceted interventions to address the pressing needs of this population (see also Westermeyer, 1989).

Community interventions have also focused on issues of public health such as acquired immune deficiency syndrome (AIDS), alcohol, and tobacco use, often employing multiple intervention components. For example, Biglan and colleagues (1996) report on a modular approach to mobilizing antitobacco influences of peers and parents in several small towns in Oregon. They employed a repeated time series design by sequentially introducing antitobacco interventions in different towns at different times, and found increased knowledge and lowered intentions to smoke among adolescents in the experimental towns. Taken together, there are an increasing number of theoretical perspectives and intervention approaches to understanding and intervening in community dynamics to improve the well-being of citizens. Additional resources on community dynamics and interventions are found in the accompanying bibliography.

Bibliography

Altman, I., & Wandersman, A. (Eds.). (1987). *Neighborhood and community environments*. New York: Plenum.

Biglan, A., Ary, D., Yudelson, H., Duncan, T. E., Hood, D., James, L., Koehm, V., Wright, Z., Black, C., Levings, D., Smith, S., & Gaiser, E. (1996). Experimental evaluation of a modular approach to mobilizing antitobacco influences of peers and parents. *American Journal of Community Psychology, 24*(3), 311–340.

Burton, L., Obeidallah, D., & Allison, K. (1996). Ethnographic insights on social context and adolescent development among inner-city African American teens. In R. Jessor, A. Colby, & R. Shweder (Eds.), *Ethnography and human development* (pp. 395–418). Chicago: University of Chicago Press.

Burton, L., Price-Spratlen, T., & Spencer, M. (in press). On ways of thinking about and measuring neighborhoods: Implications for studying context and developmental outcomes for children. In G. Duncan, J. Brooks-Gunn, & J. L. Aber (Eds.), *Neighborhood poverty: Context and consequences for children.* New York: Russell Sage.

Duck, S. (Ed.). (1997). *Handbook of personal relationships.* Chichester, UK: Wiley.

Fairweather, G. W., & Davidson, W. S. (1986). *An introduction to community experimentation: Theory, methods, and practice.* New York: McGraw-Hill.

Muñoz, R. F., Snowden, L. R., & Kelly, J. G. (1979). *Social and psychological research in community settings.* San Francisco: Jossey-Bass.

Portes, A., & Rumbaut, R. G. (1990). *Immigrant America.* Berkeley: University of California Press.

Rothman, J. (1974). *Planning and organizing for social change.* New York: Columbia University Press.

Serrano-Garcia, I., & Bond, M. A. (1994). (Eds.). Empowering the silent ranks. *American Journal of Community Psychology, 22(4),* 443–592.

Stack, C. B. (1972). *All our kin.* New York: Harper & Row.

Swartz, J. L., & Martin, W. E. (Eds.). (1997). *Applied ecological psychology for schools within communities.* Mahwah, NJ: Erlbaum.

Warren, R. L. (1977). *The community in America.* Chicago: Rand-McNally.

Westermeyer, J. (1989). *Mental health for refugees and other immigrants.* Springfield, IL: Thomas.

Edison J. Trickett

COMMUNITY PREVENTION AND INTERVENTION.

[*This entry comprises four articles*:

    Prevention with Young Children
    Prevention with School-Aged Children
    Prevention with Adults
    Prevention of Depression

For discussions related to community prevention and intervention, see Community Psychology; Intervention; *and* Prevention.]

Prevention with Young Children

Early childhood programs in the United States have emphasized the promotion of healthy development and prevention of development difficulties since their inception. Whether in government efforts early in the twentieth century to enhance children's welfare, such as the federal Children's Bureau, or in later initiatives such as the federal Head Start program, the goals of early childhood intervention have often been preventive. Large-scale early childhood intervention in the United States began with lofty hopes on the part of policy makers and some researchers regarding the scope and duration

of preventive benefits. The Head Start program, a comprehensive early childhood program targeted to low-income families, was begun in 1965 by Lyndon Johnson and members of his cabinet with the hopes of inoculating young children against all the developmental risks of poverty (Edward Zigler and Susan Muenchow, *Head Start: The Inside Story of America's Most Successful Educational Experiment,* New York, 1992). It was expected that a six-week summer program would result in a lifetime of gains among recipients in the form of increased IQ scores, school achievement, and contributions to society.

In the 1990s, such grandiose hopes have been tempered. Results of early childhood programs have rarely reached the sometimes outrageous claims of policy makers. At the same time, recognition has grown that early childhood is a crucial point in child development and a promising period for preventive intervention. Both basic developmental and intervention evaluation research show that neurological, cognitive, and social development are profoundly influenced by external environments in the first years of life. The promise of the period for intervention rests in the fact that such plasticity of development occurs at a time when children are still limited to relatively few settings (primarily home and child care or preschool), and have not begun to select their environments.

The critical questions for current development and design of interventions in infancy and early childhood include questions of outcome, focus of intervention, timing and duration, quality, and populations served. These issues will be discussed in turn.

Outcome

Most practitioners and researchers in the field of early childhood intervention would agree that the goals of such programs encompass multiple areas, including physical health and cognitive and socioemotional development. Unfortunately, research to date has not yet included the full spectrum of developmental outcomes that early childhood programs may affect. Current data show that children in poverty who attend quality early childhood education programs do go on to show higher levels of cognitive ability and school achievement in middle childhood, relative to their peers who do not, although gains may fade if enriching environments are not provided in middle and later childhood. There are, in addition, data from several demonstration programs combining early education with intensive family support that show effects in later childhood in the prevention of antisocial behavior. However, research examining the effects of early childhood intervention on social competence is still scant.

A preventive focus on reducing the impact of risk processes and strengthening protective ones that may mediate effects of early childhood programs has been adopted only recently by practitioners and researchers. Such a shift in focus requires two levels of conceptualization of outcomes: short-term or mediating outcomes, and long-term outcomes (P. J. Mrazek and R. J. Haggerty, *Reducing Risks for Mental Disorders: Frontiers for Preventive Intervention Research*, Washington, DC, 1994, and National Institute of Mental Health, *The Prevention of Mental Disorders: A National Research Agenda*, Washington, DC, 1993). For example, potential mediators of effects of early childhood programs on cognitive outcomes include parental life-course factors such as level of education or employment, or changes in aspects of the home environment such as opportunities for cognitive enrichment or parenting practices. Potential mediators of effects on socioemotional outcomes include changes in parenting practices, the parental life-course factors mentioned previously, emotion regulation, attachment style, peer-based competence, and changes in cognitive ability in the child. The assessment of mediating outcomes will continue to grow in importance as researchers in the field increasingly evaluate how, not just whether, early childhood programs can achieve long-term effects.

Focus of Intervention

The focus of intervention in infancy and early childhood has varied. Interventions can be categorized broadly as parent-focused, child-focused, and combination programs. Some aim primarily to change factors in the parent-infant or parent-child relationship. These interventions encompass such strategies as home visiting or center-based services for parents and infants. One promising approach is that of beginning nurse home visiting and family support services in the prenatal period and continuing through infancy, among first-time parents; recent evaluations suggest that such services may reduce rates of subsequent pregnancies and of injuries in infancy. Such an approach has shown promise in the prevention of child maltreatment and parent criminal behavior, as well as the reduction of welfare use.

Other programs focus primarily on child cognitive development, with less involvement of parents. One such high-quality program (the Abecedarian Project) has documented long-lasting benefits in the areas of reading and math achievement and reduced assignment to special education or grade retention, seven to ten years postintervention. A project gathering long-term follow-up data from multiple programs (mostly demonstration projects) revealed similar results (the Consortium for Longitudinal Studies).

Some programs combine child-focused educational enrichment with intensive family support services such as home visits or efforts to help parents work or further their schooling. Demonstration projects of this combination type have been promising in their ability to af-fect a range of child and family mediators in the areas of cognitive ability, parenting factors, and the parental life course. Such two-generation programs, providing services to multiple generations in a family, are an important strategy in integrating child development with economic self-sufficiency goals.

The focus of early childhood intervention thus far has been limited to the child and the family. Little attention has been paid to how goals of these programs do or do not coincide with community- or state-wide programs or policies affecting young children and families, such as neighborhood economic development or revitalization, welfare reform, managed health care, or community-wide prevention initiatives. Studies finding that neighborhood-level factors such as poverty can harm early childhood development suggest the value of exploring program effects in their wider neighborhood and policy contexts. Similarly, current prevention science notes the importance of both distal and proximal risk and protective processes in informing the development of interventions. Distal processes may include community-level economic and social processes, which should not be considered outside the purview of early childhood programs and policy. Some efforts have been made to link early childhood programs with welfare reform policies. Many questions remain, however, regarding how to integrate the two levels of intervention at local or state levels, including issues of integration of developmental with self-sufficiency goals, targeting of intensive services, adequacy of staff training, and relevance to diverse populations.

Timing and Duration

Issues of timing and duration are critical in the design of early intervention programs. Reviews of the home-visiting literature have found that quality programs began in the prenatal period and continued through the second year. Reviews of early childhood programs with effects on risks for antisocial behavior and delinquency have found that the more effective programs had in common a length of at least two years, and varied in time span across infancy and early childhood. Most researchers now consider the middle and later childhood years to be crucial to the long-term success of graduates of early childhood programs. Research on the potential of interventions in elementary school to bolster effects of early childhood programs and maintain family support services has begun, most notably through models of colocating multiple services in school settings and improving school administrative and decision-making practices.

Quality

There has been increased recognition in recent years that program quality is perhaps the most important mediator of early childhood program effects. This recognition emerged from findings that large-scale projects often do not obtain the impressive preventive results of demonstration projects, and from research demonstrating the importance of quality in child-care settings. For example, Head Start programs, based on a comprehensive model of services encompassing health, mental health, nutrition, parent involvement, and early education, have struggled to maintain quality while coping with enrollment expansion and increases in poverty-related risks among their families. Important dimensions of program quality, which have only begun to be assessed in infancy and early childhood program evaluations, include staff training, skills and compensation, staff practices, curriculum characteristics, and the degree and nature of community collaborations with other service providers in the fields of health, mental health, and child welfare.

Populations Served

Early intervention approaches have been found effective with groups varying in their definition and in their degree of risk for developmental problems. Many programs have served families at risk by virtue of being in poverty; others have served groups such as families with low-birth-weight infants or infants and children with mental retardation, Down syndrome, or other disabilities. Many of these interventions have blended clinical services and psychoeducation with more general family support services. Little information exists, however, regarding whether early intervention services are more effective for subgroups at higher risk or those at lower risk. Several rigorously evaluated programs found that their effects on children and parents were particularly strong for the higher-risk families. However, one recent large-scale program targeted to families with low-birth-weight infants (the Infant Health and Development Program) found that its positive developmental effects were stronger for the higher-birth-weight (lower-risk) infants.

Although quality early intervention programs share a sensitivity to the individual needs of their families, few have been tailored to the particular needs of racial/ethnic minority populations. The effects of culturally relevant factors, such as intervention practices tailored to a particular ethnic group, have only begun to be explored in the literature. The challenges of working with parents from multiple backgrounds speaking a variety of native languages have become increasingly clear as recent waves of immigration to the United States affect Head Start and other early childhood programs. Staff support strategies to address the needs of these populations, while widespread, have not been evaluated systematically in relation to staff, family, or child outcomes. In addition, the question of whether effects found in demonstration-project programs can be replicated when the programs expand to other populations has only begun to be explored.

Early childhood intervention has now had a rich history, stretching back to the beginning of the twentieth century. Future directions for the field as a prevention science include the following. How should programs address risk and protective processes at multiple levels, whether distal or proximal, family- or community-based, common to many outcomes or specific to one? How can early childhood interventions best be tailored to the varying needs of groups from differing cultural backgrounds? Can programs increase their preventive potential by targeting children at particularly high risk for developmental problems with enriched services? How can programs in infancy and early childhood dovetail with policy-level interventions such as welfare reform or changes in managed health care? And finally, how can long-term effects of early childhood programs be maximized through effects on short-term risk and protective processes, and through enrichment of environments—schools and neighborhoods—important in later development? Through attention to questions such as these, infancy and early childhood intervention as a preventive enterprise will continue to grow to meet the changing needs of families in the twenty-first century.

Bibliography

Campbell, F. A., & Ramey, C. T. (1995). Cognitive and school outcomes for high-risk African-American students at middle adolescence: Positive effects of early intervention. *American Educational Research Journal, 32,* 743–772.

Gomby, D. S., Larner, M. B., Stevenson, C. S., Lewit, E. M., & Behrman, R. E. (Eds.). (1995). Long-term outcomes of early childhood programs. *The Future of Children, 5(3)* (Special Issue).

Guralnick, M. J. (Ed.). (1997). *The effectiveness of early intervention.* Baltimore: Paul H. Brookes.

Lazar, I., Darlington, R., Murray, H., Royce, J., & Snipper, A. (1982). Lasting effects of early education. *Monographs of the Society for Research in Child Development, 47* (1–2, Serial No. 194). Chicago: University of Chicago Press.

McCarton, C. M., Brooks-Gunn, J., Wallace, I. F., Bauer, C. R., Bennett, F. C., Bernbaum, J. C., Broyles, S., Casey, P. H., McCormick, M. C., Scott, D. T., Tyson, J., Tonascia, J., Meinert, C. L. (1997). Results at age 8 years of early intervention for low-birth-weight premature infants. *Journal of the American Medical Association, 277,* 126–132.

Olds, D. L., Eckenrode, J., Henderson, C. R., Kitzman, H., Powers, J., Cole, R., Sidora, K., Morris, P., Pettitt, L. M., & Luckey, D. (1997). Long-term effects of home visitation on maternal life course and child abuse and neglect. *Journal of the American Medical Association, 278,* 637–643.

Olds, D. L., & Kitzman, H. (1993). Review of research on home visiting for pregnant women and parents of young children. *The Future of Children, 3(3),* 53–92.

Schweinhart, L. J., Barnes, H. V., & Weikart, D. P. (Eds.). (1993). *Significant benefits: The High/Scope Perry Preschool study through age 27.*

Seitz, V. (1990). Intervention programs for impoverished children: A comparison of educational and family-support models. *Annals of Child Development, 7,* 73–103.

Smith, S. (Ed.). (1995). *Two-generation programs for families in poverty: A new intervention strategy.* Norwood, NJ: Ablex.

Yoshikawa, H. (1994). Prevention as cumulative protection: Effects of early education and family support on chronic delinquency and its risks. *Psychological Bulletin, 115,* 28–54.

Zigler, E., & Styfco. S. (Eds.). (1993). *Head Start and beyond: A national plan for extended childhood intervention.* New Haven: Yale University Press.

Hirokazu Yoshikawa

Prevention with School-Aged Children

The central goal of primary prevention is to reduce the number and the prevalence of people affected by a disorder or unwanted occurrence, while the goal of promotion is to increase adaptive processes and outcomes. Both primary prevention and promotion programs are targeted to whole populations or settings. Early treatment programs, by contrast, target and intervene with individuals believed to be at high risk because they are already showing early signs of dysfunction; the goal is to short-circuit the dysfunctional processes that are underway in an effort to reduce their negative consequences for the individual. Regardless of the kind of intervention (prevention, promotion, or early treatment) or target (population, setting, or individual), too often the locus of responsibility for change remains with the individual. Intervention strategies in which the environment or the connections between the individual and the environment represent the target of change are far less common, yet they offer greater promise for realizing the goals of prevention and promotion.

In the last few decades, early treatment and prevention efforts among school-aged youths have focused on the prevention of a wide variety of negative outcomes including school failure, pregnancy, sexually transmitted diseases (STDs), delinquency, violence, drug use, mental illness, and suicide. Promotion efforts have focused on academic achievement, self-esteem, identity development, and empowerment. This article provides an overview and evidence of the effectiveness of early treatment and preventive, promotive interventions with

school-aged children and youths where the loci of change are in the individual, the environment, and the intersection between the two.

Early treatment or secondary prevention programs are the subject of a major debate in the field over whether they are really "preventive" since they are administered after the onset of the problems they aim to prevent. Many of these interventions target children who display early aggressive behavior, which has been linked to a trajectory of increasingly antisocial activities such as delinquency, drug use, and violence during adolescence and adulthood. For a small subset of the children, research has demonstrated that aggressive behavior patterns are stable and may be crystallized at an early age. School-based interventions attempt to identify aggressive children early and alter their developmental course. Often, aggressive children are taken out of class for special counseling sessions with mental health or para-professional staff trained to provide security, acceptance, and realistic limits. Evaluations have demonstrated improvements in school adjustment among children who have received these services.

Another approach to treatment of aggressive children is based on social cognitive research that highlights deficits in the social competence, problem-solving, and coping skills of aggressive children. After being screened, aggressive or disruptive children attend a series of curriculum-based training sessions in which they participate in structured discussions and interactive exercises to learn skills in self-control, perspective taking, resistance to peer pressure, cooperative work, critical thinking, and social problem-solving. Some programs also target parenting skills such as monitoring and discipline through an additional series of training sessions just for parents of disruptive children. Evaluation results have been mixed. They have documented improvements in the areas of teacher rated aggression, substance use, self-esteem, and problem-solving skills, but long-term effects were found only with longer intervention (over two years) and with the inclusion of parent training. Unfortunately, negative peer influences have been a problem with programs that bring together noncompliant youths. In one youth-centered program, participants ultimately reported more substance use than controls.

These early detection and intervention programs identify and single-out individual children as the problem, even when they are treated in a group context. Thus, these programs identify the child as both the source of the problem and the agent or locus of change. In this way, teachers, peers, and parents are likely to label the child perjoratively. The child in question may self-identify in the same way. In the long run, such iatrogenic effects can prove costly.

Interventions focusing on parenting skills and/or

parent-teacher communication to influence the contingencies associated with aggressive behavior have been more successful. In these interventions parents of aggressive children (referred by teachers or counselors) are trained to use specific parenting skills. Evaluations have demonstrated that parents of high-risk youths can be recruited successfully into interventions that offer parenting resources, resulting in significant improvements in family dynamics and problem behavior at school, as compared to youths randomly assigned to a no-treatment condition.

Person-centered prevention and promotion strategies of intervention do not single out individual children for treatment, but the locus of change still resides within the individual. The most popular form of prevention programs inoculate groups of children by providing them with skills, resources, and know-how to cope with future stresses, strains, and interpersonal encounters that might lead to future adjustment problems. Similar strategies are used in promotion interventions but instead they aim to enhance individual development. Many person-centered programs contain elements of both inoculation and enhancement. In these programs, recipients are less likely than in early treatment to feel blamed since everyone is receiving the intervention.

Inoculation and enhancement programs are often administered to entire classrooms as part of the educational curriculum by teachers, human service professionals, or trained volunteers. These curricula often focus on the development of social problem-solving and social competency skills, while other programs are based on principles of self-efficacy, attribution, and motivation and focus on teaching adolescents a sense of personal control and confidence about the future so that they can make better decisions and ultimately become better citizens. Staff members throughout the school are encouraged to integrate these skills into all school activities. Posters about problem-solving strategies are placed in halls. Some interventions include training for parents and community members about supporting the development of social competence in children through the use of modeling and facilitative questions. Evaluations of cognitive training interventions demonstrate consistent short-term gains in terms of problem-solving, peer relations, and social behavior. Many programs also include booster sessions in subsequent years. Effects tend to be stronger and last longer when the interventions are administered over several years.

A variant of this approach targets subpopulations of young people that are exposed to risky situations such as the death of a parent or transition into a new school. Often these programs include a focus on the application of skills in specific domains, such as resisting substance use, sex, and other health compromising behaviors, or coping with parental death or divorce. For example, substance use prevention programs include sessions that address drug-related expectancies and resistance skills regarding social influence to use drugs. Inoculation programs that target children of divorce combine cognitive skills training with the opportunity to share experiences, establish common bonds, and clarify misconceptions such as self-blame for parental divorce in a supportive group environment.

Setting-level prevention and promotion strategies of intervention focus on the dynamic patterns of social transactions (regularities) or norms as the target and locus of change within settings, such as family, school or neighborhood. A family-focused approach to prevention for populations of children who experience divorce or the death of a parent is to modify the family environment. The central component of these programs is a series of family meetings with a trained advisor who focuses upon the development and use of specific relationship skills. Controlled evaluations with random assignments yield ratings of better family relationships, communication, and discipline and lower levels of negative life events, conduct disorder, and depression for program participants than controls. Results indicated that family environment variables partly mediated the effects on mental health.

School-based interventions attempt to modify the social regularities or norms of entire classrooms, schools, or the relationships between schools and the surrounding community. To modify the social adaptational processes of classrooms, the Good Behavior Game, a team-based behavior management strategy facilitated by teachers in which classmates administer reinforcements, has been employed. When this intervention was administered to first-grade classes, improved behavior was observed relative to controls in first grade, across school transitions, and in sixth grade for males who were aggressive in first grade.

The School Transitional Environment Project (STEP) is an excellent example of a program focused upon reducing the flux in the transition to senior high school. Youth making the transition to an inner city high school were randomly assigned to either a small learning environment in one section of the school or the normal school curriculum. These students moved through all their primary classes (e.g., English, math) as a single unit and one adult was assigned to each child as a counselor. Thus, STEP students and teachers experience dramatically different social regularities. The long-term findings were impressive: 76% of the STEP youth versus only 57% of the control youth remained in school by the twelfth grade.

In the School Development Program, governance teams consisting of the principal, teachers, parents, and mental health experts are created to establish policy guidelines, carry out systematic planning, implement programs and evaluations, and work with parent groups to address curriculum, social climate, and staff development in the school. Concrete roles are created for parents in the day-to-day functioning and governance of the school. Parent engagement in conjunction with curriculum and staff development alter social norms, communicate positive expectations for low achieving students, engage students, and can improve the quality of education.

Community norms per se have been the focus of some prevention programs. One such intervention focused on the prevention of teenage smoking by targeting the actions of the cigarette sellers. As change agents, both young people and adults in the community, organized to successfully mobilize good publicity for clerks who refused to sell cigarettes to adolescents. Evaluations demonstrated reductions in tobacco sales to minors, relative to comparison communities, but these studies neglected to measure changes in teen smoking rates.

Cross-level prevention and promotion strategies of intervention attempt to modify the roles of young people within our communities; as such, they represent a promising trend. By changing youths' primary roles from service recipients to active involvement and leadership in prevention activities, such programs move beyond a purely person-centered approach and target the patterns of role relationships between the individual youths and their communities.

For example, the Teen Outreach Program (sponsored by the Association of Junior Leagues) links volunteer work in the community to classroom-based discussion on issues such as human development and decision making; some program sites also incorporate a series of discussions on sex and pregnancy prevention. Evaluations consistently demonstrate reductions in participants' pregnancy, school failure, and dropout rates by as much as 50% compared to randomly assigned comparison groups. Yet the most important element of this program is the volunteer service component; success was not related to how many of the curriculum-based components were implemented. Similarly, sites that provided youths with real choices in the type of volunteer service were the most successful. Developmentally, this program was less successful with junior high school students, perhaps because opportunities for meaningful volunteer roles in the community are less available for younger adolescents. Moreover, sites that provided youths with the greatest amounts of both autonomy and relatedness were the most successful.

Rites-of-passage programs also target the role of individual youths within the community and are typically offered during the transition from elementary to junior high school. These programs view ecological transitions as developmental opportunities rather than merely risky periods; thus, their goals are to promote health and enhance personal and cultural development rather than to prevent dysfunctional outcomes. Youths participate in a series of discussion sessions in which they consider ceremonial rites of passage and what it means to become an adult, while community members and school staff facilitate a process of youths' increasing participation in community services and activities. Central to these programs are community boards that identify key elements of the program and guide the process of integrating youths into their community in meaningful roles. The community becomes the change agent, and the loci of change include linkages between systems and the social regularities of how the community transacts with adolescents. A strength of these programs is that they can be tailor made by each community and thus move beyond cultural sensitivity to become culturally derived. For example, one such program, targeting African American adolescents, was based on the seven African principles of Nguzo Saba (e.g., Umoja—unity with the African people, Nia—purpose). Evaluations of one rites-of-passage program found improvements for participating students in the areas of family involvement, attachment to school, substance use, and delinquent activity relative to controls.

In sum, the fields of early treatment, prevention, and promotion are continuing to evolve. In assessing the efficacy or appropriateness of any given program one must pay close attention to the goals and targets of the intervention (what the program is supposed to accomplish and for whom) as well as the locus of responsibility for change (who or what must change for the program to achieve its desired outcomes). Setting- and cross-level interventions are rare and require careful collaboration between professionals and community members, but they are also more consistent with the goals of prevention and promotion compared to more individually oriented early treatment approaches.

Bibliography

Albee, G. W., & Gullota, T. P. (Eds.). (1997). *Primary prevention works.* Thousand Oaks, CA: Sage.

Cowen, E. L. (1994). The enhancement of psychological wellness: Challenges and opportunities. *American Journal of Community Psychology, 22,* 149–179.

Durlak, J. A., & Wells, A. M. (1997). Primary prevention mental health programs for children and adolescents: A meta-analytic review. *American Journal of Community Psychology, 25,* 115–152.

Felner, R. D., Felner, T. W., & Silverman, M. M. (2000). Prevention in mental health and social intervention: Conceptual and methodological issues in the evolution of the science and practice of prevention. In J. Rappaport & E. Seidman (Eds.), *Handbook of community psychology.* New York: Plenum Kluwer.

Peters, R. D., & McMahon, R. J. (Eds.). (1996). *Preventing childhood disorders, substance abuse, and delinquency.* Thousand Oaks, CA: Sage.

Edward Seidman and Daniel Chesir-Teran

Prevention with Adults

It is often thought that prevention efforts should be devoted primarily to children and adolescents, and that little preventive activity is possible for adults or the elderly. But development and change continue throughout the entire life course, although the nature of risk and protective factors changes in adulthood in a number of important ways. As the individual enters adulthood, new developmental tasks emerge revolving around family and work. Although not all adults choose all these roles, for most, establishing and maintaining committed relationships, engaging in effective parenting, and assuming occupational roles become essential to ensuring their own well-being as well as those of others. Work becomes important not only because paid employment provides material resources, but also because work can be a potent source of psychological satisfaction or distress. For some adults, the stress of financial hardship can become a critical threat to both physical and psychological well-being.

Adulthood is also a time of both planned and unplanned life transitions. Adult individuals and their families will face a number of predictable transitions, such as the transitions into working life, into marriage, or bearing children. Unplanned transitions and crises can also present significant stresses and become risk factors in adulthood. Marital conflict and divorce, unplanned childbearing without adequate support, involuntary job loss, unexpected illness, or chronic poverty can all be major risk factors in adulthood.

Both planned and unplanned transitions in adulthood present opportunities for prevention, and the systematic provision of protective support is the essence of prevention for adults. A good deal is known about protective factors that can aid adults and their families to cope with both planned and unplanned transitions. These protective factors can be found in neighborhoods and communities, such as emotional and material support from friends and family, or responsive human and medical services. Protective factors can also take the form of individual skills. For example, well-developed problem-solving skills, the ability to regulate ones emotions, cope with the demands of work, and mobilize the support from others can all help safeguard health and mental health. Prevention in adulthood is directed both at helping people to cope with the planned and unplanned transitions of adulthood, and at strengthening protective factors that provide resilience and viability through the life course.

Prevention Efforts Directed at Life Transitions in Adulthood

Marriage and committed relationships represent a major source of either protection or risk for the well-being of both adults and children. Marital distress and destructive conflict in marriage are major risk factors for a wide variety of psychological, physical, and interpersonal problems. The stress of divorce is strongly associated with higher rates of depression in adults, and conflict among spouses and partners has effects not only on members of the relationship, but also on other family members, children in particular. At its most extreme, marital conflict can result in spouse abuse or child abuse that can have enduring and severe consequences for both children and adults.

Unfortunately, not all individuals enter into a committed relationship or a marriage equipped to establish a bond of mutual support that will produce a nurturing setting for child and adult development. However, couples who are planning marriage or a committed relationship, or even those who are already married, could benefit from a prevention program intended to enhance relationships of couples. One such program teaches couples skills that have been identified by research as predicting satisfying and healthy relationships. Couples are also taught how to change behaviors that predict later marital distress, and skills for constructively handling disagreements. Research suggests that couples who go through the program and practice the communication skills they learn are much more satisfied with their relationship and have fewer relationship problems as much as five years later.

Not all marriages will thrive, however, and marital separation and divorce produce effects on both health and mental health. People who experience marital separation have been shown to have much higher levels of distress, anxiety, and depression as well as higher rates of admission to psychiatric facilities. One successful prevention program has been developed to teach people experiencing marital separation and divorce how to cope with the challenges that emerge. The program teaches people how to strengthen their own support systems, deal with single parenting, cope with legal and financial issues, housing, and homemaking problems, as well as occupational and educational challenges. The program has been shown to be effective in preventing problems of adjustment and a variety of separation related problems as well as preventing mental health problems for as long as four years after participating in the program.

Unplanned childbearing represents another adult life transition that can place both mother and child at risk. Young pregnant mothers, especially if they are unmarried, face the challenges of childbearing, as well as the challenges of their own personal development, including interrupted education and the need for paid employment. One prenatal and early infancy project used visiting public health nurses to form supportive relationships with young mothers by emphasizing their personal strengths. Nurses helped young women find job placement services, plan for child care, and advised them about job interviews and methods of family planning. This supportive service had positive effects on the likelihood of mothers being employed. They were less likely to be on public assistance in the short term. The program also improved a number of developmental outcomes for the infants.

In adulthood, involuntary job loss can become a major crisis. There is clear evidence that unemployment can increase the risk of anxiety and depression, family conflict, and substance abuse in vulnerable individuals and families. Furthermore, job loss often produces discouragement, lowered motivation, and prolonged unemployment, adding to the stress and risks in the family. Effective job-seeking skills and strong social support in the job-seeking process are crucial to negotiating the transition back into the labor market. One preventive program that not only teaches job search skills, but also how to cope with setbacks in a supportive atmosphere has been shown to be successful in improving reemployment rates, reducing economic hardship, and reducing the risk of depression.

Illness represents still another crisis that can put families at risk. When elderly parents develop illnesses and need intensive care, the burden of caregiving often falls on other family members, particularly female family members. These burdens often occur when adults in the family are still caring for their own growing children, and are also coping with the demands of working life. Preventive interventions aimed at helping adult caregivers deal effectively with these challenges can have beneficial effects on caregivers' capacity to cope and on their well-being. Typically programs to support caregivers teach a variety of problem-solving skills and increase their capacity to reach out to a variety of different sources of support in the community. These programs help caregivers learn to gain access to needed community services to increase their formal and informal support in the community, and help them gain skills in maintaining family and interpersonal relationships that often show substantial strain in dealing with the demanding tasks of caregiving.

Toward the end of life, older family members may experience the crisis of death of a spouse and bereavement. Many people experiencing loss of a spouse and widowhood are at increased risk for health and mental health problems. However, mutual help groups that aid widowed persons in coping with bereavement and loss have been shown to be effective at improving the mental health of widows.

Prevention Directed at Strengthening Protective Factors in Adulthood

Not all prevention efforts for adults are necessarily focused on planned or unplanned life transitions or crises. Some prevention programs are aimed at strengthening behaviors that reduce the risk of health and mental health problems of individuals and even whole communities. Such risk reduction efforts can help adults reduce health-compromising behavior such as alcohol abuse, reduce risks associated with cardiovascular disease, and even improve skills at managing their own mood and mental health.

Disorders of alcohol use present a substantial public health problem, and adults with drinking problems are at substantially increased risk of premature death from liver disease, cancer, and heart disease. Some estimates place the cost of alcohol-related deaths in the United States at 75 billion dollars a year. A program delivered in community-based primary care clinics provided physician advice on reducing alcohol use, and was aimed at reducing use of health care in problem drinkers. The intervention provided patients with a workbook that reviewed current health behaviors, a list of adverse effects of alcohol, and a brief visit with a physician followed by a follow-up call by a clinic nurse. Physicians engaged in behavioral contracting and education with problem drinkers and were able to help them to learn self-control techniques that reduced binge drinking and other forms of excessive drinking up to one year after participation in the program.

Over the past century, we have been able to reduce the risk of a wide range of acute infectious diseases. Yet much of the industrialized world remains at high risk for a variety of chronic diseases, particularly cardiovascular diseases. The health behaviors that are needed to reduce cardiovascular risk are well known and include exercise, smoking cessation, and dietary changes. Some prevention researchers have conducted education and behavior change programs for whole communities to stimulate and maintain changes in life style. These changes would result in a community-wide reduction in the risk of cardiovascular disease. One such program aimed at reducing obesity and hypertension, improving exercise and nutrition, and reducing smoking. The effort included a wide range of activities including the social marketing of health programs, community organization efforts, and a mass media campaign. When these community-wide efforts were supplemented with face-to-face efforts to teach better health habits, behavioral and physiological indicators of cardiovascular risk were reduced for the whole community.

Muñoz and his colleagues screened primary care low-income medical patients to identify people who showed elevated levels of depression, but who were not yet clinically depressed. These individuals were invited to participate in a course involving cognitive and behavioral methods to improve mood management to gain greater control over their moods. The course taught people about the nature of depression and how thoughts, activities, and personal interactions can influence people's moods. They were also taught how to identify and change behaviors that can have strong impact on negative moods. As a result of the course, participants became less pessimistic, had more positive and fewer negative self-punishing thoughts, and developed the ability to engage in social activities that were more likely to produce positive mood and affect, all of which led to reductions in depressive symptoms.

Bibliography

Albee, G. W., & Gullotta, T. P. (Eds.). (1977). *Primary prevention works, Vol. 6.* Thousand Oaks: Sage. A recent collection of effective prevention programs.

Heller, K. (1996). Coming of age of prevention science: Comments on the 1994 National Institute of Mental Health-Institute of Medicine prevention papers. *American Psychologist, 51,* 1123–1128. Historical and policy analysis of the IOM and NIMH reports.

Mrazek, P. J., & Haggerty, R. J. (Eds.). (1994). *Reducing risks for mental disorders: Frontiers for preventive intervention research.* Washington, DC: National Academy Press. A comprehensive review of conceptual, research, and policy issues on prevention compiled by the Institute of Medicine, National Academy of Sciences.

Price, R. H., Cowen, E., Lorion, R., & Ramos-McKay, J. (Eds.). (1988). *Fourteen ounces of prevention.* Washington, DC: American Psychological Association. A collection of model prevention programs spanning the life course.

Richard H. Price

Prevention of Depression

Treatment efforts will not significantly reduce the number of cases of highly prevalent mental disorders such as major depression because treating individuals already afflicted with the disorder does not reduce the large number of new cases. The only realistic solution to the massive impact of such disorders in our society is preventing their onset. Community psychologists such as Albee and Gullotta (1997), have argued that we must go beyond interventions limited to treatment of existing cases, which can only reduce prevalence (the total number of cases in a population). We must also implement community-based interventions to reduce incidence (the number of new cases). This article presents the arguments upon which this recommen-

dation has been based, definitional issues highlighting the differences between prevention versus treatment interventions, why depressive symptoms are a major public health problem that reach far beyond major depressive disorders themselves, the conceptual bases for community-oriented prevention approaches, and examples of community interventions that have been shown to reduce depressive symptoms in populations at risk and that are being studied to determine whether they can prevent new episodes of major depression.

The Massive Impact of Major Depression on Our Communities

Of all physical and mental disorders affecting humanity, major depression causes by far the greatest amount of disability. The World Health Organization, in a study authored by Christopher J. L. Murray and Alan D. Lopez (*The Global Burden of Disease*, Boston, 1996) reports that unipolar major depression causes 10.7% of the world's disability, more than twice the proportion (4.7%) caused by the second leading cause of disability, iron-deficiency anemia. The same report uses a measure called Disability-Adjusted Life Years (DALYs), which takes into account both disability and premature death, to estimate the relative rank of the top causes of disease burden in 1990 and 2020. In 1990, unipolar major depression was the fourth-ranked cause of disease burden worldwide, and by 2020, it is estimated to become the second-ranked, just behind ischemic heart disease.

Although major depression is not usually as severe in its consequences to the individual sufferer as, say, schizophrenia or bipolar illness, its impact on society is pervasive. Whereas schizophrenia and bipolar illness each affect about 1% of the population, unipolar major depression affects over 20% of women and 12% of men. Moreover, epidemiological studies suggest that the prevalence of major depression has been steadily increasing since the middle of the twentieth century.

During the 1900s, major advances have taken place in two key areas in the mental health field: diagnosis and treatment. However, there has been relatively little systematic attention paid to a third key area: the prevention of mental disorders. Breakthroughs in this area await the work of twenty-first century researchers and practitioners.

Why Prevention Approaches Are Crucial in the Case of Major Depression

The epidemiology of depression strongly indicates that treatment alone is unlikely to result in a reduction in its prevalence. The National Comorbidity Survey, conducted by Ronald Kessler and colleagues (*Archives of General Psychiatry*, 1994, 51, 8–19), found that 17% of adults in the United States of America suffer from at least one episode of major depression during their lives. The Epidemiological Catchment Area Project (*Psychiatric Disorders in America*, New York, 1991) found that the majority of those with major depression do not receive mental health care. For several reasons, including lack of information about depression, the continuing role of stigma toward mental disorders, and a commonly held bias that mental disorders are somehow not as "real" as physical illnesses, only about 20% of individuals who meet criteria for major depression actually receive mental health treatment in the United States. Most individuals with major depression do visit their primary care providers when they have symptoms of depression. Unfortunately, even when individuals seek health care, major depression is recognized in only a third to a half of cases. Once recognized, not all those afflicted obtain treatment, and of those who do obtain treatment, many are inadequately treated.

Treatment approaches for depression have shown remarkable advances over the last half of the twentieth century. Pharmacological and psychotherapeutic approaches focused on major depression yield improvement rates between 50 and 80%. Nevertheless, rates of recurrence are very high. The Agency for Health Care Policy and Research, in its *Clinical Practice Guideline for Depression in Primary Care* (Rockville, MD, 1993) stated that once a person developed one major depressive episode, the likelihood of having a second episode was 50%, after two, the likelihood of a third was 70%, and, after three the likelihood of another was 90%. These figures are generally cited to highlight the need for vigorous efforts to identify and treat each episode, given the chronic nature of the disorder. From a community-oriented, preventive perspective, however, these figures strongly suggest the need to prevent the first episode.

Prevention, Treatment, and Maintenance

In 1994, the Institute of Medicine of the United States of America released *Reducing Risks for Mental Disorders: Frontiers for Preventive Intervention Research* (Washington, DC). This influential document redefined the scope of preventive interventions because the earlier terminology of primary, secondary, and tertiary prevention did not sufficiently discriminate between treatment efforts and prevention. For example, secondary prevention includes early case finding and provision of treatment. The report suggested instead that the initial onset of the disorder in question be the line of demarcation between prevention and treatment. Interventions provided prior to first onset of the disorder to reduce the likelihood of its occurrence were termed prevention. Therapeutic interventions provided after the disorder is

present were categorized as treatment. Finally, interventions provided to reduce relapse or recurrence of the disorder or to rehabilitate the individual were termed maintenance.

Preventive interventions were themselves divided into three levels: universal, selective, and indicated. Universal preventive interventions are targeted to whole populations. These might include mass media presentations focused on mood management, prenatal care, and school-based interventions made available to all children, designed, for example, to help them master reading and to increase their interpersonal self-efficacy. Selective preventive interventions are targeted to subgroups in the population considered to be at higher risk than average, such as children in poor neighborhoods, elderly widows, recent immigrants, recently unemployed persons, or primary care patients actively seeking medical help. Indicated preventive interventions are targeted to those at high risk because of biological, psychological, or other factors that signal individual vulnerability to mental disorders. For example, individuals scoring high on depressive symptom scales may have problems in emotion regulation which, if they increase in duration and severity, could eventually meet criteria for a major depressive episode. Teaching them mood management skills may reduce the proportion who develop a full-blown major depressive episode.

Preventive interventions are thus most likely to occur outside of mental health offices. By their nature, they involve a community outreach component. The issue of access is crucial in prevention: universal interventions must be interesting and acceptable to the public at large, selective interventions must gain access to the higher risk subgroups, and indicated interventions require that individuals develop enough trust in the providers to allow themselves to be screened and to accept the interventions offered. The major goals of these efforts is averting exacerbation of symptoms in order to reduce the rate of onset of major depressive episodes. This contrasts with depression treatment approaches, in which the individual generally seeks or is brought in for treatment, and the therapist attempts to reduce symptoms to below clinical levels and return the patient to a normal mood state.

Delineating Differences Between Prevention and Treatment Approaches to Depression

Traditional treatment efforts focus on individuals who either come or are brought to clinical facilities because of frank disruption in their ability to function. Treatment is provided at either private offices or public sector clinics from mental health professionals or primary care physicians. A less common approach, but one that has a lot of promise, is the case-finding approach, in which screening for major depression takes place, for example, in primary care clinics. Note that this approach is still a treatment approach: The individuals identified already have the disorder in question. Case finding procedures are not intended to prevent onset of the disorder. Their goal is to provide treatment earlier than would otherwise be the case. The earlier the depressive episode is treated, generally the easier and faster it is to bring the person back to baseline functioning. Reducing the duration of the clinical episode reduces the likelihood that the person's life will suffer enduring disruptions.

Community-based prevention approaches attempt to avert onset of the disorder. The Institute of Medicine report recommended that research on programs focused on averting the first onset of the disorder should have highest priority. Such programs would clearly be preventive. However, there is controversy even among prevention advocates as to whether prevention of onset of any new episodes (first or otherwise) might not be as appropriate. The issue revolves around the conceptualization of major depression as either a disorder that can occur several times in people vulnerable to depression, or whether depression is a chronic condition, with acute exacerbations of the same underlying disorder. Currently, a person is considered to have recovered from an episode once symptoms have been absent for 6 to 12 months. Until then, exacerbation of depressive symptoms would be considered a relapse within the same episode. As an arbitrary convention, after a year or more has passed, a repeat of a major depressive episode is considered a recurrence.

Professionals doing acute treatment refer to continuation of clinical interventions as preventing relapse or recurrence. Thus, in common parlance, one reads of interventions to prevent first onset, to prevent relapse, or to prevent recurrence. Some prevention advocates would like to limit the technical term prevention for interventions designed to prevent first onset.

Why It Is Important to Define Prevention Precisely. Advocates of prevention engage in what sometimes appear to be pedantic arguments regarding what is and what is not prevention because these definitions can have very practical implications. For example, imagine that a particular mental health care system sets a policy that 10% of its efforts will be dedicated to prevention. Imagine, also that prevention of relapse is considered within this 10%. Given the recurrent nature of major depression, it is very likely that all 10% of the mental health system's efforts could easily be dedicated to clinical interventions with patients who are already in treatment for major depression. Of course, these efforts would be very worthwhile. That is not the point. The point is that such a definition could entirely exhaust resources so that programs to prevent onset are never implemented.

The dilemma faced by health professionals is how to allocate resources when acute conditions continually demand intervention, yet the only way to stem the tide is to allocate resources to prevention of new cases. Only 20% of those with major depression currently receive mental health treatment. Is it more humane to train more therapists to, say, double access to treatment to 40% of those with depression? Or should we train professionals who can develop, implement, and evaluate prevention interventions that might reduce the number of new cases by 20%? Prevention advocates argue that unless we devote a substantial amount of resources to prevention, we will never make headway against the onslaught of prevalent disorders. Bailing water out of a sinking boat becomes a more effective exercise once we plug up as many holes as possible.

Prevention of Mental Disorders Versus Promotion of Mental Health

Another source of debate has been the difference between approaches that focus on preventing mental disorders and those that focus on promoting mental health. Though there are similarities in both approaches, such as their focus on interventions occurring prior to onset of disorders, there are also areas that differ in terms of philosophy and practice.

Promotion efforts focus on healthy development and do not necessarily use the concept of pathology and disorder to define or justify their efforts. Promotion approaches are geared toward reaching a state of well-being and optimal functioning. They have been critiqued for not operationalizing positive mental health specifically enough to achieve consensus on clear promotion goals. Prevention approaches have as their goal the averting of specific outcomes, such as major depressive episodes. They have been critiqued by some promotion-oriented advocates for using a medical model of human functioning, with emphasis on pathology and clinical entities, in which health is often defined as the absence of illness. Promotion proponents prefer a more social and psychological approach to human development, which sees variation as a normal part of the distribution of mental and behavioral phenomena. They critique the preventive approach for having a fundamentally negative perspective, focusing on avoiding problems rather than promoting human potential.

Given societal tendencies to fund services that address pressing needs, neither promotion nor prevention approaches have received the kind of support that treatment approaches do. Prevention and promotion leaders have pointed out that the practical implications of the two approaches are much more similar than their philosophical differences. For example, the development of social skills, self-esteem, and self-efficacy would both promote healthy functioning and decrease the likelihood of depressive episodes.

Conceptual Bases for Community-Oriented Prevention Approaches

Mental disorders that affect large numbers of the population, are related to multiple factors that increase or decrease the likelihood of their occurrence. Risk factors increase vulnerability to onset of a disorder, protective factors decrease vulnerability. Among the many risk factors proposed for major depression are biological factors and stressful life events. Protective factors believed to play a role in averting major depressive episodes include the ability to regulate one's mood, self-efficacy, and social support.

Biological factors fall into modifiable and nonmodifiable categories. For example, genetic influences on mood regulation may place individuals at higher risk for major depression. So could other biological factors, such as external toxins (such as alcohol) or internal substances (such as imbalances in neurotransmitters, stress-related cortisol or other hormones). At present, specific genes for major depression, if any, have not been identified, and thus are not modifiable. However, the effect of harmful substances could be reduced or eliminated by abstaining from their use, or influencing their levels, for example, via stress reduction methods.

Stressful life events have been found to have a substantial impact on the onset of depression. George W. Brown and Tirril Harris demonstrated this in their classic study on the *Social Origins of Depression* (1978). Events with long-term threat were related to the onset of clinical depression in the women in their study. Chronic stresses, such as poverty, have also been found to be related to major depression (*Archives of General Psychiatry*, 1991, *48*, 470–474). It is possible that lack of power to mold one's life produces some of the elements found in clinical depression, such as hopelessness and helplessness.

Protective factors may include the ability to regulate one's mood, which has been found to reduce the likelihood of relapse in depressed patients treated with cognitive therapy. James Gross and Ricardo Muñoz have argued that emotion regulation is a skill necessary for the development of mental health (*Clinical Psychology: Science and Practice*, 1995, *2*, 151–164). A more general factor may be what Albert Bandura calls *Self-Efficacy* (New York, 1997), which involves the self-perceived ability to master specific situational demands. Self-esteem may include aspects of coping and mastery in addition to a sense of individual value.

Social support has also been found to exert a protective influence in terms of the development of disorders in general, and in the ability to cope with the consequences of such disorders. For example, in the Brown and Harris study mentioned above, having a confidant reduced the women's vulnerability to clinical depression.

Community approaches to prevention of depression focus on the reduction of risk or vulnerability factors, including biological factors and stressful life events, the strengthening of mood management skills, self-efficacy, and self-esteem, as well as the strengthening of social support networks. The goal for such interventions is preventing the development or exacerbation of depressive symptoms to the point at which they become severe enough to "cross threshold" into a major depressive episode. In other words, although fluctuations in mood states are considered normal aspects of human experience, biological, psychological, and social conditions are known to increase or decrease the probability of clinical-level mood dysregulation. Efforts to attenuate such dysfunctional mood fluctuations would be expected to reduce the number of new major depressive episodes. Such efforts might have a number of a additional public health benefits.

Depressive Symptoms as a Public Health Problem

To understand the impact of depressive symptoms in several of the major public health problems facing contemporary societies, it is helpful to consider the epidemiological concept of attributable risk, or attributable burden, that is, the proportion of the disease that would be eliminated if the causative agent were removed. For example, if all cigarettes were to disappear, some proportion of lung cancer would be prevented. That proportion is the proportion attributable to cigarettes. Similarly, if depression is responsible for some proportion of many of the major public health problems, by preventing high depressive symptoms and the onset of depressive disorders, we would be able to eliminate some yet unknown proportion of these public health problems.

McGinnis and Foege (*Journal of the American Medical Association*, 1993, *270*, 2207–2212) listed the nine major causes of death in the United States: tobacco (400,000 deaths a year), diet/activity (300,000), alcohol (100,000), microbial agents (90,000), toxic agents (60,000), firearms (35,000), sexual behavior (30,000), motor vehicles (25,000), and illicit drugs (20,000). Several of these causes of death have been found to be related to depression. For example, many people use tobacco, alcohol, or other drugs to manage their mood; activity levels and eating patterns are influenced by mood states. Sexual behavior is also influenced by mood problems: for example, Ronald Kessler and colleagues report that 15- to 19-year-old girls with affective disorders are significantly more likely to engage in sexual intercourse, to have multiple sexual partners, and to become teenage mothers (*American Journal of Psychiatry*, 1997, 154, 1405–1411). Over half of deaths due to firearms in the United States are suicides (suicides in general are more common than homicides in the United States and have been so for decades) and thus often related to depression.

Negative moods are clearly related to smoking and drinking. The 1991 U.S. National Health Interview Survey of Health Promotion and Disease Prevention obtained data on 43,732 adults aged eighteen and older. Women were more likely to report negative moods as depression, men as restlessness. Smoking, drinking, and the combination of smoking and drinking were related to negative mood. Some studies have found that smokers with high levels of depressive symptoms are less likely to quit than smokers with lower depression scores. Similarly, individuals with a history of major depression are more likely to have ever smoked and less likely to quit that those with no history of psychiatric disorder.

In sum, many people with problems in emotion regulation use maladaptive methods of mood management with massive effects on the health of our communities, such as use of psychoactive substances, unprotected sex leading to disabling disease and unintended pregnancies, and increased levels of violence (at least toward oneself) born of desperation. High levels of depressive symptoms can lead to many public health problems, only one of which is unipolar major depression. Therefore, community prevention approaches focused on teaching healthy methods of mood regulation may have a widespread positive effect on public well-being.

Community Approaches to the Prevention of Depression

Community-oriented approaches have often been conceptualized in terms of lifespan development. To organize preventive programs, it is useful to think of them as serving segments of the community going through several life stages. Community prevention is proactive, seeking out opportunities to strengthen the mental health of populations by reducing the proportion of individuals who develop major depressive episodes, maintaining depressive symptom levels low, or both. We will now illustrate interventions that fall into the three categories of universal, selective, or indicated prevention. At this stage in the development of prevention science, several types of intervention have been shown to reduce depressive symptoms. The next major step in the quest to prevent major depression is to show that reduction in depressive symptoms reduces new major depressive episodes.

Universal Preventive Intervention. The possibility of providing entire communities with information on methods to manage their mood was studied in the San Francisco Mood Survey Project by Muñoz and colleagues (*American Journal of Community Psychology*, 1982, 10, 317–329). Cognitive-behavioral methods to regulate one's mood were shown in a series of 10 television segments during the news hours for a two-week period. Reduction in depressive symptoms among those initially scoring high on depressive symptom scales were found in those who had watched at least some of the segments, compared to those who had not. However, this was not a randomized controlled study, and self-selection may have exerted an influence in the results.

The work of Sheppard Kellam and associates (in *Preventing Antisocial Behavior: Interventions from Birth Through Adolescence*, pp. 162–195, New York, 1992) is impressive in its scope and longitudinal design. This team has carried out a set of randomized controlled studies in inner city elementary school classrooms that have demonstrated that depressive symptoms are related to academic success and that interventions that increase the chances of academic success have positive effects on mood levels. The methodological perspective on which this massive research program is based, namely, developmental epidemiology, is likely to contribute significantly to the progress of prevention.

Selective Preventive Interventions. Perhaps the most clearly population-based selective prevention study conducted to date is the Hispanic Social Network Study, conducted by William Vega and colleagues (In *Depression Prevention: Research Directions*, pp. 217–231, Washington, DC, 1987). Strict epidemiological screening-enumeration methods were used to identify a sample of the population of San Diego County that was at high risk based on demographic variables: low income, Mexican American women ages 35 to 50, living in the United States a minimum of two years. Participants who did not meet criteria for a case-level psychiatric disorder or serious physical health problems were randomized into a control group or two experimental groups. The latter utilized either indigenous Hispanic natural helpers to provide individual interventions, or an educational group format. Both of the experimental groups used a social learning-based approach focused on instrumental, problem-solving techniques to cope with the stresses that low-income Hispanic women face. The subgroup with the lowest initial depression levels in the experimental groups showed significantly lower depression scores at follow-up, compared to controls. Unfortunately, evaluation of diagnostic status at one-year follow up was not carried out, so effects on prevention of clinical episodes are not available.

Bernard Bloom reports a study based on the stressful life event perspective (*Stressful Life Event Theory and Re-*

search: Implications for Primary Intervention, 1985, Washington, DC) in which newly separated individuals were recruited as being at high risk for emotional problems. They were randomly assigned to a six-month-long intervention, utilizing paraprofessionals as program representatives who contacted participants on a regular basis, developed opportunities for social interaction, and referred them to the program's study groups. Five groups were available: career planning and employment, legal and financial issues, child rearing, housing and homemaking, and socialization and personal self-esteem. Of nine measures of adjustment, five significant differences were found, favoring the experimental group, including a measure of neurasthenia. These differences persisted at 18- and 30-month follow-ups.

Richard Price and his colleagues (*Journal of Health and Social Behavior*, 1992, 33, 158–167) have carried out a set of exemplary studies in which they have recruited newly unemployed individuals and taught them a set of job-finding skills that include psychological methods to reduce hopelessness. They have not only found that individuals receiving the experimental intervention are more likely to find better jobs earlier, but they are also less likely to develop high levels of depressive symptoms.

William Beardslee has conducted a series of studies focused on children of parents with major depression and bipolar illness (*Journal of the American Academy of Child and Adolescent Psychiatry*, 1993, 32, 254–263). His approach is to educate both the parents and the children about the clinical disorder itself, help them learn to communicate about issues related to mood, and alert both to the fact that children of depressed parents are at higher risk of developing depression themselves. The intent is to help children learn to monitor and regulate their moods, and to seek help early if they begin to notice clinical levels of depression.

Irwin Sandler and colleagues have worked with children of divorce and bereavement as their high-risk group (*American Journal of Community Psychology*, 1992, 20, 491–523). For example, families of children who had experienced death of a parent were provided with a 3-session family grief workshop and 13 sessions with a family advisor who had personally experienced a similar bereavement. Children receiving the intervention improved on symptoms related to depression and conduct disorder.

The San Francisco Depression Prevention Research Project (*The Prevention of Depression: Research and Practice*, Baltimore, 1993) was a randomized control trial designed to test whether new clinical episodes of major depression could be prevented. Participants were adult English- and Spanish-speaking, public sector, primary care patients, believed to be at high risk because of their low-income, minority status and their seeking assistance in the health care system. Individuals with current depressive or other psychiatric disorders were referred for treatment and excluded from the trial. The intervention consisted of the Depression Prevention Course, eight 2-hour group sessions in which cognitive-behavioral mood management methods were taught. Participants were followed for up to one year. Depressive symptoms were significantly reduced, and symptom reduction was related to hypothesized changes in many of the cognitive and behavioral factors targeted by the intervention. Six cases of major depression were identified out of 139 individuals followed. Four were in the control condition and two in the experimental condition. Of the latter, one had attended no sessions, and the other only two. Though these figures are in the predicted direction, they are too low to provide sufficient statistical power to test adequately whether the rate of new cases was reduced significantly. The need to find even higher risk subgroups within demographically defined high-risk segments of the population is highlighted by this trial.

Indicated Preventive Interventions. Indicated preventive studies seek not only segments of the population at high risk, but actually identify individuals with characteristics that place them at even higher imminent risk for a clinical episode. Higher numbers of new cases allow prevention studies to be done with fewer numbers of participants. At this stage in the development of the prevention research field, indicated preventive intervention trials may be the most practical, because they are the most likely to show preventive effects on reduction of new episodes.

In a study by B. Raphael, conducted in Australia (*Archives of General Psychiatry*, 1977, 34, 1450–1454), out of 200 widows applying for widow's pensions, 64 were considered to be at high risk of morbidity according to four indices. The latter were randomly assigned to experimental or control conditions. The intervention consisted of one to nine (average: four) individual home sessions by a psychiatrist, using a model of "selective ego support for ego processes stressed by the crisis experience." Comparisons across conditions were done up to 13 months after the spouse's death, and are reported as being significant for better outcomes on a general health questionnaire. In addition, four control subjects (out of 33 required hospitalization for depression, compared to none of the 31 in the experimental condition.

Martin Seligman reports a series of studies done with Karen Reivich, Lisa Jaycox, and Jane Gillham, designed to prevent depression in children by teaching them optimistic explanatory styles (*The Optimistic Child*, Boston, 1995). They screened fifth- and sixth-graders and chose those with high self-reported symptoms of depression and family conflict. The comparison group was drawn from a similar school in the area. The intervention consisted of training in optimistic thinking, for example, thinking styles that attribute negative events to causes that are not stable, internal, and global, and thus increase the chances that the child will believe he or she can succeed in future efforts. The investigators report that 24% of children from both groups had moderate-to-severe depressive symptoms when the program started. At the end of the intervention, 13% in the group that received the intervention had high symptoms, compared to 23% in the school that did not receive the intervention.

The study that has come closest to showing that major depressive episodes can be prevented was carried out by Gregory Clarke and others (*Journal of the American Academy of Child and Adolescent Psychiatry*, 1995, 34, 312–321), adapting the cognitive-behavioral methods developed by Peter Lewinsohn and colleagues (*Control Your Depression*, rev. ed., New York, 1986) at the University of Oregon. This team screened high school students for major depression and referred those already meeting criteria for treatment and out of the study. They then chose from the remaining adolescents only those with high depressive symptom scores, and assigned them randomly to the experimental intervention or to a control condition. The intervention consisted of an after-school course on managing mood states. At one-year follow-ups, those in the control condition had a 26% incidence of major depression or dysthymia, compared to 15% in the experimental condition. This is the first study to actually show a difference in clinical cases of depression. One weakness in the study is a high drop-out rate in the experimental group at the one-year assessment. Nevertheless, this study points the way for other such preventive trials: individuals with high symptom levels are highly vulnerable to developing clinical episodes of depression within one year, and thus are an important target group for prevention. It is also important to obtain as complete a set of follow-up interviews in both control and experimental groups to feel confident that new cases were actually less in the group receiving the preventive intervention.

Bibliography

Albee, G. W., & Gullotta, T. P. (Eds.). (1997). *Primary prevention works*. Thousand Oaks, CA: Sage. Contains 14 chapters describing community prevention projects that have been awarded the United States National Mental Health Association's Lela Rowland Prevention Award. An introductory chapter by the authors provides a historical perspective on the evolution of the concept of prevention.

Brown, G. W., & Harris, T. (1978). *Social origins of depression*. London: Tavistock. A classic study of the social factors related to the development of depression. It describes an empirical analysis of the provoking agents, vulnerability factors, and symptom-formation factors related to serious depression in a sample of working-class women in London.

Caplan, G. (1964). *Principles of preventive psychiatry*. New York: Basic Books. A highly influential book that presents the early conceptualizations of the levels of prevention, from a crisis intervention and mental health consultation perspective.

Felner, R. D., Jason, L. A., Moritsugu, J. N., & Farber, S. S. (1983). *Preventive psychology: Theory, research, and practice*. New York: Pergamon Press.

Heller, K., Price, R. H., Reinharz, S., Riger, S., Wandersman, A., and D'Aunno, T. A. (1984). *Psychology and community change*. Chicago: The Dorsey Press.

Kelly, J. G., Dassoff, N., Levin, I., Schreckengost, J., Stelzner, S. P., & Altman, B. E. (1988). *A guide to conducting prevention research in the community: First steps*. New York: Haworth Press. A strong call to include community participants in the planning and implementation of prevention efforts.

Kessler, M., & Goldston, S. E. (Eds.). (1986). *A decade of progress in primary prevention*. Hanover, NH: University Press of New England.

Lewinsohn, P. M., Antonuccio, D. O., Breckenridge, J., & Teri, L. (1984). *The coping with depression course: A psychoeducational intervention for unipolar depression*. Eugene, OR: Castalia. A description of a widely used intervention to reduce depressive symptoms. It has been used both for preventive and treatment community approaches.

Lowry, M. R. (1984). *Major depression: Prevention and treatment*. St. Louis, MO: W. H. Green.

Mrazek, P., & Haggerty, R. (1994). *Reducing risks for mental disorders: Frontiers for preventive intervention research*. Washington, DC: National Academy Press. This major report by the United States Institute of Medicine Committee on Prevention of Mental Disorders surveys epidemiological, biological, social, and psychological perspectives on the prevention of specific mental disorders, including depression. It describes and evaluates a myriad of prevention programs and suggests promising directions for prevention research.

Muñoz, R. F. (Ed.). (1987). *Depression prevention: Research directions*. Washington, DC: Hemisphere. A collection of chapters devoted to the theoretical, methodological, and practical aspects of depression prevention efforts, including several intervention studies.

Muñoz, R. F., & Ying, Y. (1993). *The prevention of depression: Research and practice*. Baltimore, MD: Johns Hopkins University Press. An analysis of the conceptual, ethical, philosophical, and methodological issues involved in efforts to prevent major depression, together with a detailed report of the first randomized controlled trial intended to prevent new episodes of major depression.

Newton, J. (1988). *Preventing mental illness*. London: Routledge & Kegan Paul. A thoughful, evidence-based review of the historical, theoretical, research, and practical aspects of prevention efforts for depression and schizophrenia.

Price, R. H., Cowen, E. L., Lorion, R. P., & Ramos-McKay, J. (Eds.). (1988). *Fourteen ounces of prevention: A casebook for practitioners.* Washington, DC: American Psychological Association.

Rappaport, J. (1977). *Community psychology: Values, research, and action.* New York: Holt, Rinehart & Winston.

Ricardo F. Muñoz

COMMUNITY PSYCHOLOGY. [*This entry comprises four articles: an overview of the broad history of the field from its inception to the present; a survey of the principal theories that have determined the course of development of the field; a review of the methods of study that have been employed in this field; and an examination of the interventions employed in the field, including discussion of prevention.*]

History of the Field

The history of the field of community psychology is a history psychologists promoting the use of social and behavioral sciences for the well-being of people and their communities. Community psychologists promote theory development and research to increase the understanding of human behavior in its social context. The field encourages the exchange of knowledge and skills in community research and action among community psychologists, other social scientists and citizens. Community psychologists emphasize the use of multicultural and pluralistic approaches to ensure that preventive and social programs are tailored to the particular needs and aspirations of persons from different cultural, social, and ethnic backgrounds.

The knowledge and research base of the field interconnects with other disciplines, such as anthropology, sociology, and public health, and has close connections with cognitive, social, and developmental psychology. Community psychology approaches to conducting research include action research, case studies, sample surveys, various types of observational methods, epidemiologic methods, and natural experiments. Methods of analysis include a range of quantitative and qualitative methods, as well as participatory research methods, that focus on the role of research participants as partners in the entire research process. Community psychologists have pioneered research on various topics, such as social support and social competencies, that have later been elaborated upon by clinical, developmental, and social psychologists.

World War II and the 1950s

Powerful social forces contributed to the founding of the field. World War II stimulated public awareness of the country's domestic difficulties and was a catalyst to innovate mental health services. During this time, harassment of African Americans and women working in war plants on the homefront was widely communicated in the media. It was increasingly difficult for any informed citizen to deny the widespread conditions of American life such as poverty, racism, and sexism. This new consciousness contributed to an awareness among some social scientists that symptoms of personal stress were pervasive. In addition, there was an emerging consensus among investigators that social and environmental stress factors reduce autonomy, a sense of justice, and personal dignity. It also became clear in evaluating the mental health status of soldiers serving in the war that social and environmental conditions, such as being in battle and experiencing prolonged stress, contributed to a person expressing symptoms of inadequate coping and/or mental illness. Accompanying this greater realization that social factors contribute to mental health and illness was a mood of optimism in the United States as a result of the allied victory in World War II.

The postwar period of optimism, with collective attention to social issues, created an opportunity for new types of research to be carried out in the large metropolitan areas of the United States. Such large scale investigations focused in more detail than ever before on the relationships among community social conditions, cultural factors, and an individual's mental health status. It was being confirmed that a person's social environment was related to his/her expression of mental distress and subsequent treatment. Private foundations, such as the Milbank Memorial Fund, sanctioned and funded these activities and advocated community approaches to mental health and illness for the rank and file of the mental health professions. Formal and informal conversations among professionals focused on the review of these findings, and the National Institute of Mental Health (NIMH) gave priority to the creation of community approaches to the treatment of mental illness and the promotion of mental health. The climate among the mental health professions encouraged the implementation of community approaches to mental illness and health.

Accompanying the growing awareness of community and preventive approaches to mental health by foundations and professionals was widespread public anger about the status of mental health treatment. With the appearance of public investigations and journalists' reports of maltreatment and abuse of mental patients, such as the powerful newspaper accounts by Albert Deutsch, more and more citizens were informed about the plight of the mentally ill who, at the time, were being "warehoused" in large facilities. Many local citizen groups advocated change in mental health treatments and living conditions in large hospitals, where individuals were isolated from their families and communities. In this same period, the U.S. Congress, with NIMH and private foundation support, established the Joint Commission on Mental Illness and Health to review the state of the nation's mental health. Its final report, *Action for Mental Health* (1961), called for a new community perspective for treating the mentally ill.

1965–1975

The founding of the field is often identified as occurring at the Boston Conference on the Education of Psychologists for Community Mental Health at Swampscott, Massachusetts (4–8 May 1963), more commonly referred to as the Swampscott Conference. At this conference, the term *community psychology* was coined, emphasizing prevention, policy research, and the active understanding of and intervention with social problems. The role of the community psychologist was proposed as an alternative to the treatment and disease orientation of the clinical psychologist, who at that time provided services to individuals after severe and traumatic personal stress had already occurred. The Swampscott Conference was an explicit and affirmative response by the 39 psychologists in attendance to the new national mood of community-based mental health work.

The widely circulated report of the Swampscott Conference facilitated, with NIMH training support, the development of the first doctoral community training programs. Most of this training was nested in clinical psychology training programs at six universities: University of Colorado (Bernard L. Bloom); Duke University (John Altrocchi and Carl Eisdorfer); University of Michigan (James G. Kelly and Harold Raush); University of Rochester (Emory Cowen); University of Texas (Ira Iscoe); Yale University (Murray Levine and Seymour Sarason). Three programs were established independent of clinical psychology: Boston University (Donald C. Klein and Herbert Lipton); George Peabody College (J. R. Newbrough, William Rhodes, and Julius Seeman); and New York University (Isidor Chein, Walter Neff, and Stanley Lehmann).

After Swampscott, Robert Reiff of Albert Einstein Medical College was nominated by community psychologists as their spokesperson. Reiff and this new group's board of directors proposed to the members of the American Psychological Association (APA) that a new division be created. The APA Representatives accepted the proposal and the Division of Community Psychology (27) became official in September 1966.

With the acceptance of the field of community psychology by the larger psychological association, community psychologists began to explore how the knowledge of community psychology could be communicated. To facilitate publication two journals were founded: the *American Journal of Community Psychology*

(Charles Spielberger, founding editor, 1973) and the *Journal of Community Psychology* (Frederick C. Thorne, founding editor, 1973).

Since the inception of the field there has been a continuing debate regarding whether community psychology is a part of clinical psychology or a distinct and separate field. This difference in perspective reflects a number of issues, including whether the emphasis of the field should be to improve the mental health of individuals or to reduce the incidence of a social condition at the community level. This difference represents continuing debates within the field about the proper focus of research and action and whether the priority emphasis should be on the individual or the larger neighborhood or the community. This difference in emphasis is likely to remain.

1975–1985

In the mid and later 1970s, the maturity of the field was evident. Growth was reflected in the publication of several community psychology text books. The first chapter on community psychology topics appeared in the prestigious *Annual Review of Psychology*. Faculty directing doctoral training programs concerned with common curricular and training issues formed the Council of Community Psychology Training Directors. Today there are 45 members of this group who meet annually to coordinate doctoral training in the field.

While white males contributed predominately to the earlier development of the field, younger community psychologists, women, and persons of color in the mid-1970s had been strongly requesting that the Division examine the impact of race and gender on the nature of the field itself. The Austin Conference, held at the University of Texas in April of 1975, included doctoral students and recent Ph.D.s who were not only younger but who were also nonwhite. This was a major step in developing broader representation and encouraging different voices in the Division. This change in participation also increased serious attention to the role of cultural and subcultural factors in health and illness.

Following the Austin Conference, the participants began to create systematic ways to facilitate more informal communication among the members. One approach was to create a regional coordination network to develop forums for public discussion of theory, research, and practice. This mechanism is still in place today. In 1978, at Michigan State University, Deborah Bybee, William Davidson, and Donald Davis began informal faculty-student sessions away from campus to review training and professional issues. These sessions, which have evolved into student-driven regional meetings known as eco-community conferences, have served as an important resource for informal exchanges among doctoral students interested in the field.

Two major issues emerged in the second decade. One

issue was community psychologists' attitudes toward accreditation and licensing for the field. Some believed that participating in accreditation would give the field more status and provide more career options for recently trained community psychologists. In contrast, J. R. Newbrough of George Peabody College, in his 1979 Division 27 presidential address, argued that accreditation would give priority to the profession rather than the communities served by community psychologists and would inhibit interdisciplinary training. The preferred approach, as expressed by Newbrough, was that community psychologists should be a resource to various self-help and community development activities.

Another issue of rising interest for community psychologists was the desire to increase their connections to the communities in which they were situated. Irma Serrano-Garcia of the University of Puerto Rico, emphasized this issue during her later presidency (1992–1993). The earlier proposition against specialization for this field strengthened the resolve of the members ten years later to increase community-based activities advocated by Serrano-Garcia.

While members of the field were assessing and debating these issues, the field was building a strong foundation in university training programs with the establishment of new master's and doctoral degree programs. During this period, in addition to publications in the two primary journals, four more *Annual Review of Psychology* chapters were published.

1985–1995

During the SCRA presidencies of Jean Ann Linney (University of South Carolina), Dick Reppucci (University of Virginia), and Edward Seidman (New York University), 1984–1989, the field took steps toward solidifying its identity. There was wide recognition that the annual meetings of the APA were too large for informal exchanges. Biennial conferences specific to community psychology were planned to facilitate participation with undergraduate and graduate students, citizens, and members of different disciplines. The first such conference was held at the University of South Carolina in 1987.

Community psychologists also moved to rename the Division to reflect a more open, action-oriented, and interdisciplinary association. As a result of carrying out surveys of the membership, the Division was renamed the Society for Community Research and Action (SCRA) in 1987. During this period two more chapters were published in the *Annual Review of Psychology*, which has continued to cover the field's evolution and diversity.

The liveliness of the field stimulated society leadership to hold a conference in Chicago in 1988. Funded by the APA, 80 individuals attended to evaluate current research methods. Increased attention was given to creating methods that reflect the historical commitment of the field to take into account how social contexts affect human behavior. Equally emphasized were attending to the processes of designing community programs that reflect a direct and personal relationship between the investigator and informants and in addition increasing the policy connections of community research and action. Since the Chicago conference, community psychologists have been active in extending and innovating new forms of inquiry. The diversity of SCRA's activities is reflected in its varied committees and interest groups. The standing committees include APA Program Committee, Cultural and Racial Affairs, Dissertation Award, Elections, Fellowship, International, Liaison to Canadian Community Psychological Association, Membership, Nominations, Publications, Social Policy, and Women. The interest groups include aging, children and youth, community action, community health, disabilities, mutual support, prevention and promotion, rural school intervention, stress and coping, and undergraduate awareness.

Particularly since the 1980s, SCRA has facilitated active participation among community psychologists representing different interests and points of view. Additionally, community psychologists in the United States increased their communication with community psychologists around the world. For example, universities that have been particularly active in establishing community psychology training programs are located in Argentina, Austria, Australia, Canada, England, Germany, Italy, Mexico, Netherlands, New Zealand, Norway, Portugal, Scotland, and South Africa. There also has been more active participation among the practitioner and action-oriented community psychologists during the past several years. This increased participation of researchers, practitioners, and representatives from other countries has created a more dynamic organization than a solely academic, domestic U.S. organization might be. Increasingly, young people are finding that SCRA is a validating organization for their personal and career interests as they pursue the science and profession of psychology with an explicit research and action orientation to a broad range of community issues.

Conclusion

The SCRA has emerged as an active group of researchers and community action professionals. Community psychologists are proponents of a variety of community and preventive interventions, many of whom have been nationally honored and widely emulated. These programs of community research include interpersonal social problem-solving programs for young children, preventive programs for newly separated persons, heart disease prevention, and diversion from the juvenile justice system.

Information about SCRA activities, programs, and membership can be accessed from the Internet. There is a Society listserve (SCRA L@unicvm.uic.edu) and a Web page: http://www.apa.org/divisions/div27.

Bibliography

Action for mental health: The final report of the Joint Commission on Mental Illness and Health. (1961). New York: Basic Books.

Bennett, C. C., Anderson, L. S., Cooper, S., Hassol, L., Klein, D. C., & Rosenblum, G. (Eds.). (1966). *Community psychology: A report of the Boston conference on the education of psychologists for community mental health.* Boston: Boston University Press.

Iscoe, I., Bloom, B., & Spielberger, C. (Eds.). (1977). *Community psychology in transition.* Washington, DC: Hemisphere.

Levine, M., & Perkins, D. V. (1997). *Principles of community psychology: Perspectives and applications* (2nd ed.). New York: Oxford University Press.

Meritt, D. M., Greene, G. J., Jopp, D. A., and Kelly, J. G. (1998). A brief history of Division 27 and the Society for Community Research and Action. In D. Dewsbury (Ed.), *Unification through division: Histories of the American Psychological Association.* Washington, DC: American Psychological Association.

Milbank Memorial Fund. (1953). *Interrelations between the social environment and psychiatric disorders.* New York: Author.

Price, R. H., Cowen, E. L., Lorion, R. P., & Ramos-McKay, J. (1988). *Fourteen ounces of prevention: A casebook for practitioners.* Washington, DC: American Psychological Association.

Tolan, P., Keys, C. B., Chertok, F., & Jason, L. (Eds.). (1990). *Researching community psychology: Issues of theory and methods.* Washington, DC: American Psychological Association.

*James G. Kelly, David A. Jopp, George J. Greene,
and Dana Meritt Wardlaw*

Theories

Because community psychology is social problem oriented, it draws its knowledge base from both its own scholarship and from the work of researchers and scholars in other fields, in and outside of psychology. The nature of theories that have shaped the field is a joint function of the kind of problems addressed, the sort of people attracted to the field, and the historical and social realities of the day. Theory tends to be dominated by views that include more than one level of analysis, suggest open systems, reciprocal causality, respect for diversity, and social change–oriented values. Social regularities and institutions are critically analyzed, especially as they affect the most vulnerable members of society. Theory tends not to be of the classical variety with logical statements and corollaries out of which a precise program of research flows, so much as orienting frameworks for action research. An overarching theoretical inclination of community psychology, regardless of the particular theory, is to avoid a victim blaming, culturally unaware, interpretive frame. This exerts a strong influence on the design of research and on interpretation of the available empirical knowledge base.

Social Critique

As Murray and Adeline Levine have pointed out in their historical analysis, *Helping Children: A Social History* (2nd edition, 1992), there is a correlation in human services work between the general social ethos of the times and the form of help offered. Individual, biological, and internal psychological explanations tend to dominate during periods of political conservativism, while environmental and social contextual explanations are more influential in times of progressive social change. More generally, the politics of the times tend to influence the nature of social science explanations for human behavior. The same may be said for what difficulties are considered a social problem, and for what are seen as acceptable social programs and policies. (For further discussion of this point see Humphreys and Rappaport, *American Psychologist*, 1993.) Notwithstanding historical fluctuations in the social ethos, community psychology has tended to attract adherents who favor theories that emphasize environmental context and critical social analysis, including critique of the methods, and practices of psychologists. Community psychology theories are called upon to provide more than a framework for studying particular phenomena of interest. They are also expected to provide an analysis of the roles and activities of the psychologist, as well an intervention approach to social problems.

Scope of Theory

An APA-sponsored conference and publication on theory and method in community psychology (Tolan, Keys, Chertok, & Jason, 1990) identified five influential theoretical orientations, including those borrowed from other areas of the discipline (developmental, organizational, and behavioral) and those developed within community psychology (ecological and empowerment). The ecological analysis offered by James G. Kelly and Edison J. Trickett has had an enduring theoretical impact on the field. They introduced the analytic principles of social ecology, including interdependence, cycling of resources, adaptation, and succession that have served as a bridge to other systems theories. Kelly's (1990) work has also been seminal in providing a vision and a set of goals for the field, including the role of the community psychologist as boundary spanner who works with ordinary citizens and other professionals using multiple methods and epistemologies. Rappaport's 1981 and 1987 *American Journal of Community Psychology* papers introduced the idea of empowerment to the community psychology literature (see also a 1995 special issue of the *American Journal of Community Psychology*, edited by Perkins & Zimmerman).

The *Handbook of Community Psychology* section on theoretical frameworks includes chapters on prevention, empowerment, individualism and collectivism, wellness, behaviorism, social cognition, and ecological analysis. But in a field where research, intervention, and analysis are not viewed as distinct activities, it would be misleading to exclude from theoretical influence scholarship on topics such as intervention strategies and tactics, stress theory, social support, citizen participation, life span and community development, social systems, research dissemination and policy analysis, the psychological sense of community, and the creation of alternative settings, all of which make important theoretical statements.

Contextualism and Action Research

Community psychology emerged in the United States as an identifiable substantive area during the last third of the twentieth century, a time of considerable social and cultural change, with a strong interest in environmental, sociopolitical and cultural critique, including a critique of psychology practices and methods. The field has always been receptive to action research, in which theory, data collection, and intervention are reciprocal and iterative rather than linear, and in which social criticism, intervention, evaluation, and empirical research go hand in hand. This approach is embraced because the theoretical underpinnings of the field have long emphasized the principle of contextualism, i.e., that the ideal empirical research should take place in contexts about which conclusions are to be drawn. Thus, while laboratory experimental work with convenience samples is sometimes necessary, it is considered (in a reversal of traditional preferences in psychology) to be a compromise from more desirable, if difficult, work in the field. Multiple methods for empirical data collection and analysis, both quantitative and qualitative, are used.

Collaboration

Collaboration with research participants during all phases of the research process is a strongly held aspiration. Influenced early by the same historical forces that resulted in legislative change and judicial decisions accompanying the U.S. African American civil rights movement, the field has followed an outspoken concern for the rights and full participation of cultural, ethnic, and social minorities as legitimate voices in the policies and decisions (as well as the research) that affect their lives. This concern has also played itself out in the context of changes in role relationships and gender-based stereotypes. Although some scholars have argued that the field had initially neglected many issues of concern to women, others suggest that community psychology and feminism share basic insights and an agenda that is similar (A. Mulvey, *Journal of Community Psychology*, 1988).

Professional Roles

A community psychology division of the American Psychological Association was formed in 1966, and the division (later formed into a freestanding Society for Community Research and Action) has sponsored a scholarly journal (*American Journal of Community Psychology*) since 1973. Other journals where theoretical papers may be found include the *Journal of Community Psychology* and more recently the (British) *Journal of Community and Applied Social Psychology*. In addition to participation in APA, the Society holds its own biennial meeting and invites membership from professionals, students, and citizens who are not psychologists.

The field was created and influenced early by people, most of whom had been trained as clinical or social psychologists, who shared a critical analysis of the conceptual frameworks, intervention strategies, and professional roles in their own fields, especially with respect to mental illness. Initially they focused on the difficulties of reaching many people thought to be in need of human services, particularly the socially marginalized. Early on the community mental health movement, including deinstitutionalization and the prevention of mental illness, as well as a concern for how to create a human services system to better reach the socially marginalized and economically disadvantaged, was central to the field. The search for alternatives to in-the-office, one-to-one treatments of individuals by therapists led to exploration of new ways to locate and mobilize various community resources, including indigenous people, volunteers, and local citizens to promote mental health and well-being, and to prevent problems before they occur. Later, as prevention came to include the promotion of positive life circumstances, including social, educational, and economic justice, a broader perspective than mental health per se became possible.

As community psychology became much broader than an exclusive focus on mental health, research extended into areas such as education, law and juvenile justice, child welfare and domestic violence, health care and social support, citizen participation, self- and mutual help, as well as community and neighborhood organization, social advocacy, and policy. It has been widely accepted that different theoretical approaches are necessary, depending on the level of analysis at which one is working (individual, small group, organizational, institutional, community) with a search for strengths rather than deficits at every level. This way of thinking was greatly enhanced by William Ryan's now classic volume, *Blaming the Victim*, published by Random House in 1971. Ryan made clear the social process by which well-meaning helping professionals learn to blame individuals for their own problems in living, rather than to analyze the social systems and contexts that create difficulties for people. His thinking led the way to a community psychology emphasizing cultural relativity, diversity, ecological analysis, and person environment fit (Rappaport, 1977).

Sources of Help

Originally the field was closely linked to the community mental health movement, and to critiques of long-term psychotherapy. Many psychologists participated in an analysis of the failure of mental hospitals to meet the needs of the long-term mental patient (thus requiring development of alternative, community-based settings) and the lack of reach or effectiveness of human services for the economically disadvantaged (thus requiring development of alternative sources of person power and new helping, advocacy, and community organization roles for both citizens and psychologists). Both of these observations led to a variety of conceptual and theoretical approaches designed to account for why people untrained in professional practice, often working with people in their own community, usually are no worse at being helpful than professionals. The field has also been receptive to behavioral, environmental, and social systems theories, as well as to models of self and mutual help. (See, for example, Cowen, Gardner, & Zax, *Emergent Approaches to Mental Health Problems*, Appleton-Century-Crofts, 1967; Cowen, 1973, *Annual Review of Psychology* chapter; Rappaport, 1977; Christensen & Jacobson, 1994; *Psychological Science*, for a related review in the context of therapeutic services; and Humphreys & Rappaport, 1994, *Applied and Professional Psychology*, for a review in the context of self and mutual help theories and practices).

Public Health and Prevention

George Albee's *Mental Health Manpower Trends* (New York, 1959) made it clear that we would never be able to train enough mental health professionals to meet the need for treatment within a clinical services paradigm and that it is desirable to take a public health approach that seeks to prevent problems before they occur. This observation remains a basic assumption for the field. Theories forged in the fires of community mental health concerns tend to be primarily about the nature of systems for service delivery. Early influences from public health models of prevention and community psychiatry, especially the thinking of people such as Gerald Caplan, a psychiatrist who made popular the

distinctions between primary prevention (intervention targeted for an entire population intended to reduce the incidence of new cases), secondary prevention (detecting and treating a problem early in its course or in the person's life), and tertiary prevention (rehabilitation), was an important theoretical influence. Current thinking continues to use a now more sophisticated version of the public health model and this portion of the field has tended to shift toward a disciplinary practice called "prevention science." Generally, the notion of "risk" is adopted, such that depending on the nature of the analysis one speaks of people at risk, or of risky circumstances. The notion of prevention science itself tends to call for the prevention of specific diagnosable disorders through identification of hypothesized causal mechanisms, as opposed to more general efforts to improve life circumstances, living conditions, and social inequities. This is a controversial distinction and some feel that prevention science is actually less likely to create effective change than, for example, a more global approach to providing wellness enhancement for all children (Cowen, 1999)—an approach that does not posit specific mechanisms tied to specific disorders, but emphasizes reciprocal effects, such that neither the exact nature of the expression of a disorder is predictable, nor is it necessary to know the mechanism in order to correct certain obvious social inequities. (See also Albee, *American Psychologist*, 1996; Felner, Felner & Silverman, 2000, in Rappaport & Seidman's *Handbook of Community Psychology*.)

A focus on specific disorders is likely to move theory toward the biomedical disciplines, albeit with an epidemiological, public health perspective. Attention to social inequity, whether it leads to development of theories related to promotion of health, educational opportunity, neighborhood and community development, empowerment, or wellness, is more likely to be influenced by the social sciences and humanities, including critical social theory and qualitative research methods. A single unifying theory for community psychology, if possible or desirable, remains a project for the future.

Bibliography

Cowen, E. L. (1996). The ontogenesis of primary prevention: Lengthy strides and stubbed toes. *American Journal of Community Psychology*, 24, 235–249.

Cowen, E. L. (1999). Psychological wellness: Some hopes for the future. In D. Cicchetti, J. Rappaport, I. Sandler, & R. Weissberg (Eds.), *The promotion of wellness in children and adolescents*. Thousand Oaks, CA: Sage.

Heller, K., Price, R. H., Reinharz, S., Riger, S., & Wandersman, A. (1984). *Psychology and community change*. Pacific Grove, CA: Brooks/Cole.

Kelly, J. G. (1990). Changing contexts and the field of community psychology. *American Journal of Community Psychology, 18,* 769–792.

Levine, M., & Perkins, D. V. (1997). *Principles of community psychology: Perspectives and applications.* New York: Oxford University Press.

Munoz, R., Snowden, L., & Kelly, J. (1979). *Social and psychological research in community settings.* San Francisco: Jossey-Bass.

Orford, J. (1992). *Community psychology: Theory and practice.* Chichester, England: Wiley.

Perkins, D. D., & Zimmerman, M. A. (Eds.). (1995). Empowerment theory, research, and application. *American Journal of Community Psychology, 23(5).* Special Issue.

Price, R. H., Cowen, E. L., Lorion, R. P., & Ramos-McKay, J. (1988). *Fourteen ounces of prevention: A casebook for practitioners.* Washington, DC: American Psychological Association.

Rappaport, J. (1977). *Community psychology: Values, research, and action.* New York: Holt, Rinehart, & Winston.

Rappaport, J., & Seidman, E. (Eds.). (2000). *Handbook of community psychology.* New York: Plenum.

Sarason, S. B. (1974). *The psychological sense of community: Prospects for a community psychology.* San Francisco, CA: Jossey-Bass.

Seidman, E. (1988). Back to the future, community psychology: Unfolding the theory of social intervenion. *American Journal of Community Psychology, 16,* 3–24.

Tolan, P., Keys, C., Chertok, F., & Jason, L. (Eds.). (1990). *Researching community psychology: Issues of theory and methods.* Washington, DC: American Psychological Association.

Trickett, E. J. (1996). A future for community psychology: The contexts of diversity and the diversity of contexts. *American Journal of Community Psychology, 24,* 209–229.

Trickett, E. J., Kelly, J. G., & Vincent, T. A. (1985). The spirit of ecological inquiry in community research. In E. Susskind & D. Klein (Eds.), *Community research: Methods, paradigms, and applications.* New York: Praeger.

Julian Rappaport

Methods of Study

From the time of the Swampscott Conference, usually seen as the origin of community psychology, it has been clear that this new discipline would require new methods of research. Traditional laboratory methods favored by psychologists would prove inadequate to the study of people's behavior in social and cultural contexts and to understanding processes and effects of social interventions and social change.

This article discusses six principles that guide research in community psychology. Although not every project undertaken by a community psychologist demonstrates all of them, most members of the field would agree that all six are ideals. The principles are (1) research embodies social values, (2) research should be linked to action, (3) research should involve collaboration between researchers and participants, (4) research in the real world is complex, (5) research must attend to context and to multiple levels of analysis, and (6) research should be culturally anchored.

Research Embodies Social Values

Most community psychologists believe that research in the social sciences reflects social values both in the choice of topic and the approach taken. Values enter into the initial framing of a research question. For example, the question, "Why do some youths drop out of high school?" focuses attention on differences in the backgrounds, skills, and motivations of youths who complete and fail to complete high school. The question, "Why do some high schools have high drop-out rates?" focuses attention instead on the organization and financing of schools, the quality of education that they provide, and their ability to engage the youths in their charge. The first question implicitly fixes responsibility for dropping out of school on youths or their families; the second suggests that responsibility may rest with schools. The questions also imply different approaches to intervention to increase rates of high school completion, for example, tutoring to remedy youths' deficient skills, in the first case, and modifying curricula or restructuring high schools to clarify expectations and promote better relationships among students and teachers, in the second. (Other questions, with different implied solutions, are also possible.)

Community psychologists emphasize peoples' strengths rather than weaknesses. Many psychologists try to understand the particular ways that adolescents can get into trouble, by investigating the causes of high school dropout, teen pregnancy, substance abuse, delinquency, and the like. A community psychologist might ask instead how most youths, even those from poor backgrounds, manage to negotiate the shoals of adolescence and emerge as competent and contributing adults. Competence in adolescence does not involve only avoiding dropout, pregnancy, substance use, or delinquency, but also doing well in school, participating in extracurricular activities including sports, and contributing to one's family and community. Children may succeed in these realms even if they also engage in some problem behaviors. At the least, it is an empirical question whether a focus on promoting positive behaviors in adolescents is more or less effective than a focus on preventing negative behaviors in producing successful adults.

The point of these examples is not that one approach is right and another wrong. A complete understanding of adolescent development is likely to involve both individual factors and contextual ones, both strengths and problems. Rather, the point is that the choice of question in any particular study involves social values about what outcomes are most important and often unexamined premises about what predictors are most likely to explain them. Community psychologists are more likely than other psychologists to focus on people's strengths and to look for dysfunction in social environments rather than in individuals.

Research Should Be Linked to Action

Another central value of community psychology is that research should serve, ultimately, to promote human welfare. Community psychologists may work directly to develop and evaluate interventions to prevent mental health or behavioral problems or to promote well-being. For example, community psychologists have developed and evaluated programs to prevent adults who lose jobs from becoming depressed, to prevent teen smoking both by enhancing teens' skills in refusing involvement with substances and by delivering sanctions to merchants who violate the law by selling cigarettes to minors, and to enhance early development of children from poor backgrounds. In order to conduct interventions, community psychologists must first do generative research to understand the processes by which mental health problems arise or by which good outcomes ensue. For example, the program to prevent depression among workers who lose their jobs rests on research showing links between job loss and depression. Community psychologists also study processes of social change that they do not themselves instigate, including the self-help movement or community mobilization to fight environmental toxins.

Other community psychologists do research relevant to social policy. For example, studies that show that children in child care centers do better when teachers have good education and training, group sizes are not too large, and there are not too many children for each adult, can inform state regulations governing day care centers. Research that shows that homeless families who are given subsidized housing are every bit as stable as other poor families, regardless of individual problems, suggests that policies to increase the supply of affordable housing would reduce homelessness in the United States.

Community psychologists have been influenced by Kurt Lewin's model of action research (*Field Theory in Social Research*, New York, 1951), which involves a cycle of activities beginning with problem definition and research or fact finding, followed by a setting of goals and undertaking actions to reach them, followed by an evaluation of the efforts and a redefinition of the problem. In this model, research leads directly to action, which in turn leads to additional research. The model is particularly useful in working with small community organizations that can engage in multiple cycles of activity and evaluation.

Community psychologists believe not only that research should inform action, but also that action can inform theory. From this perspective, the community psychologist's social intervention is analogous to the laboratory psychologist's experimental manipulation of a variable to understand its effect. Generative research is most often correlational, and allows researchers to examine associations among variables, but not to determine causal pathways. Experimental interventions do permit us to understand causal relationships and test underlying theories.

Research Should Involve Collaboration Between Researchers and Participants

The report of the Swampscott conference described the community psychologist as a participant conceptualizer who would bring the conceptual and methodological tools of psychology to community problems but also who would be an active participant in social action in collaboration with members of the community (Bennett et al., *Community psychology: A Report of the Boston Conference on the Education of Psychologists for Community Mental Health*, Boston, 1966). Collaboration has at least two goals. First, research is likely to be better and more useful if it takes advantage of the knowledge and perspectives of research participants, including their sense of the questions that are worth asking. Second, interventions are more likely to have a lasting impact if participants make them their own. Over the years, community psychologists increasingly have taken a constructivist approach to knowledge. That is, they believe that knowledge is socially constructed, and that different participants or stakeholders may have different understandings of the same situation. For example, an intervention in a school would include as stakeholders, students, teachers, administrators, school-board members, and parents, at a minimum. Any particular intervention might include other groups. For a program to distribute free condoms in the schools, additional stakeholders might include clergy, public health officials, service providers at Planned Parenthood, and owners of pharmacies where youths might otherwise buy condoms. Different stakeholders will focus on different issues, including protection of youths from disease and unwanted pregnancy, the proper role of families and schools, sexual morality, efficiency of intervention, disruption of the school day, and economic loss. A psychologist who studies this intervention may also have a unique perspective, informed by the research literature on similar interventions and by knowledge of methodology, but this perspective is simply different, not more valid, than the others.

Even when community interventions are less controversial than condom distribution in schools, research is likely to be most useful and informative if the researcher can collaborate with local stakeholders and research participants to understand their perspectives when framing questions, and to incorporate their local knowledge in designing studies. Research that does not address participants' concerns is likely to sit on the shelf.

Further, interventions designed solely by psychologists or imported from elsewhere may meet with local resistance—even interventions that fit reasonably well with the local culture. They are unlikely to draw the same level of commitment as interventions that participants aid in designing. Designing and carrying out an intervention may be empowering and thus have greater benefits than simply participating in an intervention designed by others.

Of course, creating an intervention to obtain some desired outcome is hard work, and few interventions are successful the first time out. Rather, interventions are frequently modified and improved several times before attaining success. Thus it makes sense for people designing interventions to draw on the research literature regarding similar interventions that have worked in the past. Tension may arise between fidelity to an intervention that has been proven to work, at least under the circumstances where it was originally developed, and adaptation of the intervention to local circumstances with local ownership. Blakely and colleagues, in a large-scale study of 70 adaptations of seven different well-documented interventions, showed that modifications that changed key features of the original intervention reduced success, but that additions to the intervention to fit local circumstances enhanced it (Blakely et al., *American Journal of Community Psychology*, 1987, 15, 253–268).

Research in the Real World Is Complex

As is probably obvious by now, research in real-world contexts is often more complex than research in psychological laboratories. Laboratory experiments are designed to manipulate only a small number of variables at a time, holding all other influences on outcomes constant. Researchers who study naturally occurring processes or interventions in natural contexts do not have the luxury of isolating only a few variables to examine their effects. Community psychologists and others have made numerous creative responses to the resulting challenges.

Some researchers adopt qualitative techniques to substitute rich description of social phenomenon in a necessarily small number of people or settings for a quantitative look at a larger number of people or settings. These researchers often borrow techniques from anthropologists or sociologists, including ethnography, extensive observation, and in-depth interviewing, often

with multiple stakeholders. Observational designs, including most qualitative methods and more quantitative ones such as survey research, are particularly useful when the researcher has little or no control over the phenomenon under study. Sometimes longitudinal designs, in which researchers study the same group of people at multiple points in time, are used to tease apart relationships among variables over time.

Community researchers can also conduct true experiments in field situations, randomly assigning individuals or settings, such as classrooms, schools, or even communities, to intervention and control groups. Often the control group gets an alternative intervention, either for ethical reasons, or to motivate their continued participation in the study. In principle, if the experimental group does better than the control group on some outcome, the intervention was a success. But inferences are actually more complicated. First, researchers must be sure that the intervention was in fact delivered to the experimental group as planned. If not, the comparison is meaningless. Second, in real situations, people who are assigned to (or invited to participate in) interventions may not show up or may drop out. And those who drop out may have been doing worse than those who stayed. (For example, people may drop out of a treatment program for substance abuse because they have returned to using substances.) Comparing only people who complete the intervention with those who do not will lead to biased (misleading) results. Often researchers compare all those who were invited to participate with all those who were invited to the comparison group to avoid this bias, but other more sophisticated solutions are sometimes possible. Third, people may complete the intervention, but not the posttest. Wherever there are missing data, researchers must work to understand why, and whether they can estimate what would have happened if data were complete.

More elaborate analyses provide additional information. Follow-up data are useful in determining whether the effects of an intervention are temporary or more permanent, or even whether interventions, by altering trajectories of development, may have increasing effects over time. Researchers can bolster their conclusions by examining patterns of relationships among variables. If the theory says that an intervention to prevent college dropout works because students develop closer relationships with faculty, then it is important to test the theory to see whether closer relationships do in fact develop, and whether students with closer relationships are less likely to drop out. Finally, programs are often subjected to cost-effectiveness analysis, to see whether they are more or less effective than other programs with similar costs.

In between experimental designs where the researcher has a large degree of control and observational designs where there is little or no control, lie designs in which the investigator has some control, at least over who gets measured. A variety of clever quasi-experimental designs exploit naturally occurring variation to understand social phenomenon. If researchers cannot assign some participants at random to a control group, perhaps they can find similar people who have not been exposed to the intervention, and study them as a comparison group. Perhaps they can find measures of the outcome that extend back in time over a long period before the intervention. If the outcomes (for example, in a school setting, achievement, attendance, or drop-out rates) are quite stable for years before the intervention, and then exhibit important changes at the time of the intervention, it may be possible to infer that the intervention had an effect. Making inferences requires careful attention to other possible explanations for the phenomenon, sometimes called rival hypotheses or threats to validity. Researchers must also consider whether the phenomenon is likely to occur in the same way in other social contexts.

Research Must Attend to Context and to Multiple Levels of Analysis

A central concern of community psychologists is understanding relationships between persons and settings. Settings such as peer groups, schools, work organizations, neighborhoods, or society as a whole may influence individual behavior; people in turn can create new social settings or influence the settings they are involved in. And settings can condition or influence the nature of relationships between other variables. For example, the level of parental control that is optimal for adolescent development may depend on the level of risk in the neighborhood or the level of delinquency among the adolescent's friends. Settings may also operate in different ways for people with different characteristics. For example, police may be more likely to arrest minority adolescents than white adolescents who commit the same offense, creating different environments for the two groups. Systematic patterns of this sort are called social regularities.

Psychologists in general are far more expert in assessing individuals than in assessing social environments. Community and environmental psychologists have made considerable progress in understanding characteristics of social settings, particularly the most immediate face-to-face settings for human behavior, which Bronfenbrenner calls microsystems. [See Social Settings.] Research on characteristics of larger and more diffuse settings, such as neighborhoods, and their influence on individual behavior has burgeoned recently with new techniques for locating respondents in particular neighborhoods (known as geocoding) and then examining characteristics of those neighborhoods with census data, surveys, or observational techniques. Such research remains in its infancy, but holds considerable promise.

Failures to consider contextual effects can lead to misattributions of causality to characteristics of individuals. For example, William Julius Wilson (*The Truly Disadvantaged*, Chicago, 1987) points out that African Americans of any socioeconomic status are more likely to live in areas of concentrated poverty than are European Americans of the same socioeconomic status. If living in a poor neighborhood has adverse effects on employment (because there are fewer jobs or fewer role models) or school success (because schools are more poorly funded, have less inspired teachers, or spend more time on remedial work), researchers who ignore neighborhoods will mistakenly attribute these effects to individual race. Understanding contextual influences is thus critical to understanding the level of analysis at which a particular effect occurs. Statistical techniques can help to sort out these effects.

Research Should Be Culturally Anchored

An important context that is receiving increasing attention from community psychologists and others is culture, including values, norms, behaviors, and "blueprints for living" that may vary among groups with different national origins or, sometimes in more subtle ways, between groups defined by race/ethnicity, gender, socioeconomic status, sexual orientation, or other variables (see Hughes, Seidman, & Williams, *American Journal of Community Psychology*, 1993, *21*, 687–703). Early research by psychologists on cultural differences tended to compare some other group, most often African Americans or women, to a white male standard, with any differences seen as implying the inferiority of the other group.

Community psychologists have rejected this approach for many reasons. The values of the field preclude taking any group's characteristics as the standard of worth. Many supposedly objective categories, such as race, are in fact fluid and more dependent on perceptions than on any objective criterion. There are as many differences within particular groups (e.g., among Latin Americans from various countries of origin) as between groups. The most interesting questions may not involve comparisons between groups, but variation within groups. Even the questions may vary from group to group. For example, questions about successful adaptation to a new culture make sense only for immigrants; questions about consequences of antigay hate crime make sense only for homosexuals and bisexuals.

Other questions make sense for multiple groups, but answers may vary. For example, researchers have hypothesized that extended family, church, and informal sources of help may be more important to mental health for African Americans than for European Americans. One important class of questions concerns the extent to which prevention and intervention programs that have been shown to be effective for a particular group are also useful for other groups, or how they should be modified to be more culturally sensitive and effective. Researchers must be careful that prevention programs, such as parent training, do not simply impose the researcher's values on participants with different values.

Where similar questions make sense across different groups, it is important to understand the extent to which the underlying concepts and ways of measuring them are also comparable. If one group scores worse than another on an inventory of psychological symptoms, does the first group really have worse mental health, or are members of the first group simply more willing to acknowledge symptoms? And are mental health problems organized in similar ways for different groups?

Research is culturally anchored when it asks questions that are meaningful to the group or groups being studied, in language that makes sense to them, and with measures that are suitable for the group. Collaboration between researchers and participants may help to increase the cultural appropriateness of research efforts. Nonetheless, cultural anchoring of research remains a challenge to community psychologists, and to other psychologists as well.

In sum, although community psychology shares many methodological approaches with other types of psychology, there are important differences in emphasis. Values are central to research in community psychology and core values include linking research to action and involving research participants as collaborators. The complexities of research in the real world require clever designs and attention to the social and cultural contexts in which participants live.

Bibliography

Bryk, A. S. & Raudenbush, S. W. (1992). *Hierarchical linear models: Applications and data analysis methods.* Newbury Park, CA: Sage. Technical book that provides both a conceptual overview and statistical techniques for sorting out levels of analysis. Useful for those with a solid understanding of regression analysis.

Cook, T. D., & Campbell, D. T. (1979). *Quasi-experimentation: Design and analysis issues for field settings.* Boston: Houghton Mifflin. A bible of quasi-experimental design, explaining different types of validity and the logic of attaining each.

Fetterman, D. M., Kaftarian, S. J., & Wandersman, A. (Eds.). (1966). *Empowerment evaluation: Knowledge and tools for self assessment and accountability.* Thousand Oaks, CA: Sage. Describes and gives examples of a continuous process similar to action research to help participants improve programs via self-evaluation.

Guba, E. G., & Lincoln, Y. S. (1989). *Fourth generation evaluation.* Newbury Park, CA: Sage. Discusses qualitative approaches to program evaluation and obtaining the views of multiple stakeholders.

Rappaport, J., & Seidman E. (Eds.). (2000). *Handbook of community psychology.* New York: Plenum Press. Includes several chapters on research methods and analysis, as well as more substantive chapters.

Reinharz, S. (1992). *Feminist methods in social research.* New York: Oxford University Press. Discusses largely qualitative approaches to research from a feminist perspective; includes an extensive bibliography.

Revenson, T. A., D'Augelli, A., French, S. E., Hughes, D. H., Livert, D., Seidman, E., Shinn, M., & Yoshikawa, H. (Eds.). (in press). *Design issues in prevention and intervention research: Readings from the American Journal of Community Psychology.* New York: Plenum Press. Examples of community research, culled from the leading journal in the field.

Seidman, E. Hughes, D., & Williams, N. (Eds.). (1993). *American Journal of Community Psychology, 21* (6). Special issue on culturally anchored methodology. Essays about and examples of culturally anchored research methods.

Shinn, M. (Ed.) (1996). *American Journal of Community Psychology, 24* (1). Special issue on ecological assessment. Examples of efforts to assess social settings in community psychology.

Tolan, P., Keys, C., Chertok, F., & Jason, L. (Eds.). (1990). *Researching community psychology: Issues of theory and methods.* Washington, DC: American Psychological Association. Essays about research methods by leading community psychologists.

Marybeth Shinn

Prevention and Intervention

In the nineteenth century John Snow halted the cholera epidemic in London by removing the handle of the Broad Street water pump. By cutting off access to contaminated water, Snow managed, in a single stroke, to mount a major successful prevention effort against cholera. Neither Snow or anyone else had a very clear understanding of the mechanisms of cause and effect that were involved. Nearly a century later, in 1962 in Ypsilanti, Michigan, a high-quality preschool program for impoverished African American children was begun. The program taught basic cognitive skills and was accompanied by weekly home visits by trained teachers. This program was different in one important way. Half of the children were randomly assigned to the program and half had the usual preschool experience in their community. The children were followed for more than 20 years to learn what effects early exposure to the program might have had. As time went on, remarkable differences between the children who participated in the program and those who had not began to emerge. By primary school, children who had been in the program were much less disruptive in school, and by the time they were adolescents, the group was involved in fewer violent acts and less police contact. By the time they were 19 years old, the preschool program children had much higher rates of high school completion, lower arrest records, less placement in special education classes, and higher levels of economic achievement.

While quite different, each of these is an example of a successful prevention effort. In the case of the cholera epidemic, an infectious disease was involved. John Snow's dramatic intervention had a preventive impact, even though the reason for the success of the prevention effort was poorly understood. In the case of the preschool program, an enriching experience for vulnerable children at a critical time in their lives dramatically altered their life course, both enhancing their own life prospects and providing clear benefits for society.

More than a century after John Snow's prevention effort, our knowledge of infectious disease and our capacity to protect populations through hygienic efforts and immunization has made prevention of infectious diseases almost routine in some parts of the world. However, new challenges for prevention are emerging. Today, with the notable exception of Human Immunodeficiency Virus (HIV) and Acquired Immune Deficiency Syndrome (AIDS) and certain infectious childhood diseases such as measles, many of the targets of prevention programs are not infectious diseases. Instead they are chronic long-term recurring disorders with developmental roots and long-term trajectories such as drug abuse, failures of academic achievement, depression, conduct problems, and school failure. All of these problems have complex biological, psychological, and social roots that intertwine in the development of disorder. The field of prevention draws some of its most dramatic examples from public health, but prevention of personal, social, and developmental problems represents a common goal of many fields including education, criminal justice, psychology, psychiatry, and human development.

Risk and Protection Across the Life Course

It is helpful to think about prevention from the point of view of human development over the life course. Each developing individual is continuously changing and the risk and protective factors to which they are exposed will emerge and disappear over time. Furthermore, at every stage of the life course, certain critical developmental tasks must be accomplished, and if they are not, they will compromise development later in the life course. Early in life for example, many developmental tasks involve biological regulation, perception of the physical environment, and developing cognitive abilities. In infancy and in early childhood, critical developmental tasks involve the acquisition of language skills and the development of impulse control. Later, as the child enters school, the capacity to read and write becomes important, and social skills to get along with peers are also critical. With entry into puberty and increased freedom from parental support and supervision, new risks associated with sexuality, substance use, and health are encountered. Skills to resist peer pressure, solve complex interpersonal problems, and pursue goals in the face of setbacks become important.

Human development and risks do not end with adolescence. Indeed, as the individual moves from adolescence to adulthood, additional critical transitions emerge. The choice of an occupation and the emergence of committed relationships come to center stage. As the focus turns to the key developmental tasks of parenting, working life, and sustaining a relationship, risks associated with divorce, job loss, or disruptive parent-child relationships become salient. An important feature of risks in adulthood is that they often carry liabilities not only for the adult, but also for those with whom the adult has intimate relationships, including spouse, partner, or child. Even middle adulthood and old age expose the individual to new risks, both planned and unplanned. At the end of life, life transitions and crises associated with illness and the death of a spouse occur, still new risks emerge, and with them new opportunities for prevention.

The settings in which we live our lives, family, community, and work, can involve both risk and protection throughout the life course. Early in life, the biological and social environments of parental caregivers are critical for the development of infants and small children. Later, the school emerges as a key community setting for risk and protection. Still later, intimate relationships in family, home, neighborhood, and the community and workplace influence life trajectories. Because the social settings that are vital to human development and well-being change during the life course from clinic and nursery to school and neighborhood and finally to workplace and family, the settings most appropriate for prevention efforts change as well.

Definitions of Prevention and Classification of Prevention Efforts

Perhaps the most dramatic and successful examples we have of large-scale prevention efforts involve efforts to prevent the spread of infectious diseases. A century ago, infectious diseases such as smallpox and influenza were the leading causes of death and disability, but through the introduction of hygienic measures and immunization, these diseases had dramatically declined by 1970. Indeed, smallpox has been eradicated on a worldwide basis primarily through effective prevention efforts. Some advocates of prevention argue that no major disease has ever been eradicated through treatment.

Attempts to classify prevention efforts provide one set of organizing principles for the field. One widely recognized classification system emphasizes prevention efforts aimed at the risk characteristics of entire populations, rather than individuals. This approach, originally proposed by the Commission on Chronic Illness in 1957, defines primary prevention as efforts to reduce the rate of development of new cases (incidence) of disorder or illness. Primary prevention requires that we know enough about the early roots of disease or disorder to alter the risk factors for populations to prevent illness from occurring in the first place. This is a worthy and challenging goal made attractive by its success in earlier public health efforts with infectious diseases. Secondary prevention includes all efforts designed to reduce the number of already existing cases (prevalence) in the population. Secondary prevention can be accomplished by early and effective intervention once early signs of the problem have been identified. Finally, tertiary prevention is not actually aimed at preventing disorders at all, but instead at reducing the amount of disability and dysfunction associated with a disorder once it occurs. For example, the effort to reduce the disability associated with a serious injury, once it has occurred, is an example of tertiary prevention. This classification system focuses primarily on outcomes, but says little about how they might be achieved.

A more recent approach classifies prevention efforts in terms of how broadly they can be applied to the population with widespread benefit. For example, a universal preventive effort is one that can offer confidence to everyone in the general public where the overall benefits outweigh the risk for those who receive the program. An example of a universal preventive effort is water purification and another is smoking cessation. In each case, the benefits clearly outweigh the risks and costs, and therefore, could be provided on a universal basis. A selective preventive strategy is one that is appropriate only for people whose risk of harm is above average, and where more expensive interventions might therefore be justified. An example of a selective preventive strategy might be annual mammograms for women or special safety devices that are required for dangerous occupations. Finally, indicated preventive strategies are only appropriate for an even narrower group of people who already show a strong indication that they will develop a problem, disease, or disorder. In this case, a targeted and even aggressive intervention might be appropriate because the benefits outweigh the costs and risks, even when the cost or risk involved in the intervention is appreciable. An example might be license suspension in the case of a driver with a long record of driving while intoxicated. Here intervention with the individual could outweigh the costs and risks for society.

Recently, some researchers and community practitioners have argued that the focus of prevention may be too narrow, and that a greater emphasis should be placed on the promotion of health, mental health, and positive human development. They contend that the negative outcomes identified in prevention ignore the fact that effective promotion efforts can enhance coping ability or resistance to later disorder. There is little doubt that efforts that promote social skills, academic achievement, and personal resilience in the face of stress and adversity have substantial value in themselves. In some cases, promotion efforts may also have preventive effects, particularly for persons who are vulnerable to disorder. The distinction between prevention and promotion can be best thought of as a distinction between means and ends. Promotion efforts have a value in and of themselves, and can also be thought of as a means of preventing disorder. For example, a preschool program designed to increase social problem-solving skills may also prevent the development of disorder in children who are particularly at risk for later problems.

Strategies for Prevention Through the Life Course

Over the life course, individuals and families develop, and risks to health and well-being ebb and flow. At the beginning of life many of the risk factors are biological, and critically determine how the organism develops. Later, risks and vulnerabilities are more social in nature, both in their origins and impacts. The acquisition of language, the ability to delay gratification, to get along with peers, and to provide and care for others have both biological and social aspects.

In addition, each individual life trajectory encounters critical transitions, or milestones in development such as beginning school, entry into the world of work, the development of a committed relationship, birth of a first child, and retirement. Many of these transitions are normal and expected in society, and a number of social institutions have been developed to help negotiate these transitions. They are, nevertheless, moments of risk in the life course. Beyond these life transitions, there are numerous unplanned or unscheduled turning points in the lives of individuals and families that also present major sources of risk. These turning points can involve, for example, illness or injury in childhood, school expulsion or dropout, unplanned pregnancy, job loss or loss of a close personal relationship, bereavement or widowhood, or the death of a parent or child. In what follows, we will review a sampling of prevention efforts through the life course.

Prevention in Infancy and Early Childhood. In the development of a new life many of the risks are biological, and preventive efforts are directed at protecting the fetus and the health of the mother. High quality prenatal and perinatal care are among the most important preventive measures that can be provided at the beginning of life. Unfortunately, the availability of good prenatal care is not universal, and continued efforts are needed to make good prenatal care more widely available. The research evidence clearly suggests that a number of health and developmental complications can be avoided and healthy development can be enhanced through the simple provision of prenatal and perinatal care.

Immunization. Immunization against infectious disease shortly after birth is a second universal strategy with substantial preventive benefit. Immunization protects infants against a variety of childhood diseases, such as measles, that a century ago took a substantial toll on the health and well-being of the population. Immunization is a classic example of the traditional public health prevention model. A vaccine can confer long-term protection against a particular physical disease. For example, children not immunized against Type B influenza and meningitis can suffer long-term negative effects on the brain, resulting in learning disabilities and psychological and behavioral disorders.

An example of a successful prevention program for prenatal and perinatal care of infants focuses on working with single teenage mothers. The program uses home health visits by public health nurses to assure high quality prenatal and perinatal care. Visiting nurses also teach young mothers about risks to the infant from smoking, poor diet, and alcohol use. Visiting nurses also provide parent training and vocational guidance for the young mother as she prepares to enter the world of work. Research has shown that this program provides improved maternal diet and reduces smoking during pregnancy for teenage mothers. The program also reduces premature deliveries, and results in higher birth weight and less child abuse. In short, this prevention program uses the skills of a public health nurse to reduce a wide variety of risks for the mother and infant, and supports the transition to healthy development for both mother and child.

Prevention in Childhood. In early childhood, new developmental tasks become prominent in successful development, particularly, the acquisition of language skills and social and impulse control. When children have not yet entered school, but are learning to interact with their social world, language and social compe-

tence is critical to social development. Research has shown that programs that focus on enhancing mother-child interaction, either through home visits or through participation in a local parent-child developmental center also result in fewer behavioral problems for children, better family management practices, and higher levels of cognitive competence.

Once children enter primary school, they encounter different developmental tasks and risks. The acquisition of reading skills and the capacity to get along with peers become increasingly important in elementary school. As a community setting, the school is a major source of rewards and punishments, social models, and opportunities for skill acquisition, and a place where children spend a substantial portion of their waking life. Preventive interventions that enhance the social competence of children of elementary school age can reduce behavior problems and enhance later development. If early developmental, health, or mental health problems begin to appear in elementary school children, detection and early intervention is possible in the school setting. For example, research has shown that school based programs that teach children social and interpersonal skills can reduce early behavior problems or poor impulse control, and produce better cognitive problem solving skills.

At this age, major social transitions in home life, such as divorce, death of a parent, or severe illness in the family can present substantial risks to the child. Divorce and the conflict between parents that often accompanies it can be a significant risk factor for children. Research on a number of school-based programs have shown that weekly sessions for children that help them understand their own feelings about divorce and deal with related anxiety, anger, and interpersonal conflicts can have significant positive preventive effects on child adjustment. Although less common, children are also at risk when a parent dies. Researchers have shown that a family grief workshop followed by sessions with a family advisor can reduce school and behavior problems among children who have experienced the death of a parent.

The school is a social setting in which a wide range of childhood vulnerabilities can be ameliorated. School programs that help children master academic challenges and learn social skills to control their own behavior can have positive effects on aggressive and shy children. They can improve cognitive competence, especially among those children who have early symptoms of depression. While such school programs are not yet widely available, they have substantial promise in preventing problems for children at risk.

Prevention for Adolescents. As children move from childhood to adolescence the patterns of risk change yet again. With the onset of puberty, competent coping with sexuality becomes a major developmental

COMMUNITY PSYCHOLOGY: Prevention and Intervention 223

task. It is not only the risk of pregnancy, but also contracting sexually transmitted diseases, including AIDS, that become critical risks for young adolescents. In addition, substance and alcohol abuse become risks with very substantial potential for negative effects on development and health. Adolescence is also a time when increased risks of other problems emerge, including school failure, dropout, or behavior problems and delinquency.

A large number of drug abuse prevention programs have been developed to reduce the likelihood of alcohol or substance abuse among early teenagers. A survey of these programs suggests that successful programs have two elements. First, they encourage students to adopt attitudes against drug abuse during adolescence. Second, they involve classroom-based training to teach teenagers to identify peer and media influences to use drugs and to resist those influences. Typically prevention programs that are effective involve classroom practice at role playing to resist peer influences to use drugs, providing examples from peers and other forms of classroom instruction. Research has shown that it is possible to reduce the prevalence of cigarette smoking, alcohol, and marijuana use in adolescents through such programs.

Prevention in Adulthood. With entry into adulthood, the focus shifts yet again to new developmental tasks. In adulthood, the tasks include the establishment of committed relationships, the challenges of childbearing and child rearing, finding paid employment, and successfully sustaining a work life. There are also new risks in adulthood, including the risks associated with poverty, or the stressful burden of caring for ill or elderly family members.

Prevention programs have been designed and tested that can help adults cope with many of these key transitions and crises. For example, programs to teach couples to handle disagreements in constructive ways and to communicate more effectively have been shown to increase couples relationship satisfaction, reduce negative communication, and reduce the risk of divorce. If divorce occurs, however, the resulting conflict can negatively influence not only children in the family, but also the health and mental health of the divorcing individuals. Programs that are aimed at helping individuals cope with the multiple challenges of divorce can provide real preventive benefits. One program that provides highly specialized workshops on starting new relationships, child rearing, single parenting, and legal and financial issues has been shown to prevent depression and anxiety and enhance self-confidence and well-being.

Job loss is another unplanned life transition that can also produce significant risks for individuals and families, including increased family conflict, economic hardship, depression, and anxiety. Prevention programs have been developed to teach job search skills and skills for coping with setbacks in the job search process. The program has been shown to increase reemployment rates among participants, reduce the risk of depression, and at the same time, produce higher paying jobs for program participants.

Prevention in Later Life. Later in the life course, as chronic illness becomes more likely, family members may become responsible for the care of a parent or spouse who has become seriously ill. The caregiving task can produce a continuing stream of stressors with which the caregiver must cope. Peer and professionally led groups to support family caregivers can help people share their stressful experiences, express their support to one another, and learn tactics for coping more effectively. Caregivers who participated in these programs experience mental health benefits and better levels of knowledge about community resources that can help to relieve the caregiving burden.

At the end of life, loss of a spouse or loved one can produce prolonged bereavement with complicating health problems. Prevention efforts can be effective even for the elderly toward the end of the life course. Mutual help programs in which widows were able to share experiences and mutual support have been shown to prevent distress and depression. National networks of self-help groups for widows have been formed, and research has shown that participants greatly benefit from participation.

Evidence of Effectiveness of Prevention

The effectiveness of prevention efforts should be a concern not only to researchers, but parents and citizens as well. As the parent of a child concerned about the effectiveness of a school program to prevent drug abuse, or as a community member curious about claims of a program to prevent juvenile crime, it is natural to ask whether prevention programs are actually effective. Parents and community members should become thoughtful and demanding consumers of prevention programs, and ask for evidence of effectiveness. In the enthusiasm of public advocacy or the heat of debate, concerns for evidence of effectiveness may be lost. Yet in the long run, critical and demanding citizen consumers are essential to genuine and sustained prevention efforts in the community.

Researchers have observed that successful prevention programs have a number of characteristics in common. First, they are targeted and are informed by an understanding of the risks and problems encountered by the target group. In addition, they are designed to influence the life trajectory of people who participate in them. They are aimed at long-term change, setting individuals on a new developmental course, opening opportunities, changing life circumstances, or providing support.

What evidence should be considered in choosing a prevention program? Without doubt one of the highest standards for the evaluation of prevention programs is a study in which the program has been tested in randomized trials where both those who received the program and those who did not are followed over time to assess long-term program impact. Such studies are expensive and have been conducted only on a few of the programs that claim to prevent problems in health and human development. Nevertheless, evidence from randomized studies is very important in evaluating the worth of a prevention program.

Another kind of evidence for effectiveness is increasingly becoming available. It is called meta-analysis and involves the careful accumulation of results across multiple studies. For example, a recent meta-analysis of prevention programs reviewed 177 prevention programs designed to prevent behavioral and social problems in children and adolescents. The study found that most of the programs reviewed produced favorable outcomes, similar or greater in magnitude than those obtained in other intervention sciences. This evidence compares very favorably with that generally accepted for medical and social interventions and should be a source of considerable optimism about the effectiveness of prevention efforts. Many prevention programs actually influence a spectrum of health, mental health, and developmental outcomes, and some of the beneficial results may not appear for some time. For example, the preschool program described earlier had effects on school achievement, occupational achievement, and criminal justice outcomes. Many of these beneficial effects did not become apparent for a number of years after the end of the preschool program. This makes it clear that long-term follow-up is a critical ingredient in evaluating prevention programs.

Although developing and sustaining effective prevention programs presents challenges to the skills of psychologists and citizens alike, their costs may be small compared to the social costs of school dropout, drug abuse, depression, or delinquency. As health-care costs continue to be a national concern, we are becoming more and more aware that for every problem in development, health, and disability, someone is paying the bill in tax dollars, insurance premiums, or human suffering. Community-based programs to prevent disorders and disability promise to reduce costs to society as well as to antidote disability and human suffering.

[*See also* Community Prevention and Intervention.]

Bibliography

Albee, G. W., & Gullotta, T. P. (Eds.). (1977). *Primary prevention works.* Vol. 6. Thousand Oaks: Sage. A collection of effective prevention programs.

Commission on Chronic Illness. (1957). *Chronic illness in the United States. Vol. 1.* Published for the Commonwealth Fund. Cambridge, MA: Harvard University Press.

Durlak, J. A., & Wells, A. M. (1997). Primary prevention mental health programs for children and adolescents: A meta-analytic review. *American Journal of Community Psychology, 25(2),* 115–152. A detailed review summarizing the cumulative results of prevention programs for children and adolescents.

Gordon, R. (1987). An operational classification of disease prevention. In J. A. Steinberg & M. M. Silverman (Eds.), *Preventing medical disorders* (pp. 20–26). Rockville, MD: Department of Health and Human Services.

Heller, K. (1996). Coming of age of prevention science: Comments on the 1994 National Institute of Mental Health-Institute of Medicine prevention papers. *American Psychologist, 51,* 1123–1128. Historical and policy analysis of the IOM and NIMH reports.

Mrazek, P. J., & Haggerty, R. J. (Eds.). (1994). *Reducing risks for mental disorders: Frontiers for preventive intervention research.* Washington, DC: National Academy Press. A comprehensive review of conceptual, research, and policy issues on prevention compiled by the Institute of Medicine, National Academy of Sciences.

Munoz, R. F., Mrazek, P. J., & Haggerty, R. J. (1996). Institute of Medicine report on prevention of mental disorders: Summary and commentary. *American Psychologist, 51,* 1116–1122. Commentary on the Mrazek & Haggerty report, *Reducing risks for mental disorders.*

NIMH Committee on Prevention Research. (1995, May). *A plan for prevention research for the National Institute of Mental Health* (A report to the National Advisory Mental Health Council). Washington, DC: Author. Research policy recommendations for prevention in mental health.

Price, R. H., Cowen, E., Lorion, R., & Ramos-McKay, J. (Eds.) (1988). *Fourteen ounces of prevention.* Washington, DC: American Psychological Association. A collection of model prevention programs spanning the life course.

Reiss, D., & Price, R. H. (1996). National research agenda for prevention research: The National Institute of Mental Health Report. *American Psychologist, 51(11),* 1109–1115. Commentary on the NIMH Report.

Sandler, I. (Ed.). (1997). Meta-analysis of primary prevention programs for children and adolescents: Introduction to the special issue. *American Journal of Community Psychology, 25(2),* 111–113. Commentary on the Durlak meta-analysis.

Richard H. Price

COMPARATIVE PSYCHOLOGY deals with the study of the genesis, control, and consequences of behavior in a wide range of animal species. Behavior is viewed in a broad biological context in relation to principles of genetics, developmental biology, and evolutionary theory.

Problems of genesis concern the evolutionary and developmental histories of behavioral patterns. Those of control relate to the immediate factors, both inside and outside of the animal, affecting behavior. The consequences of behavior can be those for the animal itself, other animals, or the environment, but concern especially the reproductive success of the animal displaying the behavioral pattern. Such reproductive success, or biological fitness, feeds back to affect the evolution of the behavior and the species.

Psychology is sometimes defined as the study of human behavior. In such a context, the notion of animals as subjects of psychological study appears paradoxical. However, animal research has been a part of psychology since its differentiation as a distinct branch of inquiry and has contributed much to the field during that time.

The term *comparative psychology* has created much difficulty. Through much of the history of the field it has been used in reference to all research on nonhuman animals. The term is better used, however, only in reference to a part of that subdiscipline. Animal research targeted strictly at understanding the process of learning and that aimed at physiological mechanisms are important endeavors but are best treated as different from true comparative psychology. The term *animal psychology* can be used as an umbrella for all three.

The term *comparative* is, however, somewhat misleading in the description of the field. Some authors have proposed that in order to qualify as comparative, research must entail overt comparisons among different animal species. This perspective has been generally rejected. What is critical for research in comparative psychology is the broad biological framework in which the research is placed. Problems are framed in relation to the evolution and development of behavior conceived broadly. Some early pioneers of comparative psychology, C. Lloyd Morgan and Linus Kline, proposed that the field be termed *zoological psychology*. This term is more descriptive of the comparative psychology that has evolved because the problems studied, modes of thinking, and interpretations of comparative psychologists overlap those of many zoologists interested in animal behavior. Comparative psychologists have differed from zoologists in that their problems have often been generated and interpreted in relation to those of the psychology of human behavior. Thus, comparative psychologists have had to tread a narrow line as they work with a vision of psychological breadth, on the one hand, while placing their work in broad biological perspective, on the other.

History of the Field

Thought concerning the relationship between humans and nonhuman species can be seen early on in intellectual history. Aristotle wrote of the *Scala naturae*, be-lieving that species could be placed along a single continuum from the lowest to the highest, a view that is rejected today. Prominent among the many philosophers who addressed these issues was René Descartes, who believed there to be a fundamental dichotomy between the human soul and the reflex mechanisms governing animal behavior.

The true antecedents of comparative psychology can be seen among British scientists of the nineteenth century. The work of Charles Darwin was critical in establishing the relationship between human and nonhuman species, thus rendering a comparative psychology reasonable. Darwin's protégé, George John Romanes, and C. Lloyd Morgan followed Darwin in applying evolutionary principles to the study of behavior. They saw continuity between the instincts and intelligent acts of humans and those of other species. Also in England, Douglas A. Spalding began experimental studies of the factors important in the development of behavior.

Experimental studies in comparative psychology developed in the United States around the turn of the century. Under the influence of psychologists such as William James at Harvard and G. Stanley Hall at Clark University, psychologists such as Edward L. Thorndike, Robert Yerkes, Linus Kline, and Willard Small conducted experimental studies of animal behavior in a psychological context. Margaret Floy Washburn (1908), with a Ph.D. degree from Cornell University, wrote *The Animal Mind*, which would become the standard textbook in the field for 25 years. John B. Watson, with a University of Chicago Ph.D. degree, worked in the field of developmental psychobiology, conducted field studies of the behavioral patterns of noddy and sooty terns, and eventually developed the school of behaviorism.

After a bit of a lull during and after World War I, comparative psychology flourished during the 1930s. Robert Yerkes opened the facility that would become the Yerkes Laboratories of Primate Biology in Orange Park, Florida in 1930. It would become the leading facility for research on the great apes and attract scientists from all over the world. Among Yerkes's associates, H. C. Bingham, Henry Nissen, and C. Ray Carpenter pioneered field studies of primate behavior, thus opening the door to a productive line of interdisciplinary research. During this period T. C. Schneirla began his research, including numerous field studies, on the behavior of ants; Frank A. Beach began his long program of work on the neural and hormonal determinants of instinctive patterns in mammals; and Harry F. Harlow began work on such problems as development and learning in monkeys. Also during this period various new textbooks, such as F. A. Moss's (1934) *Comparative Psychology*, appeared. The field was in full swing.

The leaders who matured during the 1930s produced numerous students who continued to develop the field. Three post–World War II developments greatly affected comparative psychology. The first was the strengthening of ties with European ethology, as represented by Konrad Lorenz, Nikolaas Tinbergen, and their colleagues. These interactions increased comparative psychologists' interest in problems of evolution and adaptive significance and in instinctive behavior. The second was the development during the 1970s of the field of behavioral ecology/sociobiology. This approach worked from such principles as (1) natural selection works at the level of the individual animal, and (2) one's genetic interests are represented in close kin as well as in one's self. The study of animal behavior was revolutionized as a result and helped focus theory in psychology on issues of biological currency. The third was the "cognitive revolution," which resulted in a weakening of the hold of more reductionistic forms of behaviorism on the field. Although cognitive studies had always been a part of comparative psychology, they moved from the background to the foreground during this period. Today, comparative psychology flourishes as a rather diverse but productive field.

Representative Research

The main research categories in comparative psychology are four in number. They begin with efforts to identify the evolution of behavioral patterns and continue with understanding the effects of various stimuli, considering the consequences of behavior, and investigating animal cognition.

Genesis. The study of evolutionary history entails efforts to trace the history of behavioral patterns through their evolution in different species. For example, Greene and Burghardt (*Science*, 1978) traced the probable history of different patterns of constriction in ancient and modern snakes.

The development of behavior entails the continuous, dynamic interaction of genes, environment, and the organism in an epigenetic process. Studies of genetic effects on behavior have traditionally concerned inbred strains, genetic selection experiments, and hybridization. More powerful techniques have recently become available with the development of modern molecular genetics. The influence of important early experience and the changing baseline on which that experience acts have been the focus of comparative developmental research. An active research area concerns the ontogeny of bird song, where genes and environmental input interact in diverse and complex ways in different species.

Control. Many influences on behavior are contemporaneous, or nearly so, with the behavior. Many comparative psychologists study the effects of particular stimuli, such as the displays and calls of various species, on the individual of concern.

Comparative psychologists are increasingly interacting with scientists from related fields to also study internal mechanisms that control behavior. There is much interest in sensory function within the animal's skin. The study of the nervous system as it affects and is affected by behavior has become quite prominent with the development of behavioral neuroscience. Hormonal determinants and consequences of behavior have received much interest. An important trend is the ability to monitor and manipulate hormonal levels under field conditions so that effects can be examined in their full natural context.

Consequences. Although many consequences of behavior are important, effects on reproductive success have taken center stage because of their importance to evolutionary change. Such areas as prey-predator interaction and reproductive behavior have received much attention because of the obvious relationship to survival and reproductive success. In the latter case, modern techniques allow the psychologist to determine which of several possible males is the father of young animals. This enables the study of the tie between aggressive, sexual, and parental behavior and successful genetic transmission.

Animal Cognition. Studies of animal cognition have been part of comparative psychology for many years, as in the work of Wolfgang Köhler, Walter Hunter, and Robert Yerkes. In recent years, however, there has been a rebirth of interest in cognitive studies. One group of students of comparative cognition works within a behavioristic context in the study of such phenomena as attention, memory, timing, concept formation, and counting. Others, following the lead of ethologist Donald Griffin, are developing a field of cognitive ethology which advocates a return to mentalistic concepts such as consciousness, intention, and mind. Studies of language learning by chimpanzees, such as those of the Gardners with American sign language, Premack with small plastic "words," and Rumbaugh and Savage-Rumbaugh with symbols in a "Yerkish" language, and of other species, such as dolphins, parrots, and sea lions, have been especially influential in the field of animal cognition.

[*See also* Animal Learning and Behavior.]

Bibliography

Boakes, R. (1984). *From Darwin to behaviourism: Psychology and the minds of animals*. Cambridge: Cambridge University Press. A study of the history of comparative psychology with an emphasis on learning and behavioristic approaches.

Dewsbury, D. A. (1978). *Comparative animal behavior*. New York: McGraw-Hill. A textbook in comparative psychology.

Dewsbury, D. A. (1984). *Comparative psychology in the twentieth century*. Stroudsburg, PA: Hutchinson Ross. A comprehensive study of the history of comparative psychology.

Dewsbury, D. A. (Ed.). (1990). *Contemporary issues in comparative psychology*. Sunderland, MA: Sinauer. A selection of research articles by some leading comparative psychologists.

Dewsbury, D. A. (1992). Triumph and tribulation in the history of American comparative psychology. *Journal of Comparative Psychology, 106*, 3–19. A survey of the difficulties experienced and the accomplishments of comparative psychologists in the United States.

Maier, R. (1998). *Comparative animal behavior: An evolutionary and ecological approach*. Boston: Allyn & Bacon. A recent textbook in comparative psychology.

Moss, F. A. (Ed.). (1934). *Comparative psychology*. New York: Prentice Hall. A comprehensive treatment of comparative psychology as it was conceptualized in the 1930s.

Roitblat, H. L. (1987). *Introduction to comparative cognition*. New York: Freeman. A textbook in comparative cognition.

Washburn, M. F. (1908). *The animal mind: A text-book of comparative psychology*. New York: Macmillan. A standard textbook in comparative psychology during the early part of the century.

Wasserman, E. A. (1993). Comparative cognition: Beginning the second century of the study of animal intelligence. *Psychological Bulletin, 113*, 211–228. A position paper for the study of animal cognition near the end of the twentieth century.

Donald A. Dewsbury

COMPASSION. *See* Sympathy.

COMPETENCY. Clinicians are frequently called on to conduct an evaluation of an individual's competency. Although nineteenth-century conceptions equated mental illness with incompetency, the thrust of modern law reform and empirical research has been to recognize that many people suffering from mental illness, even severe mental illness such as schizophrenia, are not incompetent to engage in decision making in a variety of areas and that even when an individual is incompetent for one purpose, he or she may not be incompetent for another (Appelbaum et al., 1995; Winick, 1996). Although people found incompetent once were regarded as incompetent for all purposes, the modern approach focuses only on specific incompetency (Winick, 1996). As a result, the clinician's task is to evaluate an individual's competency to play a particular role or to perform a particular task. Clinicians also should be aware that the competency of an individual fluctuates over time.

The issue of competency arises in many legal contexts. In the criminal justice process, defendants who exhibit mental illness almost always will be evaluated for competency to stand trial (Winick, 1997a). The issue may also arise concerning the defendant's competency to waive Miranda warnings, to waive counsel, to plead guilty, to be sentenced, and to be punished, including the administration of capital punishment. In the civil context, the competency issue arises concerning a patient's ability to accept or reject treatment. It also may arise when an individual seeks voluntary admission to a mental hospital or to participate in research. The issue will frequently arise in guardianship or conservatorship proceedings in which the question is whether individuals are competent to manage their property. In addition, the issue may arise concerning an individual's competence to vote, to marry, to enter into a contract or make a conveyance of property, to exercise parental rights or serve as a guardian for minors, and to make a will.

United States constitutional history and tradition place a special emphasis on principles of individual autonomy and self-determination. We generally allow people to make important decisions for themselves, including decisions concerning their own health. We frustrate individual choice only when we think individuals lack the ability to make decisions about their own well-being. In such cases, the state may invoke its *parens patriae* power, using an incompetency label to veto such choices and to substitute the decision of another concerning what is best. Once the state applies the incompetency label, the individual generally is precluded from making decisions concerning the activity in question. Such paternalism frustrates the value of individual autonomy, but in the case of individuals who are incompetent, it is justified based on principles of beneficence. The assumption is that the injury caused by denying such people autonomy would be exceeded by the harm produced by honoring the choices of those who are incompetent. The choices of competent people are respected no matter how foolish their choices are thought to be. Alternatively, if people are determined to be incompetent, any decisions they may make are deemed invalid and without legal effect, and they are barred from playing certain legal roles, such as standing trial or pleading guilty in the criminal process or entering into contracts or managing property in the civil context.

Notwithstanding the critical importance of the competence question, no general agreement exists concerning the appropriate legal standard for ascertaining competency in many contexts, or the standard used is general and vague. Standards vary somewhat based upon state law, but certain commonalities emerge. In the treatment context, for example, a patient's competence to make treatment decisions is measured against any one or some combination of four major legal standards: (a) the ability to understand relevant information, (b) the ability to understand the nature of the situation and its likely consequences, (c) the ability to manipulate information rationally, and (d) the ability to communicate a choice (Appelbaum & Grisso, 1995; Roth, Meisel, & Lidz, 1977). These four components also form the basis for determining competency in other contexts as well, although legal language, often general and vague, may vary somewhat from context to context. For instance, the standard for measuring competency to stand trial, plead guilty, and waive counsel in the criminal process is whether the defendant has sufficient present ability to consult with an attorney with a reasonable degree of rational understanding and a rational as well as factual understanding of the proceedings against him. For guardianship purposes, the standard is often formulated as whether the individual is able to care for his or her personal safety or to attend to and provide for personal necessities, such as food, shelter, and medical care, without which physical injury would occur. The requirement that testators (those making a will) be competent is often expressed as the rule that they be of "sound mind," which usually is interpreted as whether they understand that they are making a will at the time they are making it, the nature and extent of their property, their relation to those who may assert a claim as beneficiaries, and the practical effect of their disposition. Although the formulation of the competency standard thus may differ based on context and jurisdiction, most courts in applying the standard seem to focus on one or some combination of the factors of understanding, appreciation, rationality, and ability to express choice.

The modern direction of law reform has been to erect a presumption in favor of competency, one that is applicable even when the individual is mentally ill and even when he or she has been hospitalized as a result of mental illness (Winick, 1996). This is a rebuttable presumption that places the burden of coming forward with evidence of incompetency and the burden of persuasion on the issue on the party asserting incompetency. The existence of mental illness or of any particular diagnosis will not be sufficient to overcome this presumption.

Some commentators have suggested that the competency standard should be applied differently, on a sliding-scale basis, depending on whether the individual is seeking to assent to or object to the intervention in question (such as treatment, hospitalization, or standing trial), and also on the risk/benefit ratio of the intervention in question (Winick, 1997a). Under this approach, a less demanding standard of competence would be applied when the individual seeks to assent to an intervention or choice that appears to be in the individual's best interests, particularly if it is in accordance with the recommendation of a professional having a fiduciary relationship to the individual, such as an attorney or clinician, than when the choice assented to seems risky or when the individual expresses objection to it. Other commentators have argued against this approach, suggesting the need for a uniform measure of competency.

In conducting competency evaluations, clinicians have often confused the standard for competency with the existence of psychopathology or have taken a paternalistic approach, finding individuals incompetent when this would justify an intervention thought to be in their best interests. These approaches are inappropriate. Clinicians should remember that competency is more a legal than a clinical question and should be aware of the appropriate legal standard for measuring competency in the context in question.

A number of structured and unstructured evaluation instruments are available for use in evaluating competency (Melton, Petrilla, Poythress, & Slobogin, 1997; Kapf & Mossman, 1996; Roesch, Hart, & Zapf, 1996). The most modern and valuable of these are instruments developed under the auspices of the MacArthur Network on Mental Health and the Law for its research on criminal competency and treatment competency.

Clinicians should use these instruments with caution. There are limits to the ability of psychometric measures to capture the legal concept of competency. There can be no uniform, objective, precise method of competency assessment; rather, assessment instruments can only function as screening methods to determine the need for further inquiry and to structure but not supplant clinical judgment (Kapp & Mossman, 1996). For several reasons, psychological testing is ill suited for the assessment of psycholegal statuses (Roesch, Hart, & Zapf, 1996). Psychological tests provide a structured sample of behavior for use in clinical decision making, allowing the making of descriptive, predictive, and comparative judgments about individuals. For example, they are useful in making diagnostic and treatment decisions. The law, however, has a narrower focus, dealing with the individual in a particular situation. For example, the law may wish to ascertain whether a particular individual is competent to stand trial. Psychometric instruments may be useful for providing a general framework for conducting assessments or as clinical guidelines, helping to make the assessment more systematic, but they cannot be used as objective measures of legal concepts like competency, which inevitably are context specific (Roesch, Hart, & Zapf, 1996).

Bibliography

Appelbaum, P. S., & Grisso, T. (1995). The MacArthur treatment competence study: I. Mental illness and competency to consent to treatment. *Law and Human Behavior, 19,* 105–126.

Grisso, T., Appelbaum, P. S., Mulvey, E., & Fletcher, K. (1995). The MacArthur treatment competence study: II. Measures of abilities related to competence to consent to treatment. *Law and Human Behavior, 19,* 127–148.

Grisso, T., & Appelbaum, P. S. (1995). The MacArthur treatment competence study: III. Abilities of patients to consent to psychiatric and medical treatments. *Law and Human Behavior, 19,* 149–174.

Kapp, M. B., & Mossman, D. (1996). Measuring decisional capacity: Cautions on the construction of a capacimeter. *Psychology, Public Policy, and Law, 2,* 73–95.

Meisel, A., Roth, I. H., & Lidz, C. W. (1977). Toward a model of a legal doctrine of informed consent, *American Journal of Psychiatry, 134,* 279.

Melton, G. B., Petrila, J., Poythress, N. G., & Slobogin, C. (1997). *Psychological evaluations for the courts: A handbook for mental health professionals and lawyers* (2nd ed.). New York: Guilford Press.

Roesch, R., Hart, S. D., & Zapf, P. A. (1996). Conceptualizing and assessing competency to stand trial: Implications and applications of the MacArthur treatment competence model. *Psychology, Public Policy, and Law, 2,* 96–113.

Roth, L. H., Meisel, A., & Lidz, C. W. (1977). Tests of competency to consent to treatment. *American Journal of Psychiatry, 134,* 279–284.

Winick, B. J. (1996). The MacArthur treatment competence study: Legal and therapeutic implications. *Psychology, Public Policy, and Law, 2,* 137–166.

Winick, B. J. (1997a). *The right to refuse mental health treatment.* Washington, DC: American Psychological Association.

Winick, B. J. (1997b). *Therapeutic jurisprudence applied: Essays on mental health law.* Durham, NC: Carolina Academic Press.

Bruce J. Winick

COMPETITION. *See* Cooperation and Competition.

COMPLIANCE. Compliance refers to the successful effort to alter someone's behavior through the use of direct pressure or other tactics. Most commonly, we see compliance at work when a salesperson employs the various tricks in his or her arsenal to make a sale. Although direct pressure to sell a product or secure donations is common, psychologists also have identified four effective procedures for increasing compliance in the absence of such pressure.

Jonathan Freeman and Scott Fraser introduced the first of these procedures in 1966. Experimenters using the *foot-in-the-door* procedure present participants with a small initial request to which virtually all people agree. Some time later, participants are presented with the real (i.e., target) request, one that is similar to but larger than the initial request. This procedure has been found to increase compliance to the target request beyond that found when participants are presented only with the target request. In an early demonstration of the procedure, Freedman and Fraser (1966) asked people to put a small sign in the window of their homes or to sign a petition (e.g., advocating safe driving). Two weeks later, these people were more likely to agree to placing a large sign in their front lawn advertising support of the cause than people not presented with the initial request. Dozens of foot-in-the-door studies were published in subsequent decades. However, investigators often fail to find an increase in compliance with the procedures, and on a few occasions have found the foot-in-the-door manipulation actually decreases compliance. Four meta-analyses of these studies, however, find that the effect appears more often than would be expected by chance (e.g., Beaman, Cole, Preston, Klentz, & Steblay, 1983). However, it appears the effectiveness of the procedure is affected by a number of variables. These include the length of time between requests, the similarity of requests, the size of the requests, information about normative responses, and the personality of the participant.

The most common explanation for the foot-in-the-door effect is that agreeing to the initial request alters the way people perceive themselves. According to this *self-perception* interpretation (Bem, 1967), people who sign petitions come to see themselves as the kind of people who agree with the advocated position or who help with such causes. These individuals are said to use this altered perception of themselves when deciding whether to respond to the second request. However, several investigators have challenged the self-perception explanation. In particular, researchers have had difficulty producing evidence that participants actually alter their self-perception when they comply with the initial request.

Robert Cialdini and his colleagues (Cialdini et al., 1975) demonstrated the effectiveness of a second procedure for increasing compliance, the *door-in-the-face* procedure. Experimenters using this technique begin by asking participants for a request so large most people will refuse. The experimenter immediately follows the response with a second, smaller (i.e., target) request. The procedure has been found to increase compliance compared to a control group receiving only the target request. For example, participants in one study refused a request for two years of volunteer service to a youth organization. However, when these participants were then asked to volunteer two hours of time to the same organization they were more likely to agree to the request than participants presented only with the request for two hours. Cialdini and his colleagues explain the effectiveness of the procedure in terms of a social rule known as the *norm of reciprocity*. According to this rule, we should give back something to those who have done a favor for us. In the door-in-the-face situation, participants see the second request as a concession on the part of the requester and reciprocate by "meeting the person halfway." Research findings support this interpretation. For example, Cialdini and colleagues found that the procedure is not effective when a different experimenter presents the second request or if the second request does not appear to be substantially less than the initial request. Participants in these conditions presumably perceive no concession on the part of the person delivering the second request and consequently feel no need to reciprocate.

Cialdini and his colleagues (Cialdini, Cacioppo, Bussett, & Miller, 1978) also identified and demonstrated the *low-ball* compliance procedure. Experimenters initiate the low-ball procedure by presenting a simple request. After participants agree, the experimenter raises the cost of the request. Studies find this procedure leads to more compliance to the higher-priced request than simply presenting participants with the high-priced final request from the outset. For example, students in one study agreed over the phone to participate in a psychology experiment. The experimenter then announced that participation would be more costly than the participants had imagined—the experiment would be held at 7:00 in the morning. Nonetheless, these students showed up for the early experiment more often than students told the time of the experiment before indicating their willingness to participate. Cialdini and his colleagues explained the effectiveness of the low-ball procedure in terms of commitment. They argued that by agreeing to the initial price, participants in the low-ball condition developed a commitment to perform the requested behavior. This commitment to the behavior was said to remain even at the higher price. Jerry Burger and Richard Petty (1981) subsequently demonstrated that participants actually develop a commitment to the requester, rather than to the behavior, and that this personal commitment carries over to the higher-priced request. When a different experimenter delivered the higher-priced request, or when participants were allowed to do something for the initial requester and thereby satisfy their commitment to that person, no increase in compliance was found relative to appropriate control groups.

Finally, Burger (1986) introduced the *that's-not-all* compliance procedure. Participants in these studies are offered a product at a price. However, before participants can respond, they are interrupted by the experimenter. After a few seconds, the experimenter improves the deal, either by lowering the price or adding something of value to the product. Studies find this procedure increases compliance to the request beyond that found in control groups presented only with the final offer. For example, participants told the price of a cupcake was $1.00, but then informed it was only 75 cents purchased more cupcakes than those told from the outset that the price was 75 cents. Burger introduced two explanations for the effectiveness of the procedure. First, as in the door-in-the-face procedure, participants may see the second offer as a kind of concession and may reciprocate the gesture by agreeing to the request. Second, the initial request may alter the anchor point participants use to judge whether the price is a reasonable one. After considering the $1.00 price for a cupcake, a 75-cent price seems an appropriate price for the item.

Bibliography

Beaman, A. L., Cole, C. M., Preston, M., Klentz, B., & Steblay, N. M. (1983). Fifteen years of foot-in-the-door research: A meta-analysis. *Personality and Social Psychology Bulletin, 9,* 181–196.

Bem, D. J. (1967). Self-perception: An alternative interpretation of cognitive dissonance phenomena. *Psychological Review, 74,* 183–200.

Burger, J. M. (1986). Increasing compliance by improving the deal: The that's-not-all technique. *Journal of Personality and Social Psychology, 51,* 277–283.

Burger, J. M. (1999). The foot-in-the-door compliance procedure: A multiple-process analysis and review. *Personality and Social Psychology Review.*

Burger, J. M., & Petty, R. E. (1981). The low-ball compliance technique: Task or person commitment? *Journal of Personality and Social Psychology, 40,* 492–500.

Cialdini, R. B., Vincent, J. E., Lewis, S. K., Catalan, J., Wheeler, D., & Darby, B. L. (1975). Reciprocal concessions procedure for inducing compliance: The door-in-the-face technique. *Journal of Personality and Social Psychology, 31,* 206–215.

Cialdini, R. B., Cacioppo, J. T., Bassett, R., & Miller, J. A. (1978). Low-ball procedure for producing compliance: Commitment, then cost. *Journal of Personality and Social Psychology, 36,* 463–476.

DeJong, W. (1979). An examination of self-perception mediation of the foot-in-the-door effect. *Journal of Personality and Social Psychology, 37,* 2221–2239.

Dillard, J. P., Hunter, J. E., & Burgoon, M. (1984). Sequential-request persuasive strategies: Meta-analysis of foot-in-the-door and door-in-the-face. *Human Communication Research, 10,* 461–488.

Fern, E. F., Monroe, K. B., & Avila, R. A. (1986). Effectiveness of multiple request strategies: A synthesis of research results. *Journal of Marketing Research, 23,* 144–152.

Freedman, J. L., & Fraser, S. C. (1966). Compliance without pressure: The foot-in-the-door technique. *Journal of Personality and Social Psychology, 4,* 195–202.

Gorassini, D. R., & Olson, J. M. (1995). Does self-perception change explain the foot-in-the-door effect? *Journal of Personality and Social Psychology, 69*, 91–105.

Jerry M. Burger

COMPROMISE FORMATION is a label applied to behaviors that reflect a blended interaction of contradictory aims. It often involves an apparent solution to a dilemma involving wishes that have feared consequences. The compromise blends wishful intentions, fearful expectations, and defensive operations.

One of the main aims in psychodynamic and cognitive-psychodynamic psychotherapies is to rework compromises that are maladaptive. These are often found, in such therapeutic explorations, to result from various developmental processes that have to do with character. The emergent character traits stem from the interaction of various motives. For example, a young person who intends to win out over a rival may fear hurting the rival, and compromise by seeking some other field of activity than the most desired career path. The inhibition of ambition can have maladaptive consequences such as a lack of vitality. Understanding how compromises are formed usually involves a theory about organizing networks of associations, cognitive maps, and person schemas: what the person wants and fears in relation to other people.

It is helpful to consider that a wish can be associated with threats, and can be linked by association to anticipation of dreaded states of mind. A person may anticipate a dreaded consequence of an intention and so have a wish-fear dilemma. The person arrives at a compromise. This compromise may incorporate some aspects of the wish, but it also is a way to avoid feared states of mind or the dreaded consequences of direct action. In using the concept of compromise formation, one starts by observing a pattern of repeated behaviors, and then infers the wish-fear dilemma that underlies the apparent compromise.

Compromise formation may be formulated, by an observer or the reflecting self, at the current moment by identifying the following: urges, usually for certain interpersonal transactions; emotions related to these urges; ideas about the consequences; and defensive processes used to reduce the possibility of aversive feelings. Many or all of these processes may be operative outside of awareness. Consequences might include shame or guilt at having wishes contrary to moral taboos. For example, a person who experiences a sudden urge to be noticed might have an impulse to interrupt another speaker. Realizing that this would be socially inappropriate generates a feeling of anxiety about potential embarrassment. The person then silently nods animatedly, a compromise that both gets some attention and meets the role of being polite.

Compromise formations that are more enduring traits often occur in configurations of role relationship models. In such configurations, there might be a desired, dreaded, and compromise role relationship model. The role of the self in wanting attention, behaving recklessly, and then being shamed is a dreaded role relationship model. An associationally connected desired role relationship model would be one of wanting attention, showing off real skills, and being respected and honored for the result. A compromise role relationship model is one of restraint of self-exhibitionistic impulses. Compromises can be adaptive and maladaptive. A relatively adaptive compromise could be for the self to take the role of valued audience member rather than a reckless and humiliated performer. A problematic or maladaptive compromise could be to occupy a role of sniping critic of the self-exhibitions of others, and then to be rejected as an unfair and excessive critic.

In exploratory psychotherapy, what was hidden by the compromise might be gradually clarified in a process of case formulation. Maladaptive aspects of the repeated compromise pattern in interpersonal relationships would be examined, and the reasons for them interpreted. The old wish-fear dilemma might be consciously engaged in a new, adult, and insightful manner. With such awareness, better solutions to the contradictions and problems could be forged.

Bibliography

Fenichel, O. (1945). *Character disorders in the psychoanalytic theory of the neuroses.* New York: Norton.

Hartman, H. (1958). *Ego psychology and the problem of adaptation.* New York: International Universities Press.

Horowitz, M. (1992). *Person schemas and maladaptive interpersonal patterns.* Chicago: University of Chicago Press.

Horowitz, M. (1997). *Formulation as a basis for planning psychotherapy.* Washington, DC: APPI.

Reich, W. (1949). *Character analysis.* New York: Orgone Press.

Mardi Horowitz

COMPULSIVE GAMBLING is a behavior disorder characterized by a pattern of persistent and recurrent gambling that disrupts an individual's personal, family, or occupational life. Compulsive gamblers typically show one or more of the following behaviors:

- They are preoccupied with gambling, reliving previous gambling experiences, especially big wins, planning their next venture, and ways to raise money with which to gamble.

- They enjoy the excitement and the thrill of beating the odds even more than the money that they occasionally win.
- They often need larger bets or greater risks to produce the same level of excitement.
- They are unable to control or stop the gambling behavior despite serious efforts to do so. They get fidgety and irritable when trying to cut back or stop gambling.
- They may use gambling to escape from problems or to change a negative emotional state such as anxiety, depression, or helplessness.
- They show a pattern of "chasing" the losses, using larger bets and taking greater risks to recover their losses. Although all gamblers show this behavior to some extent, compulsive gamblers persist in it, sometimes abandoning their usual gambling strategies to recover their losses all at once.
- They may lie to family and counselors to conceal the extent of their involvement in gambling.
- They may resort to illegal activities such as theft, forgery, or embezzlement to procure money to gamble.
- They may have lost a significant relationship, job, or educational opportunity as a result of involvement in gambling.
- They may have been bailed out of their gambling debts.

The American Psychiatric Association's *Diagnostic and Statistical Manual of Mental Disorders* (4th ed., 1994, *DSM–IV*), classifies pathological gambling as an impulse-control disorder. A person showing four of the behaviors mentioned above will qualify for a diagnosis of pathological gambling, the term used in medical literature. These criteria are similar to the criteria for substance abuse and for dependence in *DSM–IV*. Compulsive gambling does resemble drug addiction in some ways, but the two are independent disorders. Compulsive gambling often co-occurs with drug addictions, most commonly alcohol abuse. However, there are some basic differences between gambling and alcohol abuse. Losing money in gambling is not inherently reinforcing as imbibing alcohol, except for the thrill of placing a bet. Also, the gambler does not receive reinforcement every time he/she wagers. Compulsive gambling also shows some resemblance to the obsessive-compulsive disorder, and some attempts have been made to locate it within the spectrum of obsessive-compulsive disorders, including body-dysmorphic disorder and sexual compulsion. Body-dysmorphic disorder (in which an individual is dissatisfied with the shape of his or her body) and sexual compulsions fall on the compulsive end of the spectrum, and pathological gambling falls on the impulsive, novelty-seeking end. Compulsive gambling is more common than other impulse-control disorders. For that reason, much treatment effort has been directed toward it. Experienced clinicians using *DSM–IV* criteria can be expected to agree on a diagnosis of compulsive gambling in 80% of cases, based on the reliability information furnished. By clearly specifying the criteria for the disorder, *DSM–IV* has enhanced the descriptive validity of the diagnostic classification and to some extent its predictive validity, but the label does not provide a clue as to causation or treatment of the disorder. Prevalence rates for compulsive gambling vary from 1 to 3% of the adult population in different parts of the United States. The highest rates seem to occur in states where gambling has been legal for many years. In states where legalized gambling has been available for more than 20 years, roughly 1.5% of the adult population show a pattern of compulsive gambling. Compulsive gamblers are more likely than nongamblers to be male, non-White, unmarried, and have a lower level of education.

Causal Factors in Compulsive Gambling

A number of psychological, socio-cultural, and biological factors play a role in compulsive gambling.

Psychological Factors. One of the common explanations of compulsive gambling suggests that gamblers are seeking excitement, new experiences, and relief from boredom. What the gamblers call "being in action" provides this excitement. Studies of personality characteristics of compulsive gamblers have reported male gamblers to be antisocial, narcissistic, compulsive, aggressive, and expecting to succeed through unconventional means, and female gamblers to be dependent, submissive, and passive-aggressive. In a survey conducted by Gamblers Anonymous, wives of compulsive gamblers described their husbands as liars who were irresponsible, uncommunicative, insincere, and impulsive. Studies have also indicated that compulsive gamblers show certain kinds of distorted thinking and faulty beliefs that stem from an exaggerated sense of power and control. For example, they believe they have the skill to control the outcome of random events.

Sociocultural Factors. With the tremendous increase in the opportunity for legalized gambling, more and more people are drawn into gambling activities, and a small percentage (1–2.5%) become compulsive gamblers.

Biological Factors. Research focusing on the biological bases of compulsive gambling has found that, compared to nongamblers, pathological gamblers show a decrease in the level of the neurotransmitter serotonin, which is associated with suppression of inhibitory responses, leading to greater impulsivity. Lower levels of another biochemical, monoamine oxidase, which is a peripheral index of serotonergic function, has also been found in pathological gamblers.

Treatment Options

Because of their tendency to deny the seriousness of their problem, compulsive gamblers are not inclined to seek treatment. Only a small proportion of middle-aged White males seek treatment. A number of different types of treatment have been used to treat pathological gambling. None of them has proven to be highly effective, when used exclusively. Treatments that combine different approaches and help build coping skills have been found to be more effective. Cognitive-behavioral therapy is aimed at helping clients develop skills to manage gambling-related thoughts and behaviors and better coping skills to deal with life stresses, so they can confront problems in their lives rather than try to escape from them. Psychoanalytic therapy has focused on narcissistic personality organization and related defense mechanisms. Illusions of power and control that play a crucial role in pathological gambling are addressed in psychodynamic forms of treatment. Behavioral therapy techniques similar to those used with alcoholics, such as aversive conditioning and systematic desensitization, have also been tried in treating pathological gambling. Self-help groups, such as Gamblers Anonymous, have been modeled after Alcoholics Anonymous and are widely available to people seeking social support to overcome their compulsions. Very little research on the use of psychiatric drugs in treating pathological gambling has been reported. With gamblers who also suffered from mood disorders, lithium carbonate has been used with some degree of success. The use of drugs that prevent the reuptake of serotonin, such as clomipramine, has been reported.

[See also Addictive Personality.]

Bibliography

American Psychiatric Association. (1994). *Diagnostic and statistical manual of mental disorders* (4th ed.). Washington, DC: Author.

Angele, W. (1996). *Gambling, a family affair*. London: Sheldon Press. Presents social aspects of compulsive gambling including family relationships.

Fisher, S. E. (1996). *Gambling problems among casino patrons*. Reading, UK: Richard Kendle. Discusses the problem of compulsive gambling in Great Britain.

Galski, T. (1987). *Handbook of pathological gambling*. Springfield, IL: Charles C. Thomas.

Heineman, M. (1994). *Losing your shirt: Recovery for compulsive gamblers and their families*. Center City, MN: Hazelden. Discusses family relationships of compulsive gambler and the concept of codependency.

LeSieur, H. R. (1993). *Understanding compulsive gambling*. Center City, MN: Hazelden. Includes biographical references.

Peele, S. (1985). *The meaning of addiction*. Lexington, MA: Lexington Books.

Shaffer, H. J., Stein, S. A., Gambino, B., & Cummings, T. N. (Eds.). (1989). *Compulsive gambling: Theory, research, and practice*. Lexington, MA: Lexington Books.

Walker, M. B. (1995). *The psychology of gambling*. Oxford: Butterworth Heinemann. Deals with the psychological and social aspects of compulsive gambling.

Ajit K. Das

COMPUTERIZED ASSESSMENT. Personality appraisal is an extensive and important professional activity in contemporary applied psychology. Psychologists evaluate people in a broad range of settings and for varying purposes, for example, treatment planning, recommending applicants for employment, or determining parental suitability in child custody cases. It is imperative that personality evaluations provide reliable and valid portrayals of the individuals' current mood, symptoms, and personality features to support the conclusions and recommendations being made about people.

The validity and utility of a particular personality evaluation, however, can be influenced, not only by the characteristics of the person being assessed, but also by the personality features of the person who is conducting the evaluation. Subjectivity, an oft noted quality of human judgment, is the nemesis of personality appraisal. Unwanted, unreliable, or off-target results can lower the usefulness of personality measures in clinical decision making. Many traditional sources of personality information such as interview, observation, or response to ambiguous stimuli such as inkblots (projective methods) involve subjective analysis methods and rely to a great extent on the judgment of human interpreters. They can therefore be very vulnerable to bias.

With important decisions about people to make, psychologists have long sought methods and procedures for eliminating or reducing the influence of subjectivity in personality appraisal. The search for more reliable and valid appraisal methods has evolved along two parallel paths:

1. Through the development of objective methods of obtaining personality information from individuals and the development of explicit strategies for combining data into personality descriptions to reduce the influence of subjectivity in interpretation.
2. Through the application of automatic data processing techniques such as an electronic computer to make the assessment task faster, more comprehensive, and more reliable. For nearly 40 years, beginning with the work of H. P. Rome, W. M. Swenson, P. Mataya, and their colleagues at Mayo Clinic in 1962 (*Mayo Clinic Proceedings*) computers have been an important aid in psychological interpretation, providing rapid turnaround and more reliable evaluations to clinicians than more subjective approaches.

Development of Objective Personality Appraisal Methods

Before we explore how computer interpretation works, we need to briefly examine the data from which computer-based interpretations are drawn. Tests need to provide valid and reliable measures of the characteristics on which the personality portrayal is derived. In order for a psychological assessment procedure to be amenable to computer-based interpretation it needs to be objectively scored and possess well-defined interpretations for established test scores.

The most widely used personality scale for computer-based assessment growing out of the objective personality test tradition is the Minnesota Multiphasic personality Inventory (MMPI) and its revised version, MMPI-2. The MMPI was the first and most widely used personality instrument to be fully automated. In this article the MMPI-2 will be used to illustrate computer-based personality assessment.

How do MMPI-2 scores serve as an empirical data base for computer based interpretation? The extensive objective information that is available for the various MMPI-2 patterns makes computerized interpretation of the test relatively straightforward. Empirical scale interpretation with the MMPI-2 works as follows: An individual taking the MMPI-2 answers a series of true-false questions on the computer or a paper-pencil answer sheet that can be transferred to the computer by, for example, an optical scanner. These responses are scored according to objective rules and grouped into defined item clusters or scales. A scale is a group of items that measure particular personality characteristics. The MMPI-2 scale scores have been extensively researched and there are a number of resources, known as code books or "cookbooks" that have accumulated to provide a rich catalog of personality descriptors for the various scale patterns. This objective strategy makes it possible for individual test protocols to be effectively interpreted by electronic computer (J. N. Butcher, *Clinical Personality Assessment: Practical Approaches*, New York, 1995).

How can a computer perform the complex task of summarizing an integrated personality evaluation? Computer-based personality reports are essentially electronic reference books. Test indices along with pertinent interpretations for given levels of scale scores are stored in the computer. When the test scores for new cases are entered into the computer, the program simply "looks up" the stored information and prints out the appropriate text in a narrative format. These narratives are prototype descriptions for scales that were derived by an examination of the extensive research literature on the MMPI-2. The prototype with the closest match to the patient's profile is printed out for the client, as follows.

Case of the Depressed Reservations Agent. George W., age 50, has been employed as an airline ticket reservations agent for 21 years. He was recently recommended for a psychological evaluation and possible psychological therapy by his family physician because he has been experiencing depressed mood, chronic fatigue, and inability to function in his job since his recent divorce. His wife of 24 years recently left him without warning after their youngest child finished high school and left home—within a week of their child's departure, his wife packed up her belongings and moved out while he was at work. He has never had mental health treatment before and felt initially that his problems did not warrant a mental health referral. However, he came in for the psychological evaluation because he felt like he needed to get help for his depression. He was administered the MMPI-2 and the following computer-based narrative report was generated. The results of his testing were discussed with him and psychological treatment (cognitive-behavioral) was recommended for his depressive disorder. His MMPI-2 profile is given in Figure 1. The narrative report based on his MMPI-2 profile is as follows:

PROFILE VALIDITY
The client has presented himself in a defensive manner, attempting to show that he has few psychological problems. This pattern suggests that he needs to project an extremely virtuous image of high moral values, good self-control, and freedom from psychological problems or human weakness.

Although this profile is within valid limits, it should be kept in mind that the individual is perhaps responding in an effort to look good. The resulting MMPI-2 profile interpretation may be an underestimate of the individual's present problem situation and an overly positive view of his personal adjustment.

SYMPTOMATIC PATTERNS
The behavioral descriptions provided in this report are probably good indications of the client's present personality functioning. Correlates of D were used as the report prototype and this configuration shows high profile definition. The client has feelings of personal inadequacy and tends to view the future with uncertainty and pessimism. He tends to lack confidence in himself, is somewhat moody, is rather sensitive to criticism, and may tend to blame himself for things that go wrong. He seems to worry excessively, has low energy and a slow personal tempo, and is somewhat dissatisfied with his life. He is experiencing a depressed mood at this time. This profile may result from a stressful environment or a recent traumatic experience. The possibility of such circumstances should be evaluated.

PROFILE FREQUENCY
Profile interpretation can be greatly facilitated by examining the relative frequency of clinical scale patterns in various settings. The client's high-point clinical scale score (D) occurs in 7.2% of the MMPI-2 normative

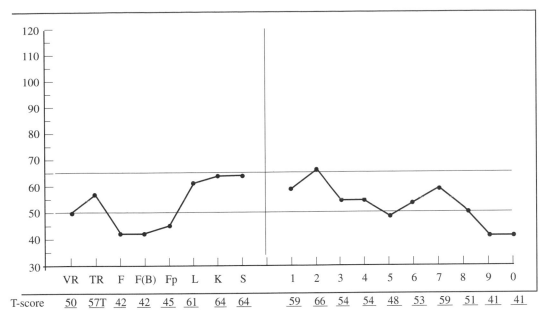

COMPUTERIZED ASSESSMENT. Figure 1. Validity and clinical scale profile for the Minnesota Multiphasic Personality Inventory (MMPI-2).

sample of men. However, only 2.4% of the sample have D as the peak score at or above a T score of 65, and only 1.1% have well-defined D spikes.

This high-point MMPI-2 score on the D scale is relatively frequent in various medical settings. In the National Computer Systems medical sample, the high-point clinical scale score on D occurs in 14.4% of the men. Moreover, 11.6% of the men have the D scale spike at or above a T score of 65, and 5.7% have a well-defined D high point in that range.

PROFILE STABILITY

The relative scale elevation of the highest scales in his clinical profile reflects high profile definition. If he is retested at a later date, the peak scores on this test are likely to retain their relative salience in his retest profile pattern. His high-point score on D is likely to remain stable over time. Short-term test-retest studies have shown a correlation of 0.75 for this high-point score. Spiro, Butcher, Levenson, Aldwin, and Bosse (1993) reported a 0.71 stability index for a large study of normals over a 5-year test-retest period.

INTERPERSONAL RELATIONS

Individuals with similar profiles tend to be hesitant and pessimistic about personal relationships and may feel rather inadequate in social situations.

DIAGNOSTIC CONSIDERATIONS

Symptoms of a mood disorder are prominent in his clinical picture.

TREATMENT CONSIDERATIONS

He may be motivated to seek and respond to therapy because of his low mood and high level of distress. Re-

sponse to psychotherapy is usually good for individuals with similar profiles.

Validity of Computer-Interpreted Tests

The validity and utility of MMPI-based interpretive programs have been widely studied. The research establishing the validity of narrative personality reports has typically involved the use of accuracy ratings by clinicians who are familiar with patients who have been tested. For example, the researcher administers the MMPI-2 to a patient in therapy and submits the answer sheet for machine scoring. Once this test is computer interpreted the report is provided to the clinician who would then rate it for accuracy and thoroughness. In one extensive study, for example (L. Eyde, D. Kowal, and F. J. Fishburne, *The Computer and the Decision-Making Process*, Hillsdale, N.J., 1993), the researchers compared the interpretive accuracy with which seven commercially available services portrayed the personality and symptomatic behavior of their patients. They found that some MMPI interpretive systems, the Minnesota Report and Caldwell Report, were judged to be highly accurate and comprehensive but that some of the systems were not sufficiently accurate to be used in clinical assessment.

The empirically based MMPI-2 correlates have considerable robustness when applied to diverse clinical samples, even across other languages and cultural groups. The MMPI-2, if adapted carefully to new cultures, can provide important information on psychopathology about patients in other cultures (J. N.

Butcher, *International Adaptations of the MMPI-2*, Minneapolis, Minn., 1996). The MMPI-2 has been widely translated into other languages and works similarly in a wide variety of countries. Computer interpretations of the MMPI-2 apply well across international boundaries. A recent study (by Butcher et al., in C. Belar, Ed., *Comprehensive Clinical Psychology: Sociocultural and Individual Differences*, New York, in press) with the MMPI-2 found that patients from Australia, France, Norway, and the United States were described with a high degree of accuracy by computer-based reports generated from American test norms and personality descriptors derived from American based research.

Values of Computer-Based MMPI-2 Assessments

The value of using computer-based reports in clinical settings can be summarized as follows:

- Test scoring by computer is more reliable than manually processed test results. Moreover, the narrative reports provided by computer programs are completely reliable, always produce the same report for the same scale elevations, unlike that what occurs with clinical interpreters who are likely to produce somewhat different results on different occasions or different from other interpreters looking at the same data.
- Computer-based assessments provide an objective summary of personality-based information that is available in the literature. Computer-based narratives provide standard interpretations of the test, such as the MMPI-2, that are based largely on actuarial data that are automatically applied for well-established test scores.
- Computer-derived reports are more comprehensive than those developed by clinicians and are usually available to the practitioner much more quickly than are manually processed evaluations. They can expedite the clinical assessment by having test information available as soon as the test is completed.
- Finally, computerized personality evaluations are more cost effective than are human processed evaluations. Manual scoring of most personality scales and indexes needed for an evaluation typically requires substantial clerical time.

Cautions and Limitations of Computer-Based Reports

For the most part, computer-based reports are "generic" personality and symptomatic descriptions based on empirical research from specific settings. Present day computer-based reports tend to be "prototypal descriptions," that is, are interpretive summaries for specific test patterns. It is important for the practitioner to determine whether the available research supports a particular application.

The practitioner needs to assure that the test data

on which the report was generated were processed appropriately and that the computerized report is relevant for the client being assessed. The practitioner needs to assure that the generated report appropriately summarizes the answers provided by the client and that the prototype used in the narrative report matches the behavior of the client. In order for this to be accomplished the practitioner needs to have a great deal of familiarity with the test being used.

The use of computer-based reports in assessment should be viewed as professional-to-professional consultations. Automated personality reports are provided to professionals who are familiar with the test being interpreted. Computer-derived reports are not recommended to be provided to the client to keep. They should be used only by practitioners who are familiar with the technical and clinical use of the instrument being interpreted.

One final consideration involves the impact that the availability of convenient and comprehensive reports can have on the diagnostic practitioner. Commercially available computer-based reports appear to be "finished" products and read like comprehensive evaluations. For the most part, however, they are not "stand alone reports." They are considered to be hypotheses that summarize the most probable interpretation for a particular test pattern. Relying solely on computer-based reports can induce an overly complacent attitude in the clinician during the diagnostic evaluation. It is important for clinicians not to become "inactive" in the diagnostic process and rely too heavily on one source of hypotheses. Practitioners need to keep in mind that the reports are summaries of likely external correlates that need to be integrated into the evaluation; a requirement that the practitioner needs to remain "in charge" and actively integrate the computer's suggestions into the final personality study.

Computer-based personality assessment is essentially a "look-up and list-out" function rather than what might be viewed as a computer-derived judgment task or "artificial intelligence" in which the computer makes judgments and produces summary evaluations. Early concerns of clinicians that the computer will replace the functioning of psychological practitioners in clinical assessment in the near future is unwarranted. That is, the computer operates largely as an electronic reference book, a stored file of interpretive statements that are indexed to various scale scores or profile elements. The computer actually makes *no* judgments except those that the psychologist-programmer has specified in establishing the system. Raymond Fowler (*Journal of Consulting and Clinical Psychology*, 1985, 53, 748–759) refers to this approach as the automated clinician because although the results are automated and follow explicit patterns and correlates that have been pre-determined, they must be evaluated by a human interpreter to be relevant and valid.

Research on computer modeling of human thought is still in its infancy but it is likely that future generations of computer-based test interpretation will assume more of an "executive" function. However, the development of a fully machine-governed computer-based personality assessment system, with all of the integrating decisions being executed by computer software, is not in the foreseeable future. Human beings and their important clinical input will likely be required in the incorporation of computer-based results into clinical assessment studies for some time.

Bibliography

Butcher, J. N. (1993). *The Minnesota Report (MMPI-2) (Revised): Adult clinical system.* Minneapolis, MN: National Computer Systems.

Butcher, J. N. (Ed.). (1987). *Computerized psychological assessment.* New York: Basic Books.

Butcher, J. N., Berah, E., Ellertsen, B., Miach, P., Lim, J., Nezami, E., Pancheri, P., Derksen, J., & Almagor, M. (1998). *Objective personality assessment: Computer-based MMPI-2 interpretation in international clinical settings.* New York: Elsevier.

Butcher, J. N., Keller, L. S., & Bacon, S. F. (1985). Current developments and future directions in computerized personality assessment. *Journal of Consulting and Clinical Psychology, 53,* 803–815.

Gilberstadt, H., & Duker, J. (1965). *A handbook for clinical and actuarial MMPI interpretation.* Philadelphia: Saunders.

Graham, J. R., Timbrook, R., Ben-Porath, Y. S., & Butcher, J. N. (1991). Code-type congruence between MMPI and MMPI-2: Separating fact from artifact. *Journal of Personality Assessment, 57,* 205–215.

Grove, W. M., & Meehl, P. E. (1996). Comparative efficiency of informal (subjective, impressionistic) and formal (mechanical, algorithmic) prediction procedures. The clinical-statistical controversy. *Psychology, Public Policy, and Law, 2,* 293–323.

Marks, P. A., Seeman, W., & Haller, D. L. (1974). *The actuarial use of the MMPI with adolescents and adults.* Baltimore: Williams & Wilkins.

Meehl, P. E. (1954). *Clinical versus statistical prediction: A theoretical analysis and a review of the evidence.* Minneapolis, MN: University of Minnesota Press.

Moreland, K. L., & Onstad J. (1985). *Validity of the Minnesota clinical report. I: Mental health outpatients.* Presented at the Twentieth Annual Symposium on Recent Developments in the Use of the MMPI, Minneapolis, MN.

James N. Butcher

COMPUTERIZED PSYCHOTHERAPY. Computers have been used in psychology for assessment, history taking, diagnosis, patient education, and clinical training. The most complex and controversial role of the computer, however, has been in the area of intervention, where the computer has been used to provide psychotherapy to individuals and groups.

The purpose of computerized psychotherapy is to make therapy more affordable, more convenient, and hence, more available to the population. If computers could be programmed to be as effective as therapists in dealing with routine problems or with particular disorders, clients with those problems could access those programs more cheaply than they could employ an individual therapist. Clients could receive therapy at any time of day and in the privacy of their own homes. Furthermore, the therapist's time would be freed to deal with more serious disorders or disorders that do not lend themselves to computer intervention. Finally, computers do not get tired, bored, or otherwise distracted. They have perfect memories and never make mistakes. Given these advantages, a computer could potentially be a more accurate therapist than a human being.

The use of computers in psychotherapy was first reported in 1966 in separate articles by Weizenbaum and by Colby, Watt, and Gilbert. These authors described software programs that allowed individuals to "talk" to computers about their personal problems. In response to a typed description of one's problem, the computer functioned as a psychotherapist by "questioning, clarifying, focusing, rephrasing and occasionally interpreting" (Colby, Watt, & Gilbert, 1966, p. 149).

Weizenbaum developed the software ELIZA, based on a client-centered approach to therapy. ELIZA used a series of rules whereby the computer received input from a subject and scanned it for key words and phrases. ELIZA responded to key words with preassigned statements that reflected the subject's feelings. Another feature of ELIZA was a forced choice tree in which the subject was required to respond to questions by choosing among several alternatives. Based on the response, the computer followed up with another question.

Although ELIZA was designed to act as a therapist, its inability to comprehend natural language prevented it from realizing that objective. After a similar attempt in 1966, Colby also concluded that these programs were handicapped by the inability to understand natural language, as well as the lack of a conceptual base upon which to relate to the client. Realizing these limitations, Wagman (1980) later suggested that by paying attention to the match between the computer's communication logic and psychotherapy communications, effective programs might be developed.

Computer therapy software operates through a series of if-then statements, which determine how the computer responds to explicit input by the client. Not all therapies, however, focus on input that can be explicitly provided by the client or have clearly defined rules that lend themselves to translation into a computer program. Psychodynamic therapy, for example, focuses on nonverbal cues and has complex and nonexplicit rules for the interpretation of behavior, both of which make it difficult to translate into computer therapy. Behavior therapy and cognitive–behavioral therapy, on the other hand, depend more heavily on the client's verbal input and have more explicit rules, which may be easily transferred to computer. Also, homework and other exercises, which are integral parts of the therapy, translate easily into computer software. Finally, computers can simulate realistic situations and objects (virtual reality), which can be useful for certain behavioral treatments based on exposure to feared situations. Behaviorally oriented computer therapy programs have been designed to treat specific problems, such as phobias, depression, smoking, obesity, and sexual dysfunction (for example, Newman, Consoli, & Taylor, 1997).

To use these computer therapy programs, the client typically works alone at the computer and follows computer-generated instructions. The therapist meets with the client at the beginning and end of the program and on an as-needed basis in between. For some programs, a therapist is available after every session with the computer to discuss the results.

In addition to programs for particular problems, more generic programs have been designed. The PLATO system (Wagman, 1980) provides individuals with counseling on dilemmas related to various choices in their personal lives. This software assists clients in formulating their problems as dilemmas and generates lists of possible solutions for those dilemmas.

Gould (1989) developed the first truly generic computerized form of psychotherapy, the Therapeutic Learning Program (TLP). TLP expanded some of the capabilities of PLATO by applying the concepts of problem formulation and solution generation to psychological problems. TLP helps clients define a problem, develop a plan of action, and resolve issues that might prevent the client from taking action. Unlike PLATO, TLP is not a stand-alone treatment. TLP consists of 10 computer sessions at the end of which the client receives a printout that serves as a basis for discussion between client and therapist.

A sparse literature exists regarding the effectiveness of computer psychotherapy compared with other modes of therapy or to no-treatment control conditions. Most studies have evaluated software packages designed to treat specific problems using cognitive-behavioral approaches. These controlled outcome studies have typically shown that participants who received computer-based treatments had equally good or better outcomes than participants in comparison groups. Other controlled outcome studies have been conducted on generic programs, such as PLATO and TLP. These outcome studies have also revealed encouraging results both in terms of participants' satisfaction with the treatment as well as on objective outcome measures (see Bloom, 1992, for a review).

The most controversial aspect of computerized psychotherapy concerns the morality of using computers to replace human therapists. Weizenbaum (1976) argues that it is immoral to use computers to supplant human functions that involve interpersonal respect, understanding, and love. Conversely, Colby (1986) argues that computerized psychotherapy is not dehumanizing and that considerable evidence suggests that clients accept and sometimes prefer interacting with computers over humans. Moreover, Colby believes that computerized psychotherapy "is consistent with the ethics of helping professions that attempt to provide effective and up-to-date care extendable to everyone in our society" (p. 415).

Computerized psychotherapy has been shown to be an effective and acceptable mode of treatment for many clients, especially for those with specific problems amenable to cognitive–behavioral interventions. But only when computers can sufficiently process natural language may the full potential of computers in psychotherapy be realized.

[See also Psychotherapy.]

Bibliography

Bloom, B. L. (1992). Computer-assisted psychological intervention: A review and commentary. *Clinical Psychology Review, 12,* 169–197.

Colby, K. M. (1986). Ethics of computer-assisted psychotherapy. *Psychiatric Annals, 16,* 414–415.

Colby, K. M., Watt, J. B., & Gilbert, J. P. (1966). A computer method of psychotherapy: Preliminary communication. *Journal of Nervous and Mental Disease, 142,* 148–152.

Gould, R. L. (1989). The Therapeutic Learning Program (TLP): Computer-assisted short-term therapy. In G. Gumpert & S. L. Fish (Eds.), *Talking to strangers: Mediated therapeutic communication* (pp. 184–198). Norwood, NJ: Ablex.

Newman, M. G., Consoli, A., & Taylor, C. B. (1997). Computers in assessment and cognitive behavioral treatment of clinical disorders: Anxiety as a case in point. *Behavior Therapy, 28,* 211–235.

Wagman, M. (1980). PLATO DCS: An interactive computer system for personal counseling. *Journal of Counseling Psychology, 27,* 16–30.

Weizenbaum, J. (1966). ELIZA: A computer program for the study of natural language communication between man and machine. *Communications of the Association for Computer Machinery, 9,* 36–45.

Weizenbaum, J. (1976). *Computer power and human reason.* San Francisco: Freeman.

Andrew Christensen and Pamela T. McFarland

COMPUTER LEARNING. Computer learning is the use or application of an electronic digital computing system to assist, mediate, or conduct a learning process. At every level of education from preschool to postdoctoral studies and beyond, computers are being used to support learning activities: a young child can learn the alphabet with the help of a special computer keyboard; a high school student can explore databases of electronic images of art and sculpture for a photo essay; an undergraduate can analyze census data using computer-based statistical software programs; and a team of doctoral students and their faculty can study computer-generated images of distant nebulae and galaxies observed through orbiting telescopes. Although based on highly complex and advanced engineering design and technology, a computer is defined simply as a system of electronic devices that accepts input, processes it according to a set or program of instructions, and produces the results as output. A computer, generally referred to as a single physical device, is actually made up of a system of electronic components that include input devices, a central processing unit, and output devices. The two major elements of every computer system are hardware and software. Hardware refers to the physical elements of a computer system such as electronic circuits, keyboards, display monitors, magnetic disk drives, CD-ROMs, and various controlling devices. Software includes the programs and instructions that direct the physical devices to perform tasks.

Computer Learning Applications

Computer learning applications can take many forms and vary significantly according to the nature of the learning activity, the age of the learner, and the expected outcomes or results. A generally accepted classification system for the various types of computer learning applications does not exist. One referenced in many general computing education textbooks is Robert Taylor's trichotomy of "tutor, tool, and tutee." In tutor mode, the computer possesses information and controls the learning environment as is the case with an intelligent tutoring system that is designed to teach specific subject matter to students, to monitor their progress, and to adjust instruction accordingly. In tool mode, the computer is used as a tool to assist in the learning activity. The use of word-processing software to teach writing composition is a common example of a tool application. In tutee mode, the learner possesses the information and controls the learning environment such as when a student learns to program a computer using a language such as BASIC or Logo to solve a mathematical problem. In many schools and colleges, all three types of learning applications are in evidence with tool applications being the most popular because of their flexibility and easy integration into other instructional activities.

Among the earliest and still most popular learning applications are word processing, electronic spreadsheet, database management, and graphics software tools. Word processing has expanded significantly into office automation applications so that students composing an essay not only have the benefits of easier editing but also can collaborate and share their work with colleagues using e-mail and group software systems. Electronic spreadsheets used extensively in business education for years can also be used for statistical analysis in the social sciences, or for experimenting with and solving mathematical and science problems. Database management systems are the foundation of most library reference areas where students can search and query databases in practically all subject areas for published articles and other information. The evolution of wide-area networks and the Internet has extended the nature of this type of searching for information to sources throughout the world. Graphics software originally designed to integrate and manipulate images with text has expanded significantly into multimedia authoring programs that can integrate text, images, sound, and full-motion video into instructional presentations.

Multimedia

Multimedia applications significantly expand the scope of many instructional activities. Students no longer simply write essays but are able to develop presentations that include text and images and other media components. Software is readily available that takes images directly from digital cameras or scans them onto magnetic disks for incorporation into a composition or article. Multimedia software can control and edit sound and images from CD-ROMs and videodiscs to develop sophisticated video presentations. Multimedia applications continue to grow in popularity mainly because they appeal to and make use of a variety of sights, sounds, and motions that stimulate the senses. Howard Gardner and other cognitive psychologists have written about and expanded the understanding of the importance of using multiple delivery mechanisms for accommodating the different learning styles of students. Multimedia learning applications, in particular, are frequently recommended for developing curricula that appeal to diverse learning styles.

Computer Networks

The latter part of the twentieth century witnessed the convergence of computer technology with communications technology. Wide-area computer networks designed to bring the power of computers into every school, business, and home are becoming a reality. The Internet exemplifies this convergence and has expanded the nature of computer learning. Computer learning applications are no longer limited to a classroom or a laboratory but can take advantage of information resources that exist throughout the world and beyond. Major universities, libraries, museums, and science research organizations are making more of their information resources available for access from home computers. Through e-mail students can collaborate with other students on any number of research projects. The popular pen-pal application has been significantly enhanced from writing a letter once or twice a month to daily e-mail and on-line discussion activities. Distance learning has taken on a new dimension and is being redefined as more and more individuals, both teachers and students, connect to the Internet at home as well as in their schools. Many students can now engage in learning activities anytime and anyplace they have access to a computer workstation.

Integrated Learning Systems

The most intensive examples of computer learning applications are represented by integrated learning systems, also referred to as intelligent tutoring systems. These systems integrate hardware, software, and curricula, and also incorporate sophisticated computer-managed instructional techniques that are able to customize or individualize material for each learner. They are designed not as an adjunct to teaching but to perform the teaching function. In schools where integrated learning systems have been implemented, teacher roles have changed or adjusted from deliverers of instruction to facilitators of instruction. The initial application of integrated learning systems has been in the basic skill areas and subjects such as reading, writing, basic mathematics, and technical training. However, these systems have the potential to reshape traditional teaching and learning as they become more advanced and are developed for a wider variety of subject areas.

The evolution of integrated learning systems has included increasing use of artificial intelligence techniques. Artificial intelligence is a field of computer science that attempts to emulate aspects of human intelligence through computer technology. It involves studying how humans think and developing similar capabilities in computers. Decision making, inference, deduction, and the ability to learn from past experience are examples of human thought processes being studied and developed for computer applications. While many artificial intelligence developments have been primarily experimental, integrated learning systems are examples of practical applications that have taken advantage of this field. For example, integrated learning

systems make decisions regarding individual student progress or mastery of subject matter, adjust the delivery of new lessons accordingly, and prescribe additional activities customized to the needs of the each student.

Future of Computer Learning

The future of computer learning will center on the continued advancement of wide-area networks and the availability of computers in homes. Learning activities will be extended beyond schools and into other places such as homes, libraries, and places of business. The computer workstation connected to the Internet or other such wide-area computer network will be the gateway to applications designed to provide aid and enhance learning. These applications will make greater use of artificial intelligence, voice recognition, and multimedia software. Virtual systems that simulate real-life activities will be available and will be designed to allow students to not only see and hear these activities but also to participate in and manipulate them.

[*See also* Artificial Intelligence; Human-Computer Interface Design; *and* Virtual Reality.]

Bibliography

Gardner, H. (1983). *Frames of mind. The theory of multiple intelligences.* New York: Basic Books. Howard Gardner's major work that presents and describes his theory of multiple intelligences.

Knapp, L. R., & Glenn, A. D. (1996). *Restructuring schools with technology.* Boston: Allyn & Bacon. Describes the role that technology can play in restructuring primary and secondary schools.

Papert, S. (1980). *Mindstorms: Children, computers, and powerful ideas.* New York: Basic Books. Seymour Papert introduces the popular Logo programming language and relates it to Piagetian theory and experiential learning.

Picciano, A. G. (1998). *Educational leadership and planning for technology.* Upper Saddle River, NJ: Prentice Hall. Provides a comprehensive overview of computer technology as used in primary and secondary schools.

Rivard, J. D. (1995). *Select topics on technology, teaching, and learning.* Needham Heights, MA: Simon & Schuster. Examines the theory and practice of technology in teaching and learning.

Taylor, R. P. (Ed.). (1980). *The computer in the school: Tutor, tool, tutee.* New York: Teachers College Press. Provides a simple classification system for computer learning applications.

Anthony G. Picciano

COMTE, AUGUSTE (1798–1857), French philosopher, sociologist. Founder of positivism and *sociology* (a term he coined), historian-epistemologist of science, and social visionary, Comte was among the nineteenth century's most influential philosophers and is now among its most neglected. His two best-known, multivolume works defined the two sides of his position and divided his early followers. Some, like Emile Littré and John Stuart Mill, embraced the theory of science presented in the earlier *Cours de philosophie positive* and rejected the utopian politics of the later *Système de politique positive*. Others, with Comte's blessing, viewed the *Cours* as merely preparatory to the *Système*'s vision of social reorganization. Mill's construal prevailed; by the mid-1900s, Comte's views seemed little more than imperfect anticipations of logical positivism. Yet recent work correctly stresses the unity of Comte's theoretical and practical teachings, and there is fresh interest in his conceptions of intellectual development, scientific methodology, and social science.

Comte's most famous idea is undoubtedly his "three-stage law," according to which human intelligence successively develops three distinct philosophical methods—the theological (fictive), metaphysical (abstract), and scientific (positive). This law depicts human development from several angles. Historically, it identifies three stages in the whole human race; epistemologically, the stages through which each science passes to realize its aim; psychobiographically, the stages of individual intellectual growth; and sociopolitically, the regeneration of economic, military, legal, and spiritual practices in response to intellectual progress. With the rise of logical positivism, this law was routinely misrepresented as claiming that science produces real knowledge, while theology and metaphysics offer only superstitious beliefs and meaningless abstractions. To Comte, however, science constitutes a transformation, not a rejection, of theology and metaphysics.

Comte's epistemology is less reductive than the phenomenalist and sensationalist theories of later positivists. Regarding scientific method, Comte does call theologico-metaphysical speculation that transcends experience "mysticism," but he also opposes any "empiricism" that depicts science as an accumulation of "bare facts." Mysticism and empiricism distort both thought and experience by perpetuating the same false dichotomy of transcendent "truths of reason" verses sense-based "truths of fact." Science, for Comte, "observes" everything from planets and atoms to social customs and language. Yet its primary interest is not observation even in this richer sense. The goal of science is rational "prevision." As in theology and metaphysics, but with better help from observation, it seeks a unified theoretical system providing for mastery of our material and social surroundings. To make scientist and citizen alike appreciate this mission, Comte resorts to history as well as logic.

Historically, science fulfills the original aim of theology and metaphysics by surpassing their ineffectual methods. Theology constitutes the necessarily spontaneous, imaginative first response to unexpectedly mysterious surroundings. Its speculations reveal that theorizing is possible, and in guiding ritual and social behavior, theology establishes the first universal praxis—a sort of primal technology. The metaphysical era is purely transitional. Reason breaks free from superstition and religious authority and discovers the power of argument and abstraction. Yet liberated reason alone offers neither effective knowledge nor improved social life. It produces competing dogmatic systems—each logically consistent but all fundamentally unconcerned about actual experience—and its preferred form of praxis is mere contemplation and love of argument. Eventually, ineffectual metaphysical rumination about life's unanswerable why's gives way to scientific exploration of the how's of observed phenomena. A hierarchy of sciences develops, from the simplest (mathematics, astronomy) to the most complex (biology, sociology), and a final form of praxis emerges—a truly global technology that controls nature and facilitates "social engineering," as humanity has desired since its earliest experiences of cosmic disruption.

Epistemologically, Comte opposes efforts like Mill's later *System of Logic* that formalize scientific procedure. Pedagogy does require such "dogmatical" accounts of science's logical structure; but absolutizing these accounts, forgetting the selectiveness and derivative character of all formal study, is a metaphysical mistake. It obscures the need for practicing scientists to shape their methods in response to their own activities, and it fosters complacency about scientific investigation as a kind of mechanical rule-following.

Comte, notoriously, claims psychology cannot be a science, because its method of "interior observation" is essentially chimerical. His point, however, is easily missed; indeed, much that he assigns to biology and sociology is part of "psychology" today. Unfortunately, his view is largely known through Mill's misinterpretation. Comte's target is not introspection, as Mill assumed, but a pseudo-method promoted by contemporaries like Victor Cousin in hopes of salvaging their metaphysics of the soul by claiming reliance on an "interior" observation just as "scientific" as external observation in natural science.

Comte is probably wrong to claim empirical warrant for his law. His "scientific" ideas often seem hopelessly dated—he proclaimed, for example, the natural inferiority of women and the rise, within a few decades, of a Religion of Humanity (with him as high priest). Regarding his positivism's general outlook, however, there is still plenty to consider. His view that mature minds are historico-critically reflective in their thinking displays striking kinship with the historicist and antiformalist epistemologies developed since positivism's demise. His contextualization of scientific theory and moral-technological interpretation of science's purpose brings him close in spirit to American pragmatism and neo-pragmatism. Finally, his opposition to "psychology," long dismissed as crudely fixated on introspection and phrenology, is today better linked with radical behaviorism's critique of traditional ideas of consciousness and will.

Bibliography

Charlton, D. G. (1959). *Positivist thought in France during the Second Empire, 1852–1870*. Oxford: Oxford University Press. A standard reference work, tracing the immediate influence of Comte in France.

Comte, A. (1830–42). *Cours de philosophie positive* [in 60 "leçons"] (Vols. 1–6). Paris: Bachelier. Reprint in 2 vols. *Philosophie prémier: Cours de philosophie positive, leçons 1 à 45* (M. Serres, F. Dagonet, & A. Sinaceur, Eds.), and *Physique sociale: Cours de philosophie positive, leçons 46–60* (J.-P. Enthoven, Ed.). Paris: Hermann, 1975. There is no complete English translation of all 60 "Lessons." Partial translations: Frederick Ferré, *Introduction to Positive Philosophy* (Indianapolis, 1988); Gertrud Lenzer, *Auguste Comte and Positivism: The Essential Writings* (New Brunswick, 1998). Ferré's translation of the two introductory lessons provides a brief overview of Comte's work as a whole. Lenzer's selections from the *Cours*, themselves sharply abridged, are from Harriet Martineau's 1853 "authorized" but very "freely translated and condensed," *The Positive Philosophy of Auguste Comte* (Vols. 1–2). (London, 1853).

Comte, Auguste. (1844). *Discours sur l'esprit positif*. Paris: Carilian-Goeury and Victor Dalmont. There is a 1903 translation, *A Discourse on the Positive Spirit* (E. S. Beesly, Trans.). London: William Reeves. Hard to obtain and not always reliable, Beesly's translation of the *Discours* nevertheless provides the most accessible account of Comte's philosophy for the general reader.

Gouhier, H. (1933–1941). *La jeunesse d'Auguste Comte et la formation du positivisme* (Vols 1–3; Vol. 3, 2nd ed., 1970). [The youth of Auguste Comte and the development of positivism]. Paris: J. Vrin. Still the most thorough and detailed study of Comte's early work, though now to be read together with Pickering (1993). Very extensive bibliography.

Haac, O. (Ed. and Trans.). (1995). *The correspondence of John Stuart Mill and Auguste Comte*. New Brunswick, NJ: Transaction. Lively, revealing exchange between two major 19th-century thinkers from 1841 to 1847, at first enthusiastic about their shared commitment to positivism and its social promise, gradually discovering deep disagreements about the desirability of formalizing the logic of science, the status of women, and the possibility of a scientific psychology.

Kremer-Marietti, A. (Ed.). (1998). Special issue bicentenary commemorating Comte's birth. *Revue internationale de philosophie*, *52*, (203). Collection of new essays by Comte specialists (English and French) from various disciplines, reconsidering Comte's legacy in light of recent revisionary scholarship and contemporary social and political issues.

Laudan, L. (1981). Towards a reassessment of Comte's *Méthode Positive*. In L. Laudan, *Science and hypothesis: Historical essays on scientific methodology* (pp. 141–162). Dordrecht: D. Reidel. One of the very few recent studies of Comte's epistemology of science, set against the background of issues and arguments in mainstream Anglo-American philosophy of science.

Mill, J. S. (1969). Auguste Comte and positivism. In J. M. Robson (Ed.), *The collected works of John Stuart Mill* (Vol. 10, pp. 261–368). Toronto: University of Toronto Press. (Original work published 1865.) There is also a separate reprint of the 1885 edition (Bristol, 1995). This is the most influential study of Comte's philosophy, written after Mill's early enthusiasm had cooled, generally favorable toward Comte's defense of science, but strongly critical of his failure to provide an "organon of proof," his attitude toward psychology, and his later social theories.

Pickering, M. (1993). *Auguste Comte: An intellectual biography* (Vol. 1). Cambridge, UK: Cambridge University Press. Definitive resource on Comte's life and thought from the early years through publication of the last volume of his *Cours* (1842). Extensive bibliography. Second volume in preparation.

Scharff, R. C. (1995). *Comte after positivism*. Cambridge, UK: Cambridge University Press. The only recent book-length study of Comte's philosophy in English. Part I includes detailed, critical comparison of Comte and Mill. Part II urges Comte's contemporary relevance, arguing that his concern for the relation between philosophy and its past makes him an ally of postpositivists like Richard Rorty, Charles Taylor, and Hilary Putnam (after 1980). Extensive bibliography.

Simon, W. M. (1963). *European positivism in the nineteenth century: An essay in intellectual history*. Ithaca, NY: Cornell University Press.

Wright, T. R. (1986). *The religion of humanity: The impact of Comtean positivism on Victorian Britain*. Cambridge, UK: Cambridge University Press.

Robert C. Scharff

CONCEPTION. *See* Human Origins.

CONCEPTS. [*To treat the term and the process of conceptual thinking, this entry comprises four articles*: An Overview; Structure; Learning; *and* Combinations.]

An Overview

Concepts are the building blocks of mental life. By *concept* we mean a mental representation of a category. Categories are the sets of entities "picked out" by concepts. For example, the concept "dog" entails any and all knowledge associated with dogs, such as the information that they generally have four paws, can make good pets, and like to chase cats. In contrast, the category "dog" consists of the set of qualified members, which in this case would include Lassie, all golden retrievers, all dobermans, and so on.

Much of the research on concepts has focused on categorization, the basic cognitive function whereby we determine whether a given item belongs to a particular category. In addition to categorization, concepts play important roles in reasoning, in learning, in the generation of new ideas through conceptual combination, and in communication and understanding. Because any complete theory of concepts must account for the full range of functions they serve, it will be helpful to start by taking a closer look at each of these functions before we go on to discuss the various models of concepts that have been proposed.

Functions

Perhaps the most fundamental purpose of concepts and categorization is *to guide inferences*, allowing us to relate new experiences to what we already know. Knowledge about a category enables us to make inferences or predictions about new instances. For example, having categorized a small, ceramic object as a mug, it is reasonable to infer that it can be lifted by its handle, may contain hot liquids, could break if dropped, and so on. Not only are new entities understood in terms of familiar concepts, but experience can also provide feedback, facilitating learning by modifying or updating previously held knowledge. For example, when expectations fail (e.g., when one encounters a handleless mug) one may need to revise the concept in question and perhaps set up subcategories (e.g., well-insulated mugs that can be grasped directly versus those that require a handle). An important issue is the question of how far an inference may be extended. A mug can be categorized at many levels of specificity: as a cup, a drinking vessel, a kind of dishware, a container, or an artifact. Should the handleless mug modify one's expectations about cups, drinking vessels, or containers in general?

The ability *to combine concepts* means that a small set of concepts can be used to generate a virtually unlimited number of novel ones. This creativity is paralleled by an impressive flexibility in our ability to understand or interpret novel combinations. How do we know that "car mug" refers to where a mug is used, while "plastic mug" refers to its material, and "coffee mug" to its contents? Another important theoretical challenge is to develop models that can explain how the combination of concepts affects or modifies our understanding of the components. For example, our concepts of "soup mug" and "coffee mug" are likely to

differ not only in terms of their typical contents, but also in terms of their probable shapes and materials.

The interrelated processes of *communication* and *understanding* affect virtually every other conceptual function. Through communication, we are able to share knowledge about a concept with others and invoke shared understanding. Since most (though not all) of our concepts have corresponding lexical terms, communication and language are closely linked; however, their precise relationship is still unclear. The interrelationship between language acquisition and conceptual development continues to fascinate not only cognitive and developmental psychologists, but linguists and philosophers as well.

With these multiple functions as background, we now turn to a brief review of the central ideas and principles behind our current understanding of concepts.

The Basic Level

How are our categories organized? Many categories exhibit a hierarchical structure, whereby a given object can be categorized at different levels of specificity (as illustrated by the mug example above). However, not all of those levels are created equal. In the 1970s, anthropologist Brent Berlin observed that across cultures, intermediate categories appeared to play a special role. Building on his work, psychologist Eleanor Rosch and her colleagues used a variety of converging measures to demonstrate the privileged status of what they termed "basic level" categories (Rosch, Mervis, Gray, Johnson, & Boyes-Braem, *Cognitive Psychology*, 1976, *8*, 382–439). These categories tend to have simple, one-word labels such as "mug," "dog," and "chair." They are the first names adults give to describe objects and tend to be the first words learned by children. Distinctive features seem to cluster at the basic level—few features are associated with more abstract categories and more specific categories do not offer much useful additional information. Treating an intermediate category level as privileged generally allows us to make a satisfactory trade-off between informativeness and efficiency. For example, in most situations, knowledge that an object is a "dog" provides us with much more useful information than knowing that it is an "animal." However, knowing that the dog is a "schnauzer" requires more cognitive processing, and the additional information provided may not be useful enough to warrant the additional effort it requires (unless, perhaps, one is a veterinarian or a schnauzer owner).

Recently, research has been conducted to determine whether the basic level may shift with expertise (e.g., Tanaka & Taylor, *Cognitive Psychology*, 1991, *23*, 457–482). In other words, perhaps (as suggested in the example above) the privileged level for a person who trains dogs is not at the level "dog," but at a more specific level, such as "schnauzer." An important question is what determines privileged status. Is it inherent to the objects that make up the category? Or is it dependent on the relationship between the category and user?

Models of Conceptual Structure

Following Smith and Medin (*Categories and Concepts*, Cambridge, MA, 1981), one can distinguish three models of conceptual structure. *The classical view* maintains that all instances of a category share defining properties, i.e., features that are singly necessary and jointly sufficient conditions for belonging to the category. For example, a triangle is a closed geometric form with three sides and interior angles that equal 180 degrees.

Although the classical view appears to handle geometric figures fairly well, a number of challenges to this view have been raised. If our use of concepts depends on defining characteristics, then specifying these characteristics should be straightforward. Yet people have difficulty doing so, even for frequently used concepts. For example, although "can fly" might seem to be a defining property of the category "bird," ostriches and penguins do not fly, while bats do. Furthermore, most people agree that the classical view is not able to explain the *typicality* findings that have been consistently obtained across studies. Typicality refers to the idea that categories are not discrete; people are able to judge different instances of categories as better or worse (more or less typical) examples of these categories. For example, robins are usually considered typical birds while penguins are not.

The probabilistic or prototype view argues that there need not be defining properties and that concepts are instead organized in terms of properties that are characteristic of category members. To continue with the example given above, birds generally fly, sing, and build nests, but there are exceptions for each of these properties. Research by Rosch and others (e.g., Rosch & Mervis, *Cognitive Psychology*, 1975, 7, 573–605) has suggested that membership in a category can therefore be graded rather than all-or-none, where the better members of the category (e.g., for birds, robins) have more characteristic properties than the poorer members of the category (e.g., penguins). Prototype theory maintains that characteristic properties are used to generate a "prototype" for each category. Potential instances of a category are compared to this representation of the average or ideal category member in order to determine category membership. Hence, probabilistic theories are able to explain typicality effects.

The exemplar view agrees with the claim that concepts need not have necessary and sufficient features but further asserts that (1) categories are represented in terms of individual exemplars and (2) potential instances are compared to known category exemplars to determine their status. For example, children seeing a pheasant for the first time might categorize it as a bird, not because it possesses birdlike characteristics, but rather because it resembles a turkey, which they know to be a bird. These comparisons may be made to a single exemplar or to a set of exemplars.

Each of the preceding three models accounts for some but not all findings and therefore each view has its proponents. There is currently no consensus about which model has the greatest capability to explain conceptual structure. Indeed, dissatisfaction with these views has led to alternative approaches to structure, outlined below.

Conceptual Models

Different as they are, the three views we have been discussing can all be described as *similarity-based models* of categorization. Consider a general model of similarity such as that proposed by Tversky (*Psychological Review*, 1977, *84*, 327–352) where the similarity of two representations is some weighted function of their shared and distinctive features. The classical view corresponds to the special case where the concept and all category members share defining features and these defining features receive all the weight. The probabilistic view conforms to a model where characteristic features are also weighted, while the exemplar view is a pure similarity model, relying on the comparison of instances to stored examples.

Similarity-based models have recently come under criticism. One concern is that the notion of similarity is not adequately constrained. Similarity can shift dramatically depending upon the weights given to particular features. For example, a zebra and a barber pole could be more similar than a zebra and a horse if the feature "striped" were weighted sufficiently. Another "constraint issue" is the problem of determining which features to use when comparing two objects. Any two objects share an unlimited number of features as well as differences. For example, both curtains and pens are man-made, can be destroyed in fire, weigh less than 200 pounds, weigh less than 201 pounds, and so on. How do we decide which attributes matter? In general, the flexibility of similarity reduces its explanatory power.

Theory-based models offer an alternative to the view that categorization depends solely on the similarity between a concept and an instance. Rather, theory-based models assert that category membership requires that an instance have the appropriate "explanatory relationship" to a concept's organizing theory. These models may address the question of why we have the categories we have, since theories can explain the coherence of a concept or category even when there is no obvious perceptual similarity among category members. For example, the category "role models" may include members as diverse as Michael Jordan, William Shakespeare, Mother Theresa, E. T., and the family pet. Despite the differences within the group, the category is still coherent because each member possesses some admirable quality (even though that quality may be quite different for each member of the category).

Theory-based models suggest solutions to some problems, but they face their own set of challenges. For example, what exactly counts as a theory and where do theories come from? For the time being, there is no convincing answer to the question of what roles theories and similarity play in categorization. Work continues to be done to try to understand their relationship.

Summary and Challenges

We have described some of the key functions, phenomena, and theories about concepts. Although research continues to be done on the categorization function of concepts, much current work focuses on other functions of concepts. For example, some work suggests that the basic level may be different for reasoning (e.g., Coley et al., *Cognition*, 1997). Other research makes the important point that the way we use concepts affects their very structure and organization (Ross, *Journal of Experimental Psychology*; 1997, *Learning, Memory and Cognition*, 1997). We believe that the pursuit of questions such as these—and the next generation of questions their answers will raise—will open an interesting chapter in the study of concepts.

Bibliography

Barsalou, L. (1985). Ideas, central tendency, and frequency of instantiation as determinants of graded structure in categories. *Journal of Experimental Psychology: Learning, Memory, and Cognition, 11*, 629–649.

Berlin, B. (1992). *Ethnobiological classification: Principles of categorization of plants and animals in traditional societies*. Princeton, NJ: Princeton University Press.

Carey, S. (1985). *Conceptual change in childhood*. Cambridge, MA: MIT Press.

Goldstone, R. L. (1994). The role of similarity in categorization: Providing a groundwork. *Cognition, 52*, 125–157.

Komatsu, L. K. (1992). Recent views of conceptual structure. *Psychological Bulletin, 112* (3), 500–526.

Murphy, G. L., & Medin, D. L. (1985). The role of theories in conceptual coherence. *Psychological Review, 92*, 289–316.

Osherson, D. N., Smith, E. E., Wilkie, O., Lopez, A. & Shafir, E. (1990). Category-based induction. *Psychological Review, 97* (2), 185–200.

Rips, L. J. (1975). Inductive judgments about natural categories. *Journal of Verbal Learning and Verbal Behavior, 14* (6), 665–681.

Waxman, S. R. (1991). Convergences between semantic and conceptual organization in the preschool years. In S. A. Gelman & J. P. Byrnes (Eds.), *Perspectives on language and though: Interrelations in development*. New York: Cambridge University Press.

Wisniewski, E. (1997). When concepts combine. *Psychonomic Bulletin and Review, 4* (2), 167–183.

Douglas L. Medin, Julia Beth Proffitt, and Hillarie C. Schwartz

Structure

A concept is the accumulated knowledge about a type of thing in the world. Thus, the concept of "car" contains someone's accumulated knowledge about cars. Such accumulations occur for many types of things in the world that are important to us. The parts of speech provide one very rough guideline for the types of concepts that people develop; for example, concepts are developed for nouns (entities), verbs (actions), adjectives (properties), and prepositions (relations). Ontological types provide another rough guideline; for example concepts are developed for living things, artifacts, events, mental states, locations, and times. Within each of these broad types, many specific concepts are developed, such as concepts for various living things (e.g., bird, rose).

Preliminary Issues

The central issue here concerns the structure of the knowledge that accumulates for a concept. As we will see, the structure of these accumulations is extremely complicated, residing at many interacting levels. Before addressing this structure, however, it is necessary to address two preliminary issues.

Active Nature of Concepts. A concept is not a passive database about a type of thing. Instead, it plays a variety of active roles in guiding cognition and action. Most generally, a concept provides inferences that go beyond perceived entities. On perceiving a car, our brains do not passively store a recording of it, as do video and audio recorders. If all that our brains did was to passively make a copy, then all we would know about a perceived car is what we sensed about it. In contrast to recorders, our brains activate a concept of "car," which becomes integrated with the perceived car. Because our concept of car contains accumulated knowledge about previous cars, it provides a rich source of inference about the perceived entity. Although we may not see an engine, we infer that the car has one. Although we may not see the car move, we infer that it can be driven away. In this manner, concepts provide expertise about the world that goes considerably beyond what we sense. For all the different types of things for which concepts accumulate, we become able to anticipate their properties and behaviors. This basic inferential capacity enters into all cognitive processes, ranging across perception, memory, language, and thought.

Representational Format. A second key issue concerns how the brain represents concepts. Since the mid-twentieth century, the dominant view has been that concepts are represented nonperceptually in something along the lines of a programming language, a statistical description, and/or a logical proof. On such views, a concept is closely related to a database about a type of thing (e.g., a symbolic description of a car's properties in a data structure; Smith & Medin, 1981). Prior to the twentieth century, however, the dominant view was that mental simulations of sensorimotor experience represent concepts (e.g., a multimodal simulation of what a car would be like if it were perceived and controlled). This view is currently making a comeback (Barsalou, 1999). Finally, a third view is that concepts are represented implicitly in dynamic systems (e.g., a pattern of activation in a neural net). Although this view has attractive qualities, it has yet to be developed as a fully functional conceptual system (McClelland & Rumelhart, 1985).

Structural Levels

The nature of conceptual structure constitutes a particularly challenging scientific problem for several reasons. First, many levels of structure exist; second, these levels interact dynamically; and third, they extend broadly into other aspects of cognition and behavior, resulting in further complex interactions. Characterizing this structure is so difficult that we lack, not just formal theories, but a complete sense of what is involved. Nevertheless, characterizing this structure is of utmost importance to a successful psychology, given the central inferential role that concepts play in virtually all psychological activity.

Features. Features constitute the most elemental level of conceptual structure. On perceiving a particular entity, features in the relevant sensorimotor systems represent the entity both unconsciously and consciously. On perceiving a car, feature maps in the brain represent its shape, color, texture, sound, feel, and so forth. According to virtually all theories of concepts, the particular features that represent a car in perception subsequently become stored in memory. Where theories vary is in what the relevant features are, how they are represented, and how they are stored. Common to all theories is the assumption that features are stored for the perceived entity, and that these features are added to the accumulated knowledge for that type of thing. Thus, features that accumulate for the concept "car" might include "shiny," "smooth," and "loud."

Unfortunately, features are no simple matter. One significant issue is *recursion*. Rather than there being a single level of features, each potential feature may have its own features. Consider "wheel": not only is "wheel" a feature of "car," it has its own features, such as "tire"

and "hubcap." In turn, these subfeatures have their own subfeatures, such as "tread" and "valve" for "tire." In turn, these subfeatures may have their own features, and so forth.

A related issue is *open-endedness*. Rather than there being a single fixed set of features, the human cognitive system creates new features on the fly (Schyns, Goldstone, & Thibaut, 1998). Thus, if attention is drawn to some new aspect of cars, such as the tapering of their hoods, this aspect can become a new feature in future cars. Or if a new goal makes some new aspect of cars relevant, it, too, can become a new feature, such as door strength in side-impact collisions.

Coming to grips with the recursion and open-endedness of features constitutes a daunting issue in the study of concepts. Until we have some means of specifying the features relevant for a concept, we will continue to be extremely limited in our understanding.

Exemplars. On perceiving an entity, more than the extraction of features occurs. Relations among features are also extracted, thereby providing an integrated representation of the entity (Hummel & Biederman, 1992). On perceiving a car, spatial relations between the wheels, doors, windows, hood, and roof are extracted, thereby integrating the individual features. Not only does this integration produce a unitary perception, it establishes a coherent representation among features in the accumulating knowledge for the category. Much work has shown that this knowledge does not just contain individual features extracted from different entities, but it also contains the interrelated features of particular entities. Thus, the concept for car contains not just typical properties of cars, but it also contains memories of specific cars (Nosofsky, 1992).

Frames. A concept does not just contain independently represented exemplars, it also contains a frame (i.e., schema) that integrates exemplars (Barsalou, 1992b). Much remains to be learned about frames, and they remain a controversial topic. Likely components of a frame are category attributes, namely, dimensions that take different forms across category members. Thus, cars take different forms on the dimensions of color, size, and weight. The knowledge that these dimensions underlie the concept of car constitutes part of the frame for car, including additional knowledge about the potential range of values on these dimensions, their distributions, and their intercorrelations. Another likely component of frames is knowledge of relations among attributes (Gentner, 1989; Goldstone, 1994). In cars, for example, wheels are generally connected to axles, which are connected to transmissions. Similarly, pressing the gas pedal causes the engine to accelerate, which causes the axle to turn faster.

Exemplars and frames constitute analogous but different levels of structure. In an exemplar, each feature and relation is an individual (i.e., token). Frames, too, contain information about features and relations but are represented as concepts (i.e., types) not individuals. Thus, frame attributes and relations are abstract descriptions of the individual features and relations likely to appear in exemplars. In "car," for example, the frame attributes for color and wheel provide abstract descriptions of individual features, and the frame relations for connect and cause provide abstract descriptions of individual relations.

Over time, a frame organizes the exemplars stored for a category. If many exemplars are encountered, a tremendous amount of information accumulates in the frame. Across different cars, different values for attributes and relations become stored, such as the different kinds of wheels that can occur in cars, as well as the different spatial relations that wheels have to car bodies. Additionally, relations among the features of particular cars remain stored, at least to some extent, so that information about particular exemplars is also available.

Conceptualizations. Concepts subserve all cognitive tasks (Barsalou, 1992a). During language comprehension, for example, concepts contribute to the meanings of words. On hearing a sentence that includes the word "car," the frame for car is accessed. The entire frame does not become active, because it contains too much information, much of which may be irrelevant. Instead, only a very small subset becomes active to represent partially the meaning of "car" (another important source of meaning comes from referent(s) in the world to which the utterance refers; Barsalou et al., 1993). The active subset of the frame is a conceptualization, namely, one particular way of thinking about the category. Such conceptualizations not only underlie language comprehension, they also underlie memory, thought, and all other cognitive processes.

The conceptualization of a concept on a particular occasion is highly context dependent, typically containing context-relevant information (Barsalou, 1987; Roth & Shoben, 1984). Thus, "car" activates different relevant subsets of "car" in the contexts of commuting (e.g., sedan), royalty (e.g., Rolls Royce), and racing (e.g., stock car).

A conceptualization may be a previous exemplar, such as the perceiver's own sedan in the context of commuting. If so, it is probably not remembered perfectly but is instead distorted in various ways. Alternatively, a conceptualization may combine information from previous exemplars, or modify information in novel ways. A particularly important conceptualization of this ilk is the prototype, or the combination of features most common across cars, which may not exist in any particular car (Hampton, 1995). Under certain conditions, the prototype may serve as a default for the category, although it is also possible that many different prototypes exist, each relevant for a different context.

Contexts. The importance of contexts in specifying conceptualizations has motivated theorists to include contexts as parts of conceptual structure. Thus, the concept of "car" is not simply an accumulated body of knowledge about cars as isolated objects, it is also an accumulated body of knowledge about the contexts in which cars occur, and the conceptualizations relevant to each.

Three different types of contexts have received the most attention: situations, intuitive theories, and taxonomies. Situations specify the locations and activities in which a concept typically occurs (Barsalou, 1991). Thus, cars occur in the situations of commuting, royalty, and racing, as well as in many others. During learning, knowledge of these situations accrues in the concept for "car," together with the relevant conceptualizations.

Intuitive theories are a lot like frames in that they provide background knowledge about the attributes and relations relevant for a concept (Murphy & Medin, 1985). They are also a lot like situations, in that they also specify the origins of a concept's exemplars, and their functions. Cars, for example, originate in the factory assembly lines, and they are used for commuting.

Finally, concepts reside in taxonomies of related concepts at both more specific and more general levels (Rosch, Mervis, Gray, Johnson, & Boyes-Braem, 1976). Thus, "car" resides in the superordinates of "vehicle" and "artifact," and it has the subordinates of "sedan" and "luxury" sedan. Many theorists have argued that taxonomic contexts create contrasts between concepts that influence their internal structure.

Summary

Concepts include many complex levels of structure, including features, exemplars, frames, conceptualizations, and contexts. Not only is each level potentially recursive and open-ended, it also interacts with other levels. Lower levels contribute to the content of higher levels during abstraction, and higher levels constrain lower levels by controlling relevance via selective attention. Characterizing this structure, its role in active cognitive processes, and its representation, constitute important and formidable scientific challenges essential to understanding many other psychological phenomena.

Bibliography

Barsalou, L. W. (1987). The instability of graded structure in concepts. In U. Neisser (Ed.), *Concepts and conceptual development: Ecological and intellectual factors in catego-*

rization (pp. 101–140). New York: Cambridge University Press.

Barsalou, L. W. (1991). Deriving categories to achieve goals. In G. H. Bower (Ed.), *The psychology of learning and motivation: Advances in research and theory* (Vol. 27, pp. 1–64). New York: Academic Press.

Barsalou, L. W. (1992a). *Cognitive psychology: An overview for cognitive scientists.* Hillsdale, NJ: Erlbaum.

Barsalou, L. W. (1992b). Frames, concepts, and conceptual fields. In A. Lehrer & E. F. Kittay (Eds.), *Frames, fields, and contrasts: New essays in lexical and semantic organization* (pp. 21–74). Hillsdale, NJ: Erlbaum.

Barsalou, L. W. (1999). Perceptual symbol systems. *Behavioral and Brain Sciences, 22,* 577–660.

Barsalou, L. W., Yeh, W., Luka, B. J., Olseth, K. L., Mix, K. S., & Wu, L. (1993). Concepts and meaning. In K. Beals, G. Cooke, D. Kathman, K. E. McCullough, S. Kita, & D. Testen (Eds.), *Chicago Linguistics Society 29: Papers from the parasession on conceptual representations* (pp. 23–61). University of Chicago: Chicago Linguistics Society.

Gentner, D. (1989). The mechanisms of analogical learning. In S. Vosniadou & A. Ortony (Eds.), *Similarity and analogical reasoning* (pp. 199–241). New York: Cambridge University Press.

Goldstone, R. L. (1994). Similarity, interactive activation, and mapping. *Journal of Experimental Psychology: Learning, Memory, and Cognition, 20,* 3–28.

Hampton, J. A. (1995). Testing the prototype theory of concepts. *Journal of Memory and Language, 32,* 686–708.

Hummel, J. E., & Biederman, I. (1992). Dynamic binding in a neural network for shape recognition. *Psychological Review, 99,* 480–517.

McClelland, J. L., Rumelhart, D. E. (1985). Distributed memory and the representation of general and specific information. *Journal of Experimental Psychology: General, 114,* 159–188.

Murphy, G. L., & Medin, D. L. (1985). The role of theories in conceptual coherence. *Psychological Review, 92,* 289–316.

Nosofsky, R. M. (1992). Exemplar-based approach to relating categorization, identification, and recognition. In F. G. Ashby (Ed.), *Multidimensional models of perception and cognition* (pp. 363–393). Hillsdale, NJ: Erlbaum.

Rosch, E., Mervis, C. B., Gray, W. D., Johnson, D. M., & Boyes-Braem, P. (1976). Basic objects in natural categories. *Cognitive Psychology, 8,* 382–439.

Schyns, P. G., Goldstone, R. L., & Thibaut, J. P. (1998). The development of features in object concepts. *Behavioral and Brain Sciences, 21,* 1–54.

Smith, E. E., & Medin, D. L. (1981). *Categories and concepts.* Cambridge, MA: Harvard University Press.

Lawrence W. Barsalou

Learning

A central issue in learning is how people acquire an understanding of concepts. Young children need to learn concepts in order to understand the world and communicate with others. Students need to learn and use new concepts to infer, predict, explain, and solve problems. Adults often are confronted with new concepts that must be acquired if they are to function effectively.

A concept is a mental representation of a class (such as students or pets) that includes how to tell if an item is a member of the class (*classification*) as well as what else we know about such things. A *category* is the set of items picked out by such a concept. This entry examines how concepts are acquired, focusing on the classification of knowledge.

Imagine the following situation: you experience a large number of very complex situations, such as visual scenes with multiple objects and motion, and are told that each contains an instance of a new concept, "dax." How do you figure out what a dax is? Although this might seem a strange task, it is actually a common one faced by children learning new concepts. This is a form of *inductive* learning in which the goal is to go beyond the information given and abstract a meaning for dax from a very large number of possibilities. The problem is that there are so many possibilities, even for what might count as a feature. In addition, each scene has multiple objects, each object has many features, and even if one knows the features, the concept may not refer to any single feature but to a set of features or relations among features. Worse than that, the concept may not refer to any object parts, but to relations among objects or even motions of objects. There are so many possibilities, how can we ever learn a new concept? The short answer is that we just do not consider all the possibilities; rather, we have a set of constraints or biases that affect what we consider to be features, what types of combinations we consider, what nonfeature information we consider, and so on.

Three general sources of constraints affect concept learning. First, there are innate constraints on what features we encode. The structure of the brain has evolved in such a way that it is sensitive to some types of features, such as visible colors and straight lines, but does not encode other types of features (e.g., infrared light). Thus, some perceptual features may be innate. In addition, we may have innate cognitive biases that affect the types of concepts that can be learned. Second, we may have a helpful "teacher" who provides additional information beyond what we can observe. The teacher may point out what the features are ("See the tail"). In some cases, people label items with concept names ("Look at the dog") and give feedback on our learning attempts ("Yes, that is a robin"). In other cases, common in formal education, the teacher may even tell us exactly what the relevant features are and how they occur in instances of the concept ("All mammals have the following properties"). Third, our concept learning is affected by what prior knowledge we bring to bear to learn a new concept, as will be discussed when examining real-world concepts.

Experimental Research on Concept Learning

Much of our understanding of concept learning comes from laboratory studies of classification in which people learn new artificial concepts. Let us consider three views of conceptual structures: classical, probabilistic, and exemplar views. The *classical view* posits that there is a definition or rule for each concept, with an item classified as an instance of the concept if it includes all the features in the rule, but not otherwise. The learning in such situations involves forming and testing hypotheses, sometimes by comparing instances of the concept to find regularities or common features. The *probabilistic view* is that we have a summary representation of the concept, a *prototype*, and classify an item as a member of that concept if it is sufficiently similar to the prototype, compared to its similarity to other prototypes. Learning for probabilistic models consists of updating the feature frequencies of the prototype. According to the *exemplar view*, we have many representations for each concept, and we classify new items by comparing them to some number of similar representations. Although these approaches are often viewed as alternatives, people probably use all of them and particular concepts may even be mixtures of all three.

The strategy people use in processing information often affects what they encode and learn. Of particular importance is the distinction between *analytic* and *nonanalytic* processing. In analytic processing, the learner "analyzes" the item, breaking it down into subparts and features, and comparing particular parts and features to stored representations (hypotheses, prototypes). In nonanalytic processing, the item is encoded more holistically and comparisons to earlier representations do not focus on particular parts or features, but on overall similarities. The analytic processing is particularly useful for finding regularities across instances, as might be found in rules, while the nonanalytic processing is more in keeping with the overall comparisons proposed in the exemplar view. The prototype view, though it can involve a large number of features, focuses only on features relevant to the concept, so requires at least some analytic processing. Again, although these strategies are often viewed as alternatives, concept learning may often require both types of processing. Perhaps in the early stages, the learner does not have a clear idea of what distinguishes the concept instances, so uses a more holistic approach, but then, with experience, begins to hone in on relevant features. One may see different strategies as a function of the type of concept, the amount of experience with the concept, plus ad-

ditional factors such as the abilities and knowledge of the learner.

A crucial part of all concept learning is the idea of comparison. In the classical view, each new instance is compared to the rule to decide classification, plus the learning may involve finding regularities across instances. In the prototype view, each new instance is compared to the prototypes to decide classification, plus the upgrading of the representation involves some comparison. In the exemplar view, each new instance is compared to a number of similar instances. Because classification necessarily involves comparisons to stored representations, the effects of such comparisons may be crucial for learning. Comparing a new instance to previous instances or even summary representations allows the noticing of regularities and also noting of contrasts or differences. Comparisons play an important role in the learning and may allow an integration of the different views. As a speculative illustration, perhaps early in the learning of a concept, people store instances due to uncertainty about the relevance of various features. To classify a new instance, they may compare it to the stored instances (the exemplar view). If the classification is correct, they may notice and encode features common to a small number of the instances ("Both these triangles have three sides and a pointed top"). With further instances and comparisons, those features that occur in many of the instances of a concept enter into more of these noticed regularities and may be viewed as more central to the concept. In addition, if a classification is incorrect, the learner may adjust the noticed commonalities and concentrate on the differences ("Oh, so the pointed top is not crucial for it to be a triangle"). Thus this possibility allows learners to use exemplars initially but then encode the regularities perhaps as prototypes or rules. If the rules are too general, further experience leads learners to specialize the rules so that they only include instances of the concept. The point is that learning may often involve multiple types of representation, with very specific information generalized by noting regularities and very general information specialized by noting additional necessary information.

Real-World Concept Learning

What are real-world concepts like? Consider natural objects, such as birds or trees. Such concepts often have highly intercorrelated feature representations. Birds not only are alike in having feathers and laying eggs, they also have wings, beaks, tend to fly, and so on. Such high similarity within these natural categories allows rich inductive inference (knowing some features allows you to predict much else), and also facilitates learning. For example, birds are so much alike (and different from other concepts) that one can form the concept with less guidance, though some unusual cases may not be initially included (ostriches) and some similar nonmembers may be (bats). Again, one might begin by storing information about particular instances, until one is more confident of the relevant features, and then form a prototype to capture those relevant features.

However, concept learning in such cases is more than comparing observable features and noticing regularities. We know much more about birds than their features. We understand how the features interrelate—how the feathers and wings are involved in flying, how flight allows nesting in trees and migration, and so on. The *theory view* is that a concept is embedded in the complex knowledge structures of a domain. The knowledge of these domains greatly affects what features are likely to be relevant, thus influencing concept learning.

In some cases, prior knowledge provides general constraints on what the relevant features are. For instance, when learning about a new animal, we believe that animals of the same type are alike in their central internal features (such as DNA), and we expect them to be similar in some respects, such as shape and eating habits. However, when learning about a new artifact, we expect the instances to have similar functions but are not surprised if they differ in shape or size. The point is that the prior knowledge we bring to bear can have a large influence on what features we think are relevant, how we compare instances, and the representations we form of the concepts.

The Effects of Greater Experience

As one gets more experience with a concept, three consequences can have interesting effects on classification. First, extended experiences lead people to notice further distinctions among concepts. For example, an expert radiologist may diagnose a problem from a small part of an X-ray that would not even be noticed by a novice. Dog handlers make far more distinctions among dog species than do most of us. Experience leads to the use of additional features and subcategories. Second, experience with a concept may lead to noting further commonalities among different concepts. Experts not only understand the many ways in which different concepts are different, but also how they are similar, and this knowledge is often useful for prediction or diagnosis. Third, with increased experience in a domain, people may learn and use different features that less experienced learners do not have available. For example, an expert problem solver may classify on the basis of deep structures of a problem (such as the principle), while a novice uses more superficial features.

Beyond the Classification Function of Concepts

This entry has focused on the classification function of conceptual knowledge, but it is important to remember that a concept includes all that we know about a class, including knowledge used to predict, infer, explain, and solve problems. Concepts are used in a wide variety of ways, and how we use them can affect how we learn about them. This effect is clear in some cross-cultural work in which the utility of objects affects the concepts formed by different groups. Experience in using objects for particular functions leads to forming concepts that capture these functions. For example, landscapers organize their tree knowledge not just by type (maples, oaks) but also by utility in landscaping (shade trees, ornamental trees). It is important to remember that concepts can help us function effectively in the world and that people are flexible enough to construct new concepts that help them do so.

Bibliography

Brooks, L. R. (1987). Decentralized control of categorization: The role of prior processing episodes. In U. Neisser (Ed.), *Concepts and conceptual development: Ecological and intellectual factors in categorization* (pp. 141–174). New York: Cambridge University Press. Discusses how regularities among instances are noted and general rules are specialized.

Bruner, J. S., Goodnow, J. J., & Austin, G. A. (1956). *A study of thinking.* New York: Wiley. A classic work in the field that began much of the research.

Estes, W. K. (1994). *Classification and cognition.* Oxford: Oxford University Press. Provides overview of several different models of artificial concept learning.

Goldstone, R. L. (1994). The role of similarity in categorization: Providing a groundwork. *Cognition, 52,* 125–157.

Malt, B. C. (1995). Category coherence in cross-cultural perspective. *Cognitive Psychology, 29,* 85–148. Provides review of anthropological research relevant to the psychology of concepts.

Markman, E. M. (1989). *Categorization and naming in children.* Cambridge, MA: MIT Press.

Medin, D. L. (1989). Concepts and conceptual structures. *American Psychologist, 44,* 1469–1481. Simple presentation of the different views of concepts.

Medin, D. L., Lynch, E. B., Coley, J. D., & Atran, S. (1997). Categorization and reasoning among tree experts: Do all roads lead to Rome? *Cognitive Psychology, 32,* 49–96.

Murphy, G. L. (1993). Theories and concept formation. In I. Van Mechelen, J. A. Hampton, R. S. Michalski, & P. Theuns (Eds.), *Categories and concepts: Theoretical views and inductive data analysis* (pp. 173–200). London: Academic Press. An in-depth discussion of the theory view of concepts.

Ross, B. H., & Spalding, T. L. (1994) Concepts and categories. In R. Sternberg, (Ed.), *Handbook of perception and cognition: Vol. 12. Thinking and problem solving* (pp. 119–148). San Diego, CA: Academic Press. Review chapter written for nonspecialists.

Smith, E. E., & Medin, D. L. (1981). *Categories and concepts.* Cambridge, MA: Harvard University Press. Very influential and readable book that provided the dominant organization for the different theories of concepts.

Wisniewski, E. J., & Medin, D. L. (1994). On the interaction of theory and data in concept learning. *Cognitive Science, 18,* 221–281. Examines different ways in which concept learning can make use of both experience and prior knowledge of the world.

Brian H. Ross

Combinations

People frequently combine familiar concepts to express new ideas or to refer to new situations. Language use is an excellent example of this process. Virtually every sentence you have ever read or heard, including this one, corresponds to a novel combination of familiar concepts. In cognitive psychology, there has been much interest in novel noun-noun and adjective-noun combinations. Recent examples include *ostrich steak* (a steak made out of ostrich meat), *zebra mussel* (a mussel with zebralike stripes), and *purple potato* (a type of potato that is purple). Once initially produced, a combination may become familiar to a language community and become part of that language as in *space shuttle*. The creation of such combinations is an important mechanism that speakers use to expand their language.

A number of challenges face any account of conceptual combination. In general, no straightforward rule describes how one concept combines with others. For example, oil combines with other nouns in many different ways: corn oil (oil made from corn), baby oil (oil rubbed on babies), lamp oil (oil for lighting lamps), or oil pan (pan that contains oil). Even an adjective can combine with nouns to produce many different meanings as in: hard exam, hard right, hard C, and hard candy. The ways that concepts combine appear limitless (Clark, 1983; Downing, 1977) despite attempts by linguists to identify a finite set of possible meanings.

Complicating the picture further is that people draw on many different sources of knowledge in understanding a combination. One source is word order. In English, the left-most term usually functions to modify the right-most or head noun. The resulting interpretation usually refers to a kind of the category named by the head noun. For example, frog bowl refers to a kind of bowl (and not to a kind of frog) that has been modified in some way by frog (e.g., a bowl that contains frogs). In other languages, such as Indonesian, the functions of the left-most and right-most terms are reversed. A second type of knowledge is the word meanings associated with the combination. For example, understanding frog bowl depends on knowledge that bowls are used to contain things. A third source of information

is the context in which a combination occurs (Gerrig & Murphy, 1992). For example, a Chicago flight could mean a flight to Chicago, a flight from Chicago, or a flight that stops in Chicago. One must rely on context to distinguish among these possibilities. So, if one hears a customer telling a travel agent that she needs to catch a plane to Chicago and the travel agent tells the customer that a Chicago flight is leaving this afternoon, then the meaning of this combination is clear. Fourth, novel combinations may be understood on the basis of how nouns have been previously combined (Gagné & Shoben, 1997). Thus, mountain fish might be understood as "fish found in the mountains," because mountain has previously combined with other nouns in a similar manner (e.g., mountain resort, mountain lion). Finally, combinations may be understood by extensional feedback—knowledge about possible referents of such terms that one has encountered (Hampton, 1987). For example, you may have never heard the term *grass carpet* but its interpretation might be influenced by having seen Astroturf.

Kinds of Interpretations

Although there are a great many ways that people combine concepts, the interpretations can be divided into three very general types (Wisniewski, 1997). In the most common type of interpretation, people link the constituents by a thematic relation, as in the familiar combinations shoe box (box that *contains* shoes) and window cleaner (cleaner that *cleans* windows). In property interpretations, the first constituent refers to a property that is applied to the head noun, as in edible mushroom and catfish. In the latter example, cat refers to one of its properties (i.e., whiskers) rather than to a cat as a whole. In hybrid interpretations, the combination refers to the conjunction of its constituents as in clock radio and houseboat. These combinations are less common than relation or property interpretations. Psychological approaches to conceptual combination can be classified in terms of whether they account for these different kinds of interpretations (see below).

Conceptual Change

Concepts change when they combine. For example, features sometimes emerge in a combination that does not appear to characterize either of the two constituents. Hampton (1997) suggests that emergent features arise in two ways—through the use of either extensional feedback or background knowledge. For example, people may not think that boiled things are "hard" or that eggs are "hard," but readily acknowledge that this feature characterizes boiled eggs that they have seen. As another example, people infer that beach bicycles have wide tires in order to ride through the sand. They derive this emergent feature not on the basis of extensional feedback (i.e., most people have never seen a beach bicycle) but rather on background knowledge suggesting that the typical bicycle tire might sink in the sand.

Even properties that are true of one constituent are changed when applied to the combination. For example, zebra refers to a striped African mammal that resembles a horse. However, in zebra clam, interpreted as a striped clam, the stripes are related to but not identical to those of the zebra. Rather, people mentally construct a new version of stripes that fit constraints specified by both the modifier and head concepts (Wisniewski, 1998). Thus, the stripes of a zebra clam might show an alternating dark and light pattern (as they do in a zebra) but be shorter and thinner than those of a zebra to be consistent with the size of a clam.

Models of Conceptual Combination

There are many models of conceptual combination. They include the selective modification model (Smith, Osherson, Rips, & Keane, 1988), which applies to some adjective-noun combinations (i.e., property interpretations such as striped apple); the attribute inheritance model, which applies to hybrids (Hampton, 1987); and the interactive property attribution model, which applies to property interpretations of noun-noun combinations (Estes & Glucksberg, in press). Other models apply to a broader range of interpretations.

The competition among relations in nominals (CARIN) and concept specialization models primarily account for how relation interpretations are derived. In the CARIN model (Gagné & Shoben, 1997), the modifier noun is assumed to activate previous combinations involving that modifier and their associated thematic relations. This information then affects interpretation. For example, mountain fish may activate the familiar combinations mountain stream, mountain resort, mountain goat, and lead to the interpretation "fish found in the mountains." In several studies, Gagné and Shoben (1997) showed that the time to judge whether a novel combination "makes sense" is a function of the relative frequency of relations associated with the modifier noun rather than with the head noun.

In the concept specialization model (Murphy, 1988), nouns are schemas consisting of slots and fillers that refer to the dimensions of the entity, along with their typical values. For example, a schema for snake may include the slot "eats" with the filler "mice." One interprets a combination by filling a slot of the head noun with the modifier noun. Thus, one might interpret robin snake by filling the "eats" slot in snake with the modifier concept "robin" to produce the meaning "a snake that eats robins." The filled slot captures a relation between the modifier and head noun concepts. To explain which slot is selected, a slot specifies preconditions that must be met by a potential filler. For example,

the filler of the "eats" slot of snake would have to be edible.

Several models attempt to capture relation, property, and hybrid interpretations. In the dual-process approach (Wisniewski, 1997), relation interpretations are derived in a manner that is similar to that described in the concept of specialization model. However, the approach uses a second process, alignment, to account for property and hybrid interpretations. In alignment, representational elements of the constituents are put into correspondence (a related process has been proposed in analogy, e.g., Gentner, 1983). The alignment indicates where a property is to be integrated into the head noun. For example, to interpret zebra horse as a horse with stripes, a person would put the bodies of the zebra and horse into correspondence. This alignment indicates that the stripes of a zebra horse should run along the body of a zebra horse just as they do in a zebra. A more recent model called constraint-guided conceptual combination attempts to account for relation and property interpretations using a single process (Costello & Keane, in press).

Summary

Conceptual combination is a fascinating mental operation that people engage in frequently and almost without effort. Current models have taken some important steps toward specifying exactly how people combine concepts. However, conceptual combination remains a challenging and important area of research.

Bibliography

Clark, H. H. (1983). Making sense of nonce sense. In G. B. Flores d'Arcais & R. J. Jarvella (Eds.), *The process of language understanding* (pp. 297–331). Chichester, UK: Wiley.

Costello, F. J., & Keane, M. T. (in press). Efficient creativity: Constraint guided conceptual combination. *Cognitive Science*.

Downing, P. (1977). On the creation and use of English compound nouns. *Language, 53*, 810–842.

Estes, Z., & Glucksberg, S. (in press). Interactive property attribution in concept combination. *Memory & Cognition*.

Gagné, C. L., & Shoben, E. J. (1997). Influence of thematic relations on the comprehension of modifier-noun combinations. *Journal of Experimental Psychology: Learning, Memory, and Cognition, 23*, 71–87.

Gentner, D. (1983). Structure-mapping: A theoretical framework for analogy. *Cognitive Science, 7*, 155–170.

Gerrig, R. J., & Murphy, G. L. (1992). Contextual influences on the comprehension of complex concepts. *Language and Cognitive Processes, 7*, 205–230.

Hampton, J. A. (1987). Inheritance of attributes in natural concept conjunctions. *Memory & Cognition, 15*, 55–71.

Hampton, J. A. (1997). Emergent attributes combined concepts. In T. B. Ward, S. M., Smith & J. Vaid (Eds.), *Conceptual structures and processes: Emergence, discovery, and change* (pp. 83–110). Washington, DC: American Psychological Association.

Kunda, Z., Mller, D. T., & Claire, T. (1990). Combining social concepts: The role of causal reasoning. *Cognitive Science, 14*, 551–577.

Levi, J. N. (1978). *The syntax and semantics of complex nominals*. New York: Academic Press.

Murphy, G. L. (1988). Comprehending complex concepts. *Cognitive Science, 12*, 529–562.

Smith, E. E., Osherson, D. N., Rips, L. J., & Keane, M. (1988). Combining prototypes: A modification model. *Cognitive Science, 12*, 485–527.

Wisniewski, E. J. (1997). When concepts combine. *Psychonomic Bulletin and Review, 4*, 167–183.

Wisniewski, E. J. (1998). Property instantiation in conceptual combination, *Memory & Cognition 26(6)*, 1330–1347.

Edward Wisniewski

CONCEPTUAL CHANGE is a type of learning in which learners actively reorganize their existing knowledge rather than simply add to it. Conceptual change involves *accommodative learning*, in which existing knowledge structures are changed to be consistent with new incoming experiences; it contrasts with *assimilative learning* in which incoming experiences are changed to fit within existing knowledge structures. In conceptual change, a person constructs a *mental model* of how something works; that is, a cognitive representation of the operation of a system, such as how a tire pump works or the formation of lightning. Generally, conceptual change occurs as an all-or-none shift in one's mental model (or as a progression of qualitatively different mental models) rather than as a gradual change in the overall amount of one's knowledge.

Example

For example, consider a situation in which an object is traveling at a constant speed along a road that leads directly to the edge of a cliff. What will be the path of the object as it goes over the cliff? According to research by Michael McCloskey (1983), the most popular answer is that the object will continue traveling horizontally along the same plane as the road for a while, but eventually will fall downward. The rationale for this answer is that the object built up momentum while it was traveling along the road, and that momentum gradually wears off after the object goes over the cliff. The underlying theory—impetus theory—is that "motion implies force," that is, if an object is in motion then some force must act on it to keep it in motion. This

view about the relation between motion and force is an example of a *misconception* or *preconception*, or of what can be called *intuitive science*.

In contrast, the correct answer based on modern Newtonian physics is that the object's path over the cliff will curve downward; it will continue to move at the same speed and direction as before in a horizontal direction while also moving downward at an accelerating speed due to gravity. The underlying theory is that an object moving at a constant speed will stay in motion unless a force acts on it.

In this case, conceptual change occurs when a student enters a physics classroom believing in impetus theory, experiences situations that directly conflict with this theory, and then changes to the Newtonian theory that is used to explain a variety of motion problems. This is an example of conceptual change because the learner completely reorganizes his or her conception of how motion and force work rather than simply adding new information to the existing conception.

Three Phases in Conceptual Change

Three phases of cognitive change are (1) recognizing an anomaly, (2) constructing a new model, and (3) using a new model.

Phase 1: Recognizing an Anomaly. The first step in conceptual change occurs when a learner recognizes that his or her mental model cannot adequately explain the observed facts; that is, when a learner realizes that he or she possesses misconceptions that must be discarded. According to proponents of conceptual change theory (Posner, Strike, Hewson, & Gertzog, 1982): "There must be dissatisfaction with existing conceptions . . . [S]tudents are unlikely to make major changes in their concepts until they believe that less radical changes will not work . . . [A]n individual must have collected a store of . . . anomalies and lost faith in the capacity of his current concepts to solve these problems" (p. 214).

Phase 2: Constructing a New Model. The second phase in conceptual change involves finding a more adequate mental model that is able to explain the observable facts; that is, replacing one model with another one. According to proponents of conceptual change theory, the new conception must be (a) *intelligible*—the learner must be able to grasp how the new concept works; (b) *plausible*—the learner must be able to see how the new conception is consistent with available observations and existing knowledge; and (c) *fruitful*—the learner must be able to use the new conception to make sense out of new areas of inquiry.

Phase 3: Using a New Model. In the third phase, the learner uses the mental model to create a solution to a new problem. In short, the new mental model allows the learner to create a novel hypothesis that was not possible using the learner's previous mental model.

Fostering Conceptual Change

Conceptual change theory suggests that students do not enter the classroom as blank slates, but rather already have built up intuitive theories based on their everyday life experiences. Research on conceptual change has had a particularly strong influence on science education. Fostering conceptual change requires helping students (1) to confront discrepancies between their conceptions and their observations; (2) to use familiar analogies to build new conceptions; and (3) to derive new hypotheses from their new conceptions.

Fostering Conceptual Change by Confronting Discrepancies. One common technique for fostering the first step in conceptual change is the predict-observe-explain (POE) method. First, a student who has a misconception is presented with a situation and asked to predict what will happen. For example, a teacher places a beaker of water and a beaker of oil on the same hot plate, places a thermometer in each beaker, and says she will turn on the hot plate until the water starts to boil. The learner's task is to predict the temperature of the oil when water starts to boil, that is, the learner must chose whether the oil's thermometer will show a lower, same, or higher temperature than the water's thermometer. A student who believes that heat is the same as temperature might answer by saying, "The oil will have the same temperature as the water because both were on the same hot plate." Alternatively, a student who believes that boiling substances are hotter than nonboiling substances might say, "The water will be hotter because it is boiling and the oil is not." Second, the experiment is carried out with the learner recording his or her observation of the results. A reading of the thermometers at the time when the water starts to boil reveals that the oil is hotter than the water. Third, the student must explain why the results conflicted with his or her predictions. In this case the learners must recognize an anomaly between their old conceptions and their new observations, which corresponds to the first step of conceptual change.

Fostering Conceptual Change by Emphasizing Analogies. Analogy and metaphor may play an important role in conceptual change, particularly in the second step in which learners search for a new conception. For example, Dedre and Donald R. Gentner (1983) found that students tended to invent one of two analogies for understanding how electrical circuits work—a water-flow model or a moving-crowd model. In a water-flow model, the wires are like pipes, the flow of electrons on the wire is like the flow of water through pipes, a battery is like a water pump, and a resistor is like a constriction in the pipe. In a moving-crowd model, the wires are like hallways or roadways, the flow of electrons is like the movement of a crowd of people or vehicles, a battery is like a loudspeaker urging the crowd to keep moving, and a resistor is like a narrowing of the hallway or roadway. Students use their models to solve problems, such as determining what happens to the rate of electron flow when a battery is added in parallel to a simple circuit. Interestingly, the water-flow model is more useful for certain types of problems (such as those involving batteries) whereas the moving-crowd model is better for other types (such as problems involving resistors).

Fostering Conceptual Change with Hypothesis Creation. In creating a new mental model, a learner may be able to invent a new explanation for a phenomenon, corresponding to the third phase in conceptual change. For example, Kevin Dunbar (1993) asked students to conduct simulated experiments in biology on a computer. Unsuccessful problem solvers were those who developed a hypothesis and then spent all their time trying to provide evidence to support it. This is an example of *confirmation bias*, i.e., the tendency to seek information that is consistent with one's hypothesis rather than information that is inconsistent. In contrast, successful problem solvers recognized a discrepancy between their hypothesis and the observed results, invented a new theory, and then tested the predictions of the new theory by creating different experiments. Rather than engage solely in hypothesis testing, students who experience conceptual change are able to participate in hypothesis creation.

Bibliography

Dunbar, K. (1993). Concept discovery in a scientific domain. *Cognitive Science, 17,* 397–344. Describes a research study on fostering conceptual change in biology.

Gentner, D., & Gentner, D. A. (1983). Flowing waters or teeming crowds: Mental models of electricity. In D. Gentner & A. L. Stevens (Eds.), *Mental models* (pp. 99–129). Hillsdale, NJ: Erlbaum. Shows how the analogies students use can influence their scientific reasoning.

Mayer, R. E. (1989). Models for understanding. *Review of Educational Research, 59,* 43–64. Describes research on how to help students build mental models of scientific systems.

McCloskey, M. (1983). Intuitive physics. *Scientific American, 248* (4), 122–130. Provides examples of students' misconceptions (or preconceptions) of motion and force.

Posner, G. J., Strike, K. A., Hewson, P. W., & Gertzog, W. A. (1982). Accommodation of a scientific conception: Toward a theory of conceptual change. *Science Education, 66,* 211–227. Provides a theoretical framework for conceptual change theory.

Vosniadou, S. & Brewer, W. F. (1992). Mental models of the

earth: A study of conceptual change in childhood. *Cognitive Psychology, 24*, 535–585. Describes a research study on conceptual change in earth science.

White, B. (1993). Thinker tools: Causal models, conceptual change, and science education. *Cognition and Instruction, 10*, 1–100. Describes a research study aimed at fostering conceptual change in physics.

Richard E. Mayer

CONDILLAC, ÉTIENNE BONNOT DE (1715–1780), French philosopher. Born in Grenoble, the son of the vicomte de Mably, a magistrate, and educated at Saint-Sulpice and the Sorbonne, Condillac took holy orders in 1740. Jean-Jacques Rousseau had been a tutor to the Mably family, and opened the salons to Condillac. They dined weekly with encylopedist and philosopher Denis Diderot, and Condillac was later elected to the Académie française under the sponsorship of Jean d'Alembert. In 1746, Condillac published his *Essai sur l'origine des connaissances humaines*. The *Traité des systèmes* (1749), and the *Traité des sensations* (1754) followed. From 1758 to 1767, Condillac was tutor to the son of the duchess of Parma, for whose instruction he wrote prolifically. He died in 1780, felled, he said, by chocolate served him by the Marquise de Condorcet. *La logique, ou, l'art de penser* (1792) and *La langue des calculs* (1798) were published posthumously.

The *Essai*, its title echoing John Locke's 1689 *Essay Concerning Human Understanding*, inaugurated Condillac's campaign to focus French philosophy upon the Lockean axiom that ideas originated in sensations. Condillac meant also to improve upon Locke's sensationism, to "do what this Philosopher forgot": to explain the crucial importance of language as the mechanism that transformed experiences into ideas. Empiricist and linguistic impulses contended and colluded in shaping Condillac's psychology.

The *Essai* traces ideas to a dual origin: sensations and the operations they occasion in the soul. Condillac gives an empiricist response to the Cartesian claim that sensations mislead, and that clear and distinct ideas are innate. He divides sensations into three parts: a perception, the "rapport" made between the perception and an external object, and the judgment that this rapport is warranted. When judgment is in error, perception and rapport can remain true and supply a source for clear and distinct knowledge without recourse to innate ideas. Turning to the second source of ideas, the operations of the soul, Condillac shifts his focus from the empirical to the linguistic origin of thought. He sketches a hierarchy of operations, from perception and attention to the higher functions of contemplation, imagination, and memory. These last involve thinking

of perceptions in the absence of the objects that occasioned them and rely upon the use of signs. To be fully at the disposal of the thinker, a sign must be "institutional," deliberately chosen, and arbitrarily related to the perception signified.

Condillac's later works elaborate the two lines, empiricist and linguistic, laid out in the *Essai*. The *Traité des systèmes*, embraced by the movement against Cartesianism as its manifesto, did not reject system-building wholesale; witness Condillac's dictum that "a well-treated science is but a well-made system." Instead, it laid down conditions for a system's validity. These were two: an analytical basis in experience, and a proper use of words. The *Traité des sensations* takes up the first, specifying the roles of the senses in founding the operations of the mind. Condillac imagines an inert and senseless statue that receives the five senses one by one, and through each, particular mental capacities. These remain self-regarding, and the statue experiences its sensations only as modifications of itself, until the sense of touch brings it an understanding of "the 'I'" as distinct from all else.

The second condition of good philosophy, a well-made language, is the subject of *La Logique*. To think, one must analyze the objects of experience verbally into classes. Here, Condillac's linguistic preoccupation carries him to his farthest remove from Lockean empiricism: he hypothesizes an innate "language of action." The Ideologues, among them P. J. G. Cabanis, the Comte Destutt de Tracy, and Philippe Pinel, later founded their science of ideas (from neurophysiology to criminal psychology) upon Condillac's philosophy.

Bibliography

Arnoux, G., & Bonnot, G., abbé de Mably. (Eds.). (1798). *Oeuvres complètes de Condillac* (Vols. 1–23). Paris. The first complete edition of Condillac's works, prepared by his brother partly from manuscripts. Contains Mably's own revisions and corrections, and the first publication of the unfinished *Langue des calculs*.

Derrida, J. (1980). *The archaeology of the frivolous: Reading Condillac*. (J. P. Leavey, Jr., Trans.). Pittsburgh: Duquesne University Press. Translation of an essay first published in 1973 together with Condillac's *Essai sur l'origine des connaissances humaines*.

Knight, I. (1968). *The geometric spirit: The abbé de Condillac and the French enlightenment*. New Haven, CT: Yale University Press. Positions Condillac's "inconsistent, even chaotic" philosophy against the "intellectual tensions of its age."

Le Roy, G. (1937). *La psychologie de Condillac*. Paris: Boivin. Traces the development of Condillac's epistemological thinking from the *Essai sur l'origine des connaissances humaines* through the *Traité des sensations*.

Le Roy, G. (Ed.). (1947–1951). *Oeuvres philosophiques de*

Condillac [The philosophical works of Condillac] (Vols. 1–3). Paris: Presses universitaires de france. Part of the series "Corpus général des philosophes français." Complete except for parts of the *Histoire ancienne* and *Histoire moderne*, from the *Cours d'études pour l'instruction du Prince de Parme*. Contains an excellent critical introduction and notes on the text.

Philip, F., & Lane, H. (Eds.). (1982). *Philosophical writings of Étienne Bonnot, Abbé de Condillac*. Hillsdale, NJ: Erlbaum.

Jessica G. Riskin

CONDITIONING. *See* Classical Conditioning; *and* Operant Conditioning.

CONDUCT DISORDER. Child conduct disorder (CD) is composed of a diverse array of troublesome antisocial acts. As noted in the *Diagnostic and Statistical Manual of Mental Disorders*, the essential feature of CD is "a repetitive and persistent pattern of behavior in which the basic rights of others or major age-appropriate societal norms or rules are violated" (American Psychiatric Association, 1994, p. 85). The 15 behaviors included in this category fall into four groupings: (1) aggressive conduct that causes or threatens physical harm to other people or animals, (2) nonaggressive conduct that causes property loss or damage, (3) deceitfulness or theft, and (4) serious violations of rules. The diagnosis is rendered if the child has shown at least three of the behaviors over the past 12 months, with at least one behavior present in the past 6 months. A second criterion for the diagnosis is that the behaviors have caused significant impairment in social, academic, or occupational functioning. Finally, CD may be diagnosed in youth older than 18 years of age, provided the criteria for antisocial personality disorder (APD) are not met. Thus the diagnostic criteria require no specific set of core symptoms, and symptoms are often exhibited in various settings, such as the home, school, or community.

Two subtypes of CD have been designated based on the age of onset. Childhood-onset type is appropriate for children showing at least one of the behaviors, commonly aggression, before the age of 10. Such individuals may exhibit other problems, such as oppositionalism and peer relationship problems, may show persistent CD, and may develop adult APD. In contrast, the adolescent-onset type is defined by the absence of any CD criteria before the age of 10. These individuals are less likely to show the types of problems mentioned for the childhood-onset type. The severity of CD may be specified as mild, moderate, or severe, depending upon the number of problems and their effects on others.

It is important to emphasize that many of these individual behaviors may be both common and problematic in their own right. Certainly, the level of severity conveyed by these individual symptoms may vary considerably, especially in terms of their potential for causing personal injury or contact with legal authorities. The chronicity of these behaviors is reflected in their high frequency, diversity, early onset, and stability across time, settings, and families, even among young children (Loeber, Farrington, Stouthamer-Loeber, & Van Kammen, 1998). Indeed, for these and other reasons, many CD children function poorly in various interpersonal contexts. Not surprisingly, then, the behaviors in CD account for a majority of clinical referrals and are among the most "referable" problems in outpatient clinics (Frick, 1998).

Several empirically derived methods that distinguish among particular behaviors or related features of the disorder have been examined for subtyping children with CD. For example, children have been classified as exhibiting overt/confrontive acts (e.g., fighting, noncompliance) or covert/nonconfrontive acts (e.g., stealing, lying). Among aggressive children, distinctions have been made between reactive (explosiveness) and proactive (bullying) acts. Developmental progressions have been identified that reflect variations in the ages of onset and behavioral manifestations of CD over time (Loeber et al., 1998). For example, certain behaviors have been found to emerge in specific sequences within such domains as overt behavior (bullying/annoying → physical fighting) and covert behavior (lying/shoplifting → vandalism/firesetting).

The correlates of CD are diverse and reflect various risk and protective factors among multiple domains (McMahon & Estes, 1997). Among child factors, patterns of diagnostic comorbidity highlight the relationship of CD to other childhood disorders, notably attention-deficit/hyperactivity disorder (ADHD), major depressive disorder, and substance abuse, with less consistent evidence for anxiety disorder. Other child correlates of CD may exacerbate this disorder, such as significant problems in interpersonal relations (peer rejection, conversational and social skill deficits), cognitive (hostile attributional bias) and problem-solving (limited generation of alternative solutions to problems) abilities, and academic (underachievement) and self-control (low frustration, empathy, or guilt) skills. CD may increase the likelihood that a child will engage in delinquent acts, illicit drug use, and violent behavior; drop out of school; have severe family conflict; and face eventual placement out of the home, which may precipitate involvement in the special education and/or juvenile justice systems.

Elements of parental and family dysfunction among CD children include psychiatric disorders, such as depression, substance abuse, and APD or criminality; ineffective parenting practices that include excesses or deficits in child management skills (e.g., few positive and many negative comments, harsh or inconsistent punishment, limited monitoring and use of contingent discipline); divorce or marital conflicts; and psychosocial disadvantages (see Kazdin, 1995; McMahon & Estes, 1997). The families of CD children may be characterized by the use of coercion and hostile interchanges to communicate and solve problems, infrequent positive or supportive behaviors, verbal and physical aggression, and a history of maltreatment.

Reliability and Validity of the Classification

Studies have examined the ability to render diagnoses of CD based on the criteria designated in *DSM–IV* and its predecessors (McMahon & Estes, 1997). *DSM–IV* diagnoses of CD have been found to possess higher internal consistency and test-retest reliability than those formulated using the next earlier method (*DSM–III–R*). Further, *DSM–IV* diagnoses also show somewhat better relationships to clinician-derived diagnoses of CD. There is also empirical evidence to support the childhood-onset type of CD. Relative to the adolescent type, the childhood type is more highly associated with heightened aggression, male gender, oppositional defiant disorder (ODD), and a family history of antisocial behavior. Finally, studies have shown how children diagnosed with CD and ODD differ in certain characteristics (level of antisocial behavior in parents, likelihood of persistence of CD). There is also significant internal validity to the symptoms associated with CD. Thus, the *DSM–IV* criteria were developed based on a series of steps consisting of literature reviews, reanalyses of existing data sets, the testing of alternative criteria in field trials, and the identification of items associated with highest clinician agreement for this diagnosis (Frick, 1998).

Prevalence and Incidence

Epidemiological studies suggest that CD is one of the most prevalent categories of mental health problems of children in this country, with rates estimated at 9% for males and 2% for females (Frick, 1998; Kazdin, 1995). The most recent evidence based on the field trials for *DSM–IV* found an overall prevalence rate of 28.6%, with rates of 22.0% and 5.0% for the childhood and adolescent types, respectively (Lahey et al., 1997). Comparable rates for the same categories based on a large household sample were 5.8% overall and 4.1% and 1.6%, respectively, for childhood and adolescent types. Other prevalence rates in individual U.S. cities have ranged from 5.6 to 8.3% across different age groups in

one study and 3.9 to 4.8% in another study. In Canada, the prevalence of CD using criteria most similar to those in *DSM–III* ranged from 6.5 to 10.4% for males and 1.8 to 4.1% for females, with an overall rate of 5.5%. More recent data from New Zealand suggest prevalence rates of 7.3% for CD. Not surprisingly, the rates for individual behaviors in the United States can be quite high. Among the behaviors with the highest rates for adolescent boys and girls, respectively, are lying and cheating (27%, 18%), cruelty and bullying (17%, 10%), and getting into fights (12%, 9%).

Studies of the incidence of CD do not appear to have been conducted, as few research articles or reviews contain such information. One longitudinal study of boys with CD found that only 33 of 65 (51%) met criteria for the disorder again in the following year (Lahey et al., 1994). Of the 65 boys who met criteria in the first year of the study, an additional 15 boys first met criteria in the second year; 7 and 10 other boys first met criteria in the third and fourth years, respectively. These figures provide some of the only information on the incidence of CD.

Treatment

Most studies of treatment and intervention have been conducted with children and youth who exhibit individual antisocial behaviors or multiple conduct problems, with fewer studies targeting patients diagnosed with CD (Brestan & Eyberg, 1998). The primary treatments have been directed toward both children and families, using an array of treatment components in clinic settings that have most recently included community and system interventions.

Child Cognitive-Behavioral Treatment (CBT) and Skills Training. CD children have been exposed to training in social or interpersonal, anger-coping and peer-coping, self-instruction, and problem-solving skills (Frick, 1998; Kazdin, 1995). For example, children have been trained to generate prosocial alternatives to personal problem situations, to inhibit impulsive responding using personalized self-instructions designed to regulate behavior, to minimize angry outbursts using relaxation training, and to develop perspective-taking abilities. Most often, children have been taught different ways to process their experiences as a means of modifying cognitive distortions or problem-solving deficits. Applications of these skills have shown reductions in parent or teacher ratings of aggression, which have been maintained at one-year follow-up. In some studies, improvements have been demonstrated in both antisocial behavior and social competence. Overall, outcome studies have shown effect sizes in the moderate range for externalizing behavior, with greater impact demonstrated on social-cognitive skills than on either social interaction skills or social adjustment. Despite these improvements, the specific mechanism of change for these interventions remains unclear.

Parent Management Training (PMT) and Family Therapy. Parents have been trained in behavior management techniques (Patterson, Reid, & Dishion, 1992), with extensions of this technology targeting parental dysfunction (e.g., depression, substance abuse), parents' communication and problem-solving skills, marital and family support, and extrafamily relationships (Frick, 1998). Thus, to improve their interactional patterns and management practices, parents have learned how to apply behavioral principles effectively (e.g., to reinforce and punish behavior), how to play with their children, and how to teach and coach the child to use new skills. Both treatment manuals and videotapes have been found to be effective in this area. Family therapy directed toward improving rule following, relationships, and family activities, and toward minimizing blame and coercive communication also has been developed for use with delinquents. Changes in children's conduct problems have been reported, with some program maintenance over long intervals that have included 3 years and 14 years in one study. In particular, high effect sizes (ES) have been reported for child outcomes, with a modest ES for parental adjustment, but limited or no effects have been found as well. Of course, not all families are ideal candidates for such interventions.

Multimodal Treatments. Some treatments have incorporated different procedures, such as child problem-solving skills training and PMT, child anger-coping training and teacher consultation, or PMT with partner-support training. Where applicable, the inclusion of medication may enhance control over aggression. The use of several components (e.g., skills training, school consultation, home visits) may facilitate efforts to target domains related to individual and family functioning, such as child maltreatment, social-cognitive repertoire, classroom conduct, parental coercion, and family instability (Kazdin, 1996). Indeed, treatment recommendations often include the use of several approaches.

Summary of Treatment Research Studies. Studies based on procedures applied in research settings have documented clinical improvements in aggression (ES = 0.42) and other conduct problems (ES = 0.49; Weisz, Weiss, Han, Granger, & Morton, 1995), mostly using cognitive-behavioral procedures, but with less impact on the maintenance of these improvements. Variables related to positive outcome have been related to the functioning of the child (reduced externalizing symptoms and hostility and internalizing attributional style), the parents (indiscriminate parenting, absence of marital problems), and the family (few negative life experiences, family decision making; see Kazdin, 1995). Heightened child and family dysfunction (e.g., severity

of antisocial behavior, adverse child-rearing practices) also predict premature treatment termination, although such findings are infrequently incorporated into outcome evaluations. Multimodal community-based interventions have been recommended to more fully address the context of CD and to enhance program maintenance (Kazdin, 1996).

Community-Based Treatment. Few clinic- or community-based studies of child treatment have been reported. Whereas early clinic-based studies revealed very minimal effects, more recent treatment studies from controlled settings that possess both research treatment and clinic treatment characteristics have reported much greater effects (see Weisz, Donenberg, Han, & Kauneckis, 1995). An emerging literature on community-based intervention has extended these positive outcomes (Dadds, 1997). For example, studies of multisystemic therapy (MST) suggest considerable benefit to conducting treatment in the child's natural environment, using a comprehensive, flexible approach that targets a range of child, parent, family, and social system factors associated with a given child's behavioral problems (Henggeler, Schoenwald, Borduin, Rowland, & Cunningham, 1998). This approach has been successful in modifying antisocial behavior and rates of restrictive placement of delinquent youth and in reducing the cost of services. Additional studies with conduct-problem children and youth have identified the benefits of conducting other treatments in the community, such as PMT groups, case management, and school intervention.

Suggested benefits of community-based programs include the flexibility to target various child and family problems in multiple domains that may maintain CD symptoms, the ability to increase access to services, the potential for minimizing obstacles to participation, and cost effectiveness. Of course, potential disadvantages also exist (e.g., difficulty in monitoring/promoting in treatment integrity, practical complications in the delivery of services, no-shows, threats to staff safety, difficulty of integrating diverse services across sites and settings, and increased costs). Certainly, studies directed toward CD youth and their families must begin to identify the right conditions under which clinical outcome and service impact in the real world are maximized (Weisz, Donenberg, et al., 1995). Treatment participation and outcome may be maximized if treatment targets the family and community context of CD, if it incorporates comprehensive and intensive services that target key participants and domains (e.g., ADHD and aggressiveness, parental adjustment and management skill, coercive family interactions, school conduct and performance problems, deviant peers), and if it is flexible with respect to the family's individual needs and service preferences.

Prevention

Prevention efforts have long been advocated to reduce the incidence of CD given the resistance of CD to treatment and the intensity of services required to produce lasting gains. Moreover, many caregivers of antisocial children may not seek services despite a long history of child problems, and, when they do, such behaviors are quite resistant to treatment and often convey a poor prognosis (Kazdin, 1995). Accordingly, many of the aforementioned treatment components have been recommended to minimize and prevent delinquency. The FAST-Track program provides an example of perhaps the most comprehensive and intensive preventive intervention being conducted in multiple naturalistic settings (home, school) directed toward children at risk for CP and antisocial behavior during a two-year period (Conduct Problems Prevention Research Group, 1992). This large-scale prevention trial incorporates several interrelated treatment components (child tutoring and classroom intervention, peer training, social-cognitive skills training, parent training, family problem solving) based on its comprehensive developmental-clinical model emphasizing multiple problems in CP families (e.g., family coercion, limited social skills, poor academic performance, peer rejection, and deviant peers). Initial data from this program highlight its clinical benefits.

Primary prevention studies have included early parent or family interventions, school-based interventions, and community-based interventions (Kazdin, 1995). Early interventions with young parents drawing upon home visits and specialized referral information have begun to report long-term benefits that include reductions in antisocial behavior and enhance child functioning, among other outcomes (less probation, fewer school problems). Likewise, improvements in antisocial behavior have been obtained following school-based and community-based programs, many of which have incorporated multiple procedures, such as child problem solving and parent training. Thus, there is emerging evidence that multiple risk factors or correlates of CD may respond to preventive interventions. Yet the long-term evidence for preventive interventions is still under investigation, and important questions exist as to which are the most effective components and when is the optimal time to intervene.

Individual Differences

It seems obvious that children with CD represent an extremely heterogeneous group, given that no single symptom or set of symptoms is required for the diagnosis. Further, children's antisocial behaviors vary across age, with young children and adolescents differing in their involvement in serious antisocial acts. Covert behaviors, for example, are much more common in adolescents than in young children. Sex differences, although poorly understood, have been found in the prevalence rates of the disorder, with boys being three to four times more likely than girls to exhibit CD. Few studies have reported consistent differences associated with socioeconomic status, racial or ethnic background, or family constellation.

Social Impact

There are several adverse consequences associated with childhood CD. The symptoms of CD are among the most frequent referrals to outpatient mental health clinics. The stability of these problems within individuals and families may contribute to behavioral difficulties experienced by these children in multiple role domains, such as academic, recreational, and social settings. CD children are a significant subgroup among those who require other costly services, such as school placement, changes in residence, and outpatient and inpatient or residential treatment. Certain children may be involved in the juvenile justice or criminal justice systems. Some evidence suggests that the costs of crime and correction for a repeated juvenile offender are extensive (ranging into six figures) and may include multiple arrests over a lengthy criminal career.

[*See also* Disruptive Behavior Disorders.]

Bibliography

American Psychiatric Association. (1994). *Diagnostic and statistical manual of mental disorders.* (4th ed.). Washington, DC: Author.

Brestan, E. V., & Eyberg, S. M. (1998). Effective psychosocial treatments of conduct-disordered children and adolescents: 29 years, 82 studies, and 5,272 kids. *Journal of Clinical Child Psychology, 27,* 180–189.

Conduct Problems Prevention Research Group. (1992). A developmental and clinical model for the prevention of conduct disorder. *Development and Psychopathology, 4,* 509–527.

Dadds, M. R. (1997). Conduct disorder. In R. T. Ammerman & M. Hersen (Eds.). *Handbook of prevention and treatment with children and adolescents* (pp. 521–550). New York: Wiley.

Frick, P. J. (1998). *Conduct disorders and severe antisocial behavior.* New York: Plenum Press.

Henggeler, S. W., Schoenwald, S. K., Borduin, C. S., Rowland, M. D., & Cunningham, P. B. (1998). *Multisystemic treatment of antisocial behavior in children and adolescents.* New York: Guilford Press.

Kazdin, A. E. (1995). *Conduct disorders in childhood and adolescence* (2nd ed.). Thousand Oaks, CA: Sage.

Kazdin, A. E. (1996). Combined and multimodal treatments in child and adolescent psychotherapy: Issues, challenges, and research directions. *Clinical Psychology—Science and Practice, 3,* 69–100.

Lahey, B. B., Loeber, R., Hart, E. L., Frick, P. J., Applegate,

B., Zhang, Q., Green, S. M., & Russo, M. F. (1994). Four-year longitudinal study of conduct disorder in boys: Patterns and predictors of persistence. *Journal of Abnormal Psychology, 104,* 83–93.

Lahey, B. B., Loeber, R., Quay, H. C., Applegate, B., Shaffer, D., Waldman, I., Hart, E. I., McBurnett, K., Frick, P. J., Jensen, P. S., Dulcan, M. K., Canino, G., & Bird, H. R. (1997). Validity of *DSM–IV* subtypes of conduct disorder based on age of onset. *Journal of the American Academy of Child and Adolescent Psychiatry, 37,* 435–442.

Loeber, R., Farrington, D. P., Stouthamer-Loeber, M., & Van Kammen, W. B. (1998). *Pittsburgh Youth Study: Vol. 1. Antisocial behavior and mental health problems: Explanatory factors in childhood and adolescence.* Mahwah, NJ: Erlbaum.

McMahon, R. J., & Estes, A. M. (1997). Conduct problems. In E. J. Mash & L. G. Terdal (Eds.), *Assessment of childhood disorders* (3rd ed., pp. 130–193). New York: Guilford Press.

Patterson, G. R., Reid, J., & Dishion, T. (1992). *Antisocial boys.* Eugene, OR: Castalia.

Weisz, J. R., Donenberg, G. R., Han, S. S., & Kauneckis, D. (1995). Child and adolescent psychotherapy outcomes in experiments versus clinics: Why the disparity? *Journal of Abnormal Child Psychology, 23,* 83–106.

Weisz, J. R., Weiss, B., Han, S. S., Granger, D. A., & Morton, T. (1995). Effects of psychotherapy with children and adolescents revised: A meta-analysis of treatment outcome studies. *Psychological Bulletin, 117,* 450–468.

David J. Kolko

CONFIDENTIALITY. There is probably no ethical value in psychology more inculcated than confidentiality. Conversely, there is probably no ethical duty more honored by its breach rather than by its fulfillment.

Confidential information can be defined as private disclosures that both the informant and the recipient expect will not be disseminated to third parties. Confidentiality is distinguishable from privacy and privileged communication, although there are commonalities. Privacy is both a civil and a constitutional right. As a constitutional right, privacy is narrowly construed, barring unreasonable intrusion by the government and by some nonpublic third parties into fundamentally private conduct and prohibiting the unreasonable gathering, storage, and dissemination of private information. Privileged communication permits clients or patients to prevent the psychologists who are treating them from testifying about certain matters in legal proceedings.

Since the time of Hippocrates (fourth century BCE), confidentiality has been a preeminent ethical value. In the latter part of the twentieth century it became a legal duty in many domestic and foreign jurisdictions as well. Many states have enacted mental health information statutes in one form or another that bar the disclosure by mental health professionals of confidential information to third parties without the informed consent of their patients.

Nevertheless, despite advocates for a deontological rule respecting absolute confidentiality, even in Hippocrates' time confidentiality was conditional and discretionary: "Whatsoever in the course of practice I see or hear *that ought never to be published abroad,* I will not divulge, but consider such things to be holy secrets" (see Adams, F., 1849, *The Genuine Works of Hippocrates*). Similarly, 2,500 years later, although psychologists are reminded that they have "a primary obligation" to maintain confidentiality in the enforceable provisions of the current APA ethics code (American Psychological Association [APA], *Ethical Principles of Psychologists and Code of Conduct,* 1992, Standard 5.02), they need take only "reasonable precautions to respect" confidentiality and are permitted to disclose private information not only when mandated by law but also for such "valid" discretionary purposes as securing professional consultations, protecting the patient from harm, or obtaining payment for services (APA, 1992, Standard 5.05).

Perhaps the greatest source of dilution of confidentiality is the decision by the California supreme court in *Tarasoff v. Board of Regents* (551 P. 2d 334, 1976). A graduate student, in the course of seeking treatment at a state university facility, told his therapist, a psychologist, that he was planning to kill a young woman he had been dating, unnamed but readily identifiable by the therapist, when she returned from her summer vacation in Brazil. After consultation with his supervisor, the therapist contacted the campus police to observe the patient for possible hospitalization. The police confronted the patient, but when he reassured them he was not serious about harming the woman, they released him. The patient never returned to therapy. Two months later he killed Ms. Tarasoff, whose family filed a wrongful-death action against the therapist and others. The California supreme court held that the parents had a legal claim against the defendants, stating:

> When a therapist determines, or pursuant to the standards of his profession should determine, that his patient presents a serious danger of violence to another, he incurs an obligation to use reasonable care to protect the intended victim against such danger. (p. 340)

It would be naive to argue for absolute prohibition of unconsented disclosures in therapy given such real-world intrusions as statutes on reporting child abuse, the many exceptions to privileged-communications laws, increasing corporatization of health care, demands for information by third-party payers (such as health care insurers), and the difficulty in preserving privacy in the ever-expanding world of electronic health care records. Nevertheless, it may be argued that fidelity to clients, patients, and research participants requires more than taking "reasonable precautions" to protect confidentiality.

In 1996, the U.S. Supreme Court had the rare opportunity to give its views on the importance of confidentiality in psychotherapy. In *Jaffee v. Redmond* (518 U.S. 1, 1996), a police officer shot and killed a man she thought was about to stab a fleeing victim. The family of the slain suspect filed a wrongful-death action against the officer. During pretrial discovery, the family learned that the officer had seen a licensed mental health practitioner about 50 times subsequent to the shooting. They sought access to the therapist's notes concerning her treatment of the officer. The Court held, however, that the notes were protected from discovery in federal trials under a psychotherapist-patient privilege. "Effective psychotherapy," it said, "depends upon an atmosphere of confidence and trust in which the patient is willing to make a frank and complete disclosure of facts, emotions, memories, and fears" (p. 10). It adopted the view, urged by the APA in its *amicus* brief, that "the mere possibility of disclosure may impede the development of the confidential relationship necessary for successful treatment" (p. 10). Protecting confidential communications not only serves the private interests of therapists and their patients but also, the Court said, "serves the public interest by facilitating the provision of appropriate treatment for individuals suffering the effects of a mental or emotional problem" (p. 11). Even in the face of a patient's disclosing a serious threat of harm to him- or herself or others, the Court asserted that the protective privilege should only give way if the harm "can be averted only by means of a disclosure by the therapist" (p. 18).

It is noteworthy that the Supreme Court may be more mindful and protective of confidentiality than are psychologists, their patients or research participants, or even the public in general. In fact, there is no definitive empirical evidence that the erosion of confidentiality has caused potential clients to refrain from seeking psychological services or that the public believes that all communications in psychotherapy are confidential. Nevertheless, fidelity to those whom psychologists assess, treat, or study is a bedrock value that differentiates psychologists from government agents whose primary duty is to protect society. It would not be unreasonable to expect that psychologists would be obliged to attempt to employ all other alternatives before they abrogate the principle of fidelity and unilaterally disclose confidential communications to third parties.

[*See also* Informed Consent.]

Bibliography

American Psychological Association. (1996). *Brief for American Psychological Association as* Amicus Curiae *in Jaffee v. Redmond*, No. 95–266 on behalf of Respondent. APA's *amicus curiae* brief citing studies and authorities on the importance of confidentiality in treatment. Available from Westlaw or LEXIS, two legal databases, or from APA.

Appelbaum, P. S., & Rosenbaum, A. (1989). *Tarasoff* and the researcher: Does the duty to protect apply in the research setting? *American Psychologist, 44,* 885–894. Asks and analyzes the question. Demonstrates that confidentiality is not solely an issue for practitioners.

Bersoff, D. N. (1999). Confidentiality, privilege, and privacy. In D. N. Bersoff (Ed.), *Ethical conflicts in psychology* (2nd ed., pp. 149–223), Washington, DC: American Psychological Association. Contains readings and commentary providing diverse views on the nature and importance of confidentiality in practice and research.

Smith-Bell, M., & Winslade, W. J. (1994). Privacy, confidentiality, and privilege in psychotherapeutic relationships. *American Journal of Orthopsychiatry, 64,* 180–193. A readable paper that provides understandable definitions distinguishing among these terms as applied to psychotherapy.

Vandecreek, L., & Knapp, S. (1993). Tarasoff *and beyond: Legal and clinical considerations in the treatment of life-endangering patients.* Sarasota, FL: Professional Resource Exchange. A comprehensive treatment of the subject, including a discussion of the ethical, as well as legal, obligations concerning confidentiality when therapists work with violent patients.

Donald N. Bersoff

CONFLICT RESOLUTION. Any reduction in the severity of social conflict is referred to as conflict resolution. It may entail deescalation of an overt struggle, reconciliation of divergent interests, or a combination of the two in which reconciliation of divergent interests leads to deescalation.

Conditions Encouraging Deescalation

Deescalation means a reduction in the severity of the tactics or negative sentiments found in a conflict. Deescalation is particularly likely to occur when there is motivational ripeness, that is, when both sides are motivated to escape the conflict. In I. William Zartman's view (*Coping with Conflict after the Cold War*, Baltimore, 1996), such motivation may result from one of three sources: a mutually hurting stalemate, in which the parties to the dispute conclude that they are suffering unacceptable costs in a struggle that cannot be won; a recent or impending catastrophe that is attributed to the conflict; or a mutually enticing opportunity that seems available if the conflict can be overcome. In addition, for parties to take action to overcome their conflicts, they must usually have some optimism about the success of this action, a condition that is frequently absent in heavily escalated conflict. Motivation to escape conflict and optimism about doing so are more likely to develop (1) in happy and/or committed relationships; (2) when attitudes are positive and there is no dehumanization; and (3) in the case of intergroup conflict, when there are crosscutting group memberships.

Research reviewed by Marilyn Brewer and Rupert Brown (*Handbook of Social Psychology*, New York, 1997), has shown that contact and communication between antagonists can encourage the deescalation of mild conflicts. However, these events may be worse than useless in severe conflicts, because they encourage the outbreak of arguments or fights.

In his classic boys' camp studies, Muzafer Sherif (*In Common Predicament*, Boston, 1966) found that the most successful weapons against escalation were superordinate goals, that is, shared objectives outside the framework of the conflict that require cooperation between the parties. Subsequent research by Stephen Worchel, Virginia A. Andreoli, and Robert Folger (*Journal of Experimental Social Psychology*, 1977, *13*, 131–140) suggests that superordinate goals must actually be achieved to ensure deescalation.

According to Charles E. Osgood (*An Alternative to War or Surrender*, Urbana, Ill., 1962), the best road to deescalation is for one of the parties to take unilateral conciliatory initiatives that encourage trust. Such initiatives are likely to be especially effective if (1) they are costly or risky to their source so that they cannot be seen as cheap tricks; (2) their source is of equal or greater strength than their target so that they cannot be viewed as signs of weakness; and (3) they are continued for a while to allow the target to think about their meaning.

The Reconciliation of Divergent Interests

The best way to reconcile divergent interests involves negotiation, in which the parties discuss the issues that divide them in an effort to reach an agreement. Negotiation tends to be unsuccessful when interests are highly divergent or the conflict is severely escalated. Unsuccessful negotiation often leads to third-party intervention, which can occur at the request of one or both disputants or on the initiative of the third party. Five forms of third-party intervention will be reviewed here: mediation, arbitration, relationship therapy, peacekeeping, and the design of conflict management systems. [*See* Negotiations.]

Mediation. The most common form of third-party intervention, mediation, takes place when the third party assists the disputants to reach their own agreement. Among the most important mediator tactics are building rapport with the disputants, facilitating communication, questioning unrealistic aspirations, reframing the issues, and encouraging disputant creativity. Several studies support a broad generalization first advanced by Jeffrey Z. Rubin (*Psychological Bulletin*, 1980, *87*, 379–391), that vigorous mediator intervention tends to be effective when the parties are hostile toward each other or lack the motivation to escape their conflict. It is counterproductive, however, when they are on good terms or there is a high degree of motivational ripeness.

Mediation is especially likely to lead to mutually satisfactory agreements when the parties are highly motivated to resolve the conflict, resource shortages are not severe, and the issues do not involve general principles. If the parties are groups or organizations, intraparty factionalism reduces the likelihood of agreement. Research by Dean G. Pruitt (*Negotiation Journal*, 1995, *10*, 365–377) suggests that the perception that fair procedures were used makes disputants more likely to adhere to mediated agreements. Mediator neutrality usually contributes to the success of mediation but is not as essential as formerly believed. Indeed, success is sometimes achieved because the mediator is closer to the side that must make the larger concessions in order to reach agreement.

Arbitration. In arbitration (which includes adjudication as a special case), the third party renders a judgment about the proper solution to the conflict. Such judgments are usually binding on the disputants but may be merely advisory. Advisory judgments are helpful when the disputants are seeking a way out of the conflict or want guidance about the probable result of binding arbitration.

Several studies have examined the impact of informing disputants that arbitration will occur if agreement is not reached in negotiation or mediation. This usually motivates the disputants to try harder to solve their dispute, because they fear loss of control over their outcomes. However, it can have the opposite effect if one (or both) of the parties is convinced that the arbitrator will rule in his or her favor. The procedure in which unsuccessful mediation is followed by arbitration is called *med-arb*. Med-arb is especially common in nonindustrial societies, with prominent members of the community rendering a binding judgment if initial efforts to reconcile the disputants are unsuccessful.

Relationship Therapy. When disputants have a distressed relationship, third parties sometimes engage in relationship therapy. Such therapy may be necessary in order to achieve success in mediation and is often essential to avoid renewal of the conflict at a later time. Relationship therapy, which has been pioneered by marital therapists, usually involves problem-solving training, in which the parties are jointly taught skills of listening, clear communication, avoiding blame, analyzing needs, and brainstorming for solutions. It may also entail an effort to identify repetitive patterns of interaction that are contributing to the conflict. Problem-solving workshops, a form of relationship therapy for intergroup and international conflict, have been pioneered by John W. Burton (*Conflict and Communication*, London, 1969) and Herbert C. Kelman (*Mediation in International Relations*, New York, 1992). Selected members of both sides meet for several days to analyze the conflict. While motivational ripeness is usually required for successful relationship therapy between individuals, problem-solving workshops may be held in advance of such ripeness, producing an informed corps of people on both sides who can spring into action once a period of ripeness arrives.

Peacekeeping. When conflicts become violent or threaten to do so, third-party intervention may take the form of peacekeeping. Examples of peacekeeping include separating fighting children, arresting abusive spouses, and United Nations operations within ethnically divided countries. Ronald J. Fisher and Loraleigh Keashly (*The Social Psychology of Intergroup and International Conflict Resolution*, New York, 1990) have proposed a normative model of third-party strategy which recommends: (1) peacekeeping for violent conflicts; (2) providing incentives to encourage motivational ripeness for heavily escalated but nonviolent conflicts; (3) relationship therapy (they call it "consultation") for moderately escalated conflicts; and (4) mediation for mildly escalated conflicts. Their model has a cascading feature in that each of these strategies is assumed to produce the conditions necessary for the success of the next strategy on the list.

Another third-party role is the design of conflict management systems for large social entities such as schools, factories, and communities. Guidelines put forward by William Ury, Jeanne M. Brett, and Stephen B. Goldberg (*Getting Disputes Resolved*, San Francisco, 1988) include identifying potentially antagonistic groups, appointing and training prospective negotiators on each side who will meet if conflict develops, appointing and training prospective mediators to help these negotiators, and agreeing to observe an immediate cooling-off period if conflict develops. Such systems work better if they provide for early warning information that allows negotiators and mediators to mobilize in advance of hostilities.

Third-party interventions other than adjudication are sometimes called "alternative dispute resolution."

Disputant Preferences Among Conflict Resolution Procedures

A number of studies have examined disputant preferences among the various procedures available for conflict resolution. A persistent finding is that arbitration is preferred to autocratic decision making. According to E. Allan Lind and Tom R. Tyler (*The Social Psychology of Procedural Justice*, New York, 1988), this shows that having a voice in the proceedings contributes to a sense of procedural justice. Preferences among negotiation,

mediation, and arbitration depend on the circumstances. For example, high time pressure enhances attraction to arbitration, presumably because it can be finished up quickly. On the other hand, people in close relationships tend to reject arbitration, presumably because of its coercive features. If conflict persists, people tend to alter their procedural preferences. A common pattern is to start with negotiation and only move to third-party intervention if negotiation is unsuccessful.

[*See also* Intergroup Relations; International Relations; Negotiation; Political Behavior; Unions; *and* War and Conflict.]

Bibliography

Deutsch, M. (1973). *The resolution of conflict.* New Haven, CT: Yale University Press. Examination of the causes of and solutions to social conflict based on psychological theory and research.

Fisher, R. J. (1990). *The social psychology of intergroup and international conflict resolution.* New York: Springer-Verlag.

Greenberg, L. S., & Johnson, S. M. (1988). *Emotionally focused therapy for couples.* New York: Guilford Press.

Kressel, K., Pruitt, D. G., & associates. (1989). *Mediation research: The process and effectiveness of third-party intervention.* San Francisco, CA: Jossey-Bass. Chapters written by the directors of 17 research projects on mediation plus an integrative overview of this and other research.

Pruitt, D. G. (1997). Social conflict. In D. Gilbert, S. T. Fiske, & G. Lindsay (Eds.), *Handbook of social psychology* (4th ed., pp. 470–503). New York: McGraw-Hill. Overview of theory and research on social dilemmas, negotiation, broader conflict, and conflict resolution.

Pruitt, D. G., & Carnevale, P. J. (1993). *Negotiation in social conflict.* Pacific Grove, CA: Brooks/Cole. Integration of the research literature on negotiation and mediation.

Rubin, J. Z., Pruitt, D. G., & Kim, S. H. (1994). *Social conflict: Escalation, stalemate, and settlement.* New York: McGraw-Hill. Research-based monograph on the origins of conflict, the dynamics of escalation and deescalation, and methods of conflict resolution.

Dean G. Pruitt

CONFORMITY consists of stating an attitude or belief or engaging in a behavior that is consistent with that of other members of a group or with other people in one's social environment. To be labeled *conformity*, this attitude, belief, or behavior represents a change from a position that was previously held or that would have been held in the absence of the influence good from other people. Extremely important in instigating the systematic study of conformity was the research of Sherif (1935, 1936) and Asch (1956). In Sherif's experiment, participants seated in a dark laboratory room observed a stationary pinpoint of light. Under such conditions, a perceptual illusion (called the autokinetic effect) occurs such that the light appears to move. Sherif's participants were required to make repeated estimates of the distance the light moved. Working in groups, participants announced their judgments out loud. Although group members' estimates initially differed considerably, after a number of trials the great majority of their judgments converged within a relatively restricted range within each group. Group members thus conformed to one another's views.

In Asch's (1956) experiment, stimuli were presented to the participants on two cards. One card displayed a single line, called the standard, and the other displayed three lines, one the same length as the standard and the other two discriminably different. On each trial, participants indicated which of the three lines was the same length as the standard line. They performed this task each as a member of a group in which all of the other group members were confederates who had been coached to give the wrong answer on certain critical trials (in criminal trials). On these trials 37% of the participants' responses agreed with those of the confederates and thus were erroneous. Participants conformed to the confederates' answers, even when these confederates' answers were blatantly in error.

These early experiments not only demonstrated the powerful impact that group members can have on each other's behavior, but also inspired analyses of how and why people conform. Distinguishing between two motivational bases of influence, Deutsch and Gerard (1955) defined *normative influence* as "influence to conform with the positive expectations of another" and *informational influence* as "influence to accept information obtained from another as *evidence* about reality" (p. 629). Thus, one reason why people are influenced by others is that they desire to gain positive outcomes from these others, including approval and liking, and to avoid negative outcomes, including rejection and personal embarrassment. A second reason for people being influenced is that they rely on others' actions and attitudes as a potentially valid source of information about the nature of reality.

The Asch experiment fostered understanding especially of the normative sources of conformity. Because the line lengths were unambiguous, participants did not need to rely on the other group members to confirm their sense impressions of the lengths of the lines. Were social influence essentially an informational process, little influence should have occurred. Therefore, interpretations of the Asch experiment took into account normative factors, such as a desire to avoid appearing deviant. In contrast, the idea that conformity can occur through informational processes provided a coherent interpretation of the Sherif (1935) experiment because

of the ambiguity of the stimuli that the participants encountered. They understandably turned to one another for additional information about the nature of reality.

The concepts of normative and informational influence drew attention to the distinction between public compliance (or outward agreement) with others' views versus private acceptance (or internalization) of these views. In a situation such as the Asch (1956) experiment in which influence probably arises largely from normative sources, participants' public agreement with the other group members would not necessarily indicate that they truly believed the views they stated. Particularly when influence has primarily normative origins, social pressure may often produce public agreement accompanied by little or no private acceptance. To the extent that influence has informational origins, however, public compliance is likely to be accompanied by private acceptance because others' views are interpreted as valid evidence about the nature of reality.

Research on conformity through group pressure became very popular after researchers invented methods for simulating the presence of other group members by portraying their opinions on a panel of lights (e.g., Crutchfield, 1955). Many of these experiments demonstrated the normative and informational origins of conformity (see review by Eagly & Chaiken, 1993). Consistent with the informational interpretation of conformity were experiments on the effects of task difficulty and ambiguity. For example, to the extent that the task that group members face was difficult or ambiguous, they were more conforming for informational reasons, because they turned to the other members to develop an interpretation of the stimuli. Other experiments supported the normative interpretation of conformity, including demonstrations that the attractiveness or cohesiveness of groups increases conformity. To the extent that other group members are attractive and desirable, winning their approval should be more rewarding and serve as a more effective incentive for conformity by means of normative processes. Also compatible with the normative interpretation of conformity is Bond and Smith's (1996) meta-analytic demonstration that in more collectivist countries, such as Japan, conformity was greater in Asch-type studies than in more individualistic countries, such as the United States and Canada.

Other research on conformity has explored the cognitive processes that underlie the tendency to agree with other group members. For example, attributional processes are important (e.g., Ross, Bierbrauer, & Hoffman, 1976) and so are the interpretations that participants give to statements by other group members in an effort to make their views seem reasonable (Allen & Wilder, 1980). Explorations into the psychological processes that underlie conformity remain an active area of research in social psychology, and various theories of social influence have important implications for understanding the processes that mediate conformity (see review by Chaiken, Wood, & Eagly, 1996; Cialdini & Trost, 1998).

Bibliography

Allen, V. L., & Wilder, D. A. (1980). Impact of group consensus and social support on stimulus meaning: Mediation of conformity by cognitive restructuring. *Journal of Personality and Social Psychology, 39,* 1116–1124.

Asch, S. E. (1956). Studies of independence and conformity: I. A minority of one against a unanimous majority. *Psychological Monographs* [Whole No. 416] *70*(9).

Bond, M. H., & Smith, P. B. (1996). Culture and conformity: A meta-analysis of studies using Asch's (1952b, 1956) line judgment task. *Psychological Bulletin, 119,* 111–137.

Chaiken, S., Wood, W., & Eagly, A. H. (1996). Principles of persuasion. In E. T. Higgins & A. W. Kruglanski (Eds.), *Social psychology: Handbook of basic principles* (pp. 702–742). New York: Guilford Press. Places research on conformity and other forms of influence in the context of research on message-based persuasion and attitudinal advocacy.

Cialdini, R. B., & Trost, M. R. (1998). Social influence: Social norms, conformity, and compliance. In D. T. Gilbert, S. T. Fiske, & G. Lindzey (Eds.), *The handbook of social psychology* (4th ed., Vol. 2, pp. 151–192). New York: McGraw-Hill. Reviews conformity research and related topics, including a range of theories of influence.

Crutchfield, R. S. (1955). Conformity and character. *American Psychologist, 10,* 191–198.

Deutsch, M., & Gerard, H. B. (1955). A study of normative and informational social influences upon individual judgment. *Journal of Abnormal and Social Psychology, 51,* 629–636.

Eagly, A. H., & Chaiken, S. (1993). *The psychology of attitudes.* Fort Worth, TX: Harcourt Brace Jovanovich. Provides a review of research on social influence, including conformity research.

Ross, L., Bierbrauer, G., & Hoffman, S. (1976). The role of attribution processes in conformity and dissent: Revisiting the Asch situation. *American Psychologist, 31,* 148–157.

Sherif, M. (1935). A study of some social factors in perception. *Archives of Psychology, 27,* 1–60.

Sherif, M. (1936). *The psychology of social norms.* New York: Harpers.

Alice H. Eagly

CONNECTIONISM. Since the pioneering work of Alan Newell and Herb Simon in the late 1950s, researchers interested in human cognitive processes have used computer simulations to try to identify general principles of cognition. The strategy is to build computational models that embody putative principles and then examine how well the models capture human performance in cognitive tasks. Until the 1980s, this effort was undertaken largely within the context of the "computer metaphor" of mind: Researchers thought of the human mind as though it were a conventional digital computer and built computational models based on this conceptualization. Indeed, this approach has led to considerable progress in modeling explicit reasoning, problem-solving, and other high-level cognitive processes.

By the late 1970s and early 1980s, however, many researchers began to think that an alternative framework was needed to capture the full range of cognitive behavior—one based more closely on the style of computation employed by the brain. The new approach, connectionist or neural network modeling, or the parallel distributed processing approach (Elman et al., 1996; McLeod, Plunkett, & Rolls, 1998; Rumelhart & McClelland, 1986), implements cognitive processes in terms of massively parallel cooperative and competitive interactions among large numbers of simple neuronlike computational units. Unit interactions are governed by modifiable excitatory and inhibitory weights on connections among the units. Although each unit exhibits nonlinear spatial and temporal summation, units and connections are not generally to be taken as corresponding directly to individual neurons and synapses. Rather, the connectionist approach attempts to capture the essential computational properties of the vast ensembles of real neuronal elements found in the brain using simulations of smaller networks of more abstract units. By linking neural computation to behavior, the framework enables developmental, cognitive, and neurobiological issues to be addressed within a single, integrated formalism.

Representation

An issue of central relevance in understanding cognition is the nature of the representations used in cognitive processes. There are two basic approaches to representation within connectionist networks. (1) In a *localist* representation, familiar entities such as letters, words, concepts, and propositions are encoded by the activity of individual units. (2) In a *distributed* representation, such entities are encoded by alternative patterns of activity over the same units, such that each entity is represented by the activity of many units and each unit participates in representing many entities. Models employing localist representations are sometimes termed *structured* networks, although this should not be taken to imply that models using distributed representations are unstructured.

Many early influential connectionist models in psychology employed localist representations. For example, the interactive activation model (McClelland & Rumelhart, 1981) consisted of three layers of units: letter-feature units, letter units, and word units. Units in each layer received excitatory connections from consistent units at other layers and inhibitory connections from inconsistent alternatives within the same layer. The resulting interactive processing played a critical role in explaining a number of context effects in perception, including the word superiority effect, in which the perception of a letter is enhanced when it occurs in the context of a word compared with when it occurs in isolation or in a random letter string. An analogous model in the domain of spoken word recognition—TRACE (McClelland & Elman, 1986)—accounts for similar phenomena.

Most recent connectionist models rely on properties of distributed representations. Although distributed representations can be less intuitive, they are attractive in part because they provide a more natural account of the richness and subtlety of the relationships among entities. The key to distributed representations is the use of patterns whose similarity relations capture similarities in the roles the patterns play in cognition, since, in connectionist models, similar patterns have similar consequences (Hinton, McClelland, & Rumelhart, 1986). Distributed representations can also be used to implement more complex, relational knowledge structures like frames and scripts if units encode conjunctions of roles and properties of role-fillers—in fact, such representations emerge naturally when networks are trained on tasks in which entities enter into multiple types of relations (Hinton, 1991).

Learning

Most distributed connectionist models place strong emphasis on learning, in part because it is difficult to hand-specify effective sets of weights in such systems. Learning in connectionist networks involves modifying the weights on connections in a way that influences the pattern of unit activations produced in response to a given input. There are three broad frameworks for learning.

1. *Supervised* learning involves changing weights so as to reduce the discrepancy between the actual output generated by the system for a given input and the correct output, which is assumed to be provided by an external "teacher."
2. *Unsupervised* learning involves changing weights based only on the input provided to the system and intrinsic biases built into the learning procedure, without any explicit feedback based on the behavior of the system.
3. *Reinforcement* learning is something of a middle ground; it involves changing weights based on minimal performance feedback—typically only a scalar

value indicating the "goodness" of outcomes that depend on the behavior of the system.

Whereas unsupervised and reinforcement learning are more directly related to known learning mechanisms in the brain, the majority of applications of connectionist modeling in cognitive psychology have employed supervised learning. This is because supervised learning is more effective at developing internal representations that can support the complex transformations involved in many forms of cognitive processing.

The most commonly employed form of supervised learning is back-propagation (Rumelhart, Hinton, & Williams, 1986). This procedure involves iteratively (1) computing activations in a forward pass from input units to output units, possibly via one or more layers of *hidden* units (so called because they are not visible to the environment); (2) computing a measure of performance error over the output units; (3) propagating this error backward through the network (using the chain rule from calculus) to determine the partial derivative of the error with respect to each weight in the network; and finally (4) changing the weights based on these derivatives so as to reduce the error. Although it is highly unlikely that the brain employs back-propagation in its literal form, there are more biologically plausible procedures (e.g., O'Reilly, 1996) which are computationally equivalent (albeit somewhat less efficient).

In an early application of error-correcting learning, Rumelhart and McClelland (1986) showed that a single network could learn to generate the past tense forms of both regular and irregular English verbs from their stems, thereby obviating the need for dual rule-based and exception mechanisms. Although aspects of the approach were strongly criticized (Pinker & Prince, 1988), many of the specific limitations of the model have been addressed in subsequent simulation work. A similar line of progress has taken place in the domain of English word reading (Plaut, McClelland, Seidenberg, & Patterson, 1996; Seidenberg & McClelland, 1989).

Processing

The *architecture* of a network refers to the numbers of units it contains, how they are organized into groups or layers, and how these layers are interconnected. There are three general classes of architecture used widely in connectionist modeling. (1) A *feedforward* network consists of a series of layers of units with a restricted pattern of connectivity, such that units project only to later layers, never within a layer or back to earlier layers. (2) A *fully recurrent* network has no restriction on connectivity, so that any unit may potentially be connected to any other unit (including itself). (3) A *simple recurrent* network is something of a hybrid: Processing is feedforward over a series of layers but the states of certain "context" input layers are set by copying the previous states of some hidden or output units. These context states allow the network to learn to be sensitive to temporal dependencies among successive inputs (Elman, 1990). In practice, many distributed models employing learning have a feedforward or simple recurrent architecture, whereas nonlearning models like the interactive activation model are typically fully recurrent. This is, however, more a computational convenience than a theoretical discrepancy, as the versions of back-propagation that are applicable to fully recurrent networks require far greater computational resources.

Even so, fully recurrent networks are increasingly being applied directly in modeling psychological phenomena. Most of these models are *attractor* networks, in which units interact to cause the network as a whole to settle gradually into a stable pattern of activity corresponding to the network's interpretation of the input. Attractor networks are particularly appropriate for modeling processes that involve selecting among alternatives, such as word recognition and comprehension (Hinton & Shallice, 1991).

Although fully recurrent networks are capable of learning to exhibit more complex temporal behavior, for reasons of efficiency it is more common to apply simple recurrent networks in temporal domains. For example, Elman (1991) demonstrated that a simple recurrent network could learn the structure of an Englishlike grammar, involving number agreement and variable verb argument structure across multiple levels of embedding, by repeatedly attempting to predict the next word in processing sentences. St. John and McClelland (cited in Hinton, 1991) also showed, for a somewhat simpler corpus, how such networks can learn to develop a representation of sentence meaning by attempting to answer queries about thematic role assignments throughout the course of processing a sentence.

Conclusion

The connectionist framework for modeling human cognition has led to the development of explicit computational models of a wide range of cognitive functions. In many cases, these models introduce new ways of thinking about the nature of the computations that are performed and the ways in which learning can give rise to the ability to carry out these computations. The models also give us new ways of relating cognitive processes to brain function. Connectionist models will play an increasingly important role in the development of cognitive theories that are both mechanistically explicit and neurobiologically realistic.

Bibliography

Elman, J. L. (1990). Finding structure in time. *Cognitive Science, 14,* 179–211.

Elman, J. L. (1991). Distributed representations, simple recurrent networks, and grammatical structure. *Machine Learning, 7,* 195–225. These two articles by Elman introduce simple recurrent networks and provide a number of demonstrations of how they can be applied in learning complex temporal tasks.

Elman, J. L., Bates, E. A., Johnson, M. H., Karmiloff-Smith, A., Parisi, D., & Plunkett, K. (1996). *Rethinking innateness: A connectionist perspective on development.* Cambridge, MA: MIT Press. Articulates and illustrates how connectionist modeling can provide important insights into cognitive development without invoking domain-specific innate constraints.

Hinton, G. E. (Ed.). (1991). *Connectionist symbol processing.* Cambridge, MA: MIT Press. A collection of important papers on applying connectionist networks to issues in higher-level cognition.

Hinton, G. E., & Shallice, T. (1991). Lesioning an attractor network: Investigations of acquired dyslexia. *Psychological Review, 98,* 74–95. The first major attempt to use connectionist networks to explain cognitive impairments due to brain damage.

McClelland, J. L., & Rumelhart, D. E. (1981). An interactive activation model of context effects in letter perception: Part 1. An account of basic findings. *Psychological Review, 88,* 375–407. A major landmark in the application of computational modeling in cognitive psychology. Many current-day models of letter and word perception retain much of the basic structure of this model.

McLeod, P., Plunkett, K., & Rolls, E. T. (1998). *Introduction to connectionist modelling of cognitive processes.* Oxford: Oxford University Press. A recent introductory text on connectionist modelling in psychology. Includes an easy-to-use software package and extensive examples for hands-on experience. A good follow-up to the Rumelhart, McClelland, and PDP Reserach Group's (1986) two-volume set on Parallel Distributed Processing.

O'Reilly, R. C. (1996). Biologically plausible error-driven learning using local activation differences: The generalized recirculation algorithm. *Neural Computation, 8,* 895–938.

Pinker, S., & Prince, A. (1988). On language and connectionism: Analysis of a parallel distributed processing model of language acquisition. *Cognition, 28,* 73–193.

Plaut, D. C., McClelland, J. L., Seidenberg, M. S., & Patterson, K. (1996). Understanding normal and impaired word reading: Computational principles in quasi-regular domains. *Psychological Review, 103,* 56–115.

Rumelhart, D. E., & McClelland, J. L. (1986). On learning the past tenses of English verbs. In J. L. McClelland, D. E. Rumelhart, & the PDP Research Group (Eds.), *Parallel distributed processing: Explorations in the microstructure of cognition: Vol. 2. Psychological and biological models* (pp. 216–271). Cambridge, MA: MIT Press. Presents one of the most influential and controversial connectionist models—applied to the generation of the past tense of English verbs.

Rumelhart, D. E., McClelland, J. L., & the PDP Research Group (Eds.). (1986). *Parallel distributed processing: Explorations in the microstructure of cognition* (Vols. 1–2).

Cambridge, MA: MIT Press. This two-volume set provided the first systematic exploration of how connectionist models could be applied effectively across a wide range of cognitive domains, as well as the theoretical and mathematical background necessary to understand the approach. Although a bit dated, it is still the best place to start in gaining an understanding of connectionist cognitive modeling.

Seidenberg, M. S., & McClelland, J. L. (1989). A distributed, developmental model of word recognition and naming. *Psychological Review, 96*, 523–568.

David C. Plaut

CONSCIOUSNESS AND UNCONSCIOUSNESS. [*This entry comprises three articles: a broad overview of consciousness and unconsciousness; a survey of their processes, including physiological and behavioral manifestations; and a cross-cultural discussion of the terms, drawing on selected examples. For a discussion related to consciousness and unconsciousness, see* Altered States of Consciousness.]

An Overview

Mind, consciousness, unconscious, subconscious, nonconscious, state of consciousness, reflective consciousness, self-consciousness: What do these terms mean, and how do they relate to each other? One of the difficulties in studying topics such as consciousness and unconsciousness is the variety of meanings that different writers have given to these terms. Not only may different writers have different meanings in mind; they may switch meanings without warning from one paragraph to the next. This article will emphasize the dominant current meanings of these terms and relate them to other common uses.

Mind

The concept of mind is broad in that it includes the conscious and unconscious mind. Philosophers and psychologists have suggested a variety of definitions. This one from Donald Hebb (1984), a prominent Canadian psychologist, captures the current emphasis: "*Mind* is the capacity for thought, and thought is the integrative activity of the brain—that activity up in the control tower that, during waking hours, overrides reflex response and frees behavior from sense dominance" (*American Psychologist*, 1974, *29*, 71–79). A more recent definition in the same spirit says, "*Mind* is the functioning of the brain to process information and control action in a flexible and adaptive manner" (Farthing, 1992, p. 5).

These definitions reflect the modern approach in taking a materialistic viewpoint on the *mind-body* problem: mind involves the activity of the living brain and it cannot exist apart from a living brain, which is a material object. People with two widely different theoretical viewpoints would object to these definitions. First, substance dualists (Cartesian dualists), who believe that mind (or consciousness) is a function of soul or some spiritual substance that can exist separately from the living brain-body. This is, of course, a religious not a scientific viewpoint. Second, some artificial intelligence (AI) researchers would agree on the basic functions of mind, but claim that mental functions could conceivably be carried out by a sufficiently complex computer system, which is a material object but not a biological one.

Meanings of Consciousness

While most scientists could probably come close to agreeing on the meaning of mind, it is harder to find agreement on the definition of consciousness. Nineteenth-century writers often used the terms *mind* and *consciousness* synonymously, but nowadays, thanks largely to the influence of Sigmund Freud, the Austrian physician who was the father of psychoanalysis, we distinguish between conscious and unconscious mind. While the term *consciousness* has been used in a variety of different ways in contexts of psychological, neurological, philosophical, and religious discussions, virtually all concepts of consciousness include *subjective awareness*, either explicitly or implicitly. I have emphasized this in my definition (Farthing, 1992):

> As a working definition, *consciousness* is the subjective state of being currently aware of something, either within oneself or outside of oneself. In this case, being aware or having awareness refers to cognizance or knowing. Consciousness is always about something. . . . Consciousness has contents. (pp. 6–7)

The contents of consciousness may include perceived objects and events, retrieved memories, thoughts in words or mental images, body sensations, emotional feelings and desires, and our own actions.

Note that the common phrase *contents of consciousness* is a visual metaphor, as if consciousness is some sort of vessel with a limited capacity but a variety of possible contents. Following this metaphor, it is often assumed that some special system of the brain (if not the Cartesian soul) is the place of consciousness, and its operations are responsible for awareness of contents. In cognitive psychological models, consciousness may be equated with working memory (Baars, 1988). This consciousness system may be attributed with certain functions, such as interpreting perceptual inputs, making decisions, or sharing information among various specialized cognitive subsystems. However, whatever the assumed functions of the consciousness system might be, in all cases the reason the word *consciousness* is applied is the underlying assumption that some sort of subjective awareness of information contents is occurring. If this assumption were not made, then there would be no reason to use the term *consciousness* to describe functions that, in most cases, could be well described in strictly objective, computer-system sorts of terms.

Thus, for example, the word *consciousness* is sometimes used to refer to a human executive control system. After all, we are commonly aware of mental activities related to choosing among goals and courses of action to reach those goals. It may seem, subjectively, that consciousness itself makes the decisions. However, modern brain research suggests that the conscious awareness system is not the same thing as the executive decision system (Schacter, 1989). Sometimes we initiate actions without awareness of what we are doing or why.

Perhaps the most common use of *consciousness* in everyday speech is synonymous with wakefulness, as contrasted with a state of sleep or coma. Thus, a conscious/awake person is aware of his or her surroundings and can initiate voluntary actions. A person who is unconscious/asleep cannot do these things. However, the conscious-unconscious dichotomy is not equivalent to the awake-asleep dichotomy. People who are awake are virtually always aware of something (though there may be an exception in cases of deep *concentrative meditation*). But while people who are in *REM sleep* are unaware of the external world, they are vividly aware of the objects and events in dreams. People who are in deep (Stage 4) sleep or coma may not be aware of anything, and thus they are truly in an unconscious state. In any case, though they are correlated (albeit imperfectly), consciousness in the sense of awareness of something is quite a different concept from wakefulness.

Self-Consciousness, Primary and Reflective Consciousness, and Introspection

Some writers equate consciousness with *self-consciousness* or *self-awareness*, which involves awareness of yourself as a unique individual, having a *self-concept* (beliefs about your personal history and personal characteristics), and also a sense of personal ownership of your thoughts, actions, and experiences. (In a different sense of the word, self-consciousness refers to a state of worry that others are critically evaluating one; this is a common aspect of shyness.) The attitude that self-consciousness is the only true consciousness is an anthropocentric view. While self-consciousness is an important aspect of normal human consciousness, in the more liberal view of consciousness as awareness, consciousness can exist in a variety of degrees and forms in different animal species, and does not necessarily require self-consciousness.

I have distinguished between primary and reflective consciousness (Farthing, 1992):

> *Primary consciousness* is the direct experience of percepts and feelings, and thoughts and memories arising in direct response to them. It also includes spontaneously arising memories, thoughts, and images, including dreams and daydreams. Within primary consciousness, sensory percepts and emotional feelings are the most primitive aspects in that they occur in animals and preverbal children. . . . *Reflective consciousness* consists of thoughts about one's own conscious experiences *per se*. In primary consciousness you are the *subject* who does the thinking, feeling, and acting in regard, mainly, to external objects and events. But in reflective consciousness your own conscious experiences—percepts, thoughts, feelings, and actions—are the *objects* of your thoughts. (pp. 12–13)

Reflective consciousness makes it possible to judge our knowledge and experiences, to interpret our feelings, to revise and improve our thoughts, to evaluate our actions, and to plan future actions. Reflective consciousness is essentially synonymous with *introspection*, or "looking inward" to examine one's own conscious experiences. While awake, people commonly switch back and forth between primary and reflective consciousness. Reflective consciousness is usually absent during sleep, though it occurs during *lucid dreaming*, when the sleeping person asks himself or herself "am I dreaming," and becomes aware that his or her conscious experiences are a dream. Reflective consciousness is necessary for developing an elaborated self-consciousness and self-concept.

Unconscious, Nonconscious, and Preconscious

According to Freud (*The Interpretation of Dreams*, 1900/ 1953), the function of consciousness is "apprehension of psychic qualities," that is, awareness of percepts, thoughts, feelings, and memories. The key criterion for consciousness for Freud, as for most writers since then, was the *introspective verbal report*: If the individual is aware of some object or event, thought or feeling, then he or she should be able to verbally report it (within the limits of the individual's capacity for verbal description). In Freud's view the *unconscious mind* contains hidden desires and repressed memories that cannot be retrieved to consciousness and reported. A main concern of psychoanalytic methods such as free association and dream interpretation was to enable the patient to obtain access to repressed memories, on the assumption that they would reveal the cause of his or her current neurosis. Freud's system also included *preconscious mind*, which contains information (such as personal memories) that is not currently the topic of consciousness but which can easily be retrieved to consciousness.

In recent years, cognitive psychologists have found extensive evidence for a *cognitive unconscious* involving a variety of *mental processes* (such as early stages of perception, attention, memory retrieval, and control of habitual actions) that operate outside of awareness and cannot be retrieved into consciousness (Kihlstrom, *Science*, 1987, 237, 1445–1456; also see Loftus & Klinger, 1992). *Preconscious processing* refers to the early stages of perceptual processing that occur before an object or event reaches consciousness. Research on *subliminal perception* shows that under some conditions a preconsciously processed stimulus can influence cognitive performance, even though it never reached consciousness (i.e., the person never became consciously aware of it).

Some writers prefer the word *nonconscious* to refer to knowledge and mental operations that are not currently the topic of consciousness, in order to avoid the connotations of Freud's dynamic unconscious with its repressed desires. I have proposed that nonconscious contents exist on a continuum of retrievability into consciousness, with some contents being easily accessible, some accessible with difficulty, and some inaccessible. Nonconscious mental contents include sensory inputs registered but not attended to, declarative knowledge in long-term memory, automatic cognitive and sensorimotor processes, and possibly nonconscious motives that influence our actions without us knowing how or why.

Characteristics of Consciousness

The idea that consciousness is about something, that it has contents, is called *intentionality* by philosophers. The intentionality of consciousness means, essentially, that it points to or relates to something (such as a perceived object, or a mental image of an object, or a thought about it). The intentionality of consciousness was one of the five higher-order characteristics of consciousness described by William James, the late nineteenth-century American psychologist and philosopher whose *Principles of Psychology* (1890/1983) is still often quoted today. Another key characteristic of human consciousness is *subjectivity*: "Every thought is part of a personal consciousness. . . . The universal conscious fact is not 'feelings and thoughts exist,' but 'I think' and 'I feel.'" Subjectivity also means that one's conscious contents, or subjective experiences, can be directly known only by the person having those experiences.

Other features of consciousness, according to James, include *change* and *continuity*. Change means that the contents and details of conscious experience are continuously changing, like the flow of an animated conversation that focuses on one topic for awhile and then abruptly switches to another topic, sometimes with, though often without, any obvious link or association between the two topics. But while the contents of consciousness are constantly changing, there is nonetheless a feeling of continuity of consciousness over time, such that we feel that the conscious contents of the previous minute or hour or day are connected with those of the present moment as thoughts of the same continuing self. In modern cognitive psychological terms, we would say that the long-term continuity of consciousness depends on *episodic memory*, and when episodic memory is disrupted, as in cases of *anterograde amnesia*, serious *depersonalization* can occur, in which one's sense of personal identity is lost. One of James's most famous phrases, "the stream of consciousness," was coined as a metaphor to describe the idea that consciousness is always changing but is nonetheless continuous.

The fifth of James's features of consciousness is *selectivity*. At any moment we are consciously aware of only a limited fraction of all of the stimuli—objects and events, internal and external—of which we might potentially be aware. The selective aspect of consciousness has been studied by cognitive psychologists under the label of *selective attention*. To a large degree we can voluntarily focus our attention. For example, in the *cocktail party phenomenon* we can selectively focus on one of several simultaneously speaking voices, and then voluntarily shift our attention to another voice, in another part of the room. But voluntary attention is imperfect. Often attention shifts involuntarily to internal stimuli (tummy rumbles) and thoughts (daydreams) or to potentially important external stimuli (such as novel stimuli, or your name spoken by a voice previously unattended to). In cognitive psychological models, selective attention is said to be necessary because of the limited capacity of *working* or short-term memory (STM), where the current contents of working memory are equated with the contents of consciousness.

States of Consciousness

The contents of consciousness, including percepts, thoughts, images, etc., change continuously throughout the day. But under some conditions the nature of our thinking and conscious experience is so drastically different from our normal waking state that it seems that either our mental functioning has changed, or that reality itself has changed. Such changes in the overall patterning of subjective experience have been termed *altered states of consciousness* (ASCs) by Arnold Ludwig, an American psychiatrist (*Archives of General Psychiatry*, 1966, 15, 225–234). ASCs may be induced by various physiological, psychological, or pharmacological means. Common examples include sleep, psychedelic drug-induced states, deep hypnosis, and meditative states, and Ludwig listed a wide variety of others such as healing trance, ecstatic trance, and sensory deprivation states.

For nineteenth-century writers like William James,

and some modern writers, the term *state of consciousness* has a narrower meaning, referring to the detailed, momentary pattern of conscious experience, such that a change in thought content or mood would be considered a different state of consciousness. James argued that a state of consciousness can never recur in exactly the same way as before, since the previous experience and intervening experiences would necessarily change the brain's activity, at least in some subtle way. Since each conscious state corresponds to a unique brain state, and a unique brain state cannot recur, a conscious state cannot recur exactly as before. The same *object* of consciousness may recur (such as a percept or image of a friend), but since its mental context and *fringe* (associations, contents in peripheral awareness) are different, the overall state of consciousness is different in its details. For example, if you see a movie for the second time, you won't experience it exactly the same way you did the first time, even though the scenes and dialog are the same.

Dissociation and Dissociative States

Pierre Janet (1889), a prominent nineteenth-century French physician, used the term *dissociation* to describe cases where there appears to be a disconnection between parts of the mental system that are normally connected. For example, in *multiple personality disorder* (MPD) the individual switches between different personalities that have different characteristic moods and motives, and the individual in one personality state does not have access to (is amnesic for) memories of what she did in an alternate personality state. Consciousness is, in a sense, divided.

Dissociative states such as MPD and psychogenic amnesia, and also extreme mood states in otherwise normal people, have characteristics similar to those of altered states of consciousness. However, in most discussions of altered mental functioning, relatively short-term, reversible conditions are called altered states of consciousness (ASC)s, whereas relatively long-term, hard to reverse or irreversible conditions are termed *psychopathology* or *neurological* cases.

In recent research, *dissociation* refers to cases where an individual registers some new stimulus or information, or performs some action, nonconsciously—without awareness—under circumstances that ordinarily would involve awareness, or without being able to consciously recall the event later, under circumstances where recall would ordinarily be possible. Clear examples come from some neurological cases. For example, in *blindsight* a patient with damage to the primary visual cortex is able to point to the location of a visual stimulus, even though he says that he cannot see it. In *implicit memory*, some *anterograde amnesia* patients can use newly acquired information to perform cognitive tasks, even though they cannot explicitly retrieve the information into consciousness or recall having learned it (Schacter, 1989). Kihlstrom (1987) proposed the term *subconscious* to refer to such cases of dissociated knowledge, that is, cases of nonconscious knowledge that cannot be readily retrieved to consciousness, but where it is possible to show by special methods that the individual did, in fact, register the information of which he or she is not consciously aware. Ernest Hilgard (*Divided Consciousness*, New York, 1977) argued that deep hypnosis is a kind of temporary dissociative state, where some actions appear to be carried out without conscious control, pain is experienced only at a subconscious level, and posthypnotic amnesia suggestions can create a temporary inability to retrieve information that could otherwise be easily retrieved.

The distinction between conscious and unconscious (or nonconscious) mind was controversial through most of the twentieth century, particularly since much of the claimed evidence for it came from the controversial theoretical interpretations of clinical cases by Freud and other psychoanalysts. Since the 1980s, however, this distinction has come to be widely accepted by psychologists as a result of controlled experimental research by cognitive psychologists and cognitive neurosychologists. The new concept of the cognitive unconscious is, however, quite different from the dynamic unconscious of the psychoanalysts.

Bibliography

Baars, B. J. (1988). *A cognitive theory of consciousness*. New York: Cambridge University Press. A cognitive-psychological theory of consciousness, along with related research. Baars gives numerous examples of comparable instances of cognitive processing with and without consciousness, to make it clear what a theory of consciousness needs to explain. A briefer, simplified version is presented by Baars in *In the theater of consciousness: The workspace of the mind* (New York: Oxford University Press, 1997).

Ciba Foundation. (1993). *Experimental and theoretical studies of consciousness*. Chichester, UK: Wiley. Ten chapters on theories of consciousness from different psychological, neurophysiological, and philosophical perspectives. Includes Nagel on the mind-body problem, Singer on the stream of consciousness, Libet on the neural time factor, Marcel on the unity of consciousness, and Gray on schizophrenia and consciousness, among others.

Ellenberger, H. F. (1970). *The discovery of the unconscious*. New York: Basic Books. A discussion of the early history of the concept of unconscious mind, including the work of Freud, Janet, and others before them.

Farthing, G. W. (1992). *The psychology of consciousness*. Englewood Cliffs, NJ: Prentice Hall. A comprehensive discussion of normal and altered states of consciousness and related topics, including the concept of consciousness and aspects of consciousness, the mind-body problem, neuropsychological research (including research on blindsight, amnesia, and split-brain patients), introspection, daydreaming, sensory deprivation, sleep and dreaming, hypnosis, meditation, and psychedelic drugs.

James, W. (1983). *The principles of psychology*. Cambridge, MA: Harvard University Press. (Original work published 1890.) This is James's classic work, which is still often quoted for its vivid descriptions and thoughtful interpretations of psychological phenomena. Chapter 9, "The Stream of Thought," is particularly recommended for its discussion of the nature of consciousness. Also see Chapter 10, "The Consciousness of Self."

Loftus, E. F., & Klinger, M. R. (1992, June). Is the unconscious smart or dumb? *American Psychologist*, 47, 761–765. This is the lead article in a series of eight articles in this issue that comprehensively discuss recent research and theory on unconscious mental processes. Other articles are by Greenwald, Bruner, Erdelyi, Kihlstrom, Merikle, Lewicki, and Jacoby.

Marcel, A. J., & Bisiach, E. (Eds.) (1988). *Consciousness in contemporary science*. New York: Oxford University Press. This book contains chapters by psychologists, philosophers, and neuropsychologists on the relationships of brain, consciousness, and behavior, and controversies about the meaning and usefulness of the concept of consciousness. Among others: Marcel on phenomenal experience, Weiskrantz on blindsight, Gazzaniga on brain modularity, and Churchland on reductionism and the neurobiological basis of consciousness.

Schacter, D. L. (1989). On the relation between memory and consciousness: Dissociable interactions and conscious experience. In H. L. Roediger & F. I. M. Craik (Eds.), *Varieties of memory and consciousness* (pp. 355–389). Hillsdale, NJ: Erlbaum. This chapter discusses research on implicit (subconscious) vs. explicit (conscious) memory in amnesic patients, puts it in the context of other dissociative phenomena, and presents Schacter's DICE model where he argues for a distinction between the conscious awareness system and the executive control system of the mind/brain. The other 19 chapters consider other aspects of memory and its relationship to consciousness.

Velmans, M. (Ed.). (1996). *Science of consciousness: Psychological, neuropsychological and clinical reviews*. London: Routledge. Nine chapters on current research and theory on consciousness and nonconscious mental processing. Includes chapters by Kihlstrom on perception without awareness, Gardener on consciousness and memory, Baars on cognitive theories, Libet on neural processes, and Velmans on conscious experience, among others.

G. William Farthing

Processes

The classification of mental processes as conscious or unconscious has a long history. Although Sigmund Freud, the founder of psychoanalysis, is often credited with first proposing the distinction between conscious and unconscious mental processes, the distinction actually predates Freud considerably. For example, in the early eighteenth century, the German philosopher Gottfried Wilhelm Leibniz wrote in his *New Essays on Human Understanding* (Cambridge, U.K., ca. 1704/1981) that "at every moment there is in us an infinity of perceptions, unaccompanied by awareness or reflection" (p. 53) and that "the choice that we make arises from these insensible stimuli, which, mingled with the actions of objects and our bodily interiors, make us find one direction of movement more comfortable than the other" (p. 166). Other examples of an appreciation of the distinction between conscious and unconscious mental processes during the eighteenth and nineteenth centuries can be found in a number of sources. These include the writings of the Viennese physician Franz Anton Mesmer who is usually credited with the discovery of hypnotism, and the writings of the German physiologist Wilhelm Wundt who, in 1879, at Leipzig, established the first research laboratory devoted exclusively to experimental psychology.

On the one hand, conscious experience is so obvious that it needs no definition, and on the other hand, it is so complex that it is difficult if not impossible to define. Definitions of consciousness usually emphasize both qualitative and functional aspects of conscious experience. The qualitative or phenomenal aspects of consciousness include subjective experiences such as our perception of colors, darkness, lightness, shape, texture, pain, hot, cold, sounds, music, tickles, tastes, or smells; our emotional feelings such as happiness, sadness, or anger; our mental images or dreams; and our sense of self. The functional aspects of consciousness refer to the psychological properties of conscious experiences. The philosopher David Chalmers (*The Conscious Mind*, New York, 1996) has described these psychological properties of conscious experiences in some detail. They include *introspection*, whereby we can access and become aware of our internal mental states; *reportability*, whereby we communicate through language the contents of our mental states; *voluntary control*, whereby we deliberately perform an action based on a prior mental state; and *self-consciousness*, whereby we are aware of our existence as an individual distinct from other individuals. In addition, the term *consciousness* is sometimes used to refer to the psychological state of *awakeness*, as contrasted with being asleep or being anesthetized, and at other times it is used to refer to *attention*, in the sense that we are conscious of something when we are paying attention to it.

Another way to think of consciousness is as a stream of thoughts. The American philosopher/psychologist William James (*Principles of Psychology*, New York, 1890) used the metaphor, the stream of consciousness, to describe how consciousness selects, shapes, and molds our thoughts so that we experience a continuous flow of ideas, sensations, and images. When consciousness is thought of as a stream of thoughts, it emphasizes that consciousness is both *continuous* and *selective*. Consciousness is continuous in the sense that we experience a continual flow of thoughts, ideas, sensations, feelings, and images with no obvious gaps in this flow of conscious experiences. Consciousness is selective in the sense that the stream of consciousness only incorporates a limited subset of ideas, sensations, and images that could in principle be consciously experienced. The selective nature of consciousness means that at any point only a limited number of thoughts, sensations, and images can be consciously experienced.

In contrast to consciousness, which is obvious in the sense that everyone experiences an awareness of being conscious, unconsciousness is obscure because no one experiences mental processes that do not lead to awareness. For this reason, unconsciousness is often defined in terms of what is lacking or absent relative to consciousness. Thus, consciousness, by definition, is associated with an awareness of our internal mental states, and unconsciousness, by definition, is associated with an *absence of awareness*. In addition, being conscious or aware of our mental states allows us to report the contents of these states, but when we are unaware of our mental states, we are *unable to report* the contents of these states; and whereas conscious mental states can lead to deliberate or voluntary actions, unconscious mental states lead to *involuntary* actions or reactions. The term *unconsciousness* is also used at times to describe the *inattention* to particular mental states and actions that can occur when a person is consciously attending to other mental states or actions.

The fact that we are aware of our conscious mental processes and unaware of our unconscious mental processes leads to an illusion. We come to believe that the limited subset of perceptions, feelings, thoughts, and images that become incorporated into our stream of consciousness reflects our most important mental processes. In fact, the illusion is so strong that even in the late 1800s, mind and consciousness were generally regarded as one and the same, and unconscious mental processes capable of influencing thoughts, feelings, or actions were either thought not to exist or were considered to be unimportant. Two major developments during the twentieth century challenged this point of view. First, Freud and others emphasized the importance of unconscious thoughts, wishes, feelings, and memories in shaping personality development. Second, experimental psychologists began studying how unconsciously perceived information can influence thoughts, feelings, and actions. [*See* Subliminal Perception.] These developments led to a new point of view. No longer are mind and consciousness considered to be one and the same. Rather, mind is now considered by the majority of psychologists to comprise both conscious mental processes which are available to awareness and unconscious mental processes which are unavailable to awareness. This view is supported by the results of many studies which demonstrate that conscious and unconscious mental processes have distinct psychological properties or functions.

Some of the more informative studies of consciousness and unconsciousness have involved patients with neurological damage. One neurological syndrome that provides a particularly good illustration of the distinct functions of conscious and unconscious mental processes is amnesia. A defining characteristic of amnesia is that a patient has difficulty recalling recent events. Although patients with amnesia seem to have what would be called normal conscious perceptual experiences, they have a great deal of difficulty in recalling these experiences once the experiences are no longer part of their ongoing stream of thoughts. However, despite the fact that patients suffering from amnesia are not able to recall previous experiences, it is possible to demonstrate that the patients have in fact memory for these experiences. For example, patients with amnesia can be taught complex skills such as mirror drawing (i.e., tracing the outline of a figure while looking at the figure through a mirror), playing a new melody on the piano, and even computer programming. After learning these skills, the patients will probably claim, if asked, that they have never done mirror drawing, or played a particular melody on the piano, or programmed a computer. However, if the patients are asked to perform the skill that they claim not to know, the patients will not only demonstrate that they have knowledge of this skill, but some patients will demonstrate a level of skill that is equivalent to the level of skill shown by neurologically intact people who receive an equivalent amount of practice. Thus, despite the fact that memory for a learned skill may be unavailable to awareness, a patient with amnesia can nevertheless use this unconscious memory to guide performance. [*See* Amnesia.]

Another neurological syndrome that illustrates the distinct functions of conscious and unconscious mental processes is visual form agnosia. Patients with visual form agnosia have severe deficits in recognizing objects and patterns. They find it difficult if not impossible to identify simple shapes such as squares and triangles, or to identify letters and digits, or to recognize drawings of common objects. However, even though these patients cannot consciously recognize objects and patterns, they often perceive considerable information regarding objects or patterns without any awareness of perceiving. A particularly informative case of visual form agnosia has been described by the neuropsychologists David Milner and Melvyn Goodale (1995). The patient, DF, is unable to describe or report the shape, size, or orientation of objects. However, despite what is clearly an absence of any conscious perception of the size or shape of objects, when DF reaches for objects, she accurately adjusts the size of her grip to accommodate different sized objects. The fact that she is able to adjust her grip size while reaching for objects shows that she has unconscious knowledge of the size of the objects, and that skilled actions can be directed toward objects even when there may be no conscious knowledge of the objects. In addition, this dissociation between DF's conscious and unconscious knowledge of objects suggests that her conscious visual perception of objects and the visual guidance of her skilled actions directed toward objects are mediated by separate visual pathways. Although DF's neurological damage has clearly affected the pathway that mediates her conscious perception of objects, it appears that this damage has not affected the pathway that guides her skilled actions directed toward these objects. [*See* Agnosia.]

The presence or absence of awareness is the most obvious difference distinguishing conscious from unconscious mental processes. However, what may be an even more important difference is that conscious mental processes allow people to perform deliberate actions, whereas unconscious mental processes often lead to actions that are more reflexive or automatic. This distinction between voluntary and involuntary actions has been studied in experiments by the American psychologist Larry Jacoby (Jacoby, Lindsay, & Toth, 1992). Imagine that you were asked to study the following list of names: Sebastian Weisdorf, Adrian Marr, and Valerie Marsh. Most likely none of these names would seem familiar. Now, imagine that you are later asked to identify the names in the following list that belong to famous people: Sebastian Weisdorf, Roger Bannister, Adrian Marr, Minnie Pearl, Valerie Marsh, and Christopher Wren. If you were told that all of the names in first list were nonfamous, then it would be relatively easy for you to distinguish the famous from the nonfamous names. However, what would happen if there was a 24-hour delay between seeing the first and second lists of names? Would you become confused at times and perhaps think that a previously studied nonfamous name (e.g., Sebastian Weisdorf) was the name of a famous person? The answer is "yes." It seems that over time people can forget that they studied one or more of the nonfamous names. However, the forgotten names may still seem or feel familiar. These feelings of familiarity reflect unconscious memories which can lead a person to decide incorrectly that a nonfamous name is famous. In contrast, if a person remembers that a nonfamous name appeared in the first study list, then the person's conscious memory of the name will guide the decision so that this previously read nonfamous name is not classified incorrectly as a famous name.

By and large, psychological studies of consciousness and unconsciousness have emphasized functional differences between conscious and unconscious mental processes (e.g., available to awareness vs. unavailable to awareness; voluntary actions vs. involuntary reactions). These studies not only establish that mind and consciousness are not one and the same, but they also reveal that conscious and unconscious mental processes often lead to different consequences because only consciousness leads to deliberate actions. There is also reason to believe that the different functions of conscious and unconscious mental processes are often mediated by separate neural pathways. However, despite the success of studies investigating functional differences between conscious and unconscious processes, other aspects of the difference between consciousness and unconsciousness remain completely mysterious. The most obvious difference is that consciousness, by definition, encompasses subjective experience. Our experiences of such things as pain, joy, sadness, the colors of a rainbow, and the taste of peppermint all have unique qualities. How can these phenomenal qualities of consciousness be explained? Why does subjective experience accompany some mental processes and not others? How do physical processes in the brain give rise to the phenomenal aspects of consciousness? These are some of the questions regarding consciousness and unconsciousness that remain to be answered.

Bibliography

Block, N., Flanagan, O., & Güzeldere, G. (Eds.). (1997). *The nature of consciousness: Philosophical debates.* Cambridge, MA: MIT Press. A collection of papers addressing both philosophical and psychological issues in the study of consciousness.

Chalmers, D. J. (1995). The puzzle of conscious experience. *Scientific American, 273,* 80–86. Discusses the issue of whether a detailed knowledge of the brain can in principle explain how the physical brain gives rise to subjective experience.

Cohen, J. D., & Schooler, J. W. (Eds.). (1997). *Scientific approaches to consciousness.* Mahwah, NJ: Erlbaum. A collection of papers written primarily by psychologists. The collection provides many examples of experimental studies investigating conscious and unconscious mental processes.

Jacoby, L. L., Lindsay, D. S., & Toth, J. P. (1992). Unconscious influences revealed: Attention, awareness, and control. *American Psychologist, 47,* 802–809.

Le Doux, J. (1998). *The emotional brain.* New York: Simon & Schuster. Written primarily for the nonspecialist. Discusses conscious and unconscious processes in emotion, with an emphasis on the neurobiology of emotion.

Milner, A. D., & Goodale, M. A. (1995). *The visual brain in action.* New York: Oxford University Press. Discusses visual deficits found in a number of neurological syndromes, with particular emphasis on visual form agnosia and the organization of the visual pathways mediating perception and action.

Reber, A. S. (1993). *Implicit learning and tacit knowledge.* New York: Oxford University Press. Overview of research investigating unconscious processes in learning, together with speculations regarding the origins of conscious and unconscious mental processes.

Roediger, H. L. III. (1990). Implicit memory: Retention without remembering. *American Psychologist, 45,* 1043–1056.

Schacter, D. L. (1996). *Searching for memory.* New York: Basic Books. Written primarily for the nonspecialist. Contains many examples of conscious and unconscious processes in memory.

Whyte, L. L. (1960). *The unconscious before Freud.* New York: Basic Books. Comprehensive history of the distinction between conscious and unconscious mental processes.

Philip Merikle

Cross-Cultural Experience

In the West, consciousness was a topic of considerable interest in nineteenth-century philosophy and the early development of psychology. The philosopher John Locke, in his *Essay Concerning Human Understanding*, defined consciousness as "the perception of what passes in a man's own mind" (1690/1959, p. 138). William James (1890/1950), in *The Principles of Psychology*, spoke of the "stream of consciousness," emphasizing the continuous and variable nature of mental content, thus viewing consciousness as a process. James also distinguished "normal, waking" or "rational" consciousness from other types. To study consciousness, nineteenth-century psychologists proceeded by means of "introspection." This method, deemed unscientific and unreliable, because it produced inconsistent findings, was rejected by J. B. Watson and other American psychologists of the behaviorist school in the early 1900s, and for more than 40 years, consciousness was not a topic of psychological study in the United States. In the 1950s diverse factors emerged in American life and science that again made consciousness a significant area of research in psychology, neurobiology, and philosophy. These factors included the development of psychoactive drugs in psychiatry and in the counterculture; experiments in psychological warfare and brainwashing as a result of the Korean War and the Cold War; studies in cybernetics and artificial intelligence; and developments in brain and sleep research, as well as interest in Eastern religions (Yoga, Zen Buddhism, and others). Intensive comparative and experimental research, some under secret governmental auspices, was carried on for some years, beginning in the 1950s. This included work with hallucinogens, particularly LSD-25, sensory deprivation, biofeedback, sleep

research, etc. Advances in technology, for example the development of the electroencephalogram (EEG) and positron emission tomography (PET), have made it possible to study some aspects of brain functioning in relation to states of consciousness.

While *awareness* is central to most current definitions of consciousness, there is no single consensus definition of the term, nor is there agreement on methodological or theoretical approaches to the subject.

With nineteenth-century interest in consciousness and introspection in psychology, and research in hypnosis, hysteria, and related phenomena in psychiatry, it became evident that mental processes exist of which the individual is not aware. As part of his system of *psychoanalysis*, Freud termed these processes *unconscious*, concluding that most mental activity is unconscious. Material that is not currently present in awareness but can be easily recalled is conceptualized as existing on a "preconscious" level. The term *unconscious* has other meanings as well: it may refer to a person who has fainted, is anesthetized or in a coma, or one who has "lost consciousness." It is also used for automatic patterning of learned behaviors, such as those in language (phonology and articulation, syntax, etc.), motor behavior (e.g., styles of walking, gesturing), or other learned skills. Most physiological processes occur below the level of conscious awareness and are "nonconscious." C. G. Jung speaks of a "collective unconscious," which is said to be inherited and shared by segments of humanity. The attribution of consciousness to inanimate matter and of humanlike consciousness to animals is referred to as *anthropomorphism*.

Some scholars (e.g., Ornstein, 1973) have distinguished two modes of consciousness, the intellectual and the intuitive. Deikman (1996) distinguishes between "instrumental" (or "object-mode") and "receptive" consciousness. Tart (1973) has proposed that ordinary consciousness is not a given but a construction, involving elements such as attention-awareness, self-awareness (i.e., awareness of being aware), volition, energy and quantity of energy, and psychological and mental structures. Importantly, these elements are variable in time, and learning plays an important role.

Ordinary waking consciousness is part of general animal and human mental activity and experience. Humans, however, are distinctive in that they are aware of being aware, a feature termed *higher order consciousness* by G. M. Edelman (1992). Such a level of consciousness requires the development of language and complex symbolic systems. Human consciousness as we know it is the product of the evolution of the species. In the individual, adult consciousness is the result of developmental processes, including significant cultural factors. Consciousness varies with states of maturation and is modified in abnormal and pathological conditions (mental retardation, sensory deficits, senility, etc.).

It is affected by training and experience. Research has shown that several sleep and dream states exist not only in humans, including neonates, but in all mammals that have been tested. The relationship between brain functions and states of consciousness, however, is a major current field for research and debate.

Concepts or discussions of consciousness exist in some other cultural traditions. For example, like William James, classical Buddhism stresses that consciousness (*Vinnana*) is not a substance, is in constant flux, and cannot exist independent of matter, mental processes, emotions, and perceptions. Concepts and theories of "consciousness" are generally part of a larger scheme of understanding of psychological functioning, including also concepts such as the self and ideas of individual identity. In Buddhism, "consciousness" is part of a system that includes ideas of death and reincarnation, and a general universal consciousness in which the individual participates. In this system the individual is viewed as a whole, whereas in the West there is a persistent dualism, involving a mind-body split, in spite of a general rejection of such a dualism by most contemporary psychological and philosophical systems. Dualism, however, has strongly affected theories of consciousness among philosophers.

Other conceptualizations of the structure of the personality and the individual's relationship to the society and the universe also exist. For example, among the Yoruba of Nigeria, the Fon of Benin, and their descendants in the Americas, as shown in the African American religions of Haiti (*Vodou*), Cuba (*Santería*) and Brazil (*Candomblé, Xangô*), the person has two "souls," one of which may be replaced when the individual is "possessed" by a spirit. The individual's behavior, self-presentation and identity, attitudes, and sensory modalities (e.g., pain threshold) typically appear to be transformed; the state is generally followed by amnesia. For the participant, however, this is not a different state of consciousness but the displacement of the ordinary self by another personality or entity. Among the peoples of Northern Eurasia and some parts of the Americas the practice termed *shamanism* has been described. An important aspect of this religious and healing system of rituals is the practitioner's "spirit journey." Here the individual, in an altered state of consciousness, experiences contact with various spirit beings, often in order to heal a patient. This state, in which the shaman may be quite insensitive to the immediate surroundings, is typically not followed by amnesia for the experience but by a report of the events of the journey.

Research in hypnosis, hallucinogens, meditation, and related matters led to the identification of altered (or alternate) states of consciousness (ASCs) and with it the identification of state-specific learning; that is, what is learned in one state of consciousness may not be accessible in another. These are states that differ in some qualitative respects, subjectively or objectively, from ordinary waking consciousness. Once systematic research in this area was undertaken, it became evident that a very large number of ASCs could be identified and classified by method of induction (Ludwig, 1972). Sleep itself involves four states or stages differentiated in EEG patterns and by subjective experience; in addition there are intermediate states between sleeping and waking. In *lucid dreaming*, the dreamer, while asleep, is aware of dreaming and able to manipulate or control the content of the dream. Some "altered" states are induced by changes in body chemistry whether through drugs, including alcohol or tobacco, infections producing high fevers, or physiological disorders, as varied as diabetic coma, epileptic auras and seizures, migraine auras, and other pathological brain states. Other types of ASC are induced by heightened or lowered stimulation or alertness. Importantly, it came to be increasingly recognized that there exist differences among various cultures in the practices associated with the intentional induction of some altered states and in the interpretation placed on the particular states, and that learning plays a major role in both the objective and the subjective dimensions of states of consciousness.

It has long been known that in classical antiquity epilepsy, called *morbus sacer* ("sacred disease") was thought to be of supernatural origins, or that during the Middle Ages in Europe certain aberrant mental states were considered to be due to diabolic possession, requiring exorcism. Indeed, beliefs in demonic possession and practices of exorcism exist today in segments of American society. Prehistoric archaeological evidence suggests that some ASCs were used ritually in Upper Paleolithic times. It has been argued that religious beliefs originated in part as attempts to interpret the experience of dreams and trances. Various of the hallucinogens Americans experimented with in the 1960s had long been used by Native Americans among whom they were taken as part of religious rituals.

It is known that virtually all preindustrialized societies and many segments of most modern societies have given ritual recognition to altered states of consciousness (Bourguignon, 1973). They do so either to intentionally induce desired states or to manage undesirable ones. For example, a number of different Buddhist and Hindu traditions have made extensive use of techniques of meditation. They differ in methods and goals, but all require considerable discipline and practice. Techniques of meditation also exist in mystical traditions of Judaism, Christianity, and Islam. Highly skilled adherents of several forms of yoga in particular have made claims for extraordinary abilities as a result of their practices. A number of these involve the autonomic nervous system and therefore were generally discounted by Western scientists until the development of operant conditioning and biofeedback. Examples are the intentional raising of body temperature, reduction of heart rate, and control of orgasm in sexual intercourse.

It is important to recognize that states and conditions intentionally induced by psychological disciplines such as yoga are positively experienced as achievements by practitioners. Comparable experiences of untrained individuals, occurring spontaneously, may be considered pathological in Western society. Castillo (1990) has given the examples of derealization and depersonalization among novice Western meditators. In spite of the existence of traditions of meditation and contemplation in Western societies, among both Christian and Jewish mystics and ascetics, there has long been a strong emphasis on and preference for conscious, rational states and a rejection of altered states as demonic or pathological. It has been suggested that the development of the scientific method, with its emphasis on skepticism and experimentation, is largely due to this orientation.

Bibliography

Bourguignon, E. (Ed.). (1973). *Religion, altered states of consciousness, and social change.* Columbus: Ohio State University Press.

Castillo, R. J. (1990). Depersonalization and meditation. *Psychiatry, 53,* 158–168.

Deikman, A. J. (1996). Intention, self and spiritual experience: A functional model of consciousness. In S. R. Hameroff, A. W. Kanziak, & A. C. Scott (Eds.), *Toward a science of consciousness: The First Tucson discussions and debates. Complex adaptive system* (pp. 695–706). Cambridge, MA.: MIT Press.

Dennett, D. C. (1991). *Consciousness explained.* Boston: Little, Brown.

Edelman, G. M. (1992). *Bright air, brilliant fire: On the matter of the mind.* New York: Basic Books.

James, W. (1950). *The principles of psychology.* New York: Dover. (Original work published 1890)

Locke, J. (1959). *An essay concerning human understanding.* New York: Dover. (Original work published 1690)

Ludwig, A. (1972). Altered states of consciousness. In C. T. Tart (Ed.), *Altered states of consciousness* (pp. 11–24). Garden City, NY: Doubleday/Anchor Books.

Ornstein, R. E. (Ed.). (1973). *The nature of human consciousness: A book of readings.* San Francisco: Freeman.

Ornstein, R. E. (1991). *The evolution of consciousness: Of Darwin, Freud, and cranial fire: The origins of the way we think.* Englewood Cliffs, NJ: Prentice Hall.

Searle, J. R. (1997). The mystery of consciousness. *The New York Review of Books.*

Tart, C. T. (Ed.). (1972). *Altered states of consciousness.* Garden City; NY: Doubleday/Anchor Books.

Varela, F. J. (1997). *Sleeping, dreaming and dying. Explorations of consciousness with the Dalai Lama.* Boston: Wisdom.

Zinberg, N. E. (Ed.). (1977). *Alternate states of consciousness: Multiple perspectives on the study of consciousness.* New York: Free Press.

Erika Bourguignon

CONSCIOUSNESS PSYCHOLOGY. *See* Psychology, *article on* Nineteenth Century through Freud.

CONSTRUCTIVISM. A range of psychological theories about learning and understanding fall under the heading of constructivism. The common element that ties together this family of theories is the assumption that people actively build or construct their knowledge of the world and of each other. This claim applies as much to perception as it does to higher-order reasoning and problem solving. Consequently, constructivists reject the view that people's perceptual experiences are direct, unmediated responses to stimuli, and instead argue that perception involves processes of interpretation that may be very abbreviated in routine instances of recognition. In addition, constructivists question the view that remembering involves the direct retrieval of information stored in memory. They instead contend that remembering is a reconstructive process in which we recall past incidents and events in terms of current understandings. Empirical support for constructivists' general claims about cognition and development come from a reasonably robust body of empirical investigations. For example, in one experiment conducted by the Swiss psychologist Jean Piaget, children were first asked to solve a task that focused on their logical reasoning capabilities. Several months later, they were interviewed for a second time and were asked to describe how they had solved the task during the first interview. Piaget and his colleagues found that children whose logical reasoning capabilities had developed between the two phases of the experiment recalled their solution attempt in terms of their newly developed reasoning capabilities and were convinced that this was how they had actually understood the task in the first interview. Piaget therefore concluded that the children's recall involved reconstructing the prior experience in terms of their current understandings.

The term *constructivism* has currency in a number of disciplines including mathematics, art, and literary criticism as well as in psychology. However, the similarities between the constructivist schools of thought in these diverse disciplines are, for the most part, superficial. The roots of constructivism in psychology can instead be found in epistemology, a branch of psychology concerned with both the historical growth of knowledge and with the justification of knowledge as true. The early eighteenth-century Italian philosopher Giambattista Vico was the first to advance an explicitly constructivist position when he argued that "the known is the made." His central contention was that in order to know a person, object, or event, we have to build up an understanding of it on the basis of experience. Vico's arguments anticipated several of the major claims that the German idealist philosopher Immanuel Kant made 80 years later. In his treatise *A Critique of Pure Reason*, Kant identified what he called the fundamental categories of thought and proposed conjectures about their origins. His central claim was that basic concepts such as number, causality, and chance are neither acquired by direct perception nor are hard wired into our mental structures as a priori ways of experiencing the world. He instead contended that these concepts are constructed on the basis of experience in order to give structure and coherence to thought and action. In his analysis, he proposed that only two basic concepts, those of space and time, are built into our way of understanding the world prior to all experience. [*See the biography of Kant.*]

Kant's philosophical analysis provided the backdrop against which the most significant contributor to constructivist theory, Jean Piaget, conducted his research. Although Piaget is typically viewed as a psychologist, he described himself as a genetic epistemologist. In this context, the term *genetic* denotes genesis or change, indicating that Piaget was interested in the process by which knowledge grows and evolves. As he explained, he ideally would have studied the origins and subsequent evolution of foundational concepts as they occurred in the history of humankind. However, as this was impossible, he attempted to gain insight into epistemological issues by studying the development of these notions in children. Significantly, the concepts that he focused on in his investigations correspond almost exactly to the fundamental categories of thought proposed by Kant 150 years earlier. However, in Piaget's work, philosophical speculation was replaced by a systematic series of investigations into the development of children's thinking.

The aspect of Piaget's work that has gained most attention among both psychologists and educators is his claim to have identified a sequence of invariant stages through which children's thinking progresses. In contrast, his explanation of the *process* by which children's thinking develops has received less attention. However, it is this process aspect of his work that is more significant from the point of view of constructivist theory. Piaget drew on his early training as a biologist to characterize intellectual development as an adaptive process of self-organization. In his theory, experienced contradictions or perturbations in reasoning serve to drive intellectual development. These perturbations might stem from differences between two children's interpretations of a situation, or from a difference between a child's anticipations about the result of an action and his or her subsequent observations. Piaget took great care to stress that, in either case, it was crucial that the differences be experienced as contradictions by the child. Only then might the child reorganize his or her reasoning processes in order to eliminate a perturbation.

Ernst von Glasersfeld (1995), one of the leading interpreters of Piaget's theory, has demonstrated that Piaget's characterization of development as a process of self-organization anticipated many of the central ideas of contemporary cybernetics. In this regard, Piaget's close collaborator Barbel Inhelder noted that Piaget was a cybernetician before cybernetics. Von Glasersfeld has also observed that Piaget went further than Kant when he addressed epistemological issues. Kant gave space and time a special status in that he regarded them as built into our way of experiencing the world. Piaget, in contrast, considered that even these elemental concepts are not given but are instead constructed on the basis of experience. Within the setting of his general epistemological concerns, the numerous books in which he reported his psychological investigations with children provide detailed accounts of the process by which these and other concepts are constructed.

Piaget's work has been the subject of a number of criticisms in recent years, the most significant of which concern the limited attention he paid to the role of social and cultural processes in intellectual development. Although he acknowledged the role of social interaction in development, he tended to cast it as an external catalyst for otherwise autonomous intellectual development. To substantiate their arguments, a number of Piaget's critics have drawn on the work of the Russian psychologist Ivan Petrovich Vygotsky (1962). Whereas Piaget's overriding interests were epistemological, Vygotsky conducted his work in the tumultuous years immediately after the Russian revolution and was primarily concerned with issues of cultural change pertaining to the creation of the "new Soviet man." Within this general orientation, Vygotsky argued that communal social processes are primary in development and that individual psychological processes are secondary. A major tenet of his sociohistorical theory of development is that an internal psychological plane of thought is formed by internalizing interpersonal social processes. For example, Vygotsky argued that children become able to monitor their thinking only after they interact with adults or more capable peers who monitor their thinking for them. In his view, children develop this capability by internalizing the monitoring process that occurs first in the interaction between themselves and the more capable other.

The emphasis that Vygotsky placed on social processes stands in sharp contrast to Piaget's characterization of development as a process of adaptive self-organization. In critiques developed from the Vygotskian perspective, Piaget's treatment of social interaction as a catalyst for otherwise autonomous development has been a focus of attack. Following Vygotsky, a number of critics have argued that not only the process of development but its products, increasingly sophisticated ways of thinking, are social through and through. In response, a number of constructivist scholars have attempted to preserve Piaget's central insights about development while locating them explicitly in a social and cultural context. As Geoffrey Saxe (1991), one of the leading social constructivist theoreticians, put it, the challenge is to explain how children's thinking becomes interwoven with the intellectual achievements of their culture. In concert with Vygotskian theory, social constructivists view a child's reasoning as an act of participating in a cultural practice. Consequently, children's activity is seen to be socially and culturally situated. However, in opposition to Vygotsky, social constructivists consider the relation between social and psychological processes to be indirect. For Vygotsky, children's developing intellectual capabilities are generated by or derived from the social and cultural practices in which they participate. In contrast, social constructivists argue that children's participation in cultural practices constitutes the conditions for the possibility of learning but that children have to reorganize their activity and thus their ways of participating in the practices. From this latter perspective, equal significance is attributed to individual and communal processes with neither being elevated above the other.

With regard to the future, there is every indication that the exchange between constructivist and Vygotskian scholars will continue to be productive for the development of theory. In addition to the relation between individual and communal processes, important issues for discussion include cultural diversity, the broader sociopolitical context within which development occurs, and the role of tools such as computers in intellectual development.

[See also the biographies of Piaget and Vygotsky.]

Bibliography

Cobb, P., & Bauersfeld, H. (Eds.). (1995). *Emergence of mathematical meaning: Interaction in classroom cultures.* Hillsdale, NJ: Erlbaum.

DeVries, R. (1997). Piaget's social theory. *Educational Researcher, 26*(2), 4–17.

Piaget, J. (1970). *Genetic epistemology.* New York: Columbia University Press.

Saxe, G. B. (1991). *Culture and cognitive development: Studies in mathematical understanding.* Hillsdale, NJ: Erlbaum.

Steffe, L. P., & Gale, J. (Eds.). (1995). *Constructivism in education.* Hillsdale, NJ: Erlbaum.

von Glasersfeld, E. (1995). *Radical constructivism: A way of knowing and learning.* London: Falmer Press.

Vygotsky, L. S. (1962). *Thought and language.* Cambridge, MA: MIT Press.

Paul Cobb

CONSTRUCTIVIST PSYCHOTHERAPY. As a philosophical position that emphasizes both personal and social processes of meaning making, constructivism has influenced several contemporary traditions of psychotherapy. For this reason it is more accurate to consider constructivism as a general approach to understanding people, conceptualizing psychological distress, and fostering human change than to view it as a distinctive "school" of psychotherapy associated with a particular theorist. Thus, constructivism is best viewed as a meta-theory that encompasses many contemporary developments in clinical theories as diverse as psychoanalysis, existential-humanistic psychotherapy, cognitive therapy, and family systems approaches. In addition, a number of novel psychotherapies have been devised along avowedly constructivist lines, from personal construct theory, which was formally set forth in the 1950s, to narrative therapy approaches that have become prominent only since the mid-1980s. Appreciating the contributions of these diverse models therefore requires a consideration of their core philosophic similarities and the range of concepts that shape their expression at the level of clinical practice.

Constructivist Philosophy

If there is a unifying theme that links constructivist forms of psychotherapy, it is at the level of their epistemology, or theory of knowledge. Although most constructivists acknowledge that a "real world" exists outside of human consciousness or language, they are much more interested in the nuances of people's construction of the world than they are in evaluating the extent to which such constructions are "true" in representing a presumably external reality. This emphasis on the active, form-giving nature of the mind dates back at least to the Italian rhetorician Giambattista Vico (1668–1744), who traced the development of thought to the attempt to understand the world by projecting upon it human motives, myths, and eventually linguistic abstractions. The German philosopher Immanuel Kant (1724–1804) likewise emphasized the transformative character of the mind, which necessarily imposes spatial, temporal, and causal order on the phenomena of experience. From these philosophers, constructivists borrowed a model of knowledge as an active structuring of experience, rather than a passive assimilation of "things in themselves," uncontaminated by human knowing.

At the threshold to the twentieth century, these themes were further elaborated by the German analytic philosopher Hans Vaihinger (1852–1933), whose *Philosophy of "As If"* asserted that people develop "workable fictions" (e.g., of mathematical infinity or God) to order and transcend the hard data of experience, and establish distinctively human goals. A similar emphasis on the distinction between our linguistic "map" of experience and the "territory" of the world was made by the Polish intellectual Alfred Korzybski (1879–1950), whose system of general semantics focused on the role of the speaker in assigning meanings to events. From these thinkers, constructivists drew the implication that human beings operate on the basis of symbolic or linguistic constructs that help them navigate in the world without contacting it in any simple, direct way. Moreover, they suggested that such constructions are *viable* to the extent that they help us live our lives meaningfully and find validation in the shared understandings of others in our families, communities, and societies.

Constructivist Psychotherapies

The first person to develop a thoroughgoing theory of psychotherapy along constructivist lines was the American clinical psychologist, George Kelly. Working in relative isolation in the 1930s and 1940s, Kelly began to experiment with novel procedures in which clients were coached to enact fictional identities in their daily lives for a limited period of time. Working from a character sketch drafted by the therapist, the client practiced the novel outlook in a series of enactments with the therapist playing various acquaintances, authority figures, and family members, while the client generalized the role to his or her daily life. At the end of this period, the role was consciously set aside, and the therapist and client discussed the extent to which the client's sense of self and social world were provisional constructions that might be lived out quite differently if viewed in alternative ways. Kelly's "fixed role therapy" was therefore the first form of brief therapy, and it foreshadowed the use of narrative strategies of change incorporated in many contemporary constructivist therapies. Eventually, Kelly drafted a comprehensive *psychology of personal constructs* that placed these procedures in a rigorous theoretical context, and suggested diagnostic, therapeutic, and research methods that continue to attract contemporary interest.

A second tradition of constructivist therapy began to gain momentum in the late 1970s as an outgrowth of cognitive therapies emphasizing the role of the person's interpretations of events in a range of disorders. Michael Mahoney, an American pioneer in the cognitive trend, began to critique the presumption that emotional adjustment was a straightforward matter of making one's cognitions realistic and in line with an observable world. In particular, Mahoney, along with colleagues such as the Italian theorist Vittorio Guidano, began to turn more attention to the "core ordering processes" by which persons construct and maintain self-schemas in a social field.

As the more relativistic philosophy of constructivism became more widespread, it began to permeate even long-standing traditions of psychotherapy, such as psychoanalysis. One harbinger of this trend was the American analyst Donald Spence, who argued that analysis could not unearth the historical truth of the patient's life, but only disclose its narrative truth in the eyes of its author, the client. In keeping with the psychoanalytic tradition, however, constructivist analysts still tend to emphasize the usefulness of accessing emotionally significant memories of one's early life, but view these less as veridical "insights" than as inventions subject to the demand for narrative "smoothing." One recent expression of this approach is the depth-oriented brief therapy developed by the American psychologists Bruce Ecker and Laurel Hulley, which uses a procedure of radical questioning to reveal the hidden implications of the client's prosymptom and antisymptom positions.

Another long-standing tradition to be influenced by a constructivist position is humanistic-existential psychotherapy, whose emphases on human choice, agency, and phenomenology or the study of experience converged with core themes of constructivist theory. One outgrowth of this convergence is the self-confrontation method devised by the Dutch personality theorist Hubert Hermans, which uses open-ended questions to elicit those "valuations," or important units of meaning that a person uses to structure a sense of her or his past, present, and future. The client then rates these synoptic life experiences on a standard list of affect terms, which yields indices of self-enhancement, union with others, negative emotions, and positivity as a method for mapping therapeutic changes in meanings over time. A second example of the infusion of constructivist themes into humanistic therapy is the dialectical approach of the Canadian psychologist, Leslie Greenberg, which emphasizes the role of internal conflict in the creation of subjective meaning. For example, therapy might attempt to synthesize two mutually contradictory internal experiences (e.g., self-contempt and the need to comfort) into a new structure (e.g., self-acceptance), by helping the client vividly attend to this complexity through the use of a "two-chair" technique. In keeping with constructivist themes, the "selfhood processes" that are the focus of these approaches are viewed as continually evolving, rather than a static "essence" to be simply discovered or actualized.

Finally, family systems therapies have been revolutionized by a social constructionist perspective, adopting a nonauthoritarian view of therapy as conversation whose goal is to alter what the American psychotherapists Harlene Anderson and Harry Goolishian termed the "problem determined system." In such approaches, the therapist functions less as an expert dispensing answers than as a conversation manager who promotes the sort of exchanges among family members that "dissolve" old problems by "languaging" about them in a new way. Other family therapists have adopted the constructivist metaphor of lives as stories, and have devised novel means of helping clients free themselves from the "dominant narratives" that originate in particular families and cultures, and that keep them from feeling like the authors of their own lives. For therapists such as Michael White in Australia and David Epston in New Zealand, externalizing the problem by reconstruing it as something separate from the client's "self" provides a useful first step toward recognizing its destructive impact on clients and the relationships in which they are engaged. Therapy can then turn toward recognizing and validating those exceptional moments when a person begins to resist the dominant narrative, and rewrite his or her life story along more hopeful lines.

Despite the contributions of constructivism to contemporary clinical practice, challenges to this postmodern perspective have been raised by realists who question what they view as its "anything goes" relativism. From the vantage point of these critics, the constructivist emphasis on multiple realities risks undermining conventional understandings of "truth" as well as "objective" procedures of research into therapy process and outcome. Tensions also arise within the perspective, particularly between personal constructivists who champion the individual's role in meaning making, and social constructionists who emphasize the extent to which meanings reside in systems of culture and language that precede any given individual. Ultimately, however, these challenges can be viewed as the predictable "growing pains" encountered by any significant new perspective that promises to help shape the future, as well as the present, of psychotherapy.

[See also Psychotherapy.]

Bibliography

Franklin, C., & Nurius, P. (Eds.). (1998). Constructivism in practice. Milwaukee, WI: Families International Press. Provides a useful overview of various forms of constructivist therapy and community practice, as well as a discussion of narrative as an integrative metaphor for such work.

Journal of Constructivist Psychology. Philadelphia: Brunner/Mazel. Quarterly peer-reviewed journal encompassing developments in constructivist theory, research, and practice, with an emphasis on clinical and counseling applications.

Kelly, G. A. (1991). The psychology of personal constructs. London: Routledge. (Original work published 1955.) The original and most systematic example of constructivist personality theory, with extensive discussion of clinical assessment and psychotherapy. However, should be supplemented by readings in contemporary personal construct theory and other related approaches listed among these annotated references.

Mahoney, M. J. (1991). Human change processes. New York: Basic Books. Provides a broad historical and philosophical survey of human development and plasticity, with a focus on its implications for psychotherapy. Although other paradigms are given some attention, constructivism emerges as the most relevant contemporary foundation for clinical practice.

Neimeyer, R. A., & Mahoney, M. J. (Eds.). (1995). Constructivism in psychotherapy. Washington, DC: American Psychological Association. Offers a conceptual introduction to constructivist thought, as well as original chapters by leading contributors to personal construct, self-developmental, systemic, and narrative therapies.

Neimeyer, R. A., & Raskin, J. (Eds.). (2000). Constructions of disorder. Washington, DC.: American Psychological Association. Critically analyzes conceptualizations of psychological distress from a range of constructivist, social constructionist, feminist, and narrative therapy traditions, and suggests how these guide practice within a generally "nonpathologizing" orientation to psychotherapy.

Robert A. Neimeyer

CONSTRUCT VALIDITY refers to the extent to which scores on a test can be shown to measure a hypothetical construct or trait (Anastasi, New York, 1988). Psychological concepts, such as anxiety, intelligence, introversion, and self-esteem are considered hypothetical constructs because they are not directly observable but rather are inferred on the basis of scientific observations of behavior. These inferences accumulate to form a descriptive theory about a particular psychological construct. The construct represented by a test of anxiety, for example, is defined by the theory of anxiety from which the test was derived and which the test scores are thought to reflect. To serve as an effective measure of the theoretical construct, then, scores on a test of anxiety must be shown to demonstrate all articulated and implied relationships proposed in the theory of anxiety.

The term *construct validity* was first officially introduced in 1954 in "Technical Recommendations for Psychological Tests and Diagnostic Techniques" by the American Psychological Association Committee on Psychological Tests (*Psychological Bulletin, 51*, 201–238). An explication of the concept was published the following year by two members of that committee (Cronbach

& Meehl, *Psychological Bulletin*, 1955, 52, 281–302) who argued that this new conception of validity constituted a radical departure from existing notions of validity, namely content and criterion validity, in that construct validation explicitly directs attention to the larger definition of the entity testers intend to measure. And although the test behaviors and their correlates are themselves considered important in construct validation, they are only considered so to the degree that they reflect the underlying theoretical construct. This is in contrast to criterion validation, for example, in which scores on a test are considered valid only to the extent that they demonstrate statistical association to some important criterion variable. For example, in the prediction of job performance as a salesperson, the criterion of units sold may be of such paramount importance to a business that a test whose scores predict this criterion may not need to be well understood to be useful. In such a case, no larger theory of an underlying construct is consulted to evaluate the meaningfulness of test scores; it is only the raw associative power of the test scores that matters. In content validation, test scores are considered valid to the degree that they represent performance on a larger universe of content from which test items are sampled. For example, scores on an algebra test are considered content valid if the test items represent a fair sampling of a specified content domain of algebra knowledge. Again, as in criterion validation, the process of content validation requires no elaboration of the theory underlying the construct of algebra knowledge; demonstration of adequate sampling of the content domain is sufficient.

Evaluation of Construct Validity

Because construct validation questions the degree to which test scores behave in a manner consistent with a number of simultaneous theoretical propositions, its evaluation is not easily summarized. Its appraisal is certainly qualitative in the sense that no discrete quantity can be assigned to represent the level of construct validity demonstrated by scores on a particular test. However, construct validation is also quantitative, at least serially, in that each theoretical proposition about the construct in question is tested against empirical data involving test scores. The process of construct validation can be said to be iterative in that the results of these empirical studies of theoretical propositions often inform construction and even modification of the construct theory. Similarly, disparity between theorized and empirical test characteristics often results in test modification, with the aim of bringing the test closer in line with the construct theory. Because this iterative process may result in the radical evolution of both construct theory and construct measurement, the process of construct validation is sometimes referred to as bootstrap-

ping, as empirical study permits poorer theory and measurement to each give way to improved versions.

The cumulative network of empirically demonstrated associations between construct test scores and scores on measurements of other constructs is known as the construct's nomological network. As research on the construct matures, this network comes to include a wide variety of associations that may take on a variety of statistical forms. These may include contrasts between groups of individuals thought to differ with regard to the construct, correlations with measures of theoretically related constructs, and especially, associations with measures of the same construct. The nomologic net extends internally as well, as test item properties such as homogeneity, content validity, and dimensionality can also be specified theoretically and tested empirically. It should be recognized that a construct's nomological net should specify not only relevant positive associations, but also negative and neutral ones as well. This distinction gives rise to the terms *convergent validity*, which refers to the demonstration of association with measures of like constructs, and *discriminant validity*, which refers to the demonstration of appropriately minimal association with measures of constructs from which the target construct is thought to be distinct.

Campbell and Fiske (*Psychological Bulletin*, 1959, 56, 81–105) articulated an influential model for the evaluation of convergent and discriminant test properties. Termed the multitrait-multimethod matrix, it involves the construction of a correlation matrix that includes multiple measures of both the target construct and competing constructs. This approach recognizes that in the measurement of a construct, scores are influenced by characteristics of the method of measuring as well as the trait. With such data, one would expect the correlations among different methods of measuring the same construct (convergent validity) to be clearly higher than correlations among different constructs measured by the same method (discriminant validity). For further verification, both of these sets of correlations should be higher than the correlations between different constructs measured by different methods, and all should be lower than reliability estimates for a given method of measuring a given construct.

Increasingly, construct validity has been recognized as a unifying concept for all types of validity evidence, in that construct validation may require a wide variety of types of validity evidence in order to test all the relational propositions specified by a theory. In a sense, this means that all statements about the validity of measurement can be seen as special cases of construct validation. This view underscores the point that there can be no measurement without some construct definition, even if the definition is implicit, or just begin-

pressing the arbitrary code of "*66" to access a telephone's call-back feature).

Many difficult-to-use designs occur because of product constraints or competing characteristics. For example, many products need to be a certain physical size which may preclude having an optimal number of separate controls or an optimal display size. For example, a cellular telephone needs to be both small enough for consumers to carry comfortably, and large enough for consumers to activate its controls and to read its display. A developer can minimize the effect of product constraints by following the six-step product development process outlined above.

Bibliography

Cushman, W., & Rosenberg, D. (1991). *Human factors in product design: Advances in human factors/ergonomics* (Vol. 14). New York: Elsevier Science.

Dumas, J. (1988). *Designing user interfaces for software.* Englewood Cliffs, NJ: Prentice Hall.

Dumas, J., & Redish, J. (1993). *A practical guide to usability testing.* Norwood, NJ: Ablex. Provides complete step-by-step guidelines on conducting usability tests.

Nielsen, J. (1993). *Usability engineering.* Boston: Academic Press. Details numerous structured and engineering methods to assess product and software usability.

Norman, D. (1988). *The design of everyday things.* New York: Basic Books. Provides an accessible, popular treatment on the matching of conceptual models to consumer product user interfaces.

Sanders, M., & McCormick, E. (1993). *Human factors in engineering and design* (7th ed.). New York: McGraw-Hill. Provides a complete textbook overview of the field of human factors, as well as sections on consumer products and warnings.

Shneiderman, B. (1998). *Designing the user interface: Strategies for effective human-computer interaction* (3rd ed.). Reading, MA: Addison-Wesley. Provides highly readable information for software user interface developers.

Wiklund, M. (1994). *Usability in practice: How companies develop user-friendly products.* Cambridge, MA: Academic Press Professional. Provides an overview of the ways that 17 companies incorporate human factors processes into their businesses.

Woodson, W., Tillman, P., & Tillman, B. (1992). *Human factors design handbook* (2nd ed.). New York: McGraw-Hill. Includes information regarding controls and displays, visual and auditory capabilities, and the use of body dimensions in product design.

David. N. Aurelio

CONSUMER PSYCHOLOGY. The study of psychological processes as they relate to the adoption, use, and disposal of products, services, or ideas is known as consumer psychology. At present, no Ph.D. degree programs offer formal degrees in this specialty. Persons associated with the discipline typically obtain a Ph.D. degree in a base discipline like social or experimental psychology and supportive coursework in marketing and advertising. Consumer psychologists are perhaps most easily identified by their membership in the Society for Consumer Psychology (SCP; Division 23 of APA) or the Association for Consumer Research (ACR) and their publications in the *Journal of Consumer Psychology* or the *Journal of Consumer Research.* Journals containing consumer psychology articles include the *Journal of Personality and Social Psychology, Personality and Social Psychology Bulletin,* the *journal of Marketing Research, Journal of Advertising,* the *Journal of Advertising Research, Psychology and Marketing,* the *Journal of Public Policy and Marketing,* and *Journal of Applied Psychology,* to name a few. The Proceedings of the Annual SCP Winter Conference and ACR conferences provide a view of current research activities and the *Handbook of Consumer Research* (Robertson & Kassarjian, 1991) includes extensive chapters on topics relevant to consumer psychology.

An examination of such publications reveals a wide range of interests and methods of inquiry. While experimental laboratory methods are still favored by the majority of consumer researchers for gaining insight into the processes underlying ultimate consumer choices, case studies, along with qualitative and exploratory studies also appear in the publications and provide fertile ground for additional theoretical development and academic debate. While relatively few psychology departments have undergraduate courses devoted solely to the topic, most business schools have courses on consumer behavior or buyer behavior. Textbooks for such courses provide a nice overview (Hoyer and McInnis, 1997; Kardes, 1999; Mowen and Minor, 1997). Consumer psychologists hold jobs as academic professors in marketing, advertising, or psychology programs as well as in federal agencies such as the Centers for Disease Control, the Food and Drug Administration, the Federal Trade Commission, and various branches of the military. Consumer psychologists also serve in research divisions of large marketing and public opinion research organizations, large corporations, independent think tanks, and consulting organizations.

The discipline of consumer psychology was formalized in the early 1960s with the founding of the Society for Consumer Psychology as Division 23 of the APA. Early leadership of the Society included psychologists who were in charge of research divisions of large advertising agencies. Businesses hired psychologists to develop research that would provide insight into the psychological processes related to consumer preferences. This interest was, in part, driven by the high productivity of U.S. companies in the early 1950s that provided consumers with many choices in the marketplace. Prior to this time, demand was so high that businesses were able to sell their complete inventories and felt little need to study the desires and interests of consumers prior to manufacturing or advertising their products. Psychologists and other behavioral scientists, with their strong training in theory, research methodology, and data analysis were recruited to help businesses understand and predict the behaviors of consumers. Perhaps not surprisingly, then, many of the issues studied by consumer psychologists then and now are similar to major issues studied in psychology in general. A recent review of the literature by Jacoby, Johar, and Morrin (1998) categorized current consumer research as focused on the general areas of (1) sensation and perception; (2) factors associated with gaining and keeping consumer attention as well as preattentive processes; (3) categorization of stimuli; (4) inference making, the development of additional beliefs based on stimulus information or missing information; (5) information search, the efforts of consumers to learn about aspects of products and services prior to purchase; (6) memory factors associated with brands; (7) research on the role of affect (8) research on attitude formation and change processes.

Consumer psychology research, like research in other areas of psychology, has witnessed increasing sophistication in theoretical and methodological approaches. Whereas early research and theory often sought to identify the "one true process" responsible for effects observed in studies, more recent theory and research focuses on understanding how different levels of situational and individual difference factors can result in similar outcomes but by way of very different kinds of processes. For example, a theory frequently employed in consumer psychology studies on the topic of attitude change is the elaboration likelihood model (ELM; Petty and Cacioppo, 1986). The ELM postulates that attitude change tends to follow one of two routes. Individuals following the central route carefully consider and evaluate information in support of a position in deriving their attitude toward a product. In contrast, individuals following the peripheral route may develop equally positive attitudes by simple associations of factors in the message (e.g, the attractiveness of a message source). Importantly, the ELM identifies a variety of situational and individual difference factors that moderate the route to persuasion. For example, high levels of personal relevance typically lead to central route processes whereas low levels of relevance increase the chances of attitudes being formed or changed via the peripheral route. Importantly, research has shown that the extent of thinking about product attributes in the formation of an attitude is associated with attitude strength—the ability of the attitude to stay positive over time, resist change in the face of attack, and predict behavior

(Petty, Haugtvedt, & Smith, 1995). The ELM and related theoretical approaches currently serve as useful guides in finding answers to research questions in both basic and applied consumer psychology.

Consumer psychologists, since their early days as consultants to businesses, have long been advocates of the appropriate use of theory and method in research. Along with their interest in helping businesses provide products that are more accurate matches to consumer needs and desires (something good for both the consumer and business), consumer psychologists have become strong advocates for the use of business and marketing techniques, along with complete consumer research, in areas like health psychology and social policy (e.g., HIV prevention, changes in dietary and exercise habits, pollution reduction, etc., Goldberg, Fishbein, & Middlestadt, 1997).

Consumer psychology is a discipline at the interface of basic and applied psychology. In a broad sense, consumer psychologists are interested in contributing to general social science understanding along with specific interests in the roles of learning, memory, attitude change, purchase decisions, product use behaviors, and interpersonal communication about products and services as they relate to the development of more efficient and effective product design and communication strategies. Consumer psychologists are also interested in the use of psychological theories and methods in the prevention of miscommunication or inappropriate influence of marketing efforts. Thus, consumer psychology expertise is also relevant to the development of product information labels and other vehicles designed to aid consumers in making choices that may be in their best interest (e.g., lower fat or lower sodium food items, etc.). Consumer psychologists are thus often called upon to develop research projects that answer specific applied questions such as "What is the best format for a nutrition label?" Answering such applied questions usually requires a thorough understanding of basic research in an area and the ability to translate such understanding into creative research designs. Attempts to answer such questions sometimes lead to the observation that the existing basic research in an area requires more development. The discipline as a whole is enhanced by sharing of efforts and expertise by persons more interested in basic processes and those more interested in answering specific applied questions.

Like many areas of psychology, there exists a constant tension between the basic theoretical development and understanding in an area and the development of research projects and papers that communicate actionable ideas to practitioners. Such a challenge makes the discipline of consumer psychology a very interesting and ever changing adventure. Consumer psychology is very much an interdisciplinary enterprise. Consumer psychologists have the opportunity to contribute to the development of basic knowledge in psychology and a variety of related disciplines, as well as the use of psychology in improving social, economic, and physical environments.

[*See also* Consumerism of Psychological Services; *and* Media Effects.]

Bibliography

Goldberg, M. E., Fishbein, M., & Middlestadt, S. E. (1997). *Social marketing*, Mahwah, NJ: Erlbaum.

Hoyer, W. D., & MacInnis, D. J. (1997). *Consumer behavior.* New York: Houghton Mifflin.

Jacoby, J., Johar, V., & Morrin, M. (1998). Consumer behavior. *Annual Review of Psychology, 49,* 319–344.

Kardes, F. R. (1999). *Consumer behavior and managerial decision making.* Reading, MA: Addison-Wesley.

Macklin, M. C. (1996). Preschoolers learning of brand names from visual cues. *Journal of Consumer Research, 23,* 251–261.

Mowen, J. C., & Minor, M. (1998). *Consumer behavior* (5th ed.). Upper Saddle River, NJ: Prentice Hall.

Petty, R. E., & Cacioppo, J. T. (1986). *Communication and persuasion: Central and peripheral routes to attitude change.* New York: Springer-Verlag.

Petty, R. E., Haugtvedt, C. P., & Smith, S. M. (1995) Elaboration as a determinant of attitude strength: Creating attitudes that are persistent, resistant, and predictive of behavior. In R. E. Petty & J. A. Kronick (Eds.), *Attitude strength: Antecedents and consequences* (pp. 93–130). Mahwah, NJ: Erlbaum.

Robertson, T. S., & Kassarjian, H. (1991). *Handbook of consumer research.* Englewood Cliffs, NJ: Prentice Hall.

World Wide Web site: www.consumerpsych.org

Curtis P. Haugtvedt

CONTENT ANALYSIS. Psychological investigations often involve making systematic, objectively specified encodings of verbal, textual, or pictorial information with a view to making reliable, valid generalizations. [*See* Reliability; *and* Validity.] Clinicians, for example, apply well-specified rules for scoring verbal responses to a standard set of inkblots. [*See* Rorschach Test.] Personality researchers score "need power," "need affiliation," and "need achievement" from stories told in response to pictures. [*See* Thematic Apperception Test.] Classic memory research by Frederic Bartlett identified what was added to a story recall and what was dropped. [*See the biography of Bartlett.*] All these procedures are forms of content analysis.

Depending on the research objectives, content analysts may measure the amount of space given to a topic, count frequency of mentions, or simply evaluate whether a document does or does not show a particular characteristic. Between-document comparisons are then made, whether of presence or absence scores, frequency counts, or inches of text. Simple presence or absence scorings can be key in identifying authorship or particular story transformations. Frequency counts may be used to evaluate overall tone or style, including classic indexes such as positivity-negativity, dominance-submission, and activity-passivity as well as measures of rational-emotional, thought-action, abstraction-specificity, or overstatement-understatement. Column inches of text are often used to measure changes in print media attention to a topic. [*See* Semantic Differential.]

Not each occurrence of a characteristic, of course, is likely to merit being assigned the same weight, but unless additional information is considered in evaluating each occurrence in its context, weightings do not usually produce enough additional yield to be worth the effort, especially when analyzing large amounts of data.

Systematic content analyses first occurred long ago (for example, in the 1640s to determine whether 90 new hymns were acceptable to Swedish Lutheranism), but content analysis was established as a tool of modern social science by World War II enemy propaganda studies by Harold Lasswell and others. Several books on content analysis appeared in the 1950s, as well as comprehensive chapters on content analysis by both Bernard Berelson and Ole Holsti in the first two editions of the *Handbook of Social Psychology* (Lindzey & Aronson, 1954, 1968).

Today, content analysis is one of the most frequently used social-science methods in applied research, especially in analyses of in-depth job interviews and open-ended survey research questions. Survey researchers, for example, study what words respondents use, rather than just their choices on multiple-choice questions. Nevertheless, the costs and time required for manual content analysis limits its use. To facilitate analyzing open-ended questions, SPSS's *Textsmart* (1998) provides content-analysis software targeted to open-ended responses in market research. For patient interviews, Louis Gottschalk (1995) has developed specific content analysis computer software to score *DSM*-related psychological states. [*See* Diagnostic and Statistical Manual of Mental Disorders.] Many scoring procedures, however, remain primarily manual, including the content analysis of verbal explanations (CAVE) procedures of Martin Seligman and colleagues or the information complexity indexes of Philip Tetlock and colleagues (Smith, *Motivation and Personality: Handbook of Thematic Content Analysis,* 1992).

Content analyses today may include highly numerical tools, such as factor analysis, cluster analysis, and time-series techniques (Weber, 1990) or, for those who prefer qualitative approaches, primarily draw upon software for categorizing and organizing information. Some content analysts study long-term trends, such as cycles in the use of primordial imagery (Martindale, *The Clockwork Muse*, 1990). No longer limited to word counting, some content-analysis software, for example, identifies word senses of high-frequency words.

The increasing importance of television and film as compared to print media and an increased interest in nonverbal communication, together with an ease of using videocameras in the field, has directed more attention to extending content-analysis capabilities beyond text to include pictures and video. Pioneering content-analysis software such as *HyperResearch* already provides an aid to conducting systematic analyses of pictures and videoclips.

Within academic research, content analysis continues to be used less in psychology than in some other social sciences. A decline in use within psychology has paralleled a decline in ideographic research such as that carried out by Gordon Allport, group dynamics, and other domains that had made considerable use of it. Content-analysis chapters no longer appear in later editions of the *Handbook of Social Psychology*. By comparison (to use a content-analysis measure), the *Encyclopedia of Sociology* (Borgotta, 1990) assigns three times more space to *content analysis* than the present encyclopedia. [*See the biography of Allport.*]

Developing objective content-analysis measures is one step; drawing valid, useful inferences from any such measures is quite another. Inferences should be carefully situated in terms of the specific context in which the information is produced and/or consumed. For example, inferences from measures of letters to stockholders should consider the business sector and economic climate in which they were written. In addition, inferences should be based upon triangulations of multiple pieces of evidence that point in the same direction, of which content-analysis measures are but one type. Not only are inferences likely to be more valid, but the research can better address underlying factors, yielding what some analysts call "latent" (in contrast to "manifest") content-analysis research.

Convenient access to desktop computing combined with appropriate content-analysis software may not only lead to more use of open-ended survey research questions, but more systematic studies of communications within social-psychological experiments as well as systematic content analyses of debriefings. An increased interest in emotional intelligence may lead to more content analyses of how people describe their feelings and how they draw upon their emotions. Future use of particular approaches to content analysis in psychology will depend on what insights, in terms of meaningful, valid inferences, they can be shown to provide.

Bibliography

Boyatzis, R. E. (1998). *Transforming qualitative information: Thematic analysis and code development.* Thousand Oaks, CA: Sage. Detailed instructions on thematic encoding based on the approach originally developed by David McClelland. Contrasts this approach with the use of thematic analysis in qualitative research.

Lindzey, G., & Aronson, E. (Eds.). (1954, 1968) Addison-Wesley. *Handbook of social psychology.* Reading, MA: Addison-Wesley.

Stone, P. J., Dunphy, D. C., Smith, M. S., & Ogilvie, D. M. (Eds.). (1966). *The General Inquirer: A computer approach to content analysis.* Cambridge, MA: MIT Press. An early general resource used by content-analysis investigators, leading to the development of shared content analysis indexes. These procedures, considerably augmented, can now be used on desktop computers.

Stone, P. J. (1997). Thematic text analysis: New agendas for analyzing text content. In C. W. Roberts (Ed.), *Text analysis for the social sciences: Methods for drawing statistical inferences from texts and transcripts.* Mahwah, NJ: Erlbaum. An overview of content-analysis issues and how they have been addressed, including their use in applied research. Changes in content-analysis objectives and capabilities are reviewed.

Philip J. Stone

CONVERSATION. A quintessentially social process, conversations emerge as two or more people try to carry out certain joint activities in which they have to coordinate with each other to accomplish their goals. Waltzing, playing poker, and playing in a string quartet are joint activities that do not require much conversation, while negotiating a deal, planning a party, and gossiping are ones that do. At first glance, conversations often seem disorderly, even chaotic, but they have a highly systematic organization that is shaped by a range of cognitive and social principles.

Conversations have three properties that are common to all joint activities (Clark, 1996). First, they have participants as distinct from nonparticipants. At any moment, the participants are the speaker, addressees, and side participants, and the nonparticipants are the bystanders or eavesdroppers. Second, conversations have public goals—mutually agreed-upon purposes for carrying out the joint activity. The overall goal may be to negotiate a deal, plan a party, or exchange gossip, and each goal has subgoals. Although some goals may be set beforehand, most get established as the participants go along. The participants also have private goals, such as maintaining face or avoiding certain topics, and the problem is how to achieve the private goals along with the public ones. Third, conversations have boundaries—distinct beginnings, ends, and transitions from one part to the next. These boundaries cannot be established by any one person alone, but must be determined by all the participants in coordination.

People trying to carry out a joint activity, therefore, have to agree at each moment on at least these issues: the participants, the joint goals, what to do next, and when. It takes coordination to reach these joint commitments and carry them out. What is remarkable is that people accomplish all of this turn by turn (Sacks, Schegloff, & Jefferson, 1974). Conversations may seem to have a global organization, but they actually emerge from local actions.

Perhaps the most basic of these actions is the *adjacency pair* (Schegloff & Sacks, 1973). Here is a spontaneous example (all conversational exchanges are from Svartvik & Quirk, 1980):

Alan   When is it,
Ben   Four-thirty tomorrow.

Every adjacency pair has two parts, by two different speakers, where part 2 is conditionally relevant given part 1. Here, in part 1, Alan *proposes* that Ben tell him when a meeting is, and in part 2, Ben *takes up* that proposal. Viewed differently, Alan proposes that (1) the participants be Ben and him; (2) their goal be the exchange of this information; and (3) their activity start with his question and end with Ben's answer. Ben agrees to all three points simply by giving the wanted answer. So adjacency pairs are perfect for coordinating. They enable people to agree on the participants, goals, beginning, end, and components of the local joint action. And they are available for a wide range of joint actions, including greetings ("Hi," "Hi"), farewells ("Bye," "Bye"), offers ("Have some cake," "Thanks"), orders ("Sit down," "Yes, sir"), and apologies ("Sorry," "Oh, that's okay") (Stenström, 1994).

Conversations cannot succeed unless the participants *ground* what they say—establish the mutual belief that the addressees have understood the speakers well enough for current purposes (Clark & Schaefer, 1989). One technique for grounding is the adjacency pair itself. When Ben says "four-thirty tomorrow," he gives evidence of how he has interpreted Alan's question. If Alan isn't satisfied with that interpretation, he can correct it; for example, by replying "No, I meant . . ." (Schegloff, Jefferson, & Sacks, 1977). Another technique is the *back-channel response, acknowledgment,* or *continuer* (Schegloff, 1982). In two-party conversations, addressees are expected to add "uh-huh" or "mhm" or "yeah" at or near the ends of certain phrases. With these, they assert that they have understood the speaker so far and imply that the speaker should continue.

Grounding is also sometimes achieved through *side sequences* (Jefferson, 1972), as illustrated here:

Alan   Now,—um do you and your husband have a j– car?
Barbara —have a car,
Alan   Yes,
Barbara No,—

Barbara hadn't heard Alan clearly, so she initiated an embedded adjacency pair, a side sequence, to clear up the problem before she went on to her answer. Side sequences can be used to clear up not only mishearings or misunderstandings, but other preconditions to taking up the first part (e.g., "Why do you want to know?").

Adjacency pairs take only two turns, but they can be used to project larger sections, as here:

Ann   Oh there's one thing I wanted to ask you,
Betty   Mhm,—
[Ann and Betty exchange ten turns as Ann describes a type of belt]
Ann   Would you like one?
Betty   Oh I'd love one Ann—

Ann's first turn is a *prequestion* (Schegloff, 1980). With it she proposes to Betty that she ask her a question, and Betty agrees to the proposal. Ann now has the freedom to take up preliminaries to her eventual question, and the two of them occupy ten turns in doing that. So prequestions project not only the eventual question, but preliminaries to that question.

Prequestions and their responses are just one of a large family of so-called presequences. Here are a few more examples:

	Part 1	Part 2
prerequests	[to waiter] Do you have hot chocolate?	Yes, we do.
preannouncements	Well d'you know what they got?	What?
preinvitations	What are you doin'?	Nothin'. What's up?
prenarrative	I acquired an absolutely magnificent sewing-machine, by foul means, did I tell you about that?	No.

Each presequence prepares the way for another joint action, and these range from simple requests ("I'll have one") to long narratives (the sewing-machine story).

Opening conversations is ordinarily achieved incrementally through a series of adjacency pairs (Schegloff, 1968, 1979). Here is an opening of a telephone conversation between two women in a British university:

Jane   (phones the Principal's office)
Kate   Hello, Principal's office

Jane	Uh this is Professor Worth's secretary, from Pan-American College.
Kate	Yes?
Jane	Um could you possibly tell me, what Sir Humphrey Davy's address is, Professor Worth thought . . . you might know . . .
Kate	Yes, we do, yeah, hang on [long pause]

First, Jane and Kate coordinate contact through a summons (the telephone call) and response ("Hello"). Next, as credentials to the projected business, they exchange official identities ("Principal's office," "Uh this is . . ."). It is only then that they establish their first joint goal, the exchange of Davy's address, and they do that in two steps. In an embedded adjacency pair, Jane asserts that Kate might know Davy's address ("Professor . . ."), to which Kate responds, "Yes, we do, yeah," and on that basis Jane asks for the address ("Um could you . . .") and Kate complies ("Hang on"). Jane and Kate couldn't launch directly into this exchange at the start. They had to establish the participants, their identities, and joint goals in increments. Similar incremental strategies are required in closing conversations and changing topics (Schegloff & Sacks, 1979).

Conversations are not merely local, but opportunistic: The paths people take depend on the opportunities made available by each local agreement. Here is an example:

| Susan | I don't know if you know the bad news?— |
| Ned | I heard. |

Susan offered to tell Ned "the bad news," but when he said he'd already heard it, they went down a different path. Susan used the preannouncement to discover how best to proceed. Speakers often make incorrect assumptions, as Helen did here:

Helen	How old were most of the children—
Sam	Well uh only a few of them, were children in fact . . . um . . . I was teaching adults.
Helen	Oh I see.

Instead of rejecting Helen's question, Sam tacitly altered it to one he *was* able to answer. In doing so, he too was being opportunistic.

People help signal which opportunities they are taking by using *discourse markers* (Schiffrin, 1987). For example, Sam used "Well" to signal that he was changing his stance to Helen's question, and she used "Oh" to signal that she was revising a previous opinion. Other discourse markers mark boundaries, such as the start of a new topic (e.g., "so," "then," "speaking of that"), the start of a digression ("incidentally," "by the way"), or the return from a digression ("anyway," "so"). All aid the participants in coordinating what to do next.

To sum up, conversations are purposive, but unplanned. They do not proceed according to a set structure, but rather emerge from people's opportunistic attempts to do things together. People have to coordinate on each local action, and for that they employ a variety of techniques. It is this flexibility that makes conversation suitable for everything from gossip to diplomacy.

Bibliography

Clark, H. H. (1996). *Using language.* Cambridge, UK: Cambridge University Press.

Clark, H. H., & Schaefer, E. R. (1989). Contributing to discourse. *Cognitive Science, 13,* 259–294.

Sacks, H., Schegloff, E. A., & Jefferson, G. (1974). A simplest systematics for the organization of turn-taking in conversation. *Language, 50,* 696–735.

Schegloff, E. A. (1968). Sequencing in conversational openings. *American Anthropologist, 70*(4), 1075–1095.

Schegloff, E. A. (1979). Identification and recognition in telephone conversational openings. In G. Psathas (Ed.), *Everyday language: Studies in ethnomethodology* (pp. 23–78). New York: Irvington.

Schegloff, E. A. (1980). Preliminaries to preliminaries: "Can I ask you a question?" *Sociological Inquiry, 50,* 104–152.

Schegloff, E. A. (1982). Discourse as an interactional achievement: Some uses of "uh huh" and other things that come between sentences. In D. Tannen (Ed.), *Analyzing discourse: Text and talk. Georgetown University Roundtable on Languages and Linguistics 1981* (pp. 71–93). Washington, DC: Georgetown University Press.

Schegloff, E. A., Jefferson, G., & Sacks, H. (1977). The preference for self-correction in the organization of repair in conversation. *Language, 53,* 361–382.

Schegloff, E. A., & Sacks, H. (1973). Opening up closings. *Semiotica, 8,* 289–327.

Schiffrin, D. (1987). *Discourse markers.* Cambridge, UK: Cambridge University Press.

Stenström, A-B. (1994). *An introduction to spoken interaction.* London: Longmans.

Svartvik, J., & Quirk, R. (Eds.). (1980). *A corpus of English conversation.* Lund, Sweden: Gleerup.

Herbert H. Clark

CONVERSION DISORDER. *See* Somatoform Disorders.

COOK, STUART W. (1913–1993), American psychologist. Stuart Cook's many-faceted career in psychology, after his doctorate from the University of Minnesota in 1938, focused on the application of research toward the understanding and amelioration of major social problems. Before he joined Col. John C. Flanagan's Aviation Psychology Program in World War II as a captain, Cook served a year as head of the Minnesota Bureau of Psychological Services. In the Air Force, he directed research concerning the selection and training of airborne radar operators. At the end of the war, shocked by emerging news of the Holocaust, he was recruited by Kurt Lewin as director of research for the Commission on Community Interrelations of the American Jewish Congress. There he conducted a program of action research combating anti-Semitism. In 1949 he moved to New York University (NYU), where he established the Research Center for Human Relations. He continued to focus on intergroup relations and prejudice, now with primary concern for Black-White issues at a time when the legal struggle for desegregation of the public schools was coming to a climax. His own background as a native-born Virginian nourished his deep personal concern with these issues. [*See the biography of Lewin.*]

In 1950 Cook became head of the NYU graduate psychology department. Recruiting such eminent social psychologists as Morton Deutsch, Richard Christie, and Marie Jahoda, he created and led a nationally prominent program that was unique in its commitment to rigorous applied research on important social issues. He led a landmark study of interracial housing as a quasi-experimental field test of the hypothesis that equal-status contact is a critical condition for the reduction of prejudice. (Later in his career he directed exemplary experimental research on this issue.) With the African American psychologist Kenneth B. Clark and his colleague Isidor Chein, he collaborated in writing the "Appendix to the Appellants' Brief" cited by the Supreme Court in the 1954 *Brown v. Board of Education* decision that outlawed segregated public schools. He and his colleagues in the Research Center drew on their common experience in writing a widely used textbook, *Research Methods in Social Relations* (Jahoda, Deutsch, & Cook, New York, 1951) which remained in print through many editions with different collaborators. [*See the biography of Clark.*]

Cook's reputation as an effective department head led to his recruitment as professor and chair of psychology at the University of Colorado, where he remained for the rest of his career. He served in a variety of leadership capacities in state, regional, and national psychological organizations. In New York, he led the legislative campaign to certify professional psychologists, a pioneering event in the history of certification and licensure. In the American Psychological Association (APA), his most enduring impact was in the development of codes of professional and scientific ethics for psychologists. He had belonged to the committee that developed APA's first code of professional ethics on the basis of an analysis of "critical incidents" of ethical dilemmas actually faced by psychologists. He brought the same empirically grounded approach to the development of *Ethical Principles in the Conduct of Research*

with Human Subjects (Washington, DC, 1973) under his leadership.

Stuart Cook was much honored for his achievements. The recognition that best encapsulates his central contributions came with the Kurt Lewin Award of the Society for the Psychological Study of Social Issues, "for research furthering the development and integration of psychological research and social action."

Bibliography

Kluger, R. (1976). *Simple justice: The history of Brown vs. Board of Education and Black America's struggle for equality*. New York: Knopf. The standard history, which includes an account of Cook's role.

Smith, M. B. (1994). Stuart W. Cook (1913–1993). *American Psychologist, 49*, 521–522. A rather full obituary.

Wilner, D., Walkley, R. P., & Cook, S. W. (1955). *Human relations in interracial housing*. Minneapolis: University of Minnesota Press. A classic quasi-experimental study of the "contact hypothesis" in the reduction of race prejudice. Characteristically, Cook put his own name last.

M. Brewster Smith

COOMBS, CLYDE H. (1912–1988), American psychologist. After finishing his degree in 1940, Clyde H. Coombs became a U.S. War Department personnel research psychologist, rising to the rank of major by the end of World War II. His design of separation and counseling programs for demobilized GIs won him the Legion of Merit. Preferring a research life, he entered academia in 1947 in the vibrant and fast-growing psychology department headed by Don Marquis at the University of Michigan. From that time until his retirement, he headed the mathematical psychology program there. He received much recognition during that time (e.g., election to the National Academy of Sciences in 1982, receipt of the Distinguished Scientific Contribution Award of the American Psychological Association in 1985).

In his work Coombs demonstrated that all psychological measurement can be conceptualized as developing spatial representations of relations between points. These relations involve *dominance* (e.g., one light is brighter than another, or a particular person's arithmetic ability surpasses that needed to solve a certain item correctly) or *proximity* (e.g., two statements express a more similar attitude than do two others, or one statement is closer to someone's attitude than is another). Moreover, points can be categorized as belonging to the same set (e.g., pairs of lights) or different sets (e.g., the item and a person's ability level). Investigators, not bound by their observations to represent them in a particular manner, choose a measurement model based on their theoretical ideas about how to map these observations into the points representing them. For example, the degree to which Morse Code signal x is identified as signal y can either be represented as a distance between them (a symmetric proximity measure) or as the relative distance of x from y, or vice versa (a conditional proximity measure). These ideas led to several articles and culminated in Coombs's book, *A Theory of Data* (1964).

Coombs's system led directly to his development of the technique of "unfolding," in which an individual's preference for one stimulus over another is modeled as a shorter distance between an ideal point (representing that person) and the first stimulus than between the ideal and the second. Given a set of such preferences from different people, it is possible to determine whether they can be "unfolded" to construct a "joint" space with points representing both the people's ideals and the stimuli. This technique, soon implemented by (hill climbing) computer programs, is so widely used in so many areas of social science that it no longer even bears Coombs's name.

A striking example is preference for family composition evaluated across cultures. Coombs and his sociologist wife Lolagene (Lo), together with their student Gary McClelland, asked subjects in more than 15 countries to state preferences for having families involving varying numbers of boys and girls. The results distinguished between a model involving an ideal number of boys and an ideal number of girls versus a model assuming one ideal for total size of family and one for its gender composition: boy minus girl. The preferences in all the countries the Coombses and McClelland examined fit the second model better than the first, and follow-up studies indicated that people's stated preferences predicted their subsequent decisions to continue having children or to stop.

At the time of his sudden death in 1988 Coombs had just finished the copyedited version of his joint book with George S. Avrunin entitled *The Structure of Conflict*. In the work, the authors used an unfolding analysis to characterize various types of interpersonal conflict; they demonstrated that the potential resolution of such conflict was dependent upon both preference and the set of options available (constituting a "Pareto efficient set" or not). They also specified the psychological importance of a zero point separating positively from negatively valued options, not just as an arbitrary origin on an interval scale representing utility. That work was the culmination of Clyde Coombs's progression ever since he "split" with his mentor L. L. Thurstone, who analyzed input numbers, whereas Coombs—consistent with fundamental measurement theory—inferred numerical or "ordered metric" representations from qualitative input. [*See the biography of Thurstone.*]

A superb teacher, Coombs also collaborated with Robyn Dawes and Amos Tversky on a textbook, *Mathematical Psychology: An Elementary Introduction* (1970), which was enthusiastically reviewed and translated into seven foreign languages. Later he prepared a small "gem," *Psychology and Mathematics: An Essay on Theory* (1983).

Bibliography

Coombs, C. H. (1964). *A theory of data.* New York: Wiley.
Coombs, C. H. (1983). *Psychology and mathematics: An essay on theory.* Ann Arbor: University of Michigan Press.
Coombs, C. H., & Avrunin, G. S. (1988). *The structure of conflict.* Hillsdale, NJ: Erlbaum.

Robyn Dawes

COOPERATION AND COMPETITION. The theme of cooperation and competition has been a prominent domain of theory and research within a variety of disciplines, including philosophy, political science, economics, sociology, biology, and psychology. The broad interest in cooperation and competition is not surprising. This theme is intimately linked to the basic views and assumptions regarding human nature and is relevant to the functioning of dyads, groups, or organizations, and even societies. Although it is often assumed that humankind is rationally self-interested, more recent theorizing and research reveals that human nature is far richer than the concept of selfishness is able to capture.

Definition and Analysis

During the past decades, the field of social psychology has developed frameworks for understanding interpersonal preferences that extend and complement the pursuit of self-interest, or the desire to enhance one's own outcomes with no or very little regard for outcomes for others. A useful typology, developed by Griesinger and Livingston (1970), distinguishes among eight distinct preferences or orientations, including altruism, cooperation, individualism, competition, and aggression, as well as nihilism, masochism, and inferiority. In this typology (see Figure 1), *cooperation* is defined by the tendency to maximize outcomes for self and others ("doing well together"), thereby assigning positive weight to both outcomes for self and outcomes for others. In contrast, *competition* is defined by the tendency to maximize relative advantage over others ("doing better than others"), thereby assigning positive weight to outcomes for self in combination with assigning negative weight to outcomes for others.

Whereas cooperation and competition include tak-

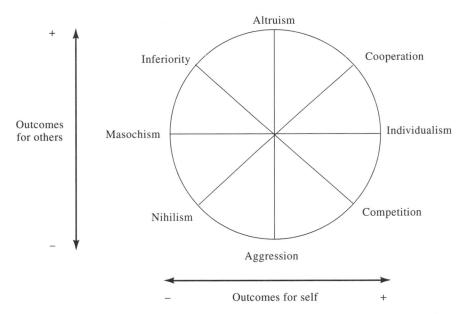

COOPERATION AND COMPETITION. Figure 1. A two-dimensional typology of interpersonal orientations (From Griesinger, D. W. & Livingston, J. W. [1973]. Toward a model of interpersonal orientation in experimental games. *Behavioral Science, 18*, 173–188.)

ing account of outcomes for self *and* outcomes for others, three other important orientations do not. *Individualism* is defined by the tendency to maximize outcomes for self, with no or very little regard for outcomes for others; *altruism* is defined by the tendency to maximize outcomes for others, with no or very little regard for outcomes for self, and *aggression* is defined by the tendency to minimize outcomes for others. The remaining three orientations of nihilism, masochism, and inferiority are interesting for conceptual purposes; yet these are exceptionally uncommon, as they involve tendencies toward minimizing outcomes for self. Cooperation, individualism, and competition represent common orientations, in that most of us probably have repeated experience with each of these tendencies, either through introspection or through observation of others' actions. Another orientation that is also quite common, yet is not represented in this framework, is *equality*—the tendency to minimize absolute differences in outcomes for self and others. Empirically, equality often goes hand in hand with cooperation: Individuals who wish to do well together tend to avoid large discrepancies between their own and others' outcomes.

Cooperation and competition represent behaviors (or behavioral tendencies) that can only be meaningfully exhibited in situations of *interdependence*, when two or more individuals' outcomes are jointly determined by one's own and others' actions. While interdependence situations can be characterized in a variety of ways (for a taxonomy, see Kelley & Thibaut, 1978), one charac-

terization centers on *correspondence of outcomes*, referring to the degree to which one's own and others' preferences correspond versus being in conflict. In two-person situations, correspondence of outcomes is high when both individuals need each other for attaining good outcomes and there is no conflict of interests—what is good for her is good for him. Correspondence of outcomes is low when two individuals can only attain good outcomes for self at the expense of outcomes for other: There is a strong conflict of interest—what's good for her is bad for him. Thus, correspondence of outcomes represents a continuum ranging from gain-gain situations or coordination situations to gain-loss situations, the most extreme situation being the zero-sum situation in which the individual's benefit equals the cost to the partner.

Situations represent a conflict between joint benefit (cooperation) and relative benefit over the partner (competition) when there is some degree of noncorrespondence. When outcomes are perfectly correspondent or perfectly noncorrespondent, considerations of joint benefit, own benefit, or relative benefit generally yield identical choices, and so there is no situational basis for cooperation or competition. When outcomes are fairly strongly noncorrespondent, then individuals may be facing dilemmas in which they have to choose whether to pursue joint benefit versus own benefit or relative benefit. Such situations are diagnostic of the presence or absence of tendencies toward cooperation. Situations in which self-interest is at odds with joint or collective interest calls for cooperation versus noncooperation. In such dilemmas, people must choose between an action that is not very good for self but very good for the collective versus an action that is good for self but bad for the collective. Such situations are often referred to as *prisoner's dilemmas*, in particular when two individuals are involved, or *social dilemmas*, in particular when more than two individuals are involved. When outcomes are somewhat noncorrespondent, then individuals may be facing dilemmas in which they have to choose whether to pursue joint benefit and/or own benefit versus relative benefit. Such situations are diagnostic of the presence or absence of tendencies toward competition, an example being the so-called *maximizing difference game*.

Basic Sources of Cooperation and Competition

Cooperation and competition have been examined in several paradigms, although such issues have received most direct attention in so-called experimental games, a methodology inspired by *game theory* (Luce & Raiffa, 1957). While game theory traditionally rests upon the assumption that people are "rationally self-interested," this view has been extended in several models and theories of interdependence. Importantly, in their *interdependence theory*, Kelley and Thibaut (1978) assume that individuals may *transform* a given situation into an effective situation, which represents preferences that take account of the outcomes for others or long-term consequences of choices. [*See* Interdependence, *article on* Interdependence Structure.] Such transformations can be promoted by preferences such as cooperation, competition, or equality. What are the basic sources of cooperative and competitive transformations?

First, tendencies to enhance collective benefit are explicated in models of *interpersonal dispositions*. One disposition, rooted in the game theoretical literature, is *social value orientation* (Messick & McClintock, 1968), revealing that individuals differ in the probability with which they seek to enhance (1) joint outcomes and equality in outcomes (prosocial orientation); (2) their own outcomes (individualistic orientation); and (3) relative advantage over others (competitive orientation). Interestingly, by approaching others in a noncooperative manner, competitors and individualists are likely to elicit noncooperative behavior from others, which may account for the fact that these individuals tend to hold individualistic or competitive beliefs regarding humankind (Kelley & Stahelski, 1970). Social value orientation tends to be shaped by prior social interaction experiences, whereby individuals have "learned" to adapt to interdependence situations in a prosocial, individualistic, or competitive manner. For example, people with prosocial orientations tend to be raised in larger families than people with individualistic or competitive orientations; yet over the course of a lifetime, most individuals tend to develop prosocial orientation (Van Lange, Otten, De Bruin, & Joireman, 1997). Examples of interpersonal dispositions that are related to social value orientation are *trust* and adult *attachment style*.

Second, tendencies toward cooperation and competition are importantly shaped by the *interdependence structure* underlying a situation or relationship. To the extent that correspondence of outcomes is higher, individuals are more likely to make cooperative (or noncompetitive) choices. When the conflict of interest becomes less intense, contributing to the collective benefit will simply be less costly, thereby removing one important barrier for cooperation to occur. Thus, interventions by which cooperation becomes structurally more attractive (reward) and noncooperation less attractive (punishment) are effective means to promoting cooperation. Another structural feature involves level of dependence on a relationship. In the context of ongoing relationships, cooperation is enhanced to the extent that individuals experience greater *commitment* to the relationship; that is, when individuals more strongly need the relationship, adopt a long-term orientation to the relationship, and feel attached to the relationship (Rusbult, Verrette, Whitney, Slovik, & Lipkus, 1991). Commitment is also important in formal organizations such that individuals are more likely to engage in extrarole behavior and less likely to engage in absenteeism to the degree that *organizational commitment* is greater.

Third, tendencies to enhance collective benefit may also be rooted in powerful *norms* that prescribe rules for dealing with specific interdependence problems and opportunities. Such norms are especially important at the global group or societal level, and often serve to (1) enhance the functioning of groups and societies, even the more microlevel forms of functioning, such as everyday rules of civility and decency, and (2) protect the "weak" from being exploited by the "powerful" and provide help to individuals who are in clear need of such help. Although often implicit, norms tend to exert fairly strong influences, are applicable to a great variety of situations, and, when violated, tend to result in disapproval by the observers and guilt in the actor. At the same time, different norms can also conflict with one another, resulting in normative ambiguity which is often resolved by adhering to norms that best serve one's personal or group interests. For example, individuals who have contributed less than average to a group's well-being tend to adhere to the norm of equality, whereas those who have contributed more than average to the well-being of a group tend to adhere to the norm of equity, claiming a proportionally greater benefit from the group in return. Also, norms tend to differ across cultures. In particular, in collectivistic cultures one may witness cooperation in response to one another's needs (e.g., *communal relationships*), whereas in individualistic cultures one is more likely to witness co-operation through the norm of reciprocity (e.g., *exchange relationships*; Clark & Mills, 1979). Finally, norms may influence not only patterns of distribution of outcomes but also the procedures used for allocating outcomes among individuals (cf. *distributive justice*; *procedural justice*; Thibaut & Walker, 1975).

Finally, tendencies toward cooperation and competition are often inspired by *beliefs or actual observations of others' behaviors*. The general rule is that cooperation tends to evoke some degree of cooperation, whereas competition evokes competition. Beliefs regarding others' cooperation and competition are strongly interrelated with one's own inclination to cooperate or compete. In the context of dyadic relationships, there is a *social-evolutionary* basis for the functionality of the so-called *tit-for-tat* strategy. This strategy, which commences a cooperative choice and subsequently imitates the other person's previous choice, is one of the most effective means for eliciting stable patterns of mutual cooperation (Axelrod, 1984). Indeed, tit-for-tat effectively rewards cooperation by acting cooperatively in turn, and punishes noncooperation or competition by acting noncooperatively in turn. Moreover, ongoing relationships are often characterized by high levels of mutuality in cooperation, such that healthy relationships tend to be characterized by high levels of mutual cooperation and less healthy relationships by lower levels of mutual cooperation (Van Lange, Rusbult, Drigotas, Arriaga, Witcher, & Cox, 1997). Finally, tit-for-tat is not only effective in dyadic relationships; small groups may also benefit from this strategy. In fact, *computer simulations* have revealed that tit-for-tat and related strategies, such as *win-stay-lose-change*, can promote collective outcomes, even in the context of large groups.

Cooperation and Competition Among Individuals and Groups

There are important psychological differences between dyadic relationships and larger group relations. To begin with, *anonymity* increases with group size. That is, unlike dyadic relationships, in larger groups one can almost never be sure who was making a cooperative or competitive choice. Also, with increasing group size, individuals tend to become substantially more pessimistic about the *efficacy* of their efforts to promote collective outcomes. And individuals tend to feel lower levels of *personal responsibility* for collective outcomes with increasing group size. For these three reasons, individuals tend to exhibit lower levels of cooperation in larger groups. Even so, cooperation in larger groups can be promoted, particularly by (1) strengthening social norms prescribing cooperation; (2) effective communication (i.e., communication about the intended choice to which they commit themselves); and (3) enhancing feelings of identity with the group or a sense of "we-ness." Alternatively, as is the case for dyadic relationships, structural factors, such as rewarding cooperation, have been demonstrated to be effective in very large groups.

Second, interactions between groups are characterized by lower levels of cooperation and higher levels of competition than are interactions between individuals (Insko, Schopler, Hoyle, Dardis, & Graetz, 1990). This so-called *individual-group discontinuity effect* can be understood in terms of (1) lower levels of trust in intergroup relations, eliciting fear of being exploited by the other group; (2) stronger levels of support group members give to each other for pursuing self-interest; and (3) lower levels of identifiability, in that responsibility for self-centered behavior is often shared in intergroup settings but not in interpersonal settings. Such evidence has been obtained in different contexts, and it is important to note that categorization in terms of "we" and "they" can yield powerful effects, resulting in *ingroup bias* or allocating greater resources or benefits to one's own group than to the other group. Indeed, *identification* with one's own group, along with feelings of "we-ness," promote cooperation within a group, and at the same time may enhance competition or even hostility with other groups. In the final analysis, conflicts between groups are powerfully influenced by the degree to which their preferences correspond or conflict. Unfortunately, the interests of one's own versus other groups often conflict—and often are believed to conflict even when they do not do so in reality—which helps us understand why interactions between groups in everyday life tend to be hostile and competitive rather than cooperative.

[*See also* Interdependence.]

Bibliography

Axelrod, R. (1984). *The evolution of cooperation*. New York: Basic Books.

Clark, M. S., & Mills, J. (1979). Interpersonal attraction in exchange and communal relationships. *Journal of Personality and Social Psychology, 37,* 12–24.

Griesinger, D. W., & Livingston, J. W. (1973). Toward a model of interpersonal orientation in experimental games. *Behavioral Science, 18,* 173–188.

Insko, C. A., Schopler, J., Hoyle, R. H., Dardis, G. J., & Graetz, K. A. (1990). Individual-group discontinuity as a function of fear and greed. *Journal of Personality and Social Psychology, 58,* 68–79.

Kelley, H. H., & Stahelski, A. J. (1970). Social interaction basis of cooperators' and competitors' beliefs about others. *Journal of Personality and Social Psychology, 16,* 66–91.

Kelley, H. H., & Thibaut, J. W. (1978). *Interpersonal relations: A theory of interdependence*. New York: Wiley.

Luce, R. D., & Raiffa, H. (1957). *Games and decisions: Introduction and critical survey.* London: Wiley.

Messick, D. M., & McClintock, C. G. (1968). Motivational bases of choice in experimental games. *Journal of Experimental Social Psychology, 4,* 1–25.

Rusbult, C. E., Verette, J., Whitney, G. A., Slovik, L. F., & Lipkus, I. (1991). Accommodation processes in close relationships: Theory and preliminary empirical evidence. *Journal of Personality and Social Psychology, 60,* 53–78.

Thibaut, J. W., & Walker, L. (1975). *Procedural justice: A psychological analysis.* New York: Wiley.

Van Lange, P. A. M., Otten, W., De Bruin, E. M. N., & Joireman, J. A. (1997). Development of prosocial, individualistic, and competitive orientations: Theory and preliminary evidence. *Journal of Personality and Social Psychology, 73,* 733–746.

Van Lange, P. A. M., Rusbult, C. E., Drigotas, S. M., Arriaga, X. B., Witcher, B. S., & Cox, C. L. (1997). Willingness to sacrifice in close relationships. *Journal of Personality and Social Psychology, 72,* 1373–1395.

Paul A. M. Van Lange

COPD. *See* Chronic Obstructive Pulmonary Disease.

COPING. It is difficult to talk about coping, or even define it, without also talking briefly about stress. Definitions of stress typically incorporate some variation on the idea that stress involves trying to meet demands from the environment that approach or exceed the person's ability to respond effectively (either due to limitations in the person's capacity or because the person's resources have been depleted). The concept of coping refers to the various ways in which people respond when confronting this situation. In general, these responses represent either further attempts to meet the demands of the situation or attempts to deal with the negative emotions that can be created by the situation. Some kinds of responses that are examined under the label *coping,* however, represent attempts to escape, in one fashion or another, from having to deal with the situation's demands.

Interest in stress and coping has had several different focuses over the years. Some people have been most interested in the psychological processes that are involved in the experience of stress and choice of coping response. People who have this focus of interest are usually concerned with issues bearing on either emotional reactions or task performances. For example, what sorts of coping responses can minimize the negative feelings that often arise when people are under stress? What variables influence the quality of people's task performances under conditions of stress? Can certain coping responses reduce the adverse effects of stress, or serve as a buffer against stress? Might certain coping responses actually make matters worse?

The interest of others has been captured by the fact that the psychological processes of stress and coping have physiological concomitants. The physiological reactions are believed to play a role in the development and progression of several sorts of illnesses and failures of the body. Accordingly, many people have become interested in questions about how the body reacts to stress, the pathways by which these physical reactions come to influence the development of physical disorder, and how the adverse physical reactions can be diminished or prevented. [*See* Stress, *article on* Definition and Physiology.]

Theory

Although several theories of coping have been proposed, the one that is employed most widely by people who study stress and coping is that proposed by Lazarus (1966) and elaborated upon by Lazarus and Folkman (1984). The theory is sometimes termed a *cognitive-appraisal* model and sometimes a *transactional model.*

Coping as a Transaction. This theory holds that the experience of psychological stress consists of the occurrence of three processes, two of which are cognitive-appraisal processes. *Primary appraisal* is the process of perceiving a threat in the environment; *secondary appraisal* is the process of deciding how to respond to the threat; *coping* is the process of executing whatever responses have been selected during secondary appraisal.

As noted, this analysis of the stress experience is also termed a *transactional model.* This term reflects the idea that the experience of stress represents a transaction between the person and the situation—it depends on both of them, rather than on just one or the other. There are at least two respects in which this is true. First, the perception of threat depends partly on the situation that the person encounters, and partly on what the person brings to the situation. For example, the sight of a spider may pose no threat to one person, but the same sight may create a severe threat to another person. This is one point at which the Lazarus model of stress intersects with the broad domain of social cognition. That is, how a given person organizes and mentally represents knowledge about the world can be expected to influence the outcomes of the person's threat appraisals.

There is also a transactional quality to the secondary appraisal process. People do not always respond reflexively and automatically to the situations they confront (or even the situations they construe). Rather, secondary appraisal often involves weighing options and considering the consequences of responding in various ways, before deciding what to do. As is true of primary appraisal, these evaluation and decision-making processes involve information from the person's memory as well as information from the situation. As a result, the outcome of the secondary appraisal process also can be expected to differ from person to person, even if people view the threat itself in the same way.

Elaborations and Further Considerations. Three further elaborations on this model should be noted before continuing: First, although these processes form a logical or conceptual sequence, they should not be assumed to operate in a strictly sequential way; rather, the outcome of one process may reinvoke a preceding one. For example, realizing that an adequate coping response is readily available may cause the person to reappraise the situation as less threatening. As another example, if the use of a coping response turns out to be less effective than was expected, the person may reappraise the level of threat or reappraise what coping reaction is most appropriate to the situation.

A second elaboration stems from the fact that the preceding description was presented entirely in terms of threat appraisal. The theory actually holds that three kinds of events can give rise to stress. *Threat* appraisal occurs when a person anticipates the possibility that something harmful or unpleasant will occur. *Loss* appraisal occurs when a harmful or unpleasant outcome occurs and cannot be undone. Examples of loss appraisal include such events as bereavement, the ending of a relationship, or returning home to find one's house burned to the ground.

In contrast to these wholly negative appraisals, *challenge* appraisal occurs when the person anticipates the possibility of acquiring a good or desirable outcome, but also anticipates that doing so will not be easy. Many of the stressful situations in life involve combinations of threat and challenge. An obvious example is the experience of preparing for and taking an examination. This situation incorporates the possibility of an unpleasant outcome (a poor score), but it also holds out the possibility of a positive outcome (a good score). Challenge appraisals appear to mobilize effort in the same manner as threat appraisals, but they do not cause negative feelings. Thus, some have questioned whether events involving only challenge truly represent stress in the same sense as events involving threat.

A final point to make here is that coping occurs under circumstances that vary greatly in duration, and they vary in the extent to which they have distinct phases. Some stressful encounters take only a few seconds (e.g., having blood drawn), others play themselves out over minutes or hours (e.g., having an auto accident or coming home to find your house burglarized, and dealing with the aftermath). Some encounters develop over more extended periods (e.g., the diagnosis of and treatment for a serious illness may take weeks or

months). Sometimes acute events such as these occur with some forewarning (e.g., radio accounts of an oncoming line of severe storm clouds; the listing of the final exam date in a course syllabus; several weeks of pain before you finally make an appointment for a medical examination). Sometimes there is no warning (as in the discovery of a burglary). This difference also changes the nature of the transaction.

Even relatively brief encounters can have reverberations across time. For example, having your home ransacked by a burglar can create an emotional reaction that is long-lasting, though the event itself (discovery of the intrusion, calling the police, creating a list for the insurance company) may be relatively brief. Some kinds of stressful circumstances have reverberations that are even longer lasting. Acute stressors (in which there is a relatively circumscribed event) are different in important ways from chronic stressors, in which the circumstance that creates the threat or loss is in place for an extended period of time. For example, having a chronic illness or chronic pain—and having had it for the past three years—is a stressful experience that is very different from having a car accident.

When the event has an anticipatory phase, a crisis phase, and an aftermath phase, people's coping responses can be expected to vary as a function of the phase currently being experienced. This principle also suggests that coping with an acute stressor (in which phases are more distinct) may differ in important ways from coping that occurs in response to a chronic stressor (in which phases are more blurred together).

Ways of Coping

It should be clear from the preceding discussion that the concepts of stress and coping can be applied to a broad range of situations. It should also be clear that the stressful situations that people experience differ from one another in several ways. For example, in some stressful situations the person can do a great deal to change the situation for the better. This is often the case in situations where threat is mixed with challenge. In such situations—and in many other situations in which only threat is present—the person can mobilize efforts to do something about the situation being confronted. In other situations there is little the person can do but endure the stressful experience. This is more likely to be the case when the stress derives from a loss experience than when it derives from threat or challenge.

Problem-Focused and Emotion-Focused Coping. Not only do situations vary in several important ways, but so do the coping responses that the situations elicit from people. Lazarus and Folkman (1984) distinguished between two broad classes of coping reactions. What they called *problem-focused coping* is any response that is aimed at doing something to alter the source of the stress—removing, defusing, or avoiding the threatening event or altering its impact on the person. *Emotion-focused coping* is any response aimed at reducing or managing the negative feelings that arise in response to the threat or loss.

Although these two categories are easy to distinguish from each other in principle, both typically occur to some degree during every stressful transaction. Indeed, the effects of these two classes of coping can be difficult to disentangle. Emotion-focused coping removes some of the distress that can interfere with problem-focused efforts and can thereby make problem-focused coping easier. Similarly, problem-focused coping can render a threat less forbidding, thereby diminishing emotional distress. Moreover, certain kinds of coping reactions have both problem- and emotion-focused aspects. For example, people can make use of their social support resources both for advice and instrumental aid (problem focused) and for reassurance and comfort (emotion focused).

There is a certain parallelism between these two classes of coping reactions and the two classes of stressful situations that were described just beforehand. Although the match is far from perfect, it has often been noted that the balance between problem-focused and emotion-focused coping reactions tends to be influenced by the kind of situation the person is confronting. When the situation is one in which something can be done to change it, problem-focused coping tends to predominate. When the situation is one that must simply be endured, emotion-focused coping tends to predominate.

The distinction between problem- and emotion-focused coping is an important one. By itself, however, it does not go far enough to distinguish among meaningful classes of coping. For example, coping reactions that are in principle emotion focused are extremely varied. They range from the use of social support to positive reframing of the situation, to daydreaming, to wishful thinking and escapist fantasy, to making jokes about the stressful event, to heightened religious activity, to alcohol and drug use, and well beyond. It is important to recognize that such diverse types of coping may also differ in the effects they have. One important goal of research is to examine these coping reactions separately, to determine what their distinct effects are.

Avoidance Coping. Studies that have examined these coping reactions separately have found that not all of these responses are effective in diminishing negative feelings. In fact, there is considerable evidence that some kinds of coping responses actually make things *worse*. Some of the responses that seem to have this adverse effect have been termed *avoidance coping*. Such reactions include wishful thinking, escapist fantasy, denial, turning to alcohol, and overeating. Another response that seems to intensify distress is self-blame. The idea that some kinds of coping reactions are dysfunctional rather than helpful is an important one. Although most people probably think of coping as responses that are somehow effective in dealing with a problem, research on the effects of coping provides just as much evidence—and indeed maybe even more evidence—that certain kinds of coping responses can work against the person.

Research Issues

How do researchers determine what effects are caused by the various aspects of coping? Determining the effects of coping is somewhat more difficult than most people may realize. The research challenges are perhaps greater in this area of study than in many other areas of psychology. Several different types of research have been conducted, but none of them is completely without problems.

There is a very large set of studies in which subjects report two things at the same time: the ways in which they are currently coping with some stressor, and their current distress levels. (Some of these studies ask people to think back and report on a stressor from the recent past.) These studies typically find that avoidance coping is related to higher distress, and they sometimes find that other aspects of coping are related to lower distress. The problem with these studies is that it is impossible to tell from them whether the coping reaction is influencing the emotional distress, or whether the emotional distress is influencing the manner in which people cope. This problem always exists when the researcher measures the coping and the emotions at the same time point.

Prospective Research Designs. The best way to get around this problem (and the best kind of research design for studying naturally occurring coping) requires measuring coping reactions and emotions at more than one point during the period of stress (i.e., "prospective" design). That way, coping at Time 1 can be used as a predictor of emotions at the later time point, while controlling statistically for the emotions that were reported at Time 1. In the same way, emotions at Time 1 can be used to predict coping at Time 2, controlling for coping at Time 1. This is one way to disentangle which came first, the emotional responses or the coping.

This prospective design often has a problem of its own, though. Sometimes the situation changes enough between the two time points that the person's emotional responses at Time 2 are more likely to reflect the change in situation than to reflect the effects of coping. This is especially likely when the person is coping with a crisis of some sort, in which there is an anticipatory period, an event period, and a subsequent period of adjustment. Shifts in the psychological meaning of the situation from one phase to another can be dramatic and the person's feelings can also shift greatly from one phase to another. When the situation changes a lot between assessments, it can be hard to be sure that the influence of the coping responses on emotions has received a fair test.

Another problem in coping research is that most studies examine how people cope naturally with whatever stressor is under investigation. That is, subjects in these studies decide for themselves how to cope. Only rarely are coping responses experimentally manipulated. As a result, most of the research on coping examines individual differences in coping and how these individual differences relate to emotional well-being (or to some other outcome). This creates the same problem as is always encountered in individual differences research: It is very hard to determine whether the coping response produced the effect in the study or whether the effect was caused by some other variable that also differed between persons and was not being directly examined. This is a limitation that is inherent in all correlational research, although this point is often ignored in discussions of the effects of coping.

Personality and Coping. It was noted earlier that coping reactions can be expected to vary from one stage to another during a stressful encounter. This variation reflects the situational aspect of coping: engaging the coping response that matches the opportunities afforded by the current phase of the encounter. (As an example, most students engage the studying response before the exam rather than right after it.) However, there is also some basis for suggesting that people have more general coping "styles" that they tend to apply to most stressful situations. This doesn't mean that their coping isn't variable across phases, only that some people have a stronger tendency toward using certain responses than other people do.

Several theorists have suggested, for example, that people vary in their general tendencies to be vigilant toward stressors. Some people are intolerant of ambiguity or uncertainty, and try to resolve ambiguities in the situations they experience as quickly as possible. These people are especially vigilant to information implying threat, whereas others are less so. These two types of people thus can be expected to function differently in any threatening situation. Another variable often discussed in conjunction with this one is the person's tolerance of emotional arousal. People who have trouble with high arousal states will be inclined to cognitive avoidance when the situation contains cues implying threat.

Another approach to individual differences in coping styles rests on assumptions about the impact of confidence and doubt on people's coping. That is, people who are confident are more likely to engage in coping efforts designed to keep them in pursuit of their goals at any given phase of a transaction than people who

are doubtful. This approach also links the notion of coping style more explicitly to an aspect of personality—optimism versus pessimism. [See Optimism and Pessimism.] There is considerable evidence that people who are relatively optimistic tend to cope in different ways than people who are more pessimistic, even at the same stage of a particular transaction. Again, this does not mean that either kind of person is insensitive to changes in situation, but simply that one is more likely to engage in certain types of coping than the other, irrespective of those changes.

Assessment of Coping. In most research on the subject, coping reactions are assessed by self-report, using one of the many measures that have been published over the past 20 years. Since many of the coping reactions that researchers are interested in are intrapsychic, some of the information gained by these self-reports cannot be obtained in any other way. However, the use of self-report rating scales raises a host of issues. For one thing, ratings are often made retrospectively, even if the study itself is prospective. That is, sometimes people are asked to indicate how they have been coping with a particular problem "over the past week." This requires the person to mentally integrate information over a substantial period of time, raising the question of how well anyone can be expected to do at this task.

Another issue that is raised concerns the nature of the response choices. Often the options are very vague, requiring a judgment on the part of the respondent about the meaning of a response choice. What does it mean to say that you used a particular coping response "a lot" during the past week? Different people have different understandings of these response choices, and this creates a problem in interpretation.

An alternative procedure makes use of paging systems that ask the person to indicate what coping responses he or she is engaged in at that moment. This has the advantage of not requiring respondents to reflect on more than a few moments in time. It has the disadvantage of possibly forcing the person to make a rating at an inopportune time. Another alternative that is less demanding but still requires some retrospection is to assess people at the end of each day regarding that day. It should be apparent that either of these alternative procedures will generate considerably more data than would a procedure that assessed once a week or once a month. The additional complexity of the data required additional complexity in the data analysis. Nonetheless, this approach seems to be more likely to be followed in the future.

Conceptions of Coping: Final Issues

Although the Lazarus and Folkman (1984) model of stress and coping has had more influence on people's work in this area than any alternative model, ideas have also been advanced by others. For example, Hobfoll (1989) proposed a view of stress that relies on a principle he calls "conservation of resources." He assumes that people strive to build, retain, and protect resources of various types, and that the potential or actual loss of those resources is threatening and stress-inducing. Resources, in this view, are anything the individual values. Resources may be objects (e.g., house, car), conditions (e.g., status, seniority), energies (e.g., time, knowledge), or personal characteristics (e.g., self-esteem, optimism). People try to hold onto their resources, and when confronting threat their goal is to minimize resource loss. One implication of this view is that actual or potential loss lies at the heart of all stress.

Coping as Self-Regulation Under Adversity. The Lazarus and Folkman (1984) model of coping was initially proposed as a way of thinking about stress and coping per se (as is also true of Hobfoll's 1989 model). Discussions of this topic typically begin with these two concepts—stress and coping—as the point of departure. In so doing, they sometimes make the topic sound as though it stands separate from the rest of psychology. Stress can seem to be an exotic event that occurs only under special circumstances; coping can seem to be a special class of actions that differs in important ways from other actions. Such a picture would be misleading, however. Stress is part of almost everyone's everyday life, and coping is in many ways no different from any other behavior.

I have argued elsewhere that the elements of experience and behavior that are emphasized in models of stress and coping are more or less the same as those that are assumed in broader self-regulatory models of behavior-in-general. Today's models of behavior-in-general tend to rely on the assumption that behavior is goal directed. They also tend to assume that people have somewhat idiosyncratic construals of the world and of the consequences of their behavior. Finally, such models typically assume that behavior varies from person to person when obstacles interfere with attainment of (or even progress toward) desired goals. In particular, people who are confident of eventual success continue, or even amplify, their task-directed efforts. Those who are more doubtful do a variety of things that reflect an avoidance of continued effort toward the goal. Sometimes those who are more doubtful even give up the goal. Giving up is often painful and difficult, however, and it sometimes takes a long time to occur.

A comparison with the theoretical description that came earlier in this entry will reveal that the conceptual elements in the preceding paragraph are very similar to the elements in the Lazarus and Folkman model of stress. The resemblance is increased by adding some brief elaboration on the meaning of threat and loss: In this view, threat occurs when the attainability of some desired goal (or the avoidability of some undesired state) is interfered with. Loss occurs when the attainability (or avoidability) has been preempted altogether.

People sometimes respond to threats with renewed effort at goal attainment, they sometimes respond by trying to relax and reduce their distress, and they sometimes respond by giving up or by engaging in avoidance coping. Avoidance coping does not help the individual figure out how to move toward a goal, however, and it may actually interfere with such movement. For that reason it ultimately can have adverse rather than positive effects. When viewed from this angle, then, coping is simply a special label for what people do every time they encounter obstacles in life, whether temporary or permanent.

[See also Defense Mechanisms.]

Acknowledgments. The author's work was supported by the National Cancer Institute (CA64710).

Bibliography

Aldwin, C. M. (1994). *Stress, coping, and development: An integrative perspective.* New York: Guilford Press. Details a conceptual model of coping and personal development.

Carver, C. S., & Scheier, M. F. (1998). *On the self-regulation of behavior.* New York: Cambridge University Press. Includes a discussion of a self-regulatory model of motivation that uses principles consistent with the pattern of findings in the literature of coping.

Hobfoll, S. E. (1989). Conservation of resources: A new attempt at conceptualizing stress. *American Psychologist, 44,* 513–524. Describes a model of stress based on the idea that stress consists of loss of resources.

Lazarus, R. S. (1966). *Psychological stress and the coping process.* New York: McGraw-Hill. Original statement of highly influential theory of stress and coping.

Lazarus, R. S., & Folkman, S. (1984). *Stress, appraisal, and coping.* New York: Springer. A theoretical statement and research summary of work conducted by the authors and their collaborators, including discussion of the distinction between problem- and emotion-focused coping.

Pearlin, L. I., & Schooler, C. (1978). The structure of coping. *Journal of Health and Social Behavior, 19,* 2–21. An early theoretical statement on differing facets of coping.

Selye, H. (1976). *The stress of life.* New York: McGraw-Hill. An early discussion of psychological and physiological aspects of stress. (Original work published 1956)

Snyder, C. R. (Ed.). (1999). *Coping: The psychology of what works.* New York: Oxford University Press. A recent collection of chapters written by experts in coping, dealing primarily with effective and positive aspects of coping, and written in a relatively nontechnical style.

Zeidner, M., & Endler, N. S. (Eds.). (1996). *Handbook of coping: Theory, research, applications.* New York: Wiley. A recent large, eclectic collection of 27 chapters written by experts in the field of coping, dealing with aspects of coping ranging from assessment, to individual differences, to what aspects of coping are adaptive and problematic.

Charles S. Carver

CORONARY HEART DISEASE. Coronary atherosclerosis is a major predisposing factor for myocardical ischemia (deficiency of blood flow to cardiac muscle), which in turn is responsible for a number of clinical states, including angina pectoris, acute myocardial infarction (MI), and sudden cardiac death. Atherosclerosis is a progressive arterial disease process that generally begins in childhood and has its clinical manifestations in middle and late adulthood. Advanced lesions of atherosclerosis involve the proliferation of smooth muscle within the inner (luminal) portion of the artery, development of a matrix of fibrous connective tissue, and an accumulation of lipids. The advanced lesion of atherosclerosis is called an atheromatous plaque. Clinical events derive either from plaques totally occluding the lumen of affected arteries or from cracks and fissures developing in a lesion leading to thromboses (blood clots) or embolisms (obstructions caused by debris from the disrupted plaque).

Angina pectoris, which is one possible manifestation of coronary heart disease (CHD), refers to a relatively brief (less than 20 minutes) episode of chest pain due to myocardial ischemia. Anginal pain occurs when oxygen demand exceeds an adequate supply of oxygenated blood to the heart. Fixed-threshold angina typically occurs when patients with narrowed coronary arteries increase their oxygen demand through exercise. In contrast, variable-threshold angina usually occurs in patients with narrowed coronary arteries, when arterial vasoconstriction causes a dynamic obstruction (vasospasm) resulting in a decreased oxygen supply to the heart. Patients with variable-threshold angina often complain of anginal pain precipitated by cold temperatures, strong emotions, or meals. The relative contribution of narrowed coronary arteries and dynamic vasoconstriction varies widely among patients.

In the United States approximately 1.5 million people annually suffer an acute MI, and about one fourth of all deaths are due to MI. Over 60% of the deaths associated with acute MI occur within an hour of the event and are attributable to arrhythmias, particularly ventricular fibrillation (chaotic rapid twitching of ventricular muscle). When time and mode of death are unexpected and natural death due to cardiac causes occurs within an hour of the onset of terminal symptoms, the term *sudden cardiac death* is often used. Almost all myocardial infarctions result from atherosclerosis of the coronary arteries, generally with superimposed coronary thrombosis.

Risk Factors

A coronary risk factor is a variable that is statistically associated with the likelihood of developing CHD. In general, the more risk factors a person possesses, the greater the likelihood of developing CHD. Individuals who are likely to develop CHD can be identified with a moderate degree of accuracy. However, the number of risk factors is large, the nature of their interactions is complex, and causes of CHD tend to be multifactorial. Constitutional risk factors include advancing age, diabetes, dyslipidemia (particularly low levels of high-density lipoproteins and high levels of low-density lipoproteins), family history, hypertension, male sex, and obesity. Some of these variables such as advancing age and male sex are not modifiable, whereas under certain conditions the risks from others such as dyslipidemia, hypertension, and obesity may be modified.

The associations between behavioral risk factors and CHD have also been widely studied and are better understood today. These behavioral risk factors may be divided into lifestyle variables, individual psychosocial characteristics, and psychosocial-sociocultural factors. The lifestyle risk factors include cigarette smoking, lack of exercise, and adverse diet. Individual psychosocial characteristics include hostility, depression, and the Type A behavior pattern. Psychosocial-sociocultural variables include low socioeconomic status, lack of social support, and occupational and social stress.

Lifestyle Risk Factors. Cigarette smoking is a major risk factor for CHD and the greatest single preventable cause of premature death in the United States. In those with established CHD, smoking reduces the effectiveness of antianginal medications and appears to compromise the long-term benefits of thrombolytic agents used to prevent and treat heart attacks.

Physical inactivity is a significant and independent risk factor for CHD. The risk of CHD among sedentary people is approximately twice as high as in physically active individuals. Reduced mortality risk is more strongly associated with increased frequency and duration of exercise than in its intensity. The CHD risk profile of active individuals is better than that of sedentary individuals particularly in terms of blood pressure, lipoproteins, fibrinolysis (process involved in blood clotting), and insulin sensitivity (facilitated uptake of blood glucose).

The relationship between the high intake of saturated fats and high serum cholesterol makes this dietary variable a risk factor for CHD. Whereas fat is a major dietary culprit affecting CHD, other dietary habits such as high consumption of fruits and vegetables may be protective, particularly because of their potassium and antioxidant content.

Being overweight also increases the risk of CHD. Research indicates that distribution of body fat, independent of overall obesity is related to CHD. Thus, research indicates that intra-abdominal obesity, frequently indexed as a high ratio of waist-to-hip circumference, is associated with angina, MI, and cardiac death.

Individual Psychosocial Characteristics. Besides health habits and lifestyle behaviors, individual characteristics related to personality and emotions have been statistically associated with CHD. Several epidemiological studies, for instance, have shown that individuals revealing the Type A behavior pattern have about twice the risk as those who do not show this pattern. Type A behavior pattern is characterized by easily aroused hostility, a sense of time urgency, extreme competitiveness, and the tendency to deal with life as a perpetual struggle. The association between the Type A behavior pattern and CHD remains intact, even after statistical adjustments are made for other standard risk factors, such as elevated cholesterol, high blood pressure, family history of CHD, and smoking.

Because the Type A behavior pattern is defined in terms of a broad constellation of behavioral characteristics, and because Type A does not appear to predict CHD under all circumstances, researchers have investigated the separate components of the Type A behavior pattern to see if some components predict CHD better than others. This research has suggested that hostility is a particularly important predictor of CHD. Thus, for example, in a reanalysis of the large-scale Myocardial Risk Factor Intervention Trial (MRFIT), it was found that one component assessed by the Type A interview, "potential for hostility," predicted CHD events after controlling for established risk factors, whereas the global Type A behavior pattern did not. Similar findings emerged from a reanalysis of the Western Collaborative Group Study, which had originally identified Type A as a risk factor.

Whereas the Type A structured interview assesses the affective (frequent and intense experience of anger) and behavioral aspects of hostility (opposition, insults, and sarcasm), several studies have shown that the cognitive (cynicism and mistrust) component of hostility also predicts CHD. Thus, several retrospective studies have found that scores on the Minnesota Multiphasic Personality (MMPI)–based Cook-Medley Hostility scale were associated with CHD severity and all-cause mortality. Finally, the Normative Aging Study, which was a prospective study that assessed cognitive aspects of hostility using the revised MMPI, found that after controlling for other risk factors, hostility predicated all-cause mortality and to a lesser degree, morbidity from CHD.

Depressive symptoms, chronic exhaustion, and emotional drain have also been implicated as risk factors for CHD. Thus, higher rates of MI have been reported among depressed than nondepressed psychiatric patients. Another study reported that major depression preceded MI in 18% and minor depression in 27% of coronary patients. In contrast, the point prevalence of major depression in community samples of comparable age and gender is only 3%. Several other studies have reported that depression is associated with increased morbidity and mortality after MI or cardiac surgery. One study that is particularly noteworthy was a prospective study that used the modified *Diagnostic and Statistical Manual for Mental Disorders* to classify patients with major depressive disorders. That study found striking evidence of a fivefold greater risk of mortality among depressed, post-MI patients than among their nondepressed counterparts. The effect of depression was independent of ejection fraction and other clinical indicators of disease severity.

Another putative risk factor that in many respects resembles depression is "vital exhaustion." Vital exhaustion is said to be a mental state characterized by unusual fatigue, a feeling of being dejected or defeated, loss of libido, and increased irritability. The proportion of individuals experiencing this syndrome prior to a coronary event has been estimated at 30 to 50%. Several studies investigating the association of vital exhaustion and CHD found it to be positively associated with stable and unstable angina pectoris. Vital exhaustion has also predicted both restenosis after successful coronary angioplasty (enlargement of the lumen by balloon compression) and incidence of angina and nonfatal MI during a 4-year period.

Psychosocial and Sociocultural Variables. Psychosocial-sociocultural variables such as socioeconomic status, job strain, and low perceived social support have been linked to CHD morbidity and mortality. At least in contemporary Western industrialized countries there is a steep social gradient in CHD mortality rate as well as in mortality rates from other diseases. The relationship between socioeconomic status and CHD mortality rates is not due simply to a relationship between poor health and poverty. Research has shown that in Western industrialized countries each increment in socioeconomic status is accompanied by an improvement in cardiac morbidity and mortality rate, even among relatively affluent classes. In the United States, where mortality from CHD has declined steadily during the past 30 years, the decline has been steepest among those of higher socioeconomic status, thereby increasing the slope of the gradient between social position and health.

Although poor hygiene, inadequate nutrition, and lack of access to medical care undoubtably help to explain the negative effects of poverty among poor people, they do not explain differences in CHD between those in the middle and higher socioeconomic strata. Moreover, even in societies in which universal health care is provided, a steep socioeconomic status gradient is seen in terms of CHD. Although the exact reasons for the gradient relating socioeconomic status and CHD risk are not known, recent research has focused upon lack of tangible material and social support, people's perceived lack of control over their personal environment, job strain, and ecological stress.

Occupational activities are an important part of daily life for most adults. Job strain occurs when individuals hold demanding jobs that offer little opportunity for employee decision-making latitude. Initial studies conducted in the United States and Western Europe indicate that men working in demanding jobs that offer few rewards for good work, such as being employed on an assembly line, are at increased risk of MI. More recent data indicate that in terms of CHD prevalence, the joint action of high demand and lack of control (decision latitude) is particularly relevant to blue-collar men, whereas the joint action of lack of control and lack of social support is more important for women and white-collar men.

Several large-scale epidemiological studies have shown that men and women who are socially isolated are more likely to die prematurely from CHD compared with their counterparts who have better social integration. The association is especially strong among men. Social support has also been linked to survival and physical recovery in CHD and in MI patients. Thus, one study found that men with CHD who have low social support reveal three times the rate of mortality as non-isolated men. Another investigation reported a greater than fourfold increase in post-MI mortality for men who have low perceived support and high life stress. In another study, living alone was found to be an independent risk factor for a major cardiac event following MI. Still other studies have found that patients who are married at the time of an MI are significantly less likely to die during hospitalization or in the following year than unmarried patients. Finally, for elderly men and women hospitalized with MI, the presence of emotional support prior to the MI has been found to be the most powerful and consistent predictor of survival after the MI.

Conclusions. Initial findings from the Framingham Study identified cigarette smoking, high blood pressure, elevated serum cholesterol, and advancing age as risk factors for CHD. However, knowledge about these risk factors, either alone or in combination, fails to predict most new cases of CHD. Subsequent research has indicated that a large number of biological, psychosocial, and sociocultural variables are associated with CHD. In order to understand the causes underlying the statis-

tical associations between risk factors and CHD, it is necessary to improve the specification of risk factors. This, of course, applies to biological as well as to behavioral variables.

Consider the metabolism of plasma lipids. Initially, total serum cholesterol, a major class of plasma lipids, was associated with an increased risk of CHD. Soon it became apparent that levels of cholesterol-bearing lipoproteins are related to the process of atherogenesis. Thus, it was found that elevated levels of low-density lipoprotein cholesterol and low levels of high-density lipoprotein cholesterol, both of which are constituents of total serum cholesterol, are individually more predictive of CHD than is total cholesterol alone.

In much the same way, initial studies of the Type A behavior pattern showed that under certain conditions the behavior pattern is associated with CHD risk. Subsequent research identified hostility as a key component conveying risk, which in turn led to further studies investigating cognitive and affective-behavioral components of hostility in relationship to CHD. The extensive research relating lifestyle, individual psychosocial characteristics, and psychosocial-sociocultural factors to CHD is likely to help us study underlying causal processes by better specifying relevant variables and the nature of their interactions.

Disease Processes and Behavior

Investigations into the causes and manifestations of symptomatic CHD usually distinguish between long-term pathogenic processes that underlie vulnerability to clinical manifestations of CHD such as atherosclerosis, and short-term acute events that constitute the symptomatic expression of CHD, such as angina pectoris, MI, and sudden cardiac death. Data suggest that behavioral factors play an important role in both the development and triggering of CHD events.

Atherosclerosis. As previously mentioned, atherosclerosis is a progressive arterial disease process that generally begins in childhood and has its clinical manifestations in middle and late adulthood. The early lesions of atherosclerosis can usually be found in children and very young adults in the form of fatty streaks. These fatty streaks consist primarily of lipid-laden macrophages (mononucleated cells that are largely scavengers, ingesting dead tissues and degenerated cells) along with lipid-filled smooth muscle cells that accumulate beneath them as the lesions increase in size. The bulk of the lipid is in the form of cholesterol and cholesterol ester, which appear to enter the fatty streak by transport of lipoproteins from the plasma via the endothelial cells that line the intimal surface of the artery. These plasma lipids taken up in the intima are ingested by macrophages and are hydrolyzed and reesterified once they are taken up. Over time fatty streaks occupy increasing areas of the coronary arteries and these sites precede the formation of advanced lesions.

The advanced lesions of atherosclerosis, which are found in mature adults, are called atheromatous plaques. These lesions consist of large numbers of proliferated intimal smooth muscle cells as well as numerous macrophages and T-lymphocytes. The macrophages and smooth muscle cells contain cholesterol and cholesterol ester; the proliferated smooth muscle cells are surrounded by collagen, elastic fibers, and proteoglycan. In individuals with elevated serum cholesterol, a fair amount of lipid is deposited in the cells and in the connective tissue. Characteristically, atheromatous plaques are covered by a fibrous cap. The principal clinical consequences of the advanced atheromas stem either from their partially or totally occluding the lumen of the artery or because cracks and fissures in the lesions lead to thrombosis or embolism.

Because atheromas take many years to develop and lead to clinical manifestations, animal models have been developed in order to study the progression of atherosclerosis. Nonhuman primates provide a reasonable model of coronary artery atherosclerosis in humans and develop the disease readily when fed high cholesterol diets. By studying the interaction of stress and diet in nonhuman primates, researchers have been able to learn a great deal about the contribution of psychosocial factors to atherosclerotic disease progression. A particularly useful model for studying behavioral contributions to atherogenesis has used cynomolgus monkeys, because interference with their ordinarily stable social group relationships is particularly stressful.

Cynomolgus monkeys normally live in small social groups, characterized by stable relationships and a dominance hierarchy. While there is an overall hierarchy led by a dominant male monkey, separate hierarchies can also be identified for males and females as well as for mature versus immature animals.

When cynomolgus monkeys are housed experimentally in separate small social groups, periodically redistributing these animals requires them to reestablish dominance hierarchies and affiliative relationships. Under such circumstances, high-status males (dominant monkeys) develop more extensive coronary atherosclerosis than do lower status animals (subordinate monkeys). Because this does not occur in dominant monkeys housed in stable colonies, the results suggest that the demands of maintaining dominant status in an unstable, stressful social environment lead to atherosclerosis.

The sympathetic-adrenomedullary (SAM) axis of the nervous system plays an important role in increasing metabolic and cardiovascular activity during stressful situations. During situations perceived as threatening, particularly those involving fight-flight, norepinephrine is released from sympathetic nerve terminals and epinephrine and norepinephrine are released from the adrenal medulla.

In order to examine the role of the SAM axis in the development of atherosclerosis in dominant male monkeys following social reorganization, reorganized animals were given chronic administration of a sympathetic nervous system antagonist (beta adrenergic blockade). It was found that administering the beta blocker propranolol to the stressed monkeys prevented the exacerbation of atherosclerosis in socially dominant monkeys. The results were apparently not due to changes in behaviors, which were carefully monitored.

Social reorganization has also been used to study the development of atherosclerosis in female cynomolgus monkeys. Interestingly, among female monkeys, social behavior is as strongly related to atherosclerosis as in males, although quite differently. Thus, among females subjected to social reorganization, it is the subordinate rather than the dominant animal that shows increased atherogenesis. The effect appears to be due to a disruption of the estrous cycle, which is induced by the social subordination.

Several studies have shown that it is the loss of ovarian function, whether it is partial, as induced by behavior, or complete, as induced by surgical removal of the ovaries, that deprives females of their protection against atherosclerosis. Conversely, research has shown that administration of oral contraceptives retards the development of atherosclerosis in female cynomolgus monkeys. This is especially the case in subordinate as opposed to dominant female monkeys living in unstable social situations. To the extent that atherogenesis in cynomolgus monkeys is similar to that in humans, the use of exogenous estrogens may retard the development of atherosclerosis.

The high cholesterol-fed monkey model has also been used to study the role of cardiovascular reactivity in atherogenesis. Thus, the monkeys that reveal the greatest heart rate responses to an external stressor develop the most extensive atherosclerosis. The association between heart rate reactivity and atherosclerosis is observed in both female and male monkeys and in both ovulating and ovariectomized females. Similar findings have been reported in an epidemiological study of Finnish men in which cardiovascular reactivity to laboratory stressors predicted noninvasive measurements of intimal medial thickness of the carotid artery, which provides an estimate of carotid artery atherosclerosis.

Myocardial Ischemia. When atherosclerosis retards blood flow through the coronary arteries it can cause myocardial ischemia, the inadequate flow of blood to cardiac tissue. Research on cynomolgus monkeys reveals that in the presence of significant atherosclerosis, chronic social stress can impair the vasomotion of the coronary arteries. Thus, when the coronary arteries of the stressed monkeys are infused with acetylcholine, which ordinarily causes vasodilation, the monkeys reveal a paradoxical constriction (vasospasm) of the arteries.

Transient myocardial ischemia has also been demonstrated in human CHD patients in response to stressors. Thus, for example, electrocardiographic monitoring of such patients has shown that mental stress during daily life can trigger transient myocardial ischemia, which is comparable to that elicited by strenuous physical exercise. Similarly, laboratory research has shown that acute psychological stress can provoke myocardial ischemia in about half of CHD patients. This ischemia mostly occurs among patients who also reveal ischemia in response to physical exercise. However, it usually occurs at a lower heart rate than the ischemia evoked by exercise, but at a comparable blood pressure level.

The relationship between angina pectoris and myocardial ischemia is not always clear. Patients may have either painful or silent episodes of ischemia or they may have both. Those with psychological traits such as anxiety or depression are more likely to report anginal pain. Depression appears to be related to a decreased threshold for anginal pain as well as to a decreased release of beta-endorphin in response to aerobic exercise. In general, aerobic exercise is more likely to trigger painful episodes of ischemia, whereas mental stress is more likely to trigger silent episodes.

Myocardial Infarction. Almost all myocardial infarctions result from atherosclerosis of the coronary arteries, usually with superimposed coronary thrombosis. In about half of patients with acute MI, no precipitating factor can be identified. However, a significant number of acute MIs occur after severe physical exertion in people who are in poor physical condition, often when they are unduly fatigued or emotionally stressed. Such infarctions could be the result of marked increases in myocardial oxygen demand, vasospasm, and/or plaque disruption in the presence of severe coronary arterial narrowing.

Emotional stressors, even in the absence of physical exertion, have often been reported to trigger an acute MI. Acute increase in oxygen demand, functional obstruction of the coronary arteries due to vasospasm, plaque disruption, and thrombus formation can be involved. Activation of the SAM system can also increase the vulnerability of the ischemic heart to ventricular arrhythmias and promote thromboses by increasing blood viscosity and stimulating blood platelet activity. Finally, the withdrawal of parasympathetic nervous system (vagus nerve) influence upon the heart can have an adverse effect upon the heart rhythm.

Research studies have revealed a pronounced circadian periodicity for the time of onset of acute MI. Peak onset occurs at about 9:00 a.m. The early morning hours are associated with rises in plasma catecholamines and cortisol, an increase in platelet aggregability, and narrowed coronary arterial lumina. This provides the background for the onset of daily activities associated with awakening, such as changes in posture, planning one's daily schedule, and hurrying to work.

Although most acute MIs are accompanied by severe and often intolerable pain, this is not invariably the case. Thus, some MIs are unrecognized by patients and are discovered only on subsequent routine electrocardiographic or postmortem examinations. Often, however, patients experience prolonged pain lasting more than 30 minutes. Frequently the pain is described as crushing, compressing, squeezing, or viselike. The pain is usually retrosternal in location, but may radiate considerably with predilection for the left side or arm. Because the pain often disappears suddenly and completely once blood flow is restored to the damaged myocardium, it has become apparent that what was initially believed to be the pain of infarction represents pain caused by ongoing severe ischemia. Thus, the immediate relief of the pain is not only a matter of comfort, but also a practical necessity.

Primary Prevention of CHD

Two theoretically different approaches have been adopted toward CHD prevention. One of these, a *high-risk strategy*, is directed toward intervening with individuals who are at high risk for CHD. The second, or *population-based*, strategy is directed toward reducing risk in an entire population.

Several clinical trials, such as the Oslo Heart Study in Norway and MRFIT in the United States, identified high-risk individuals by mass screening. They then intervened to reduce CHD risk factors and disease incidence. Both studies were successful in demonstrating evidence of risk-factor reduction associated with a significant decrease in CHD incidence when compared with population norms.

Meaningful evaluation of treatment effects in MRFIT, was compromised because many of the "high-risk" men in the control group apparently reduced risk behaviors on their own. This seems to have been a situation in which a change in the social environment—some of which seems to have been induced by media publicity surrounding the trial—and perhaps a readiness for change evidenced by those willing to volunteer for the trial, confounded the study design. In any event, MRFIT failed to show significant differences between the treatment and control groups. In contrast, the Oslo Heart Study convincingly demonstrated significant differences between the intervention and control groups, both in terms of risk-factor reduction and CHD incidence.

A wide range of techniques are now available for targeting CHD-risk behaviors. In some instances, based on the specificity of the problem and patient motivation, the clinical approach may suggest targeting a single unhealthful behavior such as smoking. In other cases, such as with sedentary, overweight patients who may be hypertensive, or dyslipidemic, a multiple risk factor intervention may be preferable. Results from such trials as the Oslo Heart Study suggest that multimodal interventions can be effective. When patients become concerned that they are at high risk, and thus seek help, a window of opportunity is opened for introducing a high-risk intervention strategy. This may occur within a primary health-care setting or within the context of secondary prevention in a cardiological venue. In either case, the intervention strategy should prominently involve changing the behaviors of high-risk patients.

In contrast to the high-risk intervention approach, the population-based strategy attempts to change the habits of an entire population, including those who are not recognized as being at high risk. Part of the justification for this population-based strategy is that most coronary events and deaths due to CHD occur in people with only moderately elevated risk. In any event, application of a population-based strategy depends on skillful use of the media and community action to communicate and encourage health-promoting knowledge and practices. Examples of this strategy include the North Karelia Project in Finland as well as the Stanford Five-City Project (California) and the Minnesota Heart Health Program in the United States. All of these projects appear to have achieved their goals, although the changes obtained in North Karelia appear to be the most dramatic and persuasive. In part, this is related to the intensity and duration of the study (more than two decades), and in part to cooperation that existed among investigators, industry, and government.

Secondary Prevention of CHD

Cardiovascular disease is the leading cause of morbidity and mortality in the United States. Almost 1.5 million Americans sustain an MI each year with more than 1 million surviving. These 1 million survivors, along with 7 million stable angina and 300,000 percutaneous transluminal coronary angioplasty (PTCA) patients, represent a pool of CHD patients who could benefit from coronary rehabilitation services.

Following MI, CABG, or PTCA, some bed rest is required although early mobilization is more common than in the past. Unfortunately, skeletal muscle mass decreases 10 to 15% within a week of bed rest. Pulmonary abnormalities include diminished lung volume and vital capacity and an increased respiratory exchange ratio. Absence of the orthostatic stress of upright posture decreases venous capacitance and blunts the normal postural vasomotor reflexes. This, in turn, leads to diminished venous return, postural hypoten-

sion, and tachycardia. However, as little as three hours daily of upright posture significantly diminishes the deconditioning effects of bed rest.

Controlled studies of cardiac rehabilitation exercise training indicate that exercise training improves exercise tolerance and decreases angina symptoms, but does not change the rate of nonfatal reinfarction. Studies of data pooled across clinical trials, however, indicate that cardiovascular and all-cause mortality are reduced by cardiac rehabilitation exercise training.

Aside from exercise training, a variety of psychosocial, educational, and lifestyle interventions have been implemented to treat CHD patients in general, and post-MI patients in particular. Although most studies have reported positive results in terms of improved quality of life and/or risk factor reductions, the small number of subjects enrolled in most studies has precluded adequate assessment in terms of reinfarction or mortality. A meta-analysis of psychosocial intervention studies, however, has reported significant decreases in morbidity and mortality rates. Thus, when psychosocial interventions are added to traditional rehabilitation regimens including pharmacotherapy, the meta-analysis indicated that there was a 46% reduction in nonfatal cardiac events and a decrease in mortality of 40% beyond that found with pharmacotherapy alone.

One randomized clinical trial included in the meta-analysis was the Recurrent Coronary Prevention Project. This trial taught post-MI patients to identify stressful situations, modify maladaptive habitual responses to these situations, and relax. The intervention was conducted in a supportive group setting. It was reported that patients participating in the intervention experienced almost a 50% reduction in recurrence of CHD events compared with patients receiving usual care.

Several studies have used multifactorial behavioral interventions to improve risk factors in patients with CHD. In some studies researchers have targeted multiple risk factors and have included multimodal interventions. Preliminary evidence indicates that an intensive behavioral program that combines stress management with dietary modification and exercise can promote the regression of coronary atherosclerosis. Because study samples have been relatively small, it is not yet known whether the reduction in risk factors observed is associated with a significant decrease in cardiovascular mortality and/or MI recurrence. Nevertheless, the results appear to be promising.

[See also Hypertension.]

Bibliography

Case, R. B., Moss, A. J., Case, N., McDermott, M., & Eberly, S. (1992). Living alone after myocardial infarction: Impact on prognosis. *Journal of the American Medical Association, 267*, 515–519. Living alone was an independent risk factor for a major cardiac event following myocardial infarction (MI).

Frasure-Smith, N., Lesperance. F., & Talajic, M. (1993). Depression following myocardial infarction: Impact on 6-month survival. *Journal of the American Medical Association, 270*, 1819–1825. Major depression was a significant predictor of cardiac mortality in post-MI patients, even after controlling for left ventricular dysfunction and previous MI.

Friedman, M., Thoresen, C. E., Gill, J. J., Ulmer, D., Powell, L. H., Price, V. A., Brown, B., Thompson, L., Rabin, D. D., Breall, W. S., Bourg, E., Levy, R., & Dixon, T. (1986). Alteration of Type A behavior and its effects on cardiac recurrences in post myocardial infarction patients. *American Heart Journal, 112*, 653–665. Post-MI patients taught to identify stressful situations, modify maladaptive behaviors, and relax showed a 50% reduction in recurrence of CHD events compared with patients receiving usual care.

Kaplan, G. A., Salonen, J. T., Cohen, R. D., Brand, R. J., Puska, P., & Syme, S. L. (1988). Social connections and mortality from all causes and cardiovascular disease: Prospective evidence from Eastern Finland. *American Journal of Epidemiology, 128*, 370–380. Lack of social ties was related to long-term mortality risk in a large-scale epidemiological study.

Kaplan, J. R., Manuck, S. B., Adams, M. R., Weingand, K. W., & Clarkson, T. B. (1987). Inhibition of coronary atherosclerosis by propanolol in behaviorally predisposed monkeys fed an atherogenic diet. *Circulation, 76*, 1364–1372. Chronic administration of a beta-adrenergic blocking agent prevented exacerbation of atherosclerosis in stressed, socially dominant male monkeys without changing behavior.

Krantz, D. S., Kop, W. J., Santiago, H. T., & Gottdiener, J. S. (1996). Mental stress as a trigger of myocardial ischemia and infarction. *Cardiology Clinics, 14*(2), 217–287. Mental stress during daily life can trigger transient myocardial ischemia in CHD patients, which is comparable to that elicited by strenuous physical exercise.

Linden, W., Stossel, C., & Maurice, J. (1996). Psychosocial interventions for patients with coronary artery disease: A meta-analysis. *Archives of Internal Medicine, 156*, 745–752. When psychosocial interventions are added to traditional rehabilitation regimens, including pharmacotherapy, significant decreases occur in morbidity and mortality rates.

Orth-Gomér, K., & Schneiderman, N. (1996). *Behavioral medicine approaches to cardiovascular disease prevention.* Mahwah, NJ: Erlbaum. This volume examines the social environment in relation to CHD risk, reviews the psychosocial and biobehavioral processes involved, and describes behavioral medicine interventions that have been applied to primary and secondary CHD prevention.

Ruberman, W., Weinblatt, E., Golberg, J. D., & Chaudhary, B. S. (1984). Psychosocial influences on mortality after myocardial infarction. *New England Journal of Medicine, 311*, 552–559. Men experiencing low perceived social support and high life stress showed more than a four-fold post-MI increase in mortality rate.

Williams, R. B., Barefoot, J. C., Califf, R. M., Haney, T. L., Saunders, W. B., Pryor, D. B., Hlatky, M. A., Siegler, I. C., & Mark, D. B. (1992). Prognostic importance of social and economic resources among medically treated patients with angiographically documented coronary artery disease. *Journal of the American Medical Association, 267*, 520–524. CHD patients who were unmarried or reported no one in whom they could confide had a significantly lower 5-year survival rate than patients who were married and/or had a confidant.

Neil Schneiderman

CORRELATION. *See* Measures of Association.

CORRESPONDENT INFERENCE. *See* Attribution Theories.

COST-BENEFIT ANALYSIS. The relationship between what a psychological procedure or program accomplishes and the value of resources consumed by that procedure or program is measured by means of cost-benefit analysis and cost-effectiveness analysis.

Cost-benefit analysis measures the outcomes of psychological procedures or programs in monetary units, such as income generated or costs saved. The net benefit of a procedure or program is calculated by subtracting costs from benefits. Other measures of cost-benefit are the ratio of benefits to costs and the time required until benefits equal costs (time to return on investment). In psychological research, the net benefit of a treatment often is calculated for each patient or client, and then is summed or averaged to describe the cost-benefit of the treatment. Often, the largest benefit assessed in cost-benefit analysis of therapy and other psychological interventions is the *cost offset*—the money saved because clients no longer need other, more costly services. The net benefit (benefits minus costs) of psychotherapy often is positive, especially for surgery preparation and prevention of health problems. If some benefits are delayed by several years, but costs are immediate, the value of delayed benefits must be discounted to show their *present value*.

Researchers can measure the cost-benefit of different psychological procedures for different clients and different problems. The cost-benefit of psychological programs for many problems, including substance abuse, anxiety, and depression, is being researched with increasing rigor. The findings of cost-benefit analysis often are used to shape policy and make decisions about whether to fund psychological services and which services to fund most. The monetary benefits of some psychological treatments have been shown to be more than worth the costs of those treatments for some clients. Although initial findings are positive, the lack of standardized procedures for measuring costs and benefits, plus the variety of psychological procedures investigated, prevent firm conclusions at present about the universal cost-benefit of psychotherapy or other psychological procedures.

In contrast to cost-benefit analysis, *cost-effectiveness analysis* measures outcomes in their "natural" units, such as decreases in anxiety or depression, improved job performance, or reduced use of medical or social services. Cost-effectiveness analysis has been used to compare the effectiveness of different treatments and programs. Effectiveness and costs of alternative treatments can be compared separately, but more useful cost-effectiveness analyses analyze the strength of relationships between specific costs, procedures, processes, and outcomes using ratios, graphs, matrices, or more complex mathematical models such as structural equation modeling or path analysis.

Careful assessment of the cost and effectiveness or benefit of each component of the therapeutic procedure enables treatment managers to adjust implementation of program procedures to maximize the effectiveness of treatment within budget (cost) constraints. With sufficiently detailed information on the costs and effectiveness of each element of treatment, it also may be possible to minimize the cost of achieving a prespecified degree of effectiveness. Data on costs, procedures, psychosocial processes, and outcomes can be used to optimize cost-effectiveness and cost-benefit using linear programming methods available in most spreadsheet software.

Bibliography

Gold, M. R., Siegel, J. E., Russell, L. B., & Weinstein, M. C. (Eds.). (1996). *Cost-effectiveness in health and medicine.* New York: Oxford University Press. Report of an expert panel appointed by the U.S. Public Health Service. Makes recommendations for improving and standardizing measurement of costs and outcomes, and the analysis of cost-effectiveness in medicine and related areas. Of particular relevance to cost-benefit analysis of psychological programs for preventing health problems and for facilitating medical service delivery.

Nas, T. F. (1996). *Cost-benefit analysis: Theory and application.* Thousand Oaks, CA: Sage. Accessible, authoritative, readable methods of cost-benefit analysis for program evaluation.

Newman, F. L., & Sorensen, J. E. (1985). *Integrated clinical and fiscal management in mental health: A guidebook.* Norwood, NJ: Ablex. Early leaders in evaluation of the cost and cost-effectiveness of mental health services provide theory, practical examples, and worksheets for using cost-effectiveness analysis in program management.

Yates, B. T. (1980). *Improving effectiveness and reducing costs in mental health.* Springfield, IL: Charles C. Thomas. The first half describes measurement of costs and effectiveness. The second half illustrates how specific operations research procedures can be used to describe and optimize cost-effectiveness in psychological services.

Yates, B. T. (1996). *Analyzing costs, procedures, processes, and outcomes in human services.* Thousand Oaks, CA: Sage. Introduction to using Cost → Procedure → Process → Outcome Analysis (CPPOA) to measure and improve cost-effectiveness and cost-benefit in a variety of psychological services.

Brian T. Yates

COUNSELING PROCESS AND OUTCOME. There are two fundamental questions for counseling researchers and practitioners: Does counseling work, and if so, how does it work? Outcome studies seek to answer the former question while process studies address the latter question. Process and outcome research are often defined in relation to one another. Outcome research attempts to address efficacy questions. Thus, outcome research is characterized by designs that compare a treatment group to a control group, or compare several different types of counseling treatments. Process research, on the other hand, attempts to characterize the changes that occur during counseling. Process research is the study of the counseling interaction that involves the counselor, the client, and the evolving relationship.

Outcome Research

In their book, *Research Design in Counseling*, Heppner, Kivlighan, and Wampold (1999) describe six types of outcome research: (1) treatment package, (2) comparative outcome, (3) client and therapist variation, (4) parametric, (5) constructive, and (6) dismantling. These types of studies are used as an organizing principle for reviewing counseling outcome research.

Treatment package studies predominated in early counseling research. Researchers compare people in a treatment condition (e.g., those receiving counseling) to those in a control condition (not receiving counseling), on a variety of outcome measures. An outcome measure is a variable (i.e., self-esteem) that is presumably affected by the counseling. While this type of research seems simple and straightforward there is a good deal of disagreement among researchers as to what constitutes an appropriate control group. Nevertheless, the pioneer counseling researchers used the treatment package studies to show that counseling was effective.

Because counseling often occurred in an educational setting, early counseling researchers frequently used measures of academic success (e.g., grade point averages) or satisfaction with counseling as their outcome criteria. In addition, these early researchers tended to study counseling generically. Contemporary counseling researchers tend to use precisely defined counseling interventions (e.g., cognitive-relaxation coping skills training) and a broad spectrum of outcome criteria. Treatment manuals and adherence measures are the hallmarks of contemporary treatment package research. Treatment manuals consist of (1) a description of the principles and techniques that characterize the particular counseling approach; (2) detailed examples of how and when to apply the principles and techniques; and (3) a scale to determine how closely the counseling conforms (adherence measure) to the principles and techniques described in the manual.

There are a number of reviews summarizing research using the treatment package strategy. These reviews conclude that counseling, in general, is effective. Specifically, the average counseled person is better adjusted and experiences less distress than the average noncounseled person.

Once researchers established that counseling, in general, was effective, they then began using the comparative outcome studies to examine the relative effectiveness of specific counseling approaches. This has usually been framed as finding the best counseling approach. In comparative outcome studies researchers compare the efficacy of two or more treatments. Early comparative outcome studies compared loosely defined treatments. For example, "client-centered permissive counseling procedures and materials" and "highly structured counselor-centered procedures" were compared (Forgy & Black, *Journal of Counseling Psychology*, 1954, *1*, 1–8). Contemporary comparative outcome studies use highly specified treatments (e.g., cognitive-relaxation coping skills training and social skills training) and treatment differentiation measures in addition to treatment manuals and adherence measures. Treatments are differentiated when they are shown to differ from each other along the dimensions that are central to their execution.

A meta-analysis by Wampold, Mondin, Moody, Stich, Benson, and Ahn (*Psychological Bulletin*, 1997, *122*, 203–215) examined all treatment comparison studies. The mean effect size for these comparisons was zero, indicating that the efficacy of bona fide treatments is roughly equivalent. Based on this finding, Wampold argued that we have spent too much time examining the least important aspects of counseling (differences among treatments) and not enough time examining the more important aspects of counseling (e.g., differences

among counselors; Wampold, *Psychotherapy Research*, 1997, *7*, 21–43).

The question posed in comparative outcome studies is probably too simplistic. As Paul initially suggested, a more appropriate question is, Which treatments delivered by which counselors are effective with which types of clients, in which settings? Client and therapist variation studies attempt to answer this question, by examining attribute by treatment interaction (ATI). ATI research systematically varies client or counselor characteristics and aspects of counseling treatments in attempting to discover optimal matches.

Unfortunately, there is not a great deal of ATI research. From a meta-analysis of counselor effects, we know that some counselors are more effective than other counselors. The source of these differential counselor effects, however, is unclear. Additionally, some research suggests that the interpersonal orientation of clients may interact with the interpersonal demands of the treatment setting to optimize treatment effectiveness. Specifically, people-oriented clients respond favorably to interactive treatment approaches while less socially oriented clients benefit from impersonal, self-directed treatments.

In parametric studies, researchers examine how variations in the structure of the treatment affect client outcome. In particular, counseling researchers have used parametric studies to examine the effects of treatment modality and treatment length. In terms of treatment modality, a number of studies compared individual versus group counseling. A meta-analysis of these studies (Tillitski, *International Journal of Group Psychotherapy*, 1990, *40*, 215–224) found that group and individual treatments had equivalent effects. Another group of studies examined the temporal aspects of counseling. These studies suggest that time-limited counseling is as effective as time-unlimited counseling and that shorter sessions are as effective as longer sessions.

In constructive and dismantling studies researchers try to identify the effective ingredients of counseling by adding to (constructive) or taking away from (dismantling) established treatment packages. Constructive and dismantling studies have generally been limited to research on social skills training. In these studies researchers have examined the relative effectiveness of modeling, practice, and feedback on the learning of social skills. These studies suggest that modeling, practice, and feedback each make an independent contribution to social skills training and that treatments are more effective when these components are delivered in combination.

While counseling outcome research has come a long way there are still a number of important issues that counseling outcome researchers have not successfully confronted. Outcome research has been dominated by treatment package, comparative outcome and to a lesser extent parametric studies. At this point in time ATI, constructive and dismantling studies have the most potential to further our knowledge of counseling outcome. There has been a significant increase in the use of treatment manuals in outcome studies. However, formal adherence measures designed for the specific treatment being investigated are rarely used. In addition, counseling research has not addressed the critical issue of counselor competence. These are just a few of the issues that counseling outcome researchers must address if this area of the discipline is to advance.

Counseling Process Studies

Process research characterizes the changes that occur during counseling. Process research is the study of the counseling interaction that involves the counselor(s), client(s), and the evolving relationship. Because process research has not been a central focus of counseling research, it is impossible to provide an in-depth review of this area. Rather, the principal topics and themes that characterize counseling process research are examined. Specifically, the major systematic investigations of counseling process are Carl Rogers's client-centered therapy, Strong's social influence model, counseling language, and the counseling relationship.

Carl Rogers is the progenitor of counseling process research. His opening up the counseling hour to recording initiated a major advance in understanding the interactions that took place between counselors and clients. More important, however, his theory of the necessary and sufficient conditions for counseling (e.g., counselor empathy, client experiencing) gave rise to both process measures and to specific testable process hypotheses (Rogers, *Journal of Counseling Psychology*, 1957, *2*, 95–103). Much of the early process literature involved measurement of these necessary and sufficient conditions.

Researchers either had outside observers rate the counselor's empathy, genuineness, and congruence or obtained the client's perception of these conditions. One of the interesting aspects of the research examining counselor empathy is the divergence of findings on the connection between counselor empathy and counseling outcome. Whereas observer ratings of empathy are generally unrelated to client outcome, client ratings of counselor empathy are moderately related to client outcome.

Rogers's theory also led to the development of several client-oriented process measures, one of which was the Client Experiencing scale (Klein, Mathieu-Coughlan, & Kiesler, in Greenberg & Pinsof, Eds., *The Psychotherapeutic Process: A Research Handbook*, New York, 1986). The Client Experiencing scale captures the essential quality of a client's involvement in counseling. More than 100 published studies have used the Client Experiencing scale to rate client behavior, group interactions, therapist behavior, and standardized assessment interviews. Studies have spanned the breadth of therapeutic orientations and examined the relationship between experiencing and personality, counselor conditions or interventions, and counseling outcome. Client experiencing is widely acknowledged as a crucial process dimension.

A second major area of counseling process research examining was initiated by Stanley Strong (*Journal of Counseling Psychology*, 1968, *15*, 215–224). Strong applied attitude change theory developed by social psychologists to the process of counseling. Specifically, he hypothesized that counseling was a two-stage process. In the first stage the counselor attempts to build up her or his power base and in the second stage she or he uses this power base to influence the client. A counselor's power or ability to influence a client was related to three counselor characteristics: expertness, attractiveness, and trustworthiness. These characteristics were operationalized in a widely used counseling process measure, the Counselor Rating Form (Barak & LaCrosse, *Counselor Education and Supervision*, 1977, *16*, 202–208.)

Expertness, attractiveness, and trustworthiness ratings have been used as both dependent and independent variables in research examining Strong's social influence paradigm. In short, a large body of research has examined the influence of various independent variables (diplomas, communication style) on client ratings of attractiveness, expertness, and trustworthiness. Another group of studies has examined the relationship of client-rated attractiveness, expertness, and trustworthiness to client outcome. A meta-analysis of these studies suggests that, as hypothesized by Strong (1968), (1) therapist cues (nonverbal behavior) are reliably related to the client's perception of the counselor as expert, attractive, and trustworthy, (2) expertness, attractiveness, and trustworthiness are strongly related to influence; and (3) the client's perception of the counselor at least partially mediates the relationship between cues and influence (Hoyt, *Journal of Counseling Psychology*, 1996, *43*, 430–447). Additionally, Hoyt showed that nonverbal cues are the most important determinant of client perceptions of expertness, attractiveness, and trustworthiness. Social influence theory has retained its great heuristic value because theoretical developments from social psychological research have continually informed the model.

Whereas the process research initiated by Carl Rogers and Stanley Strong emanates from clear theoretical positions, other process researchers have examined counseling interactions from an atheoretical perspective. An advantage of an atheoretical approach is that researchers can examine commonalities in counseling process. Client and counselor language provides a

COUNSELING PROCESS AND OUTCOME 315

atheoretical framework for examining counseling interactions. Francis P. Robinson (*Journal of Counseling Psychology*, 1955, 2, 163–169) and his students were
among the first to examine the language used by counselors and clients. Specifically, these researchers were
interested in the subordinate roles used carry out the
counselor's larger role. For example they classified
counselor verbalizations as questions about content,
questions about feelings, responses to content, responses to feelings, interpretation of content, interpretation of feelings, suggestions about content, suggestions about
feelings, and giving information. Contemporary research builds on the work of Robinson and his colleagues. For example, Clara Hill (1989) has developed
response modes systems for classifying client and counselor speech. Response mode refers to the grammatical
structure of the response for example, closed questions,
open questions, and interpretation for the counselor,
and insight, resistance, and agreement for the client.

Numerous studies have use response modes measures to examine counseling interactions. These studies
show that different schools of counseling can be differentiated in terms of the response modes used by counselors practicing a particular model. In addition, clients
seeing counselors of differing theoretical orientations
use different response modes. Other studies examined
the relationship between counselor response modes and
(1) immediate counseling outcome (client helpfulness
ratings, changes in level of client experiencing, client
reactions); (2) session outcome (client and therapist ratings of session depth and smoothness); and (3) treatment outcome (changes in anxiety, depression, and
self-concept). Consistently, the counselor response
modes of interpretation, self-disclosure, and exploration
have the greatest immediate impact. In addition, while
various counselor and client response modes are significantly correlated with measures of session and
treatment outcome, the response modes accounted for
only a small percentage of the outcome variance.

Harold Pepinsky and his colleagues developed an
alternative approach for studying the linguistic structure of the counseling interview. Specifically, they
used a computer program to classify the type of verbs
used by counselors and clients. For example, they
found that Carl Rogers, Albert Ellis, and Fritz Perls
used different types of verb phrases when interacting
with Gloria, the client, and that the verb use patterns
fit with theoretical expectations. More importantly,
however, Pepinsky and his colleagues showed that clients' verb usage converged toward counselor verb usage across counseling.

The final major area of counseling process research
is the counseling relationship. Charlie Gelso and Jean
Carter (*The Counseling Psychologist*, 1985, 13, 155–243)
provided a significant and heuristic integration of re-

search and theory concerning the counseling relationship. They defined the counseling relationship as
consisting of a working alliance, a transference relationship, and a real relationship. In a second major
analysis Charlie Gelso and Jean Carter (*Journal of Counseling Psychology*, 1994, 41, 296–306) provided specific
propositions about how these three components change
over time and how they interact among themselves.

The research on the working alliance was catalyzed
by Edward Bordin's seminal paper (*Psychotherapy: Theory, Research and Practice*, 1979, 16, 252–260) describing the working alliance as an emotional bond between
the participants and an agreement on the tasks and
goals of counseling. The working alliance represents a
robust area of counseling process research. A number
of studies meta-analytically summarized by Horvath
and Symonds (*Journal of Counseling Psychology*, 1991,
38, 139–149) support Bordin's hypothesis that a
stronger working alliance is related to enhanced counseling outcome. Moreover, the working alliance seems
to be the single best predictor of successful counseling.
More recent studies have examined client, counselor,
and interactive precursors of the working alliance.

The personal characteristics of both the counselor
and the client are important for establishing a working
alliance. Specifically, when clients and counselors have
a secure emotional attachment (i.e., believe that others
will be responsive to them when they are distressed and
believe that they are worthy of care) and an affiliative
interpersonal style, the established working alliance is
stronger. Other researchers have identified counselors'
techniques that are related to working alliance
strength. Specifically, working alliances are stronger
when counselors are challenging within a context of
empathy, are here-and-now oriented, and focus on client themes. Finally, there is evidence that it is the interaction between client and counselor attributes that
leads to an effective working alliance. Specifically, difficult clients, those with poor attachments, need more
experienced counselors, and the counselor's style of interacting needs to fit the client's expectations for counseling.

Other researchers have begun to examine the consequences of establishing a strong working alliance.
New studies suggest that the working alliance plays an
important role as a mediator and a moderator of counseling outcome. For example, changes in the working
alliance relate to changes in client social skills which
in turn relate to counseling outcome. In other research
counselor interpretation is only helpful when it is delivered in the context of a strong working alliance.
Given these promising results, it is likely that the working alliance will continue to be a productive focus for
counseling process research.

Counseling researchers have also examined the
transference relationship. In a seminal monograph,

Muller (*Journal of Counseling Psychology*, 1969, 16, special issue) coded client-counselor and client-parent interactions for indications of transference. He found that under heightened stress clients' patterns of interacting with their therapists converged on their reported interactions with family members. After Mueller's important early work, counseling process researchers seemed uninterested in investigating transference phenomena. In the 1990s, however, there was a renewed interest in studying transference. This interest is seen in both instrument development (e.g., newly developed counselor-report and self-report of measures of transference patterns) and studies examining the role of transference in counseling process. These studies examined the interrelation of transference, working alliance, and therapist techniques and the interaction of transference and insight (*Journal of Counseling Psychology*, 1997, 44, 189–221). Consistently, the amount of transference is unrelated to counseling outcome. However, the pattern of transference development over time is important. Specifically, counseling outcome is better when transference follows a low-high-low pattern of development. Additionally, transference seems to interact with client insight, with insight only being helpful in the presence of transference.

The real relationship is conspicuous by its absence for counseling process researchers. One reason for the dearth of empirical attention is the definitional and measurement problems that have plagued the study of the real relationship. Currently, there is a great deal of interest in using the working alliance and transference constructs to study the counseling relationship, so perhaps the real relationship will attract the same amount of enthusiasm.

Process Outcome Studies

Early counseling research tended to examine counseling outcome and counseling process separately. More recently, however, counseling researchers are beginning to address outcome and process within the same study. There is an increasing desire to understand what counseling process variables are linked to counseling outcome. This is an encouraging trend because the distinction between process and outcome is often arbitrary.

There are several recent examples of counseling researchers simultaneously studying process and outcome. Researchers have examined how relational control, congruence, and working alliance relate to symptom change and how transference, working alliance, resistance, and counselor technique relate to multidimensional outcomes. Process outcome will likely continue to increase as counseling researchers strive to better understand how counseling outcomes come about.

[*See also* Psychotherapy, *article on* Research.]

Bibliography

Bergin, A. E., & Garfield, S. L. (1995). *Handbook of psychotherapy and behavior change* (3rd ed.). New York: Wiley. Reviews of process and outcome studies in a variety of domains.

Brown, S. D., & Lent, R. W. (1992). *Handbook of counseling psychology* (2nd ed.). New York: Wiley. Reviews of selected areas of counseling interventions. Specifically, depression, anxiety, social interaction problems, and substance abuse.

Forsyth, D. R., & Leary, M. R. (1997). Achieving the goals of the scientist-practitioner model: The seven interfaces of social and counseling psychology. *Counseling Psychologist*, 25, 180–200. Describes the interface between social and counseling psychology.

Gelso, C. J., & Hayes, J. A. (1998). *The psychotherapy relationship*. New York: Wiley. Theory and research concerning the counseling relationship.

Greenberg, L. S., & Pinsof, W. M. (1986). *The psychotherapeutic process: A research handbook* (pp. 503–528). New York: Guilford Press. Describes and reviews the psychometric properties of several widely used process instruments.

Heppner, P. P., Kivlighan, D. M., Jr., & Wampold, B. E. (1999). *Research design in counseling* (2nd ed.). Pacific Grove, CA: Brooks/Cole. This book focuses on the major research design approaches in counseling psychology. There are chapters that specifically address outcome and process research.

Hill, C. E. (1989). *Therapist techniques and client outcomes*. Newbury Park, CA: Sage. Detailed descriptions of the process and outcome of eight cases of brief psychotherapy.

Horvath, A. O., & Greenberg, L. S. (1994). *The working alliance: Theory, research and practice* (pp. 13–37). New York: Wiley. A summary of theory and research about the working alliance.

Kazdin, A. E. (1998). *Methodological issues and strategies in clinical research* (2nd ed.). Washington, DC: American Psychological Association. This book focuses on the major research design approaches in clinical psychology.

Dennis M. Kivlighan

COUNSELING PSYCHOLOGY. [*This entry comprises three articles: an overview of the broad history of the field from its inception to the present; a survey of the principal theories that have determined the course of development of the field; and a general descriptive review of assessments and interventions used in or unique to the field. For discussions related to counseling psychology, see the entries on* Clinical Psychology; Counseling Process and Outcome; Personality Psychology; Psychoanalysis; Psychology; Training; *and various independent entries on specific psychosocial interventions.*]

History of the Field

Counseling psychology facilitates personal and interpersonal functioning across the life span with a focus on emotional, social, vocational, educational, health-related, developmental, and organizational concerns. As one of the general practice health service provider specialties, counseling psychology addresses both normal developmental issues and dysfunctional or disordered developmental issues from individual, family, group, systems, and organizational perspectives. Counseling psychology helps people with physical, emotional, and mental disorders improve their well-being, alleviate distress and maladjustment, resolve crises, and increase their ability to live more highly functioning lives.

The above description is a paraphrase of a 1998 petition by the Division of Counseling Psychology of the American Psychological Association for continued recognition as a specialty in professional psychology. The petition identified distinguishing elements of the field to be an emphasis on healthy behavior, life-span developmental issues, career and vocational as well as personality development, and a commitment to persons in the context of their environments. Core values underlying these elements, which have persisted for decades, include prevention, the importance of developmental transitions, and building on strengths. The field has favored relatively brief interventions attending to persons' assets regardless of the degree of disturbance.

Evolutionary Sources

Conceptually, philosophically, and professionally, counseling psychology evolved from several sources. Prominent among these are vocational guidance, psychometrics, and psychotherapy. Vocational guidance in the early 1900s was a movement to assist young people in their vocational adjustments through education and occupational information. The development of psychometric methods beginning with the Binet Intelligence Scales and furthered by the trade and intelligence tests created for military personnel in World War I, allowed vocational guidance to be more than giving information about jobs. Knowledge relevant to placement was greatly expanded during the Depression of the 1930s through the Minnesota Stabilization Research Institute's experimentation with psychological tests, information, and training, to assist unemployed workers to find jobs.

About this same time an interest in psychotherapy and the study of personality emerged. A highly influential contribution to this movement was Carl Rogers's work (Client-Centered Therapy, Boston, 1951). His theoretical and practical innovations offered counselors new understanding of people and their problems of ad-

justment whether the focus was on occupation, personal values, or interpersonal relations. His work also provided better understanding of counseling processes and procedures, and new methods of training for counselors.

Donald Super's 1955 article, "Transition: From Vocational Guidance to Counseling Psychology," described the merging of these streams of influence in the evolution of the field. Beginning with vocational guidance as orientation to work, then enhanced by psychometric and psychotherapeutic methods, counseling psychology became a field that assisted persons with all types of life adjustments, treating the person who needed help rather than a problem which needed a solution, and doing it in the context of the individual's world.

This evolution of a field emphasizing prevention, mental health, personal strengths, brief interventions, person-environment interactions, and life-span development occurred in a hospitable cultural context. These convictions about the field seemed in accord with societal values of the time such as commitment to change (particularly empirically based technological change), social mobility, and the emphasis on self-help or self-development.

Societal Influences

Societal events and crises also affected the evolution of the field. For example, the Army General Classification Test was developed to help assign millions of military personnel in World War I, and the economic depression in the United States during the 1930s led to new understanding of people and work and improved methods of fitting people to environments.

The 1940s and 1950s saw an emphasis on rehabilitation and restoration emerge in counseling psychology. Adapting rather than fitting people to environments became possible through research and development in methods of educational planning and guidance, physical and vocational rehabilitation, and restoration of mental health through psychotherapy or personality counseling. These methods were fostered by World War II, the Korean conflict, and the Soviet-United States competition in space research. Physical and emotional war casualties required psychological as well as medical treatment both during and following these wars. In 1944 the Veterans Administration (VA) was assigned responsibility for assisting veterans to return to civilian life by providing rehabilitation and restoration services. It became the largest employer of psychologists for inpatient treatment in its hospitals and for counseling and guidance of veterans who were using the G.I. Bill, passed by Congress, to plan for and pursue educational and career objectives. The VA contracted with colleges and universities to provide counseling and advisory services, and many student counseling centers of today originated in these VA-sponsored programs. Similarly, the space-science competition between the Eastern and Western powers led Congress to pass the National Defense Education Act which, among many other programs, funded short-term and year-long institutes in universities for training counselors for schools and colleges.

During the 1960s, counseling psychology became interested in personal enhancement. Research on self-awareness, self-actualization, phenomenonology, and existentialism was applied to psychotherapeutic methods as in Carl R. Rogers's client-centered therapy which later opened the way for other nonmedical therapies such as behavioral and cognitive-behavioral approaches. World events of the time, especially the cold war, the proliferation of nuclear missiles, and the war in Vietnam induced social consequences of discouragement, disenchantment, and for some people a sense of helplessness about an increasingly threatening environment. Methods for coping with unmanageable external threats shifted more within the person and the existential and client-centered approaches to counseling were especially compatible with this internal orientation.

In the 1970s and 1980s a concern for integration of persons and environments emerged in which theory and practice focused on individuals in a social context, an increased responsibility for environmental and social development, and the conservation of human and natural resources. Social influence theory was applied to counseling in this period and several new methods and approaches to counseling evolved, such as psychological education, peer counseling, crisis intervention, hot lines, community psychology, sensitivity training, and indigenous helping, all oriented to the development of an increased personal and environmental synchrony.

More recently counseling psychology has given greater emphasis to clinical services, and more counseling psychologists are engaged in independent practice and institutional work in health service settings. Changes in economic conditions, health-care policy, and income distribution have led counseling psychologists to be concerned about third-party payment for services, participation in managed care programs, and eligibility for Medicare reimbursement.

APA Division 17

Organizationally, the history of counseling psychology is very much the history of Division 17 of the American Psychological Association (APA) which was created by the reorganization of APA in the early 1940s. The "Reorganized American Psychological Association" was described by Dael Wolfle (*American Psychologist* 1946/1997, 52, 721–724). The origin of APA divisions was discussed by Benjamin (*American Psychologist*, 52, 725–732) and their evolution and current status by Dewsbury (*American Psychologist*, 52, 733–741).

The bylaws of the reorganized APA, published in the November 1943 *Psychological Bulletin*, defined divisions as the structure for representing special interests that lie within the Association. Nineteen charter divisions were recommended following a survey of members' opinions and Division 17, the Division of Personnel and Guidance Psychologists, was to include APA members whose primary interests were in selection, training, and guidance in schools, colleges, and guidance agencies.

A Divisional Organization Committee named temporary chairs and secretaries of the charter divisions in the May 1945 *Psychological Bulletin* including Edmund G. Williamson as chair and Catherine C. Miles as secretary for Division 17. They served the division until officers were elected and assumed office at the September 1945 annual APA meeting. The first Division 17 officers elected were Edmund G. Williamson (chair), J. G. Darley (secretary), and J. G. Darley, Alvin C. Eurich, Harold Edgerton, and C. L. Shartle (council representatives). By the following year the name of the division had been changed to the Division of Counseling and Guidance Psychologists. Its officers for 1956 to 1947 were Edmund G. Williamson (president), John G. Darley (secretary) and Hugh Bell, G. Frederic Kuder, Carroll Shartle, and Edmund G. Williamson (representatives to APA Council).

At the first business meeting of Division 17 on 5 September 1946, the bylaws drafted by Darley, as division secretary, were approved. As reported by C. Winfield Scott (1980), the purposes of the division stated in these bylaws included (1) extending techniques and methods of psychology to counseling and guidance activities; (2) promoting high standards of practice; (3) encouraging scientific and professional inquiry; (4) assisting in formulating professional standards and ethical codes for counseling and guidance; (5) promulgating scholastic and professional training requirements; and (6) collaborating with psychologists who are primarily attached to medical activities in arriving at definitions and working relationships between related psychological specialities.

The division's early structure paralleled that of APA, with standing committees for Education and Training, Scientific Affairs, Professional Affairs, and Membership. A concerted effort in the 1970s by the women members established a very active Standing Committee on Women. Except for the latter, these were three-person committees with one new member appointed each year by the president-elect to serve a three-year term, so few people could be involved in the governance of the division at any one time. Division membership increased steadily to about 2,000 in the 1970s while the number of accredited counseling psychology programs remained rather stable at about 20.

By the 1980s the number of accredited counseling psychology programs was increasing (there were 46 in

1986) and a growing concern was expressed by Division members as to how more persons could become involved in division governance. Several special-interest groups were formed in 1985 but the need for a broader and more inclusive governance became obvious. Some division members affiliated with other divisions of APA and many APA members who were counseling psychologists did not join Division 17. If the division were to remain viable it needed to become more compatible with the interests of counseling psychologists of the 1990s.

Bruce Fretz in his 1992 presidential year initiated a major restructuring to address the need for diversification of emphasis and inclusion of more members in division governance. The Executive Board designed an organizational structure which was thoroughly discussed and detailed in the presidencies of Janice Birk, Jo-Ida Hansen, and Kathleen Davis. The necessary bylaw revisions were approved at the 1995 annual business meeting. The modified structure established four elected vice presidents (Diversity and Public Interest, Education and Training, Professional Practice, and Scientific Affairs), nine appointed standing committees, and provided for the establishment of interest sections such as the Section on Women, and for the appointment of special task groups when needed (24 of the latter existed during 1995). The bylaws also established a membership category of professional affiliation for those who were not members of APA. In 1995 the number of accredited programs had increased to 69. Division membership reached a new high of more than 3,000, and more than 225 members were involved in governance activities. This dramatic increase inspired optimism that the restructuring would meet the needs of division members into the next century.

Training Conferences

Of historic importance to Division 17 were four training conferences held between 1949 and 1987. The first, though not a Division 17 undertaking, was a Conference on Training of Psychological Counselors held at Ann Arbor, Michigan, in July 1949 and January 1950. These were defined as "subdoctoral" professionals. The conference report included a description of "Counselor-Psychologists" who were persons trained at the doctoral level and whom the conferees regarded as essentially the same kind of psychologists as clinical psychologists.

The Northwestern Conference held at Northwestern University in 1951 resulted in a new name for Division 17, Counseling Psychology, which was formally approved by the members in 1951. The conference also led to the publication of "Recommended Standards for Training Counseling Psychologists at the Doctorate Level" in the *American Psychologist* in 1952 and a companion report, "The Practicum Training of Counseling Psychologists," published at the same time. In 1956 an important follow-up paper, "Counseling Psychology as a Specialty," was published in the *American Psychologist*, which included a report that the Veterans Administration had established two new positions with the title Counseling Psychologist, and that the American Board of Examiners in Professional Psychology had renamed its diploma in "Counseling and Guidance" to "Counseling Psychology."

The Greyston Conference was held in 1964 after three years of discussion and planning by the Division. Papers were presented reviewing the field's events since 1951, including the substantive bases for the specialty, work sites and activities, current assessment and innovation methods, and the nature of existing training programs. These papers and other historic documents were published in the conference report, *The Professional Preparation of Counseling Psychologists* (1964) along with a series of recommendations specifying essential areas of training for counseling psychologists and the proportions of training time for each area.

The Georgia Conference in 1987 was on "Planning the Future of Counseling Psychology." Each person attending participated in one of the following areas of discussion: Professional Practice, Public Image, Training and Accreditation, Research, and Organization and Political Issues. The report of the conference and the recommendations by the discussants was published in the July 1988 issue of *The Counseling Psychologist*.

Journals and Newsletters

Also of importance to the history of the field and an archive of division history are its publications. The first division newsletter appeared in 1948, later to be named *Counseling News and Views*, and continued until 1968. In 1969 it was replaced by *The Counseling Psychologist*, a quarterly publication, founded and edited by John Whiteley, for the purpose of critical analysis and commentary on professional problems and as a forum for professional concerns. A newsletter was reestablished by the division in 1983. Counseling psychology's primary journal, the *Journal of Counseling Psychology* was founded in 1954 by Milton Hahn, Harold Seashore, Donald Super, and C. Gilbert Wrenn, with the modest financial support of 28 stockholders (Wrenn, 1966). Its publication was assumed by APA in 1967 and its 45 volumes up to the late 1990s are a detailed history of counseling psychology's science and practice.

The field of counseling psychology today is the result of many professional movements, societal influences, and organizational developments. The accounts of its evolution can be found in its journals and newsletters and in its deposited materials at the Archives of the History of American Psychology.

Bibliography

Benjamin, L. T., Jr. (1997). The origin of psychological species: History of the beginnings of American Psychological Association Divisions. *American Psychologist, 52,* 725–732.

Bordin. E. S. (Ed.). (1951). *Training of psychological counselors: Report of a conference held at Ann Arbor, Michigan, July 27 and 28, 1949, and January 6 and 7, 1950.* Ann Arbor: University of Michigan Press.

Brown, S. D., & Lent, R. W. (Eds.). (1992). *Handbook of counseling psychology.* New York: Wiley. (Original work published 1984)

Dewsbury, D. A. (1997). On the evolution of divisions. *American Psychologist, 52,* 733–741.

Gazda. G. M., Rude, S. S., Weissberg, M., & contributors (1988). Third national conference for counseling psychology: Planning the future. *The Counseling Psychologist, 16,* 323–439.

Gelso, C. J., & Fretz, B. R. (1992). *Counseling psychology.* Fort Worth, TX: Harcourt Brace Jovanovich.

Heppner, P. P., Kivlighan, D. M., Jr., & Wampold, B. E. (1992). *Research design in counseling.* Pacific Grove, CA: Brooks/Cole.

Meara, N. M., & Myers, R. A. (1998). A history of division 17 (counseling psychology): Establishing stability amid change (pp. 9–41). In D. A. Dewsbury (Ed.), *Unification through division: Histories of the divisions of the American Psychological Association: Volume 3.* Washington, DC: American Psychological Association.

Schmidt, L. D. (1977). Why has the professional practice of psychological counseling developed in the United States? *The Counseling Psychologist, 7,* 19–20.

Scott, C. W. (1963/1980). History of the division of counseling psychology: 1945–1963. In J. M. Whiteley (Ed.), *The history of counseling psychology* (pp. 25–40). Monterey, CA: Brooks/Cole.

Super, D. E. (1955). Transition: From vocational guidance to counseling psychology. *Journal of Counseling Psychology, 2,* 3–9.

Thompson, A. S., & Super, D. E. (1964). *The professional preparation of counseling psychologists: Report of the 1964 Greyston Conference.* New York: Teachers College Press, Columbia University Bureau of Publications.

Watkins, C. E., Jr., & Schneider, L. J. (Eds.). (1991). *Research in counseling.* Hillsdale, NJ: Erlbaum.

Whiteley, J. M. (Ed.). (1980). *The history of counseling psychology.* Monterey, CA: Brooks/Cole.

Wolfle, D. (1946). The reorganized American Psychological Association. *American Psychologist, 1,* 3–6.

Wrenn, C. G. (1966). Birth and early childhood of a journal. *Journal of Counseling Psychology, 13,* 485–488.

Lyle D. Schmidt

Theories

Counseling psychology is one of four major applied specialties recognized by the American Psychological Association (APA), along with clinical psychology, industrial-organizational psychology, and school psychology. Applied specialities are developed and maintained in order to provide effective psychological services to people, based on psychological theory and research.

> Counseling psychology is a speciality that facilitates personal and interpersonal functioning across the life span with a focus on emotional, social, vocational, educational, health-related, developmental, and organizational concerns. . . . [Counseling psychology] help[s] people improve their well-being, alleviate distress and maladjustment, resolve crises, and increase their ability to live more highly functioning lives. (Continuing Education and Regional Conferences Committee of the Counseling Psychology Division of APA, 1994, *What Is a Counseling Psychologist?* [Brochure]. Washington, DC: American Psychological Association)

Counseling psychology has a long history of integrating psychological theories and theory-based research with the practice of the specialty. A few psychological theories have been unusually influential in guiding the speciality.

Eight Influential Theories

A group of experts in counseling psychology was consulted regarding the most influential theories. These experts were identified by nominations solicited from the directors of counseling psychology doctoral training programs in the United States, with self-nominations disallowed. The 29 identified experts represented age, ethnic, cultural, gender, geographic, and professional-setting diversity, reflecting the diversity in counseling psychology. Sixteen (55%) of those identified responded to an invitation to identify "the principal theories that have determined the course of development of this field." The results of this survey of experts reflect reasonable agreement on eight theories and some agreement on seven others. Newly emerging theories have not had the time to be influential and are not identified in this list, despite their potential to influence the future of the specialty.

Three of the eight theories that experts generally agreed were principally influential on counseling psychology practice, as opposed to research, are psychotherapy theories: (1) Aaron Beck's cognitive therapy theory; (2) Albert Ellis's rational-emotive therapy theory; and (3) Carl Rogers's (1951) person-centered therapy theory. Recent research in counseling psychology has only occasionally made these theories the focus of empirical investigations. The irony in this influence pattern is that Beck, Ellis, and Rogers have all championed scientific investigation as an important aspect of psychotherapeutic theorizing.

Two of the eight are theories of career development: (4) John Holland's (1973) career typology theory and (5) Donald Super's (1957) career development theory. These two theories reflect the dual missions of counseling psychology because they have strongly influenced both the practice of career counseling and research on vocational behavior. Holland's theory is the single most researched in the vocational area. In addition, it is the framework used in most standardized and computerized assessments of vocational choice. Super's theory has generated important research and influenced practice, as well, but not to the degree of Holland's theory.

Two of the theories are either directly or indirectly from social psychology: (6) Albert Bandura's (1986) social-cognitive theory and (7) Stanley Strong's social influence theory (Strong & Claiborn, 1982). These two theories have had some impact on counseling practice, but their primary influence has been on counseling psychology *research*. Bandura's theory has generated a research subspecialty on the role of self-efficacy and related social-cognitive processes in career decisions and work-related behavior. Strong's social influence theory has spawned numerous investigations of counselor factors that influence client attitudes and behavior.

Finally, a pair of racial identity development theories, those of (8) William Cross, Jr. (1991) and of Janet Helms (1990), were viewed by the experts as closely related and together as constituting the final entry in this category. These theories have generated much of the empirical research on multicultural awareness and multicultural counselor training in counseling psychology. Likewise, they have been influential in the training of counseling psychologists with regard to attitudes, beliefs, and skills necessary for sensitive and effective counseling between people of differing cultures or subcultures. So their influence on the practice of counseling is significant and growing.

Seven Additional Theories

The seven theories on which there was some, but not widespread, agreement included four theories that directly influence psychotherapy: (1) Sigmund Freud's psychodynamic theory, which has spawned such theories as attachment theory, object-relations theory, and working alliance theory; (2) B. F. Skinner's behaviorism; (3) collectively, the counseling skill development theories of Allen Ivey (Ivey & Authier, 1978), Norman Kagan (1975), and C. B. Truax and Robert Carkhuff (1967); and (4) a group of theories collectively known as feminist psychotherapy theories, because of their integration of feminist values and beliefs with counseling interventions (e.g., see reviews by Lucia Gilbert, in Brodsky & Hare-Mustin, Eds, New York, 1980; Worell & Remer, New York, 1992). Although Freud's and Skinner's theories have generated a great deal of research in other fields, within counseling psychology the primary impact of these theories has been on practice. A notable exception to that general trend has been a

group of important research investigations in counseling psychology based on theories that were themselves rooted in Freudian theory. For example, a number of studies have been reported in counseling psychology journals on the working alliance, which has its roots in Freudian theory. The skill development theories have guided much of the initial psychotherapy training of a generation or more of counseling psychologists, although the number of counseling psychology research investigations of these theories has declined in recent years. Feminist psychotherapy theories have definitely influenced counseling practice. Their impact on counseling psychology research is less pronounced, although research related to the broader construct of gender regularly appears in counseling psychology journals. [*See the biographies of Skinner and Freud.*]

The fifth entry on this list does not involve psychotherapy directly, but rather the closely related area of supervision of counselors who are engaged in psychotherapy: (5) Stoltenberg and Delworth's (1988) developmental model of psychotherapy supervision has been influential on both counseling psychology research and on the practice of counseling supervision.

The final two of these seven theories involve career development: (6) John Krumboltz's (1979) social learning theory of career decision making and (7) Nancy Betz and Louise Fitzgerald's (1987) women's career development theory. The work of Krumboltz and of Betz and Fitzgerald has influenced career development research. Krumboltz's work has paved the way for what has emerged as the social cognitive perspective in research on vocational behavior. The publication of Betz and Fitzgerald's book has helped define women's career development as a subspecialty within the area. These approaches have had less impact on counseling practice than on counseling psychology research.

Challenging Issues

Having identified these influential theories, it is important to identify several important issues that complicate the task of identifying the principal theories that have guided the specialty. One of the most common comments by experts was that the task of identifying principally influential theories was challenging. Perhaps the most important issue is that counseling psychology is not monolithic; counseling psychologists represent great diversity in demographic and cultural characteristics, work settings, age, psychotherapeutic approaches, and the like. In fact, two defining features of the speciality are its advancement of multiculturalism and of the psychology of women. So, it should come as no surprise that there is great diversity, even among the experts, regarding which theories are most influential to the field. No theory was a unanimous choice and 15 theories were thought principally influential by only one or two experts. The implication of these results is that theories other than these 8 are also influencing counseling psychology, though probably to a lesser extent.

A second, challenging issue concerns foundational theories versus derivative theories. A foundational theory is a broadly applicable psychological theory, such as Albert Bandura's social learning theory, whereas a derivative theory derives its essential intellectual character from a foundational theory and applies it more narrowly. For example, John Krumboltz's social learning theory of career decision making is derivative of Bandura's theory. What is foundational is also relative. Although Krumboltz's theory may be viewed as deriving from Bandura's, Bandura's theory itself may be viewed as deriving from the work of B. F. Skinner and John B. Watson. [*See the biographies of Bandura, Skinner, and Watson.*]

Ideas evolve, so it is sometimes difficult to identify which evolution of a theory has been principally influential. For example, John Krumboltz's theory of career counseling has led to the development of a general social-cognitive career model, championed by scholars such as Nancy Betz, Gail Hackett, and Robert Lent. Likewise, William Cross's racial identity development theory has been a foundational element in Janet Helms's racial identity development theories.

There was some disagreement among the experts regarding what constitutes a theory. For example, experts sometimes excluded intellectual products that have been influential because they did not view them as sufficiently theoretical in form or scope. For example, Betz and Fitzgerald's career psychology of women theory was viewed by some experts as more a survey of thought and research than a theoretical statement.

Some theories were viewed as sufficiently similar to each other that the experts grouped them together for inclusion as a single theoretical contribution. For example, the counseling skills theories of Ivey, Kagan, and Truax and Carkhuff were grouped together, as were the theoretical contributions of Cross and Helms.

Because so much of the work of counseling psychologists involves direct psychotherapy of individuals, couples, families, and small nonfamily groups, there is disagreement regarding whether the main influential theories should all be theories of psychotherapy, such as Carl Rogers's person-centered therapy theory, or whether the list of principally influential theories should also include theories important to counseling psychology that are not theories of psychotherapy, such as Stanley Strong's social influence theory. Psychotherapy theories in the two lists include those of Beck Ellis and Rogers, from the first list; and Freud, Ivey, Truax and Carkhuff, Kagan, and feminist therapy from the second list.

A related way of viewing this challenge is that some theories have had direct influence on the practice of counseling psychology, whereas others have stimulated counseling psychology research, but that research has not influenced the practice of the specialty. For example, Holland's and Super's theories probably have influenced the practice of vocational counseling to a greater degree than Bandura's social-cognitive theory has, although Bandura's theory has heavily influenced vocational research.

To allow the most accurate and comprehensive perspective on the speciality, both foundational and derivative theories are included in the list, as are earlier theories and their intellectual heirs. Likewise, both theories regularly used in direct psychotherapy and those not used in that context are included. From one point of view, this results in an inelegant hodgepodge. From another perspective, the list simply reflects the various differentiating characteristics of the influential ideas in the speciality.

Alternative Perspectives

Confidence in the accuracy of the list of influential theories grows when different methods produce similar lists. The opinion of experts is an important source of information regarding the identification of theories that have been influential to counseling psychology. However, a question remains regarding whether other methods produce similar lists. Next, the degree to which expert opinion coincides with coverage of the specialty's handbook (Brown & Lent, *Handbook of Counseling Psychology*, 2nd ed., 1992) and with a series of articles that have surveyed citation patterns in counseling psychology journals and texts will be detailed.

Just as there are limitations to the use of expert opinion in determining which theories are principally influential, there are also limitations to using the content of the *Handbook* and to using the results of studies of citation counts. The chief limitation of using the *Handbook* content is that it again reflects the judgments of the two experts who serve as its editors and the authors they chose to write for the *Handbook*. Although both of the *Handbook's* editors were nominated for the expert panel, their views were not included among those of the 16 judges. Only one of the 40 authors of *Handbook* chapters also served as an expert.

Regarding articles on citations, there are two main difficulties. First, these citation counts reflect impact on research, not counseling practice. Second, the data in three of the four articles that have tracked citations do so only with reference to the author and not with reference to the specific book, book chapter, or article. So, citation counts include in some cases citations of work that is not tied to the theory, or to work that is tied to a different theory from the one the experts identified as influential. For example, Albert Bandura has developed two major theories, so it would be impossible to tell in these four articles which of these theories was being cited. Finally, even if the work cited was about theory, it might have been cited for reasons unrelated to the theory; for example, because a particular method or measure was used. With those limits in mind, it is worth seeing what emerges from these other sources.

Regarding the content of the *Handbook*, the results roughly parallel those of the experts. The mean citations for theorists from the top eight was 23.6, with a range from 7 for Rogers to 42 for Holland. The mean citations for the second group was half of that for the first group (mean = 12), with a range from 3 for feminist therapy to 26 for the counseling skills theorists. The 15 theories cited as influential by only one or two experts averaged only 4.5 citations, with a range of 0 to 10. These data suggest that the distinctions made by the experts parallel the focus of the editors and authors of the *Handbook*.

Regarding the four journal articles on citations, each differed in the sources of citations, years of inclusion, and number of theories or theorists listed as frequently cited. For simplicity, if a theory or theorist was listed as frequently cited in any part of one of these four articles, it was counted as having been listed in that article. Theorists from the top-eight group were cited in 2.5 of the 4 articles on average, with a range from 1 to 4. Theorists from the second group were cited in 1.4 articles on average, with a range from 0 to 3. Theorists from the third group were cited much less frequently (mean = 0.73, range = 0–2; however, only George Kelly's personal construct theory garnered two article listings). These data, too, generally support the differences in influence that the expert panel made. The four articles were Cotton & Anderson, *Journal of Counseling Psychology*, 1973, 20, 272–274; Heesacker, Heppner, & Rogers, *Journal of Counseling Psychology*, 1982, 29, 400–405; Howard & Curtin, *The Counseling Psychologist*, 1993, 21, 288–302; and Myers & DeLevie, *Journal of Counseling Psychology*, 1966, 13, 245–246.

In summary, the judgment of experts, the citation patterns in the *Handbook of Counseling Psychology*, and the results of four journal articles on the frequency with which works are cited in journal articles and books converge in identifying eight theories as being of principal influence in counseling psychology. These three information sources also converged in demonstrating that seven additional theories also have influenced counseling psychology, but to a lesser extent. The fact that the information from these various sources, with their differing strengths and weaknesses, suggests increased confidence in the validity of the judgments experts made regarding the influential theories in counseling psychology.

Bibliography

Bandura, A. (1986). *Social foundations of thought and action: A social cognitive theory.* Englewood Cliffs, NJ: Prentice Hall. Details Bandura's theory and supportive research, which forms the basis of important vocational research in counseling psychology.

Betz, N. E., & Fitzgerald, L. F. (1987). *The career psychology of women.* Orlando, FL: Academic Press. A comprehensive survey of theory and research on women's vocational behavior, including Betz and Fitzgerald's perspectives.

Brown, S. D., & Lent, R. W. (Eds.). (1992). *Handbook of counseling psychology* (2nd ed.). New York: Wiley. The indispensable guide to current theory and research in counseling psychology.

Cross, Jr., W. E. (1991). *Shades of black: Diversity in African-American identity.* Philadelphia: Temple University Press. Describes Cross's racial identity development theory.

Helms, J. E. (Ed.). (1990). *Black and white racial identity: Theory, research, and practice.* New York: Greenwood Press. Comprehensive treatment of Helms's racial identity theory.

Holland, J. L. (1973). *Making vocational choices: A theory of careers.* Englewood Cliffs, NJ: Prentice Hall. Holland's classic statement of his theory of career choice.

Ivey, A. E., & Authier, J. (1978). *Microcounseling* (2nd ed.). Springfield, IL: Charles C Thomas. Ivey's most comprehensive description of microskills counseling training.

Kagan, N. (1975). *Interpersonal process recall: A method for influencing human interaction.* East Lansing: MI: Michigan State University. Describes Kagan's approach to counseling skills training.

Krumboltz, J. D., (1979). A social learning theory of career decision making. In A. M. Mitchell, G. B. Jones, & J. D. Krumboltz (Eds.), *Social learning theory and career decision making* (pp. 19–49). Cranston, RI: Carroll. This classic chapter describes Krumboltz's theory and related research.

Osipow, S. H., & Fitzgerald, L. F. (1996). *Theories of career development* (4th ed.). Boston: Allyn and Bacon. Latest edition of a classic survey textbook, with detailed discussions of Holland's, Krumboltz's, and Super's theories and the general social-cognitive model.

Rogers, C. R. (1951). *Client-centered therapy.* Boston: Houghton Mifflin. Rogers's theory of therapy is detailed.

Stoltenberg, C. D., & Delworth, U. (1988). *Supervising counselors and therapists: A developmental perspective.* San Francisco: Jossey-Bass. The comprehensive description of their supervision theory.

Strong, S. R., & Claiborn, C. D. (1982). *Change through interaction: Social psychological processes of counseling and psychotherapy.* New York: Wiley. Strong's most comprehensive presentation of his social influence theory.

Super, D. E. (1957). *The psychology of careers.* New York: Harper & Row. Super's comprehensive statement of his career development theory.

Truax, C. B., & Carkhuff, R. R. (1967). *Toward effective*

counseling and psychotherapy: Training and practice. Chicago: Aldine. The original text of their skills-based counseling training theory.

Martin Heesacker

Assessments and Interventions

Counseling psychology is a developmentally oriented specialty that emphasizes the integration and informed application of principles derived from basic psychological sciences such as differential, vocational, developmental, and social psychology. The practice of counseling psychology overlaps with that of clinical, industrial-organizational, management, and school psychology, making it one of the broadest and most integrative specialties in psychology.

Scientific Foundations of Counseling Psychology

Differential psychology, the study of the nature and extent of individual and group variability, and of the factors that determine or affect these differences, is one of two formative progenitors of counseling psychology. The objectives of differential psychology are to document individual differences in human attributes such as intelligence, personality, interests, and values that occur as a function of age, gender, race, and social class, and to identify the factors that contribute to those differences. Counseling psychologists share differential psychology's philosophical belief in the uniqueness of each person and this provides the philosophical rationale that guides their use of assessment techniques. In practice, counseling psychologists try to gain an understanding of how each individual thinks, feels, and acts, and their assessment practices cover the entire range of human cognitive, conative, and affective attributes.

As an applied specialty, counseling psychology evolved from the vocational guidance movement that began in the early 1900s, and the study of the effects of work on the individual continues to be an important focus of counseling psychology. Plato's notion that people should be matched to occupational environments to achieve optimal work outcomes was elaborated by Frank Parsons (1909) during the first decade of the twentieth century, and further developed by the Minnesota Employment Stabilization Research Institute during the depression of the 1930s. The person-environment fit philosophy is expressed most completely in Lloyd H. Lofquist and René V. Dawis's (1969) theory of work adjustment, which explains how matching individuals and occupational environments leads to better productivity, more satisfied workers, and job stability.

Counseling psychologists are unique among the psychological specialties in the attention they give to the measurement of vocationally relevant attributes of the individual (e.g., aptitudes, abilities, and interests) and the occupation (e.g., the demands and benefits of the job). Counseling psychology emphasizes the informed application of principles derived from basic scientific discoveries about the nature of work and of people's relations to work. John Holland's theory that there are six basic personality types and occupational environments—realistic, investigative, artistic, social, enterprising, and conventional—is used almost universally by counseling psychologists to organize information about occupational environments and vocational interests. Dale Prediger's (1982) demonstration that occupational environments differ in the extent to which they require interactions with people as opposed to things, and with data as opposed to ideas, is another heuristic that counseling psychologists use to organize knowledge about the relations between individuals and their work.

An appreciation of the relevance of developmental psychology to the discipline of counseling psychology began to emerge at midcentury. Anne Roe's (1956) theory of the effects of parent-child interactions on vocational choice, Donald Super's (1955) theory of the developmental progression of careers, and Carl Rogers's (1942) theory of personality development were instrumental in awakening counseling psychologists to the importance of developmental theory and research, and in expanding the focus of counseling psychology. An emphasis on growth, development, and prevention are core values of the specialty of counseling psychology, and many of the assessment and intervention practices of counseling psychology are intended to facilitate normal developmental processes.

Stanley Strong's (1968) interpretation of the counseling interview in terms of elemental social-cognitive processes made salient the status of counseling psychology as a form of applied social psychology. The constructs investigated by social psychologists are often the focus of counseling psychology assessment and intervention practices. Counseling psychology research and practice is concerned with the influence of social-cognitive processes on people's attitudes (e.g., in-group bias), perceptions (e.g., fundamental attribution error and unrealistic optimism), decision making (judgmental overconfidence and illusory correlation), and the effects of group processes on individual behavior (e.g., conformity, obedience, and social facilitation).

Diversity of Counseling Psychology Practice

Counseling psychologists provide services to a diverse array of clients, many of whom also are served by clinical, industrial-organizational, management, and school psychologists. Individual counseling psychologists typically specialize in one area of practice and use assessment techniques that have their greatest applicability in that area.

The work activities of many counseling and clinical psychologists are largely indistinguishable. Members of both specialties engage in psychotherapy with clients who range from the severely and chronically impaired to those suffering from situationally and developmentally mediated difficulties. The developmental orientation of counseling psychologists distinguishes their work most clearly from that of clinical psychologists and psychoanalysts. Counseling psychologists, child-clinical psychologists, and school psychologists also work extensively with children and adolescents. School psychologists work primarily in educational settings with teachers, administrators, and social workers, and they often limit their work with children to assessment. Counseling psychologists work with children and adolescents in the full range of service settings and their work typically emphasizes the use of assessment procedures as a prelude to initiating developmentally oriented interventions.

Other counseling psychologists specialize in working with clients who are similar to those served by industrial-organizational and management psychologists. Both counseling psychologists and human services personnel provide interventions such as individual counseling, individual psychological testing, career planning workshops, organizational assessment programs, formal training programs, consultation, mentoring, and developmental programs for special target groups (e.g., high-potential, terminated, female, and minority employees; supervisors; employed spouses; and parents). Industrial-organizational and management psychologists often view issues and concerns from an organizational perspective, however, and their interventions are intended to help organizations function more effectively. In contrast, counseling psychologists are concerned about the functioning and development of the individual.

Assessment Practices

The assessment practices of counseling psychologists and related specialists have been the focus of numerous studies. Psychologists have surveyed professors who teach graduate level assessment classes, and studied the assessment practices of psychologists and predoctoral interns employed in community mental health agencies; medical, Veteran's Administration, and psychiatric hospitals; internship sites that provide adult or adolescent inpatient services; counseling centers; and centers for the developmentally disabled. However, much of this research has included psychologists from multiple specialties and findings have been reported only for the aggregate group, thereby obscuring any differences in the assessment practices of the psychological specialties. Furthermore, the accuracy of the few surveys that

have focused exclusively on the assessment practices of counseling psychologists is suspect.

Evolution of Counseling Specialities. Counseling psychology expanded into new settings to treat previously underserved clients during the 1980s and 1990s, and this evolution of the specialty has not yet run its course. For these reasons, it is not possible to describe the present assessment practices of counseling psychologists with absolute precision, despite the continuing stream of research on this issue.

Time Allocated to Assessment and Diagnosis. Psychological assessment is an important activity for most counseling psychologists, regardless of the type of setting in which they work or the type of clientele they serve. A national survey of the work activities of members of the American Psychological Association Division of Counseling Psychology revealed that most of these counseling psychologists collected data about their clients (80.3%) and indentified problems and made diagnoses (76.6%). Close to 40% of the time these counseling psychologists spent in counseling activities (and over 20% of their total professional time) was devoted to assessment and diagnosis. Results from surveys consistently confirm that close to 20% of counseling psychologists' total professional time is devoted to assessment activities.

Assessment Procedures Used by Counseling Psychologists. Testing and assessment are not the same; much psychological assessment does not involve the formal use of objective or projective techniques. More than 80% of counseling psychologists report that they use interviews and observation to collect data about clients. Counseling psychologists regard using the interview as an assessment technique as central to their professional identity and they believe that is one of their most important job functions.

The tests used most frequently by counseling psychologists include objective and projective personality tests, individually administered tests of cognitive functioning, vocational interest tests, and brief scales to assess specific symptomology. The specific assessment procedures used by counseling psychologists vary somewhat as a function of the setting, client characteristics, and reason for seeking services. Projective techniques are used with greater frequency in psychiatric settings whereas interest, aptitude, and objective personality tests are used more frequently in counseling and community mental health centers. Some tests are designed for use with specific age ranges, so counseling psychologists who work with adult clients use tests that are different from the tests used by those who work with children and adolescents.

Overall, the tests that are most frequently used by counseling psychologists to measure cognitive functioning are the Wechsler Adult Intelligence Scale-III (WAIS-III), Wechsler Intelligence Scale for Children-III (WISC-

III), and the Stanford–Binet Intelligence Scale, Fourth Edition (SB). The Minnesota Multiphasic Personality Inventory-2 (MMPI-2) is the most widely used test for objective personality assessment. The Bender-Gestalt Visual-Motor Test (Bender-Gestalt) and various forms of the Draw-A-Person Test (DAP) provide projective assessments of personality and cognitive functioning. The most frequently used projective personality tests are the Rorschach Inkblot Test (Rorschach), Thematic Apperception Test (TAT), various forms of the Sentence Completion Tests (SCT), and the House-Tree-Person test (HTP). Although not ranked in the top 10 in terms of overall usage, university professors strongly advise counseling psychology students to learn to use the Strong Interest Inventory (SII), a vocational interest test, in addition to the MMPI-2 and WAIS-III. In keeping with the broad integrative nature of the specialty, counseling psychologists use a diverse array of instruments.

Many service agencies use a standard assessment battery with all who seek services. This practice insures that all clients will have the benefit of a comprehensive assessment program, and it establishes a uniform set of instruments on which the staff psychologists are expected to develop proficiency. The typical standard assessment battery includes both objective and projective tests to assess personality and cognitive functioning. The tests most commonly included in the standard assessment battery are the WAIS-III, WISC-III, MMPI-2, Rorschach, TAT, Bender-Gestalt, Figure Drawings, and SCT.

In addition to the tests mentioned above, counseling psychologists use the SII, Kuder Occupational Interest Inventory (KOIS), and Self-Directed Search (SDS) to assess vocational interests. They also have some familiarity with the Armed Services Vocational Aptitude Battery (ASVAB), the Differential Aptitude Test (DAT), and the General Aptitude Test Battery (GATB) which assess a broad sample of school and work-related aptitudes.

Other tests widely used by counseling psychologists are the Peabody Picture Vocabulary Test (PPVT) and the Wechsler Preschool and Primary Scale of Intelligence (WPPSI) to assess cognitive functioning, the Children's Apperception Test (CAT), a projective test of personality, and the Sixteen Personality Factors Questionnaire (16PF), California Psychological Inventory (CPI), and Edwards Personal Preference Schedule (EPPS), which are objective personality tests. Brief scales most commonly used for assessing specific symptomology are the Beck Depression Inventory (BDI), and Symptom Check List-90 (SCL-90). The assessment of neuropsychological functioning has not been a common work activity of counseling psychologists, but recently counseling psychologists have begun to develop expertise in that area. The tests most frequently used to assess neuropsychological functioning are the Halstead–Reitan Neuropsychological Battery, the Wechsler Memory Test, Benton Visual Relation Test, and Luria Nebraska Neuropsychological Battery.

Importance of Assessment to Professional Identity. The percentage of counseling psychologists who identify testing and measurement as their primary area of interest has declined since the mid-1970s, but counseling psychologists still rate assessment and diagnosis activities as important aspects of their work and as central to their professional identity. Work activities that are rated as important for defining the professional role of the counseling psychologist include collecting data about clients, using interviews and observations, problem identification and diagnosis, and using objective personality inventories, individual intelligence tests, vocational interest inventories, and aptitude tests. Those same work activities plus projective techniques are rated by counseling psychologists as central to their professional identity.

Unique Assessment Practices of Counseling Psychologists. Counseling psychologists are relatively unique in their use of tests to assess vocational and college major interests and in their use of information about school- and work-related aptitudes. This is illustrated by a 1980s survey, which gives the percentage of their practice that counseling psychologists devoted to specific testing activities: vocational and career (8.4%), diagnosing psychopathology (4.6%), intellectual assessment (4.3%), determining academic status (1.2%), and determining organicity (1.1%). Counseling psychologists give greater emphasis to vocational assessment and they make less use of projective tests than clinical psychologists do.

The percentage of counseling psychologists who reported using objective personality inventories (67%), occupational information (64%), vocational interest inventories (62%), individual intelligence tests (57%), aptitude tests (52%), and projective techniques (46%) in their work also illustrates their greater concern about educational and career development issues. Nevertheless, the practice of counseling psychology is broad. Counseling psychologists report that they administer an average of 7.5 objective tests and 1.8 projective tests a week; they administer objective tests to 35.9% of their clients and projective tests to 11.4%. The most frequently used tests in counseling centers, staffed more frequently by counseling psychologists than other specialists, include the SII, MMPI-2, EPPS, SCT, KOIS, Rorschach, WAIS-III, and DAT.

Counseling psychologists' emphasis on identifying the psychological attributes of work environments and integrating this information into their practice is relatively unique among the applied specialties of psychology. Counseling psychologists have pioneered the development of taxonomic systems for organizing information about vocational interests and occupational environments. Roe's (1956) theory-based classification of occupations into eight interest/personality groups, each of which was further divided into six levels of complexity, was the forerunner to Holland's Occupational Classification (HOC) system. Lofquist and Dawis's (1969) empirical description of the psychological benefits provided by occupational environments demonstrated the feasibility and advantages of classifying occupations on the basis of their effects on people. The HOC system, which classifies occupations in terms of vocational interests and level of complexity, emphasized the relation between personality and vocational interests, and it revolutionized the way in which interest test results are organized and presented. Holland's theory has achieved widespread acceptance and influenced research in personality psychology as well as theory, research, and practice in counseling psychology.

Another relatively unique assessment practice of counseling psychology is the self-administering, self-scoring, self-interpreting test. Holland pioneered this assessment procedure with his SDS, a vocational interest inventory. The rationale underlying self-interpreting tests such as the SDS is that many persons need reliable and valid information rather than counseling or psychotherapy. The self-interpreting test is intended to provide them with the information they need without involving a relatively high-priced psychological specialist. The idea underlying the self-interpreting test has now been incorporated into computer-based guidance programs such as SIGI. The use of self-interpreting tests is still largely confined to the vocational psychology subspecialty of counseling psychology, but some tests such as the Neuroticism, Extroversion, Openness Personality Inventory-Revised (NEO PI-R) have developed self-interpreting forms and other interests tests such as the Campbell Interest and Skills Survey (CISS) are developing self-interpreting forms.

Unresolved Issues

Purpose of Assessment. Investigating the practical utility of assessment procedures and their potential improvement requires a careful specification of the purposes of the assessment procedure. Actually, this issue is given scant attention by the discipline, but most counseling psychologists appear to use assessment procedures for one of three purposes. One purpose is to obtain information for making predictions. For example, counseling psychologists use assessment procedures to obtain diagnostic information that they can use in deciding how to work effectively with their clients, or to obtain predictive information that they can use in advising a client about future courses of action. Counseling psychologists also use assessment procedures to obtain descriptive information which they believe will help them understand their client better. Prediction is inherent as a secondary objective in this purpose. A

third potential application is to use assessment procedures as an intervention. For example, counseling psychologists sometimes interpret the results of the assessment procedure to their client to increase their insight into or sensitivity to important developmental issues and to stimulate their thinking about those issues.

The reasons university professors give when asked why students need to learn to use psychological tests provides a different perspective that illustrates the influence of guild issues on the discipline. University professors gave approximately equal ratings to professional reasons (i.e., provides information about personality structure, saves the therapist time, enables accurate behavior prediction, and increases client-therapist rapport) and guild concerns (i.e., satisfies legal requirements, provides a specialty, satisfies institutional demands, and enhances therapist prestige).

Each of these objectives requires that counseling psychologists be able to extract accurate information from their assessment procedures, draw accurate inferences from that information, and accurately convey the results to their clients in a manner that they can understand. There is scant evidence documenting the ability of counseling psychologists to satisfy these requirements.

Interview as Assessment Technique. The interview is the assessment technique most widely used by counseling psychologists, but psychometric assessment devices have numerous advantages over the interview. Tests possess a wealth of experience (that is incorporated into the norm groups) and they are not overly influenced by unusual or graphic cases. When used with a client, tests can be thought of as conducting a standard interview with the client, after which they report descriptive information (scores) having an approximately known level of reliability. The test scores suggest inferences having an approximately known validity. In contrast, counseling psychologists take years to amass the experience the test possesses at the beginning, conduct semistandard interviews, obtain descriptive information having an unknown reliability, draw inferences having an unknown validity (that is undoubtedly lower than the validity of the inferences drawn by the tests), and often have a backlog of clients waiting to be seen. Furthermore, the reliability and validity of tests is subjected to repeated scrutiny by both supporters and critics while the reliability and validity of the interview as an assessment device is virtually never examined.

The continued reliance of counseling psychologists on the interview as an assessment technique is undoubtedly due to three factors. First, it is not practical to use a test for everything the psychologist needs to know. Many psychologists use tests to obtain a significant part of the information they need and they use the interview to obtain information about the overall context into which the test information fits. In addition, most counseling psychologists pride themselves on being skillful interviewers, and the use of the interview to obtain diagnostic information is central to the professional identity of most counseling psychologists. Finally, while most counseling psychologists regard tests as useful but limited tools, they genuinely enjoy working with people.

Making Predictions from Tests. In 1954, Paul Meehl called attention to the fact that trained therapists are not as accurate in making predictions from tests as a statistical formula. This finding was met with considerable resistance, and today it is largely ignored by practicing therapists. To date 136 research studies have compared the ability of trained therapists to predict important future behaviors of an individual using both test and nontest information with the accuracy of a statistical formula. The statistical formula is almost always more accurate. This phenomenon is attributable to several of the factors already mentioned: Individual therapists are slow to amass experience, are prone to forget some cases, give too much weight to graphic cases, are unable to determine the proper weight to give various factors, and are likely to be influenced by irrelevant considerations.

Despite the overwhelming evidence of the superiority of actuarial predictions, the use of test information in clinical practice is virtually unchanged since the first publication of Meehl's book. A continuing challenge to counseling psychologists is to learn how to better integrate the results of assessment procedures into their clinical practice. The time is propitious for a careful examination of this issue, given the national concern about the cost effectiveness of mental health services, and the resulting movement toward managed care.

Effects of Test Interpretation. Leo Goldman cautioned in 1961 that counseling psychologists may not be very effective in interpreting test information, but counseling psychologists have largely ignored this warning. Recently, Howard E. A. Tinsley and Serena Chu reviewed 65 studies that directly investigated test interpretation outcomes. Most of the research has focused on the interpretation of aptitude and ability tests; virtually no research has examined the interpretation of vocational interest tests or the use of tests in individual psychotherapy, couples counseling, family counseling, substance abuse counseling, or any of the many other specialty areas in which counseling psychologists function. They found that few studies have been competently done or adequately reported, and that the research is fraught with methodological weaknesses (e.g., flawed criteria, use of an immediate follow-up, lack of random assignment, and lack of a control group). Consequently, they concluded that there is no coherent body of evidence demonstrating the efficacy of test interpretation as an intervention.

The research evidence provides tenuous support for only three conclusions: that the use of visual aids improves the effectiveness of test interpretation, that group test interpretation methods are as effective as individual test interpretation methods, and that the individual test interpretation interview is preferred to a group test interpretation by those receiving the interpretation. However, cost analyses reveal that individual interpretations are six times more costly than group interpretations. Given the greater cost and lack of demonstrated superiority of the individual test interpretation, there appears to be no rational basis for providing individual test interpretations in situations where group test interpretations are feasible.

A major innovation of the last three decades has been the development of self-interpreting interest inventories such as the SDS and CISS. Only seven investigations have evaluated the effectiveness of self-interpretation. The paucity of research represents a rather alarming indifference on the part of the discipline to the need to evaluate this important innovation in test interpretation. Typically, no differences among the modes of test interpretation were found.

Caveat Emptor

Despite the centrality of assessment to the work and professional identity of counseling psychologists, the incremental utility of assessment in counseling has not been established. Assessment practices rest more on folklore and assumptions of utility than on empirically demonstrated benefits. Psychology has given painstaking attention to the development of procedures for evaluating the reliability and validity of measuring instruments (i.e., tests), and training in the use of assessment devices is required for all counseling psychologists. However, insufficient attention has been given to the reliability and validity of the assessment practices of counseling psychologists. In medicine, the Food and Drug Administration has the authority to insist that the efficacy of drugs be demonstrated in rigorously controlled research studies and that the potential side-effects of the drug are evaluated before the drug is approved for use in patient care. Counseling psychology needs to adopt an analogous procedure for evaluating the efficacy of assessment techniques and practices.

Bibliography

Fitzgerald, L. F., & Osipow, S. H. (1986). An occupational analysis of counseling psychology: How special is the specialty? *American Psychologist, 41*, 535–544. Compared work functions and professional identity of counseling and clinical psychologists. Demonstrated significant overlap of the specialties.

Gottfredson, G. D., & Holland, J. L. (1996). *Dictionary of Holland occupational codes* (3rd ed.). Odessa, FL: Psychological Assessment Resources. Reference volume containing codes for more than 12,000 occupations.

Grove, W. M., & Meehl, P. E. (1996). Comparative efficiency of informal (subjective, impressionistic) and formal (mechanistic, algorithmic) prediction procedures: The clinical-statistical controversy. *Psychology, Public Policy, and Law, 2,* 293–323. Most recent summary of the research on the relative efficacy of actuarial prediction and predictions made by trained therapists.

Goldman, L. (1961). *Using tests in counseling.* New York: Appleton-Century-Crofts. Critical evaluation of the uses of tests in counseling that continues to influence the thinking of scholars to this day. It has been largely ignored by practicing counseling psychologists, but many of the issues raised by Goldman are still relevant.

Holland, J. L. (1997). *Making vocational choices. A theory of vocational personalities and work environments* (3rd ed.). Odessa, FL: Psychological Assessment Resources. Outlines theory of six personality types—realistic, investigative, artistic, social, enterprising, and conventional—and six corresponding types of occupational environments.

Lofquist, L. H., & Dawis, R. V. (1969). *Adjustment to work: A psychological view of man's problems in a work-oriented society.* New York: Appleton-Century-Crofts. Explication of the person-environment fit philosophy that guides the use of psychological tests in matching people to work environments.

Meehl, P. E. (1954). *Clinical versus statistical prediction: A theoretical analysis and a review of the evidence.* Minneapolis: University of Minnesota Press. Classic work in which the relative predictive accuracy of trained therapists and statistical formulas was first noted. Also attempted to identify the circumstances under which therapist predictions could be expected to be better than actuarial predictions.

Parsons, F. (1909). *Choosing a vocation.* Boston: Houghton. The volume that gave career counseling its first theoretical structure and advocated the use of assessment procedures in order to be able to come to a complete understanding of the individual and work environment.

Prediger, D. J. (1982). Dimensions underlying Holland's hexagon: Missing link between interests and occupations? *Journal of Vocational Behavior, 21,* 259–287. Identification of basic preferences for working with persons versus things and data versus ideas that underlie most important distinctions among occupations.

Roe, A. (1956). *The psychology of occupations.* New York: Wiley. Outlines the largely unsupported theory that early parent-child interactions influence subsequent adult vocational choices and introduces a two-dimensional occupational classification system that divides occupations among eight interest groups and six levels of complexity. The forerunner of Holland's classification system.

Rogers, C. R. (1942). *Counseling and psychotherapy.* Boston: Houghton Mifflin. Classic work that emphasizes the importance of the relationship between the therapist and patient as an important element of psychological interventions. Exerts an important influence on the way counseling psychologists communicate assessment results.

Strong, E. K., Jr. (1943). *Vocational interests of men and women.* Stanford, CA: Stanford University Press. Early scientific documentation of the feasibility and efficacy of using assessment procedures to help individuals select occupations in which they will be satisfied.

Strong, S. R. (1968). Counseling: An interpersonal influence process. *Journal of Counseling Psychology, 17,* 81–87. Influential work that conceptualizes counseling as a process in which the perceived expertness, attractiveness, and trustworthiness of therapists influence their effectiveness.

Super, D. E. (1955). Transition: From vocational guidance to counseling psychology. *Journal of Counseling Psychology, 2,* 3–9. One of the first efforts to describe the career behavior of the individual as following a normal, predictable developmental progression.

Tinsley, H. E. A., & Bradley, R. W. (1986). Test interpretation. *Journal of Counseling and Development, 64,* 462–466. Description of procedures for integrating test interpretation into the counseling interview.

Tinsley, H. E. A., & Chu, S. (1999). Research on test and inventory interpretation outcomes. In M. Savickas & A. R. Spokane (Eds.). *Vocational interests: Meaning, measurement and use in counseling* (pp. 257–267). Palo Alto, CA: Black-Davies. Comprehensive review and evaluation of research on effects of interpreting tests to clients.

Howard E. A. Tinsley

COUNTERFACTUAL THOUGHT. Humans have a compelling propensity to mentally change life's circumstances and instead to dwell on "what could have been." For example, following an automobile accident that had the consequences of $5,000 damage and a broken leg, one might think, "If I hadn't attached my seatbelt just before the accident, I would be dead." In this way, we create alternative realities, and we achieve this by mutating facts and events that were antecedent to the current situation. This tendency to imagine other possible worlds is known as counterfactual thinking, and it has become a growing area of research and theorizing since a seminal paper by Kahneman and Miller (1986).

Counterfactual thinking is important because imagining what could have been brings the realization that current circumstances were not inevitable and that things could have been different "if only—." Such a realization has significant affective, behavioral, and judgmental consequences. In other words, our feelings about current situations are determined not only by the facts of those situations but also by what did not occur, but might have occurred.

Several important questions have been raised about counterfactual thinking. The first concerns when counterfactuals are likely to be generated and what aspects of reality are likely to be changed. In general, counterfactuals are more likely to be generated following negative as opposed to positive outcomes. Thus, we are more likely to generate a counterfactual thought following an automobile accident, but less likely to imagine an alternative world after winning a lottery. Also, counterfactuals are more likely to be generated following actions that are taken as opposed to failures to act. Thus, switching an investment and losing money is more likely to lead to counterfactual thinking than is losing money by failing to switch to a new investment opportunity. In addition, unexpected outcomes are more likely to lead to counterfactual thinking than are expected outcomes. Similarly, unusual events are more likely to be mutated than are normal events. Thus, if John has an accident after leaving work at the usual time and taking a new route home, he is more likely to mentally undo the accident by mentally altering the route (changing it to the usual route) than by altering the time.

A second important issue concerns the affective consequences of thinking about "what could have been." Several specific emotions have been examined, and which emotion is experienced appears to depend on the particular type of counterfactual that is generated. People feel shame when their counterfactual involves mutations of the self ("If only I were a different kind of person"). On the other hand, people feel guilt when the counterfactual mutation involves changes to one's behavior ("If only I had acted differently").

Regret in particular has been a much studied emotional outcome of counterfactual thinking. Actions, or errors of commission, lead to greater counterfactual thinking and greater regret in the short term. However, when people think back upon their lives, the most frequent counterfactual thoughts and the greatest regret are felt for inactions. Thus, as we look back upon our lives, we feel the greatest regret for our failures to "seize the moment."

Regret and satisfaction are also related to the direction of counterfactual thinking—whether better possible worlds or worse possible worlds are imagined. It is clear that counterfactual thinking can lead us to feel either better or worse about our current situation. Again consider the automobile accident that causes $5,000 damage and a broken leg. If one thinks about a worse alternative world (being killed if the seatbelt had not been fastened), one feels relatively satisfied with current reality by comparison. Such counterfactuals are called downward counterfactuals. On the other hand, when one generates a better alternative world ("If only I had come to a complete stop at the stop sign, I would not have had the accident"), one feels unsatisfied with current circumstances. These are referred to as upward counterfactuals. By investigating the direction of counterfactual thinking and its impact on regret and satisfaction, Medvec, Madey, and Gilovich (1995) made some interesting observations about the mental states of silver and bronze Olympic medalists. Clearly, one would expect silver medalists to feel better because they have objectively performed better. On the other hand, the silver medalist is likely to think about the upward counterfactual of winning the gold medal, and thus to experience regret. Bronze medalists are more likely to generate the downward counterfactual where they won no medal, and thus their counterfactual alternative leaves them feeling satisfied. In fact, the authors found that, following the 1992 Summer Olympics, bronze medalists indeed experienced more positive emotions and greater satisfaction than did silver medalists, and such reactions were mediated by the counterfactual alternatives generated by these medal winners.

If counterfactual thoughts are so prevalent, they must serve some important psychological functions. Three such functions have been identified, all of which are beneficial and adaptive. First, there is affect regulation. Imagining other possible worlds can, as we have seen, lead people to feel better about their current reality. This function is generally served by downward counterfactuals, the alternatives that change reality to a worse one. When one feels that life could have been worse (regardless of how bad it is), one's affect is more positive.

Second, counterfactuals can give one hope for the future and can prepare one for that future. When one thinks of ways in which the past and present could have been better, if only certain steps had been taken, one is implicitly saying that things *will* be better if these steps are taken in the future. Imagining that one could have avoided an accident by coming to a complete stop may lead one to obey stop signs in the future and thus to avoid other accidents. Finally, counterfactual generation can help one achieve a feeling of controllability. By imagining how changes in what *you* did might have altered your bad outcomes, you perceive that you have control over your life and its outcomes. Even rape victims and cancer patients generate counterfactuals in which they could have prevented the rape or disease by changing some aspect of their own behavior. Although such counterfactuals lead to unnecessary self-blame, the positive feeling of control for the future seems to more than balance the self-blame.

In sum, counterfactual thinking is a ubiquitous mental activity. By imagining alternatives to reality, we realize that circumstances are not inevitable and that changes could have been and can still be made that will alter our lives and our history. Importantly, such thinking has significant impacts on our affective states and on our judgments. We should therefore strive to understand both the functional and the dysfunctional aspects of thinking about realities that might have been.

Bibliography

Gilovich, T., & Medvec, V. H. (1995). The experience of regret: What, when, and why. *Psychological Review, 102,* 379–395.

Janoff-Bulman, R. (1979). Characterological versus behavioral self-blame: Inquiries into depression and rape. *Journal of Personality and Social Psychology, 37,* 1798–1809.

Kahneman, D., & Miller, D. T. (1986). Norm theory: Comparing reality to its alternatives. *Psychological Review, 93,* 136–153.

Markman, K. D., Gavanski, I., Sherman, S. J., & McMullen, M. N. (1993). The impact of perceived control on the imagination of better and worse possible worlds. *Personality and Social Psychology Bulletin, 29,* 87–109.

Medvec, V. H., Madey, S. F., & Gilovich, T. (1995). When less is more: Counterfactual thinking and satisfaction among Olympic medalists. *Journal of Personality and Social Psychology, 69,* 603–610.

Niedenthal, P. M., Tangney, J. P., & Gavanski, I. (1994). "If only I weren't" versus "If only I hadn't": Distinguishing shame and guilt in counterfactual thinking. *Journal of Personality and Social Psychology, 67,* 585–595.

Roese, N. J. (1994). The functional basis of counterfactual thinking. *Journal of Personality and Social Psychology, 66,* 805–818.

Roese, N. J., & Olson, J. M. (Eds.). (1995). *What might have been: The social psychology of counterfactual thinking.* Mahwah, NJ: Erlbaum.

Sherman, S. J., & McConnell, A. R. (1995). Dysfunctional implications of counterfactual thinking: When alternatives to reality fail us. In N. J. Roese & J. M. Olson (Eds.), *What might have been: The social psychology of counterfactual thinking* (pp. 199–231). Mahwah, NJ: Erlbaum.

Taylor, S. E., Lichtman, R. R., & Wood, J. V. (1984). Attributions, beliefs about control, and adjustment to breast cancer. *Journal of Personality and Social Psychology, 46,* 489–502.

Steven J. Sherman

COUNTERTRANSFERENCE. Countertransference is a controversial concept in the counseling and psychotherapy literature because it suggests that counselors do not always accurately and effectively respond to clients because of their own pathology or irrational feelings, thoughts, and behaviors. Sigmund Freud (1910/1957) first used and defined this term when he noted that psychoanalysts can develop and experience their own transference reactions to their client's transference. Freud believed that all transference reactions are determined by unconscious, irrational wishes and desires based on the person's own faulty past, significant relationships, and the wishes those relationships evoked. Client transferences trigger reactions to counselors, who then may experience countertransferences. Freud argued that counselor countertransference must be recognized and rigorously avoided. Countertransference is manifested through anxiety, inappropriate and defensive behavior, and distorted perception based on counselor unconscious conflict. For example, countertransference is occurring when a counselor becomes overly harsh and uncaring toward a client. Freud argued that this reaction is caused by an unconscious and intolerable wish of the counselor to love the client, which must be defended against through distancing, punishing behavior. Understanding all counselor reactions and behaviors toward the client as countertransference became known as the "classical" approach because it narrowly limits the causes of counselor reactions to the client as pathological.

By the 1950s, psychoanalytic theorists (e.g., Heimann, 1950) began broadening the definition of countertransference to include both conscious and unconscious, rational and irrational, reactions toward the client. This "totalistic" approach argues that countertransference refers to all the feelings that the therapist experiences toward the client. These theorists found it important to include not only the counselor's unconscious and irrationally based reactions to the client's transference, but also the entirety of the counselor's feelings and attitudes toward the client. An example of this totalistic position occurs when a counselor begins to feel sorry for a client who presents with considerable guilt and worry. Rather than viewing this reaction as due to the counselor's own history, it is viewed as a realistic reaction to the client's interpersonal style.

This broadened definition of countertransference opens the door to reexamination of whether counselor countertransference reactions are always detrimental to counseling. Winnicott (1949) suggested that the objective examination of counselor attitudes and feelings toward a client will yield valuable information with regard to client pathology. In other words, countertransference reactions may help the counselor understand the client's intra- and interpersonal world. Interpersonal theorists have also begun to use the countertransference concept in their writings by drawing upon Winnicott's distinction between objective and subjective countertransference. Objective countertransference refers to those reactions that clients evoke within any counselor, as can be evidenced with an angry, hostile individual who elicits resentment and withdrawal across interpersonal situations. Subjective refers to nonuniversal or idiosyncratic counselor reactions that are embedded in counselor rather than client pathology. For example, a particular client resembles the counselor's deceased sibling, evoking strong, ambivalent reactions toward the client. A conceptual problem with these expanding definitions of countertransference is that they encompass all reactions to the client, and thus, countertransference becomes potentially meaningless other than as a term for counselor reaction.

The measurement of countertransference is highly problematic because it is theoretically linked to unconscious processes that cannot be directly observed. Contemporary psychological researchers have chosen to operationally define and measure manifestations, or observable markers, of countertransference. Three types of behaviors typically have been targeted: interpersonal distortions, avoidant behavior, and poor recall of material. Cutler (1958), for example, found that counselors had distorted perceptions of what clients discussed when the topic related to unresolved counselor conflict areas. Several researchers (e.g., Hayes & Gelso, 1991; Yulis & Kiesler, 1968) have found that counselors tend to distance themselves, or become underinvolved with clients when there is an increase in the client's emotionally laden material. A recurring problem with these research studies is the inability to link laboratory-based observations of countertransference to actual counseling settings.

Several models have been developed for understanding how countertransference feelings are managed. Reich (1960) argued that the counselor must empathize with the client to the point where the counselor has similar experiences as the client. To use this shared experience effectively, Reich advises the counselor to be alert to his or her own feelings, stop to investigate them, and then analyze what is going on (1960, p. 392). Robbins and Jolkovski (1987) attempted to clarify this model by distinguishing between countertransference feelings and countertransference behaviors. They argued that countertransference *feelings* are inevitable reactions to any interpersonal situation, but that they only become maladaptive or problematic if they are not understood. When such feelings are misunderstood or ignored they result in inappropriate *behaviors* (including interpersonal distortions and faulty recall of client material). Robbins and Jolkovski hypothesized that a counselor must first become aware of reactions toward a client, and then, second, manage these feelings through taking a cognitive perspective. They and other researchers (summarized in Gelso & Hayes, 1998) have found evidence to support the premise that awareness of countertransference feelings is a necessary but not sufficient condition for avoiding behavioral problems. Counselors must still be able to cog-

nitively "place" these reactions into a learning paradigm about the client to avoid nontherapeutic behaviors such as cognitive distortions or withdrawal of involvement.

Countertransference continues to generate considerable interest among counselors because it is recognized that irrational reactions to a client can harm the client. Conversely, if counselors are able to recognize and understand their reactions to clients, they can improve their understanding of client problems and effectively respond to the client. Surprisingly little research, however, has supported the link between counselor countertransference and therapy outcome, despite Singer and Luborsky's (1977) conclusion that uncontrolled countertransference has an adverse effect on therapy outcome. The future status of the countertransference construct will depend on whether the variety of theorists (e.g., interpersonalists, cognitive-behaviorists, contemporary psychoanalysts) using it are careful to operationally define and measure the construct, and to link it to counselor theoretical orientation, the phases of therapy, and counseling outcomes (Gelso & Hayes, 1998).

[*See also* Psychoanalysis, *article on* Psychoanalytic Psychotherapy; Psychotherapy, *article on* Research Methods; *and* Transference.]

Bibliography

Cutler, R. L. (1958). Countertransference effects in psychotherapy. *Journal of Consulting Psychology, 22,* 349–356. An early empirical study of countertransference based on psychoanalytic theory.

Freud, S. (1957). The future prospects of psycho-analytic therapy. In J. Strachey (Ed. & Trans.), *The standard edition of the complete psychological works of Sigmund Freud* (Vol. 11, pp. 139–151). London: Hogarth Press. (Original work published 1910.) This is the English translation of the complete works of Sigmund Freud.

Gelso, C. J., & Hayes, J. A. (1988). *The psychotherapy relationship: Theory, research, practice.* New York: Wiley. This book is an excellent summary of issues related to different elements of the client-counselor relationship, drawing upon theoretical and empirical literatures.

Hayes, J. A., & Gelso, C. J. (1991). Effects of therapist-trainees' anxiety and empathy on countertransference behavior. *Journal of Clinical Psychology, 47,* 284–290. An empirical analysis of the determinants of counselor countertransference behavior, distinguishing between countertransference feelings and behavior.

Heimann, P. (1950). On countertransference. *International Journal of Psychoanalysis, 31,* 9–15. An important, early effort at reconceptualizing countertransference into objective and subjective components.

Reich, A. (1960). Further remarks on countertransference. *International Journal of Psychoanalysis, 41,* 389–395. This article is a theoretical revision of Freud's original work on countertransference.

Robbins, S. B., & Jolkovski, M. P. (1987). Managing countertransference feelings: An interactional model using awareness of feeling and theoretical framework. *Journal of Counseling Psychology, 34*, 276–282. This study introduces and tests the notion that countertransference behavior is modified by a counselor's ability to first recognize, and then cognitively understand countertransference feelings.

Singer, B. A., & Luborsky, L. (1977). Countertransference: The status of clinical versus quantitative research. In A. S. Gurman & A. M. Razdin (Eds.), *Effective psychotherapy: Handbook of research* (pp. 433–451). New York: Pergamon. This is an important review of empirical versus clinical or "anecdotal" studies of countertransference behavior.

Winnicott, D. W. (1949). Hate in the countertransference. *International Journal of Psycho-Analysis, 30*, 69–75. A good description of how countertransference occurs in everyone, including mothers and therapists.

Yulis, S., & Kiesler, D. J. (1968). Countertransference response as a function of therapist anxiety and content of patient talk. *Journal of Consulting and Clinical Psychology, 32*, 414–419. An early study of countertransference using an analogue procedure.

Steven R. Robbins

COUPLES THERAPY. Broadly conceived, couples therapy includes any therapeutic intervention aimed specifically at improving the relationship between two adults. Couples therapy most commonly occurs with married couples seeking to reduce conflict or enhance emotional intimacy, although these same goals may be pursued by nonmarried or same-gender couples. Couples therapy is distinguished from both individual and family therapy by its primary emphasis on the dyadic relationship as the target of intervention. Hence, contemporary practice of couples therapy typically involves working with both partners conjointly to facilitate within-session assessment and modification of partners' patterns of interaction.

Because communication difficulties are the most common complaint of couples entering therapy, most approaches to couples therapy strive to improve partners' communication—although they may conceptualize communication difficulties differently and use distinct techniques to promote more effective or satisfying communication between partners. Common to most approaches to couples therapy are various techniques for promoting appropriate self-disclosure, enhancing each partner's experience of being understood by the other, and developing more effective means for resolving interpersonal conflict.

Couples therapy may be considered to include interventions targeting specific relationship domains. For example, anger-management training and other conflict-containment techniques may be used with couples struggling with physical aggression. Sex therapy typically emphasizes training in communication skills along with specific techniques for promoting more satisfying sexual and other physical exchanges. Other relationship enhancement techniques may be used to promote emotional intimacy through emotional expressiveness and empathy training. Couples therapy may also emphasize acquiring knowledge or skills necessary for effective collaboration between partners in managing their finances, dealing with their children or adolescents, or interacting more effectively with individuals outside their own relationship including in-laws, the public schools, and medical or legal systems.

In some applications, couples therapy may be used to promote objectives other than improving the couple's relationship. For example, in separation or divorce counseling, interventions emphasize suspending or dissolving the relationship in a constructive manner to facilitate both partners' subsequent adjustment as well as respective parental roles. Couples therapy has also been used in the treatment of individual disorders such as depression, anxiety disorders, and alcohol or other substance abuse. For each of these disorders, spouse-assisted treatment or couples therapy frequently enhances the effectiveness of interventions targeting the individual partner presenting with these difficulties.

Modalities of Couples Therapy

Couples therapy typically involves treatment sessions in which both partners are seen together or conjointly. In conjoint therapy, most treatment approaches encourage the partners to interact with each other directly, with guidance and modification of these interactions by the therapist. Less common in treatment of couples is concurrent therapy in which both partners are treated by the same therapist in separate individual sessions, but with the focus of treatment remaining the couple's relationship. Whereas concurrent therapy dominated approaches to couples treatment prior to 1970, today it is used more commonly in those situations in which partners are unable to contain their antagonism in conjoint sessions to make effective use of interventions, or instances in which one or both partners need to address significant individual concerns but do not yet feel sufficiently secure to do so in a conjoint session. More often, individual sessions with both partners may be interspersed with conjoint sessions in a combined approach.

Couples' unique circumstances sometimes require providing couples therapy in alternative formats. When one or both partners experience significant individual difficulties interfering with their relationship, they may each be seen separately by two therapists who consult with each other in a collaborative approach to treatment; such a couple might still be seen in conjoint sessions by a third therapist who consults with the other two. Group approaches to couples therapy have also been developed, ranging from relatively short-term, structured psychoeducational groups to more open-ended, experiential groups. Group couples therapy most commonly targets couples with relatively stable relationships seeking additional skills or relationship resources, but may also be provided as an adjunct to more distressed couples receiving separate conjoint treatment.

History and Development of Couples Therapy

Interest in intervening with couples experiencing relationship difficulties began in the 1930s and led to establishment of the American Association for Marriage and Family Therapy (AAMFT) (originally the American Association of Marriage Counselors) in 1942. From its inception this association has been interdisciplinary in nature, including social workers, psychologists, and psychiatrists as well as sociologists, educators, clergy, nurses, and family physicians. In 1997, AAMFT boasted more than 23,000 members. Interest in couples and family therapy as a distinct domain within psychology led to establishing family psychology as a separate division in the American Psychological Association (APA) in 1984, growing to some 2,100 division members by 1997.

Major Theoretical Approaches

Theoretical approaches to couples therapy have generally paralleled those that have evolved in individual treatment. From the 1940s well into the 1960s a psychodynamic approach to couples therapy prevailed, emphasizing relationship dysfunction as an outgrowth of individuals' maladaptive strategies for gratifying exaggerated emotional needs or defending against anticipated relationship trauma. Not surprisingly, couples therapy from this approach often emphasized concurrent and separate treatment of partners. Contemporary couples therapy from a psychodynamic perspective typically adopts a conjoint modality and emphasizes recurrent maladaptive patterns of relationship behavior based in early interpersonal experiences. Previous relationships, their affective components, and strategies for emotional gratification and anxiety containment are reconstructed with a focus on identifying for each partner similarities in their interpersonal conflicts and coping styles across relationships. In addition, ways in which previous coping strategies vital to prior relationships represent distortions or inappropriate solutions for emotional intimacy and satisfaction in the current relationship are articulated.

Systems-oriented approaches to couples therapy emerged during the 1960s as a subset of family therapy techniques conceptualizing an individual's emotional and behavioral difficulties as symptomatic expressions of broader family system dysfunction. From a systems perspective, each partner's behavior is both a cause and consequence of the other's behavior. Partners' reciprocal exchanges are examined for their function in maintaining balance in the couple's relationship. Systems-based interventions seek to alter the implicit rules that govern dysfunctional patterns of relating. Strategic techniques are used to promote more functional patterns, often through paradoxical interventions. For example, one partner's depression may be reframed as providing the other partner with a vital role as caretaker—with the subsequent directive that the caretaker should provide *less* rather than more caretaking as a means of assisting the partner in moving toward relinquishing his or her depression as a relationship-maintaining role. Other interventions from a systems perspective promote a more functional family structure: for example, emphasizing the collaborative leadership role of the parents and distinguishing the family system more clearly from broader systems involving the extended family or community.

Behavioral couples therapy emerged in the 1970s as a skills-based approach for improving couples' relationships. From a behavioral perspective, relationship difficulties stem primarily from partners' communication deficits and from ineffective strategies for influencing the other's behavior, primarily by negative or coercive means. Behavioral couples therapy assists partners in developing effective communication skills through explicit instruction, modeling, rehearsal, and modification of these skills within sessions. In addition, couples therapy from this perspective helps individuals to use positive means for promoting desired behavior from their partner in place of punishment or other aversive methods. In the 1980s, behavioral couples therapy was expanded to include interventions targeting various cognitive processes contributing to relationship distress. Cognitive components of couples therapy emphasize faulty assumptions and unreasonable standards individuals have concerning their relationship, selective attention to negative relationship events, negative relationship expectancies, and various attributional biases, including a tendency to ascribe their partner's behavior to global, enduring, negative motives or characteristics.

As in individual therapy, recent developments in couples therapy have emphasized integration of therapeutic approaches tailored to the unique characteristics and needs of individuals and their relationship. For example, some couples require direct intervention by the therapist and mobilization of additional community resources in containing disabling relationship crises involving physical aggression, substance abuse, or major psychopathology. Other couples may benefit from interventions emphasizing improved communication, basic information, and skill-acquisition in specific areas of their relationship. Still other couples appear to possess the requisite communication and relationship skills, but fail to draw on these constructively when confronted with unrealistic expectations or fears concerning the relationship or their partner's response. For these couples, more appropriate interventions might emphasize cognitive or affective processes—including those beyond partners' immediate awareness—interfering with effective use of existing relationship skills.

Effectiveness of Couples Therapy

There is considerable evidence indicating that couples therapy often produces both statistically and clinically significant effects. The average couple receiving therapy is better off at the end of treatment than 75% of couples not receiving therapy. At termination, approximately 65% of couples show significant improvement based on partners' averaged reports of satisfaction. However, using rigorous outcome criteria, in only 50% of treated couples do both partners show significant improvement in relationship satisfaction at termination. Moreover, long-term follow-up studies of couples therapy show significant deterioration among 30 to 60% of treated couples following termination.

Given the variability in couples' responses to therapy, efforts have been made to identify predictors of treatment outcome. For example, depression in one or both spouses appears to be a negative prognostic indicator—despite the finding that couples therapy may be more effective than individual therapy where both depression and relationship distress co-occur. By contrast, higher initial levels of emotional expressiveness and interpersonal sensitivity denote greater probability of positive outcome to couples therapy, as do higher levels of affection, intimacy, and commitment to the relationship.

The specific mechanisms by which couples therapy produces significant and lasting positive change remain a topic of considerable debate. There is ample evidence that teaching couples more effective communication techniques and promoting positive methods of behavior change result in increased relationship satisfaction. However, there is also growing evidence that couples treated with behavioral techniques alone remain at risk for significant deterioration in relationship satisfaction following treatment. The addition of cognitive restructuring and emotional expressiveness training to traditional behavioral couples therapy does not appear to enhance overall treatment effectiveness in promoting relationship satisfaction, although it does produce improvements on variables specifically targeted by these components. There is some evidence indicating that couples therapy approaches addressing covert affective components may produce more enduring gains in re-

lationship satisfaction, although the number of studies from this perspective remains small.

Ethical Issues in Couples Therapy

Couples therapy presents unique ethical dilemmas not typically confronted in individual approaches. Foremost among these are issues in defining the client (i.e., an individual partner, the couple's relationship, or the larger family unit) and identifying the therapist's respective responsibilities to each member. In relationships in which the two partners differ in level of individual functioning, strengthening the relationship may require suspending one partner's opportunities for individual growth or emotional fulfillment for the sake of the other. In other cases, the needs of one partner (e.g., protection from physical abuse) may demand a higher priority than preservation of a destructive relationship. Typically, the couples therapist strives to maintain neutrality and to support the relationship by facilitating exchanges and resolutions to conflict consistent with both partners' needs and values. Issues of identifying the client and therapist's responsibilities become more difficult when the modality of couples therapy switches among conjoint, individual, or family sessions. In general, the couples therapist strives to clarify from the outset the nature of his or her professional relationship with each of the persons involved.

A related ethical dilemma involves issues of confidentiality and informed consent. In general, couples therapists typically encourage an agreement from the outset that personal information or secrets are harmful to the therapy and, hence, any information provided to the therapist in any context by either partner may be incorporated or disclosed by the therapist in a subsequent conjoint session involving both partners. Informed consent occurs when all participants in the therapy are advised from the outset of the multiple possible outcomes of couples therapy, potential risks and benefits of this approach, the respective rights and responsibilities of each participant, and the opportunity to pursue alternative treatment approaches.

[See also Divorce; and Marriage.]

Bibliography

Halford, W. K., & Markman, H. J. (Eds.). (1997). *Clinical handbook of marriage and couples interventions.* New York: Wiley.

Jacobson, N. S., & Gurman, A. S. (Eds.). (1995). *Clinical handbook of couple therapy.* New York: Guilford Press.

Johnson, S. M., & Greenberg, L. S. (Eds.). (1994). *The heart of the matter: Perspectives on emotion in marital therapy.* New York: Brunner/Mazel.

Liddle, H., Santisteban, D., Levant, R., & Bray, J. (Eds.). (In press). *Family psychology intervention science.* Washington, DC: American Psychological Association.

Mikesell, R. H., Lusterman, D. D., & McDaniel, S. H. (Eds.). (1995). *Integrating family therapy: Handbook of family psychology and systems theory.* Washington, DC: American Psychological Association.

Douglas K. Snyder

COVERT CONDITIONING. Historically, the roots of covert conditioning may be found in the writings of Skinner (1953) and other behavioral researchers (Thorndike, 1911; Tolman, 1932) who addressed covert stimuli and responses. More direct influences may be identified in behavior change procedures which utilize imaginal stimuli, such as systematic desensitization (Wolpe, 1958) and implosive therapy (Stampfl & Levis, 1967). An early account of the application of reinforcement principles to covert behavior was provided by Homme (1965) who introduced the term *coverant control*—with *coverant* representing a summary term for *covert operant.* Since the mid-1960s, Joseph R. Cautela has been considered the major proponent of covert conditioning procedures, and he and his colleagues have published widely on the topic. Covert conditioning has been defined by Cautela and Kearney (1990) as "a process through which private events such as thoughts, images, and feelings are manipulated in accordance with principles of learning, usually operant conditioning, to bring about changes in overt behavior, covert psychological behavior (i.e., thoughts, images, feelings), and/or covert physiological behavior (e.g., glandular secretions)" (p. 86).

As with strategies designed to alter the expression of overt behavior, specific procedures are used depending upon whether the target behavior is to be increased or decreased. The procedures used in covert conditioning are analogous to those based on principles of reinforcement and punishment used with overt behavior. Specific procedures under the rubric of covert conditioning include the following.

Covert Reinforcement

The client imagines engaging in the target behavior and then imagines a pleasant scene or presentation of a reinforcing event. *Example:* A child imagines approaching a group of children on a playground. Then she imagines herself playing games with the other children, laughing, and having fun.

Covert Negative Reinforcement

The client imagines an aversive event which is then terminated when the client switches to imagining engaging in the target behavior. *Example:* A college student imagines that he is home alone again on a Sat-

urday night, feeling insecure and depressed. Then he switches the imaginary scene to one in which he is asking a young woman for a date and she says "yes."

Covert Modeling

The client imagines a model engaging in the target behavior and then imagines that a reinforcing (if the target behavior is to be increased) or aversive (if the target behavior is to be decreased) consequence is delivered to the model. *Example A:* A woman imagines a model (someone similar in physical and personality characteristics to herself) requesting a raise from her boss. She then imagines that the boss grants the model the raise. *Example B:* A child imagines a model (similar in physical and personality characteristics to himself) making fun of other children in his classroom. He then imagines that no one thinks this is funny and the model is rejected by his peers.

Covert Sensitization

In covert sensitization, the client imagines that he or she is engaging in the target behavior and then visualizes an aversive consequence. *Example:* A woman imagines herself smoking. She then imagines her lungs turning black, tumors forming, and blood being expelled from her mouth when she coughs.

Covert Extinction

The client imagines that he or she is engaging in the target behavior, and then imagines that the contingencies that maintain the behavior *in vivo* are no longer present. *Example:* A man imagines that he is making sexually harassing comments to his colleagues at work. He then imagines that the colleagues completely ignores his comments rather than responding with shock and engaging him in banter.

Covert Response Cost

The client imagines that he or she is engaging in the target behavior and then imagines an assessed penalty (i.e., a reinforcer that is not maintaining the behavior is withdrawn). *Example:* A child imagines that she is fighting with her siblings. She then imagines that her phone and television privileges are withdrawn for one week.

The vast majority of research on covert conditioning has been in the area of appetitive processes (e.g., cigarette smoking, alcoholism, overeating, deviant sexual arousal). Early applications primarily involved the use of covert sensitization in which an aversive physiological state (e.g., nausea) was classically conditioned to imaginal presentation of the target behavior to be decreased (e.g., alcohol consumption). Subsequently, imaginal presentation of a scene in which the individual did not consume, or turned away from, the alcohol was negatively reinforced through removal of the aversive stimulus. The use of aversive control techniques remain controversial among psychologists. However, advocates of covert sensitization emphasize that covert aversion is quite safe relative to other aversion techniques (e.g., electric shock).

Although covert conditioning procedures have been used most frequently with adult populations, these procedures have been used successfully with children and adolescents. Cautela (1982) discussed issues relevant to the implementation of covert conditioning procedures with children, including the need to ascertain the child's ability to engage in and manipulate imagery upon instruction. Due to the necessity for the client to accept and follow practitioner direction, to generate vivid imagery, and to comply with homework assignments, covert conditioning may be extremely difficult or impossible to implement with certain populations (e.g., individuals with autism, severe behavior disorders, extreme sensory deficits).

Empirical evidence for the effectiveness of covert conditioning procedures has been mixed. Although numerous case studies have documented behavioral change following covert conditioning, few reports have included an experimental control condition. In instances when an experimental control procedure has been utilized, the differential efficacy of covert conditioning has not been demonstrated consistently. Paniagua (1993) noted the following methodological problems identified in reports of the use of covert conditioning: (1) the nature of the procedure necessarily results in difficulty in assessing procedural reliability and thus the integrity of covert conditioning procedures is questionable; (2) it is difficult, if not impossible, to determine if lack of behavior change following covert conditioning is the result of inadequate instruction provided by the practitioner or rather the result of the client's difficulty or inability to obtain clear imagery; and (3) support for the efficacy of covert conditioning procedures largely has been demonstrated through the use of single-case designs, and technically what has been demonstrated is the effect of practitioner-delivered reinforcement (e.g., praise, attention) contingent upon the client's self-report rather than the effect of conditioning upon imagery *per se*. Several authors have questioned the exact mechanism by which covert conditioning results in behavior change, with the role of suggestibility (Foreyt & Hagan, 1973) and habituation processes (Plaud & Gaither, 1997) noted as potential alternative explanations.

Bibliography

Cautela, J. R. (1967). Covert sensitization. *Psychological Record, 20*, 459–468.

Cautela, J. R. (1982). Covert conditioning with children. *Journal of Behavior Therapy and Experimental Psychiatry, 13*, 209–214.

Cautela, J. R., & Kearney, A. J. (1990). Behavior analysis, cognitive therapy, and covert conditioning. *Journal of Behavior Therapy and Experimental Psychiatry, 21*, 83–90.

Epstein, L. H., & Peterson, G. L. (1973). Differential conditioning using covert stimuli. *Behavior Therapy, 4*, 96–99.

Foreyt, J. P., & Hagan, R. L. (1973). Covert sensitization: Conditioning or suggestion? *Journal of Abnormal Psychology, 82*, 17–23.

Homme, L. E. (1965). Perspectives in psychology. XXIV. Control of coverants, the operants of the mind. *Psychological Record, 15*, 501–511.

Paniagua, F. A. (1993). Anomalies in covert conditioning. *Psychological Reports, 73*, 323–327.

Plaud, J. J., & Gaither, G. A. (1997). A clinical investigation of the possible effects of long-term habituation of sexual arousal in assisted covert sensitization. *Journal of Behavior Therapy and Experimental Psychiatry, 28*, 281–290.

Skinner, B. F. (1953). *Science and human behavior*. New York: Macmillan.

Stampfl, T. G., & Levis, D. J. (1967). Essentials of implosive therapy: A learning-theory-based psychodynamic behavioral therapy. *Journal of Abnormal Psychology, 72*, 496–503.

Thorndike, E. L. (1911). *Animal intelligence*. New York: Macmillan.

Tolman, E. C. (1932). *Purposive behavior in animals and men*. New York: Appleton-Century-Crofts.

Upper, D., & Cautela, J. R. (1977). *Covert conditioning*. New York: Pergamon Press.

Wolpe, J. (1958). *Psychotherapy by reciprocal inhibition*. Stanford, CA: Stanford University Press.

Tracy L. Morris

CREATIVITY. [*This entry comprises two articles. The first article provides a broad overview of creativity. The second article presents a general survey of the psychological research conducted on the creative process. For discussions related to creativity, see* Imagination; *and* Performing Arts.]

An Overview

In the most diverse cultures, the concept of creativity arises in myths that try to explain the origins of life. The Judeo-Christian tradition is typical in this respect: the Bible starts with an account of how the supreme being created a world from chaos and crowned his efforts with the shaping of human beings. Until quite recently, creativity was assumed to be a divine prerogative. Artists or poets did not have original ideas, but were inspired by the voice of a muse. Until the Renaissance, when an artist or thinker came up with something new, it was attributed to the rediscovery of ancient knowledge rather than to an individual's unique contribution.

It is often said that in the European tradition, the first individual to be recognized as creative was Michelangelo. By the Renaissance, human agency began to be seen as having a certain freedom and independence, and thus the possibility of an individual making something new through his or her own powers became conceivable, but it was still restricted to the highest levels of human accomplishment. Ever since, the concept of creativity has expanded to cover more and more ground. As the Romantic worldview pervaded the West, every young poet or painter took on the mantle of creativity. In the late twentieth century, the finger paintings of toddlers or variations on a cooking recipe are said to be creative if they depart in some respect from conventional standards.

In psychology, creativity usually refers to the production of any idea, action, or object that is new and valued. By extension, a creative person is one who stands out from the norm by producing such ideas, actions, or objects. Such a simple definition, however, raises a number of important questions. For instance, how *new* does the product have to be? Do the most novel drawings in a kindergarten class qualify, or only those works that change the history of art? Furthermore, how *valuable* does the product have to be, and whose evaluation counts? Is it enough for the person to feel that the product is novel and valuable, or does one need the approbation of experts before a claim to creativity can be accepted? These are not just academic questions, because unless a definition is agreed upon, entirely different phenomena can be included under the term. In this article, I shall consider creativity in the stricter sense, as an idea or product that changes the culture—the way we see and understand the world, the way we act and live.

Psychological Research on Creativity

The early history of research in creativity might be dated to the second half of the nineteenth century, when the Italian physician Cesare Lombroso was struck by the relationship between genius and madness, and the British eugenicist Sir Francis Galton showed that genius appeared with unusual frequency in certain families and concluded that genius was inherited. Later investigations of creativity were, for a long time, confined to Freud and his disciples, who tried to trace the transformations of repressed libidinal content in the work of such artists as Michelangelo and Leonardo da Vinci. More empirical approaches had to wait until World War II, when the U.S. Air Force contracted with

psychologist J. Paul Guilford at the University of Southern California to develop tests for original and creative thinking. The need for such tests arose from the observation that highly intelligent and well-trained pilots did not necessarily know how to solve unexpected problems that arose when an aircraft was damaged. To be able to do this, it was assumed, something more akin to creativity was needed. [*See the biographies of Galton, Guilford, and Lombroso.*]

Guilford (1967) developed a theory of cognitive functioning that took creativity into account, and a battery of tests that measured fluency, flexibility, and originality of thought in both verbal and visual domains. His model and the tests he developed (e.g., the Brick Uses and Unusual Uses tests) are still the foundation on which much creativity testing and research is based. (e.g., Torrance, 1988). Creativity studies received a great boost in the late 1950s, when articles dealing with this topic in the psychological literature jumped from fewer than ten a year to several hundred, and then more than a thousand each year. Two separate reasons for this expansion were obviously involved. The first was Guilford's election to the presidency of the American Psychological Association and the topic of his inaugural lecture, creativity. Second, the Soviet launch of a space probe in 1957 caused a great deal of soul-searching in American society at large, and resulted in the perception that creativity needed to be enhanced in the schools, lest American science fall behind. Such effects on the development of our understanding of creativity represent not just historical curiosities, but as we shall see later, are themselves illustrations of how new forms of art, science, and technology are created. If we think of creativity research as being a valuable novelty, we see that its growth and expansion is not just the work of single individuals, but depends, to a large extent, on the contribution of social forces.

Contemporary approaches to creativity are so varied that no exhaustive description of them is possible. They range from mathematical modeling and computer-run simulations of creative breakthroughs in science as conducted by Norbert Simon and his team at Carnegie-Mellon University (Langley, Simon, Bradshaw, & Zytkow, 1987), to the intensive study of a single individual's lifelong struggle with a creative problem, such as Howard Gruber's (1981) intellectual biography of Charles Darwin. Other approaches include the historiographic method that Dean Simonton (1990) in California and Colin Martindale (1990) in Maine applied to the content of large numbers of creative works, or to a large number of biographies. Probably the majority of studies, however, are still done with schoolchildren and students, and use performance on Guilford-type tests as a criterion of creative thinking. (For reviews of work in this area, see Runco & Albert, 1990; Sternberg, 1988; and recent issues of *Creativity Research Journal* and *Journal of Creative Behavior*.)

Stages of the Creative Process

Contrary to the popular image of creative solutions appearing with the immediacy of a popping flashbulb, most novel achievements are best understood as the result of a much longer process, sometimes lasting many years. It is generally convenient to differentiate five stages of this process (Wallas, 1926), with the understanding that these stages are recursive, and may be repeated in several full or partial cycles before a creative solution appears.

Preparation. It is said that creative ideas come to prepared minds. This means, in the first place, that it is almost impossible to have a good new idea without having first been immersed in a particular symbolic system, or domain. Creative inventors know the ins and outs of their branch of technology, artists are familiar with the work of previous artists, and scientists have learned whatever there is to know about their specialty. Second, it means that one must feel a certain unease about the state of the art in one's domain. There has to be a sense of curiosity about some unresolved problem: a machine that could be improved, a disease that has to be cured, or a theory that could be made simpler and more elegant.

Sometimes the problem is *presented* to the artist, scientist, or inventor by an outside emergency or requirement. The most important creative problems, however, are *discovered* when the individual tries to come to terms with a problematic situation (Getzels, 1964). In such cases the problem itself may not be clearly formulated until the very end of the process. As Albert Einstein, among others, noted, the solution of an already formulated problem is relatively easy compared to the formulation of a problem that no one has previously recognized.

Incubation. Some of the most important mental work in creative problems takes place below the threshold of consciousness. It is not known exactly what happens at this stage, but it seems that the problematic issues identified during the preceding stage continue to be active without the person controlling the process. Presumably, the most important contribution of the incubation stage is that it allows ideas to be associated with the contents of memory more or less at random, thereby permitting completely unexpected combinations to emerge. As long as we try to formulate or solve a problem consciously, previous habits of mind will direct our thoughts in rational, but predictable, directions.

The practical implication of this phase of the process is that if one forces the mind to think only logically about problems, original solutions are less likely to result. It is, therefore, important to make time for incubation in one's schedule. There is convincing evidence that some of the best new ideas emerge after a person has been walking in the country, gardening, driving, or taking a shower: activities that occupy one's attention to a certain extent, but leave ample room for the mind to dwell on more important things.

At the same time, it is clear that incubation will not result in anything creative unless a person has become intrigued by a problem and has enough knowledge of the particular domain to evaluate the unconscious associations of ideas according to appropriate criteria. Creative individuals produce a great number of novel ideas, but they are also able to discard immediately the ones that make no sense. Nobel Prize–winning chemist Linus Pauling was once asked how he got good ideas. Pauling replied: "You have a lot of ideas, and throw away the bad ones." But because the decision as to what ideas are good or bad is made without actually thinking about it, one must have very well internalized standards to rely upon.

Insight. When a new combination of ideas is strong enough to withstand the unconscious censorship, it comes into awareness and results in a moment of illumination—the "Eureka!" or "Aha!" experience—usually thought to be the essence of creativity. Important as this moment is, no new idea or product would result from it without the long period of preparation that precedes it, and the intense work that still remains to be done.

Evaluation. The insight that emerges must then be assessed consciously according to the rules and conventions of the given domain. Most novel ideas fail to withstand critical examination. At this point, as in the preceding phases of the process, one can go wrong by being either too critical, or by not being critical enough. One of the obstacles to creativity is the perfectionism that many bright and well-trained young people have learned to apply to their profession; lacking self-confidence and expecting too much, they do not take their own ideas seriously enough to move into the last stage of the process.

Elaboration. Thomas Edison made popular the saying that creativity was 99% perspiration and 1% inspiration. Indeed, even the most brilliant insight disappears without leaving a trace unless the individual is able and willing to develop its implications and transform it into a reality. The scientific insight has to be experimentally validated, the musical idea has to be written down and orchestrated, and the visual image has to be developed on canvas.

But this stage of the creative process does not involve a simple transcription of a model perfectly formed in the mind. Most creative achievements involve drastic changes that occur as the creator ostensibly is just translating the insight into a concrete product. Therefore, it is essential to keep one's attention focused and to have an open mind in order to take advantage of unforeseen possibilities. For example, a painter may approach the canvas with a clear idea of how the finished painting should look, but most original pictures evolve during the process of painting as the combination of colors and shapes suggests new directions to the artist.

These stages can encompass many years to develop works of art or for science to change the way we see the world. Charles Darwin spent almost his entire adult life developing the theory of evolution, and Lorenzo Ghiberti spent 50 years perfecting the "Gates of Paradise" for the Baptistry of Florence. During such an extended creative process, the phases of preparation, incubation, insight, evaluation, and elaboration may recur and alternate many times.

Creativity as a Systemic Phenomenon

The question, "What is the cause of creativity?" cannot be answered by reference to the individual creator alone. No person can be creative without having access to a tradition, a craft, a knowledge base; nor can we trust the subjective report of a person to the effect that his or her insight is indeed creative. It is one of the peculiarities of human psychology that most people believe their thoughts are original and valuable. To accept such personal assessment at face value would soon deprive the concept of creativity of any specific meaning.

Creativity can best be understood as a confluence of three factors: a *domain*, which consists of a set of rules and practices; an *individual* who makes a novel variation in the contents of the domain; and a *field* composed of experts, who act as gatekeepers to the domain and decide which novel variation is worth incorporating (Csikszentmihalyi, 1996). A burst of creativity is not necessarily caused by individuals being more creative, but by domain knowledge becoming more available, or a field being more supportive of change. Conversely, lack of creativity is not usually caused by individuals who do not have enough original thoughts, but by the domain having exhausted its possibilities, or the field's inability to recognize valuable original thoughts.

Domains of Creativity. A culture consists of thousands of separate domains such as farming, carpentry, music, mathematics, religion, or gourmet cooking. Each of these is composed of a set of symbols related by rules. Most human activity involves following the rules of some domain or another. Domains are relatively stable, and are passed down from one generation to the next through learning. However, individuals are always trying out new ways to farm, new songs to sing, and new methods to compute quantities. If these are deemed to be better than the old ways, the novelty will be called creative and added to the domain.

It follows that access to a domain is essential to creativity. A person cannot be creative in the abstract, but only within the rules of some practice or idea system. It is impossible for a child living in an isolated tribe or urban ghetto to become a creative mathematician, or for an athletic young man to become a creative basketball player if that game is unknown in his culture. Domains change with time; creativity in physics, for instance, might be easier in certain periods of growth, or more difficult when the organization of the domain has become so complete that no new discovery seems possible.

Fields of Creativity. Without a group of experts who are involved in the practice of a domain, the domain will either be forgotten or become excessively rigid. In the visual arts, for instance, the field is composed of active artists, teachers, gallery owners, museum curators, critics, and collectors who decide which artists are worthy of recognition, support, and remembrance.

Members of a field can harm creativity in two ways: either by admitting every novel idea into the domain, which is likely to create chaos in the system; or by being so strict that good new ideas have no chance to be preserved. Of course, fields can also err by making wrong decisions, such as neglecting artists like Van Gogh, whom later generations recognized as having been creative. It is important to note, however, that the reason we now appreciate Van Gogh is that the field has changed its criteria, and now museums show his works, collectors pay millions for his canvases, and art historians write extensive monographs on his oeuvre. Without such a change in the judgment of the field, Van Gogh's canvases would be forgotten by now.

It is a moot question whether Van Gogh was creative all along even though he was not recognized, whether he became creative only after his paintings were appreciated, or whether he was never creative and posterity was mistaken in its attribution. Creativity is a judgment passed by society and its fields, and it is a relative judgment that holds only as long as a particular set of values lasts. It is impossible to avoid reckoning with fields, even if their judgments are reversed with time.

Thus creativity is always cocreated by the sediments of past human accomplishments deposited in the culture, by individuals bent on improving the past, and by institutions that take on the role of protecting the past from random or frivolous change. What we call creativity is the joint construction of these separate forces.

The Creative Individual

Although it has been argued so far that the individual is only one of three factors that determine creativity, it is obviously the most important one from a psychological perspective, and it is the one about which most is known. Therefore, I shall review briefly three aspects of creative individuals, namely, their cognitive processes, their personality, and their values and motivations.

Creative Thinking. For most forms of creative accomplishment, a certain amount of IQ intelligence is a prerequisite (a threshold of 120 IQ is often mentioned; Getzels & Jackson, 1962). However, the relationship of IQ to creativity is bound to vary by domain, and after a relatively low threshold, there seems to be no further contribution of IQ to creativity. The first and longest study of high-IQ children (Terman, 1947; P. Sears & R. Sears, 1980) found little evidence of adult creativity in a sample whose mean IQ as children was 152, or even in a subsample with an IQ above 170.

The most obvious characteristic of original thinkers—those whose ideas the field is likely to recognize as warranting notice—is what Guilford (1967) identified as divergent thinking, and has been popularized since as "lateral thinking" or "thinking outside the box." Divergent thinking involves unusual associations of ideas, changing perspectives, and methods of approach to problems, in contrast with convergent thinking, which involves linear, logical steps. Tests of divergent thinking are generally used to measure creativity in populations for whom no real-life evidence of creativity, such as patents, inventions, citations, awards and other forms of recognition, can be obtained.

Correlations between divergent thinking tests and creative achievement tend to be low, and some scholars even claim that the cognitive approach of creative individuals does not differ qualitatively from that of normal people except in its speed (Simon, 1988) and quantity of ideas produced (Simonton, 1990). The further conclusion some draw is that computers, which are much faster and more prolific than the human mind, will be able to achieve great creative solutions. This can only happen, however, if the computer is linked to a domain that provides questions interesting to humans, and to a field that can evaluate the computer's conclusions.

Personality and Values. One of the most longstanding concerns about the personality of creative individuals has to do with its relationship to psychopathology. In fact, some forms of mental disease, such as manic depression, substance abuse, and suicide, are more frequent among individuals involved in artistic and literary pursuits (Andreasen, 1987; Jamison, 1989), but this might have less to do with creativity than with the lack of recognition that obtains in artistic domains. At the same time, creative individuals appear to be extremely sensitive to all kinds of stimuli, including aversive ones (Piechowski, 1991), and this

might account, in part, for their higher rates of emotional instability.

Many studies have focused on the personality traits of creative individuals, and among those, the ones most often associated with creativity are openness to experience, impulsivity, self-confidence, introversion, aloofness, and rebelliousness (Getzels & Csikszentmihalyi, 1976). However, what is perhaps most remarkable about such people is their ability to be both playful and hardworking, introverted and extroverted, aloof and gregarious, or traditional and rebellious, as the occasion requires (Csikszentmihalyi, 1996). The creative person might be less distinguished by a set of traits than by the ability to experience the world along modalities, which in other people tend to be stereotyped. This also applies to the often-noted psychological androgyny of creators.

Motivation for Creativity. Given the risky and demanding nature of the creative process, a great amount of perseverance is usually required to bring a novel idea to fruition. Psychoanalysis has explained the motivation of creative individuals in terms of a sublimation of libidinal impulses that are relieved through "regression at the service of the ego" (Kris, 1952). Other explanations point to marginality and isolation in early childhood that prompts such persons to focus their energies on a divergent lifestyle.

There is no question that, for whatever reason, creative persons continue throughout life to exhibit a childlike curiosity and interest in their domains, value their work above conventional monetary or status rewards (Getzels & Csikszentmihalyi, 1976), and enjoy it primarily for intrinsic reasons (Amabile, 1983). Thus, it could be said that creativity is its own reward and needs no other explanation than the feeling of joy one gets from shaping the process of evolution.

Bibliography

Amabile, T. (1983). *The social psychology of creativity.* New York: Springer Verlag.

Andreasen, N. C. (1987). Creativity and mental illness: Prevalence rates in writers and first-degree relatives. *American Journal of Psychiatry, 144,* 1288–1292.

Csikszentmihalyi, M. (1996). *Creativity: Flow and the psychology of discovery and invention.* New York: HarperCollins.

Getzels, J. W. (1964). Creative thinking, problem solving, and instruction. In E. R. Hilgard (Ed.), *Theories of learning and instruction* (pp. 240–267). Chicago: University of Chicago Press.

Getzels, J. W., & Csikszentmihalyi, M. (1976). *The creative vision: A longitudinal study of problem finding in art.* New York: Wiley.

Getzels, J. W., & Jackson, P. (1962). *Creativity and intelligence.* New York: J. Wiley & Sons.

Gruber, H. (1981). *Darwin on man*. Chicago: University of Chicago Press.

Guilford, J. P. (1967). *The nature of human intelligence*. New York: McGraw-Hill.

Jamison, K. R. (1989). Mood disorders and patterns of creativity in British writers and artists. *Psychiatry, 52*, 125–134.

Kris, E. (1952). *Psychoanalytic explorations in art*. New York: International Universities Press.

Langley, P., Simon, H. A., Bradshaw, G. L., & Zytkow, J. M. (1987). *Scientific discovery: Computational exploration of the creative process*. Cambridge, MA: MIT Press.

Martindale, C. (1990). *The clockwork muse: The predictability of artistic change*. New York: Basic Books.

Picchowski, M. J. (1991). Emotional development and emotional giftedness. In N. Colangelo & G. A. Davis (Eds.), *Handbook of gifted education* (pp. 285–306). Boston: Allyn & Bacon.

Runco, M. A., & Albert, S. (Eds.). (1990). *Theories of creativity*. Newbury Park, CA: Sage.

Sears, P., & Sears, R. R. (1980, February). 1,528 little geniuses and how they grew. *Psychology Today*, pp. 29–43.

Simon, H. A. (1988). Creativity and motivation: A response to Csikszentmihalyi. *New Ideas in Psychology, 6*, 177–181.

Simonton, D. K. (1990). *Scientific genius*. Cambridge, England: Cambridge University Press.

Sternberg, R. J. (Ed.). (1988). *The nature of creativity*. Cambridge, England: Cambridge University Press.

Terman, L. M. (1947). Subjects of IQ 170 or above. *Genetic studies of genius* (Vol. 4). Stanford, CA: Stanford University Press.

Torrance, E. P. (1988). The nature of creativity as manifest in its testing. In R. J. Sternberg (Ed.), *The nature of creativity* (pp. 43–75). Cambridge, England: Cambridge University Press.

Wallas, G. (1926). *The art of thought*. New York: Harcourt-Brace.

Mihaly Csikszentmihalyi

Research on the Process of Creativity

It has been said that creativity is like pornography: easy to identify but difficult to define. In both cases individuals often feel that they "know it when they see it." What may be most important in that claim is the terminal pronoun: *it*. "They know it when they see *it*." In the sense that the pronoun is a substitute for a noun, this claim implies that creative *objects* or *things* are easily recognized.

Indeed, although there is no widely accepted definition of creativity, there is fair agreement about innovations, inventions, solutions to pressing problems, paradigm shifts, influential works of art, and other creative products. This agreement is reflected in the explicit theories and research on *consensual assessment* measurement techniques. To the degree that people can agree about creative works, there is a consensus.

Unfortunately, innovations, inventions, works of art, and the like do not tell us much about origins. These products may offer hints about those origins, but these hints are as likely to be relatively uninformative about the underlying process or processes that led to the creation. This is especially true when looking back, after the creative work has been completed, and when there is an attempt to infer what processes were actually used and requisite. (Significantly, judgments about creative works may be useless until a period of time has passed after the completion of the work. Some claim that it is necessary to wait for years after a creator dies before his or her impact and influence can be determined.) Retrospective and introspective analyses are sometimes used to study creativity (see Vernon's collection in *Creativity*, 1970, or Ghiselin, *The Creative Process*, 1958). Case studies are still popular (see Wallace and Gruber, *Creative Persons at Work*, 1989).

There is some experimental investigation of creativity (reviewed by Runco and Sakamoto, *Handbook of Human Creativity*, 1998), but in addition to the problem already noted—the process being completed before the creativity is recognized—there is a problem that reflects the fact that the process is protracted. Granted, some insights seem to be sudden and short-lived, but in actuality, and perhaps all of the time, insights have histories and a notable amount of time has been invested in the work. If the process requires a great deal of time—and especially if time is necessary for incubation or similar unconscious or unintentional processes—traditional experimentation on creativity is difficult and has questionable generalizability.

Some time ago all creative work was viewed as being a result of this kind of sudden insight (e.g., Kekule's famous insight about the benzene ring). This view is still implied by caricatures and cartoons which depict creative insights as a lightbulb lighting up, and you can still hear people say "the penny dropped" or "everything fell into place." Each of these implies a sudden appearance of an idea. Very likely just about everyone has had an insight experience that seemed very sudden. To the extent that creative ideas are protracted, the seemingly sudden appearance of an idea is just one's perception of the process. Yet research has suggested that even if there is a sudden "ah ha!" something has prepared the individual to have the insight. In fact, it appears that all creative accomplishment requires time and some sort of effort. It may seem at one point that we are in need of an idea, and in the next instant we have the insight, but some processing does lead up to the insight.

Models of the creative process thus assume that time is necessary. The processing itself is often broken down into stages or components. Models of the creative process differ in their inclusion of particular stages or components and in the arrangement of those stages or components. A sample of process models is given in the next section. Measurement issues are explored as they pertain to each specific model.

Models of the Creative Process

The fundamental assumption shared by models of the creative process is that there is a starting point, an end point, and intermediate steps. The starting point may be a problem, dilemma, or similar motivating situation. It may be personally motivating, as is the case when the creative process is initiated by the desire for self-expression or self-actualization. The end point of the process may be an insight, solution, or product—such as those already listed (i.e., inventions, innovations, paradigm shifts, or work of art). The intermediate steps constitute the actual process. If there was just a problem and then a solution, it would not be much of a process; but with intermediate steps, movement and actual processing must be involved.

There is a great deal of controversy and diversity and models. There are numerous theories of the creative process, and many differences among them. Some theories focus on one level of consciousness; some assume that preconscious associations of some sort occur and eventually push an insight or idea into consciousness. Some models focus entirely on intrapersonal activities; others recognize social influences. Some models describe a process with invariant stages; others include stages or components that may be employed in diverse ways. A sample of models will show the variety of perspectives.

Stage Models of the Creative Process. One of the most influential models of the creative was proposed by Graham Wallas in *The Art of Thought* (1926). Wallas reviewed a speech given by the eminent physicist Hemholtz and inferred three stages. Wallas also drew from Henri Poincaré and Thomas Hobbes and proposed one additional stage. In Wallas's model, then, creative thinking involves four stages: preparation, incubation, illumination, and verification. *Preparation* may involve collecting information for the problem at hand, changing one's perspective to obtain a new approach, or obtaining information to be used in the solution. *Incubation* occurs when progress is being made toward solution or insight, but this progress is not consciously directed. *Illumination* represents the moment of insight. *Verification* involves the testing, validation, or sharing of insights. If sharing is involved, verification takes the result of the personal stages into the social realm.

There is evidence supporting this model. Most often the evidence supports one stage rather than the entire process. In a seminal investigation of artists, Jacob Getzels and Mihalyi Csikszentmihalyi observed art students preparing to create a work of art. Artists who explored before painting produced works that were more original than those of the other art students.

Work in the 1930s by Katherine Patrick suggested that such preparation is important in other fields (e.g., poetry) as well. As a matter of fact, Albert Einstein is often quoted on this point. He believed that "the formulation of a problem is often more essential than its solution" (quoted in Einstein & Infeld, 1938, p. 83). This line of thought has blossomed such that *problem finding* is now one of the critical topics in creative studies (see Jay & Perkins, in *Creativity Research Handbook*, 1996; or Runco, *Problem Finding, Problem Solving, and Creativity*, 1994).

The other stages have also been studied, though not as extensively. Incubation has received attention in the psychological research, but there is a notable difficulty because, as noted above, incubation may be indicative of unconscious processing, and this makes it very difficult to manipulate and assess. What research has been conducted suggests that it may be related to a loosening of inhibition and censorship, and these could lead directly to original thinking. Incubation has also been tied to silent rehearsal, the dissipation of fatigue, and selective forgetting.

Illumination provides the insight, and insight is still examined in experimental research. In a significant biographical analysis Howard Gruber presented the idea, mentioned above, that insights are actually protracted; and this implies that illumination is just the time when an idea breaks into consciousness. Gruber inferred that insights were protracted from his analyses of historically significant insights, including Charles Darwin's (see Gruber, 1984, 1988; Wallace, 1991). Insight has been defined from the behavioral perspective as the *spontaneous integration of previously learned responses* (Epstein, in press).

Verification may be intrapersonal or interpersonal. Many creative efforts by artists, scientists or others suggest that individuals work after an insight to refine and confirm what they have found. The surprising thing is that some evidence suggests that creators may not be very good judges of their own work. At least this is true if you compare their judgments with a larger group, or with posterity (i.e., the works that survive in public consciousness). Yet there is an important question here, because the creative person may in fact be the best judge: he or she may have the most appropriate expertise, for example, and may know what other ideas were considered and rejected, and why. Judgments reflect the orientation and experience of the judge or judges. The question is, who is the best judge? And who is to judge the judges? These questions plague all research relying on expert or consensual judgments.

Componential Models of the Creative Process. More recent processes models are likely to focus on *components* instead of stages. Components may have replaced stages because of their allowing iterations more easily than stage models. The concept of a stage implies

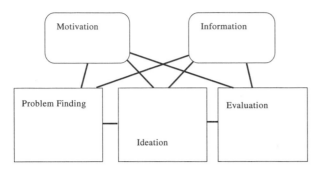

CREATIVITY: Research on the Processes of Creativity. Figure 1. One componential model of the creative process with primary components on the bottom tier and secondary components on the top.

a phase, a movement from one stage to the next, and then to the next. When working creatively it is more realistic for an individual to prepare for a while, perhaps gathering information or waiting for a clearer understanding of the problem at hand, and then to incubate for a time—but then the individual may go back and prepare a bit more. That individual may have the insight suggested by the illumination stage, but this may suggest an iteration, or at least a return to prepare yet more information. The person may produce a solution or invention, but then find some aspect during verification that requires more work. Componential models may also be more common at present than stage models because components are widely recognized within the field of cognitive science; there is, then, some generality. Componential models certainly have an advantage over stage models because they allow for extracognitive factors, and higher-order "metacomponents." These too are fashionable in the cognitive sciences.

Amabile (1990) proposed a componential model that emphasizes *intrinsic motivation, domain specific skills* (defined as technical skill and knowledge), and *creativity relevant processes* (e.g., heuristics for creative thinking and the personality traits and cognitive styles that are useful for creative work). The emphasis of this model is on intrinsic motivation, which is thought to allow the individual to move toward autonomous thought and originality. Intrinsic motivation can be contrasted with extrinsic motivation, which is thought to inhibit creative thinking, at least if it is controlling. If it provides feedback and is thereby informational, it may not be inhibitive. This model also assumes that creative ideas or products must be recognized as such by appropriate judges.

Sternberg and Lubart's model of the creative process is similar but contains additional components. Creativity-relevant skills are divided into personality

and style. Domain-specific skills include both intelligence and knowledge. The last components are environmental and motivational. The latter is task-specific but may be as general as intrinsic motivation.

A third componential model is depicted in Figure 1. This model shares features with the other componential models, though the emphases differ. This model has two tiers, one primary and one secondary. Primary components are problem finding, ideation, and evaluation. Each of these can be subdivided. Ideation, for example, was subdivided in several ways by Guilford (1968) and Torrance (in press), although most of the time only three types of ideation are recognized: fluency, originality, and flexibility. Problem finding represents problem identification and problem discovery. Evaluation can be divided into intrapersonal and interpersonal evaluations, and into those which are largely convergent and those which are more divergent. The intrapersonal evaluations and those which recognize divergence and originality distinguish evaluation in this model from that often suggested to be inhibitive of creative work. They also distinguish this kind of evaluation from social theories of verification.

Secondary components are motivational and informational. The former may be intrinsic or extrinsic, the

---

Intelligence Test Questions

How far is it from Los Angeles to Honolulu?

How many legs does a cow have?

Who was Albert Einstein?

How many dimes in a dollar?

What is the capital of Norway?

Divergent Thinking Test Questions

What strong things can you think of?
   Make a list; the more ideas, the better

What fast things can you think of?

How are a tree and a bush alike?

How are a pool and a cloud alike?

What uses can you think of for a boot?

What uses can you think of for a rock?

CREATIVITY: Research on the Processes of Creativity. Figure 2. Sample questions for a convergent (intelligence) test and from a divergent thinking test.

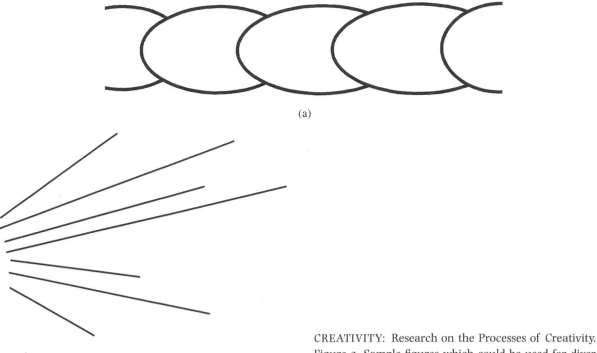

(a)

(b)

CREATIVITY: Research on the Processes of Creativity. Figure 3. Sample figures which could be used for divergent thinking stimuli.

assumption being that both can contribute to creative work. The latter may be procedural and strategic, or conceptual and declarative. These are secondary in the sense that they are less influential than the primary components. They may even result from the primary components. As an example of this causal possibility, consider the intrinsic motivation that results when an individual recognizes that they have a problem or experience in need of work. The problem identification comes first, and the motivation may follow. There is evidence for this, although there is quite a debate between those who feel that motivation and affect are causal agent or results.

There is a large amount of research on the ideational components of this model. Most of it was designed to test the reliability and validity of divergent thinking tests, independently of the knowledge and motivational components of the model. Indeed, tests of divergent thinking have become the most common assessments of creative potential.

The indices of divergent thought can be assessed with open-ended test questions. In the sense that they are open-ended, they differ from typical academic and IQ test questions (see Figure 2). A closed-ended question for an academic examination might be, "Who was the first president of the United States?" Clearly there is one correct answer to this question. A divergent thinking question from the Instances divergent thinking test is, "Name all of the things you can think of

that are strong." An examinee who gives many answers is said to be fluent with ideas, and ideas that are unique or unusual are indicative of original ideation. A variety of ideas indicates a high degree of flexibility. Data supporting the distinctiveness of divergent thinking from convergent thinking were presented by Wallach and Kogan (1965) and Runco and Albert (1985). Apparently the degree of distinctiveness depends on the testing conditions, the instructions given to the examinees, and the specific tests employed. Convergent thinking, for example, has been assessed in this area of research with IQ tests, tests of academic aptitude, and various tests of basic knowledge. Divergent thinking has been assessed with fairly artificial tests, like the Instances test (e.g., name all of the things you can think of that are square), as well as Similarities (e.g., How are a potato and a carrot alike?), Uses (list different uses for a boot), and various figural or visual tests (see Figure 3).

Categorization and Conceptualization. A very different kind of process involves the process of conceptualization. Simply put, creativity is thought to result from the (perhaps iterative) reorganization of cognitive structures (e.g., schema or concepts themselves). The conceptualization and reorganization of structures may involve analogical processes. When doing so, the individual identifies features common to categories or concepts and creates an entirely new concept or category based on those common features. It is analogical in the sense that features are shared by the new concept and the old concepts, but it is new and original in that no concept contains exactly the same features.

A great deal of anecdotal evidence indicates that many unambiguously creative achievements (e.g., the steam engine, Velcro; Davis, 1996) have been suggested by analogical thinking, and many programs intended to enhance creative thinking (e.g., the Synectics program; citation) suggest that problem solvers seek analogies. There are criticisms of the programs and concerns about that anecdotal evidence. We cannot, for example, be certain if the original insight was indeed a result of analogical thinking. Much more convincing is the experimental evidence that also supports these processes (Mumford, 1996; Ward et al., 1997). This evidence indicates that individuals who reorganize concepts efficiently are indeed more likely to produce more creative designs and solutions to various problems.

There is no widely accepted criterion of creativity. There are numerous approaches to creativity, as the sample of models reviewed suggests, and quite a bit of controversy. The debate may be more acute in studies of creativity than other fields because of the subjectivity and aesthetic basis of creative works. Certainly, there is no one criterion for the measurement of creativity. (This is the *criterion problem*, long discussed in the creativity literature.) There are several widely acknowledged correlates, such as originality, but these are at best necessary but not sufficient. As a matter of fact, if there was one criterion, many investigations would be superfluous. If one criterion was available, creative persons could be identified without using the correlates.

The varied definitions can be viewed as a virtue. This is both because there is little consensus about creativity, but also because it is quite possible that creativity is truly a *complex*. This term implies that more than one indicator would be necessary. Creativity may require a particular kind of thought, certain traits, the right attitude, and so on. Clearly, there is much that can be said about the processes underlying insight and original ideation, and the components described here constitute an important aspect of the creative complex.

Bibliography

Collins, M. A., & Amabile, T. M. (1998). Social approaches to creativity. In M. A. Runco (Ed.), *Creativity research handbook* (Vol. 2). Cresskill, NJ: Hampton Press. This chapter outlines the model, the research in support of the model, and implications for applied settings (especially organizational setting, with innovation as the objective).

Runco, M. A. (Ed.). (1994). *Problem finding, problem solving, and creativity*. Norwood, NJ: Ablex. This is a collection of chapters, each of which bears on the topic of problem finding, and each of which deals with creativity as a process. The conclusion to this volume discusses (1) commonalities among various models and (2) issues and points of disagreement. One interesting conclusion was that Wallas's model (1926), discussed above, seemed to remain useful—many models still draw from it or can fit into the same basic structure.

Runco, M. A. (Ed.). (1997). *Creativity research handbook* (Vols. 1–3). Cresskill, NJ: Hampton Press. These three volumes each cover (1) theories and approaches, and (2) special topics. Special topics include problem finding, Guilford's Structure of Intellect model (Vol. 1); suicide, affect (Vol. 2). Volume 2 also contains methodological chapters, one devoted to qualitative research, the other to the case study method.

Runco, M. A., & Albert, R. S. (1998). *Theories of creativity* (Rev. ed.). Cresskill, NJ: Hampton Press. Most articles are based on a high-level conference on the topic of creativity; several more were added to the revision. This volume presents most of the notable perspectives on the topic of creativity. It contains chapters on development, motivation, systems theory, psychopathology, personality, gender, and so on. The unique feature of this volume is that the contributors—each an influential figure in creative studies—both described their approach to creativity *and* described how that theory had developed.

Runco, M. A., & Richards, R. (Eds.). (1998). *Eminent creativity, everyday creativity, and health*. Norwood, NJ: Ablex.

Runco, M. A., & Pritzker, S. (Eds.). (in press). *Encyclopedia of creativity*. San Diego, CA: Academic Press. This encyclopedia contains over 200 articles on creativity.

Sternberg, R. J. (Ed.). (in press). *Handbook of human creativity*. New York: Cambridge University Press. This is one of several handbooks on creativity.

Sternberg, R. J., & Lubart, T. E. (in press). The role of intelligence in creativity. In M. A. Runco (Ed.), *Critical creative processes*. Creskill, NJ: Hampton Press.

Vernon, P. E. (Ed.). (1970). *Creativity*. Penguin Books. This classic contains excerpts from pioneer empirical studies, as well as introspections from Mozart, Tchaikovsky, Stephen Spender, and Henri Poincaré. Wallas's four-stage model is outlined, along with the theories of Sigmund Freud and Carl Rogers. Seminal personalities studies of Barron, MacKinnon, Cattell, and Taylor are excerpted, as are psychometric studies (e.g., Guilford, Wallach and Kogan, Hudson, and Getzels and Jackson) and suggestions for stimulating creativity (e.g., Parnes, Torrance).

Mark A. Runco

CRIMINALITY. Psychologists have studied crime and criminals for almost 100 years, including such aspects of the subject as the prevalence and nature of crime in the United States; demographics theories about crime; the relationship between intelligence, mental illness, and crime; and recidivism rates and the efficacy of rehabilitation efforts to reduce the likelihood that offenders will reoffend.

The Prevalence and Nature of Crime

At the outset, it is important to note that there are diverse views of the definition of *criminal*. Most broadly, all people who commit criminal offenses are criminals. However, when most people think of criminals they likely have a narrower definition; for example, the career offender or the individual who lives entirely off the proceeds of crime. As we review the prevalence and nature of crime, it will become clear that most crime reports employ the broadest and simplest definition of criminal noted above. By contrast, some theories of crimes that will be discussed later suggest that a criminal is generally different from others in society, and that criminals may only be considered those who repeatedly commit offenses and sometimes live off the proceeds of crime. Although it is impossible to resolve this debate here, readers should be sensitive to the scope of the definitions of *criminal* and *crime* employed here and in the literature.

Crime is a relatively frequent occurrence in the United States (U.S. Bureau of Justice Statistics, 1997a). More than 13 million offenses included in the FBI's crime index were reported to police during 1996, a rate equal to approximately one offense every 2 seconds. The incidence of property crime in 1996 surpassed the incidence of violent crime by a ratio of more than six to one. Other data indicate that the actual incidence of crime is much higher than law enforcement agency figures would suggest. For example, interviews with representative samples of Americans suggest that many crimes go unreported.

Violent crime rates demonstrated considerable variability during the 1980s and 1990s. During the late 1970s, violent crime rates increased steadily followed by a 4- or 5-year period of decline beginning in the 1980s before rising once again throughout the latter part of the decade and into the 1990s (U.S. Bureau of Justice Statistics, 1997a). Homicide, which is considered one of the most stable indicators of crime because it is relatively insensitive to changes in crime reporting or criminal justice system policies, exhibited the same general pattern as that found for other violent offenses (U.S. Bureau of Justice Statistics, 1997a). For property crime, the picture is more complicated. The reported crimes indicate that the pattern of property crime is identical to the pattern reported for violent crime. On the other hand, with the exception of motor vehicle theft, victimization surveys show a steady and consistent decline in property crime rates from the early 1970s to the mid-1970s (U.S. Bureau of Justice Statistics, 1997a).

As the discrepancies apparent between crime and victimization reports illustrate, the measurement of crime and interpretation of crime statistics is complex. One particularly troublesome issue concerns how best to define crime and individual criminal offenses of interest (Coleman & Moynihan, 1996). For example, changes or variations in arrest policies, plea bargaining, and policing levels can artificially create temporal or geographical differences in crime that are more apparent than real. In addition, many crimes do not come to the attention of law enforcement officials. Victim surveys are not hampered by the "dark figure" of officially unreported crimes; however, they are limited by the recall of respondents and the generalizability from small interview samples to the total population to which the data are extrapolated (Coleman & Moynihan, 1996).

Despite evidence that crime rates fluctuated during the 1980s and 1990s, the proportion of adults under correctional supervision has climbed steadily throughout this period (U.S. Bureau of Justice Statistics, 1997). In 1980, the percentage of American adults in custody or under community supervision was 1.1%. By 1995 this percentage had jumped to 2.8% of the population, a figure equal to more than 5.3 million people. The large majority of these offenders were on probation or parole, but by 1996 the number of inmates in federal, state, or local custody had surpassed 1.6 million people (U.S. Bureau of Justice Statistics, 1997). The burgeoning inmate population seems to be the result of a dramatic increase in the rate of admission, combined with lowered rates of release. Lower release rates do not appear to be a function of longer sentences because the average sentence length did not change during this period; however, inmates did spend more time in prison on average, suggesting a greater proportion of their sentence is now spent incarcerated. The growth in the inmate population also may be tied to America's war on drugs since the number of convicted drug offenders increased by a factor of five between 1985 and 1995.

Demographic Characteristics of Criminals

The demographic characteristics associated with criminality are remarkably consistent throughout the literature. Offenders are disproportionately male and young. Males greatly outnumber females at every stage of the criminal justice system including arrestees for violent and property crimes, inmates, and persons under correctional supervision in the community (U.S. Bureau of Justice Statistics, 1997a). Indeed, the incarceration rate for men (819 per 100,000 men) was 16 times higher than the comparable rate for women (51 per 100,000 women) in 1996 (U.S. Bureau of Justice Statistics, 1997a). Similarly, criminal offending appears to be disproportionately concentrated among the ranks of society's most youthful members. Of those persons arrested in 1996, 45% were under 25 years of age and slightly more than two thirds were under 35 years of age (U.S. Bureau of Justice Statistics, 1997a). In terms of race, Whites comprise approximately 58 to 68% of arrrestees and offenders whereas African Americans constitute roughly 28 to 32%, and Hispanics and other minority groups typically account for less than 10% (U.S. Bureau of Justice Statistics, 1997a). When each group is examined relative to the general population it is apparent that compared to Whites, African Americans are overrepresented in federal and state prisons and local jails (U.S. Bureau of Justice Statistics, 1997). There is also evidence that criminality is associated with social and occupational instability. For example, a survey of adults on probation conducted in 1995 revealed that more than 70% were never married, separated, or divorced (U.S. Bureau of Justice Statistics, 1997a).

Theories of Crime

Over time and across cultures, people have claimed that evil spirits, the devil, physical characteristics, genetics, chromosomal abnormalities, and factors in the environment are responsible for criminal behavior. Generally speaking, contemporary theories of crime focus on one of three factors (Andrews & Bonta, 1994; Blackburn, 1993, for a review): (1) biological theories, (2) sociological theories, and (3) psychological theories. Biological theories emphasize the role that genetic, physiological, and neurophysiological factors play in causing an individual to engage in criminal behavior. By contrast, sociological theories tend to focus on factors in the environment that lead people to commit crimes. Finally, psychological theories of crime attempt to identify individual differences that may lead individuals to become criminals. In particular, psychologists study the behavioral and cognitive factors that predispose people to commit crimes. Here we focus on psychology and consider psychological theories of crime.

The major psychological theories of crime fall into three categories: psychoanalytic theory, control theory, and learning theory. Sigmund Freud hypothesized about the causes of criminal behavior (Nietzel, 1979), and Blackburn (1993) noted that psychoanalytic theories of crime make three claims. First, socialization depends on the internalization of society's rules during early childhood. Second, criminal behavior is causally related to an infant's relationship with his or her parents. Those infants with impaired relationships are more likely to become criminals. Finally, criminal behavior is caused by unconscious conflicts arising from disturbed family relationships at different stages of development.

Freud essentially believed that criminals have an unconscious need to be punished. Their need to be punished stems from guilt feelings that emanate from the oedipal period when they experienced unconscious incestuous feelings. More contemporary psychoanalytic

perspectives hold that criminals have underdeveloped personalities and weak superegos (Nietzel, 1979).

In contrast to psychoanalytic theories of crime, control theories assume that everyone has the potential to engage in criminal behavior (Blackburn, 1993). Control theorists attempt to understand what processes prevent people from committing offenses. For example, Kohlberg theorized that criminal behavior is likely to occur when an individual has not developed moral reasoning (Blackburn, 1993). Other theorists, like Eysenck argue that children learn to control antisocial behavior through the development of a conscience (Blackburn, 1993).

The most influential contemporary theory of crime comes from social learning theory (Bandura, 1977) which emphasizes the interaction between the person and the environment. Social learning theorists hypothesize that people become criminals as a result of what they have learned in their environment (Andrews & Bonta, 1994; Nietzel, 1979). This theory is particularly appealing because it can explain how individuals act differently under different circumstances. For example, people are more likely to become criminals under some circumstances, and, once they have committed criminal acts, they are more likely to continue doing so if they are rewarded or reinforced.

It is impossible to know definitively what causes an individual to engage in criminal conduct because the causes of criminal behavior, as with all other behavior, are complex and involve biological, environmental, and psychological factors. With different individuals, and even with different types of crimes, each of these factors may play a different relative role in explaining why any given individual engages in criminal behavior. While social learning theory is generally accepted and is the explanation that best explains most crimes and most criminals, some specific sorts of offenders, such as psychopaths, pose further challenges to scholars attempting to understand the causes of crime.

Psychopaths are described as those individuals who do not suffer from mental disorders but who are callous, impulsive manipulators who take advantage of their environment. There is little doubt that, as a group, psychopaths "are responsible for a markedly disproportionate amount of the serious crime, violence, and social distress in every society" (Hare, 1996, p. 26). Psychopaths are more likely than others, including other offenders, to be violent, to recidivate violently, and to cause problems not only in society but in the institutions in which they are incarcerated (Hare, 1996). Furthermore, there is no evidence that psychopaths can be rehabilitated (Ogloff, Wong, & Greenwood, 1990). Indeed, they may appropriately be called, as Hare has termed them, "intraspecies predators who use charm, manipulation, intimidation, and violence to control others and to satisfy their own selfish needs" (Hare, 1996, p. 26). While relatively few criminals are psychopaths (less than 25%), it is important to consider that psychopaths do not fit easily into the conventional theories of crime.

Intelligence, Mental Illness, and Crime

It is convenient in the struggle to identify causes of crime to focus on psychological characteristics of people including their intelligence or mental illness. Considerable research attention has been devoted to determine whether people who are of below average intelligence or who suffer from mental illnesses are more likely to commit crimes than people of average intelligence and those who are not mentally ill. The relationships between intelligence and crime and mental illness and crime are complex (Douglas & Webster, 1999; Monahan, 1992; Ogloff & Schaefer, 1994). For example, while research shows that the average level of intellectual functioning of offenders is somewhat below average, does that mean that lower than average intelligence causes one to be a criminal? Similarly, research shows clearly that the prevalence of mental illness among offenders in jails and prisons is higher than we find in the general population (Ogloff, Roesch, & Hart, 1994). However, again, does that mean that mentally ill people are somehow predisposed to commit crimes?

Most researchers do not currently believe that there is a causal relationship between intelligence and crime (Ogloff & Schaefer, 1994). Two popular explanations exist for why people with lower levels of intelligence are overrepresented in the offender population. First, people with lower levels of intelligence may be more likely than those with higher levels of intelligence to be caught, arrested, and convicted. Second, people with higher levels of intelligence are more likely to obtain gainful employment and to enjoy stable lives which, in turn, lead them to be less likely to engage in criminal behavior than people with lower levels of intelligence. While the current state of research does not provide definitive support for either explanation, it must be emphasized that there is no inherent reason for intellectually impaired people to be particularly predisposed to commit crime.

Historically, it was believed that mentally ill people were more likely than others to engage in crime and to be violent (Ogloff et al., 1994). As with the relationship between intelligence and crime, though, the current state of knowledge suggests that having a mental illness, per se, does not cause one to commit crimes or to be violent. Rather, evidence now suggests that *some* symptoms of mental illness may lead people with mental illnesses to engage in criminal or violent behavior (Douglas & Webster, in press; Monahan, 1992). Indeed, when people's mental illnesses are controlled or stabilized, they are often at less risk for offending than mentally healthy people.

Taken together, the research shows that while mentally ill and mentally impaired people are overrepresented in the criminal justice system, there is no clear evidence that either being of lower than average intelligence or being mentally ill causes people to commit crimes.

Recidivism and Rehabilitation

Recidivism (i.e., committing new offenses) presents an ongoing concern for the public as well as government officials and agencies charged with the responsibility of making decisions regarding offender dispositions and release. Approximately 40 to 60% of the more than 100,000 offenders released in 1983 relapsed within three years of their release, depending upon the precise definition of recidivism used (U.S. Bureau of Justice Statistics, 1989/1997b). Specifically, 63% were rearrested in connection with a felony or major misdemeanor, slightly less than half (47%) were reconvicted, and 41% were reincarcerated. More than one out of every five offenders was rearrested for a violent offense. Although reoffense rates do vary across time, samples, and studies (Andrews & Bonta, 1994; Blackburn, 1993), two general conclusions may be drawn based on current empirical data. First, a substantial proportion of offenders relapse (20–25%). Second, offenders may remain at an elevated risk to relapse for many years, perhaps even decades after their release.

In the mid-1970s an air of pessimism surrounded the utility and efficacy of correctional rehabilitation. Following a review of correctional treatment studies, Martinson (1974) summarized the findings stating that "with few and isolated exceptions, the rehabilitative efforts that have been reported so far have had no appreciable effect on recidivism" (p. 25). Despite noting numerous studies where positive treatment effects were obtained, Martinson's central theme that "nothing works" was accepted widely without qualification and prompted many correctional treatment programs to be abandoned in favor of more deterrence-oriented models (Gendreau & Andrews, 1990).

More than a decade later, doubts over the merits of rehabilitation continued to persist in the literature, although others reviewing much the same evidence arrived at very different conclusions (Gendreau & Andrews, 1990). Andrews and Bonta (1994) reviewed the literature and argued convincingly that programs lacking demonstrable treatment gains failed to attend to three critical principles of correctional rehabilitation: risk, need, and responsivity. According to the risk principle, the intensity of correctional intervention must match an offender's risk for recidivism. Thus, offenders posing the greatest risk need to receive intensive intervention whereas the lowest risk offenders need little if any treatment. The need principle advises that correctional service must address an offender's criminogenic needs. In other words, treatment must target those risk factors amenable to change such as antisocial attitudes, procriminal peers, substance abuse, etc. Finally, the principle of responsivity dictates that correctional treatment must be delivered in a manner suitable to the cognitive abilities and learning styles of the offender.

To investigate the potential impact of these principles on treatment efficacy, Andrews et al. (1990) conducted a meta-analytic review of the literature. They found that studies involving appropriate treatment, defined as an intervention conforming to the principles of risk, need, and responsivity, had a greater impact on recidivism than did either inappropriate treatment or variations in criminal justice dispositions.

A subsequent and more extensive meta-analysis of juvenile delinquency treatment studies supports the positive benefits of correctional rehabilitation (Lipsey, 1992). Even when potentially confounding aspects of study methodology were considered, treatment still was found to have a potentially strong influence over outcome. Appropriately structured behavioral and skill-based treatments targeting specific criminogenic needs were much more effective than less structured interventions addressing offender self-esteem, anxiety, or depression. Furthermore, deterrence-oriented programs like "scared straight" or military boot camps were associated with negative effects. In terms of recidivism, Lipsey and Wilson (1993) were somewhat more conservative than Andrews et al. (1990), estimating that treatment could bring about reductions in the neighborhood of 20 to 40%.

These findings may also help to explain the generally poor treatment results associated with psychopaths in therapeutic communities. Psychopaths have generated considerable attention within correctional circles because of the disproportionate amount of crime they commit and their apparent resistance to correctional rehabilitation. Therapeutic communities embrace a wide variety of philosophies and techniques but they are typically intensive, peer-operated programs that focus on developing self-insight rather than specific behavioral or skills training (Harris & Rice, 1995). Evidence indicates psychopaths who participate in therapeutic community programs manifest higher recidivism rates than psychopaths in prison, indicating that for these offenders this treatment modality may actually raise the likelihood of recidivism (Harris & Rice, 1995). The risk, need, and responsivity principles suggest that high-risk offenders like psychopaths should be treated with intensive, highly structured programs targeting the specific criminogenic needs rather than more unstructured, humanistic approaches which are susceptible to being manipulated (Andrews & Bonta, 1994).

Conclusion

Crime is a significant factor in society, and an area to which psychology can contribute much. Beyond studying and theorizing about the causes of crime, psychologists play an important role in studying the prevalence of crime and the rate of recidivism, as well as developing and evaluating programs to rehabilitate offenders.

Bibliography

Andrews, D. A., & Bonta, J. (1994). *The psychology of criminal conduct.* Cincinnati, OH: Anderson.

Andrews, D. A., Zinger, I., Hoge, R. D., Bonta, J., Gendreau, P., & Cullen, F. T. (1990). Does correctional treatment work? A clinically relevant and psychologically informed meta-analysis. *Criminology, 28,* 369–404.

Bandura, A. (1977). *Social learning theory.* Englewood Cliffs, NJ: Prentice Hall.

Blackburn, R. (1993). *The psychology of criminal conduct: Theory, research and practice.* Chichester, U.K.: Wiley.

Bonta, P. (1996). Offender rehabilitation: What we know and what needs to be done. *Criminal Justice and Behavior, 23,* 144–161.

Coleman, C., & Moynihan, J. (1996). *Understanding crime data: Haunted by the dark figure.* Buckingham, U.K.: Open University Press.

Douglas, K. S., & Webster, C. D. (1999). Predicting violence in mentally and personality disordered individuals. In R. Roesch, S. D. Hart, & J. R. P. Ogloff (Eds.), *Law and psychology: The state of the discipline* (pp. 175–239). New York: Kluwer/Plenum Academic Press.

Gendreau, P., & Andrews, D. A. (1990). Tertiary prevention: What the meta-analyses of the offender treatment literature tell us about "what works." *Canadian Journal of Criminology, 32,* 173–184.

Hare, R. D. (1996). Psychopathy: A clinical construct whose time has come. *Criminal Justice and Behavior, 23,* 25–54.

Harris, G. T., & Rice, M. E. (1995). Psychopaths: Is a "therapeutic community" therapeutic? In L. Stewart, L. Stermac, & C. D. Webster (Eds.), *Clinical criminology: Toward effective correctional treatment* (pp. 116–127). Ministry of the Solicitor General. Toronto, Ontario.

Lipsey, M. W., & Wilson, D. B. (1993). The efficacy of psychological, educational, and behavioral treatment: Confirmation from meta-analysis. *American Psychologist, 48,* 1181–1209.

Martinson, R. (1974). What works? Questions and answers about prison reform. *Public Interest, 35,* 22–54.

Monahan, J. (1992). Mental disorder and violent behavior. *American Psychologist, 47,* 511–521.

Nietzel, M. T. (1979). *Crime and its modification: A social learning perspective.* New York: Pergamon Press.

Ogloff, J. R. P., Roesch, R., & Hart, S. D. (1994). Mental health services in jails and prisons: Legal, clinical, and policy issues. *Law and Psychology Review, 18,* 109–136.

Ogloff, J. R. P., & Schaefer, D. G. (1994). Criminality. In R. J. Sternberg, S. J. Ceci, J. Horn, E. Hunt, J. D. Matarazzo, & S. Scarr (Eds.), *Encyclopedia of intelligence* (pp. 311–315). New York: Macmillan.

Ogloff, J. R. P., Wong, S., & Greenwood, A. (1990). Treating criminal psychopaths in a therapeutic community program. *Behavioral Sciences and Law, 8,* 181–190.

U.S. Bureau of Justice Statistics. (1997a). *Sourcebook of criminal justice statistics, 1996.* Washington, DC: United States Department of Justice.

U.S. Bureau of Justice Statistics. (1997b). *Recidivism of prisoners released in 1983* (Bulletin NCJ-116261). Washington, DC: United States Department of Justice. (Original work published 1989)

James R. P. Ogloff and David R. Lyon

CRIMINAL RESPONSIBILITY. The phrase *criminal responsibility* has two meanings. It refers first to the formal criteria for criminal liability. A defendant is criminally responsible if the state can prove beyond a reasonable doubt that his or her behavior satisfied the definitional "elements" (criteria) of the crime charged and no affirmative defense of justification or excuse can be established. Criminal responsibility also sometimes refers to those characteristics of an individual agent, such as the capacity to be guided by reason, that are necessary for moral and legal accountability. Consequently, criminal responsibility is often equated with the absence of excusing conditions, such as legal insanity, that negate accountability, but this equation may be misleading. An agent can be criminally responsible in the second sense—an accountable agent—but not criminally liable or criminally responsible in the first sense because the agent's behavior does not satisfy all the definitional criteria for criminal liability. In contrast, an agent who is not accountable because an excusing condition is present will clearly not be criminally responsible in either sense: the condition establishing lack of accountability also establishes a formal affirmative defense.

Defining the legal criteria for crimes and defenses is a moral, political, and, ultimately, a legal question. Although behavioral and social science may be relevant, the issues are morally normative and rarely resolvable by empirical data.

Virtually all crimes are defined to include prohibited intentional conduct and a mental state or *mens rea* that must accompany the prohibited conduct. For example, one traditional definition of murder is the intentional killing of another human being. Any killing conduct, such as intentionally shooting at another human being, will satisfy the conduct element; "intent" is the required *mens rea*, which means that the defendant must have acted with the intent to cause the victim's death. Some crimes of so-called "strict" or "absolute" liability are defined without a mental state: formal criminal responsibility is based solely on intentionally performing the prohibited conduct. No further intent is required. Most such crimes do not involve immoral conduct and are primarily "regulatory" in nature, however, and carry light punishments and little stigma.

Even if the elements of the crime charged are admitted or proved, a defendant may avoid criminal responsibility with an affirmative defense of justification or excuse. A defendant's action is *justified* if behavior that would otherwise be a crime is legally *right* or at least *permissible* under the specific circumstances. An intentional killing in self-defense is an example. A defendant's *wrongful* action is *excused* if an excusing condition, such as duress or legal insanity, was present. For example, a defendant might be excused if she kills intentionally in response to a delusional belief that she needs to do so to save her own life. Finally, criminal responsibility is mitigated if the defendant has a partial excuse for criminal behavior. For example, an agent who kills intentionally, but in "the heat of passion" in response to especially provocative circumstances, such as finding one's spouse in the act of adultery, may be convicted of "voluntary manslaughter," a lesser degree of homicide.

The requirements of formal criminal responsibility follow from two complementary principles: Only behavior that is sufficiently harmful to warrant blame and punishment should be made criminal (the harm principle); only those agents who are sufficiently at fault (culpable) for committing the requisite harms deserve to be blamed and punished (the fault principle). Consider rudeness as an example of the former. There is no *criminal* responsibility for intentional rudeness because rudeness is not considered sufficiently harmful to warrant criminalization.

Now consider various aspects of the fault principle. A defendant's degree of responsibility depends first on the *mens rea* with which the defendant acted. For example, killing on purpose and killing simply with conscious awareness that one's conduct risks death are both sufficiently culpable to warrant criminal punishment, but the former is more culpable than the latter because intent indicates greater disrespect for the rights of others, and it would be unjust to punish both the same. If a defendant kills without fault—say, purely accidentally—the defendant will not be criminally responsible at all. Because "strict liability" offenses divorce blame and punishment from fault, most criminal law theorists condemn this type of criminal liability.

Affirmative defenses also concern fault. Punishing

an agent who has done the right or justifiable thing under the circumstances would be irrational and unjust. Nor would it be fair to blame and punish an agent for wrongful conduct either if she was not a rational agent or if she was acting in response to a wrongful threat that would cause reasonable people to yield. Finally, a partially excused defendant acts with diminished fault and therefore deserves less punishment than an agent who commits the same deed without any excuse.

Legal Insanity

There is conflict concerning the precise justification for the insanity defense. Virtually all moral and legal theorists agree that the defense is morally necessary, however, because some defendants with mental disorders are not capable of being guided by reason. And reason is a precondition for criminal responsibility in both senses, and consequently, for just blame and punishment. Legal insanity is a complete excuse. Various practical criticisms have been leveled at the administration of the insanity defense, but most are empirically or conceptually misguided or are indistinguishable from criticisms of other, uncontroversial defenses. Although all claims of legal insanity must be based in part on a threshold finding that the defendant suffered from a mental abnormality at the time of the crime, whether the abnormality affected the defendant sufficiently to warrant an excuse is a moral, political, and ultimately, a legal question.

The specific tests for legal insanity, which vary across jurisdictions, reflect the underlying rationale for the defense. In addition to a threshold mental abnormality, which in practice must usually be severe, the criteria for legal insanity require that the defendant's mental disorder must produce a cognitive impairment sufficient to excuse. For example, the famous *McNaghten* case, decided by the British House of Lords in 1843 and then followed in many states of the United States, adopted the following test: "the party accused was labouring under such a defect of reason, from disease of the mind, as not to know the nature and quality of the act he was doing; or if he did know it, that he did not know he was doing what was wrong." The influential Model Penal Code's cognitive provision reads as follows: "A person is not responsible for criminal conduct if . . . as a result of mental disease or defect he lacks substantial capacity . . . to appreciate the criminality [wrongfulness] of his conduct. . . ." Defendants unable to understand what they are doing or unable to understand the applicable moral or legal rules, are not rational agents and are therefore not morally responsible and do not deserve blame and punishment.

Some jurisdictions also provide a "control," "volitional," or "irresistible impulse" test for legal insanity. An influential state court definition of this test requires that, by reason of mental disease, the defendant, "so far lost the *power to choose* between the right and the wrong, and to avoid doing the act in question, as that his free agency was at the time destroyed." The Model Penal Code formulation requires that as a result of mental disease or defect, the defendant "lacked substantial capacity . . . to conform his conduct to the requirements of law." The control test envisions a rational agent—otherwise a cognitive test would be sufficient—who is unable to choose or conform. Such tests seem to make intuitive moral sense and many believe that they must be maintained, but the meaning of the inability to choose or to conform—independent of irrationality—is philosophically obscure, despite loose conceptualizations about lack of free will or compulsion. Such tests are also difficult to adjudicate because we cannot reliably distinguish between defendants who *could* not control themselves and those who simply *did* not. As a result of such problems, only a small minority of jurisdictions retain a control test for legal insanity.

An important issue the law now confronts is the appropriate response to claims for excuse based on newly identified syndromes that do not fit classic definitions of mental disorder, but which may nonetheless compromise a defendant's ability to be guided by reason. If the law retains a narrow view of legally insanity, such claims may be unjustly excluded or claimants may attempt to blur the boundaries of excuse and justification. In contrast, if the insanity defense is broadened too much, ordinary notions of fault may be undermined.

Legal insanity must be distinguished from "incompetence to stand trial" and from "diminished capacity." The insanity defense evaluates the defendant's responsibility for past behavior. Incompetence to stand trial criteria address whether a defendant's mental impairment at the time of trial interferes with the possibility that the defendant will receive a fair trial. There is no necessary relation between legal insanity and competence to stand trial.

Diminished capacity doctrines address whether mental abnormality prevented a defendant from forming a *mens rea* or whether mental abnormality insufficient to support a full insanity defense partially compromised the defendant's ability to be guided by reason and should at least mitigate, although not excuse, a defendant's culpability. The former type of diminished capacity is not an affirmative defense. The defendant is simply claiming that the mens rea required by the definition of the crime was lacking. Although about half the states permit such claims, they rarely succeed because even a severe mental disorder seldom prevents people from forming intentions or knowing what they are doing in a narrow sense. The latter type of diminished capacity does not deny that *mens rea* was present and is a genuine partial excusing claim, a "partial" insanity defense. Such a "partial" excuse has not been adopted in general form by any jurisdiction. In some jurisdictions, however, it is included within the law of homicide as a doctrine that reduces murder to manslaughter and claims of partial excuse based on mental abnormality are often considered at sentencing.

Bibliography

American Law Institute. (1985). *Model penal code and commentaries: Part I, Secs. 3.01-5.07.* Phildadelphia: The American Law Institute. Includes a balanced historical, doctrinal, and conceptual analysis of the insanity defense and of the foundations of the *Model penal code* proposal.

Dressler, J. (1995). *Understanding criminal law* (2nd ed.). Matthew Bender. An excellent text that covers the doctrines and theory of criminal law.

Fingarette, H., & Hasse, A. (1979). *Mental disabilities and criminal responsibility.* Berkeley: University of California Press. A detailed conceptual analysis of the criteria for criminal responsibility and a proposal for a generic excusing condition.

Goldstein, A. (1967). *The insanity defense.* New Haven, CT: Yale University Press. An outdated but still standard, invaluable historical analysis of the doctrine and operation of the insanity defense.

Hart, H. L. A. (1968). *Punishment and responsibility.* Oxford: Oxford University Press. Essays on criminal responsibility by one of the century's most influential legal philosophers, including detailed analyses of the importance of mental states.

Katz, L. (1987). *Bad acts and guilty minds: Conundrums of the criminal law.* Chicago: University of Chicago Press. An engaging, interdisciplinary analysis of the structure of criminal liability accessible to the educated lay reader.

Melton, G. B., Petrila, J., Poythress, N. G., & Slobogin, C. (1997). *Psychological evaluation for the courts: A handbook for mental health professionals and lawyers* (2nd ed.). New York: Guilford Press. Includes a comprehensive consideration of forensic practice issues concerning criminal responsibility.

McNaghten's Case. (1843). 8 Eng. Rep 718.

Moore, M. (1980). Legal conceptions of mental illness. In B. Brody & H. T. Engelhardt (Eds.), *Mental illness: Law and public policy* (pp. 24–69). Dordrecht: D. Reidel. An exceptionally deep, thorough analysis of the justification for the insanity defense and why it is morally required.

Morris, N. (1982). *Madness and the criminal law.* Chicago: University of Chicago Press. A historical analysis and influential critique of the insanity defense and related doctrines that argues that the insanity defense ought to be abolished.

Morse, S. (1985). Excusing the crazy: The insanity defense reconsidered. *Southern California Law Review, 58,* 777–836. A comprehensive evaluation of the moral and consequential arguments concerning abolition of the insanity defense.

Steadman, H. J., McGreevy, M. A., Morrissey, J. P., Callahan, L. A., Robbins, P. C., & Cirincione, C. (1993). *Before and after Hinckley: Evaluating insanity defense reform.* New York: Guilford Press. A multistate empirical study that provides the best data on the administration of the insanity defense generally and on the effects of the substantial reforms of the insanity defense laws in the early 1980s.

Stephen J. Morse

CRISIS INTERVENTION. Virtually all persons in the course of their lives will face situations in which their habitual ways of dealing with problems are no longer effective. Methods formerly used to confront and resolve problems no longer work. Frustration and anxieties mount. The individuals are at an impasse. This is the essence of a crisis.

Webster's Collegiate Dictionary defines crisis as "an emotionally significant event or change of status in a person's life, . . . an unstable or crucial time or state of affairs whose outcome will make a decisive difference for better or for worse." A crisis arises when a person, group, or institution, or even large corporation is faced with a situation it has never before encountered. With mounting concerns there is frequently a spate of ineffective coping activities including efforts to deny or avoid facing realities. A crisis is in many ways a call for some sort of action. The Chinese symbol for crisis is *opportunity*, perhaps in recognition of the possibility of using the crisis as an impetus for improvement.

A crisis is not limited to any one level of personality functions. It may occur in the mentally disturbed individual as well as a more integrated personality. Crises have a limited time aspect, distinguishing them from an epic or developmental life phase such as adolescence. Crises may be more frequent during such a phase, but developmental tasks that consitute a crisis for one individual may not do so for another.

Psychologists are interested in the myriad difficult situations or events with which individuals and institutions must contend. The pioneering work of Erich Lindemann, begun in 1944 and expanded in his book *Beyond Grief* (New York, 1979), is generally acknowledged as the seminal work on crisis and paths to its resolution. Focusing on the loss of a loved one as an inevitable crisis of living, it encouraged further research in the areas of crisis and crisis resolution.

Gerald Caplan (*Recent Development in Crisis Intervention,* 1986), in amplifying his previous pioneering work involving the relationship between crisis and mental health and the need to involve community support systems, introduced two strategies, "anticipatory guidance" and "emotional innoculation," as ways of helping to reduce or avoid the negative effects of crises. R. H. Moos (*Coping with Life Crises*, New York, 1986) broadened the field by focusing on a broad spectrum of crises. He listed five major sets of adaptive tasks needed to manage a life transition or crisis: (1) establish the meaning and understanding of the personal significance of a situation; (2) confront reality and respond to the requirement of the external situation; (3) sustain relationships with family members and friends as well as with other individuals who may be helpful in resolving the crisis and its aftermath; (4) strive to maintain a reasonable emotional balance by managing upsetting feelings aroused by the situation (the emphasis here is on the recognition that life crises arouse many powerful emotions and that it is important for the individual to maintain some hope even when the scope of the situation seems hopeless); and (5) preserve a satisfactory self-image and maintain a sense of competence and mastery. Coping efforts are strengthened when individuals have some confidence in their abilities to bring about, with some assistance, a positive outcome of the crisis situation. The concept of crisis furnishes a useful framework in which to study how individuals and institutions such as families deal with major changes in their lives, and thus is of increasing importance to the science of psychology.

Anticipatory Guidance and Crises

Anticipatory guidance involves sensitizing individuals and groups to both physical and mental stresses and changes they will encounter in conditions that they have not previously faced. Studies have demonstrated that in life-threatening situations such as open heart surgery, recovery is aided if the patient is made aware beforehand of the mechanical and rehabilitation procedures as well as the discomforts and pain that often follow surgery. Other studies have shown that orientation for individuals moving into a different culture, which generally includes a new language, different foods, and different lifestyles, helps reduce what is frequently referred to as culture shock. The learning of a few key words and use of pantomime serves to facilitate communication and reduce frustrations, reducing the possibility of an impasse or crisis.

Anticipatory guidance is not always effective. Some persons avoid facing realities. Persons who express some degree of apprehension and concern about new and possibly threatening situations do much better than those who pass them off, assuring themselves and others that they can "handle it." The recognition of the need for some sort of assistance has been shown to be a fundamental factor in successful crisis resolution.

Crises as Distinguished from Emergencies

Although the the terms *crisis* and *emergency* tend to be used interchangeably, not all crises are emergencies, and not all emergencies are crises. The major distinctions lie in the timing of interventions, the agreement regarding necessary actions, and expectancy for the future. An emergency calls for immediate and specific actions. In natural disasters such as floods and fires, persons have to be rescued, shelter provided, and the injured tended. A crisis calls for different actions. It is only after the emergency has been taken care of—victims buried or the fire extinguished—that people begin to focus on what they have lost and how they will face the future. Should the flooded home be rebuilt? Do the survivers wish to continue living in the neighborhood? How will they deal with the loss of family members, possessions, and treasures?

These are intensely personal decisions. Fortunately, agencies and services do exist that can assist persons as they begin to face the realities of their situations. In addition to personal contacts, telephone counseling services and crisis hotlines can be helpful. The act of calling for help may in itself signify the beginning of effective coping with a crisis situation.

Crisis Intervention and Counseling

Crisis counseling differs from traditional therapy in that each session should be regarded as the only session that the client will receive. It may last for several hours. The focus is on the definition of the situation as perceived by the client or family. Why is help being sought at this particular time? What are the expectancies as to the outcome? Usually several sessions are needed to clarify for the client the options and alternatives that are possible. The purpose is to "get the person off the ropes and into the center of the ring," using the coping skills and constructive intelligence that have been encouraged and even generated by the counseling sessions. The impasse that has brought about the crisis tends to lower a person's defenses, making the individual more open to new approaches.

The timing of crisis intervention is crucial to success. An intervention too soon may find persons unresponsive or defensive, as they have not yet absorbed the full significance of the events associated with the crisis. An intervention too late may not be effective because the time for appropriate action has passed and less productive coping may already have begun. Family breakup, financial setbacks, failure to obtain a promotion, and other exigencies of living can cause sorrow, pain, and distress. Reactions such as depression, lack of enthusiasm, feelings of failure, or withdrawal from friends are not unexpected. However, when they continue beyond a reasonable length of time, intervention may be indicated. Carried out appropriately, the intervention assists individuals in considering options and moving away from nonproductive activities.

Interventions may be initiated by the individuals themselves, family friends, physicians, or others familiar with the situation. The utilization of self-help groups has become an integral part of crisis intervention. Persons and groups that have experienced problems similar to those presented by the individual have been shown to be effective in providing support as well as assisting in the development of alternative coping strategies. The proliferation of problem- and issue-oriented self-help groups is testimony to their utility.

Crisis and Older Persons

The increase in longevity in the United States presents a crisis for health policy formulations at the state and national level as well as for older persons and their families. What constructive actions should be taken? Is there utility in models available from other industrialized nations? What are the responsibilities of the individual, the family, the community, and the government? The answers are not yet in.

Gerontologists have emphasized that the older population—70-plus years—is at risk for a series of crises within a relatively short period of time. Failing memory, decreased mobility, loss of autonomy, and increased financial burdens may occur almost simultaneously, overtaxing a person's coping capacities. Anticipatory guidance is urged for older persons and their families to help them become more aware of existing support systems and options. Counseling should focus on the realities of aging, emphasizing positive aspects as well as preparation for potential decreases in physical and mental functioning. In recognition of the potential crises facing an increasing number of persons, the American Psychological Association in 1997 made the study and delivery of psychological services to the aged one of its highest priorities.

Future Perspectives

Many current problems such as health care, education, and violence can be viewed as crises. Rapid technological advances, increasing cultural diversity, and lifestyle changes will create other crises. Research and practice in crisis intervention will lead to increased sophistication in crisis prevention as well as crisis resolution.

[*See also* Intervention.]

Bibliography

Abeles, N. (1997). *What practitioners should know about working with older adults*. Washington, DC: American Psychological Association.

Caplan, G. (1960). Patterns of parental response to the crisis of premature birth. *Psychiatry, 23*, 365–374. The author is one of the first to recognize prematurity as a crisis.

Caplan, G. (1964). *Principles of preventive psychiatry*. New York: Basic Books. A pioneer work dealing with prevention and crises.

Duffy, M., & Iscoe, I. (1990). Crisis theory and management: The case of the older person. *Journal of Mental Health Counseling, 12*, 303–313. Focuses on issues and problems of an aging population.

Pruett, H. L., & Brown, V. B. (Eds.). (1990). *Crisis intervention and prevention*. San Francisco, CA: Jossey-Bass. An excellent overview of the issues involved.

Sarason, S. (1996). *Revisiting the culture of the school and the problem of change*. New York: Teachers College Press. Deals cogently with the present crisis in American public schools, suggesting vital changes if schools are to succeed in their pressing mission.

Slaikeu, K. A. (1990). *Crisis intervention: A handbook for practice and research* (2nd ed.). Boston: Allyn & Bacon. A valuable guide and reference for both professionals and nonprofessionals.

Ira Iscoe

CRITICAL PSYCHIATRY, or "antipsychiatry," refers to a body of thought originally identified with the work of American psychoanalyst Thomas S. Szasz (b. 1920), British psychiatrist Ronald D. Laing (1927–1989), and Italian psychiatrist Franco Basaglia (1924–1980). Critical psychiatry challenged the disease or medical model of disturbed or disturbing behavior, mounted an enduring critique of institutional psychiatry, and sought to ethicize and politicize the twin discourse of madness and psychiatry. Early works by American sociologist Erving Goffman (1922–1982) and French philosopher Michel Foucault (1926–1984) are occasionally included in this corpus because they are among the first extensive critiques of psychiatry. The concurrent development of labeling theory in sociology also fertilized critical psychiatry. An American, Marxist-influenced "radical psychology" movement also expressed sympathy with critical psychiatry. From the mid-1960s, partly as a reaction to Laing's hold on the public imagination, a countercultural "antipsychiatry movement" flourished briefly.

The term *antipsychiatry*, coined by Laing associate David Cooper, was applied to these thinkers early on and is commonly encountered in the literature. Szasz and Laing, however, rejected it as unsuitable or absurd—they did not believe that psychiatry had to be abolished, but did expect it to emerge radically transformed if it discarded mystifying dogmas and coercive practices.

Mistakenly, Szasz's and Laing's ideas have sometimes been discussed as if they were interchangeable. Similarities include a rejection of determinism (exemplified by psychoanalysis and biological psychiatry) to explain human behavior; the idea that behavior, no matter how disturbed or disturbing, is not *disease* unless we use that term metaphorically; and the belief that psychiatry usually exercises repressive social control. Szasz, the most prolific and intellectually influential figure, remained consistent with the arguments he first set out in *The Myth of Mental Illness* (New York, 1961), extended in *Law, Liberty, and Psychiatry* (New York, 1963) and *The Manufacture of Madness* (New York, 1970), and refined in *Insanity* (New York, 1991) and *The Meaning of Mind* (New York, 1996).

Szasz's opposition is not to the disease model *per se* or its deterministic and positivistic underpinnings. Indeed, Szasz defines disease strictly as deviation from biological norms. It is the extension of the disease model to human motives and human actions, to mind, that he sees as fundamentally erroneous. A "human science" cannot be derived from measurement and mathematical calculation, the methods of biology or physics, essential for knowledge of the body. One obtains knowledge of the mind through language and the interpretation of meanings. Szasz proposed that classifying thoughts, feelings, or behaviors as diseases was a category error, or "myth," because facts from one logical category were presented in language more appropriate to another. He argued that because psychiatry sought to classify "problems in living" as diseases requiring medical treatment, psychiatric thinkers bent the rules of what, in the Western world and in the twentieth century, constitutes disease or illness.

The political foundation of Szasz's sustained criticism is classical or Jeffersonian liberalism, which emphasizes individualism. Szasz is an existential thinker and moral philosopher because of his preoccupation with individual freedom, free will, personal responsibility, and the moral dilemmas which confront human beings by virtue of their humanness and for which they wrongly seek technical remedies. His most important works are histories and critiques of psychiatry as an immensely elaborate pseudo-medical enterprise constructed to manage—by brute force or subtle indoctrination—various types of deviances after medicalizing them. In the age of science, psychiatry also serves to relieve individual guilt and provide norms of conduct. Szasz has continually denounced involuntary mental hospitalization of competent adults as "a crime against humanity."

In contrast, Laing's work provides little analysis of the mental health system, its institutions, or the power relations therein. From the start, Laing sought to understand unusual human experiences, such as schizophrenia, and to develop helping approaches to make these experiences less troubling. His first book, *The Divided Self* (London, 1959), offers a straightforward account of the experience of becoming mad, with descriptive categories derived from such existentialists as Jean-Paul Sartre and Martin Heidegger, phenomenologists such as Maurice Merleau-Ponty, and theologians such as Paul Tillich. In two books partly influenced by American research into family interactions, *Sanity, Madness and the Family* (written with Aaron Esterson, London, 1964), and *The Politics of the Family* (London, 1969), Laing argued that prolonged psychological violence and communication deviance often occurs in families, making madness intelligible in these contexts. In *The Politics of Experience* (London, 1967), his most famous and controversial work, he proposed that psychosis could—with the proper support and context—contain a healing dimension, akin to a rite of initiation involving loss of ego and emergence into a more enlightened being. This departure into new territory, coupled with an absence of articulated political principles in his calls for reform of the psychiatric system—in addition to his temporary role as a counterculture figure—has made it difficult to assess Laing's insights into the understanding of deeply troubled persons. Recent biographical studies of Laing have attempted to remedy this situation.

For his part, Franco Basaglia represents the strain of Marxist-influenced critical psychiatry that attempted to reform the mental health system as part of a collective effort for political change. Basaglia was also inspired by phenomenology and existentialism but he barely focused on the nature or experience of madness, concentrating instead on the mental hospital as society's main response to madness. For him, the hospital embodied psychiatry's central contradiction, the dual mandate of cure and control, and had to be abolished. Conceptual and spatial segregation of psychiatric patients perpetuated the false idea that our needs and those of mental patients were fundamentally different. Basaglia's reform work in Italy as director of two hospitals and leader of the "Democratic Psychiatry" movement culminated in 1978 with the adoption of the now-famous regional "Law 180," which dismantled the insane asylum, though the long-term consequences appear to have been largely diluted. The U.S. Community Mental Health movement, initially based on a new model of psychosocial care, also reached a similarly disappointing end.

To a large extent, since the remedicalization of psychiatric thought and practice in the early 1980s, critical psychiatry is no longer led by psychiatrists but by ex-psychiatric patients and social scientists, ethicists, and philosophers. There is agreement that, aside from increased user participation in mental health services, the extensive, intellectually compelling criticism generated by critical psychiatry has not yet translated into obvious political gains. However there is a renewed interest today in this approach. This validates the critical psychiatric insight that, unlike outmoded scientific hypotheses that vanish when discredited, both deterministic psychiatry and antipsychiatry may be likened to belief systems which retreat and reemerge depending on cultural needs and norms.

Bibliography

Cohen, D. (Ed.). (1990). Challenging the therapeutic state: Critical perspectives on psychiatry and the mental health system [Special issue]. *Journal of Mind and Behavior, 15* (1 & 2). Twenty authors from ten disciplines extend and refine criticisms of biological psychiatry and medicalization.

Crossley, N. (1998). R. D. Laing and the British antipsychiatry movement: A socio-historical analysis. *Social Science and Medicine, 47,* 877–889. Argues that British antipsychiatry may be considered a social movement, and explores its links to other "new social movements."

Hoeller, K. (Ed.). (1997). Thomas Szasz: Moral philosopher of psychiatry [Special issue]. *Review of Existential Psychology & Psychiatry, 23* (1, 2, & 3). Contains several well-documented articles on the meaning and impact of Szasz's entire accomplishment, including a rare discussion of his work before *The Myth of Mental Illness* (1961).

Ingleby, D. (Ed.). (1980). *Critical psychiatry: The politics of mental health.* New York: Pantheon. Marxist-influenced, mostly European strain of critical psychiatry, expressing disagreements with both Szaszian and Laingian approaches.

Kotowicz, Z. (1997). *R. D. Laing and the paths of antipsychiatry.* New York: Routledge. Presents an excellent introduction to, and contemporary reassessment of, Laing's contribution to critical psychiatry.

Scheper-Hughes, N., & Lovell, A. M. (Eds). (1987). *Psychiatry inside out: Selected writings of Franco Basaglia* (A. M. Lovell & T. Shtob, Trans.). New York: Columbia University Press. One of the few works on Basaglia available in English. Displays the breadth of his thought on various topics and discusses the extent of his radical reform efforts on behalf of mental patients in Italy.

David Cohen

CROSS-CULTURAL COMMUNICATION refers to the exchange of information between people of different cultural backgrounds. It is a well-studied field of research in several disciplines, including psychology, speech and communication, sociology, anthropology, and business.

Cross-cultural communication is highly related to a similar term, *intercultural communication.* In actuality, there is no difference between these terms in the context of communication. However, there is an important and notable difference between cross-cultural and intercultural *research.* The former refers to the comparison of two or more cultures on some variable of interest (e.g., differences between cultures A and B in the expression of emotions). The latter refers to the study of the interaction between people of two cultures (e.g., differences in how people of cultures A and B express emotions when they are with people of cultures B and A, respectively). There is yet a third term, *intracultural communication,* which refers to communication among people within a culture. The bulk of information in cross-cultural communication comes from cross-cultural research, but has considerable application to our understanding of intercultural and intracultural communication processes.

Cultural Influences on the Communication Process

These influences are at work via both verbal and nonverbal communication.

Verbal Communication. Verbal language is a system of symbols that denote how a culture structures its world. As such, by examining language, it is possible to see how a culture relates to its world. For example, some languages have words that do not exist in other cultures. The Eskimo language, for instance, has multiple words for snow while the English language has only one (Whorf, 1956). The German word *Schadenfreude* (joy in another person's misfortunes) and the Japanese word *amae* (sweet dependence), which do not exist in English, are other examples.

That the words do not exist in other languages does not mean that the concepts are nonexistent. In American culture, for example, it is very common to see people derive joy from others' misfortunes! Rather, such words reflect the fact that the concept is important enough to the culture for its language to have a separate linguistic symbol for it. In this way, verbal language is a manifestation of the larger culture within which it exists.

Another example of this manifestation is the case of self and other referents. In American English, for example, we typically refer to ourselves as "I," and to someone else as "you." There are many other languages of the world, however, that do not use such simplistic terms for self and others. The Japanese language, for instance, includes an extensive choice of terms referring to oneself and others, all dependent upon the relationship between the people interacting (Suzuki, 1978). In Japanese, you refer to your teacher as "teacher" or your boss at work as "section chief" when in English the word *you* would normally be used. In Japanese, terms denoting status are also used within the family. There are even different terms for *I,* depending on the nature of status relationships. The degree of politeness and fluency in the language and culture is dependent on the ability to use this system properly.

When people speak the language of their culture, they reinforce their concepts of culture. If you engage fluently in the Japanese use of the elaborate system of self and other referents, for example, you will reinforce your own understanding of the Japanese culture's emphasis on status relationships and interdependence. If you engage fluently in American English's "I" and "you," you will reinforce your view of the American individuality and uniqueness. Culture and language share a highly interrelated, reciprocal relationship.

That language helps to structure thought, and vice versa, is a concept that is known as the *Sapir-Whorf hypothesis*. It suggests that people of different cultures think differently, just by the very nature, structure, and function of their language. Since the early 1960s, some research has indicated that the Sapir-Whorf hypothesis may not be true with regard to the influence of lexical and semantic aspects of language (e.g., see the experiments on color names reported in Rosch & Lloyd, 1978). But, many other studies have confirmed that Sapir-Whorf is very valid with regard to the grammar and syntax of language. Also, there is a small but growing amount of evidence in research with bilinguals that supports the Sapir-Whorf hypothesis. Collectively, Sapir-Whorf suggests that people who speak different languages may interpret the same event differently because the differences in their language are associated with different thinking styles (e.g., see Matsumoto, 1996, for a review of this line of research).

Nonverbal Communication. While cultural differences in language are very apparent, there are major differences between cultures in nonverbal communication as well. In fact, ample studies have shown that the bulk of message exchange in communication occurs nonverbally; depending on the study, estimates of the contribution of nonverbal behaviors to overall communication range as high as 90%!

There are five categories of nonverbal behaviors: speech illustrators, conversation regulators, self-adaptors, emblematic gestures, and emotion signals (Ekman & Friesen, *Semiotica*, 1968, 19, 49–98). All carry some kind of communicative value and are influenced by culture. One of the most well-studied areas of nonverbal behavior is gesture, and many cultural similarities and differences have been documented (Morris, Collet, Marsh, & O'Shaunessy, 1980).

Facial expressions of emotion is another well-studied area of nonverbal communication. Research since the 1970s has shown that a small set of facial expressions of emotion are universally expressed (see review of early research in Ekman, 1972). These emotions include anger, contempt, disgust, fear, happiness, sadness, and surprise. Cultures differ, however, in the rules governing how to use these universal expressions. These

rules—called cultural display rules—are learned rules of expression management that dictate the appropriateness of emotion display depending on social circumstances. Learned from infancy, we are so adept at using these rules that by the time we are adults, we do so automatically and without much conscious awareness.

There are cultural differences in other *channels* of nonverbal behaviors, such as in gaze and visual behavior, and in the use of interpersonal space. Each of these is important in its own right, and contributes greatly to communication. Mistaken inferences about feelings and intentions easily occur because of misattributions about gaze behavior that we are not accustomed to, and interactions are often strained because they occur at spaces that are too distant or close for comfort. Collectively, the literature suggests that culture exerts a considerable amount of influence over much of the nonverbal behaviors that occur in intercultural communication episodes.

The Process of Intercultural Communication

As noted above, we all learn culturally prescribed rules that govern our expressive behaviors and language. These rules also help us to decode and interpret the behaviors of others. As display rules are heavily influenced by culture, so are our rules of decoding.

When we interact with others, a number of normal, psychological processes occur. We naturally form categories about people to help us organize the information we take in. We selectively attend to our environment, as it is impossible to attend to all possible stimuli entering our senses at any one time. We naturally appraise the actions of others around us, and make attributions about the causes of those actions. In most cases, those appraisals and attributions are heavily dependent on what we expect to be appropriate, which is related to our own learned display rules. Finally, we select attributions, appraisals, and categories to commit to long-term memory. All of these normal psychological processes underlie our own ethnocentrism (the tendency to view the world through one's own cultural filters) and stereotypes (generalizations about categories of people).

Interpreting the behaviors of others, however, is not an entirely cognitive process. It is, in fact, heavily laden with emotion and values, and extremely important to our sense of self. The display and decoding rules we learn and operate with, and the stereotypes that are formed from normal psychological processes described above, create expectations of behavior. These expectations are associated with value judgments of goodness, worth, and appropriateness. In intracultural communication, these expectations are often met, and values are reaffirmed. Positive emotions reinforce those values and our own sense of self, or self-construals. These, in turn, reinforce our own display and decoding rules, expectations, and stereotypes in a cyclical fashion.

During intercultural encounters, however, chances are greater that we interact with people whose behaviors do not conform to our expectations. When this occurs, we often interpret those behaviors, instinctively and naturally, as transgressions against our value system and morality. Consequently, they produce negative emotions, which are upsetting to our self-construals. The process of intercultural communication, therefore, is an exciting and interesting one because of the simultaneous blending of different culturally based rules of encoding and decoding. Unfortunately, because of these dynamics, it is also a source of conflict.

When negative emotions are aroused in intercultural encounters, these emotions tell us that there is a discrepancy between our expectations, stereotypes, value system, and reality. When this occurs, we can either *assimilate* our observations into our expectations (e.g., convince ourselves that our observations were a fluke and our expectations and stereotypes are correct), or we can *accommodate* our expectations to the reality (e.g., entertain the hypothesis that our stereotypes may be incorrect). Intercultural communication processes, therefore, have inherent potential for either self-growth and the development of new ways of thinking, or a crystallization of old ways of thinking, depending on how the individual deals with the challenge to self and expectations incumbent to the elicitation of the negative emotions produced by the interpretations of inappropriate behavior.

Because intercultural communication processes are laden with such unknowns, there is a considerable amount of uncertainty and anxiety attendant upon such exchanges. By understanding that such uncertainty and anxiety are natural, and by developing ways of regulating one's negative emotional reactions and channeling them toward accommodation and self-growth rather than stagnation, we can build bridges across cultures that can help to reduce intercultural conflict and produce effective communication.

Bibliography

Asante, M., & Gudykunst, W. (Eds.). (1989). *Handbook of intercultural and international communication.* Beverly Hills, CA: Sage.

Brislin, R., Cushner, K., Cherrie, C., & Yong, M. (1986). *Intercultural interactions: A practical guide.* Newbury Park, CA: Sage.

Condon, J., & Yousef, S. (1975). *An introduction to intercultural communication.* New York: Macmillan.

Ekman, P. (1972). Universal and cultural differences in facial expressions of emotion. In J. R. Cole (Ed.), *Nebraska symposium on motivation, 1971.* Lincoln: University of Nebraska Press.

Matsumoto, D. (1996). *Culture and psychology.* Pacific Grove, CA: Brooks/Cole.

Morris, D., Collett, P., Marsh, P., & O'Shaughnessy, M. (1980). *Gestures: Their origins and distribution.* New York: Scarborough.

Rosch, E., & Lloyd, B. B. (Eds.). (1978). *Cognition and categorization.* Hillsdale, NJ: Erlbaum.

Samovar, L. A., & Porter, R. E. (1997a). *Communication between cultures.* Belmont, CA: Wadsworth.

Samovar, L. A., & Porter, R. E. (1997b). *Intercultural communication.* Belmont, CA: Wadsworth.

Suzuki, T. (1978). *Japanese and the Japanese.* Tokyo: Kodansha.

Triandis, H. C. (1994). *Culture and social behavior.* New York: McGraw-Hill.

Whorf, B. L. (1956). *Language, thought, and reality.* Cambridge, MA: MIT Press.

David Matsumoto

CROSS-CULTURAL COUNSELING. Any helping relationship that assesses, understands, and evaluates a client's behavior in the multiplicity of cultural contexts where that behavior was learned and is displayed may be termed *cross-cultural counseling.* These cultural contexts may be narrowly defined to include ethnicity or nationality, but they may also be broadly defined to include ethnographic, demographic, status, and affiliation identifiers. According to the broad definition of culture, all counseling is rightly understood to be cross-cultural counseling. Culture is then a central rather than a marginal or exotic aspect of counseling, focused on the client's salient affiliation to each particular cultural context. In recent years the term *multicultural* has been preferred over *cross-cultural* counseling to emphasize the multiplicity of cultural groups and contexts in which counseling occurs.

The identification of specific competencies developed when the Division 17 Education and Training Committee of the American Psychological Association (APA) (Sue et al., 1982) published a position paper describing a three-stage developmental sequence of competence beginning with multicultural "awareness," then moving to multicultural "knowledge," and finally to multicultural "skill" competencies. This framework has been elaborated by Sue, Arredondo, and McDavis (1992) and others who specify those competencies needed to serve multicultural populations. The competency framework has since been adopted by both Division 17 of the APA and by the American Counseling Association. There is a need for defined competencies in multicultural counseling. The Basic Behavioral Science Task Force of the National Advisory Mental Health Council (1996) has identified specific examples where (1) social and cultural beliefs influence diagnosis and treatment; (2) diagnosis differs across cultures; (3) symptoms are expressed differently across cultures; (4) diagnostic categories reflect majority culture values; and (5) most providers are from the majority culture while most clients are from minority cultures.

Ponterotto, Casas, Suzuki, and Alexander (1995) provide the best single source on the contemporary issues in multicultural counseling in terms of historical antecedents, ethical guidelines, philosophical assumptions, assessment strategies, and other applications of counseling to multicultural populations. Particular emphasis is given to the range of ethnic identity models based on models of negrescence identity in the 1970s by Cross (1995). Racial and ethnic identity models for American Indians, Blacks, Hispanics, Whites, and other populations are reviewed in Ponterotto et al. (1995). More recent racial and ethnic identity models have organized the stage or state categories into a first "preencounter" stage as the level of least awareness, a second "encounter" stage, a third "immersion-emersion" stage, a fourth "internalization" stage, and a fifth "internalization-commitment" stage which is the highest level of awareness (Cross, 1995). These categories of increased awareness are important for counselors assessing their own competency as well as for defining constructive growth among clients from different cultural backgrounds.

The psychological study of cultures has always assumed that there was a fixed state of mind whose observation was obscured by cultural distortions and that there was a universal definition of normal behavior in an "absolutist" position. A contrasting anthropological science assumed that cultural differences were clues to divergent attitudes, values, or perspectives which differentiated each culture from others in a "relativist" position. Only recently has there been a serious attempt to reconcile these polarized alternatives through a synthesis in multicultural counseling theory (MCT); Sue, Ivey, & Pedersen, 1996). MCT is based on six major propositions about counseling theories as worldviews contrasted with a metatheory which emphasizes a multicultural metatheory. These propositions are as follows:

1. Each Western or non-Western theory represents a different worldview.
2. The totality and interrelationships of client-counselor experiences and contexts must be the focus of counseling.
3. A counselor or client's cultural identity will influence how problems are defined and dictate or define appropriate counseling goals or processes.
4. The ultimate goal of MCT is to expand the repertoire of helping responses available to counselors.
5. Conventional roles of counseling are only some of many alternative helping roles available in other cultural contexts.
6. MCT emphasizes the importance of expanding personal, family, group, and organizational consciousness in a contextual orientation.

More recently, multiculturalism has been described as a "fourth force" to complement the three conventional psychological forces of psychodynamics, behaviorism, and humanism (Pedersen, in press). Since all behaviors are learned and displayed in a cultural context, accurate assessment, meaningful understanding, and appropriate intervention requires that all theories need to acknowledge the central role of culture for the valid and competent application of that theory. This "culture-centered" perspective will serve to strengthen conventional counseling theories by making them more relevant to a variety of different cultural contexts. Wrenn (1962) described the "cultural encapsulation" of any counselor or theory of counseling that disregards the client's cultural context.

There is a growing awareness of changes in the ways that contemporary counseling is being perceived. Smith, Harre, and Van Langenhove (1995) contrast the new with the old paradigms. The new paradigms emphasize understanding and describing more than just measuring behavior; comprehending consequences rather than seeking causes; social significance rather than just statistical significance; language, discourse, and symbols rather than numerical reductionism; holistic more than atomistic perspectives; particularities more than universals; contextual more than context-free analysis; and the subjectivity as much as objectivity of evidential proof. These old and new rules are seamlessly connected as alternative perspectives of the same psychological phenomena. There needs to be a closer connection between theories about counseling and the practice of counseling in these necessarily multicultural contexts.

Pedersen (1997) identifies and discusses six controversies of cross-cultural counseling:

1. Is all counseling to some extent culturally encapsulated by the pervasive influence of a dominant culture on the counseling process? Until recently, the norms of healthy behavior were defined by a dominant culture.
2. Do all counseling tests and measures reflect the cultural patterns of cultural bias toward the cultural context in which they originated? Any measure which fits the exact needs of the cultural context of origin might have difficulty fitting as exactly in a completely different cultural context.
3. Should cultural identity be defined narrowly or broadly? Different cultural identities may be salient in each different situation depending on the environment.
4. Can you measure ethno-racial-cultural identity?
5. Should cross-cultural counseling emphasize similarities or differences? People or groups with similar values may display those values through very different behaviors.
6. Are ethical guidelines adequate to guide cross-cultural counselors? What is right in one cultural

context may not be as right in every other cultural context.

These and other controversies emphasize the importance of making culture central to the counseling process.

Multicultural training of counselors is a primary prevention strategy because it prevents otherwise qualified and conscientious providers from misunderstanding the behaviors of their culturally different clients. There is abundant data to document why accurate assessment, meaningful understanding and appropriate intervention requires that each behavior be interpreted with regard to the cultural context in which that behavior was learned and is being displayed.

Bibliography

Basic Behavioral Science Task Force of the National Advisory Mental Health Council (1996). Basic behavioral science research for mental health: Sociocultural and environmental processes. *American Psychologist, 51,* 722–731.

Cross, W. E. (1995). The psychology of nigrescence: Revising the cross model. In J. G. Ponterotto, J. M. Casas, L. A. Suzuki, & C. M. Alexander (Eds.), *Handbook of multicultural counseling.* Thousand Oaks, CA: Sage.

Pedersen, P. (1977). *Culture centered counseling interventions.* Thousand Oaks, CA: Sage.

Pedersen, P. (Ed.). (1998). *Multiculturalism as a fourth force.* Washington, DC: Taylor & Francis.

Ponterotto, J. G., Casas, J. M., Suzuki, L. A., & Alexander, C. M. (1995). *Handbook of multicultural counseling.* Thousand Oaks, CA: Sage.

Smith, J. A., Harre, R., & Van Langenhove, L. (1995). *Rethinking psychology.* London: Sage.

Sue, D. W. Arredondo, P., & McDavis, R. J. (1992). Multicultural counseling competencies and standards: A call to the profession. *Journal of Multicultural Counseling and Development, 20,* 644–688.

Sue, D. W., Bernier, J. E., Durran, A., Feinberg, L., Pedersen P., Smith E. J., & Vasquez-Nuttall, E. (1982). Position paper: Cross-cultural counseling competencies. *The Counseling Psychologist, 10,* 45–52.

Sue, D. W., Ivey, A. E., & Pedersen, P. B. (1997). *A theory of multicultural counseling and therapy.* Pacific Grove, CA: Brooks/Cole.

Wrenn, C. G. (1962). The culturally encapsulated counselor. *Harvard Educational Review, 32,* 444–449.

Paul B. Pedersen

CROSS-CULTURAL PSYCHOLOGY. [*This entry comprises two articles: an overview of the broad history of the field from its inception to the present; and survey of the principal theories that have determined the course of development of this field and of the methods and assessments that have been employed. For discussions related to cultures, see* Anthropology; Cultural Psychology; *and* Culture Shock.]

History of the Field

"Cross-cultural psychology is concerned with the systematic study of behavior and experience as it occurs in different cultures, is influenced by culture, or results in changes in existing cultures" (Triandis, 1980, p. 1). This broad definition includes both contemporary cross-cultural psychology and cultural psychology.

Contemporary cross-cultural psychology examines psychological phenomena in many cultures. It measures psychological constructs equivalently in different cultures. An ideal study would use an instrument that has equivalent meaning in cultures sampled from all the cultural regions of the world. One of the purposes of cross-cultural psychology is to establish the generality of psychological findings, and thus a broad sampling of cultures is appropriate. The theoretical framework is universalistic, and assumes the psychic unity of humankind.

By contrast, cultural psychology uses a relativistic framework, and examines how culture and psychological phenomena cocreate each other. Thus, it focuses on one culture at a time, and examines how psychological phenomena are modified by that culture. It does not necessarily accept the psychic unity of humankind (Shweder, 1990). There are several branches of cultural psychology (e.g., Boesch, Bruner, Cole, Greenfield, Rogoff, Shweder, Valsiner). Indigenous psychologies are related to cultural psychologies. They emphasize the explication of the meaning of key culture-specific concepts (e.g., *philotimo* in Greece, which means doing what the in-group expects one to do; and *amae*, in Japan, which means expecting great indulgence from a person with whom one is highly interdependent). Ethnic and indigenous psychologies have been developed; for example, for Mexico by Diaz-Guerrero, India by Sinha, the Philippines by Enriquez, by Yang for Taiwan, and the Chinese mainland culture (Kim & Berry, 1993).

Previous Histories

The history of cross-cultural psychology, broadly defined, started with Herodotus in the fifth century BC. In fact, two excellent histories, Klineberg (1980) and Jahoda and Krewer (1996) note that Herodotus had the insight that all humans are ethnocentric. This is a basic aspect of the human condition, because most humans are limited to knowing only their culture and thus are bound to use it as the standard for comparisons with other cultures. It is only when they have experienced several other cultures that they become sufficiently sophisticated to see both strengths and weaknesses in each and every culture.

These histories, and in more detail Gustav Jahoda's *Crossroads between Culture and Mind* (Cambridge, Mass., 1993), discuss the Middle Ages; Vico and his emphasis on culture-specific competencies; the Enlightenment; the activities of the Société des Observateurs de l' Homme (1799–1805), which developed an excellent manual for carrying out cross-cultural studies; Alexander von Humboldt (1830–1835), reporting on his explorations of South America and Siberia; Darwin and his influence on evolutionary theories, not only for species of animals but also for cultures; Wundt and his 10-volume *Völkerpsychologie* (1900–1914); and the emergence of the culture and personality field.

Tylor (1889) provided a classic definition of the term "culture" and suggested that culture can be used as the unit of analysis to study the laws of human thought across cultures. Other early pioneers included Rivers (1901), who reported on the expedition to the Torres Straits and was the first to carry out systematic experimental cross-cultural studies, and Boas (1911), who emphasized replacing ethnocentrism with the appreciation of the ways of life of others.

The middle pioneers (roughly 1920s to 1950s) included Luria (1976) and his study of culture and cognition; Bartlett (1932) and his classic study of remembering; Benedict (1935, 1945) and her studies of Japan; Vygotsky (1978) on the way the mind is shaped by culture; Dennis (1943) and his study of Hopi children; Kluckhohn's (1954) superb chapter on "Culture and Behavior"; Klineberg's (1954) social psychology text with its emphasis on ethnographic materials; and Jahoda's (1961) African studies.

History after 1967. Cross-cultural psychology emerged in the late 1960s as a self-conscious discipline, separate from both anthropology and psychology yet closely linked to both. A major turning point was the Ibadan conference, during the Christmas-New Year vacation of 1966 and 1967, at a time when the *Zeitgeist* was ready for the emergence of a separate field.

The purpose of that conference was to stimulate research that would help the economic development of less developed countries and establish mechanisms of international cooperation in social psychological research. The aim was to establish long-term research relationships, and also to help develop the skills of indigenous social psychologists and provide them with resources that would permit them to do research. The results of the conference were published by Kelman and Smith (1968).

Concerns about "intellectual colonialism" were expressed at the conference by F. Stambouli of Tunisia. He argued that collecting data in Africa and taking them to Europe or North America and publishing the results without the collaboration of indigenous scientists was morally reprehensible. Avoiding intellectual colonialism became important among cross-cultural psychologists and can be seen in books by Triandis (1972) and in the code of ethics for cross-cultural research proposed by Tapp, Kelman, Triandis, Wrightsman, and Coelho (1974). The avoidance of ethnocentrism, by searching for different perspectives on a phenomenon and developing an appreciation of culture-specific (emic) points of view, and the local standardization of psychological instruments, became central concerns of cross-cultural psychology. The development of methods that use both emic and etic (universally valid) items became one of the contributions of cross-cultural psychology. The use of multimethod approaches, the testing of rival hypotheses, and the testing of hypotheses by using data from the Human Relations Area Files (see Barry, 1980, for a description and history) as well as data obtained from participants, became important distinguishing features of cross-cultural psychology.

In the early phases of the development of the relationship of culture and psychology, a universalist viewpoint was widely used. That is, it was assumed that all psychological discoveries were valid universally, and culture provided only minor modifications of these discoveries. In the 1980s and later, however, a number of researchers assumed more relativistic positions, in some cases even denying the psychic unity of humankind. Cultural psychologies emphasized shared meanings in each culture, and these meanings may be very different from culture to culture.

During one of the sessions of the conference, we discussed the need for coordination of efforts and dissemination of information about research collaborations around the world. Thus, the *Cross-Cultural Newsletter* (1967) was born and was first edited by Triandis. It eventually became the *Cross-Cultural Bulletin*. About the same time the *Journal of Social Psychology*, edited by Leonard Doob, and the *International Journal of Psychology*, edited by Germaine de Montmollin (1966), announced policies favoring cross-cultural papers. The Human Relations Area Files began publishing a journal in 1966, which in 1992 became *Cross-Cultural Research*. It is now the official organ of the Society for Cross-Cultural Research, founded by the anthropologist Peter Murdoch in 1972, but which now includes psychologists and other cross-cultural social scientists. *The Journal of Cross-Cultural Psychology*, founded by Walter Lonner, first appeared in 1970. It became the official journal of the International Association of Cross-Cultural Psychology (IACCP), established in 1972. *The Association pour la Recherche Interculturelle* (ARIC) was established in 1984, and had a joint meeting with the IACCP in Liège, Belgium, in 1992.

The Annual Review of Psychology established chapters reviewing cross-cultural work in 1973. Significant publications included *Handbook of Cross-Cultural Psychology* (1980–1981). Significant texts included Segall (1972), Segall, Dasen, Berry, and Poortinga (1990), Berry, Poortinga, Segall, and Dasen (1992), Moghaddam, Taylor, and Wright (1992), Smith and Bond (1993, 1999), Triandis (1994).

Examples of Significant Work

Lists of significant work in cross-cultural psychology can be found in two handbooks (Triandis, 1980–1981; Berry, 1997). Limitations of space in this entry permit only one example: Berry (1980) examined members of a culture (A) who come in contact with another culture (B), and may develop a culture that uses both cultural elements (A + B), or reject their own culture and adopt the other culture (use just B, assimilation); refuse to adopt any of the elements of the other culture and thus become separated from the other culture (use just A, separation); or reject both sets of cultural elements (neither A nor B, alienation or marginalization). In the case of cultural groups that have been conquered or forced to migrate, separation is sometimes linked to "cultural opposition" (i.e., if culture B has a particular element, the separated members adopt the opposite element).

Of course, these four patterns are ideal types, and there are several intermediate possibilities. Research on the mental health of samples who have adopted these four patterns, showed that the A + B pattern was more desirable than the others. In addition, Triandis discussed acculturation in terms of "accommodation" (members of culture A acquiring elements of culture B); "overshooting" (in some cases becoming more extreme users of elements of culture B than even the members of culture B); and "ethnic affirmation" (rejecting culture B and becoming more fanatic users of elements of culture A) (Triandis, Kashima, Shimada, & Villareal, 1986). Of course, these patterns have direct relevance for the kind of ethnic identity that people develop. In some cases they see themselves as both A and B, in other cases as one or the other or neither A nor B. What applies to ethnicity also applies to race, where some African Americans adopt behavior patterns (e.g., names, hair styles) that emphasize their African ancestry, and others dress even more like the mainstream than the majority of the population.

In societies where many people adopt elements from many cultures we find cultural pluralism. An issue then is how should the educational systems be constituted to accommodate the diverse cultural elements. Depending on ideology, the more enlightened commentators suggest that we should train schoolchildren to appreciate the cultural perspectives of all cultures that have a significant presence in their country. Others emphasize national and ethnic purity and reject this view.

Current Focus of Cross-Cultural Psychology

In recent years, excitement has been generated by work on the way the self is structured in different cultures and on the corresponding cultural patterns such as individualism and collectivism (Triandis, 1995; several chapters in Berry, Segall, & Kagitcibasi, 1997). There has been much work on stereotypes and gender, moral development, culture and schooling, on values, the way in which resources are distributed (equity, equality, need), social responsibility, and cultural differences on attributions. Other important work has been done on social responsibility, the culture of honor, intercultural communication, nonlinguistic communication and behavior, emotion and culture, and culture and psychopathology. Applications of cross-cultural psychology have included work on cross-cultural training and handbooks on that topic; work on culture psychopathology as well as counseling, and the influence of culture on organizational behavior.

Graduate Training

As preparation for professional cross-cultural work in the graduate training field, graduate training has mostly been in the areas of developmental and social psychology. Those who specialize in cross-cultural psychology are encouraged to master at least one other language.

The Future

The field's origins in the 1960s were for the most part North American. In the 1970s, western European researchers began to make contributions, and in the 1980s and 1990s Asians did significant work. The next century will probably continue this trend, and will include creative integrations of cross-cultural, indigenous (e.g., Kim & Berry, 1993; Sinha, 1997) and cultural psychologies. It will profit from further contributions by psychologists from the Pacific Rim, whose work will further broaden Western psychology, and might make it a special case of the universal psychology that might be developed in the twenty-first century.

Bibliography

Barry, H. III (1980). Description and uses of the Human Relations Area Files. In H. C. Triandis & J. W. Berry (Eds.), *Handbook of cross-cultural psychology* (Vol. 2, pp. 445–478). Boston: Allyn & Bacon.

Bartlett, F. C. (1932). *Remembering.* Cambridge, England: Cambridge University Press.

Benedict, R. (1935, 1945). *Patterns of culture.* London: Routledge.

Berry, J. W. (1980). Acculturation as varieties of adaptation. In A. Padilla (Ed.) *Acculturation: theory, models and some new findings* (pp. 9–25). Boulder, CO: Westview Press.

Berry, J. W., Poortinga, Y. H., Segall, M. H., & Dasen, P. R. (1992). *Cross-cultural psychology: Research and applications*. New York: Cambridge University Press.

Berry, J. W., Segall, M., & Kagitcibasi, C. (1997). *Handbook of cross-cultural psychology* (2nd ed., Vol. 3). Boston: Allyn & Bacon.

Boas, F. (1911). *The mind of primitive man*. New York: Macmillan.

Dennis, W. (1943). Animism and related tendencies in Hopi children. *Journal of Abnormal and Social Psychology*, *38*, 21–37.

Jahoda, G. (1961). *White man*. London: Oxford University Press.

Jahoda, G., & Krewer, B. (1997). History of cross-cultural and cultural psychology. In J. W. Berry, Y. H. Poortinga, & J. Pandey (Eds.), *Handbook of cross-cultural psychology* (2nd ed., pp. 1–42). Boston: Allyn & Bacon. (Original work published 1980)

Kelman, H. C., & Smith, M. B. (1968). Social psychological research in developing countries. *Journal of Social Issues*, *24*(2), 1–287.

Kim, U., & Berry, J. W. (1993). *Indigenous psychologies: Research and experience in cultural context*. Newbury Park, CA: Sage.

Klineberg, O. (1954). *Social psychology* (2nd ed.). New York: Holt, Rinehart & Winston.

Klineberg, O. (1980). Historical perspectives: Cross-cultural psychology before 1960. In H. C. Triandis & W. W. Lambert (Eds.), *Handbook of cross-cultural psychology* (Vol. 1, pp. 1–14). Boston: Allyn & Bacon.

Kluckhohn, C. (1954). Culture and behavior. In G. Lindzey (Ed.), *Handbook of social psychology* (Vol. 2, pp. 921–976). Cambridge, MA: Addison-Wesley.

Landis, D., & Bhagat, R. S. (1996). *Handbook of intercultural training* (2nd ed.). Thousand Oaks, CA: Sage.

Moghaddam, F. M., Taylor, D. M., & Wright, S. C. (1993). *Social psychology in cross-cultural perspective*. New York: Freeman.

Rivers, W. H. R. (1901). Part I: Introduction and vision. In A. C. Haddon (Ed.). *Reports of the Cambridge anthropological expedition to Torres Straits*, Vol. 2. Cambridge, England: Cambridge University Press.

Segall, M. H. (1972). *Cross-cultural psychology: Human behavior in global perspective*. Monterey, CA: Brooks/Cole.

Segall, M. H., Dasen, P. R., Berry, J. W., & Poortinga, Y. H. (1990). *Human behavior in global perspective: An introduction to cross-cultural psychology*. New York: Pergamon Press.

Shweder. R. A. (1990). Cultural psychology—what is it? In J. W. Stigler, R. A. Shweder, & G. Herdt (Eds.), *Cultural psychology* (pp. 1–43) New York: Cambridge University Press.

Smith, P. B., & Bond, M. H. (1993). *Social psychology across cultures*. London: Prentice Hall Europe.

Smith, P. B., & Bond, M. H. (1999). *Social psychology across cultures*. Boston: Allyn & Bacon.

Tapp, J. L., Kelman, H. C., Triandis, H. C. Wrightsman, L., & Coelho, G. (1974). Continuing concerns in cross-cultural ethics. *International Journal of Psychology, 9*, 231–249.

Triandis, H. C. (1972). *The analysis of subjective culture*. New York: Wiley.

Triandis, H. C. (1980). Introduction. In H. C. Triandis & W. W. Lambert (Eds.), *Handbook of cross-cultural psychology* (pp. 1–14). Boston: Allyn & Bacon.

Triandis, H. C. (1994). *Culture and social behavior*. New York: McGraw-Hill.

Triandis, H. C. (1995). *Individualism and collectivism*. Boulder, CO: Westview Press.

Triandis, H. C., Kashima, Y., Shimada, E., & Villareal, M. (1986). Acculturation indices as a means of confirming cultural differences. *International Journal of Psychology, 21*, 43–70.

Triandis, H. C., & Lambert, W. W. (Eds.). (1980–1981). *Handbook of cross-cultural psychology* (Vols. 1–6). Boston: Allyn & Bacon.

Tylor, E. B. (1889). On a method of investigating the development of institutions. *Journal of the Royal Anthropological Institute of Great Britain and Ireland, 18*, 245–272.

Vygotsky, L. S. (1978). *Mind and society*. Cambridge, MA: Harvard University Press.

Harry C. Triandis

Theories and Methods of Study

The question of how information about the psychological functioning of various cultural and ethnic populations can be studied runs through the history of cross-cultural psychology like a thread. One tradition is based on Waitz's notion of the "psychic unity of mankind," according to which the human psyche is essentially similar across cultures. The tradition is rooted in the European Enlightenment of the seventeenth to nineteenth century, when philosophers such as Hume and Kant emphasized the basic similarity of human behavior across times and cultures and the need for cross-cultural research in identifying the principles governing this universality. In the Romantic rebellion against the Enlightenment (expressed in the work of Rousseau and Herder, among others, vast differences in the psychological functioning of different cultural populations were emphasized). Attempts to compare cultures cannot but involve peripheral aspects of psychological functioning. The tradition is noncomparative and maintains that cultures should be understood "from within." The debate between these two approaches has recurred under various disguises. Examples include the distinction between universalism and cultural relativism, cross-cultural and cultural psychology, and etic and emic approaches (a popular terminology in cross-cultural psychology, drawing on a distinction by the linguist Kenneth Pike). The distinction between a comparative and noncomparative perspective in anthropology and between the nomothetic and ideographic approach in mainstream psychology have similar roots.

Goals of the Study of Cultural Factors

Three goals of comparative and noncomparative approaches can be discerned: (1) testing the applicability of (usually) Western theories and measures in a non-Western context, (2) exploring the role of cultural factors by extending the range of variation of cultural variables, and (3) integrating culture into theories and measures in order to contribute to a truly universal psychology. These goals have an implicit temporal order. Cross-cultural psychology has enough impetus at present to conclude with confidence that important steps have been taken toward the realization of the first goal. Instruments covering various psychological domains such as intelligence, personality, and social behavior have been administered in cross-cultural studies. It has been repeatedly shown that instruments developed in Western countries are susceptible to various sources of bias, with the susceptibility tending to increase with the cultural distance between the instrument's author and the examinees. The second goal has also been well studied. Social psychology provides many examples of the former; there are ample demonstrations of the vital and not infrequently neglected influence of cultural context on social-psychological functioning.

The pervasive cross-cultural differences in the social-psychological domain have undoubtedly added to the their popularity in cross-cultural psychology. One of the best known examples of cross-cultural research aimed at the second goal such was Segall, Campbell, and Herskovits's work on illusion susceptibility (1966). In a large cross-cultural study, these authors demonstrated that in the built environment and with openness of the natural vista, illusion susceptibility is positively related to the occurrence of geometric shapes like rectangles and squares. Another example is the ecocultural framework that is frequently employed to link psychological aspects to features of the environment. In particular, food-gathering style has been studied, based on a dichotomy of nomadic hunting and food gatherers living in loosely organized societies in sparsely populated regions versus sedentary agriculturalists living in tightly knit societies in more densely populated regions. Various psychological differences of these societies have been examined, such as child-rearing patterns and cognitive style.

The second goal has also been examined from a noncomparative perspective. Two approaches are discussed here. The first is cultural psychology, a relatively young subdiscipline. It is closely related to social constructionism and aims at an in-depth understanding of psycho-logical functioning by studying *in situ* behavior, usually in only one culture. Culture and personality are taken to constitute each other in a process of mutual influences. Culture is seen as a system of meanings, with studies often focusing on how individuals gradually acquire the perspective of a culture. In line with common practice in anthropology (ethnography in particular), assessment methods are utilized that impose little or no a priori categorization on the data, such as unstructured interviews and tape and video recordings. Because of the interest in learning processes, diachronic (longitudinal) designs are often employed.

Indigenous psychologies provide another example of an increasingly popular, noncomparative approach to understanding cultural variation. It is a generic name for all types of psychologies that attempt to overcome the limitations of, in Sinha's words, "the culture-bound and culture-blind tendencies of mainstream psychology" (1997). Indigenous psychologies have been developed in various areas, such as Latin America, India, Japan, and China. The need for developing an indigenous psychology is often triggered by findings that a non-Western application of a common Western theory or instrument does not do justice to the specifics of the non-Western group. In various degrees of elaboration, these psychologies try to overcome Western biases in theory and assessment, ultimately aiming at an enhancement of the adequacy and applicability of psychological knowledge for these areas. Indigenous psychologies are not yet developed enough to have a serious effect on Western psychology. To date, the integration of cross-cultural findings and mainstream theories of psychology, the third goal of cross-cultural psychology, remains an open challenge.

Methodological Issues

The largest part of the cross-cultural knowledge base is related to the testing of the applicability of Western theories and measures. In such studies, methodological features tend to require attention. It is therefore not surprising that cross-cultural psychology has been described as a method. A good example of such a concern is the sampling of subjects within cultural populations. Whereas the anthropologist can often rely on a small number of informants who, because of their expertise, have good access to the cultural knowledge of interest, such as the indigenous taxonomy of a particular flora, the cross-cultural psychologist usually deals with psychological characteristics that vary substantially across the members of a population. The sampling procedure that is applied then has a bearing on the interpretability of the results. A comparison of two haphazardly chosen samples is susceptible to interpretation problems: Is the observed difference in psychological functioning (e.g., in locus of control) the result of an underlying cultural difference or because of sample differences in relevant though uncontrolled background characteristics, such as socioeconomic status, gender, or education?

Three popular sampling procedures represent different ways of dealing with confounding characteristics. The first is random, or probability, sampling. It assumes an available listing of eligible units, such as persons or households. If properly applied, such a sample will yield an adequate picture of the cultural population. Yet, confounding variables, which are not controlled for in this approach, may challenge the interpretation of cross-cultural differences.

The second type is matched sampling. A population is stratified (e.g., in levels of schooling or socioeconomic status) and within each stratum a random sample is drawn. Using a matching procedure, confounding variables can then be controlled, but such a sample may poorly represent a whole population. The latter may be improved by applying statistical weights to individual scores (e.g., when highly schooled people are overrepresented in the sample, these scores will get a weight that is lower than those of less educated persons). Matching is appropriate when cultural groups are not too dissimilar with regards to confounding variables, but the procedure cannot correct adequately for confounding variables when there is little or no overlap across cultures (e.g., comparisons of literates and illiterates).

The third sampling procedure combines random sampling with the measurement of control variables and enables a (post hoc) statistical control of ambient variables. The applicability of this procedure is limited only by the assumptions of the statistical technique utilized; for example, an analysis of covariance assumes equal regression coefficients of the confounding variables in the prediction of a target variable.

Cross-cultural studies also have to deal with the sampling of cultures. Again, three types of sampling can be envisaged. The first is random sampling. Because of the prohibitively large cost of a random sample from all existing cultures, it often amounts to a random sample of a particular groups of cultures (e.g., Circummediterranean cultures). The second and most frequently observed type of culture sampling is convenience sampling. The choice of cultures is then governed by considerations of availability and cost efficiency. In many studies, researchers from different countries cooperate, with each collecting data in his or her own country. The reasons for choosing a particular culture are more based on substantive considerations in the third type, called systematic sampling. A culture is deliberately chosen because of some characteristic, such as in Segall, Campbell, and Herskovits's (1966) study in which cultures were chosen based on features of the ecological environment, such as openness of the vista.

Extensive experience with the application of Western instruments (often adapted) in a non-Western context has led to a set of concepts and recommended practices. [See Cross-Cultural Test Adaptation.] Central concepts are bias and (in)equivalence. Bias refers to the presence of validity-threatening aspects of a test or inventory such as inappropriate items; a stimulus is biased if it does not have the same psychological meaning in the cultures studied. For example, endorsement of the item "[I] watched more television than usual," which is part of a common coping list, will depend on the availability of electricity and television sets, among other things. Equivalence refers to the implications of bias on the comparability of scores across cultures. [See Bias and Equivalence.]

Multilingual Studies

Cross-cultural studies are often multilingual, and recommended practices for how instruments can be translated or adapted have been developed. In an adaptation procedure, one or more parts are rewritten in order to improve an instrument's suitability for a target group. Most multilingual studies employ existing instruments. A translation, followed by an independent back-translation and a comparison of the original and back-translated version, possibly followed by some alterations of the translation is accomplished. Back-translations provide a powerful tool to enhance the correspondence of original and translated versions that is independent of the researcher's knowledge of the target language. Yet, they do not address all problems. First, back-translations put a premium on literal reproduction; this may give rise to stilted language in the target version that lacks the readability and natural flow of the original.

A second problem involves translatability. The use of idiom (e.g., the English "feeling blue") or references to cultural specifics (e.g., country-specific public holidays) or other features that cannot be adequately represented in the target language challenges translation–back-translations (and indeed all studies in which existing instruments are translated). When versions in all languages can be developed simultaneously, "decentering" can be used, in which no single language or culture is taken as starting point; individuals from different cultures develop an instrument jointly, thereby greatly reducing the risk of introducing unwanted references to a specific culture. During the last decade there has been a growing awareness that translations and adaptations require the combined expertise of psychologists (with competence in the construct studied) and experts in the local language and culture of the target culture(s). In this so-called committee approach, in which the expertise of all relevant disciplines is combined, there is usually no formal accuracy check of the translation. The committee approach is widespread among large international bodies such as the United Nations and the European Union, in which texts have to be translated into many languages.

Individual and Country-Level Studies

Cross-cultural studies can compare psychological functioning at various levels of aggregation, ranging from individuals to households, classes, schools, regions, and even whole countries. By far, most studies compare individuals, while more recently there is an increasing interest in country-level comparisons. With regards to the former, much research has been carried out in the area of intelligence and cognitive development. Factor analyses of cross-cultural applications of intellectual tasks have yielded strong support for the universality of the cognitive apparatus, with factoral structures found in Western and non-Western groups tending to be identical. On the other hand, average scores on intelligence tests in particular differ rather consistently across cultural groups, with Western individuals frequently obtaining higher scores than non-Western. The interpretation of these differences was and still is controversial, and inconclusive reasons have been offered, such as genetic origin, environmental background, and measurement artifacts (the differential suitability of the instrument).

Piagetian theory has also spurred cross-cultural research. [*See the biography of Piaget.*] The order of the stages as proposed by Piaget has been found to be universal, yet the age of onset of each stage tends to differ, with more cross-cultural variation in age found at the higher stages. Evidence for the universality of the highest stage, formal-operational thinking, is weak, although the poor applicability of formal-operational tasks in particular cultures can at least partly account for this observation. Evidence from cultural anthropology based on observations of behavior *in situ* supports the universality of formal-operational thinking.

In sum, there are no studies refuting the universality of basic features of cognitive functioning, like primacy and recency effects in short-term memory retrieval, the virtually unlimited storage capacity of long-term memory, the attainment of Piagetian conservation, and logical reasoning. Nevertheless, the area of application of certain cognitive skills may differ across cultures (and often across professional groups within cultures). Cultures can build on a set of universal "building blocks" such as long-term memory, but the kind of information that is stored (e.g., scholastic information) may vary considerably across cultures.

The second line of research attempts to establish the universality (or cultural specificity) of certain traits or personality structure in general. Eysenck's three-factor model of personality (emotional stability, psychoticism, and extroversion) and more recently, the "Big Five" model of personality (conscientiousness, neuroticism,

extroversion, agreeableness, and openness), which is based on psycholexical studies, have been the subject of cross-cultural research. Despite minor problems in both traditions (Eysenck applied a statistical procedure to demonstrate factoral stability with a low statistical power, while the fifth factor of the Big Five could not always be retrieved), the personality structure among Western subjects seems to be essentially universal. However, some non-Western studies have pointed to the incompleteness of Western models of personality. For example, in a large Chinese study it was found that a Western model of personality did not cover aspects frequently utilized in self-descriptions, such as face and harmony. The possible incompleteness of Western models of personality points to an observation often made in cross-cultural psychology: Universal aspects of psychological functioning can be found at a fairly abstract level, while a closer examination of a single group (as in the case of the Chinese study) points to the existence of cultural specifics not covered by the Western structure.

For obvious reasons, comparisons based on country scores are not numerous, yet the few large-scale studies that have been reported have been influential. The first large data base containing information about a large set of cultures was the Human Relations Area Files, published in the 1960s by George Peter Murdock, a cultural anthropologist. The data base contains scores for many variables of hundreds of (mainly nonindustrial) societies. The well-acknowledged problem of data quality (scores were obtained from a wide variety of sources ranging from trained anthropologists to missionaries, and often not applying identical criteria and with an unknown interrater agreement) is more than compensated for by the sheer size of the data base and the opportunity to compare a large set of cultures. The publication of the data base has initiated an ongoing series of publications.

In a more recent study, Geert Hofstede has compared the work-related values of over 100,000 employees of IBM branches in 50 nations. He maintains that country differences in scores can be represented along four dimensions: individualism-collectivism, uncertainty avoidance (i.e., "neuroticism at country level"), power distance (acceptance of unequal power distribution), and femininity-masculinity (gender role overlap in a country). Currently popular is the dichotomy of individualism and collectivism. Interest has increased owing to Hofstede's international comparison of work-related values, but its introduction in the social sciences goes back at least to 1887 and the work of Ferdinand Tönnies, who distinguished between *Gemeinschaft* (in which the group prevails and individuals form molar bonds characterized by an emphasis on group goals) and *Gesellschaft* (in which the individual prevails and interpersonal relationships are molecular). The impact of a country's status on the individualism or collectivism of various psychological aspects (e.g., personality and attitudes) has been extensively studied during the past decade. Much evidence has been accumulated that shows the widespread consequences of individualism. Unfortunately, many studies involve the comparisons of countries with high gross national products, which are known to show a strong positive relationship with individualism. As a consequence, confounding population differences (e.g., in schooling or income) are often poorly controlled. In another large-scale project, Schwartz asked teachers and college students in more than 80 countries to indicate to what extent each of 56 values constituted an important motive in their lives. The country differences could be represented in two dimensions: one involved an openness-conservatism dimension while the other described a continuum from self-enhancement (e.g., achievement, power) to self-transcendence (e.g., benevolence and wisdom).

Bibliography

Amir, Y., & Sharon, I. (1987). Are social psychological laws cross-culturally valid? *Journal of Cross-Cultural Psychology, 18,* 383–470. Provides an instructive demonstration showing that Western findings from experimental social psychology are often poorly generalizable in a different cultural context.

Berry, J. W. (1976). *Human ecology and cognitive style: Comparative studies in cultural and psychological adaptation.* Beverly Hills, CA: Sage. Describes the influence of ecology on psychological functioning, particularly on cognitive style.

Berry, J. W., Poortinga, Y. H., Segall, M. H., & Dasen, P. R. (1992). *Cross-cultural psychology: Research and applications.* Cambridge, England: Cambridge University Press. A textbook at advanced level, describing major theories and models of cross-cultural research.

Brislin, R. W. (1986). The wording and translation of research instruments. In W. J. Lonner & J. W. Berry (Eds.), *Field methods in cross-cultural research* (pp. 137–164). Newbury Park, CA: Sage. Gives a good overview of issues in test translations as well as a set of rules to enhance translatability.

Dasen, P. R. (Ed.). (1977). *Piagetian psychology: Cross-cultural contributions.* New York: Gardner. Summarizes the major findings of Piagetian cross-cultural studies.

Hambleton, R. K. (1994). Guidelines for adapting educational and psychological tests: A progress report. *European Journal of Psychological Assessment, 10,* 229–244. Presents an elaborate set of recommended practices in multilingual studies prepared by an international committee of psychologists. The combined efforts of psychologists and experts in the language and culture of target populations are proposed as a powerful means to safeguard accurate translations and adaptations.

Hofstede, G. (1980). *Culture's consequences: International differences in work-related values.* Beverly Hills, CA: Sage. The most frequently quoted source in cross-cultural psychology, presenting a taxonomy of differences among countries in four dimensions (individualism, power distance, uncertainty avoidance, and masculinity).

Jahoda, G. (1989). Our forgotten ancestors. In R. A. Dienstbier (Series Ed.) & J. J. Berman (Vol. Ed.), *Nebraska symposium on motivation 1989: Vol. 37. Cross-cultural perspectives* (pp. 1–40). Lincoln, NE: University of Nebraska Press. Presents a short and highly readable history of the ancestors of cross-cultural and cultural psychology, with an emphasis on seventeenth- to nineteenth-century thinkers.

Jahoda, G., & Krewer, B. (1997). History of cross-cultural psychology and cultural psychology. In J. W. Berry, Y. H. Poortinga, & J. Pandey (Eds.), *Handbook of cross-cultural psychology* (2nd ed., Vol. 1, pp. 1–42). Boston: Allyn & Bacon. Describes the intellectual roots of cross-cultural and cultural psychology.

Jensen, A. R. (1980). *Bias in mental testing.* New York: Free Press. A rich source of cross-cultural comparisons of mainly American groups.

Kagitcibasi, C. (1997). Individualism and collectivism. In J. W. Berry, M. H. Segall, & C. Kagitcibasi (Eds.), *Handbook of cross-cultural psychology* (Vol. 3, pp. 1–49). Boston: Allyn & Bacon. Presents a recent overview of individualism-collectivism studies.

Lonner, W. J., & Adamopoulos, J. (1997). Culture as antecedent to behavior. In J. W. Berry, Y. H. Poortinga, & J. Pandey (Eds.), *Handbook of cross-cultural psychology* (2nd ed., Vol. 1, pp. 43–83). Boston: Allyn & Bacon. Summarizes the main findings of the paradigms that were most influential in cross-cultural psychology.

Miller, J. G. (1997). Theoretical issues in cultural psychology. In J. W. Berry, Y. H. Poortinga, & J. Pandey (Eds.), *Handbook of cross-cultural psychology* (2nd ed., Vol. 1, pp. 85–128). Boston: Allyn & Bacon. Describes theoretical issues in cultural psychology.

Saxe, G. B. (1991). *Culture and cognitive development: Studies in mathematical understanding.* Hillsdale, NJ: Erlbaum. A good example of a the cultural-psychological approach to the study of mathematics. Both everyday and school mathematics are described and compared.

Schwartz, S. H. (1992). Universals in the content and structure of values: Theoretical advances and empirical tests in 20 countries. In M. Zanna (Ed.), *Advances in experimental social psychology* (Vol. 25, pp. 1–65). Orlando, FL: Academic Press. Describes a presumably universal structure of human values.

Segall, M. H., Campbell, D. T., & Herskovits, M. J. (1966). *The influence of culture on visual perception.* Indianapolis: Bobbs-Merrill. A good example of a theory that successfully models cross-cultural variations (of illusion susceptibility).

Segall, M. H., Dasen, P. R., Berry, J. W., & Poortinga, Y. H. (1990). *Human behavior in global perspective.* New York: Pergamon Press. A basic textbook.

Sinha, D. (1997). Indigenizing psychology. In J. W. Berry, Y. H. Poortinga, & J. Pandey (Eds.), *Handbook of cross-cultural psychology* (2nd ed., Vol. 1, pp. 129–169). Boston: Allyn & Bacon. Provides a good overview of the indigenization movement in cross-cultural psychology.

Smith, P. B., & Bond, M. H. (1993). *Social psychology across cultures: Analysis and perspectives.* New York: Harvester Wheatsheaf. A good overview of the challenges that cross-cultural studies provide to mainstream social psychology.

Stigler, J. W., Shweder, R. A., & Herdt, G. (Eds.). (1990). *Cultural psychology: Essays on comparative human development.* New York: Cambridge University Press. A rich source of information about cultural psychology.

Van de Vijver, F. J. R., & Leung, K. (1997). *Methods and data analysis for cross-cultural research.* Newbury Park, CA: Sage. Presents an overview of problems and suggested solutions of cross-cultural research.

Fons J. R. van de Vijver

CROSS-CULTURAL TEST ADAPTATION. In one early cross-cultural study, Porteus administered tests of cognitive abilities to members of various cultural populations around the world. The test he relied on most consisted of mazes drawn on paper. On the basis of the distributions of the test scores, Porteus (1937) made comparative statements about the intelligence of such groups as Bushmen and Bantu-speaking groups in Southern Africa and Australian Aborigines. He concluded that the level of intelligence, reflected in such abilities as foresight and planning (presumably measured by the maze test), was lower among the Bushmen than in any other race. Porteus discussed factors that might have affected his findings, such as absence of schooling, but these he explained away and, in the end, he accepted the validity of his findings.

Few psychologists today would share Porteus's conclusion, which implies that *culture-free* or *culture-fair* tests of intelligence are feasible, and as such this example is mainly of historical interest. However, the transfer of tests to cultural populations other than the one for which they were originally designed has greatly increased. Sometimes tests are administered without any modification except translation of verbal materials, but in most other cases there are extensive changes in item content and/or administration procedures. Any such change, including translation, is referred to as *cross-cultural test adaptation.*

The Logic of Test Transfer

A test is a standardized procedure to assess a cognitive ability, a dimension or, aspect of personality, or some other domain of behavior or aspect of psychological functioning. Here the term *trait* is used in a generic sense. Cross-cultural use of tests only makes sense if the same trait is measured in the various populations to which testees belong. If this is not the case, there is no rationale whatsoever for transfer and adaptation.

Continuing with the earlier Porteus example, the most fundamental issue is whether traits like "foresight and planning" as aspects of intelligence are meaningful concepts to explain the psychological makeup of a people like the Bushmen. A related question is whether Bushmen themselves would consider a maze task an adequate way to make an assessment of individual differences. There are traditions in psychology, such as the school of cultural psychology, that tend to see the transfer of any (Western) tests as an imposition, likely to conflict with the meaning of behavior as it is socially construed within a particular (non-Western) society (Miller, 1997). However, more common is the assumption that psychological functions and mechanisms are universal and manifestations of psychic unity. If foresight and planning are relevant scientific concepts for European American peoples, they should be relevant everywhere.

Assuming universality of foresight and planning, one may ask whether a paper-and-pencil test with mazes is an appropriate task to assess cognitive functioning in Bushmen hunter-gatherers, who only know graphical representation on ostrich egg shells, and who live in a semiarid flat environment where barriers that necessitate detours are virtually unknown. One indication of the inappropriateness of Porteus's test is that Bushmen subjects could solve more mazes when presented with a wooden version that had actual slats between the alleys (Reuning & Wortley, 1973). This example illustrates the general principle that transfer of a test presumes that the test forms an appropriate operationalization of the trait in the cultural populations concerned.

When a test provides a valid assessment of a particular trait in each of two cultural populations, there is another difficulty. It is still possible, and even likely, that the task is influenced unequally by factors that are not part of the target trait. For example, a test of arithmetic can contribute to the validity of a battery to assess intelligence in the sense of the capacity for learning and problem solving, but testees in one population on average may gain higher scores; for example, because of better quality schooling. This implies that for members of different populations an equal standing on the trait (intelligence) can be reflected by different scores, and a different standing by equal scores.

Thus, the transfer of a test requires that there is cross-cultural invariance of the relevant trait (or composite of traits), and that the operationalization is culturally appropriate; an interpretation of cross-cultural differences in score levels also requires that the test forms a quantitatively identical scale for the trait across cultural populations.

If a test does not meet these demands the scores are said to be *biased* or *inequivalent.* Effects that are likely to influence differentially all different items in a test, or at least a major proportion, are referred to as *method bias*. A well-known example for personality scales are cross-cultural differences in response styles, such as social desirability and the tendency to avoid extreme responses. An example in speeded tests of cognitive abilities are differences in speed-accuracy trade-off. In addition, reponse procedures can be mentioned, such as the multiple choice format that can lead to method bias when inexperienced testees are reluctant to guess in case of uncertainty about their answer, while testees with more experience answer more freely or make more educated guesses. A biasing effect can also be incidental to a specific item. In this case we speak about *item bias*, also called *differential item functioning*. The most common cause is a differential exposure to particular experiences and knowledge. There is a range of judgmental procedures and psychometric techniques to identify biased items, but method bias is difficult to evaluate (Van de Vijver & Leung, 1997).

The empirical record has shown that for complex behavior, such as cognitive abilities or personality traits, it is often impossible to rule out bias as an explanation of score differences, even for cultural populations that have a quite similar behavior repertoire. This imposes severe limitations on cross-cultural comparison of test scores.

Some Frequently Adapted Tests

The cognitive tests with the most extensive cross-cultural usage probably are Raven's Progressive Matrices and the Wechsler Adult Intelligence Scales (WAIS). [*See* Wechsler Intelligence Tests.] The Raven is a non-verbal test (with figural stimuli) and as such it requires no translation or adaptation of the items. It has been frequently administered to assess in a short time the "general intelligence" of testees with a low level of or no formal schooling. For quite some time this test had a reputation of being (relatively) culture-fair, although already in the 1950s it was shown that with repeated administration the last of three administrations had the highest validity for unschooled Congolese subjects (Ombredane, Robaye, & Plumail, 1956). But the most pervasive argument against culture-fairness lies in the large effects of Western-style school education on the score level.

The WAIS, which consists of verbal as well as nonverbal subtests, at the very minimum requires translation of the verbal items for non-English speaking populations. The adaptation of the WAIS, and other intelligence batteries, for a particular country involves elaborate tryouts of items and standardization studies. These batteries are rarely used for comparison of score levels between populations; the purpose is to have an instrument for assessment and diagnosis with the same qualities as in the original population.

Even more than for cognitive tests, adaptation of personality tests tends to be limited to translation of verbal items, with or without checks on the quality of this translation and the psychometric properties of the translated items. The need for more far-reaching forms of test adaptation has been recognized for a long time. For example, already in the early 1960s De Ridder (1961) published a Thematic Apperception Test (TAT) with pictures drawn for black testees in Southern Africa. However, maintaining identity of item content has been the rule.

Among the research traditions that have emerged around the cross-cultural use of specific instruments the best known example in clinical diagnosis is the Minnesota Multiphasic Personality Inventory (MMPI). Both the earlier version and the current MMPI/2 have been translated into many languages. In a number of countries the validity of diagnostic profiles originally established in the United States has been investigated. In addition, there is a literature that addresses issues of equivalence and bias (Butcher, 1996).

Another tradition, originating from the assessment of examination anxiety with the State-Trait Anxiety Inventory (STAI) and similar instruments, even has led to an international psychological association, the Stress and Anxiety Research Society (STAR). In this field cross-cultural comparison of score levels tends to be seen as problematic (Hocevar & El-Zahhar, 1992), even though it is not always avoided.

In the area of personality theory the Eysenck Personality Questionnaire (EPQ) is among the most translated instruments. Cross-cultural similarities in factor structures have been put forward as evidence for the universality of the dimensions in Eysenck's personality theory, as well as the validity of quantitative score differences (Eysenck & Eysenck, 1983). However, there have been arguments that the psychometric methods used are rather insensitive to differences in structures and effects of item bias. Recent cross-cultural research along similar lines as that of the Eysenck concerns the cross-cultural testing of the personality structure represented by the "Big Five" dimensions in the Neo-PI-R. [*See* Eysenck Personality Questionnaire.]

Evaluation

There are important reasons favoring the transfer and adaptation of tests over the construction of local new instruments. The first reason is mainly scientific and has a comparative flavor. The analysis of a trait across cultural populations can lead to new insights. But the availability of common standards is a necessary condition for precise and valid comparisons. As noted before, the Achilles heel of this type of research is the pervasive presence of all kinds of trait-irrelevant differences that collectively are referred to as cultural bias.

Other reasons for test adaptation are primarily economical and concern the local use of tests. The availability of an item set is a shortcut toward the development of a new instrument, even if this set has to be extended with locally formulated items to capture relevant manifestations of the trait not covered by the original instrument. More important, if a test does not have to undergo major changes in the process of adaptation, there is an implicit expectation that the existing literature on the original version will also be valid for the new version. There has rarely been critical examination of whether this expectation is justifiable or not, but the available evidence points to similarities in validity rather than major differences, at least for Western industrialized countries. For well-known tests like the WAIS and the MMPI, there is an extensive body of research that would be hard to replicate in any country for which these tests have been adapted.

Of the tests mentioned by name in this article none has originated in a non-English-speaking country. Two have originated in Britain (Raven's matrices and EPQ) while the others are of U.S. origin. This reflects the dominant position of Western, particularly U.S., psychology. The consequences of this situation are quite unclear, but this is a source of serious concern, particularly in the non-Western world (Sinha, 1997).

There are tendencies toward greater recognition of the cultural identity and its psychological consequences for cultural minorities within various countries, while at the same time there are movements toward internationalization of the work force and international standardization of criteria for well-being (quality of life), educational curricula, and so on. The one tendency leads to awareness of cultural bias in tests, the need for adaptation of test content and norms, and careful interpretation of test score differences. The other tendency points to the need for a further increase in cross-cultural use of tests.

A pragmatic orientation in which weaknesses and potential errors are recognized and the process of test adaptation is optimized has been reflected in a set of "Guidelines for Adapting Educational and Psychological Instruments and Establishing Score Equivalence." These guidelines, which were prepared by representatives of major international psychological associations at the initiative of Hambleton, address the various aspects of test adaptation, including the danger of over-interpretation of score differences.

[See also Back-Translation; and Testing.]

Bibliography

Andor, L. E. (1966). *Aptitudes and abilities of the Black man in Sub-Saharan Africa 1784–1963*. Johannesburg, South Africa: National Institute for Personnel Research. This bibliography is an important source for the history of mental testing and cross-cultural comparison in Africa. Unlisted references from this article can be found here.

Butcher, J. N. (Ed.). (1996). *International adaptations of the MMPI-2: Research and clinical applications*. Minneapolis, MN: University of Minnesota.

Eysenck, H. J., & Eysenck, S. B. G. (1983). Recent advances in the cross-cultural study of personality. In J. N. Butcher & C. D. Spielberger (Eds.), *Advances in personality assessment* (Vol. 2, pp. 41–70). Hillsdale, NJ: Erlbaum.

Hocevar D., & El Zahhar, N. (1992). Cross-cultural differences in test anxiety: Establishing transliteral equivalence. In K. A. Hagtvet & T. Backer Johnsen (Eds.), *Advances in test anxiety research* (Vol. 7, pp. 48–61). Amsterdam: Swets & Zeitlinger.

Miller, J. G. (1997). Theoretical issues in cultural psychology. In J. W. Berry, Y. H. Poortinga & J. Pandey (Eds.), *Handbook of cross-cultural psychology* (2nd ed., Vol. 1, pp. 85–128). Boston: Allyn & Bacon.

Porteus, S. D. (1937). *Primitive intelligence and environment*. New York: Macmillan.

Reuning, H., & Wortley, W. (1973). Psychological studies of the Bushmen. *Psychologia Africana*, Monograph Supplement No. 7. This monograph describes a fairly large number of tests that were administered in various regions of the Kalahari desert. Most of the tests are minimally dependent on language for instruction (the tasks are self-explanatory) and some are quite ingenious.

Sinha, D. (1997). Indigenizing psychology. In J. W. Berry, Y. H. Poortinga, & J. Pandey (Eds.), *Handbook of cross-cultural psychology: Vol. 1: Theory and method* (2nd ed., pp. 129–169). Boston: Allyn & Bacon.

Van de Vijver, F. J. R., & Leung, K. (1997). *Methods and data analysis for cross-cultural research*. Thousand Oaks, CA: Sage. Provides an overview of the problems of cross-cultural comparison of psychological data, including test scores.

Ype H. Poortinga

CROSS-CULTURAL TRAINING. Participation in a formal cross-cultural training program will prepare people for a successful sojourn in another country. Given the number of adjustments and the amount of potential stress that overseas assignments can entail, this approach, rather than the "sink or swim" approach is recommended (Brislin & Yoshida, 1994; Landis & Bhagat, 1996). People who live temporarily in another culture, but plan to return to their own, are known as *sojourners*, while the citizens of the culture in which they are to live are known as *hosts*. Cross-cultural training can be adapted to prepare people to interact with residents of their *own* country who belong to different cultures (Mullavey-O'Byrne, 1994a,b), in addition to its uses for training the overseas traveler or sojourner.

Goals of Training

The general goal of a cross-cultural training program is to increase the chances of success when people cross cultural boundaries. The criterion of "success" has four aspects, the first of which is that sojourners enjoy their lives in the other culture, feel that they have good interpersonal relations with hosts, and that they are as well integrated as possible into the host culture. Second, it is essential that *hosts* feel that the sojourners are making a good adjustment, have developed good interpersonal and work relationships, and are respectful of cultural norms. Third, it is essential that sojourner goals are accomplished in an effective and timely manner. Goals will vary for different people; for example, overseas students will want to obtain college degrees, businesspeople may want to establish joint ventures, and technical assistance advisers may want to introduce and to complete engineering and other projects. Then again, there are people who take a year off from their work or education to travel and broaden their interests, gain maturity, or to develop self-insight. This category of sojourners would be judged as successful or not based on accomplishment of these goals. Finally, after a period of adjustment dealing with problems captured by the term *culture shock*, sojourners should experience no more stress than they would in their own culture. Culture shock refers to the total set of stressors, experienced concurrently, that always accompany a move to another culture (Bochner, 1994). So many differences are encountered in a short time that sojourners' coping skills are challenged. Sojourners frequently report a sense of helplessness and childishness accompanying these stressors. The sense of childishness is reinforced when adult sojourners observe host 5- and 6-year-olds meeting their everyday goals and using the host language in a very efficient manner. Adults become frustrated when they think about themselves and their discomforts compared to the seemingly effortless effectiveness of young host children.

Audiences for Training

Given a concern with both international assignments and interactions with culturally different others within any one country, model training programs have been designed for many different audiences (Brislin & Landis, 1983; Landis & Bhagat, 1996). Training that involves international contact includes programs for overseas businesspeople, diplomats, technical assistance advisers, international students, and missionaries. Training within a country includes programs that assist immigrants and refugees, teachers from a rural or suburban background assigned to inner city schools (Cushner, 1994), executives and their employees in companies with a culturally diverse workforce, and clinicians and counselors who find themselves asked for assistance by people from cultures different than their own. A commonality within all these examples is that people will have extensive contact with people from other cultural backgrounds, that is, they will have numerous intercultural interactions. To be effective, people must be sensitive, knowledgeable, nonjudgmental, and they must be prepared to make adjustments in their own behavior.

Programs can be "culture general" or "culture specific." Culture-general programs are more widely usable since they deal with issues that virtually all people face. These include dealing with the loss of familiar cues and guidance for behaviors from their own culture and culture shock. Other commonalities include dealing with unrealistic expectations, challenges to attributional processes, confrontations with past prejudices, and the more mundane issues of finding food, housing, transportation, and social activities in unfamiliar settings (Cushner & Brislin, 1996). Culture-specific programs are targeted for a specific audience in a specific country or culture; for example, overseas businesspeople in China (Fang, 1999) or Native Americans seeking educational and employment opportunities in large U.S. cities (Choney, Berryhill-Paapke, & Robbins, 1995).

There are advantages and disadvantages to both approaches. Culture-general materials are more easily available (e.g., Cushner & Brislin, 1996) since commercial publishers disseminate materials with a potentially large audience. Culture-specific materials address the needs of specific people facing identifiable adjustment issues, but materials may be so limited in their focus that there is no incentive for commercial distribution. Instead, if available at all outside the organization where they were developed, they become disseminated through an inefficient and unpredictable "underground press" based on photocopying machines, library retrieval systems devoted to fugitive materials, and e-mail attachments.

Structure of Programs

Cross-cultural training programs have a number of features in common. They are designed to prepare people to live and work effectively in cultures other than their own, and they are staffed by people who are knowledgeable and experienced in training, intercultural interactions, and the life changes brought on by overseas assignments. Programs have a budget, a schedule of activities, a time and place for their implementation, and (ideally) an evaluation process to determine both program effectiveness and suggestions for improvement. Beyond these generalizations, different training directors choose different ways to structure the presentation of information and present active exercises to assist people in their upcoming intercultural interactions (Brislin & Yoshida, 1994; Triandis, Kurowski, & Gelfand, 1994). In most actual programs, a combination of different approaches is used.

Cognitive Training. Placing an emphasis on knowledge and "facts," cognitive training emphasizes giving people helpful information. It is often presented through lecture and media presentations, readings, and carefully prepared handouts that summarize key facts. Topics covered are more audience specific. Businesspeople would receive information on cultural differences in reaching decisions, ways of networking, and expectations of leaders. International graduate students would receive information on term paper preparation, ways of participating in class, and what steps mark "reasonable progress" toward degree completion.

Attribution Training. When living in another culture, people need to learn previously unfamiliar information, and they also have to learn to deal with cultural differences in the ways others think and behave. When people make judgments about the causes of other people's behavior, they are making attributions. Intercultural interactions always mean that people will observe unfamiliar behaviors. They may be tempted to make inappropriate attributions given their ignorance of the cultural context of these behaviors. Attribution training emphasizes that people should integrate knowledge of cultural differences before making conclusions about others.

Time use is one of the most frustrating sources of cultural differences (Levine, 1997). An American makes an appointment with an executive in Brazil for 11:00 A.M. The executive does not show up until 11:45 A.M. What is the American's attribution? If careless, the American might conclude that the Brazilian is unprofessional. With a knowledge of cultural differences, the American could conclude that the Brazilian is a participant in an "event time" culture where last-minute demands on a person's time are more important than a "clock time" appointment. When all people in the intercultural interactions can interpret behaviors in a similar manner, they are said to be making isomorphic attributions.

Self-Awareness Training. For many people, participation in a self-awareness training program will be the first time they have been able to examine the influence of *their own* culture on their behavior. Americans might examine the cultural background of their belief in individual liberties, the value of speaking one's mind, their distrust of centralized power, and their emphasis on individual achievements. Japanese trainees might examine the importance of group harmony, of *not* standing out as an individual, their deference to power, and the large distinctions made between the expectations of males and the expectations of females. Training sessions can become emotional given that many

people, for the first time, learn that many of their behaviors are culturally influenced and that other people from other cultures regularly engage in contrasting behaviors influenced by *their* cultures.

Experiential Training. At times, trainers can encourage program participants to "try out" a number of unfamiliar social situations that they are likely to encounter in another culture. The basic technique is role-playing: trainees act out various roles, with the support and encouragement of the training staff, and cope with different problems introduced by the trainers. Such experiential training is often more unstructured and can lead to negative reactions from participants if they are frustrated in trying to formulate appropriate responses. Such training can be general if the issues chosen are common to virtually all cross-cultural experiences. Examples include struggling imperfectly in one's second or third language, being ignored given the inability to communicate effectively, experiencing loneliness, or trying to find information about transportation, housing, food, and schooling for one's children. Experiential training can be culture specific if participants are about to encounter identifiable social situations. For international graduate students in North America, examples would be registering for classes and choosing electives, presenting ideas for thesis topics to possible committee members, and communicating a sense that one is an interesting person so as to be remembered by faculty and fellow students (Markus & Kitayama, 1991). For businesspeople in Japan, examples would be decision making *prior to* open meetings, downplaying one's tendencies to express personal opinions if they might interfere with the group consensus, and learning to read subtle cues from executives concerning policy preferences (Brislin & Yoshida, 1994).

Behavior Change. At times, trainers can introduce specific behaviors that are not naturally in a person's repertoire. Further, trainers can argue that if participants engage in these behaviors in another culture, they can increase their chances of success. Since the behaviors are unfamiliar, they often have to be practiced during the training program. A trainer must make sure that participants are comfortable with the new behaviors, see no ethical qualms, and that they understand the rationale behind them. Returning to the example of punctuality or its absence in Brazil, participants might practice previously unfamiliar behaviors related to "waiting patiently" for the executive. Participants do not want to show irritation, and in fact want to show an understanding of the demands on executives' time and resources. Participants can show an understanding of clock and event time by starting their own events. They might chat with and get to know others in the executive office suite since in many event time cultures, goals are accomplished and red tape is assaulted through the insiders that a person knows well.

Some behaviors will be more comfortable to some people than others. For example, trainers might explain that in some Asian countries, gifts are a social lubricant and signal the development of good working relationships. Gifts do not have to be extremely expensive. Ideal gifts are personalized according to the recipient: Compact discs or videotapes featuring a favorite singer or actor are possibilities. Practice would include ways of identifying such personalized gifts, presenting them with proper modesty, accepting gifts offered, and determining whether one opens the gifts now or later. Training can emphasize that there are not always simple solutions to decisions involving behavior change. In some countries, and for some individuals in countries where small gifts are often appropriate, much larger gifts of money will be expected. Returning to the discussion of attributions, large gifts will be seen as "commissions" by some people and as ethically unacceptable "bribes" by others. A good training program provides an opportunity for people to think about such ethical dilemmas and to receive guidance concerning possible responses.

Bibliography

Bochner, S. (1994). Culture shock. In W. Lonner & R. Malpass (Eds.), *Psychology and culture* (pp. 245–251). Boston: Allyn & Bacon.

Brislin, R., & Yoshida, T. (1994). *Intercultural communication training: An introduction.* Thousand Oaks, CA: Sage.

Choney, S., Berryhill-Paapke, E., & Robbins, R. (1995). The acculturation of American Indians: Developing frameworks for research and practice. In J. Ponterotto, J. Casas, L. Suzuki, & C. Alexander (Eds.), *Handbook of multicultural counseling* (pp. 73–92). Thousand Oaks, CA: Sage.

Cushner, K. (1994). Preparing teachers for an intercultural context. In R. Brislin & T. Yoshida (Eds.), *Improving intercultural interactions: Modules for cross-cultural training programs* (pp. 109–128). Thousand Oaks, CA: Sage.

Cushner, K., & Brislin, R. (1996). *Intercultural interactions: A practical guide* (2nd ed.). Thousand Oaks, CA: Sage.

Fang, T. (1999). *Chinese business negotiating style.* Thousand Oaks, CA: Sage.

Landis, D. & Bhagat, R. (Eds.). (1996). *Handbook of intercultural training* (2nd ed.) Thousand Oaks, CA: Sage.

Landis, D., & Brislin, R. (Eds.). (1983). *Handbook of intercultural training* (Vols. 1–3). Elmsford, NY: Pergamon.

Levine, R. (1997). *A geography of time.* New York: McGraw-Hill.

Markus, H., & Kitayama, S. (1991). Culture and the self: Implications for cognition, emotion, and motivation. *Psychological Review, 98* 224–253.

Mullavey-O'Byrne, C. (1994a). Intercultural communication for health care professionals. In R. Brislin & T. Yoshida (Eds.), *Improving intercultural interactions: Mod-*
ules for cross-cultural training programs (pp. 171–196). Thousand Oaks, CA: Sage.

Mullavey-O'Byrne, C. (1994b). Intercultural interactions in welfare work. In R. Brislin & T. Yoshida (Eds.), *Improving intercultural interactions: Modules for cross-cultural training programs* (pp. 197–220). Thousand Oaks, CA: Sage.

Triandis, H., Kurowski, L., & Gelfand, M. (1994). Workplace diversity. In H. Triandis, M. Dunnette, & L. Hough (Eds.), *Handbook of industrial and organizational psychology* (2nd ed., Vol. 4, pp. 769–827). Palo Alto, CA: Consulting Psychologists Press.

Richard W. Brislin

CROSS-DRESSING. *See* Transvestism.

CROWD BEHAVIOR. Crowd events have played a central role in both celebrating and challenging many different communities and societies. Crowd behavior both reflects the ideology of these collectivities and seeks to change them. One has only to think of the civil rights demonstrations, the mourners at Princess Diana's funeral, the masses listening to the Pope outside the Vatican, and those who gathered to demolish the Berlin Wall, in order to be aware of this and also to be aware of how diverse crowd behavior can be. But, in the main, authorities, the media, and academics have only been interested in crowds to the extent that they threaten the social order, and this has led to a very distorted understanding of the phenomena. In the United States, there was an upsurge of research on crowds after the urban disturbances of the 1960s and 1970s. The same happened in Britain after the inner-city riots of the 1980s. However, crowd psychology was born in late nineteenth-century France in response to a series of upheavals that were seen to endanger the very existence of society.

Throughout the Western world, industrialization had led to the formation of large urban masses. What is more, in contrast to village society, the working masses lived separately from and were increasingly anonymous to the social elite. In this context, a great fear arose amongst this elite that the masses might rise up to challenge the existing order. Susanna Barrows shows how crowds were seen as the vehicle of that uprising and therefore became a primary focus of fear (*Distorting Mirrors*, New Haven, CT, 1981). Due to the fragility of its regime, all these concerns were particularly acute in France. Born out of defeat in the Franco-German war of 1871, the Third Republic was buffeted by mass opposition from populist movements, from clericalist campaigns, and, most importantly, from rising industrial and radical unrest. The major concern of crowd psychology was not so much to understand the general phenomenon as to deal with the particular danger. Indeed, the first debate in crowd psychology was between two criminologists, Gabriel Tarde and Scipio Sighele, and the issue of who was responsible for crowd unrest (everybody involved or just the leaders?) and therefore who should be arrested in order to prevent unrest.

While these early theorists have been largely forgotten, one name stands out. Gustave Le Bon is undoubtedly the best known of all crowd psychologists and his book *The Crowd*, first published in 1895, is possibly the most influential psychology text of all time (*The Crowd: A Study of the Popular Mind*. London, 1947). It influenced such figures as Hitler and Mussolini and, as Serge Moscovici has pointed out, went as much to create as to explain the mass behavior of the twentieth century (*The Age of the Crowd*, Cambridge, 1985). For Le Bon, there are three stages to crowd psychology. The first is *submergence*: by virtue of becoming an indistinguishable part of the mass, people lose a sense of their individual self, lose all sense of responsibility, and gain a sense of invincible power. The second stage is *contagion*: having lost their selves and hence their ability for rational judgment, crowd members uncritically follow the ideas and (particularly) the emotions of others in the crowd. The third and final stage is *suggestion*: the ideas and emotions that influence the crowd principally emanate from the racial unconscious—a common primitive mental substrate which unites members of a "race." The resulting portrait of crowd behavior is deeply unflattering. Because the "racial unconscious" goes back to a precivilized age, so crowd behavior is inherently uncivilized. For Le Bon, the crowd member is a barbarian, one who descends "several rungs on the ladder of civilization" and crowds are powerful only for destruction.

The most obvious problem with this approach is that it suggests that all crowds behave in a similarly mindless and negative manner and therefore ignores the evidence of the diverse and socially meaningful nature of crowd action. More generally, Le Bonian theory ignores the context in which crowds act. Thus the behaviors that result from the particular social conflicts of Le Bon's age are turned into the timeless characteristics of all crowds. Moreover, insofar as one cannot see how these behaviors make sense given their setting, they are portrayed as irrational and mindless. In this way, crowd theory serves its ideological purpose, for violence becomes ascribed entirely to crowd pathology and there is no space to question the social background to conflict. Martin Luther King, Jr. once described crowds as "the voice of the powerless." Le Bon's approach serves to silence that voice.

Conceptually, this approach is underpinned by an individualistic view of selfhood. The self is seen as a singular and unique property of the individual and as the basis for rational control over one's behavior. Social factors play no part in determining the nature of this self, they only determine how clearly it operates. Thus, crowds serve as the "off switch" for identity and entail a loss of behavioral control. What is missing from this account is any consideration of the possibility that identity may be formed by social factors and hence that there may be a social basis to the control of behavior. It is at this conceptual level that Le Bon's approach has continued to exert a significant influence over crowd theory in particular and social psychology more generally.

The most direct example of his influence comes from work on deindividuation, which was originally inspired by the notion of submergence. Following earlier experimental work by Leon Festinger and others, Zimbardo proposed a model of deindividuation whereby antecedent factors—most notably anonymity in a group—leads to a weakening of controls based on guilt, shame, and concern for self-evaluation. This in turn leads to the expression of antisocial behaviors (Zimbardo, "The human choice: Individuation, reason and order versus de-individuation, impulse and chaos," in W. J. Arnold & D. Levine (Eds.), *Nebraska Symposium on Motivation*, Lincoln, NE, 1969). Subsequent models discarded the idea that deindividuated behavior is always antisocial. Rather they suggested that factors such as "perceptual immersion in a group" lead to a lowering of awareness of one's internal standards and hence to increased domination of behavior by external cues. However, all variants of deindividuation theory share with Le Bon the assumption that collective behavior involves both loss of self and loss of control.

Paradoxically, even those who most vehemently opposed Le Bon's theory helped perpetuate his underlying assumptions. Floyd Allport, one of the pioneers of American social psychology, rejected the notion of a racial unconscious, or group mind as "a metaphysical abstraction" and "a babble of tongues." He wrote his foundational social psychology text largely as a response to the French theorist (Allport, *Social Psychology*, Boston, 1924). Rather than proposing that selfhood is lost in collective settings, Allport is best remembered for proposing precisely the opposite: "the individual in the crowd behaves just as he would behave alone only more so" (p. 295). The distinctive predispositions of particular people are, if anything, accentuated in collective settings. This insight underlies so-called "convergence" models of crowds. People of similar predispositions come together in crowds and crowd behavior reflects such similarities. Violent behavior reflects the violent tendencies of participants. However, such views are not supported by the empirical evidence. For instance, those involved in the American urban riots of the 1970s were, if anything, less likely than their nonparticipant peers to have previous convictions. Moreover, while the convergence approach may allow for different crowds to behave differently as a function of those who compose them, it still cannot account for the socially meaningful nature of such action. This is because Allport, like Le Bon, retains an individualistic view of self. The difference between them is that, while Le Bon considers that selfhood is attenuated in collective contexts, Allportians consider it to be accentuated. Even so, the latter like the former exclude the social determination of self and social action.

In the last few decades, a number of attempts have been made to overcome these limitations. From a microsociological background, Ralph Turner and Lewis Killian have proposed emergent norm theory (*Collective Behavior*, Englewood Cliffs, NJ, 1987). They suggest that, while crowd behavior may look homogenous to outsiders, actually there is little unity at the outset. It takes a period of "milling," during which prominent members ("keynoters") suggest appropriate actions, for norms to form and for a basis for common action to emerge. This account stresses the importance of debate and discussion amongst crowd members. It also stresses that crowd behavior is not random or mindless but rather is based on shared understandings of what is appropriate. However, it suggests that every crowd creates new norms from nothing and it fails to explain the basis on which, when different "keynoters" say different things, certain suggestions will predominate over others. Because the model fails to link situated crowd norms to wider ideological understandings it still has difficulty in explaining the socially meaningful nature of crowd action.

Within social psychology, the social identity tradition has given rise to a rather different approach (Turner, Hogg, Oakes, Reicher, & Wetherell, *Rediscovering the Social Group*, Oxford, 1987). Social identity theorists start from a conception of the self as a complex system rather than a singular construct. People can see themselves in terms of their personal identity—that which makes them distinctive compared to other individuals. However, they may also see themselves in terms of social identity—the groups to which they belong. We all have a number of possible social identifications and different ones will be salient in different contexts. The person who thinks of herself as an American at a patriotic rally may think of herself as a Christian while in church and as a Democrat at a primary rally. What is more, when we act in terms of any given social identification, our behavior is guided by the meanings associated with the relevant category—what it means to be an American, a Christian, or a Democrat. So, when people go from acting as individuals to acting as members of a group, they do not lose identity and hence behavioral control. Rather, they shift from personal to social identity, and hence their behavior comes to be controlled by the standards associated with the relevant group rather than those associated with their personal identity. Moreover, when a large number of people identify with the same social category, they will act on the basis of the same collective understandings and hence, even without overt direction, they are likely to behave in similar socially meaningful ways. Of course it also follows that different collectivities will behave differently as a function of their different social identities.

As applied to crowd behavior in particular as opposed to groups in general (Reicher, "Crowd behaviour as social action," in J. Turner, M. Hogg, P. Oakes, S. Reicher, & M. Wetherell (Eds.), *Rediscovering the Social Group*, Oxford, 1987), social identity should be seen as a framework rather than a rigid determinant of action. This is because crowds often occur in ambiguous and novel situations. Instead of simply following preexisting norms, crowd members need to determine what it means to be a member of their given social category within the given situation—for instance, what does it mean to be a civil rights demonstrator when attacked by racists? Sometimes there is time for debate and discussion as emergent norm theorists stress, sometimes one has to act quickly and can only infer norms from the actions of fellow group members. However, whichever is the case, situational creativity is bounded by the definition of social identity. One will only act in ways that are consonant with the broader meanings associated with the category. Thus the above mentioned civil rights demonstrators may adopt a number of strategies but only within the agreed philosophy of nonviolence. To put it more generally, there will be limits to situational norm creation in terms of the broader category ideology. That is why crowd behavior can be creative while remaining socially meaningful.

While this model recontextualizes crowd behavior, it can be criticized for only going half way. On the one hand, it places crowds in relation to wider social ideologies but it fails to examine the immediate context in which crowds act. Crowd events are predominantly intergroup affairs: the crowd faces another crowd, the police, or even the army. On the other hand, the model explains how crowd behavior reflects society but not how it can change society. Recent extensions of the social identity model suggest that these two facets are interlinked: only by examining how the intergroup dynamics of crowd events unfold over time is it possible to see how change occurs. In particular, where there is an asymmetry between the way crowd members understand their social identity and the way it is understood by the outgroup, and where members of the outgroup are powerful enough to impose their understanding on the crowd, then crowd members may find their social position changed and their relationship to the social order radically altered as a result of their initial actions (Reicher, "Social identity and social change: Rethinking the context of social psychology," in P. Robinson (Ed.), *Social Groups and Identities: Developing the Legacy of Henri Tajfel*, London, 1997). For instance, demonstrators who think of themselves as respectable citizens exercising the right to protest can be seen as dangerous by the police and hence be impeded in their actions and harshly treated. This in turn can lead such demonstrators to see the police as illegitimate and can thereby entrain a process of radicalization in which they unite with other oppositional groups and enter into an escalating series of challenges to the social order.

Clearly, psychologists still have a long way to go in unravelling the complexities of crowd behavior. However, after nearly a hundred years of misrepresentation it is possible to state two things with confidence. In the first place, far from the traditional image of crowd behavior as primitive and irrational (and hence of minor importance to an understanding of "normal behavior"), it is actually subtle and complex. Indeed, crowd behavior is simultaneously determined by and determining of society. In this sense it represents a context in which to address the fundamental paradox of human sociality. In the second place, it is clear that any adequate theoretical model must analyze crowds in context: both the broad social background and the immediate intergroup setting. Crowd theory points the way toward a historical and interactive social psychology.

[*See also* Social Identity.]

Bibliography

Crowds in History

Davis, N. Z. (1978). The rites of violence: Religious riot in sixteenth century France. *Past and Present, 59,* 59–91.
Thompson, E. P. (1971). The moral economy of the English crowd in the eighteenth century. *Past and Present, 50,* 76–136.

Early Crowd Psychology

Nye, R. A. (1975). *The origins of crowd psychology.* London: Sage.
van Ginneken, J. (1994). *Crowds, psychology and politics. 1871–1899.* Cambridge, U.K.: Cambridge University Press.

A Critique of the Le Bonian Tradition

Reicher, S. (1996). "The crowd" century: Reconciling practical success with theoretical failure. *British Journal of Social Psychology, 35,* 535–553.
Reicher, S., Spears, R., & Postmes, T. (1995). A social identity model of deindividuation phenomena. In W.

Stroebe & M. Hewstone (Eds.), *European Review of Social Psychology* (Vol. 6, pp. 161–98). Chichester, U.K.: Wiley.

The Social Identity Tradition

Hogg, M. A., & Abrams, D. (1988). *Social identifications: A social psychology of intergroup relations and group processes.* London: Routledge.
Turner, J. C., Oakes, P. J., Haslam, S. J., & McGarty, C. (1994). Self and collective: Cognition and social context. *Personality and Social Psychology Bulletin, 20,* 454–463.

Empirical Studies Using the Social Identity Model of Crowds

Reicher, S. (1984). The St. Pauls riot: An explanation of the limits of crowd action in terms of a social identity model. *European Journal of Social Psychology, 14,* 1–21.
Reicher, S. (1996). The Battle of Westminster: Developing the social identity model of crowd behaviour in order to deal with the initiation and development of collective conflict. *European Journal of Social Psychology, 26,* 115–134.

Stephen Reicher

CROWDING. The experience of crowding is an adverse psychological response that occurs when the need for space exceeds the current supply. Thus crowding, a psychological construct, can be distinguished from density, an objective index of the amount of space available (Stokols, *Psychological Review,* 1972, 79, 257–277). High density is a necessary but not sufficient condition for crowding to occur. Crowding has behavioral consequences. High density has been linked, both in laboratory and in naturalistic settings, to negative behavioral outcomes. These include psychophysiological stress, impaired task performance, negative interpersonal relationships, motivational deficits, and psychological distress.

Psychological research on crowding has operationalized the construct in objective terms, typically measuring density as people per room in the field or manipulating the number of people per square meter in the laboratory. The measurement of density is important for theoretical and practical reasons. Theoretically, a distinction can be drawn between social density, changing the number of people while holding space constant, and spatial density, changing the amount of space while holding the number of people constant. Most research on crowding and human well-being has investigated social density. Although there are some trends indicating that social density is a more potent stressor than spatial density, several studies have shown that changes in people per room, for example, while holding family size constant, still predict negative outcomes. There are also several laboratory studies where manipulations of spatial density proved potent. Not withstanding, some critics of residential crowding research have argued that crowding reflects nothing more than the negative effects of family or group size. Interestingly, the obverse criticism, that family or group size effects simply reflect density, has not been acknowledged. Nonetheless, the obvious collinearity between family size, numbers of children, group size, and density should be kept in mind. Concern that density correlates actually reflect some third variable like social class are probably not well founded. Many studies of density in the field control for income and laboratory studies with random assignment have produced negative effects.

Policy makers rely on household density (people per room) as an indicator of housing quality in conjunction with measures of structural deficiencies. As the latter have dramatically improved in the United States, household density has taken on an increasingly major role in defining housing quality. Rates of substandard housing, in turn, are a key mechanism in several federal funding programs to states. The percentage of U.S. households with more than one person per room (the official U.S. census definition of overcrowding) dropped continuously from 1940 to 1980, then took an upturn, standing at 5.18% of households in 1990. Obviously the percentage of crowded households is dramatically influenced by income. For example in 1990, 12.8% of households were crowded among those living $\leq$ 0.75 of the federal poverty line; whereas 1.10% of households were crowded among those living at 4.0 times the poverty line. Various indicators of crowding capacity are also used in decision making about construction of prisons, schools, hospitals, and many other building facilities.

Research on the impacts of household density indicates that people per room is the critical metric and that measures such as people per square foot, household units per block or building, or more areal indices of density such as people per acre, people per census tract, or buildings per acre, explain little or no variance in pathology. The reason for this appears to be that what makes density aversive is unwanted social interaction. When privacy, the ability to regulate social interaction, is interfered with by the close presence of others, crowding results (Altman, *The Environment and Social Behavior*, Monterey, CA, 1975). This is why sharing a large room with considerable space is experienced by most people as more crowded than having one's own, extremely small cubicle.

Early works in public health and sociology evidencing little or no relation between crowding and various indices of pathology failed to appreciate the psychologically meaningful distinction between experiencing close, unwanted social encounters within the residence versus counting how many people lived in a given geographic area. Much of this early work also included people living alone in density calculations. This causes two difficulties: Crowding requires the close presence of others as a necessary prerequisite. Second, living alone is positively correlated with psychological distress. Another unfortunate legacy of early crowding research is the popular but mistaken belief that there are clear cultural differences in crowding tolerance. While data indicate interpersonal spacing behavior (personal space) varies systematically with culture, there is no body of scientific knowledge either supporting or refuting the concept of cultural variability in tolerance of crowding.

Although there is reasonable convergence among experimental and field studies on several outcomes related to crowding, field research on density has not incorporated sufficiently rigorous designs to warrant definitive conclusions, particularly about suspected impacts on psychological or physical health. Only one study of crowding and health has utilized a prospective design (Lepore, Evans, & Schneider, *Journal of Personality and Social Psychology*, 1991, 61, 899–909). Results indicated no correlation, controlling for income, between residential density (people per room) and a standard index of psychological distress during the initial period of occupancy; whereas 6 months later there was a clear and positive correlation between density and psychological distress. This study is important because it refutes a reasonable, alternative hypothesis for the residential density/pathology link, namely that persons in poorer psychological health choose or involuntarily wind up living in poorer quality housing, including more crowded living quarters.

Several laboratory studies and a few field studies have linked high density to elevated cardiovascular and neuroendocrine activity, indicative of heightened psychological stress. The preponderance of data indicates elevated blood pressure. Fewer studies have examined neuroendocrine, stress hormone measures. Research on crowding and physical health is inconclusive. There are a large number of methodologically flawed studies and a host of contradictory findings. Some reasonably consistent evidence for small, negative health correlates of crowding emanates from studies of institutionalized individuals; for example, in prisons or on board ships (Evans, In Baum, Revenson, & Singer, Eds., *Handbook of Health Psychology*, Hillsdale, NJ, 2000).

Research on crowding and psychological distress is difficult to characterize because of the plethora of different density metrics used and frequent reliance on nonstandardized psychological distress indices. Moreover with the exception of one study, all are cross sectional. With these caveats in mind, trends indicate a modest correlation between density and psychological health when chronic residential density is operationalized as people per room (Evans, in press).

Laboratory and field studies reveal more negative interpersonal social interactions under high-density conditions in comparison to low-density conditions. Outcomes have included hostility, irritability and negative affect, aggression, and familial conflict. Crowding may also adversely impact task performance, although only when the tasks are of sufficient complexity to pressure cognitive capacity (Evans & Cohen, In Stokols & Altman, Eds., *Handbook of Environmental Psychology*, New York, 1987). There is insufficient data on crowding and cognitive development or elementary school children's academic performance to draw firm conclusions, but studies both with infants and elementary-aged schoolchildren reveal disturbing trends warranting further attention. Infants in more crowded homes show several signs of delayed cognitive development (Wachs & Gruen, *Early Experience and Human Development*, New York, 1982). Elementary-aged schoolchildren from crowded homes manifest more behavioral problems at school and impaired academic achievement vis-à-vis their low density counterparts (Saegert, In Baum & Singer, Eds., *Handbook of Psychology and Health*, Hillsdale, NJ, 1982; Evans, Lepore, Shejwal, & Palsane, *Child Development*, 1998, 69, 1514–1523).

The current direction of research on the psychological consequences of crowding is focused primarily on underlying, explanatory processes to account for why/how crowding has its apparently negative impacts on people. Two promising lines of inquiry indicate that social support and control, respectively, are mediating mechanisms that may serve as explanatory processes for the links between residential crowding and psychological distress. Our work has shown in the field and in the laboratory that chronically crowded individuals seem to cope with high density by socially withdrawing from one another. This withdrawal appears to cause the deterioration of socially supportive relationships in high-density homes. The inability to formulate and maintain social bonds, in turn, leads to greater psychological distress (Evans & Lepore, *Journal of Personality and Social Psychology*, 1993, 65, 308–316). Note that social support in these studies functions as an underlying, mediating mechanism between density, an environmental stressor, and psychological health. This runs counter to the predominant conceptualization of social support as a protective mechanism that buffers the harmful effects of stressors. In this case the stressor, crowding, deteriorates the coping resource, social support.

High residential density also appears to be associated with frequent, uncontrollable social interactions which if prolonged foster learned helplessness. Residents of more crowded college dormitories over time manifest increasingly strong symptoms of helplessness indexed by self-report and by interpersonal behaviors, measured in the laboratory (Baum, Gatchel, Aiello, & Thompson, In J. Harvey, Ed., *Cognition, Social Behavior, and the Environment*, Hillsdale, NJ, 1981). Residents of crowded dormitories show a marked drop in competitive behaviors in a prisoner's dilemma game around the fifth week of occupancy. This decrease in competitiveness is mirrored by a corresponding increase in withdrawal strategies. Of further interest, these behavioral trends, indexed in the laboratory, are matched by self-report data on residents' perceptions of control over dormitory living. Children living in more crowded environments also appear more vulnerable to the induction of helplessness (Rodin, *Journal of Experimental Social Psychology*, 1976, 61, 564–578).

Research priorities for the future include prospective, longitudinal field studies of crowding and both psychological and physical health along with investigations of early cognitive development and school performance; careful cross-cultural work on crowding tolerance and possible variability in coping processes; incorporation of additional variables into performance studies such as duration of exposure, effort, and simultaneous psychophysiological monitoring. More research is required on underlying processes to better understand why crowding impacts behavior. Research on crowding in work and daycare settings and among elderly residents is of high priority given current sociodemographic trends.

Residential crowding is frequently accompanied by an array of other physical and social stressors related to poverty. The analytic precision achieved by statistically isolating the effects of density apart from the natural context in which it is embedded may have led us to underestimate the potentially harmful effects of chronic, crowded living conditions, particularly on vulnerable subgroups, such as children. Another priority area of future research is to examine the potential multiple stressor effects of crowding, noise, inadequate housing, and the psychosocial ravages of poverty, as they interrelate to impinge upon psychological well-being. Finally, research is necessary on the potential role of environmental design to ameliorate the negative impacts of crowding. While it may not always be feasible to provide people with more spacious living, daycare, or working accommodations, it is likely that designers can create better environments of equivalent size.

[*See also* Environmental Design Research.]

Bibliography

Baum, A., & Paulus, P. (1987). Crowding. In D. Stokols & I. Altman (Eds.), *Handbook of environmental psychology* (pp. 533–570). New York: Wiley.

Baum, A., & Valins, S. (1977). *Architecture and social be-*

havior: Psychological studies of social density. Hillsdale, NJ: Erlbaum.

Calhoun, J. B. (1962). Population density and social pathology. *Scientific American, 206*, 139–148. Classic paper showing links between crowding and pathology in rats reared in the laboratory.

Evans, G. W., & McCoy, J. (1998). When buildings don't work: The role of architecture in human health and well-being. *Journal of Environmental Psychology, 18*, 85–94. Presents a conceptual framework for thinking about how design might impact human health.

Gove, W. R., & Hughes, M. (1983). *Overcrowding in the household*. New York: Academic Press.

Paulus, P. (1988). *Prison crowding*. New York: Springer-Verlag.

Wohlwill, J. F., & van Vliet, W. (Eds.). (1985). *Habitats for children*. Hillsdale, NJ: Erlbaum. Reviews research on children and crowding.

Gary W. Evans

CULTS. The term *cult* originally denoted a religious movement, and implied deviance from established belief, and sometimes transcendental experiences. Some contemporary cultlike groups have been called new religious movements, however, to imply their potential for finding a place in the religious mainstream. In recent colloquial use, the concept of a cult adds an additional connotation of a more problematic deviancy, and rejection of participation in the majority culture. Recent decades have brought many cultic groups to the fore, much to the concern of the general public, although the phenomenon is clearly not a new one. Attention was focused on cultlike youth movements in the 1970s like Hare Krishna and the Unification Church, particularly because their members were drawn away from family ties and engaged in practices which appeared bizarre and even harmful to themselves. The startling mass suicides of 914 followers of Jim Jones in isolation in the Guianese jungle in 1978 lent a more ominous note to the potentially lethal outcome for cult members. It later became clear that cultic psychology could yield attempts at mass murder as well, when members of the Aum Shinrikyo cult in Japan were responsible in 1995 for the deaths of 12 people and the injury of many more by a poison gas attack in the Tokyo subway. Significantly, even members of that group living in the general community retained fidelity to it after the nature of the attack was revealed, as is common among cult dropouts. Suicidal acts among the Branch Davidians outside Waco, Texas in 1993 and the Heaven's Gate members outside San Diego in 1997 only reinforce our appreciation of the intense influence of such groups.

In a generic sense, the term *charismatic group* has been used by Galanter in *Cults: Faith, Healing and Coercion* (New York, 1989) to describe most contemporary cults as well as many similar nonreligious zealous groups. A charismatic group is characterized by (1) a high level of social cohesiveness; (2) an intensely held belief system; and (3) a profound influence on members' behavior. It is charismatic because of the commitment of members to a fervently espoused, transcendent goal; this goal is generally articulated by a zealous leader or ascribed to the progenitor of the group. Charismatic groups, by means of their intense psychological influence, can relieve certain symptoms associated with psychopathology, but they precipitate problematic symptoms as well.

In the charismatic group, these forces generally operate to compel behavioral conformity and modulate affect, without overt coercion. To understand this process of social control, it is useful to contrast these groups with the influence observed in *brainwashing*, a term applied to the experience of Western prisoners who were forcibly confined by the Communist Chinese during the Korean War. In both brainwashing and cultic groups, those directing the process of social control manage all communications in order to infuse ideas of their choosing and prevent the expression of perspectives contrary to their own. In the brainwashing setting, however, participants are typically imprisoned and physically coerced. There is generally no physical coercion in charismatic groups because of the efficacy of their implicit social controls. Instead, psychological forces reinforce the members' attribution of new meaning and values to their experiences and to the adoption of prescribed behaviors.

How does this reinforcement take place? Findings on the role of these forces suggest the operation of a "relief effect" in the psychological impact of charismatic groups. That is to say, both recruits and long-term members experience a relief from emotional distress when they feel more closely affiliated with the group, whereas a decline in affiliative feelings results in greater distress. This reinforcement, both positive and aversive, continually operates on the members, reinforcing their commitment to the group and its ethos.

Intense conversion to the group's beliefs is often a central feature. In *The Varieties of Religious Experience: A Study of Human Nature* (New York, 1902) William James wrote about religious conversion as a process through which an individual, "divided and consciously wrong, inferior and unhappy," becomes "unified and consciously right, superior and happy" as a consequence of achieving a hold on his or her religious reality. The process may otherwise be described as one in which a person comes to adopt an all-pervasive worldview, and this applies to people joining cults as well. Transcendental or mystical experiences are often important in the conversion process. This may be central to the resolution of personal conflicts, even to the point of precipitating acute hallucinatory episodes in both nonpsychotic and psychotic individuals.

The potential restitutive function of conversion may also be considered. It can be likened to the crystallizing role of an "experience of significance" that can occur at the onset of delusion formation, wherein an idiosyncratic meaning is attributed to the circumstances encountered by a person under intense pressure. But delusion formation *per se* generally occurs in the face of disruption of a pathological and much more severe nature. Whatever the magnitude of the preceding disruption, such religious experiences may be considered as part of the coping system that provides ego integration for the individual.

Cognitive dissonance theory, developed by Festinger and others, emerged from a body of research that can contribute to our understanding of cultic behaviors. This theory has shown how individuals cannot easily dismiss a belief or attitude they hold, even when the attitude is directly contradicted by evidence or events. People will sooner adopt farfetched ideas to explain events than relinquish their preconceptions. In so doing they avoid having to face the dissonance between what they see and what they have long believed. The dismissal of plain reality can take place when people are confronted by challenges to their ingrained patriotism, their prejudices, or their religious values, and their cult-induced beliefs as well. Under these circumstances, they may ignore cruelty, hypocrisy, or incompetence, or create elaborate rationalizations rather than challenge the principles espoused by their leader. Thus, once fully inducted, cult members may not only accept the validity of a leader's deviant views, but may also develop rationalizations to sustain them. For example, they may take his idiosyncrasies as evidence of his divine inspiration, rather than as a reason to question his judgment. To have questioned it would have shaken the foundations of their acquired beliefs, and created intolerable conflict within the cult member. Furthermore, as demonstrated by Stanley Milgram in *Obedience to Authority* (New York, 1975), people will respond to designated authority, even to the point of subjecting others to painful stimuli. All this redounds to a psychological basis for the acceptance of some of the more adverse impositions which cults may impose on nonmembers.

The unusual behaviors observed in cultic groups may also be clarified by recourse to their operation as systems. Such systems are characterized by boundary control, whereby the potential components of the system (people and beliefs, in this case) are either defined as part of the system or kept outside. In cultic groups, this is particularly important because of conflicts between the group's perspectives and those of the general population. Thus, individuals' acceptance of unusual beliefs may be puzzling in terms of their antecedent personalities, and the panoply of ideologies observed in these groups bears little obvious relationship to the psychological or social needs of one group's individual members. With regard to system's needs, however, such ideologies do serve as a cognitive basis for the group's boundary control function—to differentiate the group's own members from nonmembers. The system's function of boundary control may also help to explain puzzling behaviors observed among members of these groups. For example, some observers of these groups have described the glazed and withdrawn look of certain sect members, similar to that observed in a dissociative reaction. Although this response may appear pathologic when observed in a given individual, it may be quite adaptive for sustaining membership in the group. It may facilitate the members' avoidance of influence from outsiders and can thus be understood as a component of the group's boundary control function, evinced as a demand characteristic of the group. Such responses may be engendered through membership in the group, but may emerge only in settings that threaten the group's integrity. Thus, an observer who is perceived as antagonistic to the group would be more likely to report this response than one who is not.

The process of deprogramming needs further investigation. It generally refers to a set of techniques for removing persons from cultic groups and involving them in a rigorous and even coercive resocialization process in order to get them to renounce their beliefs and accept a mainstream perspective. The legalities of court-mandated intervention along these lines are important but may be confusing to the mental health clinician and the family of a cult member. The appointment of a conservator by the court is one device which can be used to sequester adult members for deprogramming. A conservator (or guardian) is a person appointed to care for any adult who by reason of illness or mental weakness is likely to be deceived or imposed upon by others' manipulations. Many states have temporary conservatorship laws that permit signing of the court order in case of an emergency without giving any notice to the proposed conservatee. This has sometimes permitted parents to obtain the help of local police in apprehending their adult children without warning and then forcibly detaining them for a designated period of time.

Bibliography

Galanter, M. (1990). Cults and zealous self-help movements: A psychiatric perspective. *American Journal of Psychiatry, 147,* 543–551.

Proudfoot, W., & Shaver, P. (1976). Attribution theory and

the psychology of religion. *Journal for the Scientific Study of Religion, 14,* 317–330.

Marc Galanter

CULTURAL DISINTEGRATION. The term *culture* has been variously defined, but there is general agreement that, whatever the concept entails, it serves as (1) the "glue" which keeps groups of individuals together as distinct entities, and (2) the means by which individuals adapt to the group and maintain a sense of identity and psychological stability. Cultural disintegration, then, can have a dual impact: it can cause a cultural entity to cease to exist and can also have a disruptive effect on the emotional adjustment of the individual.

There is not further consensus that cultures are static; cultures arise to enable a group to adapt to the demands of their surroundings and, as the context changes, the form and content of culture will also change. In the normal course of events these changes are slow and likely may not even be recognized within the lifetime or cultural memory of individuals. Thus, while there may be an appearance of sameness, over the longer course, substantial changes can occur with the culture remaining substantially intact and individuals retaining a sense of belonging and good psychological health.

Cultures rarely exist in isolation for any great length of time. With increasing worldwide population and mobility, the opportunity for contact between cultures has increased substantially, thus increasing the potential for more rapid cultural change. In the *Handbook of Cross-Cultural Psychology* (Boston, 1997, Vol. 3) John Berry and David Sam described four adaptational strategies that can be employed by individuals when cultural groups are faced with change (the usual paradigm of change occurs when a smaller group encounters or becomes immersed in a larger, more dominant cultural group). *Integration* occurs when individuals retain a value for their traditional culture but also desire participation in the dominant society. *Assimilation* comes about when there is a desire to become a member of the dominant culture and there is no attachment to the original culture. *Separation* is the opposite of assimilation, where the total commitment is to the original culture and a rejection of the dominant culture. Lastly, *marginalization* occurs when the traditional culture is lost and there is no attachment to the dominant culture. The first two of these strategies involve the least stress on individuals, while the latter two would be expected to result in some psychopathological sequelae. [*See* Cross-Cultural Psychology; Ethnic Identity; *and* Marginalization.]

The term *acculturative stress* has been used to describe the psychological effects that occur whenever an individual encounters cultural change. This stress is assumed to operate on a continuum and its intensity is linked to a number of factors in the cultural change process including (1) the circumstances of change (e.g., voluntary or forced); (2) the level of similarity between the original and assumed cultures; (3) the psychological stability of the individual in the process of change; and (4) the acceptance of the host culture of cultural differences. Using this model one would expect to find a wide range and intensity of emotional disorders that are related to either acute or chronic stress.

Other models of cultural adaptation do not posit an inherent stress factor. In particular, models that incorporate the possibility of bicultural (or multicultural) modes of functioning avoid the inevitability of stress. In fact, individuals who can successfully navigate the demands of two or more cultures are seen as cognitively more complex and to have better overall psychological adjustment. There are several requirements for the development of biculturalism (LaFromboise, Coleman, & Gerton, *Psychological Bulletin*, 1991, 114, 395–412): (1) an adequate knowledge of cultural beliefs and values of both cultures; (2) positive attitudes toward both cultures; (3) trust in one's ability to function in both cultures; (4) language competency in both cultures; (5) behavioral repertoires appropriate to each culture; and (6) supportive social networks in both cultures. The more of these qualities one possesses the lower the likelihood that stress will accrue.

Cultural disintegration implies a circumstance at the extreme end of the acculturation process and thus is likely to have the most profound negative effects on individuals. Disintegration is more likely when (1) the impetus for change is external to the group; (2) the change is exceptionally large; (3) the change is rapid; and (4) the cultural group has little control over the change process. A contemporary example wherein all of these conditions are present is the removal of all of the inhabitants of Bikini Island in the South Pacific. In the late 1940s the U.S. government wanted the island for use as a nuclear test site and relocated the island's population. The government made the decision, the move was to a totally new environment, it occurred in a very short period of time, and the Bikinians had no choice in the immediate or subsequent attempts to ameliorate the ensuing problems. The result was a substantial loss of the original culture, serious demoralization among the people, and a great deal of stress with which individuals continue to cope with varying success.

A range of emotional disorders have been associated with extreme degrees of acculturation stress accompanying the disintegration of a culture. The more recent literature describes varying levels of posttraumatic stress disorder (PTSD) as being common among those that have been displaced or have experienced severe trauma due to war or natural disasters. In these instances individuals must not only deal with the physical and psychological effects of trauma but also with the possible loss of cultural surround that would normally provide coping strategies and a basis of support. Numerous studies of children who have experienced a wide range of traumas have concluded that the variable that determined whether or not children will develop PTSD was the continued presence of a strong cultural base during and following the traumatic events. Viktor Frankl (*Man's Search for Meaning*, New York, 1984) focused more on the inner strength of individuals as the key factor in determining psychological survival both during and following extreme cultural trauma; those who are able to maintain a sense of "meaning in life" can endure extreme conditions. Ultimately, however, this sense of "meaning" is determined by one's cultural learning and values and the degree to which the individuals are identified with their culture.

Where the loss of culture is more gradual, or does not involve traumatic events, the expression of psychological problems is less clear and more difficult to characterize. A major problem in this regard is the definition of emotional disorders across cultures; what may be seen as problematic in one culture is not so in another. Since most of the research in this area has been done from a Western perspective, most of the labels that are used have distinct Western psychological flavor. With this caveat in mind, various expressions of anxiety and depression disorders have been found where cultures have been disrupted, especially in refugee populations. Similar to the findings from the PTSD research, the presence of a supportive ethnic cultural community has been found to ameliorate the intensity of anxiety and depression disorders. To the extent that refugee populations exist in sufficient numbers and conditions allow the expression of traditional values, beliefs, and behaviors, individuals will fare much better from a psychological standpoint.

Identity disorders or problems are another potential outcome of cultural disintegration. One's personal identity is developed within and supported by the cultural milieu, and when the milieu is disrupted or the person is rapidly removed from it, the central sense of one's self may be in jeopardy. This is more likely among the young or those who have not developed a strong sense of identity in their traditional culture.

During periods of rapid cultural change some individuals may become marginalized (see Berry and Sam's typology above). These are people who have been only somewhat successful in their traditional culture and who cannot (or choose not to) make the transition to the demands of the new culture. In Robert Merton's terms (*Social Theory and Structure*, Glencoe, IL, 1957)

these people are in a state of anomie. Such individuals lack the means to achieve success in either culture and are prone to resort to deviant means to meet their basic or perceived needs. Further increasing the chance of deviance is the lack of identification with either culture. Thus there is nonadherence to norms and the sanctions applied against deviance from either culture, which are now meaningless. A similar, but not necessarily pathological, condition can occur when one's traditional culture has been eradicated (by war or other disaster), and thus cannot meet one's needs, and access to success is blocked in other cultures. Forced emigration, including slavery, with subsequent prejudicial treatment, are examples. In these instances people may have strong allegiance to their traditional culture and may make more or less successful attempts to recreate that culture, including maintenance of norms and the invocation of sanctions against deviant individuals.

The destruction of an intact culture often results in the deterioration in a variety of health and social indicators among those affected. Health status may decline, leading to a shorter lifespan, educational and other training opportunities may be restricted, thus reducing employability, and deviance, including alcohol and other substance abuse disorders, may increase (once again, the caveat of the dangers of cross-cultural definitions must be invoked in these circumstances). To the extent that these conditions deviate from what was present in the original culture, they can be attributed to the absence or removal of functional cultural elements. For example, in all cultures mechanisms are developed to address injury and disease and these become acceptable and familiar to members of a culture. When these approaches no longer exist (e.g., traditional medicine people or medicines are not available), there is a reluctance to seek out, or engage in, the medical practices of a new culture. Thus general health care will decline. Likewise, immersion in a new culture may bring circumstances or customs, which the traditional culture had no experience with or social controls for. The indigenous populations of North America and their experience with alcohol provide an example. When the indigenous cultures were supplanted by colonization, alcohol was introduced, a substance with which the tribal cultures had little or no experience. There were no customs regulating alcohol use, no beliefs about moderate use, and no sanctions for abuse. The subsequent toll taken on the indigenous peoples of North America is a well-known story.

The term *culture shock* is often discussed in the literature on extreme culture change. This concept shares some of the elements of cultural destruction but contains an important difference. Culture shock describes the individual's response to a rapid and total immersion in another culture. However, it is usually reserved for those circumstances where an individual voluntarily moves to another cultural environment and has the freedom to return to their original culture. Missionary work, the Peace Corps, or short-term employment are typical circumstances where culture shock can occur. While the immersion is voluntary in nature, the effect on the individual can be quite intense and may resemble what occurs among individuals in more coercive situations. Familiar values, beliefs, and behaviors are no longer applicable, the usual support systems and coping strategies are not available, one's sense of identity comes into question, and emotional responses of anxiety, depression, and anger may emerge. While the situation may be time limited, there is a perception of permanency about it. With time, however, the many strategies discussed previously can be employed to adjust to the new cultural environment.

In summary, culture is the means by which groups of individuals survive in and make sense out of their environment. Additionally, culture provides a means of survival and nurturance for the individual. Clearly, major disruptions of culture, or cultural disintegration, can have a serious and lasting impact on the quality of life, or even life itself for the individual. The extent of the impact is dependent upon the nature, degree, and rapidity of conditions that radically alter an individual's cultural context, the cultural integrity and psychological health of the individual, and access to the use of a variety of coping strategies.

[See also Culture, article on Culture and Mental Health.]

Bibliography

Bammer, A. (1994). *Displacements*. Indianapolis: Indiana University Press. Various essays on the reconstruction of cultural identity among displaced people.

Berry, J. (1980). Social and cultural change. In H. Triandis & R. Brislin (Eds.), *Handbook of cross-cultural psychology: Vol. 5 Social psychology* (pp. 211–279). Boston: Allyn & Bacon. Discusses psychological factors preceding and resulting from change, including a good discussion of acculturative stress.

Betancourt, H., & Lopez, S. (1993). The study of culture, ethnicity and race in American psychology. *American Psychologist, 48*, 629–637. Makes useful distinctions between the three concepts that are commonly garbled in much of literature.

Fagan, B. (1984). *Clash of cultures*. New York: Freeman. An account of the process and results of colonization of twelve indigenous cultures from 1488 to 1900.

Oetting, E., & Beauvais, F. (1990–1991). Orthogonal cultural identification theory: The cultural identification of minority adolescents. *The International Journal of the Addictions, 25*, 655–685. Provides theory and measurement of bicultural and multicultural identification.

Pedersen, P. (1995). *The five stages of culture shock*. Westport, CT: Greenwood Press.

Phinney, J. (1990). Ethnic identity in adolescents and adults: Review of research. *Psychological Bulletin, 108*, 499–514. Describes the nature and function of ethnic identity as a psychological construct.

Tanaka-Matsumi, J., & Draguns, J. (1997). Culture and psychopathology. In J. Berry, M. Segall, & C. Kagitcibasi (Eds.), *Handbook of cross-cultural psychology: Vol. 3, Social and behavior applications* (pp. 449–491). Boston: Allyn & Bacon. A thorough treatment of the problems involved in cross-cultural diagnosis.

Wallace, W. L. (1997). *The future of ethnicity, race and nationality*. Westport, CT: Praeger. An extensive review of human culture development, stages and cultural change and various types of cultural contact and consequences of contact.

Williams, C., & Westermeyer, J. (1986). *Refugee mental health in resettlement countries*. New York: Hemisphere.

Fred Beauvais

CULTURAL DIVERSITY. [*This entry describes how social class and subcultural variables affect research and intervention in communities.*]

Cultural diversity is a central feature of community psychology. It derives from a general psychological focus on the naturally occurring diversity among people within a context and between groups of people who are a part of different contexts. Implicitly, most theories and practices of psychology have inferred ordinal distinctions among people in a context and ordinal distinctions between people of different contexts (Jones, 1994). In contrast, community psychology assumes that diversity reflects nominal and not ordinal differences among people.

Definition and Conceptual Perspective

At first glance, *cultural diversity* appears to be a redundant phrase: *Culture* and *diversity* are two words that both connotatively and denotatively refer to the state of uniqueness and variety. More precisely, Lonner and Malpass (1994) stated that culture is defined as the distinct and significant explanation of differences observed among different groups of people. Culture characterizes the many complex ways in which peoples of the world live, and through which they tend to pass along to their offspring significant meanings about the world. Diversity is defined as differing from one another, to make diverse, or to increase variety. Diversity implies appreciating the plurality of views and experiences in our society (Anderson & Collins, 1996). Thus, a closer examination reveals that cultural diversity reflects the sentiment of community psychology's notion of promoting resilience and strength by acknowledging and availing an already existing variety of attributes among people and, more important, between groups of peoples. Hence, the research and practice of community psychology require an analysis and accounting of cultural diversity.

Cultural Diversity and Ecological Perspective

As a fundamental principle in community psychology, cultural diversity fits neatly within an ecological viewpoint of research and intervention. Cultural diversity substantiates the notion that significant meaning contained in an environment is reflective of the unique perspectives held by different populations about the way the world works and their understanding of their place in that world (Gibson & Ogbu, 1991; Lonner & Malpass, 1994). Therefore, cultural diversity is consistent with the theoretical perspective outlined by Kurt Lewin (1935/1977). Lewin offers a formula that illustrates the interdependence between the nature of human functioning and the context, the structure of the context, and the processes taking place between them. The formula $B = f(P, E)$ conceptualizes this relationship, such that human behavior evolves as a function of the interplay of the person and her environment.

In addition, activity within a context can occur at multiple levels of that context (Bronfenbrenner, 1979). For example, Bronfenbrenner (1979) conceptualizes social networks as several concentric circles of ever-increasing environmental influence around an individual, including settings in which he or she either participates, or never enters, and the generalized patterns of societal, institutional, and cultural interaction. A broader understanding of and a closer approximation to the reality of one's social environment is obtained by examining the dialectical influences of interlocking and interacting networks (Bronfenbrenner, 1979). More important, everyone is presumed to be involved in a complex and complicated set of human contexts. Behaviors cannot be measured and interpreted without considering contextual influences. The contextual parameters of cultural diversity are evident by the existence of significant meaning and life perspective, relevant behavioral activities and patterns, beneficial associations and networks, and productive and resilient consequences in human contexts.

Cultural Diversity and Strategies of Research and Interventions

Psychology in general and psychological science in particular acknowledge the mutuality in the relationship between the individual and the context. However, the usual scientific practice is to account for and control relevant but extraneous contextual effects, of which, cultural diversity is a representative. Thus, with few exceptions, Lewin's symbolic equation seldom guides the enterprise of most psychological research. Often, researchers either attend to the individual's behaviors in isolation, or may attribute behavior to the context while ignoring the interdependence between the person and the contextual variables.

Harrison and her colleagues noted that ethnic minority status has potent meaning and experiences of cultural diversity because of the difficulties such culturally diverse groups have experienced in attempting to coexist with the European American culture (Harrison, Wilson, Pine, Chan, Buriel, 1990). These difficulties shape part of the meaning of being a member of a culturally diverse group in the United States and form external environmental forces operating on the functioning of diverse groups. That is, ethnic minorities who have traditionally experienced persistent discrimination, exclusion, and oppression in American society make their ethnicity qualitatively different from all other ethnic groups that have immigrated to the United States. In addition, Boykin (1984) has asserted that ethnic minority people hold several competing frames of references including the majority, a minority, and bicultural frames of reference which merge majority and minority references. Boykin suggests in this triple quandary hypothesis that the minority person's experience of the world reflects a complex and complicated perspective and status in society. These experiences have influenced beliefs about what it means to be a member of an ethnic minority group. It is widely held that beliefs form an important psychological guide to action (Siegal, 1983). A cultural diversity perspective must assess and account for the variety of relevant meanings and understandings of the target group's or individual's environment and the subjective meaning of that group's and individual's place in particular environments. In other words, human functioning must be understood both in terms of the behaviors themselves, as well as the contextual containment of human functioning. Because community psychology assumes that intervention and research necessarily involve work with contextually relevant diverse groups, it is important to assess the meaning, activity, situation, and consequences of human contexts. Incorporating a culturally diverse perspective in research and intervention means that the relevant population's frame of reference or contextual understanding is included in the project.

Assumptions of Group Heterogeneity and Heterogeneity of Groups

Culturally diverse groups of people must be understood from their contextual perspective and experiences. Race, ethnicity, gender, and class are the usual categories of cultural experiences in which aspects of human life are structured. Thus, two general assumptions concern the relationship of diverse groups of people. First, although it is generally agreed that people may be exposed to a similar context, that context will be experienced differently by each and every person. Second, not only are people in a similar context different but different contexts and contextual influences on people will differ. In order to compare any two groups of people we must make assurance that instruments of comparison are reflective of the relevant and similar meaning, activity, situation, and consequences within each group.

However, research is often conducted in a way that diminishes the importance of diversity. Past research has assumed homogeneity among participants of a particular population and cultural equivalence between populations. Indeed, race, ethnicity, class, gender, and sexual orientation have been so confounded by the assumptions of group homogeneity and cultural equivalence that egregious blunders are made. For instance, past research on lower socioeconomic African Americans was assumed to represent all classes of African Americans.

Failure to acknowledge cultural diversity and other contextual variables within a research population ultimately raises questions about generality and the validity of results. Thus, it is important to assess not only individual differences among a population of people but examine carefully contextual differences. Usually, it is experimentally convenient and expedient to assume contextual equivalence homogeneity and cultural equivalence among categories of people such that legitimately comparisons can be assessed in terms of a common standard. In addition, the existence of hierarchal relationships among people reflects a socially constructed variation where the primary purpose is subordination.

It is important to remember that a context is conceptualized validly in research under two conditions (Bronfenbrenner, 1979). First, the researcher must know the subjective meaning that the context carries for the individual. The researcher must understand the context in the terms of the experiences and the meaning for the individuals that are a part of that context. This subjective meaning may change over time. Second, the subjective meaning of the research context must correspond to the context to which the researcher wants to generalize the findings.

Community Research and Action

In addition to research, a major tenet of community psychology is action. Oftentimes, action takes the form of intervention efforts. Here the accurate assessment of contextual influences proves invaluable to successful efforts. Intervention programs are based on an understanding of a problem and proposed solutions for that problem, or the problem definition. Definitions structure our approach to social issues, and are inherently embedded in our own views of human behaviors and our value systems. As a discipline, community psy-

chology encourages scientists to operate from a clear framework that integrates values, research, and action (Rappaport, 1977). The fundamental premise of recognizing the values of both the researcher and the target community promotes the establishment of an intervention program that encompasses the interest of all parties.

Throughout the research and action process, values must be made explicit and include respect for diversity because this will facilitate the development of a common purpose, plan, and program, and will increase the intervention's likelihood of success. This approach becomes increasingly important when working with culturally diverse groups of people and with groups whose cultural practices differ from those of the mainstream culture. Indeed, failure to ensure the congruence between the values implicit in a proposed program and the cultural beliefs and practices of people who are directly affected by the efforts, may result in harm to the very population intended to help. One general and fundamental strategy for addressing the issue of varying values is to always define and address problems through collaboration with the members of the community, as this will ensure that the intervention is valid for that context and promote community support to secure the success of the program.

Conclusions

Cultural diversity is a valued aspect of humanity. Its social implications are dramatic and far-reaching in that the key to viable solutions may lie in the diversity of our peoples. Community psychology places cultural diversity as a hallmark to understanding and finding solutions to problems in living (Rappaport, 1977; Trickett et al., 1994).

Bibliography

Anderson, M. L., & Collins, P. H. (1996). *Race, class, and gender* (3rd ed.). Belmont, NY: Wadsworth.

Boykin, A. W. (1984). Reading achievement and the social frame of reference of Afro-American children. *The Journal of Negro Education, 53,* 464–473.

Bronfenbrenner, U. (1979). *The ecology of human development.* Cambridge, MA: Harvard University Press.

Gibson, M. E., & Ogbu, J. U. (1991). *Minority status and schooling.* New York: Garland.

Harrison, A. O., Wilson, M. N., Pine, C. J., Chan, S. Q., & Buriel, R. (1990). Family ecologies of ethnic minority children. *Child Development, 61,* 347–362.

Jones, J. M. (1994). On similarities are different: Toward a psychology of affirmative diversity. In E. J. Trickett, R. J. Watts, & D. Birman (Eds.), *Human diversity* (pp. 27–48). San Francisco: Jossey-Bass.

Lewin, K. (1977). *Principles of topological psychology.* New

York: Holt Rinehart, & Winston (Original work published 1935)

Lonner, W. J., & Malpass, R. (1994). *Psychology and culture.* New York: Allyn & Bacon.

Rappaport J. (1977). *Community psychology: Values, research and action.* New York: Holt Rinehart, & Winston.

Siegal, I. E. (1983). The ethics of intervention. In I. E. Siegal & L. Laosa (Eds.), *Changing families* (pp. 2–22). New York: Plenum.

Trickett, E. J., Watts, R. J., & Birman, D. (1994). *Human Diversity.* San Francisco: Jossey-Bass.

Melvin N. Wilson and Felicia D. Hall

CULTURAL PLURALISM is a form of cultural diversity in certain countries where cultures can still maintain their unique qualities and combine to form a larger richer whole. In many countries, including the United States, the term *multiculturalism* is used synonymously or in place of *cultural pluralism*.

According to Newman (1973, p. 29), societies can range from those that are monistic (composed of one group) or dyadic (composed of two groups) to those that arc pluralistic (composed of many groups). He goes on to point out that "societies that are customarily described as culturally pluralistic are those composed of numerous groups that, either by virtue of coalitions between minorities or on the basis of their own critical size, are able to resist being lumped into an undifferentiated mass" (p. 29). Finally, Newman noted that "cultural pluralism may be expressed in the formula $A+B+C = A+B+C$, where A, B, and C represent different social groups that, over time, maintain their own unique identities" (p. 67).

Stent, Hazard, and Rivlin (1973) provide a similar definition by proposing that:

[Cultural pluralism] is a state of equal co-existence in a mutually supportive relationship within the boundaries or framework of one nation of people of diverse cultures with significantly different patterns of belief, behavior, color, and in many cases with different languages. To achieve cultural pluralism, there must be unity with diversity. Each person must be aware of and secure in his own identity, and be willing to extend to others the same respect and rights that he expects to enjoy himself. (p. 14)

A key feature of these definitions of cultural pluralism is their contrast to the earlier approach to cultural diversity in countries, namely assimilation as the desired and inevitable process. This process of assimilation assumes a unidirectional pattern of cultural change whereby new immigrant and refugee groups would eventually become more and more like the dominant group in the host country. In the United States, this process of assimilation was referred to as the "melting pot" notion whereby all cultural groups would eventually melt in the same pot that is the United States and the result would be Americans, Indistinguishable from each other. Critics of the assimilation model or the "melting pot" idea quickly pointed out that the actual process of cultural change was not the development of a new cultural identity for all who lived in the United States. Instead, the assimilation model involved the imposition of Western European cultures on all non-European groups with the accompanying loss of these groups' unique cultural heritage. According to Newman's mathematical model (1973), assimilation would be represented by "$A+B+C = A$, where A, B, and C represent different social groups and A represents the dominant group" (p. 57).

Given this perspective on assimilation and the dangers of cultural monopoly where the dominant cultural group can impose its attitudes, values, beliefs, and customs onto the smaller or less powerful cultural groups, a key ingredient in the cultural pluralism perspective is the recognition, maintenance, and ultimately respect and appreciation of the uniqueness and distinctiveness of different cultures. To return to the earlier metaphor of the "melting pot" which represents the assimilation perspective, others have proposed the "salad" or "tapestry" as good metaphors for the cultural pluralism perspective since both involve the creation of a unified item which maintains the unique and distinctive qualities of the separate elements contained within the item. Berry (1997) has proposed acculturation as a useful framework for understanding different forms of cultural adaptation in a culturally pluralistic society. [*See* Culture.]

On the other hand, cultural pluralism can also be described from many different social science perspectives using different levels of analysis. In one sense, cultural pluralism can be viewed psychologically in terms of an individual's cultural orientation or multicultural ideology. At the same time, cultural pluralism is a demographic trend in many countries including the United States, occurring as a result of increasing cultural diversity of the population in a particular country. In another sense, cultural pluralism can also be viewed as a national policy. For example, many international social scientists who have traveled to both the United States and Canada have commented on how cultural pluralism is an explicit part of the national policy in Canada but not the United States. Relatedly, it can be analyzed from the perspective of social psychology and political science. For example, what political factors have created the ethnic conflict and warfare between the cultural groups in Yugoslavia which have occupied much of the 1990s?

Given the increasing cultural diversity of the population in most countries, it can also become an educational philosophy on how we can and should educate the children of a country who come from many different cultural backgrounds. Finally, cultural pluralism has also become an issue of concern in organizations to the extent that cultural differences between workers and between workers and managers can lead to conflicts and misunderstandings that negatively affect productivity and morale. These last two perspectives on cultural pluralism have received the most attention from psychologists and will be discussed later in the current article.

Next, it would be useful to delineate some psychological barriers to the achievement of cultural pluralism. Berry (1997) provides a useful conceptualization of the barriers to achieving cultural pluralism and recommends examining three levels, namely the national, institutional, and individual levels. At the individual level of analysis, Berry (1997) recommends examining the multicultural ideology of individuals. These attitudes and beliefs can serve as barriers to the achievement of cultural pluralism in day-to-day interactions and encounters. One important example of the barriers created by individual social cognition is ethnocentrism. [See Ethnocentrism.]

Many cross-cultural psychologists have pointed out that ethnocentrism is a natural and widespread phenomenon. Ethnocentrism is the belief that the customs, norms, values, and practices of one's culture represent the correct way of ordering society, and are, indeed, superior to those of other cultures (Triandis, 1994). Scholars studying cultural pluralism have pointed out that ethnocentricism is responsible for much of the resistance to the establishment of policies, practices, and procedures in educational and organizational settings based on cultural pluralism. Within the United States, ethnocentrism has been proposed to be primarily manifested as a Eurocentric bias since White European Americans dominate the country politically, economically, and demographically. In response to this Eurocentric bias, some scholars from Black studies have proposed an Afrocentric curriculum for African American children. This Afrocentric approach would embed not only the content but also the process of education in the African-centered experiences of African Americans.

Barriers at the national level can be manifested in explicit policies or official laws and procedures. Examples of national policies that serve as a barrier to the achievement of cultural pluralism include the contrast between Canada and the United States. As mentioned earlier, multiculturalism is an explicit national policy in Canada (Berry, 1997) while it is not in the United States. Many international visitors have observed that due to this difference in national policy, Canada does a better job of respecting and integrating the members of different cultural groups into its society than the United States. Some authors have pointed out that another example of policies that seek to undermine cultural pluralism were attempts in the 1990s to pass laws in the state of California making English the official language. These authors argue that while English is the dominant language in the United States, passing a law to make English the official language would in effect encourage neglect and even discrimination against recent immigrants and refugees who have not yet mastered the English language.

At the institutional level, cultural pluralism has also become an important policy and practice issue in both work organizations and educational institutions. In educational settings ranging from elementary school to colleges and universities, the issue of cultural pluralism as an educational approach or educational philosophy has received increased attention during the last decade. Given the increasing cultural diversity of student populations in schools and universities, pressures to attend to the cultural differences, and sometimes cultural conflicts, created by these changes have been mounting. How to create a classroom and a general educational environment that promotes cultural pluralism have been discussed increasingly in many educational institutions. These discussions have occurred in student affairs conferences, continuing education workshops for teachers, courses in schools of education, and seminars for university administrators. The content of these discussions has ranged from policies about appearance and dress for students, to the underrepresentation of faculty of color in various university departments, to how many and what type of courses focusing on various cultural groups should be included in the curriculum.

The results of some of these discussions have sometimes been quite controversial. For example, there was an uproar at Stanford University when faculty selected mainly Western European works as the basic required material that Stanford undergraduates should be exposed to during their years in college. At the University of California-Berkeley, certain Asian American groups filed a lawsuit when they perceived the change in university policy about the cut-off scores for admission was changed selectively to discriminate against Asian Americans. The university had raised cut-off only on the verbal and not the math scores on the SAT for admission which these Asian American groups perceived as targeted at them. Asian Americans tended to have lower verbal scores which they make up for with their high math scores, and many were getting admitted into the university based on the total score approach. The use of specific minimum cut-off scores for math and verbal meant that many Asian Americans would no longer be accepted into the university. In some school districts in the United States, heated debates have resulted from the African American community leaders' demand for Afrocentric schools as alternatives to the regular school systems which they perceive as ignoring or minimizing the educational coverage of the cultural heritage of their children. At the same time, many ethnic minority and cultural groups have perceived a backlash against the cultural pluralism movement in the schools with the attack on affirmative action programs in universities.

Within work organizations in the United States, the cultural pluralism movement has had a somewhat different track from that of educational institutions. The integration of a cultural pluralism approach has been a less contentious issue in organizations. This is due to the fact that organizations are perhaps more oriented toward effectiveness and the impact of ineffectiveness on the bottom line of productivity and profits. Starting around 1987 with the *Workforce 2000* report (Johnson & Packer, 1987), organizations in the United States began to realize that a culturally diverse workforce was inevitable and that attention to cultural differences in the workplace was essential. With this recognition, many organizations began hiring consultants and trainers to help them deal with this cultural diversity issue. Not surprisingly, there was a parallel increase in the number of books and journal articles dealing with the issue of managing cultural diversity in organization (Triandis, Kurowski, & Gelfand, 1993). Many of these interventions involve providing training workshops and seminars for various levels of managers and supervisors on how to interact and communicate more effectively with the increasingly culturally diverse workers. Some critics of this approach to cultural pluralism in the workplace have accused organizations of making only superficial attempts at changes in the form of transient interventions such as workshops and seminars rather than structural changes (e.g., hiring more cultural and ethnic minorities as managers and supervisors). The cultural pluralism movement in organizations is still relatively new and we will need more time to accurately determine if long-lasting changes have been effected with these current sets of interventions.

In summary, cultural pluralism is an issue which will remain central for many years to come and there is a great need for more cross-cultural studies to form the basis of the cultural pluralism movement. As pointed out by Berry (1997):

> [A]ll contemporary societies are now culturally plural. There are no longer any societies that can claim to be homogeneous with respect to objective cultural markers (such as ethnic origin, language, and religion) or subjective indicators (such as one's ethnic identity or personal expressions of one's culture). Such diversity elicits a variety of responses at a number of levels: national societies, institutions, and individuals can celebrate or deny it; they can share it or isolate it; they can accommodate it or attempt to squash it. Whatever the attitude or course of action, however, both history and contemporary experience provide compelling evidence that cultural pluralism is durable, even if its forms and expressions evolve over time. . . . (p. 17)

Bibliography

Berry, J. W. (1997). Individual and group relations in plural societies. In C. S. Granrose & S. Oskamp (Eds.), *Cross-cultural work groups*. Thousand Oaks, CA: Sage.

Johnson, W. B. & Packer, A. H. (1987). *Workforce 2000*. Indianapolis, IN: Hudson Institute.

Newman, W. M. (1973). American pluralism: A study of minority groups and social theory. New York: Harper & Row.

Stent, M. D., Hazard, W. R., & Rivlin, H. N. (1973). *Cultural pluralism in education: A mandate for change*. New York: Appleton-Century-Crofts.

Triandis, H. C. (1994). *Culture and social behavior*. New York: McGraw-Hill.

Triandis, H. C., Kurowski, L. L. & Gelfand, M. J. (1993). Workplace diversity. In M. D. Dunnette & L. Hough (Eds.), *Handbook of industrial and organizational psychology* (2nd ed., Vol. 2, pp. 769–827). Palo Alto, CA: Consulting Psychologist Press.

Frederick T. L. Leong

CULTURAL PSYCHOLOGY is an interdisciplinary extension of general psychology regarding those psychological processes which are inherently organized by culture. As a discipline, cultural psychology relates to cultural anthropology, sociology, semiotics, language philosophy, and cultural studies. Within psychology, cultural psychology relates to cross-cultural, social, developmental, and cognitive issues. [*See* Anthropology; *and* Culture.]

Systemic Focus

Cultural psychology is a heterogenous class of perspectives which share an interest in explaining how human psychological functions are culturally constituted through various forms of relations between persons and their social contexts. Different trends in cultural psychology can be contrasted to cross-cultural psychology. Cultural psychology looks for systemic explanation, attempting to include in the explanatory system the notion of culture or its derivates (meaning, semiotic mediating devices, folk models, social representations). For such systemic analysis, direct empirical comparisons between different societies are useful but not necessary. In contrast, cross-cultural psychology is largely concerned with the empirical investigation of differences between societies across a broad spectrum of psychological topics and exemplified by different psychological methods. [*See* Cross-Cultural Psychology.]

History

Cultural psychology antedates experimental psychology (1879), the first professorship in folk psychology (Völkerpsychologie) having been established in 1860 at the University of Bern, Switzerland. In general, cultural psychology is rooted in the nineteenth-century German *Völkerpsychologie* tradition (Moritz Lazarus, Heyman Steinthal, Hermann Paul, Wilhelm Wundt), as well as on the language philosophy of Wilhelm von Humboldt. In parallel, it is based on the semiotics of Charles Sanders Peirce in the United States, and in the action theory of Pierre Janet in France.

In the first half of the twentieth century, cultural psychology relates to the sociology of Georg Simmel and Emile Durkheim, the anthropology of Richard Thurnwald and Lucien Lévy-Bruhl, the genetic logic of James Mark Baldwin, John Dewey's pragmatism, and the social psychology of George Herbert Mead. Frederick Bartlett's constructionist look at folk stories in the 1920s in England, and Muzafer Sherif's analyses of construction of social norms, have laid the foundation for understanding the ways in which people reconstruct the social stimulus world. The cultural-historical theory of Lev Vygotsky and Alexander Luria in Russia (Vygotsky & Luria, 1930/1993, 1930/1994), the communication theory of Karl Bühler in Germany and William Stern's personalistic psychology, are further roots for the contemporary reappearance of cultural psychology.

Contemporary Directions

Versions of cultural psychology differ from one another in the definition of the role of the person in the cultural-psychological analysis. The person is either denied as a unity and human psychological processes are viewed as merged with the cultural context (e.g., directions that emphasize *appropriation* of social input), or the person is viewed as an autonomous agent, who is nevertheless interdependent with the social environment.

Ernst E. Boesch's Symbolic Action Theory. Boesch (1991) has developed a system of cultural psychology that integrates concepts from the developmental constructionism of Jean Piaget and Pierre Janet with basic psychoanalytic insights, in clearly personological ways. Working between Germany and Thailand since the mid-1950s, his theory includes a basic focus on complex psychological phenomena (e.g., aesthetic objects) which a person experiences through personal generalized symbols (*fantasms*) which are based on socially available *myth* stories. His focus on the symbolic nature of action allows for analysis of the ways in which persons move from myths to actions via personally relevant fantasms. Boesch's focus is in many ways parallel to the explanation of conduct through the notion of social representation of French social psychologist Serge Moscovici, yet it builds new concepts of a personal-subjective kind (e.g., *Heimweh* or longing for home).

Lutz H. Eckensberger's Action Theory. A direct descendant of Boesch's symbolic action theory that was developed in Saarbrücken, Eckensberger's action theory builds on Boesch's work in a number of ways. Originally formulated within the cross-cultural psychology perspective, Eckensberger has moved on to construct a dynamic theoretical perspective of cultural psychology of human action and thinking (Eckensberger, 1990). The emphasis on *persons' goal-directed actions* and their *emerging reflexive abstraction* are the cornerstone of Eckensberger's cultural view of mental processes. Boesch's agency notion is carefully retained, and it is seen to both construct "action barriers" and negotiate those in the domain of action and reflexive abstraction. By concentrating on the emergence of higher levels of actions in the mental sphere, Eckensberger manages to solve the complex problem of integration of intentionality into his theoretical scheme.

Gananath Obeyesekere's (1990) "Work of Culture." Building on the basis of Freudian psychoanalysis and the cultural phenomena of South Asian societies, Obeyesekere has demonstrated how persons organize their personal life course through meanings-based participation in cultural rituals, and how human conduct is *overdetermined by meanings*. Obeyesekere's version of symbolic anthropology is close to Boesch's theoretical system in its ideas.

Hubert Hermans's (1995) Dialogic Self Theory. Based on the notion of traditional research on motivation, and on the dialogical approaches of Martin Buber and Mikhail Bakhtin, Hermans has formulated a view of the self which builds upon the relationship between different meanings (or "voices") that take different forms (e.g., those of agreement, disagreement). His theory of dialogical self is connected with phenomena of psychotherapy, and with his *valuation theory* (Hermans & Kempen, 1993), in conjunction with a measurement system for personal valuations.

Alfred Lang's Semiotic-Ecological Approach. Uniting historical thinking about the human condition which begins with the work of Johann Gottfried Herder, Lang's approach also links the semiotics of C. S. Peirce with a Lewinian focus on the personal sense of the life space (Lang, 1993). Taking from Kurt Lewin the notion of developmental lines, and linking up with Boesch's symbolic action theory, Lang overcomes the dualism of the inner and outer psychological worlds by way of considering the constant process of movement of sign processes between the person and the world. This focus is similar to Dewey's efforts to create models of dynamic relations between organism and environment.

Pablo del Rio's Focus on the Dynamic Nature of Human Activity. Based on the analysis of human life environments, and on Vygotsky's cultural-historical theory del Rio's focus has led to the development of the notion of the *zone of syncretic representation* (ZSR) which allows the del Rio and Alvarez to conceptualize the dynamic nature of person-environment relations. There is *continuous help* from the external operators to the internal, and vice versa in a person's relating to his or her culture. One can start an internal plan of action ("Want to do X"), which passes to another plan that is externally activated in the cultural space ("It is good to do Y"). Human actions are personal and freely initiated, but their organization is syncretic in the common territory of distributed operations of our internal-and-external mind (Del Rio & Alvarez, 1995). Del Rio emphasizes the role of general idea complexes (similar to Boesch's fantasms) in the organization of the person-environment relations.

Ivana Markova's Dialogical Approach. This view integrates the cognitive and language functions in the process of analysis. Relying on the traditions of the Prague Linguistic Circle (Markova, 1992), Markova also brings the notion of Hegel's dialectics home to the reality of analysis of dialogues (both inter- and intrapersonal). Within her analytic scheme, the concentration on the emergence of novelty in dialogue becomes highlighted, as she develops a three-step analytic unit (at time 1 two opposites, A and B are in a relationship that leads to the transformation of at least one of these into a novel form—e.g., A becomes C—at time 2).

Michael Cole's Work. Historically indebted to the thought of Alexander Luria, and through him to Lev Vygotsky, Cole's version of cultural psychology emerges from his studies of cultural tools, paired with an explicit interest in the historical nature of cultural processes (Cole, 1996). His theoretical construction is based on *cultural practice theory.* The problem of relationships between microgenetic (situationally emerging) and ontogenetic phenomena in human development is central to the cultural practice theory. The main mechanism by which culture and person are related is that of *mutual interweaving.* This interweaving reflects the general process in which the culture becomes individual and the individuals create their culture—the culture and cognition are *mutually constituted.*

Richard A. Shweder. His version of cultural psychology is based on his experiences with the moral reasoning of persons in Orissa, India. He has demonstrated the relevance of both the person and the social world for cultural organization of human conduct. His cultural psychology relates the intentional worlds of human cultural environments, with the actions, feelings, and thinking of intentional persons. Persons and their cultural worlds interpenetrate each other's identities, and set the conditions for each other's existence and development, while jointly undergoing change through social interaction (Shweder, 1990, p. 25).

James V. Wertsch. Dewey/Leontiev activity approaches underlie Wertsch's version of cultural psychology along with the notion of semiotic mediation through "voices of the mind" (Wertsch, 1991), and Bakhtin's emphasis on dialogicality, whereby the analysis of "voices" affords the treatment of the complexity of messages. The result is a consistent return to the study of ambivalences embedded in communicative messages—in the form of *polyphony of voices* or *heteroglossia.* Different "voices" can be seen in utterances in ways that "interanimate" or dominate each other in the act of speaking in situated activity contexts. Bakhtin's legacy allows Wertsch to advance his theory of communication into the realm of conceptualizing *processual relations* between the components in a dialogue (i.e., different "voices"). "Privileging" in relations between "voices" (i.e., the "foregrounding" of voice X while voice Y is simultaneously being "backgrounded") is a central issue for Wertschian analysis. Wertsch is interested in society's macrolevel dialogues (such as the dialogicality involved in school history textbooks, leading to different forms of national identity).

Barbara Rogoff's Ethnography of Guided Participation. Rogoff's focus is mostly ethnographical, which allows her to take into account the complexities of the culture-embedded mentality in action. Rogoff provides a solution to the problem of the context—it is the *sociocultural activity* which involves *active participation* of people *in socially constituted practices* (Rogoff, 1990, p. 14). Within that activity, persons are interacting on problem solving (rather than being involved in lengthy intrapersonal contemplations or soul searching). The active (but not always persistent) social guidance by others to the person is complemented by the person's own constructive role in his or her own development. The person is always an *active* apprentice who *participates* in *socially guided activity settings.*

International Representation

Cultural psychology is an international discipline. Apart from the directions described above, there are a number of others which focus on specific issues. In Britain, the promotion of discursive analysis (Edwards, 1997) by Michael Billig, Derek Edwards, Jonathan Potter, and David Middleton at Loughborough University has carved out a new methodological road for some of cultural psychology. Russian transformations of the German focus on activity in the form of Alexel N. Leontiev's activity theory have been instrumental in the advancement of activity-centered cultural psychology of Yrjö Engeström in Finland. Different thought systems close to cultural psychology (but not necessarily labeled as such) can be found in Norway (Ragnar Rommetveit's philosophy of communication), Estonia (Peeter Tulviste's cultural-historical approach to human action). South Africa (Ronnie Miller's semiotic approach), India (Veena Das's cultural sociology), and Australia (Anna Wierzbicka's efforts to build a universal semantics). Pierre Bourdieu's sociological analysis of *habitus* has had an impact upon cultural psychology, and Serge Moscovici's focus on *social representations* has been a basis for social psychologists' tackling of complex cultural phenomena. An extension of the Bakhtin-Wertsch line of thought has provided a productive basis for research in the area of education in Brazil (Smolka, Góes, & Pino, 1995).

In the United States, cultural psychology emerged in the social sciences of the 1980s, largely in dialogue with cognitive science. The focus on internal mechanisms of cognition was replaced by calls to study human actions in culturally organized settings. Led by Markus, Kitayama, and others, William James's analysis of the self has become a target of recent empirical analyses of the cultural organization of human selves. Jerome Bruner (1990) has suggested his approach to meaning making; Jaan Valsiner (1998) has focused on semiotic regulation of human conduct. Such semiotic regulation entails the use of signs as *cultural regulators* of conduct. Regulators operate by way of creating *temporary constraints* upon the flow of psychological processes. Human conduct is regulated *redundantly*, by way of action constraints and signs that operate as constraints on the meanings used to guide action.

Methodological Challenges

Cultural psychology deals with psychological phenomena which cannot easily be studied by the use of standard psychological methods. The focus on meaningfulness of psychological phenomena in cultural psychology requires the construction of new methodology, which is slowly appearing in the 1990s (Ratner, 1997; Valsiner, 1998). Since cultural psychology deals with systemic, complex phenomena, its contemporary methodological innovation continues the traditions of holistic traditions of the past (*Gestalt psychologie, Ganzheitspsychologie*) and rules out the primacy of statistical techniques in inference making.

[*See also* Anthropology; Cross-Cultural Psychology; *and* Culture.]

Bibliography

Boesch, E. E. (1991). *Symbolic action theory and cultural psychology*. New York: Springer.

Bruner, J. (1990). *Acts of meaning*. Cambridge, MA: Harvard University Press.

Cole, M. (1996). *Cultural psychology: A once and future discipline*. Cambridge, MA: Belknap/Harvard, University Press.

Del Rio, P., & Alvarez, A. (1995). Directivity: The cultural and educational construction of morality and agency. *Anthropology and Education Quarterly, 26,* 4, 384–409.

Eckensberger, L. H. (1990). From cross-cultural psychology to cultural psychology. *The Quarterly Newsletter of the Laboratory of Comparative Human Cognition, 12,* 37–52.

Edwards, D. (1997). *Discourse and cognition*. London: Sage.

Hermans, H. J. M. (1995). Voicing the self: From information processing to dialogical interchange. *Psychological Bulletin, 119,* 31–50.

Hermans, H. J. M., & Kempen, H. J. G. (1993). *The dialogical self: Meaning as movement*. San Diego, CA: Academic Press.

Lang, A. (1993). Non-Cartesian artefacts in dwelling activities: Steps towards a semiotic ecology. *Schweizerische Zeitschrift für Psychologie, 52,* 138–147.

Markova, I. (1992). On the structure and dialogicity in Prague semiotics. In A. H. Wold (Ed.), *The dialogic alternative: Towards a theory of language and mind* (pp. 45–63). Oslo: Scandinavian University Press.

Obeyesekere, G. (1990). *The work of culture*. Chicago: University of Chicago Press.

Ratner, C. (1997). *Cultural psychology and qualitative methodology: Theoretical and empirical considerations*. New York: Plenum.

Rogoff, B. (1990). *Apprenticeship in thinking*. New York: Oxford University Press.

Shweder, R. A. (1990). Cultural psychology—What is it? In J. W. Stigler, R. A. Shweder, & G. Herdt (Eds.), *Cultural psychology* (pp. 1–43). Cambridge, UK: Cambridge University Press.

Smolka, A. L. B., Góes, M. C., & Pino, A. (1995). The constitution of the subject: A persistent question. In J. Wertsch & B. Rogoff (Eds.), *Sociocultural studies of the mind*. Cambridge, UK: Cambridge University Press.

Valsiner, J. (1998). *The guided mind*. Cambridge, MA: Harvard University Press.

Vygotsky, L. S., & Luria, A. R. (1993). *Studies on the history of behavior: Ape, primitive, and child*. Hillsdale, NJ: Erlbaum. (Original work published 1930)

Vygotsky, L. S., & Luria, A. R. (1994). Tool and symbol in child development. In R. van der Veer & J. Valsiner (Eds.), *The Vygotsky reader* (pp. 99–174). Oxford: Blackwell. (Original work published 1930)

Wertsch, J. V. (1991). *Voices of the mind*. Cambridge, MA: Harvard University Press.

Jaan Valsiner

CULTURE. [*This entry comprises three articles: a broad introduction on the cultural foundations of human behavior; a survey of the cultural dimensions of mental health; and a review of the models of cultural influences on human development. For discussions related to culture, see Cross-*

Cultural Psychology; Cultural Psychology; Determinants of Intelligence, *article on* Culture and Intelligence; Gender, Sex, and Culture; *and* Military Culture.]

Cultural Foundations of Human Behavior

Marshall McLuhan is quoted as saying that "It's a cinch fish didn't discover water." Just as clearly, psychologists didn't discover culture. Any context for human behavior that is so all-encompassing as culture is for the developing individual is likely to be ignored, or if noticed, to be taken for granted. And just as quickly as the fish out of water discovers its importance, so too has psychology recently had to contend with culture as an important foundation for the discipline. As national societies become increasingly diverse and international contacts become common, psychologists can no longer assume an acultural or a unicultural stance.

Problems of an Acultural Psychology

Until recently, most of psychology has been both *culture blind* and *culture bound*. The first claim can be supported by examining textbooks and journals for treatments and studies that take culture into account (Lonner, 1990). For example, most introductory textbooks have a chapter entitled "The Biological Basis of Behavior"; but there is no parallel chapter on "Cultural Foundations," even in texts that emphasize culture as an important context (e.g., Westen, 1996).

The reduction of this culture-blind situation has required the systematic incorporation of cultural factors influencing, and being influenced by, individuals in the course of their development. This has produced a "cultural psychology," similar to the earlier appearances of "social psychology" or "environmental psychology," where these other surroundings have been established as significant frameworks within which to understand the development and display of individual human behavior.

The second claim (that psychology is culture bound) can be supported by examining the same texts and journals for their incorporation of authors, concepts, and data from the available worldwide cultural diversity. One can also examine this encyclopedia and conclude from all these examples that psychology is limited to a Western (European American) worldview, primarily rooted in universities (with their academic, rather than mundane, interests), and committed to a narrow scientific method (rather than incorporating other systems of knowing that are prevalent in many other cultures). The discipline can be characterized as Western Academic Scientific Psychology (WASP), which is locked into a small corner of the psychological world. The reduction of this culture-bound situation has produced a broadly comparative approach known as "cross-cultural psychology."

Taken together, the recent introduction of the cultural and the comparative dimensions to the discipline has provided considerable evidence for how culture and human behavior are related. Substantial documentation of these relationships is now available in handbooks (Berry, Dasen, & Saraswathi, 1997; Berry, Poortinga, & Pandey, 1997; Berry, Segall, & Kagicibasi, 1997; Triandis et al., 1980), textbooks (e.g., Berry, 1992; Segall, Dasen, Berry, & Poortinga, 1999), a book of readings (e.g., Goldberger & Veroff, 1995); and journals (e.g., *Journal of Cross-Cultural Psychology, Culture & Psychology*). A recent review of the development, implications, and applications of cross-cultural psychology is readily available (Segall, Lonner, & Berry, 1998). Interested readers should consult these sources for details about many topics discussed in the balance of this article.

Meanings of Culture

The concept of culture in anthropology was introduced by Tylor in 1871: "culture is that complex whole which includes knowledge, belief, art, morals laws, customs and any other capabilities and habits acquired by man as a member of society." Since that time, there have been hundreds of refinements and elaborations, most emphasizing it as a shared feature of human groups, created and transmitted by them to others (usually their descendants); in short, culture is a shared way of life among a group of people.

This original view of culture as an observable feature of social groups, existing prior to the arrival, and influencing the development, of individuals, was refocused by Clifford Geertz, who emphasized meanings and symbols that are communicated between people and across generations. The earlier view of culture as a relatively concrete context for individual development has now been supplemented by a more abstract or symbolic view, with an emphasis on interaction among individuals and groups (Jahoda, 1992).

The earlier conception of culture was contemporary with the development of the comparative study of culture and behavior, and hence is often associated with "cross-cultural" psychology. The more recent conception has become associated with the "cultural" perspective. However, formal definitions of the two branches only partially capture this difference in emphasis:

Cross-cultural psychology is the study of similarities and differences in individual psychological functioning in various cultural and ethnic groups; of the relationships between psychological variables and sociocultural, ecological, and biological variables; and of current changes in these variables. (Berry et al., 1992, p. 2)

Cultural psychology is, first of all, a designation for the comparative study of the way culture and psyche make each other up. Second, it is a label for a practical, empirical, and philosophical project designed to reassess the uniformitarian principle of psychic unity and aimed at the development of a credible theory of psychological pluralism. Third, it is a summons to reconsider the methods and procedures for studying mental states and psychological processes across languages and cultures. (Shweder & Sullivan, 1993, p. 498)

While distinguishable, these two definitions do not suggest that the "cultural and "cross-cultural" approaches are incompatible. Indeed, recent discussions have attempted to achieve unity or convergence between them (e.g., Poortinga, 1997).

Theoretical Issues

At the present time, the field faces three conceptual issues.

Within and Across. The first issue is where to look for relationships between human behavior and the cultural context in which it was nourished. Quite early on it was evident that certain problems must be faced when studying human behavior across cultures.

The emic-etic distinction was prominent in these early writings. The consensus was that *both* perspectives were necessary to the developing field: local knowledge and interpretations (the *emic* approach) were essential, but more than that perspective was required to relate variations in cultural context to variations in behavior (the *etic* approach). These two approaches became elaborated. First came the notion of *imposed etic* which served as the starting point for comparative research, because it was obvious that all psychologists necessarily carry their own culturally based perspectives with them when studying other cultures; these perspectives were initial sources of bias (usually European American), to be confronted and reduced as work progressed in the other culture(s). Second came the *emic* exploration of psychological phenomena, and their understanding in local cultural terms; this provided the important culturally based meanings that were most probably missed when making the initial *imposed etic* approach to psychological phenomena in various cultures. Third came the notion of the *derived etic* which might possibly be discerned following extensive use of *emic* approaches in a number of cultures; it was expected that some similarities in psychological phenomena might be derived by the comparative examination of behavior in various cultures.

These three concepts, in turn, gave rise to three goals of cross-cultural psychology to *transport and test* our current psychological knowledge and perspectives by using them in other cultures (the imposed etic approach), to *explore and discover* new aspects of the phenomenon being studied in local cultural terms (emic); and to *integrate* what has been learned from these first two approaches in order to generate a more nearly uni-

versal psychology, one that has panhuman validity (the derived etic approach). The existence of *universals* in other disciplines (e.g., biology, linguistics, sociology, anthropology) provided some basis for the assumption that we would be able to work our way through to this third goal with some success.

Finally, these three goals have become identified with three theoretical orientations in cross-cultural psychology: *absolutism, relativism*, and *universalism* (Berry et al., 1992). The absolutist position is one that assumes that psychological phenomena are basically the same (qualitatively) in all cultures: "honesty" is "honesty," and "depression" is "depression," no matter where one observes them. From the absolutist perspective, culture is thought to play little or no role in either the meaning or display of human characteristics. Assessments of such characteristics are made using standard instruments (perhaps with linguistic translation) and interpretations are made easily, without taking into account alternative culturally based views. This orientation resembles the *imposed etic* approach.

In sharp contrast, the *relativist* approach assumes that all human behavior is culturally patterned. It seeks to avoid ethnocentrism by trying to understand people in their own terms. Explanations of human diversity are sought in the cultural context in which people have developed. Assessments are typically carried out employing the values and meanings that a cultural group gives to a phenomenon. Comparisons are judged to be conceptually and methodologically problematic and ethnocentric, and are thus virtually never made. This orientation resembles the *emic* approach.

A third perspective, *universalism*, lies somewhere between the first two positions and assumes that basic human characteristics are common to all members of the species (that is, they constitute a set of psychological givens in all human beings) and that culture influences the development and display of these characteristics (by playing different variations on these underlying themes. Assessments are based on the presumed underlying process, but measures are developed in culturally meaningful versions. Comparisons are made cautiously, employing a wide variety of methodological principles and safeguards, and interpretations of similarities and differences are attempted that take alternative culturally based meanings into account. The orientation resembles the *derived etic* approach.

Different approaches can be distinguished according to their orientation to this issue of within or across. Although few today advocate a strictly absolutist or imposed etic view, the relativist emic position has given rise to numerous approaches: ethnopsychology, societal psychology, indigenous psychology, and to some extent cultural psychology (Cole, 1996). And the derived etic view has given rise to a universalist psychology (Berry et al., 1992). A mutual compatibility between the emic and derived etic positions has been noted by many. For example, Berry et al. (1992, p. 384) have claimed that indigenous psychologies, though valuable in their own right, serve an equally important function as useful steps on the way to achieving a universal psychology, using a cross-indigenous approach.

To summarize this first issue, there has been widespread acceptance by most psychologists of the necessity for *both* the *within* and *across* approaches to understanding relationships between cultural context and human experience and behavior. In my view, it is not possible to be "cross-cultural" without first being "cultural"; but to be only "cultural" (or to pretend that it is possible to be so), seriously undermines the possibility of attaining the general principles to which all sciences aspire.

Culture Contact. The second issue involves the recognition that cultures are not static, but change for a variety of reasons. One reason for this view is that when cultures come into contact with each other, *acculturation* occurs. This process involves changes in both *group* or *collective* phenomena (for example, language, politics, religion, work, schooling, social relationship) and *individual* or *psychological* phenomena (for example, identity, beliefs, values, attitudes, abilities). A good deal of early cross-cultural psychological work took place by comparing people who were not in contact with each other; indeed, this was a methodological necessity for comparisons requiring independence of cases. However, some early work also took place in situations of intercultural encounters, often as a result of colonization, migration, or the continuation of culturally distinct communities living side by side in plural societies.

Over the years many cross-cultural psychologists have adopted the view that *both* these kinds of work are legitimate and important ways of understanding human behavior as it is influenced by the cultural context in which it occurs. One major difference between these two lines of influence is that psychological phenomena during contact may be more difficult to understand and interpret than those in noncontact situations because, in the contact setting, there are at least two sources of cultural influences; hence comparative studies may be even more important here in order to tease out the relative cultural contributions to psychological phenomena. A second major difference is that opportunities to create new cultural forms may be greater during the process of acculturation.

This interest in psychological phenomena resulting from culture contact has given rise to the suggestion that there could be an *ethnic psychology* or *psychology of acculturation* concerned primarily with group and psychological acculturation phenomena. Another field to emerge has been that of *psychologie interculturelle*, studied primarily by French researchers (Camilleri & Vi-

sonneau, 1996). As intercultural contacts increase, this area of psychology will almost certainly grow in importance.

Culture: Given or Created. The third and final issue stems from the change in the conceptions of *culture*. As we have seen, an early view was that culture was "out there" to be studied, observed, and described; culture was a shared way of life of a group of socially interacting people; and culture was transmitted from generation to generation by the processes of enculturation and socialization. That is, culture was viewed as a *given* that preceded in time the life of any individual member.

This view of culture has had a major influence on thinking in cross-cultural psychology. The main task was to understand how the established culture *influenced* the psychological development of individuals, and *guided* their day-to-day behaviors. However, along with more recent cognitive approaches in many branches of psychology, individuals have come to be viewed, not as mere pawns or victims of their cultures but as cognizers, appraisers, and interpreters of them (Boesch, 1991). Thus different individuals experience different aspects of their culture in different ways. One example of this more cognitive orientation is in the framework for analyses of cultural contexts (Berry et al., 1992) in which more subjective and individual "experiential" and "situational" contexts were distinguished from more objective and shared "ecological" and "cultural" contexts.

A sharp contrast to this perspective on the nature of culture is advanced by those adopting a "social construction" perspective. From this perspective culture is not something that is given but is being interpreted and created daily through interactions between individuals and their social surroundings. This view is one espoused by those identifying with *cultural psychology*.

This core idea, however, has been a part of the cross-cultural approach for some time. There are numerous examples of interactions between context and person (for example, in ecocultural frameworks) and of reaction to contact (as one form of adaptation associated with acculturation). This reciprocal relationship between person and culture, leading to the modification and creation of new cultural forms as a result of acculturation, has been of long-standing interest in the field.

Methodological Issues

With these theoretical and conceptual issues as a foundation, I turn to some methodological issues and propose some standards against which we can judge empirical research. The starting point is the distinction between the group and the individual level of analysis outlined earlier. The former provides the context for individual human development and action and is studied primarily through ethnographic methods (including key informant, observational, and archival data sources); the latter is considered to be the psychological outcome for particular individuals. The key methodological issue is how can we demonstrate valid linkages between these two levels?

In the past few decades, most cross-cultural researchers used the "Jack Horner" research strategy, characterized in this rhyme:

> Little Jack Horner,
> Sat in a corner,
> Eating his Christmas pie,
> He stuck in his thumb,
> And pulled out a plum,
> And said "What a good boy am I."

In other words, this strategy consists of collecting convenient data, deriving some statistical outcomes, and declaring a favored interpretation. The two hallmarks of this strategy are the use of *unguided search* and of *post hoc interpretation.*

In recent years cross-cultural psychologists have moved more and more to a research strategy in which cultural groups that provide *varying contexts* for psychological development and human behavior are *selected in advance* (on the basis of known characteristics based on ethnographic descriptions and national indicators). Individual outcomes are then *predicted*, using some theory that links psychological phenomena to their cultural background. *Independent* conceptualization and measurement of phenomena at the *group* and *individual* levels are required in order to establish nontrivial links between cultural and psychological phenomena.

In order to establish valid linkages between context and outcome, prediction and verification need to be based upon appropriate sampling of the group and individual phenomena of interest. There are four kinds of populations from which samples can be drawn and two types of sampling (*strategic* and *representative*); each sampling strategy has a characteristic goal (to *test* and to *generalize*, respectively) (see Berry et al., 1992, chapter 9).

Considering the two suggested goals first, if the goal of a cross-cultural study is to *test* a particular hypothesized relationship between a cultural and psychological phenomenon, then a few strategically well-chosen cultural contexts may suffice. However, if the goal is to produce a *generalization* about a culture-behavior relationship (perhaps eventually with the status of a universal law), then a representative (and larger) sample would be required.

Considering the four populations from which samples can be drawn, *cultural groups* are typically the largest unit with which we are concerned, although broader *cultural areas* are also of some interest (south-ern Asia or eastern Europe, for example). In some cases, *societies* or *nation-states* are also of interest to a researcher. The crucial points here are to know and declare the goal of the study (to test or generalize) in advance and to select cultures in order to meet this goal.

Because most groups (whether societies, nations, or cultures) are heterogeneous, the selection of which *communities* within those groups to work with can be crucial. Once again they should be selected according to the goal of the study (to test or to generalize) and with all the earlier points in mind (that is, their qualities known in advance).

Individuals may also be a sampling problem in cross-cultural studies. Who can provide a valid test of a prediction and who can be the basis for a generalization may well vary from culture to culture. Variations in a person's status as a *carrier* of the culture are known to exist according to a number of factors (for example, whether the person lives in slavery or freedom and is male or female, schooled or unschooled, oppressed or oppressor). These variations will necessarily render individuals differential exemplars of the hypothesized relationship between culture and behavior.

Finally, *behaviors* sampled should have a known relationship to the population of behaviors nurtured in individuals in the cultures selected. Any preselected set of behaviors may or may not match the developed array of behaviors (the *repertoire*) among individuals living in communities that are part of the cultures selected. There needs to be some match between the behaviors the researcher wishes to study and the behaviors actually present in the population.

Cultural Influences

With the stage set by the discussion of definitional, conceptual, and methodological issues, following is a review of selected domains of behavior in relation to culture. Since separate articles are included on gender, health, and intelligence these domains are not considered here. Instead, the focus is on six areas: human development; perception; cognition; language; values and acculturation.

Human Development. It is a truism that culture necessarily is part of the developmental process: without engagement between the human organism and its environment, there can be no development; and as noted earlier, a substantial part of the environment of any group is "manmade" (that is, it is cultural). This fundamental fact is explored, and evidence for it is provided in numerous syntheses of the field (Berry, Dasen, & Saraswathi, 1997).

Often linked to studies of development has been an interest in the process of enculturation or socialization; in what ways can culture come to influence the developing child, and shape the emerging behaviors? One basic position is that this process of cultural transmission is an integrated part of the surrounding culture, and that both are adaptive to the broader ecological context.

An early question was whether human development is a standard one, a set of changes that are the same in all children, independent of culture. An impressive set of evidence has shown that the course of human development is very much influenced by cultural factors. As a result, the question changed to *how* culture interacts with developmental processes to yield the magnificent diversity that is found around the world.

To illustrate how this second question has been approached, the concept of *developmental niche*, can be employed. This integrative framework is rooted in the views about linkages among ecology, culture, and socialization noted above. The developing child is part of an organized system that includes three interrelated components: the physical and social settings in which the child lives; the culturally regulated customs of child care and child rearing; and the psychology of the caretakers. These three components are thought to function to mediate the individual's developmental experience within the culture. They operate together, usually in consonance with one another; they are embedded in the overall ecological setting of the group; and there is *mutual* adaptation between each component and the developing child, such that the individual and group influence each other.

Of particular recent interest has been the last of these three components: parental beliefs about their children (their potentialities, goals, achievements). These have become known as "parental ethnotheories," since they are clearly rooted in other aspects of their culture. Parents' views have been revealed for virtually every domain of behavior: intelligence, emotions, social relations, morality, as well as for developmental "milestones" for each behavior.

Thus, the initial interest in whether culture played any role in human development has itself developed into a number of complex questions, about how, in respect to which behaviors, and at what periods in the developmental course of a child life.

Perception. A similar issue stimulated the first studies of perception across cultures; was it really possible that people perceive the world differently, guided by their cultures; or did everyone perceive in the same way, and with the same resultant perceptions? The classic studies were carried out by Rivers at the end of the nineteenth century in Melanesia, and covered visual acuity, color vision, and illusion susceptibility. Of these areas, subsequent work explored how the perception of illusions might be similar or different across cultures (reviewed by Segall et al., 1999).

The major study of this issue (Segall, Campbell, & Herskovits, 1966) employed a standard set of illusion stimuli distributed to colleagues in seventeen different parts of the world. They hypothesized that since perception is functional (allowing people to perceive in ways that are adaptive), individuals are likely to learn to interpret visual cues differently in different visual ecologies. To illustrate, people whose culture has produced a "carpentered environment" (one in which straight lines, right angles, and planes predominate) will learn that their visual world has a high probability of being made up of such features, and will hence "see" visual displays in terms of these probabilities. When presented with visual illusions, people continue to use these learned probabilities and to "see" the illusions in these terms. In the case of the well-known Müller-Lyer illusion (the "arrowhead" illusion, in which the lengths of two lines are to be compared) people who live in carpentered environments tend to interpret the acute and obtuse angles of the "arrowheads" as right angles, producing high susceptibility to this illusion. In contrast, those who have not lived in a carpentered environment could not have learned this interpretation, and will be less susceptible to this illusion. The finding of Segall et al. (1966) to a large extent supported their hypothesis: groups did vary across this dimension of carpenteredness, with those most susceptible being from Western urban settings.

In general, cultural influences on perception are typically found when there is some plausible theoretical link between experiences in a particular culture, and a specific perceptual phenomenon (such as illusions). However, for many basic perceptual functions (such as visual or auditory acuity) there is little evidence for variations across cultures.

Cognition. Much of the attention in the area of cognition has been focused on human abilities, especially on the notion of *intelligence*. However, there is substantial information on other abilities, and on other aspects of cognition (such as cognitive development and cognitive processes). The basic question is whether there are fundamental similarities or differences in the cognitive life of people living in different cultures.

For it is now clear that cognitive abilities, like many other behaviors, show variation across cultural groups. Such variation is usually related to what people need to do well in order to live in particular ecological and cultural circumstances. This functional view avoids the political baggage that constrains the discussion of intelligence, since there is not just one entity which can be large or small ("smart" or "stupid"), but many abilities that are organized in the service of successful daily living.

For example, spatial ability is now known to be adaptive for, and highly developed among, nomadic hunting and gathering peoples. Visual disembedding and analysis are also essential for hunting, and are similarly well developed. These abilities are patterned into a cognitive style that works well for these populations, but is not particularly useful for agriculturalists, who develop other patterns of cognitive abilities that are useful to them (such as conservation of quantity or number).

With respect to cognitive processes and development, the universalist perspective has prevailed: evidence strongly suggests that all basic cognitive processes are present in all human populations, but that during the course of development in different cultures, they are directed toward differential outcomes. For example, all research to date has shown that people everywhere engage in categorization, and can sort objects in their world into categories. But the underlying principles used, the explanations provided, and the elements placed in each category vary by culture. Similarly, memory processes are present in every culture, but the strategies used in storing and recall vary, particularly between literate and nonliterate peoples.

With nonliterate populations, a recent interest has been in their "everyday cognition" (Berry, Dasen, & Saraswathi, 1997). This development has grown from the realization that much of the world's population has not been formally schooled, and cannot read or write. Yet they carry out complex cognitive tasks needed to engage in daily communication and problem solving. How do they do such mundane activities as remembering, reasoning, and arithmetic calculations without the tools provided by schooling? Evidence clearly reveals that many are proficient at such tasks, and that they develop (and share) their own strategies. For example market children can readily count, calculate the amount owed, and make change; but when they are taken out of their daily context, and put in a formal school setting, they are much less able to do "mathematics."

Language. Intimately related to cognition is language; and as an integral part of a group's culture, language can serve as a vehicle for understanding links between culture and cognition. Since all cultures have a language, and virtually all members of a culture learn their language, we are dealing with both a cultural and a psychological universal. Moreover, most people in the world learn two or more languages, providing an opportunity to examine the psychological correlates of bilingualism or multilingualism, and in particular to dispose of the notion that there is some disadvantage or handicap associated with knowing more than one language.

Early work on language acquisition was more concerned with similarities than with differences across cultures, largely influenced by the views of Chomsky. More recent work, while accepting the existence of some underlying linguistic universals, has been concerned with variations across cultures. Since language is socialized, and (as we have seen) socialization practices vary across cultures, variation is to be expected, and indeed has been found. For example, cultural and environmental factors influence the sequence and range of vocabulary acquisition. And the "communicative style" (expressive or referential) may also be culturally linked, depending on the group's emphasis on whether social relations or environmental interactions are given the greater importance during socialization.

The knowledge and use of two (or more) languages does more than "double up" one's language activity. The cultural setting of multiple language use is also more complex than earlier believed: In some situations, growing up multilingual is normal and natural, in others it is threatening and undermines the vitality of the group; while in others, it may be a vehicle for exploring the world beyond one's borders. This psychological and situational complexity has led to a burgeoning of research with multiple-language users, attempting to understand the personal consequences.

First, with respect to cognitive outcomes, early research showed poor academic achievement of bilinguals, compared to monolinguals. However, such children were often socially disadvantage, and the studies did not control for the potential effects of immigration, status or mother tongue. More recent controlled studies have reversed this earlier picture, and it is now known that bilingualism accords an advantage in flexible thinking, creativity, and intellectual attainment. Moreover, bilinguals have superior "metalinguistic awareness," such as understanding ambiguity, and sensitivity to intonation and to rules governing language use.

Second, social consequences of bilingualism are also now well documented. Integrative attitudes (the desire to know about and participate in the other culture), and often greater social awareness and acceptance of "the other" are established consequences. Thus, far from being a handicap, bilingualism is now seen as an advantage, both cognitively and socially, when the cultural context is taken into account.

Values. Intuitively, the values that people hold are intimately linked to the dominant themes of one's culture. While values were an early interest among anthropologists, the psychological study of values in relation to national cultures really began with the work of Hofstede (1980). This area has assumed major importance, particularly the value dimension of individualism/collectivism (Berry, Segall, & Kagitcibasi, 1997), which was one of the four basic dimensions identified by Hofstede.

In his 50-nation study, Hofstede isolated (in addition to individualism/collectivism), power distance (the extent to which there is inequality or "pecking order" in social systems); uncertainty avoidance (lack of tolerance of ambiguity and need for formal rules); and masculinity (an emphasis on goal attainment and assertiveness over interpersonal relations and nurturance).

However, it is the first dimension that has dominated the study of values. It is defined as a concern for one-self as opposed to concern for the collectivity to which one belongs, as valuing "loose" social relations as opposed to more tightly knit ones. The list of meanings suggested for these two terms continues to expand, so that the value dimension is in danger of losing its core meaning, or at least losing a consensus about its meaning.

Paralleling this expansion in meaning is a widening network of factors, both cultural and psychological, that are empirically related to an individual's and country's position on the individualism-collectivism dimension. At the individual level, many psychological attributes of individualism are claimed: emotional detachment from one's ingroup, the primacy of personal goals, use of confrontation, self-reliance, independence, and experience of loneliness. For collectivism attributes claimed are acceptance of hierarchy and search for harmony in one's ingroup, acceptance that one's behavior should be regulated by ingroup norms, self is defined in terms of the group, acceptance of obedience and duty, sacrifice for one's ingroup, and need for social support and interdependence. Skepticism and criticism about how one dimension can cover so much psychological territory has appeared recently, even while more and more research is carried out, almost as a fashionable wave.

At the cultural or national level, individualism/collectivism is claimed to be related to economic development, social complexity and stratification, population density, cultural homogeneity, little occupational role differentiation, and so on. It is apparent that there is no end to this list.

Acculturation

Perhaps the most active area of research in the filed is the study of how individuals and groups relate to study of how individuals and groups relate to each other following contact, and their long term mutual accommodations. As noted previously, the cultures of the two groups involved can influence the psychological adaptations made.

With respect to the larger or dominant society, the national policies, and expectations by the general population, can lead the members of the non dominant group to adapt in various ways: societies that encourage *assimilation* may induce nondominant groups to change their behaviors (language, dress) and their identities in order to merge with the dominant society. However, reaction to such pressures toward cultural loss may lead to behaviors that seek *separation*, in which cultural maintenance away from the dominant society is the main strategy. In contrast, a national policy of *segregation* may lead to ghettoization, and when com-

bined with cultural loss, to *marginalization*. In this latter case, many social and psychological problems are frequently observed. A generally preferred option is that of *integration* in which members of the nondominant group seek to maintain important features of their culture and identity, while participating fully in the larger society; this option obviously requires the dominant group to accept the right of others to live in culturally diverse ways, and not to discriminate against them because of it. [*See* Marginalization.]

Not only are there variations in these strategies across dominant and nondominant groups in contact, there are also large individual differences in these acculturation strategies. These occur within groups, within communities and even within families, often creating a source of conflict. Moreover, individuals are known to explore how they prefer to relate to members of their own and other groups, leading to the dynamic, culture-creating dimension noted earlier.

Conclusions

It is no longer possible to think of behavior as "culture free"; there is now substantial evidence that the culture of a group and the behavior of its members are intimately entwined. The sampling of theoretical, methodological, and empirical evidence for this claim that has been provided in this article should dismiss once and for all the view that individuals are independent of culture, or that psychology can remain acultural.

Bibliography

Berry, J. W., Dasen, P. R., & Saraswathi, T. S. (Eds.). (1997). *Handbook of cross-cultural psychology: Vol. 2. Basic processes and human development.* Boston: Allyn & Bacon.

Berry, J. W., Poortinga, Y. H., & Pandey, J. (Eds.). (1997). *Handbook of cross-cultural psychology: Vol. 1. Theory and method.* Boston: Allyn & Bacon.

Berry, J. W., Poortinga, Y. H., Segall, M. H., & Dasen, P. R. (1990). *Cross-cultural psychology: Research and applications.* New York: Cambridge University Press.

Berry, J. W., Segall, M. H., & Kagicibasi, C. (Eds.). (1997). *Handbook of cross-cultural psychology: Vol. 3. Social behavior and applications.* Boston: Allyn & Bacon.

Boesch, E. (1991). *Symbolic action theory in cultural psychology.* Berlin: Springer.

Camilleri, C., & Visonneau, G. (1996). *Psychologie et culture: Concepts et méthodes.* Paris: Armand Colin.

Cole, M. (1996). *Cultural psychology: A once and future discipline.* Cambridge, MA: Harvard University Press.

Goldberger, N., & Veroff, J. (Eds.). (1995). *The culture and psychology reader.* New York: New York University Press.

Hofstede, G. (1980). *Culture's consequences.* Beverly Hills, CA: Sage.

Jahoda, G. (1992). *Crossroads between culture and mind.* London: Harvester Wheatsheaf.

Lonner, W. J. (1990). The introductory psychology text and

cross-cultural psychology. In D. Keats, D. Munro, & L. Mann (Eds.), *Heterogeneity in cross-cultural psychology* (pp. 4–22). Liss, UK: Swets & Zeitlinger.

Poortinga, Y. H. (1997). Towards convergence? In J. W. Berry, Y. H. Poortinga, & J. Pandey (Eds.), *Handbook of cross-cultural psychology: Vol. 1. Theory and method*. Boston: Allyn & Bacon.

Segall, M. H., Campbell, D. T., & Herskovits, M. J. (1966). *The influence of culture visual perception*. Indianapolis: Bobbs-Merrill.

Segall, M. H., Dasen, P. R., Berry, J. W., & Poortinga, Y. H. (1999). *Human behavior in global perspective* (3rd ed). Boston: Allyn & Bacon.

Shweder, R., & Sullivan, M. (1993). Cultural psychology: Who needs it? *Annual Review of Psychology, 44,* 497–523.

Triandis, H. C. (Ed.). (1980). *Handbook of cross-cultural psychology* (Vols. 1–6). Boston: Allyn & Bacon.

Westin, D. (1996). *Psychology: Mind, brain, and culture*. New York: Wiley.

John W. Berry

Culture and Mental Health

The study of culture and psychopathology is concerned with understanding the relationships of cultural factors to the etiology, assessment, diagnosis, classification, and treatment of psychopathology. Interest in the study of cultural variables is relatively new although the importance of examining and comparing psychopathology across cultures was first acknowledged in 1904 by the father of modern psychiatry, Emil Kraepelin. During the course of a world tour introducing his new psychiatric classification system which distinguished between dementia praecox and the manic-depression psychosis, Kraepelin reported difficulties diagnosing cases among Southeast Asian people and various American Indian tribes. This led him to propose the study of *Vergleichende Psychiatrie* (comparative psychiatry). He wrote:

> The characteristics of a people should find expression in the frequency as well as in the shaping of the manifestations of mental illness in general; so that comparative psychiatry shall make it possible to gain valuable insights into the psyche of nations and shall in turn also be able to contribute to the understanding of pathological psychic processes. (Kraepelin, 1904, p. 9)

Today, numerous subdisciplinary specialities are concerned with cultural aspects of psychopathology (e.g., psychiatric anthropology, transcultural psychiatry, culture and mental health, cultural psychiatry). I have traced the history of the field from its modern roots in the mid-eighteenth century to contemporary times (Marsella, 1993).

The Growing Popularity of Culture and Psychopathology

I have pointed out that ethnocentric and cultural bias in psychiatry and related mental health sciences and professions was fostered, in part, by twentieth-century beliefs that considered non-Western values and lifestyles as inferior, primitive, and unimportant, while Western science and knowledge were considered to be universally valid. However, in the last few decades, this viewpoint changed in response to social, political, and professional dynamics including

1. more international collaborative and comparative studies (e.g., the World Health Organization *Pilot Study of Schizophrenia*) that demonstrated ethnocultural variations in psychopathology;
2. increases in the number of ethnic minority and non-Western psychiatrists and related mental health scientists and professionals;
3. disaffection of ethnic minority and non-Western psychiatrists and related mental health professionals with the ethnocentrism and cultural and racial bias of Western psychiatry;
4. increases in political and social awareness of the pathological sequalae of racism, sexism, imperialism, colonialism, and other "isms" producing powerlessness, marginalization, and underprivileging among sizable population sectors;
5. awareness of the multiple and interactive determinants of psychopathology (e.g., biological, psychological, cultural, sociological, spiritual, environmental); and
6. proliferation of scientific and professional communication networks and outlets promoting interest in the topic through societies (e.g., World Federation of Mental Health; Society for the Study of Psychiatry and Culture; World Association for Social Psychiatry), and professional-scientific journals (e.g., *Transcultural Psychiatry; Culture, Medicine, and Psychiatry; Culture and Mental Health*).

These changes have generated a number of critical questions: Should ethnic and racial minorities and non-Western people be evaluated according to Western (i.e., White, Anglo-Saxon, Protestant, male) standards of normality and abnormality? Should they be tested with culturally insensitive and ideologically based instruments, such as the Minnesota Multiphasic Personality Inventory (MMPI), or the Wechsler Adult Intelligence Scale (WAIS)? Should they be diagnosed according to culturally insensitive and ideologically based classification systems, such as the *Diagnostic and Statistical Manual of Mental Disorders (DSM)* or the *International Classification of Diseases (ICD)*? Should they be treated with culturally insensitive and ideologically based therapies (e.g., psychoanalysis, cognitive behavior therapy, client-centered therapy)? Should they be treated with psychopharmacological medications that may have a multiplicity of effects, dynamics, and consequences across cultures as Lin, Poland, and Nakasaki (1993) reported in *Psychopharmacology and Psychobiology of Ethnicity*? These questions have increased the popularity of culture and psychopathology as a subdisciplinary specialty.

Critical Concepts and Issues

Ethnocentrism and the cultural construction of reality are key issues.

Ethnocentrism. The fundamental assumption underlying the study of culture and psychopathology is ethnocentrism and cultural bias. The term *ethnocentrism* refers to the "natural tendency or inclination" among people everywhere to view reality from their own cultural experience and perspective. In the course of doing so, the traditions, behaviors, and practices of people from other cultures are often considered inferior, strange, abnormal, and/or deviant. Obviously, when a decision must be made regarding a person's sanity and treatment, ethnocentrism can have destructive consequences.

Most of our basic conceptual, methodological, and professional assumptions and practices regarding mental health are derived and validated within the historical and cultural contexts of northern European and North American societies. As such, they are ethnocentric and culturally biased. They are rooted within ideological worldviews that favor individualistic, materialistic, democratic, and scientific perspectives. As a result, the essential concepts of personhood, normality and abnormality, illness and health, consciousness, and personal choice and responsibility that guide Western psychological and psychiatric thought and practice bear little relevance and/or applicability to people from non-Western cultures and traditions.

This fact has been well known for many years but has only recently become a major concern for both Western and non-Western people. For example, a quarter century ago, Clifford Geertz, an American cultural anthropologist, wrote (*The Interpretation of Culture*, New York, 1973):

The Western conception of the person as a bounded, unique, more or less integrated motivational and cognitive universe, a dynamic center of awareness, emotion, judgment, and action, organized into a distinctive whole and set contrastively—both against other such wholes and against social and natural background—is, however incorrigible it may seem to us, a rather peculiar idea within the context of the world's cultures. (p. 34)

More recently, Ajita Chakraborty (*Lancet*, 19, *337*), an Indian psychiatrist, wrote:

Even where studies were sensitive, and the aim was to show relative differences caused by culture, the ideas and tools were still derived from a circumscribed area of European thought. . . . Research is constrained by this view of psychiatry. . . . Psychiatrists in the developing world . . . have accepted a diagnostic framework developed by western medicine, but which does not seem to take into account the diversity of behavioral patterns they encounter. (p. 1204)

Cultural Construction of Reality. But, most important, Western psychiatrists and mental health scientists and professionals are beginning to accept the view that culture constitutes the context in which our different worldviews are shaped and differentiated (i.e., the cultural construction of reality). I noted (1982) that since our realities are culturally constructed, how can we expect universality in psychopathology? I wrote:

We cannot separate our experience of an event from our sensory and linguistic mediation of it. If these differ, so must the experience differ across cultures. If we define who we are in different ways (i.e., self as object), if we process reality in different ways (i.e., self as process), if we define the very nature of what is real, and what is acceptable, and even what is right and wrong, how can we then expect similarities in something as complex as madness. (p. 363)

This new awareness of the importance of culture helped encourage the American Psychiatric Association to include an entire section on culture-specific disorders in the fourth edition of the *Diagnostic and Statistical Manual of Mental Disorders* (*DSM–IV*; American Psychiatric Association, 1994). Indeed, some psychiatrists are now proposing a new diagnostic axis for ethnocultural factors for the fifth edition of the *DSM*. [*See* Culture-Bound Disorders.]

Key Questions in the Study of Culture and Psychopathology

The study of culture and psychopathology is concerned with the following key questions:

1. What is the role of cultural variables in the etiology of psychopathology? How do cultural variables interact with biological, psychological, and environmental variables to influence psychopathology?
2. What are the cultural variations in standards of normality and abnormality?
3. What are the cultural variations in the classification and diagnosis of psychopathology?
4. What are the cultural variations in the rates and distribution of psychopathology according to both indigenous and Western categories of psychopathology?
5. What are the cultural variations in the phenomenological experience, manifestation, course, and outcome of psychopathology?
6. Are all psychiatric disorders culture bound?

Some Critical Issues and Research Findings

The roles of biology and culture in psychopathology, cultural concepts of illness, equivalence in clinical assessment, and epidemiology are the main areas under discussion.

Biology and Culture in Psychopathology. The greatest ethnocultural variation is in normal behavior because this is where learning and acquired experience exercise their greatest influence. As we begin to enter the realm of severe psychopathology and biological factors also come to play an influential role, the ethnocultural variation will diminish but will still not be absent. Thus, normal behavior, though obviously a function of biological substrates, has the widest latitude of variability across cultures. As the nervous system becomes more directly implicated, as is the case in neurological diseases, cultural variability decreases. However, even in the most severe neurological diseases or disorders, cultural influences still occur since the individual's interpretation and experience of the disorder, its behavioral referents, and the social response to these referents is influenced by culture.

Concepts of Illness and Disease. In a survey of concepts of health and illness across cultures, Murdock (1980) identified Western and non-Western views of disease causality. He reported that Western scientific views were based on naturalistic views of disease causation including infection, stress, organic deterioration, accidents, and acts of overt human aggression. In contrast, many non-Western societies believe in disease causation models based on supernatural causes (i.e., any disease which accounts for impairment of health as a consequence of some intangible force) including (1) theories of mystical causation because of impersonal forces such as fate, ominous sensations, contagion, mystical retribution; (2) theories of animistic causation because of personalized forces such as soul loss and spirit aggression; and (3) theories of magical causation or actions of evil forces including sorcery and witchcraft. Although a patient's conception of the causes of their disorder is critical for treatment because it implicates cooperation and treatment compliance, non-Western notions of disease causality are seldom used by professionals.

Equivalence in Clinical Assessment. If cross-cultural studies are to be valid, there must be linguistic, conceptual, scale, and normative equivalency of the instruments. This means the instruments will not be biased against certain populations because of their cultural differences. Clearly, the use of Western diagnostic instruments and clinical assessment methods (e.g., interviews) in which the language, content, scales, norms, and expectations are based on Western culture constitutes a serious validity problem for both research and clinical practice.

Epidemiology. The distribution of disorders is referred to as epidemiology. Typically, the emphasis is on identifying the number of people who have a particular disorder at a specific point (i.e., prevalence) and/or the number of people who are likely to develop a disorder in a given time period (i.e., incidence). Cross-cultural psychiatric epidemiological studies have been reviewed for many disorders including posttraumatic stress disorder (PTSD) (e.g., DeGirolamo & MacFarlane, 1996), depression and anxiety disorders (e.g., Kleinman & Good, 1986), and schizophrenia (e.g., Marsella et al., in press). However, major problems in case definition and identification, cultural bias in diagnosis and classification, and lack of familiarity with the population make it difficult to compare findings. Future cross-cultural epidemiological studies should (1) use relevant ethnographic and anthropological data in designing a study, especially in determining what constitutes a symptom or category; (2) develop glossaries of terms and definitions for symptoms and categories; (3) derive symptom patterns and clusters using multivariate techniques rather than relying on a priori clinical categories; (4) use similar or comparable case identification and validation methods; (5) use culturally appropriate measurement methods which include a broad range of indigenous symptoms and signs that can be reliably assessed; and (6) establish frequency, severity, and duration baselines for indigenous and medical symptoms in both normal and pathological populations.

Research Strategies for Studying Culture and Symptomatology Relationships

One of the most important research areas in culture and psychopathology is the study of symptomatology differences across cultures. I recommended a variety of research strategies for this task (Marsella, 1982) including (1) matched diagnosis studies (i.e., comparing patients from different cultures with similar diagnoses); (2) matched sample studies (i.e., comparing patients from different cultures who are similar in age, social class, religion, etc.); (3) international surveys (i.e., profiling symptoms across large samples from many different countries); (4) culture-bound disorder studies (i.e., investigating culture-bound patterns of disorder such as *latah, koro, susto, mali-mali, shinkeishitsu, amok*); and (5) multivariate studies (i.e., generating symptom clusters based on statistical analyses rather than clinical perceptions and experiences).

Regardless of the research strategies that have been used to study the expression of psychiatric disorders across cultures, results have consistently indicated variations in the experience, manifestation, and prognosis of psychiatric disorders across cultures.

Ethnocultural Parameters of Psychopathology

Research findings have revealed that there are ethnocultural variations across many parameters of psychopathology including perceptions of the causes, nature, onset patterns, symptom expression, disability levels, idioms of distress, course, and outcome. This has been true for even the most severe forms of psychopathology including depressive disorders (e.g., Kleinman & Good, 1986), PTSD (e.g., Marsella, Friedman, Gerrity, & Scurfield, 1996), and schizophrenic disorders (e.g., Marsella et al., in press).

Depressive Disorders. Ethnocultural variations in basic symptom patterns of depressive disorders are evident, including a relative absence of guilt, suicidal tendencies, withdrawal, and negative self-image. Although extreme sadness and grief are present in non-Western cultures, the situations that elicit them, their perceived meaning and implications, their expressions, and the social response to them often varies. Sometimes the distress is expressed in somatic symptoms rather than existential and/or cognitive-symbolic complaints since the latter modes of expression may be alien to non-Western experience.

Schizophrenia. In the case of schizophrenic disorders, often considered to be the most universal of the psychoses in expression and clinical parameters, research conducted by the World Health Organization (WHO); Jablensky et al., 1992) reports some similarities in core symptoms, but also considerable variations in secondary symptoms, the course and outcome of the disorders, and the rates of the disorders. Marsella et al. (in press) identified a number of ethnocultural determinants of schizophrenic disorders. [*See* Schizophrenia.]

Posttraumatic Stress Disorder (PTSD). In a review of the cross-cultural studies on PTSD, Marsella, Friedman, Gerrity, and Scurfield (1996) concluded that while there appears to be a universal biological response to extreme stressors and traumas (e.g., arousal of the hypothalamic-pituitary adrenal axis with associated biological and psychological changes) and elicitation of the general adaptation syndrome (GAS; i.e., arousal, resistance, and exhaustion), there are considerable cultural variations in the perceptions of a traumatic event and in the expressions and experience of the disorder.

PTSD can be diagnosed across cultures, but only if considerable care is taken to contextualize the problem within the cultural milieu of the patient. One reason for this is that many ethnic minority and non-Western people have been exposed to multiple traumas as a result of daily life problems (e.g., poverty, exposure to crime, violence, natural disasters) and collective group traumas (e.g., wars). These problems are often exacerbated because of the absence of mental health services. It has been suggested that the term *complex PTSD* may be a more appropriate diagnostic term across cultures because of its inclusion of multiple traumas and dissociative and somatization symptoms.

Cultures as Causative of Psychiatric Disorders

It is important to recognize that cultural factors may play an important role in causing psychiatric disorders.

This can occur via a number of mechanisms including the following:

1. *Stress.* Culture can be a source of stress by confronting individuals and/or groups with environmental demands that exceed their ability to cope. A typical example of this is the rapid social change that characterizes contemporary life and the serious problems associated with urbanization and urban lifestyles. Other culture-related stressors include institutional racism, cultural disintegration, cultural dislocation, cultural abuse, and industrial developments that introduce toxins and environmental pollution. The massive social changes accompanying technical and industrial development can be both sources of stress and sources of positive change (Desjarlais, Eisenberg, Good, & Kleinman, 1995).

2. *Normality and Abnormality.* Culture determines the standards for normality and abnormality. Problems in defining the limits in these areas can lead to serious problems regarding deviancy and conformity. The main issue here is the balance between tolerance and suppression. There can be no doubt that certain cultures insist on absolute conformity while others permit acceptable levels of deviancy. One of the continuing challenges facing the study of culture and psychopathology is the identification of "universal" normal and abnormal behaviors, as well as culture-specific normal and abnormal behaviors (Ackerknecht, 1942).

3. *Coping and Resources.* Culture determines rates of certain disorders such as depressive dysfunctions by posing certain stressors and limiting certain supportive mechanisms. For example, politically repressive cultures may limit individual or group choice and may punish certain behaviors resulting in learned helplessness. Further, certain cultures may have few or ineffective coping resources to mediate stress (e.g., religious beliefs, social support networks, personal predispositions).

The causal relationships between culture and psychopathology are far more complex than can be discussed in the present entry. However, the prior examples help demonstrate the many impacts that culture can have upon mental disorders by virtue of the stressors it fosters, the resources it offers, and the particular concepts of personhood, normality, and social process it socializes.

Bibliography

Ackerknecht, E. (1942). Psychopathology, primitive medicine, and primitive culture. *Bulletin of the History of Medicine, 14,* 30–67. An early paper calling attention to cultural relativity of normality and abnormality. Suggested empirical efforts be launched to identify pannormal and panabnormal and heteronormal and heteropathological problems.

American Psychiatric Association (1994). *Diagnostic and statistical manual of mental disorders* (4th ed.). Washington, DC: Author. Official diagnostic and classification system of the American Psychiatric Association. Reflects Western biomedical ideology and assumptions about the nature and patterning of mental disorders. Numerous validity problems because of inconsistent nosological principles and ethnocentric biases.

Comas-Diaz, L., & Griffith, E. (Eds.). (1988). *Clinical guidelines in cross-cultural mental health*. New York: Wiley Interscience. Popular textbook for the study of culture and mental health with specific chapters devoted to different ethnic minority groups and to various issues. Dated but still a valuable introduction to the research and clinical literature.

DeGirolamo, G., & MacFarlane, A. (1996). The epidemiology of PTSD: An international review. In A. J. Marsella, M. Friedman, E. Gerrity, & R. Scurfield (Eds.), *Ethnocultural aspects of PTSD: Issues, directions, and clinical applications* (pp. 33–86). Washington, DC: American Psychological Association Press. Most thorough and exhaustive international coverage of epidemiological studies of PTSD, with special attention paid to methods and prevalence rates.

Desjarlais, R., Eisenberg, L., Good, B., & Kleinman, A. (1995). *World mental health: Problems and priorities in low-income countries*. New York: Oxford University Press. Reviews current knowledge on the relationship between poverty and mental health in developing countries. Examines the sources of the high rates of mental disorders and makes suggestions for intervention and prevention programs.

Jablensky, A., Sartorius, N., Emberg, G., Anker, M., Korten, A., Cooper, J., Day, R, & Bertelsen, A. (1992). Schizophrenia: manifestations, incidence, and course in different cultures: A WHO ten-country study. *Psychological Medicine, 20* (Suppl.), 1–97. Reports results of the World Health Organization twelve-country study on the determinants of outcome of severe mental disorders including schizophrenia. Findings indicate international variations in rates and patterns of schizophrenia and psychosis.

Kleinman, A., & Good, B. (Eds.). (1986). *Culture and depression.* Berkeley: University of California Press. Considered the best single resource on cross-cultural studies of depression. Raises serious questions about the cultural biases accompanying Western research and clinical efforts. Chapters cover studies of depression among numerous ethnocultural groups.

Kraepelin, E. (1904). Vergleichende psychiatrie. [Comparative psychiatry]. *Centralblatt für Nervenherlkande und Psychiatrie, 15,* 433–437. Important historical publication that documents Kraepelin's difficulties in diagnosing non-Western people (i.e., Southeast Asians, American Indians) according to his classification system (i.e., dementia praecox, manic depression) and his suggestion that a field of comparative psychiatry be established.

Lin, K., Poland, R., & Nakasaki, G. (1993). *Psychopharmacology and psychobiology of ethnicity*. Washington, DC: American Psychiatric Press. Pioneering effort describing ethnocultural and racial variations in response of psychopharmacological medications including differences in dosage level responses, circulating plasma levels, side effects, and therapeutic effects.

Marsella, A. J. (1982). Culture and mental health. In A. J. Marsella & G. White (Eds.), *Cultural conceptions of mental health and therapy*. Boston: Reidel Press. Early overview of cross-cultural psychiatry studies. Thorough discussion of research findings and issues with excellent bibliography. Calls attention to cultural bias in psychiatry and psychology.

Marsella, A. J. (1993). Sociocultural foundations of psychopathology: A pre-1970 historical overview. *Transcultural Psychiatric Research Review, 30,* 90–142. Detailed review and discussion of the historical roots of culture and psychopathology studies from the seventeenth century to 1970. Key personalities, studies, and events are noted.

Marsella, A. J., Friedman, M., Gerrity, E., & Scurfield, R. (Eds.). (1996). *Ethnocultural aspects of PTSD: Issues, research, and clinical applications*. Washington, DC: American Psychological Association Press. Considered most thorough and comprehensive review of ethnocultural aspects of PTSD. Chapters address basic issues, rates, and patterns of PTSD among different ethnic groups and special populations.

Marsella, A. J., & Kameoka, V. (1989). Ethnocultural issues in the assessment of psychopathology. In S. Wetzler (Ed.), *Measuring mental illness: Psychometric assessment for clinicians* (pp. 229–256). Washington, DC: American Psychiatric Press. Concise discussion of major issues associated with the assessment of psychopathology across cultures. Addresses emic-etic, ethnic identity, and measurement equivalence problems (i.e., linguistic, conceptual, normative, and scale equivalence). Raises serious problems about cultural bias in application of Western instruments to non-Western and minority populations.

Marsella, A. J., Suarez, E., Leland, T., Morse, H., Scheuer, A., & Digman, B. (in press). Cross-cultural studies of schizophrenia: Issues, research, and directions. *British Journal of Psychiatry.* Comprehensive review of cross-cultural studies of the epidemiology, etiology, expression, and course-outcome of schizophrenic disorders across cultures. Raises serious questions about the validity and applicability of Western concepts and methods to non-Western and ethnic minority populations. Includes more than 160 references.

Murdock, R. (1980). *Theories of illness: A world survey*. Pittsburgh: University of Pittsburgh Press. Considered classic text in medical anthropology. Discusses different theories of illness found among more than 170 ethnic groups based on data from the Human Relations Area Files (i.e., notes from most anthropological field studies and ethnographies).

Anthony J. Marsella

Culture and Development

Human development takes place in the interaction of a child and the culture in which he or she matures. Culture can be conceived of as knowledge, skills, practices, and values that are created and shared by groups of people. Processes of development and processes of culture are inextricably intertwined. An important aspect of psychological development is the acquisition of cultural knowledge, which children are exposed to from birth. Children actively acquire cultural knowledge from the cultural surroundings. There are important methodological and theoretical issues to be considered in any discussion of culture and human development.

Methodological Approaches

In the study of culture and human development, there are two different methodological lines of inquiry: cross-cultural and cultural (e.g., Shweder, 1990). Each methodological approach is associated with a way of thinking about culture. In cross-cultural research, culture is most often thought of as a group label (e.g., Chinese, African American). Applied developmentally, cross-cultural methodology leads to comparisons of behavior at different ages across different cultural groups.

In cultural methodology culture is, by contrast, most often thought of as a psychological process. Culture is part and parcel of the individual psyche (Shweder, 1990). Human development is an important part of cultural psychology (Cole, 1996): human beings are seen as creatures who acquire culture through learning and apprenticeship. Cultural learning occurs by means of language, modeling, and participation in cultural activities.

A distinguishing feature of cross-cultural psychology is that an experimental procedure or test that has been developed in one culture can be carried, with translation and other minor modifications, to another culture, to make cross-cultural comparisons (Berry, Poortinga, Segall, & Dasen, 1992). Classical examples in the study of cognitive development revolve around testing the universality of Swiss psychologist Jean Piaget's theory of cognitive development (Dasen, 1977).

In contrast, the methodological ideal of the cultural psychologist is to derive procedures for each culture to be studied by observing the practices and modes of communication in that culture. Whereas cross-cultural psychology tends to derive its problems and procedures from established psychological research paradigms, cultural psychology derives its problems and procedures from a unique analysis of each individual culture. Methodologically, cultural psychology represents an integration of methods from psychology and anthropology.

Conceptual Approaches

Major conceptual approaches to culture and development emphasize social interaction, cultural practices, symbolic tools, ecological adaptation, cultural values, and intergroup influences on development. The first three are key concepts in the sociohistorical tradition, to be discussed first.

Sociohistorical Tradition. The sociohistorical research tradition in developmental psychology is derived from the work of the Russian psychologist Vygotsky (e.g., 1962). It emphasizes that human development is constructed through social interaction, cultural practices, and the internalization of symbolic cultural tools. An example of a cultural tool that is internalized is money; each culture's system of currency influences the development of certain mental strategies for doing mathematics (Saxe, 1991). Cultural practices and tools are developed over long periods of time; they therefore have an important historical dimension.

Researchers in the sociohistorical tradition have studied parent-child interaction, sibling, and other kinds of peer interaction, and teacher-child interaction (e.g., Tobin, Wu, & Davidson, 1989; Zukow, 1989). Social interaction influences both cognitive development and social development.

Cultural practices involve everyday experiences and education, both informal and formal. Practices such as candy selling (Saxe, 1991) are linked to cognitive development. A review of the everyday practices approach is found in Schliemann, Carraher, and Ceci (1997).

Ecocultural Approach. This approach emphasizes adaptation to the environment and derives from the work of John and Beatrice Whiting, U.S. psychological anthropologists. The Whitings (Whiting & Edwards, 1988) used a cross-cultural approach to study how behavior is influenced by societal characteristics such as urbanization and social complexity. Weisner (1984) has developed a theory in the Whiting tradition which considers how aspects of the ecocultural environment such as subsistence patterns, assigned roles for men, women, and children, and child-rearing practices affect behavior.

Ethnotheories of Development: Individualism and Collectivism. Systems of developmental goals and values which guide child rearing and socialization for particular parents or groups of parents are called parental ethnotheories of development (Harkness & Super, 1996). This approach focuses on cultural models, emphasizing how a diversity of child-rearing goals and values influence familial child-rearing practices and the resulting trajectory of development. Two particularly important models, derived from social psychology, are individualism and collectivism (Triandis, 1988), also known as independence and interdependence (Markus & Kitayama, 1991). These alternative cultural frameworks are particularly basic and generative; they constitute unspoken assumptions that guide socialization practices and child behavior in a myriad of specific domains and situations (Greenfield & Suzuki, 1998). In individualism, the preferred endpoint of development is independence (Greenfield & Cocking, 1994). The primary goal of socialization in this model is an autonomous, self-fulfilled individual. In collectivism, the preferred endpoint of development is interdependence (Greenfield & Cocking, 1994). The primary goal of socialization in this model is for the mature person to be embedded in a network of relationships and responsibilities to others; personal achievements are ideally in the service of a collectivity, most importantly the family. With these cultural goals in mind, many researchers have examined the influence of individualistic and collectivistic goals on parenting styles and child development.

Intergroup Contact. Intergroup contact is a major source of diverse developmental pathways in multicultural societies such as the United States, Canada, and Australia. Often the emphasis in this approach is on racially distinctive ethnic groups. (The developmental pathway of the dominant majority tends to be taken for granted as normative, rather than as cultural.) Intergroup contact raises ethnic identity to the forefront of developmental issues (Phinney, 1996) and produces more complex processes of cultural learning such as bilingual and bicultural development.

One source of diverse developmental pathways are the specific values that ethnic groups maintain from their ancestral cultures. The notion is that the distinctive patterns of socialization and development manifest in various groups in the United States and other multicultural societies derive to a great extent from ancestral values. Ethnic groups are compared with groups in their ancestral homelands, not merely with groups in the host society (Greenfield & Cocking, 1994).

The theory and research of Ogbu (1978) on minority status emphasizes intergroup contact and identity issues. Ogbu, an anthropologist who grew up in Nigeria focuses on the importance of the history and power relations between minority and majority groups within a given society. He identifies two major classifications of minority groups: involuntary and voluntary. Involuntary minorities become incorporated into a nation through conquest, slavery, or colonization. They define themselves and their culture in opposition to the values of the majority and thus feel that they cannot adopt any of the majority's ways without losing their own. Voluntary minorities become incorporated into a nation through voluntary immigration. They maintain their preexisting cultural values and view positively institutions such as schools as places where they can be helped to improve their opportunities for success in their new country. In terms of development, this theoretical distinction has been used mainly to understand differing patterns of school achievement.

Conclusion

Development is universally influenced by symbols, tools, values, and complex social relations. These are universally present, yet vary in their form from culture to culture. Cultural differences arise from adaptations to diverse ecological niches and sociohistorical traditions. The two main approaches to the study of the psychological interaction of culture and development are cross-cultural and cultural psychology. Cross-cultural psychology puts the emphasis on universal dimensions of culture; it treats culture as something in the environment. Cultural psychology, in contrast, focuses on local values and ecocultural factors in development such as people's use of tools, their minority or majority status, and cultural history; it treats culture as something inside the individual. The role of culture in behavior is pervasive and should be carefully considered in any examination of human development.

Bibliography

Berry, J. W., Poortinga, Y. H., Segall, M. H., & Dasen, P. R. (1992). *Cross-cultural psychology*. Cambridge, UK: Cambridge University Press.

Dasen, P. (1977). *Piagetian psychology: Cross-cultural contributions*. New York: Gardner Press.

Greenfield, P. M., & Cocking, R. R. (1994). *Cross cultural roots of minority child development*. Hillsdale, NJ: Erlbaum.

Greenfield, P. M., & Suzuki, L. K. (1998). Culture and human development: Implications for parenting, education, pediatrics, and mental health. In W. Damon (Series Ed.) and I. E. Siegel & K. A. Renninger (Volume Eds.), *Handbook of child psychology: Vol. 4. Child psychology in practice* (5th ed., pp. 1059–1109). New York: Wiley.

Harkness, S., & Super, C. M. (1996). *Parents' cultural belief systems: Their origins, expression, and consequences*. London, England: Guilford Press.

Markus, H. R., & Kitayama, S. (1991). Culture and the self: Implications for cognition, emotion, and motivation. *Psychological Review, 98*, 224–253.

Ogbu, J. U. (1978). *Minority education and caste*. New York: Academic Press.

Phinney, J. S. (1996). Understanding ethnic diversity; The role of ethnic identity. *American Behavioral Scientist, 40*, 143–152.

Schliemann, A., Carraher, D., & Ceci, S. J. (1997). Everyday cognition. In J. W. Berry, P. R. Dasen, & R. S. Saraswath (Eds.), *Handbook of cross-cultural Psychology: Vol. 2: Basic processes and human development* (2nd ed., pp. 177–216). Needham Heights, MA: Allyn & Bacon.

Shweder, R. A. (1990). Cultural psychology: What is it? In J. W. Stigler, R. A. Shweder, & G. Herdt (Eds.), *Cultural psychology: Essays on comparative human development* (pp. 1–46). Cambridge, UK: Cambridge University Press.

Tobin, J., Wu, D., & Davidson, D. (1989). *Preschool in three cultures: Japan, China, and the United States*. New Haven, CT: Yale University Press.

Triandis, H. C. (1988). Collectivism vs. individualism: A reconceptualization of a basic concept in cross-cultural social psychology. In C. Bargley & G. K. Verma (Eds.), *Personality, cognition, and values: Cross-cultural perspectives of childhood and adolescence.* London: Macmillan.

Vygotsky, L. S. (1962). *Thought and language.* Cambridge, MA: MIT Press.

Weisner, T. S. (1984). Ecocultural niches of middle childhood: A cross-cultural perspective. In W. A. Collins (Ed.), *Development during middle childhood. The years from 6 to 12.* Washington, DC: National Academy Press.

Whiting, B. B., & Edwards, C. P. (1988). *Children of different worlds: The formations of social behavior.* Cambridge, MA: Harvard University Press.

Zukow, P. G. (1989). *Sibling interactions across cultures: Theoretical and methodological issues.* New York: Springer-Verlag.

Patricia M. Greenfield, Ashley E. Maynard,
and Lalita K. Suzuki

CULTURE-BOUND DISORDERS. Psychological disorders considered specific to particular ethnocultural groups because of distinct cultural factors influencing the etiology, meaning, expression, and/or treatment of the disorder are referred to as culture-bound activities. The term is used in contrast to those psychological disorders considered to be "universal." In its *Diagnostic and Statistical Manual of Mental Disorders (DSM–IV)*, the American Psychiatric Association (1994) states:

> Culture-bound syndromes are generally limited to specific societies or culture areas and are localized, folk, diagnostic categories that frame coherent meanings for certain repetitive, patterned, and troubling sets of experiences and observations. There is seldom a one-to-one equivalence of any culture-bound syndrome with a DSM diagnostic entity. (p. 844)

Types of Culture-Bound Disorders

The most thorough discussion and listing of culture-bound disorders can be found in Simon and Hughes (1986). In *DSM–IV*, the American Psychiatric Association (1994) describes a number of known culture-bound disorders. Table 1 lists some of the well-known culture-bound disorders with their associated locations and risk populations.

A number of researchers proposed subclassification systems for the culture-bound disorders based on common behavioral and psychological expressions. For example, Ari Kiev (1964) suggested they could be classified as anxiety states (e.g., *koro, susto*) phobic states (e.g., *mal ojo, voodoo* death), depressive disorders (e.g., *hiwa itchk*), hysterical disorders (e.g., *latah*). Simons and Hughes (1986) classified the culture-bound syndromes according to different taxons (i.e., taxonomy categories): startle-matching taxon (e.g., *latah, imu*), sleep paralysis taxons (e.g., *uqamairineq*), genital retraction taxon (e.g., *koro*), sudden mass assault taxon (e.g., *amok, cathard, negi-negi*), running taxon (e.g., *pibloktoq*), fright illness taxon (e.g., *susto, saladera*), cannibal compulsion (e.g., *windigo*).

Kiev (1964) and Simons and Hughes (1986) acknowledge the distinct cultural influences shaping each disorder; however, they also wanted to provide generalizable taxonomical principles by which the disorders could be reconstructed within Western conceptual models of psychological disorders. Thus, for them, *koro* can be considered an anxiety disorder, *latah* could be considered a hysterical disorder. Although this approach is viable (i.e., proceeding from emic to etic categories), many researchers now believe there is no one-to-one equivalence of culture-bound disorders to the Western psychiatric disorders represented in *DSM–IV* and the *International Classification of Diseases* (ICD–10). This has become a major issue in psychiatry because it raises questions about the universality of Western psychiatric disorders and about the principles used for constructing Western psychiatric classifications.

Historical Origins

I noted in an earlier work that over the past century, culture-bound disorders have also been termed *culture-specific disorders, exotic disorders, culture-bound reactive disorders, ethnic psychoses, esoteric disorders, hysterical psychoses,* and *atypical disorders/psychoses* (Marsella, 1996). The variations in terms applied to culture-bound disorders reflect some of the important issues associated with their conceptualization in Western psychiatry. Terms such as *exotic* and *esoteric* reflect the ethnocentric bias that has accompanied efforts to understand culture-bound syndromes. It must be asked, why it is that non-Western people have "exotic" or "esoteric" disorders while Western people have the real thing? The answer, of course, is simple: Western psychiatry is part of the Western political, economic, and social domination of the world over the past centuries; with dominance comes privilege. Western psychiatry believed its assumptions and practices were "true," and as such, "universal." It has only been within recent years, that psychiatry has acknowledged "relativism" as a competing knowledge paradigm, and accepted psychiatry's ethnocentric roots and ideologically biased foundations.

Culture-bound disorders entered Western psychiatric literature in the late nineteenth century as Western physicians working in colonies in Asia, Africa, and South America reported strange and "exotic" disorders that appeared distinct from disorders reported in Europe or North America. However, reports of these disorders have actually been traced to the historical journals and reports of sixteenth-century European travelers, explorers, and adventurers to distant shores. For example,

CULTURE-BOUND DISORDERS. Table 1. Examples of culture-bound disorders

Name	Definition and Location
amok	A sudden outburst of explosive and assaultive violence preceded by period of social withdrawal and apathy (Southeast Asia, Philippines).
ataque de nervios	Uncontrollable shouting and/or crying. Verbal and physical aggression. Heat in chest rising to head. Feeling of losing control. Occasional amnesia for experience (Caribbean Latinos and South American Latinos).
hwa-byung	Acute panic, fear of death, fatigue, anorexia, dyspnea, palpitations, lump in upper stomach (Korea).
latah	Startle reaction followed by echolalia and echopraxia, and sometimes coprolalia and altered consciousness (Malaysia and Indonesia).
koro (shook yong)	Intense fear following perception that one's genitalia (men/women) or breasts (women) are withdrawing into one's body. Shame may also be present if perception is associated in time with immoral sexual activity (Chinese populations in Hong Kong and Southeast Asia).
phii pob	Belief that one is possessed by a spirit. Numbness of limbs, shouting, weeping, confused speech, shyness (Thailand).
pissu	Burning sensations in stomach, coldness in body, hallucinations, dissociation (Ceylon).
suchi-bai	Excessive concerns for cleanliness (changes street clothes, washes money, hops while walking to avoid dirt, washes furniture, remains immersed in holy river (Bengal, India—especially Hindu widows).
susto (espanto)	Strong sense of fear that one has lost one's soul. Accompanied by anorexia, weight loss, skin pallor, fatigue, lethargy, extensive thirst, untidiness, tachycardia, and withdrawal (Latinos in South and Central America, Mexico, and Latino migrants to North America).
taijin kyofusho	Intense fear of interpersonal relations. Belief that parts of the body give off offensive odors or displease others (Japan).
tawatl ye sni	Total discouragement. Preoccupation with death, ghosts, spirits. Excessive drinking, suicide thoughts and attempts (Sioux Indians).
uquamairineq	Hypnotic states, disturbed sleep, sleep paralysis, dissociative episodes and occasional hallucinations (Native Alaskans: Inuit, Yuit).

H. B. M. Murphy (1973), in his scholarly article on culture-bound disorders noted that *amok* was first reported in 1552 by Portuguese travelers to Southeast Asia who described religious zealots willing to sacrifice their lives in battles with the enemy.

Conceptual Issues

The distinction between "culture-bound" and "universal" disorders has provoked considerable controversy. Essentially, the major issue is whether all mental disorders should be considered *culture-bound* or whether the term should be reserved for those disorders judged by Western-trained scientists and professional to be localized or folk disorders. For example, some researchers have suggested that anorexia nervosa is specific to in-

dustrialized cultures (*DSM–IV*; APA, 1994, p. 844) because of the excessive valuation of personal control and beauty associated with thinness in these cultures. However, other disorders such as schizophrenia continue to be considered universal. Among the major questions that are still being debated are the following:

1. Should culture-bound disorders be considered neurotic, psychotic, or personality disorders?
2. Should these disorders be considered variants of disorders considered to be "universal" by Western scientist and professionals? (e.g., is *susto*, soul loss, merely a variant of depression?)
3. Are these disorders variants of common "hysterical," "anxiety," "depression," or "psychotic" processes that arise in response to severe tension, stress,

and/or fear, and present with specific culture content and expression?

4. Are there taxonomically different kinds of culture-bound syndromes (i.e., anxiety syndromes, depression syndromes, violence-anger syndromes, startle syndromes, dissociation syndromes)?

5. Do some culture-bound disorders have biological origins (e.g., *pibloktoq*—screaming and running naked in the Arctic snow—has been considered to result from calcium and potassium deficiencies because of dietary restrictions; *amok* has been considered to result from febrile disorders and neurological damage)?

6. Are all disorders "culture-bound" disorders since no disorder can escape cultural encoding, shaping, and presentation (e.g., schizophrenia, depression, anxiety disorders)?

Why Are Culture-Bound Disorders Important for Western Psychiatry?

The existence of culture-bound disorders raises important issues about Western classification systems.

The Nature of Western Psychiatric Classification. Culture-bound disorders raise fundamental questions about the nature of Western psychiatric disorders and their classification. Through the years, Western approaches to psychiatric classification have relied primarily on symptomatology, etiology, and/or treatment responsivity as the basis of classification. This approach is consistent with medical approaches to disease classification. However, these approaches have been subject to considerable criticism because the same etiology can lead to different disorders, different etiologies can lead to the same disorder, and similar treatments are used for disorders with different etiologies and expressions.

These problems are magnified when applied to disorders found in different cultures because different etiologies, symptom patterns, and treatment responsiveness may be operating. Can a common etiology be responsible for *amok* in Southeast Asia, *cathard* in Polynesia, and *negi-negi* in the New Guinea Highlands? Can different etiologies lead to similar explosive and violent behavior in Sweden, Southeast Asia, Polynesia, and the New Guinea Highlands? Is each disorder (explosive violence in Sweden, *amok* in Southeast Asia, *negi-negi* in the New Guinea Highlands) unique in its etiological foundations and expressive symptomatology and meanings? These questions go to the core of psychiatry's foundations as a science and profession. What is a universal disorder? What is a culture-bound disorder?

Decontextualizing Symptoms and Disorders. Taking symptoms and disorders out of their cultural context is a common but unfortunate practice in psychiatry. *Koro*, the fear that one's sexual organ is shrinking or withdrawing into one's body, assumes a different meaning when considered within the context of Chinese cultural views regarding the balance of *yin* (female) and *yang* (male) forces in the etiology of disease and the promotion of health. The loss of semen—whether through masturbation, frequent intercourse, or problematic anatomy—assumes a different meaning and consequence in Chinese society than it does in the West. The disorder cannot be extracted from its Chinese cultural context and interpreted in Western society as simply a delusion that occurs in hysterical personalities. The explanatory power of the latter is limited and biased because context is excluded. Imagine the reverse: Based upon treating more than 1,000 Yoruban (Nigeria) women, a Yoruban folk healer considers a severely agitated "depressive" episode in a Western middle-class housewife to be *asinwin* (i.e., a Yoruban disorder often found in women), and suggests that violations of ancestral spiritual taboos have caused the problem.

The universality view held by many in Western psychiatry is ethnocentric. It is rooted in the assumption that Western science and medicine have discovered universal truths and facts about a universal reality. This can be contrasted to emerging relativistic views that consider reality to be culturally constructed and determined. The latter view argues that each culture constitutes a distinct experiential context in which normal and psychopathological behavior originate, elicit meaning, find expression, and are responded to by culture members. The decontextualization of symptoms or disorders represents a serious conceptual and ethical error that emerges from intellectual bias and the abuse of power rather than the validity of the conclusion.

Cultural Determinants of Psychopathology. Once we acknowledge the existence of culture-bound disorders, it becomes clear that cultural factors constitute critical determinants of the etiology, expression, and treatment responsivity of psychopathology. This fact forces us to reconsider existing views of psychopathology that currently favor biological and/or psychological factors as the essential determinants, independently of the cultural context in which the disorder arises, is experienced, shaped, and treated. The acceptance of the culture-bound disorder as a fundamental reality in psychopathology encourages Western scientists and professionals to broaden their conceptual models to include cultural, environmental, and spiritual forces, and to explore the utility and value of indigenous models of psychopathology.

Cultural factors, including values, beliefs, socialization practices, ways of knowing (i.e., epistemologies, ontologies), consciousness patterns, personality, and social-role expectations all influence psychopathology. In addition, certain cultures may present particular stressors that help shape psychopathology such as cultural disintegration, cultural dislocation, racism, and sexism. Finally, psychopathology in particular cultures may be shaped through preferred breeding patterns, nutritional practices, climate, and other biologically related factors. In brief, culture-bound disorders compel us, as scientists and professionals, to consider cultural factors in our case conceptualizations and deliberations. It is as important to conduct culturological interviews as it is to conduct conventional psychiatric and psychological examinations.

Bibliography

American Psychiatric Association. (1994). *Diagnostic and statistical manual of mental disorders* (4th ed). Washington, DC: Author. Includes a glossary of 25 culture-bound disorders with brief descriptions of symptomatology and risk populations. Important because it represents the first APA acknowledgment of culture-bound disorders in the diagnostic manual.

Kiev, A. (1964). *Magic, faith, and healing.* New York: Free Press. Classic introduction, though now dated, to cross-cultural psychopathology and therapy. Includes a chapter on culture-bound disorders that attempts to classify them according to certain on features that are also common to Western disorders.

Marsella, A. J. (1996). Culture-bound syndromes. In R. Corsini & A. Auerbach (Eds.), *Concise encyclopedia of psychology* (2nd ed., pp. 223–224). New York: Wiley. Concise summary of history, types, and classifications of culture-bound syndromes. Includes discussion of major conceptual issues associated with the concept. Argues that all disorders, including Western disorders, may be culture-bound disorders since it is impossible to escape the influence of culture.

Murphy, H. B. M. (1973). History and evolution of syndromes: Amok and Latah. In M. Hammer, K. Salzinger, & S. Sutton (Eds.), *Psychopathology* (pp. 33–53). New York: Wiley. Scholarly and in-depth discussion of history and issues associated with two culture-bound disorders, *latah and amok.*

Simons, R., & Hughes, C. (1986). *The culture-bound syndromes: Folk illnesses of psychiatric and anthropological interest.* Boston: D. Reidel. Considered to be the most authoritative source on the topic of culture-bound disorders. Detailed glossary and description of more than 50 culture-bound disorders is provided. Favors the idea that different culture-bound disorders can be classified according to a finite number of different taxons (moves from etic to emic).

Yap, P. M. (1969). The culture-bound reactive syndromes. In W. Caudill & T. Lin (Eds.), *Mental health research in Asia and the Pacific* (pp. 33–53). Honolulu: University Press of Hawai'i. One of the early publications that attempted to link culture-bound syndromes to Western psychiatric disorders by identifying similar features and categorical dimensions.

Anthony J. Marsella

CULTURE SHOCK. Some of the earliest records of human culture describe people traveling to foreign lands for trade or conquest. Today people travel in order to find work, to study or teach. They make brief trips (e.g., for vacations) or settle permanently in a country other than their own. Such travel inevitably involves personal contact between culturally dissimilar individuals, and in the case of visitors, exposure to unfamiliar physical and social settings. As anyone who has traveled will acknowledge, this can be an unsettling experience, particularly if the transition from old to new is sudden.

The journals of Captain Cook, Marco Polo, and Christopher Columbus provide very good descriptions of what will be referred to in this article as culture contact. Modern-day examples include employees of international organizations, guest workers, overseas students, tourists, immigrants, refugees, missionaries, and peacekeepers.

During the last 40 years, the migration rate across national boundaries has greatly increased. This has been fueled by mass access to air travel, the globalization of industry, education, and leisure, and natural and human-made disasters such as floods, famine, and regional conflicts.

The coining of the phrase *culture shock* has been attributed to the anthropologist Kalervo Oberg, who in an article in 1960 used it to describe how people react to strange or unfamiliar places. But snappy titles should be treated with caution, and the term *culture shock* provides a good illustration of this rule. Certainly, it captures some of the feelings and experiences of travelers. However, the use of the word *shock* draws excessive attention to the *negative* aspects of coming into contact with novel situations, ignoring the fact that such experiences may also have consequences that benefit the participants. Over the years, *culture shock* has become a widely used and misused term, both in popular language as well as in cross-cultural psychology.

Culture Contact

Culture shock can best be understood by placing it conceptually within the wider process of culture *contact*, the term used to describe the (usually first-time) meeting of people who come from different cultural or ethnic backgrounds. Two types of culture contact have been distinguished: within society and between society.

Within-Society Contact

Within-society cross-cultural contact is a defining characteristic of life in multicultural societies. Successful multicultural countries may contain many diverse ethnic groups, which are unified by institutional structures and values that produce a common sense of nationhood. The United States from its earliest days has exemplified such a social system. As people go about their daily lives, they will inevitably encounter others who are dissimilar to them in appearance, heritage, values, and practices. In countries which value ethnic diversity, such cross-cultural contact enriches the lives of its citizens. The opposite is the case in countries where intergroup relations are based on ethnocentric principles.

Between-Society Contact

Between-society culture contacts refer to the category of individuals who go abroad for a particular purpose and for a specified period of time, and the relationships they establish with members of the host society. The term *sojourner* has been used to describe such culture travelers, implying that they are temporary visitors, with the intention of returning home after achieving their aims.

Most of the research on culture shock has studied between-society contact, because the sojourner experience involves a transition from familiar to unfamiliar settings that is highly focused and usually quite abrupt. For instance, prospective overseas students may leave Kuala Lumpur in Malaysia by plane in the morning, arrive in Sydney, Australia 12 hours later, and suddenly become immersed in a set of circumstances which are totally strange to them, and for which they may not have been prepared. One of the terms Oberg used was "buzzing confusion" to describe such an experience. Furthermore, most sojourners cannot realistically opt out of contact with significant host members, unlike minority groups in multicultural societies, who can effectively segregate themselves from contact with the wider society if they so wish.

The other reason why sojourners have been the center of attention is that culture shock in this area has economic consequences. It costs a lot of money to send business executives (or students) abroad, and if their performance is impaired by their inability to cope with their new environments, this has adverse consequences for the all-important financial bottom line.

Culture as Shared Meanings

The concept of culture is very slippery. For instance, in the 1950s the anthropologist C. Kluckhohn (Kroeber & Kluckhohn, 1952) reviewed 150 definitions, all somewhat different in what they denoted. In our own work on contact, we have found it useful to regard culture as a set of shared meanings that characterize a particular group, and which distinguish it from other groups. This definition is sufficiently general to cover broad, nationwide societal structures, but it can also be used to refer to subcultures within societies. It is also increasingly used to describe corporate cultures. And although the definition emphasizes cognitions, it does not rule out values and behaviors, as these too can be expressed in terms of the meaning the actor and perceiver ascribes to them. Historically, different cultures have evolved unique philosophical systems about the meaning of life and how it should be conducted. In many instances, there exist large between-culture differences, which may be diametrically opposed to each other, so that what is a virtue in one society could be offensive in another.

The Similarity-Attraction Hypothesis

Theory and empirical research in social psychology has shown that people prefer others who are similar to themselves. People can be similar in a variety of ways, all of which can have an effect on how they respond to each other. Thus, individuals are more likely to seek out, enjoy, understand, want to work and play with, trust, vote for, and marry others with whom they share important characteristics. These include interests, values, religion, group affiliation, skills, physical attributes, age, language, and most other aspects on which human beings differ.

The reason for this in-group bias is that the similarity of another person is reassuring. The social world contains many choices and alternatives. Furthermore, values often tend to be unclear and ambiguous, leading people to seek guidance as to their conduct. At one end of the spectrum people may consult traditional religious works, and at the other, books on etiquette. But a more common way is to look at how other people have responded to the problem, the technical term for this process being *consensual validation*. A person with similar views and practices to our own will provide support which confirms that our opinions, behaviors, and decisions, are safe, virtuous, and correct. Conversely, a dissimilar person may threaten such a self-image.

The Culture-Distance Hypothesis

It follows from the definition of culture as shared meanings that contact between culturally diverse people will inevitably occur between individuals who are dissimilar, often with respect to important, deeply felt issues. Research has shown that the greater the cultural distance separating two individuals, the more difficulty they will have in establishing mutual understanding and effective communication.

The Determinants of Culture Shock

There are a number of determinants of culture shock, including social-cognitive factors, differences in core values, and others.

Social-Cognitive Factors. Social psychologists (for instance Michael Argyle, 1994) regard interpersonal encounters as a skilled performance in which the participants engage in a reciprocal process requiring them to respond to each other's signals and cues on a continuing basis. It is a bit like waltzing, which can either be executed smoothly or awkwardly, depending on how well the dancers coordinate their movements. In social episodes, the main vehicle for communication is spoken language. However, nonverbal aspects of communication also play a vital role, in particular gestures, turn-taking, tone of voice, posture, proximity between the communicators, and touching. These behaviors are regulated by a set of socially constructed rules and conventions, and participants who have similar backgrounds will have a better understanding of what is expected. In cross-cultural meetings, or for that matter, in contact between members of different subcultures, those involved may not share the assumptions, perceptions, or interpretations of each other's behavior, and often may not even be aware that they are at cross-purposes. This can lead to misunderstanding, interpersonal awkwardness, confusion, uncertainty, and ultimately to hostility.

The anthropologist E. T. Hall (1966) called these nonverbal and contextual cues the hidden dimension of communication, hidden because they are generally not attended to until a rule is broken. In cross-cultural communication, they are a potential source of trouble, because they are much less accessible to the outsider, and by definition, cross-cultural contact is between outsiders. For instance, most Westerners would regard a smile as a sign of warmth, but in some cultures it may be a way of indirectly conveying disapproval. Indeed, cultural differences in direct or indirect expression of emotion constitute a major barrier to cross-cultural understanding. For example, in many cultures it is impolite to explicitly refuse a request. Uninitiated members of direct cultures do not understand that a "maybe" means "no," and "indirect" individuals may be offended by an overt refusal, no matter how politely it is phrased.

Differences in Core Values. Culture distance in values is another major source of culture shock. Contact between members of societies diametrically opposed on core issues is fraught with difficulty. For instance, the inferior status of women in some societies attracts deep disapproval in cultures that value nondiscriminatory gender relations. On the other side of this coin, members of male-dominated societies regard the occupational and sexual freedom which women enjoy in many Western cultures as distasteful and immoral. Similar disparities in what is regarded as correct and proper can be found in many other domains, such as religion, attitudes to the natural environment, age versus youth, dietary preferences, attitudes to punctuality, respect for status, and formal versus informal forms of address.

Reducing or Preventing Culture Shock. There is very little that can be done to facilitate communication between participants who differ in core values that cannot be reconciled, other than to alert those involved that these differences exist, that each party is sincere in its beliefs, and that people should agree to differ. Other techniques that have had modest success in preventing or reducing culture shock include selecting persons for overseas assignment on the basis of personality characteristics deemed to assist in coping with the unfamiliar, such as flexibility, self-efficacy, tolerance for ambiguity, and a nonprejudiced outlook, or racial color blindness as it is sometimes called. Predeparture briefing about salient physical, economic, and political aspects of the new setting is also useful, as are details about the customs, values, and social practices of the people, particularly with respect to any major differences between the sojourners' and the host cultures. And because disconfirmed expectations contribute to culture shock, it is important to provide accurate information about the negative aspects of the destination.

Most culture contact situations contain a pragmatic element, in the sense that it is in the interests of both sojourners and their immediate hosts to come to some kind of accommodation. Overseas students or expatriate executives may harbor fundamental objections to some aspects of the host culture they find themselves in, but they have a job to do, and most sojourners will consciously follow practices that contribute to those aims. Likewise, host counterparts may be less than impressed with some of the foreigners they have to deal with, but will restrain themselves and make allowances, in the interests of achieving goals that require a cooperative relationship. Sojourners unable to make the necessary adjustments will find the going tough, both personally and professionally, will probably not last the distance, and become part of the minority of travelers who return early, disappointed, and hostile toward their erstwhile hosts. However, the vast majority of sojourns are successful, and contribute to international understanding, both at the personal and institutional level.

Conclusion

Culture shock is an inescapable consequence of culture contact, particularly when a significant distance separates the sojourners' culture of origin and the culture of the visited country or culture. However, in most instances, culture shock can be reduced by providing culture travelers with useful predeparture information, making them aware of and sensitive to cultural differences, teaching them specific, culture-relevant social skills, and giving them systematic social support during the sojourn.

[See also Cross-Cultural Psychology; and Culture, article on Culture and Mental Health.]

Bibliography

Overview

Argyle, M. (1994). *The psychology of interpersonal behaviour* (5th ed.). Harmondsworth, UK: Penguin.

Bochner, S. (1994). Culture shock. In W. J. Lonner & R. Malpass (Eds.), *Psychology and culture*. Needham Heights, MA: Allyn & Bacon.

Furnham, A., & Bochner, S. (1986). *Culture shock: Psychological reactions to unfamiliar environments*. London: Methuen.

Hall, E. T. (1966). *The hidden dimension*. Garden City, NY: Doubleday.

Kroeber, A. L., & Kluckhohn, C. (1952). Culture: A critical review of concepts and definitions. *Papers of the Peabody Museum* [Special issue] 47(1).

Oberg, K. (1960). Cultural shock: Adjustment to new cultural environments. *Practical Anthropology, 7,* 177–182.

Smith, P. B., & Bond, M. H. (1998). *Social psychology across cultures* (2nd ed.). Hemel Hempstead, UK: Prentice Hall Europe.

Torbiorn, I. (1994). Operative and strategic use of expatriates in new organizations and market structures. *International Studies of Management and Organizations, 24,* 5–17.

Triandis, H. C. (1996). The psychological measurement of cultural syndromes. *American Psychologist, 51,* 407–415.

Similarity-Attraction Hypothesis

Byrne, D. (1969). Attitudes and attraction. In L. Berkowitz (Ed.), *Advances in experimental social psychology* (Vol. 4). New York: Academic Press.

Consensual Validation

Bennis, W. B., & Shepard, H. A. (1956). A theory of group development. *Human Relations, 9,* 415–438.

Festinger, L. (1954). A theory of social comparison processes. *Human Relations, 7,* 117–140.

Culture-Distance Hypothesis

Babiker, I. E., Cox, J. L., & Miller, P. (1980). The measurement of cultural distance and its relationship to medical consultations, symptomatology, and examination performance of overseas students at Edinburgh University. *Social Psychiatry, 15,* 109–116.

Furnham, A., & Bochner, S. (1982). Social difficulty in a foreign culture: An empirical analysis of culture shock. In S. Bochner (Ed.), *Cultures in contact: Studies in cross-cultural relations*. Oxford: Pergamon.

Interpersonal Communication as a Mutually Organized, Skilled Performance

Argyle, M., & Kendon, A. (1967). The experimental analysis of social performance. In L. Berkowitz (Ed.), *Advances in experimental social psychology, Volume 3*. New York: Academic Press.

Stephen Bochner

CUMULATIVE RECORD. A record that shows total responses plotted as a function of time and that thereby makes the patterning of behavior in time easy to see is

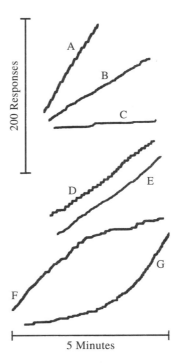

CUMULATIVE RECORD. Figure 1. Sample cumulative record. These illustrate different but relatively steady response rates in A, B, and C; differences in grain in D and E; and the difference between negatively and positively accelerated responding, respectively, in G.

known as a cumulative record. A pen or marker moves horizontally at a constant rate across a paper or some other display, and each response (e.g., a pigeon's key peck or a rat's lever press) moves the marker vertically a fixed distance. When the marker reaches the top of the paper or display, it automatically resets to the bottom to start a new segment of the record. Pips or other indicators are often added at appropriate places along the record to represent other events, such as reinforcers or stimulus onsets and offsets.

In a cumulative record, the faster the rate of responding the steeper the slope. Moment-to-moment changes in slope correspond to the detailed changes in response rate. Sample cumulative records are shown in Figure 1. Records A, B, and C all indicate relatively steady response rates, but the rate in A is highest of the three and the low rate in C includes several extended horizontal segments during which no responses occurred. The average rate for A is about 60 responses per minute and that for B is about 20; at this scale, individual responses are not visible. Response and time scales are typically chosen to make the most common response rates produce a slope of about 45 degrees, because at that slope a given percentage change in rate produces the biggest and therefore most easily visible change in angle. A cumulative record cannot have a negative slope, because the marker can record responses only by moving upward across the display.

The response rates in records D and E are about equal, but the patterns of responding are different: D is steplike, indicating periods of responding alternating with pauses; E is smoother, indicating relatively steady responding. This difference is sometimes referred to as grain: D has rougher grain than E.

Records F and G show how cumulative records can make gradual changes in rate over time easily visible. In F the rate of responding is negatively accelerated: it decreases as time passes; in G the rate is positively accelerated: it increases as time passes. Various temporal patterns of responding are characteristically produced by the different ways in which consequences can be arranged for responses (schedules of reinforcement). Those who work with schedules distinguish among many such patterns as they appear in cumulative records (e.g., the scalloping or gradual increases in rate that occurs between reinforcers in fixed-interval schedules, and the break-and-run pattern that occurs as the pause after a reinforcer is followed by a rapid transition to a high rate in fixed-ratio schedules).

The cumulative recorder was invented by the American experimental psychologist, B. F. Skinner (1904–1990). Its earliest version was a modification of the kymograph, a rotating cylinder then in common use in physiological recording. As the cylinder rotated, the record was made by a stylus that scratched a line on a smoked paper attached to the cylinder; the record was preserved by coating the smoked paper with shellac. Skinner created devices that raised the stylus a fixed distance with each response, thereby cumulating responses over time. These early devices were soon supplanted by recorders in which a roll of paper was threaded around a motor-driven roller so that the paper fed out at a constant speed. A pen or other writing device rested on the paper as it passed over the roller, and each response moved the pen a small distance at right angles to the movement of the paper. Most contemporary cumulative records are produced by computer.

[See also the biography of Skinner.]

Bibliography

Catania, A. C. (1998). *Learning* (4th ed.). Upper Saddle River, NJ: Prentice Hall. Shows how cumulative records operate, and uses many examples of records in presenting data from the psychology of learning.

Ferster, C. B., & Skinner, B. F. (1957). *Schedules of reinforcement.* New York: Appleton-Century-Crofts. A survey of the effects of reinforcement schedules that presents virtually all of its findings in the form of cumulative records.

Skinner, B. F. (1930). On the conditions for elicitation of certain eating reflexes. *Proceedings of the National Academy of Sciences, 16,* 433–438. The first paper to provide data in the form of cumulative records.

Skinner, B. F. (1938). *The behavior organisms.* New York: Appleton-Century-Crofts. This classic work, in which cumulative records played a major role, established rate of responding as a crucial measure of behavior.

Skinner, B. F. (1956). A case history in scientific method. *American Psychologist, 11,* 221–233. Includes an account of the invention of the cumulative recorder.

A. Charles Catania

CURIOSITY. Described as a desire for information in the absence of any extrinsic benefit, curiosity has been identified as a critical motive in human behavior. It is seen as a driving force in child development, educational attainment, entrepreneurship, scientific discovery, and consumer behavior. It is also seen, less positively, in behavior disorders such as a voyeurism and nonsanctioned behaviors such as illicit drug use. As a research topic, curiosity occupies a critical position at the crossroads of cognition and motivation.

Canadian psychologist D. E. Berlyne, who did pioneering research on curiosity, classified different forms of curiosity on two dimensions: one extending between "perceptual" and "epistemic" curiosity and the other spanning "specific" and "diversive" curiosity. Perceptual curiosity was intended to describe the exploratory behavior observed in animal studies. Epistemic curiosity referred to a desire for knowledge and applied mainly to human behavior. Specific curiosity referred to the desire for a particular piece of information, as epitomized by the attempt to solve a puzzle. Diversive curiosity referred to a more general seeking of stimulation, which is closely related to boredom.

Most research on curiosity occurred in two waves. The first, during the early 1960s, addressed the question of its underlying cause. One influential account, inspired by striking similarities among curiosity, hunger, and sex, viewed curiosity as a type of drive (Berlyne, 1960). Researchers advocating this account showed that curiosity did, indeed, display drivelike qualities: it has strong motivational force, can be "satisfied," intensifies over some interval if not satisfied, and produces arousal if not satisfied (see Loewenstein, 1994, p. 81). A later account proposed by Hunt (1963), which was inspired by the earlier work of Hebb and Piaget, saw curiosity as a response to violated expectations or perceived environmental incongruity, both of which signal an incomplete understanding of the environment. Berlyne's and Hunt's accounts share the assumption that curiosity exhibits an inverted U-shaped relationship to environmental complexity or incongruity, where low levels of complexity produce boredom, middle levels produce curiosity, and high levels produce fear or confusion. An alternative account, which viewed curiosity as a manifestation of intrinsic motivation, was proposed by White (1959) and expanded upon by Deci (1975). More recently, Loewenstein (1994) proposed an "information-gap" theory of curiosity which draws on Gestalt psychology and behavioral decision theories.

The second wave of curiosity research, in the late 1970s, focused mainly on the problem of measuring individual and group differences in curiosity. A variety of scales were developed to measure individuals' curiosity traits (e.g., Day, 1971). An important finding from this line of research is that items measuring curiosity and those measuring boredom typically load on separate, largely uncorrelated dimensions. Other attempts to measure curiosity relied on teacher evaluations, peer evaluations, and self-evaluations (Maw and Maw, 1968). One study examined children's tendency to explore curiosity-evoking items, such as a box with windows, lights, and protruding knobs (Coie, 1974). These studies have yielded often contradictory relationships between curiosity and age, gender, and other demographic factors, perhaps because they share a fundamental limitation. Inevitably, to measure a person's curiosity, one has to measure curiosity about *something*, but different people are curious about different things. Thus, for example, if older people seem more curious as measured by a particular scale, it may be simply because that scale includes items that are especially curiosity-evoking for that age group.

The least developed area of curiosity research, in which there is the most pressing need for further exploration, comprises the situational determinants of curiosity. Berlyne attempted to relate curiosity to stimulus complexity by measuring how long subjects looked at geometric shapes that varied in novelty and complexity. Later, however, he repackaged this line of research as an investigation of aesthetics. In a study that employed diverse and innovative dependent measures of curiosity, educational psychologists Lowry and Johnson (1981) found that students' curiosity was enhanced by having them participate in discussion groups that encouraged argument and epistemic conflict. Loewenstein (1994) obtained evidence confirming the importance of several situational determinants of curiosity (i.e., the desire to fill a specific gap in one's knowledge) increases with the accumulation of background information.

Bibliography

Berlyne, D. E. (1960). *Conflict, arousal, and curiosity*, New York: McGraw-Hill.

Coie, J. D. (1974). An evaluation of the cross-situational stability of children's curiosity. *Journal of Personality, 42*, 93–117.

Day, H. I. (1971). The measurement of specific curiosity. In H. I. Day, D. E. Berlyne, & D. E. Hunt (Eds.), *Intrinsic motivation: A new direction in education* (pp. 99–112). Ontario, Canada: Ontario Institute for Studies in Education.

Deci, E. L. (1975). *Intrinsic motivation*. New York: Plenum Press.

Hunt, J. McV. (1963). Motivation Inherent in information processing and action. In O. J. Harvey (Ed.), *Motivation and social interaction* (pp. 35–94). New York: Ronald Press.

Loewenstein, G. (1994). The psychology of curiosity: A review and reinterpretation. *Psychological Bulletin, 116*, 75–98.

Lowry, N., & Johnson, D. W. (1981). Effects of controversy on epistemic curiosity, achievement, and attitudes. *Journal of Social Psychology, 115*, 31–43.

Maw, W. H., & Maw, E. W. (1968). Self-appraisal of curiosity. *Journal of Educational Research, 61*, 462–465.

Naylor, F. D. (1981). A state-trait curiosity inventory. *Australian Psychologist, 16*, 172–183.

White, R. W. (1959). Motivation reconsidered: The concept of competence. *Psychological Review, 66*, 297–333.

George Loewenstein

CURRICULUM DEVELOPMENT is a broad-based enterprise with three major interacting dimensions. These include a normative dimension concerned with articulating and justifying the values and aims of the programs of study employed in schools; an analytic dimension intended to identify the meaning of key concepts within the curriculum field and the formulation of new concepts designed to guide the study and creation of curricula; and an empirical dimension consisting of studies intended to assist curriculum developers and those concerned with assessing the effects of educational programs employed in schools and other agencies.

The term *curriculum* itself has more than one meaning, and it is important to make those meanings explicit at the outset. The term *curriculum* most often refers to the course of study employed in an educational institution. This conception of curriculum is often referred to as "the explicit curriculum" and it involves those formal plans and content areas that constitute the "course to be run." It should be noted that the explicit curriculum has managerial consequences. Teachers are hired to teach in those content domains defined by the explicit curriculum, tests are often employed to measure student progress, grades are assigned to students for performance within those content domains, and transcripts are kept to certify each student's competency and to issue diplomas and other forms of certification.

A second conception of curriculum refers to the informal institutional and organizational practices within a school that have a significant impact on what students learn. This curriculum is often referred to as "the implicit curriculum" (Eisner, 1994) or in some circles, "the hidden curriculum." For example, the implicit curriculum determines what students learn by virtue of the way in which content areas are divided, how time is allocated to various subject matters, and the scheduling of subjects within the school day. In addition, the ways in which students are rewarded for learning, the tacit and covert values that are implicit in the social roles and processes employed in school, and the ways in which competition or cooperation is promoted among students all constitute aspects of the implicit curriculum. The implicit curriculum, some argue, is far more powerful than the explicit curriculum because it is more pervasive and enduring.

A third conception of curriculum is something of a paradox. If the curriculum can be conceptualized in general as a program of studies intended to influence what students learn under the aegis of the school, what schools *do not* offer is also a part of the curriculum and can also be a powerful source of influence. The absence of content diminishes the scope of learning opportunity. This absence is regarded as constituting "the null curriculum" (Eisner, 1994); it is a curriculum consisting of what is *not* taught.

There is an additional distinction related to curriculum that is worth making. This distinction has to do with the curriculum *in vitro*, which is the curriculum as a set of materials—syllabi, instructional resources, and so forth—provided to teachers for their use in the classroom, compared to the curriculum *in vivo*, the curriculum as it actually unfolds in the classroom. Thus, like other fields, when one looks carefully at curricula they often emerge in a more complex form than initially conceived.

Curriculum development, that is, the process of designing curriculum materials to be used in a particular classroom or school, school district, or throughout the nation, occurs in a variety of ways. First, there are commercial publishers who employ teachers, graphic designers, curriculum writers, and sales representatives to develop new curriculum materials to be marketed for adoption by the various states in the United States. These commercial companies are often very skilled in producing visually attractive materials having various levels of substantive quality. Adoption of a curriculum by a state assures the company of a wide market for their product. Most of the major curriculum programs in reading, mathematics, and writing are conceptualized, developed, tested, and disseminated by commercial companies.

At a less macro level, school districts will, from time to time, appoint curriculum development committees to create curricula that are particularly suited for use in their school district. Content areas for which commercial curriculum resources are not adequate relative to the district's view of what should be taught, often become the focus of such an enterprise. Teachers are often given release time or they are provided with extra income for working during the summers to develop and implement new curriculum programs in their school districts.

At a microlevel, teachers informally develop programs for use in their own classrooms when they have the option of developing their own approach to the teaching of a subject. Furthermore, virtually all teachers interpret and implement curricula in distinctive and unique ways since no body of curriculum materials can adequately address all of the contingencies and adjustments that must be made if they are to be used effectively in the classroom.

What role does psychology as a field play in conceptualizing and developing curricula? The classic and still enduring statement on this matter is to be found in the work of Ralph W. Tyler (1950), a curriculum theorist and social scientist who was professor of education at the University of Chicago in the 1940s. According to Tyler, psychology has a major role to play in determining, for example, the psychological developmental capacities of the children and adolescents who are to be engaged by the curriculum. Developmental considerations must be taken into account when designing learning activities and in defining the content that students are supposed to learn. Contrary to Bruner's (1960) observation that a child can be taught anything in an intellectually honest way at any age, Tyler believed that some ideas and tasks were beyond the ken of children of particular age levels and, therefore, developmental considerations were not at all irrelevant.

Developmental considerations, however, are by no means the only considerations in designing learning experiences. Since one general aim of the curriculum is to promote higher levels of thinking, psychological theory plays an important role in defining those cognitive skills that curriculum activities are intended to stimulate, develop, and refine. For example, if one aim of the curriculum is to promote ideational fluency, curriculum activities must be formulated that will make it possible for students to utilize such a mode of thought. The concept of ideational fluency is derived from J. P. Guilford's (1967) work and is one feature in his conception of the structure of intellect. Psychological considerations also influence the ways in which curricular sequence is determined in the development of a program of studies. A term that is currently employed in the psychological literature in education is *scaffolding*. The fundamental idea of scaffolding is that the teacher will mediate the activities provided to students so that these activities function within the student's zone of proximal development (Cole, John-Steiner, Scribner, & Souberman, 1978). By making appropriate pedagogical adjustments, it is more likely that the student's cognitive growth will be fostered.

There is also an increasing interest in phenomenological psychological considerations in curriculum development and implementation. Educators increasingly are becoming interested in the phenomenological character and quality of learning experiences of students in the classroom (Van Mannen, 1990). Experience is regarded as the primary educational medium. It is what students actually experience within a curriculum that makes the difference in their lives, not merely the intentions of curriculum developers or even teachers.

Attention to phenomenological experience is easier to recommend than to provide. Nevertheless, it has become an important consideration when thinking about the ways in which educational growth occurs. Aided by a philosophical constructivist view of knowledge, what has become salient in educational discourse is the idea that meanings are constructed psychologically by individuals situated in contexts, and that unless teachers and curriculum developers can take into account the meanings the situation has for the individual, the probability of optimizing his or her cognitive growth is small. Thus, there is a move away from behavioristic criteria into "lived experience" (Van Mannen, 1990).

The legal control of curricula in American schools is from a formal perspective rooted in each of the 50 states. The Tenth Amendment to the U.S. Constitution gives states the responsibility for areas not mentioned explicitly as belonging to the federal government. Because education is not mentioned in the constitution, it is considered a state responsibility. The definition of curriculum goals, content, and, in some states, the amount of time allocated to each of the content areas at each grade level, are normally a part of the state education code. States are the primary agents responsible for defining the curriculum for schools under their aegis. At the same time, the formal specification of responsibility is not always replicated at the local level. In the United States, there are about 16,000 local school boards. Each school board has jurisdiction over local educational matters, including curriculum, within the parameters established by the states; that is, local school districts can define programs at the local level as long as they are in compliance with state expectations. Thus, in a nation that is as diverse as the United States, there is substantial local variation not only in what is taught, but how teaching is to occur, and what particular local values are to animate the program.

In describing local variation, variability should not be overemphasized, although clearly it is there. At the same time, it must be acknowledged that publishing companies themselves have a major homogenizing influence on school programs. This is accomplished by large-scale adoption of textbooks and other kinds of materials which often serve as the curricular hubs around which teaching occurs. The character of a curriculum is often shaped significantly by the materials, and especially by the testing agencies whose tests influence the public's opinion of the quality of its schools. Here too, the field of psychology has a major influence on curricula since psychological theory and, especially, measurement theory, provides the methodological framework for test construction. Measurement theory helps in determining which test items are retained, which are discarded, whether the test is norm or criterion referenced, what conditions must be met to create statistically reliable instruments, which are all-important considerations in meeting psychological test standards. These considerations, when they serve as criteria for test construction, in turn, influence both the form and content of tests. The form of the test and its content, in turn, influence how schools, students, and teachers are appraised. What is counted, someone once said, counts. Thus, psychological considerations in assessment practices also have a significant impact on what schools teach and thus on what students learn.

One development in assessment, "authentic assessment" (Gifford & O'Conner, 1992), emerged in the 1990s. It affords students opportunities to demonstrate their knowledge and skills in settings that are intended to approximate the situations in which those skills are normally used in schools.

Under traditional assessment circumstances, students are given formal examinations, often objective in character, in which they may be required to complete answer sheets that are later scored by an optical scanner. There has been criticism in recent years that such a form of assessment is unique to schools and that the primary aim in assessment should be to create conditions that are likely to have better predictive validity than traditional tests. The implicit criticism is that traditional forms of assessment are inauthentic.

Combining the notion of authentic assessment with the concept of situated cognition (Greeno, 1997), it is evident that psychological theory has an emerging impact on ways in which curriculum programs in schools are defined. Clearly, the aim of schooling is to enable students to do well not only in school, but in the life they lead outside the confines of school. Situated cognition is a tacit recognition of the importance of this aim, and authentic assessment is a practice designed to reflect the importance of assessing skills and knowledge within the contexts in which they are to be used.

Finally, the role of theory in the curriculum field may vary depending on what is meant by theory. If theory refers to a set of interrelated propositions that define empirical relationships which can be tested within specified boundary conditions, then the curriculum field has few, if any, theories that meet those criteria. If, however, theory refers to a set of beliefs or values that give direction to an educational enterprise, then the curriculum field has a number of important "theories."

Since the 1970s, the curriculum field and education theory and its usefulness or application in actual practice have been brought increasingly into question (Schwab, 1969). The development of theory has long been regarded as the fundamental intellectual objective of both the natural and the social sciences. Educators, although confronted with practical problems riddled with unpredictable contingencies, have also sought to create or adopt theories that can ultimately guide, even prescribe practice. What has become apparent is that the problems faced by curriculum developers, teachers, and school administrators are problems that do not submit easily to theory. Scientific theories are idealizations of relationships that make it possible to explain those relationships within a given set of specified parameters. Although educators have long desired such intellectual tools, practical life is filled with uncertainties.

The practical tasks related to curriculum development and teaching are to make sound and responsive instructional decisions. To do this, considerations having to do with prudence and feasibility, appropriateness and ethics must be brought to bear. Life in classrooms and the teaching-learning process are far more complex and contingent than the kind of matters that, say, physicists address in the laboratory. As a result, in recent years theory has been assigned a more marginal position in curriculum development than it once enjoyed. It is not that theory has no utility, rather, theory is no longer expected to provide rules for teachers and curriculum developers to follow. In addition, there is no single theory that is likely to be adequate for addressing the complexities of classroom practice. Thus, theory as an epistemological vehicle is one of many resources that individuals who develop and implement curricula for diverse learners can use.

As was suggested earlier, theory in the curriculum field, emphasizes the aims or orientation of the curriculum, is more value laden than the concept of theory in the natural sciences. For example, in recent years there has been considerable interest in the cognitive consequences of different forms of representation or various symbol systems as they are employed by students to perceive, understand, and represent some aspect of the world (Eisner, 1994). To use one example, educational scholars realize that poetry makes meanings possible that differ from those of prose. Mathematics creates meaningful structures that the visual arts cannot replicate. These, in turn, require particular modes of thinking. If an aim of education is to diversify the forms of meaning that individuals are able to achieve in their lives, and if the curriculum is viewed as the primary vehicle through which the cognitive skills necessary to use different forms of representation or symbol systems are cultivated, then the school curriculum needs to provide students with opportunities to encounter and practice such skills. The implication of this general orientation is to build curricula in which students are invited to engage in tasks that "exercise" cognitive processes related to different forms of representation. The acquisition of such competencies constitutes a conception of multiple forms of literacy, where literacy refers to the ability to decode and encode different kinds of meanings, the meanings that different forms of representation make possible.

Clearly, the orientation just described is rooted in cognitive theory, as well as in the philosophical work of Ernst Cassirer (1953), Suzanne Langer (1957), and Nelson Goodman (1978). Concerns about the provision of diverse types of representation of content or knowledge also appeal to matters of educational equity. Educational equity, in turn, is related to aptitude. By building curriculum programs that are diverse with respect to the forms of representation students can use, opportunities for learning among students whose aptitudes are congruent with those forms are increased. When all students are confined largely to literal language and numeric forms of representation, aptitudes that reside in, for example, the aesthetic treatment of sound or visual image or in areas of movement as they exist in choreography are marginalized and handicapped. Psychological theory, in this sense, provides a major basis for what many regard as a more equitable approach to the curricular provisions of the school.

Bibliography

Bruner, J. (1960). *The process of education.* Cambridge, MA: Harvard University Press.
Cassirer, E. (1953). *Philosophy of symbolic forms.* New Haven, CT: Yale University Press.
Cole, M., John-Steiner, V., Scribner, S., & Souberman, E. (Eds.) (1978). *L. S. Vygotsky.* Cambridge, MA: Harvard University Press.
Eisner, E. (1994). *Educational imagination* (3rd ed.). New York: Macmillan.
Eisner, E. (1994). *Cognition and curriculum reconsidered.* New York: Teachers College Press.
Gifford, B., & O'Conner, M. (1992). *Changing assessments.* Boston: Kluwer Academic.

Goodman, N. (1978). *Ways of world making.* Indianapolis: Hackett.

Greeno, J. et al. (1997). Theories and practice of thinking and learning to think. *American Journal of Education, 106,* 85–126.

Guilford, J. P. (1967) *The nature of human intelligence.* New York: McGraw-Hill.

Langer, S. (1957). *Problems of art.* New York: Scribner's.

Schwab, J. (1969). The practical: The language for curriculum. *School Review, 78,* 1–23.

Tyler, R. W. (1950). *Basic principles of curriculum and construction.* Chicago: University of Chicago Press.

Van Mannen, M. (1990). *Researching lived experience.* London, Ontario: The University of Western Ontario.

Elliot W. Eisner

D

DALLENBACH, KARL M. (1887–1971), American psychologist. Dallenbach was born in Champaign, Illinois, the son of John Dallenbach and Anna Mittendorf, farmers. In 1906, he entered the University of Illinois as an undergraduate with the intent of going into law. In his second year, however, he took a course in psychology from John Wallace Baird, who had come to Illinois from Cornell where he had studied under Edward B. Titchener. Baird's lectures and Titchener's *Textbook* (1910) interested Dallenbach, and he later took other courses in psychology at Illinois. Dallenbach's laboratory notes in Baird's experimental psychology course were so impressive that Baird had them bound. Later, when Titchener came to Illinois to give a lecture, he saw the notes and suggested that Dallenbach come to Cornell for his doctorate in psychology. In the meantime, after graduating from Illinois in 1910, Dallenbach received his master's degree in 1911 from the University of Pittsburgh. He then went to Cornell to study under Titchener. He received his doctorate in psychology in 1913 with a dissertation on the topic of attention. Titchener's influence would stay with Dallenbach through the remainder of his career.

After a summer in Germany studying with Oswald Külpe, then in Bonn, Dallenbach returned to America and took an appointment at the University of Oregon. The following year he went to Ohio State University. Then, in the fall of 1914, he returned to Cornell as a faculty member, where he would teach until 1948.

During World War I, Dallenbach served in the newly established Psychological Testing Corps commanded by Robert M. Yerkes. He was offered an applied position in personnel testing after the war but chose to return to Cornell and academic life.

It was in the early 1920s that Dallenbach, believing he was negotiating for a consortium of Cornell professors, purchased the *American Journal of Psychology* from G. Stanley Hall, the journal's founder. Dallenbach soon discovered that the others did not have liquid assets, including Titchener, and so had to borrow against his inheritance to purchase the journal. Titchener became its editor and Dallenbach its business manager. It was a grand gesture on Dallenbach's part in honor of his major professor and became a commitment for the remainder of his career. Titchener resigned as editor in 1925 in a dispute with Dallenbach; thereafter, the journal continued in a joint editorship that included Dallenbach.

Dallenbach continued his research on attention in which he became a world authority. With John G. Jenkins, he carried out the experiment on the effect of sleep versus activity on the retention of learned material. It was the crucial experiment on the interference versus disuse theories of forgetting.

Dallenbach also conducted research in the field of tactual sensation, involving the mapping of various sensory areas on the skin, including pain and temperature. He invented a temperature stimulator that became standard laboratory equipment which bears his name. In the 1940s and early 1950s Dallenbach and his students produced classical studies on the localization of objects in space by the blind (Supa, Cotzin, & Dallenbach, 1944). This research disproved William James's "facial vision" hypothesis and led to the modern research in auditory localization and lateralization. During World War II Dallenbach did psychological testing and served as chair of the Emergency Committee in Psychology of the National Research Council.

After the war, he returned to Cornell, where he became the Sage Professor of Psychology. In 1948, Dallenbach left Cornell and went to the University of Texas, where he served as chairman of the department of psychology. He obtained a new building for psychology and designed its laboratories. In 1958, he stepped down as chair and returned to teaching until his retirement in 1970, although he continued his research work. In 1965, he published an experimental article on single-trial learning.

Dallenbach is noted especially for his stewardship of the *American Journal of Psychology*, which he edited and coedited faithfully from 1926 until 1968.

Bibliography

Boring, E. G. (1958). K. M. Dallenbach. *American Journal of Psychology, 71,* 1–40.

Dallenbach, K. M. (1923). Some new apparatus. *American Journal of Psychology, 34,* 92–94.

Evans, R. B. (1972). Karl M. Dallenbach: 1887–1971. *American Journal of Psychology, 85,* 462–476.

Jenkins, J. G., & Dallenbach, K. M. (1924). Obliviscence during sleep and waking. *American Journal of Psychology, 35,* 605–612.

Supa, M., Cotzin, M., & Dallenbach, K. M. (1944). Facial vision: The perception of obstacles by the blind. *American Journal of Psychology, 57,* 133–183.

Titchener, E. B. (1910). *A textbook of psychology.* New York: Macmillan.

Rand Evans

DANGEROUSNESS. *See* Violence Risk Assessment.

DARWIN, CHARLES R. (1809–1882), English naturalist. Darwin's 1859 book, *On the Origin of Species by Means of Natural Selection, or the Preservation of Favoured Races in the Struggle for Life,* transformed the life sciences. Although the notion of evolution or "transmutation" of species had been proposed by earlier figures including Jean-Baptiste Lamarck (1744–1829) and Charles's grandfather Erasmus Darwin (1731–1802), it had not seriously challenged the traditional belief in the independent and separate creation of all species. By offering in-depth support for natural selection as a plausible mechanism or natural process by which transmutation might occur—something earlier evolutionary theories had lacked—the *Origin* literally demanded that evolution be taken seriously.

Briefly summarized, the theory of natural selection rests upon two key assumptions: (1) that a broad range of small but inheritable variations exists within every breeding population, on innumerable characteristics including size, shape, coloration, and conformation of organs; and (2) that within every breeding population more individuals are born than will live to reproduce, so there is a competition for survival and procreation. Darwin reasoned that, within differing environments, differing patterns of variations will inevitably offer slight advantages or disadvantages for survival and procreation. Thus, "nature" will preferentially "select" different adaptive characteristics to be propagated within the different environments, in somewhat the same way domestic animal breeders select and mate only the best representatives of the breeds they are developing or maintaining. Carried on over countless generations, such a process should result in distinctly different populations derived from originally identical stock, who have diverged sufficiently from each other to become separate species. There are no absolute standards of best or worst in this process, only differing degrees of adaptation to particular environmental circumstances. And since those circumstances are subject to change, both geographically and over time, constant pressures are in place for the gradual change and evolution of all species. Assuming an evolutionary past of many millions of years, Darwin argued that the present great diversity of life forms could be accounted for in this way.

Virtually all of Darwin's examples in the *Origin* dealt with physical characteristics and were drawn from non-human species, but he wrote prophetically in the book's Conclusion: "In the distant future I see open fields for far more important researches. Psychology will be based on a new foundation. . . . Light will be thrown on the origin of man and his history" (Darwin, 1859, p. 488). That future was actually not so distant, as both Darwin himself and several of his followers quickly took up his lead. Psychology, particularly in Great Britain and America, took on a distinctly Darwinian cast, which it retains today.

Darwin's Early Life

Charles Darwin was born into a wealthy and distinguished family in Shrewsbury, England, on 12 February 1809. His father, Robert Darwin, ranked among the most highly paid of all English provincial physicians, following in the footsteps of his eminent father Erasmus (who besides promoting evolution had been a famous physician, inventor, poet, and general man of science). Charles's mother, Susannah Wedgwood Darwin, came from the famous chinaware manufacturing family. An indifferent classical scholar, young Charles languished at the local Shrewsbury school, but developed a strong extracurricular passion for natural science. Two years of medical training in Edinburgh provided some useful scientific background, but he could not bear to be present at operations performed without anaesthesia, and abandoned medicine. He went to Cambridge in 1827, expecting to prepare for a career as a country parson. Again he failed to shine in the required classical and mathematical subjects, taking his nonhonors degree in 1831. Darwin participated vigorously in Cambridge's extracurricular scientific activities, however, and became friendly with such scientifically oriented faculty as the geologist Adam Sedgwick (1785–1873) and the botanist John Stevens Henslow (1796–1873).

In 1831, Henslow recommended Darwin for "by far the most important event in my life" (Darwin, 1969, p. 76)—an opportunity to sail aboard the surveying ship H.M.S. *Beagle* as an unpaid "naturalist" and dining companion to its captain Robert FitzRoy, on what became a five-year voyage. While circumnavigating the globe with extended stays along the coasts of South America, and stopovers at the Galapagos Islands, Tahiti, New Zealand, Australia, and South Africa, Darwin honed his scientific skills. He sent home specimens and observational reports from these exotic locales that immediately established his reputation as a gifted naturalist.

His geological reports offered crucial support for the disputed theory of uniformitarianism—the notion that the earth's primary geological features are the result of gradual and relatively "uniform" processes extending over vast stretches of time. The competing and then dominant theory of catastrophism attributed the earth's major geological features to a relatively small number of massive cataclysms such as the Flood. Darwin found fossilized sea shells high in the Andes and personally experienced an earthquake that raised some Chilean coastal features a few feet higher than they had been before. Surely the elevation of the fossils was more likely the result of a large number of similar earthquakes occurring over vast ages of time, than of a single, cataclysmic event. Darwin also proposed that the geology of many oceanic islands was best accounted for by gradual uniform processes such as undersea volcano eruptions, coral growth, and the slow rising or subsidence of the ocean floor. Besides turning the tide of British geological opinion toward uniformitarianism, these findings accustomed Darwin himself to assuming a very extended history for the earth, marked by gradual change and development.

Darwin also made important biological observations, the full implications of which he did not appreciate until after his return. He found the fossilized remains of extinct creatures with skeletal structures similar to modern sloths, armadillos, and llamas—and although he doubted FitzRoy's assertion that these were remains of animals who had been left off Noah's ark, he had no alternative explanation for them at that time. Darwin also observed peculiarities in the geographical distributions of similar but distinct living species, such as giant tortoises with slightly differing shells and finches with differently shaped bills, in the Galapagos Islands.

The Origin of *Origin of Species*

After his return to England in late 1836, Darwin's published accounts of his *Beagle* observations and adventures established him as a leading naturalist and popular travel writer. Thoughts of ordination disappeared when he realized he would have sufficient independent income to devote his life to scientific pursuits. In 1837, he began seriously and systematically reflecting upon the implications of his *Beagle* observations for various biological issues, including that "mystery of mysteries," the origin of species. The traditional, creationist answer to that mystery relied heavily on the argument from design—the assertion that the vastly divergent species were so wonderfully adapted to their particular environments that they could only have been separately and deliberately designed by an omniscient Creator. Darwin's alternative answer—the hypothesis of natural selection—occurred to him in the autumn of 1838, after he had been reading the economic theorist Thomas Malthus's (1766–1834) argument that most human beings are destined to live in poverty because their rate of reproduction will always eventually outstrip the rate at which they can produce food to sustain themselves. This idea led Darwin to the thought that for any species, many more individuals are conceived than can survive to reproduce. Further assuming a range of inheritable variations within each species and a variety of environments in which differing characteristics will prove adaptive, Darwin had the essentials for his theory of evolution by natural selection.

Knowing that this theory would encounter stiff and emotional resistance from upholders of the traditional creationist view, Darwin held back from publishing his theory until he had collected an enormous amount of supporting argument and documentation. Only in 1856 did he begin writing *Natural Selection*, a work he projected to be several thousand pages in length. In 1858, however, he received a short paper from Alfred Russel Wallace (1823–1913) outlining a theory virtually identical to his own. This precipitated a meeting of the Linnean Society at which Wallace's paper was read, along with brief extracts from two of Darwin's earlier unpublished works describing the theory. This first public presentation of natural selection failed to make much impression, however, being (as Darwin expected) much too brief and schematic to fully illustrate the theory's power. Nevertheless, Darwin now rushed to prepare an intermediate-length "abstract" of the theory: the 490-page *Origin of Species*, which duly appeared in late 1859. This proved sufficient to show that Darwin had seriously grappled with the argument from design and other major objections to the theory and immediately made evolution a concept to be taken seriously. The retiring Darwin shied away from the clamor aroused by his unstated but clearly implied assumption that humans are descended from apelike creatures, but his cause was vigorously taken up and defended by supporters such as the botanist Joseph Hooker (1817–

1911) and, most spectacularly, "Darwin's bulldog" Thomas H. Huxley (1825–1895).

Darwin's Influence on Psychology

Within a decade much of the clamor had subsided, and in the 1870s Darwin published three works that helped lay his promised "new foundation" for psychology. *The Descent of Man* (1871) argued that virtually all human characteristics—including such "higher" and psychological qualities as courage, kindness, and reasoning—can be found in rudimentary form in many "lower" species; hence there is no reason not to see them as having evolved. *The Expression of the Emotions in Man and Animals* (1872) made the complementary case, namely, that human beings' emotional expressions betray many remnants of an inherited ancestral "animality." And with his 1877 paper, "A Biographical Sketch of an Infant," Darwin pioneered the genre of "baby biography" while describing his young son's psychological development as an approximate recapitulation of the evolutionary past of the human species.

Darwin's evolutionary perspective directly stimulated many important developments in psychology. His theoretical emphasis on variation and adaptation lent particular new significance to the identification and measurement of individual differences and their role in adaptive behavior. Following this lead, Darwin's cousin Francis Galton (1822–1911) proposed the development of what we now call intelligence tests to measure hereditary individual differences in "natural ability." In his controversial efforts to demonstrate the hereditary determination of intelligence, and his promotion of the eugenics movement, Galton also defined the modern "nature/nurture" issue and laid many of the foundations for the modern field of behavior genetics. Darwin's insistence that human beings are related by evolution to other species lent new theoretical importance and relevance to the study of animal behavior, and he actively encouraged his young friend George Romanes (1848–1894) to launch the new discipline of comparative psychology.

Darwin's general influence became especially strong on British and American psychologists, who focused heavily on issues of process, adaptation, function, measurement, and individual differences. The "pragmatic" psychology of William James (1840–1910) was one example of this trend, followed by the functionalism of James Angell (1869–1949), John Dewey (1859–1952), Edward Thorndike (1874–1949), and Robert Woodworth (1869–1962), among others. G. Stanley Hall (1844–1924) adapted the recapitulation hypothesis from Darwin's "Biographical Sketch," while pioneering "developmental psychology" as a major subdiscipline at Clark University. The school of behaviorism explicitly relied on the Darwinian theory of evolution, while arguing for the relevance of animal studies for human beings.

A school of "social Darwinism" arose shortly after Darwin's death in 1882, promoting unbridled competition and laissez-faire capitalism on the grounds that "survival of the fittest" would inevitably hasten social and economic, as well as biological progress. The school actually owed much more to Herbert Spencer (1820–1903) than to Darwin, however; for, unlike Spencer, Darwin denied that evolution could be equated with "progress" in any ultimate or moral sense. For him, evolution was a conseqence of adaptation pure and simple, devoid of any other values.

In more recent times, a sometimes controversial approach known as sociobiology has attempted to account for the evolution of social behavior. To explain the persistence of such apparently nonadaptive characteristics (for individual survival) as altruism, sociobiologists have proposed one important shift in emphasis from Darwin's. Whereas Darwin identified the basic reproducing unit in evolution as the individual organism, sociobiologists have hypothesized that it is the individual gene—a concept that did not even exist in Darwin's time. Richard Dawkins's conceptualization of the "selfish gene" as a self-replicating mechanism is perhaps the most influential presentation of this idea. Dawkins also proposed the concept of the "meme" as a unit of cultural evolution corresponding to the gene in biology. Cognitive psychologists and computer scientists have provocatively combined these ideas with developments in the fields of computational theory and artificial intelligence (e.g., Dennett, 1995). Steven Pinker (1997) has interpreted the human mind as a collection of mechanistically operating, computational "modules," each one independently evolved to meet survival needs in the not too distant past. Whatever the ultimate fate of specific ideas such as these, Darwin's general concepts of adaptation, competition, and evolution will surely continue to influence psychological theorizing for the foreseeable future.

Bibliography

Works by Darwin

Darwin, C. (1859). *On the origin of species by means of natural selection, or the preservation of favoured races in the struggle for life.* London: Murray.

Darwin, C. (1871). *The descent of man, and selection in relation to sex.* London: Murray.

Darwin, C. (1872). *The expression of emotion in man and animals.* London: Murray.

Darwin, C. (1877). Biographical sketch of an infant. *Mind, 2*, 285–294.

Darwin, C. (1969). *The autobiography of Charles Darwin 1809–1883* (N. Barlow, Ed.). New York: Norton.

Works about Darwin

Bowler, P. (1989). *Evolution: The history of an idea* (Rev. ed.). Berkeley, CA: University of California Press.

Browne, J. (1995). *Charles Darwin voyaging: A biography.* Princeton: Princeton University Press.

Dawkins, R. (1976). *The selfish gene.* Oxford: Oxford University Press.

Desmond, A. and Moore, J. (1991). *Darwin.* New York: Warner Books.

Dennett, D. C. (1995). *Darwin's dangerous idea: Evolution and the meanings of life.* New York: Touchstone.

Gruber, H. E. (1974). *Darwin on man: A psychological study of scientific creativity.* London: Wildwood House.

Pinker, S. (1997). *How the mind works.* New York: Norton.

Richards, R. J. (1987). *Darwin and the emergence of evolutionary theories of mind and behavior.* Chicago: University of Chicago Press.

Raymond E. Fancher

DASHIELL, JOHN FREDERICK (1888–1975), American psychologist. A pioneer in the experimental study of learning and author of the first introductory text in psychology based on behavioral principles (*Fundamentals of Objective Psychology, 1928*), he was the founder and head of two departments of psychology (at the University of North Carolina at Chapel Hill in 1920 and at Wake Forest University in 1958). He served as president of the American Psychological Association in 1938 and was the recipient in 1958 of the Gold Medal Award for a lifetime contribution to psychology from the American Psychological Foundation. As an editor Dashiell was instrumental in founding the *Psychological Monographs* as well as establishing a long series of distinguished volumes on psychology published by McGraw-Hill. More than twenty volumes were issued under his editorship. He published widely on experimental studies of learning in rats, based on complex mazes of his own design. Dashiell also developed the first teaching manual in laboratory procedures for undergraduate psychology majors.

Dashiell was born on 30 April 1888 in Southport, Indiana, the ninth child in a family of 12 children of John W. and Fannie S. (Myers) Dashiell. His father was a Methodist minister who frequently moved his family around the state of Indiana. As an undergraduate at Evansville College, Dashiell earned both a bachelor of literature degree in 1908 and a bachelor of science degree in 1909. He was outstanding in college sports as well as in academic work and briefly considered a career in professional sports, trying out as a pitcher with the New York Yankees baseball team.

After graduation, Dashiell entered Columbia University to study philosophy and psychology. There he worked with R. S. Woodworth, John Dewey, E. L. Thorndike, and J. McK. Cattell. He completed a master's degree in 1910 and a Ph.D. degree in 1913. Upon completion of his doctorate, Dashiell served on the philosophy faculties of Princeton University, the University of Minnesota, and Oberlin College before joining the department of philosophy at the University of North Carolina in 1919. In 1920, Dashiell was named head of an autonomous department of psychology. He was named Kenan Professor in 1935 and continued to serve as head of the department until 1949. After retiring in 1958, Dashiell was named a Whitney visiting professor at Wake Forest University in Winston-Salem, North Carolina, where he undertook the establishment of their department of psychology. Subsequently he served on the faculty of the department of psychology at the University of Florida before his final retirement to Chapel Hill. He died on 3 May 1975.

[*Many of the people mentioned in this article are the subjects of independent biographical entries.*]

Bibliography

Dashiell, J. F. (1967). (John Frederick Dashiell.) In E. G. Boring & G. Lindzey (Eds.), *A history of psychology in autobiography* (Vol. 5, pp. 95–124). New York: Appleton-Century-Crofts.

Dashiell, J. F. (1928). *Fundamentals of objective psychology.* Boston: Houghton Mifflin.

Dashiell, J. F. (1931). *An experimental manual in psychology.* Boston: Houghton-Mifflin.

Dashiell, J. F. (1935). Experimental studies of the influence of social situations on the behavior of individual human adults. In C. Murchison (Ed.), *A handbook of social psychology* (pp. 1097–1158). Worcester, MA: Clark University Press.

Dashiell, J. F., & Stetson, R. H. (1919). A multiple unit system of maze construction. *Psychological Bulletin, 16,* 223–230.

W. Grant Dahlstrom

DATA ANALYSIS. The physicist Stephen Hawking has defined a scientific theory as "a model of the universe, or a restricted portion of it, and a set of rules that relate quantities in the model to observations that we make." Psychologists use a wide variety of models to explore human behavior and thinking. For example, mathematical models have been developed to represent basic processes in vision and learning. Similarly, psychologists have developed computer models of such diverse phenomena as associative learning and personality. However, the type of model most widely used in psychological research is represented by the class of statistical models. This class is especially useful in studying human behavior and thought because a distinguishing characteristic of statistical models is that they are stochastic, which means that the model includes a probabilistic component reflecting the inherent uncertainty of the data. As will be described in greater detail later in this chapter, this feature has two important advantages in psychology: it acknowledges the unique nature of individuals, and it provides a foundation for making inferences beyond the specific individuals included in any single study.

As Hawking's quote suggests, statistical models can be used to derive information from observations. Most often, statistical models are applied to quantitative observations, such as scores on a personality inventory or reaction times on a cognitive task. In some cases, however, even when the observations are qualitative rather than quantitative, statistical models can still be used. For example, females and males might be compared to one another on their preferences during a forced-choice task in which the available choices differ from one another along purely qualitative grounds. [*See* Analysis of Counts.] Regardless of whether observations are quantitative or qualitative, statistical models can help researchers examine relationships among variables, which Kerlinger has defined to be the primary goal of behavioral research.

Statistics is often conceptualized as consisting of two distinct but related sets of methods for obtaining information from data. First, descriptive statistics consists of methods for organizing data through numerical summaries and ways of describing data through graphs. The last decade has seen increasing interest in exploratory data analysis as a collection of methods for investigating various properties of data, especially understanding the nature of the relationships between variables. [*See* Exploratory Data Analysis.] Second, inferential statistics consists of methods for making inductive inferences about the extent to which observed properties of data might be expected to maintain themselves in populations over and above the properties displayed in a sample of individuals. Inferential methods are especially important in psychology, because psychologists typically observe relatively small samples of research participants but hope to generalize conclusions to a broader universe of potential individuals. Statistical methods use probability theory to make such inductive inferences possible.

Psychologists employ a wide variety of statistical models in their research because the discipline explores such a vast array of research questions. As Cronbach (1957/1975) pointed out, scientific psychology has developed from two largely unrelated historical traditions. One tradition, the experimental approach, tends to examine situational factors that are presumed to have a consistent influence on individuals. The correlational approach, on the other hand, tends to examine consistent differences between individuals. Thus, psychological methods and statistical models have often developed along two different trajectories, the first designed to identify environmental influences that make individuals behave similarly to one another, and the second designed to identify characteristics of individuals that make them different from one another.

Parameter Estimation and Inference

Regardless of whether the ultimate goal involves situational effects or personal characteristics or some combination of the two, a statistical model is usually formed to represent the presumed relationship among two or more variables. For example, one of the simplest research designs involves randomly assigning individuals to either a treatment group or a control group, and then measuring each individual on some characteristic of interest subsequent to the experimental manipulation. The ensuing question involves the relationship between scores on the characteristic of interest (referred to in this context as the dependent variable) and group membership (referred to as the independent variable). The most typical statistical model for data arising from this design is $Y_{iT} = \mu_T + \varepsilon_{iT}$ for individuals in the treatment group and $Y_{iC} = \mu_C + \varepsilon_{iC}$ for individuals in the control group. The uppercase letter Y on the left side of the equation represents the dependent variable, i.e., the characteristic whose value may depend on the experimental condition. The subscripts (either iT or iC) show that each individual i may have a distinct value of Y. Potential influences on Y are shown on the right side of the equation. This simple model includes only two types of influence. First, μ_T and μ_C are parameters that represent the mean value of Y in the treatment and control conditions, respectively. Second, ε_{iT} and ε_{iC} are random (or stochastic) terms that acknowledge that the Y score of any specific individual i may well be different from the mean score (i.e., either μ_T or μ_C) for that group.

One of the major goals of data analysis is to estimate the parameters of the presumed statistical model. In the example given above, observations are collected in order to estimate μ_T, the mean of a treatment group, and also μ_C, the mean of the control group. The values of these parameters generally are unknown even after collecting observations, because observations are obtained for a sample, which is typically only a very small subset of the entire population of interest. For example, if a treatment is designed to alleviate depression, the population of scientific interest may consist of all depressed individuals in the world (perhaps even including those not yet born), but it is clearly impossible to include all such individuals in a single research study, which might make one doubt the point of collecting data in the first place. However, one of the major contributions of statistics is that it provides methods for using a sample of individuals to obtain estimates of the population parameters of a statistical model. Furthermore, it is often possible to prove mathematically that certain methods provide optimal estimates of parameters contingent on specific additional assumptions. In particular, when the data are normally distributed, the sample mean is the best estimator of the corresponding population mean. (However, when the data are not normal, other estimators may be superior to the sample mean, and, indeed, the search for estimators that perform well under a wide range of distributions is a current research area in statistics.)

Suppose the sample means in our simple example turn out to be 46 for the treatment condition and 50 for the control condition. If lower scores indicate less depression, our best estimate is that μ_T is 4 points less than μ_C, which would imply that the treatment produces an average 4-point improvement on this measure of depression. In order to interpret this difference, two questions must be addressed. First is whether a difference of this magnitude is important from a scientific and/or practical perspective. While this is ultimately a question of content and not methodology, methodologists have nevertheless developed a number of indices of "effect size" to help researchers address this issue. Second, without some indication of the precision of the estimates of the two parameters μ_T and μ_C, it is difficult to know how much confidence to place in this estimated four-point effect. In particular, even if the treatment has no effect in reality whatsoever, the specific sample of individuals in the treatment group could simply be less depressed than the sample in the control group, even in the absence of any true effect produced by the treatment. No matter how sophisticated the research design, this possibility cannot be entirely eliminated. Fortunately, statistical methods allow a researcher to stipulate the precision of the estimated effect, and in particular to test whether the observed effect can truly be distinguished from zero, that is, a null effect. [See Hypothesis Testing.]

Statistical methods allow a researcher to specify a level of confidence to be associated with an interval surrounding the single best estimate of the difference between the parameters. Psychology and most other disciplines that use statistics have adopted a common standard of 95% confidence. After having specified this level of confidence, an interval can be formed based on the observed data. The width of the interval depends on three factors: the level of confidence desired, the variability of scores within each group, and the sample size of each group. To help understand the implications of forming such an interval, suppose that in our hypothetical study this procedure produces an interval estimate of the treatment effect ranging from 0.5 points to 7.5 points.

The fact that this interval does not contain zero is especially important, because it implies that a zero treatment effect is implausible in these data. Forming this confidence interval provides the information needed to test a (null) hypothesis that the difference between μ_T and μ_C equals zero. In these data specifically, this null hypothesis would be rejected because the confidence interval does not contain zero. While forming a confidence interval provides one mechanism for testing the null hypothesis, a t-test can also be performed to test the hypothesis. The t-test rejects the null hypothesis (or yields a statistically significant result) if and only if the confidence interval does not contain zero, so in this respect the confidence interval communicates all of the information contained in the hypothesis test. Regardless of how the test is conducted, this rejection is necessarily probabilistic because the entire population has not been observed. However, the formation of a 95% confidence interval controls the probability of incorrectly rejecting the null hypothesis when it is true at 5%. Unless the entire population is observed, there is always some risk of rejecting the null hypothesis when it is really true, but statistical methods allow researchers to set this probability at some prespecified value, typically 5%. Rejecting the null hypothesis when it is true is referred to as a type I error, and the corresponding probability of committing a type I error is typically denoted α.

Notice that such an interval is centered around the single best estimate (in our example, this is 4 points), but acknowledges that the 4-point estimate is not entirely precise. Upon reflection, however, it is also true that the interval from 0.5 to 7.5 points is not entirely precise, because one cannot be 100% certain that such an interval contains the value of the true population difference between the parameters. The level of confidence can be increased beyond 95% but it can never reach 100% unless the entire population is observed. Furthermore, once the data have been collected and a method of analysis is chosen, the only way to increase the level of confidence is to increase the width of the interval. For example, for a total sample size of 30, the corresponding 99% confidence interval for these data would be from −0.7 points to 8.7 points.

The interval from −0.7 to 8.7 points has the advantage that a higher level of confidence can be attached to it. As a result, the probability of a type I error has been reduced from 5% to 1%. However, the new interval is 35% wider than the original interval, displaying the inevitable trade-off (all other things being equal) between confidence and precision. It is especially noteworthy that the 99% interval, unlike the 95% interval, contains zero. Thus, the 99% confidence interval does not provide sufficient grounds for rejecting the null hypothesis, that the true treatment effect is zero.

From the perspective of testing the null hypothesis,

researchers are at risk of making either of two types of errors. The first type, already mentioned, is rejecting the null hypothesis when it is true. The other possible error is failing to reject the null hypothesis when it is false. This is referred to as a type II error. Notice that by increasing the level of confidence from 95% to 99% (and thereby reducing α from .05 to .01), it has become more difficult to reject the null hypothesis. In fact, in our hypothetical example, the null hypothesis was rejected for 95% confidence but was not rejected for 99% confidence. Thus, all other things being equal, reducing the probability of a type I error necessarily raises the probability of a type II error.

Fortunately, the situation is not so bleak as it may seem because all other things do not have to be equal. In particular, by changing the research design or by increasing the sample size, it is possible to reduce or at least maintain the type I error rate at a desired level while simultaneously lowering the probability of a type II error. Researchers often prefer to conceptualize this issue in terms of statistical power, which is simply the probability of rejecting the null hypothesis when it is false. As such, power is the probability of correctly rejecting the null hypothesis, and simply equals 1 minus the probability of a type II error. Methodologists have devoted considerable attention to procedures for increasing power, especially by developing procedures for calculating necessary sample sizes to achieve a desired level of statistical power for a wide variety of research designs.

While specific models should be chosen according to the research design and the scientific questions to be addressed, the overall goals of statistical analysis remain much the same. Arguably the most basic goal is to assess the adequacy of the model. Even a simple independent-groups t-test assumes that data are normally distributed, that scores are equally variable within the two groups, and that scores are independent of one another. In some cases violations of such assumptions call into question any model inferences, while in other cases procedures have been shown to be robust to violations of assumptions. When assumptions may be doubtful and robustness is questionable, other methods such as nonparametric approaches can be advantageous. [See Nonparametric Statistics.]

After having assessed the adequacy of the model, the next goal typically involves estimating parameters of the model. While the meaning of such parameters clearly depends on the specific model and the research design that generated the data, the overall structure of the statistical phase of the research nevertheless tends to remain much the same. In addition to estimating the parameters of the model, researchers usually also hope to infer model characteristics for the population. This step typically consists of forming confidence intervals and/or testing null hypotheses about model parameters, either individually or as a group. While simultaneous inferences about multiple parameters can be useful for making inferences about the global characteristics of models, it is almost always important to conduct more focused investigations of individual parameters as well.

Additional Examples of Statistical Models

The specific example discussed up to this point involves comparing the means of two groups of individuals. Even within the restricted domain of comparing means, methodologists have developed a wide array of research designs and accompanying statistical techniques. In general, analysis of variance refers to a collection of statistical models whose parameters represent population group means. [See Analysis of Variance.] In the simplest extension of the example presented earlier, there might be a second treatment group, potentially necessitating an additional parameter in the model. More generally, analysis of variance models allow a variety of structures among groups, including factorial and nested designs, as well as repeated measures designs, in which each individual is measured on more than one occasion. Repeated measures designs are especially important in psychological research for two independent reasons. First, by repeatedly observing the same individual over a variety of treatment conditions, statistical power can be increased without having to increase the number of research participants. Second, many psychological questions involve a consideration of how individuals change over time, so repeated observations of the same individual over time may be of interest, frequently leading to a repeated measures design. In the latter case, notice that repeated observations are pertinent because individuals may naturally be changing over time, whereas in the former case repeated observations are obtained because the experimenter has chosen to vary the treatment condition to which each individual is exposed. Both cases lead to a repeated measures design, or a within-subjects design, as it is sometimes called. Analysis of variance encompasses a wide variety of designs and thus can serve as a viable statistical model for a wide range of statistical questions. However, a potentially serious disadvantage of analysis of variance models is that all variation within a group is regarded as error, when in most psychological studies a substantial component of within-group variability may reflect true individual differences. Analysis of covariance provides an extension of the analysis of variance that allows the inclusion of one or more individual-difference variables.

While mean comparisons are central to some psychological investigations, oftentimes the research question leads to other types of statistical methods, necessitating approaches other than analysis of variance and analysis of covariance. One such method is multiple regression analysis. Both analysis of variance and analysis of covariance models can be viewed as special cases of the multiple regression model, which expresses scores on a dependent variable Y as a linear additive function of one or more predictor variables. For example, the following model states that the score for individual i on variable Y can be expressed as a weighted linear combination of the three predictor variables X_1, X_2, and X_3.

$$Y_i = \beta_0 + \beta_1 X_{1i} + \beta_2 X_{2i} + \beta_3 X_{3i} + \varepsilon_i$$

The weights β_0, β_1, β_2, and β_3 then become model parameters to be estimated based on sample observations. The multiple regression model is much more flexible than it might appear, because one or more of the X variables can be reexpressions of the original predictor variables. For example, some or all of the X variables can be coded to represent group membership, which is why the model subsumes analysis of variance and covariance. Furthermore, an X variable as entered in the model can be a transformation of an original variable. For example, instead of using reaction time as a predictor of some Y variable, a researcher might decide to use the logarithm of reaction time as the X variable in a regression model. Or, the researcher might choose to enter both reaction time and the square of reaction time as predictors in the model. Thus, the model can represent a variety of nonlinear forms of relationships among variables. Similarly, although the model may appear to be restricted to additive relationships, a single X variable might in truth be the product of reaction time and number of errors, which allows for a specific form of nonadditive (i.e., interactive) relationship.

The multiple regression model itself can be generalized in any of several ways. In particular, psychological research often involves the simultaneous consideration of multiple dependent variables. The general linear model expands the multiple regression model by allowing for multiple Y variables. For example, if there are p Y variables, the model includes p β_0 parameters, p β_1 parameters, p β_2 parameters, and so forth. The general linear model then encompasses a wide variety of procedures as special cases, such as analysis of variance, analysis of covariance, multiple regression, multivariate analysis of variance, multivariate analysis of covariance, and discriminant analysis.

The general linear model can in turn be generalized in two important ways. First factor analysis expands on the general linear model by allowing unmeasured latent variables to be included in the model. Notice that the general linear model and all its special cases outlined above require that at least one Y variable and at least one X variable be observed. Furthermore, a numerical score is obtained for each individual on each variable, although in some cases a variable may arbitrarily be coded to reflect group membership (e.g., individuals in a treatment group are coded 1 on X, while individuals in a control group receive a score of 0). However, in 1904 Charles Spearman developed a model called factor analysis, whereby the predictor variables are neither observed nor measured. For example, with four dependent variables this model might be written as:

$$Y_{i1} = \beta_{10} + \beta_{11} F_i + \varepsilon_{1i}$$

$$Y_{i2} = \beta_{20} + \beta_{21} F_i + \varepsilon_{2i}$$

$$Y_{i3} = \beta_{30} + \beta_{31} F_i + \varepsilon_{3i}$$

$$Y_{i4} = \beta_{40} + \beta_{41} F_i + \varepsilon_{4i}$$

Although this model has the same appearance as the general linear model, there is a crucial difference because the F variable is not measured. Instead, it is a latent variable, or a factor. Even though scores on F are not observed, under certain specified conditions it is nevertheless possible to estimate the β parameters in the model and test relevant null hypotheses. For example, the model shown above would allow a researcher to test a hypothesis that a single latent variable explains common individual differences observed on the four Y variables. Factor analytic models have received much attention from psychologists over the years in part because, as Cronbach pointed out, the study of individual differences has been one of the two main traditions of scientific psychology. In recent years latent variable models have received additional attention also because of the realization that most theoretical constructs in psychology cannot be measured perfectly.

Second, although the general linear model allows simultaneous investigation of multiple dependent and multiple independent variables, it sometimes is not flexible enough to serve as an appropriate statistical model. One potentially major limitation is that it requires each variable to serve as either an independent variable or a dependent variable. However, it does not allow a variable to appear on both sides of the equation. In reality, however, a researcher may conceptualize some variables as both causes and effects in a broader system of variables. Structural equation modeling (also referred to as covariance structure modeling) generalizes the general linear model by allowing some variables to be included on the left side of an equation (thus constituting a dependent variable) but also on the right side of one or more other equations (thus constituting an independent variable in this context). Such models are especially useful for studying intervening relationships where one variable is thought to mediate the relationship between two others. For example, in a simple case, X_1 might be hypothesized to cause X_2, which in turn is thought to cause X_3, so in this system X_2 plays the role of both cause and effect. Structural equation modeling has the important added benefit that it allows latent variables as well as observed variables to serve as both causes and effects.

Another recent generalization of the general linear model is multilevel modeling, also referred to as hierarchical linear modeling. Like the general linear model and the structural equation model, the multilevel model allows more than one equation. The distinguishing characteristic of the multilevel model is that the multiple equations pertain to different levels of data. For example, one popular application of the multilevel model is to longitudinal data, in which multiple individuals may be measured over multiple points in time. The multilevel model expresses such data in terms of two distinct equations. The first equation models the pattern of each individual's changing scores over time. In this idiographic model, one or more parameters are estimated for each individual. These parameters then essentially become dependent variables in another set of models based on between-individual characteristics. Multilevel models can be useful not only for modeling change over time, but also for studying individuals in environmental contexts. For example, an educational psychologist might be interested in studying individual-level and school-level correlates of math achievement.

Summary

The diversity of psychological inquiry and the complexity of behavioral research requires a sophisticated array of methodological tools. The development of new statistical methods allows psychological researchers to explore old scientific questions from new perspectives, as well as to point out entirely different ways of conceptualizing research questions. While psychological methodology is ever changing, basic principles of research design, measurement, and data analysis serve to unite the vast diversity of questions addressed by the discipline of psychology.

[See also Analysis of Counts; Analysis of Variance; Exploratory Data Analysis; Hypothesis Testing; Nonparametric Statistics; and Statistical Significance.]

Bibliography

Bentler, P. M., & Dudgeon, P. (1996). Covariance structure analysis: Statistical practice, theory, and directions. *Annual Review of Psychology, 47*, 563–592.

Bollen, K. A. (1989). *Structural equations with latent variables.* New York: Wiley.

Bryk, A. S., & Raudenbush, S. W. (1992). *Hierarchical linear models: Applications and data analysis methods.* Newbury Park, CA: Sage.

Cohen, J. (1988). *Statistical power analysis for the behavioral sciences* (2nd ed.). Hillsdale, NJ: Erlbaum.

Cronbach, L. J. (1957). The two disciplines of scientific psychology. *American Psychologist, 12,* 671–684.

Cronbach, L. J. (1975). Beyond the two disciplines of scientific psychology. *American Psychologist, 30,* 116–127.

Freedman, D., Pisani, R., Purves, R., & Adhikari, A. (1991). *Statistics* (2nd ed.). New York: Norton.

Hays, W. L. (1994). *Statistics* (5th ed.). Fort Worth, TX: Harcourt Brace.

Johnson, R. A., & Wichern, D. W. (1992). *Applied multivariate statistical analysis* (3rd ed.). Englewood Cliffs, NJ: Prentice Hall.

Jones, L. V., & Appelbaum, M. I. (1989). Psychometric methods. In M. R. Rosenzweig & L. W. Porter (Eds.), *Annual review of psychology* (Vol. 40, pp. 23–43). Palo Alto, CA: Annual Reviews, Inc.

Judd, C. M., & McClelland, G. H. (1989). *Data analysis: A model-comparison approach.* San Diego: Harcourt Brace.

Judd, C. M., McClelland, G. H., & Culhane, S. E. (1995). Data analysis: Continuing issues in the everyday analysis of psychological data. *Annual Review of Psychology, 46,* 433–465.

Kenny, D. A. (1996). The design and analysis of social-interaction research. *Annual Review of Psychology, 47,* 59–86.

Maxwell, S. E., & Delaney, H. D. (1990). *Designing experiments and analyzing data: A model comparison perspective.* Belmont, CA: Wadsworth.

Scott E. Maxwell

DATA COLLECTION. [*This entry comprises two articles*: Field Research *and* Laboratory Research. *Included for each article is an overview of the concept and its purpose, importance, and role in the field of psychological research, including its historical development, methodology, and various types. See also* Artifact; Assessment; Case Study; Data Analysis; Direct Observation; Qualitative Research; Sampling; Statistical Significance; *and* Survey Methodology.]

Field Research

The term *field research* refers to a systematic investigation that is carried out in the field, as opposed to in a laboratory. There are numerous methods that can be categorized as field research, including experiments in naturalistic settings, ethnographic fieldwork, systematic observational methods, field surveys and interviews, and the use of unobtrusive methods.

Methods of Research

Ethnographic fieldwork aims to describe a society's culture. It identifies what people must have learned in order to participate acceptably in the activities of the society. It describes also how people deal with one another. To do this the researcher first learns the language of the people in that setting and then categorizes the people, things, and events to which individuals in a given society respond. The investigator examines the dimensions that distinguish these categories, the distribution of the categories on those dimensions, and often describes how people govern themselves, ritual performances, and methods of conducting local affairs. To do a good job the ethnographer must keep good notes of daily observations, and store and retrieve the data in the field to form generalizations about the culture. Upon returning to their base, researchers often write a book (an ethnography) that summarizes the data and their generalizations.

Systematic observations in naturalistic settings specify how behavior is taking place in a particular setting. This approach requires specification of the units of study, such as categories of people, behavior, and settings. Systems of data recording vary on two dimensions: all-inclusive description (e.g., videotaping of social behavior) versus selective description (e.g., recording only who asks questions of whom), and behavioral replicas (e.g., films) versus transformations (e.g., trait ratings). Crucial issues include how to sample people, settings, and events. Should one record behavior rates or proportions of different types of behavior? How should interactional sequences be recorded? Should one record only motor behavior, verbal behavior, or both? Should the observer use instrumental aids (e.g., a written protocol and shorthand) or some coding system such as checklists? Coding has to specify time intervals, behavior boundaries, theoretical bases, breadth or detail of coverage. Distortions may be introduced while coders work, because they are susceptible to shifts in their levels of adaptation. For example, if they have coded a very large number of aggressive behaviors, a mildly aggressive behavior may be coded as neutral.

Surveys and interviewing examine the beliefs, attitudes, and values of samples of a population. Sampling of people, questions, and response formats are important issues. Questionnaires (administered to groups of people or through the mail) and face-to-face interviews have similar problems. Social disclosure is often problematic. [See Research Methods, article on Concepts and Practices.] The authenticity of the survey reflects the capability of the interviewer to get unbiased and genuine responses from the respondent. Authenticity depends on who the interviewer is (affiliation, image, similarity to interviewee, respondent relevance for the topic under investigation, interviewer bias); what the setting is (how relevant to the topic, social desirability of the setting, capacity to reach depth, length, and structure of the interview or questionnaire). It also includes respondent factors (gap between private and public opinions, previous experience with similar methods, saturation with studies, response sets), and cultural factors (norms for giving answers, reticence, game playing with interviewers who are perceived as out-group members). The interviewers usually must be trained, and the preparation of a booklet that discusses the problems of interviewing is recommended in order to minimize artifacts. [See Artifact, article on Artifact in Assessment.]

Tests and inventories are used to measure abilities, personality, and attitudes. Projective techniques can also be used to measure motives. Many of the issues discussed under surveys and interviews are also relevant with tests and projective techniques. Construct validation where the measurements of the antecedents and consequences of a construct conform to the expectations of theory are especially important. [See Attitudes, article on Attitude Measurement; Projective Methods; Construct Validity; and Data Analysis.] Issues of data analyses, such as the comparability of the measurements across samples, must be considered.

Unobtrusive methods in which the participants are unaware that they are being studied, usually examine attitudes. These methods are especially appropriate when the issue under investigation is taboo, embarrassing, or the issue is subject to incompatible normative pressures. The classic description of these methods was presented by Eugene J. Webb and associates in *Unobtrusive Measures: Nonreactive Research in the Social Sciences* (Chicago, 1966/1981) and are discussed elsewhere in detail. [See Unobtrusive Methods.]

Concerns have been expressed about the ethical acceptability of unobtrusive methods, on the grounds that there is no informed consent. For example, the "lost letter technique" involves dropping 400 or so letters in a wide sample of locations in a city. The assumption is that people who see the letters would mail them. If they favor the recipient (addressee) they will be more likely to mail the letter than if they object to the recipient. Half the letters are addressed to a socially controversial recipient (e.g., a proabortion committee) and the other half, randomly determined, to a neutral recipient. The difference in the rate of return of the two sets of letters is used as an indicator of attitudes toward the controversial addressee. For example, if 100 of the 200 letters to the neutral recipient are mailed, but only 50 of the 200 letters to the controversial recipient are mailed, this would imply a substantial opposition to the controversial recipient. However, if people had heard of this method, the results would be distorted. That is, people who knew about the method would become suspicious if they found a letter that had been dropped near a mailbox; they might not mail it, even if the letter was not part of an experiment. Thus, a further ethical concern is that a socially desirable act (mailing the letter that did not get into a mailbox) may not occur.

General Problems of Field Methods

All field methods raise issues of sampling, authenticity, reliability, and validity. Sampling people ideally should be done in such a way as to obtain a representative sample of the population to which the researchers wish to generalize. For example, one might use area probability sampling to represent the population of a city. This can be done by listing all the blocks of the city and taking a random sample of these blocks. Then in each block one can list all the addresses, and take a random sample of these addresses. Then at each address one can list all the individuals who are normally living or working at that address, and take either a random or systematic sample (e.g., all voters) of the people or study all these individuals. This method of sampling has the advantage that the error of measurement can be calculated at each step and the total error of measurement can be estimated for the particular survey. However, some individuals do not wish to be surveyed, which is especially true for those who are members of disadvantaged populations, do not speak the language of the interviewer, have a criminal record, or are trying to hide from the authorities (e.g., illegal immigrants). [See Reliability; Validity; and Sampling.]

Sampling a universe of questions that captures the important aspects of a construct is also important. Constructs can be broad or narrow. If the construct is broad (e.g., intelligence), then one should sample the various kinds of intelligence (verbal, quantitative, emotional, memory, creativity, etc.). The broader the construct, the less internal consistency there will be in its measurement. Ideally one needs to measure each of the different aspects of the construct separately. Thus the fidelity of measurement is usually inversely correlated with the breadth of measurement. If one examines a narrow aspect (e.g., memory for faces) one can get high levels of reliability, but the measure will be unrelated to other aspects of intelligence. If one measures the construct broadly (i.e., different aspects of intelligence), the internal consistency of the measurements (say, memory for faces would not correlate with verbal intelligence) will be low.

Sampling the response formats is also important. One can ask people to perform a variety of tasks, such as rate, rank, remember, freely associate, complete sentences, write stories that correspond to a picture, push buttons, recognize, interact with others, and so on. Again issues of breadth and fidelity will have to be considered. Rating may not correlate with ranking as well as one might expect. Two rating tasks will be correlated with each other because they require the same type of response. This similarity suggests reliability, but it does not guarantee that one has obtained an adequate, useful measure.

The dissimilarity of interviewee and interviewer can introduce distortions. It can reduce authenticity (see above) and can result in avoidance of the interviewer. In some cultures women cannot be interviewed by male researchers. In some cultures it is mandatory to lie to an outsider, and one entertains one's friends by mentioning what lies one has told to the outsider.

Response sets such as social desirability, acquiescence (saying "Yes" or "Agree" to all questions), extreme response style ("Very Strongly Agree/Disagree"), or moderate style (using the middle of a scale, no matter what the question) can distort the results. [See Social Desirability.] Sometimes these response sets can be overcome by methodological strategies, but experts are concerned that some strategies can introduce their own distortions and artifacts.

Bibliography

Triandis, H. C., & Berry, J. W. (Eds.). (1980). *Handbook of cross-cultural psychology* (Vol. 2). Boston: Allyn & Bacon. Contains detailed descriptions of the procedures mentioned in this article, and other methods of data collection in field research.

Webb, E. J., Campbell, D. T., Schwartz, R. D., Sechrest, L., & Grove, J. B. (1981). *Nonreactive methods in the social sciences* (2nd ed.). Boston: Houghton Mifflin. (Original work published 1966.) Revision and update of Webb et al.'s classic text, *Unobtrusive measures: Nonreactive research in the United States.* This book also discusses the ethical dilemma arising from the use of such methods.

Harry C. Triandis

Laboratory Research

Data collection is a critical phase in all laboratory research. The term refers to many different kinds of activities, because data come in many different forms. Depending on the questions asked and the research techniques used, the data collected from participants may be responses on questionnaires, reaction times to stimuli presented on computer screens, recall or recognition of events that were recently experienced, physiological measures such as heart rate, or dozens of other measures designed by psychologists to explore behavior. The critical quality that researchers desire is for data to be unbiased, so that the hypothesis or question posed by the research can be put to a fair and accurate test. [See Data Collection, *article on* Field Research.]

In *Unobtrusive Measures* (Chicago, 1966), Webb, Campbell, Schwartz, and Sechrist pointed out that one central dimension of data is whether they result from direct (obtrusive) or indirect (unobtrusive) measures. If participants are aware that the responses they produce are being measured, the data are said to be collected by direct or obtrusive measures. If other aspects of behavior are measured (e.g., speed of walking from the lab, or eye contact during an experimental session) without the participants' awareness, the measures are said to be indirect or unobtrusive. Direct measures are often appropriate. For example, if a researcher wants to test a person's recollection of recent events, the person must be made aware of this purpose in order to participate. However, in other cases, indirect measures may be appropriate, especially when a participant's behavior may change if he or she knows that observation is occurring. [See Hawthorne Effect; Artifact, *article on* Artifact in Assessment; *and* Unobtrusive Measures.]

Data collection is typically arranged to be as free as possible from bias. One type of bias is fraud: Researchers may discard data that disagree with their hypothesis, or they may fudge data in slightly less obvious ways. Many famous examples of fraud exist in science. However, because of the self-correcting nature of science, in which replication and confirmation of results by other researchers is part and parcel of the process, outright fraud (although reprehensible) may not, in the long run, pose too much danger to the scientific enterprise. Therefore, although cases of outright fraud do exist and must be guarded against, the typical problem of bias in data collection is more subtle [See Artifact, *article on* Artifact in Research.]

We consider several problems that can compromise data collection: (a) the effects researchers can unintentionally exert on data analysis; (b) experimenter expectancy effects; and (c) effects of participants and their expectancies on research. During data collection, many opportunities exist for bias to creep in. Some are very simple. If the experimenter collects the data by hand, he or she may simply misrecord what the participant did or said. (Automated research procedures, especially those using computers, make this error less likely). In a related vein, researchers may relax their criteria for collecting data over the course of the research, becoming more casual in the systematic and rigorous application of the procedure, and they may be unaware of doing so. This practice may change the data as they are collected over time.

More subtly, researchers may set criteria for elimination of participants' data that do not meet certain conditions of the experiment. For example, there may be a manipulation check to ensure that the experimental variable has had an effect. This practice is often a good one, and if it is applied in the same way to all conditions of the experiment, no bias should occur. However, if the criteria are applied slightly differently to the various conditions, then more participants may be dropped from one condition than another, thereby influencing the results. Similarly, researchers measuring reaction times often drop responses that are outliers (those that are very different from the mean of the group). The idea is that the participant's attention may have wandered (or he or she may have fallen asleep) on that trial, and therefore the data should be discarded as unrepresentative. This seems fair, but if one condition of the experiment actually does produce more variable responding than does another condition, then more responses might be excluded from this first condition. The result is that behavior in the two conditions might look more similar than is really the case, because the outlying responses were eliminated from the first condition.

These subtle biasing factors are difficult to eliminate completely; after all, they are often produced by the desire to remove bias in the data, such as by eliminating outliers that are unrepresentative of the data. The best strategy is to provide multiple approaches to data analysis (different cutoffs for outliers, different criteria for excluding participants) to see if the same conclusions hold under all sets of assumptions. To the extent that the same conclusions hold across various practices, then the researchers may have more confidence in accepting the findings as valid.

Another problem is the experimenter expectancy effect, discussed by Robert Rosenthal in *Experimenter Effects in Behavioral Research* (New York, 1966): If an experimenter testing participants knows the condition in which they are being tested, the experimenter may behave differently in subtle ways and influence the outcome of the research. For this reason, research is often conducted under conditions in which the experimenter is unaware (or "blind") with respect to the condition in which the individual participates. This practice minimizes or eliminates experimenter expectancy from influencing the outcome of the research. In some computerized studies in cognitive psychology, the computer administers the various experimental manipulations without intervention of the researcher, which also circumvents the problem. When it is not possible to make the experimenter unaware of conditions, then he or she should work diligently to treat all participants in all conditions as similarly as possible; only the experimental manipulation should vary. [See Expectancy Effects.]

A third type of bias in data collection is that exerted by the expectancies of the participants themselves. For example, a procedure or strategy might be hypothesized to improve participants' memories in one condition (an experimental condition) relative to another (the control condition). However, if participants in the experimental condition know or expect that the procedure may improve memory, then they may try harder in this condition than do those participants in the control condition, therefore introducing a confounding factor and biasing the data collection. It is difficult to guard against this problem in all types of research, because participants in psychological research often must be made aware of the topic of study in order to be tested. When participants can be rendered unaware of the condition of the experiment, they are also said to be blind to the condition of the experiment. An example occurs in testing the effects of drugs. If a drug is tested to improve mood in depressed individuals, it is necessary to have at least two conditions. Both groups are told that the study is about whether a particular drug elevates mood, but those in one group receive the actual drug, whereas those in the other group receive an inert substance (a placebo) that does not influence mood. The participants will not know if they are assigned to the drug or the placebo condition. Even the placebo control group's moods will probably improve during the course of the experiment, due to the expectancy or placebo effect; therefore, the question at issue is whether moods of those in the experimental group receiving the drug will improve more than the moods of those in the control group. If so, the conclusion could be drawn that the drug is effective. The placebo condition overcomes the pitfall of participant expectancy effects hampering conclusions that can be drawn from the data [See Demand Characteristics; and Placebo Effect in Research Design.]

In some cases it is possible to overcome both experimenter expectancy effects and participant expectancy effects simultaneously by using procedures in which both parties are unaware of the assigned condition of the participant. In these cases, the experiment is said to be conducted under "double-blind" conditions. Because neither the experimenter nor the participant knows what condition is being tested in double-blind studies, some third person keeps records as to the assignment of participants to conditions.

Data collection in the laboratory is a central aspect of most psychological research. Careful researchers provide safeguards so that the data will be unbiased and permit a valid test of the issue under study. Researchers must be on constant guard to show that the forms of bias discussed here do not cloud interpretation of their results.

Bibliography

Barber, T. X. (1976). *Pitfalls in human research: Ten pivotal points.* New York: Pergamon Press. A brief, excellent overview of ten pitfalls that can hamper interpretation of research results.

Boring, E. G. (1961). The nature and history of experimental control. *American Journal of Psychology, 67,* 573–589. This article provides attempts in experimental psychology to gain experimental control.

Broad, W., & Wade, N. (1982). *Betrayers of the truth.* New York: Simon & Schuster. A book about fraud in science, including some fascinating cases.

Elmes, D. G., Kantowitz, B. H., & Roediger, H. L. (1998). *Research methods in experimental psychology* (6th ed.). Pacific Grove, CA: Brooks/Cole. A textbook providing an overview of naturalistic, correlational, and experimental research methods.

Hyman, R. (1964). *The nature of psychological inquiry.* Englewood Cliffs, NJ: Prentice Hall. An excellent book outlining the process of psychological research.

Rosenthal, R., & Rosnow, R. L. (Eds.). (1969). *Artifact in behavioral research.* San Diego, CA: Academic Press. This important book includes chapters by experts on sources of artifact in research and ways to overcome them.

Henry L. Roediger III and Erik T. Bergman

DATE RAPE. *See* Rape.

DAY CARE. Three major, often conflicting, purposes for day care create the dilemma we see today. First, day care supports maternal employment, which is a necessity for individual families and for the economy. Second, child care (a term preferred over day care) serves children's development, which can be enhanced by high-quality early childhood programs, whether or not their mothers are employed. Third, child care has been used throughout the twentieth century to socialize economically disadvantaged and ethnic minority children to the cultural mainstream (Scarr & Weinberg, 1986).

The roots of child care are in the welfare and reform movements of the nineteenth century. Day nurseries, which evolved into the child care centers of today, began in Boston in the 1840s to care for poor and immigrant children, whose mothers had to work (Scarr & Weinberg, 1986). The primary purpose of day nurseries was to keep the children of the poor safe and fed while their mothers worked. Other benefits, such as early education, were secondary. By the late 1960s, educators and child development researchers recognized the value of nursery schools for poor children, who needed the stimulation and learning opportunities that such early childhood settings afforded children from affluent families.

By contrast, kindergartens and nursery school began in the early twentieth century with the purpose of enhancing the social development of middle- and upper-class children. For a few hours a week, the children could play with others and experience an enriched learning environment under the tutelage of trained early childhood teachers. Nursery schools existed to serve the developmental needs of middle- and upper-class children, whose mothers were not employed

(Scarr & Weinberg, 1986). Now that the majority of middle-class mothers are employed, distinctions between day care and early education are blurred.

In 1995, 62.3% of mothers with children under six years were employed. This rate was up more than 2% from 1994 and nearly 5% from 1993. Among mothers with children under two years, 57.9% were working in March 1995, up 3.5% from 1993. The ideal of a non-employed mother remained strong, however. One legacy for working mothers of the baby boom generation and beyond is guilt about their employment.

Varieties of Child Care Arrangements

When the focus is on early childhood education, whether for higher- or lower-income children, the setting is usually a center or preschool. When the focus is on care while parents work, the setting is often a home.

Family Day Care Versus Center Care. Family day care providers care for children in their own homes. The provider's own children are often included in the mix of ages from infants through schoolage children who come before and after school. Most family day care homes accommodate 6 or fewer children with one caregiver. Some larger homes care for 6 to 20 children and employ aides. States generally regulate larger homes.

Child care centers provide group care for children from infancy to school age in age-segregated groups with smaller ratios of children to adults at younger ages. Facilities vary from church basements to purpose-built centers with specialized spaces and equipment. The most notable differences between homes and centers are educational curricula and staff training, which centers are required to provide and homes are not. Parents prefer center-based care for preschool children and use more home care for infants and toddlers.

Licensed Versus Unlicensed Care. In all states child care centers must be licensed by a state department of social services or its equivalent. (In 11 states, church-sponsored child care is exempt from all but health and safety licensure.) Licensure includes regulations on health and safety, ratios of children to adults, group sizes, staff training, and often required play materials. Regular inspections are done in semiannual or annual visits, and more frequent visits if problems have been noted.

Most family day care providers care for fewer than six children and are therefore exempt from any state regulation or inspection. Availability of federal food subsidies to licensed homes, however, has encouraged more family day homes to seek licensure or registration. Family day care homes are rarely visited by state regulators.

Nonprofit Versus For-Profit Centers. In the United States, child care centers are sponsored by churches, nonprofit community groups, public schools, Head Start, employers, for-profit independent providers, and corporations. The mix of public provision and private enterprise in U.S. child care reflects the ambivalence Americans feel about whether child care is primarily a publicly supported service for children or a business expense for working. Should tax dollars be used to supply child care only to poor children, or should all children be eligible for publicly supported child care? Should family day care and privately owned centers *profit* from the child care business, or should child care be a public service like primary education?

Where Are Children Today?

In 1995, there were nearly 21 million children under the age of 5 who were not yet enrolled in school. Of these, about 40% were cared for regularly by parents, 21% by other relatives, 31% in child care centers, 14% in family day care homes, and 4% by sitters in the child's home. These figures total more than 100%, because 9% of children have more than one regular care arrangement (Hofferth, 1996).

In 1965 only 6% of children were cared for in centers; by 1995, 31% were (Hofferth, 1996). Children from more affluent families and those from families on welfare were most likely to be enrolled in centers rather than cared for in homes. Families with more than $50,000 annual income can afford center-based programs; those below the poverty line receive subsidies for child care. Working families with incomes below $25,000 per year are the least likely to afford center-based care.

A Labor Force Perspective on Child Care Research

Today, 48% of workers are women; 80% of those women are mothers. Mothers (and fathers) are employed because their families need or want the income to enhance their standard of living. Two thirds of mothers are working to keep their families out of poverty (Scarr, Phillips, & McCartney, 1990). With welfare reform, this proportion has increased.

Gender Equality. Another reason for maternal employment is to promote economic, social, and political gender equality. The major reason for women's lesser compensation and career achievements is due to family responsibilities that fall more heavily on women, especially when there are small children in the home. Unequal child care responsibilities lead mothers to be less motivated to maintain continuous, full-time employment, which is the key to income advances. Income inequalities between men and women are largely explained by the lower labor force participation of mothers in their child-bearing years. In 1995, *childless* women in their 20s and 30s earned 98% of men's wages (*Wall Street Journal*, 1997).

If child care costs were more reasonable, national

surveys show that 10 to 20% more mothers would return to the labor force after giving birth. Accessibility and cost determine the impact of child care on parents (Prosser and McGroder, 1992). Travel time to a child care setting directly affects how likely a mother is to stay in the labor force. Middle- and upper-income mothers are much more likely to keep their jobs if they use day care centers, whereas labor force participation among low income mothers depends on the availability of relatives to care for children, because they cannot afford to pay market rates for child care (Collins & Hofferth, 1996).

Since the late 1980s, married mothers have been working at the same rate as single mothers (Scarr, Phillips, & McCartney, 1989). By the mid-1990s, public empathy for mothers supported by Aid for Families with Dependent Children (AFDC) to stay home with their children had evaporated. Reform of the welfare system rose to the top of the political agenda and was passed in 1996. Child care is *the* essential ingredient in welfare reform and mothers' employment.

Absenteeism and Productivity Effects. When child care arrangements break down, employed parents are more likely to be absent, to be late, to report being unable to concentrate on the job, to have higher levels of stress and more stress-related health problems, and to report lower parental and marital satisfaction. Breakdowns in child care arrangements are frequent and stressful; in a Portland study, 36% of fathers and 46% of mothers who used out-of-home care reported child care–related stress. Leading causes of child care breakdown are child illness and a provider who quits (Galinsky, 1992).

A Child Development Perspective on Child Care Research

Since child care can extend from birth through adolescence, research involves a complex array of factors.

Infant Care. Nonmaternal infant care is the most controversial issue in child care research. From the mid-1980s to the present, dramatic claims have been made about the damaging effects of early entry into day care on infants' attachments to their mothers (Belsky, 1992). The NICHD Early Child Care Research Study (NICHD, 1997) of more than 1,000 infants shows no relationship between age at entry or amount of infant care and attachments, measured by the Strange Situation (for reviews, see Scarr, 1998). Naturally, less sensitive, less well-adjusted mothers are more likely to have insecurely attached infants. Several interaction effects suggest that higher quality day care may help to offset poor mothering (NICHD, in 1997).

Dimensions of Quality. Child care researchers and practitioners around the world agree that quality child care consists of warm, supportive interactions with adults in a safe, healthy, and stimulating environment, where learning opportunities and trusting relationships combine to support individual children's physical, emotional, social, and intellectual development. Poor care is unresponsive to children's needs, not deliberately cruel.

Quality of day care in the United States varies from excellent to dreadful and is, on average, mediocre (NICHD, 1996; Scarr, Phillips, McCartney, & Abbott-Shim, 1993). Quality is measured in units that are regulated (such as ratios of teachers to children and teacher training) and in observations, such as adult-child interactions and appropriate activities. Although quality is a multifaceted concept, commonly used measures have similar dimensions (Scarr, Eisenberg, & Deater-Deckard, 1994).

Effects of Poor Quality. Poor quality child care has been reported to put children's development at risk for poorer language and cognitive scores and lesser ratings of social and emotional adjustment (for a review, see Scarr & Eisenberg, 1993). Measures of child care quality account for 1 to 2% of the variation in child measures, a small effect. The implications of even small effects are not straightforward, however, because the quality of care selected by parents is correlated with parents' personal characteristics (Bolger & Scarr, 1995), thereby complicating interpretations of any effects of child care per se.

Long-Term Effects of Day Care. Parents and policy makers want to know if quality differences in early child care have lasting benefits or detriments for children. Low-income children definitely benefit from quality child care, which has been used successfully to improve their early development (Field, 1991; Ramey & Ramey, 1992). For children from middle- and upper-income families, the long-term picture is far less clear. Long-term effects of day care quality were reported in longitudinal studies by Vandell, Henderson, and Wilson (1988) and Howes (1988), but recent studies fail to confirm those results. Our research group has conducted four longitudinal studies of child care quality and family effects on children's development from infancy to school age, with null results in all cases (Chin-Quee & Scarr, 1994; Deater-Deckard, Pinkerton, & Scarr, 1996; McCartney, et al., 1997; Scarr, Lande, & McCartney, 199; Scarr, Phillips, McCartney, & Abbott-Shim, 1993; Scarr & Thompson, 1994).

Conclusion

Within a broad range of safe environments, the effects of quality variations in child care on most children's development are small and temporary. These results do not apply to children from low-income homes, for many of whom quality child care programs supply missing elements of emotional support and intellectual opportunities. Quality variation within the range of centers studied does not have a major impact on the development of children from ordinary homes. Given the learning opportunities and social-emotional support that their homes generally offer, child care of mediocre to good quality is not a unique or lasting experience for them. For most children, parents supply the genes and the home environments, which correlate with the care they select for their children outside of the home.

[See also Fathering; and Preschool Education.]

Bibliography

Belsky, J. (1992). Consequences of child care for children's development: A deconstructionist view. In A. Booth (Ed.), *Child care in the 1990s: Trends and consequences*. (pp. 83–94). Hillsdale, NJ: Erlbaum.

Bolger, K. E., & Scarr, S. (1995). Not so far from home: How family characteristics predict child care quality. *Early Development and Parenting, 4,* 103–112.

Chin-Quee, D., & Scarr, S. (1994). Lack of longitudinal effects of infant and preschool child care on school-age children's social and intellectual development. *Early Development and Parenting, 2,* 103–112.

Deater-Deckard, K., Pinkerton, R., & Scarr, S. (1996). Child care quality and children's behavioral adjustment: A four-year longitudinal study. *Journal of Child Psychology and Psychiatry, 37,* 937–948.

Field, T. (1991). Quality infant day-care and grade school behavior and performance. *Child Development, 62,* 863–870.

Galinsky, E. (1992). The impact of child care on parents. In A. Booth (Ed.), *Child care in the 1990s: Trends and consequences* (pp. 159–171). Hillsdale, NJ: Erlbaum.

Hofferth, S. (1996). Child care in the United States today. *The Future of Children, 6,* 41–61.

Howes, C. (1988). Relations between early child care and schooling. *Developmental Psychology, 24,* 53–57.

McCartney, K., Scarr, S., Rocheleau, A., Phillips, D., Eisenberg, M., Keefe, N., Rosenthal, S., Abott-Shim, M. (1997). Social development in the context of typical center-based child care. *Merrill-Palmer Quarterly, 43,* 426–450.

NICHD Early Child Care Research Network (1997). The effects of infant child care on infant-mother attachment security: Results of the NICHD Study of Early Child Care. *Child Development, 68,* 860–875.

Prosser, W., & S. McGroder (1992). The supply and demand for child care: Measurement and analytic issues. In A. Booth (Ed.), *Child care in the 1990s: Trends and consequences* (pp. 42–55). Hillsdale, NJ: Erlbaum.

Ramey, C., & Ramey, S. (1992). Early educational intervention with disadvantaged children—to what effect? *Applied and Preventive Psychology, 1,* 131–140.

Scarr, S. (1998). American child care today. *American Psychologist, 53,* 95–108.

Scarr, S., & Eisenberg, M. (1993). Child care research: Issues, perspectives, and results. *Annual Review of Psychology, 44,* 613–644.

Scarr, S., Eisenberg, M., & Deater-Deckard, K. (1994). Measurement of quality on child care centers. *Early Childhood Research Quarterly, 9,* 131–151.

Scarr, S., Lande, J., McCartney, K. (1989). Child care and the family: Cooperation and interaction. In J. Lande, S. Scarr, & N. Guzenhauser (Eds.), *Caring for children: Challenge to America*. Hillsdale, NJ: Erlbaum.

Scarr, S., Phillips, D., & McCartney, K. (1989). Working mothers and their families. *American Psychologist, 44,* 1402–1409.

Scarr, S., Phillips, D., & McCartney, K. (1990). Facts, fantasies, and the future of child care in the United States. *Psychological Science, 1,* 26–35.

Scarr, S., Phillips, D., McCartney, K., & Abbott-Shim, M. (1993). Quality of child care as an aspect of family and child care policy in the United States. *Pediatrics, 91(1),* 182–188.

Scarr, S., & Thompson, W. (1994). Effects of maternal employment and nonmaternal infant care on development at two and four years. *Early Development and Parenting, 3,* 113–123.

Scarr, S., & Weinberg, R. A. (1986). The early childhood enterprise: Care and education of the young. *American Psychologist, 41,* 1140–1146.

Vandell, D. L., Henderson, V. K., & Wilson, K. S. (1988). A longitudinal study of children with day-care experiences of varying quality. *Child Development, 59,* 1286–1292.

Wall Street Journal. (1997). Women's figures. 15 January, p. A15.

Sandra Scarr

DAYDREAMS. Daydreams are part of the stream of thoughts and images that occupy most of a person's waking hours. Some are fanciful mental episodes, such as those about special achievements, heroic rescues, hair-raising escapes, unrealistic athletic or supernatural feats, romantic or sexual escapades, uncharacteristic assertiveness, and improbable aggressive acts. More often daydreams are more or less realistic although unintentional thoughts about the daydreamer's real life, as in mind wandering or brief periods of inner distraction. Researchers have defined them in at least three different ways: (1) as unrealistic, fanciful thoughts (as implied by psychoanalysts since Sigmund Freud); (2) as thoughts unrelated to the immediate environment or tasks one is performing (as proposed by psychologist Jerome L. Singer, the pioneer of modern daydreaming research, and his colleague John Antrobus); or (3) as spontaneous, "undirected" or "respondent" thoughts that flit into and back out of consciousness unbidden with no apparent purpose (as I once proposed; Klinger, 1971). However, these definitions have been shown to refer to three largely independent properties of thought. For present purposes, daydreams are defined as *either* nonworking (unbidden, apparently purposeless) *or* fanciful thoughts, whether spontaneous or intentional.

These are usually distractions from whatever the day-dreamer is doing.

Much has been learned about daydreams during the past century, much of it contrary to previous beliefs. The first work based on extensive observation of daydreaming, in this instance the author's own daydreams, was by the Dutch psychologist Julien Varendonck (*The Psychology of Day-Dreams*, London, 1921), who anticipated many of the general conclusions reached later with other methods. The next major advance was Singer's classic 1966 book *Daydreaming*, and since then, investigators have contributed both major theory and a great deal of data to an understanding of daydreams.

Most of the data have been collected with retrospective questionnaires, such as Singer and Antrobus's Imaginal Processes Inventory (Princeton, N.J., 1970) and psychologists Sheryl C. Wilson and T. X. Barber's Inventory of Childhood Memories and Imagining (in E. Klinger, Ed., *Imagery*, New York, 1981), or by means of thought sampling (also called consciousness or experience sampling, developed independently during the 1970s by psychologists Mihalyi Csikszentmihalyi, Russell Hurlburt, and Eric Klinger). In thought sampling, beepers or pagers interrupt research participants at unexpected times, at which point they report the thoughts, feelings, and activities that occurred just before each signal. Sometimes, they write down daydreams whenever they become aware of them. Sampling methods, though labor intensive, depend far less than retrospective questionnaires on the accuracy of the reporters' memories, but they sample only a tiny proportion of participants' thoughts.

About half the sampled thoughts of college students are daydreams. Psychologist Leonard Giambra, using the Imaginal Processes Inventory and experimental methods, found that daydreaming peaks in young adulthood and then gradually subsides, especially in extreme old age and especially if the daydreams are sexual, heroic, or hostile. In experiments by Singer, Antrobus, and colleagues, people daydreamed less while engaged in difficult tasks or when the stakes were high, but no experimental conditions they tried eliminated it.

Most daydreams are related to the goals daydreamers are pursuing, whether lofty or mundane, long-term or immediate, positive or aversive (Klinger, 1971, 1990). In Singer's terms, daydreams are about unfinished business. Experiments have shown that daydreams are triggered by the person encountering some cue associated with a goal pursuit, either external, such as something read or heard, or internal, such as one's own ongoing thought stream. If the individual can reasonably take overt action then toward the goal, he or she will; if not, the impulse becomes a purely mental response, often a daydream. Goal-related cues may depend for their daydream-triggering effect at least partly on their evok-ing emotional responses. Therefore, emotion-arousing cues such as reminders of a pleasant vacation just ended or of a distressing failure may also trigger daydreams. Inasmuch as goal-related cues can interfere with other cognitive activity and, during sleep, can shift the course of dreams, the response to them appears to be involuntary and probably inexorable.

Views of the worth of daydreams have changed sharply. Daydreaming has traditionally been viewed as counterproductive, and, after Freud, as infantile, regressive symptoms of neurosis. Until the 1960s and beyond, textbooks for prospective teachers warned against allowing children to daydream lest they become so entranced by their daydreams that they retreat into them and become schizophrenic. None of these judgments has been borne out by empirical evidence. There is no consistent relation between enjoying daydreaming and any form of mental illness. Similarly, contrary to Freudian theory, people with the most active sex lives do the most sexual daydreaming, and even daydreaming about sex during sexual activity is virtually unrelated to mental health or overall satisfaction with one's partner. People who most need to escape into fantasy—for example, the depressed, the lonely—have daydreams that are on average more depressive or lonely and are therefore unattractive havens. Depressed individuals daydream on average more than others while ruminating or worrying about their troubles, which is no escape.

"Fantasy-prone" nurses studied by Wilson and Barber had by and large been a well-functioning professional group with normally satisfying social relationships. Psychologists Steven Lynn and Judith Rhue (*American Psychologist*, 1988, 43, 35–44) similarly found few links between mental disability and fantasy-proneness, although the most extreme group had modestly more encounters with the mental health system and with dissociative phenomena. However, the inventory they used also measures some behaviors other than daydreaming frequency that may be associated with mental illness.

Very little is known about the developmental course of daydreaming during childhood. There is, however, some agreement that it picks up where overt play leaves off. In that case, children's imaginative play is the precursor of fanciful daydreaming. Psychologists Jerome and Dorothy Singer (*The Child's World of Make-Believe*, New York, 1973), Roni Tower (*Imagination, Cognition, and Personality*, 1984–85, 4, 349–364), and colleagues have found the most imaginative children to be more confident, resourceful, self-controlled, assertive, and socially skilled, and less aggressive or distressed.

Researchers, beginning with Singer and Antrobus, have identified three ways in which individuals' daydreaming styles differ: positive-constructive daydreaming (which daydreamers enjoy having), guilty and fearful daydreaming, and poor attentional control. These daydreaming styles reflect the daydreamers' overall tendencies toward positive emotion, negative emotion, and other personality traits. German psychologists Julius Kuhl and Jürgen Beckmann (1994) have identified individual differences in "action orientation," the ability to put rumination aside and take action. Daydreamers who focus mainly on desired outcomes rather than how to attain them may, according to studies by German psychologists Peter Gollwitzer and Gabriele Oettingen (1997), be less successful in attaining them.

Daydreams probably perform important, even central, functions in human life. While a person is absorbed in one particular task they serve as continual reminders of the rest of the person's agenda. People gain knowledge by spontaneously reviewing their past experiences in daydreams and rehearsing for future situations. Daydreams appear to generate creative solutions to difficult problems. They are linked with greater empathy for others. They may be spontaneous but not entirely idle.

[See also Dreams; and Fantasy.]

Bibliography

Hurlburt, R. T. (1990). *Sampling normal and schizophrenic inner experience.* New York: Plenum Press.

Hurlburt, R. T. (1993). *Sampling inner experience in disturbed affect.* New York: Plenum Press.

Klinger, E. (1971). *Structure and functions of fantasy.* New York: Wiley.

Klinger, E. (1990). *Daydreaming.* Los Angeles: Tarcher.

Kuhl, J., & Beckmann, J. (Eds.). (1994). *Volition and personality: Action versus state orientation.* Göttingen: Hogrefe & Huber.

Martin, L. L., & Tesser, A. (1996). Some ruminative thoughts. In R. S. Wyer, Jr. (Ed.), *Advances in social cognition* (Vol. 9, pp. 1–48). Hillsdale, NJ: Erlbaum.

Mueller, E. T. (1990). *Daydreaming in humans and machines: A computer model of the stream of thought.* Norwood, NJ: Ablex.

Oettingen, G. (1997). *Psychologie des Zukunftsdenkens* [The psychology of future-oriented thinking]. Göttingen: Hogrefe.

Singer, J. L. (1966). *Daydreaming: An introduction to the experimental study of inner experience.* New York: Random House.

Singer, J. L. (1975). *The inner world of daydreaming.* New York: Harper & Row.

Eric Klinger

DAY TREATMENT. Partial hospitalization programs were first developed in the Soviet Union in the 1940s as a low-cost alternative to inpatient psychiatric care. The concept of day hospitals was first brought to North America in 1946 when the first of its kind was developed by D. Ewen Cameron at the Allan Memorial Institute in Montreal. This program was designed as an alternative to inpatient treatment for patients with acute illnesses. Shortly thereafter, a number of partial hospitalization programs were developed in both the United States and England as a solution to a shortage of inpatient resources. The first American partial hospitalization program was established at the Menninger Clinic in 1958.

Such programs remained scarce in the United States until the 1960s, at which time the development of partial hospitalization programs grew rapidly. Several factors contributed to their growth, including the development of more efficacious psychotropic agents, the development of group treatment techniques, milieu therapy, and the idea of the therapeutic community. The civil rights movement resulted in deinstitutionalization policies by both the American and Canadian governments, thereby increasing the demand for alternatives to inpatient care of psychiatric patients. In 1963, the U.S. Congress passed the Mental Retardation Facilities and Community Mental Health Center Construction Act, which made partial hospitalizations a mandated service in the community.

Although many partial hospitalization programs were developed in the 1960s with the expectation of being widely used, these programs have had a history of underutilization. The intent of the deinstitutionalization movement was that outpatient programs would grow as inpatients were discharged into the community. Most states, however, gradually decreased their funding for partial hospitalization programs, and third party reimbursement has been low relative to more traditional inpatient and outpatient services, resulting in the failure of these programs to be utilized as widely as was originally hoped. This underutilization was also reflected in the decrease in the number of publications pertaining to partial hospitalization programs during the 1980s.

Instead of being defined by their own qualities and strengths, partial hospitalization programs have often been referred to as an economical alternative to inpatient care. These programs have traditionally had a difficult time defining and establishing themselves as a beneficial therapeutic modality in their own right. The lack of clear definitions has resulted in confusion in the literature.

In an effort to provide a clear description of such programs, the American Association for Partial Hospitalization (AAPH) published, in 1982, a definition of partial hospitalization programs that emphasized the multidisciplinary nature of care within a setting less restrictive than inpatient hospitalization. In 1991, the AAPH modified this definition to include the ideas of time-limited treatment and a stable therapeutic milieu. The definition now reads:

> Partial Hospitalization is defined as a time-limited, ambulatory, active treatment program that offers therapeutically intensive, coordinated, and structured clinical services within a stable therapeutic milieu. Partial hospitalization is a general term embracing day, evening, night, and weekend treatment programs which employ an integrated, comprehensive schedule of recognized treatment approaches. Programs are designed to serve individuals with significant impairment resulting from a psychiatric, emotional, or behavioral disorder. They are also intended to have a positive impact on the identified patient's support system. (Block & Lefkovitz, 1991, pp. 1–2)

Partial hospitalization programs have been described as "half time in plus half time out" (Weil, 1984). These programs strive to provide comprehensive treatment while permitting patients to remain in contact with their community, including family, friends, and work settings. The balance of intensive multidisciplinary treatment and community living is unique to this therapeutic setting.

Partial hospitalization programs can be divided into three broad categories according to their function: day hospitals, day care centers, and day treatment programs. Day hospitals are most closely tied to inpatient psychiatric hospital units because they provide the same types of services to acutely ill patients. In addition, day hospitals are designed to accommodate patients who are transitioning from inpatient to outpatient care. Day-care centers focus primarily on the maintenance of chronically ill patients. Although these patients do not need to be hospitalized, they require a more rigorous treatment program than can be provided by traditional outpatient services. Typically, patients in a day-care program are over the age of 50, suffer from schizophrenia, and are primarily dependent on family and social services. Finally, day treatment programs treat patients who are in remission from an acute psychiatric illness. The goal of day treatment is to reduce patients' symptoms and to enhance their overall functioning. Despite repeated calls in the literature, this nomenclature has not been widely used by psychiatrists and other mental health professionals, and there is little consistency across states—and even among programs within a given state—in the way partial hospitalization programs are described.

The AAPH specifies that the majority of programming at partial hospitalization programs should consist of active treatment that targets the presenting problems of the population (Block & Lefkovitz, 1991). Suggested treatment includes individual psychotherapy, psychoeducational therapy groups, family therapy, and medication evaluation and maintenance. Adjunctive therapeutic activities are also included in these programs, such as instruction in personal hygiene, social activities, and budgeting. Each individual in such a program has a designated staff member who coordinates the patient's entire treatment and monitors progress throughout his stay. The importance of a stable therapeutic community for a partial hospitalization program cannot be overstated. Efforts to create this therapeutic milieu include the establishment of scheduled activities and client and staff continuity. Activities such as daily community meetings and patient government also aid in the development of a therapeutic community.

Some programs have come under fire for failing to live up to these standards. Most criticism has focused on longer-term facilities serving chronically ill patients; some of which have failed to provide sufficient goal-oriented treatment and rehabilitative services, offering participants little more than pharmacotherapy in quasi-institutionalized settings.

Despite the wide variety of programs described in the literature and methodological problems inherent in much of the research in this area, there are some consistent research findings from which general conclusions may be gleaned. In terms of symptom improvement, familial adjustment, and relapse prevention, partial hospitalization programs have generally been found to be more effective than standard community-based treatment and equally effective as traditional inpatient settings for equivalent patient populations. For example, Rosie, Azim, Piper, & Joyce, (1995) evaluated the effectiveness of a model program from Edmonton, Canada, using a treatment versus delayed-treatment design to assess the progress of 60 matched pairs. The results demonstrated that patients in the treatment condition improved significantly more than those in control conditions on measures of symptomatology, life satisfaction, self-esteem, and interpersonal functioning. These treatment effects were maintained at a follow-up assessment conducted eight months later. There have been mixed findings as to whether partial hospitalization programs produce greater improvement in social functioning relative to traditional inpatient programs.

Research has consistently demonstrated that partial hospitalization programs are significantly less expensive than inpatient programs (for example, Endicott, Herz, & Gibbon, 1978). In terms of suitability, research indicates that anywhere from 15 to 72% of patients referred to partial hospitalization programs who might otherwise be referred to an inpatient setting were deemed appropriate for partial hospitalization programs (Klar, Frances, & Clarkin, 1982; Gudeman, Dickey, Evans, & Shore, 1985). The dropout and nonattendance rates at partial hospitalization programs are relatively high, ranging from a low of 20% to a high of 50%.

Specialized partial hospitalization programs have been developed to meet specific community needs, including treatment for diabetic, borderline, schizophrenic, eating-disorder, chronic-disease, mentally retarded, and substance-abusing patients. Stout (1993) described a therapeutic day-school program for children unable to function in traditional school settings. The program utilized the elements of partial hospitalization programs to help foster children's social, physical, academic, and emotional growth. The program provided academic services in addition to psychological services, including psychoeducational testing, behavioral-modification plans, and individual, family, and group therapy.

Critics of partial hospitalization programs have argued that most of the functions of such programs can and should be assumed by intensive outpatient treatment and assertive community rehabilitation programs (Hoge et al., 1992). These critics argue that the typical length of stay in partial hospitalization programs is greater than needed to stabilize symptoms yet not long enough to affect significant strides in psychosocial rehabilitation. Even the critics, however, acknowledge the usefulness of short-term day hospitals for acutely symptomatic patients. In addition, most criticism has focused on programs that treat primarily schizophrenic patients, and that rely on verbal psychotherapies as a primary therapeutic modality. There appears to be a growing recognition of the utility of traditional partial hospitalization programs for other disorders, including severe personality and mood disorders (Rosie et al., 1995).

There is significant diversity among partial hospitalization programs. Programs often specialize in treating specific populations, such as patients of a certain age or with a specific diagnosis. Staffing can also vary, with various combinations of social workers, teachers, counselors, psychologists, art therapists, music therapists, movement therapists, and psychiatrists. Programs differ in terms of their length of stay. In some programs, the length is predetermined, while other programs have more flexible time limits. Partial hospitalization programs also differ in terms of their function, with some programs focusing primarily on treatment whereas others emphasize rehabilitation.

The future of partial hospitalization programs is uncertain. Although there will likely continue to be a role for short-term programs serving acutely ill patients, the role of longer-term programs is increasingly being assumed by intensive outpatient services. The ultimate survival of this unique mode of treatment and rehabilitation will depend not only on further research demonstrating clinical effectiveness but more important on the ability to provide effective services that are economically competitive with alternative settings.

[See also Impatient Treatment.]

Bibliography

Block, B., & Lefkovitz, P. (1991). American association for partial hospitalization standards and guidelines for partial hospitalization. *International Journal of Partial Hospitalization, 7,* 3–11.

Cameron, D. E. (1947). The day hospital: An experimental form of hospitalization for psychiatric patients. *Modern Hospital, 69,* 60–62.

Endicott, J., Herz, M., & Gibbon, M. (1978). Brief versus standard hospitalization: The differential costs. *American Journal of Psychiatry, 135,* 707–712.

Goldman, D. (1990). Historical notes on partial hospitalization. *International Journal of Partial Hospitalization, 6* (2), 111–117.

Gudeman, J., Dickey, B., Evans, A., & Shore, M. (1985). Four-year assessment of a day hospitalization program as an alternative to inpatient hospitalization. *American Journal of Psychiatry, 142,* 1330–1333.

Hoge, M., Davidson, L., Hill, W., Turner, V., & Ameli, R. (1992). The promise of partial hospitalization: A reassessment. *Hospital and Community Psychiatry, 43,* 345–354.

Klar, H., Frances, A., & Clarkin, J. (1982). Selection criteria for partial hospitalization. *Hospital and Community Psychiatry, 33,* 929 933.

Piper, W., Rosie, J., Joyce, A., & Azim, H. (1996). *Time limited day treatment for personality disorders.* Washington, DC: American Psychological Association.

Rosie, J., Azim, H., Piper, W., & Joyce, A. (1995). Effective Psychiatric Day Treatment: historical lessons. *Psychiatric Services, 46,* 1019–1025.

Stout, C. (1993). Day treatment alternative: A model of innovation. In M. Squire, C. Stout, & D. Ruben (Eds). *Current advances in inpatient psychiatric care.* Westport, CN: Greenwood Press.

Weil, F. (1984). Day hospitalization as a therapeutic tool. *Psychiatric Journal of the University of Ottawa, 9,* 165–169.

Whitelaw, C., & Perez, E. (1987). Partial hospitalization programs: A current perspective. *Administration in Mental Health, 15,* 62–72.

James D. Herbert and Suzanne G. Goldstein

DEAFNESS AND HEARING LOSS describe a physical condition with significant psychological implications. Physically, hearing losses are defined by the severity, type, and cause of hearing impairment. Severity refers to the degree to which a sound must be amplified to be heard. The type of hearing loss describes the physiological malfunction (e.g., conductive, sensorineural) that leads to the hearing loss. Hearing losses are unilateral (one ear) or bilateral (both ears). Finally, hearing loss is identified by etiology (e.g., maternal rubella, genetic syndrome).

Psychologically, the functional characteristics of hearing loss are more important than its physical characteristics. Two features of hearing loss affect a person's functioning: (1) the severity or degree of hearing loss with appropriate amplification, and (2) the age of the person at hearing loss onset.

Severity or Degree of Hearing Loss with Amplification

Typically, the degree of hearing loss is associated with response to amplification. People with less severe (i.e., mild to moderate) hearing loss are more likely to benefit from amplification than people with more severe (i.e., severe to profound) hearing loss. However, individuals vary in response to amplification. For some, amplification can virtually eliminate functional difficulties, whereas for others, amplification is of no functional value in mitigating the impact of hearing loss.

Age at Onset

The timing of a hearing loss influences psychological and social development. Although physicians typically distinguish between congenital (i.e., present at birth) and adventitious (i.e., acquired after birth) losses, psychologists distinguish between prelingual (i.e., onset before acquisition of oral language) and postlingual (i.e., onset after acquisition of oral language) hearing loss. Postlingual losses may be further classified as late-adult onset losses, which are typically associated with aging.

Hearing loss onset and severity largely, but not entirely, determine how a person with a hearing loss will function in society. Three functional categories describe people with hearing losses: (1) hard-of-hearing, (2) deaf, and (3) deafened. Hard-of-hearing people have mild to moderate hearing losses with onset at any age. Deaf people have severe to profound hearing losses with prelingual onset. Deafened people have severe to profound losses with postlingual onset. Because people with hearing losses generally prefer disability-first language (e.g., "deaf people" is preferred to "people with deafness"), disability-first language is used in this entry.

Prevalence

The prevalence of hearing loss varies primarily by age, and by gender and ethnicity. Although 8.6% of the U.S. population has a significant hearing loss, 1.8% of children 3 to 17 years of age have a hearing loss, versus 15.4% of people over 65 years of age. Gender and age interact with hearing loss; whereas approximately equal numbers of males and females below seventeen years of age have a hearing loss, twice as many males as females 65 years or older have hearing loss. Likewise, the prevalence of hearing loss within people younger than 18 years of age is approximately equal for Whites and Blacks, but among people 65 years or older, hearing loss is nearly twice as common in Whites than

Blacks. If one defines "deaf" as a person who, at best, understands words shouted into the better ear, only 0.10 to 0.12% (i.e., about 1 in 1,000) of people under the age of 45 years are deaf; 2.48% of those over 65 are deaf (or, more precisely, deafened). Only 5.4% of deaf people experience onset prior to 3 years of age (i.e., prelingually), and about three in four have a hearing loss onset after 18 years of age.

There are four psychological issues related to deafness: (1) acquisition of language and culturally specific knowledge; (2) cognitive development and intelligence; (3) behavioral and emotional adjustment; and (4) social identity. Each of these issues raises the question of whether the relationship between deafness is best described as a deficit or a difference. Historically, the "deficit" orientation has dominated by framing deafness as a deficit in hearing, and by exploring how deaf people compare to people with normal hearing on various psychological measures. In the 1990s, scholars adopted a difference, not deficit, orientation, and so examined deafness and psychology primarily from a qualitative (not ordinal) difference orientation.

Culturally Specific Knowledge

Prelingually deaf children have substantial difficulties acquiring fluency in oral/auditory language. About nine in ten prelingually deaf children have two normal-hearing parents. Delays associated in identifying deafness, choosing responses to deafness, and the time needed to implement communication accommodations typically delay a deaf child's introduction to language. Many deaf children are not diagnosed until they experience significant delays in speech; consequently, educational interventions often start at an age where normal-hearing peers have already acquired basic grammar, syntax, and working vocabularies in the hundreds or thousands of words. Special accommodations to assist language learning (e.g., signing to the child, amplification) are often delayed and inconsistently applied due to technical, resource, and motivational obstacles. Consequently, prelingually deaf children frequently experience delayed, nonstandard, and inconsistent language exposure during their critical language development years (birth to 6 years of age). The vast majority of prelingually deaf children consequently show significant and persistent deficits in oral speech, reading, and writing throughout their life span.

Because prelingually deaf children have limited oral language bases, and limited communication channels, they exhibit significant and substantial delays in knowledge acquisition. For example, normal-hearing children learn to read by associating visual images (letters, words) with their existing auditory language base (phonemes, speech). In contrast, deaf children can see letters and words, but have no auditory language base.

Therefore, for deaf children, learning to read is often learning a language.

Acquisition of other knowledge also suffers. Deaf children exhibit substantially lower academic achievement than their normal hearing peers in all domains, but especially in language arts. The achievement gaps between deaf children and normal-hearing peers increase with age. The majority of high-school graduates served in special education programs for deaf and hard-of-hearing youth have achievement levels below functional literacy (i.e., the fourth grade level). However, deaf and hard-of-hearing children may acquire language and knowledge specific to deaf cultures, but such knowledge is not formally measured.

Cognitive Development

The impact of deafness on intelligence and cognitive development is mixed. Although deafness inhibits culturally specific knowledge and reasoning skills (i.e., crystallized intelligence), it has little impact on nonverbal reasoning skills (i.e., fluid intelligence). Deaf children show the same ordinal Piagetian development stages as normal-hearing peers, although they may achieve stages somewhat later in age. Deaf children apparently use information processing (e.g., memory) strategies similar to normal-hearing peers, but they may be less efficient in invoking and using strategies.

Other researchers suggest deaf children have different (not less efficient) information processing frameworks. Factor analyses of intelligence tests suggest that young deaf children organize cognitive tasks quite differently from their normal-hearing peers, but they become more similar to their normal hearing peers with age. The debate between those who argue deficits (e.g., deaf children have lower verbal knowledge or reasoning skills) versus differences (e.g., deaf children have similar knowledge and skills, but these skills are based in sign language and are not tapped by intelligence tests) is unresolved. There is much less debate about the relative lack of influence of postlingual deafness on cognitive abilities. Because postlingually deafened people have a well-developed internal language base, the impact of deafness on their cognitive abilities and development is generally limited to an inability to "overhear" (i.e., acquire incidental information).

Behavioral/Emotional Adjustment

Deaf children exhibit higher rates of externalizing behaviors, and externalizing disorders, than their normal-hearing peers. Whether these behaviors reflect insufficient internal regulation, or an adaptive response to communication difficulties, is a hotly debated issue. Deaf and normal-hearing adults have similar rates of psychoses (e.g., schizophrenia), but mild behavioral and psychological disorders (particularly externalizing or impulse-control disorders) are slightly more frequent

among deaf adults. Psychologists used to believe that paranoia was more common among deaf and deafened people (because their hearing impairment would lead them to believe that people were talking about them). However, paranoia is no more common among deaf people, although it may be a short-term reaction to recent hearing loss among deafened people.

Normal social-emotional development, especially the development of autonomy in young children, may be inhibited by limited communication between child and parent. Additionally, factors affecting all children with disabilities (e.g., parental denial, grief, guilt regarding the child's disability; altered family relationships) may affect the emotional development of deaf children. Once again, there is a continuing debate over the interpretation of behavioral and emotional differences between deaf and normal-hearing people, with some researchers viewing differences as evidence of elevated pathology, and others viewing the differences as adaptive responses to deaf people living in a normal-hearing world.

Social Identity

The timing and severity of hearing impairment influence social identity. People who are hard-of-hearing and postlingually deafened (especially late adult onset) identify with normal-hearing culture(s). However, prelingually deaf people with severe to profound hearing losses often identify with Deaf culture. These individuals use American Sign Language (ASL) as their primary mode of communication, and they share linguistic, historical, and cultural traditions based on ASL. Ironically, somebody who is deaf (that is, has a severe hearing impairment) is not necessarily Deaf (that is, a member of the Deaf community).

Deafness is unique in two ways. First, it is the only disability whose members share a common language different from the dominant (normal-hearing) society. Second, it is the only cultural group whose membership and language is not learned from the family. Most deaf children are socialized into the Deaf community via educational programs (especially residential schools for deaf students) and social and fraternal organizations (such as the Junior National Association of the Deaf).

However, a minority (about 4%) of deaf children have two deaf parents. These families use ASL, and they socialize their deaf children into the Deaf community. Research shows that deaf children of deaf parents have higher academic achievement scores, better social-emotional adjustment, fewer behavior disorders, and higher nonverbal IQs than deaf children of hearing parents. Although these differences may be due to language acquisition, parenting, and cultural assimilation, genetic factors may also enhance outcomes for deaf children of deaf parents.

Societal Responses to Deafness

The question of how society should best respond to deafness is extremely controversial. Educators vehemently disagree about the benefits of oral/aural approaches (that emphasize listening/speech), total communication approaches (that emphasize concurrent signing and speaking of English), and bilingual/bicultural approaches (that emphasize teaching ASL before English). Deaf community advocates oppose full inclusion of deaf students in general education and cochlear implants to cure deafness, because these initiatives seek to assimilate or eliminate deafness. In contrast, hard-of-hearing and deafened people welcome these initiatives as providing better access to normal-hearing culture. Because the debate regarding how society should respond to deafness is more often controlled by ideology than research, it is likely to continue unresolved for the foreseeable future.

[*See also* Auditory Impairment; Hearing; *and* Rehabilitation Psychology.]

Bibliography

Holt, J., & Hotto, S. (1994). *Demographic aspects of hearing impairment: Questions and answers* (3rd ed.). Washington, DC: Center for Assessment and Demographic Studies, Gallaudet University. This book provides information about demographic aspects of deafness. This information, and other information, is also available at the Gallaudet Graduate Research Institute website: http://gri.gallaudet.edu/

Lane, H., Hoffmeister, R., & Bahan, B. (1996). *A journey into the deaf-world.* San Diego, CA: Dawn Sign Press. This book provides an overview of issues related to deafness from the perspective of Deaf culture advocates.

Marschark, M. (1993). *Psychological development of deaf children.* New York: Oxford University Press.

There are many Internet resources addressing deafness and hearing loss. The Alexander Graham Bell Association (http://www.agbell.org/) promotes oral/aural responses to hearing impairment; the American Speech and Hearing Association (http://www.asha.org/) represents speech pathologists and audiologists; the (U.S.) National Association of the Deaf (http://www.nad.org/) and the British Deaf Association (http://www.bda.org.uk/) are fraternal organizations representing deaf people; the Center for Hearing Loss in Children (http://www.boystown.org/chlc/) and the (U.S.) National Institute on Deafness and Other Communication Disorders (http://www.nih.gov/nidcd/) are federally funded information sites; Deaf World Web (http://dww.deafworldweb.org/) links deafness-related Internet sites; Cued Speech (http://web7.mit.edu/CuedSpeech/) provides information about supplementing speech with hand cues to improve communication; and the National Technical Institute for the Deaf (http://www.

isc.rit.edu/~418www/) and Gallaudet University (http://www.gallaudet.edu/) are institutions of higher education devoted to serving deaf and hard-of-hearing adults.

Jeffery P. Braden

DEATH AND DYING. Psychology is usually regarded as a social and behavioral science. It is also a life science, however, and, as such, cannot encompass its subject matter without considering death. How could we hope to understand children's constructions of reality without learning what they make of withered plants and dead birds? How could we understand adolescent behavior without attention to the risk-taking behavior that all too often puts their lives in jeopardy? How could we understand an adult's disposition toward depression and disabling fear of relationship loss without recognizing that it might represent the enduring effects of childhood bereavement? How could we understand why people sometimes withdraw from friends who are terminally ill or bereaved? How can we understand why physicians have sometimes abandoned their terminally ill patients? How can we understand thought and language without attention to the diverse ways in which death is symbolized? How can we comprehend intimate relationships without insight into the fear of loss?

Nevertheless, for many years the human encounter with death had little place in psychological theory, research, education, or services. The cultural taboo against acknowledging mortality encompassed scholars and professionals as well as the general public. Psychologists, physicians, and clergy often completed their professional training with little guidance for discussing death or interacting with dying and grieving people. The subject of death was to be evaded in thought and conversation. Those who were frequently exposed to death-related situations had to rely upon a repertoire of stereotyped responses, usually marked by distancing body language and stock phrases. "Death," "dead," "dying," and "cancer" were among the words that could not be uttered. Even more unfortunately, people who had been touched by death were also to be avoided: "I wouldn't know what to say," was one typical apprehension; another was, "If I said the wrong thing, she would just lose all hope—it would be awful." So it was that at midcentury, psychology was still proceeding as though life could be understood without death.

Today, however, psychology contributes to the understanding of the human encounter with death in many ways. Some of this work is carried out within the established boundaries of psychology. Most studies of death anxiety and of children's understanding of death, for example, have been conducted by psychologists. However, psychologists also collaborate with

DEATH AND DYING. Table 1. Stages of death comprehension in childhood (Nagy, 1948)

Stage	Age Range	Interpretation of Death
1	3–5	Death is separation. The dead are less alive. Very curious about death.
2	5–9	Death is final—but one might escape it! Death takes the form of a person.
3	9–adult	Death is personal, universal, final, and inevitable.

health care professionals and scholars from a variety of other disciplines, for example, in the study of death-bed scenes or the training of hospice volunteers.

Death in Everyday Life

What is death? How should we cope with death? These two questions are closely related. The person who conceives of death as the transition to a spiritually evolved plane of being may live by a different set of rules than the person who fears death as punishment for sin, and both may differ from the person who believes that personal existence vanishes with the last breath. The mass suicide of Heaven's Gate members in 1997, for example, was predicated upon an unusual belief system that combined biblical with science-fantasy elements. The relationship between conception of death and behavior is far from simple, however, because belief systems themselves are products of complex individual and societal interactions.

Thinking about Death

Whatever else death may be, it is a thought, a mental construct. Adult conceptions of death require the ability to grasp abstractions that are considered beyond the cognitive scope of young children. These abstractions include:

- Futurity. Time is independent of our own experiences and desires. Things will change. We will change. Time will give and time will take away.
- Inevitability. Life will end no matter what one thinks, says, or does.
- Temporal uncertainty. One is always vulnerable to death, and death is certain to occur, but the time is uncertain.
- Universality. All that lives will die.
- Personal inclusion. It is not just that everybody else will die, I will die, too.
- Permanence. The dead stay dead.

Each of these concepts requires a degree of cognitive maturity and experience that is not present in early childhood and that is not granted to all adults. Furthermore, it is necessary to coordinate all these separate concepts to achieve the basic adult construct of death. The gap between juvenile and adult conceptions of death can be illustrated by the basic presence–absence paradigm. Infants and young children live in a here-and-now world. When mother leaves the immediate time–space field there is no way to measure her distance except by response to a forlorn cry. The yearling cannot differentiate between mother's spatial displacement to the backyard or another city—or between a separation that will last for just a few minutes or forever. Adults are better equipped to withstand absences that they understand are temporary, whereas the young child responds to a departure with the anxiety adults usually reserve for extended or permanent separation. Something of the child's survival-oriented separation anxiety remains in adult life when people respond to a brief leave-taking with what would seem to be disproportionate apprehension and sorrow.

Acceptance of the basic adult model of death requires more than cognitive maturity: It also requires the willingness to surrender faith in magical control. Observations suggest that, even among adults, this surrender often is not complete. Stressful circumstances may lead us to revert to the belief that we can alter unwelcome reality through denial and the substitution of wish-fulfilling fantasies.

Research has confirmed the propositions that children's understanding of death is related to their general level of cognitive development, age, and experiences with death-related phenomena. Age is a helpful but rough guide to charting children's ideas about death. By early adolescence, if not before, children with normal intellectual endowment generally have mastered the set of constructs identified here. General level of cognitive development provides a more refined index, however. Children of the same chronological age differ to some extent in their grasp of such concepts as time, causality, and constancy. As one might expect, those children who have a more advanced command of basic concepts also have a more advanced understanding of death.

Field studies have added support for the influence of experience as well as age and developmental level. For example, Bluebond-Langner (1996) observed that children with chronic life-threatening illness and their healthy siblings often have a much more realistic view of dying and death than parents and caregivers realize.

Precisely how does the child's understanding of death develop? The most influential answer derived from a study by Hungarian psychologist Maria Nagy (1948) who interviewed children and asked them to draw death-related pictures. "Auntie Death," as she was affectionately called, found a stage-like progression, as summarized in Table 1.

These findings provide a useful database for contemporary studies although personifications of death in childhood have been relatively uncommon in subsequent studies, and the variables of developmental level and personal experiences with death have received more attention.

Five other points are worth consideration in comprehending the child's orientation toward death.

1. Even the youngest children are aware of separation and its threat to their survival. One does not have to understand the mature adult model of death in order to respond to the experience of loss.

2. Young children do occasionally express spontaneous insight into the finality of death, as when encountering a dead animal or withered plant; however, there is often a retreat from this realization and a return to more limited and wish-fulfilling ideas.

3. Children have a lively curiosity about death, leading at times to questions or little experiments that can unsettle adults (e.g., taking a caterpillar apart to see if it can be put back together again and made to go). The brightest and most observant children usually show the most curiosity.

4. Adults often exclude children from death-related conversations and respond to their questions with evasion and anxiety. A rule of silence regarding death applies in many homes, and with particular force to children.

5. Adults who are committed to preparing children for life should themselves be prepared to serve as mentors and guides as children encounter death in either reality or fantasy. Many parents have reported their discomfort in trying to help their children deal with death-related questions and experiences because they had so little guidance in their own childhood.

Adolescents' improved understanding of death often becomes part of a general anxiety about the future: All that one seeks lies ahead, but so does the risk of embarrassment, disappointment and failure, and the certainty of death. It is not uncommon for adolescents to develop a protective sheath of attitudes and a repertoire of behaviors designed to cope with the newly perceived vulnerability to death. An exaggerated sense of invulnerability may be expressed, coupled with risk-taking behavior that appears to taunt death (followed by the pleasurable experience of relief after escape). "Slash-and-gash" horror films and comic books draw most of their aficionados from the ranks of young men, although adolescents share this enthusiasm. Concern about body image and the increasing salience of sexuality may lead to intense and troubled interpretations of death. There may also be highly insightful and imaginative interpretations. With their newly enlarged perspectives on life and death, some youth have created memorable poetry (including, for example, the 17-year-old William Cullen Bryant's "Thanatopsis").

The basic adult model of death identified here is not favored by all people. Buddhist and Hindu conceptions of life and death offer alternative perspectives. The "new age" construction of death is viewed as one transition among others: "Death is just a change of clothes"; "Death is only a door we pass through." Such characterizations represent a selective borrowing from Eastern religions, coupled with an optimistic meliorism that is distinctively American.

There is no firm line between cognitive understanding and belief system, but it is useful to distinguish between those who do not comprehend universality, inevitability, permanence, and related concepts on the one hand, and those who comprehend but reject those ideas.

Attitudes and Coping Strategies

How do we move through life with knowledge of our mortality? "Anxiously" is the answer that has been proposed by influential observers and theoreticians. It is asserted that we are highly anxious about death as individuals and as a society. This anxiety leads us into avoidance and denial strategies, as though death will cease to exist if we stop thinking and talking about it. These propositions are often linked with advocacy for accepting death as a natural condition of life. Our focus will therefore be on death anxiety, denial, and acceptance, but we will also identify other attitudes and coping strategies.

Two extreme positions have been staked out by theorists. The early psychoanalytic approach rejected the idea that it is even possible to fear death. Freud heard many people express death-related fears, but he regarded those as disguised expressions of some other source of concern (e.g., a derivative of castration anxiety or a general loss of security). Why are we unable to fear death? Because death is an idea that does not translate into the language and modus operandi of the unconscious. Furthermore, we have never had the experience of death, so how can we fear it?

> Our own death is indeed quite unimaginable, and whenever we make the attempt to imagine it we can perceive that we really survive as spectators. At bottom nobody believes in his own death, or to put the same thing in a different way, in the unconscious every one of us is convinced of his own immortality. (Freud, 1917/1959, p. 304)

These comments by Freud were seized upon by many others who were reluctant to deal straightforwardly with death-related fears. In his later years Freud took death far more seriously as a crucial issue, but it is the earlier formulation that proved more influential.

The existential position could hardly be more different, as articulated by Becker (1973). Fear of annihilation is said to be the root of all human anxiety. A person who faces this terror without shield or illusion is in danger of psychosis. Becker believed that schizophrenia is an attempt to make a heroic response to the naked confrontation with mortality. Many other disturbed patterns of thought and behavior are also attributable to death anxiety. Moreover, according to Becker, when we do keep ourselves "normal," it is because we are conforming to societal patterns of denying death. It is much easier to deny death if we are all in the game together. Many other observers joined Becker in characterizing the United States as a society with a long-standing tradition of controlling death anxiety through denial. Indeed, one of the first tasks of the death awareness movement, which took hold in the 1970s, was to encourage people to break the anxious silence and enter into dialogue. The increased openness to discussion of dying and death created a more favorable climate for the introduction of hospice programs for palliative care of terminally ill people.

Despite their marked differences, psychoanalytic and existential approaches have important areas of agreement as well. Both hold that evasion and denial are not effective strategies. Psychoanalysts emphasize the expensive investment in keeping death-related thoughts under wraps, whereas existentialists point to a lack of authenticity in human relationships when people cannot accept and express their mortal fears. Both sides are joined by researchers and clinicians who emphasize the distortions, gaps, and misunderstandings in communication that occur when people cannot bring themselves to share their thoughts and feelings about death. Furthermore, there is a widespread belief that death anxiety, whatever its source, exists at a disturbingly high level in the United States.

Neither the psychoanalytic dismissal nor the existential enthronement of death anxiety have proven susceptible to definitive research. In fact, most of the abundant studies of death anxiety have been atheoretical. The typical study has employed fixed-choice questionnaire measures in a one-time sampling of available respondents. These studies have numerous limitations, including reliance on verbal self-report, lack of demonstrated relationships to behavior in real-life situations, and uncertainty regarding the meaning of low scores (low anxiety or high defensiveness?). Despite these limitations, four consistent findings have emerged from the numerous academic studies of death anxiety.

1. There is only a moderate level of self-reported death anxiety in the general population, usually well below the established scale midpoint. This finding is at odds with the assumption that most people in the United States are highly anxious about death. A tempting explanation is that most people are well defended against death anxiety, hence the relatively low scores. This ex post facto explanation, however, raises its own questions, including the purpose of using death anxiety scales in the first place if one reserves the right to ignore the findings.

2. Death anxiety scores are consistently higher for women. The interpretation most in accord with research findings and field observations is that women are more aware both of their feelings and of psychobiological imperatives. It has long been evident in the death awareness movement that women provide services to terminally ill and grieving people much more frequently than men, and also comprise the majority of people who enroll in death education courses. The relatively higher self-reported death anxiety for women appears, in general, to be a motivating rather than a disabling influence.

3. Death anxiety does not necessarily increase with advancing age. Most studies either find no age-related differences or lower levels of anxiety among older adults. This finding serves as a reminder that objective distance from death and subjective interpretation of mortality cannot be assumed to correspond.

4. Fears of pain, helplessness, dependency, and the well-being of surviving family members are usually more salient than anxiety about annihilation. Most people are less concerned about the ontological nature of death than about the palpable ordeal that might be experienced during the end phase of life. The theoretician's death anxiety is replaced by individual and family concerns about the dying process.

Clinical reports supplement these findings with the observation that death anxiety increases when people are overwhelmed by stress from any source. For example, death may become a symbol for the sense of having lost value, esteem, and control when an important relationship has been sundered. This condition (with its indirect support for the psychoanalytic hypothesis) often subsides when the person again feels worthwhile and in control. Concerns about death may represent either an actual crisis regarding mortality and loss, or a symbolic way of expressing one's sense of abandonment, dread, and overwhelming stress.

A few studies have examined death anxiety at two or more levels of assessment (e.g., self-report, perceptual response to death words or images, projective tests, and psychophysiological responses). Those studies indicate that people frequently have a more intense response to death-related signals outside their awareness than what appears in verbal self-reports. When Feifel and Branscomb (1973) posed the question, "Who's afraid of death?" the emerging answer was "Everybody!"—once we move past verbal self-report.

The role of death anxiety in everyday life has been illuminated by research to some extent. For example, Sanner (1997) has found that people who donate blood are also more willing to donate their bodies for organ transplantation. The blood/body donors seemed to have less anxiety about death, as well as less fear of physical injury and loss of control. There are probably many other ways in which people with higher and lower levels of death anxiety differ in their decision making. It has also been found by various studies that both high self-esteem and a well-developed sense of humor are associated with a less anxious response to death-related stimuli and situations.

Perhaps it is useful to step back from the two grand theories of death anxiety, the psychoanalytic and the existential, and consider a commonsensical alternative. The creatures who will live to see another day are those who will overcome various threats to their continued existence. It might not be justifiable to speak of a survival instinct within the context of today's evolutionary biology, but there is abundant evidence for the existence of a vigilance orientation that is followed by both general and particularized stress-adjustment responses. The chances of survival are improved by vigilance, and vigilance has some of the experiential and behavioral characteristics of anxiety. On this view, it would not be useful to impair the organism's ability to detect possible threats to its survival, just as it would not be useful to be paralyzed or disorganized by excessive and prolonged vigilance. In other words, some death anxiety may be a necessary condition for continued survival.

The emphasis on anxiety as a response to death has somewhat obscured the other ways in which people orient themselves toward mortality. There are often feelings of sorrow, regret, and resignation. The prevailing mood is not one of hyperalertness and apprehension, but, rather, sadness in contemplating the prospect of life's end. Individual variations on this theme are often subtle and unique. We learn about sadness, regret, and resignation from conversation and personal documents rather than fixed-choice questionnaires. With death in prospect, people often review their entire lives, attempting to affirm and discover meaning. These narratives and diaries can tell us much about the perceived shape of a completed life, as well as one's interpretation of death.

Quite a different type of response occurs along a dimension ranging from peaceful acceptance to ecstatic fulfillment. These responses have been lodged primarily in cultural and religious belief systems that have not often been studied empirically. Studies of death personification, however, have yielded pertinent findings. The image of a gentle comforter has been the most prevalent representation of death as a person in studies conducted in the 1970s and repeated in the 1990s (Kastenbaum, 2000). This image is most often presented as a firm but kind elder who places mortals at ease before escorting them from life. Terrifying images of death are not uncommon, but are consistently outnumbered by the gentle comforter. The more extreme positions on the acceptance dimension often take the form of anticipated reunion with a loved one or being gathered to the bosom of God. Of particular interest are the sexualized versions in which death is conceived as the opportunity for ecstasy that has been denied on earth. There have been episodes in cultural history in which sexualized death was celebrated in literature and drama and may have encouraged suicidal behavior. Romantic and erotic transformations of death can be found today, most obviously in some areas of youth culture, but have not yet been studied systematically.

That we live more fully and wisely when we have come to terms with our own mortality is a proposition that has strong support from all major schools of thought and is consistent with the available research findings.

Confrontations with Dying and Death

The emphasis shifts here from thinking about death in the midst of everyday life to those situations in which death has become a salient and immediate concern. Particular attention will be given to the communicational interactions through which we exchange either guidance and comfort, or pain and confusion.

Barriers to Death-Related Communication. Several barriers to death-related communication have been documented repeatedly since social and behavioral scientists turned their attention to this topic shortly after 1950:

1. Weak response repertoire in death-related situations. What should we say to a person who has been given a terminal diagnosis? To a person who is actively dying? To the family? At a funeral? Many people are at a loss in such situations. Mainstream culture has provided little in the way of guidance or effective models for interacting with people in the shadow of death. It is common to fall back upon homilies and evasions.

2. Fear of saying or doing the wrong thing. The lack of effective preparation that many people bring with them into death-related situations contributes to exaggerated concern about the possible effects of their own interactions. Afraid that one slip of the tongue might destroy the other person's hope, there is a strong tendency to keep conversation within narrow limits if it cannot be avoided entirely. In turn, the resulting tension and artificiality increases the discomfort of both parties.

3. Development of rigid defensive strategies. Those who interact repeatedly with terminally ill, dying, and grieving people have often adopted coping techniques to protect themselves from the anxiety associated with limited ability to control the situation and reminders of their own mortality. Physicians have most often been criticized for limiting themselves to brisk and perfunctory interactions that do not respond to their patients' cognitive and emotional needs. Psychiatrists have been found to have particularly high levels of death anxiety.

The defense against what might be called *secondary death anxiety* has itself become recognized as a source of stress and disordered communication.

4. Institutionalized patterns of evasion. It is not just the individual who often has difficulty interacting in death-related situations. Organizations have also maintained implicit rules against open communication. For example, workplaces have frequently invoked a code of rigid protocol and near silence when a colleague becomes terminally ill, has died, or has lost a loved one. Educational systems from grade school to graduate school tend to look the other way when a death occurs particularly if by suicide. The most elaborate network of techniques for avoiding and minimizing death-related interactions has been documented in health care facilities. In their classic field studies, Glaser and Strauss (1966, 1968) identified many types of institutional evasion that made open communication almost impossible to achieve in hospitals. For example, mutual pretense was a common arrangement: both staff member and patient acting as though the other did not know the grim truth. Unfortunately, recent studies have found that institutional evasion remains standard procedure in some of the nation's major teaching and research hospitals.

5. Uncertainty about the status of the dying person. Family and care providers are experiencing more difficulty in deciding if they are dealing with a dying person, and therefore adjusting their expectations and interactions. People are now more likely to spend a longer period of time in the interval between decline and death. Neither "dying" nor "terminal" quite fit the variety of situations in which people find themselves. Health care professionals have come to recognize the end phase or end stage as a distinct situation: The major physical systems have failed and death is imminent. But many people live with their eventually terminal conditions for months or years, and, as a society, we have not yet learned how to comprehend and address this phenomenon. The fact that *dying* has become an increasingly imprecise term is contributing to ambiguity and hesitations in death-related communications.

Improvements to Death-Related Interactions. Psychologists and their colleagues in related fields have been discovering effective approaches to improving the quality of communication, and therefore the quality of care, in death-related situations:

- Education and role-playing to improve perspective-taking and empathic skills. Training exercises have proven valuable in helping the various professionals involved in terminal care to respect each other's viewpoints as well as appreciate the situation of patients and their families.
- Developing strategies for preserving a sense of control and efficacy on the part of all people involved in the terminal care situation. This includes a shift from an authoritarian medical model to shared responsibilities and a more open communication network.
- Encouraging peer support groups for families coping with chronic and terminal illness and the grief of bereavement. Professional guidance is helpful in establishing support groups and assisting them over difficult episodes, although much of the benefit is provided by the members themselves.
- Developing increased resourcefulness in dealing with death-related situations. A growing research base and active death education programs provide the opportunity for people to analyze situations, discover alternative approaches, and offer a wider variety of responses. For example, students of psychology and related fields often develop a quantum leap in their understanding when exposed to family members' reports of responses that were helpful and not helpful.
- Recognizing that a moderate level of death anxiety is not only acceptable, but useful. It has been found that empathy, openness, and the willingness to help vulnerable and suffering people often is associated with a discernible level of death anxiety. Preoccupation with concealing or denying one's death anxiety seems to interfere with responsiveness to other people's needs.
- Improving our understanding of pain and suffering will also improve communication and effective interventions. It is now agreed that pain cannot be comprehended adequately from an objectivistic standpoint alone. The same is true for the general sense of suffering and despair that may be experienced in dying and grieving. Phenomenological and gestalt/holistic traditions in psychology can provide the dimension that was too often neglected in the past.

Additionally, studies suggest that whatever strengthens a person's sense of purpose in life and connection with enduring values also improves one's ability to withstand the stress of terminal illness, grief, and offering services to those so afflicted (Schneider & Kastenbaum, 1993; Viswanathan, 1996). The current revival of interest in the role of emotions and values in human behavior is in keeping with the experiences of those who work with the dying and bereaved.

The Psychologist and Death

There is no turning back from the realization that psychology must address the human encounter with death. The general public, professionals, researchers, educators, lawyers, clergy, and policy makers are all engaged with death-related issues along a broad front. Assisted suicide is the spotlight issue with all its ethical and legal aspects. Nevertheless, it is palliative care for the dying and counseling for the bereaved that affect a larger number of people.

Psychology's constructions of death have taken several forms (Kastenbaum, 2000). Most prevalent was the implicit belief that death is irrelevant, except for occasional use of mortality statistics. This approach has usually been associated with a disconnect from natural time and situational context. The focus of psychology in the United States has often been on characteristics of individuals taken as individuals, rather than on people moving through their life course in a biosocial context. The first pass at including death within psychological theory has been its construction as a "task" to be completed in the later adult years. Although not without value, this approach imposes a work–achievement ethos, and establishes a kind of protective ghetto by isolating death as a concern primarily of the aged. The popularity of developmental task theory has yet to be earned through confirmatory research or contribution to everyday dealings with dying and death. Pop psychology has created a fantasy meld in which nineteenth-century romancings of death are embodied within the wrappings of modern media images. Depictions of death as an inspiring adventure are greatly removed from the experiences of most people who are coping with the stress of terminal illness or grief.

Psychology has yet to offer a compelling, comprehensive, and realistic framework for understanding our relationship to death. This is a major challenge for the future. When this challenge is adequately met, it will be one of the finest hours in the history of psychology as a natural, as well as a human, science.

Bibliography

Becker, E. (1973). *The denial of death.* New York: Free Press.

Bluebond-Langner, M. (1996). *In the shadow of illness.* Princeton, NJ: Princeton University Press.

Bregman, L., & Thiermann, S. (1995). *First person mortal.* New York: Paragon.

Byock, I. (1997). *Dying well.* New York: Riverhead Books.

Cushing, S. (1994). *Fatal words.* Chicago: University of Chicago Press.

Feifel, H. (Ed.). (1959). *The meaning of death.* New York: McGraw-Hill.

Feifel, H. (Ed.). (1977). *New meanings of death.* New York: McGraw-Hill.

Feifel, H., & Branscomb, A. B. (1973). Who's afraid of death? *Journal of Abnormal Psychology, 81,* 282–288.

Freud, S. (1959). Thoughts for the times on war and death. In *Sigmund Freud, Collected Works* (Vol. 4, pp. 288–317). London: Hogarth. (Original work published 1917)

Glaser, B., & Strauss, A. (1966). *Awareness of dying.* Chicago: Aldine.

Glaser, B., & Strauss, A. (1968). *Time for dying.* Chicago: Aldine.

Glaser, B., & Stroebe, M. S., Stroebe, W., & Hansson, R. O. (Eds.). (1993). *Handbook of bereavement.* Cambridge, England: Cambridge University Press.

Hafferty, F. W. (1991). *Into the valley. Death and the socialization of medical students.* New Haven: Yale University Press.

Kastenbaum, R. (2000). *The psychology of death* (3rd ed.). New York: Springer.

Kastenbaum, R. (1998). *Death, society, and human experience* (6th ed.). Boston: Allyn & Bacon.

Kastenbaum, R., & Kastenbaum, B. K. (Eds.). (1989). *The encyclopedia of death.* Phoenix: Oryx Press.

Nagy, M. (1948). The child's theories concerning death. *Journal of Genetic Psychology, 73,* 3–27.

Neimeyer, R. A. (Ed.). (1994). *Death anxiety handbook.* Washington, DC: Taylor & Francis.

Nuland, S. B. (1993). *How we die.* New York: Knopf.

Sanner, M. A. (1997). Registered bone marrow donors' views on bodily donations. *Bone Marrow Transplantation, 19,* 67–76.

Schneider, S., & Kastenbaum, R. (1993). Patterns and meanings of prayer in hospice caregivers: An exploratory study. *Death Studies, 17,* 471–486.

Strack, S. (Ed.). (1997). *Death and the quest for meaning.* Northvale, NJ: Aronson.

Vachon, M. L. S. (1987). *Occupational stress in the care of the critically ill, the dying, and the bereaved.* Washington, DC: Hemisphere.

Viswanathan, R. (1996). Locus of control, and purpose in life of physicians. *Psychosomatics, 37,* 339–345.

Weisman, A. D. (1972). *On death and denying.* New York: Behavioral Publications.

Robert Kastenbaum

DECEPTION is the deliberate misrepresentation of facts through words or actions. Although someone may unintentionally misrepresent the truth, the psychologist is concerned with discriminating between the person who is trying to tell the truth and the one who is deliberately lying. Clinical psychologists must be alert that a client may intentionally misrepresent his or her psychological state. For example, a depressed person may try to deceive a clinician about the depth of his or her depression. Forensic psychologists often provide assessments of individuals for law enforcement (e.g., lie detection tests), the courts (e.g., whether a person is insane or just "acting"), or a parole board (a risk assessment). In each of these contexts the person being assessed may engage in deception. It should be noted that a client or witness may unintentionally misrepresent the truth (e.g., through a mistaken belief), but such factual errors are not included in the definition of deception.

Ekman (1992) noted that deception may occur in emotional, opinion, or factual domains. One can misrepresent, through behavior or dialogue, a true emotional state, a true belief, or factual information. Factual deception can be of two types: (a) denying an experience when it actually occurred (e.g., a defendant falsely denying his guilt); or (b) reporting an experience that did not occur (e.g., a complainant falsely claiming to be a victim of a crime). Despite popular misconceptions, there is no single behavior or indicator that is diagnostic of either of these types of deception across individuals. Thus, detecting deception is a profoundly difficult task. Psychologists have focused research and practice in three domains to detect deception: (a) behavioral cues, (b) verbal cues, and (c) tests of malingering.

Behavioral Cues to Deception

Research on behavioral cues to deception has included physiological responses, facial expressions, body language, and voice pitch.

Physiological Measures. The most popular, and widely researched, technique to assess deception is the polygraph, or lie detector test. The polygraph records physiological responses that vary with stress, typically heart rate, skin conductance (related to sweating), and respiration (and sometimes blood pressure). These measures are recorded while the individual is asked a series of questions. With the control question test, responses to the critical questions are compared to responses to stressful questions unrelated to the crime. Alternatively, the guilty knowledge test involves assessing the individual's reaction to questions concerning aspects of the case that would be known only to someone connected with the case (e.g., the use of an ice pick as a murder weapon). It is difficult to apply this version of the polygraph when the media have reported critical aspects of the case.

The polygraph depends upon the assumption that a person will have an emotional response when lying, reflecting a fear of detection and/or guilt about lying. Lying is also thought to place demands on cognition that may be another source of physiological change. Although the polygraph is a useful investigative tool, it has the same problem that exists in most detection techniques: There is no lie response, only a stress response. It is assumed that stronger responses to critical questions are due to guilt, but they could be due to fear of false arrest, or some other emotion felt by an anxious but innocent person. Thus, the polygraph test is prone to false-positive errors (wrongly concluding that a person is lying). It is also possible for deceptive individuals to beat the test (false-negative error) by means of countermeasures (e.g., cognitive effort during the control questions). The extent of such errors is a matter of considerable debate among researchers.

There have been recent attempts to identify more reliable physiological indicators of deception. Electrical and blood flow activity in the brain have been examined as possible cues to deception. The necessary research on these cues has yet to be conducted but they offer some intriguing future possibilities.

Demeanor. The demeanor of a liar has often been proposed as a clue to deception and has received some empirical support. Demeanor includes changes in facial expressions, body language, and voice pitch. For example, microsecond changes in facial expressions have been recorded in individuals misrepresenting their emotional state. The rate and nature of some hand and arm movements have been found to change when a person is lying. Also, voice pitch may rise when a person is being deceptive. However, most observers cannot reliably detect these behavioral changes. Scores of experiments have found that people, usually undergraduate students, perform only slightly better than chance when asked to discriminate lying from truthfulness on the basis of demeanor. However, much of the research has two weaknesses: (a) there is little at stake for the liars, which may reduce behavioral cues to deception; and (b) the cues are compared between individuals (e.g., it is possible that spending time with a person may reveal personal, idiosyncratic demeanor cues to deception). In any event, although training and experience may enhance detection of deception, no one has yet demonstrated what training or experience is required.

Verbal Cues to Deception

A relatively recent development in deception research has examined whether the content of what a person says can reveal deception. Beginning in the 1950s, German psychologists developed the first systematic approach to analyzing statements. Although originally developed for use with children, the procedure came to be applied to the statements of adults as well, particularly to the statements of adults alleging a sexual assault or sexual abuse as a child. With statement analysis the trained assessor applies a set of 19 criteria to the content of a statement(s). The criteria are based upon an assumption (the Undeutsch hypothesis) that the description of memories for directly experienced events is qualitatively different from the description of invented or coached memories. Research completed with child and adult witnesses indicates that the procedure performs better than chance at discriminating the descriptions of actual experiences from deceptions, although there are some limitations with younger children.

Tests of Malingering

Malingering is the intentional distortion or misrepresentation of psychological symptoms for personal gain or to avoid negative consequences (e.g., incarceration). There have been a number of attempts to detect malingering with validity scales on pencil-and-paper tests, such as the Minnesota Multiphasic Personality Inventory (MMPI). It is recognized that people malingering will often endorse items that exaggerate the seriousness of pathology compared to people with a genuine mental disorder. Another recent approach to identifying a malingering patient is symptom suggestion, in which a psychologist suggests a false symptom to a suspected malingerer. These clinical tools are often described as useful aids to clinicians in interpreting responses to pencil-and-paper tests. However, to date, there are no reliable, valid tests of malingering.

Bibliography

Ekman, P. (1992). *Telling lies*. New York: Norton. An authority on deceit provides a thorough review; the text also provides a detailed examination of the circumstances that make lies difficult or easy to detect.

Graham, J. R. (1993). *MMPI-2: Assessing personality and psychopathology*. New York: Oxford University Press. An overview of the most widely employed personality test with information on how it handles the problem of deception with validity scales.

Lykken, D. T. (1981). *A tremor in the blood: Uses and abuses of the lie detector*. New York: McGraw-Hill. An overview of the polygraph by one of its strongest critics.

Memon, A., Vrij, A., & Bull, R. (1998). *Psychology and law: Truthfulness, accuracy and credibility*. New York: McGraw-Hill. An overview of the field of credibility assessment; the chapters vary in quality from excellent to poor.

Raskin, D. (1986). The polygraph in 1986: Scientific, professional, and legal issues surrounding the application of polygraph evidence. *Utah Law Review, 12*, 29–74. An overview of the polygraph by one of its strongest advocates.

Rogers, R. (Ed.). (1988). *Clinical assessment of malingering and deception*. New York: Guilford Press. The best available review of the problems related to the detection of malingering.

Yuille, J. C. (Ed.). (1989). *Credibility assessment*. Dordrecht, The Netherlands: Kluwer. This volume includes chapters by the presenters at the first international conference devoted to the detection of deception.

John C. Yuille and Stephen Porter

DECISION MAKING. People face a great variety of decisions in their lives. Some are fateful, such as whom to wed, what to study, which causes to defend, and how to handle medical crises. Some have limited scope, such as where to dine or shop, what to read or eat, and how to exercise or continue an unrewarding conversation. Some decisions involve clear-cut choices, while others are shrouded in uncertainty. Sometimes that uncertainty concerns what will happen; sometimes it concerns what one really wants and values. Sometimes there are opportunities to learn from experience; sometimes one must get it right the first time. Some decisions offer time for deliberation; others must be made in an instant.

Given the diversity of decisions, how could one hope to develop systematic general knowledge about decision-making processes? Psychologists have adopted two converging strategies in order to address this challenge. One strategy relies on the statistical analysis of multiple decisions, involving complex tasks drawn from a single domain. The second relies on the experimental manipulation of simple decisions, looking at elements that recur in many different decisions (e.g., uncertainties, trade-offs).

The former strategy achieves greater ecological validity, in the sense of placing people in circumstances more closely approximating their actual decision making. However, it uses such complex situations that it can be hard to tell which factors are driving people's choices. The latter strategy isolates factors. However, it also creates the inferential challenge of generalizing from the small world of the experiment to the real world of actual decisions. Combining these strategies offers the opportunity for a relatively balanced perspective on what is—and what can be—known about decision-making processes.

A balanced perspective is essential to fulfill a goal shared by both approaches: helping people to make better decisions. That goal is ill-served by exaggerated claims of any sort. Practical concerns have also made evaluating decision-making performance a focus of both research traditions. In some cases, the standard is achieving a real-world objective (e.g., predicting an event, achieving a return on investment). In other cases, the performance standard is demonstrating consistency with a principle of decision theory (e.g., having transitive preferences, ignoring irrelevant features of tasks).

Statistical Models of Decision Making

Psychology won its stripes (as worthy of public funding) by its ability to process large numbers of people in wartime. During World War II, that processing included diagnosing soldiers' mental conditions. After the war, interest grew in how effective those efficient decisions were. The study of such clinical judgment began by examining the performance of psychologists deciding, say, whether clients were psychotic or neurotic. It gradually expanded to consider the judgments of such diverse experts as radiologists sorting images of tumors into benign and malignant, auditors deciding whether loans were "nonperforming," and admission committees choosing graduate school applicants.

When many predictions of a particular type are characterized on a common set of cues, one can create statistical models predicting either the clinicians' own choices or the real-world event, using the information at the clinicians' disposal. Many such studies have consistently found (a) simple statistical models do a good job of predicting judgments that clinicians describe as the result of complex inferential processes; and (b) somewhat different but still simple statistical models do at least as good a job as clinicians in predicting actual events.

These are challenging results, with provocative implications for how such decisions should be made. Much research (statistical and experimental) has gone into explaining them, leading to some fundamental findings of decision-making research. One result is that people often have limited insight into their own cognitive processes. Particularly when asked to summarize multiple judgments, they may confuse what they did with what they wanted to do or with what people generally do. They may misremember their own judgmental processes, confusing in hindsight what they saw (and said) in foresight. They may underestimate the "treatment effect" created by their own predictions (which can shape subsequent events in their own image). They may remember only an unrepresentative subset of their decisions, leading them to exaggerate their past consistency and success.

A second line of evidence arose from growing recognition of the predictive power of simple (linear) statistical models. If one can identify and measure the cues that individuals consider, then one can often mimic their summary judgments quite well with simple additive models. However, the arithmetic rules for combining those cues need not bear any direct relationship to the underlying cognitive processes. Indeed, one can often predict well with a model that assumes that people simply count the number of factors favoring and opposing each option and then choose the alternative with the best overall tally. And one can also do quite well with a model using variables correlated with those that directly occupy decision makers.

Although the power of linear models is good news for those hoping to predict people's choices, it is bad news for those hoping to explain them. There may be many models that predict equally well, even though they incorporate different variables—and hence represent different theories of the choice process. As a result, it may be hard, and even impossible, to determine which of a set of competing models really captures how people make their choices. Without that knowledge, one may lack the insight needed to help people improve those processes. How researchers have attempted to circumvent these fundamental limits is an interesting and important story. So is the reluctance of decision-making institutions to replace clinical judgment with demonstrably superior statistical procedures.

Experimental Studies of Decision Making

The complementary approach asks whether people have the basic cognitive skills needed to make effective decisions. Those skills include assessing the probability that different actions will lead to different outcomes, and evaluating those outcomes in terms of their rela-

tive attractiveness (or aversiveness). Successful probability assessment is evaluated in terms of (a) accuracy, how well people's beliefs agree with statistical estimates; (b) coherence, how well the relationships among beliefs follow the axioms of probability theory; and (c) calibration, how well people understand the limits to their own knowledge. Successful outcome evaluation requires (a) accuracy, people's predicted (dis)pleasure should correspond to their actual experience, (b) consistency, people should evaluate different representations of the same problem similarly, and (c) articulation, people should be able to translate their general values into preferences for specific choices.

In both respects, experimental work has found a mixture of strengths and weaknesses. Overall performance is, perhaps, about as good as could be expected, considering how little training people receive in decision-making processes and what poor conditions the world offers for learning on their own (e.g., unclear and delayed feedback). A widely accepted account holds that people respond to complex, uncertain decision-making tasks (and their limited information-processing capacity) by using heuristics. These are rules of thumb that are generally helpful, but can lead one astray when used outside their domain of validity.

For example, people may judge the probability of an event by the availability (in memory) of examples of its occurrence. Generally speaking, commonly observed events should be more frequent than rarely observed ones. Moreover, people are good at keeping a rough count of the frequency of the events that they observe, even when they do not expect to be asked. However, there are cases when an event is disproportionately available for reasons that people do not realize or whose effects they cannot undo (e.g., the crime rate as revealed by local TV news). If so, then its probability will be overestimated.

The most widely accepted normative standard for combining probabilities and values into a choice is utility theory. The pillar of modern economics, utility theory evaluates options in terms of their expected utility, defined as the sum of the utilities associated with the different outcomes (e.g., how much money will the person have, how much respect, how much prestige), weighted by their probabilities. Psychological research has found that people are sensitive to features missing from utility theory and insensitive to ones in it. Some of the most dramatic demonstrations have shown framing effects, in which formally equivalent descriptions of a decision elicit different choices (e.g., describing a civil defense program in terms of the lives it will save or the lives that will still be lost; describing the payment for an insurance policy as a "premium" or a "sure loss."

The central role of performance standards in decision-making research has been a source of often productive controversy. It has encouraged thinking hard about the fairness of tasks, sharpening their formulation. It has created an obligation to develop interventions designed to overcome apparently robust judgmental limitations. It has prompted the creation of alternative normative accounts, sometimes involving economists, philosophers, management scientists, and others. Finally it has involved psychologists in public policy debates focused on people's competence, such as adolescents' control of their reproductive choices and citizens' involvement in environmental policy.

[*See also* Illusory Correlation; Political Decision Making; Thinking, *article on* Problem Solving.]

Bibliography

Connolly, T., Arkes, H., & Hammond, K. R. (in press). *Judgment and decision making: An interdisciplinary* (2nd ed.). New York: Cambridge University Press. A diverse collection of articles sponsored by the Society for Judgment and Decision Making.

Dawes, R. (1988). *Rational choice in an uncertain world.* San Diego, CA: Harcourt Brace Jovanovich. A synthesis with special emphases on ethical issues, formal underpinnings, and clinical judgment.

Fischoff, B. (1999). Why (cancer) risk communication can be hard. *Journal of National Cancer Institute Monographs,* 25, 1–7. An introduction to research on health decisions.

Fischhoff, B., Lichtenstein, S., Slovic, P., Derby, S. L., & Keeney, R. L. (1981). *Acceptable risk.* New York: Cambridge University Press. Decision-making research applied to the management of risks in society.

Hammond, K. R. (1997). *Human judgment and social policy.* New York: Oxford University Press. A comprehensive approach, emphasizing regression methods.

Kahneman, D., & Tversky, A. (1979). Prospect theory introduces a local psychological alternative to utility theory. *Econometrica,* 47, 263–291.

Kahneman, D., & Tversky, A. (Eds.). (in press). *Choice, values and frames.* New York: Cambridge University Press. Articles on the formation and measurement of values.

Plous, S. (1993). *The psychology of judgment and decision making.* New York: McGraw Hill. An accessible introduction, with good treatment of related results in social psychology.

Raiffa, H. (1968). *Decision analysis: Introductory lectures on choices under uncertainty.* Reading, MA: Addison-Wesley. A seminal analysis of prescriptive decision making, systematically incorporating judgment.

Simon, H. (1957). *Models of man: Social and rational.* New York: Wiley. The classic analysis of coping strategies for dealing with information-processing limits.

Thaler, R. (1991). *Quasi-rational economics.* New York: Russell Sage Foundation. Articles from the *Journal of Economic Perspectives,* describing psychological phenomena challenging standard economic theory.

Tversky, A., & Kahneman, D. (1974). Judgment under uncertainty: Heuristics and biases. *Science,* 185, 1124–1131. A well-known summary of heuristics approach.

von Winterfeldt, D., & Edwards, W. (1986). *Decision analysis and behavioral research.* New York: Cambridge University Press. An integrated approach to normative, descriptive and prescriptive decision making.

Yates, J. F. (1990). *Judgment and decision making.* New York: Wiley. An authoritative upper-division text.

Baruch Fischhoff

DEFENSE MECHANISMS are patterns of feelings, thoughts, or behaviors that are relatively involuntary. They arise in response to perceptions of psychic danger or conflict, to unexpected change in the internal or external environment, or in response to cognitive dissonance (American Psychological Association, 1994). They obscure or diminish stressful mental representations that if unmitigated would give rise to depression or anxiety. They can alter our perception of any or all of the following: subject (self), object (other), idea, or feeling. There is increasing evidence that choice of defensive styles makes a major contribution to individual differences in response to stressful environments (Vaillant, 1992). As in the case of physiological homeostasis, but in contrast to so-called coping strategies, defense mechanisms usually are deployed outside of awareness. The use of mechanisms of defense usually alters perception of both internal and external reality. Often, as with hypnosis, the use of such mechanisms compromises other facets of cognition.

Adaptation to psychological stress can be divided into three broad classes of coping mechanisms. One class consists of voluntary cognitive or coping strategies, which can be taught and rehearsed; such strategies are analogous to consciously using a tourniquet to stop one's own bleeding. The second class of coping mechanisms is seeking social support or help from others; such support seeking is analogous to calling 911 in response to one's own bleeding. The third class of coping mechanisms are the involuntary defense mechanisms. Such coping mechanisms are analogous to depending on one's own involuntary clotting mechanisms in order to stop bleeding.

Nineteenth-century medical phenomenologists viewed pus, fever, pain, and coughing as pathological; twentieth-century pathophysiologists have learned to regard these same processes as evidence of the body's healthy, if involuntary, efforts to cope with physical or infectious insult. In analogous fashion, many of the mental symptoms that phenomenologists classify as mental disorders can be reclassified by those with a more psychodynamic viewpoint as manifestations of the brain's involuntary adaptive efforts to cope with mental stress. In recognition of the close association between psychological homeostasis and psychopathology, the latest edition of the *Diagnostic and Statistical*

Manual of Mental Disorders (*DSM–IV*; APA, 1994), has included a Defensive Functioning Scale as a proposed diagnostic axis for further study.

Defenses operate in four major arenas. First, they can provide individuals with a period of respite (denial) to master changes in self-image that cannot be immediately integrated; such changes in reality might result from leg amputation (e.g., "But I still have both my legs."). Second, defenses can deflect or deny sudden increases in affective states (e.g., "I'm not angry—just perturbed."). Awareness of forbidden or conflicting "wishes" is usually diminished; alternatively, antithetical wishes may be passionately adhered to. Third, defenses can keep anxiety, shame, and guilt within bearable limits during sudden conflicts with conscience and culture. Finally, defenses enable individuals to mitigate and alter internal representations and unresolved conflicts with important people, living or dead (e.g., "My mother gave me a perfect childhood.").

Choice of mental defensive mechanisms is a major consideration in understanding differential responses to environmental stress. Defenses are mental mechanisms that alter the relationship between self and object, and between idea and affect, in rather specific and differentiated ways. For example, the defense of projection enables someone conflicted over expressing anger to change "I hate him" to "He hates me." In addition, defenses dampen awareness of and response to sudden changes in reality, emotions and drives, conscience, and relationships with people. For example, some people respond to danger or loss in a surprisingly stoic or altruistic fashion, whereas others become phobic or get the giggles or project responsibility. These responses can be differentiated by assigning different labels to the mechanisms underlying the responses. While cross-cultural studies are still sorely needed, socioeconomic status, intelligence, and education do not seem to be causal predictors of maturity of adult defensive style (Vaillant, 1992).

Freud's Discovery of the Concept of Defense

That emotions were significant to humans had been known since ancient times, but our understanding of their modulation through unconscious mechanisms of defense originated with Sigmund Freud, who was trained in both neurology and physiology. In delineating the nature of defenses, Freud not only emphasized that upsetting affects, as well as ideas, underlay psychopathology; he also suggested that no experience "could have a pathogenic effect unless it appeared intolerable to the patient's ego and gave rise to efforts at defense" (Freud, 1906/1964, p. 276).

Over a period of 40 years, Freud described most of the defense mechanisms of which we speak today and identified five of their important properties:

1. Defenses were a major means of managing impulse and affect.
2. Defenses were unconscious.
3. Defenses were discrete from one another.
4. Although often the hallmarks of major psychiatric syndromes, defenses were dynamic and reversible; they were states, not traits.
5. Finally, defenses could be adaptive as well as pathological. Freud conceived of a special class of defense mechanisms—sublimations—that could transmute conflicting affect not into a source of pathology but into culture and virtue. (1905/1964, pp. 238–239)

Freud also introduced the concept of an ontogeny of defenses. Like projection, repression, and sublimation, defenses not only lay along a continuum of relative psychopathology but along a continuum of personality development. With the passage of decades, the defense acting out (e.g., impulsive self-detrimental sexuality) could become the parent of reaction formation (sex is bad, celibacy is good) and a potential grandparent of altruism (teenage mothers are troubled and deserve help).

Modern Conceptualizations of Defense in *DSM–IV*

From the beginning, defenses have posed a problem for experimental psychology. First, there is no clear line between character (enduring traits) and defenses (shorter-lived responses to environment), behavior and mental mechanisms, symptoms (psychopathology) and unconscious coping processes. Conflict-driven adaptive aberrations of a normal brain (defenses) cannot always be distinguished from the symptoms of neuropathology. Second, defense mechanisms can serve other purposes; conversely, any of the mind's functions, not just standard defenses, can be employed in the service of defense. Third, in any effort to produce a comprehensive list of defenses there will be enormous semantic disagreement.

Differentiated mechanisms of defense are clearest when one can study the psychopathology of healthy everyday life in detail. Our appreciation of the defensive nature of mature behavior awaited studies of normal populations, such as those by Ernst Kris, Robert White, Heinz Hartmann, David Hamburg, and Anna Freud (1936). Every one of these investigators, however, presented a different nomenclature; no one supplied mutually exclusive definitions; few sought rater reliability or provided empirical evidence beyond clinical anecdote. Over the last 30 years, several empirical studies (e.g., Haan, 1977; Vaillant, 1977; Perry, 1994) that are well reviewed by Cramer (1991), Skodol and Perry (1993), and Conte and Plutchick (1995) have clarified our understanding of defenses with experimental and reliability studies. By offering a tentative hierarchy and glossary of consensually validated definitions, *DSM–IV* sets the stage for further progress.

DEFENSE MECHANISMS. Table 1. Defense levels and individual defense mechanisms (adapted from *DSM–IV*)

I. Level of Defensive Deregulation. This level is characterized by failure of defensive regulation to contain the individual's reaction to stressors, leading to a pronounced break with objective reality. Examples are
- delusional projection (e.g., psychotic delusions)
- psychotic denial of external reality
- psychotic distortion (e.g., hallucinations)

II. Action Level. This level is characterized by defensive functioning that deals with internal or external stressors by action or withdrawal. Examples are
- acting out
- apathetic withdrawal
- passive aggression
- help-rejecting complaining

III. Major Image-Distorting Level. This level is characterized by gross distortion or misattribution of the image of self or others. Examples are
- autistic fantasy (e.g., imaginary relationships)
- splitting of self-image or image of others (e.g., making people all good or all bad)

IV. Disavowal Level. This level is characterized by keeping unpleasant or unacceptable stressors, impulses, ideas, affects, or responsibility out of awareness with or without a misattribution of these to external causes. Examples are
- denial
- projection
- rationalization

V. Minor Image-Distorting Level. This level is characterized by distortions in the image of the self, body, or others that may be employed to regulate self-esteem. Examples are
- devaluation
- idealization
- omnipotence

VI. Mental Inhibitions (Compromise Formation) Level. Defensive functioning at this level keeps potentially threatening ideas, feelings, memories, wishes, or fears out of awareness. Examples are
- displacement
- dissociation
- intellectualization
- isolation of affect
- reaction formation
- repression
- undoing

VII. High-Adaptive Level. This level of defensive functioning results in optimal adaptation in the handling of stressors. These defenses usually maximize gratification and allow the conscious awareness of feelings, ideas, and their consequences. They also promote an optimum balance among conflicting motives. Examples of defenses at this level are
- anticipation
- affiliation
- altruism
- humor
- self-assertion
- self-observation
- sublimation
- suppression

All classes of defenses in Table 1 are effective in "denying" or defusing conflict and in "repressing" or minimizing stress, but they differ greatly in the psychiatric diagnoses assigned to their users and in their consequences for long-term biopsychosocial adaptation. At level 1, the most pathological category, are found denial and distortion of external reality. These mechanisms are common in young children, our dreams, and psychosis. Such a definition of denial is a far more narrow but specific use of the term than making the term *denial* synonymous with all defense mechanisms. Level 1 defenses rarely respond to simple psychological intervention. To breach them requires altering the brain by neuroleptics or waking the dreamer.

More common to everyday life are the relatively immature defenses found in levels 2 to 4. They are often associated with what *DSM–IV* calls Axis II disorders. Immature defenses externalize responsibility and allow individuals with personality disorders to appear to refuse help. These categories are associated with adolescents, immature adults, and individuals with personality disorders. It includes the paranoid's projection, the schizoid's autistic fantasy, and mutual passive-aggression (the sadistic drill sergeant and the infuriating recruit). Like cigarette smoking in a crowded elevator, such behavior may seem innocent to the user and deliberately irritating and provocative to the observer. Such defenses are consistently and negatively correlated with global assessment of mental health and profoundly distort the affective component of interpersonal relationships.

Defenses in this category rarely respond to verbal interpretation alone. They can be breached in two ways. First, by confrontation—often by a group of supportive peers—or by highly focused but empathic psychotherapy. Second, immature defenses can be breached by improving intrapsychic competence by rendering the individual less anxious and lonely through empathy, less tired and hungry through rest, less intoxicated through abstinence from alcohol, or less adolescent through maturation.

The third class of defenses, those at level 6, are often associated with what *DSM–IV* calls Axis I anxiety disorders and with the psychopathology of everyday life. These include mechanisms like repression, intellectualization, reaction formation (i.e., turning the other cheek), and displacement (i.e., directing affect at a more neutral object). In contrast to the "immature" defenses, the defenses of neurosis are manifested clinically by phobias, compulsions, obsessions, somatizations, and amnesias. Such users often seek psychological help, and neurotic defenses respond more readily to interpretation. Such defenses cause more suffering to the individual than to those in the environment.

The fourth and theoretically most mature class of defenses includes those at level 7: humor, altruism, sublimation, and suppression. These mechanisms still distort and alter feelings, conscience, relationships, and reality, but they achieve these alterations gracefully and flexibly. These mechanisms allow the individual consciously to experience the affective component of interpersonal relationships, but in a tempered fashion.

While mature defenses are arguably more conscious and certainly more "coping" than immature defenses, to dichotomize defenses as either "coping" or "defending" has proven both arbitrary and not helpful. The defense most highly associated with mental health is suppression, a defense that modulates emotional conflict or internal and external stressors through stoicism, by postponing but not ignoring wishes, and by subjectively minimizing but not ignoring disturbing problems, feelings, and experiences.

Implicit in the concept of defense is the conviction that it is not only genetic vulnerability and life stress but also the patient's idiosyncratic defensive response to such vulnerability and stress that shapes psychopathology. Thus, despite problems in reliability, the validity of defenses makes them a valuable diagnostic axis for understanding psychopathology. By including defensive style as part of the mental status or diagnostic formulation, clinicians are better able to comprehend what is adaptive as well as maladaptive about their patients' defensive distortions of inner and outer reality. They may also learn to view qualities that initially seemed most unreasonable and unlikable about their patients as human efforts to cope with conflict.

[*See also* Coping; Learned Helplessness; Optimism and Pessimism; Repression; Self-Consciousness; *and* Stress.]

Acknowledgments. This work is from the Division of Psychiatry, Department of Medicine, Brigham and Women's Hospital and the Study of Adult Development, Harvard University Health Services. It was supported by research grants MH 00364 and MH 42248 from the National Institute of Mental Health.

Bibliography

American Psychiatric Association. (1994). *Diagnostic and Statistical Manual of Mental Disorders* (4th ed.). Washington, DC: Author.

Conte, H. R., & Plutchik, R. (1995). *Ego defenses: Theory and measurement.* New York: Wiley.

Cramer, P. (1991). *The development of defense mechanisms.* New York: Springer Verlag.

Freud, A. (1936). *The ego and mechanisms of defense.* London: Hogarth Press.

Freud, S. (1964). Three essays on the theory of sexuality. In J. Strachey (Ed.), *Standard edition* (Vol. 7, pp. 130–243). London: Hogarth Press. (Original work published 1905)

Freud, S. (1964). My views on the part played by sexuality in the etiology of the neuroses. In J. Strachey (Ed.) *Standard edition* (Vol. 7, pp. 271–279). London: Hogarth Press. (Original work published 1906)

Haan, N. (1977). *Coping and defending.* San Francisco: Jossey-Bass.

James, W. (1890). *The principles of psychology.* New York: Henry Holt.

Perry, J. C. (1994). Defense mechanisms and their effects. In N. Miller, L. Luborsky, J. Docherty, & J. Barber (Eds.), *Psychodynamic research.* New York: Basic Books.

Skodal, A., & Perry, J. C. (1993). Should an axis for defense mechanisms be included in *DSM–IV*? *Comprehensive Psychiatry, 34,* 108–119.

Vaillant, G. E. (1977). *Adaptation to life.* Boston: Little, Brown (reprinted by Harvard University Press).

Vaillant, G. E. (1992). *Ego mechanisms of defense: A guide for clinicians and researchers.* Washington, DC: American Psychiatric Press.

George E. Vaillant

DEINDIVIDUATION is a psychological state of reduced self-awareness and a reduced sense of personal identity resulting in behavior that is influenced by current situational or group norms, rather than by personal or societal norms. Deindividuation is most likely to occur when individuals are submerged in a group, but may also occur outside a group when situational cues draw attention away from the self. Deindividuation may help explain many forms of collective antisocial behavior. For example, rioters may feel faceless and unaccountable in the midst of a lynch mob, and sports fans may yell obscenities at a referee when submerged in a crowd of similar others. However, deindividuation does not necessarily produce antisocial behavior, and can lead to positive consequences if the group or situation creates positive standards for behavior. Indeed, people sometimes deliberately seek out potentially deindividuating experiences such as parties, dances, and religious gatherings in the hope of enhancing positive emotions and feelings of closeness.

Historical Background

In 1895, French theoretician Gustave Le Bon (*The Crowd*, London) proposed that a crowd of people can become a unified entity that operates as though guided by a collective mind, with emotions and behaviors that are easily transmitted from one person to the next. Festinger, Pepitone, and Newcomb (1952) first coined the term *deindividuation* and described it as a phenomenon in which individuals become so submerged in a group that they engage in disinhibited, deviant behaviors. These ideas were expanded and refined in later years by a variety of American and European social psychologists. A variety of theories have been developed, and more than 60 laboratory and field experiments have identified important factors that can lead to deindividuation. Although deindividuation research has provided much insight into collective behavior, it has also produced some inconsistencies and unanswered questions. Future research is needed to determine more precisely the conditions under which deindividuation is likely to occur and to produce positive and negative consequences, as well as the specific mechanisms through which deindividuation alters the behavior of individuals.

Key Factors Contributing to Deindividuation

Research has identified a number of factors that influence the occurrence and magnitude of deindividuation.

Group Size. As the size of the group or crowd increases, so does the potential for deindividuation. Mullen (1986) illustrated the importance of group size in a content analysis of newspaper accounts of 60 lynchings committed in the United States between 1899 and 1946. Mobs were more likely to engage in savagery and commit atrocities when the size of the mob increased relative to the number of victims.

Anonymity. A number of studies suggest that anonymity plays an important role in deindividuation. For example, Zimbardo (1969) found that women who were clothed in oversized lab coats and hoods were more willing to administer supposed electric shocks to another person than were women who wore normal clothes and name tags. Similarly, in an anthropological study of 27 cultures, Watson (1973) found that warriors who hid their identities during battle by using face and body paint or masks were significantly more likely to torture or kill enemy prisoners than were warriors who could be readily identified. However, anonymity does not always result in negative behaviors. For example, in a conceptual extension of Zimbardo's experiment, Johnson and Downing (1979) found that anonymity only enhanced aggression when the costumes bore a resemblance to Ku Klux Klan outfits, but actually reduced aggression when the costumes resembled nurse uniforms.

A clever study by Diener and colleagues (1976) of Halloween trick-or-treaters in Seattle further illustrates the importance of anonymity. A greeter asked the children to take just one piece of candy, then left the room. Half of the children were asked to provide their names and say where they lived. Hidden observers noted that the anonymous children were more than twice as likely to take extra candy than were the identified children.

Reduced Self-Awareness. Experiences that diminish self-awareness can also contribute to deindividuation. A number of studies have found that, compared with self-aware people, deinidividuated people behave in a manner that is less self-regulated, less consistent with their own attitudes and values, and more easily influenced by situational cues. Thus, factors that can reduce self-awareness, such as alcohol, arousal, and distraction, can enhance one's responsiveness to situational norms. However, factors that increase self-awareness, such as mirrors, cameras, name tags, and bright lights, increase self-regulation, enhance the consistency between personal attitudes and behaviors, and serve as potential remedies to deindividuation.

Group Identification. Reicher, Spears, and Postmes (1995) suggested that deindividuation occurs when individuals shift their attention from their personal identity to a more social or collective identity, and therefore attend more to group norms and social norms in the immediate social context than to personal norms. Consistent with this logic, a recent meta-analysis by Postmes and Spears (1998) found that individuals' behavior in deindividuation experiments appears to be influenced more by situation-specific norms than by general social norms. Whether changes in self-identity rather than other potential sources of deindividuation produce these patterns is currently unclear.

Bibliography

Diener, E. (1980). Deindividuation: The absence of self-awareness and self-regulation in group members. In P. B. Paulus (Ed.), *The psychology of group influence* (pp. 209–242). Hillsdale, NJ: Erlbaum. Provides a review of early research and presents the first self-awareness theory of deindividuation.

Diener, E., Fraser, S. C., Bearnan, A. L., & Kelem, R. T. (1976). Effects of deindividuating variables on stealing among Halloween trick-or-treaters. *Journal of Personality and Social Psychology, 33,* 178–183.

Festinger, L., Pepitone, A., & Newcomb, T. (1952). Some consequences of de-individuation in a group. *Journal of Abnormal and Social Psychology, 47,* 382–389. Presents the first deindividuation experiment and offers a theoretical treatment.

Johnson, R. D., & Downing, L. L. (1979). Deindividuation and valence of cues: Effects on prosocial and antisocial behavior. *Journal of Personality and Social Psychology, 37,* 1532–1538.

Mann, L. (1981). The baiting crowd in episodes of threatened suicide. *Journal of Personality and Social Psychology, 41,* 703–709. An archival analysis of the role deindividuating variables may have played in a number of cases in which onlookers verbally encouraged a person to jump from a building or bridge.

Mullen, B. (1986). Atrocity as a function of lynch mob composition: A self-attention perspective. *Personality and Social Psychology Bulletin, 12,* 187–197.

Postmes, T., & Spears, R. (1998). Deindividuation and antinormative behavior: A meta-analysis. *Psychological Bulletin, 123,* 238–259. Synthesizes 61 publications on deindividuation and reviews prior theories.

Prentice-Dunn, S., & Rogers, R. W. (1989). Deindividuation and the self-regulation of behavior. In P. B. Paulus (Ed.), *The psychology of group influence* (2nd ed., pp. 86–109). Hillsdale, NJ: Erlbaum. Presents a comprehensive self-attention theory of deindividuation.

Reicher, S., Spears, R., & Postmes, T. (1995). A social identity model of deindividuation phenomena. In W. Stroebe & M. Hewstone (Eds.), *European review of social psychology* (Vol. 6, pp. 161–198). Chichester, England: Wiley.

Watson, R. (1973). Investigation into deindividuation using a cross-cultural survey technique. *Journal of Personality and Social Psychology, 25,* 342–345.

Zimbardo, P. G. (1969). The human choice: Individuation, reason, and order vs. deindividuation, impulse, and chaos. In W. J. Arnold & D. Levine (Eds.), *Nebraska Symposium on Motivation* (Vol. 17, pp. 237–307). Lincoln: University of Nebraska Press. Presents an influential process theory of deindividuation and explores its implications for a wide range of social problems.

Steven J. Karau

DEINSTITUTIONALIZATION was intended as a process in which institutional psychiatric care would be reduced but improved where necessary or replaced by comprehensive, community-based services encompassing treatment, rehabilitation, and support (Government Accounting Office, 1977). In common understanding, however, deinstitutionalization has simply meant reductions in the census of public mental hospitals.

The magnitude of deinstitutionalization can only be appreciated through statistics. Increasing steadily since the early 1900s, the resident population of state/county mental hospitals peaked in 1955 at 558,922 patients. By 1980, this figure was one-quarter of its previous high. Interestingly, the number of hospitals stayed constant during this time period; admissions rose through 1970 and then declined. The major effect of deinstitutionalization was on the number of beds per hospital and length of stay.

The process of deinstitutionalization was driven by a confluence of social forces—conservative and liberal. Operation of public mental hospitals was an economic burden borne mainly by state governments. By 1955, costs were consuming politically indefensible state revenues, for example, 38% of New York State's budget (R. J. Isaac and V. C. Armat, *Madness in the Streets*, New York, 1990). Exposés of deplorable conditions in state hospitals combined with this economic burden to heighten state concerns.

The "discovery" of antipsychotic medications is frequently cited as the major cause of deinstitutionalization. Anne Johnson in *Out of Bedlam* (New York, 1990) points out, though, that adoption of neuroleptic drugs resulted primarily from promotions by entrepreneurial pharmaceutical companies, invested heavily in marketing strategies targeted at state legislatures to increase hospital drug budgets. Medication-based treatments were attractive to fiscal conservatives as they promised to reduce institutional costs.

Deinstitutionalization was also driven by humanitarian concerns. Rights protections, initiated through civil rights cases, were extended to other disadvantaged groups, including psychiatric patients. Gerald Grob in *The Mad Among Us* (New York, 1994) notes that mental health systems were also a focus for academic sociologists, positing deviance as a social construction enhancing group cohesion in times of social change. The function of psychiatric diagnosis was to reify and legitimate the existing social order. In this antipsychiatry movement, mental illness, if it existed at all, was created by the social institutions designed to cure it. Eliminating mental hospitals would therefore eliminate mental illness.

Psychological theories recognizing the influence of parenting practices on child development and later adult outcomes contributed to rejection of illness and hospital treatment models. Effective interventions needed to be in vivo, social and educational in nature. The mental hygiene movement espoused the potential of early interventions with families, schools, and communities to prevent mental illness; in the future, hospitals would not be needed.

In response to these social and economic concerns, the U.S. Congress created the Joint Commission on Mental Illness and Health. In its 1961 report, *Action for*

Mental Health, Congress recommended upgrading state hospitals to therapeutic levels, increasing psychiatric treatment in general hospitals, and developing community mental health centers to divert persons with mental illness from hospitals and provide aftercare for those discharged yet incompletely recovered. The Community Mental Health Centers (CMHC) Act (1962) was the legislative response. The act and its associated regulations, however, placed an emphasis on prevention and included no mechanisms or funding to improve conditions in state hospitals—contrary to National Institutes of Mental Health assurances in congressional hearings. The act also ignored the state's role in implementation or monitoring CMHCs. Thus, state authorities were still without legitimate means to address the responsibility of state hospitals.

Deinstitutionalization, representing an economic and political mandate, nevertheless, was already proceeding. Its immediate implementation, however, was seriously flawed in most locations. Community facilities were not adequate to provide appropriate care for discharged and/or diverted patients. CMHCs had no function nor any staff with training or interest in long-term mental illness. Their focus was on prevention and services to less seriously disturbed individuals; therefore, rather than diversion or step-down programs, less appropriate mechanisms were used to reduce state hospital census.

Deinstitutionalization is seen as a failed policy or a failure to implement policy by most. Many unintended, negative results have been attributed to deinstitutionalized patients allegedly discharged before they were ready, transferred or discharged to inappropriate sources, or refused admission in order to decrease hospital utilization. The burden of care for these individuals was consequently borne by other sectors, resulting in the following:

- *Homelessness:* released patients without a home and/or capabilities to care for themselves wind up living on the streets or discharged to shelters;
- *Transinstitutionalization:* older patients transferred directly from state hospitals to nursing homes (through federal Medicaid funding), where care is inadequate for serious psychiatric problems; others sent to board and care homes, funded through Supplemental Security Income;
- *Criminalization:* unable to receive treatment through hospitals when needed, individuals with mental illness engage in bizarre behaviors and/or illegal acts necessary for survival (for example, loitering, stealing food, breaking or entering to obtain shelter, and so forth). Their resulting treatment is jail;
- *Family burden:* families that still have connections to ill relatives have no choice but to care for them or turn them out on the street. This increases the family's own stress and economic vulnerability, since it usually receives no assistance from public authorities.

These processes reflect states' shifting their costs in operating mental hospitals. Transinstitutionalization shifts costs to federal government revenues, homelessness and criminalization to local governments, and family burden to personal or private sources. But, of course, the largest effect is on quality of care. Rather than receiving appropriate attention in a hospital, patients live alone, stigmatized in the community and unable to obtain jobs. Such conditions can exacerbate symptoms, producing the revolving door phenomenon. Ironically, attempts to protect rights instigated by advocacy groups (for example, mental patient liberation advocates including young, public interest attorneys focused on eliminating civil commitments, ending unnecessary detention, and upholding rights to refuse treatment) may have exacerbated these negative outcomes by limiting treatment options even further.

Some statistics have been amassed in support of these allegations. E. Fuller Torey and colleagues in *Criminalizing the Seriously Mentally Ill* (Washington, D.C., 1992) provide data on the sizeable population of persons with mental illness in local jails. Research on homelessness indicates that about 20 to 30% of homeless populations have experienced long-term serious mental illness. However, as persuasive as the advocates are, none of the documentation on homelessness, family burden, or criminalization can establish that without a deinstitutionalization policy, these individuals with mental illness would have been cared for adequately anyway.

While the short-term failures of deinstitutionalization are readily visible, the long-term positive consequences are not often identified. Deinstitutionalization has at least contributed to the development and expansion of innovative organizational forms (psychiatric rehabilitation, clubhouses, assertive community treatment), more humanistic treatment (rights protection guarantees), and a social movement (former-patient advocacy, self-help groups for persons with serious mental illness, and consumer-run programs). Examples can be found of well-planned state hospital closures, accompanied by exemplary treatment that is completely community-based (Northampton State Hospital in Massachusetts). Long-term data on mental health service utilization (from 1970 to 1986) does resemble more the comprehensive definition of deinstitutionalization. Only 24% of episodes are inpatient (compared to 77% in 1986); the number and size of public mental hospitals and additions to their census have decreased; and the resident population has been reduced by another two-thirds. Finally, despite allegations of poor and/or unsafe community treatment, consumer preferences are almost uniformly in favor of community residence rather than hospitalization (see Davidson et al., The experiences of long-stay patients returning to the community, *Psychiatry, 58,* 122–132, 1995).

While deinstitutionalization presents a complicated story of causes and effects, it also contains many lessons to learn. Deinstitutionalization was not a policy; despite its significance, it just happened. Probably because of extreme polemics, planning was totally inadequate, driven by dogma and self-interest rather than patient concerns. Policy implementation did not match policy intent, but there were no checks or balances to monitor this. Local programs needed oversight to assure policy congruence, but federal authorities could not do this; involvement of states or local constituencies was needed. Furthermore, for meaningful change, all components of a system must be prepared to change—which requires adequate funding upfront and a long time frame. Most of all, deinstitutionalization needed an integrated and meaningful federal policy on treatment of mental illness.

Deinstitutionalization is still underway with downsizing and state hospital closures. As of 1995, the number of resident patients in state and county mental hospitals was 69,177: 12.4% of the 1955 peak and 20% of the 1970 census. The need for national policy and social science involvement in deinstitutionalization still exists.

Bibliography

Bachrach, L. L. (1996). The state of the state mental hospital in 1996. *Psychiatric Services, 47* (10), 1071–1078. Updates the author's 1976 monograph on deinstitutionalization. Reviewing and integrating available data, the author concludes that individual state mental hospitals vary in the composition of their resident populations, the content of their services, and the overall quality of care. Although superseded by community-based service structures in some places, they continue to occupy a critical place in systems of care.

Center for Mental Health Services. *Mental Health, United States, 1996.* R. W. Manderscheid & M. A. Sonnenschein (Eds.). DHHS Pub. No. (SMA)96–3098. Washington, DC: Supt. of Docs., U.S. Govt. Print. Office. This seventh edition of this document presents mental health epidemiological data for adults and children, data on mental health service utilization and staffing, information on geographical distribution of mental health services, and chapters on managed behavioral health care, as well as mental health in Medicaid/Medicare.

Fisher, W. H., Simon, L., Geller, J. L., Penk, W. E., Irvin, E. A., & White, C. S. (1996). Case mix in the "downsizing" state hospital. *Psychiatric Services, 47* (3), 255–262. Examined trends in case mix over a fourteen-year-period at two Massachusetts state hospitals, differing in levels of community-based services. The authors conclude that while alternative treatment settings allow diversion of many types of patients, some patient subgroups have not been diverted, e.g., recidivists and patients who are behavioral risks. Further deinstitutionalization and/or privatization must include a focus on these patient groups.

Grob, G. N. (1991). From hospital to community: Mental health policy in modern America. *Psychiatric Quarterly, 62* (3), 187–212. A succinct summary of Grob's thesis presented more fully in his book, *From Asylum to Community: Mental Health Policy in Modern America* (Princeton, 1991). The article reviews the fundamental changes in mental health policy in the United States from World War II through the 1970s. The legitimacy of institutional care was undermined by individuals and groups committed to an environmentalist psychodynamic and psychoanalytic psychiatry and to community-oriented programs. The consequences of the policy changes during these decades, however, differed in significant respects from the goals and intentions of those who favored innovation.

Kiesler, C. A., & Sibulkin, A. E. (1987). *Mental hospitalization: Myths and facts about a national crisis.* Newbury Park, CA: Sage. The authors present a reanalysis of national data on inpatient psychiatric utilization and expenditures. They analyze the overall system of mental health hospitalization and other institutional substitutions, e.g., nursing homes, as well as the changing patterns of utilization and care. The book also reviews national policies concerning mental health treatment and establishes the argument that mental health policy in the United States is de facto rather than de jure.

Lewis, D. A., Shadish, W. R., & Lurigio, A. J. (1989). Policies of inclusion and the mentally ill: Long-term care in a new environment. *Journal of Social Issues, 45* (3), 173–186. Inclusionary policies refer to the fact that deinstitutionalization, and all the policy changes associated with it, resulted in the forcible inclusion back into society of patients formerly excluded by institutional placement. This compelled both society and the patient to change in profound but often unpredicted ways. This conceptualization can explain and unite many phenomena associated with deinstitutionalization, for example, how its problems resemble those of racial desegregation, why it results in increasing differentiation of types of patients, and how it turned what had formerly been a mental health problem into a broader welfare problem. Future research topics implied by this conceptualization are suggested.

Okin, R. L. (1995). Testing the limits of deinstitutionalization. *Psychiatric Services, 46* (6), 569–574. Reports on the distribution and funding of services in western Massachusetts, where a comprehensive community-based mental health system was established to replace entirely Northampton State Hospital. Data indicate very low utilization of inpatient services and/or nursing homes. Total expenditures were similar to the rest of the state but reflected higher per capita spending on residential, emergency services, and case management. The author concludes that under certain conditions, state hospitals can be completely replaced.

Steadman, H. J., Morris, S. M., & Dennis, D. L. (1995). The diversion of mentally ill persons from jails to community-based services: A profile of programs. *American Journal of Public Health, 85* (12), 1630–1635. In a national mail survey to all U.S. jails with a rated capacity of 50 or more (resulting in a sample of 1,106), slightly more than a third indicated they had a formal diversion program for mentally ill offenders. Eighteen of these were selected for on-site interviews. Programs were categorized and key factors found among the most effective were identified.

Witkin, M. J., Atay, J., & Manderscheid, R. W. (1996). Trends in state and county mental hospitals in the U.S. from 1970–1992. *Psychiatric Services, 47* (10), 1079–1081. Documents changes in state mental hospitals from 1970 to 1992 in four areas: the number of hospitals, the average daily census, expenditures, and the number of staff. The authors conclude that state hospitals will continue to reduce their populations, although at a slower rate than in the past, and will continue to care for individuals due to involuntary admissions or lacking alternative living arrangements.

Carol T. Mowbray and David P. Moxley

DELBOEUF, JOSEPH-RÉMI-LÉOPOLD (1831–1896), Belgian psychologist. Joseph-Rémi-Léopold Delboeuf can be considered as the first significant Belgian psychologist. He earned a doctorate in philosophy in 1855 and in physical and mathematical science in 1857 from the University of Liège. After working in the area of geometry and logic, he was named professor of Philosophy at the University of Ghent (1863–1866). As a philosopher and a mathematician, he naturally took an interest in then current scientific work in psychology and more specifically in perception and psychophysics.

An encounter with the physicist Joseph Plateau apparently oriented Delboeuf toward the question of optical illusions. He advanced the concept of muscular strength in order to put forward a theory applicable to all optical illusions (changes in muscular sensations enable us to judge differences in extent). He tested his theory empirically in 1865 on a new optical illusion known now as "Delboeuf concentric circles," which consists in a change in the perceived size of one circle in the presence of a circle of a different size.

The first experimental researches by Delboeuf in the domain of psychophysics were executed at the University of Ghent between 1865 and 1866 before he was nominated to the University of Liège as a philologist. These studies led him to compile two important memoirs and several articles where, with considerable originality, he defended the famous Fechner's logarithmic law relating sensation strength to stimulus strength. His work in this area is characterized on the one hand by an amendment to Fechner's formula and on the other hand by the utilization of a psychophysical technique based on brightness contrast (bisection method).

Although viewed by Fechner himself as an opponent of his beliefs, Delboeuf was actually one of his least virulent critics and the only psychologist of the era to have adopted a logarithmic law.

In his later career Delboeuf gradually devoted more of his time to research on a variety of subjects including philology, philosophy, biology, and above all at the end of his life, hypnotism, a subject he had been interested in since 1850. It was in the context of a book he published in 1885 on sleep and dreams in connection with memory that he decided to study hypnotism. He visited the famous hypnosis researcher Jean Charcot in 1885 in order to verify a phenomenon widely accepted at the time: the total loss of memory *after* hypnosis for events that took place *during* hypnosis. For Delboeuf, this memory loss was not a characteristic of the hypnotic state and he cleverly showed that memories created under hypnosis can, in fact, be evoked. On his return home he practiced hypnotism and published a book on the Salpêtrière school showing that many of the regularly observed characteristics of hypnosis really were due to influences unconsciously transmitted. Delboeuf's major conclusion about the role of suggestion was also consistent with many of the early observations made at Nancy by investigators such as Liébault, Bernheim, and Liégeois. Delboeuf's ideas are now considered as precursors of modern ideas on both hypnotism and clinical psychology.

Bibliography

Duyckaerts, F. (1992). *Joseph Delboeuf: Philosophe et hypnotiseur* [Joseph Delboeuf: Philosopher and hypnotist]. Paris: Delagrange.

Nicolas, S. (1995a). On the concept of memory in the works of Joseph Delboeuf. *Psychologica Belgica, 35,* 45–60.

Nicolas, S. (1995b). Joseph Delboeuf on visual illusions: A historical sketch. *The American Journal of Psychology, 108,* 563–574.

Nicolas, S., Murray, D. J., & Farahmand, B. (1997). The psychophysics of J. R. L. Delboeuf. *Perception, 26,* 1237–1315.

Wolf, T. H. (1964). Alfred Binet: A time of crisis. *American Psychologist, 19,* 761–762. Describes Delboeuf's visit to Charcot's hypnosis laboratory.

Serge Nicolas

DELGADO, HONORIO (1892–1969), Peruvian psychiatrist and philosopher. Born in Arequipa, the second largest city in Peru, Delgado studied medicine at San Marcos University in Lima where he became a disciple of psychiatric pioneer Hermilio Valdizán (1884–1929). In 1915, while still in medical school,

Delgado published an article in the newspaper *El Comercio* (Lima) entitled "El psicoanálisis," one of the first articles written in Spanish about psychoanalysis. In 1918 Delgado earned his medical degree and wrote a dissertation with the same title. During that same year, Valdizán and Delgado founded the *Revista de Psiquiatría y Disciplinas Conexas* (Review of Psychiatry and Related Disciplines). Until 1930, Delgado dedicated much effort to the dissemination of Freudian theory in Latin America. During a trip to Europe in 1922, Delgado met Freud, as well as Adler. Freud (*History of Psychoanalytic Movement*, 2nd ed.) described Delgado as an important representative of psychoanalysis in the Spanish-speaking world, and the *Revista* as the regional publication of his movement.

After 1930, Delgado gradually grew more and more disassociated from psychoanalysis, finally becoming one of its most bitter critics in Spanish-speaking psychiatry. Instead, he developed a keen interest in German, philosophically oriented psychologies, especially those of Karl Jaspers (1883–1969) and Nicolai Hartmann (1882–1950). Delgado viewed psychology as a *Geisteswissenschaft* (a social or cultural science, as opposed to a natural science), and tried to demonstrate the importance of Hartmann's ideas for psychopathology. His critical attitude toward psychoanalysis grew increasingly apparent when he became chair of psychiatry at San Marcos University after Valdizán's death. Delgado's papers and books diminished the diffusion of psychoanalysis in Peru.

Delgado was active in a number of academic societies, and in 1938 joined J. Oscar Trelles (1904–1990) in founding the *Revista de Neuropsiquiatría* (Review of Neuropsychiatry). He also served as psychiatrist at Víctor Larco Herrera Hospital, an institution devoted to the treatment of psychiatric patients. He was appointed Minister of Education (1948), Dean of the San Marcos University Faculty of Medicine (1961), and was the first rector (1962–1966) of the University of Medical and Biological Sciences (the current name of the university is Cayetano Heredia University), which he helped to found.

Delgado was a prolific author. Among his most important books are *Sigmund Freud* (Lima, 1926), *Psicología* (with M. Iberico; Lima, 1933), *La formación espiritual del individuo* (The spiritual formation of the individual; Lima, 1933), *La personalidad y el carácter* (Personality and character; Lima, 1943), *Curso de psiquiatría* (The textbook of psychiatry; Lima, 1953); *Enjuiciamiento de la medicina psicosomática* (Critical evaluation of psychosomatic medicine; Barcelona, 1960), *De la cultura y sus artífices* (Of culture and its artifices; Madrid, 1961), and *Contribuciones a la psicología y a la psicopatología* (Contributions to psychology and psychopathology; Lima, 1962).

Bibliography

Alarcón, R. (1968). *Panorama de la psicología en el Perú* [An overview of psychology in Peru]. Lima: Universidad Nacional Mayor de San Marcos.

Alarcón, R., & León, R. (Eds.). (1996). *Tiempo, sabiduría y plenitud. Estudios sobre la vida y obra de Honorio Delgado* [Time, wisdom, and completion. Studies on the life and work of Honorio Delgado]. Lima: Universidad Peruana Cayetano Heredia.

León, R., & Zambrano, A. (1992). *Honorio Delgado: Un pionero de la psicología en América Latina* [Honorio Delgado: A pioneer in psychology in Latin America]. *Revista Latinoamericana de Psicología, 24*, 401–423.

Mariátegui, J. (1989). La psiquiatría en el Perú [Psychiatry in Peru]. In J. Mariátegui (Ed.), *La psiquiatría en América Latina* (pp. 163–182). Buenos Aires: El Ateneo.

Ramón León

DELINQUENCY refers to the commission of acts prohibited by the criminal law, such as theft, burglary, robbery, violence, vandalism, and drug use, by persons aged under 18. The minimum age for delinquency varies in different places but is rarely less than seven. There are many problems in using legal definitions of delinquency. The boundary between what is legal and what is illegal may be poorly defined and subjective, as when school bullying gradually escalates into criminal violence. Legal categories may be so wide that they include acts that are behaviorally quite different, as when robbery ranges from armed bank robberies carried out by gangs of masked men to thefts of small amounts of money perpetrated by one school child on another. Legal definitions rely on the concept of intent, which is difficult to measure, rather than the behavioral criteria preferred by psychologists. Also, legal definitions change over time; however, their main advantage is that because they have been adopted by most delinquency researchers, their use makes it possible to compare and summarize results obtained in different projects.

Delinquency is commonly measured using either official records of arrests/convictions or self-reports of offending. The advantages and disadvantages of official records and self-reports are to some extent complementary. In general, official records include the worst offenders and the worst offenses, while self-reports include more of the normal range of delinquent activity. The worst offenders may be missing from samples interviewed in self-report studies. Self-reports have the advantage of including undetected offenses but the disadvantages of concealment and forgetting. By normally accepted psychometric criteria of validity, self-reports of offending are valid. Fortunately, the worst offenders according to self-reports (taking account of frequency and seriousness) tend also to be the worst offenders according to official records, and the predictors and correlates of official and self-reported delinquency are generally very similar.

Epidemiology

The most useful information about epidemiology and risk factors for delinquency is obtained in prospective longitudinal surveys of delinquency based on large community samples. For example, over 400 South London boys were followed up from age 8 to age 40 in the Cambridge Study in Delinquency Development, and over 1,500 Pittsburgh boys were followed up from ages 7 to 25 in the Pittsburgh Youth Study.

Most research concerns males, because the prevalence of delinquency is greater for males than for females. About three times as many boys as girls are arrested in the United States for the more serious "index" crimes, and about six times as many boys as girls are arrested for violent index crimes (murder, rape, robbery, and aggravated assault). There are also ethnic/racial disproportionalities in arrest rates. Over five times as many African American juveniles as Caucasian juveniles per capita in the United States are arrested for violent index crimes. The gender and ethnic/racial disproportionalities are generally lower in self-reports than in official records.

Even according to official records, the cumulative prevalence of delinquency is high. In a Philadelphia follow-up study of over 27,000 children born in 1958, Paul Tracy reported that the prevalence of juvenile arrests for nontraffic offenses was 42% of African American males, 23% of Caucasian males, 19% of African American females and 9% of Caucasian females. According to self-reports, most juveniles commit delinquent acts. David Huizinga, in a longitudinal study of over 1,500 Denver children, found that 94% of boys and 90% of girls reported that they had committed a delinquent offense before age 18. In the large-scale Denver, Pittsburgh, and Rochester studies, almost half of 17-year-old boys admitted committing at least one "street crime" (such as burglary, serious theft, robbery, and aggravated assault) in the previous year.

While the overall prevalence of delinquency is high, especially in the inner-city samples that are commonly studied, a small fraction of the population (the "chronic offenders") accounts for a large fraction of all serious delinquencies. In the 1958 Philadelphia birth cohort study, 7% of the males accounted for 61% of all the offenses. Terrie Moffitt of London University has suggested that it is important to distinguish between the more committed "life-course-persistent" offenders and the less committed "adolescence-limited" offenders.

Generally, delinquents are versatile rather than specialized in their offending. Most juveniles who commit violent crimes are persistent offenders who appear to commit different types of crimes almost at random during their criminal careers. As demonstrated in the Cambridge study, delinquents disproportionally tend to commit many other types of deviant acts, including heavy drinking, substance use, drunk driving, heavy smoking, heavy gambling, and promiscuous sexual behavior.

Generally, there is significant continuity between delinquency in one age range and delinquency in another. In the Cambridge study, 73% of those convicted as juveniles were reconvicted as young adults, and there was continuity for self-reported offending and for antisocial behavior in general. An early age of onset of juvenile offending predicts a large number of juvenile offenses and a high probability of persisting into an adult criminal career.

Risk Factors

Literally, thousands of factors differentiate significantly between official delinquents and nondelinquents and correlate significantly with self-reports of delinquency. The major problem is to establish which risk factors have causal effects. There are many biological, individual, family, peer, school, and community risk factors for delinquency, only a few of which can be mentioned here.

Hyperactivity and impulsivity are among the most important personality or individual difference factors that predict later delinquency. Related concepts include poor attention, a poor ability to defer gratification, and a short future-time perspective. The most extensive research on different measures of impulsivity was carried out by Jennifer White in the Pittsburgh Youth Study. This showed that cognitive or verbal impulsivity (for example, acts without thinking, unable to defer gratification) was more strongly related to delinquency than was behavioral impulsivity (for example, clumsiness in psychomotor tests).

Low IQ and low school attainment are important predictors of delinquency. In a prospective longitudinal survey of about 120 Stockholm males, Hakan Stattin found that low IQ measured at age 3 significantly predicted officially recorded offending up to age 30. Frequent offenders (with four or more offenses) had an average IQ of 88 at age 3, whereas nonoffenders had an average IQ of 101. Similarly, Paul Lipsitt reported that low IQ at age 4 predicted court delinquency up to age 17 in the Collaborative Perinatal Project. Delinquents often do better on nonverbal performance IQ tests, such as object assembly and block design, than on verbal IQ tests. This is concordant with other research suggesting that they find it easier to deal with concrete objects than with abstract concepts.

The classic longitudinal studies by Joan McCord in Boston and Lee Robins in St. Louis show that poor parental supervision, harsh discipline, and a rejecting parental attitude are all important predictors of delinquency. In the Cambridge study, the presence of any of these family background features at age 8 doubled the risk of a later juvenile conviction. Also, there seems to be significant intergenerational transmission of violent behavior from parents to children, as Cathy Widom found in a follow-up of over 900 abused and about 700 control children in Indianapolis. Children who were physically abused up to age 11 were significantly likely to become violent offenders in the next 15 years.

Many studies show that broken homes or disrupted families predict delinquency. In a follow-up of 1,000 children born in Newcastle-upon-Tyne, England, Israel Kolvin reported that marital disruption (divorce or separation) in a boy's first 5 years predicted his later convictions up to age 32. Similarly, in a follow-up of over 1,000 children born in Dunedin, New Zealand, Bill Henry found that children who were exposed to parental discord and many changes of the primary caretaker tended to become antisocial and delinquent. Generally, boys from homes broken by death are not particularly likely to be delinquent, in contrast to boys from homes broken by divorce or separation due to disharmony. Joan McCord's research showed that boys reared in single-parent families with affectionate mothers were less likely to become delinquent than those reared in two-parent homes characterized by parental conflict, suggesting that the quality of family relationships was more important than the number of parents.

Criminal parents tend to have delinquent children. In the Cambridge study, the concentration of offending in a small number of families was remarkable. Less than 6% of the families were responsible for half of the criminal convictions of all members (fathers, mothers, sons, and daughters) of all 400 families. Having a convicted mother, father, brother, or sister significantly predicted a boy's own convictions. Furthermore, convicted parents and delinquent siblings were related to a boy's self-reported as well as official offending.

Large family size is another important predictor of delinquency. In the British National Survey of over 5,000 children, Michael Wadsworth found that the percentage of boys who were officially delinquent increased from 9% in families containing one child to 24% in families containing four or more children. Large family size, together with hyperactivity, impulsivity, low school attainment, poor parental supervision, parental conflict, an antisocial parent, a young mother, a broken family, and low family income, all proved to be replicable predictors of delinquency in England in the 1960s (in the Cambridge study) and in the United States in the 1990s (in the Pittsburgh Youth Study).

Interventions

The major methods of reducing delinquency involve developmental, community, situational, and criminal justice prevention. The focus here is on developmental prevention, that is, interventions designed to prevent the development of delinquency potential in individuals, targeting risk and protective factors discovered in studies of human development. Developmental prevention can be demonstrated most convincingly in randomized experiments with reasonably large samples. Only the most significant experiments can be mentioned here.

Delinquency can be prevented by intensive home visiting programs. In New York State, David Olds randomly allocated 400 mothers either to receive home visits from nurses during pregnancy, or to receive visits both during pregnancy and during the first two years of life, or to a control group who received no visits. The home visitors gave advice about prenatal and postnatal care of the child, about infant development, and about the importance of proper nutrition and avoiding smoking and drinking during pregnancy. The results showed that, especially among socioeconomically deprived mothers, home visits caused a decrease in child physical abuse, in the mother's offending, and in the child's delinquency.

One of the most successful early prevention programs has been the Perry preschool project carried out in Michigan by Lawrence Schweinhart. This was essentially a "Head Start" program targeted on disadvantaged African American children. The experimental children attended a daily preschool program, backed up by weekly home visits, usually lasting two years (covering ages 3 to 4). The aim of the "plan-do-review" program was to provide intellectual stimulation, to increase thinking and reasoning abilities, and to increase later school achievement. This program led to decreases in school failure, delinquency, and other undesirable outcomes. For every one dollar spent on the program, seven dollars were saved in the long term.

Behavioral parent management training, as developed by Gerald Patterson in Oregon, is also an effective technique. Patterson's careful observations of parent-child interaction showed that parents of antisocial children were deficient in their methods of child rearing. They failed to tell their children how they were expected to behave, failed to monitor their behavior to ensure that it was desirable, and failed to enforce rules promptly and unambiguously with appropriate rewards and penalties. The parents of antisocial children used more punishment (such as scolding, shouting, or threatening) but failed to make it contingent on the child's behavior. Patterson trained these parents in effective child-rearing methods, namely noticing what a child is doing, monitoring behavior over long periods, clearly stating house rules, making rewards and punishments contingent on behavior, and negotiating disagreements so that conflicts and crises did not escalate. His treatment was shown to be effective in reducing child stealing and antisocial behavior over short periods in small-scale studies.

The set of techniques variously termed cognitive-behavioral interpersonal social skills training have also proved to be quite successful. The "Reasoning and Rehabilitation" program developed by Robert Ross in Ottawa, Canada, aimed to modify the impulsive, egocentric thinking of delinquents, to teach them to stop and think before acting, to consider the consequences of their behavior, to conceptualize alternative ways of solving interpersonal problems, and to consider the impact of their behavior on other people, especially their victims. It included social skills training, critical thinking (to teach logical reasoning), values education (to teach values and concern for others), assertiveness training (to teach nonaggressive, socially appropriate ways to obtain desired outcomes), negotiation skills training, interpersonal cognitive problem solving (to teach thinking skills for solving interpersonal problems), social perspective training (to teach how to recognize and understand other people's feelings), role-playing and modeling (demonstration and practice of effective and acceptable interpersonal behavior). This program led to a large decrease in reoffending in a small sample of delinquents.

Multimodal programs including both skills training and parent training are likely to be more effective than either alone. An important multimodal program was implemented by Richard Tremblay in Montreal. He identified about 250 disruptive (aggressive/hyperactive) boys at age 6 for a prevention experiment. Between ages 7 and 9, the experimental group received training to foster social skills and self-control. Coaching, peer modeling, role playing, and reinforcement contingencies were used in small group sessions on such topics as "how to help," "what to do when you are angry," and "how to react to teasing." Also, the parents of the boys were trained using Patterson's techniques. This prevention program was quite successful. By age 12, the experimental boys committed less burglary and theft, were less likely to get drunk, and were less likely to be involved in fights than those in the control group. At every age from 10 to 15, the experimental boys had lower self-reported delinquency scores than the control boys.

An important school-based prevention experiment was carried out in Seattle by David Hawkins. This combined parent training, teacher training, and skills training. About 500 first grade children (aged 6) were randomly assigned to experimental or control classes. The children in the experimental classes received special treatment at home and school, which was designed to increase their attachment to their parent and their bonding to the school, on the assumption that delinquency was inhibited by the strength of social bonds. Their parents were trained to notice and reinforce socially desirable behavior in a program called "Catch Them Being Good." Their teachers were trained in classroom management, for example, to provide clear instructions and expectations to children, to reward children for participation in desired behavior, and to teach children prosocial (socially desirable) methods of solving problems. This program was effective in reducing violent delinquency and heavy drinking up to age eighteen.

Much has been learned from longitudinal studies about development and risk factors, and much has been learned from randomized experiments about effective interventions. More efforts are needed in future to coordinate longitudinal and experimental studies to advance knowledge about causal influences and to ensure that the interventions are solidly grounded in theory and empirical knowledge.

[See also Gangs.]

Bibliography

Farrington, D. P. (1996). The explanation and prevention of youthful offending. In J. D. Hawkins (Ed.), *Delinquency and crime: Current theories* (pp. 68–148). Cambridge: Cambridge University Press. Reviews knowledge about continuity and versatility in delinquency careers, risk factors for delinquency, and experimental interventions to reduce delinquency.

Loeber, R., & Farrington, D. P. (Eds.). (1998). *Serious and violent juvenile offenders: Risk factors and successful interventions*. Thousand Oaks, CA: Sage. Contains detailed chapters about delinquency development, risk factors, and interventions, with special emphasis on serious and violent delinquency.

Loeber, R., Farrington, D. P., Stouthamer-Loeber, M., & Van Kammen, W. B. (1998). *Antisocial behavior and mental health problems: Explanatory factors in childhood and adolescence*. Mahwah, NJ: Erlbaum. Describes the Pittsburgh Youth Study and focuses especially on a wide range of risk factors and comorbid conditions.

McCord, J., & Tremblay, R. E. (Eds.). (1992). *Preventing antisocial behavior: Interventions from birth through adolescence*. New York: Guilford Press. Contains chapters on prevention experiments by leading researchers.

Raine, A. (1993). *The psychopathology of crime: Criminal behavior as a clinical disorder*. San Diego: Academic Press. A wide-ranging text including extensive reviews of biological factors in offending.

Rutter, M., Giller, H., & Hagell, A. (1998). *Antisocial behavior by young people*. Cambridge: Cambridge University Press. A wide-ranging text, including reviews of risk/protective factors, gender differences, and prevention.

Snyder, H. & Sickmund, M. (1995). *Juvenile offenders and victims: A national report*. Washington, DC: Office of Juvenile Justice and Delinquency Prevention. Provides basic statistical information about juvenile delinquency in the United States, including types of offenses and demographic characteristics of delinquents.

Stoff, D. M., Breiling, J., & Maser, J. D. (Eds.). (1997). *Handbook of antisocial behavior*. New York: Wiley. Contains many chapters on development, biology, and prevention.

Thornberry, T. P. (Ed.). (1997). *Developmental theories of crime and delinquency*. New Brunswick, NJ: Transaction. Contains chapters by leading scholars reviewing developmental theories of delinquency.

David P. Farrington

DELUSIONAL DISORDER. *See* Paranoid Disorder and Delusional Disorder.

DELUSIONS have the essential feature of being reality distortions or unrealistic ideas or beliefs. A delusion can be defined as an improbable, often highly personal, idea or belief system, not endorsed by one's culture or subculture. This idea or belief is held with a high degree of conviction despite the availability of more probable or more coherent hypotheses and is often maintained in the face of direct evidence to the contrary (Altman & Jobe, 1992). As can be seen from three clinical cases, delusions can range from the simple and disorganized to the highly complex and precisely reasoned:

> A 24-year-old male salesman, with a diagnosis of delusional disorder, reported that "I am being followed by the C.I.A. and I know they are after me."
> A 26-year-old female patient with bipolar disorder recently admitted for an acute manic episode reported that "my right ear can receive messages from outer space, which helps direct my mission here on earth."
> A 38-eight-year-old male patient with a diagnosis of schizophrenia, reported that "the bison overpower buffalo with tyromean ultraforce for world domination."

Some available data suggest that rather than a patient being exclusively delusional or nondelusional, there are gradations, and the extent of delusional belief may fit on a continuum with normal beliefs. This phenomena, called "double awareness," represents an in-between state (Sachs, Carpenter, & Strauss, 1974).

Classification and Reliability and Validity

There are countless ways to classify pathological beliefs, such as delusions. A large number of pathological beliefs are (1) persecutory/paranoid, (2) delusions of reference, (3) grandiose delusions, (4) nihilistic delusions, (5) delusions of influence, (6) somatic delusions, and (7) delusions of metamorphosis. All of these types usually relate directly to the person having the delusion and are personally relevant to the life history of that individual. Thus, patients may have delusions that people are following them, or people are trying to influence them, but one rarely finds patients, for example, who have delusions about isolated window shades, or about railroad trains, without any reference to the patient or his concerns.

Kenneth Kendler and colleagues in their article "Dimensions of Delusional Experience" (1983), delineated five different dimensions of delusionality: (1) conviction, (2) the degree of certainty by which the belief is maintained, (2) extension, the degree of the patient's life experience that is absorbed by the belief, (3) bizarreness, the degree of improbability of the belief, (4) disorganization, the degree of coherence of the belief, and (5) pressure, the degree of urgency to action arising from the delusion. Other investigators also have analyzed delusions by studying separate dimensions of delusions (Garety & Hemsley, 1944; Harrow, Rattenbury, & Stoll, 1988).

Prevalence and Incidence

Delusions have come to represent one of the most important defining factors in classification systems of diagnostic categories. Some researchers believe that delusions may be the most important symptom of schizophrenia.

The overall incidence and prevalence of delusions is dependent upon the type of disorder, or the diagnostic group in which the patient belongs. For example, the percent of schizophrenia patients with delusions at the acute phase of hospitalization is approximately 80% while the percent of bipolar manic patients with delusions at the acute phase is over 60%.

The question of the prevalence and incidence of delusions raises the issue concerning whether delusions are a traitlike feature or just a one-time aberration in which the patient has at one period in his life a series of pathological beliefs. Longitudinal evidence suggests that delusions tend to recur for both schizophrenics and for other psychotic disorders as well (Harrow, MacDonald, Sands, & Silverstein, 1995). Thus, for most schizophrenics and many psychotic affectively disordered patients, delusions are not a one-time aberration but recur over time and appear to represent a traitlike feature.

Treatment of Delusions

For schizophrenia and delusional disorder, neuroleptic agents that block dopamine, and specifically the D2 receptor, have been effective, particularly in treating acute delusions. Clozaril and other atypical neuroleptics, which block both dopamine and serotonin 5HT-2 receptors, have also been effective in treating delusions as well as other features known as negative symptoms. In general, treatment with neuroleptics is not diagnosis specific; rather, treatment with neuroleptics is specific to certain symptom groupings, which include delusions. Thus, the treatment of delusions cuts across diagnosis and is not specific to a single diagnostic group. Persistent or chronic delusions are impacted by medications, but less so than acute delusions.

Theories of Delusions

The study of delusions has prompted more theories than hard data. The theories include psychoanalytic views of repressed impulses in paranoid delusions, alteration of the view of one's self-structure, effects of personality characteristics, existential factors, learning deficits, management of hostility, effects of social humiliation, effects of abnormal reasoning, effects of abnormal perceptions, and effects of cognitive styles. From among these views, many promising theories about the genesis of delusions have arisen (Bentall, Kinderman, & Kaney, 1994; Butler & Braff, 1991; Garety & Hemsley, 1994; Oltmanns & Maher, 1988).

The perceptual deficit theory of delusions proposes that abnormal perception leads to the formation of delusions to explain how these perceptions occurred. Using this scheme, delusions could evolve out of abnormal perceptions that then lead to "reasonable" explanations of how such perceptions came about. This may be the genesis of delusional beliefs for select patients, however, it is rare. Empirical assessments of this view have produced mixed results (Garety & Hemsley, 1994). On the other hand, a more promising lead for understanding delusions is in terms of the misinterpretation of normal perception, which is due to background motives/goals and associated emotions. In other words, the interpretation or perception of the environment is influenced by one's background motives/goals/ plans (Lazarus, 1991) and associated concerns and needs (Harrow et al., 1988). The ideas or beliefs that result are generated from these background motives/ goals and associated emotions as a guiding force for interpretation.

Data suggest delusions are not primarily logical errors but are derived from emotional material. Under high cognitive arousal, memories from the patient's affective past, and wishes and preoccupations from current affective life, thrust themselves into, or are intermingled with the person's ongoing thinking (Harrow, Lanin-Kettering, Prosen, & Miller, 1983). The intermingling becomes more prominent in a state of high tension and heightened cognitive arousal, when cognitive disruption occurs. Under such circumstances, the guiding motives/goals, wishes, and preoccupations also influence and temporarily bias components of longterm memory that, under normal circumstances, would help to self-monitor one's own ideas and beliefs (Harrow, Lanin-Kettering, & Miller, 1989). The delusions can be-

come "real," vital, and intense to the patient. After an individual becomes delusional, the delusions often become mixed up, and their origin becomes difficult to recognize.

Other unknown factors are also involved in the generation and maintenance of delusions, since both disturbed and normal people have motives/goals that influence their perception. However, only select people are vulnerable to major reality distortions and delusions over a sustained period of time. We still do not understand the biological factors involved in the generation, control, and regulation of aberrant thoughts and beliefs. It may be that amygdaloid influences on frontal-temporal ideas, beliefs, and thinking become stronger, or there may be weakened frontal inhibition, or disinhibition, with poorer cognitive monitoring.

This explanation, however, cannot completely explain why many normal people who regularly jump to conclusions do not become delusional. Research (Harrow et al., 1988, 1989) suggests that faulty self-monitoring is involved in delusion formation. Faulty self-monitoring, that is based on ineffective use of stored knowledge (stored in long-term memory) about what types of ideas are socially appropriate may be an important component of almost all psychotic symptoms, including delusions, although other unknown factors are also involved.

Manfred Spitzer, partly modifying a theory by Ralph Hoffman (1987), emphasizes the importance of self-organizing neural networks. This type of network has a local learning rule that changes the strengths of connections between neural elements without the need for an instructor and provides a more brain-related model of delusions (Spitzer, 1995).

Overall, many aspects of delusions are still poorly understood. More empirical research is needed regarding the formation and persistence of delusions and the relationship between delusions and other forms of psychopathology such as thought disorder and hallucinations (for example, most sustained hallucinations include some delusional beliefs). New techniques such as brain imaging may play a role in helping to provide additional insight.

Bibliography

Altman, E., & Jobe, T. H. (1992). Phenomenology of psychosis. *Current Opinion in Psychiatry, 5*: 33–37.

Bentall, R. P., Kinderman, P., & Kaney, S. (1994). The Self, attributional processes and abnormal beliefs: Towards a model of persecutory delusions. *Behaviour Research and Therapy, 32* (3): 331–341.

Butler, R. W., & Braff, D. L. (1991). Delusions: A review and integration. *Schizophrenia Bulletin, 17* (4), 633–647.

Garety, P., & Hemsley, D. R. (1994). *Delusions: Investigations into the psychology of delusional reasoning.* Institute of Psychiatry, Maudsley Monographs, No. 36, Oxford University Press.

Harrow, M., Lanin-Kettering, I., & Miller, J. G. (1989). Impaired perspective and thought pathology in schizophrenic and psychotic disorders. *Schizophrenia Bulletin, 15,* 605–623.

Harrow, M., Lanin-Kettering, I., Prosen, M., & Miller, J. G. (1983). Disordered thinking in schizophrenia: Intermingling and loss of set. *Schizophrenia Bulletin, 9,* 354–367.

Harrow, M., MacDonald III, A. W., Sands, J. R., & Silverstein, M. L. (1995). Vulnerability to delusions over time in schizophrenia, schizoaffective, and bipolar and unipolar affective disorders: A multi-followup assessment. *Schizophrenia Bulletin, 21,* 95–109.

Harrow, M., Rattenbury, F., & Stoll, F. (1988). Schizophrenic delusions. In T. Oltmans and B. A. Maher (Eds.). *Delusional beliefs: Interdisciplinary perspectives* (pp. 184–211). New York: Wiley.

Hoffman, R. E. (1987). Computer simulations of neural information processing and schizophrenia-mania dichotomy. *Archives of General Psychiatry, 44,* 178–188.

Kendler, K. S., Glazer, W., & Morgenstern, H. (1983). Dimensions of delusional experience. *American Journal of Psychiatry, 140,* 466–479.

Lazarus, R. S. (1991). Cognition and motivation in emotion. *American Psychologist, 46,* 352–367.

Oltmanns, T., & Maher, B. A. (Eds). (1988). *Delusional beliefs: Interdisciplinary perspectives.* New York: Wiley.

Sacks, M. H., Carpenter, W. T., Jr., & Strauss, J. S. (1974). Recovery from delusions: Three phases documented by patient's interpretation of research procedures. *Archives of General Psychiatry, 30,* 117–120.

Spitzer, M. (1995). A neurocomputational approach to delusions. *Comprehensive Psychiatry, 36* (2), 83–105.

Thomas Jobe and Martin Harrow

DEMAND CHARACTERISTICS is the term given for the totality of cues and mutual role expectations that inhere in a social context (for example, a psychological experiment or therapy situation), which serve to influence the behavior and/or self-reported experiences of the research participant or patient. The expression was adapted by the first author in 1959 (*Journal of Abnormal and Social Psychology, 58,* 277–299) from a related concept—*Aufforderungscharaktere,* which refers to the "demand value" that the psychological environment exerts upon the behavior of an individual—derived from Kurt Lewin's field-theoretical analysis of personality (*A Dynamic Theory of Personality: Selected Papers,* New York, 1935). The behavioral impact of the demand characteristics of a given situation will vary with the extent to which they are perceived, as well as with the motivation and ability of the person to comply.

Scientific experiments seek to explain phenomena (represented by systematic differences in some dependent variable, or DV) by expressly manipulating the hypothesized causal variable (that is, independent variable, or IV) while holding constant or equating any other potential contributory conditions. If variation in the IV produces corresponding changes in the DV to an extent that is probabilistically greater than the natural, random variation of the DV in the population, then a causal relation can be inferred. Unfortunately, the experimental method may be compromised when the subject of investigation is a sentient, reasoning organism, capable of perceiving (or misperceiving) the purpose of the research. The usual prescription for identifying causation is inadequate because of the investigator's inability to control the degree to which the participant's behavior may be contaminated by expectations and responsiveness to situational cues relevant (or irrelevant) to the experimental hypothesis.

In a research context, a volunteer enters into a social contract with the investigator to assume the role of "subject" for the purpose of advancing scientific knowledge. Under these circumstances, the behavioral scientist is likely to elicit behaviors that are not typical for the participants under investigation. We have observed, for example, that research volunteers are willing to perform clearly meaningless tasks for several hours—such as completing successive sheets of 224 addition problems, only to follow instructions to tear up each sheet before proceeding to the next. When queried by an independent investigator about their perceptions of the purpose of the study, participants invariably impute considerable meaning to their endeavors, viewing their activities as a test of endurance or something similar.

The demand characteristics of an experiment can be subtle—personnel in white laboratory coats, the reputation of the senior investigator, the wording of informed consent documents, as well as the expectation that one's participation will contribute toward the understanding of an important scientific problem. Nevertheless, they can affect not only the external validity (i.e., generalizability beyond the laboratory) of an investigation but its internal validity as well (that is, how confident one can be that the IV was uniquely responsible for the observed changes in the DV). The use of quasi-control procedures, such as a postexperimental inquiry carried out by a second investigator who is unaware of the assigned experimental condition and corresponding performance of the participant, is one way of detecting the contribution of demand characteristics in social and behavioral research. [*See* Artifact, *article on* Artifact in Research.]

Although generally regarded as artifact by the scientific community, demand characteristics remain a potent, and often unrecognized, source for therapeutic change in the clinical context. Rather than relegating demand characteristics to the realm of artifact, they should be acknowledged as a pervasive influence upon all human interaction. Both researchers and clinicians can benefit from determining what meaning an individual attributes to the totality of cues in any given situation.

Bibliography

Orne, M. T. (1962). On the social psychology of the psychological experiment: With particular reference to demand characteristics and their implications. *American Psychologist, 17,* 776–783. Outlines the potential contribution of demand characteristics to experimental outcomes in psychological research.

Orne, M. T. (1969). Demand characteristics and the concept of quasi-controls. In R. Rosenthal & R. Rosnow (Eds.), *Artifact in behavioral research* (pp. 143–179). New York: Academic Press. Discusses the role of demand characteristics in psychological research as well as methods for detecting their presence.

Orne, M. T., & Bauer-Manley, N. K. (1991). Disorders of self: Myths, metaphors, and demand characteristics of treatment. In J. Strauss & G. R. Goethals (Eds.), *The self: Interdisciplinary approaches* (pp. 93–106). New York: Springer-Verlag. Articulates the often unrecognized role of demand characteristics in the context of psychotherapy.

Rosnow, R. L., & Rosenthal, R. (1997). *People studying people: Artifacts and ethics in behavioral research.* New York: W. H. Freeman. Provides a concise and contemporary overview of artifacts in behavioral research.

Martin T. Orne and Wayne G. Whitehouse

DEMENTIA. *See* Alzheimer's Disease.

DEPENDENT VARIABLES. *See* Research Methods.

DEPRESSANTS, SEDATIVES, AND HYPNOTICS. These categories of drugs all depress central nervous system (CNS) activity. Some are nonselective, while others are more selective in their actions and effects on the CNS and behavior. Sedatives, more typically termed anxiolytics, are drugs indicated for the treatment of anxiety and hypnotics for insomnia. Depressant is an older term used prior to introduction of the benzodiazepines in the 1960s. Currently, the term is used to refer to older, non-CNS selective drugs including barbiturates, alcohol, and alcohol-aldehyde–based drugs.

These drugs, used as sedatives and hypnotics in the past, are now rarely used as their margin of safety is narrow, tolerance to their effects develops rapidly, and most have a relatively high abuse liability.

The drug class of choice for treatment of insomnia is the benzodiazepine receptor agonist. The class name is derived from the recognized site of action of the drugs. Some have the benzodiazepine chemical structure, while others do not. All share the characteristic of occupying benzodiazepine receptors on the gamma-amino-butyric-acid (GABA) receptor complex, with receptor occupation opening ion channels and thereby facilitating GABA, the predominant inhibitory neurotransmitter. This drug class also remains the mainstay in treatment of anxiety disorders, although some tricyclic antidepressants and specific serotonin reuptake inhibitors have been used with success in panic disorder, mixed anxiety and depression, and generalized anxiety disorder.

Many placebo-controlled studies have shown the efficacy of benzodiazepine receptor agonists for insomnia. All hasten sleep onset, reduce wakefulness after sleep onset, and reduce the amount of light (that is, stage 1 nonrapid-eye-movement) sleep. This has been demonstrated in insomniacs and in individuals experiencing transient sleep problems. The drugs differ in their pharmacokinetic profiles and metabolic pathways. Most have a rapid onset of action (that is, $Tmax \leq 2$ hrs) and effectively induce sleep. All the short- (that is, $T1/2 \leq 5$ hrs) and intermediate-acting (that is, $T1/2 = 6–12$ hrs) drugs sufficiently maintain sleep for seven to eight hours. Those that are long-acting or have long-acting metabolites (that is, $T1/2 \geq 12$ hrs) have the potential of producing residual sedation the following day. The characteristic pharmacokinetics of oxidated drugs are altered in elderly and in liver disease as seen by an increased area under the plasma concentration curve. With some drugs this occurs by increasing the peak plasma concentration and others by extending the duration of action, or both. Those drugs metabolized by conjugation are potentially safer for aged patients or patients with liver disease as their pharmacokinetics do not change.

The sedative action of the benzodiazepine receptor agonists is the desired effect in anxiety disorders. Anxiolytic effects are achieved at lower doses than doses producing hypnotic effects. Although a given benzodiazepine receptor agonist may have an anxiolytic indication, at higher doses it will have hypnotic effects and vice versa. Again, many placebo-controlled studies have demonstrated the efficacy of these drugs in various anxiety disorders. However, the therapeutic dose differs for the various disorders. Parenthetically, it should be noted that these drugs also have muscle relaxant and anticonvulsive effects. The primary issues in the use of benzodiazepine receptor agonists as anxiolytics and hypnotics are their side effects and abuse liability.

In some insomnia conditions, residual sedation the following day is an undesired side effect, while in anxiety disorders it is the desired effect. The duration of action, determined by the drug's half-life and dose, predicts the likelihood of residual sedation for that drug. Another side effect related to dose and half-life is rebound insomnia. Upon discontinuation, sleep may be disturbed beyond that of baseline for one to two nights. Rebound insomnia occurs after high doses (that is, above the therapeutic range) and is avoided by dose tapering or long half-life drugs. An oft-mentioned corollary to rebound insomnia is rebound anxiety, but it has not been scientifically demonstrated. Rebound insomnia is not the expression of a withdrawal syndrome or physical dependence. It is a single symptom that can even occur after a single night of a high-dose short-acting drug.

Amnesia is another well documented effect of benzodiazepine receptor agonists. It is desirable when these drugs are used as premedicants for surgery and other invasive medical procedures. Its clinical significance when used for insomnia and anxiety depends on patient characteristics and circumstances. The extent of tolerance to this effect is not known. The amnesia is found after both IV and oral administration, is anterograde in character (that is, events occurring after, but not before, drug administration), and is dose related. In dispute is whether the amnesia is secondary to the sedative effects of these drugs or to their direct effects on hippocampal memory systems or to both.

Finally, of concern is the abuse liability (that is, the likelihood of physical and behavioral dependence) of the benzodiazepine receptor agonists. Both epidemiological and laboratory studies suggest it is relatively low. Survey data indicate a 1 to 3% annual prevalence of non-medical use; it is rare in the general population but more frequent in identified drug abuse populations. Surveys of medical use indicate the majority of patients use sedatives and hypnotics for two weeks or less. However, a percentage of individuals use hypnotics nightly (14%) and anxiolytics daily (25%) on a chronic basis yet with no dose escalation. Whether this pattern of medical use reflects addiction (that is, physical and/or behavioral dependence) is disputed. Although there are reports of physical dependence at therapeutic doses in long-term daytime anxiolytic use, no study of long-term hypnotic use has been done. Daytime studies of the reinforcing effects of these drugs indicate they have a low behavioral dependence liability. Studies of their behavioral dependence liability in the context of their use as hypnotics have come to a similar conclusion. Hypnotic use by patients with insomnia is therapy-seeking behavior, does not lead to dose escalation, and

does not generalize to daytime use (that is, does not occur outside of the therapeutic context).

Clinicians generally agree that pharmacotherapy alone rarely "cures" insomnia or anxiety disorder; it is symptomatic treatment. Cognitive-behavioral therapies are typically used to treat some insomnia and anxiety disorders. The role of adjunct pharmacotherapy is highly debated. One view is that pharmacotherapy, in either insomnia or anxiety, blocks or delays the necessary "unlearning" required in treating the specific disorder. The other view is that the drug can in the short term relieve symptoms and the burden of the disorder and reinforce the behavior therapy. There are few well-conducted outcome studies that resolve this question.

[See also Drugs; and Drug Abuse.]

Bibliography

Curran, H. V. (1991). Benzodiazepines, memory and mood: A review. *Psychopharmacology, 105,* 1–8. Reviews amnesic effects of benzodiazepines in relation to mood and arousal state and discusses their beneficial or harmful effects as adjuncts to psychological therapies.

King, D. J. (1992). Benzodiazepines, amnesia, and sedation: Theoretical and clinical issues and controversies. *Human Psychopharmacology, 7,* 79–87. Reviews amnesic effects of benzodiazepines in the context of hypnotic use and relates the amnesic effects to the sedative actions of the drugs.

Roehrs, T., Vogel, G., & Roth, T. (1990). Rebound insomnia: Its determinants and significance. *American Journal of Medicine, 88,* 39S–42S. Reviews the determinants and clinical significance of rebound insomnia.

Roth, T., Roehrs, T. A., Vogel, G. W., & Dement, W. C. (1995). Evaluation of hypnotic medications. In R. F. Prien & D. S. Robinson (Eds.), *Clinical Evaluation of Psychotropic Drugs, Principles and Guidelines* (pp. 579–592). New York: Raven Press. Reviews the efficacy and side effects of hypnotic medications and provides tools to critically evaluate the literature.

Rickels, K., Schweizer, E., Case, W. G., & Greenblatt, D. J. (1990). Long-term therapeutic use of benzodiazepines I and II. *Archives of General Psychiatry, 47,* 899–915. Clinical studies of patients discontinuing long-term benzodiazepine use.

Woods, J. H. & Winger, G. (1995). Current benzodiazepine issues. *Psychopharmacology, 118,* 107–115. Reviews and discusses the adverse effects of benzodiazepines and specifically reviews their abuse liability.

Timothy A. Roehrs and Thomas Roth

DEPRESSION has been one of the most intensely studied mental disorders. Theorizing about depression began in ancient times. Early concepts were generally physical in nature, and this emphasis continued into the nineteenth century. Some early speculations about depression viewed it as a general debility of the excitatory vascular system of the brain (Benjamin Rush) or a disturbance of nutrition to the cerebral cortex (Richard von Krafft-Ebing). With the development of Sigmund Freud's ideas, however, there was a distinct shift toward psychological paradigms of depression.

One of the most important conceptual advances was made in the early twentieth century when Emil Kraepelin noted that depression and mania were closely associated. He viewed these as alternative manifestations of the same disease process, and he brought them together under one diagnosis. Leonhard (1957) later emphasized the importance of distinguishing between unipolar and bipolar depression because of differences in the courses of the disorders, degrees of genetic transmission, and premorbid temperament. He defined bipolar depression as a mood disorder having a course that included episodes of mania during the individual's lifetime.

Epidemiology

Depression and mania affect a significant number of persons in our society, with a point prevalence in the United States of 3% for unipolar major depression and 0.7% for bipolar depression. Based on data from the Epidemiologic Catchment Area Study, 6% of persons in the United States have had unipolar major depression at some point in their lives. The likelihood of having depression is higher for women than for men by a ratio of approximately 2 to 1. The prevalence of depression among individuals presenting to primary care physicians has been demonstrated to be as high as 25%. Despite improved treatments for depression, there is evidence that the incidence of affective disorders is increasing with each generation.

The presence of increased levels of stressful events preceding the onset of depression has received considerable empirical support (e.g., Brown & Harris, 1978); nevertheless, the actual variance accounted for by stressful events in predicting depression is only about 10%. In order to understand the relationship between the two better, investigators have increasingly examined the role of moderating variables, such as coping style, social support, and personality (Cronkite & Moos, 1995). At least 50% of individuals who recover from an episode of depression have a recurrence of symptoms within one year. When there has been more than one episode, the probability of recurrence rises still further. The key to treating depression appears to lie in aggressive treatment. Early intervention has been shown to shorten the duration of new episodes.

Data on the long-term course of bipolar disorder is inconsistent. Emil Kraepelin followed cases at the turn of the nineteenth century and found that 45% of persons with manic depression have only single episodes, even though his follow-up periods lasted up to 40 years. More recent studies have found a much higher incidence of recurrence. This may reflect that biological or social changes are increasing patients' proneness to relapse, or it may simply reflect methodological inadequacies in early studies.

Mood disorders may coexist with almost any other psychiatric disorder. Some of the most common of these are anxiety disorders, substance abuse, and eating disorders. Depression with psychiatric or physiological comorbidity has a poorer prognosis than depression without accompanying disorders. There is a high level of comorbidity between major depression and panic disorder, and to a lesser degree, between major depression and other anxiety disorders such as social phobia. Mood disorders are also very commonly associated with psychoactive substance use disorder (PSUD). They account for one half of all Axis I disorders accompanying PSUD, and approximately one fourth of PSUD patients are at risk to have a mood disorder.

Psychological Theories of Depression

Modern psychological theorizing about depression may be said to have begun primarily with Freud, who developed a complex formulation comparing depression to mourning. Freud theorized that an early disappointment in the depressed person's life, particularly the loss of a relationship, led to reconstructing and substituting an image of the desired person within, resulting in an ambivalent emotional cathexis of the lost person (i.e., both longing for and anger toward him or her). Since the image of the desired person had been taken into the self as a way of compensating for the disappointment, anger was also turned inward at the self. With the loss of a love object in adulthood, anger again was experienced and directed inward toward a representation of the recently lost love object, thus causing depression.

Modern analytic theory has significantly departed from this conceptualization. One of the most influential neoanalytic theorists regarding depression was Edward Bibring. He viewed depression as resulting not from intrapsychic conflict but from loss of self-esteem caused by environmental loss. Arieti and Bemporad (1980) hypothesized that reactive depression results from an overreliance either on a dominant other or a dominant goal for a sense of meaning and self-worth. When these external supports to self-esteem are lost, a drastic loss of self-esteem ensues. They also theorized that a third type of depression, characterological depression, results when the individual cannot find pleasure, meaning, or self-worth from any source—internal or external. All three types of depression share in common "anxiety over the direct attainment of pleasure . . . fear that spontaneous activity will result in rejection or criticism from others" (p. 1363). In addition, all three types of depressed persons "overvalue the opinions of others, and . . . overestimate their own effects on the inner lives of others" (p. 1363). This analytic formulation shows some convergence with cognitive theories of emotional disorders.

One theory that has stimulated a great deal of research has been the theory of "learned helplessness," developed by Seligman (1975). Seligman used an animal analog model from the laboratory to study depression. Dogs exposed to inescapable shocks were less able to learn to avoid future aversive events than dogs exposed to similar levels of escapable shock. Hiroto and Seligman (1975) showed that the helplessness effect could occur in humans also, and subsequent research focused on similarities between depressed persons and persons subjected to a learned-helplessness induction in the laboratory. Later, a model was constructed that incorporated human cognition as a moderator of helplessness effects in humans. This revised learned-helplessness model generated considerable research, examining attributions made by persons in uncontrollable, unpleasant situations, and also attributions made by depressed individuals. According to the revised model, once persons perceive their situation as uncontrollable, they begin to make attributions to explain their loss of control (Abramson, Seligman, & Teasdale, 1978). Attributions for helplessness are either internal (believed to be due to characteristics of the person) or external (due to the environment); global (applying to many situations) or specific (applying to a limited range of situations); and stable (persisting over time) or unstable (limited in time). Loss of self-esteem is theorized to occur when persons decide that their helplessness is due to personal deficiencies rather than to reasons that would universally affect almost anyone in that situation. Stable, global, and personal attributions for helplessness and/or failure have generally been found to produce the greatest degree of depressive deficits.

Subtypes of Depression

Depression is now actually known to be a heterogeneous group of disorders that require multiple alternative treatment strategies. Awareness of the characteristics of the subtypes can enhance recognition of depression in general as well as lead to improved decision making in treatment planning.

Some types of depression have been shown to have very strong biological foundations. Bipolar disorder, for example, is closely linked to biological causes. Although there is a wealth of evidence demonstrating this conclusion, one particularly convincing piece of data is the very high monozygotic concordance rate (70%) for bipolar disorder. With unipolar depression, the picture is somewhat more complex. Whereas some unipolar depressions may be almost purely endogenous (i.e., presumably biological) on the one hand, or exogenous (reactive to the environment) on the other, the overall evidence regarding the nature of unipolar depression suggests that both physical and psychological processes are involved. The causal sequence that brings about an initial episode of unipolar depression remains somewhat obscure, but appears to include psychological, biological, and environmental processes.

The nature of dysthymia (chronic mild depression) is somewhat less well understood than major depression. It is not known if it is primarily a disorder of the personality or a mild variant of clinical depression. The concept of double depression has gained increasing attention. Double depression is defined as a major depression superimposed on dysthymia. Some studies have shown that persons with double depression (as opposed to simple unipolar depression) have greater impairment, more depressive symptoms, greater comorbidity, and more personality disturbance. They are also less likely to recover fully and are more likely to relapse into depression.

Another highly studied subtype has been atypical depression, which includes symptoms such as oversleeping, overeating, marked decrease in energy ("leaden paralysis"), and rejection sensitivity. This type of depression appears to respond preferentially to monoamine oxidase inhibitors over tricyclic antidepressants.

Psychotherapy for Depression

Modern psychological research into depression treatment began in two ways: in studies about behavior therapy in the 1970s conducted by Peter Lewinsohn (e.g., Lewinsohn, Biglan, & Zeiss, 1976) and Lynn Rehm (e.g., Rehm, Fuchs, Roth, Kornblith, & Romano, 1979), and in three studies funded by the National Institute of Mental Health (NIMH). The NIMH studies tested interpersonal therapy (Klerman, DiMascio, Weissman, Prusoff, & Paykel, 1974), group therapy, and marital therapy.

Similar to some other behaviorists, Peter Lewinsohn hypothesized that when persons encountered a lack of response-contingent positive reinforcement, a decrease in adaptive behaviors was likely to result. The reasons for a lack of positive reinforcement might be poor social skills, environmental changes, or failure to engage in activities that would be pleasant and rewarding. Thus, one strategy was to provide feedback to depressed persons on their interpersonal skill deficits. Because evidence had demonstrated a positive covariation between participation in pleasant events and positive mood, and between aversive events and negative mood, both of these were targeted in his behavioral therapy. Participants were coached to increase pleasant events in their lives. Social skills training was also emphasized (e.g., assertiveness training).

One of the most intensely studied of all psychological treatments of depression has been cognitive therapy (Beck, Rush, Shaw, and Emery, 1979). It is based on the theory that negative cognitions are critical in the development and maintenance of depressive symptoms. The roots of cognitive therapy for depression can be traced at least as far back as Alfred Adler, who asserted that behavior arises from beliefs. Cognitive techniques were further developed by Albert Ellis (1962), who also emphasized the need for individuals to change their irrational attitudes about life. But it was Aaron Beck who applied cognitive principles most systematically to depression. Beck guided individuals to test negative expectations and specific self-statements as well as to work on their underlying beliefs. He advocated a Socratic method, termed *collaborative empiricism*, of leading the individual to examine negative thinking in a logical manner. According to Beck, the judgment of self-worth and of the meaning of situations is accomplished with the aid of an enduring, implicit cognitive structure termed the *schema*. The schema acts as a template to make sense of incoming information. In depression, the schema is generally a negative view of self, world, and future. Examples of schemas causing vulnerability to depression would be excessive requirements for approval or for achievement in order to deem oneself worthwhile.

Another major psychological therapy of depression is interpersonal psychotherapy (IPT). Klerman, Weissman, Rounsaville, and Chevron (1984) based the treatment on traditional psychotherapy techniques and on the results of epidemiological studies. Paykel et al. (1969) found that undesirable life events and events involving exits or losses in the social field of the individual (marital separation, children growing up and leaving home) were more frequent in the recent histories of depressed than nondepressed persons. Partially for this reason, IPT was focused on recent rather than remote events. In clinical trials for acute depression, it was found to be generally as effective as tricyclic antidepressants and as effective as cognitive-behavioral therapy. IPT theory posited that there were four major areas of interpersonal disruption accompanying depression: role transitions, interpersonal disputes (e.g., marital arguments), unresolved grieving, and interpersonal deficits. In addition to being an effective treatment for the acute phase of many depressions, there is also evidence that it has a delayed beneficial impact on social functioning, which may appear 6 to 12 months following the end of acute treatment. When given as a maintenance treatment, it also appears to extend the time until relapse.

The value of family therapy for depression has been increasingly explored. Family stress, conflict, and loss have been shown to be associated with the onset of, and relapse into, depressive disorders. Depressed persons have difficulty fulfilling their roles as both parents and spouses. The children and spouses of depressed persons are at increased risk for psychological distress and psychiatric problems.

The NIMH Treatment of Depression Collaborative Research Program

With the development of cognitive, behavioral, and interpersonal therapies for depression, the National Institute of Mental Health (NIMH) decided to test psychotherapies of depression through a collaborative investigation involving several treatment sites at the end of the 1970s. This study is highlighted because of the great care taken methodologically and because of its very large sample size. Cognitive-behavioral therapy and interpersonal psychotherapy were chosen to be compared with imipramine plus clinical management, and placebo plus clinical management. Analysis of acute treatment results revealed no significant differences among the three active therapies after 16 weeks of treatment, but there was a statistically significant difference between imipramine plus clinical management and placebo plus clinical management (Elkin et al., 1989). Imipramine was more effective than the psychotherapies at 8 and 12 weeks, but not at the 16-week termination point. (A later analysis using random regression analysis suggested that imipramine plus clinical management had in fact been statistically more effective than either of the two psychotherapies.)

The Problem of Nonsignificant Differences

One of the perplexing issues facing depression researchers is the lack of strong differences in efficacy among various psychological treatments. Only rarely have studies comparing cognitive-behavioral, interpersonal, and short-term analytic therapies found significant differences. A similar perplexing finding has been that combinations of psychological treatments and medications do not consistently lead to better outcome than individual treatments alone. In addition, despite the differing theoretical bases of the psychotherapies, treatments sometimes fail to differ significantly from each other, even in areas of functioning that are directly and differentially targeted.

One explanation for these findings is that most treatments have several elements in common: (a) they are directive in encouraging clients to work on changing their perceptions, their thoughts, their social participation, or some other central aspect of depression; (b) they generally utilize a one-to-one therapist-client relationship; and (c) they emphasize the importance of the client making attempts to change depressive behavior from very early on in therapy. Another possible explanation for the similarity in effectiveness is that for many persons depression may be a relatively unstable homeostasis. Negative cognitions, inefficient coping behaviors (e.g., social withdrawal), altered brain biochemistry, and negative feedback from the social environment may all serve to reinforce each other. For many depressed persons, these are abnormal conditions, and so the positive feedback loops supporting these negative conditions are likely to be somewhat fragile. Given an adequate therapeutic relationship and sustained assistance in altering any one of these conditions, the homeostasis may begin to deteriorate. This would not be true for chronic depressions, however.

Biological Processes in Depression

Numerous biological processes have been found to be altered in major depression. Any final theory will undoubtedly include numerous physiological factors in the distal and/or proximal causality for severe depression. Nevertheless, at the end of the twentieth century it is still very difficult to establish particular biological processes as being essential causes of depression rather than merely being concomitant processes.

Most biological research has focused on the neurotransmitters norepinephrine, and serotonin. These are monoamines, and the hypothesis that dysregulation of one or both of these neurotransmitters causes depression is termed the *monoamine hypothesis.* Most antidepressants have a demonstrable effect on the presynaptic or postsynaptic receptors for one or more of these transmitters. The monoamine hypothesis states that either there is a deficiency in the neurotransmitter at the synapse or that there is some disturbance in the ability of neurons to chemically transmit stimulation received from monoamines in order to lead to further neural firing.

Another major area of biological research has been in the area of sleep. Sleep in depressed persons is often disturbed—not only in the form of insomnia, but also in basic sleep architecture. Depressed persons have a shortened rapid eye movement (REM) latency, and most somatic treatments of depression will suppress REM to some degree.

Positron emission tomography (PET) has been used to study cerebral metabolism in depression. Such studies have generally shown a decrease in frontal activity in persons with severe depression. This generally improves as the depression remits. Another area of biological research in depression has focused on the hypothalamic-pituitary-adrenal (HPA) axis. Approximately one half to three fourths of hospitalized depressed patients have elevated glucocorticoids. Through feedback mechanisms, these high levels may in turn negatively affect HPA axis functioning.

The Role of Pharmacological Treatment

In the 1990s, the primary antidepressants in use have been the selective serotonin reuptake inhibitors (SSRIs; e.g., Paxil, Zoloft, and Prozac). These have a reduced frequency of side effects (e.g., anticholinergic effects, orthostatic hypotension) and a lower incidence of cardiotoxic effects. They may also be safer when patients attempt to overdose compared to the tricyclic antidepressants. On the other hand, many of the newer agents have a few side effects that still pose problems, such as inhibition of sexual functioning.

One of the most interesting, and clinically pressing, issues in treatment research is whether psychotherapy or pharmacotherapy is more efficacious in the acute treatment of major depression. A detailed analysis of this topic would be beyond the scope of this article. However, there is no consistent finding that can easily be summarized here. The same may be said of comparisons between treatments combining psychotherapy and pharmacotherapy versus treatments using psychotherapy or pharmacotherapy alone. The most that can be said with considerable certainty is that there is no evidence that psychotherapy and pharmacotherapy conflict with or undermine each other when used together. The combination of psychotherapy with pharmacotherapy appears to be a generally effective treatment, but there are no consistent data that it is more effective than psychotherapy alone or pharmacotherapy alone. Psychotherapy and pharmacotherapy both tend to be efficacious. Although current research yields some clues about which individuals may respond best to these two general classes of treatment, no firm conclusions can yet be drawn. It is likely that severity of depression and other variables will determine the relative efficacy of these two major types of treatment.

[See also Mood Disorders; and Seasonal Affective Disorder.]

Bibliography

Abramson, L. Y., Seligman, M. E. P., & Teasdale, J. D. (1978). Learned helplessness in humans: Critique and reformulation. *Journal of Abnormal Psychology, 87,* 49–74. Contains the revision of the learned helplessness theory as it applies to humans.

Arieti, S., & Bemporad, J. R. (1980). Psychological organization of depression. *American Journal of Psychiatry, 137,* 1360–1365. A modern psychoanalytic view of depression.

Beck, A. T., Rush, A. J., Shaw, B. F., & Emery, G. (1979). *Cognitive therapy of depression.* New York: Guilford Press. One of the first treatment manuals for depression, containing practical as well as theoretical information about cognitive therapy of depression.

Beckham, E. E., & Leber, W. R. (1995). *Handbook of depression*. New York: Guilford Press. A comprehensive handbook of psychological knowledge regarding depression.

Brown, G. W., & Harris, T. (1978). *Social origins of depression: A study of psychiatric disorders in women.* New York: Free Press.

Cronkite, R. C., & Moos, R. H. (1995). Life context, coping processes, and depression. In E. E. Beckham & W. R. Leber (Eds.), *Handbook of depression* (2nd ed., pp. 569–587). New York: Guilford Press.

Elkin, I., Shea, M. T., Watkins, J. T., Imber, S. D., Sotsky, S. M., Collins, J. F., Glass, D. R., Pilkonis, P. A., Leber, W. R., Docherty, J. P., Fiester, S. J., & Parloff, M. B. (1989). National Institute of Mental Health Treatment of Depression Collaborative Research Program: General effectiveness of treatments. *Archives of General Psychiatry, 46,* 971–982. A major and extremely well-designed study comparing psychotherapy and pharmacotherapy for depression.

Ellis, A. (1962). *Reason and emotion in psychotherapy.* Secaucus, NJ: Citadel.

Hiroto, D. S., & Seligman, M. E. P. (1975). Generality of learned helplessness in man. *Journal of Personality and Social Psychology, 31,* 311–327.

Klerman, G. L., DiMascio, A., Weissman, M. M., Prusoff, B. A., & Paykel, E. S., (1974). Treatment of depression by drugs and psychotherapy. *American Journal of Psychiatry, 131,* 186–191. One of the first outcome studies of psychotherapy of depression.

Klerman, G. L., Weissman, M. M., Rounsaville, B. J., & Chevron, E. (1984). *Interpersonal psychotherapy of depression.* New York: Basic Books. An excellent introduction to interpersonal psychotherapy for depression.

Leonhard, K. (1957). *Aufteilung der Endogenen Psychosen* [The classification of endogenous psychoses]. Berlin: Akademieverlag. Contains the proposal to split manic–depression into unipolar and bipolar disorders.

Lewinsohn, P. M., Biglan, T., & Zeiss, A. (1976). Behavioral treatment of depression. In P. Davidson (Ed.), *Behavioral management of anxiety, depression, and pain* (pp. 91–146). New York: Brunner/Mazel.

Paykel E. S. (Ed.). (1992). *Handbook of affective disorders.* New York: Guilford Press. A handbook of depression with a medical and psychiatric emphasis.

Paykel E. S., Myers, J. K., Dienelt, M. N., Klerman, G. L., Lindenthal, J. J., & Pepper, M. P. (1969). Life events and depression: A controlled study. *Archives of General Psychiatry, 21,* 753–760.

Rehm, L. P., Fuchs, C. Z., Roth, D. M., Kornblith, S. J., & Romano, J. M. (1979). A comparison of self-control and social skills treatments of depression. *Behavior Therapy, 10,* 429–442.

Seligman, M. E. P. (1975). *Helplessness: On depression, development, and death.* New York: Freeman. A groundbreaking book proposing an experimental analogue of depression.

Thase, M. E., & Howland, R. H. (1995). Biological processes in depression: An updated review and integration. In E. E. Beckham & W. R. Leber (Eds.), *Handbook of depression* (2nd ed., pp. 213–279). New York: Guilford Press. An excellent overview of biological research into depression.

E. Edward Beckham

DEPRIVATION. *See* Poverty, *article on* Childhood Poverty.

DEPTH PERCEPTION. One of our most remarkable perceptual capacities is our ability to recover the three-dimensional structure of our environments. All of our actions rely on the ability to recover information about the positions, shapes, and material properties of objects and surfaces as they exist in three-dimensional space. In vision, the term *depth perception* refers to the ability to recover depth from the two-dimensional images projected to our two eyes. The information used to recover depth can be divided into two broad kinds: information from a single view of a scene (so-called pictorial depth cues); and information available when two or more views of a scene can be compared (for example, the slightly different views from the two eyes or the results of motion).

Many pictorial depth cues arise when the three-dimensional world is projected onto the backs of our eyes. As distance from an observer increases, parallel lines on a ground plane appear to converge in the two-dimensional image (linear perspective, Figure 1). Texture becomes increasingly compressed and more dense along the line of sight, creating texture gradients (Figure 2). For example, when a circular disc is tilted away from the observer, it projects the image of an ellipse. The aspect ratio of the ellipse depends on the degree of tilt relative to the observer's line of gaze, and the size of the ellipse depends on both object size and viewing distance. If a series of circles are placed on the ground and viewed from an angle, the circles will project a series of ellipses that become smaller and "flatter" as distance from the observer increases, producing a texture gradient. Contrast decreases from atmospheric haze, commonly referred to as aerial perspective.

Shading and shadows can also provide vivid impressions of depth in images (Figure 3). The amount of light reflected from a surface to a point of observation depends on the surface properties of the reflecting surface, and the angle formed between the light source and the surface. In general, surfaces have complex reflectance properties with varying degrees of scatter and specularity. These properties determine whether sur-

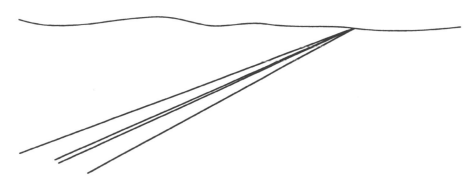

DEPTH PERCEPTION. Figure 1. Linear perspective.

faces look hard, soft, squishy, flaky, smooth, rough, and so forth. For example, if the surface is matte or dull in appearance, the light striking that surface will be scattered and reflected in many different directions. For a purely specular surface (like a mirror), light will essentially bounce off of the surface like a billiard ball, generating the familiar law of optics ("the angle of incidence equals the angle of reflection"). This optical law relating the angle at which light strikes and bounces off of surfaces is also responsible for shading: the amount of light reflected to a point of observation depends on the surface's orientation relative to the direction of the light source. Our visual systems can use patterns of shading to infer the three-dimensional shape of surfaces.

The interruption of more distant surfaces by nearer occluding surfaces also provides information about the depth order of objects in a scene (also known as interposition). However, unlike other sources of monocular depth information, monocular occlusion information does not provide any explicit information about the size of the intervals separating the near and more distant surfaces.

Finally, the size of familiar objects also provides information about depth: if the true size of an object is known, then the angular size of the object on the retina can provide information about the distance to that object.

One of the most powerful sources of information about depth is provided by the parallax generated from multiple views of a scene. Parallax refers to the apparent change in relative position of objects when they are viewed from different positions. The apparent shift in the relative positions of objects in the two views generated by binocular parallax can be experienced by alternately opening and closing your two eyes. The impression of depth generated from binocular parallax is known as stereopsis. The importance of binocular parallax in giving precise information about depth can be seen by the fact that virtually all animals that have stereopsis are predators. This ability comes at a cost, however, since this requires viewing the same region of the world from two perspectives, and hence, a frontal placement of the eyes. In contrast, most prey have laterally placed eyes, which sacrifices the high resolution depth information afforded by stereopsis in favor of a

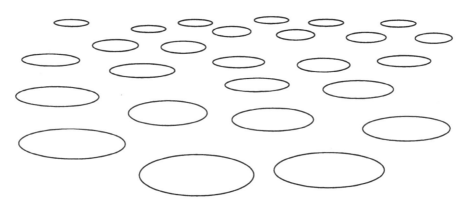

DEPTH PERCEPTION. Figure 2. Texture gradients.

DEPTH PERCEPTION. Figure 3. Shading and shadows.

larger visual field but has the distinct advantage of being able to spot a predator coming from all directions.

In order to extract depth information from binocular parallax, the visual system must determine how to combine or fuse the two images into a single three-dimensional representation. When binocular fusion occurs, an impression of a single, three-dimensional world is experienced. A failure to fuse images can produce diplopia (or double vision) or binocular rivalry, a perceptual battle between the two monocular images. Fusion requires that the images in the two eyes must be brought into "correspondence." To understand this problem, imagine that the retinal images have been copied onto two transparencies. Your goal is to line up the images as best as possible. Because of the shift of the relative position of the objects caused by binocular parallax, the images can never be perfectly aligned, but the overall difference between the positions of objects in the two images can be made larger or smaller. Binocular fusion and stereopsis only occur when the differences between the two images are less than some value, known as the fusion limit.

The images are brought within the fusion limit by appropriately "crossing" or "uncrossing" the eyes (known as vergence movements). Once appropriate eye movements have been made, there remains the problem of extracting depth from the two views. Some of the regions in the two images will correspond to a common portion of an object's surface seen from two slightly different positions. The relative difference in retinal position of these surface regions is known as binocular disparity, which gives rise to a vivid sense of depth. The region that is binocularly fixated will fall on the fovea in both eyes and has zero disparity. Nonzero disparity has a size and a sign. The size of the disparity is pro-

portional to an object's distance in depth from the fixation point. The sign determines whether a feature appears closer or farther than the fixation point. If the image in the left eye is to the right of the image in the right eye, disparity is crossed and the feature appears closer than fixation. If the image in the left eye is to the left of the image in the right eye, disparity is uncrossed and the feature is more distant than fixation.

In addition to disparity, the binocular viewing of solid objects provides information about stereoscopic depth by generating features that are visible to only one eye. You can observe this by alternately opening and closing your left and right eyes while attending to the right edge of this book. Notice that your right eye can see a portion of the area behind the edge of the book that is not visible to your left eye. The opposite is true along the left side of the book: the left eye sees more of the background than the right. These monocular (or half-occluded) regions provide information about the presence of occluding contour that the visual system uses to separate objects from backgrounds.

There are strong parallels between the depth from binocular parallax and the depth from motion parallax. When an observer moves, she acquires a continuous stream of new views. In stereopsis, the multiple views are always in a fixed spatial relationship relative to one another, since the eyes are in a fixed relative position in our heads. However, since we are capable of moving in three dimensions, the same is not true for motion parallax. The amount of motion parallax generated by an observer depends on how fast the observer is moving, whereas the maximal amount of binocular parallax is limited by the distance between the eyes. Moreover, a variety of different motion patterns can be generated by motion parallax, and these patterns impart different experiences of depth. The parallax field most similar to that generated by binocular vision occurs when an observer moves his head laterally to the left or right. For example, if you fixate any object in a scene and move your head laterally to the right, the objects closer to the point of fixation appear to move the left, whereas those farther than the fixation appear to move to the right. The speed that a surface patch moves relative to the point of fixation will increase as distance from the fixation point increases. The difference in the relative velocities of objects is analogous to the disparity differences generated binocularly. Moreover, just as binocular parallax generates features that are visible in only one eye, motion parallax generates features that appear (or accrete), and features that disappear (or delete) behind occluding surfaces. This accretion and deletion of partially occluded objects provides compelling information about three-dimensional structure. Motion parallax can therefore provide information about relative depth in much the same way as binocular disparity.

However, motion generates more than one kind of parallax field that imparts a sense of depth. When an observer walks through a three-dimensional world and looks straight ahead, a global optic flow pattern is generated: The entire visual field appears to expand and flow out of the point of fixation and around the observer. Under natural conditions, this pattern of optic flow only occurs when an observer moves relative to his environment and therefore provides an unambiguous source of visual information about self-motion. Indeed, when this flow pattern is reproduced in an artificial environment and shown to stationary observers, an extremely compelling sense of self-motion through a three-dimensional world is experienced. Note that this type of parallax field is unique to motion: one eye would have to be placed well in front of the other to generate a similar parallax field in binocular vision.

In addition to the parallax generated by a moving observer, the relative motion of regions within a moving object can also provide information about relative depth, even for stationary observers. The kinetic depth effect (or KDE) refers to the experience of depth generated by the relative motion of surface regions within an object. An example of this effect can be constructed with the aid of a piece of white paper, a bright flashlight (or projector), and wire (such as a paper clip). Bend the wire into a random three-dimensional shape, hold it up behind the sheet of white paper, and use a flashlight to cast a shadow of the paper clip on the paper. If you rotate the paper clip, this will create a two-dimensional image in which the portions of the paper clip move with different velocities. Nonetheless, we are able to use the differential velocities in the image to recover the shape of a three-dimensional object rotating in depth. The shadow stimulus is ambiguous. It

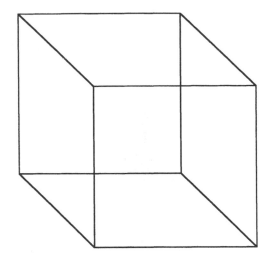

DEPTH PERCEPTION. Figure. 4. Necker cube.

will appear to rotate first one way and then the other even when no changes occur in the physical rotation. The multistability of the KDE occurs because the motion information is consistent with two plausible reconstructions of the three-dimensional world. This is just one of many examples where a depth cue is ambiguous (see, for instance, the Necker cube in Figure 4).

There are two main schools of thought about how a three-dimensional structure is recovered by our visual systems. One perspective assumes that the visual system acts as a kind of detective. Different visual "cues" are independently measured. Each provides some evidence that is used to make an educated guess about the true three-dimensional structure. The need for such detective work arises from the "underconstrained" nature of the two-dimensional image. Returning to the Necker cube (Figure 4), the two-dimensional image is consistent with an infinite number of three-dimensional realities. For instance, the lines that look like a cube could actually represent a flat pattern on a page. To overcome this ambiguity, assumptions must be made about the likely cause of a given image, and the different cues to depth must be combined into a single, three-dimensional representation.

The other school of thought asserts that depth perception does not rely on ambiguous "cues" in images to recover depth. Rather, depth is recovered by directly sensing complex relationships between optical properties that uniquely specify the three-dimensional relationships between surfaces (Gibson, 1979). In this theoretical framework, the starting point of visual processing is not the images formed on the eye, but rather the three-dimensional optical structure formed by the reflections of light from surfaces into the optical media (air). This perspective assumes that our experience of depth arises from the presence of invariants that have a one-to-one correspondence with the three-dimensional structure of our environments. All that is putatively required is a system capable of sensing these invariant patterns; no visual "detective work" is needed. Instead, the problem is to understand how nature equipped us with "sensors" that respond directly to these complex, invariant patterns.

Bibliography

Anderson, B. L. (1994). The role of partial occlusion in stereopsis. *Nature, 367,* 365–368.

Anderson, B. L. (1997). A theory of illusory lightness and transparency in monocular and binocular images: The role of contour junctions. *Perception, 26* (4), 419–454.

Anderson, B. L., & Julesz, B. (1995). A theoretical analysis of illusory contour formation in stereopsis. *Psychological Review, 102,* 705–743.

Clowes, M. B. (1971). On seeing things. *Artificial Intelligence, 2,* 79–116.

Huffman, D. A. (1971). Impossible objects as nonsense sentences. *Machine Intelligence, 6,* 295–323.

Gibson, J. J. (1979). *The ecological approach to visual perception.* Boston: Houghton Mifflin.

Guzman, A. (1968). Decomposition of a visual scene into three-dimensional bodies. In A. Grasselli (Ed.), *Automatic interpretation and classification of images.* New York: Academic Press.

Malik, J. (1987). Interpreting line drawings of curved objects. *International Journal of Computer Vision, 1,* 73–103.

Nakayama, K., & Shimojo, S. (1990). DaVinci stereopsis: Depth and subjective occluding contours from unpaired image points. *Vision Research, 30,* 1811–1825.

Rogers, B., & Graham, M. (1982). Similarities between motion parallax and stereopsis in human depth perception. *Vision Research, 22,* 261–270.

Wallach, H., & O'Connell, D. N. (1953). The kinetic depth effect. *Journal of Experimental Psychology, 45,* 205–217.

Barton L. Anderson

DERMATOLOGICAL DISORDERS. The contribution of psychological factors to dermatological disorders was first discussed by Wilson in his book about diseases of the skin published in 1842. Modern psychosomatic research in dermatology began in the 1930s, when a number of physicians wrote about the relationship between specific skin diseases and unconscious conflictual and personality constellations (Koblenzer, 1987). The psychological aspects of skin disease appear infrequently in the literature but this is slowly changing with the publication of specialty journals such as *Psyche and Cutis.* However, what has been published consists primarily of clinical case examples and theoretical speculation, rather than systematic empirical and experimental observation.

In a prevalence study conducted through the Health and Nutrition Examination Survey of 1971–1974, it was estimated that one third of the U.S. population had one or more significant skin conditions. Among the most common complaints mentioned were psoriasis, atopic dermatitis, acne, and contact dermatitis. One third of the respondents felt that their skin condition posed a social handicap, and one tenth believed it affected their employment or housework. In 1992 there were a total of 29 million visits to dermatologists in the United States; in addition, it was estimated that 18.3% of all visits to primary care physicians were for skin complaints.

Dermatological patients are extremely reluctant to accept a referral to a mental health professional because there is still a stigma associated with mental illness and because such patients, by consulting a dermatologist, have defined themselves as having a medical, rather than an emotional or psychological, illness (Koblenzer, 1987). A variety of studies has found that the incidence of psychological symptoms is higher in dermatological disorders than in a normal population. It appears that depression, anxiety, and obsessive-compulsive disorders are among the most common symptoms. However, the exact type of psychological disorder and the true prevalence of these disorders in dermatological patients are still unknown. Much of the clinical literature suggests that the incidence of psychological difficulties is higher among women, although this is based on clinical treatment studies rather than true epidemiological data. Specific information on ethnic, racial, or age-related differences is rarely reported.

Spitz (1965), in his classic studies of institutionalized infants, found that early impairment in mother-child relationships led to an increase of infantile eczema. His work is an early example of a model postulating an interaction between biological vulnerability and environmental stressors in dermatological disorders. Since this early clinical observation, clinical research has demonstrated that psychological disorders can lead to an increase in dermatological disorders, and psychological disturbances can result from having a dermatological disorder.

Early theories for understanding the etiology and course of psychocutaneous disease relied on psychoanalytic and behavioral models. Contemporary research emphasizes the diathesis-stress model in which genetically vulnerable individuals may develop dermatological diseases under stress due to allergies and/or psychosocial stressors (Gatchel & Blanchard, 1993).

A classification of psychocutaneous disorders (Koblenzer, 1987) for use by clinicians includes three categories: (a) conditions strictly psychological in origin (e.g., delusions as they relate to the skin, delusions of parasitosis); (b) dermatological conditions in which psychological factors are purported to be involved in etiology and maintenance (e.g., urticaria or hives); and (c) those conditions dependent on genetic, environmental, and stress factors (e.g., acne, psoriasis, and eczema).

Case studies have suggested the usefulness of behavioral treatment for a wide range of dermatological disorders. Techniques such as relaxation training, biofeedback, and for child cases, behavioral procedures such as noncontingent attention for scratching, have been utilized. These interventions are based on the speculation that emotional reactions in dermatological conditions may lead to altered autonomic activity resulting in peripheral vascular changes, a lowering of itch thresholds, and the development of a vicious itch–scratch cycle. Behavioral procedures have been developed to combat different aspects of this theory. The clinical literature also has a number of reports on the usefulness of supportive and dynamic psychotherapy for individuals suffering with dermatological disorders.

In summary, there is a relatively large body of literature implicating stressful life situations in precipitating or exacerbating dermatological disorders. The literature is marked by clinical case reports and theoretical speculation with very few well controlled outcome studies. Dermatological disorders of all types can cause an untold amount of suffering for the afflicted. Psychological factors such as stress play an important role for a significant proportion of such individuals. An important new direction is to view dermatological disorders in a truly comprehensive diathesis-stress model. Health psychologists are just beginning to answer some of the fundamental questions that have long existed in the dermatological literature. Psychologists can have a major impact in the lives of countless individuals and, at the same time, contribute to an understanding of the relationship between psyche and soma.

Bibliography

Gatchel, R. J., & Blanchard, E. B. (Eds.). (1993). *Psychophysiological disorders: Research and clinical applications.* Washington, DC: American Psychological Association. A state-of-the-art review of health psychology with a chapter on dermatological disorders.

Koblenzer, C. S. (1987). *Psychocutaneous disease.* New York: Grune & Stratton. A comprehensive review by a leading dermatologist-psychiatrist in this field that discusses disorders, theory, and treatment.

Spitz, R. A. (1965). *The first year of life: A psychoanalytic study of normal and deviant development of object relations.* Madison, CT: International Universities Press. A classic in the literature on human development.

Wilson, E. (1842). *A practical and theoretical treatise on the diagnosis, pathology, and treatment of diseases of the skin, arranged according to a natural system of classification and preceded by an outline of the anatomy and physiology of the skin.* London: J. Churchill. A difficult to obtain but interesting historical volume.

Steven Friedman

DE SANCTIS, SANTE (1862–1935), Italian psychologist and psychiatrist. De Sanctis studied under Cesare Lombroso and Giuseppe Sergi but departed from their positions by adhering to the ideal of the philosophical impartiality of scientific inquiry. Referring to himself as a "medical psychologist" he maintained in his autobiography that he was "above all and essentially a physician" (de Sanctis, 1936).

In 1899, de Sanctis founded the Asili schools for the assistance and social rehabilitation of mentally handicapped children and adolescents. In 1905, he received the first chair in the history of Italian psychology in experimental psychology. Then, for 25 years (1906–1931), he directed the Psychology Institute of the Faculty of Medicine of the University of Rome, dedicating himself to both teaching and research in various fields of psychology. He introduced clinical and psychopathological methods through his contributions to general and experimental psychology, educational psychology, judicial psychology and criminology, the psychology of religion, and above all, psychotechnics and child psychopathology. He strongly defended the autonomy and the scientific status of experimental psychology, upon which applied psychology and psychopathology should be founded. Yet it was in the field of psychotechnics—grounded in vocational psycho-physiology and concerned with the study of the human "biopsychical personality"—that de Sanctis, recognizing the importance of mental tests, made significant contributions. He devised a number of tests to assess the degree of mental retardation in children and adolescents and promoted the translation and the Italian adaptation of Binet's and Simon's well-known test.

With his 1925 volume *La neuropsichiatria infantile*, de Sanctis gave rise to the new discipline of child neuropsychiatry. In this work, he identified the *dementia precocissima* syndrome and suggested a scheme for the identification and classification of abnormal children that Kraeplin acknowledged as a novel and relevant contribution.

In 1929, de Sanctis published a treatise on experimental psychology in two volumes—the first of its kind in the history of Italian psychology. Written for Italian scholars who wished to extend their knowledge of psychology in order to achieve practical results, the treatise attempted "to prove that it is possible to conceive a modern, scientific and generally acknowledged psychology." De Sanctis thus advocated the necessary separation of scientific psychology—"an autonomous discipline by intent and method"—from the philosophical disciplines. In its attempt to create "a scientific representation of human psychophysical activity," scientific psychology, de Sanctis further maintained, could not adopt a specific gnoseological perspective.

His unique attitude toward psychoanalysis and the psychoanalytic movement should be emphasized. In 1899 he had, in fact, published his work *I sogni, studi clinici e psicologici di un alienista* (Dreams: Clinical and Psychological Studies of an Alienist), and he had continued extending and refining this theme in the following years, considering the Freudian innovations. Sante de Sanctis had established a correspondence with Freud in 1900, and he supported the growing Italian psychoanalytic movement. He refused, however, to adhere to the movement, seeking to "defend his freedom of thought." Nevertheless, he hoped that psychoanalysis would officially become part of psychology and psychopathology, asserting that "Freudism" should be acknowledged in the history of the two disciplines. Hence, in de Sanctis's view, experimental psychology would, after due consideration, control, test, or confute psychoanalysis by subjecting it to methodological, and therefore comparable, observation, and perhaps even to pure experimentation.

Bibliography

De Sanctis, S. (1899). *I sogni, studi clinici e psicologici di un alienista*. Turin, Italy: Bocca.

De Sanctis, S. (1925). *Neuropsichiatria infantile: patologia e diagnostica*. Rome: Stock.

De Sanctis, S. (1929). *Introduzione alla psicologia sperimentale*. Scuola Positiva.

De Sanctis, S. (1931). Visual apprehension in the maze behavior of normal and feebleminded children. *Journal of Genetic Psychology*.

De Sanctis, S. (1934). Psicologia e psicopatologia. *Rivista di Psicologia*.

De Sanctis, S. (1936). In C. Murchison (Ed.), *A history of psychology in autobiography* (Vol. 3, pp. 83–120). Worcester, MA: Clark University Press.

Nino Dazzi

DESCARTES, RENÉ (1596–1650), French philosopher and mathematician. Descartes attempted a total reform of philosophy, especially metaphysics and natural philosophy (the science of all natural things). Drawing on contemporary theory and his own dissections of animal parts, he advanced a speculative physiology of the whole organism, including major vital, sensory, and motor functions. In metaphysics he proposed that mind and body are distinct substances, a position subsequently known as mind-body dualism.

Life and Works

Descartes was born at La Haye (later renamed Descartes), near Tours in the Poitou region of France. His mother died when he was 13 months old. He lived with his maternal grandmother before entering the newly established Jesuit college at La Flèche, where he studied from 1606 to 1614. The standard curriculum included grammar, rhetoric, literature, logic, mathematics, natural philosophy, ethics, and metaphysics. In 1616, he received a law degree from the University of Poitiers, where he probably also studied medicine. Two years later, while traveling as a gentleman soldier, Descartes met the Dutch natural philosopher Isaac Beeckman, who kindled his interest in mathematical approaches to nature. He dedicated his first written work to Beeckman, the *Compendium musicae* (published posthumously in Holland in 1650), which was translated as *Compendium on Music* (Rome, 1961).

In November 1619, while in Germany, Descartes recorded three powerful dreams that he believed confirmed his quest for a new scientific system. During the 1620s, living in Paris, he discovered the sine law of refraction (also discovered by Willebrord Snel). He started a book on universal mathematics, which contained examples from optics and also a rudimentary theory of cognition and the senses, but abandoned the project in 1628. The incomplete draft was published as *Regulae ad directionem ingenii* (Amsterdam, 1701), or *Rules for the Direction of the Mind*. In 1629, Descartes moved to the Netherlands, where he lived for the next 20 years, with frequent changes of address. That same year his attempts to understand parhelia (appearances of multiple suns) led him to expand his studies to all of natural philosophy, including human physiology and sensory psychology.

From 1629 to 1633, Descartes worked on *Le Monde*, or *The World*, which was to comprise three treatises: on light (covering the physical world), on man (meaning human beings in general), and on the soul. He had nearly completed the first two treatises when, in 1633, he learned of Galileo's condemnation by the Roman Catholic Inquisition. He abandoned these works and they were published posthumously as *Le Monde, ou Le Traité de la lumière* (Paris, 1664), translated as *The World, or Treatise on Light* (New York, 1979), and *L'Homme* (Paris, 1664), translated as the *Treatise of Man* (Cambridge, Mass., 1972). The first work contained the elements of Descartes's physics, including his theory that matter is constituted by small corpuscles of inert, extended stuff, varying only in size, shape, and motion; his three general laws of motion, including an early statement of the principle of rectilinear inertia; and his cosmological theory of the formation of the solar system and the earth. The second work contained a speculative physiology of the human body, including the role of sensory stimulation in initiating and guiding movements of the whole organism.

In 1637, Descartes published, anonymously, his *Discours de la méthode* (Leiden), or *Discourse on the Method*, which summarized the development of his philosophy and described the need for hypotheses and empirical confirmation in natural science. It served as a preface to his essays, the *Geometry*, which applied algebraic techniques to geometrical problems, the *Meteorology*, which examined atmospheric phenomena, including the rainbow, and the *Dioptrics*, which examined the general properties of light and the physiology and psychology of vision, including size and distance perception. Descartes's most significant metaphysical work was the *Meditationes de prima philosophia* (Paris, 1641), or *Meditations on First Philosophy*. It contained his celebrated inference from "I think" to "I exist," offered as an instance of certain knowledge, and his argument for mind-body dualism.

In 1644, Descartes published *Principia philosophiae* (Amsterdam), or *Principles of Philosophy*, summarizing his metaphysics and physics. During this time he retained interest in physiology and medicine, and worked on *La Description du corps humain* (published posthumously in Paris in 1664), or *Description of the Human Body*. The final work published in his lifetime, *Les Passions de l'ame* (Amsterdam and Paris, 1649), or *Passions of the Soul*, was written in response to queries from Princess Elizabeth of Bohemia. It contained a general theory of the emotions, their physiological causes, functions, and relationships to one another, along with means for their control. In 1649, Descartes moved to Stockholm at the behest of Queen Christina of Sweden, and died of pneumonia the next year. His *Lettres*, published in three volumes (Paris, 1657–1667), contained discussions of his philosophical, mathematical, and scientific works, as well as much pharmaceutical and medical advice for his friends.

Mind and Psychology

As a theorist about mind, Descartes is best known for asserting that mind is wholly distinct from body. This theory contradicted the dominant Aristotelian view of his time, according to which the soul is the animating and organizing principle of the body and all of its functions, from digestion to rational discourse. The Aristotelian theory did not sharply divide physiological from mental processes. Descartes postulated a strict division of mind and body into distinct substances, each capable of existing independently of the other. He was the first to articulate clearly the view that the mental is defined by the contents of consciousness, so that pains, sensations, imaginings, present memories, acts of will, and intellectual thoughts are all part of a single domain, which he called the domain of thought (by contrast with the domain of extension, i.e., of matter). According to his dualistic position, some thoughts, such as acts of will or intellect, can occur without any brain activity. Other thoughts, such as sensations or willings of bodily motion, require that mind and brain interact.

Descartes's metaphysical writings on mind focused largely on the theory of cognition, especially on the means for achieving true cognition. He argued that the most fundamental and secure knowledge is gained independently of the senses. Knowledge of geometry, of one's own mind, and of an infinite deity were his paradigm cases of purely intellectual cognition, devoid of sensory content. He held such knowledge to be innate in the sense that it is available to the intellect independently of sensory experience, and he believed that intellectual cognition can yield the fundamental tenets of metaphysics and physics. But he did not think that all of science can be known independently of sensory observation, nor did he consider sensory cognition to be generally deceptive or faulty. In the sixth of his *Meditations*, and in parts 1 and 4 of the *Principles*, he described the function of the senses as providing guidance for avoiding bodily harm and locating benefits. He also wrote in the *Discourse* (part 4), *Principles* (part 4), and *Letters* (from 1637 and 1638) that sensory perception was essential for testing alternative hypotheses in science.

Descartes was notorious in the seventeenth century for his claim that (nonhuman) animals are soulless machines. He compared the animal body to a complicated hydraulic machine, driven by a rapidly moving, vaporous bodily fluid called the animal spirits. He held that the blood is heated in the heart and passes through the arteries to all parts of the body, while its most subtle parts (material animal spirits) are filtered out in the brain, where they are shunted into various nerves and ultimately cause muscles to inflate, grow taut, and contract in length. He believed all animal behavior could be explained in these terms and applied the same purely mechanical analysis to the human body. Contrary to common doctrine, he maintained that bodily processes such as digestion and growth can be explained mechanistically (in terms of matter in motion), and that most sensory-motor processes can occur without mental intervention. In the *Treatise of Man* he described mechanisms for the reception of sensory stimulation, the storage of sensory patterns in memory, the control of behavior to seek food and avoid danger, and learned changes of behavioral pattern. Consonant with his hydraulic theory, he postulated a clever sensory-motor control device in the brain. Famously, Descartes held that the pineal gland (in the center of the brain) is the seat of mind-body interaction, but he postulated that the gland also serves to mediate between sensory and motor processes in a purely mechanical way. The animal spirits that inflate the muscles spew forth from the pineal and make their way to the muscles through hollow neural tubes (nerves were usually conceived as hollow tubes at the time). They enter one nerve or another depending on which nerves are open (Figure 1). This, in turn, depends on activity in the sensory portion of the nerves.

Descartes envisioned sensory functions to be carried out by thin fibrils running in neural tubes from the sense organs to the surface of a cavity surrounding the pineal gland in the center of the brain. A pattern of activity at a sense organ—say, on the retina of the eye—causes motion in the nerve fibrils; this motion causes the nerve tubes lining the central cavity to open in a corresponding pattern; animal spirits then flow down the tubes and cause the muscles to contract in one way or another, leading to a bodily motion, such as pointing (Figure 1). Descartes asserted that purely mechanical changes in the brain can account for the behavioral manifestations of learning and memory in both humans and animals.

Although Descartes described elaborate mechanical processes for the control of behavior, he held that human mental life cannot be explained in a purely mechanical way but requires the postulation of an immaterial mental substance. In his view, mind was necessary to explain three aspects of human psychology: conscious experience, general reasoning ability, and linguistic ability. He accounted for conscious sensory experience through mind-body interaction at the pineal gland, with the mechanical pattern caused at the pineal by sensory stimulation serving as the basis for perceptual experience. In vision, the shape of the pineal pattern leads to a corresponding imaged shape, and the mechanical characteristics of the stimulation cause the experience of various colors.

To explain size and distance perception, Descartes hypothesized purely psychophysical mechanisms, as well as judgmental processes. He called the use of convergence to perceive distance "natural geometry," since it involves determining the altitude of a triangle (the distance to an object) from two angles and the length of a side (the angles of convergence of the eyes, and interocular distance). He postulated mechanical brain correlates of accommodation and convergence that directly cause the idea of distance in the mind and further theorized that distance can be judged by relating image size to known size, and that size can be judged from image size and perceived distance (yielding size constancy). Descartes later explained that such judgments occur rapidly and habitually, and so go unnoticed (*Meditations*, Sixth Replies). Unnoticed judgments must nonetheless count as conscious for Descartes, given his theoretical stance that all mental events are conscious.

In the *Passions of the Soul*, Descartes examined the physiological causes and mental expression of the emotions. He divided the emotions into six primitive types:

wonder, love, hatred, desire, joy, and sadness. In a 1647 letter to his friend Pierre Chanut he related adult emotions to prenatal and childhood associations between emotions and bodily functions, holding that joy, love, sadness, and hate were the only prenatal emotions. Before birth, they were "only sensations or very confused thoughts, because the soul was so attached to matter that it could not yet do anything else except receive various impressions from it. Some years later it began to have other joys and other loves besides those which depend only on the body's being in a good condition and suitably nourished, but nevertheless the intellectual element in its joys or loves has always been accompanied by the first sensations which it had of them, and even by the motions or natural functions which then occurred in the body" (Descartes, *Philosophical Writings*, vol. 3, p. 308).

Descartes's theoretical commitment that all mental phenomena are conscious did not lead him to propose that we explicitly notice all our thoughts and mental processes. As in the case of unnoticed perceptual judgments, habitual or rapidly occurring emotional factors may go unnoticed.

Influence on Subsequent Psychology

Descartes's work had the immediate influence in psychology of encouraging examination of the neural conditions of sensory experience and other mental phenomena. An example of this influence is the discussion of sensory perception and the moon illusion in Pierre Regis's *Physique* (Lyon, 1691) or *Physics*. Descartes's mechanistic physiological approach to behavior helped inspire Julien La Mettrie's *L'Homme machine* (Leiden, 1748), or *Man a Machine* (Indianapolis, 1994). In *Science and Culture*, the nineteenth-century biologist Thomas Henry Huxley praised Descartes as a physiologist of the first rank.

In the twentieth century, Descartes has been invoked as both a hero and a villain. He was a hero for those committed to the reality of mental phenomena and the need for mental explanations in psychology—even if his admirers did not accept substance dualism. He was portrayed less favorably by those needing a symbolic target for an attack on mentalism and was sometimes as a pure metaphysician who had no interest in natural science and who denied the need for empirical observation. More recently, his contributions to the rise of modern science and his discussions of scientific method have become more widely known.

Descartes's deepest and most lasting influence on psychology is twofold. First, he proposed that the contents of consciousness reveal a unified domain of mental phenomena, ranging from pains and tickles to abstract thoughts. In effect, he discovered the concept of the mental as a unitary natural kind. Second, he initiated a long tradition of explaining sensory-motor phe-

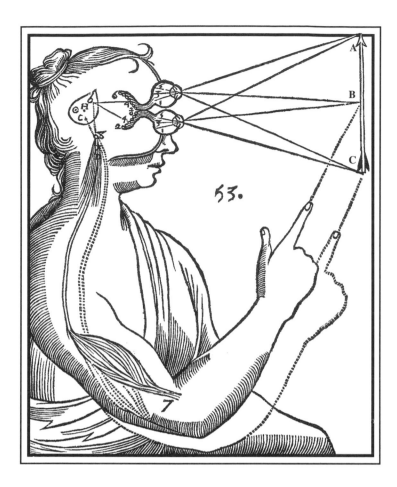

DESCARTES, RENÉ. Figure 1. Sensory motor processes according to Descartes. External object ABC causes retinal pattern 1-3-5, which is conveyed by the optic nerves to the internal cavity of the brain at 2-4-6. Animal spirits leaving pineal gland H from point b proceed to point 4 and also into tube 8, which leads to muscle 7, which the spirits cause to inflate and contract, causing the arm and finger to point at location B. When animal spirits go from point c to tube 8, the muscle is inflated so that the arm points at C. The pineal flow from points b and c (and intermediate points) causes the soul to experience external objects at B and C (and in between). (From *L'Homme*, 2nd edition, 1677, 104.)

nomena by appealing to physiological mechanisms and processes. Thus he stands behind both the mechanistic and the mentalistic traditions in the history of modern psychology.

Bibliography

Cottingham, J. (Ed.). (1992). *Cambridge companion to Descartes*. Cambridge: Cambridge University Press. Contains many helpful interpretive essays, including a chapter on Descartes's physiology and psychology.

Cottingham, J. (Ed.). (1994). *Reason, will and sensation: Studies in Descartes's metaphysics*. Oxford, England: Clarendon Press.

Descartes, R. (1972). *Treatise of man* (T. S. Hall, Ed. & Trans.) Cambridge, MA: Harvard University Press. (Original work published 1664.) Contains extensive annotations by Hall on Descartes's physiology.

Descartes, R. (1984–1991). *Philosophical writings* (Vols. 1–3, J. Cottingham, R. Stoothoff, D. Murdoch, & A. Kenny, Trans.) Cambridge, England: Cambridge University Press. The standard translation, containing full or abridged versions of Descartes's major philosophical and scientific works, and excerpts from his letters.

Gaukroger, S. (1995). *Descartes: An intellectual biography.* Oxford, England: Clarendon Press. Emphasizes the scientific motivation and content of Descartes's work.

Hatfield, G. (1995). Remaking the science of mind: Psychology as a natural science. In C. Fox, R. Porter, & R. Wokler (Eds.), *Inventing human science* (pp. 184–231). Berkeley, CA: University of California Press. Discusses the reception of Descartes's writings on mind and the formation of psychology as a natural science.

Hatfield, G., & Epstein, W. (1979). The sensory core and the medieval foundations of early modern perceptual theory. *Isis, 70*, 363–384. Discusses Descartes's theory of perception in relation to its predecessors and successors.

Huxley, T. H. (1884). *Science and culture.* New York: Appleton.

Rosenfield, L. C. (1940). *From beast-machine to man-machine: The theme of animal soul in French letters from Descartes to La Mettrie.* New York: Oxford University Press.

Voss, S. (Ed.). (1993). *Essays on the philosophy and science of René Descartes.* New York: Oxford University Press.

Wolf-Devine, C. (1993). *Descartes on seeing: Epistemology and visual perception.* Carbondale, IL: Southern Illinois University Press.

Gary Hatfield

DESENSITIZATION. *See* Systematic Desensitization.

DESPAIR. *See* Emotion.

DESSOIR, MAX (1867–1947), German psychologist. Born in Berlin, the son of Ludwig Dessoir, a famous classical actor, Dessoir attained a doctorate in philosophy in 1889 at Berlin, a medical doctorate in 1892 at Würzburg, and an assistant professorship in philosophy at the University of Berlin in 1897, where he remained for over forty years. One of Wilhelmine Germany's elite academicians, he was a colleague of some of the most prominent German intellectuals of his time including Ernst Cassirer, Wilhelm Dilthey, and Georg Simmel. A prolific scholar equally sympathetic to philosophy, psychology, history, and art, Dessoir's primary activities were teaching philosophy and system building in aesthetics. In 1906 he established a journal, the *Zeitschrift für Ästhetik und allgemeine Kunstwissenschaft*, and in 1909 a professional society, the *Gesellschaft für Ästhetik und allgemeine Kunstwissenschaft*, both of which successfully promoted the scholarly study of aesthetics and related psychological issues for many years. Dessoir was an influential member of the intellectual establishment whose students entered all areas of German cultural and academic life, including German psychology as it developed from a philosophical specialty to its autonomous applied-scientific phase in the 1930s (Geuter, 1992). He suffered a complete interdiction of his scholarly activity by the Nazis in 1940, survived the war in Germany, and published his memoirs (1947a).

Dessoir's influence on American psychology was less direct than that of his contemporaries. The relatively few American psychologists who studied at Berlin preferred his more experimentally oriented colleagues. His aesthetics, largely descriptive and based on ideas of classic beauty, receded into the background in an era in which revolutionary art movements succeeded each other almost yearly. Other German psychologists who proposed explicit explanatory mechanisms for aesthetic experience, for example Lipps or the Gestalt psychologists, fared better with functionalist Americans. Dessoir began his career by publishing on then-fashionable topics, a bibliography on hypnosis (1888) followed by a study of dissociation (1890). But he soon turned toward philosophy while, at the same time, American interest in hypnosis began to wane (Hilgard 1987). Probably his most important influence on American psychology was his history of German psychology (*Geschichte der neueren deutsche Psychologie*, Berlin, 1894) whose shorter version in 1911, the *Abriss einer Geschichte der Psychologie* (Heidelberg, 1911) appeared in English translation the next year as *Outlines of the History of Psychology* (1912). Dessoir's history, concurrent with that of G. S. Brett, offered a comprehensive, erudite account of psychology's philosophical background and reinforced the idea held by many turn-of-the-century psychologists that psychology was an established, respectable field with fundamental connections to classical philosophy. Though many disagreed, most notably E. G. Boring, this is still the standard view of the history of psychology today. [*See the biography of Boring.*] Beyond this, Dessoir was deeply interested in psychic phenomena and was credited by many—including himself (Stuttgart, 1931, p. vii)—for introducing the term *parapsychology* (Ger. "Parapsychologie") into psychology in 1889 to refer to events outside of ordinary mental experiences that can be studied systematically. He wrote extensively on such subjects throughout his career: his last work, *Das Ich, Der Traum, Der Tod* (Self, dream, and death, Stuttgart, 1947b), is concerned with, among other things, the survival of bodily death. Yet few modern "parapsychologists" cite him, as he was, regarding paranormal phenomena, a fierce though tolerant skeptic.

Bibliography

Dessoir, M. (1888). *Bibliographie des modernen Hypnotismus* [Bibliography of modern hypnotism]. Berlin: C. Duncker.

Dessoir, M. (1890). *Das Doppel-Ich* [The duplicate I]. Leipzig: E. Gunther.

Dessoir, M. (1912). *Outlines of the history of psychology* (D. Fisher, Trans.). New York: Macmillan.

Dessoir, M. (1931). *Vom Jenseits der Seele: Die Geheimwissenschaften in kritischer Betrachtung* [From the far side of the soul: A critical examination of the occult]. (6th ed.). Stuttgart: F. Enke.

Dessoir, M. (1947a). *Buch der Erinnerung* [Memory's book]. (2nd ed.). Stuttgart: F. Enke.

Dessoir, M. (1947b). *Das Ich, Der Traum, Der Tod* [Self, dream, and death]. Stuttgart: F. Enke.

Geuter, U. (1992). *The professionalization of psychology in Nazi Germany*. New York: Cambridge University Press.

Hilgard, E. (1987). *Psychology in America: A historical survey*. San Diego, CA: Harcourt Brace Jovanovich.

David C. Devonis

DETERMINANTS OF INTELLIGENCE. [*This entry comprises six articles:*
    Heritability of Intelligence
    Socialization of Intelligence
    Culture and Intelligence
    Schooling and Intelligence

Heritability of Intelligence

Heritability (h^2) is the proportion of phenotypic variance in a population attributable to genetic variation.
Narrow heritability (h_N^2) is the proportion of phenotypic variance due to additive genetic variance. Narrow
heritability indexes genetic variability that breeds true
and is of most use to agricultural breeders. Broad heritability (h_B^2) includes all sources of potential genetic
variability and is the indicator of greatest interest in
the behavioral sciences. Discussion here will be confined to broad heritability.

Figure 1 is a diagram of potential sources of genetic
and environmental variance. The phenotype refers to
any measurable characteristic like height or intelligence.
For many psychological phenotypes, error of measurement can be substantial and will reduce estimates of
heritability. Genotypic variation is due to differences in
our genes. The 23 pairs of human chromosomes are
composed of genes, which can be thought of as individual packets of information that code the genetic portion
of our phenotype. Humans are estimated to have
100,000 genes and half of those may be involved in
brain function. Genetic variation exists because each
gene has alternate codes, called *alleles*, which occur with
different frequencies in a population. New alleles can
arise through the process of mutation, which is one way
of ensuring genetic variation in a species.

Genetic variance can be divided into two main categories: additive and nonadditive. Additive genetic variance is the phenotypic result of all of the simple, additive effects of the alleles. Nonadditive genetic variance
is the interactive effects of dominance and epistasis.
The two alleles of a gene at homologous sites on paired
chromosomes may have an effect beyond what would
be predicted from each allele alone. This is known as
dominance. Epistasis is similar to dominance except the
alleles that affect each other are at different locations
on the chromosome.

One of the most important reasons for understanding the genetic contribution to a trait is to separate it
unambiguously from the environmental contribution.
For example, a child's vocabulary has been related to
the parents' vocabulary (the words a child hears and
books in the home are among other variables). Although such studies are useful for descriptive purposes,
it is impossible to tell what the cause of vocabulary
development is without explicitly separating environmental from genetic causes. What the child hears, how
often the child is read to, and other assumed environmental variables could be the only determinants of the
child's vocabulary. On the other hand, parents who
have large vocabularies could pass along genes that allow their children to acquire large vocabularies. Unless
environmental and genetic sources of variation are explicitly identified, it is not possible to determine which
of these alternatives is correct. In the history of psychology, failing to separate genetic and environmental
sources of variation is one of the most frequent and
serious errors made. This error partly explains why the
nature-nurture issue has been such a persistent debate.

When heritability is assessed, it is possible to identify
two broad sources of environmental influence. The first
type is environmental influences common to a particular family. These influences are the same for all members within a family, but differ across families and are
called *between-family* or *common environmental influences*. They make members of a family more alike. The
second type of environmental influence is called *unique,
specific*, or *within-family environmental effects*. These influences make family members different and arise from
unique experiences specific to a single family member.

Two other sources of variation can be identified.
These are the interaction or correlation of genetic and
environmental influences. The first of these is a genotype by environment interaction. Certain environments
may be more favorable to specific genotypes. For example, dairy cows bred over many generations for milk
production in Wisconsin will not be outstanding milk
producers when they are moved to Texas because of
differences in grass characteristics in the two places.
The second potential source of variation is the covariance or correlation of the genotype and environment.
Tall boys in the United States may be more likely to
seek out opportunities to play basketball than short
boys, thereby providing themselves with better environmental chances to become good at basketball.

How Is Heritability Measured?

One way of estimating heritability would be to know
which genes contribute to intelligence, allowing exact
specification of an individual's genotype. This is within
the realm of possibility but still far from reality. Of the
many genes that could potentially affect intelligence,
one has been identified (Chorney et al., 1998). The
gene, IGF2R on chromosome 6, is for insulin-like
growth factor-2 receptor. It was identified by showing
that frequencies of the alleles at the location of this
gene were different in people of high and average intelligence. Though this result is very encouraging, it
will take some time to identify directly all the genes that
make major contributions to intelligence.

Current estimates of heritability are less direct than
identifying the specific genes involved. Because each offspring receives half of its genes from each parent, the
expected genetic relationship of individuals can be estimated. This knowledge of genetic similarity, along

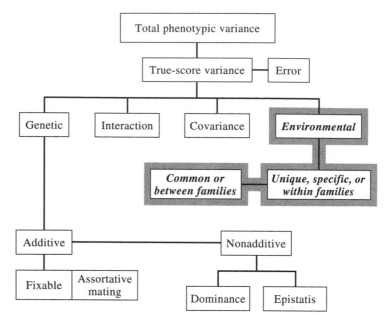

DETERMINANTS OF INTELLIGENCE: Heritability of Intelligence. Figure 1. The puzzle of nongenetic variance. A representation of total phenotypic variance into potential components,. These components can be estimated using quantitive genetic technique. (Modified from Jensen, 1997. Copyright 1997 by Cambridge University Press.)

with some special situations like adoption and twins, allows an estimate of heritability. If a trait like intelligence is heritable, the more closely individuals are related, the more similar they should be on the trait. By correlating scores on the trait, it is possible to compare the correlation actually obtained to what would be expected from predictions based on genetic similarity.

Specifically, siblings, who have the same parents, will, on average, have half their genes in common. Since each child gets a random half of the parent's genes, it is only possible to say that siblings will have an average of half their genes in common. They could have anything from all genes in common to no genes in common but, on average, would share half. Similarly, half-siblings would share one quarter of their genes and cousins would share one eighth of their genes, on average.

A very special case is monozygotic or identical twins. Because they result from a single egg and sperm, monozygotic twins are genetically identical. On the other hand, dizygotic or fraternal twins each result from a separate egg and sperm and are no more genetically similar than other siblings. A comparison of the correlations between monozygotic and dizygotic twins on a trait can be used to obtain a rough estimate of heritability. Broad heritability is about twice the difference in the correlation between monozygotic and dizygotic twins.

Obviously, siblings who have been raised in the same home not only share genes in common but share a common environment. An important control for environment is adoption. Children adopted away from their biological parents early in life show what happens when persons with similar genetic heritage are raised in different environments. Monozygotic twins reared apart are an important example of the adoption method. Since adopted monozygotic twins share all of their genes in common, any similarity between them can only be due to genetic differences (or selective placement, which, at least in more recent studies, is carefully measured). The phenotypic correlation between monozygotic twins provides a direct estimate of heritability. Monozygotic twins reared apart are rare; fewer than 200 cases have been reported in the literature.

Nonadditive sources of variation can be estimated with studies of inbreeding depression and hybrid vigor. When genetically related individuals like cousins mate, they are more likely to have similar genes including deleterious recessive genes. The offspring of related individuals are, therefore, more likely to have two genes that together produce a negative effect on the trait, referred to as depression. Outbreeding produces just the opposite effect. If members of two formerly independently breeding groups mate, there is a lowered probability of matching two deleterious genes and there will be a positive effect on the trait in their offspring, called hybrid vigor. Both inbreeding depression and hybrid vigor are known to exist for intelligence, providing evidence for nonadditive genetic effects.

Although estimates of heritability can be obtained from monozygotic twins reared apart, a comparison of monozygotic and dizygotic twins, or almost any other genetic relationship, the best way to obtain an estimate is through model fitting. The models used are complex and beyond the scope of this discussion. The advantage of these mathematical models is that they use all available data and include most, if not all, of the factors that can affect estimates of heritability.

Predictions assume random mating, but people mate nonrandomly for intelligence. Individuals select mates of similar intelligence and this phenomenon is known as *assortative mating*; typically, the correlation between mates is .33. When significant assortative mating occurs and is not controlled for, estimates of heritability will be inflated.

What Is the Evidence Regarding the Heritability of Intelligence?

Bouchard and McGue (1981) compiled all the world's literature on the correlation of IQ for genetically related individuals either raised in their family environment or adopted away. There were more than 200 studies including over 50,000 pairs of individuals of various relationships surveyed. Some average correlations were: monozygotic twins raised together (.86), monozygotic twins raised apart (.72), dizygotic twins raised together (.60), siblings raised together (.47), single parent-offspring together (.42), adopted-biological siblings reared together (.29), and adopting parent-adopted sibling (.19). The ordering of these correlations is strongly suggestive that intelligence is a heritable trait. Doubling the difference between the correlation for monozygotic and dizygotic twins [2(.86−.60)] produces a heritability of .52. This is lower than the .72 estimate obtained from monozygotic twins raised apart, but most individuals in that group were adults when tested.

Chipuer, Rovine, and Plomin (1990) used Bouchard and McGue's (1981) compilation of data to fit a multivariate genetic model, simultaneously accounting for assortative mating, nonadditive and additive genetic effects, and common and unique environmental influences. Figure 2 shows the results for the best-fitting model for siblings. Broad heritability (the sum of additive and nonadditive genetic components) is .51. Although this is probably the best single estimate of heritability, nearly all other results can be characterized as finding heritabilities between .40 and .80. Intelligence appears to be the most heritable of all psychological traits.

Is Heritability Different for Different Groups?

Since heritability is a population estimate, the heritability obtained will depend on the population used. Heritability is not necessarily fixed and unchangeable. It is important to remember that heritability reflects the particular conditions that exist in a particular population at a particular time. When conditions change, heritability can change.

Is there any evidence that heritability actually does change for intelligence? The studies summarized by

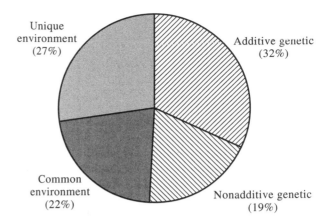

DETERMINANTS OF INTELLIGENCE: Heritability of Intelligence. Figure 2. The distribution of environmental and genetic sources of variation for siblings obtained by model fitting.

Bouchard and McGue (1981) were heavily weighted with children and adolescents. When examined by age, heritability is found to increase substantially in adulthood, approaching .80. This increase in heritability of intelligence is accompanied by a decrease in common environment to levels approaching zero. This finding makes sense because, when young adults leave home, family environment should have decreasing impact. The increase in heritability with age confirms the old saying that we become more like our parents as we grow older. At the other end of the age range, heritability of IQ for children under six is close to .40, with common environment also being about .40. At all ages, unique environmental influences are constant at about .20.

What Heritability Is and Is Not

Some cautions must be kept in mind when interpreting any estimates of heritability. Heritability does not mean fixed or unchangeable. If conditions change, heritability can change. Furthermore, genes turn on and off during the course of development. Heritability does not apply to a particular individual. It is a population average and, like all averages, there may be no person in the population who exactly represents that average. A heritability of .51 cannot be interpreted as meaning that a particular person's intelligence is 51% due to genetic influences.

Even with these caveats, heritability is an extremely important statistic. It provides a map of the terrain that must be explored to know what causes differences in intelligence. It also provides a methodology for the explicit identification of various sources of variance, both genetic and environmental. In the future, the genetic methods used to estimate heritability may find their most important application in the identification of environmental variables that affect intelligence. Currently, there are few environmental variables that have been unambiguously identified as affecting intelligence, although it is known that common and unique sources of environmental variance contribute to its development.

Acknowledgments. Parts of this work were supported by Grant No. HD07176 from the National Institute of Child Health and Human Development, Office of Mental Retardation.

Bibliography

Bouchard, T. J., Jr., & McGue, M. (1981). Familial studies of intelligence: A revision. *Science, 212,* 1055–1058.

Chipver, H. M., Rovine, M. J., & Plomin, R. (1990). LISREL modeling: Genetic and environmental influences on IQ revisited. *Intelligence, 14,* 11–29.

Chorney, M. J., Chorney, K., Seese, N., Owen, M. J., Daniels, J., McGuffin, P., Thompson, L. A., Detterman, D., Benbow, C., Lubinski, D., Eley, T., & Plomin, R. (1998). A quantitative trait locus associated with cognitive ability in children. *Psychological Science, 9,* 159–166.

Jensen, A. R. (1997). The puzzle of nongenetic variance. In R. J. Sternberg & E. L. Grigorenko (Eds.), *Heredity, intelligence, and environment* (pp. 42–88). Cambridge, England: Cambridge University Press. A brief review of behavior genetics and speculation on sources of nongenetic variance.

Jensen, A. R. (1998). *The g factor: The science of mental ability.* Westport, CT: Praeger. A comprehensive review of the literature on general intelligence including a discussion of behavior genetics and intelligence.

Plomin, R., Defries, J. C., & McClearn, G. E. (1990). *Behavioral genetics: A primer* (2nd ed.). New York: Freeman. A general introduction to behavior genetics, including modeling.

Plomin, R., & McClearn, G. E. (1993). *Nature, nurture, and psychology.* Washington, DC: American Psychological Association. A discussion of behavior genetics and environment.

Douglas K. Detterman

Socialization of Intelligence

From the 1960s through the 1980s, the major approaches to understanding intellectual development emphasized basic cognitive processes with little attention to the content or context of cognitive processing. In the late 1980s, however, theories of intellectual development began to consider seriously the influence of context on cognition (e.g., Ceci; 1990, Rogoff, 1990; Sternberg, 1985). Stephen J. Ceci, a prominent cognitive psychologist, suggested that "the basic psychological and biological processes are the 'engines' that drive intellectual development and context provides the fuel and steering wheel to determine how far and in what direction it goes" (1994, p. 404). This article considers the ways in which children's social context (e.g., families, schools, and cultural groups) facilitates and hinders their intellectual development.

Family Influences

Two major approaches have been employed to examine parental influences on children's intellectual development. One approach has been to study specific aspects of parental beliefs and behaviors and their relations to children's performance on cognitive tasks thought to be directly related to those aspects of parenting (e.g., the way parents talk to their children and children's verbal ability). A second tack has been to look at the relations between children's cognitive performance and global assessments of parenting or the home environment. Both types of studies have garnered evidence that what parents do is related to their children's intellectual development.

A landmark longitudinal study (Hart & Risley, 1995) in which specific aspects of parents' behaviors have been linked to children's intellectual development, focused on the ways in which parents in 42 midwestern families interacted with their young children and the relations between parenting and children's language learning, and IQ. The young children were observed for one hour every month from the time they were 6 months old until they were 3 years old. Multiple aspects of parenting were assessed including (a) the diversity of parent language (e.g., number of different words spoken by parent during an hour); (b) the affective quality of the parent-child interactions (e.g., expressions of approval); (c) the emphasis parents placed on telling children about objects and events; (d) the ways in which parents prompted and corrected children's behaviors; and (e) parents' responsiveness to the child. Using very specific, detailed descriptions of parent behaviors with their children over a long period of time, Hart and Risley were able to highlight the cumulative difference in parenting behaviors. For example, there was a vast range in the amount the parents talked to the child from a low of about 50 utterances per hour to a high of approximately 800 utterances per hour when the children were 11 to 18 months of age. In addition, the amount the parent talked to the child when the child was an infant was highly correlated with the amount the parent talked to the child at age 3 ($r = .84$). This consistency in parenting behavior leads to a cumulative difference in children's environments. If a child hears 50 utterances an hour for an average of 14 waking hours per day, that child will be exposed to about 700 utterances each day. On the other hand, if parents address their child 800 times per hour, the child will hear more than 11,000 utterances each day. Hart and Risley argued that cumulative differences in parenting behaviors can lead to profound differences in children's intellectual development. They found, for example, that (a) greater diversity in parents' language was associated with more rapid growth in children's vocabulary; (b) more positive affect during parent-child interactions was associated with higher IQ scores at age 3; and (c) the ways in which parents guided and corrected their children's behavior were related to children's IQ scores. In a regression analysis, the five aspects of parenting were able to account for 59% of the variance (or individual differences) in children's IQ scores. When the children were in third grade, 29 of the original children were given language development tests. Parents' interactions with their children at ages 1 and 2 were related to children's language development at ages 9 and 10. By third grade, family socioeconomic status (SES) explained 30% of the variance in children's language scores. In contrast, parenting variables accounted for 61% of the variance in language scores. This study demonstrates that the language environment that surrounds the child during the first three years of life can have long-term consequences for the child's verbal ability.

Studies examining the relations between parenting style and children's development take a broader view of the nature of parenting. Parenting style is an analysis of parenting behavior including discipline, responsiveness to child, structure, and warmth with child. Developmental researchers have found that parenting style is related to children's intellectual development. In studies with children and adolescents, researchers have found that authoritative parenting (a parenting style in which parents have high expectations for their children, cultivate warm, nurturing relationships with their children, and help develop children's autonomy) is associated with higher performance on cognitive tasks and school achievement.

The Home Observation for Measurement of the Environment Inventory (HOME) is another widely used global assessment of parenting and the home environment. It measures multiple dimensions of the home environment including maternal responsiveness to child, maternal acceptance of child, provision of appropriate play materials for the child, language stimulation, and encouragement of social maturity. Several researchers have found that scores on the HOME inventory are related to children's current and subsequent cognitive performance. For example, Bradley, Caldwell, and Rock (1988) found that HOME scores taken when children were 2 years old were related to children's school achievement test scores at age 10.

Finally, strong correlations between parenting and children's cognitive performance are *not* necessarily the result of what parents do with and for their children. The correlations may be a function of parents' genetic contribution to their children's development. Some researchers have used measures of parents' intelligence (e.g., IQ scores) to take parents' genetic contribution into account. Studies examining the relations among children's intelligence, home environment, and maternal intelligence have yielded mixed results. Luster and Dubrow (1992), however, demonstrated that when multiple aspects of the home environment are measured and children are assessed at younger ages (i.e., when the home environment should have a stronger influence on intellectual performance relative to other experiences, such as school), then home environment predicts children's cognitive performance after controlling for mothers' IQ scores. Their work provides evidence that parenting influences children's intellectual development beyond what is explained by genetic inheritance.

Educational Influences

Developmental psychologists have posited that quality and amount of schooling help explain individual differences in intelligence test performance, and that schooling shapes the way individuals reason about information. Both arguments are discussed below. (For excellent reviews of this research, see Ceci, 1990, and Rogoff, 1981.)

Researchers have consistently found strong correlations between IQ scores and years of schooling. Some have interpreted these correlations to mean that people with higher intelligence are better able to complete more years of education; others have argued that more time in school boosts IQ scores. Whereas no single study has definitively resolved this debate, consideration of multiple types of studies provides sufficient evidence to argue that educational context affects intellectual development.

1. Swedish psychologists, for example, have capitalized on mass IQ testing of children in third grade and subsequent IQ testing of young men in military service. When third-grade IQ scores and SES were controlled, men who had more years of schooling had higher IQ scores.

2. Comparisons of children whose birthdays were immediately before and after their school entry cutoff dates have shown that children who have had one year more schooling by a given age (e.g., age 8) have higher IQ scores than their peers who just missed the school entry cutoff date.

3. A consistent finding over several studies is that IQ scores drop after summer vacation, particularly for low-income children. Researchers have hypothesized that the drop occurs primarily for low-income children because their summer activities are least likely to be related to academic tasks.

4. Studies in the mid-1900s documented that when African American families migrated to northern cities, children's IQ scores rose relative to their

southern peers. Researchers attributed the improvement in test scores to differences in quality of schooling.

5. Finally, studies in the early 1900s of children who had little or no schooling (e.g., children of gypsies in Great Britain, children raised in isolated communities in the Blue Ridge Mountains of the United States) have shown that the average IQ scores of younger children (4 to 6 years old) were only a little below normal (e.g., IQs of 90), but the average IQ scores of older children dropped to the retarded range (e.g., IQs of 60). Psychologists have maintained that the lower IQ scores of the older siblings reflect the cumulative effect of the lack of schooling.

Taken together, these data provide evidence that time in school affects children's intellectual development as measured by IQ tests.

Researchers have also argued that formal schooling develops specific types of cognitive abilities. In a critique of research on the impact of education on intellectual development, Rogoff (1981) suggested that among other skills, formal education improves children's abilities to memorize unrelated pieces of information, to organize objects according to taxonomic rules rather than functional rules, to interpret two-dimensional drawings, and to do Piagetian formal operational problems. Schooling provides experience and practice in specific types of problem solving. The importance of these skills depends on their relation to the types of problems children encounter outside school and later on as adults. Much cognitive research today focuses on individuals' ability to transfer skills learned in one setting (e.g., school) to other settings (e.g., work).

Cultural Influences

Cultural context shapes intelligence in a multitude of nontrivial ways. In a review of research on cultural influences on intellectual development, Okagaki and Sternberg (1991) concluded that cultural context functions in four ways to shape intellectual development: (a) provides the content—the objects and ideas—of our thinking; (b) sets the functions or ways in which these ideas and objects are normally used; (c) establishes the social contexts in which we act and shapes our expectations within these settings; and (d) specifies what constitutes an acceptable answer. A classic cross-cultural study conducted by Alexander Luria (1976), a Russian psychologist, demonstrates one of the ways social context shapes intellectual performance. In the 1930s, Luria presented a variety of cognitive tasks to groups of Russian peasants. One task called for the individual to generate spontaneously three questions on any topic. Of the 21 illiterate peasants, 13 politely refused to ask any question: "I can't imagine what to ask about—I only know about spadework, nothing else . . . to ask

questions you need knowledge" (p. 138). For those Russian peasants, the social context of an experimental interview simply did not permit them or help them to ask questions. Whether or not those adults had a role in their society in which they spontaneously sought information from authority figures was unclear. Whatever the case, in the strange social context of an experimental interview in which the researcher asked them to perform odd tasks for no apparent reason, the social expectations and behaviors the peasants carried with them from their everyday social contexts did not give them the clues to decipher and comply with the experimenter's request.

Finally, a series of cross-national studies by Harold Stevenson, an American developmental psychologist, and his colleagues highlights the impact that differences in cultural values, home environment, and schooling have on children's intellectual performance. Based on their comparisons of students from multiple nations (e.g., Chen, Lee, & Stevenson, 1996; Stevenson et al., 1990), Stevenson and his colleagues posited a cultural-motivational theory of academic achievement. They proposed that a general cultural emphasis on education and a general cultural belief in the importance of effort in intellectual achievement, as opposed to innate ability, create an environment in which children develop a high level of motivation and achievement-related behaviors, which in turn yield better intellectual performance. These cultural beliefs are translated into specific parenting and educational practices that affect intellectual development. For example, in a study of first-grade children in the United States, Japan, and Taiwan, U.S. children did not do as well in math as the East Asian children did. However, there were virtually no overall differences among the three groups on basic cognitive tasks (e.g., spatial reasoning, perceptual speed, and verbal memory), and in reading, the U.S. children did better than Japanese first graders did, but not as well as the Chinese students. Thus, although basic cognitive abilities, such as perceptual speed, did not differ across groups, their performances on math and reading tests did. Aside from providing evidence that the amount and type of school instruction in math and reading contributed to these differences, Stevenson and his colleagues maintained that parents' beliefs affected children's performance. U.S. parents were more satisfied with both their children's schooling and with their children's performance than were other parents. When the children were in eleventh grade, a 10-year follow-up was conducted. In all three countries, children's home environment during first grade (including parental involvement in child's learning and overall home intellectual environment) was positively correlated with eleventh-grade math, reading, and general knowledge test scores. These cross-national studies bring together the multiple influences of parenting, education, and culture on children's cognitive development.

Bibliography

Bradley, R. H., Caldwell, B. M., & Rock, S. L. (1988). Home environment and school performance: A 10-year follow-up and examination of three models of environmental action. *Child Development, 59*, 852–867.

Ceci, S. J. (1990). *On intelligence . . . more or less: A bioecological treatise on intellectual development.* Englewood Cliffs, NJ: Prentice Hall. Includes discussions of the roles of heredity and environment in shaping intelligence.

Ceci, S. J. (1994). Contextual trends in intellectual development. *Developmental Review, 13*, 403–435.

Chen, C., Lee, S., & Stevenson, H. W. (1996). Long-term prediction of academic achievement of American, Chinese, and Japanese adolescents. *Journal of Educational Psychology, 18*, 750–759.

Hart, B., & Risley, T. R. (1995). *Meaningful differences in the everyday experience of young American children.* Baltimore: Paul H. Brookes.

Luria, A. R. (1976). *Cognitive development: Its cultural and social foundations* (M. Lopez-Morillas & L. Solotaroff, Trans.; M. Cole, Ed.). Cambridge, MA: Harvard University Press. Luria, a Russian psychologist, provided classic examples of the way in which cultural context shapes individuals' thinking.

Luster, T., & Dubrow, E. (1992). Home environment and maternal intelligence as predictors of verbal intelligence: A comparison of preschool and school-age children. *Merrill-Palmer Quarterly, 38*, 151–175.

Okagaki, L., & Sternberg, R. J. (1991). Cultural and parental influences on cognitive development. In L. Okagaki & R. J. Sternberg (Eds.), *Directors of development: Influences on the development of children's thinking* (pp. 101–120). Hillsdale, NJ: Erlbaum.

Rogoff, B. (1981). Schooling and the development of cognitive skills. In H. C. Triandis & A. Heron (Eds.), *Handbook of cross-cultural psychology: Developmental psychology* (Vol. 4, pp. 233–294). Boston: Allyn & Bacon.

Rogoff, B. (1990). *Apprenticeship in thinking: Cognitive development in social context.* New York: Oxford University Press. A sociocultural approach to understanding cognitive development.

Steinberg, L., Dornbusch, S. M., & Brown, B. B. (1992). Ethnic differences in adolescent achievement: An ecological perspective. *American Psychologist, 47*, 723–729.

Sternberg, R. J. (1985). *Beyond IQ: A triarchic theory of human intelligence.* Cambridge, England: Cambridge University Press. This theory brings together information-processing, psychometric, and contextual views of intelligence.

Stevenson, H. W., Lee, S., Chen, C., Stigler, J. W., Hsu, C., & Kitamura, S. (1990). Contexts of achievement: A study of American, Chinese, and Japanese children. *Monographs of the Society for Research in Child Development, 55*, (1–2, Serial No. 221).

Lynn Okagaki

Culture and Intelligence

The adaptation of the human species relies on transformation of the natural environment by means of culture accumulated over the course of history. As a result of their different social histories, human groups around the world vary considerably in the particular system of practices, artifacts, and symbols that makes up their culture. Cross-cultural variation is thus related to intelligence in several ways: as a system of meanings, each culture informs the way in which intelligence is conceptualized; as a nurturant environment for personal growth, it places particular demands on the development of an individual's intelligence; and as a forum, each culture frames its own debates about the significance of intelligence in terms of a particular set of topical concerns.

The web of meanings that informs people's lives in a given community defines the cluster of mental characteristics that qualify for the designation *intelligent*. In contemporary, industrialized societies, intelligence is strongly associated with individual excellence on literate, mathematical, or scientific tasks emphasized by academic curricula. However, in a community without schools, those indicators have no indigenous meaning. Several studies in subsistence, agrarian societies of Africa have found that indigenous conceptualization of intelligence focuses on social productivity, and cognitive alacrity is only valued as a mental trait when it is responsibly applied to benefit society.

Even within the United States, members of the general public generally place greater emphasis on social competence in their conceptions of intelligence than do expert researchers, as reflected in published theories, standardized tests, and responses to surveys. Alternative theories responding to this challenge have proposed a distinction between the normative view of academic intelligence and other dimensions such as practical, social, or emotional intelligence. Critics object that this obscures important technical distinctions between cognition and motivation, between ability and disposition, and between general competence and special talents. But the popularity of these texts suggests that they resonate with widely held preoccupations of contemporary Western culture.

According to Piaget, intelligence is a state of equilibrium in which understanding approximates closely to the world as it really is, which the developing individual gradually constructs over time through active exploration and experimentation. This extremely influential theory rests on several philosophical premises that have purchased for Western science a certain clarity at the expense of other types of understanding: a dualistic separation of mind from body, prioritization of detached contemplation over emotional and moral engagement, a mechanistic orientation, and a teleological theme of progress toward an ideal end state. Given this sociohistorically situated character of Piaget's theory, critics have questioned whether the cognitive stages he described mark a process of substantive discovery and enlightenment about the world as it is, or rather the progressive assimilation of a particular cultural perspective on the interpretation of experience.

Empirical investigations designed to assess the cross-cultural validity of Piaget's theory have generally replicated the basic sequence of stages that he postulated, but the rate at which children progress from one stage to the next is highly variable across cultures. Indeed, even the stage of concrete operations, characteristic of eight-year-olds in Geneva, was not found among a majority of the adults tested in several less industrialized countries. More precisely focused studies have shown that the ecological press for children to develop an understanding of different domains varies across desert, forest, and city cultures with predictable consequences for their rates of cognitive development in each particular domain.

Other cross-cultural studies of perceptual and mathematical skills conclude that decontextualized tests of performance generally afford an invalid estimate of general competence. Different human communities organize the physical and social environment so differently for their children that behavioral adaptation can only be understood and evaluated with reference to the constraints of an ecoculturally particular, developmental niche. The context of human development is not merely a source of external stimulation, but constitutes an incorporating system of social activity, informed by a cultural system of meanings. According to Vygotsky's cultural-historical perspective, Bronfenbrenner's ecological theory and others, the developing child appropriates the system of meanings encoded in language and other shared cultural resources by participating in structured activities. Cognition arises from interactive processes such as intersubjectivity and coconstruction, which support the growth of competence within the child's zone of proximal development.

The study of developmental change in cognition is relevant to an understanding of the nature of intelligence, and as a frame of reference for evaluating individual differences. Yet very little of the theoretical conceptualization of cognitive development is explicitly reflected in the design of the most widely used intelligence tests. Instead, the rationale of these tests is generally phrased in speculative terms, combined with statistical evidence of psychometric reliability and empirical correlations with external criteria, such as scholastic achievement, as evidence of validity.

Intelligence testing is an historically situated cultural practice, whose formal procedures and instruments reflect not only their manifest psychological functions, but also the institutional arrangements within which those functions were conceptualized. The pioneering design of intelligence tests was constrained by considerations of speed, affordability, simplicity, and reliability. Background assumptions included the age-graded school curriculum of institutionalized public basic schooling, so that intellectual aptitude was indexed in a manner that corresponded closely with scholastic precociousness. Thus, individuals introduced to literacy at a relatively late age, and/or socialized in a cultural tradition that places a lower premium on speed, may appear relatively incompetent on these tests.

In the early 1970s a great debate erupted in the forum of American society about the degree to which an individual's intelligence is open to influence by educational and other cultural experiences, and to what extent it is determined by genetic endowment. The debate has continued over ensuing decades and will probably continue to command public attention, given the volatile nature of race relations in the United States. Although various ideological commitments have contributed to both sides of the debate, one of the central issues at stake remains what is meant by intelligence and the methodology of assessing it. Defenders of a mainstream orthodoxy contend that the technology of psychometrics has established valid and reliable methods for measuring intelligence. Many critical researchers, however, have advanced alternative conceptions of intelligence and how it should be measured, which may generate a quite different cultural consensus in the future. Meanwhile, the general public tends to encounter professional assessments of intelligence with respect to decisions on resource allocation for individuals at the two extremes of a continuum from low to high intelligence.

The condition of severe intellectual disability or *mental retardation* is widely recognized across most of the world's societies, and is attributed by contemporary biomedical science to organic impairment that gives rise (unless secondary preventive measures are taken) to functional disability, which in turn places the individual at risk for handicap. The degree to which a functional disability is handicapping depends on social factors, including cultural beliefs and practices. Thus, individuals with severe mental retardation are stigmatized as incompetent in the cultural context of institutionalized schooling, but may be effortlessly included in the everyday social life of some subsistence agricultural communities, and are even accorded special privileges within the religious institutions of some societies.

Milder degrees of learning difficulty have been the subject of intense controversy. Placement of children in special educational programs designed to support their learning sometimes incurs social stigma, leading some parents to resist assiduously such placement. Ethnic and cultural minority groups in the United Kingdom and the United States are significantly overrepresented in such special programs. Given the questionable cross-cultural validity of the measures used to classify students, the arbitrariness of the cutoff points between categories, and the rarity with which those labeled with special needs are readmitted to the mainstream, critics and political activists have argued that intelligence testing serves to legitimate oppressive discrimination against culturally different minority groups by restricting their educational opportunities.

The use of intelligence and aptitude tests for educational selection has been equally controversial. One rationale invokes the elitist principle that scarce instructional resources should be invested in those persons with the greatest potential payoff. Empirical validation of measures used to assess potential in this context is hindered by the tendency for selection to match students' intellectual abilities and dispositions with the character of the curriculum, generating a circular pattern of mutual confirmation between selection criteria and curriculum development. The rationale of matching modes of instruction to the learning characteristics of individual minds implies a need for mutual adaptation by both students and educational programs. Since different kinds of intelligence are demanded by the different eco-cultural settings that exist or are planned for the next generation in different societies around the world, educational selection using tests standardized with reference to past experience in Western industrialized societies is liable to restrict in culturally conservative ways the range of intellectual traits in the pool available to the professions. For non-Western societies, the use of such tests implies a commitment to the Western pattern of socioeconomic transformation methods determining placement of children are open to the charge of cultural hegemony.

The concept of cultural bias in intelligence tests has been interpreted in several different ways. From a psychometric perspective, a test shows no *predictive bias* against a given group if its correlation with outcomes on a validation criterion such as educational achievement is similar to that found for relevant comparison groups. Although this is the case for African Americans with respect to several standardized IQ tests, the sociopolitical reality of their massive underrepresentation in the educational programs and professions to which such tests serve as admission criteria constitutes prima facie evidence of *outcome bias*. The inconsistency between these two conceptions of bias can perhaps be resolved with reference to the notion of *sampling bias*. The tests that currently dominate psychometric practices in the United States derive their legitimacy from their predictive power within educational and industrial settings, which are overwhelmingly informed by the meaning system of mainstream Western culture. They therefore sample skills, styles, and attitudes valued in that mainstream (and promoted within the develop-

mental niche that it informs) more thoroughly than those valued and promoted in minority cultural groups.

Some practitioners attempt to counter the cultural bias of existing tests by adjusting the standard criteria for individuals from disadvantaged groups. However, the practice of simply adding points or lowering the bar lacks scientific validity. Culturally appropriate tests need to be sensitive both to the task demands of future educational and occupational contexts, and to the learning opportunities of the testees' antecedent learning contexts. Development of such culture-specific tests has been attempted in some third-world countries and U.S. cultural minority groups, with an emphasis on distinctive dimensions of intellect valued in the indigenous meaning systems, on skills widely promoted in indigenous activity settings, and on caution in the use of performance in Western-origin school settings as validation criteria. Such tests should be of particular value to practitioners for identifying individual strengths and supportive resources in the home and community.

Whenever an intelligence test standardized on a culturally different population is used for assessment, great caution is needed in interpreting the scores, including an estimate of the direction and degree of error likely to arise from taking them at face value. It is especially hazardous in such cases to summarize assessment in the form of a single score such as an IQ, which misleadingly implies the availability of a technically valid frame of reference for ranking the individual relative to others. A culturally sensitive report would present each test score, with a suitably moderated interpretation, as part of a multidimensional profile of strengths and needs, together with suggestions for how these can best be responded to by resources available in the context for which assessment is being conducted.

The psychometric practices standardized in the twentieth century are informed by a view of intelligence that reflects three broad themes of contemporary Western culture: decontextualization, quantification, and biologization. Restricting the definition of intelligence in this way has perhaps enabled Western industrialized societies to address some of the pressing needs of their particular historical circumstances, but it has also narrowed the field in ways that need to be unpackaged and reformulated in much broader, less definitive terms for application to the concerns and needs of other social groups in other places and in other times.

[*See also* Cross-Cultural Psychology; *and* Culture.]

Bibliography

Bronfenbrenner, U., & Ceci, S. J. (1994). Nature–nurture reconceptualized in developmental perspective: A bio-ecological model. *Psychological Review, 101,* 568–586.
Church, A. T., & Katigbak, M. S. (1988). Imposed -etic and

emic measures of intelligence as predictors of early school performance of rural Philippine children. *Journal of Cross-Cultural Psychology, 19,* 164–177.

Dasen, P. R. (1984). The cross-cultural study of intelligence: Piaget and the Baoule. *International Journal of Psychology, 19,* 407–434.

Dent, H. E. (1996). Non-biased assessment or realistic assessment? In R. L. Jones (Ed.), *Handbook of tests and measurements for Black populations* (Vol. 1, pp. 103–122). Hampton, VA: Cobb & Henry.

Gardner, H. (1993). *Frames of mind: The theory of multiple intelligences.* New York: Basic Books.

Laboratory of Comparative Human Cognition. (1982). Culture and intelligence. In R. J. Sternberg (Ed.), *Handbook of human intelligence* (pp. 642–719). Cambridge, England: Cambridge University Press.

Neisser, U., Boodoo, G., Bouchard, T. J., Boykin, A. W., Brody, N., Ceci, S. J., Halpern, D. F., Loehlin, J. C., Perloff, R., Sternberg, R. J., & Urbina, S. (1996). Intelligence: Knowns and unknowns. *American Psychologist, 51* (2), 77–101.

Serpell, R. (2000). Intelligence and culture. In R. J. Sternberg (Ed.), *The handbook of intelligence* (pp. 549–577). New York: Cambridge University Press.

Serpell, R., & Boykin, A. W. (1994). Cultural dimensions of cognition: A multiplex, dynamic system of constraints and possibilities. In R. J. Sternberg (Ed.), *Handbook of perception and cognition. Vol. 12: Thinking and problem solving* (pp. 369–408). San Diego, CA: Academic Press.

Serpell, R., Zaman, S. S., Huq, S., Ferial, S., Silveira, M. L. M., Dias, A. M. C. de S., Campos, A. L. R. Narayanan, H. S., Rao, P. M., Thorburn, M. J., Halim, A. J., Shrestha, D. M., Hasan, Z. M., Tareen, K. I., Qureshi, A. A., & Nikapota, A. D. (1988). Assessment criteria for severe intellectual disability in various cultural settings. *International Journal of Behavioural Development, 11*(1), 117–144.

Robert Serpell

Schooling and Intelligence

The benefits of staying in school are pervasive. Over their lifetimes, high school graduates will earn $212,000 more than nongraduates, college graduates will earn $812,000 more than high school dropouts, and graduate students with professional degrees will earn nearly $1,600,000 more than college graduates (Bronfenbrenner, McClelland, Wethington, Moen, & Ceci, 1996). School attendance is also associated with lower rates of teen pregnancy, welfare dependency, and criminality (Bronfenbrenner et al., 1996).

Why does schooling increase income or decrease criminality? To some, it is because schooling is a marker for intelligence. High school dropouts tend to score lower on intelligence tests and earn less than those who graduate (Bronfenbrenner et al., 1996). High correlations are found between measures of intelligence and the amount of schooling one receives, ranging from .6 in Herrnstein and Murray (1994) to .9 in Ceci's (1991) review of 16 studies.

Although positive relationships among schooling, intelligence, and life outcomes are agreed upon by researchers, the causal relationships are not. Historically, the relationship among these three factors has been explained as the influence of innate intelligence as measured by IQ on schooling and earnings, a position in accord with Herrnstein and Murray's (1994) analysis. IQ has been posited to affect earnings directly (i.e., intelligent workers are rewarded for the skills they display), and indirectly through years of schooling (i.e., people who get more schooling are more intelligent before they even enter school, thus are more likely to stay in school, and through the additional schooling they obtain the minimum entry-level educational standards required for getting certain jobs; e.g., Scarr, 1992). According to these researchers, after considering intelligence, very little of the variance in job success is accounted for by schooling (Gottfredson, 1997, p. 86).

We will briefly review seven types of evidence suggesting that staying in school elevates IQ. Because of space constraints, we cannot supply all the methodological details or citations supporting our analysis (see Ceci, 1991, for a review and references).

Historical Evidence for the Effects of Schooling on IQ

The following discussion outlines seven effects of schooling on intelligence.

1. Intermittent School Attendance. Around 1900, the London Board of Education commissioned Hugh Gordon to study children who had very low IQs. Some children were in London classrooms, others attended school only intermittently, either because of physical disabilities or their status as children of gypsies, canal boat residents, and so on. As reported by Freeman (1934):

> Intelligence quotients of children within the same family decreased from the youngest to the oldest, the rank correlation between the intelligence quotients and chronological age being −.75. Not only that, but the youngest group (4 to 6 years of age) had an average IQ of 90, whereas the oldest children (12 to 22) had an average IQ of only 60, a distinctly subnormal level. . . . The results of the investigation suggest that without the opportunity for mental activity of the kind provided by the school—though not restricted to it—intellectual development will be seriously limited or aborted. (p. 115)

Thus, the longer youngsters stayed out of school, the lower their IQs became.

In 1932, Sherman and Key studied children reared 100 miles west of Washington, D.C., in hollows that rim the Blue Ridge Mountains. Sherman and Key selected four hollows with differing levels of isolation. Colvin, the most remotely situated hollow, had only three literate adults, no movies or newspapers, and virtually no access roads to the outside. There was a single school, but it had been in session only 16 of 127 months between 1918 and 1930. The other three hollows had intermediate levels of contact with the outside world.

Sherman and Key (1932) observed that the IQ scores of the hollows' children fluctuated systematically with the level of schooling available in their hollow. Advantages of 10 to 30 points were found for the children who received the most schooling. As with the gypsy children, IQ decreased dramatically with age. Six-year-olds' IQs were not much below the national average, but by age 14 the children's IQs had plummeted into the retarded range. Similar cumulative deficits in IQ with age have been reported among African American and British working-class children (Ceci, 1991).

2. Delayed School Start-Up. In South Africa, Ramphal (1962) studied the intellectual functioning of Indian children whose schooling was delayed for up to four years because of the unavailability of teachers. Compared to children from nearby villages who had teachers, these children experienced a decrement of five IQ points for every year of delay.

Schmidt (1967) reported similar results in his analysis of a different South African community of East Indian settlers. Schmidt measured the impact of schooling on both IQ and achievement within children of the same age, socioeconomic status (SES), and parental motivation. When age, SES, and motivation were removed from the picture, the correlation between the number of years of school attended and IQ ranged from .49 to .68 depending on the measure of intelligence used.

Schmidt (1967) also found that years later, those who began school late had substantially lower IQs than those who began school early: another instance of a cumulative deficit. Finally, Schmidt reported that the relationship between the number of years of schooling completed and achievement test scores was no stronger than between schooling and IQ. This suggests that IQ scores are as influenced by schooling as is something explicitly taught in school, namely, academic achievement.

Another instance of delayed school start-up occurred in the Netherlands during World War II. Nazi occupation forced school closures, which resulted in many children entering school several years late. Those children's IQs dropped approximately seven points, probably as a result of their delayed entry into school.

These results strongly suggest that schooling affects IQ independent of parental motivation. Moreover, none of the findings supports the proposition that the IQ–schooling relationship can be attributed to intelligent children beginning school earlier or staying there longer.

3. Remaining in School Longer. What systematic factor could be responsible for men born on, say, 9 July 1951 being more intelligent than men born on, say, 7 July 1951? No ready explanation springs to mind. Consider, though, that toward the end of the Vietnam War, a draft priority score was established with each day of the year being assigned a number, from 1 to 365. If a man's number was low, his chance of being drafted was heightened if he did not have a student deferment or a medical exemption. Thus, staying in school was a sure way to avoid being drafted. It is well established that men born on the first draft date (9 July 1951) stayed in school longer, on average, than their peers born on the last draft date (7 July 1951).

Men born on 9 July 1951 earned approximately a 7% rate of return on their extra years of schooling (Angrist & Krueger, 1991). This figure of 7% rate of return is very close to the estimates derived from studies of being born early or late in a given year (see Neal & Johnson's study as cited in Heckman, 1995). Although these data do not demonstrate a direct causal effect of schooling on IQ, they imply such a link because IQ was presumably the same for both groups prior to their divergence in schooling.

4. Discontinued Schooling. Researchers have demonstrated the detrimental effect of dropping out of school before finishing. In his study of Swedish boys, Harnqvist (1968) randomly selected 10% of the Swedish school population born in 1948 who, at the age of 13, were given IQ tests. In 1966 at the age of 18, 4,616 of these Swedish boys were retested as part of their country's national military registration. Harnqvist compared children who were comparable on IQ, SES, and school grades at age 13, and determined the impact of dropping out of school. He found that for each year of high school (gymnasium) not completed, there was a loss of 1.8 IQ points, up to maximum of nearly 8 IQ points difference between two boys who were similar in IQ, SES, and grades at age 13, but who subsequently differed in the amount of schooling completed by up to four years of high school. (Similar findings have been reported by others using different samples and analytic procedures.)

5. Summer Vacations. Two independent studies have documented, with large samples, the systematic decline in scores that occur in American children over summer. With each passing month away from school, children lose a small but consistent amount of ground from their end-of-year scores on both intellectual and academic tests.

6. Early-Year Birth Dates. Consider the effect on intelligence of being born early versus late in the year. Most states restrict the minimum age of school entry, and mandate compulsory attendance until age 16 or 17. Because of these laws, individuals born in the last 3 months of the year are likely to miss the age cutoff for school entry and enter school a year later than their birth-year cohort. These individuals reach the end of mandatory attendance (16 or 17) when they have been in school one less year then the rest of their birth-year cohort. Upon coming of age, some individuals decide to leave school. Hence, late-year births are likely to stay in school one year less than early-year births because they reach the age for school-leaving after one less year of school attendance.

Given the random nature of birth dates, we can assume that the genetic potential for intelligence is the same in these groups. However, late-year births, as a group, have lower IQ scores than early-year births. Neal and Johnson's study (citied in Heckman, 1995) showed that, for each completed year of schooling, there is an IQ gain of approximately 3.5 points. Angrist and Krueger (1991) found that those who spent an extra year in school earned between 7 and 10% more than their peers who dropped out a year earlier but at the same chronological age. These lower IQs and lower incomes among late births are entirely a function of being more likely to attend one less year of school than their early-birth peers.

7. Cross-Sequential Trends. Baltes and Reinert (1969) randomly sampled 630 children from 48 elementary schools in Saarbrucken, Germany. Three groups of 8- to 10-year-olds, who were separated in age by 4-month intervals, completed a German version of the Primary Mental Abilities. Because the German school system at that time required entering children to be 6 years of age by 1 April, it is possible to compare same-aged children who had received up to a year of difference in schooling. For example, we can compare a child born on 15 March to a child born on 15 April (after the cutoff) who entered school 1 year later. The former child would have one additional year of schooling by the time he or she was 8 years old despite only a 1-month difference in chronological age. Baltes and Reinert found a substantial correlation between the length of schooling completed and intellectual performance among same-aged, same-SES children. In fact, highly schooled 8-year-olds were actually closer in mental abilities to the least-schooled 10-year-olds than they were to the least-schooled 8-year-olds! Similar findings have been reported by Cahan and Cohen (1989) and Morrison, Griffith, and Frazier (1996).

Conclusion

Due to space constraints, we have not discussed some variables that might complicate our argument. For example, we were not able to delve into the possibility that schooling may not be static. It may be that as IQ changes over the life course, it influences decisions to stay in school. Hence, what looks like a schooling effect on IQ may in actuality be an influence of changes in IQ on the decision to remain in school (e.g., individuals who experience an elevation in IQ may decide to remain in school longer than individuals who experience a decline). Resolution of these issues must await future research.

Bibliography

Angrist, J., & Krueger, A. B. (1991). Does compulsory school attendance affect schooling and earnings? *Quarterly Journal of Economics, 106,* 979–1014.

Baltes, P., & Reinert, G. (1969). Cohort effects in cognitive development in children as revealed by cross-sectional sequences. *Developmental Psychology, 1,* 169–177.

Bronfenbrenner, U., McClelland, P., Wethington, E., Moen, P., & Ceci, S. (1996). *The state of Americans.* New York: Free Press.

Cahan, S., & Cohen, N. (1989). Age versus schooling effects on intelligence development. *Child Development, 60,* 1239–1249.

Ceci, S. J. (1991). How much does schooling influence general intelligence and its cognitive components?: A reassessment of the evidence. *Developmental Psychology, 27,* 703–722.

Freeman, F. (1934). *Individual differences.* New York: Holt.

Gottfredson, L. S. (1997). Why "*g*" matters: The complexity of everyday life. *Intelligence, 24,* 79–132.

Harnqvist, K. (1968). Changes in intelligence from 13 to 18. *Scandinavian Journal of Psychology, 9,* 50–82.

Herrnstein, R., & Murray, C. (1994). *The Bell curve: Intelligence and class structure in American life.* New York: Free Press.

Morrison, F. J., Griffith, E. M., & Frazier, J. A. (1996). Schooling and the 5 to 7 shift: A natural experiment. In A. J. Sameroff & M. M. Haith (Eds.), *The five to seven year shift: The age of reason and responsibility* (pp. 161–186). Chicago: University of Chicago Press.

Ramphal, C. (1962). *A study of three current problems in education.* Unpublished doctoral dissertation, University of Natal, India.

Scarr, S. (1992). Developmental theories for the 1990s: Developmental and individual differences. *Child Development, 63,* 1–19.

Schmidt, W.H.O. (1967). Socio-economic status, schooling, intelligence, and scholastic achievement in a community in which education is not yet compulsory. *Paedogogica Europa, 2,* 275–286.

Sherman, M., & Key, C. (1932). The intelligence of isolated mountain children. *Child Development, 3,* 279–290.

Stephen J. Ceci and Livia L. Gilstrap

Teaching of Intelligence

Can people learn—can they be taught—to be more intelligent? How one answers this question must depend on how one defines intelligence, how one assesses it, what one takes learning or teaching it to mean, and what one is willing to consider as evidence that it has increased. If intelligence is defined as the cognitive potential with which one is born, then, clearly, it cannot be modified by training, but if it is taken to be the capacity to learn at any time throughout the life span, then its mutability is not ruled out as a matter of definition. If one's score on a standardized IQ test is taken to be a reliable measure of the amount of intelligence one has, then the question of whether that amount can be increased by training is easily answered by testing; however, if one considers intelligence to include capabilities, qualities, or characteristics not fully captured by such tests, answering the question is not so easy.

Most theoretical treatments of intelligence stress its multidimensional, or multicomponent, nature, although they do not all identify the same dimensions or components. Even among psychologists who stress the multifaceted nature of intelligence, many recognize a general ability component that is believed to support intellectual performance across a broad variety of contexts, especially those involving complex information processing. Some views distinguish different types of intelligence or different intelligences (Gardner, 1983). One widely accepted distinction is that between crystallized intelligence, which is assumed to relate more directly to intellectual performance on the kinds of formal tasks typically imposed in educational contexts, and fluid intelligence, which is more closely associated with reasoning and problem solving in novel situations that call for flexibility and creativity in response.

A major limitation in our knowledge of intelligence stems from the fact that most of the studies about it have taken place in classrooms and psychological laboratories, and the extent to which the findings generalize to other situations more representative of those encountered outside these contexts is not clear. Problems used to study or measure intelligence in the laboratory typically are well defined, self-contained, and have known solutions, whereas many of those encountered in everyday life are not well defined, lack essential information, and their solutions are unknown. The differences between the kinds of challenges represented by traditional tests of intelligence and those presented by real life have been considered sufficiently great by some investigators to justify a distinction between academic and practical intelligence: the former being what is needed to do well on academic tasks, and the latter what is required to cope effectively outside the classroom (Sternberg & Wagner, 1986).

The relative importance of heredity and environment as determinants of cognitive capability has been explored in many ways, notably through the study of genetically unrelated (e.g., adopted) children raised in the same environment and identical twins reared apart. Interpretation of the results of such studies can be quite complicated; in the aggregate they make it clear that both heredity and environment contribute to adult intelligence, but the relative importance of the two factors remains an ongoing debate. The pendulum representing the predominant view has swung from a position emphasizing heredity to one emphasizing environment, and back, several times since the 1820s, but the swings have become progressively less extreme and the pendulum now appears to be resting in the middle position (Plomin & Petrill, 1982).

With respect to environmental influences on intelligence, we should distinguish between the question of how intelligence is influenced by environmental factors during the first few years of life, and whether it can be increased later through formal instruction.

The idea that one's intellectual development can be greatly influenced by environmental factors during one's infancy and preschool years has been widely held among developmental psychologists. The fact that average IQ, as represented by scores on standardized tests, has been increasing by about three points per decade over the last half of the twentieth century has been seen as evidence that performance on such tests is subject to environmental factors (e.g., nutrition, schooling, child-rearing practices), inasmuch as changes in genetic effects would not be expected to occur over such a short time (Neisser, 1997).

The question of whether intelligence can be increased by explicit efforts to raise it through instruction has become of interest recently, as it relates to the cognitive demands that people may face in the workplaces of the future. Whether those demands will be greater, on balance, than they are today is an open question. Given the rapidity of technological development, projecting how the cognitive requirements of jobs are likely to change even over a few decades is very difficult and experts do not present a unified view.

Beyond its implications for work, high intelligence is generally considered advantageous, especially in a competitive world. It is assumed that the higher one's intelligence, the greater the range of opportunities one is likely to have, and the greater one's chances of success are. This assumption motivates interest in the possibility of raising intelligence through instruction, but it also suggests a rephrasing of this question: Can people learn whatever is necessary to increase the range of opportunities they will have and their chances of success at whatever they choose to do? This is a different question than whether or not people can learn to improve their scores on IQ tests. There are many books that assure readers that they will be able to raise their scores on such tests if they learn what the authors have to teach about the structure and contents of IQ tests and follow their advice in taking them. There is little reason to doubt that the promise of improved test scores can be realized in many cases; there is considerable evidence that one can learn to improve one's performance on academic tests, conventional tests of intelligence included. Whether what they learn as a consequence of efforts to improve their test scores transfers as more intelligent behavior in practical situations is less clear. On the other hand, people can learn to behave in ways that would be perceived as more intelligent in practical situations, but whether what is learned in this case will be reflected in higher scores on formal tests of intelligence is also not certain.

The question of greatest interest for present purposes is this: What, if anything, can be done in the context of formal education to increase the ability of people to behave in what are generally considered intelligent ways? The evidence supports several answers to this question.

1. To the extent that intelligent behavior in specific contexts is dependent on domain-specific knowledge and technical skills, it can be increased by increasing such knowledge and skills. Probably no one doubts that this can be done. A person with experience in carpentry, or journalism, or surgery will function more intelligently as a carpenter, or journalist, or surgeon than will one who lacks that experience. Some researchers have argued that the importance of domain-specific knowledge and skills to high-level cognitive performance is generally underestimated, and that the teaching of them deserves more emphasis than many programs to enhance intellectual performance give them (Glaser, 1984).

2. Much of the knowledge and many of the skills on which effective cognitive functioning in modern society depends are layered in the sense that the development of knowledge or skills at one level of complexity depends on the existence of more foundational knowledge or skills. Knowledge of arithmetic is basic to the learning of higher mathematics, for example, and the ability to read is essential to the acquisition of numerous other capabilities. The acquisition of foundational knowledge and skills enables the development of higher level capabilities, and failure to acquire them early puts one at a serious disadvantage.

3. People can improve their learning skills: They can learn to learn. Educational psychologists have identified a variety of learning strategies that can be goals of instruction, and have presented evidence of their effectiveness in facilitating learning (Weinstein & Underwood, 1983).

4. Training in the use of mnemonic methods has a long history and is demonstrably effective in enhancing both short- and long-term memory. Descriptions of a variety of mnemonic techniques can be found in most texts on human memory; self-help books on how to improve one's memory, written for a general audience, abound.

5. The idea that training in logic improves the way in which people deal with cognitively demanding problems in daily life has had few strong supporters among psychologists since Thorndike contested it over 80 years ago. However, evidence has been obtained in recent years that performance on deductive reasoning tasks can be improved by training in certain "pragmatic reasoning schemas" that people appear to have in their repertory (Cheng, Holyoak, Nisbett, & Oliver, 1986).

6. Much of the reasoning that is required in everyday life is probabilistic in nature, involving the need to deal with uncertainties of various sorts. Many studies have documented ways in which probabilistic thinking goes astray. Studies have also shown that training in statistics and probability can be effective in improving the way in which people approach problems of reasoning under uncertainty (Nisbett, Fong, Lehman, & Cheng, 1987).

7. Teaching heuristic strategies has been prominent in many approaches to the enhancement of problem-solving ability. Strategies include finding effective ways to represent a problem, breaking down a problem into manageable subproblems, finding analogous problems that are familiar or relatively easy to solve, working backward from a goal state to the initial state, and considering extreme examples of a problem type. Brief descriptions and examples of some of these heuristics, which have been shown to work in various contexts, are given in Nickerson, Perkins, and Smith (1985).

8. Teaching self-management and other metacognitive skills and techniques has been stressed by some investigators, and the effectiveness of this approach has been demonstrated in several studies. An increasing emphasis on metacognition has been seen as a distinctive way in which approaches to the teaching of thinking and problem solving have changed over time (Presseisen, 1987).

There are many factors that are not usually considered causally related to intelligence that unquestionably help determine the effectiveness with which people meet challenges, including those that have major cognitive or intellectual components. Motivation is a case in point: it may be a determinant, among others, of course, even of performance on intelligence tests, and is clearly susceptible to change. Social and organizational skills, which are not necessarily associated with high academic intelligence, can be important to success in the workplace and in everyday life, and these too deserve attention as targets for improvement (Organ, 1994).

The importance of beliefs about the malleability of intelligence as determinants of behavior has been demonstrated in many studies. The belief that one's intelligence is unchangeable can demotivate students from making an effort to learn, whereas the contrary belief that one's cognitive capabilities can be enhanced through learning can motivate effort (Dweck & Eliot, 1983). Thus, one's belief regarding the mutabilty or immutability of intelligence can become a self-fulfilling expectation.

Success in the workplace and in everyday life depends on a variety of competencies, not all of which are cognitive. A high level of general intelligence, as evidenced by performance on IQ tests, is unquestionably an asset, but it appears to be neither a necessary nor a sufficient cause of success. The goal of raising intelligence through education and other environmental means is not an unreasonable one, although it is one that we do not yet know how best to realize, and it should not be pursued at the cost of neglecting to develop other competencies and character traits that are important to a meaningful and productive life.

When intellectual performance has been improved through training, it may not be possible to determine conclusively whether intelligence has been increased, or the individuals involved have become better at tapping the intelligence they have. For practical purposes, this distinction is not very important. What is important is that performance can be enhanced: People can learn to act more intelligently in dealing with the problems and opportunities of everyday life.

Bibliography

Cheng, P. W., Holyoak, K. J., Nisbett, R. E., & Oliver, L. (1986). Pragmatic versus syntactic approaches to training deductive reasoning. *Cognitive Psychology, 18*, 293–328.

Dweck, C. S., & Eliot, E. S. (1983). Achievement motivation. In P. H. Mussen (Series Ed.) & E. M. Hetherington (Vol. Ed.), *Handbook of child psychology: Vol. 4. Socialization, personality, and social development* (4th ed., pp. 643–691). New York: Wiley.

Gardner, H. (1983). *Frames of mind: The theory of multiple intelligences.* New York: Basic Books.

Glaser, R. (1984). Education and thinking: The role of knowledge. *American Psychologist, 39*, 93–104.

Neisser, U. (1997). Rising scores on intelligence tests. *American Scientist, 85*, 440–447.

Nickerson, R. S., Perkins, D. N., & Smith, E. E. (1985). *The teaching of thinking.* Hillsdale, NJ: Erlbaum.

Nisbett, R. E., Fong, G. T., Lehman, D. R., & Cheng, P. W. (1987). Teaching reasoning. *Science, 238*, 625–631.

Organ, E. W. (1994). Organizational citizenship behavior and the good soldier. In M. G. Rumsey, C. B. Walker, & J. H. Harris (Eds.), *Personnel selection and classification* (pp. 53–67). Hillsdale, NJ: Erlbaum.

Plomin, R., & Petrill, S. A. (1997). Genetics and intelligence: What's new? *Intelligence, 24*, 53–77.

Presseisen, B. Z. (1987). *Thinking skills throughout the curriculum: A conceptual design.* Bloomington, IN: Pi Lambda Theta.

Sternberg, R. J., & Wagner, R. K. (Eds.). (1986). *Practical intelligence.* Cambridge, England: Cambridge University Press.

Weinstein, C. E., & Underwood, V. L. (1983). Learning strategies: The *how* of learning. In J. Segal, S. Chipman, & R. Glaser (Eds.), *Thinking and learning skills: Relating instruction to basic research* (pp. 241–258). Hillsdale, NJ: Erlbaum.

Raymond S. Nickerson

Nutrition and Intelligence

Many studies have shown that children who are well nourished have better cognitive skills than children who are poorly nourished. However, the interpretation of the link between nutrition and intelligence is difficult because many factors, such as family income, illness, and genetic background, are correlated with both the adequacy of nutrition and children's cognitive skills. For this reason, the often-noted small, but significant, association between children's physical size, a marker of nutritional adequacy, and their intelligence could be due to these related factors. In this case, good nutrition would be a correlate, but not the cause, of higher intelligence.

The most powerful research evidence that nutrition contributes directly to cognitive development comes from supplementation studies in which kilocalories, protein, vitamins, and minerals have been provided. The abilities and achievements of children with enriched diets were contrasted with those of children who had nonsupplemented or less fully supplemented diets. The most consistent beneficial effect of supplementation on young infants has been on their motor skills. Supplementation also improved mental abilities in older infants, preschool, and school-age children, although the effects were smaller than the effects on motor abilities, and were more inconsistent both within and across studies. The strongest, long-term results came from a study in Guatemala in which supplementation was carried out for the first seven years of the children's lives, and the effects of supplementation were found many years later in arithmetic skills, vocabulary, reading achievement, and overall knowledge.

Whereas such studies suggest that nutrition is causally related to academic achievement, some of the critical components of good nutrition are not identified for two reasons. First, most of the well-executed studies have been conducted in developing countries where the level of malnutrition is fairly severe. Thus, the effects of more limited forms of malnutrition are less well understood. Second, intakes of calories and protein were not manipulated independently from intakes of vitamins and minerals. For this reason, the separate contribution of calories, protein, and micronutrients could not be assessed.

An extensive body of research shows that iron deficiency anemia has serious consequences in child development. Moreover, the effects of early iron deficiency anemia may not be completely reversible because children who were iron deficient in infancy often have lower cognitive abilities than comparison children many years after their anemia has been treated successfully. The other evidence for the importance of vitamins and minerals comes from a study, carried out in Egyptian, Kenyan, and Mexican communities in which caloric and protein intakes were generally adequate. The level of intake of animal products, an important source of vitamins and minerals, was related to cognitive skills in young children even when potentially confounding factors of parental IQ, family income, and child health were statistically controlled. These results suggest that children need to have adequate vitamins and minerals to acquire good cognitive skills.

One theory proposed to account for the effects of nutrition on cognitive development is that early inadequate nutrition causes neurological damage that limits children's capacities to learn. This hypothesis does not account for the recovery from short-term malnutrition often shown by children whose diets and quality of life improve, although these children may have mild impairments not evident on many cognitive assessments. A second theory is that the small stature and limited motor skills caused by nutritional insufficiency leads these infants to be treated as less mature, which interferes with their learning experiences and cognitive achievements. Some support for this theory comes from the demonstration that nutritional supplementation and family intervention in combination made a significantly greater contribution to children's cognitive functioning than either experimental manipulation alone. Additional support is derived from the observation that the quality of schooling interacts with nutrition in influencing cognitive achievements. The results of these studies suggest that the link between nutrition and cognition is functional rather than structural; hence, the effects of malnutrition can be reversed with combined dietary and educational mediation.

Bibliography

Grantham-McGregor, S., Powell, C. A., Walker, S. P., & Hines, J. H. (1991). Nutritional supplementation, psychological stimulation, and mental development of stunted children: The Jamaican study. *Lancet, 338*, 1–5.

Lozoff, B., Jimenez, E., & Wolf, A. (1991). Long-term developmental outcome of infants with iron deficiency. *New England Journal of Medicine, 325*, 687–694.

Pollitt, E. (1995). Functional significance of the covariance between protein energy malnutrition and iron deficiency anemia. *The Journal of Nutrition, 8S*, 2272S–2278S.

Pollitt, E., Gorman, K. S., Engle, P., Martorell, R., & Rivera, J. (1993). Early supplementary feeding and cognition: Effect over two decades. *Monographs of the Society for Research in Child Development, 58* (7, Serial No. 235).

Sigman, M. (1995). Nutrition and child development: More food for thought. *Current Directions in Psychological Science, 4*, 52–55.

Sigman, M. & Whaley, S. E. (1998). The role of nutrition in the development of intelligence. In U. Neisser (Ed.), *Intelligence on the rise? Secular changes in IQ and related measures* (pp. 155–183). Washington, DC: American Psychological Association.

Wachs, T. D. (1995). Relation of mild-to-moderate malnutrition to human development: Correlational studies. *American Journal of Nutrition, 125*, 2245S–2254S.

Marian D. Sigman